DICTIONARY OF
LITERARY
THEMES
AND MOTIFS

DICTIONARY OF LITERARY THEMES AND MOTIFS

A – J

JEAN-CHARLES SEIGNEURET,
EDITOR

A. Owen Aldridge, Armin Arnold, and
Peter H. Lee,
EDITORIAL BOARD

Madeleine G. Demers,
RESEARCH CONSULTANT

Kabimbi John Kalubi,
EDITORIAL ASSISTANT

GREENWOOD PRESS
NEW YORK • WESTPORT, CONNECTICUT • LONDON

Library of Congress Cataloging-in-Publication Data

Dictionary of literary themes and motifs.

 Includes indexes.
 1. Literature, Comparative—Themes, motives—
Dictionaries. I. Seigneuret, Jean-Charles.
PN43.D48   1988   809'.933'0321   87–12004
ISBN 0–313–22943–0 (lib. bdg. : alk. paper)
ISBN 0–313–26396–5 (lib. bdg. : alk. paper: vol. 1)
ISBN 0–313–26397-3 (lib. bdg. : alk. paper: vol. 2)

British Library Cataloguing in Publication Data is available.

Library of Congress Catalog Card Number: 87–12004
ISBN 0–313–22943–0 (set)
ISBN 0–313–26396–5 (v.1)
ISBN 0–313–26397–3 (v.2)

First published in 1988

Greenwood Press, Inc.
88 Post Road West, Westport, Connecticut 06881

Printed in the United States of America

The paper used in this book complies with the
Permanent Paper Standard issued by the National
Information Standards Organization (Z39.48–1984).

10 9 8 7 6 5 4 3 2 1

CONTENTS

//

PREFACE

— // —

When a *Survey of Research Tool Needs in French Language and Literature*, which I conducted for the National Endowment for the Humanities in 1977–1978, revealed that the need for a thematic dictionary of European literature ranked third among twenty-one essential research tools listed in an interdisciplinary section, I offered to assist my colleague at Washington State University, Professor Lester Shepard, an expert in comparative literature, in producing a dictionary of themes and motifs in world literature. After much preliminary work, a contract was signed with Greenwood Press in 1980. By examining recent bibliographical references, we were able to identify more than 600 scholars who had written articles or books of thematic significance. They were contacted and invited to contribute entries to the future *Dictionary of Literary Themes and Motifs*. Faced with the need to expand their expertise to world literature, many potential contributors turned us down. Others had made previous commitments for the near future. Approximately one hundred scholars accepted our invitation, but even those who declined welcomed our proposed endeavor.

To assist our collaborators, Madeleine G. Demers, Lester Shepard, and I read summaries of more than 4,500 works of literature and identified three or four major themes per work. In addition, another 600 Slavic works were examined by Eva Kagan-Kans, Associate Professor of Slavic Languages and Literatures at Indiana University, and her team of colleagues and graduate students, Maria Carlson, Henry Cooper, Andrew Durkin, Steve Gititsky, Joanne Innis, Irene Kiedrowski, Tim Larson, Ronald Meyer, Nadia Peterson, Teddy Robertson, Andrea Rogers, and Eric Stinebring. Printouts by keywords were made available and were meant to assist, not to replace, conventional research. We asked that authors approach their topics, whenever possible, in a historical manner and that efforts should be made to include discussion of non-Western literatures. A number of entries included such discussion; others did not, primarily because the authors involved felt that these literatures were outside their expertise. Our work therefore stresses Western literatures with a special emphasis on England and the United States. There is an obvious need for a thematic dictionary devoted exclusively to the non-Western world.

In 1982, as entries began to arrive, Lester Shepard had to withdraw from the project and I decided, with great trepidation, to take it over and bring it to fruition. I was extremely fortunate to obtain the services of three internationally known experts in comparative literature who would form an editorial board. The board was small enough to facilitate speedy evaluation of manuscripts, yet representative of both Western and Eastern literatures. To Professors A. Owen Aldridge, University of Illinois; Armin Arnold, McGill University; and Peter H. Lee, University of California, Los Angeles, go my deepest thanks. I was fully guided by their comments as far as content is concerned, and contributors were strongly encouraged to revise their entries accordingly. The final responsibility for content of the entries remains, of course, with the authors.

During the next two years, entries continued to trickle in, though as often happens with a work dependent on the voluntary contributions of a large number of scholars, many entries were abandoned along the way, and suitable replacement authors had to be found, mostly by seeking nominations from active participants. Beginning in 1984 a concerted effort was made to secure entries on topics considered essential, with the final outcome being 143 entries written by 98 scholars. Most major themes are included directly or indirectly, along with a number of minor topics that reflect the expertise of some of our contributors and serve as examples of a broad range of narrower themes that could not, at this time, be covered to any extent (e.g., Bear, Butterflies, Lion, and Unicorn representing the animal and insect worlds; Philately and Mountaineering serving to illustrate hobbies and sports).

The word "dictionary" in our title should not be construed as implying completeness. Far from it. Our work is meant to grow over the years and to reflect current research interests while filling out the gaps of this first edition. It contains almost three times the number of entries of Elisabeth Frenzel's *Motive der Weltliteratur* (1962, rev. ed. 1980), yet does not pretend to replace it but to expand on it. There is no question that authors writing on themes also found in Frenzel's work are extremely indebted to her previous research. Following Frenzel's examples, we decided to limit the topics of this present work to concrete and abstract common nouns. Proper nouns, such as literary characters, persons, and places, merit separate treatment.

There are at least as many potential themes and motifs in literature as angels on the head of a pin. Hence, this "dictionary" will remain in a constant state of being. For an expert discussion of themes, motifs, and thematology, the reader is invited to turn to the Introduction, written by Professor François Jost of the University of Illinois, whose work on comparative literature has achieved world recognition. Other important sources on this subject are listed in the bibliography appended to Jost's Introduction.

Readers seeking information on a particular theme or motif in these volumes should first ascertain if the topic is listed in the table of contents as an entry. If the topic is not listed, or for additional information, the reader is invited to consult the Cross-Index to Themes and Motifs following the last entry. Whenever an entry discusses, in a meaningful way, a secondary theme or motif, this related "keyword" can be found in the Cross-Index. Keywords are listed there in alphabetical order and are followed by the titles of the entries in which they are illustrated or discussed.

Entries begin, in general, with a short definition of the headword and, when appropriate, briefly sketch in the origin and historical background of the theme or motif involved. For the most part, the approach is chronological but, when the logic of the subject so requires, the material is grouped according to geographical area, genre, style, or a combination of these. Analysis and interpretation are allotted space and presented depending on the contributor's perception of the significance and character of the topic. Each entry concludes with cross-references to related entries, where appropriate, and a brief bibliography (three or four items at the most, with the exception of lengthy entries such as Travel).

Bibliographical and literary references follow the format recommended by the Modern Language Association of America (1984). Foreign titles alluded to in the entries are transliterated when appropriate and, when first mentioned, are followed by their English titles or the titles they are known by in English. None is listed if the title is identical in both languages or if no English title exists. I chose to transliterate Greek titles rather than give only their Latin titles, as is common practice among classicists, for the sake of consistency and because recent reference works follow this practice. Subsequent references within the same entry may list foreign works by their English translations or their original titles. The traditional spellings of Russian authors have been used. Genre and date of publication (sometimes performance in the case of plays) are given in parentheses if they are not explicit in context. Rather than decide which works did not require notification of genre (Shakespeare's *Hamlet*, for example), I chose to treat all literary works equally: better to sin by commission than by omission. The most time-consuming editorial task undertaken in the preparation of this dictionary was the checking of all titles and dates for accuracy. For the sake of consistency, I chose to normalize dates (known or assumed) and titles of English translations throughout the work, and I take full responsibility for changes made to contributors' entries. When faced with an approximate date (noted as "c." for *circa*) the reader should not assume that *all* scholars agree with it. It represents my considered judgment. Preparing the index and verifying titles and dates were facilitated by my editorial assistant, Kabimbi John Kalubi, a doctoral candidate in French literature, to whom I am very grateful.

I am also indebted to the Department of Foreign Languages and Literatures at Washington State University and the Department of Romance Languages and Literatures at the University of Cincinnati for supplies and clerical assistance. Most of all, I wish to thank the members of my editorial board and my contributors, many of whom must have wondered if the work would ever go to press; my mother, Madeleine G. Demers, research consultant par excellence;

my wife, Sue Seigneuret, who assisted me and encouraged me when I was ready to give up; and my children, Bernard, Hélène, and Madeleine, who kept asking me, as the years went by, ''Are you not finished yet?''

JEAN-CHARLES SEIGNEURET

INTRODUCTION

——————— // ———————

The history of literary motifs and themes is an essential part of a contemporary academic discipline known as thematology or thematics. This Dictionary meets an urgent need of the literary-oriented world at large, and especially of the English-speaking community, which has been deprived so far of authoritative reference books in this domain. Some twenty years ago, it is true, Sith Thompson completed his related six volume *Motif-Index of Folk Literature*, which may have encouraged, if not inspired, present-day critical endeavors. The work renders mainly ancillary services, however, to researchers engaged in the study of letters. Closer to our concerns are Elisabeth Frenzel's two books, *Stoffe der Weltliteratur* and *Motive der Weltliteratur*. Although directly accessible only to German-speaking scholars, they are valuable and have been consulted by some of the contributors to the present publication. Individual studies on various themes have also been systematically pursued during the last fifty years. Hundreds of monographs and articles about multifarious motifs and themes, from Potiphar's wife to the Flying Dutchman, have found their way to the shelves of academic and public libraries and enriched the cash registers of various publishing houses and bookstores. The entries of this Dictionary, however, do not reproduce indiscriminately reference cards stocked in the Library of Congress. A choice had to be made among thousands of theoretically eligible items. The criteria for selection were their relevance to a broad and prominent body of literary works, their significance for the evolution of cultural history, and their vitality as measured by the interest shown by presently active researchers. The focus points to the West, although scores of entries reveal the universal interests of their authors.

Two factors may explain the rise of the thematological method: its interpretive potentialities and its intrinsic congruency with the history of ideas. Influential literary authorities, moreover, have considered it an efficient antidote against primarily aesthetic movements such as "progressive Universalpoesie," a formula first used in 1800 by Friedrich von Schlegel in the *Athenäum* which he published with his brother August Wilhelm. The concept has been revamped by Verlaine with his dedication to "De la musique avant toute chose," [Music before everything], the first line of his famous "Art poétique," [The Art of Poetry] written in 1874. For centuries, literature has been considered a compound of two elements, form and substance, words and thoughts, just as water is composed of oxygen and hydrogen. In literature the two ingredients, obviously, are not measured by definite proportions like atomic weights in chemistry. While quality remains an obligatory constituent of any product of art, science is uniquely based on quantities. The autopsy of some defunct critical theories of temporary vogue sadly reveals the cause of their demise. An overdose of form has to be blamed for the fatal anemia. The anatomy of long-lived practices, on the contrary, testifies to the fact that only a balance of values between flesh and spirit can guarantee intellectual health. Recent German criticism has overreacted to aestheticism by creating and propagating the word and the notion of "Literatur-*wissenschaft*" (science), although "Literatur*kunde*" (knowledge) would be a more appropriate expression. Indeed intuition and sensibility may prevail over, or at least challenge, historical data and controllable events.

Literary lexicographers seek to list appropriately selected keywords accompanied by adequate commentaries concerning related developments and opinions. Transcending the notion of bare inventory, the present volumes contain or suggest conclusive judgments. The bringing together of similar topics in various cultures and in diverse circumstances provides insight not only into the mechanism of the literary clockwork, but also into the process of establishing and defining aesthetic values. The reader is invited to examine the function and artistic significance of textual elements within the overall framework of different, but factually and intellectually kindred writings. A straight enumeration might occasionally be necessary in order to demonstrate and illustrate briefly the diffusion or popularity of specific motifs and themes. Characteristic prototypes, "proto-motifs" and "protothemes," preferably identified in masterpieces, are here assigned their proper role in literary history and criticism. Nonetheless this publication is primarily intended to serve as a thesaurus of reference.

German critics have been most concrete and specific in defining the various components of thematology. Their views are widely adopted in the West and tend to prevail over all other suggestions. They use the term *Stoff* for logically or chronologically arranged parts of literary matter pertaining to human existence or fragments of events. In narrative genres, *Stoff* consists of a self-sufficient story or meaningful episode; it constitutes a rationally comprehensible whole born out of an organizing principle. In Flaubert's novel *Madame Bovary* (1856) the diverse incidents are logically and psychologically tied together; in the *Life* (1791) of Johnson they are cemented primarily by chronology. The intelligibility of these and similar works is based on a cause-effect or past-present relationship. Obviously a drama and a poem also have a theme since both are usually treating a more or less precisely delineated topic or plot. Thus *Stoff* is the intelligible subject matter of a literary work of fiction. Indeed *Stoff* and theme are identical.

Beyond the facts and feelings and their narrative or poetic expressions endowed with their intrinsic value and meaning, there might loom a fundamental problem of which one specific work is just one single and unique illustration. This all-pervading, deeper meaning (which may be psychological, philosophical, political, moral, sociological, or religious in nature) is precisely the thematological element that we call "*motif.*" Flaubert delivers a clear message: romantic dreamers are marked for decline and fall. Boswell, in the preface to the second edition of his biography of Johnson, compares his work to Homer's and quotes the following lines from Horace: "To show wisdom and what sense can do / The Poet sets Ulysses in our view." The task of identifying thematical and motival aspects in a work devolves upon the reader. At one place in one of Tolstoy's novels, the nephews of Anna Karenina are playing with little boxes representing cars in a train. The episode has tragic overtones for the critic who knows the outcome of the novel. It is, at least indirectly, affiliated with one of the virtual motifs of the story—adultery does not pay—since Anna quits her lover forever by committing suicide by throwing herself under the wheels of a locomotive. Events sometimes carry several issues expounded on different levels; thus, often more than one lesson is dispensed. The Russian novel embodies at *least* two other motifs. Society crushes whoever defies its rules; whoever yields to the spell of a femme fatale or of an "homme fatal" sadly seals his destiny forever.

The rationale of the system may be easily comprehended, though the proposed terminology has not been so far universally adopted. There is no international consensus—there is no Parliament in the Republic of Letters—to regulate the vocabulary of thematics. One critic may call *motif* what another designates as *theme*. Both words are occasionally used interchangeably, and some examples of this synonymity are given in this Dictionary. We should remember, however, that contributors may deal with works in which the two concepts overlap; furthermore, they are conscious of the fact that they have to be concerned with themes as defined here, and only indirectly with motifs. The difference between the two notions cannot be specified in the individual articles and thus is taken up in this Introduction.

Common sense combined with elementary philosophy and simple semantics often proves to be a wise and accurate judge in disputes over terminology. This is the case of "motif" as a thematological concept. It has developed from the Latin *movere*, to set forth ideationally, not factually, to stimulate and spur, prompt and urge, or to cause something to happen and to move forward. It explains or justifies a motion or a development on a theoretical level. It is *Beweggrund*. According to a growing number of scholars, the motif is intellectual by nature; it expresses a process of reasoning about men's conduct of life and, as a consequence, does not concern itself with the analysis of individual characters or extraordinary happenings. An unspecified agent is engaged in a certain type of action and similar results are achieved, thanks to similar conditions and circumstances—one of the meanings of agency. The motif, therefore, represents what Ernst Robert Curtius calls "Urbedingungen des Daseins" ("Prime conditions of existence"). Gottfried Keller states in his novelle *Romeo und Julia auf dem Dorfe* (*The Village Romeo and Juliet*, 1856) that fables, basic human situations, reappear ceaselessly "in neuem Gewand," and "zwingen alsdann die Hand, sie festzuhalten:" nothing new except the garnment, the theme. Thus a person (agent) living with vain dreams and wishes (agency, instrumentality) brings his own downfall (action and consequence). The motif is abstract and reflects teleological thinking. The theme, on the contrary, is practical and concrete. It represents one out of countless incarnations of the same motif. Emma and Werther as well as an infinity of other fictional characters belong to the same family of themes. Similarly *Don Quijote* (*Don Quixote*, novel, 1605, 1615) remains but one single actualization of innumerable possibilities. Cervantes' hero is unique (theme), while his message (motif) is familiar to readers of every continent. Such types are walking in our streets (motif), where, however, there are no windmills (theme). In short, the theme is a specific expression of a motif, which is universal in essence. Its individualization is the result of the passage from the general to the particular (Raymond Trousson). It is usually embodied in a plot. As far as the motif is concerned, it represents the quintessence of fictional narrative, its soul, its transcendence. The motif bridles and guides the imagination of authors of masterpieces. It is the post to which they tie their capricious fantasy. One may conclude that motifs are subject to be incarnated in universal types.

Half a century ago, Paul Van Tieghem, considered the official godfather of modern comparatism and one of the most apodictic prophets of the discipline which he helped promote, distinguished five sectors in thematology: themes, types, legends, ideas, and sentiments. Strangely enough, some contemporary reflections on thematology do not reach much further than those of the French scholar, even though in recent decades studies in motifs and themes have assumed international and interdisciplinary dimensions. Thematology holds an eminent position not only in comparative literature, but in other areas of the liberal arts such as text interpretation and linguistics, history and musicology. The reason why a discipline that is an integral part of the humanities still suffers from an equivocal terminology may be perceived in the fact that some undisciplined proponents of that discipline delight in exhibiting their intellectual freedom.

A majority of eminent scholars properly identify themalogical concepts. While at work with notions, however, some of them are still at play with words. Yet continuing efforts, although with limited results, are being made in the Anglo-American world specifically, in order to dispel contradiction and confusion. In his essay "Thematics and Criticism" Harry Levin identifies basic aspects of the dichotomy *Stoff-Motif* (*Stoff* meaning "theme"), though without offering clear-cut definitions. "The adjective *thematic*," he writes, "has generally had to do with meaning as distinguished from techniques." True, but hardly a conclusive statement, since both the motif and the theme have in one way or the other to do with meaning. For numerous scholars a theme remains "something named by an abstract noun or phrase: the futility of war, the mutability of joy, heroism, inhumanity" This statement from Monroe C. Beardsley's *Aesthetics* (p. 403) obviously induces the reader to conclude that theme means subject matter. The futility of war, for instance, has been for decades a sterile subject of conversation between superpowers, but the theme, in our thematological sense, that is, a demonstration of how and why wars *actually* are futile, has been treated in *Voĭna i mir* (*War and Peace*, 1865–1869), and in scores of lesser known novels.

Other scholars explain that the theme consists in the ideas that emerge from the particular structure of textual elements such as action, observations revealing states of mind, feelings, or gestures. "Such textual elements I designate by the term *motif*; the idea that emerges from motifs by means of abstraction I call the theme" (Eugene H. Falk). Elsewhere we read: "Discovering themes or meanings in a work involves us in making connections between the work and the world outside it. These connections are meanings" (Robert Scholes). In our language this specific meaning is the motif, provided that the "world outside it" refers to generalization and depersonification. Scholes's views are shared mainly by disciples of what one may call the Anglo-American school of thematics, although other explanations and comments abound in any part of Western criticism. *A Handbook to Literature*, after asserting that *theme* (see entry) is the central or dominating idea in a literary work concludes that "in poetry, drama, and fiction it is the abstract concept which is made concrete through its representation in person, action, and image in the work" (Holman, Thrall, Hibbard). In its first part this ambiguous statement seems to allude to the motif, in the second to the theme. There is a way out of the maze. When we are concerned with ideas and notions, born from human life, and illustrative of anybody's biography, we are in the domain of the motif. Yet with concepts by themselves, good and evil, virtue and vice, prosperity and poverty, happiness and distress, love and death, we are in the realm of simple topics or of metaphysics. Thematics is not primarily concerned with speculative philosophy. Quite a few scholars have grown tired of the semantic bedlam created by a host of individualistically minded thematologists and are tending toward allegiance to a firm system, to a creed professing that the motif remains the permanent and the impersonal, the theme, the transitory and the personal. According to that faith, the motif is the soul that undergoes a continuous thematic metapsychosis passing into countless individual literary bodies, the works. Writers are the midwives in multiple rebirths. Today the list of motifs is probably closed, while that of themes will be open until the universal judgment.

One may ask whether a novelist or a playwright first invents a theme and imposes upon it a motif, or vice versa, just as scholars in operatics are bustled by the dilemma "prima le parole, poi la musica" [first the words, then the music]. The question is perhaps irrelevant for our theoretical discussion, but quite intriguing for the biographer of an author. Why did Melville narrate the destiny of a whale? is an intriguing question. *Moby-Dick* (1851) transcends by far the adventurer's cetacean experiences. It is in part an allegorical account of the author's life—its crucial phase—and he endowed it with a motif. Whoever loves danger, as the Ecclesiast warns, shall perish through danger, or at least run a high risk of perishing through it. This is the motif or one of the plausible motifs of the novel. First, it seems, the actual, immediate motivation for writing the work was Melville's thrilling experiences at sea; then came the philosophical motif endowing the work with a meaning beyond its particular story, beyond the theme.

Why did Samuel Johnson write *Rasselas* (novel, 1759)? He had to foot the bills for the funeral of his mother. Why did Voltaire write *Candide* (novel, 1757)? He wanted to air his wrath against Frederic, his scorn for Rousseau, and his contempt for Leibniz. Here we are concerned with factual motivations, with concrete reasons. Let us return to thematics. If we depersonalize Voltaire's story, we notice that he means to deliver an overall valid message, namely, that whoever organizes his existence according to foolishly optimistic principles ends up by being a fool himself. This very same motif, identifiable only in the abstract and on the ethical level, may be found in a host of novels in universal literature. The theme of each of them, however, is unique. Only in one work may we find a narrative combination involving the rape of Cunégonde, an auto-da-fé at Coimbra, a Jesuit in Paraguay, a garden in Constantinople, and a crop of pistachios, while in hundreds of works we may find types like Candide.

As a consequence of these remarks, we notice that the number of themes is theoretically unlimited, that of motifs, limited. As we read in *Gespräche mit Eckermann* (*Conversations with Eckermann*, 1836–1848), Goethe noticed that the Italian playwright count Carlo Gozzi, who was the first critic to statisticize the basic meanings of European drama, maintained that the tragedy knows only thirty-six primary situations. Goethe reported Gozzi's statement to Schiller, who disagreed. Yet, after some reflection and investigation, Schiller was not even in a position to cite an amount of examples equalling Gozzi's proposed number. The commedia dell'arte offers some twenty motifs and hundreds of themes. Lope de Vega credits himself with 1,500 plays—while Calderón wrote "only" 120. And even a book entitled *Les 200.000 situations dramatiques* (E. Souriau, 1950) has seen the light of day. But the Spanish dramatists were repeating their own motifs, and obviously the French author was alluding to particular circumstances within similar plots. In neither France nor Spain is there a question of producing the suggested abundance of instances revealing a fundamental sense of life, of motifs, but rather of developing illustrations, or individual junctures of various contingencies of themes.

Around the literary stars of first magnitude we have seen glittering in the themalogical firmament, several planets are circling in diverse orbits. The *leitmotiv* illustrates the motif in its thematic materialization. The word was first used by composers. Wagner attached a specific salient musical motif (that is the smallest melodic unit) to some of his major characters. The sound of that motif, which he called "leitmotiv," announces to the audience that the hero is about to appear on stage or refers implicitly to some incident of the plot. In painting, the motif is a striking element identified in several pictures of an individual artist or in a vast collection of works. It may function as leitmotiv, since it can guide and lead through parts of an artist's or of a group of artists' achievements. Literary criticism uses the term leitmotiv almost as a synonym for a recurring image and may also relate it to the objective correlative. Tolstoy and Melville once more provide illustrations. The numerous allusions to the railroad throughout *Anna Karenina* (1877) foreshadow the heroine's suicide, which epitomizes the intellectual substance of the novel, the motif. All references in *Moby-Dick* to Jonas, to sea monsters, to their bones, to endangered species symbolize the whale's and the hero's destiny. Western literatures abound with leitmotivs or comparable thematological components. In Dickens' novel *Bleak House* (1853) all birds belong exclusively to crazy Miss Flite, and in Fielding's novel *Tom Jones* (1749) only Mrs. Western, Sophia's aunt, ceaselessly declares that she "knows the world." The leitmotiv is comparable to, though *not identical* with, the Homeric epithet: only in the *Ilias* (*Iliad*, epic, c. 8th century B.C.) do we find "swift-footed Achilles" and "white-armed Hera," and only in the *Odysseia* (*Odyssey*, epic), "bright-eyed Athene" and "Menelaos dear to Ares." These particular adjectives and phrases are monopolized by individual characters.

The *topos*, on the contrary, that originated with ancient grammarians, is a stock figure or expression, a suggestive cliché that may be found in any context. *Locus amoenus*, for example, designates a place offering well-defined geographical and climatic "amenities." The phrase conveys to the reader the image of a certain landscape, the actual description of which would need considerable space. Finally, if we wish to complete the inventory of the thematological arsenal, we must remember literary types; their two groups consist of the *archetypes*, the prime samples or oldest known representatives of specific human patterns of behaviors, attitudes, or actions, and the *prototypes*, the most prominent model for these deeds or ways of living. We recognize in Tirso de Molina's drama *El burlador de Sevilla* (*The Libertine of Seville*, 1630) the archetype of the Don Juan motif, while Molière's play (1665), Mozart's opera (1787), or Byron's poems (1818–1823) may be considered prototypes—whichever work comes first to the objective critic's mind. Evidently a celebrated archetype may also be a prototype.

The permanent problem criticism has to face is the balance between the two constitutive elements of literature, the idea and its incarnation, the *fond* and the *forme*, The *Gehalt* and the *Gestalt*. It has been explained that the motif represents the abstract substance of a work, while the theme is its concrete treatment, its application to various particulars or striking happenings, its illustration. The former reflects the overall human significance of a work, and the latter, thanks to a series of devices that have just been mentioned, constantly reminds the reader of the ultimate meaning of a specific human situation or events. The motif does not depend upon linguistics or poetics, metaphors or allegories. It concerns itself with intellectual esthetics, that is to say, with the intrinsic beauty of thoughts, of logically verifiable truths, or of intuitively perceived and objectified truths. The theme uses all the resources offered by handbooks of stylistics and semiotics, rhetoric and poetry. It has to generate tangible values by materializing one of the thousand potentialities of the motif with imaginary accounts or with lived experience. Beauty is made flesh. Understood in this manner, thematology represents a compendium of literature itself. Although in theory it distinguishes between the two prime elements, in practice it asserts and confirms their indissoluble alliance, their *indivisa unitas*.

It is not to be expected that the difference between these two literary components be formally made in the individual articles of this Dictionary, since its main purpose is to trace the history and scholarly implications of important themes. The distinction is of prominence, however, even if here and there it is left to the reader to disentangle various notions and concepts. The final purpose of criticism, to be sure, is to help to understand the mechanics or trade secrets of literary beauty. If it is hard labor to detect them, one may find some solace by rereading the last phrase of Plato's second Hippias Dialogue: "for beauty is a difficult thing."

Bibliography

Beardsley, Monroe C. *Aesthetics, Problems in the Philosophy of Criticism*. 2d ed. Indianapolis: Hackett, 1981.

Bisanz, Adam J., and Raymond Trousson. *Elemente der Literatur: Beitrage zur Stoff-, Motiv-, und Themenforschung*. 2 vols. Stuttgart: Kröner, 1980.

Bodkin, Maud. *Archetypal Patterns in Poetry: Psychological Studies of Imagination*. 1934. New York: AMS Press, 1978.

———. *Studies of Type Images in Poetry, Religion, and Philosophy*. London: Oxford University Press, 1951.

Burke, Kenneth. *A Grammar of Motives and a Rhetoric of Motives*. Cleveland: World Publishing Co., 1962.

Calvet, Jean. *Les types universels dans la littérature française*. 1926. 2 vols. Paris: Lanore, 1964.

Clemente, José Edmundo. *Los temas esenciales de la literatura*. Buenos Aires: Emece, 1959.

Curtius, Ernst Robert. *European Literature and the Latin Middle Ages*. Trans. Willard R. Trask. [New York]: Princeton University Press, 1953.

Ehrenpreis, Irvin. *The "Types Approach" to Literature*. New York: King's Crown Press, 1945.

Falk, Eugene H. *Types of Thematic Structure; the Nature and Function of Motifs in Gide, Camus, and Sartre*. Chicago: University of Chicago Press, 1967.

Fokkema, D. W., and Elrud Kunne-Ibsch. *Theories of Literature in the Twentieth Century: Structuralism, Marxism, Aesthetics of Reception, Semiotics*. London: C. Hurst, 1977.

Frenzel, Elisabeth. *Motive der Weltliteratur: ein Lexikon dichtungsgeschichtlicher Längsschnitte*. 2d ed. Stuttgart: Kröner, 1980.

———. *Stoffe der Weltliteratur: ein Lexikon dichtungsgeschichtlicher Längsschnitte*, 6th ed. Stuttgart: Kröner, 1983.

———. *Stoff- und Motivgeschichte*. 2d ed. Berlin: Schmidt, 1974.

Holman, C. Hugh, William Flint Thrall, and Addison Hibbard. *A Handbook to Literature*. 5th ed. New York: Macmillan, 1986.

Jeune, Simon. *Littérature générale et littérature comparée, essai d'orientation*. Paris: Lettres modernes, 1968.

Jost, François. "Grundbegriffe der Thematologie" in *Theorie und Kritik: zur vergleichenden und neueren deutschen Literatur*. Bern: Francke, 1974.

————. *Introduction to Comparative Literature*. Indianapolis: Pegasus, 1974.

Kayser, Wolfgang. *Das sprachliche Kunstwerk*. 1948. Bern: Francke, 1983.

Kohlschmidt, Werner, and Wolfgang Mohr. *Reallexicon der deutschen Literaturgeschichte*. 2d ed. 4 vols. Berlin: De Gruyter, 1958–1984.

Körner, Josef. "Erlebnis, Motiv, Stoff." *Vom Geiste neuer Literaturforschung. Festschrift für O. Walzel*. Ed. Julius Wahle and Victor Klemperer. Potsdam: Akademische Verlagsgesellschaft Athenaion, 1924, 80–90.

Levin, Harry. "Thematics and Criticism." *The Disciplines of Criticism*. Ed. Peter Demetz et al. New Haven: Yale University Press, 1968: 125–145.

Marino, Adrian. *Kritik der literarischen Begriffe*. Trans. Bernd Kolf. Cluj: Dacia Verlag, 1976.

Muschg, Walter. *Tragische Literaturgeschichte*. 1948. München: Francke, 1983.

Pickett, Ralph E. *Recurring Themes in Art, Literature, Music, Drama, and the Dance as Found in Various Episodes of Classical Mythology, Religion, and History*. Rev. ed. [New York]: R. E. Pickett, 1961.

Scholes, Robert, ed. Introduction. *Elements of Fiction. An Anthology*. By Scholes. Rev. ed. New York: Oxford University Press, 1982.

Sperber, Hans, and Leo Spitzer. *Motiv und Wort, Studien zur Literatur-und Sprachpsychologie*. Leipzig: O. R. Reisland, 1918.

Stanzel, Franz. *Narrative Situations in the Novel*. Trans. James P. Pusack. Bloomington: Indiana University Press, 1971.

Thompson, Stith. *Motiv-Index of Folk Literature*. Rev. ed. 6 vols. Bloomington: Indiana University Press, 1955–1958.

Trousson, Raymond. *Un problème de littérature comparée: les études de thèmes; essai de méthodologie*. Paris: Minard, 1965.

Van Tieghem, Paul. *La littérature comparée*. 4th ed. Paris: A. Colin, 1951.

Weber, Jean-Paul. *Domaines thématiques*. Paris: Gallimard, 1963.

Weisstein, Ulrich. *Comparative Literature and Literary Theory, Survey and Introduction*. Bloomington: Indiana University Press, 1973.

Wilpert, Gero von. *Sachwörterbuch der Literatur*. 6th ed. Stuttgart: Kröner, 1979.

FRANÇOIS JOST

2

DICTIONARY OF
LITERARY
THEMES
AND MOTIFS

A

//

ADOLESCENCE

Adolescence generally denotes the transition from childhood to adulthood, but more accurately it refers to a process (rather than to a stage) whereby maturing youth struggles to achieve some measure of integration with society. The struggle for integration almost always involves the education of the heart, often its death, or at best a Pyrrhic victory as a more prosaic world triumphs over the heart's poetry (to paraphrase Hegel).

Until the mid-eighteenth century adolescence was neither a predominant literary motif nor a subject of much concern. In fact adolescence and childhood were often interchangeable terms. With Rousseau, however, adolescence came to denote an increasingly distinct state or condition. In late-eighteenth-century Germany the concept was fueled by the development of such genres as the *Bildungsroman* (or novel of development) and of the related *Entwicklungsroman* (or novel of education) and *Künstlerroman* (or novel of the developing artist). By the first decade following World War I, the novel of adolescence crested in popularity, and the twentieth century became known as the century of adolescence. As Justin O'Brien points out, in France alone "more than half again as many novels of adolescence appeared during the decade of 1920–1930 as during the preceding years, or, for that matter, as during the whole course of French literature until then."

Early representative types include the Bible's Prodigal Son and his literary descendants (see John Lyly's *Euphues: The Anatomy of Wit* [treatise, 1578], or Robert Greene's *A Groatsworth of Wit, Bought with a Million of Repentance* [pamphlet, 1592]); figures of early Greek myth and drama; the questing hero of chivalric literature (Sir Gawain, Parzival); the courtly lover (Troïlus); the picaresque heroes of Spain, France, and England (El Buscón, Françion, Gil Blas, Tom Jones); the hero of moral allegory, from *Humanum Genus* of *The Castle of Perseverance* (15th-century morality play) to John Bunyan's Christian; the

Renaissance man, eager to integrate fully his talents; and the reconstituted self of autobiography (St. Augustine, Jean-Jacques Rousseau).

The Beginnings to the Eighteenth Century

Humankind has always recognized the transitional nature of adolescence (it is neither childhood nor adulthood), but not all ages have found it a worthy subject for detailed exploration. To the Greeks and Romans, for example, who valued maturity for its possibility of rational perfectibility, the adolescent was but an imperfect, sexually ambiguous being who at fourteen was only just beginning to develop his faculty for reasoning. Only partially capable of compassion and understanding, he was not in himself particularly interesting. Nevertheless, a passage from Plato's dialogue *Timaios* (*Timaeus*, 4th century B.C.) describes the challenge to youth that subsequent centuries and cultures reiterate with only few modifications: "And now if some right nurture lends help towards education, he [the adolescent] becomes entirely whole and unblemished, having escaped the worst of maladies; whereas if he be neglectful, he journeys through a life halt and maimed and comes back to Hades uninitiate and without understanding." With increasing intensity subsequent generations document this tension between the struggle for wholeness and understanding and the threat of failed or unregenerate initiation.

Without providing a gallery of adolescents per se, antiquity does, however, offer a gallery of psychologically acute precursors. Indeed any discussion of adolescence today owes much of its significant vocabulary to Greek myth. When Freud described adolescence as a revival of the Oedipus crisis, for example, he drew on Sophocles' king to focus attention on the role of the family in orienting human desire and destiny. Arguing that each of us "was once a budding Oedipus in phantasy," Freud maintained that the adolescent, relinquishing powerful (and incestuous) familial ties for social ones, must rerout that desire or fail to mature. From Henry Fielding and *Tom Jones* (1749) to D. H. Lawrence and *Sons and Lovers* (1913), novelists concerned with growing up have intentionally or unintentionally reworked the Oedipus myth for comic or tragic ends.

And when psychoanalysis maintains that adolescence brings with it a recrudescence of narcissism, it draws on the most famous of Ovid's tales to describe a powerful concomitant of the structure. Perhaps literature's first true adolescent, Narcissus cannot tear himself away from his compelling reflection. His death fortells the fate of many literary adolescent relatives whose own narcissism keeps them in thrall—for example Goethe's Werther, for whom the self-engendered ideal becomes more powerful and seductive than the real.

A more easily recognized precursor than either Oedipus or Narcissus is Telemachus, son of Odysseus and Penelope. Homer's epic poem *Odysseia* (*Odyssey*, c. 8th century B.C.) details the stages of his initiation: his initial helplessness in the face of his mother's suitors and in imagining his father's great strength; his adventure-filled quest for a lost father and for a father's spirit (and by extension his quest for his own identity); his initiation into manhood through bloodshed, as father and son rout the enemy from their home. In many ways Telemachus' dark double, Orestes, son of Agamemnon and Clytemnestra, also comes to manhood in a blood-letting ceremony, but by slaying his mother and her lover, Aegisthus. If the matricide may be taken as metaphor, Orestes enacts the stuff of primitive puberty ritual, giving birth to himself as the all-male warrior-hero (according to Sven Armens and other critics) whose initiation into the world of men means a vanquishing or purging of the female world that marks his birth and infancy.

Notable in history's gallery of daughters are Antigone, whose allegiance to familial law—"woman's law," according to Creon—means defying the patriarchal state and ultimately brings her death; Iphigenia, sacrificed by her father for the state; and Persephone or Kore, whose abduction by Hades has come to serve as metaphor for female psychosexual history.

Another precursor, Tristan, comes originally by way of Celtic myth, the legend passing through the hands of Chrétien de Troyes and Gottfried von Strasburg, among others. Having drunk from the magic philtre "not of love alone, but love and death together," Tristan and his lover Iseult exemplify a host of descendants who suffer, as Denis de Rougemont (*Love in the Western World*, 1956) has phrased it, "the anguish of being two." The blurring of boundaries between self and other, the embrace of fluidity and flux, the loss of one's singular identity—these become increasingly predictable features of adolescent crisis (see Shakespeare's drama *Romeo and Juliet* [c. 1596], for example) as the theme develops.

Most works of adolescence involved both a quest and an education, and in this sense Wolfram von Eschenbach's nearly 25,000-line epic *Parzival* (completed around 1210) is an early representative of the form that over the centuries crystalized into the *Bildungsroman*. His name deriving perhaps from the Arabic *Parsch-Fal* ("pure or guileless fool"), Parzival dons a fool's cap and bells and sets off from his secluded home in the forest to join the knights of the Round Table. A series of adventures leads him by a circuitous path through loss of faith and despair to wisdom and maturity.

With the development of the picaresque tradition, the adolescent's induction into the world becomes an occasion for satire. In subverting the chivalric romance, in replacing the idealized knight with the low-life *pícaro*, the genre thereby introduced the first juvenal delinquents to literature. Generally told as autobiography (a cynical old man looks back on his idealistic youth), the picaresque is a loosely constructed, episodic narrative in which a young man of low birth goes out into the world to seek his fortune. Over the years he receives his "education" at the hands of various masters, all hypocrites, charlatans, and thieves. In Spain, where the genre developed, the most notable early example is *Lazarillo de Tormes* (1554). The appearance of young Lazaro anticipates his even more famous relative, Pablos, of Francisco Gómez de Quevedo's *La vida del Buscón* (*The Swindler, 1626*). The son of a thief and a witch, "El Buscón" begins his apprenticeship determined, like Dickens' Pip some two hundred years later, to become a gentlemen. In Germany the genre is represented by Hans Jacob Christoffel von Grimmelshausen's *Der abenteuerliche Simplicissimus* (*The Adventurous Simplicissimus*, 1669) (Simplicissimus also follows the path of the Prodigal Son), and in France by Lesage's *Histoire de Gil Blas de Santillane. (The Adventures of Gil Blas of Santillane* (1715–1735).

The Eighteenth Century

In general, modern interest in adolescence evolved from the new spirit of inquiry—essentially ego- or man-centered—ushered in with Locke, Newton, and Descartes. Specifically, it owes its shape to the two burgeoning forces of (primarily French) romanticism, largely confessional and autobiographical in tone, and the German *Humanitätsideal* later in the century. As much as anyone, Rousseau shaped what remains to a large degree our current understanding of adolescence. Concerned that "nothing is known about childhood," Rousseau wrote the novel *Emile* in 1762 as a corrective to those who, in his words, "keep looking for the man in the child, not thinking of what he is before he becomes a man." In outlining what he calls the natural development of the child, Rousseau characterizes adolescence as "the second birth," beginning at age sixteen with "The Age of Friendship" in which "we are born twice over; the first time for existence, the second for life; once as human beings and later as men or women." Whereas the child is androgynous, says Rousseau, the adolescent is distinctly male or female. Whereas childhood is characterized by self-love, adolescence marks the birth of self-esteem. And whereas the task of children is to study the physical world, like Robinson Crusoe on his island, adolescence provokes a new awareness of oneself as a moral being inextricably related with others in a network of social relations.

According to the prevailing convention of his time, however, Rousseau offers the development of the young woman within the novel of seduction. Influenced by *La vie de Marianne* (*Marianne's Life*), Marivaux's novel begun in 1731 of a young girl of unknown parentage and her initiation into love and society, and by Samuel Richardson's novel *Clarissa Harlowe* (1748), Rousseau wrote the epistolary *La nouvelle Héloïse*, (*The New Heloise*, 1761) one of the most influential novels of the century. Only vaguely resembling the medieval tale of Héloïse and Abélard to which the title refers, the novel offers an education on the purification of adolescent passion and on the spirit of female renunciation and sacrifice that Rousseau says should greet the end of those turbulent years.

By 1770 Rousseau had finished a new sort of inquiry into human nature, the autobiographical probing into the self. By way of answering "Who is Jean-Jacques Rousseau?" the philosopher devotes fully one-half of the *Confessions* (1781–1788) to an analysis of his own adolescence— "This period of my youth . . . of which I have the most confused idea." The result is a stunning portrait of youth recounted with all the advantages that the autobiographical mode affords. "I was restless, absent-minded, and dreamy; I wept and sighed and longed for a pleasure which I could not imagine but of which I nevertheless felt the lack," he writes, recounting the bewildering feelings that accompany sexual awakening. Of particular interest is the emotional climate—by turns idyllic and melancholic, intense, and incestuous—that surrounds the pivotal relationship of his youth, his liaison with Mme de Warens.

Reflecting the influence of Rousseau, Choderlos de Laclos produced the enormously popular *Les liaisons dangereuses* (*Dangerous Acquaintances*, 1782), another novel of education by seduction (Vicomte de Valmont seduces young Cécile and Mme de Merteuil seduces Cécile's young lover, Chevalier de Danceny); in 1787 an admirer of Rousseau, Bernardin de Saint-Pierre, launched the perhaps even more popular utopian novel, *Paul et Virginie* (*Paul and Virginia*), which sees youth as essentially innocent, adulthood essentially corrupt. In this work the idyllic life of the children on the island of Mauritius gives way to catastrophe as adulthood approaches and civilization intrudes.

In Germany the debate about human nature and human potential was filtered through two of literature's most famous adolescents, Johann Wolfgang Goethe's young Werther and Wilhelm Meister. In *Die Leiden des jungen Werthers* (*The Sorrows of Young Werther*, 1774), Goethe adopted the epistolary method begun by Richardson and developed by Rousseau to afford the fullest possible view of the psychological workings of the dark side of romanticism. Goethe was to describe the adolescent Werther as "a young man, gifted with deep, unspoiled sensitivity and penetrating insight, who loses himself in visionary dreams, undermines himself by empty speculations until finally, deranged by unhappy passions he experiences, especially an unending love, he puts a bullet in his head." Considered a document of the romantic *Sturm und Drang* movement of Johann Gottfried Herder, Goethe's novel influenced among other works Ugo Foscolo's novel *Le ultime lettere di Jacopo Ortis* (*The Last Letters of Jacopo Ortis*, 1802), and Chateaubriand's novel *René* (1802). In its portrait of death sought at the moment of consummation, it looks to André Gide and nineteenth-century romanticism.

The adolescent was also a vehicle for articulating Germany's particular brand of late-eighteenth-century bourgeois humanism and its concern with *Werden*, or "becoming." Is a coherent, integrated self possible? Such a question lies at the heart of Christoph Martin Wieland's *Agathon* (1766–1767), a novel in which the young hero seeks harmony between head and heart, spirit and flesh, a theme that would dominate the nineteenth century. The question is reiterated in Goethe's *Wilhelm Meisters Lehrjahre* (*Wilhelm Meister's Apprenticeship*, 1795–1796), the archetype of the *Bildungsroman* and one of the most influential novels ever written. "To put it in a word," remarks Wilhelm Meister, "to develop myself, entirely as I am, that was obscurely my wish and intention from childhood." It was also the aim of many an eighteenth-century hero. Appearing almost simultaneously with *Wilhelm Meister* was Johann Friedrich Hölderlin's *Hyperion* (1797–1799), the tale of a young romantic whose search for an ideal community ends in failure and in his own self-imposed isolation. In Novalis' *Heinrich von Ofterdingen* (*Henry of Ofterdingen: A Romance*, 1802), the fragment of an apprenticeship novel, the young hero finds redemption in the world of the imagination rather than in Wilhelm Meister's practical world.

The Nineteenth Century

From Chateaubriand's *René* to André Gide's novel *Les cahiers d'André Walter* (*The Notebook of André Walter*, 1891), the adolescent was an indispensable figure for exploring the romantic legacy and, in particular, the psychology of love and longing and the melancholic pursuit of unassailable—and inaccessible—purity. As did Werther before him, René came to embody the romantic *mal du siècle*, as "a young man," or so the narrator describes him, "with neither strength nor moral courage, who finds the source of his torments within himself." In its detailed understanding of both the attraction and tyranny of incestuous longing, it resembles other works of the century, notably Richard Wagner's opera *Siegfried* (1876), and even to a degree George Eliot's novel *The Mill on the Floss* (1860), which is usually classified as a *Bildungsroman*. Wertherism directly inspired Etienne Pivert de Sénancour's novel *Obermann* (1804), and Alexander Pushkin made the "superfluous young man" a theme of Russian literature with his novel in verse, *Evgeni Onegin* (*Eugene Onegin*, 1823–1831).

Similarly, Gustave Flaubert used the sexual awakening of youth in his novels—particularly the romantic passion of a young man for an older woman—to describe, as he phrased it, "the moral history, or rather the sentimental history, of the men of my generation." Beginning with *Mémoires d'un fou* (*Memoirs of a Madman*, 1836), Flaubert pursued the theme through *Novembre* (*November, 1840–1843*), and two versions of *L'éducation sentimentale* (*The Sentimental Education*, 1845, 1869).

In contrast, English romanticism may be represented by Byron's epic *Don Juan* (1819–1824), which owes its form to the epic of the Italian renaissance and the picaresque of Spain and to William Wordsworth's poem *The Prelude* (1799–1805), in which adolescence provides a map to "the growth of the poet's mind."

In an age dominated by introspection and self-revelation, mention should be made of the contribution of nineteenth-century autobiography in exploring the adolescent self. Tolstoy's *Detstvo* (1852), *Otrochestvo* (1854), and *Yunost'* (1857) (*Childhood, Boyhood*, and *Youth*) reflect his indebtedness to Rousseau, whose portrait the Russian artist wore around his neck at sixteen. Other examples include Ernest Renan's *Souvenirs d'enfance et de jeunesse* (1883) and George Moore's *Confessions of a Young Man* (1888).

The Nineteenth Century Bildungsroman

The theme of the youth who, though innocent of the tangles and snares of the world, must somehow navigate its dangers and come to an understanding of society and of the inward self is virtually ageless. In the hands of late-eighteenth-century writers, however, the theme became transformed into the pre-eminent novel of youth, the *Bildungsroman*. The *Bildungsroman* owed its genesis, of course, to the Germany of Goethe, Schiller, and Wilhelm von Humboldt, advocates of self-cultivation of the individual. But by the nineteenth century the genre dictated both in Germany and England the predominant shape of the novel. By turning his attention to adolescence, to the singular change that occurs between childhood and maturity, the artist could focus on the organic evolution of the self and thereby articulate the tension between limitless human potential and the unrelenting, prosaic demands of civilization.

The plot has been documented almost to the point of cliché. Constrained either intellectually or emotionally by the provinces in which he grows up (the hero is nearly always "he"), and at odds with the family who fails to understand him, the adolescent sets out for the city to make his fortune. After a series of encounters—both with life and with love—the hero comes to some sort of understanding of himself and of his environment.

The endless variations of the plot are reflected in such early and diverse works as Karl Philipp Moritz's *Anton Reiser* (1785–1790) and Jean Paul's *Titan* (1800–1803). Thomas Carlyle's *Sartor Resartus* (1833–1834) blends philosophy, mysticism, and the *Bildungsroman* genre to argue the interrelatedness of all things and to present a searching definition of the self. By following the progress of young Teufelsdröckh as he falls from the Edenic "happy season of childhood" into the despair that characterizes adolescence, Carlyle charts the severe diminishment of self that leads to spiritual rebirth, to the famous "Everlasting Yea." Adalbert Stifter's *Der Nachsommer* (*Indian Summer*, 1857) describes young Heinrich Dreudorf's return from the grand tour to the Rose House of his teacher, Risach, to demonstrate the wholeness that is, paradoxically, made possible only through constraint, through self-limitation. On the other hand, Gottfried Keller depicts—according to Martin Swales—the uneasiness that afflicts bourgeois idealism by tracing the deadening and psychologically dislocating process that attends the initiation of *Der grüne Heinrich* (*Green Henry*, 1854).

By the latter half of the century, a change takes place in the genre, which begins focusing with greater intensity on the dissonance between generations. Youth in conflict with familial authority is, of course, an ancient and well-documented theme. What is new, Susanne Howe points out, is the psychological intensity the writer brings to bear on the subject. Ivan Turgenev's *Otśy i deti* (*Fathers and Children*, 1862) for example, pits the adolescent nihilist against the romantic aristocracy. An example of what might be called an anti-*Bildungsroman*, George Meredith's *The Ordeal of Richard Feverel* (1859) documents the wrong sort of education a youth receives at the hands of his misogynistic father. Samuel Butler's *The Way of All Flesh* (1903) dramatizes the debilitating tyranny of the family.

The rise of naturalism, too, leaves its mark on the genre, as Stephen Crane uses a young woman's suicide to illustrate poverty's devastating effects on the soul (see *Maggie: A Girl of the Streets*, 1893). The extreme flexibility of the genre by the end of the century may be seen in Mark Twain's *The Adventures of Huckleberry Finn* (1884), whose episodic wanderings resemble those of the

pícaro rather than anything else. Huck's trip down the river is an occasion for
Twain's biting social satire and unforgettable gallery of rogues, an acid-etched
portrait of American civilization. Significantly, Huck rejects it.

The Twentieth Century

In retrospect it seems inevitable that the twentieth century should become
known as the century of adolescence. Romantics bequeathed an on-going impulse
for self-revelation; naturalism, a concern for understanding our social and economic conditioning. German pietism and its interest in the inner life and feeling,
as well as the subjectivism of Bergsonian thought, contributed to the growing
cult of the ego and increasing concern with "Moi." The adolescent becomes
the natural reflection of these concerns.

More to the point, however, is the burden the adolescent suddenly is asked
to bear. What Ihab Hassan remarks about the adolescent in American fiction
might well be true of the motif in general: by the twentieth century interest in
adolescence signals a transition from the idylls of innocence to the burden of
experience. In a century that has seen the unprecedented devastation of two
world wars before it was half over, the adolescent has come to symbolize our
doubts about the very viability of initiation into adulthood. Both Huck Finn's
rejection of society as well as Daisy Miller's "refusal to compromise" (Hassan's
phrase) are prophetic.

A few trends may be discerned early in the century. Henry James' technique
of making the adolescent the novel's center of consciousness (*What Maisie Knew*,
1897; *The Awkward Age*, 1899) and the attention given, for example, to Romain
Rolland's monumental *Jean-Christophe* (1904–1912), which won the Prix Fem-
ina-Vie heureuse, reflect increasing interest in adolescence for its own sake. In
1906 Hermann Hesse's novel *Unterm Rad* (*Under the Wheel*) foreshadows works
to come by pitting a sensitive youth against the crude educational system that
crushes him, as, for example, Ramón Pérez de Ayala would do in his school-
room novel, *AMDG* in 1910. And in a novel that challenges the romantic legacy,
Gabriel Miró's *Las cerezas del cementerio* (1910) shows how the romantic
sensibility of Felix Valdivia makes him incapable of seeing life as it is.

With the Great War came not so much a new sensibility as an intensification
of the sentiments of the prewar era. The last bastion of innocence before the
harsh ugliness of experience, adolescence invited one to linger indefinitely, as
does the hero of one of the most influential novels of the century, Alain-Fournier's
Le grand Meaulnes (*The Wanderer*, 1913). Following Fournier, Henry de Mont-
herlant's novel *La relève du matin* (1920) eulogizes adolescence, that singular
period during which, says the writer, the soul is born and dies. In postwar France
in general the novel was devoted to exploring adolescence, from Raymond
Radiguet's *Le diable au corps* (*The Devil in the Flesh*, 1923) to the works of
François Mauriac (*L'enfant chargé de chaînes* [*Young Man in Chains*, 1913];
La robe prétexte [*The Stuff of Youth*, 1914]; *La chair et le sang* [*Flesh and
Blood*, 1920]; *Le désert de l'amour* [*The Desert of Love*, 1925]) and Jacques de

Lacretelle (*La vie inquiète de Jean Hermelin*, 1920). In England, with D. H. Lawrence's *Sons and Lovers* (1913), considerable attention is given to the psychological, rather than the aesthetic, evolution of the self, and the ending of that novel reflects the general inconclusiveness of "awakening" and dawning maturity.

Thomas Mann's *Der Zauberberg* (*The Magic Mountain*, 1924), however, deserves special attention for its reflection of postwar disillusionment. Mann described his novel as "a story that, in a queer, ironical, almost parodistical way, attempts to renew the old German 'Bildungsroman' of the Wilhelm Meister type, this product of our great bourgeois epoch," and declared *Der Zauberberg* the story of an epoch before World War I. Hans Castorp does indeed undergo an education—a widening of sensibility and a growing philosophy of life—but it takes place in a rarified atmosphere, the sick world of the sanitorium. His education is unrelated to the world of social discourse—and world catastrophe— below. As Martin Swales points out, world history is ultimately more powerful in directing destiny than is the individual, and despite his humanistic gains, Castorp ends up as "cannon fodder."

The dark mood of the age is reflected in a bumper crop of 1929 classic novels, such as Alberto Moravia's *Gli indifferenti* (*The Time of Indifference*). The failure of adolescence to result in the rebirth of a Carlylean "Everlasting Yea" is seen in both William Faulkner's *The Sound and the Fury*, in which the self-enclosed, suicidal world of Quentin Compson is a metaphor for the alienated American South, and Jean Cocteau's *Les enfants terribles* (*The Holy Terrors*), whose adolescent world is dominated by necrophilia, incest, and the tyrannical dynamics of lordship and bondage—potent drugs that lock youth in an intensely imagined but singularly passive world marked by withdrawal and eventually death. In the 1930s James T. Farrell relied on the naturalistic tradition to show how the environment of Chicago gradually destroys Studs Lonigan, whose adolescence is spent in drinking, fighting, and hustling and whose adulthood is spent in trying to reclaim the days of his youth (see *Studs Lonigan: A Trilogy*, 1935).

By World War II and in the decades to follow, rejection of the adult world has taken two forms: the paralytic ennui of Holden Caulfield, cult figure for a generation, and the angry, violent rebellion of the Angry Young Men (see, for example, John Wain's novel *Strike the Father Dead*, 1962). Once stripped of the veneer of civilization, the adolescent comes to symbolize, not innocence, but the locus of all violence, and in William Golding's novel *Lord of the Flies* (1954) young Ralph stands "with filthy body, matted hair, and unwiped nose . . . [weeping] for the end of innocence, the darkness of man's heart."

It may be that the traditional (and largely male) novel of adolescence has reached something of a dead end. Nevertheless, the modern novel of female development has breathed new life into the genre. Arguing that within the process of cultural assimilation men and women are unequally socialized or constrained, recent feminist inquiry has turned to the ever proliferating works of confessional literature and adolescence by women to understand the dynamics of female disenfranchisement and to chart a newly emerging social consciousness. Old classics, for example Christina Stead's *The Man Who Loved Children* (1940), have been revived, and renewed interest in female sexual initiation has similarly resuscitated such works as Edith Wharton's *Summer* (1917) and Ellen Glasgow's *The Sheltered Life* (1932). With such works as Gwendolyn Brooks's *Maud Martha* (1953), Toni Morrison's *The Bluest Eye* (1970), and Maya Angelou's *I Know Why the Caged Bird Sings* (1970), black women writers have depicted a particular kind of disenfranchisement, one based on color, and lesbian literature has chronicled the alternative sexual awakening of female youth (see Rita Mae Brown's novel *Rubyfruit Jungle*, 1973).

It may also be true that the feminine fictions of female development—for example, Doris Lessing's *Children of Violence* sequence (1952–1969), which goes far beyond the adolescence represented in *Martha Quest* (1952)—have brought us anew to the threshold of maturity. It remains to be seen, however, whether we soften our obsession with adolescence and cross the threshold.

See also Family, Great Father, Incest, Marriage, Parents and Children, Psychoanalysis of the Self, Search for Father.

Selected Bibliography

Buckley, Jerome Hamilton. *Season of Youth: The Bildungsroman from Dickens to Golding*. Cambridge, Mass.: Harvard University Press, 1974.

Howe, Susanne. *Wilhelm Meister and His English Kinsmen: Apprentices to Life*. New York: Columbia University Press, 1930.

O'Brien, Justin. *The Novel of Adolescence in France*. New York: Columbia University Press, 1937.

Swales, Martin. *The German Bildungsroman from Wieland to Hesse*. Princeton, N.J.: Princeton University Press, 1978.

ANDREA GALE HAMMER

AFTERLIFE

Afterlife is a state of life after death either specific (limbo, hell, purgatory, the Celtic Brittia) or vague (the Greek Hades) where the dead live on in a neutral state (limbo), suffer punishment (the Greek Tartarus, hell), undergo purgation (purgatory), or experience bliss (the classical Elysium, paradise).

The Greek Afterlife

The early Greeks believed that at the moment of death one's psyche—a two-dimensional representation of the self, airlike but without flesh, bones, and sinews—would escape from the mouth and depart for Hades (literally, "unseen"), a shadowy realm usually beneath the earth and entered by a cave. Since myths tend to be confused and contradictory, a poetic tradition of the afterlife developed alongside the popular and assigned a specific location to Hades. In his epic poem *Odysseia* (*Odyssey*, 11.13–9; c. 8th century B.C.), Homer placed Hades in the far west, beyond Ocean, the stream surrounding the earth, in the misty and fog-bound land of the Cimmerians. Originally there was no corporeal punishment in Hades since the unsubstantial psyche could not experience physical pain. Of later origin is the tradition of punishment of the wicked after death in the bottomless pit of Tartarus deep within the earth. Although the end of Book 11 of the *Odyssey*, the first book of the dead in Western literature, recounts the punishment of Sisyphus, Tantalus, and Tityus, the section is a later addition. The Homeric view of the psyche as a noncorporeal second self would make the psyche impervious to physical pain (*Odyssey* 11.218–22). In addition to Hades, there was Elysium (also known as the Islands of the Blessed and the Fortunate Islands), where favored mortals went after death. Elysium was an earthly paradise where there was neither rain nor snow but only the refreshing breezes of the west wind (*Odyssey* 4.561–68).

A characteristic of the afterlife found in *Odyssey* 11 is grouping by class, a concept on which Virgil elaborated in his epic poem the *Aeneis* (*Aeneid*, 19 B.C.) and which Dante perfected in his epic poem *La divina commedia* (*The Divine Comedy*, c. 1320). In the *Odyssey* the heroes of the Trojan War were grouped separately; similarly, the women who died for love. Even in the interpolated ending of *Odyssey* 11, the damned occupied a separate quarter of Hades.

The afterlife that Plato described at the end of his dialogue, *Politeia* (*The Republic*, c. 380 B.C.), in the Myth of Er, was considerably more detailed than Homer's. After death the souls proceeded to the meadow of judgment. The just ascended for 1,000 years of happiness; the unjust descended to Tartarus for 1,000 years of pain and purgation if they were guilty of murder, betrayal, impiety, or tyranny. Thus Plato extended the notion of Tartarus to include a place of purgation. After the 1,000-year period of bliss or purgation, the souls journeyed to the pillar of light, the axis on which the heavenly system revolved with the earth in the center. They looked upon the light, which took the form of the spindle of Necessity, causing all the orbits to revolve, with staff and hook of adamant and a whorl of adamant and other material; as a combination of the changing and the unchanging, the spindle suggested that choice was a combination of chance and free will. The souls were given a view of the cosmos from the outside: a model of concentric rings with the fixed stars, Saturn, Jupiter, Mars, Mercury, Venus, the sun, and the moon revolving around the earth. Next the souls saw the three fates: Lachesis, Clotho, and Atropos. They came before Lachesis to choose their next form of life; all kinds of future lives were available, including rebirth as an animal. Once they chose, they proceeded to Clotho, who ratified their choice, and then to Atropos, who made it irreversible. Finally they travelled to the plain of oblivion, where they drank from the river Lethe and forgot their previous existence.

The Roman Afterlife

The afterlife depicted in book 6 of Virgil's *Aeneid* was more complex than Homer's Hades. Virgil's was an imaginative interpretation of the cliched "house of Hades.'' The Virgilian underworld was a shell of a house with a threshold and doors leading to an interior of ''unsubstantial realms'' (*inania regna*) and a road leading to the river Acheron, one of the four rivers of the underworld— the others being Cocytus, Phlegethon, and Styx. Virgil's was a highly stratified afterlife with separate regions for the damned and the blessed and specific types occupying specially designated areas. Outside of Hades proper were children who died in infancy, those unjustly condemned to death, and suicides—all encircled nine times by the river Styx. Other sections included the Fields of Mourning, where unhappy lovers dwelled in thickets of myrtle that probably symbolized their illicit passion; the fields of the heroes; Tartarus, which Aeneas did not see but which was described as a city surrounded by three walls, guarded by the fury Tisiphone, and encircled by the river Phlegethon. In Tartarus sins of fraud, disrespect for one's parents, avarice, murder, waging an injust war, bribery, and incest were punished. Finally Aeneas came to Elysium, a place of laurel groves and dazzling light, where he met his father Anchises. Elysium was also the dwelling place of priests and artists, as well as of certain heroes who suffered wounds while defending their country.

The Medieval Afterlife

Medievel descriptions of hell include many of the same motifs found in the classical afterlife: the guide accompanying the traveller (Michael the Archangel accompanying St. Paul in the third century *Visio Sancti Pauli* [*Vision of St. Paul*], just as the Sibyl accompanied Aeneas in the *Aeneid*); Cerberus as hound of hell; physical torments; the foul smelling river; grouping according to type of sin and punishment suited to the nature of the offense (e.g., immersion to the knees in a foul river for slander, to the navel for adultery and fornication).

Numbers, especially seven, three, and multiples of three, played an important part in the medieval hell: a furnace with seven separate flames (*Vision of St. Paul*), St. Brendan's nine pains of hell, the 144,000 torments that Michael told Paul existed in hell. The medieval hell was more lurid than anything depicted in classical literature. The tortures were bizarre, often sexual. The descriptions of Satan were grotesque; in one account he was a black beast with a hundred hands, each hand with twenty fingers and lancelike nails of iron.

Although the chief difference between purgatory and hell was one of temporal as opposed to eternal punishment, some descriptions of purgatory such as *Tractatus de purgatorio Sancti Patricii* (*St. Patrick's Purgatory*) (12th century) are as horrifying as those of hell. The medieval depiction of paradise was similar to that of the Garden of Eden, probably because it was commonly believed that the location of paradise would coincide with the scene of man's creation. Thus the Tree of the Knowledge of Good and Evil, originally in Eden, was also in paradise. Located in the east, paradise was portrayed as a fragrant garden with jewelled houses and rich fruit; it was situated on a mountaintop where the Tree of Life was watered by the four rivers of Eden: Phison, Gehon, Tigris, and Euphrates.

The Dantean Afterlife

By the time of Dante (1265–1321), the tradition of an afterlife based on hierarchical grouping and correlation of crime and punishment, with the degree and nature of punishment determined by the seriousness of the sin, was well established. Dante's outstanding achievement in the *Comedy's Inferno* (*Hell*) was his synthesis of the classical underworld and the Christian hell within a coherent system. It was a two-part synthesis consisting of mingling characters from classical mythology (e.g., Ulysses, Chiron the centaur, Minos the judge of the underworld, Charon the ferryman of the dead, Cerberus) with historical figures; and adapting Aristotle's threefold classification of evil dispositions (not really sins)—incontinence (uncontrolled appetite), violence or bestiality (perverted appetite), fraud or malice (abuse of reason)—to a Christian context where sins of incontinence were the least serious and those of fraud and malice the most serious. Sins of incontinence (lust, gluttony, avarice, prodigality, and anger) were more numerous, and therefore less serious, than sins of violence; thus they were punished in upper hell. More serious than sins of incontinence, but less serious than fraud and malice, were sins of violence, which Dante subdivided into violence against humankind; against the self (suicide); against one's substance (profligacy); and against God (blasphemy), nature (sodomy), and art (usury). The most serious, and therefore least numerous, sins were those of fraud (e.g., seduction, flattery, divination, graft, hypocrisy, and theft) and malice (treachery and betrayal) because they were peculiar to humankind and because they were deliberately intended and deliberately carried out. Thus sins of fraud and malice were punished in lower hell.

To explain the origin of hell and purgatory, Dante invented a myth at the end of the *Inferno*. At the time of creation, sea and land had not been separated. When Satan fell, the land occupying the Southern Hemisphere, fearing contact with Satan, fled to the Northern Hemisphere as the ocean flowed in to fill the void. The bowels of the earth rushed to the south and formed Mount Purgatory, leaving a cavity in the middle of the earth that became hell. Thus the Northern Hemisphere was the hemisphere of land; the Southern of water.

One must conceive of Dante's hell as a conical cavity in the center of the earth and consisting of nine circles of decreasing size, in all but the first of which a specific sin is punished. There is no real punishment in the first circle (limbo), the abode of the virtuous pagans; their greatest sorrow is that they can never see God. But the punishments in circles two through nine follow Dante's law of symbolic retribution, in which the punishment reflects the nature of the sin. The lustful are tossed forever in a howling wind; the violent are immersed in blood; grafters are sunk in boiling pitch and flatterers in excrement. Sodomites, blasphemers, and usurers, all of whom have sinned against nature, are relegated to a burning plain where blasphemers lie face down, usurers squat, and sodomites roam unceasingly.

In his *Purgatorio* (*Purgatory*) Dante envisaged purgatory as a mountain rising from an island antipodal to Jerusalem and consisting of an antepurgatory and seven terraces or ledges, on each of which one of the seven capital sins was purged. Common to these seven sins was the misuse of love; misdirected love (pride, envy, wrath); insufficient love (sloth); and excessive love (avarice, gluttony, lust).

Although the earthly paradise was on top of Mount Purgatory, it was not the abode of God, who dwelled in the empyrean, the tenth and outermost sphere. Before Dante could proceed through the nine heavens (Moon, Mercury, Venus, Sun, Mars, Jupiter, Saturn, Fixed Stars, Primum Mobile) to the empyrean, he had to drink of the waters of Lethe to erase all memory of former sins. The *Paradiso* (*Paradise*), which depicts Dante's ascent to the empyrean, culminates in his vision of the Celestial Rose with the blessed seated on its petals, and finally of the Trinity as three circles of the same circumference but different colors.

Common Features of the Afterlife

One should expect a certain amount of repetition in accounts of the afterlife, regardless of the era or culture that is represented. Like any archetype, the afterlife is made up of a limited number of recurring images and details that have evolved into literary conventions and symbols. The following motifs are common to descriptions of the afterlife:

1. Islands. The other world was often an island: the Islands of the Blessed, which the Romans identified with the Canary Islands; Dante's Purgatory; the Celtic Brittia, the home of the dead, which was thought to be the Isle of Man or possibly Denmark; Leuke (the "white island") in classical mythology where some mythographers said Achilles went after death.

2. Rivers. There can be rivers in the afterlife whether it is located below or above the earth: the four subterranean rivers of the classical underworld, the four rivers of Eden and paradise. The Celtic *sid* was an underground Elysium with streams flowing with wine and mead.

3. Bridges. The bridge was not a feature of the classical underworld, but it is found in Persian mythology, where the souls crossed over to the other world on a bridge that was broad for the good, narrow for the wicked. In the medieval tradition, the bridge was one of the trials in the afterlife where, in some accounts, the souls must walk across a bridge spanning a river of boiling pitch. The reefs of stone spanning the eighth circle of Dante's *Inferno* resembled drawbridges connecting the moats surrounding a castle.

4. Mountains. In the Summerian *Epic of Gilgamesh* (c. 2000 B.C.), the way to Kur, the underworld, was through a mountain. Dante's purgatory was a mountain; the medieval paradise was atop a mountain.

5. Journeys. Alone (Gilgamesh); with a guide (Aeneas and the Sibyl, Virgil and Dante); by ship (Odysseus, the medieval voyage to the other world).

6. Mist and fog. The land of the Cimmerians was fogbound and perpetually without

sunlight. Dante began his descent on the evening of Good Friday in the "brown air" (*l'aere bruno*).

7. Cities. Virgil conceived of Tartarus as a city; Dante depicted lower hell as a city with moat and drawbridge. In *Paradiso* 30 Dante was given a vision of the city of God. The motif ultimately derived from the tradition of the other world as a kingdom with its own rulers (Hades and Persephone in Greek mythology).

8. Obstacles. Shades and mythological creatures menaced Aeneas; three beasts terrorized Dante.

9. The waste land (*terre gaste*). The waste land tradition, in which a knight must traverse a waste land to reach the Grail chapel, while not directly associated with the afterlife, includes infernal motifs such as the desolate landscape, the narrow bridge, the mist barrier, the terrible river, the ferryman's boat, and so forth.

The Post-Dantean Tradition

The portrait of the afterlife, begun by the ancients, culminated in Dante, whose extraordinary visual imagination and synthesizing power enabled him to depict an afterlife that has never been rivaled. Subsequent writers have drawn on the archetypes and conventions of the afterlife without adding much to them. Even those who depict the present as hell are harking back to Dante, who, by a clever manipulation of time at the end of the *Inferno*, limited Dante the pilgrim's stay in hell to a twenty-four-hour period, suggesting that he witnessed a typical day, the only difference being that it was rendered allegorically. Even Goethe's use of heaven as the scene of a debate between the Lord and Mephistopheles in *Faust*, part 1 (1808), was not particularly original; nor was the discussion of hell, heaven, the life force, and the superman in the third act of Shaw's *Man and Superman* (1903), commonly known as "Don Juan in Hell." Aristophanes initiated the practice of having intellectual discussions in the afterlife in his comedy *Batrachoi* (*The Frogs*, 405 B.C.), where the underworld was the scene of a debate between the tragedians Euripides and Aeschylus. Once a tradition is established, it can be recreated (Elysium in Gluck's opera, *Orfeo ed Euridice* [*Orpheus and Eurydice*, 1762]), or burlesqued (Hades in Offenbach's operetta, *Orphée aux Enfers* [*Orpheus in the Underworld*, 1858]). It can also be reinterpreted, as some modern writers have done, who view the twentieth century as a waste land and who use otherworldly motifs and images to portray a world of cultural and moral sterility.

In his poem *The Waste Land* (1922), T. S. Eliot described a modern inferno inhabited by the living dead who discarded the past, reducing it to "a heap of broken images" that are reflected in the echoes from earlier literature that reverberate throughout the work. Eliot drew on such conventions as the infernal city (London); the infernal river (Thames); grouping by class and type (the Thames Maidens as betrayed women, the habitués of the pub); the collective dead (the crowds flowing over London Bridge); the individual dead (Madame Sosostris, the typist, the young man carbuncular, Mr. Eugenides); the mist barrier ("brown fog"); the journey (from London to the banks of the Ganges); the knowledge derived from visiting the other world ("Give, sympathize, control").

In his novel *La nausée* (*Nausea*, 1938), Sartre called his infernal city Bouville ("Mud town"). Sartre inverted the Dantean pattern of descent/ascent as well as the traditional distinctions between hell, purgatory, and heaven by having his hero, Roquentin, ascend by tram to a park on top of a hill (a combination of purgatory, heaven, and hell), where he came to grips with the agonizing question of existence, rejecting the past and realizing that there was nothing before existence.

Ezra Pound's epic poem "Hell Cantos," cantos 14–16 in *A Draft of XXX Cantos* (1930), offers a world perverted by politicians, purists, and profiteers. Pound's is a modern hell governed by a Dantean logic by which those who have inverted the natural order are punished accordingly. Politicians wear their faces on their backsides; purists who scorn colloquial language sport soiled collars around their legs; profiteers drink blood sweetened with excrement; betrayers of language plunge jewels in the mud, howling when they find them unstained.

T. S. Eliot's play *The Cocktail Party* (1949) extended the living hell into the overly civilized realm of the drawing room where "hell is oneself" (specifically one's loveless self) and where salvation consisted of accepting the world or divesting oneself of it. If hell is oneself, hell can also be other people—a point Sartre made in his play *Huis clos* (*No Exit*, 1944) in which three people were doomed to a hell of repetition because of their moral apathy. Although Sartre set the action in the afterlife, it was merely to show that people in bad faith would act the same way in any mode of existence. Unlike Dante's dead, who knew the future, Sartre's knew the past as well as the present, since they could see the living. However, they could not prophesy, since they had no future. Their future was their past, which they must continually relive—a punishment that is thoroughly Dantean in principle.

To delineate a world in a state of entropy, losing moral as well as physical energy, Thomas Pynchon in his novel *V* (1963) inverted the traditional motifs, making the infernal river a sewer and transforming the mist barrier into the "brown light" in which "bodies milled." The shades were people so enamored of the inanimate that they behaved like automata. Paris in 1913 was a waste land parched by lack of rain, its decadence complementing its desiccation. In his novel *The Crying of Lot 49* (1965), Pynchon continued to explore the implications of the world as waste land, now locating the *terre gaste* in California, where the disaffected despaired of conventional means of communication and resorted to an underground system.

Unlike hell, purgatory and paradise have had only a minor influence on modern writers. Dante's *Purgatorio* was the point of departure for Eliot's conversion poem *Ash Wednesday* (1930), in which the speaker underwent a purgation of sense and spirit, suffering emptiness and detachment until the process had been completed. Eliot incorporated the Dantean themes of humility (where the pilgrim, now the penitent, must descend before ascending, as in the *Purgatorio* where one must start at the shore before climbing the mountain); the paradox of haste (souls must hasten to climb the mountain yet must not be too hasty); and the need to remain undistracted (the souls were distracted by Dante's shadow; the speaker in Eliot's poem must learn "to sit still"). In the poem *Four Quartets* (1943), Eliot offered an alternative to life as hell/purgatory through a synthesis of time and eternity, death and life, present and past, love of God and poetry ("this Calling") so that ultimately "the fire and the rose are one"; and human and divine love, natural and spiritual love, are inseparable.

The most famous portrayal of purgatory in modern literature occurs in Thornton Wilder's play *Our Town* (1938), the third act of which was set in purgatory, where the dead bide their time, waiting to enter heaven. First they must lose their memory of the past, as did the souls in Plato's *Republic*, when they drank of the waters of forgetfulness (as Dante also did at the end of the *Purgatorio*). In *Our Town* the dead knew the present, since they were on stage with the living; they also knew the past, but not the future. They were awaiting their future— eternity.

Most contemporary versions of Elysium and paradise are parodies or inversions. In Thomas Mann's novelle *Der Tod in Venedig* (*Death in Venice*, 1912) Aschenbach's infatuation with the youth Tadzio caused him to view reality mythically, confusing a plague-ridden Venice with Elysium. In his novel *Free Fall* (1959), William Golding inverted the Dantean tradition; his solipsistic hero was Sammy Mountjoy of Paradise Hill, whose Beatrice was a neurotic who finally went mad. Golding created an even greater contrast between the two Beatrices. Just as Dante first saw Beatrice dressed in red at the age of nine, Sammy saw Beatrice Ifor at a red light when both were nineteen.

The Popular Afterlife

The afterlife featured in much fiction and drama is not so much classical or Christian as it is an anomalous other world in which the dead live on and which they frequently leave to involve themselves in human affairs because (1) the author is exploring the tension between illusion and reality by having the living and the dead intermingle (Strindberg's play *Spöksonaten* [*The Ghost Sonata*, 1907] Jean Anouilh's play *Eurydice* [*Point of Departure*, 1941]. Robert Nathan's novel, *Portrait of Jennie*, 1940); (2) the author is exploiting the romantic potential of a relationship between a mortal and a ghost (R. A. Dick's novel *The Ghost and Mrs. Muir*, 1945) or the comic possibilities of a ghost that can only be seen by the protagonist (Noel Coward's play *Blithe Spirit*, 1941); (3) the author is challenging the accepted view of the afterlife as a place of perfect justice by placing murderers in heaven and the good in hell (Elmer Rice's play *The Adding Machine*, 1923) and by having hell go on strike because heaven is pardoning sinners (Max Frisch's play *Biedermann und die Brandstifter* [*Biedermann and the Firebugs*, 1958]; (4) the author is using the dead as a means of dramatic foreshadowing in order to foretell the fate of the living (Caesar's apparition to Brutus in Shakespeare's *Julius Caesar*, act 4, sc. 3 [c. 1599]; the ghosts that appear at the end of Shakespeare's *Richard III*, act 5, sc. 3 [1591–1594]). Since the dead have traditionally had prophetic powers, authors often use them for that purpose. The prophesying shade is as old as Homer. Significantly, in *Odyssey* II, the shade of Teiresias foretold Odysseus' further adventures as well as the circumstances of his death in the same narrative context as Odysseus' voyage to the land of the dead, thereby establishing a connection between the afterlife and the prophetic powers of those dwelling there. Thus the reason for a mortal's journey to the other world was to acquire knowledge of self and ultimately an appreciation of the divine order.

See also: Dance of Death, Death and the Individual, Demonic Musician and the Soulbird, Descent into Hell.

Selected Bibliography

Knight, W. J. Jackson. *Elysion: On Ancient Greek and Roman Beliefs concerning a Life after Death*. New York: Barnes & Noble, 1970.

Matthews, Honor. *The Hard Journey: The Myth of Man's Rebirth*. New York: Barnes & Noble, 1968.

Owen, D.D.R. *The Vision of Hell: Infernal Journeys in Medieval French Literature*. New York: Barnes & Noble, 1971.

Patch, Howard Rollin. *The Other World, According to Descriptions in Medieval Literature*. Cambridge: Harvard UP, 1950.

BERNARD F. DICK

ALCHEMY

There are three kinds of alchemist: (1) the scientist, (2) the mountebank, and (3) the mystic. This is not to say that elements of all three classes may not be found in the same individual, a wizard-figure such as the Arthurian Merlin has evolved into, as in Mark Twain's *A Connecticut Yankee in King Arthur's Court* (satiric novel, 1889). The scientific alchemists were, for the most part, very poor and were contemptuously called "puffers" for their grimy use of the bellows to fire their furnaces. As the stakes were large—the changing of "base" metals into "noble" ones (silver, gold)—these puffers concealed their formulas, equations, and proceedings under a veil of symbols. They delighted also in the use of conundrums, fables, and enigmas. One of the earliest known alchemical enigmas is provided in the Formula of the Crab in the Greek writings of Zosimos of Panopolis (third or fourth century A.D.) and represents a putative method for making imitation gold. The second symbol of this cryptic Formula has been said to refer to "the all," or universal matter; the crab to fixation; the tenth symbol to the Philosopher's Egg; with the appropriate ending, "Blessed is he who gets understanding." With the advent of Robert Boyle and the publication of his *The Sceptical Chymist; or Chymico-physical Doubts and Paradoxes* (1661), the Aristotelian "four elements" and the Paracelsian "Tria Prima" (three "hypostatical principles''), upon which the puffers had raised the edifice of their practice, were routed from the stage. According to Boyle, "The four Elements, or the three Hypostatical Principles, do not evince what they are alledg'd to prove.'' With that, scientific alchemy became modern-day chemistry.

The mountebank alchemists were quick to see their chance in so ill-defined an area as pre-Boylian chemistry, whether this entailed astrology, clairvoyance, necromancy, palmistry, counterfeiting, or mesmerism, all of these as Egyptian as alchemy in origin. The object was to prey upon susceptible minds. A good historical example of the mountebank alchemist was Giuseppe Balsamo (Cagliostro), born at Palermo June 8, 1743, who, after picking up the rudiments of chemistry and medicine while assistant to the apothecary of the monastery of Caltagirone, wandered in Greece, Egypt, and Asia, then married Lorenza Feliciani, a very pretty twenty-year-old, whom he passed off as really sixty while peddling his "elixir of immortal youth.'' Cagliostro borrowed the word "elixir'' from the alchemists.

The mystical alchemist, although not always identified as such, is the most literarily germane of the three; but only because the mountebank or rogue alchemist is not really an alchemist, literally or metaphorically. The mystical alchemist is often referred to as esoteric, one of the relatively few guardians of "the secret.'' Since *Khem* was the ancient name for Egypt, the country of the dark soil, the biblical Land of Ham, and *al* is the Arabian definite article, Egypt is frequently held to have given birth to alchemy, the "art of the dark country.'' The alchemists of the Middle Ages learned their art from the Arabs in Spain and southern Italy, who in turn had adopted it from the Greeks, who again had developed it on Egyptian soil in the fourth century B.C. Thus, alchemy extends its roots into the tombs and labyrinths of Egyptian religion, with its aten-solification myths and monstrous hybrid gods and goddesses. Indeed, the Hellenistic figure of the alchemically tutelary Hermes Trismegistus, who is the model for the medieval Mercurius, derives ultimately from the Egyptian Thoth, god of mathematics, science, and writing. Hermes/Mercury/Thoth, combining the dual roles of messenger to the gods and divine sponsor of writing, is of key importance to the understanding of Hermetic, or alchemical, creative writing.

Esoteric Alchemy

As a mystical system of transubstantiation (the code formula being "to change lead into gold''), esoteric alchemy's apparent interest in metallurgy translated to apocalyptic symbolism whereby the four elements were sublimated into a species of Aristotelian *prima materia* (prime matter) or quintessence (fifth essence) by means of a potent transmuting agent, known variously as *aqua vitae* (water of life), *elixir vitae* (elixir of life), *filius philosophorum* (the son of the philosophers), and the Philosopher's Stone. This "medicine of the metals'' was held capable of curing the imagined diseases of the base metals, thereby ennobling them to the perfect metals, silver and gold. In alchemy there were seven bodies: sun (gold), moon (silver), Mars (iron), Mercury (quicksilver), Saturn (lead),

Jupiter (tin), and Venus (copper). As a sophisticated and mystical Theory of Humors, alchemical metallurgy, then, may be appreciated as a means of curing life itself by enhancing or ennobling one's character or nature. The secret understanding of the word "metal" was that it joined two ideas that were key to esoteric alchemy: "beyond" (*meta*) and "other" (*allon*). The "other" is the world of phenomena; what lies "beyond" is the fifth essence, variously interpreted. One improves one's mettle (metal) by seriously applying the principles of esoteric alchemy to one's life.

As a mystical discipline, alchemy attracted to itself and absorbed whatever life had to offer, including the "Doctrine of the Two Contraries," which was later refined to the "Theory of the Four Elements." Alchemy's intent was to unite contraries and to "cure" all base combinations of the "four elements" "allo"-pathically. As the resolved harmony of all things, the "fifth being" (quintessence) is, inter alia, hermaphroditic, spiritually speaking, and the "Sons of Hermes" are, ideally, simultaneously also the "Daughters of Hermes." In Jungian terminology the *animus* (male principle) and *anima* (female principle) are at one (at-onement, or atonement for Christian esoteric alchemists). The paradoxical result of such unity is not licentiousness but the perfect chastity of sincere virginity.

Neo-Platonism and Genesis appealed to the alchemists, because in their view the substance of this complex of doctrines amounted to not only the four Aristotelian elements but the Mosaic *prima materia* (the "nothing" of Genesis), itself sublimated (creation humanly perfected) so as to accord with Divine Omneity. To organize phenomena properly was an act of visionary piety. What was thus "precipitated" Paracelsus called the *Archeus* (seminal Reason or the Logos), familiar enough today to the initiated in archetypal literary criticism. In addition to Neo-Platonism, Pythagoreanism played a key role in esoteric alchemy. The origin and interpretation of the Cosmos might be expressed numerically. Number came into alchemical prominence partly from the Greek schools of thought and partly also from the doctrines of the Hebrew Cabbala. There was a cabbalistic system of expressing words in numerical terms, according to which, for example, the name of gold had the value $(1 \times 2 \times 3 \times 4)8$, or 192. Had they possessed a knowledge of atomic weights, alchemical mystics would no doubt have pointed out that this number falls within a few units of the atomic weight of gold (196.9665). Cabbalism also maintained the ancient importance of the number four, in such mystical quaternions as the corners of the earth, the elements, the winds, spirits, guardian angels, and rivers of Paradise. Among certain Jewish Gnostics, this quaternion extended even to the Godhead, with the addition to the more traditional Trinity of Barbhe-Eloha, God the Mother. In American literary criticism, the New Critics, though they often thought of themselves as Aristotelian, were, in effect, esoteric alchemists in their close attention to numerical symbology. The contemporary Yale Critics are squarely in that camp, some (J. Hillis Miller) with and others (Harold Bloom) without tellingly Christian interpretations.

Classical Antiquity and the Middle Ages

Ovid, in his epic poem *Metamorphoses* (c. A.D. 2–17), "transmuted" the lead of apparently idle stories into the gold of moral and psychological allegory; but his Roman outlook caused him to condemn the Egyptian implications of the Hermaphroditus-Salmacis story. Hermes and Aphrodite, at their transformed son's implorations, poison the nymph's pool with an *incastum medicamen* (unholy drug), thus projecting an Ovidian verdict on today's splinter, esoteric, alchemical, psychedelic literary cults. They ruinously induce the loss of manhood. Largely influenced by the esoteric alchemical thinking of Averrhoës (1126–1198), the hermeneutical critics of the Middle Ages and early Renaissance, among them St. Thomas Aquinas (1225–1274), Dante Alighieri (1265–1321), and Giovanni Boccaccio (1313–1375), perceived Ovid's mode of writing to be not only legitimate ("figurative") but, indeed, tactfully prudent, "because thereby divine truths are the better hidden from the unworthy" (St. Thomas Aquinas, *Summa theologica* [c. 1266–1274], "The Nature and Domain of Sacred Doctrine," Ninth Article).

The Philosopher's Stone appears in many disguises in the Middle Ages, most notably that of the grail which, nonetheless, sometimes occurs as both stone and grail, as in the heroic romance *Parzival* (1210) by Wolfram von Eschenbach. Here Wolfram presents, by way of the hermit's account, "gallant Templars" who "serve the Grail at Monsalväsch" (bk. 9, lines 234–35; trans. Jessie L. Weston, 1894). "Men call it *Lapis Exilis*—by its magic the wondrous bird, / The Phoenix, becometh ashes, and yet doth such virtue flow / From the stone, that afresh it riseth renewed from the ashes' glow" (9.240–42). "And this stone all men call the Grail" (9.250). The Gnostic, Manichaean, Albigensian, and Catharist implications of Wolfram's grail mythology are made clear by Leonardo Olschki in his *Il castello del Re Pescatore e i suoi misteri nel Conte del Graal di Chrétien di Troyes* (1961; translated by J. A. Scott and edited by Eugene Vinaver in 1966 as *The Grail and Its Mysteries*). The "daily bread" of these "grail knights" is the phenomenological world that they "supersubstantiate" into their own brand of Eucharist or *epiousia* (Gr. for *panis quotidianus*, daily bread).

In his contribution to the didactic poem *Roman de la rose* (*The Romance of the Rose*, c. 1275) entitled "Nature," Jehan de Meung subordinates the Phoenix (96) to "God's command" (109) and "Dame Nature" (110). As for Alchemy (184–192): "Or if of alchemy Art learn / So much that he can metals turn / To varied colors, ne'er can he / Work them so that they changéd be / Unless he by his skill may lead / Them back to that whence they proceed; / Not working deftly till he die / Can pierce the subtle mystery / Of Nature."

But the non-Catholic esoteric alchemists sought not to complement nature anagogically but to destroy it and replace it apocalyptically with the congenial artifice of a private or "humanistic" ideal. This is why Dante, in part 1 of his epic poem *La divina commedia* (*The Divine Comedy*, c. 1320), places Tiresias, "who by his arts/ succeeded in changing himself from man to man" (*Inferno*, 20.40–41), damnable as he is, much higher in Hell than the alchemists (29; see line 137: "Che falsai li metalli con alchìmia"; "who falsified the metals with alchemy," in the words of Capocchio). The altered Tiresias is still Tiresias. He corrupted his nature but did not, unlike the alchemists, radically attack the very principle of identity. Geoffrey Chaucer agrees with the severity of Dante's judgment (*The Canon's Yeoman's Tale*, *The Canterbury Tales* [c. 1380–1400], lines 1476–79): "For whoso maketh God his adversarie,/ As for to werken any thynge in contrarie/ Of his wil, certes, never shal he thryve,/ Though that he multiplie terme of his lyve." Multiply is an alchemical term referring to the transmutation of a base metal into a noble.

The Renaissance, Reformation, and Seventeenth Century

The significance of Paracelsus (Theophrastus Bombastus von Hohenheim, 1493–1541) to alchemy lies not in his quest for gold but for a universal panacea. This is set forth in the *Opus paragranum* (1565, published posthumously). The circumstances of his vagabond existence, however, invested this Swiss alchemist with an aura of diabolic resourcefulness and dangerous subterfuge. How else could a man so arrogant and insolent have survived for long? It behooved an arrant mountebank such as he was popularly perceived to be to have the security of a pact with the devil. So it was that Samuel Butler observed of him in his satirical poem *Hudibras* (1663–1678): Bombastus kept a devil's bird/ Shut in the pommel of his sword,/ That taught him all the cunning pranks/ Of past and future mountebanks.

Unlike his monkish namesake Roger Bacon (1214–1294), who believed in the Philosopher's Stone and was hardly sympathetic to the notion of a precipitated universal panacea, or nostrum, Francis Bacon (1561–1626) declared himself, in his *Instauratio magna* (1605-never completed, *The Great Instauration*), a scientific treatise of more than six books, "a true priest of sense (from which all knowledge in nature must be sought, unless men mean to go mad." Of the alchemists, he wrote (*Novum organum* [second part of *Instauratio magna*], 64, 1620): "through the premature hurry of the understanding to leap or fly to universals and principles of things, great danger may be apprehended." Sir Thomas Browne went off on a different tack, one entirely in keeping with the mysticism of esoteric alchemy. In the anthropological tract *The Garden of Cyrus* (part 3, 1658), he noted with approbation the theophantic work of "the Egyptian embalmers" and "the cruciated character of Trismegistus, or handed crosses" (corpse's hands placed to form an 'x'). What he called "decussation" (mystical significance of the Roman numeral X), a pattern repeated endlessly and universally in nature, fascinated him: the bottom part betokening "Nullity," the upper "Omneity." In part 4 he comments on Justin Martyr's "Learned Observations of Egypt, where he might obviously behold the Mercurial characters, the handed crosses, and other mysteries," "Cabalisticall Technology," "Cabalisticall Doctors," and "the Oneirocriticall Masters." In the posthumously published ethical tract *Christian Morals* (section 15, 1716), Sir Thomas discusses "the *Archetypal Sun*, or the Light of God, able to illuminate intellectual Eyes, and make unknown visions." In part 1 of the autobiographical religious meditation *Religio medici* (*The Religion of a Doctor*, 1643), having protested against Paracelsus' "receipt to make a man without conjunction" (cf. today's test-tube baby), he goes on to say, "I am half of the opinion that Antichrist is the Philosopher's Stone in Divinity." Ben Jonson had already reprised these esoteric alchemical motifs, and more, in his brilliant satiric comedy *The Alchemist* (1610); for example, the cabbalistic hermaphroditism expressed by Epicure Mammon in the phrase "Madam Rabbi."

In religion Martin Luther (1483–1546) made monergistic grace the Philosopher's Stone, the panacea. Robert Browning was to explore the outrageous implications of such reductionism in his poem "Johannes Agricola in Meditation" (1836). The Catholic view, that of synergistic grace, is presented by Christopher Marlowe's play, *The Tragical History of Dr. Faustus* (1604): "See, see where Christ's blood streams in the firmament!/ One drop would save my soul—half a drop: ah, my Christ!" Faustus is not saved because, despite the available reservoir of redemptive grace, he does not will to be saved. Velleity, or impulse, is not good enough. It is, by its very nature, quaquaversal.

Such idle metastasis is illustrated in Shakespeare's tragedy, *Romeo and Juliet* (c. 1596). Mercutio is alchemical in that one of the alchemists' favorite metals for "multiplication" was mercury (quicksilver). What Mercutio does by means of his wit is multiply variations on a thesis in the manner of the Scholastic Philosophers, only much more quickly than they. The metaphysical wit of John Donne was also mercurial. In the sardonic poem "Loves Alchymie" (c. 1600), Donne appraises sexual love as the panacea, the *elixir vitae* proposed by the "New Physic" of Paracelsus (in vogue c. 1600), and finds the "pregnant pot" (the alchemical crucible, furnace, or Philosopher's Egg; in this case, sexual activity) "imposture all."

The Eighteenth Century

The so-called Age of Reason (Enlightenment, Éclaircissement, Aufklärung) produced more madmen among creative writers than any other era. The pre-Romantics, disoriented by cultural preoccupations with the Industrial Revolution, shortcircuited into various enthusiasms or dream-states. With the exception of William Blake, the trappings associated with scientific alchemy were either dropped or ignored. Blake's apocalyptic poems "The Tiger" (1794) and "The Lamb" (1794) were meant, alchemically, to precipitate the Logos, to reveal the Two Contraries united in a single spiritualized *prima materia*. The "furnace" (line 14) of the first poem, when prescinded from other details that evoke a smithy, is gnomic (Gnostic, Vulcan's workshop) in intent; hence, alchemical. The tiger is quintessential "gold." As such, it is equal to the value attached to the lamb of the second poem, presented as a "name" (line 13) of the Logos (ostensibly Christ).

Among the English and German Graveyard Schools of poetry, the mere "furniture" that they borrowed from such a Senecan drama as *Hamlet* (c. 1600) fuses in the intense internalized heat of the psyche *qua* Hermetic vessel and are really etherealized, or volatilized, into the paradigm of the graveyard coitus of alchemy (nigredo), where the woman-element of the Hermaphroditic psyche (anima) rules while the burial of the man-element (animus) endures. This is to say that silver (the passive imagination as symbolized by the moon) prevails while gold (reason as symbolized by the sun) is swallowed up in darkness (the "rationalistic" but not reasonable spirit of the age). One of the noble metals of alchemy still adds lustre to the "landscape," reflecting "the *Archetypal* sun" (Sir Thomas Browne) of what Jung will call the Collective Unconscious. This is the meaning of the poem "The Rime of the Ancient Mariner" (1798) by Samuel Taylor Coleridge.

What Coleridge has to say about alchemy is of such cardinal importance to this transitional stage in literature that it is well worth quoting. His most sustained statement about Paracelsus is found in a note in the margins of the collected essays *The Holy State and the Profane State* (1642) by Thomas Fuller on Fuller's *Life of Paracelsus* (bk. 2, ch. 3):

The Potential (*Logos Theanthropos*), the ground of the Prophetic, directed the first *Thinkers* (Mystae) to the metallic bodies, as the Key of all natural Science. The *then* Actual blended with this instinct all the fancies, and fond desires, and false *perspective*, of the Childhood of Intellect. The *essence* was truth, the *form* was folly: and this is the definition of Alchemy. —Nevertheless, the very terms bear witness to the veracity of the original Instinct/ The World of Sensible Experience cannot be more luminously divided than into the modifying powers, *to allon*—that which *differences*, makes this *other* than that: and the *met' allon*, that which is beyond or deeper than modification. Metallon is strictly "the *Base* of the Mode": and such have the Metals been determined to be by modern Chemistry.

The Nineteenth Century

In the drama *Faust*, part 1 (1808), by Johann Wolfgang von Goethe, a Spinozan/Jungian Earth Spirit serves as the universal solvent; that is, as an etherealized chthonic impulse toward pantheism; but, as we have seen with Marlowe's Faustus, velleity is not enough. Gretchen, later, is introduced to act as the anima hailing the animus—the sensate (Lockean rationalist) Faust. The Romantics are beginning to incarnate the spirit of esoteric alchemy in their writings without being consciously aware of it. Some, however, are. In the poem *Alastor, or the Spirit of Solitude* (1816), Percy Bysshe Shelley cries out: "O, for Medea's wondrous alchemy" (line 672); "the dream/ Of dark magician in his visioned cave,/ Raking the cinders of a crucible/ For life and power" (681–84); "the brave, the gentle, and the beautiful,/ The child of grace and genius" (689–90). The alchemist is beginning to be assimilated by the Magus and the Witch, as in Shelley's long poem, *The Witch of Atlas* (1824), where the witch shapes a companion for herself out of snow and fire. She calls her creature Hermaphroditus.

In the novel *Madame Bovary* (1856; "Bovary" obviously means "cowshed," the dung that harbors the alchemical scarab), Gustave Flaubert makes use of the color blue as the menstruum (the universal solvent), with Emma incarnating the anima (moon, revery) and Charles the animus (sun, if only in eclipse). Opposed to the possibilities of this kind of romantic alchemy is the chemistry of Homais, whose jars, containing pickled foetuses, gleam luridly by artificial light in his shop window and jangle thematically against the archetypal vitality of the implied idea of the Philosopher's egg, to whom, at the end of the story, the Legion of Honor, with its Gadarene resonance, is accorded. These foetuses are the thwarted "dragons" unable to be born, for "rationalistic" reasons, from the alchemist's "egg" (the Collective Unconscious), the dragons of whom D. H. Lawrence was to write in his essay *Apocalypse* (1932). That Charles dies in sunlight with a blue sky above him indicates an alchemical union of the Two Contraries, since when he first met Emma she was wearing a blue dress. In a less graceful way, the androgynous hero/heroine of the novel *Séraphita* (1835) by Honoré de Balzac had also represented a reconciliation of the Two Contraries, but not along alchemical lines. As a result, whereas *Madame Bovary* is a classic, *Séraphita* is a bizarre literary oddity.

In England, it was Gabriele Rossetti, the Italian Republican patriot living in exile, who, while proclaiming himself "un buon cattolico" ("a good Catholic") to his anxious wife and surrounded by heaps of books on alchemy, Freemasonry, and Brahmanism, referred now to Emanuel Swedenborg (1688–1772), now to the Kabbala, and wrote commentaries on the "pensier di Dante/ Pensier d'Eleusi e Menfi" ("thought of Dante, thought of Eleusis and Memphis" from the poem *Veggente in solitudine* [*Seer in Solitude*, 1846]). That he transmitted a goodly amount of alchemic lore to his son Dante Gabriel Rossetti (1828–1882) is clear from many of the latter's poems and paintings. The presence of the *senhal* (screen-lady) in the paintings and, indeed, the virtual, almost funeral-parlor aspect of a good deal of English Pre-Raphaelite pictures reflected the anima-figure in the poetry of William Morris (1834–1896) and Algernon Charles Swinburne (1837–1909), both of whom wrote poems that echoed the alchemic motif of Swinburne's poetic drama *Atalanta fugiens—Atalanta in Calydon* (1865) and Morris' "Atalanta's Race" (1868). A moonlit seascape and an appeal to an indeterminate "love" supply both the menstruum and the anima-figure in the poem "Dover Beach" (1867) by Matthew Arnold, who, animus-ridden by ("Stanzas from the Grand Chartreuse," 1855) "rigorous teachers" who "seized my youth,/ And purged its faith, and trimm'd its fire" (lines 67–68), finds himself "Wandering between two worlds, one dead,/ The other powerless to be born" (85–86); that is, with no *meta allon*, no ground for a figure. In contrast to this kind of submerged esoteric alchemy, we find drunkenness proposed as the menstruum in the collection of quatrains *Rubáiyat of Omar Khayyám of Naishápúr* (mostly original translation from the Persian, 1859; by Edward Fitzgerald; qua-train 59): "The Grape that can with Logic absolute / The Two-and-Seventy jarring Sects confute: / The sovereign Alchemist that in a trice / Life's leaden metal into Gold transmute."

In his essay "The Poet" (*Lords of Life*, 1841–1843), Ralph Waldo Emerson, referring to "Pythagoras, Paracelsus, Cornelius Agrippa, Cardan, Kepler, Swedenborg, Schelling, Oken, or any other who introduces questionable facts into his cosmogony, as angels, devils, magic, astrology, palmistry, mesmerism, and so on," describes their achievement as "a new witness . . . the magic of liberty." In France, as Wallace Fowlie observes (*Mallarmé*, 1953),

Baudelaire, Rimbaud and Lautréamont are alike in this respect. . . . Their writings appear to us now as heroic attempts to understand the world and to efface the frontiers of the real world by means of a *metaphorical intelligence*, which in its very nature is limitless. They are diametrically opposed to the rationalist tradition of the seventeenth and eighteenth centuries, and take their place beside the gnostic writers and the masters of the occult tradition.

What they were practising was verbal alchemy. Gérard de Nerval wrote his *Les chimères* poems (*The Chimeras*, 1854), a book saturated with alchemy; for example, in "Horus," he writes "C'est l'enfant bien-aimé d'Hermès et d'Osiris!" ("He is the beloved infant of Hermes and Osiris!") The graveyard coitus of alchemy is involuted here; both Hermes and Osiris are males. The sterile coupling of the psychopomp and the god of the dead brings forth Horus (Nerval's suicide).

The Swede August Strindberg actively practised the "science" of alchemy and tells us in his autobiography (*Inferno*, 1897) that sometimes he precipitated a few particles of gold in his "heated crucible"; but, although he admits to being attracted to the "Catholic Symbolists of Paris," alchemy had another meaning for him, Illuminism, as when he says, "The next instant I was illumined by a vision displaying the secret of gold before my eyes." The basic ideas of Illuminism can be traced back through Swedenborg to the Caballa and to Oriental mysticism (Brahmanism and Taoism), and forward through Baudelaire, Rimbaud, and the Symbolists. Illuminism flourished in the Middle Ages with the grail cultus. Robert Browning expressed its archetypal character in the dramatic poem *Paracelsus* 1835; 726–37):

> Truth is within ourselves; it takes no rise
> From outward things, whate'er you may believe.
> There is an inmost centre in us all,
> Where truth abides in fulness; and around,
> Wall upon wall, the gross flesh hems it in,
> This perfect, clear perception—which is the truth.
> A baffling and perverting carnal mesh
> Binds it, and makes all error; and to KNOW
> Rather consists in opening out a way
> Whence the imprisoned splendour may escape,

Than in effecting entry for a light
Supposed to be without.

Opposing Paracelsus' gnosis (knowledge) is Festus, the spokesman for "love."

Alchemic premises undergird the poetry of Edgar Allen Poe. In his short story "Von Kempelen and His Discovery" (1840), the successful practice of "scientific" alchemy provides the main character with enough gold to threaten the nation's monetary stability. A thorough knowledge and application of esoteric alchemy is operative in Poe's short story (closer to a novella in length) "The Gold-Bug" (1843) where the negro slave Jupiter, the skull, and the *scarabaeus* (the *cervus fugiens* of alchemy) play key roles.

Also noteworthy is the drama *Paracelsus* (1897) by Arthur Schnitzler. When Freud read this work, he remarked that he had not thought an author could know so much.

The Twentieth Century

When Sigmund Freud published *Die Traumdeutung* (*The Interpretation of Dreams*, 1900), he proved himself to be one of Sir Thomas Browne's "Oneirocriticall Masters." He also proved that he had not read Schnitzler's *Paracelsus* in vain. Within a purely human context, the menstruum, for him, was the libido. He narrowed the archetypal "primordial" to the "primal" and related this, in the main, to psychosexual trauma. He provided writers with a Philosopher's Stone guaranteed to transmute the ordinary into the prurient, as in D. H. Lawrence's stories *The Horse Dealer's Daughter* (1963) and "The Prussian Officer" (1914); but Lawrence's autobiographical novel and masterpiece, *Sons and Lovers* (1913), while evincing some Freudian touches, is overwhelmingly Jungian and alchemical. So are the Keatsian novels by F. Scott Fitzgerald, *The Great Gatsby* (1925), utilizing the Hermetic nightingale symbol, and *Tender Is The Night* (1934). The color symbolism of the former resonates the first line of Keats's sonnet "On First Looking into Chapman's Homer" (1816): "Much have I traveled in the realms of gold," the gold being the book's exquisitely accomplished mythopoesis.

Stephen Dedalus, in the pseudo-autobiographical novel *A Portrait of the Artist as a Young Man* (1916) by James Joyce, who catechistically declares that he no longer believes in the Catholic Eucharist, is an alchemist of the Archetypal *Logos Theanthropos* (see Coleridge, earlier), "a priest of eternal imagination, transmuting the daily bread of experience into the radiant body of ever-lasting life." Stephen's "song" is a "fabulous" anagram, dear to the alchemical tradition: "O, the green wothe botheth," the 'O' being the ouroboros, the symbolic tail-eating serpent of alchemy; "the green rose" being the "black art" (green) of sacramental carnal love (rose), and "botheth," when unscrambled, being the alchemical mandate "Be Thoth." The name "Dedalo" is also mentioned by Griffolino D'Arezzo, an alchemist condemned to Hell (Dante's *Inferno* 29, line 116). "A sense of fear of the unknown moved in the heart of his weariness, a fear of symbols and portents, of the hawklike man whose name he bore soaring out of his captivity on osierwoven wings, of Thoth, the god of writers, writing with a reed on a tablet and bearing on his narrow ibis head the cusped moon.'' Joyce's alchemical interest surfaces again in the novel *Finnegans Wake* (1939) with references to ''the mutthering pot'' (20.5; Hermetic vessel) and ''the Mutther Masons'' (223.3: the Freemasons).

Alchemy and Gnosticism pervade both the poetry and prose of William Butler Yeats. In *Explorations* (essays, 1962), Yeats refers to his stories ''Rosa Alchemica'' and ''The Adoration of the Magi'' and foretells the universal reign of the ''harlot''; that is, ''by the Third Person of the Trinity,'' which translates to Barbhe-Eloha, the Eternal Feminine, the bringer of gnosis, frequently in the manifestation of a sexually initiating woman. In *A Vision* (1925), he describes yielding to God as characterized by ''complete passivity, complete plasticity,'' ''liquefaction,'' ''pounding up.'' Apart from the albedo and calcination of alchemy, which features the pulverized stone of albefication, this evokes Yeats' poem ''Leda and the Swan'' (1923) in an alchemical parody of the Incarnation, Leda symbolizing the anima and the Swan the Archetypal Divine Splendor, or Leda (moon) being ''multiplied'' by the swan (sun).

A kaleidoscopic psychic tychism derived principally from Marx and Freud, which nevertheless still claimed ''verbal alchemy'' as its modus operandi was surrealism. In *Manifeste du surréalisme* (*What Is Surrealism?*, 1924), André Breton made it clear that the beyond, considered solely as sensate extravagance, was within. By letting words collide, one came up with a new, hopefully bemusing, molecule of mental atoms. The Philosopher's Stone of this stillborn alchemy was ''the vertiginous descent within ourselves, the systematic illumination of hidden places and the progressive obscuration of other places, the perpetual promenade in a completely forbidden zone.'' The Abyss of the Gnostic alchemists became a titillating or startling possibility, a ploy of sensate consciousness. The esoteric alchemists, observing this method of psychic onanism, would have echoed Virgil's epic poem *Aeneis* (*Aeneid*, 19 B.C.), where he states: ''facilis descensus Averno'' (''easy is the descent to Avernus'') (6.126). A traditional authoritarian Christian might say the same about alchemy.

Carl Gustav Jung (1875–1961), in *Psychologie und Alchemie* (*Psychology and Alchemy*, 1944), writes,

The efficacy of dogma, however, by no means rests on Christ's unique historical reality but on its own symbolic nature, by virtue of which it expresses a more or less ubiquitous psychological assumption quite independent of the existence of any dogma. There is thus a ''pre-Christian'' as well as a ''non-Christian'' Christ, in so far as he is an autonomous psychological fact. At any rate the doctrine of prefiguration is founded on this idea. In the case of the modern man, who has no religious assumptions at all, it is therefore only logical that the Anthropos or Poimen [shepherd; ruler] figure should emerge, since it is present in his own psyche.

This, morally speaking, is like fitting a blind man with dark glasses that have had eyes painted on them. This kind of wanton pneumaticism is fully persuaded that the Incarnation, as a unique historical event, is wholly irrelevant to elite souls. It is clear that to speak of Christ-figures in literature is an assimilative effort on the part of conscious Gnostico-alchemical critics to etherealize even the historical Jesus to the status of one of many, not to say universal, manifestations of "the *Archetypal* sun," variously understood to be The Abyss (the Ineffable God).

T. S. Eliot understood the alchemical menace to traditional, authoritarian Christianity as early as the poem "The Love Song of J. Alfred Prufrock" (1917), where the sensibility of Prufrock, disassociated and projectively creative, is presented as a meandering "yellow fog," as both touchstone and Philosopher's Stone (proof-rock) with regard to the quality of the "gold" it precipitates. Eliot shrewdly relates animus to animus in this poem, as Nerval had done, albeit less prudently, in the "chimerical" poem cited. He uses a troubadour setting to make his point about the morally suicidal character of Albigensian and Catharist *amour courtois* (courtly love): "lonely men in shirt-sleeves, leaning out of windows" (line 42). The lady *qua* "other" is replaced by a mirroring animus. One of the tactical effects is to render Prufrock effeminate—castrated like the Fisher King in *Parzival*.

The reign of this emasculated King Amfortas, whose name, etymologically considered, means weak, infertile, and who is generally pictured as having lost his "sacred spear," is widespread today—a latter-day Catharism (Purism; *catharos* in Greek meaning "pure"—undefiled by earthly dross or carnality, which frequently enough shortcircuits into its opposite, licentious idiocy). His subjects include, bizarrely, the Jean Genet who wrote the novel *Notre-Dame des fleurs* (*Our Lady of the Flowers*, 1943) and the Italian exponents of *Graalismo* (Grailism) who in their manifesto (R. Cervo, ed., *La lirica contemporanea*, 1951, p. 236) profess that "Il Graalismo fa della Poesia una coppa simbolica che soltanto mani pure possono elevare verso il cielo per raccogliere le lacrime delle notti umane e il sangue delle aurore divine" ("Grailism makes of Poetry a symbolic cup which only pure hands can raise toward the sky to gather the tears of human nights and the blood of divine dawns").

Northrop Frye is an alchemical "creative critic" of the first rank. His *Fearful Symmetry: A Study of William Blake* (1947), *The Anatomy of Criticism* (1957), and *Fables of Identity* (1963) are lodestars on the contemporary Gnostico-alchemical literary scene. In "Quest and Cycle in *Finnegans Wake*" (*Fables of Identity*, 257), he writes, "In Joyce too the concrete universal, the identity of individual and total man, is the organizing principle of the symbolism." We are back, *mutatis mutandis*, to Paracelsus' panacea by way of a misreading of Joyce's strategic deployment of epiphany. The panacea is "creative imagination, . . . imaginative catholicity"; that is, the puppetry antics of "the *Archetypal* sun."

The panacea of Paracelsus was, indeed, laudanum, and the use of it by Coleridge, Thomas De Quincey (1785–1859), and D. G. Rossetti resulted in many a unitary high or adequately subjective psychophany. All literature that uses drugs as the menstruum is alchemical; for example, that of the beats William

Burroughs (1914–) and Jack Kerouac. Beat here is taken to mean beatitude, as in Kerouac's autobiographical picaresque novels *On the Road* (1957), *The Dharma Bums* (1958), and *Satori in Paris* (1966); ignorance (shortcircuiting chemically to gnosis and thereby transmuting a sot into a hipster), incoherence, and illiteracy are beatific, crime is lovely, do as you want, get stoned, learn to be naïve, attain sweetness and light. Marijuana, LSD, and other herbal and chemical *filii philosophorum* serve to transform the metaphorical lead of the harried, detribalized modernistic conscience into the "gold" latent in "Acapulco gold," "prime weed," the all-wise gatekeeper, the *janitor pansophum*, the primary oocyte or spermatocyte as it endows the dreaming *ovum humanum* (human egg) spaced out regressively, a singular universal, in a prenatal Beyond. This psychedelic Philosopher's Stone is acknowledged in the phrase "stoned out of one's mind."

It is precisely this kind of banalized "Eucharistic" precocious senility on the part of "alchemists" who have lost their authentic scientific footing that prompts the Catholic realist Marshall McLuhan (1911–1980) to describe "a juvenile activist" popping "a pellet into the metropolitan water supply" and ending "a city as readily as could an atom bomb" as "The Return of the Alchemist" (*Take Today: The Executive as Dropout*, 1972; p. 175). McLuhan replaces the "Native" of the title of Thomas Hardy's novel here with "Alchemist" to show how modern technology has so radically alienated mankind from the earth through the process of artificialization that one is no longer in nature, no longer born to the earth (native) but prearranged to commit any enormity; that is, wilfully to transmute what ought to be naturally real and sustaining to an opportunity for an involuted hypercosmic pattern of poisonous spite; to assert one's humanity, one's spirit, only by way of vengeful reaction.

When piety lacks a proper object, Bedlam is adored. The "singular universal" (Bernard Henri Lévy's essay *La barbarie à visage humain* [*Barbarism with a Human Face*, 1977]) is idolized, elevated to the status of a manifestation of the Gnostic Pleroma (The Abyss, The Fullness of the Ineffable God). Is one to imagine an innate "charity" as the characteristic of the elite? If not "charity," what then is the menstruum? This is the principal problem facing the "science" of the French New Philosophers—André Glucksmann (1937–), Jean-Paul Dollé (1939–), Guy Lardreau (1947–), Bernard Henri Lévy (1949–), and Christian Jambet (1949–)—whose vision of reality is, professedly, as alchemical as that of Don Quixote when he perceived that the windmills were, in accordance with the laws of a higher logic, really giants. In the words of Guy Lardreau ("On the Death of Science," from *Le singe d'or* [*The Ape of Gold*, 1973; the ape was an alchemical symbol for Thoth]), "Concretely: to say that alchemy and astrology *in the Occident* are manifestations of a 'pre-scientific', 'pre-logical', or even 'non-scientific' mode of thought has, we believe, no interest, except that these labels block the means of understanding them. They are, on the contrary, profoundly scientific." Given the ambiguity of the word *science* in French, meaning both "science" and "knowledge" in English, what Lardreau in the context of his thought is saying is this: alchemy is "profoundly scientific"; that is, in its surviving ontological/behavioral form, both Gnostic and Quixotic.

See also: Science.

Selected Bibliography

Coburn, Kathleen. *Experience into Thought: Perspectives in the Coleridge Notebooks*. Toronto: University of Toronto Press, 1979.

Fabricius, Johannes. *Alchemy: The Medieval Alchemists and Their Royal Art*. Copenhagen: Rosenkilde and Bagger, 1976.

Sivin, Nathan. *Chinese Alchemy*. Cambridge: Harvard University Press, 1968.

Taylor, Frank Sherwood. *The Alchemists: Founders of Modern Chemistry*. New York: Schuman, 1949.

NATHAN A. CERVO

ALIENATION

The Latin term *alienatio* signified (1) the transference of property, (2) a state of insensibility, (3) mental derangement, and (4) the act of becoming hostile or estranged. "Alienation" in English usage and *aliénation* in French retain the ideas of estrangement, of madness, and, in legal contexts, of transference of property. Alienation as a literary theme may be described as the estrangement of the literary character or persona from something with which he/she has been, should be, or would like to be in conformity and consonance. In contrast, the resolution of the problem of alienation, the theme that stands in opposition to it, is reconciliation. The theme of alienation is related to that of rebellion in the sense that alienation is often that which gives impulse to acts of defiance and rebellion; nevertheless, alienation may not, indeed often does not, give rise to rebellion. Clearly, the figure of the Underground Man is integrally linked to alienation, since he is the personification of impotent alienation. Conceived by Dostoevsky, who discovered him in embryo form in the works of Gogol, the Underground Man is the negation of the Romantic rebel. The relationship of alienation to the theme of solitude consists in the solitary, often ostracized circumstance of the alienated figure. However, solitude may be shown to have positive aspects—peacefulness, the opportunity to commune with nature or God, the conditions that foster creativity—which have nothing to do with alienation.

We may establish six basic types of alienation based on the entity from which the individual is alienated. (1) The alienation may be from the physical environment: from the sea, as in Horace's *Carmina* (1.3 or 1.14; *Odes*, c. 23 B.C.), or from the modern city, for example, Baudelaire's *Tableaux parisiens* (*Parisian Scenes*, 1861). (2) It may be from one's own epoch, as in T. S. Eliot's poem, *The Waste Land* (1922). (3) Often literary characters experience estrangement from the community of others and/or the values and mores of their society. Some form of social alienation can be considered the norm in Western literature from the flowering of romanticism to the present, although this theme can certainly also be found in earlier works. (4) A fourth kind of alienation is the separation from the Creator and the cosmic order. (5) The conception of alienation from self, or the divided self, derives ultimately from the Latin meaning of madness or derangement but receives considerable impetus from modern philosophy and psychology. In literature this kind of alienation has traditionally been expressed by such devices as the soliloquy and, symbolically, by doubling or metamorphosis. (6) Perhaps the most profound kind of alienation is the existential, that is, estrangement from the condition of being human. This is not simply estrangement from some aspect of the external world or a split in the self in terms of which one seeks reconciliation; it is, rather, the inability to rationalize and conform to one's essential nature, to adapt to the limits of humanness. This latter kind of alienation is probably most powerfully explored in the work of the so-called Existentialists from Kierkegaard to Dostoevsky to Sartre. In general one can expect alienation to be a prevalent theme in periods in which faith in God or in reason is shaken or challenged or in periods unusually preoccupied with mutability (either instability or decline).

Generic Considerations

Certain literary genres and modes lend themselves particularly to the expression of alienation or to the creation of situations that produce alienation. Lyric poetry, because it is individual and solitary, given to the intimate expression of personal thought or emotion, gives appropriate form to a subjective exploration of alienation. In drama both tragedy and the modern Theater of the Absurd create situations that are almost inevitably paradigms of alienation. In tragedy this is because the tragic hero suffers a rupture with the social order that precipitates his or her decline but allows that order to survive. The Theater of the Absurd belongs here for its propensity to pose problems arising out of threats to the self that derive from the modern perception of radical estrangement from the Other.

Three modes that lead to the development of the novel are particularly relevant' to the theme of alienation: satire, the pastoral, and the picaresque. Clearly, satire is defined in terms of its opposition to, or alienation from, a society, a culture, or the vices to which human nature is seen to be prone. Nevertheless, the satirized object has fallen short of an ideal the existence of which calls into question the reading of satire as a totalizing expression of alienation. The pastoral, on the other hand, although it is characterized by tones of longing and nostalgia (the myth of the Golden Age never being quite lost in spirit) creates a sense of a distancing and a remoteness from contemporary civilization in such a way as to suggest an implied alienation from all that civilization represents. In the picaresque mode, many of society's flaws are exposed, and, in addition, the protagonist becomes the outsider even though the work itself may be either satirical or, on the other hand, a conservative piece exonerating society at the expense of the rascally, nonconforming *picaro*. The novel, then, as heir to these three modes, assumes patterns and stances that give body to the sense of alienation.

Indeed, Carlos Fuentes has stated that "without alienation there would be no novelist. Alienation is at the source of the novel" (Luis Harss and Barbara Dohmann, *Into the Mainstream: Conversations with Latin American Writers*, 1972, p. 306). The novel is given, then, to the expression of alienation, especially because of its concern to depict both the individual in relation to his/her circumstance and because this relation is always seen as problematical. This is not to say that the novel will always project alienation; it is to say, rather, that the novel is fertile ground for the growth and fostering of alienation in one or many of its forms.

The Bible

The fact that alienation is a predominant theme in Western literature since romanticism does not mean that it does not occur throughout the history of the tradition. In the Bible the estrangement of man from God begins with the temptation, the eating from the tree of knowledge, and the expulsion from Eden. The separation of man from man is symbolized in Cain's killing of Abel, and a further distancing from God is accomplished by the condemnation of Cain to become a fugitive and a wanderer. The rivalry between Cain and Abel to win God's favor by their gifts establishes one of the major sources of alienation in the Old Testament, which is the estrangement from God arising out of involvement in culture. God favors Abel's gift of the lamb over Cain's cultivated products just as He will later destroy cities, the centers and symbols of human civilization and culture. Knowledge is that which distances and estranges. The prophets, seeing man's social and cultural efforts as vain and futile, feel themselves isolated. "So I came to hate life, since everything that was done here under the sun was a trouble to me; for all is emptiness and chasing the wind," says the Speaker in Ecclesiastes (2:17), who has been a seeker after wisdom. In the New Testament, reconciliation comes through the death and resurrection of Christ. Jesus himself establishes the connection between temptation (symbolized by Satan) and alienation (in the form of madness) when he cures a madwoman and specifically refers to her madness as possession by Satan. Not only does Jesus overcome the alienation worked by Satan, he also preaches reunion with the Gentiles, thus attempting to bridge the spiritual and cultural distances between the Jews and their neighbors. Finally, his death on the cross makes possible the reconciliation of man with God. Nevertheless, St. Paul's doctrine of justification in the Epistles points out the predicament of even the most faithful of believers. Even those who know the law do not always keep it. All are thus sinners and inevitably alienated in terms of the great distance between what they know they must do and what they do. Faith is what justifies the sinner and, in effect, reconciles him/her with God.

Greek Antiquity

In general one can recognize in Greek literature, from Homer and the early poets to Plato, a search for cause and effect in the physical, moral, and spiritual domains and a need to acknowledge and participate in the perceived order. In Homer's epic poem, *Ilias* (*Iliad*, c. 8th century B.C.), the most powerful instance of alienation may be the wrath and revolt of Achilles. Indeed, by withdrawing from the battle, Achilles distances himself from the divine will and from the Greeks and their cause. The reconciliation of Achilles to gods and men, brought on by the death of Patroclus, and to the moral order, by his releasing Hector's body to Priam, typifies the movement in Greek literature toward harmony. No less quintessentially Greek is the process of revenge and reconciliation in Aeschylus' trilogy of plays, *Oresteia* (458 B.C.), from Clytemnestra's killing of Agamemnon, to the pursuit of Orestes by the Erinyes (the avenging furies), to the trial at the end of the trilogy in which the Erinyes become transformed into the gracious Eumenides; and peace, harmony, and justice are established by Athena. In contrast to the alienation from culture expressed in the Old Testament, the Greeks found hope and optimism in converting the ancient *daimones* (originally nature gods) into civic-minded deities. Similarly, Sophocles' Oedipus, condemns himself to blindness and to exile in the play *Oidipous tyrannos* (*Oedipus Rex*, c. 429 B.C.), but ends by being buried in hallowed ground and revered as though immortal in the play *Oidipous epi Kolōnō* (*Oedipus at Colonus*, c. 406 B.C.). Antigone, his daughter, dies alienated in an effort to preserve ancient custom, and her death sets in motion the fall of Creon and the restoration of the natural order in the play *Antigonē* (c. 441 B.C.).

Generally in early Greek poetry, misfortune is to be met by resignation and endurance. Nausicaa, for example, counsels Odysseus that it is Zeus who dispenses happiness to men, and man must endure his lot (*Odysseia* [*The Odyssey*], c. 8th century B.C.). Nevertheless, certain poets occasionally express an anger and hostility that border on alienation; for example, Archilochus in his vengeful satires; Mimnermus, whose pessimism approaches despair; and Theognis ("Best of all things/ is never to be born"). Yet even Archilochus writes a poem on moderation, and his counsel of a measured response to victory or defeat typifies another Greek ideal, which is perhaps most fully elaborated in Aristotle's treatise *Ēthika Nikomacheia* (*Ethics*, 4th century B.C.).

The tragedies of Euripides bring to prominence one of the most powerful and ubiquitous techniques for the expression of alienation, the soliloquy. Both his Medea and his Phaedra proclaim their madness, that is their alienation from their true selves. Medea (*Mēdeia* [*Medea*, 431 B.C.]), the stranger in a foreign land, outcast and about to be exiled again, protests the condition of being a woman: "We women are the most unfortunate of creatures." And this is because women must marry, must abandon their families and homes, must bind themselves to one who may become indifferent. Her schism of self is manifested in her conflict with her own heart and hand as she is about to murder her children. Phaedra (*Hippolytos* [*Hippolytus*, 428 B.C.]) remonstrates with herself over the dilemma of her love for her stepson and the pain brought on by her passion. Like Medea, she is a self divided, and her alienation is so profound as to require her death.

Roman Literature

Perhaps the mode that most surely provides a transition for the theme of alienation from the literature of ancient Greece to that of Rome is satire, for satire continues to be written through the Hellenistic period, for example, by Theophrastus, Ennius, Menippus, Lucilius, Varro, and others. Some satire does not rely on a spirit of alienation, but many satirists, in their ferocity and violence, do indeed convey a profound sense of alienation. Horace's satire falls into the former category, since in his didactic passages he reveals a belief in the possibility of human moderation and goodness. Petronius and Juvenal, on the other hand, belong to the latter class. The theme of alienation in Roman literature, then, arises most convincingly in the work of some satirists and in other writers of the Augustan Age and beyond who decry the decline of the morals and culture of their times.

The Golden Age of Roman literature displays an energy and vigor, a sense of its own greatness, a robust delight in the senses and a classical sense of proportion that preclude the intrusion of alienation. Nevertheless, the end of the Roman republic and the accession of Augustus coincide with a tendency to alienation that will continue in Roman writing until the fall of the empire. Petronius' novel *Satyricon* (A.D. 60) stands out as a ribald examination of the vulgar excesses and the seamier aspects of society under Nero. Furthermore, by the manner in which he undercuts with irony his protagonist/narrator, Encolpius, Petronius implies that there is neither relief nor escape from the ugliness and viciousness of human society. Similarly, Juvenal, in his vituperative *Satirae* (*Satires*, c. A.D. 100–127), manifests anger and outrage at a society so depraved that, as he says, it is difficult *not* to write satire.

The Middle Ages

If alienation can be said to occur in the literature of the Middle Ages, it is linked to the contempt for the material world and the flesh found in the writings of some of the saints, hermits, and church fathers. As A. O. Lovejoy has shown, the medieval conception of the dichotomy between this-worldliness and other-worldliness has its origins in Plato (*The Great Chain of Being: A Study of the History of an Idea*. Cambridge, 1964). The alienation from the material world may involve a denial of realness and importance to things perceived by the senses, a condemnation of its temporal character and incompleteness, or its characterization as random, fragmentary, and imperfect. In addition, the world of the senses is the embodiment of temptation, and intercourse with it leads inevitably to perdition (Lovejoy, p. 26–29). St. Peter Damiani, one of the most authoritative exponents of asceticism, writes that true mortification springs from delight in contemplation of the Creator: "This is how it happens that a man, bearing his Redeemer's cross, seems dead to the world, . . . he searches and takes pleasure in remote and lonely places; as far as he can, he avoids all human contact" (*De perfectione monachorum*, ch. 3 [*On the Perfection of Monks*, c. 1065]). Nevertheless, in Damiani, as in the majority of medieval ascetics, the negative and alienated qualities exhibited in the contempt for the world are overshadowed by the positive values of faith in the divine order and belief in salvation. The dominant medieval vision of the *summum bonum* only becomes seriously marred in the decline of the Middle Ages, and this tendency is perhaps best exemplified in the work of François Villon. Here we find the pessimistic tone typical of the fifteenth century, the *ubi sunt* motif, and a pungent, gritty social satire arising not out of piety but out of despair. The recourse to vulgarity, to explicit sexual reference and double-entendres, the thematization of hunger, crime, pestilence, war, and death recall Petronius and give a renewed continuity to a realism that forms an undercurrent during the later Middle Ages and which bursts into the open in the fifteenth and sixteenth centuries.

Renaissance and Baroque Literature

Renaissance optimism, the faith in the grandeur and perfectability of man, as manifested, for example, in Pico della Mirandola's vision of the compatibility of the Hebrew, classical, and Christian intellectual traditions (*Oratio de hominis dignitate* [*Oration on the Dignity of Man*, 1486]), or the achievement of virtue by the soldier/poet/courtier through service to the beloved woman in Baldassare Castiglione's treatise *Il cortegiano* (*The Courtier*, 1528), or the discovery of a harmony of the word, nature, the spirit, and the cosmos in the poetry of Fray Luis de León maintains itself as a major strain in Western thought for a relatively short period. Furthermore, during this period much important writing reveals diverse sources of alienation. Niccolò Machiavelli argues for a hardened, pragmatic political philosophy that is motivated by his disillusionment with courtly ideals. The figure of paradox, informing the writings of Desiderius Erasmus, François Rabelais, Torquato Tasso, and many others, mounts a serious challenge to the efficacy of human reason. And the novel *Lazarillo de Tormes* (anonymous, 1554) and its picaresque progeny create and give impulse to a tradition of an antihero so distanced from the social and spiritual ideals of his society that he is an embodiment of social alienation.

The period of the Counter-Reformation or the baroque rivals the romantic and postromantic periods as a time in which alienation is a supreme and dominant characteristic of literary expression. The exuberant confidence of Renaissance man wanes and is gradually replaced by an existential doubting and questioning as profound and terrible as anything the twentieth century has produced. Alienation in this period expresses itself in the revelation of the flaws and weaknesses of the hero as well as the human species in general, of the realization of the human being's inability to discern truly what is real, and of the insecurity arising out of an obsession with mutability. Montaigne, in the "Apologie de Raymond Sebond" (*Essais*, 2.12 ["Apology for R.S.," *Essays*, 1580–1588]), attacks man's anthropocentrism and vents his rage at the hubris of those who consider man as the center of creation. Vanity, according to Montaigne, is emptiness, appearance, illusion. In the last half of the essay, Montaigne raises questions of epistemology by casting doubt on the power of reason, science's instrument, and by pointing to the perpetual contradictions in human thought, to human impotence in the determination of moral law, and to the imperfections of the senses. Shakespeare's magnificent heroes end in ignominy and defeat for their vanity (Macbeth and Othello), their impotence (Hamlet), their moral blindness (Lear). Don Quijote's idealism is madness, and he is reviled and mocked as he enters Barcelona at the climax of Miguel de Cervantes' novel (*Don Quijote* [*Don Quixote*, 1605, 1615]). He dies the humbled, chastened Christian, redeemed yet diminished. Pedro Calderón de la Barca sums up one important aspect of baroque ethos in Segismundo's lament in his play *La vida es sueño* (*Life is a Dream*, 1635): "All of life is a dream, and dreams are only dreams." It can be argued that beneath the moral and metaphysical anguish of the baroque period lies a solid foundation of faith. Nevertheless, the anxieties of the age are so profound as to suggest a sense of terrible crisis, not only of optimism and confidence, but of a faith to which thinkers and writers desperately cling. The absoluteness and certainty with which literate men and women had viewed their condition on earth and in the divine scheme is irremediably shaken. Perhaps the most significant representation of alienation in the seventeenth century is Tirso de Molina's Don Juan in the play *El burlador de Sevilla* (*The Libertine of Seville*, 1630). So alienated is Don Juan that he mocks the social codes of his society, the honor of women and the family, the king and his father, innocence, friendship, charity, death, God and, finally, hell. The very conception of Don Juan testifies to the fear, general to the period, of terrible estrangement from man and God that threatens the individual.

The Enlightenment

The writers of the Enlightenment proclaim their confidence in the human being's ability to attain freedom, virtue, and social reform through science and reason and by the rejection of superstition and Christian history. This is an age of turbulent yet rational inquiry and a dogmatic optimism, yet it produces, as well, one of history's most brilliant exponents of alienation, Jean-Jacques Rousseau. Rousseau's alienation, expressed forcefully in the *Confessions* (1781–1788) and explicated in his attacks on society and civilization throughout his work, arises out of his belief that the natural and instinctual tendency to goodness of the human being becomes stifled and corrupted by education and the social structure. Profoundly disturbed by social inequality, by the snobbishness and hypocrisy of the educated classes, by divisiveness and factionalism in human relations, Rousseau constructs an anthropology and a theory of human development (especially in *Discours sur l'origine et les fondements de l'inégalité parmi les hommes* [*Discourse on the Origin and Bases of Inequality among Men*, 1754] and the novel *Emile* [1762]), which portrays man as estranged from his essential and original nature. And in the second half of his novel *La nouvelle Héloïse* (1761, *The New Heloise*), he depicts a utopian model of a hierarchized yet harmonious and just society. Rousseau's *Confessions* especially break new ground in the expression of alienation by means of an often bitter and tormented tone and a relentless analysis of disillusioning experiences and failed relationships.

Romanticism and Symbolism

In its break with neoclassical restraints, its celebration of the imagination and individualism, and its probing of the darker impulses and instincts of the human psyche, the romantic movement brings to full prominence a range of alienated literary types. The vigorous romantic challenge to reason, its belief in emotion as the key to the apprehension of beauty, truth, and the hidden self, results in a radical instability, for romantic emotion is necessarily unbridled and leads to anguish if not madness. Thus the romantic age lends new depth and richness and new refinements to the tradition of alienation in Western literature. Lord Byron's Manfred (the hero of a dramatic poem by that name, 1817) can be seen as a prototype of the romantic hero. Unwilling and unable to form bonds with others because of his terrible secret, his superior sensibilities, the inability on the part of others to comprehend or share his unique suffering, the aristocratic Manfred, inhabiting an isolated mountain tower, transcends the limits of the human, communing with the supernatural and dying a death reserved for the tormented few. It is suggested that his secret is a forbidden love, probably incestuous, ending in the death of the beloved. His estrangement, like that of many romantic heroes, is the result of a rebellious, supremely individualistic personality whose highly charged imagination finds its nourishment in nature rather than in society. He is both an outsider and, implicitly, an outcast, since his crime sets him beyond the limits of tolerance of bourgeois society. Like Manfred, François René de Chateaubriand's René, (novel, 1802) exhibits the melancholy, the tortured soul, the solitude, the longing for oblivion of the true romantic. In addition, he is the wanderer who can find neither peace nor a place to which he feels an attachment. Herman Melville's Ahab, in the novel *Moby-Dick* (1851), embodies the hubris of the alienated romantic hero as he dares to challenge the very symbol and incarnation of nature, the white whale, and is thereby destroyed.

On the other hand, the outsiders of Nikolai Gogol's Petersburg tales—"Shinel' " ("The Overcoat," 1842), "Nos" ("The Nose," 1836), or *Zapiski sumasshedshego* (*The Diary of a Madman*, 1835), for example—are anything but superior and transcendent. They are tortured but small souls, plagued by the meanness and indifference of the city and human hypocrisy and menaced by vague supernatural phenomena. Victimized even by the witty spite of their narrators, they exhibit pain conveyed at a level of intensity newly felt in Western literature. They lead directly to the Underground Man, Dostoevsky's quintessential formulation of modern alienation.

Before considering Dostoevsky, however, it is necessary to note briefly some contributions of German philosophy to the modern conception of alienation.

G.W.F. Hegel, in *Phänomenologie des Geistes* (*Phenomenology of Mind*, 1807), explores the ontology of self and other as two completely discrete entities that depend ultimately on each other for validation and identity. The consciousness of self passes through two stages, each involving a form of alienation. At the moment of self-knowledge, according to Hegel, consciousness loses temporarily the immediate presence of the other. The next movement, however, is the loss of difference and otherness, a return to unity with the sensible. In social philosophy Karl Marx conceives alienation (his term is *Entfremdung*, after Hegel) as a state created by a process in which the human being turns himself into an object by selling his labor (*Economic and Philosophical Manuscripts of 1844*). And Friedrich Nietzsche's ideal of the *Übermensch*, delineated in the prose poem *Also sprach Zarathustra* (*Thus Spoke Zarathustra*, 1883–1892) could be said to reflect a form of alienation to be actively striven for, since he willingly breaks both with the morality that has weakened and rendered the human race helpless and with the characteristics which bind human beings to each other emotionally.

In the novel *Zapiski iz podpol'ia* (*Notes from Underground*, 1864), Dostoevsky creates a character who is at the same time a synthesis of the romantic literary and philosophical outsider and the rebel against that conception. The Underground Man is "sick," tortured by an overacute self-consciousness, knowing, vaunting, and yet despising his own malignant nature. He refuses to be objectified, to be played like the keys of a piano. He cuts himself off from others by a sado-masochistic process that he analyzes but cannot escape. In him are intertwined pride and humiliation, reason and will overcome by pain, self-sufficiency and a desperate need to relate to others. The depiction of social, psychological, and existential alienation in this character reaches a new level of sophistication, and it clearly anticipates Freud and modern psychology as well as the twentieth-century figure of the alienated individual. The metaphysical dimension seems strangely absent from this work, which is seminal to the creation of Dostoevsky's subsequent novels, and that is because religious references were excised by the censor. In the novel *Prestuplenie i nakazanie* (*Crime and Punishment*, 1866), Dostoevsky posits pride and the absence of faith as those factors that underlie alienation.

Charles Baudelaire's poems *Les fleurs du mal* (*The Flowers of Evil*, 1857) make ever more acute the themes of alienation from the modern city, the special sense of estrangement felt by the artist ("L'albatros" ["The Albatross"]) and the quest for experience, spiritual or aesthetic, as yet unconceived—*le nouveau* ("Le voyage" ["The Voyage"]). The comte de Lautréamont's (pseud. of Isidore Ducasse) Maldoror (the protagonist of his prose poem *Les chants de Maldoror* [*Maldoror*, 1868–1869]) mounts violent attacks against the Creator and his creation, man (and in effect challenges the romantic cult of creativity). The Symbolists, heirs to Baudelaire, further develop the theme of alienation in two directions. Arthur Rimbaud's assertion, "Je est un autre," implies a psyche dislocated from its self by the special hallucinatory state obtained by taking drugs and other means and further suggests the uniquely self-reflexive mental and spiritual state necessary to the creation of poetry. In Stéphane Mallarmé, on the other hand, the idealization of, and the movement toward, pure poetry aims to produce an artistic experience in a mode of other-worldliness and symbolism that constitutes a remoteness from ordinary human sensual, social, and spiritual life approximating the mystical.

The Twentieth Century

In twentieth-century literature expressions of alienation follow patterns established already in the nineteenth century, and yet these become ever more searchingly analyzed and deeply experienced. The philosophical movement known as existentialism takes ''alienation'' as one of its central terms. The figure of the outsider, the isolated and alienated protagonist, becomes one of the predominant types in fiction. The Theater of the Absurd studies the enormous distances between the individual and otherness. And the emergence of oppressed peoples from colonialist and subjugated systems creates a range of minority, Third World, and feminist literatures of alienation and protest.

In a gesture deeply meaningful to the Modernist spirit, the mediocre writer/protagonist of Thomas Mann's novelle *Der Tod in Venedig* (*Death in Venice*, 1912) surrenders himself to certain death of cholera in order not to abandon his shattering, ultimate encounter with Beauty (in the form of the boy, Tadzio). In this story, as well as in many works of the early twentieth century, the suggestion of homosexuality marks the protagonist as an outsider, as one who refuses to conform to bourgeois restraints and is the bearer and symbol of an alternate vision. In his novels Marcel Proust's protagonist/narrator writes *A la recherche du temps perdu* (*Remembrance of Things Past*, 1913–1927) in search of a lost unity, or indeed to impose an unattainable temporal and aesthetic unity on his life and that of his society. So powerful is his fear of oblivion and of irremediable alienation that he achieves a new level of complexity in the structuring of time in the novel and in the novelistic exposition of consciousness by interweaving tiny strands of sense-induced memory through fifteen volumes. Robert Musil's novel *Der Mann ohne Eigenschaften* (*The Man without Qualities*, 1930–1943) portrays the dilemma of the man of integrity who cannot participate in the grand designs of his society because of an instinctual grasp of their falsity and futility. Like many, perhaps most, modern literary protagonists, he knows that he does not and cannot conform to the temper of his age. In James Joyce's novel *Ulysses* (1922) Stephen Dedalus and Leopold Bloom spend a lifetime in a day engaged in a spiritual search for each other. The artist (Dedalus) and the Jew (Bloom), two archetypal exiles in modern literature, making only the most tentative contact at the end of their odyssey, illustrate the near impossibility of human bonding in twentieth-century literature. *Ulysses* stands as the foremost example of the tasks that Modernist writers set for themselves: the study of the workings of consciousness, the objectification and re-creation of poetic language, the discovery of the ontology and function of art in its relation to modern experience and the portrayal of the individual as fragmented and dehumanized by the environment. Franz Kafka's characters—Gregor Samsa in the story "Die Verwandlung" ("The Metamorphosis," 1915) or Joseph K. in the novel *Der Prozess* (*The Trial*, 1925)—fall prey to the nightmarishly literalized forces in modern life that brutalize, degrade, dehumanize, and deform the individual.

Modernist alienation expresses itself just as surely and profoundly in the objectifying visions of such poets as T. S. Eliot and Ezra Pound. Pound, in the *Pisan Cantos* (1948), not only mourns the passing of what was for him a utopian dream and evokes the beauty and power of past civilizations, but he derides modern culture for its superficiality, ugliness, and stupidity. Pound's *Cantos* recalls the definitive poem of the twentieth century, T. S. Eliot's *The Waste Land*, charged as it is with the archetypal myths that underlie European civilization, now fragmented and emptied of any but the most trivial content. The fragmentation and reassemblage of diverse species of discourse into a cubist mosaic in both poems typifies the twentieth-century preoccupation with the ruptures that are perceived to occur in language as it tries to convey human experience. The sense of the betrayal of language itself is one of the most prevalent aspects of twentieth-century alienation.

Another source of concern with alienation is that strain of existentialist phenomenology (with its roots in Hegel) that culminates in French Existentialism. Jean-Paul Sartre, in the novel *La nausée* (*Nausea*, 1938), chronicles the growing alienation of his protagonist Roquentin in terms of his increasingly acute awareness of the facticity, the "thingness," of the phenomena that constitute reality. As he does his unwitting phenomenological analysis, Roquentin comes to realize the absolute absence of coherence and meaning at the root of existence. Nevertheless, Sartre offers hope, not in the possibility of reconciliation—for the absurdity of existence is irremediable—but in the human imagination, which can create works of art endowed with coherence and internal necessity, and in the human power and freedom to choose. Albert Camus, in the novel *L'étranger* (*The Stranger*, 1942), again poses the problem of the random universe, the world in which the laws of cause and effect do not exist. Like Kafka's characters, Camus' Meursault is acted upon by forces that he cannot rationalize or understand. Camus' antidote to despair, however, consists in recourse to the pleasures of the senses, which are so compelling as to make life unbearably desirable.

Twentieth-century theater also confronts the problem of alienation. Luigi Pirandello, in *Enrico IV* (1922) and other plays, creates characters who can only be themselves while disguised, and thus he, too, like Sartre, Camus, and many others, focuses on the problem of precarious and threatened individual identity. The Theater of Cruelty, propounded by Antonin Artaud in *Le théâtre et son double* (*The Theater and its Double*, 1938) finds part of its inspiration in the special alienation of the surrealists. André Breton, in his essay *Manifeste du surréalisme* (*What Is Surrealism?*, 1924), and other members of this group proclaim estrangement from the rational mind and consciousness, seeking new paths to creativity and freedom in manifestations of the unconscious. Artaud then proposes a theater that will return to its ritualistic origins and display the human being's unconscious tendencies to violence and anarchy.

Finally, alienation engendered by oppression, neocolonialism, and the established literary canon emerges during the twentieth century in a host of important writings by peoples of color, citizens of developing countries, and by women. Forcing a new awareness of the politics of literature and supported by groundbreaking work in the field of anthropology (which acts to foster understanding of and interest in non-European cultures), black and Latin American writers come to prominence in literature and in the expression of alienation. The literary/political movement known as *négritude* includes both Africans, for example, Leopold Senghor, and people of African descent in the Americas. The major work of many black writers is semiautobiographical and aimed at the creation of a specifically black cultural consciousness, for example, Aimé Césaire's poems *Cahiers d'un retour au pays natal* (*Return to My Native Land*, 1939) or Richard Wright's *Black Boy* (1945). Conscious of the alienating effects of expressing themselves by means of the colonizer's language, black poets like Nicolás Guillén and Langston Hughes experiment with African words and rhythms that create a native, non-European texture in their verse. Ralph Ellison's novel *The Invisible Man* (1952) incorporates into the picaresque tradition the thematics of black alienation and creates an archetypal image of the disinherited minority outsider.

Latin American writers gain recognition as a powerful voice, both introducing innovations in the art of the novel and speaking for colonized peoples throughout the world. Pablo Neruda's epic poem *Canto general* (1950) combines the lament of the alienated individual inhabiting the modern world with the chronicle of the struggles of the colonized to overthrow their oppressors and find their spiritual roots. Alejo Carpentier, in such novels as *El reino de este mundo* (*The Kingdom of this World*, 1949), *Los pasos perdidos* (*The Lost Steps*, 1953) and *El siglo de las luces* (*Explosion in a Cathedral: A Novel*, 1962)—and other writers associated with Magic Realism—study the history and culture of Latin America by means of the dialectics of indigenous culture and values in opposition to colonized culture. In the novel *Cien años de soledad* (*One Hundred Years of Solitude*, 1967) García Márquez demonstrates the destructive effects to the sense of community caused by egocentric individualism, bureaucracy, capitalism, and the selfish interests of the church and the United States.

In opposition to thousands of years of patriarchal domination, the feminist movement brings to the forefront the literary woman and the woman's traditional exclusion from the literary canon. Virginia Woolf's essay *A Room of One's Own* (1929) demonstrates the perennial difficulties socioeconomic restrictions impose on women who would write. Simone de Beauvoir's essay *Le deuxième sexe* (*The Second Sex*, 1949) narrates a history of woman's marginalization in society and literature. And feminist poets, such as Anne Sexton, Sylvia Plath, Julia de Burgos, and Alfonsina Storni, explore, with tragic vision, the poignancy and despair of the woman whose alienation is so profound and implacable that she must finally end her own life.

See also: Existentialism, Feminism, Nihilism, Rebellion, Theatrical Absurdity, Tragicomic Hero, Underground Man.

Selected Bibliography

Abood, Edward F. *Underground Man*. San Francisco: Chandler and Sharp, 1973.

Barrett, William. *Irrational Man: A Study in Existential Philosophy*. Garden City, N.Y.: Doubleday, 1958.

Schacht, Richard. *Alienation*. Garden City, N.Y.: Anchor Books, 1970.

Wilson, Colin. *The Outsider*. Boston: Houghton Mifflin, 1956.

NANCY GRAY DÍAZ

AMAZONS

Female warriors are described in many cultures. Take, for instance, the Germanic Brunhild of legend and history or the British Boadicea (or Boudicca), queen of the Iceni, who led her warriors in a revolt against Roman rule. China has the ballad of Mulan (c. 220–588), a girl who disguised herself for years as a male warrior and accomplished such feats of arms that the Khan was willing to reward her with a powerful administrative position. But because of the formative Greek tradition, the word "Amazon" has come to refer to a woman living in a society in which women are dominant and go to war, not in disguise but usually in recognizably female attire. The pendulum of opinion about the historicity of Amazons has swung back and forth and might itself yield interesting material for the anthropologist. However, the most recent studies of Amazons (William Blake Tyrell, *Amazons: A Study in Athenian Mythmaking* and Abby Wettan Kleinbaum, *The War against the Amazons*) show little interest in this particular question. Tyrell says programmatically: "My reading of the myth begins with the observation that there is no way, through modern historical methods, to affirm or deny the Amazons' existence, since the evidence we have pertains only to myth and not to the Amazons *qua* Amazons. . . . The existence of the Amazons remains moot." While there are many cities of the ancient Greek world whose history and culture are said to be linked to Amazons, archeologists and historians do not seem to have conclusive proof of the existence of a female warrior culture. On the other hand, a mere opposition of "myth" (or "literature") versus "reality" is naïve. Ever since the seminal (and now much criticized) study of Bachofen, *Das Mutterrecht* (*Mother Right*, 1861), Amazons have been scrutinized *qua* myth as to what they reveal about reality in the classical and preclassical periods. Moreover, it may be said that like the legends of Faust and of Hamlet, the concept of the Amazon has importance beyond the intent of those who first reared it. While the questions raised since the nineteenth century about the factual core of ancient myths and legends certainly deserve rethinking, the Amazon legend after the Classical Age has had a life of its own in imaginative literature. Though this life is not independent of the classical image of Amazons, it deserves attention for its own sake.

Since armed confrontation between male and female almost invariably elicits authors' comments about male and female roles, such accounts in historical and fictional works of the past yield significant insight into the sensibility of those periods. For our times Kleinbaum reports that an increasing number of women "feel irresistibly drawn to the idea of Amazons. Its core is the image of a free and autonomous community of women." This is so although the very origin of the idea is, as she thinks, male: "The Amazon is, after all a dream of the past, a vision originated by men. As surely as no spider's web was built for the glorification of flies, the Amazon idea was not designed to enhance women, but to serve the needs of its male creators." In this view she is not far removed from Tyrrell, who, scrutinizing in detail an array of political and cultural implications of Greek Amazon lore, at one point concludes: "The Amazon myth was developed by men in charge of the media."

Antiquity

To the ancients Amazons were barbarians usually thought to derive from the Scythians; they were meat eaters and experts at the bow (see Aeschylus' play, *Hiketides*, 1.287 [*The Suppliants*, 463 B.C.], where the king says to the female refugees that if they were armed with bows he would take them for "man eating" Amazons). They were supposed to have carried moon-shaped shields, and were sometimes thought to have but one breast, their name being explained as *a* (no) + *mazos* (breast) ("but it is more likely that the name accounted for the condition," Tyrrell states).

Some of the major Greek heroes connected with Amazons are Herakles, Theseus, Achilles, Bellerophon, and Alexander. The ninth of Herakles' Twelve Labors was the task of winning a girdle from the queen of the Amazons, for which feat he was sometimes called Amazonius, a title adopted for that reason by the Roman Emperor Commodus. According to the mythology of Apollodorus (*Bibliothēkē* [*Bibliotheca*, 2d century B.C.]) Herakles was sent across the sea to get the girdle, a warrior's belt and token of prowess in war; Hippolyta promised to give him the girdle, but Hera stirred up strife. In the commotion that followed, Herakles killed Hippolyta and took the girdle. Tyrrell has shown that as Herakles takes by force the girdle (for which the word used is *zoster*, phonically and semantically related to the word *zone*, a woman's girdle) he symbolically rapes Hippolyta. In Euripides' play *Hēraklēs* (*Heracles*, c. 417 B.C.), the chorus recounts Herakles' Amazonian exploits. Theseus is sometimes said to have participated in Herakles' exploit and sometimes is imagined to have gone on a quest alone. Since there is some uncertainty about the name of the Amazon (Hippolyta, Antiope, Menalippe, and Glauce are mentioned), it has been surmised that this myth is not truly ancient. According to Plutarch, Theseus invited one of the Amazons (later called Hippolyta) on board his ship and seduced her. This act led to the war of the Amazons, in which Athens was besieged for three months. Finally a peace treaty was negotiated with the help of Hippolyta. Plutarch knows also about a version (which he characterizes as fable) according to which the Amazons came to avenge Theseus' rejection of Hippolyta in favor of Phaedra.

To later European literature (up to Kleist's tragedy *Penthesilea* [1808]) possibly the most popular Amazon episode is Achilles' slaying of Penthesilea in battle before Troy; he falls in love with her when he takes off her helmet as she lies dying. The episode appears to derive from the epic *Aethiopis*, which has not come down to us. According to Quintus Smyrnaeus, who many centuries later (4th century A.D.) elaborated on the scene in his epic on the fall of Troy, (*Ta meth'Homeron* [*Posthomerica*]), Penthesilea had come to seek fame at the side of the Trojans. Depicting the reaction of women to Amazons, Quintus Smyrnaeus also renders the rousing speech of the Trojan "feminist" Tisiphone, who watches the Amazons fight side by side with their husbands and urges the Trojan women to do likewise; she is dissuaded by the wise Theano who points to the Amazons' intensive training in warfare and horsemanship. While Bellerophon's combat with Amazons has no sexual overtones (the Amazons are merely warriors whom he overcomes, as he overcomes the Chaemera and the Solymi), the episode of the beautiful Amazon queen Thalestris visiting Alexander in order to conceive a child by this most renowned warrior has excited the imagination of many readers and writers, although it was already discounted by the ancients. Plutarch reports that when an officer of Alexander's command heard the story, he laughed and asked: "And where was I at the time?"

Through Quintus Smyrnaeus and, even more importantly through Dares and Dictys, whose reports of the fall of Troy (translated in Latin c. 4th or 5th century A.D.) were thought in the Middle Ages and the Renaissance biased but authentic (while Homer and Virgil were considered poetic) until they were shown to be invented, the Amazon matter (and particularly the Penthesilea story) kindled the imagination of medieval and Renaissance writers. In Dictys' *Ephemeris belli Troiani*, purportedly told from the Greek perspective, Penthesilea is no match for Achilles, who overcomes her in the first battle—she is then dumped, still half-alive, into the Scamander and drowned as punishment for transgressing "the bounds of nature and her sex" (bk. 4, ch. 3). This is consistent both with Greek resentment for an enemy and more specifically with Greek animosity against such female warriors, who, as Tyrrell has shown, in many ways represented the very opposite of what male and family-centered Greek society held dear.

According to Dares, whose equally fictitious account *De excidio Troiae historia* became even more popular because the Latin speaking West approved of his Trojan bias, Penthesilea's battle is expanded to huge proportions, until she is finally slain by Neoptolemus. Dio Chrysostomos (c. A.D. 40–112) criticized Homer in his eleventh oration for not including the expedition of the Amazons, and seems to confirm Dares' version when he reports that an unusually ferocious

Amazon tried to set fire to the Greek ships and was killed by Neoptolemus with a naval pike.

The Medieval and Renaissance Period

Dares' narration became an epic poem in the late twelfth century, the *Roman de Troie* (c. 1165) by Benoît de Sainte-Maure, which was closely read by Boccaccio, who included sections on Amazons in his biographies *De claris mulieribus* (1360–1362, *On Famous Women*) and was paraphrased in Latin prose by Guido delle Colonne in his *Historia destructionis Troiae* (c. 1285). Though there is in Dares' account no indication of Penthesilea's motives in defending Troy, and Dictys says her motive is simply mercenary, Guido states that she acted "ob amoris Hectoris." This is also reported by Boccaccio, who goes on to elaborate that Penthesilea did deeds of valor to please Hector, a courtly love situation in reverse (*De claris mulieribus*, ch. 30). In his *Troy Book* (1412–1420), poem based on Guido's version, Lydgate presents this "romantic" motive in characteristic fashion, saying that she "loved with al hir hoole herte / Worthy Hector."

Although Christine de Pisan derives her stories from the same traditional material, in her works Amazons begin to serve feminist purposes. In the allegory *Le livre de la mutacion de fortune* (1403) she applies the heroic qualities of "fortitudo et sapientia" (fortitude and wisdom) to Penthesilea and, giving the word "homme" full semantic content, says of her: "En tout le monde on ne savoit / Homme qui tant eust proece" (11.17568–69, ed. Suzanne Solente). In the prose work *Cité des dames* (1405), translated as *City of Ladyes* (1521), Christine even says that Penthesilea's courage inspired her to practice life-long virginity: "This lady was of so hyghe courage that she dysdeyned never to be coupled to man but was a mayde all her lyfe." This idea, which Christine also uses to characterize another Amazon queen, Synope, runs counter to the opinion, commonly held by the ancients, that Amazons lived rather promiscuously, seeking out men at certain seasons in order to have offspring, an opinion that led Boccaccio (in a curious conflation with the Alexander-Thalestris story) to report as a possible interpretation that Penthesilea came to Troy in order to have a child by Hector. Christine's Amazons fight valiantly; if tradition dictates that they finally succumb, they usually do so as the result of male cowardice or treachery.

To the Renaissance, Amazons were a significant source of imaginative interest. Kleinbaum has described how the discovery of the West Indies amplified the interest in Amazons by Europeans long since exposed to such fantastic accounts (as Sir John Mandeville's): "For two hundred years European literature, first Spanish and Portuguese, then Italian, French, German, and English, was laced with Amazon dreams." Encountering unheard of races and civilizations, the Portuguese and Spanish conquistadores saw them through the spectacles of ancient and contemporary descriptions of Amazons. The name "California" derives from Queen Califa who in *Las sergas de Esplandián* (1510), Montalvo's sequel to the popular romance *Amadís de Gaula* (*Amadis of Gaul*), which he compiled and published in 1508, was imagined to live with her Amazons and griffons on an island abounding with gold and precious stones (see Kleinbaum, ch. 3).

Renaissance writers frequently explored the ambiguity of gender disguise. We should distinguish these characters of prose and verse fiction who disguised their gender from the Amazons, because the difference can sometimes become thematic: female warriors (in male disguise) are brought into opposition, even martial confrontation, with Amazons. Quite in agreement with the late classical and medieval tradition, Amazons are usually depicted as monstrous in the Renaissance, like the proud Erifilla who, saddled on a wolf, attacks Ruggiero in Ariosto's epic *Orlando furioso* (1516), or as in Spenser's epic poem, where Queen Randegund, who after overcoming Artegal through a ruse, puts him to the "sordid office" of the distaff and hangs his companion (*The Faerie Queene*, 1590–1596). It will be up to the female warrior Britomart, who is disguised as a male (and in Spenser's allegory stands for the power of chastity in action), to lop off the cruel Amazon's head after a long fight, in which Britomart herself receives a gashing wound, and thus to free Artegal from female rule and abject bondage.

Spenser's account of the Britomart-Radegund confrontation can be seen as a tight version of Ariosto's fanciful report of the killer women, which draws together many elements of the Amazon myth, including speculations about their origin (*Orlando furioso*, cantos 19–20). The killer women subject any male newcomer to bondage (making him work at spindles or shuttles) or kill him unless he is able to vanquish ten men in combat and, then, in the same night, please ten women. Ariosto describes how a group of noble travellers, shipwrecked in the perilous city of the Amazons, is drawing lots in order to determine who will have to take upon himself the dreaded test, and then wryly makes the female warrior Marfisa (who wears male disguise) insist that she be included in the lottery—and he has Marfisa win. It is Marfisa finally who will overcome the "unnatural" Amazon society and lead her companions to freedom.

There is at least a suggestion in some Renaissance romances that through subjection to women, even by infatuation, men become effeminate. The few males that live with Ariosto's killer women wear long skirts, while Spenser's Artegal, by being moved to pity by Radegund's beauty, falls into the subjection in which he is forced to wear women's clothes. The most curious episode of this type is in Sidney's pastoral romance, *Arcadia* (1590), where Pyrocles puts on an elaborate Amazon disguise in order to be close to the lady with whom he has fallen in love. Mark Rose has interpreted this episode as expressing vividly the Renaissance commonplace that falling in love makes a man "womanish" ("Sidney's Womanish Man," *Review of English Studies* 15 [1964]:353–63), and this is indeed what Pyrocles' friend is charging ("This effeminate love of a woman doth so womanize a man"). But Pyrocles will reject the charge saying that he is adopting the disguise for the sole purpose of proving himself a man.

Although it seems that Queen Elizabeth appeared in armor as she reviewed her troops at Tilbury in 1588, the association of Amazons with unnaturalness was so strong that her contemporaries rarely called her one. In the anonymous and satirical *Mundus alter et idem* (1609), the Amazon society described is an explication of the topos of the world turned upside down. Jean Gagen has shown that many seventeenth-century plays finally end with ex-Amazons giving up their rule for the love of a man (*The New Woman*, 1954).

The Seventeenth Century to the Present

As opposed to an imaginative and literary interest of early seventeenth-century writers (e.g., Ben Jonson in his play *Masque of Queens* [1609] and Thomas Heywood in *Gynaikeion*, known as *The History of Women* [1624]), the late seventeenth and eighteenth centuries began to take a scholarly or at least an antiquarian collector's interest in Amazons: Pierre Petit's scholarly and elaborately illustrated *De amazonibus dissertatio* (Amsterdam, 1687) was followed by Claude Marie Guyon's *Histoire des amazones anciennes et modernes* (Paris, 1740), and Joseph Towers draws on both works in his *Essay on the Antient Amazons* (London, 1785). Guyon's description of Penthesilea may give a notion of how contemporary (male) views conditioned that Amazon's eighteenth-century image: "The blackness of her hair and eye-brows brought out the whiteness of her skin. Spirit and vivacity sparkled in her eyes. Her grace tempered their fire. Her modesty and reserve demanded respect. Her affability and graceful smile made her lovable. Penthesilea knew how to unite the sweetness of her sex with the appearance and virtues of a warrior." Joseph Towers, who with more than conventional modesty calls his essay "an inquiry of no great importance" and chiefly "a matter of literary curiosity," lacks Guyon's enthusiasm for Amazons and his ability to combine such a wide spectrum of fashionable qualities in martial women. In his concluding paragraph he quotes Rousseau, apparently with approval, as saying, "The empire of the woman is an empire of softness, of address, of complacency. Her commands are caresses, her menaces are tears," and complements this ideal with Dr. Johnson's view that the Amazons' courage was deformed by ferocity. "The hand could not be very delicate," he quotes from the essays, *The Idler* (1758–1760), "that was only employed in drawing the bow and brandishing the battle-axe."

To the twentieth century the concept of an Amazon society has become both a topic of feminist studies and a source of popular spectacle of Broadway and screen productions (see Kleinbaum's chapter "Understanding Them/Joining Them"). Before this, however, Heinrich von Kleist created the powerful tragedy *Penthesilea*. The Amazon queen's hate-love, partly generated by the conflict between her love for Achilles and her attachment to her female subjects, drives her into a manic fit in which she mauls her lover to death. Like her dogs, she sinks her teeth in his flesh. After his death she only gradually returns to her senses and to the terrifying realization of what she has done: "Did I kiss him to death?" This line, called "by far the silliest of the play" (Kleinbaum), is consistent with Kleist's interest, and that of the romantics in general, in the nexus of sex, sadistic perversity, and love in male-female relationships.

In Tennyson's poem "The Princess" (1857–1861), the lecturer "Lady Psyche," surveying the history of the human race and of female oppression "glanced at the legendary Amazon / As emblematic of a nobler age," an intent (as Mary R. Lefkowitz has shown so persuasively) not unlike that of some modern feminists reviewing and reinterpreting the Amazon matter to make a statement about contemporary society (Lefkowitz, "Princess Ida, the Amazons and a Women's College Curriculum," *Times Literary Supplement*, 27 Nov. 1981, 1399–1401; Mary Lefkowitz refers to accounts of Amazons in Helen Diner, *Mothers and Amazons: The First Feminine History of Culture* [1965; German ed., 1932] and Phyllis Chesler, *Women and Madness* 1972]). For anyone seriously interested in the emergence of the thinking about Amazons, the sobering accounts by such classicists as Lefkowitz and Tyrrell will be food for thought, the more so since both are in basic agreement.

See also: Feminism, Utopia.

Selected Bibliography

DuBois, Page. *Centaurs and Amazons: Women and the Pre-History of the Great Chain of Being*. Ann Arbor: University of Michigan Press, 1982.
Kleinbaum, Abby W. *The War against the Amazons*. New York: New Press, 1983.
Tyrrell, William B. *Amazons: A Study in Athenian Mythmaking*. Baltimore, Johns Hopkins University Press, 1984.

WINFRIED SCHLEINER

ANDROGYNY

Androgyny derives from the Greek roots *andros* (male) and *gyne* (female). The term has frequently been considered a synonym for hermaphroditism and bisexuality. The more expanded definition of androgyny, however, suggests a spirit of reconciliation and cooperation between the male (the rational) and the female (the intuitive) aspects of the human psyche, between socially imposed traits and modes of behavior for the male and female sexes, or between the masculine (analytical) and the feminine (synthetic) approaches to reality. In this sense, androgyny means the experience of wholeness or perfection symbolized by the fusion of male and female or masculine and feminine traits and attitudes within the individual and within the culture or society. More broadly, then, androgyny is defined as the ONE that contains and balances the TWO—the male and female or the masculine and feminine opposites.

Androgyny as Archetype

Researchers who have explored the idea of androgyny maintain that it is an archetype deeply rooted in the human psyche. In *Androgyny: Toward a New Theory of Sexuality* (1976) June Singer describes androgyny as "the oldest archetype of which we have any experience" and which "appears in us as an innate sense of primordial cosmic unity." Similarly, Carl G. Jung, in "The Special Phenomenology of the Child Archetype" (*Psyche and Symbol*, ed. Violet S. de Laszlo [1968], explains the concept of the androgynous being as a "projection of unconscious wholeness" that refers back to a primitive state of mind in which differences were either completely merged or barely separated and that has become a "unifying symbol," a "symbol of the creative union of opposites." Two books by Erich Neumann, *The Great Mother* (1963) and *The Origins and History of Consciousness* (1971), follow Jung's theories. Neumann shows that the earliest mythmakers perceived their original and ideal human state as androgynous. They projected their preconscious existence in mythic images of "the uroborus, the circular snake biting its tail" (an androgynous symbol frequently appearing in literature). The "archetype" of the "One" or the "All," the uroborus is the "Great Round" representing a perfect state of being that contains the opposites and which is therefore self-sufficient, content, and independent.

The round gives birth to the primal dualities, male and female. In various cultures this symbolic split in the human psyche was further intensified by an increasing dominance of the masculine, patriarchal view of the world, which came to associate the male side of the duality with man and the female with woman and which assumed the superiority of the male and the inferiority of the female. Thus, woman was relegated to a subordinate position in human society; man denied the female in himself and suppressed the feminine impulse in society.

The separation of the male and female or the masculine and feminine opposites represents a loss of wholeness and harmony that humankind strives to recapture. According to Neumann, the symbols through which human beings sought to grasp the beginning in mythological terms have persisted throughout the ages. As long as human beings shall exist, Neumann says, "the Primal Deity who is sufficient unto himself, and the self who has gone beyond the opposites, will reappear in the image of the round," of the androgynous being. For, in addition to symbolizing the perfect beginning in which "the opposites have not yet flown apart," the round also represents the perfect end because in it "the opposites have come together again in a synthesis" (*Origins*). The distant goal of humankind's development is to find again the primal wholeness that was lost with the separation of the opposites and the increasing clarity of consciousness.

The human quest for wholeness and perfection, for androgyny, described by Neumann and Jung, is ever-present in myth, ritual, art, and literature. Joseph Campbell discloses it in *The Hero with a Thousand Faces* (1949) as he explores worldwide representations of androgynous gods and as he examines the androgynous, mythic experience of the hero. Also, in *The Masks of God: Occidental Mythology* (1970), Campbell identifies the androgynous impulse permeating world mythology. Norman O. Brown, in *Life against Death: The Psychoanalytical Meaning of History* (1959), demonstrates the persistence of androgyny in all the dreams of mysticism. And an essay by A. J. L. Busst, "The Image of the Androgyne in the Nineteenth Century," which appears in *Romantic My-*

thologies edited by Ian Fletcher (1967), analyzes the different images of the androgyne prevalent in the works of a number of nineteenth-century artists and authors. In *The Denial of Death* (1973), Ernest Becker asserts that such themes and images evince "a striving for wholeness, a striving that is not sexual but ontological. It is the desire of being for a recapture of the (Agape) unity with the rest of nature, as well as for a completeness in oneself. It is a desire for a healing of the ruptures of existence, the dualism of self and body, self and other, self and world."

Imaginative literature, perhaps more than any other form, presents a superb embodiment of the eternal quest for the lost ideal of androgyny. Two books of literary criticism, both published in 1973 and influenced in many ways by feminist theory, explore themes of androgyny in literary works. Carolyn Heilbrun's *Toward a Recognition of Androgyny* shows the "hidden river" of androgyny appearing and reappearing in European literature throughout the ages as "a continuing human ideal." And Nancy Bazin's *Virginia Woolf and the Androgynous Vision* examines the novels of Virginia Woolf in light of Woolf's belief that the work of art must be androgynous; it must capture and harmonize both the masculine and feminine opposites. Both Heilbrun and Bazin seek to show that in societies where the claims of the masculine, patriarchal view of the world became ever more insistent, literary artists committed themselves to a search for stability and unity of being. These authors further demonstrate that abiding works of literature exemplify a longing for wholeness and harmony, for androgyny, and a struggle to reintegrate the masculine and feminine opposites both in individuals and in the society.

To illustrate the persistence of androgyny as "a continuing human ideal" in literature, the remainder of this entry seeks to unfold the presence of themes related to androgyny in selected ancient creation myths and in representative literary works by authors from Western culture. Because it flows through literature as a "hidden river," androgyny as a theme may not appear as an obvious motif in many literary works. Thus, careful interpretation is often necessary to disclose its presence. Such interpretation, guided by an awareness and understanding of androgyny as an ancient concept, is not meant to supplant but to provide an added dimension to traditional, already widely accepted interpretations. Interpretations included in this entry rely heavily on the ideas and theories presented in Carolyn Heilbrun's book *Toward a Recognition of Androgyny*.

The Background of Androgyny in Ancient Creation Myths

The idea of androgyny first appears in the creation myths found in the religions of various cultures. Such myths usually begin with an androgynous godhead that gives birth to the male and female or the masculine and feminine opposites. Taoism, the system of beliefs through which the ancient Chinese sought to explain the world, embodies a clear expression of androgyny. In Taoism, the Tao—the Middle Way, the undivided unity lying behind all earthly phenomena—gives rise to the Yin (female, passive) and Yang (male, active) principles that signify the duality of nature. According to ancient Chinese thought, the harmonious interaction of Yin and Yang in the universe and in human beings resolves all the conflicts of nature and brings prosperity to the world.

Well-known versions of the creation from Greek mythology also represent an androgynous deity in the union of Mother Earth and Father Sky—a union responsible for all the duality and multiplicity in the universe. Likewise, both the Purānas (compiled c. 4th–11th century) and the Upanishads (c. 10th–7th century B.C.) in Hindu mythology contain accounts of the separation of the originally androgynous godhead. In Genesis (1:27) God created man in his own image, "male and female," *before* Eve was taken from Adam's body. This indicates that the Judeo-Christian God is androgynous. The supreme being in American Indian creation mythology also represents an androgynous whole from which male and female are created. The Cheyenne creation myth "How the World Was Made," for example, describes Maheo, the All Spirit, who fashions man from a rib taken out of his right side and woman from a rib taken out of his left side. Not only do ancient stories of the creation reveal a separation of the originally androgynous One into Two, but many also disclose the halves, thereafter striving unceasingly to reunite, to restore the primal state of wholeness. In the familiar story recorded in Plato's dialogue *Symposion* (*Symposium*, c. 384 B.C.), for example, the parts of the initially round (androgynous) man-woman being split in half by Zeus continually strive to reunite, to become whole again.

Themes of Androgyny in the Epics and Tragedies of Ancient Greece

Themes of androgyny are readily apparent in the epic poems and tragic dramas of ancient Greece. Homer's epic poems *Ilias* and *Odysseia* (*Iliad* and *Odyssey*, c. 8th century B.C.), for instance, embody a contrast between two different worlds. The world of the *Iliad* is one of manly work, of war and violence, of men who perform monstrous acts with matter-of-fact efficiency and of women whose fate depends on the outcome. It is a world dominated by the masculine principle. In the world of the *Odyssey*, however, the feminine principle prevails. The poem chronicles the long voyage of the hero Odysseus, as he, guided or detailed by female influences, searches for and finally reaches home and the warmth and sensitivity of the feminine principle that awaits him there. In the *Odyssey*, the masculine and feminine opposites are reunited in peace and harmony.

In a society where women were severely restrained and accorded subordinate status, ironically, the dramatists of ancient Greece portrayed women in androgynous roles. Such writers as Euripides, Sophocles, and Aeschylus created powerful and assertive women characters like Clytemnestra, Cassandra, Medea, and Antigone who are not totally defined or encompassed by their sex. Contrast, for instance, the daring and defiant yet warm, loving, and instinctively human Antigone with her sister Ismene, the appropriately submissive and obedient lady. Carolyn Heilbrun suggests that if we reverse the roles of Antigone and Haemon in Sophocles' play *Antigonē* (c. 441 B.C.), we can readily perceive the "androgynous quality" of the work, for "it is in those works where the roles of the male and female protagonists can be reversed without appearing ludicrous or perverted that the androgynous ideal is present."

The Greek tragedies are peopled with characters who exhibit androgynous traits. Dionysus in Euripides' play *Bakchai* (*The Bacchants*, c. 405 B.C.), for instance, represents, in a sense, the androgynous being. In him the masculine and feminine opposites are united. Though male, Dionysus was treated and educated as a girl and grew up to be effeminate. To Thomas G. Rosenmeyer, Dionysus "presents himself as woman-in-man, or man-in-woman, the unlimited personality" within whom "strength mingles with softness, majestic terror with coquettish glances. To follow or to comprehend him we must ourselves give up our precariously controlled, socially desirable limitations" ("Tragedy and Religion: The Bacchae," *Euripides*, ed. Erich Segal [1968]). For June Singer, however, "Dionysus is not the true androgyne . . . for he has not come to peace with his feminine side. His masculine and feminine aspects are not fused, they are merely confused."

If not Dionysus, then Tiresias, the blind but uncannily wise prophet who appears in several of the Greek tragedies, epitomizes the androgynous existence. Tiresias has experienced life as both man and woman. His blindness and his intuitive knowledge are symbolic. Although he has lost the facility of external sight, associated with the masculine principle, he has gained strength and wisdom, which spring from his inner vision, a quality of the feminine. In Sophocles' *Oidipous tyrannos* (*Oedipus Rex*, c. 429 B.C.) the blind Tiresias embraces a vision of what is to come and offers Oedipus a warning that Oedipus does not heed. Only after his self-blinding does Oedipus perceive the truth, which has always been apparent to Tiresias. Significantly, too, Oedipus' daughters are the faithful ones who care for him in his blindness and lead him to redemption. Thus, Oedipus also emerges as an androgynous character who reigns heroically in a world of manly courage and valor and then retires to the comforts and saving graces of the feminine principle. Oedipus lives, like Tiresias, first in light and then in darkness.

The story of Tiresias appears again in book 3 of Ovid's epic poem *Metamorphoses* (c. A.D. 2–17). T. S. Eliot also uses Tiresias as a character in his poem *The Waste Land* (1922). According to Eliot's own analysis, what Tiresias "sees" is the substance of the poem. Eliot also says that Tiresias unites all other characters in the poem; all the men blend into one man, all the women into one woman, and "the two sexes meet in Tiresias" (*Collected Poems, 1909–1962* [1963]). Thus, in both ancient and modern literature, Tiresias stands as a literary embodiment of the androgynous ideal.

Shakespeare's Androgynous Vision

During the Renaissance, William Shakespeare emerges as the chief exponent of the androgynous vision. Like the Greek writers, Shakespeare portrays characters in androgynous roles. In his play *The Tempest* (1611), for instance, the lively little sprite Ariel, who defies final sexual identification, is fully androgynous. Shakespeare also skillfully exploits the Renaissance tradition of depicting girls disguised as boys and boys disguised as girls in such plays as *The Two Gentlemen of Verona* (c. 1594) and *As You Like It* (c. 1599). Many times, actors played the role of women in Shakespeare's dramas, for no English women are known to have performed in the public theater of Shakespeare's time. Carolyn Heilbrun comments on the androgynous quality of the male/female disguise in Shakespeare's plays. Few realize, she says, "that the beautiful ease of the passage from boy to girl is part of the point, if not the whole point," for Shakespeare. She further states that "disguise for Shakespeare is not always falsification." Rather, it "may be another indication of the wide spectrum of roles possible to individuals if they can but find the convenient trappings of another persona." Like the Greek tragedies, Shakespeare's dramas also embody an interplay between the masculine and feminine opposites. They further demonstrate the necessity for a proper balance between these two opposing principles if chaos and destruction are to be averted.

The Symbolism of Plato's Androgyne

An androgynous motif that appears throughout Western literature in a multiplicity of guises is the mystical union (or the innate desire for such a union) of two persons into a oneness. The description of the origin of the sexes and of romantic love found in Plato's *Symposium* seeks to explain this seemingly inevitable need for human conjoining that defies rational explanation. In the *Symposium*, Aristophanes describes the original man-woman being (the androgyne) as round on all sides and uniting within itself the two sexes. Out of anger, Zeus created the male and female when he cut this being in half "like a sorb apple which is halved for pickling." Ever after, the two halves chased each other trying to get back together; for they wanted desperately to be whole again, to be restored to their original double nature "which was once called androgynous." This longing for total merging often appears in literature as a kind of symbiotic relationship, a relationship of mutual dependence in which each person fulfills basic needs for the other.

Book 4 of Ovid's *Metamorphoses* presents the story of Salmacis, which may serve as one example of the desired androgynous union that Aristophanes describes in Plato's *Symposium*. In the story, the nymph of Lake Salmacis falls in love with the son of Hermes and Aphrodite. She clings to him so tightly that they become one being. (Of particular interest also is the story of book 10, which relates a quite different androgynous transformation. This story tells of the daughter of Telethusa, who is reared and dressed as a boy, who falls in love with a girl and is changed by an Egyptian goddess into a boy who experiences love and happiness thereafter.)

The famous medieval lovers, Tristan and Isolt in Gottfried's romance *Tristan* (c. 1210), provide another example of an androgynous union between lovers.

In the love that exists between Tristan and Isolt, Carolyn Heilbrun sees "a metaphor for the androgynous condition, the need of a merging of the masculine and feminine with equal passion." According to Heilbrun, the love potion that these lovers mistakenly drink "joins them in a union necessary to their very survival." Shakespeare's unforgettable lovers, Romeo and Juliet, are significant as well in this connection.

John Donne also pictures the androgynous merging of lovers in such poems as "The Canonization" (1635), "The Extasie" (1635), and "An Epithalamion" (1613). He frequently portrays lovers in a sexless two-in-oneness as in "The Undertaking" (1635), "The Relique" (1635), and "Elegy to the Lady Bedford" (c. 1614). (Of interest also is the androgynous motif in Donne's sermons. In several of these, he pictures his own soul as feminine; he depicts the believers in Christ as androgynous, and he represents the godhead as containing both masculine and feminine qualities.) Likewise, in Emily Brontë's novel *Wuthering Heights* (1847), Catherine and Heathcliffe's love represents the androgynous state. But these lovers desert the oneness that they find with each other and become engaged in an eternal search for the ideal love, each in quest of the other half that has been denied.

Often in literature, androgynous mergings occur between male-female twins. Carolyn Heilbrun comments on the "identity" of opposite-sex twins as a persistent symbol in literary works: "Throughout European literature, from the Greeks onward, the 'identity' of these twins has been continually stressed, as have in more outspoken periods, the incestuous impulses of the pair." The creation myths of many religions depict the original human pair as male-female twins who experience a miraculous birth and who are destined to join or to merge in wholeness. Ovid's *Metamorphoses* shows a female twin passionately in love with her brother. In book 3 of the epic poem *Faerie Queene* (1590–1596), Edmund Spenser describes opposite sex twins enclosed in their mother's womb displaying an urge toward union with each other. (In addition, we cannot ignore Spenser's hermaphroditic Venus—a veiled man-woman, who, according to William Nelson in *The Poetry of Edmund Spenser* symbolizes "conflict resolved" as does the snake, which binds her legs together, "its head and tail 'fast combined'." "She is the binding, generative power that holds together mother and child, man and woman, friend and friend, subject and sovereign, the diversity of a nation, the great globe itself.")

Among other literary works that portray the strong attraction between opposite sex twins, Heilbrun mentions John Barth's novel *The Sot-Weed Factor* (1960), in which Anna is driven toward fusion with her twin brother, Ebenezer. Anna evokes a comparison from Burlingame (another character in the story) with Aristophanes' version of the ancient split of the whole into parts that eternally seek each other:

Your sister is a driven and fragmented spirit, friend; the one half of her soul yearns but to fuse itself with yours, whilst the other half recoils at the thought. 'Tis neither love nor lust she feels for you, but a prime and massy urge to coalescence. . . . As Aristophanes maintained that male and female are displaced moieties of an ancient whole, and wooing but their vain attempt at union, so Anna . . . repines willy-nilly for the dark identity that twins share in the womb, and for the well-nigh fetal closeness of their childhood.

In similar manner, Byron's Manfred (dramatic poem, 1817) sees his own likeness in his twin sister. For her only does Manfred express a passionate love. And Mann's story "Wälsungenblut" ("Blood of the Walsung," 1921) depicts Siegmund and Sieglinde who ultimately find themselves in sexual embrace.

The Androgynous Impulse in Selected British and American Novels

The novel, in Carolyn Heilbrun's words, is "the great androgynous form." In it the ancient concept of androgyny has found a "new, perhaps ultimate, manifestation." Not all novels written can be said to embody the androgynous impulse. But many novels by British and American writers reveal the age-old quest for androgyny, for balance and harmony between the masculine and feminine opposites, for wholeness in both individuals and the society. Themes of androgyny in such works are apparent in the centrality of female characters who are not defined or confined by the conventional ideas of femininity prescribed for the female sex. Overtones of androgyny are also evident in the author's representation of equality between the male and female sexes and of, to again quote Heilbrun, "the peculiar human need to join the sexes in a shared destiny" ("The Masculine Wilderness of the American Novel," *Saturday Review*, 29 Jan. 1972, 43).

Daniel Defoe's *Moll Flanders* (1722) perhaps paved the way for the portrayal of a woman protagonist who is not encompassed by the traditional female role but who pursues diverse outlets for her energy. As Defoe was one of the first writers to use the novelistic form, so Moll Flanders served as a precursor of the woman as a central character portrayed in an androgynous role. Following her in Samuel Richardson's 1748 novel is Clarissa, who triumphs at the end of her story in the achievement of a near-androgynous spiritual identity. Clarissa's approach to wholeness, to androgyny, is conveyed through the snake that she chooses for her coffin. As previously indicated, the snake is an ancient androgynous symbol. "To Clarissa, it represents eternity, being circular, but because it contains in itself the male and female members, it is also androgynous: male in its serpent shape, female in its mouth which receives and surrounds" (Heilbrun, *Toward a Recognition of Androgyny*). Resembling Clarissa in many ways is Hester Prynne in Nathaniel Hawthorne's novel *The Scarlet Letter* (1850). The androgynous quality of Emily Brontë's *Wuthering Heights*, represented in the lovers Catherine and Heathcliff, has already been mentioned. Carolyn Heilbrun calls *Wuthering Heights* "a pure, androgynous novel": "the sense of waste, of lost spiritual and sexual power, of equality of worth between the sexes, is presented with no specific cry for revolution, but with a sense of a world deformed" (*Toward a Recognition of Androgyny*).

The works of three major twentieth-century British novelists reflect a similar "sense of a world deformed." In their writings, D. H. Lawrence, Virginia Woolf, and E. M. Forster demonstrate an imbalance and desire for harmony between two opposing approaches to reality, or ways of seeing, which they associate with the male and female sexes. In their essays and in their novels, these writers reveal a cry for wholeness and unity of being, for androgyny, in both personal and social life. Woolf and Forster were members of the "Bloomsbury Group," which Heilbrun writes of "not as the apotheosis of the androgynous spirit, but as the first actual example of such a way of life in practice." They lived "as though reason and passion might be equal ideas" (*Toward a Recognition of Androgyny*).

Lawrence's interest in defining and harmonizing the masculine and feminine opposites runs throughout his essays. In "Apropos of *Lady Chatterley's Lover*" (*Phoenix II*, ed. Warren Roberts and Harry Moore, 1968), for instance, he observes that human beings have two ways of knowing: "knowing in terms of apartness which is mental, rational, scientific, and knowing in terms of togetherness, which is religious and poetic." His "Study of Thomas Hardy" (*Phoenix*, ed. Edward McDonald, 1936) links these two ways with the two sexes. To the male he assigns such qualities as multiplicity, activity, time, change, intellect, spirit, rationality, and light. To the female he attributes oneness, stability, permanence, sensuousness, instinct, intuition, and darkness. Life, according to Lawrence, is "Two-in-One, Male and Female. Nor is either part greater than the other." Lawrence believes that all creativity depends upon the fruitful interaction of these two principles. Writing of Michelangelo and the "joy" of his pictures, Lawrence describes the moment of consummation, the androgynous moment, as "the perfect stable poise . . . the perfect combination of male and female in one figure." Through his pictures, Michelangelo, Lawrence says, seeks "the moment of consummation, the keystone, the pivot, in his own flesh. For his own body is both male and female."

Virginia Woolf's nonfiction also expresses her concern for unity and balance between the male and female principles. In *A Room of One's Own* (1929) for example, she writes of "two sexes in the mind corresponding to the two sexes in the body" which "require to be united in order to get complete satisfaction and happiness." In each of us, she says, "two powers preside, one male, one female." "The normal and comfortable state of being is that when the two live in harmony together, spiritually cooperating . . . Coleridge perhaps meant this when he said that a great mind must be androgynous. It is when this fusion takes place that the mind is fully fertilized and uses all its faculties."

In their novels both Lawrence and Woolf portray characters in search of what Lawrence calls "the moment of consummation," a point of wholeness, of unity, stability, and peace. This quest is communicated through the depiction of the opposition between the male and female or masculine and feminine principles and through a central character, in many instances a woman, who seeks to harmonize these opposing ways of seeing. In Lawrence's *Sons and Lovers* (1913),

Paul Morel struggles to achieve androgynous being—to integrate the masculine and feminine, the best qualities of his mother (whom Lawrence associates with the male view) and the best qualities of his father (whom Lawrence associates with the female), within himself. *Lady Chatterley's Lover* (1928) embodies a similar struggle in Constance Chatterley as she vacillates between the masculine world (the "mental consciousness") of Clifford Chatterley at Wragby Hall and the more feminine world (the "blood consciousness") of Oliver Mellors in the woods surrounding Wragby. It is with Mellors that Constance finds peace, serenity, and wholeness. In Virginia Woolf's *To the Lighthouse* (1927), the artist, Lily Briscoe, cannot complete her painting until she understands and appreciates the relationship between the opposing approaches to reality represented by Mrs. Ramsay (the feminine) and Mr. Ramsay (the masculine). Only then does she achieve the perfect point of balance that permits her to produce the "androgynous" work of art. *The Waves* (1931) shows each of Virginia Woolf's central characters, three male and three female, searching in his or her own way for integration and harmony. At the same time each of the three is a part of Woolf's androgynous whole. While neither character achieves the androgynous vision, the novel represents an androgynous whole in its design and rhythm. The androgynous impulse is also evident in Virginia Woolf's *Orlando* (1928), a fantasy biography in which the hero lives as a woman for half of his life.

Like Lawrence and Woolf, E. M. Forster links the two opposing approaches to reality to the two sexes. In the novel *Howards End* (1910), for instance, he associates the masculine with the Wilcoxes, whose house is predominantly male; and in the Schlegels, whose household is primarily female, he represents the feminine. The Wilcoxes represent the acquisitive, competitive approach to life, the outer, seen aspects of existence. The Schlegels represent the unseen, the inner, private life. *Howards End* focuses on connecting the seen and the unseen, the outer and the inner, the public and the private aspects of life represented by the two families. Chiefly through Margaret Schlegel and Mrs. Wilcox, Forster shows a struggle to unite the two into one, an attempt to achieve the androgynous whole. In the novel *A Passage to India* (1924), he demonstrates a similar urge toward connection and wholeness through Mrs. Moore and her spiritual essence, which pervades the novel even after her death.

Works by more contemporary novelists of the twentieth century also evince the urge toward androgyny. For example, Ursula Le Guin's *The Left Hand of Darkness* (1969) is a science fiction novel that presents the Gethenans who "do not see one another as men or women." "There is no division of humanity into strong and weak halves, protective/protected, dominant/submissive, owner/chattel, active/passive. In fact the whole tendency to dualism that pervades human thinking may be found to be lessened, or changed, on [the planet] Winter." Doris Lessing, especially in her later novels, issues an adamant plea for wholeness. Influenced by the doctrines of Sufism, Lessing speaks to illuminate the Sufi truth that "life is One." In such novels as *Briefing for a Descent Into Hell* (1971), *The Summer before the Dark* (1973), and *The Memories of a*

Survivor (1975), she depicts her central characters in search of harmony and integration with self and with all creation. In the novel *Meridian* (1976), Alice Walker's Meridian also progresses toward harmony and wholeness, toward androgyny. Through the full range of her experiences, Meridian creates a new self, an androgynous self. Her androgynous quality is communicated through a passage near the end of the novel when she visits a prison and the inmates ask, "Who was that person? That man/woman person with a shaved part in close-cut hair? A man's blunt face and thighs, a woman's breasts." Here, Meridian appears as one who has creatively united the masculine and feminine opposites and achieved a state of unconscious wholeness. Shug Avery in Alice Walker's *The Color Purple* (1982) is also an androgynous character.

Themes related to androgyny permeate world literature. This entry merely seeks to provide some representative examples of the portrayal and exploration of this theme in selected literature primarily from Western culture.

See also: Love in Greek and Roman Literature, Metamorphosis, Sex (Heterosexual, Erotic).

Selected Bibliography

Eliade, Mircea. *The Two and the One*. New York: Harper and Row, 1965.

Harding, Mary Esther. *Woman's Mysteries Ancient and Modern: A Psychological Interpretation of the Feminine Principle as Portrayed in Myth, Story, and Dreams*. New York: Bantam, 1971.

Warren, Barbara. *The Feminine Image in Literature*. Hayden Humanities Series. Rochelle Park, N.J.: Hayden, 1973.

Women's Studies: An Interdisciplinary Journal 2 (1974) (A special issue on androgyny).

ALMA S. FREEMAN

ANTI-HERO

Frequently confused with the rogue of the picaresque novel, the anti-hero is distinctively a phenomenon of modernism, the principal tenet of which is that there is no such thing as essence since the times are changing and we are being changed in them. Therefore, when an author uses an anti-hero, either to express his own philosophy directly or to advance a thesis-novel by which he plans to refute modernism in some way, he postulates that traditional values are irrelevant to his character. Keeping in mind that an author may not agree with his anti-hero's expressed views and conduct, what Seán O'Faoláin writes on the subject in his collection of critical essays, *The Vanishing Hero* (1956), is quite helpful:

This personage is not a social creation. He is his own creation, that is, the author's personal creation. He is a much less neat and tidy concept, since he is always presented as groping, puzzled, cross, mocking, frustrated, and isolated, manfully or blunderingly trying to establish his own personal, supra-social codes. He is sometimes ridiculous through lack of perspicacity, accentuated by a foolhardy if attractive personal courage. He is sometimes intelligent, in the manner of Julien Sorel or Stephen Dedalus. Whatever he is, weak or brave, brainy or bewildered, his one abiding characteristic is that, like his author-creator, he is never able to see any Pattern in life and rarely its Destination.

Fine as this is, not to insist upon the vital connection between the anti-hero and modernism is to stray from the truth of the matter, which is that, far from "trying to establish his own personal, supra-social codes," the anti-hero is always a displaced person and, in relation to society, infrasocial. His self-centeredness makes him not only unheroic but anti-heroic. In his *Anatomy of Criticism: Four Essays* (1957), Northrop Frye deplores the widespread loss of heroism, which he contrasts as a "decisive act of spiritual freedom" to the "bondage, frustration, or absurdity" characteristic of the ironic anti-hero. The anti-hero is bound by the *Zeitgeist*, which usurps his personhood and changes him into its *persona*, or mask. The frustration involved is that of complete human being. Instead of acting on principle, the anti-hero reacts to the main chance or opportunity.

In the wake of the decline of what Marshall McLuhan has described as the audile-tactile participatory roundness of medieval culture, the anti-hero emerges from a debris of linear-sequential typographical functional units that are engineered to be repeatable, replaceable, and impressive ("striking") in the production of visual artifacts. He takes his image from that debris, repeating his tics, knowing that he is eminently replaceable, and inclined to violence ("striking"), whether through verbal irony or his fists. His idea of freedom is breaking out of this pattern; hence, his unpredictability.

Unable to perceive or share in the larger active patterns of human existence, the sense of a meaningful life, the anti-hero is the prisoner of his own sensibility. He has no motive for acting that does not directly relate to that aspect of the self which Aristotle called *to krinon* (the "sorter") and St. Thomas Aquinas the *sensus communis*, the "common sense"; and, indeed, that is not confined to it. The anti-hero is keenly aware of his environment, but he is alienated from intellectual and religious traditions. He is, perforce, a lone wolf, what the Italians call *un cane sciolto* ("a stray dog"). In a signification of the term not fully appreciated by the average reader, the anti-hero lives not so much by his wits, as does the *pícaro*, as by the sensate acumen (he is "street-wise") of "common sense." This common sense is really "the common sense," the "sorter" that centrifugally seeks out stimuli by means of the external senses and distinguishes the environment only as a mosaic of sensation. Within the sphere of pure sensibility, the sorter is complemented by the imagination (phantasy), the estimative power (akin to instinct in animals), and the memory. The sorter is self-reflexive as a power, though the data it acquires and sifts vary from moment to moment. When Guy de Maupassant, in the preface to his novel *Pierre et Jean* (1888), wrote that "every theory is the generalized expression of a temperament asking itself questions," he fixed on the self-reflexive "temperament" (sensibility) as the critical faculty of creative modernism, which, of course, is not creative at all but diaphanous.

In the light shed by the above remarks, an anti-hero may be defined as a temperament interfacing or, more accurately, in osmosis with its environment.

The Background in Antiquity

In Homer's epic poem *Ilias* (*Iliad*, c. 8th century B.C.), Thersites, the ugliest and most scurrilous of the Greeks besieging Troy, is an anti-hero, a temperament uncontrolled by what Marshall McLuhan has called "*ratio*-nality." The demented Lotos-Eaters and some of the suitors of Penelope (Homer's epic poem *Odysseia* [*Odyssey*, c. 8th century B.C.]) are temperaments disenfranchised of will power and intellect. In other words, they are brutish and brutal. The animals in Aesop's fables (sixth century B.C.) utilize cunning that is indistinguishable from the estimative power of the sensibility. The quaquaversal Socrates, presented by Aristophanes in the comic drama *Nephelai* (*The Clouds*, 423 B.C.) as a sophist inhabiting an air-borne basket, is infrasocial, thanks to his skeptical temperament. Theophrastus (c. 370–288 B.C.) exhibits a gallery of temperaments (precursors to the Elizabethan humors) in his *Charaktēres* (*Characters*, n.d.). Hermaphroditus, his sexuality dissolved and confused in the pool of the nymph Salmacis, is temperamentally labile and "impressionable," as is true of other characters in Ovid's epic poem *Metamorphoses* (c. A.D. 2–17). In the *Satyricon* (A.D. 60), the satirical romance in prose and verse by Petronius, Trimalchio, a wealthy tasteless upstart, gives a fantastic dinner in keeping with his temperament, upon which F. Scott Fitzgerald (1896–1940) patterned the entertainments offered his guests on his estate by the parvenu Jay Gatsby in his novel *The Great Gatsby* (1925).

The Dark and Middle Ages

In the Anglo-Saxon epic poem *Beowulf* (c. 8th century), the brutish (villainous) Grendel and his dam subvert the courtesy exemplified by Heorot Hall by their nocturnal forays. In *Hell*, part 1 of his epic poem *La divina commedia* (*The Divine Comedy*, c. 1320), Dante Alighieri (1265–1321) describes the damned as those "who have lost the good of intellect" ("ch' hanno perduto il ben dello intelletto": *Inferno*, 3.18). Among them he situates the trimmers, "these wretches who were never alive" ("questi sciaurati, che mai non fur vivi": 3.64), who took their shape from their chances. In canto 21, Dante introduces a grotesque rout of boorish devils led in their Wild Hunt by Alichino (French, *Harlequin*), who foreshadows the anti-heroic spirit of the times in Nathaniel Hawthorne's short story "My Kinsman, Major Molineux" (1851), figured by a rabble-rousing "Lord of Misrule," who has half his body painted red, the other half painted black. Knead the devils of the Grotesque Cantos into human form and the result is Sebastian Brant's satire *Das Narrenschiff* (*The Ship of Fools*, 1494), upon which Katherine Anne Porter patterned her novel *Ship of Fools* (1962). In "Ballade de la grosse Margot" (1461, "Ballad of Fat Margot"), François Villon sounds the rallying cry of the anti-heroes (36–37): "Nous deffuyons onneur, il nous deffuit,/ En ce bordeau ou tenons nostre estat'' (''We flee from honor, it flees from us,/ In this bordello where we manage our affairs'').

The Renaissance, Reformation, and Seventeenth Century

Retaining the lubricity of the *fabliaux*, Boccaccio (1313–1375) polished and refined the ''dirty joke,'' often sacrilegious in character (e.g., the story of Rustico the monk and the would-be hermitess), to high art. In 1532, Franc͵ois Rabelais published *Pantagruel*, and with Pantagruel, Gargantua, and the Abbey of The͵-le`me, whose motto was ''Fais ce que voudras'' (''Do whatever you want''), enormous sensuality was unleashed, mostly of a gluttonous and libidinous kind. In Germany there appeared from an unknown hand the merry prankster Till Eulenspiegel, who was to be enshrined in a tone-poem by Richard Strauss (1864–1949). Much coarser than Till is Grobianus, another peasant and the subject of Friedrich Dedekind's satire (*Grobianus*, 1549). The desire for self-gratification knew no limits, and *Die Historia von Dr. Johann Faust* (published anonymously in Frankfurt in 1587) tells of a magician so ambitious that he sold his soul to the devil.

With the publication of the novel *Lazarillo de Tormes* (1554), the knight errant of chivalry gave way to his proletarian counterpart, the resourceful vagabond. This tramp was accompanied by a partner whom he initiated in the ''ways of the world.'' It was Cervantes' point in the satiric romance *Don Quijote (Don Quixote*, published in two parts, 1605, 1615) that chivalry was passe͵. Sancho Panza, the lout, survives Don Quixote, the knight who wore a barber's basin for a helmet and romanticized an increasingly drab world. Cervantes said that he wrote the book ''to diminish the authority and acceptance'' of books of chivalry. Alain-Rene͵ Lesage published volumes one and two of *Gil Blas* in 1715. These were followed by volumes three (1724) and four (1735). A clever and well-meaning but vain Spaniard, Gil Blas relates the story of his adventures while engaged in various occupations, some of them of a bad or questionable character.

In England, John Milton published the epic poem *Paradise Lost* (1667). The city built by the devils in hell, Pandemonium, presided over by a tarnished but attractive Satan, is a ''ship of fools'' stranded on burning marl and strident with demonic malice; but William Blake (1757–1827) and Percy Bysshe Shelley (1792–1822) reflected the antinomianism of the times when, respectively, they adjudged Satan to be the real hero of *Paradise Lost* and morally superior to Milton's rendition of God. A new, awesome *Beau Ide͵al* was given to the world. In addition, the intense angelic temperaments of Moloch, Belial, and Mammon replaced the Elizabethan humors as the constituents compounding one's identity: demonic furies (1, 454–57), ''Whose wanton passions. . . . / *Ezekiel* saw, when by the Vision led / His eye survey'd the dark Idolatries / Of alienated *Judah*.''

The Eighteenth Century

The fragmented, private-point-of-view, angelic intelligences (self-reflexive temperaments) found superficially urbane but superciliously violent voices among the wits and satirists of the eighteenth century. The central socially destructive idea of La Rochefoucauld's *Maximes* (*Maxims*, 1665); paved the way; namely, that each human being is motivated exclusively by self-interest, "l'amour propre." The shrewd observer of mankind deduces such axioms as these: "Nous sommes si accoutumés à nous déguiser aux autres, qu'à la fin nous nous déguisons à nous-mêmes" ("We are so used to disguising ourselves in relation to others that we end up disguising ourselves in relation to ourselves"), and "Les personnes faibles ne peuvent être sincères" ("Weak persons cannot be sincere"). La Rochefoucauld postulates here that we become divided selves through subterfuge and that, for the powerless masses, duplicity is the order of the day. This is the scandalously "perceptive" voice of the seducer Lord Henry Wooten in Oscar Wilde's novel *The Picture of Dorian Gray* (1891); Wilde is quick to utilize the motif of the divided self in this work. Temperamental suspiciousness teaches us that, as a rule of thumb, things are never what they seem to be.

If temperament is an osmotic accretion, an age that lacks the unifying theological virtue of charity is liable to suicidal pique, as in the case of John Wilmot, Earl of Rochester, who wrote ("A Satyr against Mankind," 1675), "I'd be a Dog, a Monkey or a Bear,/ Or any thing, but that vain Animal,/ Who is so proud of being rational." Jonathan Swift continued the haughty attack on the canaille, whom he contemptuously branded as "yahoos" in his satiric journey tale (*Gulliver's Travels*, 1726).

The Nineteenth Century

What it means to survive only according to the flesh is the subject of Mary Wollstonecraft Shelley's novel *Frankenstein* (1818), in which a golem is pieced together from matter collected by ghouls and "granted" life by a yahoo scientist. Electricity replaces the God of Genesis, and the monster takes its first steps toward the advanced cybernetics of our Electronic Age. Less sensationally, but intimating that modern society is a golem sutured from dead fragments, William Makepeace Thackeray wrote the satiric novel *Vanity Fair* (1847–1848), "a novel without a hero," in which the parasitic Amelia Sedley and the unscrupulous Becky Sharp are accorded as much stature as anybody else in the book.

In English poetry the dramatic monologue abounds with anti-heroes; for example, Robert Browning's " 'Childe Roland to the Dark Tower Came' " (1852–1855) and "Andrea del Sarto" (1855).

In France Gustave Flaubert fashioned two full-fledged anti-heroes in the novel *Madame Bovary* (1856), the chemist Homais and Madame Bovary, lost in the mazes of her sensibility. The principal character in Guy de Maupassant's novel *Bel-ami* (1885) is an unmitigated cad. The delirious monk Paphnutius in Anatole France's novel *Thaïs* (1890) illustrates La Rochefoucauld's maxim about disguising ourselves.

In Italy the anti-hero of Antonio Fogazzaro's novel *Il santo* (*The Saint*, 1905) knows who and what he is, but the people do not, and they acclaim him a saint.

In the United States Stephen Crane (1871–1900) and Frank Norris (1870–1902) turned to naturalism, the anti-hero genre par excellence, to delineate the plight of cosmic waifs; such as the prostitute in Crane's *Maggie: A Girl of the Streets* (1893) and the wife-murdering dentist in Norris' *McTeague* (1899). These American novelists followed the principles set forth by Emile Zola in his critical essay *Le Roman expe'rimental* (*The Experimental Novel*, 1880). So did Theodore Dreiser who, in one of his chapter headings in the novel *Sister Carrie* (1900), described his antiheroine as "a waif amid forces."

The Twentieth Century

Zola's purest successor in this century is Alberto Moravia (1907–), but more metaphysical currents have entered the stream—somewhat more than paranoia, somewhat less than spiritual. The Czech Franz Kafka introduced and explored the motif of a betrayed or missed orientation in the novel *Der Prozess* (*The Trial*, 1925) and suggested that the anti-hero is the victim of a conspiracy as in his novel *Das Schloss* (*The Castle*, 1926). The anti-hero cannot participate because he is kept ignorant of the rules governing the game. Gradually becoming aware of his plight, he grows frantic. Alienated not only from society but from a transcendental source of comfort as well, conscious that his center is threatened by depletion, he copes, or tries to prevail minimally, by taking his psychic and "moral" shape from a labyrinthine circumference. Jean-Paul Sartre sees mankind as trapped in "viscosity." His semiautobiographical novel *La nause'e* (*Nausea*, 1938) isolates existence itself as the cause of contemporary man's profound malaise and disgust.

Some writers who include anti-heroes in their novels are Albert Camus (e.g., Meursault, in *L'e'tranger* (*The Stranger*, 1942), Evelyn Waugh (Tony Last, *A Handful of Dust*, 1937), Graham Greene (Pinky, *Brighton Rock*, 1938), Ernest Hemingway (Frederic Henry, *Farewell to Arms*, 1929), Elizabeth Bowen (Stella Rodney, *The Heat of the Day*, 1949), Virginia Woolf (Clarissa Dalloway, *Mrs. Dalloway*, 1925), James Joyce (Leopold Bloom, *Ulysses*, 1922), Joyce Cary (Gulley Jimson, *The Horse's Mouth*, 1944), D. H. Lawrence (Ursula Brangwen, *The Rainbow*, 1915), Rosamond Lehmann (Mrs Jardine, *The Ballad and the Source*, 1945), John Wain (Charles Lumley, *Hurry on Down*, 1953), Kingsley Amis (Jim Dixon, *Lucky Jim*, 1954), and Joseph Heller (Yossarian, *Catch–22*, 1961). In drama, among a plethora of anti-heroes, there are Blanche Du Bois (Tennessee Williams, *A Streetcar Named Desire*, 1947) and Willy Loman (Arthur Miller, *Death of a Salesman*, 1949).

See also: Alienation, Anti-Intellectualism, Nihilism, Picaresque, *Pi'caro* in American Literature, Scapegoat, Tragicomic Hero.

Selected Bibliography

Beuchat, Charles. *Histoire du naturalisme franc,ais*. 2 vols. Paris: Corre^a, 1949.
Jung, Carl Gustav. *Modern Man in Search of a Soul*. New York: Harcourt, Brace, 1933.
McLuhan, Marshall. *The Gutenberg Galaxy*. Toronto: University of Toronto Press, 1962.

O'Faoláin, Seán. *The Vanishing Hero: Studies in Novelists of the Twenties*. London: Eyre and Spottiswoode, 1956.

NATHAN A. CERVO

ANTI-INTELLECTUALISM

The anti-intellectual impulse in literature gives pleasure by exposing the folly of the wise and of their so-called wisdom. As a literary tactic, it logically complements encomiums to the wisdom of fools. Since anti-intellectualism (a-i) is a recent term—its vogue in America dating from the McCarthy era—it has not been used by most writers who have exploited the impulse. Even so, literati from the earliest of times to the present have found inspiration in the glaring deficiencies not only of knowledge and reason, but also of empirical science and particular intellectual doctrines. Contempt for the life of the mind is deeply ingrained in Western culture, where it serves as a counterbalance to such awesome intellectual enterprises as philosophy and science. Speculation, curiosity, intellectual play, impartiality, and incredulity are characteristics of intellectuals that have been perennially unpopular with nonintellectuals. Yet intellectuals themselves—writers, scholars, teachers, scientists, ideologues, clerics, and so forth—have been among the most vigorous exponents of a-i.

As the term itself suggests, a-i delimits not only a subject matter of literature—intellectuals and intellectual pursuits; it also dictates a certain attitude toward these subjects. Since this attitude is negative, ranging from the vituperative to the condescending, the favorite, though not exclusive, literary mode of a-i is satire. A prime target of literary a-i has always been the figure of the intellectual himself, who enters literature under many guises, as investigator (scholar, philosopher, scientist), author, educator, or consultant (expert, ideologue). Intellectuals appear in a host of unflattering ways, as madmen, megalomaniacs, bunglers, charlatans, terrorists, pedants, parasites, weirdos, heretics, dreamers, and malcontents, which shows that the kinds of intellectual foolishness are astonishingly various. By thinking too much or by meddling with the secrets of nature, intellectuals are shown to produce an array of laughable or tragic results harmful to themselves or to their fellow humans. Thus the treatment of the intellectual, though still negative, may go beyond satiric derision and become tragic or pathetic and elicit compassion for his fate as a misfit or martyr.

The Background in Antiquity and the Middle Ages

The archetypal stories of Pandora, Oedipus, Icarus, and Prometheus point up the importance and antiquity of a-i in Greco-Roman culture. The fate of the latter two illustrates the hazards of applied knowledge. In the play *Oidipous tyrannos (Oedipus Rex*, c. 429 B.C.) Sophocles presents the hero's compulsion to know-at-all-costs as a kind of intellectual pride, tragic in consequences, though it leads to a higher wisdom born of terrible experience. Also in the 5th century B.C., one of the first intellectuals, the pre-Socratic thinker Thales, becomes the butt of anti-intellectualist humor. According to a libelous legend Socrates helped spread in his dialogue *Theaitētos* (*Theaetetus*, c. 368 B.C.), Thales fell into a well while studying the stars. Socrates' point: philosophers are always good for a laugh because they combine arrogance with an ignorance of matters at hand. Socrates tried to avoid both by declaring he was wise only in his knowing how little wise he was (*Apologia* [*Apology* c. 4th century B.C.]), a favorite topos among later anti-intellectualist poseurs. But Socrates' prudence proved futile, for he too became a laughing stock both in Aristophanes' comedy *Nephelai* (*The Clouds*, 423 B.C.) and much later in Lucian's satiric dialogue, *Biōn prasis* (*Philosophers Up For Sale*, 2d century A.D.). Aristophanes, who completely misrepresents Socrates for purposes of discrediting intellectual inquiry and Soph- ism, portrays him as a parasite, a deceiver, and a corrupter of youth. Socrates undermines morality so much that his student tries to justify beating his own father with sophistical arguments. In Lucian's funny dialogue, Socrates states his views on love of youth, community of women, and the Forms so simple- mindedly that they seem immoral and ludicrous. The setting is a sale of philos- opher-slaves who are quizzed by the buyers; Pythagoras, Diogenes, Democritus, Heraclitus, an Epicurean, a Stoic, a Peripatetic, and finally a skeptic are bur- lesqued. Lucian knows that the mere juxtaposition of so many conflicting phi- losophies suffices to discredit philosophy in general. Thus the very richness of ancient thought becomes an embarrassment when exploited by a satirist like Lucian. Though the skeptic too is savaged, Lucian's own views seem closest to Pyrrhonist skepticism, which produced a subtle, highly knowledgeable critique of the idea that man could know anything for certain. For every proposition a counterproposition seems equally true, or, in Lucianic terms, for every laughing Democritus, there is a weeping Heraclitus. For later writers wishing to attack intellect by intellectual means, Lucianic satire and epistemological skepticism proved useful resources.

Less playful or cerebral than that of the ancient Greeks, the a-i of early Christianity and its Hebrew sources is more deeply rooted. The Jews were the "people of the book," but the Adam and Eve myth identifies the attainment of wisdom with sin and human misery (Genesis, 2.9), a recurring doctrine in the Old Testament, where it occurs most eloquently in the Wisdom literature. Job's sin, for example, comes not from moral wrongdoing but from his arrogant need to investigate God's ways; but God denies Job the right of an explanation. In Ecclesiastes the Preacher teaches the impotence of reason. Fools and the wise share the same fate and "knowledge increases sorrow" (1.16–18; 2.12–16). Isaiah proclaims that the wisdom of the wise will perish (29.14). St. Paul, who quotes this passage (1 Cor. 1), is the pre-eminent source of early Christian a-i. In Col. 2.8 he warns against the philosophers, and in 1 Cor. 1 he asserts that God has "made foolish the wisdom of the world"; that He let Himself be known through the folly of the cross; and that He chose the foolish, that is, ignorant apostles, to "shame the wise." This chapter, along with 1 Cor. 4.10: "We are fools for Christ's sake," exerted an immense influence on later literature, whose a-i grew out of Christian fervor. Yet the medieval church, though paying lip service to the Pauline line, built its doctrine on Augustine and Aquinas, who valued humane learning and rational inquiry. True, unlimited inquiry was condemned, as is shown by the fate of Dante's Ulysses, damned for going beyond the Gates of Hercules in search of worldly knowledge. Even so, a-i plays a subdominant role in medieval culture, where its finest expression is in the literature of the mystics. In reaction to the prevailing scholastic intellectualism, they embraced the *via negativa*. Ignorance becomes the precondition for oneness with God. Jacopone da Todi's fine lyric (c. 1300) "Como è sommo sapienzia . . . " ("How it is highest wisdom to be known as a fool for the love of Christ") is typical. It concludes that Paris, center of scholasticism, has yet to see so great a philosophy as divine folly. *The Cloud of Unknowing* (English, 14th century), Thomas à Kempis' *De imitatione Christi* (*Imitation of Christ*, c. 1418), and Nicolaus Cusanus' *De docta ignorantia* (*Of Learned Ignorance*, c. 1440) all movingly extol the spiritual benefits of voluntary ignorance.

The Renaissance

The real heyday for a-i in literature is the Renaissance, especially the sixteenth and early seventeenth centuries. Faust and Hamlet, two prototypes of the modern Western intellectual, emerge and come to represent the tragic dimensions of intellectuality. Hardly a major writer neglects to assail reason or learning on the basis of one or more of the four anti-intellectual currents of the period—the humanist, the religious, the skeptical (Pyrrhonist), and the occultist. Renaissance a-i arose from a deep uncertainty about what constitutes knowledge and from the corresponding temptation to find truth by such nonintellectual means as revelation, tradition, magic, or commonsense experience.

The invention of printing made available to the educated a bewildering amount of learning that drove home how contradictory were the views of the learned on nearly every issue. Thus in book 3 of Rabelais' novel *Tiers livre* (*Gargantua and Pantagruel*, 1546) Panurge interviews savants from all branches of learning to find out if he should marry. The contradictory views he gets cancel each other out and seem to discredit learning in general. Furthermore, important ancient texts recovered by the humanists ratified a-i. First came the treatises *Corpus hermeticum* (*The Hermetic Writings*, c.100–300) which favored the occult over traditional learning and magic over reason. In scene 1 of Marlowe's *Doctor Faustus* (1604), the hero, "glutted . . . with learning's golden gifts," reviewing the deficiencies of human knowledge, sees that *magia* offers what learning lacks—omnipotence. "Philosophy is odious and obscure," he cries, "Tis magic, magic that hath ravished me." Next came the skeptical or Pyrrhonist writings of Sextus Empiricus, whose major claim was that neither reason nor the senses were adequate means of reaching certain knowledge; one should therefore suspend all judgment. Montaigne, in his *Essais* (*Essays*, 1580–1588), is the greatest literary Pyrrhonist of the age, especially in his "Apologie de Raymond Sebond" ("Apology for R.S.," 2;12), where he wittily uses reason and much learning to demonstrate the vanity of learning. Montaigne's influence was extensive, and Hamlet, if not Shakespeare, seems a Pyrrhonist. Hamlet, a university scholar, repeatedly poses the problem of certain knowledge, and for every proposition he makes, he seems able to find a valid counterproposition. "And thus the native hue of resolution / Is sicklied o'er with the pale cast of thought."

The discovery of the New World with its "noble savages" also cast all received knowledge in doubt. Contrasting the virtues of South American Indians to the vices of lettered Europeans, Montaigne in his essay "Des cannibales" ("Of Cannibals," 1.31) could identify ignorance with wisdom, literacy with decadence. A related development is the rise of the wise fool. From Erasmus' Stultitia, the first of the lot, through Lear's fool, to Cervantes' Sancho, who as an illiterate governs better than the lettered, the wise fool is a main outlet of Renaissance a-i. In Erasmus' essay *Moriae encomium* (*The Praise of Folly*, 1511), Folly herself proves that through her rather than through wisdom come all good things: forgetfulness, sexuality, feeling, and so forth. The wise, who reject these, are cold, pedantic, life-denying, and inhuman.

The reform and humanist movements were chiefly anti-intellectual in their reaction to Scholasticism. Humanists, such as Thomas More, Erasmus, and Rabelais, ridiculed the logic-chopping, metaphysical inquiries of medieval philosophy, and the schoolman became a stock figure of humanist satire. Generally, the humanists tried to discredit *scientia* (learning) by distinguishing it sharply from *sapientia* (wisdom, moral virtue). Thus Sir Philip Sidney, in his essay, *A Defence of Poetry* (1595), complains that astronomers and mathematicians may know their subjects but lead crooked lives all the same. And Montaigne, continually correlating a full memory with hollow judgment, elevates self-knowledge through experience over book learning, which enervates the citizenry. The Protestant reformers, too, rejected scholastic intellectualism. Much of their a-i, resembling that of the medieval mystics, harks back to St. Paul and the Pauline folly for Christ. Erasmus, a reformer who stayed in the church, concludes his *Moriae encomium* with a brilliant Pauline defense of Christian a-i.

The Seventeenth and Eighteenth Centuries

Though the scientific revolution is the main incitement to a-i in these centuries, conventional satire of foolish pedants and scholars, a legacy of the Renaissance, throve, especially on the stage. Tirso de Molina's *El melancólico* (c. 1611), Cyrano de Bergerac's *Le pédant joué* (1654), and Chevalier's *Le pédagogue amoureux* (1665) often draw their humor from the scholar's failure to deal with his feelings or the claims of love. Molière introduces a new twist in *Les femmes savantes* (*The Learned Ladies*, 1672), which makes fun of the superficial learning and bossy habits of some early bluestockings, who, for instance, sack a first-rate maidservant for making a grammatical error.

The Copernican revolution, whose real impact occurred in this period, cast all in doubt and raised an intense debate over the authority of inherited ideas and methods of learning. Bacon's inductive method and Descartes' methodical doubt mandated the questioning of traditional learning. The scientific successes of Newton contributed to the ''Quarrel of the Ancients and Moderns,'' wherein the Moderns claimed that Newton and Kepler had overthrown Aristotle and Ptolemy and shown the falsity of inherited learning. Even so, the Ancients, or their friends, proclaimed the vanity of the new learning. The critics of science and of the Moderns wished to save the authority of both classical antiquity and Christian faith. In book 8 of his poem *Paradise Lost* (1667) Milton shows his mistrust of the study of external nature, especially cosmology. When Adam quizzes the Archangel on celestial motion, the latter advises that ''heav'n is for thee too high/ To know what passes there; be lowly wise. . . . Dream not of other worlds.'' And Pascal, in his *Pensées* (*Thoughts*, 1670), speaks of the feebleness of reason in the face of the infinite cosmos.

The prevailing tone of the Age of Reason can hardly be called anti-intellectual, yet its grandiose claims, that reason, science, and education would result in moral and social progress, invited satirical treatment. Taking to task the silly scholar thus remains in vogue. Swift, in the Third Voyage of his satire *Gulliver's Travels* (1726), mocks absent-minded intellectuals in the Laputians (Cartesians?), who live up in the air on a floating island. Their attention can only be got by flapping their ears with inflated pig bladders. In the Academy of Lagado, a travesty of Bacon's House of Solomon, Swift ridicules attempts to gain sunlight from cucumbers, food from feces. Here the experimental method of Bacon and the Royal Society is shown to lack a rational basis and a clear sense of purpose. With Swift and Pope there arises a new genre: the mock heroic satire of intellect. In prose Swift's satire *Battle of the Books* (1704) literally sets in battle modern books against ancient ones, who win the day: ''Then Aristotle, observing Bacon advance . . . let fly his arrow, which missed the valiant modern . . . ; but Descartes it hit.'' In verse, Pope's several *Dunciads* (1728–1743) glory ironically in the monumental dullness of pedantry and obscure learning.

Later in the century, Samuel Johnson, in the novel *The History of Rasselas* (1759), shows that the study of higher things, such as astronomy, leads to madness and estrangement, but the unfortunate astronomer is portrayed sympathetically rather than satirically. Not so Dr. Pangloss in the novel *Candide* (1759). Voltaire makes fun of the blindness of intellect, and more particularly Leibnizian philosophy, by confronting the arch-optimist Pangloss with one calamity after the next. Finally, J.-J. Rousseau (d. 1778) adumbrates the Romantics' rejection of enlightened reason. In the tradition of Montaigne, his *Discours sur les sciences et les arts* (*Discourses on the Sciences and Arts,* 1750) eloquently denounces the age's identification of knowledge and moral advance and praises instead the ignorant but noble savage.

Romanticism and the Nineteenth Century

The a-i of the Romantics came from a deep mistrust of the rationalistic, mechanistic thinking of the seventeenth and eighteenth centuries, which seemed to limit intolerably the self-determination, creative expressiveness, and unique subjectivity of the person. Rather, the Romantics assigned to Imagination that priority which the eighteenth century had given to Reason. Among the Romantics, William Blake and William Wordsworth are the most militantly anti-intellectual. In the poem *The Book of Urizen* (1794) Blake denounces Urizen or Reason in favor of Los or Inspiration, and in "Mock on, mock on Voltaire, Rousseau" (*Poems from the Note-Book*, 1800–1803) and the poem *Milton* (bk. 2; 1804), he assails Newton, Locke, and Bacon. One finds in Wordsworth's writings typical romantic motifs with anti-intellectual implications: the apotheosis of childhood; poetry as subjective feeling; a veneration of humble, illiterate folk; and a taste for the wild and unbounded in nature. His most memorable verses from *The Tables Turned* (1798) condemn the analytic mind: "Our meddling intellect/Misshapes the beauteous forms of things:/ We murder to dissect."

Romantic fiction gives us the first full treatment of the Faustian intellect, especially as it appears in the mad scientist. Though Goethe's play *Faust* (1808) reflects other aspects of romantic a-i, the mad scientist motif is only touched on with Wagner's laboratory creation of a homunculus. The archetypal story of Faustian intellect is Mary Shelley's novel *Frankenstein* (1818), in which an obsessed scientist creates in the laboratory a humanoid monster that returns to persecute him. The destructive consequences of scientific inquiry appear in a number of romantic tales that strikingly resemble Shelley's. In E.T.A. Hoffmann's "Der Sandmann" ("The Sandman," 1817) a mad scientist, who creates a female robot, persecutes and destroys the protagonist. Hawthorne, in "The Birth-Mark" (1846), presents an obsessed scientist who kills his beautiful wife in trying to remove by scientific means a blemish from her skin. And Balzac's Balthazar Claes isolates himself in his laboratory in the novel *La recherche de l'absolu* (*The Quest of the Absolute*, 1834); in so doing he ruins himself and his family. In all these works science is treated as occult and demonic; a dark, seductive pursuit. Though they see science negatively, these romantics insist on viewing the unfortunate scientists in tragic or pathetic, rather than satiric terms.

The rest of the century, however, shows that pedantry and intellectual folly had somehow survived all the ridicule heaped on them through the ages. Writers use satire as never before, especially to criticize the union of intellect with bourgeois values. Nietzsche, in his treatise *Jenseits von Gut und Böse* (*Beyond Good and Evil*, 1886), contrasts the genius to the mere scholar whom he compares to an old maid, respectable but sterile. In George Eliot's novel *Middlemarch* (1871–1872), an indictment of both pseudo-intellect and a-i, Casaubon is such an old maid: preoccupied with solar deities he has become indifferent to sunlight, nor do his intellectual labors amount to anything. Flaubert's *Bouvard et Pécuchet* (*Bouvard and Pécuchet*, 1881) and Samuel Butler's *Erewhon* (1872) are satirical novels that demonstrate in entirely different ways that learning in a philistine civilization must always be a vanity. In Erewhon, genius is a criminal offense. These disparate works share a loathing of the pettiness and sterility of middle-brow, middleclass intellectual endeavors. The true intellectual must transcend or renounce conventional, philistine learning, but in doing so he becomes an outcast.

The second half of the nineteenth century witnesses the rise of the intellectual hero, or anti-hero, in the realist novel, where intellectual alienation is often a strong motif. These intellectual protagonists find themselves in the center of conflicts made to test enlightened claims about the moral usefulness of reason and intellectual inquiry and to test the compatibility of thought and experience. The nineteenth-century Russian novel realizes this pattern more profoundly than any other, mainly because the Russians were so preoccupied with the moral and cultural consequences of introducing Western intellectual forms into their society. From Turgenev's short story "Gamlet shchigrovskogo uezda" ("Hamlet of the Shchigrovo," 1852) to Dostoevsky's novel *Brat'īa Karamazovy* (*The Brothers Karamazov*, 1880) the "superfluous" intellectual is a central figure of the Russian novel. In the novel *Zapiski iz podpol'īa* (*Notes from Underground*, 1864), Dostoevsky reveals the underlying baseness of the human quest for intellectual mastery, and in all his works shows the lack of access that the rational mind has to a fundamentally irrational world. Ivan Karamazov's intellectual gifts, for instance, reach an impasse in self-destructive pride and finally brain fever. In the novel *Anna Karenina* (1877) Tolstoy shows that Koznyschev's intellectual preoccupations preclude a satisfying relationship with women or nature and lead him to make dubious political commitments. Levin, a main protagonist and a closet intellectual, needs to grapple continually with ideas because for him they are "so vivid that they must be brought into conformity with other ideas and with reality." Yet Levin is unable to make his own irrational impulses or the inexplicable needs of his peasants conform to his own rational ideas. In the end he renounces the life of the mind to find salvation in the irrational. Overall, the Russian novel presents an influential indictment of the Western intellect.

The Twentieth Century

By the end of the nineteenth century the new currency of the terms "intelligentsia" (from the Russian) and "intellectual" (brought into vogue by the Dreyfus affair, 1898) indicates a heightened awareness of the difficult role of the intellectual in society. In the twentieth century intellectual despair among intellectuals reaches a zenith. This condition can be traced to a sense of guilt over the simultaneous impotence and exceptional responsibilities of the intellectual.

Though the idea that existence is at bottom irrational goes back to Kierkegaard and Dostoevsky, it does not reach full force until the intellectual revolution led by Freud, Jung, and Bergson. The absurd, disastrous conduct of civilized nations in World War I confirmed the idea. In this context, rationality seemed like a deviation from the norm or even a disease. The writings of Kafka and Pirandello explore this paradox with humor and pathos. Croce observed that Pirandello's theater was based on the inability to reason in a logical way. *Cosi è se vi pare* (*It Is So, If You Think So*, 1917) is a play about the futility of knowing anything.

Contradictory stories are given about the identity of a Signora Frola, who, appearing at the end of the play, claims that both stories are true, thus leaving the audience in a complete quandary. For Pirandello the disjunction between intellect and existence is ineradicable. The sense of the irrational as a source of a-i is a major motif in Thomas Mann's novel *Der Zauberberg* (*The Magic Mountain*, 1924), where Naphta represents the new intellectual who despises intellect. Contemptuous of knowledge for its own sake, he sides with the church against Galileo and would subordinate all science to dogma. He eloquently insists on the humanly degrading consequences of free inquiry and mass literacy. Such self-destructive a-i culminates in his death by suicide. Yet Mann readers of the thirties and forties evidently felt that Naphta the irrationalist was more convincing than his opponent, Settembrini the rational humanist. In the novel *Doktor Faustus* (1947), Mann's parable of German culture before and during National Socialism, the composer Adrian Leverkühn is an intellectual genius who finds in disease and barbarism the sources of intellectual creativity. The basic opposition between health/sanity and intellect is stressed. Real intellectual power is gained only by connivance with those irrational, daemonic powers that govern human existence.

A second feature of literary a-i in this century is the bitter self-recrimination of intellectuals in the face of their failure at political engagement and social solidarity. The attempts of intellectuals to realize ideas in the *vita activa* appear in literature as tragic or pathetic. Political commitment became a pressing issue forced on the intellectual with the rise and triumph of such totalitarian ideologies as Soviet communism, Italian Fascism, and German National Socialism, and with the need for resistance or collaboration in the World-War-II period. Intellectual neutrality seemed morally indefensible. The plight of the intellectual is most extensively treated in French literature from 1930–1950, particularly in the fiction of André Malraux and Jean-Paul Sartre. In the latter's novel *L'âge de raison* (*The Age of Reason*, 1945) and in Simone de Beauvoir's novel *Les mandarins* (*The Mandarins*, 1954) the intellectuals are cast in a poor light because of their bad faith and their sense of complicity in social crimes. They long for, but cannot reconcile themselves to, vital human values and humanitarian politics and programs. Their failure comes from an inborn elitism, an ingrained distrust of mass movements, and a compulsive need for impartiality.

Given the twentieth-century intellectual's felt impotence in either interpreting or engaging in life, it is ironic that the most recent wave of literary a-i stems from the enormous impact on life of the work of natural scientists, particularly nuclear physicists. The development of nuclear weapons, their use on Japanese cities in 1945, and now the likelihood of their destroying the world have heightened the urgency of such issues as the intellectual's social responsibility and the negative consequences of the quest for truth. Hence the mad scientist motif remains prominent. Dr. Strangelove is a cultural anti-hero of our time. Because of the power of the demonic element in human affairs, many intellectuals think that the quest for truth through scientific investigation will be catastrophic for civilization. This problem is the subject of much post-World War II literature.

Friedrich Dürrenmatt's play *Die Physiker* (*The Physicists*, 1962) is representative, yet it should be seen in the context of other works, such as Brecht's play *Leben des Galilei* (*The Life of Galileo*, 1947—revised version). Like *Oedipus Rex,* on which it is modelled, *Die Physiker* demonstrates that the road to truth, though paved with good intentions, leads to disaster. Of three supposedly mad physicists in an insane asylum, Moebius, the protagonist, pretends to be King Solomon in order to discourage people from using his dangerous scientific discoveries. The other two are also faking it, because they are really secret agents of opposing world powers who are out to pick Moebius' brain. In portraying Moebius sympathetically, Dürrenmatt turns the mad scientist motif on its head, but Moebius' ploy fails, and we are left to understand that humanity cannot really control the effects of its intellectual discoveries. Finally, from America is Walter Miller, Jr.'s *A Canticle for Leibowitz* (1959), a postnuclear catastrophe novel that portrays the world six hundred years later. Nearly all intellectuals have been killed by the survivors, and all books burned, in order to prevent a recurrence of the holocaust. This too fails, for the intellectual quest proves to be so inevitable that no humanitarian prudence can stop it. In these pessimistic works, the critique of the Faustian intellect achieves, perhaps, its most prophetic expression.

See also: Epistemology, Fool, Noble Savage, Reason, Science.

Selected Bibliography

Brombert, Victor. *The Intellectual Hero: Studies in the French Novel 1880–1955*. Philadelphia: J. B. Lippincott, 1961.
Gilson, Etienne. *Reason and Revelation in the Middle Ages*. Scribner's, 1954.
Jones, R. F. "The Background of the Attack on Science in the Age of Pope." *Eighteenth-Century English Literature: Modern Essays on Criticism*. Ed. J. L. Clifford, New York: Oxford University Press, 1959.
Kolakowski, Leszek. "Intellectuals against Intellect." *Daedalus* 101 (1972): 1–15.

JON THIEM

ANTI-SEMITISM

The word anti-Semitism, although first used in the late nineteenth century to combat the perceived influence of Jews in European society, generally describes anti-Jewish attitudes that have been endemic in Western literature for millennia. As a specific term, anti-Semitism appears in Wilhelm Marr's *Der Sieg des Judenthums über das Germanenthum* (1879) as a foil to the concept of Teutonism or Aryanism, which signified the attempt of Germanic-speaking people to find a new identity and unity for themselves grounded in a belief in German racial, national, and cultural superiority. Anti-Semitism has a specific contextual meaning in nineteenth- and twentieth-century usage reflecting the prevalent ideology of race. Anti-Semitic literature is characterized by false descriptions of Jewish beliefs and customs and an attack against the loyalty of Jews to the societies in which they lived. Anti-Semitism in general has to be studied against the spirit of a contemporary period with manifestations of philo-Semitism, tolerance, and apologetics by Jews and non-Jews coexisting as a logical foil. In the extant classical Greek and Latin literature, for example, there is almost as much curiosity about Jews as animosity. Anti-Semitic literature also reflects the stress of radical changes within societies with the Jews perceived as an identifiable and politically vulnerable scapegoat.

The Jewish emphasis upon the unity of God and the Bible's intrinsic rejection of polytheism put this minority people on a collision course with all of ancient civilization. Hostile classical authors considered Jews to be atheists and antisocial because they refused to accept polytheism; moreover, the Jewish code of holiness (e.g., dietary laws and ritual clothing) precluded participation in many aspects of the majority society. In the biblical Book of Esther, Haman, the archenemy of the Jews, mouths the classic summary of animosity toward Jews: "There is a certain people scattered abroad and dispersed among the peoples in all the provinces of the kingdom; and their laws are diverse from those of every people; neither keep they the king's laws; therefore it profiteth not the king to suffer them" (5:8).

Antiquity and the Medieval Period

History in the Hellenistic and Roman periods was expressed as ethical and moral literature, but was also the vehicle to defend ethnic self-identity. Thus Manetho's *Aigyptiaka* (3d century B.C., *History of Egypt*) and Tacitus' *Historiae* c. A.D. 100–110, *Histories*) slander the Jews as part of their partisan treatment of their respective nation's relationships with the Jews. The slanderous allusions of classical rhetoricians (Cicero and Apion) continued to influence scholars through the centuries, especially Cicero, who became the standard for Latin style. An anthology with refutations of classical anti-Semitism was edited by the first-century Jewish priest and historian Joseph ben Matityahu (Josephus Flavius) in his *Contra apionem*. These and other texts have been edited and annotated by M. Stern in *Greek and Latin Authors on Jews and Judaism* (1974).

The New Testament added a new dimension to anti-Semitism even though its contents reflect intra-Jewish rivalries of the first century. As these texts were adopted by gentiles who did not understand their background, all the hostile references to Jews took on a new meaning that was exacerbated by the sermons and commentaries of the church fathers. Eusebius introduced the distinction between the Old and New Testament, meaning that the former was abrogated with the Resurrection of Jesus as the Christ. All biblical curses were reinterpreted to denigrate the Old Israel while all the blessings were applied to the New Israel. The word "Jew" eventually came to be used pejoratively against any heterodox Christian. The Jews themselves were defined as deicides or Christ-killers and increasingly persecuted once Christianity gained political power and became the exclusive religion of the Roman Empire. This Christian animosity permeates

Byzantine and other eastern Orthodox literatures in Europe and the East. During the Middle Ages two new elements were added: an economic hostility that was based upon rivalry between Christian and Jewish merchants; and the growing indebtedness of Christians to Jewish moneylenders. Roman Catholic society prohibited Christians to lend money at interest. The condemnation of Jews as usurers is a recurrent theme in ecclesiastical and secular literature.

On the popular level a Christian society began to equate the Jew with the devil and to attribute to Jews responsibility for such ills of society as crop failure, child disappearance, and even plague. Later the Talmud, the repository of Jewish law, custom, and ethics, was judged blasphemous by an inquisitional trial in 1240 and burned. Within a decade, minnesingers parodied the Talmud, and Jews were described as poisoning both the body and the mind. A typically coarse disputation is the thirteenth-century Spanish *Disputa entre un cristiano y un judio*. Successive papal bulls, from the twelfth century on, denounced these charges. Still these themes, particularly ritual murder, became quite popular in plays such as the German *Endiger Judenspiel* (15th century), Geoffrey Chaucer's "Prioress's Tale" (*Canterbury Tales*, c. 1380–1400) and contemporary French poetry of the Low Countries. Medieval theater in general and mystery plays of the fourteenth and seventeenth centuries in particular were openly hostile to the Jews who are depicted as usurers, desecrators of the host, ritual murderers, and deicides, as in the *Oberammergauer Passionsspiel* (*The Passion Play of Oberammergau*, 1634), the *Alsfelder Passionsspiel* (15th century), Arnould Gréban's *Mystère de la Passion* (c. 1450), and *Il miracolo di Bolsena* (14th century). In the sixteenth century Erasmus, summarizing the popular medieval and Renaissance feeling, expressed his own dislike of Jews: "If hating Jews is Christian, then all of us are exceedingly Christian."

From the fifteenth century to the present, each national or linguistic group expressed its hostility to the Jews in open persecution and literary insult sometimes developing new themes but always alluding to the basic animosities inherited from the ancient and medieval periods. The words "Jew" and "Judas" became in general pejorative terms in European languages; Spanish *judio* and French *juif* have the meaning of moneylender. The English and American jibe "to Jew" was already anticipated in the twelfth century by Bernard de Clairvaux's *iudaizare*, both expressions later meaning usurer and heretic. Therefore, while there are patterns that are perceivable across generations as in earlier periods, the next sections of this entry will follow national and geographic areas. Such a diachronic approach can show developmental patterns as opposed to synchronic parallels.

Spain and Germany

In Spain continued massacres of Jews, forced baptisms, and conversion out of fear gave rise to a significant number of New Christians who were to generate a new facet of anti-Jewish sentiment: racist exclusion. Old Christians called them *marranos* (swine) and demanded that they be restricted to separate quarters in the fifteenth century. Modern scholars believe that the national Inquisition instituted by Ferdinand and Isabella in the fifteenth century was really intended to vitiate the power of the New Christians, many of whom were considered false converts to Christianity.

Anti-Jewish slurs appear in Juan Alfonso de Baena's poetic anthology *Cancionero* (1445). Francisco Gómez de Quevedo y Villegas (1580–1645) consistently satirizes Jews, especially his play *La hora de todos* (*The Hour of All Men,* 1635). The concept of *limpieza de sangre* ("purity of blood"), which distinguished between Old and New Christians, would dominate the Golden Age of Spanish literature in the sixteenth century. This theme is central in the works of Lope de Vega, while anti-Jewish allusions in Tirso de Molina's play *El burlador de Sevilla* (*The Libertine of Seville,* 1630) and other works were clear to contemporaries. Tirso's play *La prudencia en la mujer* (*The Wife's Discretion,* 1634) accuses converso doctors of killing their Christian patients.

The Protestant Reformation in Germany initiated by Martin Luther was at first favorable to the Jews (cf. his *Dass Jesus Christus ein geborener Jude sei* [*Jesus Christ Was Born a Jew,* 1523]); however, for a number of reasons, lack of enthusiastic support and conversion to his new faith being primary, Luther later wrote a number of virulently anti-Jewish tractates, in particular his *Von den Juden und ihren Lügen* (1542, *On the Jews and Their Lies*). His literary and anti-Jewish influence prevailed in the Lutheran church and even in Nazi propaganda.

By the end of the sixteenth century a particularly scurrilous tract emerged that spread throughout every European land and was translated with adaptations into every European language. Beginning in Italy, *The Curse of the Twelve Tribes* rapidly crossed the border into Germany and France, where it received a popular welcome. Essentially a parody of Genesis 49 (Jacob's blessing to the Twelve Tribes), the text denigrates pornographically each tribe of Israel for its part in the crucifixion of Christ and may be seen as the mirror opposite of the symbol of redemption that the theme of the rediscovery of the Ten Lost Tribes had for both Jews and some Christians. The popularity of this theme in European literatures and the related one of the Wandering Jew has been traced by George K. Anderson, *The Legend of the Wandering Jew* (1965).

England and France

In England the image of the Jew as usurer is immortalized in Shakespeare's play *The Merchant of Venice* (c. 1595), by Shylock, an image that has a long history. Originally a philo-Jewish description of a Jew who is loaned money by a pagan Roman with God as his guarantor (Babylonian Talmud: Nedarim 50a), the theme was soon Christianized with the sympathetic Jew lending money to a Christian with Christ as guarantor. Later this story devolves into the hostile usurer theme. Shakespeare's contemporary, Christopher Marlowe, depicts a vicious image of a Jewish moneylender in his play *Jew of Malta* (c. 1589). These and similar images (e.g., George Lansdowne's play *The Jew of Venice*, 1701) continue in plays and stories throughout the seventeenth and eighteenth centuries.

In addition to the traditional themes of ritual murder and usurer noted here, other familiar anti-Jewish stereotypes appear in eighteenth- and nineteenth-century English literature. Daniel Defoe depicts a Jew as an ugly criminal in his novel *Roxana* (1724); Tobias Smollett's novel *The Adventures of Roderick Random* (1748) castigates the Jew as usurer in the portrayal of Isaac Rapine; while Maria Edgeworth elaborates on many such images in her *Moral Tales* (1801). Other stock anti-Semitic images in nineteenth-century English novels include the notorious Fagin in Charles Dickens's *Oliver Twist* (1837–1838) and the figure of Scrooge in the latter's immortal *A Christmas Carol* (1843). The devil Svengali, a Jew, was created by George du Maurier in his novel *Trilby* (1894). Still before World War I such conservative Catholics as Hilaire Belloc and G. K. Chesterton exploit medieval images. George Bernard Shaw too revives these themes in his plays and indulges in hostile imagery in his *Man and Superman* (1903), *Major Barbara* (1905), *Saint Joan* (1923), and *The Doctor's Dilemma* (1906). Slurs against rabbis can even be found in *The Pearl*, that popular journal of nineteenth-century underground Edwardian erotic literature.

The French Enlightenment contributed to anti-Jewish sentiment through the *philosophes*, in particular Voltaire, who unearthed classical anti-Jewish images as part of his attack against both the medieval Catholic church and its power in France and also the Jews who represented something alien in his new rationalist society. The sheer volume of Voltaire's denigrating statements about Jews and Judaism in his essays provide a lasting legacy to his readers in every age. The Marquis d'Argens promoted an ambivalent attitude toward Jews, hostile to the unenlightened while positive toward the enlightened whom he expected to convert to Christianity. His *Lettres juives* (*Jewish Letters*, 1736–1738) and *Lettres cabalistiques* (1737–1741) were quite influential in their depiction of Jews as usurers. The huge volume of anti-Jewish pamphlets in seventeenth- and eighteenth-century England and France should also be noted.

Nineteenth-century French literature is replete with pro-Jewish and anti-Jewish images. The latter include stereotypes such as the greedy banker and art collector in Honoré de Balzac's multivolume series *La comédie humaine* (*The Human Comedy*, 1842–50), the corrupting heroine in the novels of Edmond and Jules de Goncourt, *Manette Salomon* (1867) and Alphonse Daudet, *Les rois en exil* (*Kings in Exile*, 1879), unsympathetic Jews in the novels of Paul Bourget, *Cosmopolis* (1892), Guy de Maupassant, *Mont-Oriol* (1886) and Emile Zola, *L'argent* (*Money*, 1891). Victor Hugo satirized Jews as usurers in his dramas *Cromwell* (1827) and *Marie Tudor* (1833), but sympathized with Jews as victims of persecution in *Torquemada* (1882).

Anti-Semitism as a racially expressed ideology emerged in the wake of the Dreyfus affair. Works were written to reflect the hostility of the extreme conservatists and ultranationalists. Though not belles-lettres, the very popular *La France juive* by Edouard Adolphe Drumont (1885) was extremely influential among anti-Semites in the twentieth century. Its main theme was the control of French society by the Jews. (This theme was well parodied by the sharp pen of Roger Peyrefitte, *Les Juifs* [*The Jews*, 1965], subtitled in the English translation *A Fictional Venture into the Follies of Antisemitism*). Novels that exploit the theme include Paul Adam's *L'essence du soleil* (1890), Léon Cladel's *Juive-errante* (1897), Léon Daudet's *Le pays des parlementeurs* (1900) and *La lutte* (1907), and Maurice Donnay's play *Le retour de Jérusalem* (*The Return from Jerusalem*, 1904).

Central and Eastern Europe

During the nineteenth century, at first mainly in Germany and Austria and later in Russia, anti-Semitism became a full-fledged political and ideological attempt to resolve various internal social problems. Much anti-Jewish sentiment was added to the endemic hostility of Christian society by those Jews who, upon converting to Christianity, justified their rebirth, as had their apostate predecessors during the Middle Ages, by a denigration of Judaism. Karl Marx is perhaps the most obvious example, although it was his father who had converted him. The crux of nineteenth-century anti-Semitism was the rejection of the emancipation of the Jews and the attendant opportunities available to them as individual citizens to integrate fully and without converting into Western society in the wake of the French Revolution and the Napoleonic conquests, which shattered the older corporate structure of medieval catholic society. The rejection manifests itself in the literary, historical, and political works of the old guard of conservatives, who were incapable of adjusting to the dynamic changes that revolutionized the nineteenth-century West from Russia to America.

Nineteenth-century German literature expressed the hostility toward Jews that was developing in the political and cultural arenas. Anti-Jewish images can be found in numerous novels: Gustav Freytag's popular *Soll und Haben* (*Debit and Credit*, 1834), Jeremias Gotthelf's (Albert Bitzius) *Uli der Knecht* (*Uli the Servant*, 1841), Felix Dahn's *Ein Kampf um Rom* (*A Battle for Rome*, 1876), and Wilhelm von Polenz's *Der Büttnerbauer* (*Farmer Büttner*, 1895). (Positive Jewish images can be found in Freytag's and Dahn's other works.) Each of these novels depicts an evil Jew who is untrustworthy and commits acts against the German people and who therefore cannot be civilized. This type of Jew had already appeared in the pro-Jewish tract of Christian Wilhelm von Dohm, *Über die bürgerliche Verbesserung der Juden* (*On the Civil Improvement of the Jews*, 1781), which argued that the emancipation of the Jews would overcome all the vicissitudes of their lack of civilized character, a theme that goes back to the Marquis d'Argens and ultimately to the proselytizing propaganda of early and medieval Christianity. Emancipated Jews developed this theme in their treatment of East European Orthodox Jewry, which they disparaged as ignorant (of *Hochdeutsch*) and uncultured.

Nineteenth-century Polish literature, while portraying positive images of Jews, does so against the background of anti-Semitism in Polish society. Overtly anti-

Jewish works are written by conservatives at the end of the century such as Władysław Stanisław Reymont's novel *Ziemia obiecana (The Promised Land,* 1899), which denounces the exploitations by Jewish and German capitalists of Polish workers, a theme that negatively interprets the economic situation that had existed in Poland since the late medieval period.

The chaos at the time of the late nineteenth-century retreat of the Ottoman Empire from Eastern Europe led to increasing attacks against Jews as aliens, enemies of society, and commercial usurpers in addition to repetition of medieval Christian canards. The rampant anti-Semitism in nineteenth-century Rumania encouraged ultranationalists such as Vasile Alecsandri to exploit anti-Jewish themes in his plays; for example, the greedy Jewish innkeeper in *Lipitorile satului (The Village Leeches,* 1860), the cowardly Jewish peddler *Herşcu boccegiul (Herschel the Peddler,* 1851), the same in *Surugiul (The Postillion* 1861), and the exploitive merchant in *Ion Păpuşarul* (1864). The poetry of Mihail Eminescu (1850–1889), Bogdan Petriceicu Hăşdeu (1838–1907), and Costache Negruzzi (1808–1868) continued the attacks. Only occasionally does anti-Jewish sentiment appear in nineteenth-century Bulgarian literature; Ivan Vazov's drama *Kŭm propast (Toward the Abyss,* 1910) blames the Jewish wife of Czar Ivan Alexander for the Ottoman conquest of Bulgaria in the fourteenth century.

The rise of nationalism in Hapsburg Czeckoslovakia added a new note to anti-Semitism by identifying Jews with their German antagonists. The poems of Viktor Dyk, Peter Bezruč (pen name of Vladimir Vašek), and Antonín Sova raised this theme to the laureate level. Anti-Jewish images predominate in the plays of Ladislav Stroupežnický, Jaroslav Hilbert, and F. F. Samberk, and in the novels of František Pravda, Alois Mrštík, Vilém Mrštík, Josef Holeček, Jindřich Baar, Rudolf Medek, and Emil Vachek.

Russia

Anti-Semitism in Russia and the Soviet Union has gone through several stages since its inception in the Middle Ages. Originally an import with Byzantine Christianity, early records reflect ecclesiastical rivalry with Judaism, which held a strong position due to the influence of Jews and Judaism in southeastern Europe emanating from the Judaized Khazar Empire that held sway as far west as Kiev until the late tenth century. The last Judaizing movement was extirpated from Russia at the end of the fifteenth century and the Jews themselves banned from Russia until their reappearance in massive numbers due to the partition of the Polish kingdom at the end of the eighteenth century. At that time commercial interests coupled with deep seated national and religious animosities forced the czar to restrict these Polish Jews to the newly acquired western provinces. Nineteenth-century government policy aimed at converting the Jews or forcing them to emigrate. By the end of the century government-sponsored pogroms attempted to hasten that process. Nineteenth-century Russian anti-Semitic literature has to be seen against this background of an unwanted minority gained through conquest.

Anti-Jewish images can be found in Mikhail Lermontov's drama *Ispantsy* (The Spaniards) (1830), Ivan Turgenev's short story "Zhid" ("The Jew," 1847), Nikolai Gogol's novella *Taras Bulba* (1835, rev. 1842), Dostoevsky's novel *Zapiski iz mërtvogo doma* (*Memoirs from the House of the Dead*, 1860–1862). While Leon Tolstoy condemned anti-Semitism on Christian principles, his occasional references to Jews were extremely negative. Paralleling the rise of anti-Semitism in the West, Jews are portrayed as anti-Russian, anti-Christian and as revolutionaries in such works as Vsevolod Krestovskiĭ's *T'ma egispetskaĭa* (Egyptian Darkness, 1899).

The United States

In the United States the rich literature of the nineteenth century emphasized a number of traditional and contemporary anti-Semitic themes. Popular revivalist Christians of the period produced a wave of well-received novels about New Testament times hostile to Jews and Judaism. These include James Clarke's *Legend of Thomas Didymus, The Jewish Sceptic* (1881) and Elbridge Brook's *A Son of Issachar: A Romance from the Days of Messias* (1890). Jewish stereotypes are criticized in Edgar Saltus' *Mary Magdalen: A Chronicle* (1891), Mary Jennings' *Asa of Bethlehem and His Household* (1895), and Caroline Mason's *The Quiet King: A Story of Christ* (1896). Jews are designated as ugly, slaves to the law, haters of Christ, and his crucifiers. These themes stem from a literal reading of the anti-Jewish sentiments embedded in the New Testament. Other novels denigrate Jews but laud intermarriage and conversion, which represents an independent American adaptation of traditional medieval and contemporary themes in Christian Europe.

Jews as criminals, usually committing nonviolent crimes such as fraud and arson, is a theme that mirrors European images adapted to the American scene. It was given impetus at the time of the mass arrival of East European Jews in the United States and parallels negative attitudes toward other immigrants. The thieving Jewish pawnbroker appears in Horatio Alger's *Ben, The Luggage Boy* (1870) and *Paul, the Peddler* (1871). The very popular and influential crime novels produced a stereotypical thieving Jew found in any neighborhood from slum to Wall Street. The character is invariably a coward. The professionalizing of anti-Semitism has been attributed to Telemachus Timayenis, who founded the Minerva publishing house that disseminated anti-Jewish works. His own anti-Jewish novels include *Judas Iscariot* (1889) and *The Original Mr. Jacobs* (1888). His survey of Greek history emphasized the definition of civilization as Hellenic and Christian, which may explain his bias. By the end of the century the linking of immigrant Jews to criminality was exploited by popular and serious novelists and pulp media from *Puck* to *Life* magazine.

The theme of usurer and parasite painted in unsympathetic strokes can be found in James Fenimore Cooper's *The Bravo* (1831), J. B. Jones' *Border War* (1859), and Julia Ward Howe's 1857 play, *The World's Own*. This image of an ugly Jewish moneylender is prevalent in the novels of Henry James as a scapegoat for the vicissitudes of the patrician merchant class, which in the period 1884–1902 was being replaced by an immigrant merchant class. The theme even appears emphasized in the rhymes of *Mother Goose*. This patrician backlash portrayed the Jew as corruptor of American Christian society in such early twentieth-century novels as Willa Cather's *The Professor's House* (1925), F. Scott Fitzgerald's *The Great Gatsby* (1925), and T. S. Eliot's poem "Burbank with a Baedeker: Bleistein with a Cigar" (1920).

Other end-of-the-century themes that appear in American literature include the Jew as alien who cannot be assimilated and the Jew as enemy of society who disdains non-Jews and exploits them. The legend of the Wandering Jew crossed the ocean and became interwoven with the theme of a world conspiracy, a cabal, as most popularly outlined later in George S. Viereck and Paul Eldridge's novel *My First Two Thousand Years* (1928). These themes proliferate in novels such as Francis M. Crawford, *A Roman Singer* (1884), George Gossip, *The Jew of Chamant* (1899), Richard Henry Savage, *The White Lady of Khaminavatka* (1898), Frank Norris, *McTeague* (1899), and Ignatius Donnelly, *Caesar's Column* (1890). Whatever contemporary problems and evils that non-Jews feared or contemplated were explained as a Jewish plot. Such externalizations of psychological and social problems recall the medieval image of the Jew as devil and, both in Europe and America, helped set the stage for the greatest Jewish tragedy in that people's long history, the Holocaust of World War II.

The Twentieth Century

In the twentieth century the forces of ultraconservatism dominated Europe politically and adversely affected the literary attitude toward Jews. The theory of world conspiracy (whose modern version was *The Protocols of the Learned Elders of Zion* plagiarized in the 1890s from a French polemic against Napoleon III and translated into Russian by Sergei Nilus circa 1905) has dominated twentieth-century anti-Semitic literature in Russia and elsewhere. In the United States it was popularized by Henry Ford in *The Dearborn Independent* (serialized until 1927). At the same time the voices of radical revolution found in the image of the Jew a convenient stereotype against which to depict their hostility to the old order. A world in flux found the Jew a convenient (by tradition) scapegoat for every ill from capitalism to communism.

The center for anti-Semitism during the interwar years was Nazi Germany, where it proliferated in belles-lettres, journalism, scholarship and governmental decree. Adolph Hitler's autobiography *Mein Kampf* (*My Battle*, 1925–1927) summarized much of the earlier hatred (the German translation of *The Protocols of the Elders of Zion* appeared in 1920) and set the tone for most anti-Jewish propaganda. These Nazi-developed themes spread throughout conservative Europe and affected historians like the Rumanian Nicolae Iorga and other professors. Anti-Jewish and anti-Communist themes appear among Rumanian authors like Nae Ionescu, Nicolae Davidescu, Octavian Goga, Cezar Petrescu, Ionel Theodoreanu, and Panait Istrati. Nazi influence on French literature is evidenced in the novels of Louis-Ferdinand Céline's *Voyage au bout de la nuit* (*Journey to the End of the Night*, 1932), his racist *Ecole des cadavres* (*School of Corpses*, 1938) and Pierre Drieu la Rochelle's *Gilles* (1939).

The defeat of Nazi Germany and the general revulsion in the West following the discovery of the mass murder of 6 million Jews during World War II discredited anti-Semitism as a legitimate literary theme. A recently developed tool of literary criticism called deconstructionism, which is derived from the application of cabbalistic terminology and methodology, has uncovered new dimensions of anti-Semitism embedded in post-war French literature in the works of Maurice Blanchot, Léon Bloy, Jean Giraudoux and André Gide.

During the Soviet period anti-Semitism was officially condemned and in the years immediately after the Revolution severely prosecuted. Hostility to the Jews, Judaism, and Zionism is, however, a prominent part of official Soviet literature, and one may argue that the center for a dissimulated anti-Semitism in the post-Nazi world is in the Soviet Union. Ivan Shevtsov's novel *Liubov' i nenavist'* (*Love and Hate*, 1970) which is replete with vituperative anti-Semitism and anti-Zionism, was praised by the Soviet academy. Igor Beliaev's novel *S chernogo khoda* (*By the Back Way*), published in the journal *Znamya* (1972), is also virulently anti-Zionist. The most strident attack on this official policy is Evgenii Evtushenko's renowned poem *Babii Iar* (*Babi Yar*, 1961, Russian censored edition, 1966), and its novelization by Anatoli Kuznetsov (1966). The official government and literary line is still hostile as evidenced in the state-sponsored literature summarized by Y. Tsigelman's "Anti-Semitism in Soviet Publications (Belles Lettres and Feature Stories)," in *Anti-Semitism in the Soviet Union: Its Roots and Consequences*, ed. Theodore Freedman (1984) and *The Image of the Jew in Soviet Literature: The Post-Stalin Period* (1984), by Jakub Blum (on Soviet Russian literature) and Vera Rich (on Belorussian texts).

Arabic and Muslim Literature

Anti-Semitism (a more euphemistic term is Judeophobia [i.e., fear leading to hatred and oppression] since, as Arabs correctly argue, they too are Semites) in Arabic and Muslim literature is based upon two factors: a rivalry with Judaism on the part of Muslim theologians and the search for a new self-identity on the part of Arabic-speaking non-Jews lost in the maelstrom of post-World-War-I political and cultural changes. The former takes its cue from Mohammed's polemical remarks in the Koran, while the latter is a direct import from Christian, Nazi, and Soviet sources. In both aspects hostility to Jews and Judaism (although tolerated officially) and to Israel and Zionism arises from the disunity that has afflicted the Arab peoples since medieval times. Christian and Muslim religious stereotypes permeate modern Arab anti-Semitism.

The themes introduced by Mohammed include hostility of Jews to their own prophets and ipso facto to himself as the "soul of prophecy," falsification of the holy scriptures, and deadly animosity to Muslims. These themes *mutatis mutandis* permeate all subsequent Islamic literature. Later Christian themes such as Jewish domination and the blood libel are introduced during the nineteenth century. Shakespeare's *Merchant of Venice* was translated into Arabic at the end of the nineteenth century, and his Shylock portrait is much quoted. The twentieth-century Egyptian play *Ilah Isrā'īl* (*The God of Israel*) by 'Alī Aḥmad Bākathīr (published in Cairo, c. 1963) depicts Jews as demons and devils who are descendants of unholy unions between demons and women. All traditional sources are interwoven into the polemics of governments, journalists, theologians, and authors, which reflect the wide-ranging ramifications of the Arab-Israeli conflict of the twentieth century. One of the most popular of such Western treatises is *The Protocols of the Elders of Zion*, which is handed out by Arab leaders to foreign dignitaries and is required reading for politicians and soldiers.

Conclusion

The ignorance of the consequences of anti-Semitism allows it to remain a popular theme in post-World-War-II literature and other arts. The admission by the Second Vatican Council of 1965 that Jews are not guilty of deicide has not affected the perpetuation of that canard. That decision, in any event, has been overshadowed by the United Nations resolution in 1975 that Zionism is a form of racism. Zionism as a synonym for racism has become a denigrating codeword for Third World peoples. Zionism as synonymous with Nazism and along with hostility to Judaism has become a predominant theme in Soviet propaganda and has spilled over into legitimate literature as well. Neo-Nazi sympathizers, with the support of academics, are attempting to deny that the Holocaust of European Jewry during World War II ever occurred. Contemporary East European literature simply avoids mention that Jews were victims, a concomitant of the Soviet policy of writing Jews out of history. In many Western countries, attacks on Jews, Judaism, Zionism, and Israel by Jews, non-Jews, and anti-Semites proliferate as acceptable themes where a corresponding attack on any other racial or religious group would be publicly denounced by concerned citizens or responsible officials. This leads to the conclusion that anti-Semitism, no matter under what euphemism it is disguised, remains an accepted facet, as it has been for the past two-and-a-half millennia, of world literary expression.

See also: Alienation; Banker, Financier and Usurer; Christianity versus Christendom.

Selected Bibliography

Dobkowski, Michael N. *The Tarnished Dream. The Basis of American Anti-Semitism.* Westport, Conn.: Greenwood Press, 1979.

Low, Alfred D. *Jews in the Eyes of the Germans from the Enlightenment to Imperial Germany.* Philadelphia: Institute for the Study of Human Issues, 1979.

Poliakov, Léon. *The History of Anti-Semitism.* 4 vols. New York: Vanguard Press, 1965.

Rubin, Abba. *Images in Transition. The English Jew in English Literature, 1660–1830.*
    Westport, Conn.: Greenwood Press, 1984.

STEVEN BOWMAN

ANXIETY

Anxiety is a generalized, often debilitating apprehension of impending personal
destruction. The most widely accepted psychoanalytic understanding of anxiety
is based on Sigmund Freud's 1926 study, *Hemmung, Symptom und Angst (Inhibitions, Symptoms and Anxiety)*, a revision of his earlier theories. Unlike fear
or, perhaps, worry, anxiety is unfocused, lacking a clearly identifiable internal
or external object; whereas we "fear" or "worry about" this or that fact or
possibility, we are anxious without being able to say why. Because it supposes
full destruction as opposed to mere harm, anxiety is intense to the point of being
nearly overwhelming. It absorbs, as it were, all reason, attention, and energy.
It includes strong psychosexual components: literally, the feared loss of mother,
father, or spouse may be involved in anxiety; more often, anxiety symbolically
incorporates a sense of the loss of love, which deprivation participates either in
the expected personal destruction or in its apparent causation.

Background

Both as a human distemper and as a literary theme, anxiety is essentially a
twentieth-century phenomenon. First, it is most likely to occur in times of
uncertainty and rapid change; secondly, and perhaps more significantly, some
amount of psychoanalytic sophistication is required to recognize anxiety and to
distinguish it from similar disturbing emotional conditions such as fear. Yet
Freud and Jung regularly disclaimed credit for "discovering" psychological
patterns and conditions, affirming instead that they were exploring and codifying
discoveries made and communicated by the great poets and dramatists.

Sophocles' tragedy *Oidipous tyrannos* (*Oedipus Rex*, c. 429 B.C.) represents
a very interesting early expression of anxiety. Ironically, the protagonist Oedipus
is infected with hubris of such potency that one could hardly imagine his ever
experiencing even the shortest anxious episode; however, the community itself
is thoroughly anxiety-ridden, fearing that absolute destruction is imminent and
associating this communal threat with such specifically sexual causes as incest
and parricide. A message of Sophocles' powerful praxis is that we are forever
in danger of ignorantly corrupting love and its institutions—and thus of bringing
total destruction upon ourselves, our families, and our communities.

William Shakespeare's *Macbeth* (1605–1606) is a tragedy with a psychosexual
dynamic akin to that of *Oedipus Rex*. Much emphasis is placed upon the opposition of natural and unnatural forces, and the mood of the play from the outset
is surely characterized by anxiety. Macbeth himself, unlike Oedipus, is plagued

by anxiety, but in most of his behavior he is run by motors other than his own thoughts, feelings, or emotions. It is possible to assert that Macbeth is not the central figure in the drama—but that he and Lady Macbeth together function as a kind of compound protagonist. Alone, neither is sufficient in humanity, and neither alone is sufficient for tragedy. Yet what each lacks is available in the other, and precisely in such quantity that together they own a couple's full share, though it is improperly distributed. Shakespeare seems to have focused this imbalance in the area of their sexuality. Macbeth is in many ways not a man, according to his spouse, but most specifically he is not *male*, having excessive "milk" of human kindness; and Lady Macbeth is enough of a male to wish to have her unsexing completed so that the masculine gender of her motives and methods might not be belied by her breasts, her female form. Thus the anxiety that pervades *Macbeth* is related to a destruction that seems almost to be in progress, with a severe psychological disharmony in the one flesh of husband and wife.

The Nineteenth Century

Artistic genius infers long in advance what science eventually describes. In the nineteenth century artistic genius and science converge in what sometimes amounts to a fascination with anxiety—so that by the dawn of the twentieth century anxiety has become a major artistic preoccupation.

Edgar Allen Poe would have been hard pressed to choose between art and science had he been required to abandon one or the other. He is forever speculative and expressive, and though his subject is most commonly thought to be horror, it is perhaps more specifically anxiety: fear of destruction and the loss of love. See almost any of his best-known tales or poems, notably the poem "The Raven" (1845), perhaps the best known of all, in which death and the loss of love are explicitly the chief themes. Yet possibly the story "The Fall of the House of Usher" (1839) is artistically the supreme example of Poe's explorations of anxiety, beginning with a description in which nearly each word is dark and full of foreboding and ending, quite literally, in a kind of destruction that most anxiety barely adumbrates. The sexual hints in "The Fall of the House of Usher" point toward incestuous goings-on, presumably to stave off loneliness and the end of a family line—corruptions of love that destroy both love and lovers, as well as the hope of future generations.

In the novel *Moby-Dick* (1851) Herman Melville's Ahab is one of the great anxiety-haunted characters of literary history. He has abandoned love, having deserted his young wife in pursuit of a monster by whom he has been wounded (sexually wounded, it seems clear) and by whom he will finally be destroyed. Ahab's appalling greatness in the reader's eyes no doubt depends largely upon the fact that although he is sick with anxiety (he sleeps with his fingernails digging into his palms) he persists—which makes him a cut more amazing than the tragic hero who plunges on toward destruction without any suspicion that he is in danger; Ahab even exceeds the romantic hero who knowingly attempts the impossible, in that most such heroes do not carry Ahab's freight of anxious torment but fight on blissfully innocent of self-doubt, yea perhaps mindlessly. Ahab knows and Ahab feels—and is still destroyed, reminding us that when the anxiety-plagued hero fears destruction he is not necessarily wrong in being thus afraid. It would not be possible to be truly anxious, indeed, if we did not know of examples of the destruction even of anxious persons.

Because naturalism is often characterized by violence, literature of the late nineteenth century seems full of anxiety, yet often what we perceive is not general, unfocused anxiety but more properly an unusual quantity of ordinary fear. Even so, Dostoevsky (who, incidentally, denied having any truck with any of the forms of realism) seems especially well attuned to the sources of anxiety. For example, in reading the novel *Prestuplenie i nakazanie* (*Crime and Punishment*, 1866) it may be more difficult to believe that Raskolnikov murders from a compulsion to evade moral law than it is to believe that he is, ironically, driven by deep anxiety to act out evils that he fears within himself. If so, he is acting in the direction of suicide; in being saved by love he emphasizes for us the prominence of love as a key feature of the anxiety paradigm.

The Twentieth Century

Anxiety is so much a major theme in literature after 1950 that we are in danger of missing the forest while in search of the trees. Perhaps anxiety is the medium in which many or most people live and think in the later twentieth century—as it was the medium in which Franz Kafka lived and wrote in the earlier years of the century.

Kafka may be the one writer to date for whom anxiety has served as a central theme. His story "Die Verwandlung" (The Metamorphosis, 1915) demonstrates how beneath a brilliantly executed overglaze of wit and satire (which in retrospect seem increasingly ghastly, a controlled hysteria) Kafka probes deep psychological wounds. Gregor Samsa, as he explores the range of uses to which he can put his new insect body, indeed plays pranks on his family and their lodgers—but he is never truly light-hearted. More to the point, he is almost continuously tormented with shame, guilt, and loneliness. At the beginning of the story, Gregor is concerned that he may lose the respect and love of his mother and may disappoint his father; at the story's end he has been dead, central character or not, for several pages—and the family not only do not miss him but are nearly ecstatic. Indeed, his sister, his sole sibling, whose having cared for him throughout the story has approximated genuine sympathy, positively blooms in his absence as if his living had been keeping her from air and sunlight. To say that Gregor's self-image, that of a roach with a festering sore inflicted by his own father, is negative and anxious is to make a laughable understatement. Such is the literary power of Kafka when dealing with the theme of anxiety.

T. S. Eliot's poem *The Waste Land* (1922) perhaps can be said to function more as an evocation of those things that work to produce modern anxiety than as a description or evocation of anxiety itself. If so, its main themes perhaps include anomie more than anxiety; and entropy seems more the fate of the universe than some more cataclysmic destruction. Similarly, Samuel Beckett's play *En attendant Godot* (*Waiting for Godot*, 1952) is an artistic document of anxiety chiefly by its showing such aftereffects of prolonged anxiety as apathy and alienation. Indeed, *most* literature of the later twentieth century that treats upon anxiety may be said to treat upon it indirectly, as if anxiety has become a part of the environment.

A subcategory of twentieth-century literature in which anxiety is prominent is literature dealing with alcoholism, probably because alcoholism and anxiety function symbiotically. A masterpiece in this category is Malcolm Lowry's novel *Under the Volcano* (1947), in which destruction seems foreordained for the protagonist Geoffrey Firmin, whose addiction to alcohol works simultaneously as cause and effect of his sense of being doomed. W. Somerset Maugham's novel *The Razor's Edge* (1944) contains in the minor character of Sophie an example of an anxiety-tormented alcoholic who eventually in effect commits suicide by placing herself in the company of low-life drifters, one of whom cuts her throat and throws her into the sea. Yet Maugham's contribution consists in his showing, by contrast with Sophie perhaps, how his major characters manage with varying degrees of success to skirt the dangers presented by selfishness and materialism.

See also: Dream, Existentialism, Horror, Terror.

Selected Bibliography

Freud, Sigmund. *The Standard Edition of the Complete Psychological Works of Sigmund Freud.* Trans. and ed. James Strachey in collaboration with Anna Freud. 24 vols. London: The Hogarth Press and the Institute of Psycho-analysis, 1955.
Rickman, John, M.D., ed. *A General Selection from the Works of Sigmund Freud.* 1937. New York: Doubleday, 1957.

HALE CHATFIELD

APOCALYPSE

The word apocalypse comes from the Greek word *apokalypsis*, to uncover or reveal (the root is *kalypto*, to cover or conceal) and is eschatological in nature (the root here being *eschatos*, furthest or uttermost), concerned with final things, with the end of the present age, the Day of Judgment, and the age to follow. Apocalypse is a revelation of spiritual realities in the future, realities that are given temporal sequence and historical embodiment by the apocalyptist. This projection of the way in which time will progress toward its end is essentially linear and teleological (*telos* being the Greek word for goal). One event after another is described, each event belonging to a definite pattern of historical relationships that will not repeat itself in the cyclical manner of Oriental myth but which will move toward its goal at the end of history. Thus, "apocalypse" is a synonym for "revelation" (*not* for "disaster," though it is often misused as such), a Judeo-Christian mythic vision of the beginning and end of history, expressed in recognizable narrative and symbolic literary conventions.

The basic narrative structure of apocalypse begins to develop from the Judaic prophetic tradition during the century or so preceding Christ. With the growth of the great empires of Persia, Greece, and Rome and the consequent political powerlessness of the Hebrew people, the contradiction between the prophetic ideals and the actual experience of the nation became more and more apparent. The prophets' vision of their history as moving toward the establishment of a community based on a special relationship with Yahweh seemed less and less realizable in view of their contemporary historical situation. The apocalyptists began to replace the prophets, insisting that only a radical change or break in history would be enough to rectify present conditions. The present age would have to end before God's kingdom could begin, and only the righteous would survive the eschatological revolution. Whereas prophecy focuses on the earthly destinies of men and on their specific, present behavior as they attempt to fulfill their appointed role as God's chosen people, apocalypse emphasizes future events and exhorts men to endure their present suffering with the assurance of a blessed future life. Both prophecy and apocalypse look forward to the future, but the prophet sees the future as arising out of the present, whereas the apocalyptist sees the future as breaking into the present. The beleaguered early Christians found the apocalyptic mode suitable for the expression of their oppressive earthly situation, as had the Hebrews before them. Indeed, it is likely that to some extent Christ's great appeal has been his assurance, first to his disciples and then to all his followers, that the end of this world and the beginning of his messianic kingdom are near.

There are many examples of apocalypses in both Hebrew and Christian writings: Ezekiel, Daniel, and Zechariah are foremost examples of testamentary Hebrew apocalypses; the Gospel of St. Mark and the second Epistle of St. Peter contain apocalyptic passages and, above all, the revelation of St. John of Patmos exemplifies Christian testamentary apocalypse. Noncanonical apocalypses also exist in abundance. Apocalypse is concerned with the nature of history and the nature of time itself. The apocalyptist's narrative point of view is ostensibly beyond the end of time, a point of view that allows him to recount the past, present, and future, to relate the beginning of God's plan for history to its end, to describe history in its totality. In Revelation St. John responds to God's urgent command to write what he has seen and heard. The events that he describes include a catalogue of natural disasters and civil chaos presided over by the Antichrist, Gog and Magog, and other symbolic embodiments of evil; a thousand-year reign by Christ and his martyred followers; a "last loosing" of Satan from the bottomless pit where Christ has cast him; the final triumph of Christ in the battle of Armageddon; and the Last Judgment, the ultimate destruction of this world and the descent of the eternal city, the New Jerusalem. For the traditional apocalyptist the future is recounted as if it were past. Thus St. John describes the projected end of time in a strange mixture of tenses, for the rest of history lies revealed before him. Apocalypse projects the patterns of creation, growth, decay, renewal, and catastrophe onto history, encompassing the beginning and the end of time within its vision. Time itself becomes a vehicle of divine purpose.

Apocalyptic thinking is dualistic, envisaging human history as a kind of dialectic between two opposing forces, both personal and cosmic in character, which vie for control of the world. Although malign powers are considered to be in control of this evil, temporal, limited age, they are soon to be overcome by the direct intervention of God. This age will end abruptly, and God will then initiate a timeless kingdom that will be perfectly righteous. The progression of events within this historical dialectic may vary from one apocalypse to another, but all describe the alternation of evil and good as the forces of the Antichrist and those of God engage in their cosmic battle for ultimate supremacy. This dualism of ethical forces, ages, and worlds implies the view that history is radically discontinuous. After the final cosmic struggle between Satan's forces and God's, time will cease, heaven and earth will become one for eternity, and the faithful will enter the holy city. If the end of time is catastrophic for some, it is a glorious consummation of God's plan for those who have faithfully maintained their eschatological conviction. Thus, it should be clear that the current use of the word ''apocalypse'' as a synonym for ''disaster'' or ''cataclysm'' is only half correct. The myth comprehends both cataclysm *and* millennium, tribulation *and* triumph, chaos *and* order, and it is the creative tension, the dialectic, between these opposites that explains in part the myth's enduring relevance. The extent to which various ages have emphasized the pessimistic or the optimistic side of apocalypse differs greatly, of course. That our own age has focused primarily upon the cataclysmic aspect of the myth is evident in the subsequent discussion of contemporary literature.

Apocalyptic thinking is also fundamentally deterministic. The apocalyptist, speaking from a point beyond the future, reveals a definite time schedule that God himself has predetermined. The vision of things to come, listed in apocalyptic literature, provides a metaphoric itinerary for God's inevitable victory over evil. But despite the assumption of a predetermined progression of events toward a given end, men's actions are not necessarily predetermined. Apocalypse developed, as stated here, out of the Judaic prophetic tradition as a mode of exhortation, of encouragement to those suffering persecution. It urges struggle, will, tenacity, loyalty, even martyrdom for the cause of God's kingdom; it promises reward to the faithful and vengeance to the wicked, those who fail to act for the achievement of the kingdom of God. Thus, apocalypse describes men's actions and God's reactions. It is this expression of confident expectation of divine justice that has given apocalypse its great appeal during periods of oppression, affliction, and persecution.

Apocalyptic visions are expressed in hermetic symbols and coded (often numerological) references. Addressing himself to a persecuted minority, the apocalyptist felt himself forced to use a kind of cryptic language, allusive and obscure. It is this political expedient, as well as the sense that the message being revealed is beyond simple description, that explains the rich poetic content of apocalyptic archetypes, allusions, and symbolic patterns. The Revelation of St. John provides the most complete example of apocalyptic imagery, beginning with the vision of God and the Lamb on the throne, surrounded by four beasts and a sea of glass like crystal, from which issue lightning, thunder, and voices. There are the visions of the seven seals on the book of destiny or doom which, when broken, produce the four horsemen of the apocalypse (war, oppression, famine, and death); the cosmic woes of earthquakes, falling stars, a blackened sun, and a bloody moon; the seven trumpet woes; the swarms of locusts; the red dragon with seven heads and ten horns; the whore of Babylon—all expressing man's awe of divine retributive power. Such visions of violence have always exerted an intense fascination, and there is, of course, a profound relationship between eschatological insight and private fantasies of vengeance. The Revelation of St. John concludes with the vision of Christ Triumphant upon a white horse, his vesture dipped in blood, the songs in heaven, and the New Jerusalem with its pure river of the water of life, its tree of life with leaves for the healing of the nations. Such imagery expresses man's most ardent hopes for the realization of God's just rule on earth. Drawing from Psalms and Isaiah and many other Old Testament sources, the apocalyptist attempted to understand and communicate the spiritual purpose in history.

Medieval History and Literary Uses of Apocalypse

Whereas the Revelation of St. John, written during the reign of Domitian, probably between A.D. 94–96, expects the imminent return of Christ and the end of this world, expectation of the second coming of Christ began to be less urgent by the middle of the second century. Responding to scoffers who question Christ's delay in returning to initiate his kingdom, the author of the second Epistle of Peter explains that Christ may forestall the Last Judgment until all men have accepted his word. During this period, Christian apocalypses, which had hitherto enjoyed canonical authority, were deprived of it, for the millennium began to seem a remote rather than an impending event. The third century saw the first attempts to discredit apocalyptic visions. Origen, one of the most influential theologians in the ancient church, whose writings greatly influenced subsequent doctrine, asserted that the millennium was not to be conceived of as an event that would occur in the world, but rather as a spiritual event that would occur in the individual soul. In the fourth century, as the Catholic church accrued power and position, visions of an earthly paradise that would supplant the world of a suffering Christian minority seemed anachronistic and even seditious. Early in the fifth century, St. Augustine reinterpreted the apocalyptic strain of the church in accordance with the new official position of Christianity. In *De civitate Dei* (*The City of God*, 413–426) St. Augustine asserts that the Revelation of St. John is to be read as an allegory, that the millennium had begun with Christ and was fully realized in the church. The Council of Ephesus, in A.D. 431, condemned belief in a literal millennium as a superstitious aberration. After this time, millennial movements persisted, and indeed persist into the present, but literal expectation of the second coming of Christ was placed outside of official church sanction.

The most important apocalyptic visionary of the Middle Ages was Joachim of Fiore (c. 1130–1202), an Italian abbot from Calabria who applied the symbol of the Trinity to history, dividing time into three periods, based upon the three persons of the Trinity. In his *Expositio in Apocalypsim* (c. 1200) Joachim proposes that the three ages of history, the ancient (corresponding to the Father), the medieval (corresponding to the Son), and the modern (corresponding to the Holy Spirit), are characterized by intelligible increases in spiritual fulfillment. Joachim felt that the third age, which had not yet begun, was to be initiated imminently, sometime between 1200 and 1260. During the transitional period immediately preceding and requisite to the third age, certain specified events were to occur. A new religious order would appear to preach the new gospel; from this new order of spiritual men, twelve patriarchs would emerge who would convert the Jews; an emperor for the last days, an angelic pope, would show the world the way to leave off materialistic concerns and attend to spiritual ones. Joachim predicted that exactly three-and-one-half years before the initiation of this third age, the last world emperor would destroy the corrupt and worldly church, overthrow the Antichrist, and then inaugurate the millennium. Joachim's concept of a nucleus of "spiritual men" was seized on by various groups to justify their own historical importance. Although the Spiritual party within the Franciscan order is the most noteworthy example, many other religious movements identified themselves at one time or another with the hoped-for remnant of spiritual men who would form the seed of the rulers of the third age of the Holy Spirit. Likewise, secular leaders, most notably Frederick II (1194–1250), found it politically useful to link themselves to this last emperor myth, although it is clear that Joachim envisioned not a political agent but a holy pope who would subdue the Antichrist and begin the third age. (During the Reformation, Joachim's terms were exactly reversed. For Martin Luther and other reformers, the pope was identified with the Antichrist, not with his opponent.) Joachim's pattern of three progressive stages of historical development came to dominate the age and to influence the secular schematas of progressive history that developed in the eighteenth and nineteenth centuries, for example, those of Vico, Comte, Prudhon, Hegel, and Marx. A recent vestige of Joachim's apocalyptic vision of a third age of future perfection is the Third Reich of Hitler's Germany.

The most notable medieval literary exponent of Joachimist apocalypticism is Dante (1265–1321). Dante was a fervent believer in an earthly beatitude under the rule of a single emperor. In his letter to the Princes and People of Italy in 1310, Dante showed his political messianism, hailing Emperor Henry VII as God's chosen vessel and expressing his belief that the true potential of mankind could be realized through the harmony of one world government. In his epic poem, *La divina commedia* (*The Divine Comedy*, c. 1320) one senses clearly the eschatological expectation of a great ruler who would restore order to the world. Indeed, Dante honored Joachim himself as a great prophet, placing him in the *Paradiso (Paradise)* as one endowed with the spirit of prophecy; furthermore, Dante uses two of Joachim's symbolic figures to express his hope for the apocalyptic transformation of this world into a new order of spiritual blessedness. Contemporary literary use of Joachimist thought has been made implicitly by American novelist, Walker Percy, in *Lancelot* (1977) and *The Second Coming* (1980), and explicitly by Mexican novelist, Carlos Fuentes, in *Terra nostra* (1975).

The medieval apocalyptic vision of the radical transformation of this world into "a new heaven and new earth" (Rev. 21:1) is fully embodied not only in Dante's *Divine Comedy* but also in William Langland's English narrative poem, *Piers Plowman* (c. 1362–1387). *Piers Plowman* is fundamentally concerned with the problem of Christian perfection, and Piers is an eschatological figure, able to lead the way into the kingdom of God. It has been argued, in fact, that in the fourteenth century, social thinking on the subject of perfection had to be apocalyptic. The transcendence of society to a new level was thought by many to be the only way out of the crushing dilemmas of the time. The sad state of the contemporary church could be explained only on the grounds that God was planning, if not a new age, at least a renewal of the good and the just. The evil of the times was seen as a necessary prerequisite to God's renewal, the birth throes of the new order. Thus, the prologue of *Piers Plowman* presents an apocalyptic setting of social decay that requires renewal, just as St. John of Patmos catalogues the disasters of the present age to suggest the necessity—the inevitability—of divine intervention in history. Throughout the poem, the very presence of Antichrist is actually evidence for the imminence of renewal and fundamentally a hopeful sign. Furthermore, there appears an ideal pope or spiritual leader who is a multidimensional symbol. These two figures of late medieval apocalypticism—the angelic pope and ideal king—are united in the figure of Christ as conqueror, king, and judge. Individual perfection becomes in the last analysis a problem of social perfection, and social perfection to a convinced Christian of the time meant the kingdom of God, an apocalyptic event.

Given this fourteenth-century attitude and its extension into the fifteenth century, it is not surprising that the discovery of America inspired much apocalyptic fervor. Might this pristine land be the site that God had prepared for his kingdom? Christopher Columbus, reaching the coast of South America, quoted passages from Revelations and Isaiah, which tell of "a new heaven and a new earth," and he wrote to his royal patrons, "I deeply feel within me that there, where I have said, lies the Terrestrial Paradise." In his journal the explorer explained that the world is pear-shaped like a woman's breast and that the terrestrial paradise lies on the spot corresponding to the nipple, from whence flow the waters of the rivers of Eden. Citing scripture and his own observations, Columbus at length concluded that his voyage and God's historical purpose were one. The New

World's promise exerted irresistible attraction upon many Europeans, who came to convert the Indians; to find that golden New Jerusalem called El Dorado; to exercise the religious, political, and economic freedom impossible in the Old World. Given such eschatological pressure on the very idea of America, American literature was bound from its first appearance to be the frequent repository of apocalyptic visions.

The Renaissance in European and American Literature

In North American Puritan literature, Increase Mather's "New Jerusalem," written in 1687, is an interpretation of St. John's account of the last days of the world in terms of New England's history, even suggesting that New England was to be the site of the fulfillment of God's promise to his chosen people. In 1727, Samuel Sewall published *Phaenomena quaedam apocalyptica . . . (The New Heaven . . . upon the New Earth)*, in which he proposed America as the site of the triumphant culmination of world history. In general, however, second and third generation Puritan settlers were not so optimistic. Sermons based on the cataclysmic rather than the millennial imagery of Revelation became standard fare. For example, Jonathan Edwards' series of sermons, *A History of the Work of Redemption* (delivered in 1739, published in 1786), is informed by apocalyptic thinking. And although the apocalyptic literature of the seventeenth and eighteenth centuries in North America is primarily in histories and sermons, the Reverend Michael Wigglesworth chose to supplement his sermons with poetic expression of the impending cosmic disasters and the future new world. In the poem "The Day of Doom" (1662), Wigglesworth sought to popularize the subject that he felt to be of the most urgent importance, God's impending judgment of sinful mankind.

As in New England, millennial hopes accompanied the settlement of New Spain in the sixteenth century, and apocalyptic fervor motivated the colonization of Spanish America. Because it was believed that the kingdom of God could not be initiated until the gospel had been preached to all men (including the newly discovered populations of the Indies, as Spain referred to its American territories), the conversion of native populations to Catholicism was viewed as being of utmost urgency and described in apocalyptic terms in the early chronicles of New Spain. Apocalyptic drama was common in what were referred to as *auto-sacramentales*, plays for the purpose of the religious education of the Indians. An example is *El día del juicio final* (1573), by Fray Andrés de Olmos (which played in Mexico City in 1982).

In England, the great seventeenth century epic, *Paradise Lost* (1667), by John Milton, draws directly on the Book of Revelation. The War in Heaven, treated in books 1 through 4, and in 9, and referred to as the "heavenly" or "celestial cycle," is based on four verses in Revelation (12:4, 7–9). Although it has been asserted that the celestial cycle in *Paradise Lost* is best understood in terms of epic or classical literature, Milton also used well-known sixteenth-and seventeenth-century commentaries on Revelation to inform his epic poem, and a large proportion of his imagery is derived from Revelation. For Milton, the Book of Revelation contained an explanation of God's hidden or secret decrees, which were fore-ordained and published before the foundation of the world.

Since the Renaissance the term "apocalypse" has been largely shorn of its biblical overtones. Subsequent use of the word has tended to refer not to the vision of St. John and others of a transformed heavenly kingdom and the future, but rather to secular and humanistic phenomena, whether political or psychic tranformation (as the English Romantics used the word), or simply to upheaval, chaos, doom.

The Romantics and Apocalypse

The English Romantic poets were essentially social revolutionaries, and their rhetoric was often biblical, so apocalypse came to suggest not a vision of the divine intervention in history, but one of social renovation. Apocalyptic change seemed promised by the social projects of the French and American Revolutions. William Wordsworth and Samuel Taylor Coleridge regarded the early stages of the French Revolution in what Martin Buber has described as an "inverted apocalyptic," that is, "an optimistic modern apocalyptic" (of which, according to Buber, the chief example is Marx's theory of history). But when the French Revolution aborted into meaningless violence, the transformative power of the poetic imagination, rather than revolutionary reform, came to be regarded as the source of apocalypse. Disillusioned when historical developments in France proved less than expected, the Romantics turned to what have been termed "apocalypses of imagination," that is, to the achievements of poetry rather than to the actualities of social change. Political action had failed to bring about the apocalypse, but the force of poetic vision might still prevail, the millennium might still be achieved. Percy Bysshe Shelley, at the end of his lyrical drama, *Prometheus Unbound* (1820), proposes that "hope" creates "from its own wreck the thing it contemplates"; Wordsworth, in the didactic poem *The Excursion* (1814), mixes Virgilian and biblical millennialism; and Blake, in the poem *The Four Zoas* (1797), creates an epic fragment that has been described as the most spectacular and sustained apocalyptic set-piece since the Book of Revelation. Blake celebrated not the apocalypse itself, but a revitalized human society that he considered the apocalypse to have created. Blake's late epics, which are referred to as the "prophetic books," are thus more accurately called apocalyptic. These two phases of Romantic apocalypticism, the revolutionary and the poetic, represent a progression of the kind that occurs when the expected apocalypse is disconfirmed, that is, when the changes originally projected fail to occur.

Nineteenth- and Twentieth-Century American Apocalyptic Literature

The apocalyptic visions that inspired the exploration and settlement of the New World in the sixteenth and seventeenth centuries have often appeared in American literature, and, indeed, in almost every aspect of American intellectual

life. Proof of the centrality of apocalyptic thinking in the United States is represented in the fact that several major indigenous American religious groups
have been based on urgent expectation of the second coming of Christ: for
example, the Seventh Day Adventists, the Latter Day Saints, the Jehovah's
Witnesses, and more recently the "Jesus people," in a variety of fundamentalist
manifestations. Nevertheless, as has already been suggested, by the nineteenth
century, the American apocalyptic mentality had become largely secularized,
just as the reasons for settling America had become secular; the religious impulse
that brought the Puritan settlers to America in the seventeenth and eighteenth
centuries no longer predominated. And in the twentieth century the optimistic
side of apocalypse, the promise of a transformed future world, has been largely
subsumed by visions of doom.

During the nineteenth century in the United States, the spirit of progress and
expansion inspired visions of beginnings rather than ends. From the American
Revolution to the mid-nineteenth century, there are only occasional glances
toward the negative side of apocalypse, few symbolic equivalents to the seven
trumpet woes, the seven vials of God's wrath, the Day of Judgment. The major
exception is Edgar Allan Poe, who, in a cosmological prose poem entitled *Eureka*
(1848) explains in scientific fashion the annihilation of the world; in the poem
"Al Aaraaf" (1829), the tale "The Masque of the Red Death" (1842), and in
metaphysical prose dialogues such as "The Conversation of Eiros and Char-
mion" (1839), "The Colloquy of Monos and Una" (1841), and "The Power
of Words" (1845), Poe takes for his theme the cataclysmic end of the world.
However, visions of an ecstatic future predominate in this period; there was no
major American writer at this time who did not write some science fiction or
utopian romance based upon an apocalyptic vision of a brave new world.

In the twentieth century, however, the emphasis of American literature has
been on the cataclysmic side of apocalypse. The novels of William Faulkner
embody a sense of doomed history that is based on the author's extreme consciousness of the racial and economic exploitation of the once pristine and
promising New World; the South becomes a prime example of the decline and
decay of the millennial potential that once inhered in America. Injustice to blacks
and the destruction of the wilderness through personal greed are the sins of the
fathers now visited upon the sons. The South in Faulkner's novels is a world
defeated by its excesses, doomed by its pride and pretensions and most of all
by its terrible moral heritage of slavery. *The Sound and the Fury* (1929), *As I
Lay Dying* (1930), *Light in August* (1932), *Absalom, Absalom!* (1936), and *The
Hamlet* (1940) are all part of Faulkner's tightly knit chronicle of degeneration.
The tragic past of the South renders men's struggles futile, dooming their present
and their future.

Pessimism about America's destiny and visions of America's end are embodied
in Nathanael West's novels, *Day of the Locust* (1939) and *Miss Lonelyhearts*
(1933), Kurt Vonnegut's novel *Cat's Cradle* (1963), Joan Didion's novel, *Play
It as It Lays* (1979). Didion's essays are collected under the title *Slouching*

towards Bethlehem (1968), a phrase based on W. B. Yeats' poetic vision of apocalypse, "The Second Coming," (1921). Further examples are novelists Norman Mailer's *An American Dream* (1965), Flannery O'Connor's *The Violent Bear It Away* (1960), Thomas Pynchon's *The Crying of Lot 49* (1965), Robert Coover's *The Origin of the Brunists* (1966) and *The Universal Baseball Association, J. Henry Waugh, Prop.* (1968).

On the other hand, Walker Percy's novels, *Love in the Ruins* (1971), *Lancelot*, and *The Second Coming*, are informed by a traditional Catholic apocalyptic eschatology that does, in fact, hold out the hope of a tranformed future world. William Goyen's novel *Come the Restorer* (1974) also treats the existential transfiguration of the old into the new, a lyrical apocalypse that is symbolic, transcendental.

A contemporary variation on the apocalyptic vision is provided by the metaphor of entropy. Like apocalypse, entropy is an eschatological vision; it is based on the second law of thermodynamics, which describes the gradual leveling of energy in the universe and the molecular equilibrium called heat death at the end of the process. Entropy posits a world moving toward its extinction inexorably and irreversibly; the end is not to be orchestrated with the great crescendo of apocalyptic cataclysm but rather with the decrescendo of entropic chaos. This eschatology is far more pessimistic than is conventional apocalyptic eschatology. The end is not caused by man's action and God's reaction, but is produced by decomposition, disintegration, and gradual loss of energy and differentiation. The anthropomorphism of the traditional apocalypse, with its implicit sense of purposeful history responding to human as well as to divine actions, yields to the bleak mechanism of a purely physical world that is irreversibly running out of energy. Whereas the apocalyptic vision sees a causal relationship between past, present, and future, the law of entropy, when applied to human affairs, negates such rational, temporal continuity. History does have a direction as it moves toward heat death, but it admits no human influence, no logical relationship between cause and effect. The use of the metaphor of entropy to describe the end of time appears throughout the fiction of Thomas Pynchon, William Burroughs, Norman Mailer, and James Purdy.

Contemporary Spanish American Apocalyptic Literature

Visions of the end of time are found throughout contemporary Spanish American fiction. Gabriel García Márquez's short stories and novels consider the end of history, whether cosmic or personal. A "biblical hurricane" sweeps away Macondo, the fictional world of *Cien años de soledad* (*One Hundred Years of Solitude*, 1967), and the political abuses of the ancient dictator in *El otoño del patriarca* (*Autumn of the Patriarch*, 1975) would seem to presage the apocalypse, although the world in fact survives his long-awaited demise. Carlos Fuentes' *Terra nostra* is set in both the old and the new worlds of the sixteenth century, as well as on the last day of this millennium, 31 December 1999. In the historical sections of the novel, we follow the activity of medieval, heretical, apocalyptic sects such as the Brethren of the Free Spirit, a group that flourished in Europe along with related sects of Adamites, Waldensians, and Cathars. These groups of revolutionary chiliasts are juxtaposed by Fuentes to the millennialism surrounding settlement of the Indies. The novel seems to suggest that it is human fate to dream of heaven and create hell. Nevertheless, the novel ends on a note of tentative expectancy. Mario Vargas Llosa's *La guerra del fin del mundo* (*The War of the End of the World*, 1981) is concerned with the late-nineteenth-century messianic uprising in northern Brazil of Antonio Vicente Mendes Maciel, "Antonio Conselheiro," and his followers, and is based in turn on a treatment of that uprising by Brazilian novelist Euclides da Cunha in his novel, *Os sertões* (*Rebellion in the Backlands*, 1902). Ernesto Sábato takes the title of his most recent novel, *Abaddón el exterminador* (*Abbadón, the Exterminator*, 1974), from the Book of Revelation: Abaddón is an avenging angel and, not surprisingly, the novel is a bleak portrait of contemporary society, written from a nihilistic, existential point of view. Other works informed by a contemporary apocalyptic perspective are José Donoso's *El obsceno pájaro de la noche* (*The Obscene Bird of Night*, 1970), Julio Cortázar's short story "Apocalípsis en Solentiname" ("Apocalypse at Solentiname," 1978), which in turn evokes the apocalyptic poetry and social philosophy of Nicaraguan poet/priest, Ernesto Cardenal.

It seems inevitable that with the approach of the year 2000, visions of apocalypse in literature will continue to appear. The symbolic importance of that date, plus increasing global anxiety about nuclear holocaust, population explosion, decreasing world resources, pollution and ecological perturbations, worldwide economic instability and financial uncertainty are likely to keep images of apocalypse in plain sight in our literature for some time to come.

See also: Christianity versus Christendom, Dream, Religion in Science Fiction.

Selected Bibliography

Charles, R. H. *Eschatology: The Doctrine of a Future Life in Israel, Judaism and Christianity.* 1891. New York: Schocken Books, 1963.

McGinn, Bernard. *Visions of the End: Apocalyptic Traditions in the Middle Ages.* New York: Columbia University Press, 1979.

Mounce, Robert H. *The Book of Revelation.* The New International Commentary on the New Testament 17. Ed. F. F. Bruce, Grand Rapids, Michigan: Eerdmans, 1977.

Zamora, Lois Parkinson, ed. *The Apocalyptic Vision in America: Interdisciplinary Essays on Myth and Culture.* Bowling Green, Ohio: The Popular Press, 1982.

LOIS PARKINSON ZAMORA

APOLOGY (SELF-DEFENSE OF SATIRISTS AND HUMORISTS)

Laughter has often been regarded as subversive. It threatens with ridicule and insignificance men and institutions that take themselves, and are taken by many, seriously. Since comedy and satire, unlike epic and tragedy, have often run into censure, comic writers have felt a need, not shared by their tragic counterparts, to enter into their works justifications of themselves and of their craft.

The Classical and Medieval Period

The first great comic writer in the West, Aristophanes, was also one of the most outspoken personalities. In his earliest extant play, *Acharne͂s (The Acharnians*, 425 B.C.), the hero apologizes for speaking about Athens in a comedy, but "what is true even comedy can tell/And I shall utter startling things but true." As he proceeds to give a critique of recent Athenian policy, the chorus, won over by his speech, heaps praise on the playwright for fearless, witty, truth-telling satire that has undermined the duplicities of orators and politicians. The comic poet works for the greatness of the state and the happiness of the people, neither bribing nor catering to the lowest taste with cheap jokes. A Persian ruler is even said to marvel that a Greek state has a "wonderful poet . . . as its stern and unsparing adviser," one who makes those he lashes with his satire wiser and harder to beat in war.

This is a high vision of the comic poet's calling, a proud declaration, at the beginning of the long history of comedy, that its enterprise involves not just entertainment but the highest moral and national goals. The theme is continued in other plays, in the middle of which the chorus addresses lines directly to the audience. In the *Sphekes (The Wasps*, 422 B.C.), Aristophanes (through the chorus) accuses the audience of ingratitude to the solicitous comic poet who is a Herculean purifier of the state and attacker of the monstruous. In the *Nephelai (The Clouds*, 423 B.C.), he claims credit for his purifying work on comedy and for raising its level.

The candor of Aristophanes was cited centuries later by Horace (*Satirae [Satires*, 37–30 B.C.]) in defending his own satire from the charge of malice. His subjects, contends the Roman, are not innocent people, who have nothing to fear, but only obsessive people who are examples of vices to be avoided. So also does Juvenal (*Satirae [Satires*, c. 100–127]) insist that, with injustice, vice, arrogance, and absurdity rife in Rome as never before, he is justified in attacking with pen and indignation. Writing about Achilles and Aeneas is a safe ploy other poets resort to because naming the names of the guilty in satire is dangerous.

The other great Greek comic writer, Lucian, faced the hostility not of society but of the class of philosophers and intellectuals. In the *Halieus e anabiountes (Fisherman*, 2d century) dialogue, Philosophy remarks to a sullen Plato that she takes terrible chaffing from Comedy at the festival of Dionysus yet still considers her a friend, for jokes "never do any harm" and rather make a thing of beauty stand out the more. In one of the *Nekrikoi dialogoi (Dialogues of the Dead*, 2d century), Diogenes the philosopher accuses Lucian of making people despise philosophy and its practitioners. Lucian replies that the issue is not the accusation itself but its validity; the blame should fall on those hypocritical pseudo-philosophers whose misbehavior makes the criticism just and besmirches philosophy, not on the satirist who simply submits evidence. Having heard this debate, Philosophy announces the verdict of not guilty and adjudges Lucian to be "one of us."

In his novel *Satyricon* (A.D. 60) Petronius raises an issue that was to become important during the Christian era—obscenity. He wonders why "every nagging prude" must cry "shame" and "lewd" about his "simple, modern book." He asserts in turn his "purity of speech" and, especially, his candor in writing of the things that "living men say and do." What is, moreover, shameful about sexual experience, which brings delight? Not his writings but people's "preconceptions," "ready made opinions," and "sham morality" are silly and false.

A millenium later, a man with similar temperament confronted a prudery based on Christian ethics. In his novellas, *Il decamerone* (*Decameron*, c. 1350), Boccaccio has one of his storytellers preface her scabrous tale of a lustful monk by dismissing monks as hypocritical, prone to attack in others what are really their own vices, and acting as if they owned paradise. Another storyteller, noting that the author is accused of trying too hard to please the ladies, responds that the author and women, who brought him so many hours of pleasure, were made to please each other. In other words, instead of writing love poems to some imaginary or etherealized Beatrice or Laura, he tells stories in which the joys of the flesh are celebrated and which are inspired by his own erotic experiences with women and by the pleasure women actually take in reading such material. Earthly love is natural, moreover, and to attempt to resist nature often results in stress and baneful consequences. So here the argument has turned into a defense of a dissenting moral philosophy, not just of the literary genre of satire.

The "Author's Conclusion" enters into the issue in great detail. To the charge that the stories are nonsensical and therefore improper for a serious thinker, he responds by citing the sermons of friars, which are filled with jokes and foolishness. Nor is levity out of place in tales whose avowed purpose is to drive away a lady's melancholy. As to the manner of narration, his response is that he is only a faithful reporter giving the tales "as they were told." Still, to meet every last moral objection, Boccaccio invites his sensitive reader to skip the ones he might find offensive and, in order to help the reader do so, provides a summary at the beginning of each tale. This maneuver disarmingly turns the tables on his critics since, having been forewarned, if they read on at their own peril, they betray an interest either in that which they were so quick to condemn as salacious or in condemnation for its own sake.

Besides, Boccaccio continues, nothing is indecent if required by the nature of the subject matter, if recited in the "proper words," and if not told in a church or a philosophy class. Nor is anyone forced to read these tales. Furthermore, some people use obscene words in normal conversation, others are more concerned with words and seeming than with deeds and being, and still others perform the very thing that they decry in the tales. Above all, the tales are, like wine or fire, harmful or useful according to the circumstances. Just as good words are useless to a corrupt mind, so corrupt words cannot contaminate a healthy mind. The holiest of words are in Scripture, yet many have perversely misinterpreted them and damned themselves thereby.

Some of these agile and cunning arguments are echoed in the work that is thought to have been influenced by the *Decameron*, Chaucer's *Canterbury Tales* (c. 1380–1400). At the close of the "General Prologue," Chaucer apologizes for speaking bluntly. The cause is not lack of good manners but (as Boccaccio had said) the need for accuracy. This defense is a mixture of good sense and sophistry. It helps create the illusion of verisimilitude and realism, the sense that the tales are not fictitious but accurate descriptions of what happened to actual people. Chaucer's ironic sophistry becomes deliberately and amusingly outrageous, however, when he proceeds to cite as role models Plato and Jesus; for Plato may indeed have wanted words to reflect reality, but he was, after all, the first man to give a philosophic legitimacy to the age-old censorship of literature on moral grounds, and Jesus certainly spoke "candidly, critically, openly" (one meaning of Chaucer's word, "brode") but not "lewdly, coarsely" (the other meaning), which is the charge against Chaucer.

The Renaissance

In the prologue to the play *Clizia* (1520) Machiavelli asserts that he himself is a moral man who would be offended if someone thought the plot obscene. His excuse is the conventional rationale for literature—to teach delightfully. Comedies are instructive (in accurately exhibiting the weaknesses, excesses, and vices of people) and entertaining. And what entertains is not dignified dialogue but words that are "either silly, blasphemous, or salacious." In the play *Mandragola* (*The Mandrake*, c. 1512–1520), he meets the charge that the play is too light for a serious person by implying that the function of levity is to provide relief from life's anxieties. A similar charge—that his novels seem to be frivolous, mocking, foolish—is met somewhat differently by Rabelais, who insists that they have "substantial marrow" and important ideas about "our public and private life." They have, in fact, outsold the Bible during the months of their existence and are the proud contribution to the war effort of one unable to help out physically. Like Aristophanes, Rabelais presents the comic as actually a patriot.

Shakespeare's play *As You Like It* (c. 1599) contains both the standard attack on and defense of the satirist's role, albeit with vigor and comprehensiveness. The melancholy Jaques wishes that he were a "fool" and had the license to speak freely; those victimized by even the random shots of his privileged speech "most must laugh" or else confess themselves to be the real fools by showing their guilt and consequent pain. Given such a license, he would "cleanse the foul body of the infected world." The Duke, on the other hand, thinks that Jaques would, in chiding sin, be sinning himself, for he accuses Jaques (as many critics accuse writers they consider unsavory or pessimistic) of having been a loose man who now would "disgorge into the general world" the evil consequences of his prior life; in other words, that Jaques is guilty of projection, of compensating for his imperfect life by presuming to drag everyone else down to his level rather than by reforming his own ways.

Jaques conveniently ignores this charge and rather replies that the world is already corrupt and that any accusation he himself makes of ostentatious dress or prodigality is not aimed at particular individuals. If an individual is stung by taking what is general as if it were personal, he should vent his anger rather on himself for having provided the occasion and the material for the satiric thrusts than (as Lucian had complained) on the messenger, who merely holds up the mirror. If, on the other hand, he is innocent, the satirist's words fly harmlessly past him. To take umbrage at the satirist is therefore to give oneself away. The Duke, in short, is saying that the satirist describes only himself, while Jaques is saying that the satirist describes (and hurts) only the guilty, who have no grievance, and that those who attack the satirist incriminate themselves.

As one who more than Shakespeare self-consciously adopted the role of stage satirist, Ben Jonson often found himself besieged. In his plays *Every Man in His Humour* (1598) and *Everyman out of His Humour* (1599), he defended himself on the grounds that he deals with follies, not crimes; rather than flatter, he will strip the follies of the time with a whip of steel and laugh them out of popularity. In the play *Volpone* (1607), he answers the charge of "sharpness" and bitterness. He has been personal against no prominent individual, only against those who deserve censure. Besides, anything written can be construed negatively by those with malice. And in the poem, "An Ode to Himself" (1640), dismissing "our dainty age/[Which] cannot endure reproof," he vows to turn away from the stage.

A specific target is at issue in Dryden's preface to the *Fables* (1700), as it had been in Lucian's dialogues. Dryden approves of Boccaccio's and Chaucer's satire of the clergy, for the "scandal which is given by particular priests reflects not on the sacred function." The vices of clerics are too important to be left to them for eradication, as their impartiality is in doubt; hence the satirist, being "the check of the layman on the bad priests," has a noble function. Like Shakespeare and others, he argues also that critics of satirists seem to have a guilty conscience and, under the guise of public concern, are really trying to conceal their own vices.

When it comes to lewd language, on the other hand, Dryden retreats from the advanced position established by Boccaccio and Chaucer. He disowns anything profane and "loose" that may have crept into his translations. He even cites the two medieval authors' apologies for "broad speaking" and "very gross ribaldry," only to dismiss them. Had the two been asked why they introduced in the first place characters in whose mouths "obscene words were proper but very indecent to be heard," they would have had no valid answer, and therefore Dryden refrains from translating their ribald tales.

One of the greatest of dramatic satirists, Molie`re, facing the hostility of some of the most powerful noblemen and clergymen in France, had to even write short plays in self-defense. In *La critique de l'e´cole des femmes* (*Criticism of the*

School for Wives, 1663), the ironic point is made that Clime`ne, a strong objector to Molie`re's satire of the "pre´cieuses" ladies, is herself an example of one; she objects to the term but not to the thing that she is from head to toe—that is, a uniquely affected woman. Clime`ne now enters and rails at Molie`re's *L'E´cole des femmes* (*The School for Wives*, 1662) for being filled with filth. Uranie, one of the commonsensical women, remarks that Clime`ne must have an eye for filth that others lack, for she herself did not see anything wounding. Nothing is as ridiculous as seeing something heinous in the most innocent things. Women making such a fuss seem to be more chaste in their ears than in the rest of their bodies. When Clime`ne cites Molie`re's allegedly salacious use of the article "the," Dorante, the mouthpiece of Molie`re, observes that prudes disfigure the language, wrench the meaning of words, and find virtually any word arousing. He then supplies the psychological underpinnings by remarking that too much ado over honor is made by aging beauties who look to "the grimaces of a scrupulous prudery" to replace the delights they indulged in when young.

Later Uranie voices the standard defense. All satires on stage should be seen without chagrin, for they are "general censure" and "public mirrors" from which one should profit without showing that it has any relevance to oneself. To take offense is to accuse oneself. When Clime`ne is angered that Molie`re seems to call the ladies animals, Uranie hastens to point out what is often overlooked by critics of the drama (or novel)—that it is "a ridiculous character" in the play who makes the statement and that the statement reflects on the character who utters it, not on the ladies or on the author. Dorante concludes that writing tragedy is easier than comedy because it involves grand postures and noble sentiments, whereas comedy necessitates a look at the ridiculous side of man, the lifelike representation of the defects of the men of one's day, and painting from nature rather than letting one's imagination soar.

In *L'impromptu de Versailles* (*The Impromptu of Versailles*, 1663), Molie`re returns to the question raised in the *Critique*. Comedy portrays the defects of contemporaries, hence it is impossible for him to create any character that does not correspond to someone in society. If he will be accused of having directed his shafts at individuals, he will have to cease writing comedy altogether. He has no fears, though, that he will run out of material because people furnish him richly, and what he has done so far is only a trifle of what remains to be satirized. Despite his satire, mankind goes its way without improvement, thus leaving him even more material to work on. He insists on writing plays that everyone feels compelled to see and in which people are so well portrayed that everyone recognizes himself. If he wrote like a contemporary hack, he would have no enemies—and no audience. The best response to his critics is to write another successful comedy. And in *Tartuffe* (1664) Molie`re's comic portrayal of a hypocritical exploitative clergyman is complemented by the important speech to the effect that contempt for a hypocrite, far from being a sign (as many think) of an antireligious attitude, is, on the contrary, part of a genuine religious dedication and concurs with the highest respect for those who are sincerely and unobtrusively pious. Numerous examples abound of such truly devoted souls who keep their piety private and do not attack others' every little foible. Molière's defense here parallels Aristophanes's contention that he is a patriot while attacking certain Athenians and Lucian's that he is a philosopher while attacking certain "philosophers."

The Eighteenth Century to Modern Era

A different outraged group put Congreve, author of the play *The Double Dealer* (1694), on the defensive. Women were offended that some of their own kind are portrayed by him as vicious and affected, but the comic poet must "paint the Vices and Follies" of the human race and women are part of the race. Since the virtuous are only made better looking by such portraits and the guilty ones can pass for virtuous by ignoring the satiric thrust, he has thus actually done all of them a service. Addison and Steele, in their essays *The Spectator* (1711–1712), make the conventional remarks about aiming at types and follies, not at individuals and vices. But one of the greatest of all satirists, Swift, with typical detachment and secretiveness, makes no apologia in any of his major writings—though in a famous letter to Pope he declares it his goal to vex rather than divert the world and proclaims his love for individuals and hatred of groups. A few years later, Fielding, in the preface to his novel *Joseph Andrews* (1742), defends burlesque (writing in a high style about low matter) as doing a better job of putting audiences into "good humor and benevolence" than do tragedy or lectures. His characters are drawn from nature—that is, experience and observation—but are so altered as to injure no individual. In the novel *Tom Jones* (1749) he invokes the spirit of comedy that inspired the other masters, asking it to make the reader see through the layers of self-deception by means of this comic novel written with learning, experience, and sympathy.

More persistently on the defensive than most is Byron in *Don Juan* (1819–1824), a long comic poem with numerous gibes. He asks the reader not to complain prematurely that his "gay" story is not moral; in any case the poet plans to show "the very place where wicked people go." His lovers, Haidee and Juan, were not married; Byron whimsically shifts the blame from himself to them—meaning that fidelity to reality requires that the characters in the story act as they would have in life. He is using Chaucer's excuse of merely writing exactly as events dictate. Later, taking note of those who see in every part of the poem an attack on "the creed and morals of the land," he denies any intention other than supplying brief merriment. Such writing for entertainment may seem strange to Englishmen, he adds sarcastically.

When the plot brings him to a delicate point, Byron notes that some readers took exception "at the first two books having too much truth" and therefore he will move on, leaving the reader "to the purer page/Of Smollett, Prior, Ariosto, Fielding." (In a letter he wrote that *Don Juan* will come to be appreciated for what it is, "a satire on abuses and not an eulogy of vice," and that he could not help its being occasionally voluptuous, something that Ariosto, Smollett, and Fielding were more guilty of.) In the prose preface to cantos 6–8, he quoted

Voltaire to the effect that modesty, having fled from men's hearts, now resides on their lips and that the more that morals become corrupt, the more correct does speech become, as people hope to regain in language what they have lost in action. This witticism is the only answer that the "degraded and hypocritical" public deserves. Hirelings daily use words of abuse like "Blasphemer," "Radical," and "Jacobin" without realizing that their victims join the select company of Socrates, Jesus, and others who tried to oppose abuses "of the name of God and the mind of man."

Later he declares that he will be "immoral" only by showing "things really as they are,/Not as they ought to be." Until one sees reality, one is far from improvement. Women, who in youth enjoy themselves, gain not only knowledge of the world and awareness of the consequences of erring but also are wiser in their warnings "against the woe / Which the mere passionless can never know." The prude compensates for her burdensome virtue by railing at passions she envies but does not know and by seeking rather to hurt than to save. The daughters of women who know the world "by experience rather than by lecture" turn out much better wives than those "bred up by prudes without a heart." Hence his work is moral "if people would but see its real drift," but they will not because all "gentle readers" have "the gift of closing 'gainst the light their orbs of vision."

One of the founding fathers of modern Russian literature, Gogol, also facing hostile criticisms, issues in his novel *Me"rtvye dushi* (*Dead Souls*, 1842) a sort of realist manifesto, in which the stress is on the loneliness of the writer of comedy and satire. The man who ventures to portray that which is always before our eyes and which we consequently fail to perceive—the trivia of daily life, the chilly depth of normal people—need expect no applause, enthusiasm, or the love of girls. He will rather receive "hypocritically callous judgment," will have his work called "mean and insignificant," will be assigned a despicable niche with those "who have affronted humanity," and will have attributed to him personally the qualities of the characters in his books. For "contemporary judgment" does not understand careful scrutiny of and fidelity to reality or see that the "high laughter of delight" is worthy of a place next to "lofty lyrical emotion" and differs greatly from circus clowning.

At one satiric juncture he must leave two women nameless lest he rouse anger as on previous occasions. He now gives the old lament of satirists. If he invents a name, there is bound to be someone in the vast Russian Empire whom it will fit and who will complain of having been spied upon by the author. Reference to a person's rank exacerbates the situation. People are so touchy that any fictional character is liable to be taken for a living person. One need only say that there is a stupid man in some town, and at once someone will jump up and assert that he is a man "and therefore stupid."

Gogol acknowledges that his hero is not virtuous. He insists the portrayal was deliberate, as the words "virtuous man" and the character the words stand for have been overworked in literature. The reader might call Chichikov a rogue, but that is current rigidity for there are no such people any more, "only well-intentioned and agreeable people" who talk of virtue. The hero is an acquisitive man.

That may make him repulsive, and the reader who in everyday life gets along well with such a person will suddenly object if he turns up as the protagonist of a literary work. Gogol is less worried that readers dislike his hero than they secretly like him. If the author had not probed and revealed the depths of Chichikov, they would have rejoiced in him as an interesting man, for the readers "would rather not see human poverty exposed." Life is full of depressing things, they say, and they would prefer beautiful, comforting images; why go out of one's way to describe the wretchedness of life? Why should the author, sick of his own imperfections, make them central in his book? Thus they who are busy exploiting others for the sake of money are aroused—as soon as a book reflects some bitter truth—over letting foreigners see Russian weakness and lack of patriotism. Such patriotism Gogol dismisses as a façade for a fear of looking at anything beneath the surface. If an author does not do so, who will? Another ploy is for the reader to dismiss Chichikov as a droll, roguish eccentric to be found in some provinces. A reader with Christian humility, however, might acknowledge to himself that there is something of that rogue in himself rather than, when someone else passes by, being quick to condemn the passerby as a Chichikov.

Thus it is that the charges Aristophanes had to respond to were still raised and answered a few thousand years later, for comedy and satire are high-risk occupations, never as edifying and respectable as tragedy. Perhaps all these writers have finally won their case, at least in intellectual circles if not with the middlebrow and lowbrow public. Perhaps in the corrosive modern climate of skepticism, relativism, and cynicism, the value of comedy and satire has become self-evident. Or perhaps the mingling of the grave and the light in that predominantly modern genre of tragicomedy gives enough respectability to the comic component. Whatever the reason, the great modern masters of levity—such men as Chekhov, Joyce, Proust, Waugh, Shaw, Faulkner, and Heller—no longer find it necessary to incorporate such apologias in their major works.

See also: Comedy (Comic Hero), Laughter.

Selected Bibliography

Burns, E., and T. Burns, eds. *The Sociology of Literature and Drama*. Baltimore: Penguin Books, 1973.

Davis, Leonard. "A Social History of Fact and Fiction." *Literature and Society*. Ed. Edward Said. Baltimore: Johns Hopkins University Press, 1980.

Pratt, W. W. *Byron's Don Juan*. 4 vols. 2d ed. Austin: University of Texas Press, 1971.

Schücking, Levin L. *The Sociology of LiteraryTaste*. Trans. E. W. Dickes. London: K. Paul, 1944.

MANFRED WEIDHORN

ARCADIA

Arcadia was a country in central Peloponnesus surrounded on all sides by mountains. The Arcadians were regarded as among the most ancient peoples in Greece, having retained the possession of their country when the remainder of the Peloponnesus was conquered by the Dorians. Consequently they experienced fewer changes than the other peoples of Greece and became the model for an isolated, changeless, and idyllic existence. Their chief occupations were hunting and herding and their chief deity Pan. Isolation and an inland location has been so associated with the Arcadian moment and Arcadian poetry that doubt has been expressed that a seafaring people devoted to fishing could provide an Arcadian setting. This is obviously not the case, for the 19th-century German painter Hans von Marées (1837–1887) created a marine Arcadia for the German Marine Biological Station in Naples, which is one of the pre-eminent depictions of the Arcadian moment.

Arcadia, however, is a state of mind rather than a geographical location. Since the beginning of literature in the Mediterranean and Near Eastern world, Arcadia as a place and the pastoral as a literary genre have provided avenues of escape from a landscape or a situation filled with tension and unavoidable conflict. Arcadia and the pastoral landscape by definition are free of alienation, sin, conflict, instinctual renunciation, and contradiction. It is the land of heart's desire and the "Big Rock Candy Mountain." It is the world as it came fresh from the hand of God, untainted by sin and uncorrupted by time's enmity to the harmonious, the beautiful, and the noble.

Arcadia is ruled by the pleasure principle; happiness is achieved without remorse, and passion satisfied without melancholy and regret. Life takes the form of a Watteau painting of a courtly picnic. Since Arcadian life is devoid of consequence, it is not surprising that dalliance rarely produces children and that those who dwell in Arcadia are usually youthful or in middle years. Pornographic literature, because it deals with remorseless passion and aimless sexuality, often has a pastoral structure and an Arcadian setting.

The sources of the Arcadian impulse are various. The impulse may derive from the flight from urbanization and technology. Its earliest manifestations were often an attempt to escape the social patterns of settled agriculture and to return to a herding and hunting society. It may involve an effort to escape class conflict or widespread warfare. The effort to transcend the limitations and denials contingent on daily life inspires the flight to Arcadia. The tensions need not be, and frequently are not, socioeconomic or political. Thus for A. E. Housman (1859–1936) the conflict to be avoided was located in tensions produced by the homosexual content of the poet's imagination and his thematic material. By shifting the location of his setting into the Arcadian and pastoral landscape, conflict is avoided and the thematic content legitimated. Thus, while the transformation of the mode of production and class conflict may be the source of much of the Arcadian theme, this explanation is not exhaustive. Nor is it necessarily true that pastoralism is essentially "aristocratic" as a literary mode. One could hardly describe Sarah Orne Jewett's book of tales *Country of the Pointed Firs* (1896) as aristocratic in its sensibility. It is none the less true that the Arcadian vision is a backward-looking one and that its protagonists are apt to say of the past or the present moment, "Stay, thou art so sweet." There is in the Arcadian vision a fear of change, transformation, and conflict.

The Arcadian vision derives from two separate traditions, the Greek myth of the Golden Age and the biblical account of the Garden of Eden. These two myths are fused by the Church Fathers and medieval and Renaissance poets. Nonetheless, they constitute separate and different traditions.

The earliest record of the Greek myth is an eighth-century B.C. poem of rural life known as *Works and Days* (Hesiod's *Erga kai hēmerai*). It was composed by a Boetian peasant-poet and provides us with the classical locus of a landscape inhabited by a "golden generation of mortal people" living under the benign reign of Kronos and spending their days in feasting and merrymaking. This poem is the source of the cycle of the metallic races moving in a declension from an age of gold to one of iron. This cycle of the races came, in time, to be welded into the Near Eastern-Mediterranean concept of the millenial year or the "great year" as it is depicted in Virgil's Fourth Eclogue, "The Golden Eclogue" (*Bucolica*, 42–39 B.C.).

In Hesiod's Golden Age the Arcadian themes are nearly all present. The earth gives its fruit without the labor of tillage, life is free of violence and pain. The evils of old age are unknown, and one passes from life to death in the manner of falling into a slumber. The conflict of sexuality is unknown as the reign of Saturn antedates the myth of Pandora. The free satisfaction of sexual inclination need not be a necessary aspect of the Arcadian mode. In many respects this mode echoes Homer's depiction of country life in book 18 of the epic *Ilias* *(Iliad*, c. 8th century B.C.), in which he describes the gathering of the vintage as depicted by Hephaistos on Achilles' shield.

Hesiod and Homer engage in unconscious pastoral. The Hellenistic poets Theocritus (c. 300–c. 260 B.C.), Moschus (fl. c. 150 B.C.) and Bion (fl. c. 100 B.C.) made pastoral poetry a self-conscious literary form and influenced directly and indirectly nearly all later pastoral poetry. These bucolic poets are typical of the mood of withdrawal and escape from the megapolitan city and the conflicts of the Hellenistic monarchies into an idyllic world of shepherds and nymphs, pan pipes and choral contests, summer and the pleasures of the Arcadian landscape. This poetry is overwhelmingly a poetry devoted to homosexual love, though the contemporary erotic romance, *Ta kata Daphnin kai Chloēn* (*Daphnis and Chloe*) by Longus (2d century?), while borrowing the pastoral theme and setting of Theocritus, presents the story of heterosexual awakening and fulfillment.

Death is the one unsolvable problem, the single unbanishable evil of the Arcadian landscape. Nowhere is this more acutely noted than in the seventeenth-century painting by Nicolas Poussin *Et in Arcadia ego* (*I Am Even in Arcadia*). Consequently one of the persistent themes is elegy. From Theocritus through Milton's poem "Lycidas" (1637) to A. E. Housman, the elegiac note mingles with the shepherd's choral contests. It is interesting to note that pastoral poetry becomes a formal literary genre just at the time when the first Utopias were framed.

It is this Alexandrian, Hellenistic Arcadian mode that Rome inherited and transformed. The bucolic poetry of imperial Rome, the *Eclogues* and *Georgica* (*Georgics*, 29 B.C.) of Virgil and the epic poem *Metamorphoses* (c. A.D. 2–17) of Ovid had a decisive influence on the development of the medieval and Renaissance conception of Arcadia. Of greatest importance and influence was Virgil's Fourth Eclogue. In it, Virgil announces the arrival of "the final age of Sibylline song" and the renewal of the millenial cycle. The rule of Saturn will return and mankind will once more dwell in an Arcadian age of gold. Here the age of gold is shifted out of the past and into the future. This future orientation made it possible to identify the prophetic content of the Fourth Eclogue with Christian revelation, and thus to bridge the gap between the pagan and the Christian vision. Astraea is identified with the Virgin, and the poem was thought to herald the Nativity. Milton's ode "On the Morning of Christ's Nativity" (1629) is a direct echo of Virgil's Eclogue.

The Hebrew-Christian component of the Arcadian vision is part of a Near Eastern mythological tradition that extends back at least to the second millenium B.C. in the Tigris-Euphrates Valley. The extent to which the Judaic-Christian conception of the Garden of Eden is unique is much contested by scholars, but the biblical account of the Garden of Eden accorded well with the classical Greco-Roman conception of the age of gold. The first equation of the Greek *paradeiosis* with *Gan Eden* is to be found in the Septuagint translation of the Old Testament. Both Jewish apocalyptic thought and Christian millenarianism anticipate the restoration of a paradisial state after the coming of the Messiah or at the end of the great millenial week of seven days. Medieval Jewish and Christian literature is filled with these expectations, which culminate in Cabbala and the twelfth-century prophecies of Joachim of Fiore. These conceptions, in combination with notions of classical Arcadia, led fifteenth- and sixteenth-century explorers to anticipate the discovery of tribes of men living in a prelapsarian "age of gold."

Nevertheless, as Renato Poggioli has so eloquently pointed out, the Arcadian vision is nearly incapable of reconciliation with the Christian vision of man's experience in history as a time of testing in which the individual is invited to take up his cross and follow Christ on the way of the Passion. At best Christian literature provides only, to use Poggioli's phrase, "pastoral oases," Arcadian interludes in an otherwise unarcadian commonplace. Such "oases" appear in Dante's epic poem *La divina commedia* (*The Divine Comedy*, c. 1320), Tasso's epic *Gerusalemme liberata* (*Jerusalem Delivered*, 1581), Ariosto's poem *Orlando furioso* (1516), Cervantes' novel *Don Quijote* (*Don Quixote*, 1605, 1615) and Shakespeare's comedy *As You Like It* (c. 1599). They are interruptions of the everyday world, and their object is the depiction of bliss rather than blessedness.

The garden either as nature perfected and ordered by the hand of man or the garden as an Arcadian oasis in a chaotic and disordered world comes increasingly to act as a substitute for a return in time to the unspoiled innocence of the Golden Age or Eden or the attainment through redemption to a "new heaven and a new earth." The garden thus becomes a means to human perfection, and nature, impinging on the human spirit, purifies and orders it. Thus gardening is the means to perfection in both Rousseau's novel, *La nouvelle Heloïse* (*The New Heloise*, 1761) and Goethe's novel *Die Wahlverwandtschaften* (*Elective Affinities*, 1809). The New World, as A. Bartlett Giamatti has noted, was conceived of as a "great unspoiled garden." Arcadia is thus translated into the supposedly attainable perfection of the garden. Thus the New World became for many, and this is particularly marked in literature, as Leo Marx has said, "a kind of Vergilian pasture."

Dante, in *The Divine Comedy*, reconciles the images of the garden and the city held in opposition since the bucolic poets of Hellenistic Greece. Civility becomes a dimension of innocence and redemption. The natural man and the political man are one and the same. Even in the city of Dis nature is not overthrown. Eden thus does not become an end in itself but a means to a greater perfection.

Though the penalty of Adam abolishes the possibility of earthly perfection, Renaissance writers seek to restore the Arcadian life through artifice, fiction, and magic. The medieval land of Cockaigne, "a poor man's golden age" as Harry Levin so aptly puts it, is transformed into Rabelais' Abbaye de Thélème in the novel *Gargantua* (1534). The motto of the abbey, "Do whatever you like," is certainly an Arcadian sentiment. The fictions, magic, and artifice of Renaissance Arcadias are always unbelievable. They have much in common with the masque. They are a series of stately and edifying postures and whether the poem is Ariosto's *Orlando furioso* or Spenser's *The Faerie Queene* (1590–1596) the art of the writer is a self-consciously illusionistic one.

The last and greatest of the Renaissance poets, Milton, attempts to write both a Hellenist Arcadian elegy in "Lycidas" and a Christian pastoral in his poem *Paradise Lost* (1667). Only St. Augustine could exclaim, with Milton, "O felix culpa" after reading *Paradise Lost*. It is a pastoral lost, and the amending *Paradise Regained* (1671) fails, like the edifying illusions of earlier Renaissance pastorals, to carry much conviction of Arcadia restored.

The ambiguity of feelings concerning Arcadia is best exemplified in Shakespeare's *As You Like It*. Ostensibly Arcadian, "They say he [the Duke] is already in the forest of Arden, and many merry men with him; and there they live like the old Robin Hood of England. They say many young gentlemen flock to him every day, and fleet the time carelessly, as they did in the golden world," it in actuality verges on the antipastoral. The Duke and his followers flee to the forest of Arden. They do not deliberately choose a pastoral life. Arcadia is an interlude, and its leafy joys are balanced by the pains and inconvenience of country life.

Vladimir Lenin was not the first to speak of "rural idiocy." At best, *As You Like It* may be described as an Arcadian interlude. It is more aptly viewed as a satirical treatment of pastoral enthusiasms.

At first sight the Arcadian and pastoral theme in the eighteenth and nineteenth centuries seems very different from that of the sixteenth and seventeenth centuries, though an identifiable common tradition links them together. The cult of sensibility and the inherent pantheism of the Romantics tended to expunge the imperfections of Christianity's fallen world. The restoration of man to his original perfection and well-being, the return to the age of gold, is to be achieved by a return to nature, the natural, and the unaffected. The noble savage, the child of nature, whether American Indian or Polynesian, lives still in the age of gold because he has not put on civilization's artifices and corruptions. The *Jesuit Relations* and Louis-Antoine de Bougainville's travel account *Voyage autour du monde* (*A Voyage around the World*, 1771) were read by many as accounts of Arcadian man.

The revolution in epistemology and theology that ushered in romanticism was accompanied by a revolution in garden architecture. The picturesque garden in England, France, and Germany aimed at the restoration of Arcadian life. Alexander Pope (1688–1744) was both a revolutionary in garden architecture and a major pastoral poet. Queen Marie Antoinette and her shepherds and milkmaids, disporting themselves at the Petit Trianon, were acting out the conventions of Arcadian poetry in the poses of the French painters Boucher and Watteau.

The short step to full blown romanticism was taken by Jean-Jacques Rousseau, who philosophically and emotionally justified the Arcadian vision. In his long prose poem, *Rêveries du promeneur solitaire* (*Daydreams of a Solitary Stroller*, 1782), the self and a sensibility, derived from and merged in nature, became one. Rousseau's work seeks to heal the alienation of man from nature and to return even civil man to the Arcadian state. In his powerfully influential second discourse, the *Discours sur l'origine et les fondements de l'inégalité parmi les hommes* (*Discourse on the Origin and Bases of Inequality among Men*, 1754), Rousseau rejects the "state of nature" as the Golden Age and asserts rather that the Golden Age lies at that point in human development at which the division of labor and the differentiation of sex roles have not yet eventuated in the exploitation of one man's labor by another and the expropriation by the powerful of the common store of the earth's wealth. In short, the ideal state, the Golden Age, is that of the Caribbean Indian and the Polynesian native.

This new vision of Arcadian man reflected itself in a spate of popular literature. Already in 1719 Daniel Defoe had published *Robinson Crusoe*, about which Rousseau said, "Since we must have books, there is just one which, to my mind, furnishes the finest treatises on education according to nature." Many later novels followed the pattern of *Robinson Crusoe*, and *Der schweizerische Robinson* (*Swiss Family Robinson*, 1812–1827) by Johann Rudolph Wyss, enlarged and strengthened the Arcadian content of *Crusoe*. It is no exaggeration to say that the numerous novels of life among the Indians on the American frontier follow in the wake of these novels. "Li'l Abner," in Al Capp's famous twentieth-century comic strip, is a kind of Dog Patch *Emile* (1762) and owes far more to Rousseau than American newspaper readers commonly recognized. The cowboys who animate the pages of so many "Western" novels are often the herdsmen of Hellenistic poetry brought up to date.

Nonetheless, the pagan Golden Age was never really regained even in imagination. The dialectical poetry and philosophy of romanticism (M. H. Abrams, *Natural Supernaturalism*, 1971) sought through "sublation" to transcend alienation and achieve the reconciliation of opposites and the return to paradise at a higher level. This pattern lies at the root of the Marxist vision. It is equally the source of William Wordsworth's (1770–1850) effort to transcend alienation and achieve the unity with nature and supernature that exists in the unclouded mind of the child.

Not every treatment of the Arcadian theme is an affirmation of the pastoral vision. The relationship of Johann Wolfgang von Goethe is a case in point. It is debatable that the poem *Hermann und Dorothea (Hermann and Dorothea*, 1797) can be described as "a bourgeois pastoral" (Renato Poggioli). The pastoral interludes in the play *Faust* (1832), part 2, while cloaked in the imagery of Arcadia, are, if anything, antipastoral in content. Thus the figures of Philemon and Baucis borrowed from Ovid's *Metamorphoses* represent the abolition and destruction of the Arcadian rather than its affirmation. Goethe's drama *Torquato Tasso* (1790) is a rejection of the Arcadian dream of free love. Eleanora voices Goethe's sentiment when she says, "My friend, the golden age is really past. . . . That which is seemly is permitted." In these words Goethe rejects the love-ethnic of Tasso and the motto of Rabelais' Abbaye de Thélème.

Puritanism found little space for the Arcadian dream. The Puritan image of nature was that of the ruined garden. But many Americans stood aside from the Puritan vision of nature. Thomas Jefferson (1743–1826) read Theocritus in the original Greek and fashioned his yeoman farmer, his American common man on the ancient Arcadian model. Henry David Thoreau (1817–1862) enacted the pastoral life at Walden pond. Herman Melville thought he had discovered paradise anew in the South Seas until, as he tells us in the novel *Typee* (1846), he discovered the cannibalism of the natives. Walt Whitman (1819–1892) divorced the Arcadian from its usual hostility to technology and the machine. The American Adam, homosexual as the shepherds of Theocritus, lives in a paradise whose amplitude has been extended and whose wonders have been intensified by the machine.

In Europe the middle years of the nineteenth century, dominated as they were by materialism and realism, were not hospitable to nor productive of Arcadian literature. The onset of neoromanticism and symbolism in the 1870s alters this mood. The romantic revival of myth, which had begun with the thought of Schelling and Creuzer, led at the end of the century to the rebirth of Pan, who was reputed to have died at the birth of Christ. Pan and his entourage of fauns and nymphs became favorite themes of literature, music, and art. Stéphane

Mallarmé's poem *L'après-midi d'un faune (The Afternoon of a Faun*, 1876) is not only one of the greatest of symbolist poems but the most complete modern evocation of the Arcadian mood. Slighter as literature but equally important as significant cultural statements are Kenneth Grahame's fantasy *The Wind in the Willows* (1908), and William Henry Hudson's novel *Green Mansions* (1904). In both, the Arcadian interlude is merged in a tension-filled world and, as in Christian literature, appears as an oasis.

D. H. Lawrence, in the novel *Lady Chatterley's Lover* (1928), presented his contemporaries both with a description of the Arcadian moment in the love affair of Connie and Mellors the gamekeeper, a kind of Daphnis and Chloe brought up to date, and a recipe for the restoration of pastoral. In his novel, *The Rainbow* (1915), the lyrical representation of life on the farm approaches Arcadian poetry.

In the course of the cultural revolution of the 1960s and 1970s, the drug culture and the pastoral and Arcadian ideal were united. Alienation was to be overcome and man reunited to nature and to his fellow man in the world of a drug-induced Arcadia. In the world of communal agricultural life, at one with nature, and with human unity expressed in polymorphic sexuality, drugs seemed to induce that sense of cosmic harmony that was, perennially, the substratum of pastoralism. No great literature emerged from this period, but Gurney Norman's *Divine Right's Trip: A Folk-Tale* (1972) is in every way representative of the drug induced Arcadia.

The Arcadian vision is a perennial dream that, in spite of its remoteness from reality, continues to captivate the mind of Western man. It is a part of the larger dream of harmony that looks beyond discord and alienation to the reconciliation of man with nature and man with man. Little wonder that some of our greatest poetry is animated by this vision.

See also: City and Literature, Noble Savage, Psychic Landscape, Utopia.

Selected Bibliography

Giamatti, A. Bartlett. *The Earthly Paradise and the Renaissance Epic*. Princeton, N.J.: Princeton University Press, 1966.

Levin, Harry. *The Myth of the Golden Age in the Renaissance*. Bloomington: Indiana University Press, 1969.

Marx, Leo. *The Machine in the Garden, Technology and the Pastoral Ideal in America*. New York: Oxford University Press, 1964.

Poggioli, Renato. *The Oaten Flute: Essays on Pastoral Poetry and the Pastoral Ideal*. Cambridge, Mass.: Harvard University Press, 1975.

STEPHEN J. TONSOR

ARTIST IN LITERATURE THROUGH THE RENAISSANCE

In his essay "Tradition and the Individual Talent" (1917, 1932), T. S. Eliot argues that we must know not only the past (the "tradition") but also how the present (the "individual talent") may alter the past. The conclusion Eliot draws from this view is central to the present attempt to formulate the image of the artist from earliest times through the Renaissance: "The difference between the present and the past is that the conscious present is an awareness of the past in a way and to an extent which the past's awareness of itself cannot show" (part 1). If this is so, our inquiry must take us not only into what the images of the artist have been in the past, but also into what these have become. Together in these images, we find the temporal and the timeless.

In *The Secular Scripture* (1976), Northrop Frye formulates an important view of what the whole shape of literature is: "Romance is the structural core of all fiction: . . . it brings us closer than any other aspect of literature to the sense of fiction, considered as a whole, as the epic of the creature, man's vision of his own life as a quest" (p. 15). Central to Frye's view is the independence and relatedness of man's two "scriptures":

The secular scripture tells us that we are the creators; other scriptures tell us that we are actors in a drama of divine creation and redemption. . . . Identity and self-recognition begin when we realize that this is not an either-or question, when the great twins of divine creation and human recreation have merged into one, and we can see that the same shape is upon both (p. 157).

In his poem *The Waste Land* (1922), T. S. Eliot imaged for us the Emmaus figure in the secular scripture, the ghostly Logos figure that he believed we sense near us, but we are not ourselves in any sense we can understand. In the poem *Notes Toward a Supreme Fiction* (1942), Wallace Stevens tells ephebe, the apprentice poet (and us), that for the artist "The major abstraction is the idea of man," but that in reality the idea or nature of man is not an abstraction but our most intimate companion, a *real presence* (in theological terms), a present presence: "Logos and logio," "Beau linguist," "Fat girl, terrestrial, my summer, my night," "my fluent mundo." The "idea" of man, the Logos presence, is, in Frye's terms, the Creating Word of Stevens' secular scripture, whether we think of that as the artist, or the god, the Muse, in whom the artist participates.

It is this image of the artist as we may understand it in our own time that sends its resonance backward to the images that are more strictly our concern in the present essay, the central archetype of which is Orpheus, not Christ.

True Poets and False Poets

From earliest times, there has been the important distinction between the false poet and the true poet. In secular literature, the *locus classicus* for this distinction is Plato's dialogue *Phaidros* (*Phaedrus*), where Socrates (470–399 B.C.) tells us of the four divine madnesses, which are the greatest gifts of the gods, he says, but that also have their demonic counterparts. Poetry is only one of these four, strictly speaking, but we shall not be mistaken if we think of each as a possible form of poetry. *Love* is a gift of the gods, but *lust* is its demonic form; *prophecy*, a gift from the gods, has a demonic form in *lunacy*; mysticism comes from the gods, but has as its opposite *drunkenness*; and *poetic madness* comes from the gods, the Muses, but in its demonic form "poets praise tyrants." These find their answering formulation in Frye's presentation in *Anatomy of Criticism* (1957) of the central major character types in literature, the *eirons* or self-deprecators, who correspond to those who take their divine madness, or inspiration, from the gods (but who may be simply the visionaries of the human spirit), and the *alazons* or impostors ("though it is more frequently a lack of self-knowledge than simple hypocrisy that characterizes them") who claim to have a knowledge or a power that they do not have, or who have a demonic parody of it (cf. p. 172).

In his *Anatomy* also, Frye formulates the different conceptions of the artist in the five historical modes of literature, which we may take to "predict" the images of the artist in literature. The five modes are myth, romance, high mimetic works, low mimetic works, and irony. In each mode the artist may have an encyclopedic voice (as he is a spokesman for his society) or an episodic voice (as he emphasizes the separateness of his vision) (pp. 33–35, 52–67). References will be made at times in what follows to these differences.

Homer and Plato

Homer (c. 8th century B.C.) as artist appears at the beginning of his two epics as a self-effacing eiron who prays to the Muse to sing in him the two great themes of wrath and of *polytrophon*, or craft or cleverness (the quality that, with Athena's aid, brings Odysseus home from the Trojan War at last). It is the Muse of epic poetry, the daughter of Zeus, who can sing with the more than mortal knowledge that tells us of the wrath that destroys not only the civilization of one's enemy, but also one's dearest friends and ultimately one's self and the way of life and civilization that is being fought for. And it is also the daughter of Zeus who can sing with more than mortal knowledge of the struggle to return home and regain one's life and the civilization in which that life has meaning. Man does not know these things; only the gods can tell of mysteries as profound. In that sense, the image here is of the inspired artist.

There are (at least) three images of the artist in *Odysseia* (*Odyssey*): Demodocos, the blind bard of the Phaeacians; Odysseus himself, who for the Phaeacians remembers and tells the story of his travel homeward; and the son of Terpes, Phemies, the singer in Odysseus' own hall, whom Odysseus spares when he is slaying those who betrayed him and the hospitality of his house. All three are presented as entertainers of a high order, with a knowledge that has the greatest importance to a people. The stories of great men and deeds are the treasure of a people from the god who inspires a singer to tell of them. They are an encyclopedic knowledge "regarded sacramentally," in Frye's terminology. But when Odysseus must tell his own story, he presents most clearly the image of the artist whose function "is primarily to remember," as it is in the mode of romance, but it is remembering with a difference: the resonance and poignancy of living experience.

But if romance presents the secular analogy of scripture, we see the high mimetic, episodic, image of the artist in Plato's *Phaedrus*, where a more clearly human voice presents the very broad topic of the language arts in general, which are "an art of influencing the soul through words." Chief among these arts are rhetoric, philosophy, and poetry. In the dialogue, Socrates argues that only the artist who sees true reality can write or speak well, and thus nourish the soul by "the divine nature which is beautiful, wise, good, and all such qualities." This true-seeing comes from one or another of the inspirations of divine madness, the greatest gifts of the gods, the chief being love. The man who can thus best nourish the soul is a philosopher-lover-poet. Here we are more clearly in the realm of the secular, rather than the revealed, scripture.

The demonic parody of this, the portrait of the false artist in the high mimetic mode, is in Plato's dialogue *Politeia* (bks. 2, 3, and 10; *The Republic*, c. 380 B.C.), and the key to this view is the one indicated in the *Phaedrus*: when "poets praise tyrants," they are false. The "tyrant," ultimately, is the diseased or tyrannical soul, of which Socrates presents several versions, contrasting them with the just and virtuous "Republic," or healthy state and state of the soul.

The Tiresias Figure in Eliot, Homer, and Sophocles

In *The Waste Land*, T. S. Eliot presented Tiresias, the Greek prophet, as an image of the artist with all the males melting into one character and all the females into another, and Tiresias combining the two sexes and "uniting all the rest" (Eliot's note to 1.218). As such, Tiresias is the image of the artist with encyclopedic knowledge, a secular Logos figure of a type who has oracular, prophetic knowledge of all life, whether or not he understands that knowledge. Pre-eminently, for Eliot, Tiresias remembers (but does not understand) that the "fire of desire and passion" of life is a purgatorial fire from which God may ultimately deliver a man. Similar figures appear in William Butler Yeats' late poem "Under Ben Bulben" (1939) as the (African) Witch of Atlas and the (Irish) superhuman horsemen near Ben Bulben mountain near Sligo, both of whom are presented as figures whom Yeats once said "can see the reality of things," at the culmination of their lives. Indeed, Yeats' request that he be buried "under Ben Bulben" indicates he, no less than Eliot, wishes to be associated with this figure as the achievement of his vision.

Thus instructed by Eliot, we can return to the special image of the artist, the Tiresias figure, in Homer, and also in Sophocles. We spoke of three images of the artist in *The Odyssey*: Demodocos, Odysseus, and Phemios. The fourth is Tiresias, who (Eliot suggests) knows from experience. From the underworld, Tiresias can tell of what has happened and will happen in the areas of life with which Odysseus is concerned. This is a Tiresias in the mode of romance, the image of the artist who not only knows but also understands what he knows, who has the human equivalent of oracular knowledge. We know nothing of the source of Tiresias' prophetic knowledge other than Circe's explanation that "to him alone even when dead did Persephone grant a mind that could understand," but Tiresias tells of the trials and alternatives in what lies ahead for Odysseus. So much of life does he "understand."

The two Theban plays (in the high mimetic mode) we will deal with of Sophocles are the late *Oidipous tyrannos* (*Oedipus Rex*, c. 429 B.C.) and the very late *Oidipous epi Ko⁻lono⁻* (*Oedipus at Colonus*, c. 406 B.C.). In the former, the blind Tiresias is summoned by Oedipus to reveal the murderer of Laius, the last king, so that the plague on life in Thebes can be overcome. Tiresias comes only reluctantly, but when Oedipus threatens him, he responds with a mysterious statement about the guilt he himself has and shares with Oedipus. The implication seems to be that while Tiresias and Oedipus share some of the same guilt, only Tiresias knows his own; Oedipus has yet to learn about his. In thus having learned about others from understanding his own experience, Tiresias is like the Tiresias in Hades of *The Odyssey*, only more "realistically" portrayed as the possessor of his "understanding." In this, Tiresias is also like the artist-image of Odysseus in the halls of the Phaeacians, who knows the price of his kind of understanding.

There is no Tiresias in *Oedipus at Colonus*. The play tells of Oedipus coming to the Grove of the Eumenides (the Furies) at Colonus, the "doorsill of . . . great Athens." Here Oedipus is to die in peace at last, with the gods showing him great favor in his death that he did not find in the central events of his life. It is Oedipus himself who is the seer and prophet, the artist image, in this play; indeed, he becomes one of the Furies at the end of his own life, pronouncing his curses on Creon and his own two sons for attempting to use him, after so many years of rejection, when he is valuable for their own political schemes. Oedipus prophesies the returning plague on the land of Thebes, for which they are, in turn, responsible, and which will surely (he says) destroy them. At the end of his long life, Sophocles thus presents the artist-seer with the understanding of Tiresias and the experience of Odysseus—only Oedipus' understanding comes too late for him to have the joy of regained life that Odysseus has when he overcomes, in his way, the blight on his land.

Aristophanes and Plato

Aristophanes presents poets in two of his plays, *Ornithes* (*The Birds*, 414 B.C.) and *Batrachoi* (*The Frogs*, 405 B.C.), and presents Socrates, the philosopher-critic of poets, in *Nephelai* (*The Clouds*, 423 B.C.). The poets in *The Birds* are depicted comically, and from them we get a portrait of what the poet should not be. Two elderly Athenians, Peisthetaerus and Euelpides, leave their city to go to live with the birds and establish "Cloudcuckoobury" (a parody of Plato's Republic) that will establish sovereignty over the world. No sooner do they have the new state founded and named, than there appears a nameless Pindaric poet, come to sing the praises of the new state. The priest, who has a jerkin and a tunic, is forced to give the poet his jerkin for bounty, but the poet will not leave until he has the priest's tunic too. And part of the further "plague" that begins coming to Cloudcuckoobury is a dithyrambic poet, Cinesias, who is jeered at and sent away in scorn.

The Frogs portrays poets comically also, but is ultimately sympathetic. The humor comes from what they think of one another, not from what they are themselves. In Hades, there is a row between Aeschylus and Euripides over who is the better artist and thus entitled to have his dinner in the assembly hall at the side of Pluto. Pluto has resolved to have a tournament to decide which is the better poet. Aeschylus is a high mimetic tragedian, writing in an aristocratic spirit as a spokesman for his society, and his work is full of heroic men and women and high sentence. Euripides is a low mimetic tragedian, also a spokesman for his society, writing in a democratic spirit of more ordinary and "realistic" men and women; his style is clear and witty. The "mob" in Hades likes Euripides, but Aeschylus thinks them "trash and nonsense to judge poetic wits"; the two poets agree to have Dionysus be the judge of which of them is the better artist. But even before the contest, the Chorus knows what will happen: each has great, but different, gifts. On one thing they are agreed—what the things are for which a noble poet is praised. Aeschylus accepts Euripides' formulation: "For his ready wit, and his counsels sage, and because the city folk, he trains to be better townsmen and worthier men."

In *The Clouds* Aristophanes presents Socrates as a sophist who takes money to teach students to make the worse cause seem the better. The foolish Strepsiades, an Athenian, puts his son Phedippides under Socrates' tutelage to learn the Worse Logic he hopes his son will use to deny his father's just debts. Instead, Socrates teaches Pheidippides to deny the gods, to be a law unto himself, and to justify his beating of his father and his intention to beat his mother.

The image of the true artist in Aristophanes, then, is of the man who is the true teacher of Athens; the false artist is the false teacher, among whom might be the man who seeks primarily wealth or fame instead of the good of his society, or a man who speaks nonsense; worse, the false artist might be a man who, like Socrates or the sophists, is a present danger to his society.

Strangely, when we examine the *Symposion* (*Symposium*, c. 384 B.C.) dialogue of Plato, where Aristophanes is characterized, the criticism of poets is that they are not true artists, not true teachers of Athens. The *Symposium* presents a series of speakers on the set topic of the god Eros, at the end of a banquet in honor of Agathon, the writer of tragedies, who has just had his first poetic success. Aristophanes sets out to live up to his reputation as a professional comic, and he presents a brilliant parody of Eros as, in the words of A. E. Taylor (*Plato: The Man and His Work*, 7th ed., 1960), "the great primitive cosmic force," in a tale of humans long ago being split in half by the fearful gods and now looking for their other halves. But, as Taylor further says, Aristophanes "has no conception of any worthier life than that of the 'lover of honours.' "

An even more important image of the artist in the *Symposium*, a companion piece to the one of Aristophanes, is Plato's carefully drawn self-revelation by Agathon, the prize-winning artist whose success is being celebrated on this occasion. Agathon speaks in praise of Eros for what he is, both beautiful and virtuous. By beauty, Agathon means the softness and tenderness, adaptability and flexibility, and comeliness of youth, but he instances no beauty of maturity of the sort a writer of tragedy might be expected to be concerned with. And so also with virtue. What one notices most are Agathon's clever and pretty phrases rather than a developing insight into the reality of love, in which he seems to have no real interest.

Socrates' speech establishes a definition of Eros as the soul seeking for a good that is beyond her; this is the beginning point for his discourse. He believes that, although noble intermediate goals of the desirous spirit (Eros) may be to engender deathless spiritual offspring like the poems of Homer and Hesiod or the laws and institutions of Lycurgus and Solon, the longing for an eternal good is not satisfied short of participation in the eternal beauty, the eternal good. As Taylor says, "The 'deiform' do not 'think about' God, they live Him." To put it another way, "we can best describe the purpose of the speech in the language of religion by saying that it is the narrative of the pilgrimage of the soul on the way to salvation, from the initial moment at which it feels the need of salvation to its final 'consummation'." It is not for nothing that *The Odyssey* begins at the "initial moment" when Odysseus feels most acutely his need and desire to return "home."

In the morning, the only three men awake are Aristophanes, Agathon, and Socrates, the latter trying to persuade the other two that the man who can compose a tragedy "by his art" (*tekhnē*, or understanding of what he is doing) can also compose a comedy. Taylor annotates the ironic implications of this: "Both [Aristophanes and Agathon] are the instruments of 'genius' which masters *them*, not wielders of a tool of which they are masters."

Again we see that Tiresias, Homer, and the aged Sophocles are (as T. S. Eliot suggests) the greater artists, knowing Odysseus and Oedipus in a way that these men do not know themselves. It is an achievement to return from savagery to a regained or achieved identity, and it is an achievement to die in old age honored by the gods at the doorsill of Athena's city, but (as Homer knew) there is a fleet of ships filled with men who perish when only a single Odysseus returns. There must be some better way to know what Odysseus (and Oedipus) knows at the end, the achievement of his pilgrimage, than experiencing all that he has experienced.

What this survey of ancient images of the artist indicates is that it is not Socrates alone who condemns the artist who is not a great teacher; The artists themselves tell us this.

The Psalms

We may turn for a moment to the Psalms in the Old Testament, to see what they say about the third who walks always beside us, the Logos or the achieved wisdom of a people, that of which the Psalmist sings. The "third" is presented in different images—as the true Jerusalem, as the anointed one of God, as the house of the Lord, as man (or Adam) as God created him.

In the moment where *The Odyssey* begins, we find Odysseus longing for his home (and all that it means) in Ithaca. In the imagery of the Psalms, this Ithaca is Jerusalem, and the image of the artist that emerges is the one who, for his people and for himself, functions to remember this true home of man: "By the rivers of Babylon we sat down and wept when we remembered Zion. . . . If I forget you, O Jerusalem, let my right hand wither away" (137:1, 5). And thus is presented Ithaca, or the place where Socrates lives: "Happy are those who dwell in thy house; they never cease from praising thee" (84:4).

Finally, the Psalms present the artist as the man who knows that all tyrannies which seek to enslave man are as one voice of tyranny struggling against that "third" beside us, which is the one chosen or anointed by God: "Why are the nations in turmoil? Why do the peoples hatch their futile plots? The kings of the earth stand ready, and the rulers conspire together against the Lord and his anointed king. . . . Of me he says, 'I have enthroned my king on Zion my holy mountain' " (2:1–2, 6). The false suitors that struggle to replace Odysseus and tyrannize over his house, the men who make the land infertile and put a blight on human life, are variants of the tyrant true poets do not praise; true poets praise, we might say, since their vision does not fail them, the truly anointed one of the gods, or of God, who is the "third" beside us. They praise the authentic form of our own humanity, what in religious terms is called the *real presence* in our midst and in ourselves, what Wallace Stevens calls "Fat girl, terrestrial, my summer, my night," "Beau linguist." It should not be altogether surprising that in ancient myth Orpheus, the type of the poet, was torn to pieces by the "race" of "Bacchus and his revellers" (Milton's poem, *Paradise Lost* [1667] 7.33). "The nations" and "the peoples" "conspire together against" Odysseus and Socrates as well as Jesus of Nazareth.

Jesus of Nazareth

The New Testament presents Jesus of Nazareth as both the theme of artists, whose function it is to remember and tell of his origin, nature, work, and life, and as an artist himself. The beginning of John's Gospel tells us all we need to know about Jesus, that he is the Logos, the Word of God (and the Word of man), finally come to define what man is (what we are invited to believe we are, that the grave cannot hold) and to reveal God. In the Acts, Paul made this clear when he spoke at the Court of Areopagus in Athens (17:23–24, 27–28). In Paul's view, it is Jesus that Greek poetry speaks of, Jesus who lives as a presence in our lives. To this extent, it is Paul himself who claims that the theme of the secular scripture (the literature we are surveying here) is the song of the Logos, or Jesus.

In the Gospel stories of the crucifixion of Christ, we find a reformulation of what it is that the Achilles in us destroys, how the blight on the land and human life comes, what the Athenian jurors condemn when they vote to put Socrates to death, and what Odysseus must overcome (in himself and his world) to return to Ithaca.

Taking Jesus of Nazareth not as a theme of artists but as an artist himself, we find him pre-eminently a man who knows, and is in communion with, the good about which he teaches man, just as we have seen the true artist is, who composes by *tekhnē,* or understanding, in the Tiresias figure and (pre-eminently) Socrates. Thus, while Jesus is in communion with God, he is not "inspired" by God, not in the power of a genius that is not his own. So far as Jesus' teaching is concerned, we find he speaks principally in parables, stories that instruct. Among the greatest of these parables is that of "The Prodigal Son."

In this parable, we see the man who takes his heritage and leaves his home, where that heritage is best defined, wastes it in a Babylon or land of Calypso, where when it is almost too late he realizes the value of the home or identity he has abandoned—the Jerusalem, the House of the Lord, the Ithaca, the Colonus, or the Athens. He returns home, as Odysseus did, but Achilles could not, to live "in the house of his father," which he understands as if for the first time. His father receives him joyfully. The "real meaning" of this parable is to tell us what Taylor calls "the pilgrimage of a soul on the way to salvation, from the initial moment at which it feels the need of salvation," as evidently Odysseus and Oedipus do.

In this sense, then, Jesus of Nazareth is presented as the true Tiresias, the true Homer, the true Socrates, the insistent presence of the "third" who walks always beside us, or a presence in which we may participate. In Taylor's terms, Jesus "lives God."

Moses, Isaiah, Mohammed, and Caedmon

Just as in Greek literature there is a strand of images of divine inspiration of the poet, and thus the image of the poet as a servant to his god, so we may trace the same theme from the Old Testament times to the Middle Ages. As often as not, this is an image of a fool or naïve or illiterate person being transformed into a wise, prudent, literate artist. We see this in India in Kālidāsā (fl. 400), the author of the drama *Śakuntalā (Shakuntala),* who received the gift of poetry from the Mother Goddess. In the Bible, we see this in the stories of the calling of the prophets Moses and Isaiah. In the Middle Ages, we see this in the story of the calling of Mohammed and in the tale of the gift of poetry given to Caedmon, narrated by Bede (c. 673–735).

In Exodus 3 and 4, we have the calling of Moses to lead his people out of bondage in Egypt, which might be said to be the beginning of Israel's own spiritual pilgrimage, her own attempt to "live God." God speaks to Moses, a shepherd, telling him He intends to deliver His people out from Egypt into a land flowing with milk and honey, and Moses will be His Servant. Moses protests that no one will believe or listen to him. At that, God shows Moses the miracles he can perform as signs from God. But Moses still protests: "O Lord, I have never been a man of ready speech, never in my life, not even now that thou hast spoken to me; I am slow and hesitant of speech.'' To which God replies: ''Who is it that gives a man speech? Who makes him dumb or deaf? Who makes him clear-sighted or blind? Is it not I, the Lord? Go now; I will help your speech and tell you what to say'' (4:10–12). Of course, Moses is to be the specially-chosen servant of God; but the passage suggests all good gifts come from God, so that Moses is not so much a man apart from other poets as an archetypal figure who points to the meaning of all artistry that truly serves man and God. We have this same kind of story of divine inspiration in the narrative of the calling of Isaiah (Isaiah 6:1–9).

A similar story is told of the prophet Mohammed (570–632). In the Koran (Surah 96, 1–5), God is also the true teacher, the teacher of truth, for whom the prophet is the spokesman and the inspired servant. This indicates the real distance between those whom Socrates says are ''inspired'' and those who ''understand.'' Bede's story of Caedmon tells a similar tale, one perhaps inspired by this tradition, perhaps even by the account of the calling of Mohammed.

Dante and Chaucer

We find more human (less ''inspired'') singers in two other works of the Middle Ages, in the images of the artist given by Dante and Chaucer. In Dante's epic *La divina commedia* (*The Divine Comedy*, c. 1320) the central images of the artist are the Roman Virgil, the author of *Aeneis* (*The Aeneid*, 19 B.C.) the epic poem of the founding of Rome by Aeneas, a survivor of Troy and the Trojan War; and the further portrait, on which the poem focuses, of Dante himself, the persona. In middle life, Dante finds himself lost in the dark Wood of Error, and the poem tells of his journey, with the direction of Virgil, through Hell and Purgatory, and—with a new guide, Beatrice, the woman Dante loves— beyond these through Paradise to the final beatific vision. Thus, the story is, in Taylor's words about the *Symposium* presentation by Socrates, ''the narrative of the pilgrimage of a soul on the way to salvation, from the initial moment at which it feels the need of salvation to its final 'consummation.' '' Dante is writing in the mode of romance or epic, as a spokesman for his society, articulating for that society the vision that is latent or needed in it. The persona Dante is the image of the possibilities of the soul returning to its home (in the terms of *The Odyssey* and the story of ''The Prodigal Son''); of the purification and recovery from the blight on human life (imaged in *Oedipus Rex* and *Oedipus at Colonus*); or (in the imagery of the second Psalm) of being chosen as the anointed child of God in a world otherwise lost in tyranny and rage.

Of Virgil, the other image of the artist, Dorothy Sayers tells us: ''In the allegory, Virgil is the image of Human Wisdom—the best that man can become in his own strength without the especial grace of God. He is the best of human philosophy, the best of human morality; he is also poetry and art, the best of human feeling and imagination.'' While Virgil cannot enter Heaven or bring anyone else there, as Dante presents him, he can awaken us to the need of salvation (our sense of lostness, of being far from ''home'') and can guide us, as he does Dante, through "Hell" and "Purgatory," to the point where we may be open to what Dante presents as "the God-bearing image" (*Theotokos*)— which for Dante was Beatrice, the woman he loved (Dante, *Hell*, trans. by Dorothy Sayers, 1949, 67–68).

The temper of Geoffrey Chaucer could hardly be more different from that of Dante, but *The Canterbury Tales* (c. 1380–1400) is literally framed in the context of another religious pilgrimage. A group of pilgrims on their way to the Shrine of St. Thomas à Becket at Canterbury meet together and agree to tell stories to one another to amuse themselves on the way to (and back from) that saint's shrine. Chaucer is characterized in the General Prologue, in which he talks directly to his audience, and in the two Prologues and Tales where the persona Chaucer appears.

The pilgrimage to Canterbury is presented realistically, not ideally, and we see a range of devotion, from the pious Parson, through the Wife of Bath, who likes to go on fancy outings, to the Pardoner, who may have come along only to profit from piety by selling his "pardons" of sins. In the portraiture of the pilgrims in the General Prologue, Chaucer is a sensitive observer of man, and we see this also in the dramatic self-revelation in the individual tales. This breadth of knowledge marks his poetic voice as a romantic one in which he is encyclopedic in the sense that he presents to his society a portrait of itself on its pilgrimage through life. So far as the persona Chaucer is concerned, we see a self-deprecator who may nonetheless be much wiser and more sophisticated than he pretends to be.

In the Middle Ages, then, we see no less variety than in ancient times. There is still the strain of the image of the artist as inspired by God, as in Mohammed and Caedmon, but emerging more clearly is the image of the poet as simply a human being, as in the more sustained work of Dante and Chaucer, and as a human being much more frail than the poet-philosopher, such as Socrates. That frailty would be even more obvious if we were to trace the full variety of "artists" in *The Canterbury Tales*. We know this strain also from the poems (c. 8th century) *The Wanderer* and *The Seafarer*, and from numerous little complaints written by monks in the margins of medieval manuscripts.

Sidney

Sir Philip Sidney presents an image of the artist in *A Defence of Poetry* (1595) and the sonnets *Astrophil and Stella* (written 1580–1584). The principal achievement of the *Defence* is the formulation of man's creatorness, his being created in the image of his Maker, as the source and origin of his work. In this conception, then, Sidney defines the Logos or Word in human terms, insofar as it relates to secular poetry, creatorness being the sine qua non of man's spirit. In this way, the artist may present visions and works that are wholly human in origin, the product of man's "erected wit," or "purified understanding," as he calls it later. Thus, Sidney opens the way to the formulation of a secular scripture (and to understanding past literature as part of that scripture) that is man's revelation of himself, of the human Logos, which Northrop Frye indicates results in the epic or quest of the human spirit.

In *Astrophil and Stella*, Astrophil is the hero-poet who writes of his experience of love of his lady, Stella. In Sidney's cosmos, a hierarchy of values is presented, with Stella, embodying Virtue and True Beauty, at its zenith; below that is what Astrophil calls the "skies" of the "Heroicke minde" (sonnet 25). Below that is the fallen world. Man's "Heroicke" impulse to unite himself with the divine (Sidney greatly admired Plato) is the expression of the "divine breath" within him and is his chief glory.

In Sonnet 85, Astrophil is on the threshold of succumbing to the tyranny of a narrowly conceived desirous love, which asks what he has called Virtue and True Beauty to be something less than these, asks his god to sacrifice itself for him; and so he falls (whatever his lady's response is). The poet-hero pays a price for his wisdom, and the price is his awareness of how far he is from his Ithaca, his Colonus, his father's house, or what Astrophil himself calls "our countrey" (Sonnet 5). In Sonnet 107, he embraces his star with his mind, as he has learned he must do, and asks her to release him to the "great cause" he believes she wills for him. At the end of the work, Astrophil knows what Virtue and True Beauty he values and loves, and he turns to the larger, fallen world, which he hopes these will help to shape and reform through his work, whatever work that may be.

The image of the artist in Sidney is a union, at last, in which the imaginative vision of the wholly human spirit joins the conception of man that makes the human experience of questing, as that vision guides him, into what might truly be called a secular scripture.

Spenser

Edmund Spenser followed his friend Sidney in writing a sonnet sequence, *Amoretti* (1595), but his was about his courtship of Elizabeth Boyle, the woman whom he married, and he added to the sonnets a spousal hymn for her, the *Epithalamion* (1595). In the *Amoretti* Spenser writes as a poet and a lover, as did Sidney. But though Spenser complains at times of his lady as cruel and proud, he reasons that she is his "sweet saint" (22) and "the glorious image of the Maker's beauty" who is justified in scorning "base things" like himself (61). Eventually, however, he wins her, when "her own good will her firmly tied" (67). Nonetheless, he can read her a lecture on what true beauty is: "The true fair . . . is the gentle wit and virtuous mind." To the extent she has these, she is "divine and born of heavenly seed," derived from the Holy Spirit, which is the source of all true beauty (79). The artist, then, is the lover of things immortal, and he sings to memorialize these. As a high mimetic poet, Spenser means to teach virtue to the court, and so his is an encyclopedic voice, one formulating what his society is at its best, and what it ought to be.

This alliance of the poet with divinity, in what he loves and sings, is the crown of Spenser's *Epithalamion*, his wedding song for his new wife, which is the true culmination of the *Amoretti*. In the first few lines, he asks for the inspiration of the Muses, but it is clear throughout that he is singing as a man, of what he understands and loves. His lady is the real inspiration of the poem, and she is a human Logos figure that is not beyond his understanding. Spenser describes her physical beauty and the beauty of the world on their wedding day, and then, in the stanza just before the wedding vows, he indicates that what he marries is "the inward beauty of her lovely sprite" (1.186).

But Spenser's most developed formulation of "the third" who walks always beside us is his romantic epic, *The Faerie Queene* (1590–1596), dedicated to Queen Elizabeth, and presenting what at best England is and ought to be. Spenser is "a spokesman for his society," and in him "a poetic knowledge and expressive power which is latent or needed in his society comes to articulation" (*Anatomy*, 54). The central image of the poem, the one that comprehends all the others, as Tiresias does in *The Waste Land* for Eliot, is Arthur, or Magnificence, in search of Gloriana, the Faerie Queene, or True Glory. Thus, the poem aims to present Magnificence joined with True Glory, neither *eiron* nor *alazon*. The first six books, along with a fragment of the seventh, are all that Spenser ever wrote, and each of these six books deals with a constituent virtue that is part of Magnificence: Holiness, Temperance, Chastity, Fidelity, Justice, and Courtesy. Not only can the Logos of the secular scripture be known, but it could be analyzed and formulated for teaching and imitation.

Clearly the poet like Spenser is a teacher, but it is not clear whether Spenser's model is Orpheus or Christ, so closely have they become related. But the invocation of the Muse and of Venus in *The Faerie Queene*, and Spenser's indication that he is inspired by Queen Elizabeth also, places him clearly within the frame of the secular scripture, with a claim to no more knowledge than that of a man. He is a teacher, but a teacher of the highest kind, who both instructs and delights our souls, so much is his what Sidney calls "a heart-ravishing knowledge."

Shakespeare

In the *Sonnets* (1609), William Shakespeare presents three chief figures: the poet persona; a married "dark lady" with whom he is sexually involved; and a fair young man whom the poet loves, who is, in Hallet Smith's words, "of superior beauty and rank but of somewhat questionable morals and constancy" (*Riverside Shakespeare*, ed. G. Blakemore Evans, 1974, 1745–46). There is also a "rival poet" who is spoken of in a few poems by the poet persona. In this way, Shakespeare's *Sonnets* combine (to put it simply) the elements of lawless passion we find in Sidney's *Astrophil and Stella* and the fruitful and productive relationship we find in his *Amoretti*. The poet here is largely a self-deprecator, an *eiron*, who thinks himself unworthy of the noble young man and thinks his poetic skill less than that of the rival poet. But at the same time, he seems to be preoccupied with the theme of the parable of the talents (Matthew 24:14–30), as for example in Sonnet 94, where he tells the fair young man that what is worst is the corruption of the best: "Lilies that fester smell far worse than weeds." At times he can speak of the immortality of his lines memorializing the fair young man: "Not marble nor the gilded [monuments] of princes shall outlive this pow'rful rhyme . . . the living record of your memory" (55.1–2, 8). At other times, he is filled with self-doubt: "O how I faint when I of you do write, knowing a better spirit doth use your name" (80.1–2).

The greatest of the *architectus*, or artist, figures in the plays is Prospero, in *The Tempest* (1611). Prospero tells Miranda, his daughter, that all his care is for her, the tempest that drives Alonso and the court party to his island raised only for her. He wishes her to know who and what she is (lessons there is no Sunday School to teach her). A White Magician, Prospero sets about to use the brief time his powers have to work in order to fashion and guide Miranda's experience so that she will understand unfallen man (the True Adam, Authentic Man) and love him.

The characters in *The Tempest* are divided into two groups, the educable and the uneducable. The former are Alonso, Ferdinand, Miranda, and Caliban (and perhaps Ariel and Prospero himself). The latter are Antonio, Sebastian, Trinculo, and Stephano; they must simply be restrained from the evil that they would do. Of the educable, Alonso must learn penitence for his sins against Prospero, the deposed Duke of Milan, and his own family (he was prepared to use his children as political pawns). Miranda and Ferdinand, on the other hand, are given the opportunity to fall innocently in love, taking each other for possessed of the divine. Alonso, King of Naples, is not *made* to feel guilt, but is accused of his real sins and responds with a nearly suicidal despair in which he is cared for by the good Gonzalo. The climax of Ferdinand and Miranda's education is also the vision of real happiness offered to Alonso, a real return of the Prodigal, for him. Without hesitation, he joys in the vision when Prospero draws the curtain from his cell to reveal the innocent love of Miranda and Ferdinand, who treat each other as the true holy. And Miranda at last has her vision of the nature of unfallen man, the true Logos of the secular scripture: "How beauteous mankind is! O brave new world that has such people in't" (5.1.183–184). Those who are given the opportunity to learn, and can learn, envision a Milan and Naples, a Jerusalem, an Ithaca, something more than a Colonus, that is well worth the effort to reach. Shakespeare's voice here is high mimetic in the sense that he thinks of his function "in relation to social or divine leadership, the theme of leadership being at the center of [this] fictional mode" (Frye, *Anatomy*, 58).

In the tragedies, there is something of the *architectus* figure in Iago (*Othello*, c. 1604), the bad, the dangerous, artist who works to bring about the tyranny he wants to teach and praise (to destroy, in Plato's terms, the "Republic"). Ultimately Iago is defeated by the essential goodness of his wife Emilia, the person he thought himself best able to control.

Perhaps it is possible to say, then, that in Shakespeare the image of the artist is of one who is inspired not by the gods and powers beyond his own genius, but by his own vision of the home—in Sidney's term, the "golden world"—

he wants his prodigals to return to or to find; or, if short of that, to value properly. And not only his prodigals, but his innocents, as well, he wishes to grow in understanding of and love for (to use another of Sidney's terms) "our countrey." Paradoxically, the artist of the *Sonnets* lives in both Babylon and Jerusalem.

Milton

In "Lycidas" (1637), John Milton develops the image of the artist as a shepherd who tends his flock in a manner supported and approved by both the spirit of Cambridge University (the river Cam) and St. Peter, the latter contrasting such poets as Lycidas with false shepherds who instead of nourishing their flocks destroy them with rot and contagion (11.103–31). The ease with which Milton moves between pagan and Christian imagery is a measure of the extent to which he thinks Christianity fulfilled rather than replaced not only Old Testament thought but also that of Greece and Rome. The Logos of the one, Milton thought, is the developing Logos of the other.

In *Paradise Lost*, Milton presents an image of the artist in the four invocations, at the beginning of books 1, 3, 7, and 9. He develops parallels in his first invocation (11.1–26) between Achilles and Adam, who are destroyers of civilization and their own peace, Achilles through wrath, Adam through disobedience; and between Odysseus and Aeneas, and the Messiah, who restore civilization as it should be. Thus while Virgil sings of one man, Aeneas, Milton will sing of two, as did Homer. Milton asks the "heavenly Muse" to sing of this "loss of Eden, till one greater man restore us." He identifies this heavenly Muse with the one who inspired Moses on "Sion hill" to be a shepherd and also gave him the Law on "Mount Oreb," inspiring him to be a prophet. Thus Milton offers himself for either the priestly or the prophetic role. The "heavenly Muse" is apparently the Son, the divine Logos (the second person of the Trinity). Milton regards himself as a type of Moses, a second Moses (11.1–16). He goes on to a further invocation, now clearly addressing the Holy Spirit (the third person of the Trinity): "And chiefly thou O Spirit, that doest prefer before all temples the upright heart and pure" (11.17—18).

In this way, Milton presents the Holy Spirit as (properly understood) the inspiring "Muse" for all true poets, to image and lead man to the Logos, in the past, the present, and the future. Milton's purpose in *Paradise Lost*, then, is to present disobedience (departure from the Logos, which is both God's nature and man's own nature) as the destroyer of the true human civilization God intends for man, his Ithaca, Colonus, Republic, Jerusalem, or Paradise. He wants to show man has no opportunity to come out of his "fallen world," his Troy, Thebes, Egypt, or Inferno, until the divine Logos (which is also the human Logos of man's secular scripture) is restored as the model or guide for man to live by or "to come to himself" in (and thus for man, in Taylor's terms, to "live God"). Thus would the prodigal return to the home of his father.

In book 3, in his invocation to his source of inspiration (11.1–55), Milton is again addressing the Son, the "Holy light," but his voice is a personal one, as if to a "third" beside him. His focus is personal and intimate and ultimately centers on the experience of inspiration he both has had, as a living presence in his life, and prays he will continue to have, to illuminate the powers of his mind and pen.

In his invocation of his Muse in book 7 (11.1–39), Milton both indicates a lower flight of his imagination, one he welcomes, and finally gives a name to his Muse, "Urania." Again we have the portrayal of his sense of the closeness of the source of his inspiration, again the personal note, but now a sense of relief that the remainder of his work will deal with things accessible to human understanding and experience—with the world of the more clearly human Logos. For the source of his inspiration, he accepts the classical name Urania, Muse of Astronomy, but questions if this is her true name. "The meaning, not the name I call," he says, insisting again that Christianity does not reject ancient wisdom, but fulfills and informs it. Thus he does not deny the power of Homer's evident inspiration, for example, but insists he now knows better, that we now know better, the power that Homer was touched by and did not very well understand.

The last invocation is in book 9 (11.1–47), as preface to the remaining four books, which depict the fall of Adam and Eve and its results. These books present the judgment on Adam and Eve, and their eventual learned penitence, and turn back toward a partial restoration both of their own former relationship and of their relationship with God. And these books present their instruction in a faith and a promise of a Charity that will give "a paradise within thee, happier far" than the one they have lost (12.587). The paradox of this invocation is involved in the extent Milton is here an *eiron*, a self-deprecator. On the one hand, he speaks of his "celestial patroness" visiting him nightly to dictate to him sleeping or to inspire "easy my unpremeditated verse." On the other hand, he evidently knows very well what he is doing. For example, he knows his talent is not to indite wars and battles, knightly furnishings, and feasts in great halls, but "that which justly gives heroic name to person or to poem," that is, spiritual struggle (11.40–41): "the better fortitude of patience and heroic martyrdom unsung" (11.31–33), which is the especial focus of the epic poem *Paradise Regained* (1671), where Jesus' overcoming temptations in the wilderness is the type of the "regaining" of Paradise.

The image of the artist as Milton presents himself is of a man with vast learning, with a respect for both the classical age and the biblical ones (as well as the literature, philosophy, and theology of the Middle Ages and the Renaissance), who brings this learning to bear on the profound themes of loss and return that have inspired some of the greatest thinkers in every age and culture. A respecter of other literary masters (the "tradition"), he has labored to make their work his own and to reinterpret them (the "individual talent") as experiences with the God who he believes is a persistent presence in our lives, encouraging us to find our health, our wholeness, and our selves in Him. This real presence, the true (creative) artist finds as both his inspiration and theme in his work, as well as the goal of his quest, whether that quest be for Ithaca, Colonus, the Paradise or Republic within, or the shrine of St. Thomas à Becket at Canterbury.

Conclusion

In every age there is the problem of distinguishing the true artist from the false one. The true artist, whether philosopher-lover, mystic, prophet, or "artist" more narrowly defined, is among the greatest benefactors of mankind. But the false artist may be more dangerous than the fool who pretends to know more than he does and is obviously absurd or who depends on a superstitious deference to those of his craft, though the false artist may also be these. The danger is the lustful man, the drunken man, the lunatic, or the "artist" who praises tyranny, persuading man to accept "rot" and "contagion" in place of those things that truly nourish the soul.

But distinguishing the true artist is not so easily done, as the outcomes of Orpheus, Socrates, and Jesus of Nazareth show.

The true artist may compose by what the Greeks called *tekhnē* (art), by knowing what he is doing, as the philosopher-lover does. But he may also compose by an inspiration that is beyond his own understanding, and others may be able to understand his greatest works better than he does, though all great artists perhaps transcend themselves to some degree. If we are not to have such artists, as Plato (Socrates) sadly urges, then clearly we are not to have men and artists who are learning from their own experience. We may have Homer, but not Achilles and Odysseus; Sophocles, but not Oedipus; the martyr St. Peter, but not the disciple Peter; the Prodigal at home, but not the Prodigal on his journey; the shrine of Becket at Canterbury, but not the pilgrims on their way to inspect it.

Also to some extent the true artist is almost always an *eiron*, a self-deprecator, rather than an *alazon,* an impostor, as we see in Milton, Mohammed, Socrates, Isaiah, and Homer, if he is humbled and awed by the source of his inspiration and the nature of his vision.

The artist may be imaged as entertainer, or seer; a man who has come to live with the Furies and be one himself, or a lover of man; an opportunist, or a fool; a philosopher, or a tyrant or slave of tyranny; an observer of the passing scene, or an actor in it; an ignorant man, or an inspired prophet; a martyr, or a criminal; a teacher and a theme for teachers, or an impostor and a would-be tyrant; an inmate of the fallen world, or a man seeking Magnificence that will be joined with True Glory; a shepherd, or a hireling; a Miranda and a Prospero, or an Iago; a man created in the image of God, or a lawless man bent on seducing the faithful wife of another man long gone on a spiritual journey.

See also: Artist/Poet in Drama since the Renaissance, Autobiographical Impulse, Literature within Literature.

Selected Bibliography

Curtius, Ernst Robert. *European Literature and the Latin Middle Ages*. Trans. Willard R. Trask. New York: Princeton University Press, 1953.

Foster, Leslie D. "Poetry Both Sacred and Profane: The History of the Conception of the Artist from Plato to Sidney's *Defence.*" *Michigan Academician* 7, no. 1 (1974): 57–74.

Hathaway, Baxter. *The Age of Criticism: The Late Renaissance in Italy*. Ithaca, N.Y.: Cornell University Press, 1962.

————. *Marvels and Commonplaces: Renaissance Literary Criticism*. New York: Random House, 1968.

LESLIE D. FOSTER

ARTIST/POET IN DRAMA SINCE THE RENAISSANCE

In addition to "poet," the term "artist" is used here to describe creators of works having aesthetic value in areas such as music, architecture, sculpture, painting, and imaginative literature other than poetry; only plays in which the poet/artist's creativity is central to his whole existence as well as to the dramatic conflict are mentioned.

Prior to the second half of the eighteenth century, artists do not appear as main characters in drama. With the advent of romanticism, however, dramatists turn to concerns of artists in an increasingly bourgeois society. Although still dependent on patronage to some degree, artists are now able to support themselves by their art because a broader segment of the population has developed a taste and an appreciation of the arts in general and of theater in particular.

Romanticism

Romantics demand the freedom to follow impulse, to live life to the fullest, to champion rebellion against any form of oppression, to revel in their emotions and express them in their work. Eccentricities and excesses are frequently tolerated and excused as being part of the "artistic" temperament. Not surprisingly, Romantic artists (as well as their successors of the later modern period) indeed differ from their more sedate and pedestrian fellow citizens and, as a result, are apt to come in conflict with those around them. At the same time, believing themselves to be distinct and special, they develop a strong sense of kinship with one another and become interested, even absorbed, in their own problems as suitable subject matter for drama. Having become less dependent on individual patronage, they are now able to express their views more freely and critically.

The first fully developed play with an artist as main character is Goethe's *Torquato Tasso* (1790). The madness of the Italian poet fascinated Goethe, but his fictional Tasso does not actually lose his sanity. Instead, he is depicted as a supremely sensitive person, a walking wound, as it were, who is incapable of developing ordinary relationships. His desire for recognition and for emotional involvement is invariably thwarted by his doubts regarding the true value of his work and therefore his worth as an artist and as a human being. He is thus driven to inescapable isolation and loneliness. The Austrian Franz Grillparzer finds his material in the legendary love of the Greek poet for the youth Phaon in the tragedy *Sappho* (1818). The somewhat older Sappho loses her young lover to an ordinary young girl because Phaon cannot bear the feeling of inferiority he suffers vis-à-vis the famous poet. Sappho, realizing that she is unfit for a normal life, takes a suicidal leap from a rock. In Russia, Pushkin, relying on rumors about the alleged murder of Mozart by his jealous artistic rival, writes the short verse play *Mofsart i Sal'eri* (*Mozart and Salieri*, 1830). Although the ostensible motive for the poisoning is envy, the two characters are starkly contrasting personalities. Salieri, who has gained fame through diligent study, hard work, and respect for art, rebels against the injustice of Mozart's easy rise because the latter seems to him to profane art. Salieri sees his murder as a service to all "serious" artists. Shortly thereafter, the Frenchman Alfred de Vigny is moved by the suicide of the young Thomas Chatterton to write a play about the young poet, *Chatterton* (1835). The fictional poet is driven to his death by a combination of an unappreciative world and by his own inability to function within it. His belief in his own genius causes his arrogant rejection of a job he considers beneath him. Even the love and devotion of a woman are not enough to make life worth living for this *poète maudit*.

What is striking about these romantic plays is that all of them are based to a larger or lesser extent on the lives of actual persons. To be sure, the dramatized characters are partly inventions and partly transformations of the originals. But it is certainly worth noting that the authors apparently needed such a connection with historicity and that a purely fictional artistic character presumably lacked authenticity or credibility. All characters are drawn with sympathy and under-standing. Even when their actions cannot be condoned, they are given redeeming qualities or placed in unbearable situations. Their predicaments are the result of their artistic temperaments or their dedication to art.

The Modern Period

Modern drama is generally said to have begun with the Norwegian Henrik Ibsen, for in the 1870s he was the first to successfully combine the realistic treatment of serious contemporary subjects with the form of the well-made play. The status of the artist in an increasingly middle-class society continued to fascinate dramatists and in fact intensified their interest. The self-image of the artist as someone special was given an extraordinary boost by Nietzsche's concept of the *Übermensch*, an, in every respect, superior individual, a precursor of a higher type of human being, who to that end must reject the constraints of conventional laws and morality. The doctrine proved quite seductive to many artists, who saw themselves as superior because of their talent, their keenly critical perception of the life around them, and their ability to express themselves through their art. At the same time, they chafed under the social demands for conformity endemic in the bourgeoisie as well as under the difficulty to have their work accepted on their own terms. Thus their attitudes and experiences were rife with conflict and therefore eminently suitable for a dramatic treatment. As a result, almost all established dramatists of the period wrote plays about artists, dealing with the latters' internal and external problems in a wide variety of ways and forms.

The Artist and His Muse. One type of tension in the artist's life is caused by his relationship with his muse when she is a woman. In Germany, Gerhart Hauptmann in a poetic fairy-tale play *Die versunkene Glocke* (*The Sunken Bell*, 1896) creates a bell founder who attempts suicide because the stifling quotidian atmosphere of his village has caused his creative powers to atrophy. He is saved by a wood nymph who miraculously restores his vitality and becomes his inspiration. Yet life with her in the woods is marred by his guilt for having deserted his wife and children. When he is told that his wife killed herself, the idyll is shattered, and he turns against the nymph. Left alone to pine away, he is briefly reconciled with the nymph but dies without having created his masterwork.

The sculptor in the Italian Gabriele D'Annunzio's *La Gioconda* (1898) faces a similar problem. He fully appreciates his devoted wife but is irresistibly drawn to his model and mistress, whose graceful body enables him to give almost living form to marble. After his wife saves him from an attempted suicide, he is determined to remain with her, a much better person than the mistress who tries to break his latest statue in a jealous rage. The wife, in a supreme sacrifice to save his work, breaks the statue's fall and has her hands crushed. Yet the sculptor cannot live without his work and without the woman who inspires it; so he abandons his wife for good, being painfully aware of his cruelty to her.

Almost simultaneously, Ibsen writes his last play, *Naar vi døde vaagner* (*When We Dead Awaken*, 1899) in which an aging sculptor meets the model of his early days and is surprised to learn that she left him because he did not return her love. He admits that she was to him an ideal object of beauty and his inspiration, but also that he was devastated by her desertion and never again produced work of the same quality, even though he is now rich and famous and married to a young and vivacious wife. But neither his art nor his personal life has brought happiness. He now realizes that his former model is his true soul mate, and they climb a mountain to consecrate their renewed commitment, a sort of union of art and life. The futility of their hopes is revealed when they are swept to their deaths by an avalanche. It is either too late for those who have been inwardly dead for years, or such an ideal union is impossible to attain.

In all three plays there is no happy or even satisfactory solution. In the first two, the artists are unable to dismiss their obligations and responsibilities as easily as they would wish in order to pursue their creative work. In the third, missed opportunities cannot be reclaimed.

The Artist as an Exploiter of Life. Some artists are so obsessed by their art and so driven by the urge to create that they treat their own and others' lives as mere source material for their work. Such an artist is the successful writer in the Russian Anton Chekhov's *Chaĭka* (*The Sea Gull*, 1895). By his own admission, he goes through life making mental notes of scenes, situations, and people. He even tells the young girl, whom he will make his mistress and then abandon, in advance what her fate is more or less likely to be. He belittles his own success and admits that his work gives him no true satisfaction because his life is a treadmill of superficial sensations and experiences, all of which are forgotten as soon as they are fictionalized in his writing. He is a compulsive scribbler, rushing to start the next piece as one is finished. There is no time and no desire for commitment to another human being or any lasting interest in the fate of the people who have provided him with a temporary inspiration. The person has been consumed by the artist's creative urge.

An even more heightened situation is seen in the Austrian Arthur Schnitzler's short play *Die Frau mit dem Dolche* (*The Woman with the Dagger*, 1902). It is a play-within-a-play, framed by a visit to an art gallery where a painting of such a woman is viewed by a visitor who then has a vision of how the picture may have originated. There appears the wife of a Renaissance painter with his pupil whom, in her husband's absence, she has taken as her lover because of his physical beauty, but whom she tells openly that the affair means nothing to her. Neither her own nor her husband's infidelities matter as their relationship is based on their joint dedication to his art. When the husband returns, he refuses to be provoked by the pupil's confession or by his challenge to a duel. But when the humiliated younger man threatens to destroy the husband in some way, the enraged wife stabs the former to death. As she stands with a bloody dagger over the corpse, the husband instantly decides to paint the scene. (The result is the painting in the frame part of the play.) Genuine love, fidelity, even murder lose significance unless they inspire the painter's creativity. Dedication to art has produced demonic qualities.

The Price of Success. In Sweden, Strindberg demonstrates both the fickleness and corrupting force of success in *Brott och brott* (*There Are Crimes and Crimes*, 1899). When the writer's play is finally accepted by a theater, he turns into a scoundrel by abandoning his long-time mistress and their child and starting an affair with the lover of his best friend with whom he spins plans of luxurious living and wishes his daughter would die so as not to stand between them. Only after his euphoria is dashed by a scandalous accusation of murder does the chastened dramatist, cleared of suspicion, realize that success has its dark side.

More recently, success has come to be associated with a selling out. In *Epitaph for George Dillon* (1958) by the Englishmen John Osborne and Anthony Creighton, the writer struggles for many years, even accepting the support of a kindly family. But he achieves success only when he agrees with the suggestion of a smooth agent to change his play to bring it more in tune with popular taste. The collapse of his physical health is simultaneous with his agreement to give up his integrity, and the material success is also the death knell of true artistic creativity. In both instances success is a corruptor.

The Artist as Jealous Rival. Strindberg examines the presence of ill-will among artists in terms of his favorite topic, the struggle between the sexes. In *Kom-*

raterna (*Comrades*, 1887) both husband and wife are painters. All is well as long as he basks in the certainty of his superior talent; he even helps her with advice and recommendations. But when her picture is accepted by a salon while his own is rejected, he flies into a rage, humiliates his wife and mocks her efforts, and ends the relationship. The thought of her surpassing him is unbearable, and the wife and comrade becomes an enemy.

In England, Peter Shaffer returns to the relationship between Mozart and Salieri in *Amadeus* (1980). In his old age, Salieri remembers his recognition of Mozart's talent, his disdain for the younger man's character, and presumably just imagines having committed the murder. Both men are seen with their faults and weaknesses in an ironic study of their respective characters.

The Artist as Superman. The most exalted picture of the artist is presented by those most influenced by Nietzsche. But with his exquisite sense of irony the Anglo-Irishman George Bernard Shaw deflates the notion. In *The Doctor's Dilemma* (1906), a tubercular painter claims the last vacancy in a sanatorium because of his talent. At the same time, he flaunts his contempt for conventional ethics by borrowing without returning, by breaking contracts and promises, and by becoming a bigamist. He gets away with such behavior by using charm, wit, and sheer brazenness, but fails to convince the doctors to give him preference.

A more solemn "superman" is the German Georg Kaiser's poet in *Noli me tangere* (1922). Imprisoned for unexplained reasons, he is befriended and advised by a Christlike fellow prisoner, who clearly sees him as special and facilitates his escape. Their conversation revolves around the difficulty of being a teacher-prophet in order to improve humanity, without alienating the masses by getting too far ahead of them. The allusion to the fate of Christ is unmistakable. The play is expressionistic and the figures purely symbolic. No satisfactory synthesis between the lofty intentions and the practical execution is offered.

In Ireland, William Butler Yeats' poet takes on the powers that be in *The King's Threshold* (1904). Having been banished from the king's council, the poet sits down on the palace threshold and commences a hunger strike because he is the representative of all arts, which must not be excluded from the nation's life. He stubbornly refuses all attempts at reconciliation and rejects the pleas for compromise. In fact, he is prepared to bring down the social structure to make his point, for a people without the arts is not worth saving. When he dies, the shaken king releases the other poets he had imprisoned in an effort to break the will of the striker, and an apocalyptic upheaval is avoided in this poetic play set in the legendary Irish past.

The Retrospective Artist. The emotional death experienced by some artists has been mentioned earlier. But the ultimate enemy is the aging process and physical death itself. A re-examination of one's life is undertaken by Ibsen's architect in *Bygmester Solness* (*The Master Builder*, 1892). When his creative powers diminish, he tries various means to keep productive, not all of them honorable. Yet his whole life seems hollow as he looks back. He has challenged God by refusing to build churches, but the homes he built for people's pleasure have not made them happy. In fact, happiness is impossible on earth, he decides. Accepting the challenge of a young seductress to start anew, he climbs a tower despite his dizziness, only to fall to his death. His life appears to him as a waste and a failure.

Another aging artist is undone not by the loss of creative ability but by social pressures that stifle it. In the Italian Luigi Pirandello's *Quando si è qualcuno* (*When One is Somebody*, 1933), a famous poet manages to escape into hiding, write poetry in an innovative style, and have it published under another name. The poetry is enthusiastically accepted by the young people who turn against him, however, when the author's identity is revealed. His family also insists on his maintaining the position of a celebrated national institution. The tyranny of the public will not tolerate any deviation from the aesthetic "norm" he himself helped create. In a stunning image, the honored poet is gradually transformed into a petrified figure. The living artist has turned into a monument, a statue of stone.

The Artist as a Celebrator of His Art. In each of the works discussed here, the artist's lot is not a happy one. Indeed, the overwhelming majority of dramatists clearly feel that way. However, there are some exceptions. In Austria, the young Hugo von Hofmannsthal writes a dreamlike poetic verse play *Der Tod des Tizian* (*The Death of Titian*, 1892). Although the painter is ninety-nine years old and near death, he is still busily at work. He does not appear on stage, and the play is a tribute to him expressed by his assembled pupils. The purpose is to create an aesthetic ambiance, a paean to beauty and its servant, art. One of the youngsters describes his walk through the lovely Italian garden, producing a synesthetic effect, caressing the ear with the poetry while evoking images of nature in the mind. When the painter's death is announced, there is no sense of grief, for he has long since been immortalized in his work.

In France, the neo-Romantic Edmond Rostand writes the play *Chantecler* (*Chanticleer*, 1910), which is also a lyrical fable. The poet here is the legendary rooster. He delights in his companions, in the loveliness of his beloved, in the beauty of nature, and most of all in his ability to make the sun rise by his song. He bears no malice toward those who goad him into an unequal fight, and he shows no envy when told that the nightingale's song is superior to his; on the contrary, he appreciates it and is crushed to see the bird shot. Even the disillusioning realization that the sun will rise without his summons does not produce a lasting misery. He contentedly resumes his place among the flock that loves and appreciates him. There is no trace of alienation in this artist who is in complete harmony with all creation.

In the last decades the artist in drama appears less self-centered. One reason may well be that the notion of a Nietzschean superman was badly tarnished by the National Socialists in Germany. The expressionists, many of whom were dedicated pacifists, had to watch helplessly the devastation of first one and then another world war. This could not but bring the humbling realization that their ability to influence, let alone shape, events or human behavior was negligible.

Many remain alienated, but their preoccupation with their own lot clearly lacks universality. Thus the absurdists have turned to the basic existential questions common to all men. Some artists have turned to the investigation of the process of creation, rather than of the creator. But that subject is inherently undramatic and has been treated more successfully by novelists.

See Also: Artist in Literature through the Renaissance, Autobiographical Impulse, Literature within Literature.

Selected Bibliography

Dietrich, Margret. *Das moderne Drama: Strömungen, Gestalten, Motive.* 3d ed. Stuttgart: Alfred Kröner Verlag, 1974.

Gregor, Joseph, Margret Dietrich, et al. *Der Schauspielführer.* 12 vols. Stuttgart: Hiersemann Verlag, 1953–1982.

Kienzle, Siegfried. *Modern World Theater: A Guide to Productions in Europe and the United States since 1945.* Trans. Alexander Henderson and Elizabeth Henderson. New York: Frederick Ungar, 1970.

IRENE SUBOCZEWSKI

AUTOBIOGRAPHICAL IMPULSE

For millenia, literature consisted of stories that do not appear to have had anything to do with the life of the writer. Homer was not a leading warrior, nor was Shakespeare a dispossessed Danish prince. The invisible writer forged an objective narrative and kept himself out of the picture. With the passage of time, however, two changes took place. The writer came to think the story of his own experiences worthy of interest to others. Or he came to tell a story as seen from inside someone, and, in the consequent first-person narrative, a fictional character addressed a reader as if he were making a confession. At issue here is not so much actual self-revelation as books and passages written in a self-revelatory manner. After all, some modern works (*The Education of Henry Adams*, 1907), written in the objective-sounding third person, are clearly autobiographical, and others are accompanied by denials of any personal relevance, in the face of the known facts. If a literary work or passage, therefore, feels and sounds autobiographical—if it is personal or only pseudo-personal—it can qualify as an expression of the autobiographical impulse, whether or not it is demonstrably so.

Autobiography may be written either because the author has a special story to tell (e.g., St. Augustine) or because he has a writing itch but no interest in or talent for inventing stories (e.g., Proust), or both. It may spring from the need to confess or to exhibit oneself, to rationalize or to justify oneself, from reasons of vanity or guilt. Whatever the provenance, the autobiographical impulse manifests itself in five forms: simple or overt; veiled; intermittent; indirect or allegorical; feigned. The overt autobiographer (St. Augustine) tells the story of his life, albeit sometimes with suppressions and distortions. The veiled autobiographer (Proust) pretends to write fiction but draws heavily on the events of his own life. The intermittent autobiographer (Milton) injects autobiographical passages—overt or veiled—into nonautobiographical works. The indirect autobiographer (Melville in the novella *Bartleby* [1853]) is more problematic; neither the character nor the plot of the story directly relates to him, but the emotions or the symbolism in it in some way may, depending on which critic or scholar one reads. The feigned autobiographer (Defoe) simply writes a work of fiction in the first person, a confession of an individual who never existed and who has nothing in common with the author.

Antiquity and the Middle Ages

Whether something is in fact autobiographical is not always easily ascertained. The problem does not arise with ancient literature because it deals mainly with mythology, because the first person narrative is almost nonexistent, and because resort by the reader to extraliterary sources (something that at least one school of critics finds impermissible) is rendered impossible by paucity of reliable historical information.

The first real person to write about himself, however briefly, is Hesiod, who, in his poem (*Erga kai hēmerai* [Works and Days, 8th century B.C.]), decries the loss to a voracious brother of his portion of an inherited farm. Little else can be found—besides a few self-descriptive passages in the choruses of his comedies by Aristophanes, and Lucian's short allegorical *Enupnion* (*Somnium*, 2nd century). Two prominent, articulate Athenians whose patriotism and probity were under attack defended themselves with memorable courtroom orations in which they justified their own characters and careers: Socrates (Plato's dialogue *Apologia* [*Apology*, 4th century B.C.]) and Demosthenes, in the oration *Peri tou stephanou* (*On the Crown*, 330 B.C.). Plato also has some interesting things to say about his own life—if the *Seventh Letter* (c. 350 B.C.) be indeed his. So does very briefly Xenophon in the historical *Anabasis* (c. 386–377 B.C.). The first famous extant ''feigned'' autobiographies or first-person narratives are Petronius' *Satyricon* (A.D. 60), the picaresque tale of a sexual, intellectual, and social drifter; and Apuleius' *Metamorphoses* (*The Golden Ass*, c. 150), an odyssey from donkeyhood to ritual purity and holiness.

A parallel odyssey is at the heart of the next work. Just as Western literature in general and the epic in particular came into being at one fell swoop with the first and still greatest example (Homer's *Ilias* [*Iliad*, c. 8th century B.C.]), so the genre of overt autobiography was initiated with a work still to be improved upon, St. Augustine's *Confessiones (Confessions,* c. 397–400). Paul had provided some autobiographical sentences in his epistles, but the story of his conversion remains sketchy. It is not until St. Augustine that one obtains a detailed picture of what goes on in the mind of someone finding his way, through the valleys of the divided self and related agonies, to unification within and to rest in the truth. Here is, in fact, the first literary work to portray the subjective self. All earlier literature, even when containing rich portraits, never presented the thought processes and undivulged feelings of the subjective self. The alteration was due to Christianity or to the change in outlook of which Christianity was a symptom. What Jesus meant by fulfilling the Law was made clear by his various remarks leaning toward a spiritualizing or internalizing of meaning and reality. Paul continued this drift by abrogating the mere mechanical, technical, physical observance of the ceremonial Law. Christianity thus made the inner mental processes more important than the external physical realm, and it elevated motive over action.

St. Augustine was the first to follow through upon that new perspective in a literary way (though Petronius' and Apuleius' feigned autobiographies may have been parallel responses to the *Zeitgeist*). His *Confessions* is, in effect, more autopsychography than autobiography. The external world hardly exists. He discusses only those personal facts that bear upon his spiritual pilgrimage or illustrate theological points. As a result we see the complexities and anomalies of the mind, as never before and as rarely since. The work is a love letter addressed to God and circulated among men; or, alternatively, a confession to men in the presence of God. Springing from the Christian injunction to confess one's sins, it parallels the emergence of the confession as a sacrament. By telling his tale to everyone, St. Augustine confronts his own depravity, holds the mirror up to fellow sinful Christians, gives them hope that they too may yet find their way, and celebrates the grace and the glorious working—gradual and invisible though it be—of God in human affairs. Looked at one way, it is too tendentious to be an autobiography in the modern sense; looked at another way, it is the greatest of autobiographies because it records only the things that matter.

A short but compelling document is Pierre Abélard's *Historia calamitatum* (c. 1134), the story of a public figure, a controversial philosophy teacher who allowed the imperatives of the private life to overtake him. His affair with a student having catastrophic consequences for his life, his autobiography is a cry from the heart in an age when authors and artists not only did not tell about themselves but often were content to remain anonymous. Or if they spoke out, they did so in the idealized and semiallegorical fashion of a Dante walking only partly in St. Augustine's footsteps. For, though hitherto rare, the autobiographical impulse is ubiquitous in the epic poem *La divina commedia* (*The Divine Comedy*, c. 1320) as many of the characters in the next world address to the pilgrim brief descriptions or synopses of their lives. More important is the framework, which offers the confessional mode of St. Augustine reduced to essentials. At the beginning of the book and far more so in the center of it, when he meets Beatrice, Dante reveals that, like St. Augustine, he had lost his way, having been distracted by profane love and secular philosophy. Also like in St. Augustine's book, a woman in his life, who is already where the pilgrim will someday be, functions as both a magnet and a cheering audience. But unlike in St. Augustine (and alien to the teachings of Jesus and Paul), that woman is not his mother, but a love object, Eros transmuted into Agape. (The origin of that love had been given in an earlier brief autobiographical work, *La vita nuova*, c. 1295, which combines sonnets and commentary.) The *Commedia* ends with the beatific vision, the ultimate experience for a Christian soul; all that is left for the corporeal pilgrim still in this world is to sit down and write the story from the beginning (more or less), as St. Augustine had and as, in a secular vein, Proust and Joyce would. That this work, however idealized and allegorized, is in some sense autobiographical is made clear by its author's other writings, some external documentation, the pilgrim's being called once by his name, "Dante," the historical events cited in the long speech made by Dante's ancestor Cacciaguida, and by the fact that the narrator is a writer who discusses his craft with Homer and others; he is also repeatedly urged in the hereafter to tell the world all he has seen.

The Renaissance and Neoclassical Period

Autobiographical elements may be found in some of Boccaccio's works, while Petrarch's *Secretum* (1342), a dialogue with St. Augustine, shows the imprint of the Latin master. A work perhaps the equal of St. Augustine's *Confessions* is Montaigne's *Essais* (*Essays,* 1580–1588), an intermittent autobiography. Though written in the essay form and often constituting reflections on current or past events or on something read, and though lacking order, chronology, or structure, the book is an autopsychography. In one of the most candid expositions of man's inner self ever written, Montaigne expresses his thoughts and feelings on almost everything, including his temporary impotence and his taste in fruits. He insists that he and his book are congruent, consubstantial. He began to expose himself thus because, regarding himself sui generis, he thought the reader might find such an odd person amusing. He ended by coming to the conclusion that he was, with all his idiosyncracies, terribly normal and representative and that he had written a self-portrait of everyman. He is so unique as to be everyman and so like everyone else—only, as he would say, more so—as to be unique.

His work differs from St. Augustine's in that the saint tells, chronologically though selectively, of a pilgrimage, despite many zig zags, to a goal, a rise to the mountain top of truth; Montaigne describes, chaotically but all-inclusively, a journey through life, with destination (as it is in most adventures) unknown, a wandering in and out of philosophic positions, an errancy signalled by the fact that a portion of a sentence may express an early stoic view and another portion of the same sentence may express a later skeptic or epicurean one. St. Augustine, writing from a religious vantage point, is feverish and judgmental about everything; Montaigne, secular and psychological, is detached and tolerant. St. Augustine needs to see hierarchies, design, and meaning, Montaigne is content to take life in discrete particles. St. Augustine, as a good Christian, indulges in theological paradoxes but, as a fine philosophic mind, eschews logical self-contradiction; Montaigne is at ease over owing a greater allegiance to truth than to mere consistency. One man who appears to have been strongly tempted by the autobiographical impulse was Milton. Like Dante, he did not number modesty among his vices. In prose or poetry, he can drop the issue at hand and go off on a tangent about himself. When, as was common in the polemics of that time, personal attacks were made on him, the earnest Milton was plunged into soul-searching and self-justification. He turned to the "intermittent" spiritual auto-biographical mode because of his ego and, as a child of the syncretist Renaissance, because of his awareness of the two sorts of role models: the Christian confessional example of St. Augustine and Dante, and the classical self-justifications of Socrates and Demosthenes. The results are three personal digressions in his prose polemical pamphlets. In *The Reason of Church-Government* (1642), he presents himself as a man who feels called upon to drop poetic ambitions and youthful successes in order to adopt the role of prophet and social critic. This is his proud response to the question, "Just who do you think you are?" In the *Apology for Smectymnuus* (1642), he offers something rare then and now—a detailed scholarly exposition of the intellectual phases (Ovidian; Dantesque-Petrarchan; chivalric-romantic; Platonic; and lastly, like St. Augustine and Dante after wayfaring in philosophy, Christian) of his own artistic career so far. Having been accused of frequenting brothels, he shows how he rather spends his time. In the *Defensio secunda* (1654), he offers a conventional though brief autobiographical passage, beginning with parents and birth and ending with pride over having joined the English Civil War by writing on the "three species of liberty which are essential to the happiness of the social life—religious, domestic, and civil." So deep was this strain in Milton that he even had the temerity to tamper with the epic form of his beloved Homer and Virgil and to introduce into *Paradise Lost* (1667) autobiographical lines for which no counterpart can be found in *Iliad* or *Aeneis* (*Aeneid*, 19 B.C.): In the proem to book 3 is a moving passage on his blindness (echoed in his drama poem *Samson Agonistes*, 1671; and in *Sonnets* 19, 22, and 23, 1655–1658); in the proem to 7 are lines on his living in dangerous isolation. And always he harps on his night-time inspiration.

The Romantic and Modern Period

Romanticism brought with it a new interest in the self and in subjectivity, much as Christianity had done, except that now the thrust was mainly secular. Rousseau's *Confessions* (1781–1788) was symptomatic; the age of the obligatory autobiography was beginning. Wordsworth's *Prelude* (1799–1805), the story in verse of the making of a poet, elaborates that love of nature and feeling which mark Rousseau's book (and Goethe's novel *Werther* [1774]), adding more theoretical scaffolding (in the name of antitheory!). Wordsworth anticipates Proust in his talk of "spots in time," his thesis that sensuous experience conjures up in all their vividness incidents from long ago, and in his consequent melding of events from different periods of his life. Highly selective, he is more reticent than St. Augustine or Rousseau about his amatory life. Works that deal with a phase of one's life, with one obsession or value, or with a personal experiment in forms of escape are Hazlitt's *Liber amoris* (1823), on an amatory infatuation; De Quincey's *Confessions of an English Opium Eater* (1822), on drug addiction and visions; and Thoreau's essays *Walden* (1854), on living alone in nature for a time.

One epiphenomenon of the increasing subjectivity and inwardness in the nineteenth century is the tendency toward veiled or unacknowledged autobiographical passages and works. Early literature had dealt almost exclusively with mythology. Medieval and Renaissance literature had derived its plots from scripture, chivalric and romance traditions, or (as in Shakespeare's tragedies and chronicle-plays) history. From the eighteenth century on, writers invent stories, and originality becomes a value. Yet just as plots were so opened up that only the author's imagination limited him, some writers chose rather to contract the narrative scope by writing about themselves—something that, so far as we know, Homer, Sophocles, Virgil, Wolfram, Shakespeare, and Fielding had not done. Dickens is one of the first, when he inserts a strong autobiographical element in his novel *David Copperfield* (1850). Intermittent and veiled autobiographic portraiture by Tolstoy can be found in those seekers of the truth, Andrey and Pierre in the novel *Voǐna i mir* (*War and Peace*, 1865–69) and Levin in *Anna Karenina* (1877). Dostoevsky's *Zapiski iz mërtvogo doma* (*Memoirs from the House of the Dead*, 1860–1862) is at the juncture of fiction and reportage.

A parallel occurrence is the proliferation of the feigned autobiography, the first-person confessional narrative à la Petronius and Apuleius, as in Swift's satire *Gulliver's Travels* (1726), nearly all of Defoe's novels, and both of Sterne's. The difficulty of defining the autobiographical impulse is never so manifest as in Dostoevsky's *Zapiski iz podpol'ïa* (*Notes from Underground*, 1864). Written in the first person, it is so searing as to sound like an authentic confession, and yet the "I" is a persona, a creature of fiction. The subject matter is self-revelation of the candid sort— structurally like Montaigne's, substantively like St. Augustine's and Rousseau's—but Dostoevsky is even more daring and self damning. (The persona dismisses Rousseau for not being candid enough.) The work expresses a misanthropy, self-contradictoriness, and perversity that none before or since have exhibited. By now permanently sulking in his lair in isolation from the world, the Underground Man is three-fourths insane and yet somehow, as mad people never can be, riveting. The work triumphs precisely because it carries the confessional impulse to its logical conclusion. Just as a character in Dante's *Inferno (Hell)* admits that he confesses to the pilgrim only because no one else is listening (an admission that T. S. Eliot used as epigraph for the autobiographical-sounding poem "Love Song of J. Alfred Prufrock," c. 1917), so are we privy to information about the self that is never talked or written about and that we would be happier not to confront. We overhear a soul communing with itself, a perverse Iago-like, Hitlerite soul that yet, strangely, seems representatively human. This forbidden, unsettling material, whose philosophical ramifications undermine the whole of modern rationalist, meliorist, technological society, makes for a unique work in world literature. A century later Camus tried for the same effect in *La chute (The Fall*, 1956), a fine pseudo-psychographical novel that could never have been written without the example of Dostoevsky.

A related and controversial development is the indirect autobiography, the work of literature that allegedly presents material from the author's life in poetic, symbolic, or disguised form. Scholars have speculated that Melville's *Bartleby the Scrivener* is an allegory about the author and his intellectual isolation. Similar interpretations have been made of, among many other works, Kafka's major tales as fables of the author's estrangement from his father or from God. And each of the Karamazov brothers is thought to represent a facet of Dostoevsky's personality.

More curious perhaps is the ubiquitous autobiographical impulse, veiled and intermittent, in twentieth-century fiction. It is a phenomenon that borders on solipsism and which bespeaks a pessimism as to the reality or relevance of the outside world, that glittering objective presence so royally and confidently depicted by Homer, Virgil, Dante, and Shakespeare. Samuel Butler's novel *Way of All Flesh* (1903), like Mann's novel *Buddenbrooks* (1901)—as well as the latter's story "Tonio Kröger" (1903) and novelle *Der Tod in Venedig* (*Death in Venice*, 1912)—have numerous personal elements, notably the family background of the heroes. Conrad's novella *Heart of Darkness* (1902) is paralleled by notebooks and personal documents. D. H. Lawrence's novel *Sons and Lovers* (1913), perhaps his finest book, is so close to the author's life as to almost be a third-person memoir. Literally true-to-life are many of the 3,000 pages of Proust's novels, *A la recherche du temps perdu* (*Remembrance of Things Past,* (1913–27). The work is concurrently the story of his preparation for his artistic vocation as well as the record of the life experiences that were to be transmuted into literature. As in Dante's *Commedia*, the first person narrator has the same Christian name as the author and is called by that name only once or twice; but where the medieval Italian vision work is autobiographical only in the framework and in an idealized reconstruction of events, the modern French novel is demonstrably true-to-life in character, incident, and locales; only the names have been changed. Marcel is, to be sure, a persona, for Proust was half Jewish and wholly homosexual and Marcel is neither. Yet, for a typical Frenchman, Marcel does have a suspiciously large number of Jews and homosexuals among his acquaintances. Furthermore, when Marcel hears that one of his acquaintances had spoken of him behind his back as a "hysterical little flatterer," the characterization does not quite fit Marcel but exactly fits Proust.

Joyce's *Portrait of the Artist as a Young Man* (1916) is, like Lawrence's contemporary novel, nearly a nonfiction, third-person memoir. The novel *Ulysses* (1922), with Bloom as a main character, cannot be overtly autobiographical, yet Bloom's somewhat bizarre sexual tastes were not unlike the author's, and the portrayal of the "artist," Stephen Dedalus, is a continuation from the earlier book. At one point, someone says that in ten years or so Stephen will be ready to write a great book; this is exactly the period between the time of the statement, 1904, and the time that Joyce began *Ulysses* itself, 1914. The work is also allegorically autobiographical in that it dramatizes how Stephen, a haughty esthete in flight from family and society, came to have contact with the decent human norm in the person of the outsider Bloom; this contact, we are to understand, constitutes the stuff of experience and the raw material of literary art. Some such encounter, some such recognition of the dignity lurking in the normal bourgeois existence he had been disdaining till now, must have drawn Joyce from a barren fin-de-siècle estheticism into creativity. Just as Dante, having reached the end of his journey with the beatific vision, must now sit down and write the story of the journey, and Proust, having through a climactic involuntary memory at long last discovered his vocation to be the setting down of the experiences in society, love, and art garnered while seeking a vocation, so Dedalus-Joyce, having had his epiphany through the encounter with Bloom, has been transformed into the person who will eventually be able to write about his wasted sterile years (in a Dublin that is in some sense like the *Inferno* and like Parisian high society) and about the occasion of his self-discovery. The *Commedia*, the *Recherche*, and *Ulysses* thus reveal how and why they came to be written, and, in celebrating the making of the artist and of the work, these books, however obliquely, manifest the autobiographical impulse.

Virginia Woolf's novel *To the Lighthouse* (1927) deals with, among other things, the difficulty of relating to an intellectual, remote father, something we know to have been the author's predicament as well. Hemingway's novel *A Farewell to Arms* (1929) is close to the author's World-War-I experiences; the novels *The Sun Also Rises* (1926) and *For Whom the Bell Tolls* (1940) present the Hemingway of the 1920s and 1930s. Similar in thrust are Fitzgerald's novels *Great Gatsby* (1925) and *Tender Is the Night* (1934); Henry Miller's autobiographical works *Tropic of Cancer* (1934) and *Rosy Crucifixion* (1949–1960); Mailer's novel *The Naked and The Dead* (1948); Styron's novel *Sophie's Choice* (1979); and many of Philip Roth's novels. Whether for good or ill, the autobiographical impulse has never been so ubiquitous and peremptory.

See also: Literature within Literature, Psychoanalysis of the Self.

Selected Bibliography

Morris, John N. *Versions of the Self*. New York: Basic Books, 1966.

Pascal, Roy. *Design and Truth in Autobiography*. Cambridge: Harvard University Press, 1960.

Spengemann, William C. *The Forms of Autobiography: Episodes in the History of the Literary Genre*. New Haven, Conn.: Yale University Press, 1980.

Weintraub, Karl Joachim. *The Value of the Individual: Self and Circumstance in Autobiography*. Chicago: University of Chicago Press, 1978.

MANFRED WEIDHORN

B

—— // ——

BANKER, FINANCIER, AND USURER

The word *banca* referred to the tradesman and moneychanger's bench or stall. Translated as *baunche* or *baunck* in Old English charts and wills, as *bancour* in Old French, and as *bankwere* in Old German/Nordic, it appears in legal documents since the mid-twelfth century.

"Financier" is derived from the Old French *finer*: to "refine" or render payment in metals, found in Old French texts as early as 1160. Medieval English defined "fynaunce" as tax collection. In France between 1549 and 1789, "financier" specifically designated an agent of public finances or a landowner who reported on fiscal matters to the king. The English teller or exchequer is named a "financier" in Blount's dictionary in 1656.

Usurier, derived from the Latin noun *usura* meaning money lent at interest, appears in Old French around 1170.

In Europe the terms "banker" and "financier" are used in an administrative context throughout the Middle Ages in commercial, legal, and religious tracts; however, in literature only the "usurer" can be found until the seventeenth century. Semantic and historical confusion between usurer, moneylender, and banker continues through the end of the Renaissance. For example, English sermons in the sixteenth century translate Jesus' words in Luke as "the bankers' tables" or the "moneylenders' tables." By 1680 in France, *banquier* also denotes the moneykeepers for the gambling tables. Italian documents distinguish moneylenders (*banchi*) from moneychangers (*cambio*), which becomes the root of the French term for currency traders, (*cambistes*). However, in fourteenth-century Florence *cambio* is synonymous with *banchi grossi*, or important bankers.

After the publication of *Das Kapital* (*Capital*) in 1867, the term "financier" is often treated as analogous to Marx's usage of capitalist or industrial capitalist. By the 1850s the use of the term "usurer" becomes less frequent in European texts, reflecting the bankers' and banks' legalized absorption of the usurer's function of lending to individuals, which relegated the usurer to the lower economic and societal level of pawnbroker or loanshark.

Sources in Antiquity

The earliest treatment of banking in antiquity is procedural. Hammurabi's Code (1728–1686 B.C.) devotes more than 150 paragraphs to technical rules governing interest, guarantees, loans, and other transactions. By contrast, the Bible did not seek to codify an accepted practice. Instead, it provides the source for the ethical and theological condemnation of the banker and moneylender that pervades medieval European literature. The prohibition, "Thou shalt not lend upon interest" is reiterated in Exodus, Leviticus, Deuteronomy, and Luke. In the biblical view, moneylending is a sterile activity that does not involve productive labor but instead reaps a profit through the mere passage of time and contradicts ethical principles that advocate a direct casuality between an individual's efforts and the reward of his labors.

Aristotle condemns interest-bearing transactions and in his essays states "The profession of handling money is justly hated" (*Politika* [*Politics*, 4th century B.C.]).

Comical or satirical literature in Athens treats with derision individuals who deal or handle money as a profession. The historian Herodotus portrayed moneylenders as so avaricious that they devised methods of enforcing debts by forbidding the most natural of human impulses—the need to bury one's dead:

In the reign of this king, money being scarce and commercial dealings straitened, a law was passed that the borrower might pledge his father's body to raise the sum whereof he has need. A proviso was appended to this law, giving the lender authority over the entire sepulchre of the borrower, so that a man who took up money under this pledge, if he died without paying the debt, could not obtain burial either in his own ancestral tomb, or in any other, nor could he during his lifetime bury in his own tomb any member of his family (*Historiai*, bk. 2 [*History*, 5th century B.C.]).

In Latin literature during the Empire, references to bankers or moneychangers appear in Cicero's *Ad Atticum* (*Letters to Atticus*, 68–44 B.C.), Petronius, and Juvenal. In the novel *Satyricon* (A.D. 60), attributed to Petronius, Trimalchio regards moneychanging as the most difficult profession after literature and medicine because its practitioners must detect true value among falsehood and illusion. Juvenal's *Satirae* (*Satires*, c. A.D. 100–127) make scornful references to fraudulent lending practices, embezzlement, payment of interest, and the supposed propensity of Jewish merchants to hoard money.

Later, the Hebrew Talmud, compiled during the third century A.D., returns to rule-making procedural concerns and imposes specific conditions on the borrowing and lending of money.

Medieval Sources

Throughout the Middle Ages, literary treatments of the banker and usurer betray a dialectical tension between economic realism and moral considerations.

In the tenth and eleventh century feudal hierarchy of Europe, the banker or moneylender (often synonymous with the merchant) is relegated to a marginal societal role. He is allowed to deal only with the small ruling faction, who tends to deny or minimize their relationship in order to avoid religious and moral censure. During the twelfth and thirteenth centuries, the prevailing view of mercantile activities reflected Saint Jerome's axiom: "The mercantile man can hardly, if ever be pleasing to God," a motto repeated by Aquinas and other theologians. However, during that time the papacy itself introduced greater leniency in its treatment of merchants and moneylenders.

This evolving attitudinal shift occurred contemporaneously with the economic impact of the first three Crusades (1096, 1146, 1189) and the creation of the first banks in Genoa and Venice in 1171 and 1177. The development of commodity markets in the Mediterranean; financial dealings between Italian merchants, Crusaders, and French kings; changes in European currency standards; and royal restrictions on minting privileges, *droit de frappe*, created new transactional methods and concepts. By the mid-thirteenth century, merchants and bankers began to take on well-defined roles in their societies.

Thus, the courtly novel *Galeran de Bretagne*, attributed to Renault (c. 1210–1220), dedicates a passage to moneychangers in Metz who deal in silver, gold, and precious metals. By 1250 Italian documents in Lombardy, Genoa, and Venice discuss transactions employing banking instruments such as bills of exchange, overdrafts, loans with concealed interest called *nutuum gratis et amore* (in English, "free and loving" notes), and *lettres de change* often involving parties in different countries. In Italy and Flanders during the late thirteenth century, a hierarchy could be discerned among the usurers (usually Lombards or Jews), who dealt in short-term loans; the cambio, who changed money; deposit bankers, who received and lent in ordinary business contexts; and the great merchant-bankers, who lent at long term to monarchs, the church, or the papacy.

In practice, the individual in need of a loan had recourse only to the usurer, who was typically a Jew denied the right to practice a different profession or to work the land. As a foreigner in the religious and cultural context, the usurer was often subjected to hatred and scorn. The image of the moneylender came to include physical deformity, ugliness, or moral perversity—an archetypal negative stereotype that had not been laid to rest even by the end of the nineteenth century. Thus, in Jehan de Meung's continuation of the didactic poem *Roman de la rose* (*Romance of the Rose*, c. 1275) Faux Semblant (False Seeming) indicts usurers for hoarding hidden reserves of gold; and *The Prioress' Tale* in Chaucer's *Canterbury Tales* (1380–1400) describes a Jewish quarter "for foul usury and love of villany."

In the *Inferno* (*Hell*), canto 17 of Dante's epic poem *La divina commedia* (*The Divine Comedy*) (c. 1320), usurers are placed in the seventh circle of Hell with wealthy popes and cardinals. In that canto, usury is symbolized both by the Gerydon, a Griffin-clawed, half-human monster, and the money pouches perpetually hung around the condemned usurers' necks. In Dante's perspective, all forms of moneylending are usurious and symptoms of excessive concern with material, as opposed to moral or spiritual, well-being.

Unlike Dante, Boccaccio's novellas *Il decamerone* (*Decameron*, c. 1350) mentions but does not explicitly condemn wealthy Jews who lend "at usurance." Boccaccio also refers favorably to "a punctual repayer of loans," whose prompt repayment of the loan (presumably minimizing the interest thereby) mitigates the usurious nature of the transaction.

The papal councils of Lateran (1179), Lyon (1274) and Vienna (1311) condemned the usurer to excommunication without the benefit of Christian burial. However, by the late thirteenth century, when the typography of Purgatory began to be mapped, authors proved willing to mitigate the usurers' torments and condemned them to the lower levels of Purgatory, instead of the more horrible regions of Hell.

The Renaissance and the Seventeenth Century

By the mid-fifteenth century French and English currency was standardized, at least nominally, public banks were established in Italy, and real estate speculation expanded in the form of land bonds. In consequence, relationships between money in its function as a medium of exchange and the commodities that it purchased became increasingly indirect.

In the literature of the Renaissance, there are only occasional reflections of those evolving concepts and modes of exchange. Bonaventure des Périers' *Nouvelles récréations et joyeux devis* (tales, 1558) makes occasional references to misuse of funds, poor investments, or poor debts, always in the context of negative themes of fraud or self-deception. In Pierre de Larivey's *Les esprits* (*The Spirits*, play, 1579) the protagonist is the greedy usurer Severin. In England the theme of usury as a vice became a popular subject in the Elizabethan theater, with Marlowe's *The Jew of Malta* (c. 1589), Shakespeare's *Merchant of Venice* (c. 1595), Thomas Middleton's *A Trick to Catch The Old One* (c. 1605), and the portrayal of shady dealings, greedy creditors, and the superstitious voluptuary financier, Sir Epicure Mammon, in Ben Jonson's *Alchemist* (1610).

Shakespeare dealt with economic conflicts and transactions in *A Comedy of Errors* (c. 1594). In *The Merchant of Venice*, Shylock represents the anti-Semitic archetype of the Jewish usurer, whose ostracism from the Gentile community is reflected in his physical appearance. To an Elizabethan audience, Shylock personified the medieval usurer: a societal pariah whose venality, avarice, and desire for the humiliation of Christians justify his downfall. Yet he is not only a figure to be scorned. He is also endowed with positive qualities, such as commercial acumen and love for his family, which make him function as a tragic figure rather than merely an object of contempt. On a more representational level, his clients, the Christian merchants Bassanio and Antonio, personify the developing merchant class embroiled in speculation and long-term borrowing based upon risky and unpredictable maritime ventures.

During the seventeenth century, literary themes of banking and moneylending were fashionable in France, where a rapidly prospering urban bourgeoisie attained and often surpassed the economic power of the declining aristocratic classes. Subtle shifts in attitude away from earlier condemnation of bankers can be glimpsed in the theater and early forms of the novel. For medieval and Renaissance historiographers, or philosophers like Montaigne, economic issues had no legitimate function in political or historical analysis. By contrast, as early as the 1630s the *comédie de moeurs*, such as Corneille's *Place royale* (1633), began to include realistic financial and commercial terms and situations in a theatrical context.

In Molière's theater, a character's psychology is often derived from his financial or social status. In *L'avare* (*The Miser*, 1668), Harpagon's miserliness and obsession with gold is juxtaposed against his social pretentions and his desire to impress an aristocrat. His occupation as a usurer reflects a hatred for himself and his station, as when (in repudiation of his paternal instincts and duty) he lends money to his own son under a pseudonym. In *Dom Juan* (*Don Juan*, 1665), a creditor is an economically impotent object of mockery in the scene between Monsieur Dimanche, the merchant, and the dissipated aristocrat. The disdain shown by Don Juan for Dimanche in refusing to honor his debt play upon Dimanche's bourgeois subservience and combine to make Dimanche unable to enforce his economic rights. The formal clichés of Don Juan's aristocratic discourse distract Dimanche from the economic reality of his situation and precipitate his retreat for the palpably foolish reason that, "it is true that he shows me so many considerations and gives me so many compliments that I could not ask him for money." In *Le bourgeois gentilhomme* (*The Would-Be Gentleman*, 1670), the wealthy tradesman Jourdain becomes a figure of farce as he seeks to purchase prepackaged social graces and aristocratic skills to sublimate his economic identity and to integrate himself into an unwelcoming aristocratic class.

Between 1680 and 1715, financiers, tax collectors, and usurers appear in numerous French plays dealing with themes of bankruptcy, moneylending, public utilities schemes, and gambling debt. Two of the most successful were Champmeslé's *La rue St. Denis* (1682), set on a street of retail trade in Paris where a prosperous Jewish usurer, Sabatin, receives stolen goods, and N. de Fatouville's *Le banqueroutier* (1687), where the financier Persillet is involved in fraudulent operations, removal of assets, and tricking creditors, abetted by his notary, M. de la Ressource. These works helped to incorporate financial and commercial terminology into literary discourse, while, from a psychological perspective, Furetière's *Roman bourgeois* (novel, 1666) and La Fontaines' *Fables* (1668–1694) consider the tension between the search for personal happiness and the approbation of society on the one hand, and the acquisition of wealth on the other, through their treatment of financiers.

The Eighteenth Century

The establishment of the Bank of England (1694), joint stock companies, royal charters for trade monopolies, and a sharp increase in land and stock speculation made banks and bankers more accessible to the general public.

Literary references to finance and banking similarly reflect a state of evolution and redefinition. In many works, the bourgeois as financier becomes reconciled to and even proud of his nonaristocratic identity. For the first time, merchants called *négociants* are praised or criticized for their economic achievements or conduct, instead of being condemned *ab initio* because their activities violate moral or theological proscriptions. And in contrast to the previous century, where earning a livelihood through finance was seen as invidiously defining one's social class, financial transactions are presented as a means of achieving social mobility in a slowly disintegrating hierarchal society.

In his novel *Moll Flanders* (1722), Daniel Defoe depicts the protagonist's pursuit of her career through the use of economic terms such as "dues," "shares," "commodities," and "prices." Moll Flanders' activities, including her numerous marriages, are defined as transactions in which she is treated as a commodity and is evaluated strictly in terms of the profit that she can generate for her marriage partner.

French novels such as Prévost's *Manon Lescaut* (1731), Sade's *Justine* (1791), and Restif de la Bretonne's *Nuits de Paris* (*Nights of Paris*, 1788–1793) also examine the female protagonist's function within the economic structure. In Sade's work, Juliette's body is described as a commodity: "the same merchandise was sold to 80 persons who paid." *Manon Lescaut* underscores the dialectical tension between Des Grieux's ignorance of and scorn for the acquisition of money, and Manon's knowledgeable manipulation of the corrupt bankers and financiers who "keep" her. In these works, personal relationships are expressed in the semantics of exchange in which persons and objects interrelate according to their current market value, and even a character's downfall can be cushioned by previous financial dealings. Manon's wealth—like that of Moll Flanders, acquired through fraud, larceny, or prostitution—is used to secure better living conditions even when she falls into prison.

Between 1700 and 1730, political and economic events culminating in the devaluation of the French *louis d'or*, the circulation of paper money, and "agiotage" (speculation based upon fluctuating relative values of gold and paper currency) are reflected in the theater. The newly wealthy merchant, the usurer, and poor and conniving aristocrats are presented on stage in Dancourt's *Agioteurs* (1710), and Lesage's *Turcaret* (1709). In *Turcaret* the plot is based on a series of transactions involving letters of credit, unpaid debts, and dubious loans.

Popular literature in France, including journals, diaries, and pamphlets, described the banking scheme of John Law, who established the first national bank system in France. The Royal National Bank merged with the Compagnie des Indes, a trading company that sold shares in future development of French colonies in America. Speculation in the shares of the Compagnie des Indes and the fortunes that were made or lost in those shares attracted every social class to the Rue Quincampoix exchange, bringing aristocrats and valets into direct financial contact with one another. But Law's creation failed in 1720, leaving many shareholders penniless while providing others with sudden fortunes. The crisis created by the failure of the Compagnie des Indes left in its wake a new mistrust of banking institutions and negotiable instruments such as paper money.

Nevertheless, the financier-merchants Aurelly and Melac in Beaumarchais' *Les deux amis ou le négociant de Lyon* (1770) are endowed with qualities (such as altruism, a sense of honor, and generosity) that were previously attributed to members of the aristocracy. Beaumarchais' play incorporates a broad spectrum of financial terminology, which the playwright evidently expected to be understood by a general audience. Slightly earlier, Sedaine's *Le philosophe sans le savoir* (1765) also presented the banker as a sympathetic figure in the character of Vanderk, a nobleman by birth who chooses to be a financier and takes pride in his chosen profession. In the face of his son's protests, he defends his calling and praises his fellow practitioners as "the silken threads" who link nations together.

The Nineteenth Century

In the early nineteenth century, the continued expansion of the London and Paris Stock Exchanges, increases in trade and urban industrialization, and creation of credit unions and commercial banks propelled the banker and the bank as an institution farther into the public's consciousness. By the 1840s, a financial press offering stock quotations, tips for speculators, and general economic and business information had began to develop in the capitals and provinces of France, England, and the United States. Yet, in the same period, and especially during the French Restoration (1814 to 1830), a resurgence of reactionary aristocratic biases revived the image of the banker and financier as an exploiter and outsider.

The works of Balzac, Goethe, and Dickens reflect their societies' ambivalent attitudes toward finance, banking, and money. Balzac and Dickens returned to and recodified a series of negative physical and moral stereotypes that then dominated those themes for most of their century. For the novelist Balzac, financial transactions are simply variants of usury, as in the rural setting of *Les paysans* (*The Peasants*, 1844), where Rigou and Soudry purchase land in order to subdivide it for resale at usurious rates to their debtors. In *Illusions perdues* (*Lost Illusions*, 1843) the hero-victim Lucien de Rubempré's perennial status as a debtor is cause for a lengthy diatribe against banking, which Balzac attacks as a "formidable royalty invented by the Jews in the 12th century and which today dominates thrones and people."

To Balzac, bankers are international conspirators in league with accountants, notaries, and the civil judiciary. Far from acting as "silken threads" among nations, in *Le père Goriot* (*Father Goriot*, 1834), *Eugénie Grandet* (1833), *La maison Nucingen* (*The House of Nucingen*, 1838), *Gobseck* (1830), and *Un homme d'affaires* (*A Man of Business*, 1845), banking functions solely for the purpose of enriching the individual banker. Financial profit and emotional satisfaction became complementary themes, where characters act and speak in a context of values based upon financial accumulation: dowries, bonds, debts, real estate. Like the outsider Shylock, the baron de Nucingen, with his Alsatian accent, emphasizes the perception of the banker as a menacing and grotesque foreigner. On a physical level, Balzac's bankers conform to a common type: male, middle-aged or older, rotund, and sedentary.

Balzac and Goethe both compare the financier's knowledge of commissions, interest, and collateral—in short, the ability to convert intangible assets into gold—with the powers of the alchemist. In Goethe's play *Faust*, part 2 (1832), Mephistopheles comes to the Imperial Palace as financial advisor to remedy the kingdom's lack of liquid funds. Mephistopheles' diabolic solution is paper money, with which, to the emperor's surprise, he proposes to pay the state's public debts and settle the emperor's personal accounts. Mephistopheles' advocacy of paper currency is a metaphor for Goethe's criticism of the paper money circulated in Germany in the 1790s to supplement gold reserves and as a means of meeting military and state payrolls.

To Dickens, financial transactions such as speculation in stocks and currency fluctuations are symptoms of moral corruption. The novels *Dealings with the Firm of Dombey and Son* (1846–1848), *Nicholas Nickleby* (1838–1839), *A Christmas Carol* (1843), and *Hard Times* (1854) present the acquisition of wealth as inimical to emotional fulfillment or moral worth. In those works, the financier is an impotent and solitary figure who finds solace only in his worldly possessions. Josiah Bounderby is cruel and tyrannical, Ebenezer Scrooge only shows affection for his bill-discounting business, and Dombey only regains his ability to experience the sentiments of fatherhood when he becomes bankrupt and leaves the financial community. Nicholas Nickleby's Uncle Ralph is a notorious usurer who corrupts and defrauds in order to increase his hoard of riches.

Similarly, Mr. Merdle's "wonderful bank" in *Little Dorrit* (1855–1857) grew out of usurious interest loans and shady speculations. Here again, the financier's moral defects of narcissism, megalomania, and arrogance are reflected in his hypocritical and dishonest business dealings. When Mr. Merdle dies, even his commercial life is proven to be hollow—his banking empire consists of fraudulent accounts and illusionary assets. (Merdle's end is echoed in Dickens' *American Notes for General Circulation* [essay 1842] where he says of Wall Street that, "Many a rapid fortune has been made in this street and many a no less rapid ruin.")

In Dickens' moral dialectics, the speculator/financier often comes to a justifiably miserable end. Dostoevsky's novel *Prestuplenie i nakazanie* (*Crime and Punishment*, 1866) adopts this theme in its characterization of the female usurer, a unique, desexualized person whose physical appearance, spinsterhood, and avarice negate her inherent womanhood. To Raskolnikov, the act of murder can be justified because of the evil and destructive economic character of his victim.

In French literature from the 1840s through 1914, anti-Semitic attacks formerly directed against the usurer because of exorbitant interest charges are transferred to bankers and financiers. Religious prejudice aside, the view of the banker as foreign, anti-French, and yet in a position of authority able to monopolize France's financial resources had some basis in certain historical realities. The influence and power of the Jewish Rothschild family and of the financier Jules

Mirès over the political and economic power structure were consolidated during the July Monarchy and the Second Empire from 1830 through 1870. During that time, despite the government's official support for economic and financial growth, the banker remained an image shrouded by mystery, whose wealth was assumed to have been ill-gotten, and who was thought to thrive upon an international network of conspiratorial relations and a mystical ability to control the flow of money.

In 1857 Jules Vallès, a radical journalist, published a satirical diatribe against the stock market, mockingly dedicated to the Jewish financier Jules Mirès, and entitled *L'argent: rentiers, agioteurs, millionnaires*. In that work, Vallès defined the Parisian stock market as the new "City Hall of the New Republic" where knowledge of financial operations, brokerage, deals, and money markets would replace all humanistic values.

Karl Marx's lectures on economic theory compiled in *Das Kapital* formally codified a vocabulary describing the relationships among money, commodities, and societal structure. For Marx, the banker is a "hoarder" of unnecessary reserves of capital who acquires wealth produced by the labor of the exploited working class. His function as intermediary destroys the direct transactional relationship between the producer and the user of commodities. Marx's economic semantics influenced all subsequent portrayals of the banker. After Marx, the banker becomes a target for leftist writers as the personification of abhorrent capitalist concepts, while for the right, he is condemned as a democratizer of money and commerce.

Flaubert's novel *L'éducation sentimentale* (*The Sentimental Education*, 1869) describes French society during the Revolution of 1848. It presents Dambreuse, the banker and speculator, as a person without principles who vacillates politically "like a barometer constantly expressing the latest variations." Flaubert's verdict (recalling Dickens' treatment of Merdle) is that bankers like Dambreuse are inherently frauds and hypocrites.

Dumas fils' play *La question d'argent* (*The Money-Question*, 1857), Edmond About's play *Ces coquins d'agents de change* (1861), and Maurice Barrès' novel *Les déracinés* (1897) attack the banker from the viewpoint of the political right. Barrès' debunking of republican ideology holds that finance is contrary to the interests of France and "no longer may be in solidarity with French destinies." According to Barrès, the attempt to rise above one's social class by any form of financial wheeling and dealing or speculating in stocks necessarily ends in a disaster of crime and moral corruption.

Jules Claretie's *Le million* (1882), Alphonse Daudet's *Le nabab* (The Nabab, 1877) and Emile Zola's *L'argent* (*Money*, 1891), all novels, dealt with the realm of finance as a mythic battlefield of conflicting moral and theological values. In *L'argent*, inspired by the success and rapid failure of the Union Générale Bank created in 1887 by Catholic aristocrats as a counterweight to Jewish and Protestant French banks and supported by the Gambetta government, the Stock Exchange (La Bourse) becomes both a cult and a temple where Saccard, the Gentile creator of the Banque Universelle, attempts to defeat Gundermann, the wealthy Jewish banker, but is himself defeated. Zola's novel, like Jean-Richard Bloch's *Et cie* (1917) and Anatole France in *L'île des pingouins* (*Penguin Island*, 1908), includes anti-Semitic tirades and digressions that emphasize the Jewish banker's supposed international contacts, excessive venality and greed, and subversive beliefs. *L'argent* focuses upon the interplay of stock exchange operations and tensions (described in accurate trading and banking terminology) and the descending spiral of financial success and stock manipulations, followed by rapid reversals leading to the collapse of markets and accusations of fraud and later by bankruptcy, trial, and disgrace. Zola's linear narrative progression sets a pattern that later reappears in numerous French and American novels on finance.

American banks and bankers functioned in a decentralized structure based on regulation by the states in an environment that emphasized the individual's ability to create new markets and generate new wealth through speculation and investment. The image of the banker as adventurer and pioneer acquiring wealth through skill, daring, and shrewd financial manipulation forms part of the American myth of the individual's power to transcend or control the existing authority structure. True to that image and myth, banks as institutions may be criticized or condemned, but the banker himself is largely treated as a positive figure. Unlike in France and England, where the individual who deals in money is considered to be tainted by moral, theological, or racial defects, such social, religious, or political biases are not often stamped upon the figure of the banker and financier in American literature. In that regard, the prevailing Protestant ideology in which the acquisition of wealth could coexist with theological virtue stands in direct contrast to the French and Italian Catholic disjunction between moral rectitude and economic pragmatism.

Henry James' creation of the "American abroad" hero or heroine emphasizes cultural conflicts between American and European values. His characters, such as Newman in *The American* (novel, 1877) or Bender in *The Outcry* (novel, 1911), are self-made "commercial men" who are unable to integrate themselves into the French and English aristocratic milieux. In contrast to Dickens' characters, James creates a new type of financier—young, physically attractive, and virile—who personifies a synthesis of qualities previously treated as mutually exclusive. Generous, honest, and forth-right, James' financiers are also endowed with business acumen, an ability to gamble and speculate successfully, and a total commitment to gain and profit. Reconciled to their identity and persuaded of their beneficient social function in a growing country, they are closer to the eighteenth-century French image of the financier than to the caricaturized, negative stereotypes of the nineteenth century.

The Twentieth Century

Theodore Dreiser and Frank Norris find a topographical, psychological, and semantic field of study in the vast expansion of American financial and commodity markets and brokerage houses, and land, railroad, and mining investments.

The saga of Frank Cowperwood in Dreiser's novels, *The Financier* (1912) and *The Titan* (1914), spans forty years of economic growth in Philadelphia and Chicago. Cowperwood's ascent from bookkeeping, to brokering, to note brokerage (the selling of municipal notes), and then to investment banker (a new and more prestigious occupation than commercial banking because of its power to create and direct financial undertakings) is followed by the downward spiral of misappropriation of city funds, desperate financial scheming, and inability to meet loans called after the Chicago Fire panic of October 1871, which leads to his bankruptcy, trial, and imprisonment, and (in striking contrast to *L'argent*) culminates in his pardon and return to the market in 1873 with new ventures in land and lease speculation in Chicago (*The Titan*). Dreiser's portrayal of the financier combines respect for his skills and adaptability with an acceptance of the amorality that permeates his political, business, and sexual standards. To Dreiser, the financier can be a noble figure: "He was a financier by instinct and all the knowledge that persisted to that great art was as natural to him . . . as the subtleties of life are to a poet."

Norris' novel *The Pit* (1903) uses the grain market exchange and brokerage houses in Chicago as the setting for the financier Jadwin's ascent and failure. Jadwin's fascination with speculation in wheat prices leads him to ignore his family and, eventually, to evade every commitment or responsibility other than the "wheat pit." His obsession finally culminates in his emotional wreckage. Like Zola's Bourse, Norris' Board of Trade Building, "black, grave, monolithic" mythifies the topos of speculation.

By the beginning of the twentieth century, banking and the stock market became increasingly technical professions, requiring schooling in economic theory and statistics and a formal apprenticeship in a hierarchical corporate structure. At the same time, literature began to reflect with greater specificity the practical distinctions among commercial or investment bankers, brokers, dealers, and traders. Moreover, as the banking field became more institutionalized and regulated, the individual was no longer seen to have the same degree of power as his predecessors to generate or control vast sums of money.

In Europe and in the United States, the representation of the banker or financier takes on heightened political and psychological overtones. As a character, he personifies capitalist goals to writers of socialist or Marxist orientation. To writers generally, he becomes more introspective as an individual in defining his identity in professional, societal, and personal terms. Subjective emotions of loss, ambivalence, and disillusionment color or interfere with his financial success.

The character of Undershaft in Shaw's play *Major Barbara* (1905) revises Dickens' moral and economic dialectics by attacking what Shaw described in his preface as the Victorian glorification of poverty. Undershaft, a capitalist producer of gunpowder, considers his profits to be entirely justifiable in a world where all social entities, including the Salvation Army, depend on money in order to survive.

Thomas Mann, in his novel *Buddenbrooks* (1901), and Proust, in his novels *A la recherche du temps perdu* (*Remembrance of Things Past*, 1913–1927), emphasize generational conflicts between monetary and aesthetic values. Mann's hero must transcend the merchant class with its narrow financial goals to enter into the realm of art. Similarly, the father of Swann, the esthete and art critic, was an *agent de change* or broker. However, Proust does not condemn the financier. As he subtly implies in his description of the Princesse de Parme's genealogy (*Le côté de Guermantes* [*Guermantes Way*, 1920]), the continuance of humanistic or aristocratic values depends upon the existence of financial support systems. The family history juxtaposes early Christian patriarchs with the blessings of an excellent stock portfolio containing "most of the shares of the Canal of Suez and three times as many Royal Dutch as Edmond de Rothschild."

Later in the century, Larbaud's *A. O. Barnabooth* (1913), Maurois' *Bernard Quesnay* (1926), and Mauriac's *Nœud de vipères* (*The Vipers Tangle*, 1932), all novels, treat the theme of the inability of monetary success or accumulation of wealth in a competitive society to provide sufficient emotional or spiritual sustenance. Fitzgerald's novel *The Great Gatsby* (1925) analyzes acquisition and possession of material wealth in terms of deception, disillusion, and futility. The narrator, "a bond man," finds his own profession formalized in textbooks and stripped of glamour, while Gatsby's attempt to live up to his persona of the mysterious financial adventurer and speculator ends in suicide.

For Marxist and socialist writers of the 1920s and 1930s, the banker reverts to the Balzacian moral and physical stereotype. He becomes a physical caricature and a symbol of the exploitation and manipulation of the worker and the underprivileged in Aragon's *Cloches de Bâle* (*Bells of Basel*, novel, 1934) and of rural orchard pickers in Steinbeck's novel *In Dubious Battle* (1936). In Bertolt Brecht's *Die Dreigroschenoper* (*The Threepenny Opera*, 1928), bankers in morning coats post the bail for their new director, McHeath, king of the underworld.

Before the Great Crash of 1929, banking and Wall Street brokerage or insurance firms were considered to be gentlemen's professions, practiced by a network of Ivy League schools and men's clubs. After that time, even when the bank itself retains its apparent veneer of prestige and stability, that image is betrayed by intimidations of corruption, failure, and possible betrayal of trust involving the misappropriation of depositor's funds. John Kenneth Galbraith, in *The Great Crash, 1929* (1955), described the banker's loss of reputation at the hands of an American public outraged by the depression, "For the next decade they were fair game for congressional committees, courts, the press and the comedians."

John Dos Passos, in his novel *The Big Money* (1936), presents a narrative in the form of a fragmented collage or "camera eye" of historical and fictional events. The United States is defined as consisting of "holding companies, trade

unions, radio networks . . . stock quotations rubbed out and written in . . . USA
is a set of big mouthed officials with too many bank accounts.'' To Dos Passos,
financial transactions and the desire to make a "killing in the market" are a
sublimination of primitive urges toward aggression and violence.

In later novels, the "descending spiral" narrative structure of fraudulent speculation, trial, and disgrace becomes a medium for reappraisal of American ideology linked to a loss of faith in the banker's honesty, societal role, and prestige.
Robert Penn Warren's *At Heaven's Gate* (1943) and Louis Bromfield's *Mrs.
Parkington* (1943), develop a parallel conception of the American financial world
in terms of corporate rivalry, intrinsic violence, and a hypocritical obsession
with social status.

John P. Marquand's *Point of No Return* (1949) analyzes the banker's profession in terms of societal function, corporate ambition, and the ambivalence
between an individual's conception of himself and his institutional role. The
protagonist, Charles Grey, must return to his hometown and undergo a ritual
purging of past traumas, including his father's suicide during the October 1929
Crash, in order to reintegrate his adolescent ideals into his adult values, goals,
and sense of self-worth.

In Marquand's novel the bank itself has the trappings of a medieval citadel,
with its tellers' cages, underground vaults, and secret chambers from which only
the initiated (the bank's officers) control the flow of money. However, the
apparent strength and prestige of the Stuyvessant bank cannot guarantee the
banker's own security or sense of identity and self-worth.

In the 1930s, the image of America as the embodiment of free markets,
capitalist ventures, and economic opportunity became mythified in European
literature. Céline's novel *Voyage au bout de la nuit* (*Journey to the End of the
Night*, 1932) follows Bardamu's journey to New York and Detroit, the antipodes
of capitalism and socialism. Wall Street is portrayed as a secular church dedicated
to the sacred ritual of "the Dollar, a true Holy Ghost, more precious than blood,"
but the sanctuary of the bank is also the scene of ritualistic use of public toilets
and defecation. Kafka, in his novel *Amerika* (1927), describes a fantasmagoric
journey where the hero, Karl, meets Mr. Pollunder, a New York banker and
symbol of American efficiency. Karl's experiences with finance and exchange
of commodities are dehumanized, anonymous transactions within a bureaucratic
robotlike structure.

Returning to a European scene, Christina Stead's novel *House of All Nations*
(1938) presents a collage of bankers, financiers, and corrupt speculators in a
private Parisian bank. Stead's image of the Jewish banker Bertillon again incorporates anti-Semitic connotations, but here the foreign influence decried is
an economic dependence on American (not European) financial markets. Banking
itself is described as mere façade for fraud and misrepresentation, part of the
"immorality as well as the mythomania of the financial world."

André Malraux's novel *La condition humaine* (*Man's Fate*, 1933) places the
dialectics of state finance and individual power in an existentialist context. Ferral,

the protagonist head of the French financial consortium in Indochina, rebels against his reactionary, decrepit, and impotent colleagues; who define banking only in terms of riskless, secured, short-term loans; whose vocabulary is "a totally numerical language"; and whose view of success is based not on productive work or efficiency but commissions. Ferral attacks them for considering only narrow economic factors in withdrawing their investments while ignoring the wider lessons, needs, and demands of history.

In the 1950s through the 1970s, the earlier thematic typology of the banker as the aggressive male adventurer raping women and institutions reappears in such American novels as Cameron Hawley's *Cash McCall* (1955) and Ayn Rand's *Atlas Shrugged* (1957). In this same period, Faulkner's *The Town* (1957) caricatures the profession and institution of banking. *The Town*'s debunking of hypocritical mores, fraudulent financial schemes, and embezzling bank presidents in the Old South incorporates such grotesque characters as the child named Wall Street Panic by his mother (his teachers rename him Wall Snopes) whose life's ambition is "to learn how to count money." In *The Town*, respect for the bank as a symbol of wealth, power, and potency coexists with a fear of the institution's lack of security, "like an Elizabethan Inn" where travelers (depositors) fear for their lives and possessions.

Louis Auchincloss' 1966 novel *The Embezzler* is a psychological study of financial mores in 1936 where the embezzlement scheme of Guy Prime, a playboy-broker, leads to a discussion of business amorality, in which larceny of negotiable instruments can be rationalized as not a crime, but rather as a reapportionment of available resources.

More recent popular American novels, such as Arthur Hailey's *The Money Changers* (1975), Emma Lathen's (pseudonym of Mary Latis and Martha Hennisart) mystery series involving John Putnam Thatcher, the conservative "wasp" banker-detective (1961) and *Cashing In* by Antonia Gowar (1982) incorporate the mechanics and concepts of high-technology banking and depersonalized administrative structures, as well as the specialized terminology and jargon of computerized trading centers and board rooms.

The Gowar and Hailey works also present a new phenomenon, the woman banker and banking executive. But Hailey's Edwina d'Orsay or Gowar's Lisa Gould do not change the basic image of the banker; instead, they merely graft the traits of monomanical ambition, amorality, and disillusion onto a female character. Unlike in eighteenth and nineteenth century literary works, whose themes treated women as merely another form of commodity, assets, or profit, or as a tangible prize for the male financier, women in these latest novels move from objective to subjective status. Yet they do not transform the genre—they merely reverse sexual roles and update the stereotype.

Current politico-economic instability, new currencies and markets, electronic transfers of funds, computer theft, and the growth of international financial corporations are contributing to another redefinition of capitalism and banking. Increased dependence on electronic equipment and hyper-specialized, technical knowledge are creating new semantic fields and new forms of financial experts and manipulators. These evolving factors will soon be reflected in and impose their thematic varients upon themes of bankers and banking in the literature of the future.

See also: Anti-Semitism, Capitalism, Money.

Selected Bibliography

Braudel, Fernand. *The Mediterranean and the Mediterranean World in the Age of Philip II*. New York: Harper and Row, 1972.

Le Goff, Jacques. *Marchands et banquiers du Moyen-Age*. Paris: PUF, 1956.

Shell, Marc. *Money, Language and Thought*. Berkeley: University of California Press, 1982.

IRÈNE FINEL-HONIGMAN

BEAR

The bear is found in all kinds of literature as an easily recognized symbol of ferocity, sloth, intelligence, playfulness, lust, and of other attributes as well. Its large size made it conspicuous among wild European and North American animals. Its curious resemblance to humans when it stands or walks on its hind legs made it a figure of fun or pathos. When captured young it could be tamed as a pet or trained to dance and perform tricks. Various traits of the wild animal were observed from the earliest times: hibernation, the fierce and dangerous protectiveness of the mother bear with cubs, the shuffling gait, the rough pelt, the animal's solitariness, and its craving for berries and honey. Any one of these traits or a combination of them could be emphasized for literary purposes.

Ancient naturalists, mainly following the authority of Aristotle, described the birth of bear cubs with details that were based on false observations or deductions but that were believed to be authoritative. The cubs were thought to be the smallest among animals in proportion to the mother's weight. When new-born, the cubs were believed to be blind, hairless, and shapeless. Some said that the lustfulness of the females caused them to expel the fetuses prematurely. The mother accordingly had to give her cubs their features by licking them, using her tongue as a sculptor uses his tools. This supposed process, together with the unusually long period of growing up that the young spend with their mothers, gave rise to the image of the nurturing mother bear.

In Greek myth and legend the bear has several important connections. Salmoxis was a rather obscure oracle-divinity among the Thracians, perhaps worshipped in the form of a bear, his periods of hibernation in underground dens giving him contact with sources of special knowledge (Herodotus, *Historiai* [*History*, 5th century B.C.]). Artemis, the Olympian goddess who was patroness of young animals in general, was closely associated with bears at her cult-site in Brauron, a small town on the coast of Attica east of Athens. Young girls made pilgrimages there dressed in specially colored robes. They were called *arktoi* (bears), and archaeological investigations of the site have shown that bear-masks and statues of the animal were part of the equipment of the ceremonies, which were probably in the nature of a rite of passage marking a certain stage in the maturity of the initiates. The myth of Callisto, told most elaborately by the Roman poet Ovid (*Metamorphoses*, epic poem, c. A.D. 2–17), but well known in fifth-century Athens, is also associated with Artemis (Diana in Roman mythology). Callisto, one of the band of virgin girls who accompanied Artemis in the wild, aroused the desire of Zeus, king of the gods (Roman Jupiter). He disguised himself as Artemis, approached Callisto when she was alone, induced her to trust him as Artemis, and then seduced her as Zeus. When her pregnancy revealed that she had violated her vow of virginity, Callisto was expelled from the group of Artemis' attendants. She gave birth to a son, Arcas (Bear-boy), but Hera (Zeus's wife, Roman Juno) punished her by transforming her into a bear. Callisto, whose name means "Most Beautiful," becomes most ugly. Later, when Arcas grew up and became a hunter, he met his bear-mother in the woods and was about to kill her when Zeus intervened and changed both mother and son into the constellations of the Great and Little Bears (Ursa Major and Minor; the Big and Little Dipper). Transformations of humans into bears or humans born from bear-mothers or from human women impregnated by bears are narrative possibilities all touched upon in this myth and they recur frequently elsewhere.

Bears are not infrequent in Roman literature, owing to the display of large numbers of the animals in the games or *venationes* (animal-hunts) at Rome and throughout the Empire. They were baited as an entertainment, killed in mock hunts, or paired with bulls and other large animals for fights. An episode in Apuleius' novel *Metamorphoses* (*The Golden Ass*, c. 150) tells the story of some robbers who kill bears that are being gathered for such a display in the arena, skin the bears, and, wearing the skins, imitate the animals as a means of escaping capture themselves. The fabulists Aesop and Babrius use bears, though not frequently, as one of the beasts in the world of fable, starting a long tradition in which the modes of literature and folklore overlap. The Roman poet Virgil, in an often-repeated anecdote, compared his slow process of composing verses to the way a mother bear licks her cubs into shape.

Although bears are not frequently referred to in the Bible, they were given important symbolic values by the interpretations of the Church Fathers and other early Christian writers. As a ferocious predator, the bear symbolizes the Devil or evil in general. David slays a bear and a lion that were preying on his father's flocks, a proof of his strength, which he uses to persuade Saul to let him fight Goliath (1 Sam. 17:34–37). In the Book of Daniel (7:5) a bear with three rows of teeth symbolizes the ferocity of the enemies of Israel. As an animal of overwhelming strength, the bear can symbolize the punishments of an angry God. The children who mock the prophet Elisha are immediately eaten, all forty-two of them, by two she-bears in answer to the prophet's curse (2 Kings 2:24).

In the lives of the saints the bear is typically mollified and tamed by the holy man and becomes a helpful companion, as was the case with St. Columban, St. Gall, St. Corbinian, and St. Romedius, all of whom have a bear as their emblem.

The wild bear has its ferocious side but also can be attractive and amusing, as it harvests berries, searches for honey, and escorts its playful cubs. The dual nature of the bear is summed up in the figure of the animal displayed by an itinerant bear leader, who makes his companion dance and perform tricks to amuse on-lookers. Exhibition of the animals like this should be considered as a more or less continuous source of images of the bear. References to performing bears occur as early as the fourth century B.C. in Athens, and there are numerous representations of bears harnessed and on leashes in all periods of Western art. The control of the human over the wild animal is given a visual symbol, while the almost human configuration of the standing bear is reinforced, a possibility that is heightened if, as often, the bear is dressed in human clothes. At the same time, the image of the dancing bear may be pathetic, insofar as a strong animal out of the wild has been forced to perform trivial tricks.

The presence of the bear in folklore and in oral traditions is very widespread. The songs of the Ainu people in northern Japan have the bear as one of their principal figures. A bear ceremony among these people, involving the capture, feeding, and ritual killing of the animal, was an important communal religious event. Tangun, the legendary founder of Korea, the land of Bright Morning, was the son of a heavenly god and she-bear. Finnish traditional poetry, collected in the *Kalevala* by Elias Lönnrot (1835), includes legends of the origin of bears, tales of bear hunts, and the texts of bear charms. This tradition appears to be very old and to show a close connection between humans and bears. The myths and tales of the natives of the Pacific Northwest use both the black bear and the grizzly among their important animal figures. The legend of the female berry-picker who, after mocking a bear, is abducted by him and gives birth to a bear-son is a basic narrative pattern. In the Old Norse (Icelandic) *Hrólfs saga kraka* (*King Hrolf's Saga* c. 1250–1350) the hero, Bothvar Bjarki (Warlike Little Bear), is the son of Bjorn (Bear) and Bera (She-bear). Bjorn is a bear by day and a human by night. The folktale motifs that underlie this story are also present to some extent in the Anglo-Saxon epic *Beowulf* (c. 8th century), whose hero's name may possibly mean Bee-wolf, that is, enemy to bees, the honey-loving bear. The best known of the medieval beast epics is Reynard the Fox, in which Bruin the Bear plays a large role. His craving for honey causes him to be cruelly tricked by the wily fox.

Bear-baiting as a spectacle was popular from the early Renaissance both in Europe and in England. Noble families obtained and kept bears in pits for this purpose. The spectacle was also a public entertainment, most famously in the Beargarden in London that was near Shakespeare's Globe Theater and competed with it for customers. Among numerous references to bears in Shakespeare's plays, allusions that would have gained in vividness from the popularity of bear-baiting, Macbeth's lines (*Macbeth*, 5.7; 1605–1606) comparing himself in defeat to a bear tied to a stake are the most powerful, while the famous stage-direction, "Exit, pursued by a bear" (*The Winter's Tale*, 3.3; 1611), is the most intriguing. From the early Renaissance onward bears appear commonly in emblems, heraldry, and popular imagery. Spenser exploits much of this in his poems; there are ten bear-images in *The Faerie Queene* (1590–1596), and the animal appears as an allegorical figure in the narrative. The French novel *Valentin et Orson* (*Valentine and Orson*, 1489) was extremely popular for several centuries. Orson, one of the brother-heroes, is lost by his mother in a forest as a baby and is raised by a bear-family, living with them for no less than fifteen years.

The seventeenth and eighteenth centuries produce few striking examples of the literary use of the bear, although there are constant minor uses of it as an example of savagery and roughness. Samuel Johnson, for instance, was compared to a bear because of his unkempt appearance and gruff manner. Robinson Crusoe's man Friday overcomes a bear in an amusing but not very convincing fight when he is brought back to Europe.

The nineteenth century is rich in examples of the literary bear, the impulse coming from the romantic interest in nature, the wild, and the primitive. The Grimm's collection of folk stories (1812–1822) has several in which the bear appears as a friendly creature, and their publication set the fashion for other similar national collections and imitations. In von Kleist's *Über das Marionettentheater* (*On the Puppet-Theater*, 1810) the narrator, visiting an estate in Russia, defeats his host's sons in fencing but cannot defeat a bear that is kept on the estate and that fences with its paws. This defeat, in the context of the essay, can be seen as the failure of art before the strength and natural abilities of a natural creature. Robert Southey's *The Three Bears* (1837) is famous as a literary tale that achieved the status of a folktale. His source appears to have been a family tradition. A private manuscript version of the same tale was composed and illustrated by Eleanor Mure in 1831 but was not published until 1967. Versions of *Goldilocks and the Three Bears*, as the tale came to be known, have been written and illustrated virtually without interruption since Southey's time. Tolstoy's version was published in 1875 in a collection of tales for children. The story can be seen to introduce children to the problem of the relationship between civilization and the wild.

Heine's verse epic *Atta Troll* (1847) elaborates the fable of the dancing bear that escapes back to the wilderness. Set in the Pyrenees, the poem has a bear as hero. He is humanized by being given a wife and several children and by being made to ruminate intellectually. The poem's bear-story is largely the framework for literary satire and political commentary. Atta Troll is finally hunted down while his wife ends up in a Paris zoo.

In Tolstoy's "Okhota pushche nevoli" ("The Bear-Hunt," story, c. 1872), the narrator goes hunting along with a peasant bear-tracker. The narrator's sophisticated and casual attitude toward the bear is contrasted with the peasant's knowledge of, and sympathy with, the animal. At the climax the narrator fails in his attempt to shoot the bear, which then attacks him. He is saved by the peasant, who talks to the bear and tells it to go away. The almost mystical closeness of peasant and bear reveals the educated frivolity of the narrator. (Like much of his fiction, "The Bear-Hunt" has a basis in autobiography; Tolstoy is known to have been mauled by a bear during a hunt.) Chekhov's one-act farce, whose title, *Medved'*, is usually given as *The Bear* (1888), introduces the theme of the socially uncouth, rough-acting man who can nevertheless win the affection of a refined woman. In Ibsen's last play, *Naar vi døde vaagner* (*When We Dead Awaken*, 1899), Maia, the wife of a sculptor, is attracted to a bear-hunter and, abandoning her husband, finally goes away with him to the mountains to find freedom. Ulfheim, the bear-hunter, shares some of the qualities of his prey: solitariness, independence, and unrepressed sexuality.

To the traditions based on the European brown bears were added in the nineteenth century the traits of the North American grizzly. This largest and most feared of American animals generated a tradition of its own based on encounters in the wild reported in explorers' and travellers' accounts. Grizzly Adams became a folk hero along the lines of Davy Crockett or Daniel Boone. Adams was written up widely in books and pamphlets, and he eventually exhibited tamed grizzlies with P. T. Barnum in New York. He and others generated a plethora of hunting and survival stories in which the grizzly epitomizes the savagery of the frontier as it is pushed back by civilization. At the same time the respect and totemic reverence for the bear and the activities of the bear-shamans among some American native peoples were observed and recorded. Theodore Roosevelt's *Hunting the Grisly* (1893) was a late and sophisticated version of this kind of material, with the addition of a well-respected naturalist's observations of the animal in the wild. These accounts are still highly regarded.

The popularization of the teddy bear is associated with Roosevelt. This nursery toy, although hardly literary in itself, works along with such tales as *Goldilocks* to perpetuate the amusing and cuddly aspect of ursine imagery. Although bear-baiting was outlawed in England in the 1830s and in California in the 1860s, the exhibition of trained bears in circuses and of collections of the animals in public zoos continued to supply force to the popularity of the bear as an acceptable wild animal for very young children. The teddy bear becomes a speaking character in *Winnie-the-Pooh* (1926) by A. A. Milne and in *The House at Pooh Corner* (1928). In E. Waugh's *Brideshead Revisited* (1945) Sebastian Flyte carries a stuffed toy bear while he is an undergraduate at Oxford, a sign of his social flippancy and of his delayed maturity. Other such children's bears are innumerable in popular literature. Paddington Bear is also a stuffed toy, while the Little Bear in a series of books illustrated by Maurice Sendak is a sensitively humanized creature. The reduction of the bear to a prevalent nursery figure may be the adult's way of indicating to the child that children must be tamed and civilized in the same way that the fierce beast has been transformed into a plaything or harmless companion. Many other interpretations of the phenomenon could obviously be advanced.

William Faulkner's *The Bear* (1942) is the classic among modern stories about the animal. It richly exploits many themes associated with the bear within the typically American hunter's tale. The youth Ike McCauslin learns courage in a rite of passage, advances further into adulthood, and has an encounter with the mystery of reality. The shadowy and numinous bear of the story is at once frightening, noble, and pathetic, the last representative of the wilderness receding before civilization and a symbol of primordial intelligence violently destroyed. Many literary uses of the bear that follow Faulkner's story can be more or less explicitly related to it. In Marian Engel's *Bear* (novel, 1976), a Toronto librarian goes to an old house on a remote island, where, living by herself, she befriends a real bear. The gradual weakening of her urban frustrations leads her to fall in love with the animal, with whom she engages in sexual activity but whom she must desert to return to the city. The sexes of such a relationship are reversed in Stanley Elkin's novella *The Making of Ashenden* (1973). A wealthy, blasé young man's life is quite changed when he encounters a she-bear in a game-park and copulates with her. Norman Mailer's *Why Are We in Viet Nam? A Novel* (1967) has two young heroes who go on a hunt for grizzlies in Alaska and have a vision of nature undisturbed as they watch bears grazing above the Arctic Circle. John Irving has a theme of bears running through several of his novels, while humans who disguise themselves as bears appear in Edzard Schaper's novel *Das Tier* (*The Dancing Bear*, 1958) and in Sławomir Mrożek's play *Vatzlav* (1970). The bear as the conventional emblem of Russia lends some contemporary European writing in which bears occur a clear political implication.

See also: Hunt, Metamorphosis, Monsters, Werewolf.

Selected Bibliography

Edinger, Harry G. "Bears in Three Contemporary Fictions." *The Humanities Association Review* 28 (1977): 141–150.
———. "Episodes in the History of the Literary Bear." *Mosaic* 4 (1970): 1–12.
Jones, Gwyn. *Kings, Beasts and Heroes*. London: Oxford University Press, 1972.
Storer, Tracy I., and Lloyd P. Tevis. *California Grizzly*. Lincoln: University of Nebraska Press, 1978.

                                                                HARRY G. EDINGER

BEAT GENERATION

The beat generation was a group of American writers, primarily novelists and poets, emerging after World War II and characterized by their own mutual friendships, by a set of political and social attitudes roughly held in common, and by their appearance in particular literary outlets, rather than by congruent stylistic and philosophical approaches. "Beat" in this usage encompasses for the members of this coterie a variety of meanings and implications, including the following: beaten down, hopelessly alienated and discouraged; the rhythmic beat of musical composition, especially of contemporary jazz; the beating of the heart as a symbol of love and vitality; and the beatific, spiritual quest for meaning and value in life. As a strong, visible, and cohesive literary movement, the beat generation thrived between 1956 and 1961, but its leading figures (Jack Kerouac, William S. Burroughs, Allen Ginsberg, and Lawrence Ferlinghetti) have been artistically productive well beyond that period, and the group has influenced subsequent writers in subject matter and style.

History

Although several important novels by beat generation writers appeared in the early 1950s (Kerouac's *The Town and the City* in 1950, John Clellon Holmes' *Go* in 1952, and Burroughs' *Junkie* in 1953) and Holmes had focused attention on the group in an article, "This Is the Beat Generation," appearing in the *New York Times* in 1952, the literature and life styles of the beats did not begin to have a national impact until 1957, when Kerouac's novel *On the Road* appeared and Ginsberg's *Howl and Other Poems* (1956), published by Ferlinghetti's City Lights Books, was on trial in San Francisco on obscenity charges. The next few years witnessed a torrent of significant publications by beat generation writers and the emergence of periodicals offering quality outlets sympathetic to the movement, notably *Evergreen Review* in 1957 and *Big Table* in 1959, the latter founded to publish Kerouac's poem "Old Angel Midnight" and sections from Burroughs' novel *Naked Lunch*, which had been planned for publication in the *Chicago Review* but had been suppressed by university officials. Response to the writings of the beat generation was sharply divided. They were greeted by a hysteria that seemed common both to their admirers, who viewed them as literary and societal saviors, and to their detractors, who saw them as scourges of literature and society. The unconventional behavior and attitudes of the beats often seemed calculated to arouse polarized reactions, and their writings cultivated public controversy and consternation. By 1961 the beat generation movement had begun to disintegrate. Kerouac had already composed his major works, Burroughs was in Tangiers, Ginsberg had left for India, and *Big Table* had ceased publication. The individual social and political stances of the beat generation caused internal frictions and led to animosity and estrangement. Ginsberg became aligned with the emerging hippie culture. In 1968 Neal Cassady, a Byronic adventurer who had served as a model and prototype for many of the beat generation writers, was found dead, and Kerouac died in 1969, in effect marking the end of the beat generation.

Political and Social Attitudes

Although the writers of the beat generation cannot be described as endorsing a systematic program of political or social beliefs, their writings share significant attitudes toward government and society. Often accused of being un-American, they exhibited an idiosyncratic patriotism, subscribing enthusiastically to the ideals upon which America was founded, the spirit Kerouac described in *On the*

Road as "the wild yea-saying overburst of American joy"; at the same time they decried what they considered a contemporary nightmare of racism, poverty, capital punishment, overpopulation, and the threat of atomic warfare. The majority of beat writers professedly assumed apolitical and amoral stances, but they found themselves repeatedly addressing the critical issues of the day. For the most part, the beat generation seemed to adhere to Walt Whitman's advice, "Resist much, obey little," condemning contemporary society for violating and deadening the imaginative capacity, poisoning the wellsprings of vitality in the individual, and even alienating human beings from their own bodies. They advocated a new social order and the creation of a new consciousness, which virtually forced them into a position of rebellion against the established figures of authority and the concomitant castigation of these figures. They were outspoken and adamant in their distrust and criticism of governments, of the machinations of politics, and of the entangling networks of the bureaucratic system.

One of the most frequent clarions in their work is the call for the dissolution of nationalism in favor of internationalism, yet this is a call that can only be considered viable through the highly developed systems of communication and transportation nurtured technologically within nationalistic structures. Their common outbursts against police forces stem at least in part from the paranoia that accompanies their violation of the law, particularly in the forms of theft, homosexuality, and drug use. The bitter criticisms by the beat generation must be viewed alongside America's lionization of them and its proselytism, however unintentional, of their concerns and beliefs. The rebellion of these writers is, thus, necessarily tempered by a grudging affection, a simultaneous attraction and repulsion portrayed by Ginsberg in his poem "Howl": "we hug and kiss the United States under our bedsheets the United States that coughs all night and won't let us sleep." Assuming that the undermining of positive humanistic values in America has resulted from dependence on intellection and logical systems, the beat generation celebrates the attractiveness of alternative states of consciousness, especially the subconscious and unconscious, imagination, visions, mysticism, and drug-induced hallucinations. Both in their literature and in their lives, they abjure restraint, tirelessly and recklessly cultivating "kicks" and ecstasies, subjecting their bodies to the vagaries of the weather, to the lower reaches of poverty, to alternating bouts of drunkenness and abstention and of sexual promiscuity and celibacy, and to extreme varieties and dosages of drugs. They tramp across the country from coast to coast and back again and beyond the American borders to Mexico, Europe, Northern Africa, India, and Russia, searching always for vitality, energy, and excitement, but only managing to discover that ecstasy dissolves into ennui, debilitation, and desolation.

Major Writers and Literary Contributions

Jack Kerouac, who coined the epithet "beat generation," was its leading literary spokesman and cataloguer of the beat life style. His first novel, *The Town and the City*, a sprawling chronicle in the tradition of Thomas Wolfe, lays the foundation for the spirit of discontent and rebellion that informs the later novels. *On the Road*, which, according to Ginsberg, was once "a magnificent single paragraph several blocks long," was edited into a more conventional form and established Kerouac's reputation. The novel consists of five sections, the first four of which spring from gloom and boredom, swell to an exhilarating joie de vivre, and then crash to broken images and rhythms; the last section provides a brief, lyrical epilogue concluding with serene and graceful sadness. The novel traces the adventures of a group of rootless, adventurous young adults as they roam across America and into Mexico searching for some sense of meaning and significance in their lives. The protagonists court a world of sensation, rejecting conventional mores and standards, pursuing frenetic but directionless activity, jazz, drugs, sex, and petty thievery—all without apology. The novel's prose style, though presumably severely attenuated by editorial changes, retains a subtle, fluid elasticity that Kerouac saw as paralleling the rhythms of improvisational jazz.

The Subterraneans (1958), which was Kerouac's first novel to be published without editorial modifications, is emancipated in style, moving swiftly, powerfully, with streaming, convoluted sentence patterns building to an abrupt conclusion which culminates both the novel and the complex romantic affair that is its subject. The story rushes along in extended bursts of spontaneous prose designed to capture both excitement and psychological honesty without the supposedly contaminating intrusion of artistic self-consciousness and artifice. Kerouac's purpose was to capture as accurately as possible the qualities of spoken language uttered without design, simply plunging into narrative, description, and reflection with no restraint, an embodiment of the reckless pursuit of experience typical of the characters in the novel. *Visions of Cody*, written in 1951–1952 but published in its entirety only in 1972, focuses on a prototype of the energetic and convention-flouting mid-century American hero, physically robust, open to experience of every kind, and throbbing with sheer intensity of feeling and sensation. The prose is experimentally daring, "following free deviation (association) of mind into limitless blow-on-subject seas of thought, swimming in sea of English with no discipline other than rhythms of rhetorical exhalation and expostulated statement, like a fist coming down on a table with each complete utterance, bang! (the space dash)." The novel is a massive, rambling, allusive prose reverie incorporating stylized transcriptions and imitations of taped conversations. The result is a charged and expressive exploration of the heights and depths of undisciplined life, variously evocative of the meaningless boredom of daily existence and of the intensities of life spent in quest of experience.

The prose works of William S. Burroughs raised considerable controversy because of their stylistic and structural experimentation and their focus on violence, scatology, sexual perversion, and drug addiction. His major novels can be divided into three phases. *Junkie* and *Naked Lunch* (1959), his first published books, establish his themes, style, and structure. In these novels the world of drug addiction is used to symbolize all forms of domination and control in contemporary society, including mass media, politics, capital punishment, racism, sadomasochism, and sexuality in any form. His prose style combines the flat, clipped succinctness of hard-boiled detective fiction with a fragmented, descriptive lyricism, structurally episodic, at times modular, with rapid fade-outs and cuts, coherence emerging by indirection, juxtaposition, and thematic overlay rather than through plot or continuity. The second phase includes *The Soft Machine* (1961), *The Ticket That Exploded* (1962), and *Nova Express* (1964), a trilogy of radical and often bewildering experiments. These novels pursue the theme of addictive control and the death-sex-domination links to a galactic level, projecting human weaknesses and limitations as imposed by viral agents from beyond this planet who inflict on humanity physiological and verbal dependency. These agents assert their control biologically and stunt the human evolutionary process at a point where reversion to lower life forms happens uncontrollably.

In the novels of this period, Burroughs' prose style is professedly designed to destroy verbal tyranny, to "cut word lines" that dictate human behavior and attitudes. To effect this attack, he employs the "cut-up" and "fold-in" techniques: in the cut-up, pages of manuscript are literally cut into sections, rearranged, and then incorporated into the text; in the fold-in, pages are folded vertically down the middle and aligned to form a composite page. The result of each device is aleatory creation, arbitrary juxtapositions that violate conventional syntactical patterns and expectations and disturb the usually comfortable reaction of the reader to the page, while often disturbing too clarity and intelligibility. The third phase of Burroughs' development includes *The Wild Boys* (1971), *Exterminator!* (1973), *Port of Saints* (1973), and *Cities of the Red Night* (1981), fantasy novels of interpenetrating time sequences, spatial leaps, and character shifts. These later novels are much more accessible than those of the second phase because Burroughs, alternating experimental sections with straight narrative passages, exercises more control over his innovations rather than allowing them to assert their own chaotic autonomy. The novels continue to explore the themes of power and control and to project futuristic alternatives to the culture and institutions of contemporary society. Thus, the wild boys comprise a voluntarily international and an entirely male community determined to dissolve the family, the nation, and the word. They are no longer earth-bound, word-bound, flesh-bound, or death-bound, a self-sufficient humanoid species invulnerable to what Burroughs sees as alien penetration and manipulation of the human nervous system.

Allen Ginsberg's poetry comprises a virtual record of radical American protest since the mid–1950s, together with an intensely personal concern for alternative choices for individual self-realization and for community development. *Howl and Other Poems* employs an adaptation of the Whitmanesque long line in poetic structures ranging from the dithyrambic protests of "Howl" to the conversational humor of "America," a poetry drawing upon natural language, imagery, and rhythms ("to recreate the syntax and measure of poor human prose") in the common American rather than English idiom. "Howl" begins with a litany, an ecstatic and surreal celebration of individual innocence ("angelheaded hipsters") driven to darkness and despair by society and its values: "I saw the best minds of my generation destroyed by madness." Part 2 of the poem constitutes a jeremiad against a cannibalistic, destructive force of capitalistic bureaucracy ("Moloch") that oppresses individuality, an excoriation made in impassioned exclamations and fragments. The third section of the poem returns to the litany structure in an affirmation ("the soul is holy and immortal"), with the responses to the fixed base growing gradually longer and culminating in a rhythmic, prophetic conclusion. "Footnote to Howl" attempts to exorcise the Moloch demon by proclaiming in starkly physical terms the holiness of life even in suffering. "Sunflower Sutra" again employs the long line stanza, this time in a spontaneous poem that balances the images of grimy mechanical corruption in a railroad yard against those of organic nature and Blake's "naked human form divine." "America" offers a more variable structure filled with street diction and language providing both a refusal to accept contemporary values and a reminder of the country's identity and glory, together with the speaker's commitment to work toward the refurbishing of those ideals. *Kaddish and Other Poems* (1961) opens with the poet's attempt to come to terms with his mother's madness and death, exploring "the broken consciousness of mid twentieth century suffering anguish of separation from my own body and its natural infinity of feeling its own self one with all self," and focusing, especially in the latter poems of the volume, on the role of drugs as a catalyst in achieving that unity insofar as they allow the poet to "Widen the area of consciousness." In *Planet News* (1968), the tensions of the earlier volumes are resolved in "The Change: Kyoto-Tokyo Express," where the poet finally comes to an acceptance of self and physical being, despite all the betrayals of the frail human body and the sordid desolation of human awareness. In "Wales Visitation" the visionary embrace of the natural crests in a rhapsodic intermingling of the human body and the earth in a mystical union Ginsberg later calls "man wedded to Earth." In "Wichita Vortex Sutra," the stage expands from the personal to the political front, registering protest against the war in Vietnam and the manipulation of Americans by the mass media's distortion of language toward commercial and inhumane ends. *The Fall of America* (1972), an epic travel commentary, offers Ginsberg's most controlled and ambitious criticisms. The poet begins with an American locale and proceeds to an associative analysis of the character of the United States. Road signs, advertisements, newspaper headlines, popular songs, and historical data all emerge from the setting and are incorporated in the poem, providing through their accumulation and interplay a critical evaluation, with selected images combining to elicit a cultural statement.

In the spring of 1957, Lawrence Ferlinghetti and Kenneth Rexroth engaged in a series of experiments reading their poetry to a jazz accompaniment in a San Francisco nightclub, The Cellar. Although the experiments were not entirely successful, their significance cannot be denied. They reveal the poets and their audiences straining against the restrictions and confines of the printed word.

They also reveal two crucial aspects of Ferlinghetti's poetry: his concentration on the sound of his poems and his attraction to improvisational spontaneity in oral presentation. His first volume, *Pictures of the Gone World* (1955), is a collection of lyrics with a strong emphasis on sound, and alliteration and assonance play a dominant role. In addition, these poems show the influence of e e cummings, as Ferlinghetti uses typographical delineation, the patterns the lines take on the page, to reflect the swing of the rhythm, to graph the beat, or to portray the meaning in visual emblematic terms. *A Coney Island of the Mind* (1958) continues these experiments in poems that tend more and more toward political and social commentary. He also sharpens his focus on language and literature. For example, "sometime during eternity . . ." translates the story of Christ's life into hip jargon, and "Constantly risking absurdity . . ." creates an extended comparison between acrobats and poets. The volume also contains seven poems identified specifically as "Oral Messages," conceived for jazz accompaniment and designed for spontaneity, "still in a state of change." *Starting from San Francisco* (1961) continues Ferlinghetti's social concerns and introduces "Tentative Description of a Dinner to Promote the Impeachment of President Eisenhower" and "One Thousand Fearful Words for Fidel Castro," which the poet describes as populist broadsides in the genre of the "political-satirical tirade," forms he later used also in *Tyrannus Nix?* (1969) and "Where Is Vietnam?" in *Open Eye, Open Heart* (1973).

The compositions of the beat generation writers are distinctly individual, but they share three basic characteristics: loose literary construction; colloquial, slang diction and rhythms; and a cultivated appearance of spontaneity. The writers offered their works as an alternative to what they saw as the anemic and sterile academic literature governing twentieth-century American prose and poetry. Their projection of themselves as primitive, natural artists, together with their rejection of formal conventions of punctuation, grammar and syntax, spelling, and logical patterns, gained them reputations as anti-intellectuals or, in Norman Podhoretz's phrase, "Know-Nothing Bohemians." However, most of the writers were college-educated, several even having pursued advanced graduate studies, and had studied under and been encouraged by such eminent university scholars and critics as Mark Van Doren and Lionel Trilling. The quarrel of the beat generation writers was not with the intellect or the academy but with the narrow road of logical conservatism to which they felt these forces were prone at the expense of imagination and sensitivity. As a means of delimiting rational behavior and attitudes, their works embrace surrealism and sensuality, focusing in a highly emotional manner on intensely personal material. As with most highly subjective literature, the quality of their writing encompasses extremes, ranging from self-indulgent depictions of whining self-pity or nugatory delight to passionate embodiments of exhilaration or despair.

See also: Hippie, Rebellion, Utopia.

Selected Bibliography

Bartlett, Lee, ed. *The Beats: Essays in Criticism*. Jefferson, N.C.: MacFarland, 1981.

Nicosia, Gerald. *Memory Babe: A Critical Biography of Jack Kerouac*. New York: Grove, 1983.

Parkinson, Thomas, ed. *A Casebook on the Beat*. New York: Thomas Crowell, 1961.

Tytell, John. *Naked Angels: The Lives and Literatures of the Beat Generation*. New York: McGraw-Hill, 1976.

MICHAEL SKAU

LA BELLE DAME SANS MERCI

The phrase *La Belle Dame sans Merci*, meaning the beautiful lady without pity, was popularized in the nineteenth century when John Keats borrowed the title for his literary ballad (1820) from a medieval poem (1424) of the same name by Alain Chartier. A study of analogues to Keats's poem reveals, however, a potential ambiguity in the meaning of the words. Some stories tell of a woman whose seduction of her lover displays a ruthless disregard for his well-being or for the fate of the persons or even nations that depend on him. But another group of tales depicts a similar woman whose motive for attaching herself to him involves some punishment that only he can abate or a deficiency which can only be made up for in a union with him. Then it is she who must be pitied and *merci* may be the grace that only her lover can bestow. As a term now in popular use, *La Belle Dame sans Merci* is often used interchangeably with *femme fatale* (fatal woman) to describe a dangerous seductress who destroys the man who loves her. It is, however, useful to distinguish between two kinds of literary figures and see *La Belle Dame sans Merci* as the supernatural enchantress whose magic realm is as symbolically important as she, the theme merging with that of the Earthly Paradise or Enchanted Garden. In contrast, the *femme fatale* is mortal, although the psychology behind the two motifs is often similar, as are the story patterns in which supernatural and mortal women appear. Both motifs are ubiquitous in the folklore, legend, and literature of the world, reflecting as they do complex attitudes toward women and the feminine attributes of the human capacity to fantasize about that which the real world does not yield.

Folklore

The *Belle Dame sans Merci* theme has many of its roots in the virtually universal popular belief that beyond the human realm there exists another world peopled by creatures who physically resemble humans and who mate with them. The fairies who attach themselves to human lovers can be divided into malevolent and benign beings, although the two are not readily distinguishable by the unwary mortal—an ambiguity that later writers would exploit to depict their own ambivalent attitudes toward the realm of the imagination. The evil fairies are often interpreted as emissaries of a demonic world who entice humans into their realm, sometimes because the human soul represents a tithe paid to the devil in whose service they are. Behind the Middle English popular ballad, "Thomas Rhymer," later expanded into the medieval romance of *Thomas of Erceldoune* (2nd half of 13th century), lies such folklore. Similar themes inform the Irish stories of Oisin and Connla and the German Tannhäuser. The more benign fairies seek a mortal man to compensate for some deficiency in their own existences. In the sixteenth century, Paracelsus offered an explanation of their quest when he explained the nature spirits (e.g., the undines) who resemble humans in all aspects except in the possession of a soul, and who consequently are willing to surrender their carefree lives to marry a mortal, experience human suffering, and thereby win spiritual immortality. Paracelsus' explanation influenced later writers, particularly the nineteenth-century German, Friedrich de la Motte Fouqué, whose tale *Undine* (1811) was the source of Hans Christian Andersen's "Den Lille havfrue" ("The Little Sea Maid," 1837) and the twentieth-century French play by Jean Giraudoux, *Ondine* (1939). These works are also reflected in Thomas Mann's novel *Doktor Faustus* (1947), in which the fairy's world becomes the unreal realm of the artist cut off from humans' social concerns. Closely related to this folk and literary motif are the stories of the Animal Brides in which the *Belle Dame sans Merci* is sometimes an animal or reptile who awaits disenchantment by her lover. Again, the motif can take a malign form, as in the stories of the serpentine Lamia (also, popularized by Keats), or a benign form, such as that known by the world through the story depicted in the ballet *Swan Lake* (1876). The Animal Bride motif is also associated with the Loathly Lady theme, perhaps known best in Chaucer's *The Wife of Bath's Tale* (c. 1380–1400), in which the hero weds an ugly hag only to see her transformed into a beautiful woman when he has come to accept the meaning of the answer to the riddle of what it is that women most want: domination over their husbands. Finally, folklorists frequently distinguish between two types of fairy mistresses, the aggressively imperious ones typified in Celtic lore, and the more passive Swan Maiden type associated with German mythology.

Demonology

Because of the malign characteristics of the *Belle Dame sans Merci*, she is often portrayed as a witch, vampire, revenant, succubus, or other creature from the hellish regions of the dead or damned. It is easy to see how popular notions that temptresses in league with the devil would seduce mortals to steal their souls could merge with the belief in witchcraft, since witches were often conceived of as paramours of the devil who similarly tempted men into the service of unholy powers. A bizarre twist to this theme has to do with the succubus. According to ideas whose source has been traced to various places, even the Bible, the devil could assume the form of either male or female to copulate with mortals. In the form of the incubus he often impregnated women, who, depending on the particular account, gave birth to monsters or heroes. As a succubus the devil gathered the necessary sperm. (Again, there are more benign versions of this motif, and the goddess Thetis can be seen as a *Belle Dame sans Merci* who gave birth to Achilles after her union with the mortal Peleus.) The succubus appeared to men in their sleep in order to have sexual relations with them, often making such excessive demands as to lead to their lovers' deaths. More, however, has been written about the incubus than the succubus, probably because during the witchcraft craze of the fifteenth through seventeenth centuries, more women than men were indicted for witchcraft and the masculine fantasies of their inquisitors were better satisfied by the women who confessed to consorting with their incubi. As the succubus motif merged with other demonic aspects of the *Belle Dame sans Merci* theme, it fed the gothic atmosphere of the late eighteenth and nine-teenth centuries. As demon, vampire, or revenant, the fairy shows up in such works as Goethe's ballad "Die Braut von Korinth" ("The Bride of Corinth," 1797), Coleridge's "Christabel" (poem, 1816), and Poe's "Ligeia" (story, 1840). In the decadent literature of the late nineteenth century, images of vam-pirism or necrophilia would be used in portraits of *femmes fatales* in the works of Flaubert, Gautier, Swinburne, and others.

Biblical Literature

Insofar as there is a virtually universal tendency to polarize women and see them as whores or saints, temptresses or redemptresses, punishing or good mothers, it can be claimed that the *Belle Dame sans Merci* and *femme fatale* are daughters of Eve. To attribute all evils in the world to figures such as Eve or Pandora reflects a pervasive view of women as destructive of the masculine order. As a significant ancestress of *La Belle Dame sans Merci*, however, Lilith is still more compelling. According to the Talmudic tradition, she was the first wife of Adam, expelled from Eden, supposedly for her refusal to accept Ad-am's dominant role. In Jewish folklore, Lilith preys on mothers, killing their children, and is thus associated with the lore of the vampire and the Greek Lamia. Lilith appears in Goethe's play *Faust* (1808), and in Mann's *Der Zauberberg* (*The Magic Mountain*, 1924) she is associated with Clavdia Chauchat, the *Belle Dame sans Merci* of that novel. But it is in Dante Ga-briel Rossetti's poem, *Eden Bower* (1881), that many of the associations with Lilith converge. She is depicted as entwined with a serpent, making love to it, promising herself to it if it will help her revenge herself on Ad-am's new wife, Eve. Thus it is Lilith who initiates the fall of man.

The Classical Period

The *Belle Dame sans Merci* and *femme fatale* motifs can be found in the Greek and Roman epics. In his epic *Odysseia* (*Odyssey*, c. 8th century B.C.), Homer portrays some of the most famous temptresses, Circe, the Sirens, and Calypso. Again, it is possible to see more or less malign and benign facets of the motifs operating. Circe is the witch who turns her victims into beasts after their orgies of pleasure in her domain. But Calypso is dangerous for Odysseus only insofar as his enthrallment impedes his journey back to Ithaca where he must assume his responsibilities as ruler, husband, and father. (*La Belle Dame sans Merci* is frequently pitted against the hero's mortal wife or sweetheart, whose rival she is. So popular is this pattern that when Georges Bizet wrote his opera *Carmen* (1875), he added a character absent in Prosper Merimée's tale (1845), Micaela, Don Jose's virtuous sweetheart.) Playing a role similar to Calypso's is Virgil's Dido, from whom the hero of the epic *Aeneis* (*Aeneid*, 19 B.C.) must wrench himself to fulfill his destiny to found Rome. And from the classical period would also come the *femme fatale*, Cleopatra, although it would await Shakespeare to place her in the tradition of Homer's and Virgil's seductresses. And, finally, there is the archetypal *femme fatale*, who from the Trojan legends on had captured the literary imagination as a symbol of the allure of ideal beauty: Helen. As *femmes fatales* go, however, the Greek Helen is a rather passive temptress, although in later centuries she would at times assume the more aggressive and demonic attributes of *La Belle Dame sans Merci*, for example in D. G. Rossetti's poem *Troy Town* (1881).

When the Christians sought to convert heathens, they did not preach that the pagan deities were mere fictions. Rather they convinced their converts that they were demons, falsely worshipped as gods. From this position comes the demonic Venus of two popular legends. First, there is the goddess beloved by Tannhäuser, who dwells in the Venusberg until fear for his soul impels him to leave his supernatural mistress and journey to Rome, where the knight fails to win forgiveness from the pope and must dwell with the demonic goddess until Judgment Day. Second, there is a group of stories that tell of a youth, an athlete, who places his wedding ring on a statue of the goddess while participating in the games celebrating his marriage. Venus interferes between him and his bride when he attempts to consummate his marriage, and her power over him can only be broken through exorcism rites. These legends concerning Venus come long after the classical period, of course, but they reveal a link to a much older source and Christianity's lingering ties to the pagan tradition out of which it was partially born. In the nineteenth and twentieth centuries, the Tannhäuser story was widely told in England and Germany by William Morris, Swinburne, Heinrich Heine, Richard Wagner, Thomas Mann, and others. The less popular Venusring legend is found in Joseph von Eichendorff's story *Das Marmorbild* (*The Marble Statue*, 1819), Merimée's tale *La Vénus d'Ille* (*The Venus of Ille*, 1837), Henry James's short story "The Last of the Valerii," (1874) and recently by Anthony Burgess in *The Eve of St. Venus* (novel, 1964).

The Middle Ages

The *Belle Dame sans Merci* motif in the Middle Ages can be found in four quite distinct areas. There are the dangerous witches, Vivien and Morgain la fée of the Arthurian tales. Second, there are also the famous adulteresses, whose tales would be told for centuries, Iseult and Guinevere, although it would take the English Victorian imagination to turn them into full-fledged *femmes fatales*, Guinevere to Camelot what Eve was to Eden. Third, there are the fairy mistresses of the *Lais* (short romances, c. 1170) of Marie de France; the romances of

Chrétien de Troyes (in the *Contes del Graal*, [*Story of the Grail*, c. 1190], Orguelleuse de Logres is specifically referred to as a *pucele sanz merci*), whose mortal heroines have been traced back to the Celtic fairies; and the German romance *Peter von Staufenberg* (c. 1310), in which is a motif frequently associated with *La Belle Dame sans Merci*. Staufenberg's fairy mistress enters into a relationship with him subject to a condition (taboo) that he fails to live up to, thereby losing her. A taboo is similarly a primitive motif in the popular medieval tale of *Mélusine* (*Romance of Melusine*, c. 1390) by Jean d'Arras. Because of a punishment she is suffering, Melusine must assume one day each week the shape of a serpent, and she warns her husband not to spy on her during her periodic seclusion. When curiosity over the mysterious nature of his wife overcomes him, he defies this condition to learn what happens to her during this time, and Melusine loses her chance for an immortal soul as well as release from her beastly form. Shrieking horribly, she leaves her house and family in the form of a fifteen-foot serpent. Melusine is associated with the Celtic Banshee, the Lamia motif, and stories of Loathly Ladies.

The fourth *Belle Dame sans Merci* in the Middle Ages is the adored object of the Courtly Lover. This subject has to be treated separately; it is worth noting, however, that the lady in Courtly Love literature is often as passive as Troy's Helen (for example, the heroine of Chaucer's *The Franklin's Tale* [c. 1380–1400]). But that her lover pines away or is driven to desperate acts out of passion for her makes her an ancestress of the crueller women of later periods, the indifferent Carmens or Manons who are willing to exploit their lovers for their own ends and then cast them aside.

The Renaissance

The most famous Renaissance *Belles Dames sans Merci* can be found in the great literary epics of the period: Alcina in Ariosto's *Orlando furioso* (1516) and Armida in Torquato Tasso's *Gerusalemme liberata* (1581) were among the influences that helped create Acrasia in Edmund Spenser's *The Faerie Queene* (1590–1596). In these epics, the enchantress inhabits a magic realm, an enchanted garden named by Spenser the Bower of Bliss, a false paradise into which the hero is lured, and whose destruction is necessary, for it represents the temptations that the Christian soul must reject. The lover fast asleep in Acrasia's embrace as his armor lies nearby unused provides a gloss on Shakespeare's *femme fatale*, Cleopatra, for whom Antony neglects his duties. Behind this pairing of *La Belle Dame sans Merci* and her soldier lover is the myth of Mars and Venus, caught in their illicit liaison by Vulcan's net as the other Olympian gods jeered at them. It was the tendency of the Renaissance to allegorize this classical motif, and the net symbolizes the internal traps into which man falls when he becomes prey to *La Belle Dame sans Merci*.

The Romantic Age

In an age noted for the growth of empirical sciences, enlightenment, and political satire, fairy mistresses in enchanted gardens are less likely to be popular subjects for literature. Alexander Pope's mock epic, *The Rape of the Lock* (1712), contains in effect a mock *femme fatale*, Belinda, whose temper tantrums replace the danger or fury—or even the sorrow—of a Venus, a Lilith, a Melusine, a Lamia, or Keats' Faery Child. After the Renaissance, the *Belle Dame sans Merci* motif suffered an eclipse, overshadowed as she was by the victimized woman, the descendents of Richardson's *Clarissa* (novel, 1748), which had an enormous influence throughout the continent. But in the nineteenth century *La Belle Dame sans Merci* experienced a powerful rebirth. A profound change in philosophical ideas focused the artistic imagination on the inner world of the creative beings whose dreams of a perfection not to be known on earth were suddenly endowed with psychological validity as the line between reality and fantasy was blurred. The fairy mistress now ruled over a shadowy realm whose values could no longer be summarily dismissed but whose danger was not thereby any the diminished. At the same time, in a world made gray by the growth of science and technology, the Philistine interests of a rising middle class and utilitarian philosophies, all of which reduced the world of fantasy to triviality, artists sought in art itself a way of escaping the ordinary life. *La Belle Dame sans Merci* thus became one of the romantic muses, and the domain of the fairy became what Alfred Lord Tennyson would later call the Palace of Art. But whether the supernatural mistress was a demon who lured the writer from a healthy life based on a firm rooting in the reality principle or a pathetic Undine or Lady of Shalott seeking her salvation in the artist's power to make art itself a viable force in the real world depended upon the writer who told her tale and his particular view at the time he told it. In Germany Keats's contemporaries told tales analogous to his: Ludwig Tieck's novelle *Der Runenberg* (1804) and E.T.A. Hoffmann's *Die Bergwerke zu Falun* (*The Mines of Falun*, 1819) treated themes also found in the work of Hugo von Hofmannsthal, Richard Wagner, L. Achim von Arnim, and Novalis. In England, Keats's successors focused on the Tannhäuser story, while the Irish poet William Butler Yeats wrote about the analogous *Wanderings of Oisin* (poem, 1899). In France, despite the Celtic origins of many fairy mistress tales and the popularity of *Mélusine*, the *Belle Dame sans Merci* motif did not enthrall writers as it had in England and Germany (with the exception of Gérard de Nerval). French writers concentrated instead on the *femme fatale*. Merimée introduced to the world perhaps the most famous of all, Carmen, and both French and Italian opera borrowed from the eighteenth-century novel by l'Abbé Prévost, *Manon Lescaut* (1731). Again, the *femme fatale* motif merged with others, for another form of escape from mundane reality was a total commitment to the life of the senses, and the sensual pleasures offered by the fatal woman brought back into literature the excesses associated with vampirism, occultism, witchcraft, necrophilia, demoniac possession, and other forms of demonology. In England Aubrey Beardsley wrote the *Story of Venus and Tannhäuser* (often called *Under the Hill*, 1959), and the equivalent of Keats's elfin grot became a pornographic fantasy.

Modern Literature

The realism of modern literature has effected a shift away from the *Belle Dame sans Merci* toward the kind of *femmes fatales* depicted in the novels of F. Scott Fitzgerald. The love of Gatsby for Daisy in *The Great Gatsby* (1925) fuses the theme of the fatal woman with that of the American Dream. It is, however, probably most profitable to study both kinds of temptresses in negative terms, that is, to look at their demise in literature. Modern feminism does not look kindly at the polarization of woman into her antithetical types, since the male obsession with feminine evil is seen as but the other side of the coin of the so-called idealization of woman—a supposedly civilizing force. But perhaps the most fatal blow to be dealt to the *Belle Dame sans Merci* motif comes from the dulling of the human imagination itself in a world given over to what Wordsworth called the dreary intercourse of daily life and the light of common day. Prufrock, in T. S. Eliot's poem "The Love Song of J. Alfred Prufrock" (c. 1917), fears that he is so representative of modern man that the mermaids will not bother to sing to him. Even more devastating is the less famous sonnet by C. Day Lewis, "Nearing Again the Legendary Isle" (1933). The voices in the poem are modern-day mariners travelling the route of Odysseus, persons for whom the sirens are but "chorus-girls . . . surely past their prime." Is there any worse commentary on modern life that such men need no longer be tied to the mast and can pass on without either stopping their ears or averting their eyes from the sirens?

See also: Incubus and Succubus, Love in Greek and Roman Literature, Seduction.

Selected Bibliography

Fass, Barbara. *La Belle Dame sans Merci and the Aesthetics of Romanticism*. Detroit: Wayne State University Press, 1974.

Giamatti, A. Bartlett. *The Earthly Paradise and the Renaissance Epic*. Princeton, N.J.: Princeton University Press, 1966.

Praz, Mario. *The Romantic Agony*. New York: Meridian Books, 1956.

BARBARA FASS LEAVY

BIRTH OF THE HERO

The theme of the birth of the hero from a god (Achilles, Theseus, Aeneas, Jesus) or his having in some way a divine origin (Adam and Eve, Tennyson's Arthur) is related to the attitude that heroism is a gift from the gods, not least when the hero's is a spiritual heroism. This attitude is expressed in the mysterious origin (or the mystery about the origin) of the hero in literature as divergent as the stories of the Gautama Buddha and the American Western (Jack Schaefer's *Shane* [1949], Owen Wister's *The Virginian* [1902], with the archetype going back to

Natty Bumppo in James Fenimore Cooper's *Leatherstocking Tales* [1823–1841]). It is the recognition that the genesis of heroism, whether historical, spiritual, or psychological, perhaps eludes us and cannot be accounted for on natural grounds alone. Allied to this theme is the further theme that because the hero represents a higher order of reality he threatens the order into which he is born and so must be protected until he matures.

The theme of the birth of the hero developed here is made especially clear by relating it to the biblical creation stories, a central archetype in Western culture, and a version of the theme that can illuminate its use in secular literature. Illustrations over the range of literature (especially in English) will indicate the importance of the theme in its hold on the human imagination and man's questing spirit. More developed examples will be drawn from Spenser, Shakespeare, Sterne, and Tennyson to show the power of the theme among the greatest, more mature writers.

Folklore tells us the stories of births of culture heroes associated with divinity in Irish, Samoan, and Greek myth. Births from virgins are reported in Buddhist myth and legend of India, and stories of children born in answer to prayers are found in Spanish, Italian, Jewish, Indian, Chinese, Japanese, Korean, and West India lore. Immaculate conception stories of culture heroes are also told in Hawaiian and South American Indian legend, as well as in Roman Catholic literature of the Virgin Mary (see Stith Thompson, *Motif-Index of Folk-Literature*, 1955–1958).

Greek mythology has many stories of heroes born from the gods, among them Helen of Troy, born from Leda and the Swan (Zeus); Theseus, born of Aethra and Poseidon; Persephone, born of Demeter and Zeus; Dionysos, born of Semele and Zeus; Heracles (Hercules), born of Alcmena and Zeus; Achilles, born of Peleus and Thetis (a Nereid); and Aeneas, born of Anchises and Aphrodite.

Matthew Arnold says "terms like grace, new birth, justification . . . terms, in short, which with St. Paul are literary terms, theologians have employed as if they were scientific terms" (*Literature and Dogma*, 1873, 1.1). Of course it is in birth as a literary theme that we are interested. The theme is expressed by Sophocles: "Nobly to live, or else nobly to die, befits proud birth" (*Aias [Ajax*, play, c. 441 B.C.]).

Northrop Frye (*Anatomy of Criticism*, 1957) says that the birth of the hero "is often associated with a flood, the regular symbol of the beginning and end of a cycle" (198; cf. 51). We find the theme of a child floating on water in the stories of Perseus and Moses and in the beginning of the epic *Beowulf* (c. 8th century). Noah's ark is the image of new life after the flood, and baptism as the time of giving a (Christian) name is part of the same theme. In Shakespeare's play *Twelfth Night* (c. 1600), there are suggestions of Viola as a Venus Aphrodite figure, being born from the sea.

The Biblical View

The *locus classicus* for the miraculous birth theme is in the Bible, in the creation of Adam and Eve described in Genesis, and supremely in the two versions of the origins of Jesus in the New Testament, the first in Matthew and Luke, and the second in John. Whatever they are historically or theologically, these are notable literary images that have influenced the presence of the birth theme in secular literature and illuminate those images where influence is unclear. These three stories are artistically paralleled, with Matthew and Luke having in mind Genesis, and John having in mind Matthew and Luke as well, each writer interpreting and reformulating the ones before him.

In Genesis, Adam and Eve, the progenitors of all mankind, are created by God in his own image. Thus, man is defined as fundamentally a (created) creator and maker, as Sir Philip Sidney recognised in his essay *A Defence of Poetry* (1595), and John Milton portrayed in the poem *Paradise Lost* (1667). Man's sense of self-fulfillment is thus inextricably bound up with his being true to his "creatorness," which is his God-given nature, according to this view. Thus too, all men are called to be heroes, to be "themselves," by their being invited to share and participate in creating the world, in the divine creativeness and tendence activity, which is man's own concern as well as God's. This seems to be a central purpose of the Genesis story, as it is a central theme of Milton's *Paradise Lost*.

The parallelism of the "new creation" story of the New Testament in the nativity of Jesus told in Matthew and Luke reinforces and interprets Genesis. Jesus, the New Adam (and the New Mankind), is born of the Holy Spirit and a virgin and so is nobly born and has a noble heritage. Paradoxically, his birth in humble circumstances at Bethlehem, laid in a manger for cattle in a stable behind an inn, enforces a theme of the humble majesty of the divine serving mankind, indicating that God's nature in man is meant to serve man, and suggests also how little man attends to his nature, his gift from God. It is the simplest people, the shepherds, who recognize the Christ immediately; the Wise Men, the great and scholarly, take longer to come to worship at the manger, having perhaps travelled months or even years to honor him. At the same time, however, the Wise Men know to warn of his enemies, which the shepherds know nothing about.

His names, Jesus and Emmanuel, which mean "savior" and "God is with us" (Matt. 1:21–23), indicate Jesus' heroic work in its two aspects, combined in the divinely appointed leadership and service. He saves mankind by representing God and man among his people, presenting what man is to believe in. He also represents mankind and its legitimate aspirations. The theme could hardly be stated more simply, yet more profoundly: God's nature—man's own nature—works to save mankind.

The threat to the newborn hero is represented in the Flight into Egypt; but it is a threat that continues throughout Jesus' life, ending with his crucifixion.

John's simpler, in some respects, and theological rather than historical presentation develops the same theme. The consummation of all wisdom (from God) is incarnated in human life, expressing the meaning and direction of human nature: "In the beginning was the Word, and the Word was with God, and the

Word was God. He was in the beginning with God; all things were made through him and without him was not anything made that was made. In him was life, and the life was the light of men. . . . And the Word became flesh and dwelt among us, full of grace and truth" (John 1:1–4, 14, Revised Standard Version). "Word," of course, is the Greek "logos" or "reason"; it has a central position in the culmination of Greek philosophy, and it had come to have a distinct existence in the Old Testament, as in "the Word of God."

For John, all that Matthew and Luke had to say in their conventional and highly poetic nativity stories, as well as the meaning of the Genesis story, is summed up briefly: "And the Word became flesh and dwelt among us." The birth theme is the same as in Matthew and Luke. Jesus' origin was mysterious and brought about by God. John's hero too is "God is with us."

In a surprising late development of the theme, the Genesis and New Testament creation and nativity stories are brought together strikingly by John Masefield in an image which asserts (what is implied by the parallelism in the Bible) that *all men* are born with God's image, born to heroism and greatness: "she who gives a baby birth brings Saviour Christ again to Earth" (*The Everlasting Mercy*, narrative poem, 1911). In John Milton's dramatic poem *Samson Agonistes* (1671), the Israelite hero Samson has similarly had his birth foretold by an angel. And his breeding, Samson says, was "ordered and prescribed as of a person separate to God." When, restored to "himself" and to God's favor, Samson pulls the temple down upon the tyrannical Philistines, the people of Israel can say again, "God is with us."

The Culmination of the Theme in the Renaissance

Early in the Renaissance, Rabelais develops a complex and outlandish parody of the heroic birth theme in his masterpiece, *Gargantua et Pantagruel* (*Gargantua and Pantagruel*, novels, 1532–1564). In his introductory lines to his reader, Rabelais warns that his book tells of no birth of any value except for mirth. And in his prologue, he says he more values works that smell of wine than those that smell of the lamp. Pantagruel and his father, Gargantua, come from the ancient line of giants. (In Greek mythology, the giants were a monstrous race that challenged the gods. In the Bible, the Hephilim of Gen. 6:4 were monstrous children of "the sons of God," perhaps fallen angels, and the daughters of men; they are used to explain man's growing evil, which led to the Deluge.) In Rabelais, who has been called "the Father of Laughter," Gargantua and Pantagruel both have monstrous appetites, as is indicated by the name "panta-gruel," and they also have prodigious tastes for mirth-provoking monstrosities. In the eleventh month of his mother's pregnancy, Gargantua is born from his mother's ear when her feasting on tripe leads to her having "the runs" so bad that Gargantua disdains the normal route of delivery.

But in "L'Allegro" (poem, 1632), Milton gives "heart-easing Mirth" two alternate, but noble, sets of parents. She may be the child of Venus and Bacchus, sister to Brightness and Bloom; or, she may be the child of spring, begot by

"Zephyr with Aurora playing." But whether in Rabelais or Milton, the effect is to valorize the origins of a human quality, human mirth.

More clearly to the point is the sonnet sequence *Amoretti* (1595), where Edmund Spenser tells his future wife her "gentle wit and virtuous mind" indicates ("argues") that she is, like Christ, born of the Holy Spirit.

In the epic poem *The Faerie Queene* (1590–1596), Spenser presents Queen Elizabeth as derived from the fabulous Prince Arthur, who is himself looking for the great and virtuous Gloriana, "the Faerie Queene," another compliment to Elizabeth. Spenser tells Elizabeth she is "descended farre from mightie kings and conquerours in war." In the allegory, Arthur is *magnificence*, the embodiment of all virtue and a Logos figure, in search of *true glory*. In book 2 of *The Faerie Queene*, Arthur and Guyon recover from their preliminary struggles and prepare for their greater heroic efforts in the House of Temperance (Castle of Alma, or soul). In a tower room of the castle, they find the sage Eumnestes (Good Memory), where Prince Arthur reads from the book *Briton moniments*, and Guyon reads from *Antiquitie of Fairie londe*, each to find out about his origins.

Guyon, an Elfin knight who serves the Faerie Queene, Gloriana, learns of how all the Elfin race was descended from "Elfe, Quick" (i.e., a living thing), whom the god Prometheus made, and who met and wed in the Gardens of Adonis "a goodly creature, whom he deemed in mind to be no earthly wight, but either Spright, or Angell." From them was directly descended not only all men (again all men are born of the gods) but especially the Faerie Queene, in whose service Guyon, the knight of Temperance, finds meaning and purpose. "God is with us," again.

Prince Arthur, on the other hand, is also reading about his (historical) ancestors. He is the "foster Childe" of Briton, as are all her kings who trace themselves back beyond Donwallo, the first British king, who succeeded to the throne first held by Brutus, or Brute, himself a great-grandson of the Trojan Aeneas. And (as also in Virgil's epic poem *Aeneis* [*Aeneid*, 19 B.C.]) Aeneas was the son of Anchises and the goddess of love, Aphrodite. Thus Prince Arthur will sit on the throne established by the lineage of Brutus, great-grandchild of the love goddess. In short, he is the heir of divinity. The compliment also carries forward to Queen Elizabeth, Arthur's descendent in the legend. *Magnificence* and *glory* are thus Elizabeth's heritage, and indeed of all the "foster children" of Briton. It is of all these that Spenser sings in *The Faerie Queene*. Nobility is what Spenser asks of his readers (including his queen), and their ancestry is traced to the gods in Venus and Prometheus, from whom their divine gifts come. Again, "God is with us."

The theme of the miraculous origin of the hero is present also in Medieval hagiography, where sterile women get pregnant through the intercession of the saints. And it is present in vestigial form in the anonymous Medieval story of *Havelok the Dane* (romance, c. 1250), where Havelok is marked at birth with a shining cross on his shoulder, and this and the light that is sometimes seen around him or which shines from his mouth when he is sleeping enlist aid for him to restore his and his wife's lost kingdoms of England and Denmark.

But "God is (not) with us" in a medieval Russian work, which presents the demonic inversion of the heroic birth theme, the heroic epic *Slovo o polku Igoreve* (*Lay of the Host of Igor*, c. 1187), Russia's *Iliad*. There, Igor is spoken of as swaddled and provided for as an infant by martial trumpets, spears, and helmets. In his maturity, Igor was foolhardy, sought glory dishonorably, and provoked fratricidal wars.

In less mythic, more mimetic or "realistic" literature, the theme is more "displaced," in Northrop Frye's term, modulating into the phase of the hero having an uncertain or masked origin, like Cinderella, appropriate to a more secular age and audience, perhaps.

The literal noble birth theme was not always congenial to audiences (though it persists in some form down to our own time). The objection is clearly stated in John Fletcher and Philip Massinger's play *The Prophetess* (1647): " 'Tis virtue, and not birth that makes us noble: great actions speak great minds, and such should govern." This, of course, does not deal clearly with the question of where "virtue" and "great minds" come from. And Shakespeare can be deeply ironic in using this birth theme, as in his play *Henry IV, Part 1* (1597), where Glendower tells Hotspur of the portents at his birth and how the earth "Shak'd like a coward"; Hotspur rejoins: "Why so it would have done at the same season if your mother's cat had but kitten'd." Still, irony at times left untouched the theme of the birth of the hero, as in Milton's "Nativity Ode" (1629) and in Richard Crashaw's "In the Holy Nativity" (1652).

Ultimately, Shakespeare, standing on the threshold of the brave new world, was sympathetic to the theme of the noble or divine birth setting the hero apart. The play *The Tempest* (1611) can be seen as Prospero's effort, in the midst of a secular world, to give his daughter her Confirmation lessons about what her true heritage is, what is the nature of man she shares. Prospero realizes the time has come for her maturity when she responds with compassion and insight as she witnesses the danger the tempest has brought to King Alonso's ship and guesses it contains within it some noble person. The "tempest" in the play seems to be a symbol of the vicissitudes of the storm of time, and thus it is appropriate that time lesson Miranda. In the first act of her maturity, Miranda tells her father: "O! I have suffered with those that I saw suffer. . . . Had I been any god of power, I would have sunk the sea within the earth or ere it should the good ship so have swallow'd." If Miranda is old enough to imagine herself participating in divinity, she is old enough to know who she is and whence she comes. Prospero says "the hour's now come" for her to learn her true, divine, heritage.

Living alone on the island, Miranda has seen no human other than her father and Caliban, the half-animal who tried to rape her. But aboard this "good ship" is Ferdinand, King Alonso's son, whom she is destined to marry. Almost fifteen years old, Miranda has been on the island with her father for twelve years. She remembers only that she came from a place of nobility, which she perhaps misunderstands as wealth. Though she understands there is evil in the world, Prospero leads her to understand her mother "was a piece of virtue," and her paternal grandmother, though she bore one bad son, perhaps, was another. Miranda reasons it out: "Good wombs have borne bad sons."

But as she learns more of the evil that brought Prospero and her to the island and of the good Gonzolo who was charitable to them, Miranda falls asleep. It is the tempest of life that must teach Miranda the rest of her catechism. As Prospero controls the evil plotters on the island, Miranda and Ferdinand are left to work out their own visions of the nature of man. As is common enough in romantic works, each sees divinity in the other, but denies it in himself. It is not enough to say they feel beloved of, and blessed by, the gods, that for them "God is with us." Of Ferdinand, Miranda says: "I might call him a thing divine, for nothing natural I ever saw so noble." And so the familiar story goes, with the romantic partner the God-bearing image (*Théotòkos*), until finally Miranda sees all the men on the island and marvels at her vision of man:

> O wonder!
> How many goodly creatures are there here!
> How beauteous mankind is! O brave new world
> That has such people in't!

Fortunate is the girl (or boy) in the brave new world who is so persuasively lessoned in the creation stories of Genesis, Matthew and Luke, and John. Without this, what can it mean to her to learn, as she will, of the Fall, and even the Crucifixion? Is this what Shakespeare says to us? There is far less irony than is often supposed in Prospero's response to Miranda's vision of the brave new world: " 'Tis new to thee." For Prospero has bent his whole effort to make possible this image of the birth of a new world and two souls into that world— to make it "new to thee." But it is not Prospero's art that has finally made possible this vision; it is likewise dependent upon the virtue and real love and respect of Miranda and Ferdinand for one another that is revealed when Prospero draws the curtain from his cell disclosing them in their simple, virtuous joy in one another, a sight that greatly affects the penitent Alonso (Ferdinand's father, who had feared he had destroyed his son, as he perhaps had done to his daughter).

Shakespeare, then, recognizes the problems inherent in the brave new world of the theme of birth associated with the gods, but he contrives to present the same theme and catechize us all. "God is with us" even at the threshold of the new age.

The Eighteenth and Nineteenth Centuries

The eighteenth and nineteenth centuries bring the theme of the association of the birth of the hero with the divine or with divine will into the area of generally less mythic, more "realistic" portrayal, but nonetheless it persists, and indeed thrives, as can be seen from works as diverse as those by Wordsworth, the

Brothers Grimm, Longfellow in his use of American Indian lore, Tennyson, and many others, though it is useful to take up first the parody of the theme by Sterne to show the temper of the times under which the theme did continue to flourish.

Laurence Sterne perhaps hoped to lay to rest, once and for all, the theme of the birth of the hero that is *set apart* (and thus "sacred") in his novels *Life and Opinions of Tristram Shandy* (1759–1767), in which he generally satirizes the epic form, which especially lends itself to the theme of divine or mysterious birth. Tristram has his own annunciation and nativity, to which the first three volumes of the work are devoted, with Tristram born only in volume four and largely disappearing afterward from this most eccentric novel.

From the habits of Walter Shandy, Tristram's father, we know that he wound the thirty-one-day clock and took care of other "household duties" on the first Sunday of each month. The exact moment of Tristram's conception, on the first Sunday of March 1718, was marked by Mrs. Shandy asking her husband if he had wound the clock. A good-natured but rather simple woman, Mrs. Shandy was very aware of the pattern of her husband's habits, and naturally associated one thing with another.

Tristram's nativity was likewise neither miraculous nor mysterious. He was born at Shandy Hall on November 5, 1718, the place called for in the Shandy marriage contract, though Mrs. Shandy had nonetheless earlier gone to London, at some expense to Mr. Shandy, for her lying-in. The night of the birth, the angels did not sing in the fields to shepherds keeping watch over their flock. But Dr. Slop sat in the parlor of Shandy Hall listening to Mr. Shandy expatiate, while a midwife was upstairs with Mrs. Shandy. When the moment for the birth came, Dr. Slop attended the woman long enough to smash Tristram's nose with a forceps, a mark he bore the rest of his life. Tristram's name was another misadventure. He was supposed to be called "Trismegistus," after Mr. Shandy's favorite philosopher, but when the careless maid Susannah ran to the curate to give the name for the sickly baby, all she could remember was "Tris-," and the curate assumed the child should be given his own name, Tristram. ("Trismegistus" refers to the "thrice-greatest" Hermes in the Greek, and refers to Thoth, ancient Egyptian god of wisdom and the art of writing, later associated with the god Hermes.) Nor was there any miracle or mystery about Tristram's circumcision, which occurs when the window sash falls while Tristram is relieving himself out the window. Nor is his education a mystery, since Mr. Shandy designs a "Tristra-paedia" for him, in imitation of the education designed for Cyrus the Great by Xenophon.

Perhaps it is best to understand Tristram as an anti-hero—a figure, common in our own age's literature, having the opposite of heroic qualities and characteristics. And yet he is not entirely that, though a humble figure. His family, including the lovably innocent Uncle Toby who plays soldier, and Toby's devoted servant Corporal Trim, along with Parson Yorick (a wholly innocent man), as well as other figures, are such originals that one may wish to call them "God's plenty" or at least "God's very own." But whatever Sterne's intention about the noble birth theme, Sterne certainly did not succeed in ridiculing it out of existence.

Along this line, a frankly demonic form, or parody, of the theme of the birth of the hero is in Goethe's play *Faust* (1808, 1832), where the *Homunculus* figure, the being created by Wagner, is a monster. A similar, but more complex, demonic parody of the theme of the birth of the hero associated with divine origins is *Frankenstein* (1818), the novel by Mary W. Shelley. The nineteen-year-old author's romantic sympathies are with the nameless monster created by Victor Frankenstein, a young German student of philosophy who is obsessed with a desire to be a creator of life. What he creates in his hubris, however, is a monster who makes his life a misery and ultimately destroys him. The novel invites us to sympathize with the rebellion of the monster, who initially is amiable and most of all wants love and companionship. But Frankenstein has visited charnel houses to create him and has made him hideous in appearance, so that all who see him fly from him in horror. We hear echoes of Milton's Satan (in *Paradise Lost*) as the monster pleads for Frankenstein to create a mate for him: "Everywhere I see bliss from which I alone am irrevocably excluded. . . . I was benevolent and good; misery made me a fiend. Make me happy, and I shall again be virtuous." When Frankenstein cannot create that mate because he feels revulsion at the thought of a race of such monsters, the monster devotes himself to revenge. The general theme Mary Shelley may be said to explore is the revenge of a being against the society that rejects him. But she has said in the novel she wanted to create a tale "which would speak to the mysterious fears of our nature." The context of this present entry perhaps illumines what Mary Shelley has also done here: explored our dark fears that we are not the children of a benevolent God, but a monstrous progeny. It is the very theme which the birth of the hero motif we trace here seeks to avert.

Before Sterne, we see the mysterious birth (or mystery about birth) theme developed by Henry Fielding in his novel *Tom Jones, a Foundling* (1749), where only at the end do we find Tom to be born to a station (approximately) appropriate to the character he has and develops, and he weds the virtuous Sophia Western and becomes Squire Allworthy's heir. We find the theme also used by Charles Dickens, in the novel *Oliver Twist* (1837–1838), where Oliver's birth and real heritage are kept from him and are discovered only at the end of the novel, a form of the theme probably derived from Greek New Comedy formulas. And Thomas Hardy in the novel *Tess of the D'Urbervilles* (1891) plays centrally over what is or is not a noble creature and a noble heritage, with Tess greater than all her fellows and nobly born, but tragically misunderstood, and in the end put to death.

In "Ode: Intimations of Immortality from Recollections of Early Childhood" (1807), William Wordsworth frankly invents a birth myth to explain why the child we all were, so eagerly, so earnestly, plays at being grown-up, trying on different identities to see what will suit him. Wordsworth views this childhood "play" as part of man's search for his true identity, a search which eventually leads him to realize that he is only the foster-child of Nature and this world, and that his longings are immortal. One finds this focused best in the child, "over whom thy Immortality broods like the day." It is this delight in exploring his heritage by the child that Wordsworth can find imagery for only in a birth myth: "Not in entire forgetfulness, and not in utter nakedness, but trailing clouds of glory do we come from God, who is our home." Wordsworth finally sings in praise in this ode of a two-fold blessing: man's "high instincts" of search for his true home; and the ability of his soul to know what that home is and is not. The exact words are important, for they formulate the blessing that the birth-myth is a means of explaining. Wordsworth sings in praise of "those first affections, those shadowy recollections, which, *be they what they may*, are yet the fountain-light of all our day, are yet the master-light of all our seeing" (italics mine). What the child has is the experience of the "Soul's immensity"; what the years bring is the mature man's understanding of himself, that he has an immortal soul. The divine birth image for Wordsworth is a kind of fiction that presents the profound and mysterious reality of what man is. Again, "God is with us," the more we are ourselves, and this is what it means to know ourselves.

The fairy tales collected by Jakob Grimm (1785–1863) and his brother Wilhelm (1786–1859) regularly associate moral goodness with supernatural powers or protection, and this is sometimes developed in imagery of birth from God, though the more common, realistically "displaced," presentation of the theme is in birth from noble kings and queens, themselves part of a world perhaps bordering on the miraculous and the supernatural to men and women far below that station.

In "Die Nelke" ("The Pink," 1812), a queen who had not been "blessed" with children prays every day for a child, until one day an angel promises she will have a son with the power of wishing. The child born to her is indeed finally a blessing to his mother. The wicked cook steals him away and accuses the queen to the king of allowing the boy to be killed by a wild animal, and she is walled up in a high tower without food so that she will pine away. Until she can be exonerated, two angels from heaven, in the "displaced" form of white doves, bring her food twice daily for the seven years she will not be fed. But when the divinely gifted boy, now a prince, reaches an age when he can understand and does learn what has happened to his mother, he goes back and reveals the great error the king, his father, has made because of the wickedness of the cook. But when the king releases the queen, she will no longer eat or drink. Now that her long ordeal is over, she says the merciful God who preserved her life for this day will release her. She dies in three days, and the white doves hover over her grave. The wicked cook is torn into quarters, and the king dies shortly after, his heart filled with grief and remorse. But the good prince marries the beautiful maiden who helped protect him from the cook and helped uncover the treachery, sending the prince back to reveal, as heaven wished, the innocence of his mother.

We see the birth by heaven's will also in the tale "Rapunzel" (1812); and while Snow White is born as a result of a queen's wish only, she is saved by the miraculous power of human love—that of a prince.

In Japanese folktales, we see also the association of moral goodness with supernatural origins. In "Momotarō" ("The Peach Boy") the devoted wife of an honest old woodman finds a peach floating in the river and brings it home to him. But when he is about to eat it, it splits and bears a child. The couple call him "Momotarō" and raise him as their own child. One day the son resolves to carry off the riches from the island of the ogres. We see he has his foster-parents' virtue when on his journey to the island he enlists the aid of an ape, a pheasant, and a dog by sharing his fine millet dumplings with them. His virtue is rewarded when together they overcome the ogres and carry away all their treasure. Like the good son he is, Momotarō carries this wealth home to his foster-parents, who enjoy peace and abundance for the rest of their days. Again we see water imagery associated with an important new beginning. And again the artistic problem is of how to present the mysterious origins of human virtue.

In the narrative poem *Hiawatha* (1855), Henry Wadsworth Longfellow depicts an American Indian culture hero who is, like all men (it appears), the child of Gitche Manito, "the Master of life," "the creator of nations," "the Great Spirit." Hiawatha's immediate origins are likewise linked to supernatural spirits. His father is Mudjekeewis, who is the Wind and the father of the winds, and later becomes Kabeyun (the West-Wind, which he keeps for himself). Nokomis, the daughter of the moon, is Hiawatha's maternal grandmother, whose first-born is Wenonah, Hiawatha's mother, who is said to have the beauty of the moonlight and the starlight. Hiawatha himself after his death will become the master of the Northwest-Wind, the "home" wind.

Long ago, Gitche Manito called the nations—the tribes—of men together, summoning them from warfare and asking them to live together in peace as brothers. At that time, he promised man a "Prophet" and "Deliverer of nations" who would guide and teach him in the ways of peace and its fertility and prosperity. Longfellow presents two figures who might be that deliverer, neither of which is explicitly identified as such. The chief candidate, of course, is Hiawatha, whose life story the poem tells. The second figure is Jesus Christ, son of the Virgin Mary, the God whom the missionary at the end of the poem offers the Ojibway tribe Hiawatha leads.

Hiawatha is notable throughout his life for his efforts toward civilization and peace. At his maturity, he prays "for profit of the people, for advantage of the nations." He is the benefactor who brings the blessing of maize (corn) to his people; he also brings writing and painting, and the use of herbs and medicines, antidotes, and cures; he encourages music, dancing, and story-telling. From the first, Hiawatha is seen to be not chiefly a warrior, like the other Indian leaders, but a divinely gifted man who leads his people in the way of the Master of Life, the way of peace.

It is this heritage that Hiawatha leaves his people and the new Christian missionary to whom at his own death he allies his people and with whom he makes a compact of peace. Thus, the poem invites the reader to consider Hiawatha as the precursor and type of Christ, both then one Deliverer. Or—just as possible as an interpretation—the god the white man *actually* brought may stand in silent, ironic contrast with the true teacher and peacemaker, Hiawatha. From the introductory stanzas of the poem, we know Longfellow preferred the first view; from the final section of the poem, however, we know Longfellow left the poem to speak for itself.

In Hiawatha, Longfellow combined two figures, "Hiawatha," the Indian culture hero, and "Manabozho" (the name varies), the Indian divinity, who was the figure born of the Wind. For the portrait, Longfellow undoubtedly also drew on the *Kalevala*, the Finnish national epic, whose origins may go back before Homeric times, though it is believed parts of it came from the Middle Ages and later. The hero, Väinämöinen, is born of an Air Spirit mother made pregnant by the wind. She is the mother of the water and has been responsible for the creation of the earth, the heavens and the clouds, and headlands, bays, and shores. She is also called a Virgin of the Air and a Nature Spirit. Väinämöinen is renowned for cultivating the earth and for his knowledge and the charms he casts as a singer of songs. In his singing contest with the jealous young Joukahainen, he makes clear that the greatest singer is the one who can sing of the profound origins of things. The child of a creator-figure, he is himself especially identified with generation and cultivation, that is, with the knowledge of a creator and the mysterious power that this gives him.

It is worth pausing a moment more over another longer work, Alfred Lord Tennyson's *The Coming of Arthur* (1869), from his poems *Idylls of the King* (1859–1885), to see what concerns continue to dictate the use of the theme of divine or mysterious birth, even in a mimetic or "realistic" age. The *Idylls* tells of the failure of the Round Table, undercut by widening evil; but *The Coming of Arthur* is from the earlier, more hopeful phase, as indeed is the birth theme generally.

Leodogran, king of Cameliard, had a daughter, Guinevere, his only child. His kingdom ravaged by beasts and beastly men, Leodogran calls on Arthur for help, though Arthur's legitimacy was questioned by some, who said he was not the son of the good King Uther, and thus his rightful heir. Nevertheless, Arthur comes to Leodogran's aid and defeats his beastly enemies, whereupon he asks Leodogran to give him Guinevere as his wife. Leodogran debates much in his heart, saying he does not know how he can give his only child to a man other than a king or a king's son. He questions Arthur's knights, Ulfias, Brastias, and Bedivere, asking if Arthur was the son of Uther, and the first two tell him "Aye." But Bedivere, the first man knighted by Arthur, sets out the facts for Leodogran:

> There be those who hate him in their hearts,
> And call him baseborn, and since his ways are sweet,

> And theirs are bestial, hold him less than man:
> And there be those who deem him more than man,
> And dream he dropped from heaven.

Bedivere then relates that Ygerne, faithful wife of Gorloïs, was beloved of Uther, and Uther and Gorloïs fought a war over her, with Gorloïs dying. The victorious Uther took Ygerne as his wife, but died himself not many months afterward, mourning for a son and heir, "lest the realm go to wrack." The night Uther died, "the night of the new year," Ygerne in grief brought forth Arthur "all before his time." Merlin took him away from those who would kill him and gave him to Anton to raise. When Arthur had grown to maturity, Merlin brought him forward as Uther's son and had him crowned as king.

Still debating within himself "if Arthur were the child of shamefulness," Leodogran questioned Ygerne's daughter by Gorloïs, Bellicent, who had always treated Arthur as a brother. Bellicent tells of Arthur's nobility and how once he spoke to his Round Table "with large, divine, and comfortable words" and all saw his likeness to the king, and a light beam came down through the casement and through the cross of "the Crucified" and smote Arthur. Still questioned more by Leodogran, Bellicent tells him of her deep love for Arthur, and she also knows the story Bleys, master of Merlin, told her on his deathbed, of he and Merlin on the night Uther died receiving the infant Arthur from a fiery ship coming from the clouds; they caught the child and cried "The king! Here is an heir for Uther." But when Bellicent later questioned Merlin about the truth of his tale, Merlin only sang to her a riddle about how the *young* may not have mature judgment and the *old* may have wandering wits. Bellicent counsels Leodogran to fear not to give Arthur "thine only child."

Still, undecided, Leodogran rejoices, doubts, and drowses. In his sleep he sees Arthur crowned in heaven, and he awakes and sends to Arthur his "Yea."

"God is with us," again, insistently. But insistently also come the "realistic" queries Tennyson raises: "Where?" and "How shall I know him?" Tennyson's Leodogran must ultimately decide for himself what is noble and comes from heaven and has its blessing. And so must man generally, Tennyson indicates.

The Twentieth Century

Both heros and anti-heros are present in the poems of W. B. Yeats. Yeats identified the anti-hero at times with the "anti-Christ" figure of 1 John (2:18–22, 4:3), and he wrote of his birth, his coming, in our own time (as every age has believed he has come in theirs): "The blood-dimmed tide is loosed. . . . The best lack all conviction, while the worse are full of passionate intensity. . . . And what rough beast, its hour come round at last, slouches towards Bethlehem to be born?" ("The Second Coming," 1921). But Yeats prayed for a far different birth for his own daughter, one in genuine innocence, which he still believed possible: "And may her bridegroom bring her to a house where all's accustomed, ceremonious; for arrogance and hatred are the wares peddled in the thoroughfares. How but in custom and in ceremony are innocence and beauty born?" ("A

Prayer for My Daughter,'' 1921). Here, Yeats is speaking of his own infant daughter and yet speaking of a mysterious, secluded birth for her.

Stephen Spender also wrote of the divine birth of the true hero in lines untouched by irony or satire common in our age: ''I think continually of those who were truly great, . . . the names of those who in their lives fought for life, who wore at their hearts the fire's centre. Born of the sun, they travelled a short while toward the sun, and left the vivid air signed with their honour'' (''I Think Continually of Those,'' 1933).

The Academy Award-winning motion picture *Chariots of Fire* (1980), by Colin Welland, has been described by Vincent Canby as a ''very clear-eyed evocation of values of the old-fashioned sort that are today more easily satirized than celebrated'' (*New York Times*, 25 September 1981, sec. c, p. 14). The story is of two Olympic runners (1924), one of whom, Harold Abrahams, is said to ''run like a god.'' The other, Eric Liddell, who will not run on the sabbath, is appealed to to run by the Prince of Wales, who says they are both ''children of the race''; implicitly, Liddell's refusal is because of his over-riding loyalty as a 'child of God.' Earlier, he has told his sister, a fellow-missionary: ''God made me devout and—He made me fast.''

Less ''old-fashioned'' and more ''modern'' is the American poet Wallace Stevens, who believed ''poetry is the supreme fiction, madam'' (''A High-Toned Old Christian Woman,'' 1923). In ''The Idea of Order at Key West'' (1935), he wrote of a singer who was in some way the spirit of poetry, ''the spirit that we sought'':

> We
> As we beheld her striding there alone,
> Knew that there never was a world for her
> Except the one she sang, and singing, made. . . .
> Oh! Blessed rage for order, pale Ramon,
> The maker's rage to order words of the sea,
> Words of the fragrant portals, dimly-starred,
> And of ourselves and of our origins,
> In ghostlier demarcations, keener sounds.

Man is even yet a ''maker.'' Here is a more tentative ''God is with us'': ''words . . . of ourselves and of our origins.'' What are we? from where do we come?

A Special Note on Modern African Literature

In modern African literature, we see an especial interest in the theme of the birth of the hero associated with the divine and the divine will, for example in the Nigerian *Ozidi Saga* and the play based on it by J. P. Clark, in Wole Soyinka, and in some of the novels of Ngugi.

In his first novel (published second), *The River Between* (1965), Ngugi Wa Thiong'o (formerly James Ngugi, b. 1938, Kenya) develops the theme of a divine peace and promise, when the god Murungu ''in the beginning'' created Gikuyu and Mumbi, the father and mother of the Kenyan ethnic group, the

"Gikuyu people." On the mountain Kerinyaga ("He-who-shines-in-Holiness"), and later in a sacred grove on the mountain Kameno, Murungu gave his people all the land they could see, "*tene na tene*, world without end." (But the white man was later to take it over, until the struggle for an independent Kenya triumphed, after the time of the novel.) In the sacred grove on Kameno, when he has come of age, Waiyaki, the hero of the novel, is told by his father, Chege, that he is descended from Gikuyu and Mumbi, thus from the god Murungu, and, further, that he is descended from a special line, from the prophet Mugo wa Kibiro, who told that one day salvation would come from his own offspring. Chege tells his son, Waiyaki, that he is the last of this line, which will bring forth a "savior" for his people.

Waiyaki attends a mission school and develops, on his own, a vision of peace in the deeply troubled valley (called "the valley of life") between the mountains Kameno (associated with familiar tribal ways) and Mukuyu (associated with stranger Christian ways). Waiyaki is also influenced by Muthoni, a Christian girl who seeks to combine her religion with the tribal ways of "circumcision" to be "a woman," and he is greatly affected by her death from infection after this tribal ritual, when he takes her too late to the mission hospital. Waiyaki identifies himself with education and with "the river between" these mountains, the River Honia, which means "cure, or bring-back-to-life." At the end of the novel, the reader is left in doubt whether Waiyaki and his betrothed, Nyambura (Muthoni's other sister), who shares his vision of peace and brotherhood in "the valley of life," are being (as they seem to be) taken away to be crucified for their work in support of that vision. Is the way of the Gikuyu savior The Way of the Cross?

In his second novel, *Weep Not, Child* (1964), Ngugi recurs to the special birth theme, but more allusively. The novel is developed again in the context of Murungu, the Creator-god, who creates the parents of the tribe, Gikuyu and Mumbi, and gives them the free and beautiful land. Njoroge, the hero, also a "Gikuyu," is followed from when he begins primary school to the time when he is twenty years old. He is, clearly, a "child of God," but he is developed more explicitly as "the son of the land."

Njoroge is another of Ngugi's figures who believe in the saving power of education. But ultimately education comes in this novel to be associated with the feminine: his mother, Nyokabi, who sends him to school; his beloved, Mwihaki, who believes in his hope in education when he has abandoned it; and his own desire to stay above the late-colonial strife in Kenya and pursue his education. Against this feminine is the masculine (if we may call it that) of hatred, physical strife, and murder associated with his father, Ngotho; his brother, Boro; Jacobo, the Judas who betrays his tribe; pre-eminently the demonic white man Howlands, who comes to stand more generally for white colonial rule in Kenya; and even the Mau Mau, the native revolutionary group. Njoroge is a failed-savior whose "hope of a better day was the only comfort he could give to a weeping child."

At the end of the novel, Njoroge has been tortured by Howlands and threatened with castration (a maiming carried out on his father); has seen his father tortured and ultimately left to die; and has seen both his brother Boro, who killed Howlands, and his brother Kamau, who had paid Njoroge's school fees, imprisoned for Howlands' murder. By then, Njoroge has lost faith in education, in God, and in himself; but his life (for what it is worth) is rescued by the feminine. When his beloved, Mwihaki (daughter to the slain Judas figure), his "last hope," cannot "save" him, as he asks her to do, but instead takes up his own former theme of "a new day" and their "duty" to serve the Gikuyu people, Njoroge attempts to commit suicide; but his mother, Nyokabi, prevents him. As he returns home with her, he tells himself, in almost the last words of the novel, "I am a coward." This, apparently, is where education has brought him in this time of national strife. It was his mother, also, who, in the first words of the novel, thrilled him by telling him that his family would sacrifice to send him to his first (primary) school.

Both Waiyaki in *The River Between* and Njoroge in *Weep Not, Child* are presented as "God with us," but there are no Wise Men to warn them of their enemies and give them time to come to maturity.

Elsewhere in African literature, in the oral *Ozidi Saga* of the Ijaw region of Nigeria, Ozidi is a cultural hero who avenges the murder of his father and overcomes the forces, both natural and supernatural, that oppose his people. The Ijo tend to be a matrilineal society, and their supreme god, the single source of life (and thus of Ozidi's life, of course) is female, called Oyin ("Our Mother") and Tamara ("She Who Cares"). Ozidi is greatly dependent, in his heroic deeds, on his maternal grandmother, Oreame, who is indeed "she who cares" for Ozidi, and she is a powerful witch; thus she is not only his lineal support and link to the supreme god but also his direct source of assistance in conquering the natural and supernatural forces that are a danger to his community.

The uneven but ground-breaking play *Ozidi* (1966), by J. P. Clark (b. 1935, Nigeria), a student and translator of the *Saga*, transforms this oral work presented over seven days to written literature in a five-act play. While Clark's version substitutes some tragic elements for the epic and heroic of the oral original(s), Clark maintains the mythic and divine links of Ozidi. The word *ozidi* is the Ijo term for "warrior," and in the *Saga* (for which there is no entirely consistent version among storytellers) the link of warrior heroism to divine birth and divine and supernatural gifts is central. In the play, however, Clark essays at times to explore the especially modern topic of the use and abuse of divine power, the interrelation of warrior energies and sexuality, and (to use terms of Milton's *Paradise Regained*) the problem of the hero's uncertain poise in the trial of standing by his own human powers at the high pinnacle of the temple. In this way, Clark wishes to have both mythological portraiture and psychological realism to reconcile "God and sinners" (to use a Christian image) in a wholly African traditional framework.

As these works suggest, and as does also the important symbolic play *The*

Strong Breed (1963), by Wole Soyinka (b. 1934, Nigeria), which is too complex to be presented in brief compass, African literature has the potential for profoundly enriching our understanding of the association of the birth of the hero with the divine and the divine will. Here too "God is with us," though where and how is the problem, suggested already by Tennyson, that calls upon our own greatest gifts of recognition and understanding.

From this sampling of the theme of the birth of the hero as it appears in Western literature, it should be clear that man still explores his nature and his origins, and the theme continues to be developed, as it has been since *The Iliad* and Genesis. Whether artists will continue to use this resource in their work is for the future to tell.

See also: Anti-Hero, Christian Hero, Comic Hero, Leader, Monsters, Social Status of Hero, Tragicomic Hero.

Selected Bibliography

Campbell, Joseph. *The Masks of God*. 4 vols. New York: Viking Press, 1959–1968.
Leeming, David Adams. *Mythology: The Voyage of the Hero*. 2d ed. New York: Harper and Row, 1981.
Raglan, Fitz Roy R.S., baron. *The Hero: A Study in Tradition, Myth, and Drama*. 1937. Westport, Conn.: Greenwood Press, 1975.
Rank, Otto. *The Myth of the Birth of the Hero and Other Writings*. Ed. Philip Freund. 1914. New York: Johnson Reprint, 1970.

LESLIE D. FOSTER

BRAGGART

The braggart has been a stock character in comic drama dating from antiquity. Originally a soldier whose grandiose boasts of prowess mask a fundamental cowardice, the braggart, a man of ordinary talents, aspires to appear extraordinary not by performance but by linguistic hyperbole. Although the single-minded purpose of this self-assigned hero of imaginary victories is to persuade others of his uncommon valor, his rousing rhetoric and bombastic egocentricity provoke only obvious contempt (the typical reaction of the braggart's parasitic "confidant") or benign amusement. Lustful, vain, mildly hedonistic, the braggart is as convinced of his sexual virility and attractiveness to women as he is of his physical strength. Such belief is unwarranted, however, and the bachelor braggart remains ever frustrated throughout the drama, or, should he be married, finds himself repeatedly cuckolded.

Greek and Roman Prototypes

The model for subsequent imitations of the braggart soldier appears initially in Greek and Roman comedies, wherein he constitutes a contemptuous object of satire, a caricature of the mercenary soldier who makes his fortune fighting in foreign wars. That the general population found such soldiers of fortune to be generally reprehensible is apparent in the remarks of characters in Menander's *Kolax* (*The Flatterer*) and *Sikyōnios* (*The Man from Sicyon*), both written after 321 B.C. A boorish figure whose wealth is often disproportionate to his merit, the braggart on stage appears notably lacking in breeding, elegance, intelligence, and sensitivity. Consequently, he must resort to telling incredible tales in order to attract the attention he feels his status so richly deserves. Obsessively materialistic, he hopes to lend authenticity to his mythical victories by compounding both their quality and quantity, but the end result runs comically counter to his every expectation. In the final scene, the braggart is properly humiliated, moralistically repentant, ignominiously alienated.

Throughout antiquity, the braggart defines himself by excess. He overstates his skills, his triumphs in battle, his potential, and his heritage with grandiose abandon and wanton inaccuracy. In his eagerness to glorify the self, the braggart unflinchingly relates surrealistic details to an audience of scornful skeptics. Hyperbole is not, however, merely a linguistic phenomenon. The braggart's mode of comportment, his gestures, manner of dress, manner of speaking, all are painstakingly overdrawn. From entrance to exit, the braggart appears fanatically extreme. Sword prominently displayed, hat and uniform symbolically oversized, stride ultra-militaristic, he attempts to camouflage an all too apparent lack of substantive ability with an equally apparent surficial excess. His name proves no less ostentatious than his manner, an unlikely amalgamation of incompatible sounds that provoke a comic response either by sound alone or by a denotative significance thoroughly at odds with the characteristics of the persona so designated.

Plautus' plays contain the most representative and well-sketched braggarts to be found in this literary period. With tongue-twisting names (Polymachaeroplagides in *Pseudolus* [191 B.C.] and Therapontigonus Platigadorus in *Curculio* [n.d.] for example) and mind-boggling feats of prowess (see, for example, the deeds of Antamonides in *Poenulus* [*The Little Carthaginian*, n.d.] or of Pyrgopolinices in *Miles gloriosus* [*The Braggart Soldier*, c. 204 B.C.]), the braggart in Plautus embodies virtually all of the requisite characteristics of the archetypal model. Pyrgopolinices is so successful as a dramatic creation that the title of the play in which he appears has come to signify the type of character itself. Although Plautus does excel in this sort of portraiture, he is merely continuing a tradition inherited from earlier dramatists. In Greek comedy, both Aristophanes (*Acharnēs* [*The Acharnians*, 425 B.C.], *Batrachoi* [*The Frogs*, 405 B.C.], *Ornithes* [*The Birds*, 414 B.C.]) and Menander (*Misoumenos* [*The Hated Man*, n.d.], *Perikeiromenē* [*The Shorn Girl*, n.d.]) depict braggart soldiers.

While most braggart soldiers remain remarkably similar and technically consistent throughout classical literature, certain variations prove significant for subsequent development. The braggarts of Aristophanes, for example, appear slightly more clever and prove more successful than their counterparts in this literary period, a tendency that reoccurs in Terence's braggart, Thraso, in *Eunuchus* (*The Eunuch*, 161 B.C.). In *The Eunuch*, Terence downplays the militaristic component, accentuating instead more humanistic, less reprehensible, qualities. As the braggart begins to take less pride in his warrior capabilities and endeavors instead to draw praise for mental agility and quick-wittedness, he becomes less a farcical caricature than a dramatic creation endowed with limited sensitivities. As such, in the waning years of the Classical Age, the braggart appears occasionally as a sympathetic, almost vulnerable figure, who, despite his immense ego, seems somehow to sense his own insignificance and constitutes less a literary echo than a potential source of inspiration for centuries to come.

The Medieval Period

Braggarts, of course, are the hallmark of medieval epic poetry. In fact, the epic hero is recognized by the very overblown rhetoric that seasons the comical diatribes of the comic braggart in Greek and Roman comedy. The difference between hero and braggart is one of substance rather than style. The epic hero ultimately establishes the perfect synonymy between action and articulation so comically absent in the figure of the comic braggart. Despite this obvious difference, however, the very hyperbolic nature of the epic hero's bold assertions lends itself to humorous parody, resulting in a satirical body of literature wherein braggarts figure prominently. For example, in works such as Sir Thomas Malory's prose romance *Morte d'Arthur* (c. 1469), in *Le franc-archier de Baignollet* (c. 1468), a dramatic monologue, and in the indecent French fabliau "Bérengier au lonc cul" ("Long-Assed Berenger," 13th century), the braggart recalls such legendary heroes as Roland in the epic poem *La chanson de Roland* (*The Song of Roland*, c. 1100) and Fierabras in *Fierabras*, a twelfth-century epic. Braggarts can be found also in Chaucer's *Canterbury Tales* (c. 1380–1400), in Boccaccio's *Il decamerone* (*Decameron*, novellas c. 1350), and in European Jocuse poetry (the thirteenth-century poet Rustico de Filippo offers an excellent illustration in his bestiary sonnets). Although not a comic figure, Rodomont, Moorish king of Algiers in Italian chivalric literature, supplies many languages with a noun to describe a boastful tirade. Matteo M. Boiardo provides a well-sketched depiction of Rodomont in his epic *Orlando innamorato* (*Orlando in Love*, books 1 and 2 written in 1483; complete edition in 1495).

Braggarts appear not only in parody in Medieval literature but in more serious works as well, most notably in mystery and morality plays. Here the braggart actually has a dual function. He serves to relieve the dramatic sobriety, and he is instrumental in rendering the villains of the play as contemptible as they are odious. Braggart characteristics can be found in soldiers and/or gravewatchers in fourteenth- and fifteenth-century liturgical representations of the crucifixion (*The Guarding of the Sepulchre* in the Ludus Coventriae cycle; the *Ordo Paschalis* from Klosterneuberg; the fifteenth-century poem *The Northern Passion*) as well as in the figure of Herod (14th and 15th centuries, miracle plays and mysteries: *York, Towneley and Digby Plays*).

In the English morality play, the braggart resembles even more closely the type established in Greek and Roman comedy. It is perhaps logical that a body of literature so heavily influenced by Christian morality would seek to condemn such vices as pride, vanity, and egocentrism in allegorical literature, especially in light of the fact that such notorious Christian villains as Herod and Pilate are occasionally portrayed as braggarts themselves in the mystery plays. In the morality play, the braggart becomes the personification of such vices, and his presence contributes to the establishment of a tone far less serious than the didactic theme would normally project. Like classical braggarts, the vice/persona possesses an unfounded belief in his own superiority, strikes a studied pose of confidence to mask a fundamental inadequacy, and finds himself moralistically defeated in the closing moments of the drama. Morality plays continue well into the sixteenth century, but early examples wherein braggart models occur are the Macro plays *The Castle of Perseverance* (c. 1425), *Wisdom* (c. 1460) and *Mankind* (c. 1471), and in the play of Henry Medwall, *Nature* (c. 1500).

The Sixteenth Century

It was in the sixteenth century that the writers of Western Europe most fully exploited the possibilities offered by the braggart soldier in comic drama. In the early days of the Renaissance, the braggart appears as but the slavish imitation of the Greek and Roman original, grounded in classical prototype and practice. Self-impressed, blundering, and generally ridiculous, he is often used, as were the braggarts of antiquity, to satirize soldiers, specifically foreign soldiers, in an attempt on the part of the author to lodge a literary protest against an unwelcome military presence invading his native soil. Italian resentment against the Spanish best exemplifies such a modus operandi, revealing itself in such plays as Lodovico Domenichi's *Le due cortigiane* (1563), Alessandro Piccolomini's *L'amor costante* (1540), and Giovanni Maria Cecchi's *I rivali* (1561). Like classical braggarts also, those of the Renaissance bear extravagant and ironically misinformative names and relate incredible accomplishments with astonishing sobriety, of which Capitano Spavento in Girolamo Parabosco's *Il pelligrino* (*The Pilgrim*, 1552), Trematerra in Raffaello Martini's *Amore scolastico* (1568), Dentifrangolo in Giambattista Della Porta's *La Trappolaria* (*Trappola's Comedy*, 1596), Frangipietra in Luigi Pasqualigo's *Fedele* (1576), Brumandilón in Sancho de Muñón's *Lisandro y Roselia* (1542), Capitaine Taillebras in Jean-Antoine de Baïf's *Le brave* (1567), and Brisemur in Pierre de Larivey's *Le fidèle* (1611) constitute illustrious examples.

Later Renaissance braggarts begin to develop vital distinguishing characteristics. To begin with, the soldier is markedly less financially well-off than in classical comedy and frequently bemoans his impoverished state. *I gelosi* (1545) of Vincenzo Gabiani; *Il martello* (1585) of Giovanni Maria Cecchi; *La tabernaria* (*The Tavern Play*, 1612) of Della Porta; *Il Travaglia* (1546) of Andrea Calmo; *Tragicomedia de Calisto y Melibea* (*Celestina, or The Spanish Bawd*, 1499–1502) partially attributed to Fernando de Rojas; and *La talanta* (1542) of Pietro Aretino depict such soldiers without fortunes. More significant perhaps, the braggart in sixteenth-century comedy seems to benefit from the general enlightenment pervading all of sixteenth-century Western Europe. Whereas in Greek and Roman drama the braggart appears to be little more than a foolish dolt, in Renaissance drama he is decidedly more learned, even though he appears equally foolish when demonstrating such knowledge. The braggart occasionally makes reference to mythology; demonstrates a knowledge of history, geography, art, or literature; and frequently alludes to people, places, and topics of contemporary interest in Sancho de Muñón's *Lisandro y Roselia*; Aretino's *La talanta*; Lodovico Dolce's *Il capitano* (*The Captain*, 1545); Martini's *Amore scolastico*; G. B. Marzi's *La fanciulla* (c. 1570); Sforza Oddi's *Erofilomachia* (1572); Belisario Bulgarini's *Gli scambi* (1574); and Cecchi's *Il martello*.

Contemporary references place the braggart in more familiar surroundings, enabling authors to satirize local customs as well as personalities. The duel, for example, is particularly exploited for comic effect and is widely used as a device to uncover the braggart's cowardly nature. Well-versed in the elaborate codification of the duel's ritualistic format, the braggart is ever ready to provide excuses to avoid so risky a contest and decline a challenge he more than likely initiated (or, at least, provoked) himself. Such refusal places the comic emphasis on the dramatic discrepancy between the braggart's boast and his subsequent behavior, between his surficial confidence, and substantive incompetence rather than on the verbal outlandishness of his rhetoric. This discrepancy is highlighted in plays such as Gigio Arthemio Giancarli's *La cingana* (*The Gypsy*, 1545); the English miracle play *The Trial of Treasure* (1567); Lope de Rueda's *Medora* (1567); Ulpian Fulwell's *Like Will to Like* (1568); W. Wager's *The Longer Thou Livest, the More Foole Thou Art* (c. 1568); Della Porta's *L'Olimpia* (*Olympia*, 1588) and his *La fantesca* (*The Maid Servant*, 1592); and Cecchi's *I rivali*.

The Seventeenth and Eighteenth Centuries

After the Renaissance years, the braggart begins to lose his soldier status. Braggart soldiers do continue to people comic drama well into the seventeenth century, however, in plays of such successful dramatists as Pedro Calderón de la Barca (*El principe constante* [*The Loyal Prince*, 1629] and *La puente de Mantible* [*The Bridge of Mantible*, 1632] among others); Pierre Corneille (*L'illusion comique* [*The Comic Deception*, 1636]); Antoine Mareschal (*Le véritable Capitan Matamore* [*The Real Captain Killmoor*, 1640]); and George Farquhar (*The Recruiting Officer*, 1706), but the braggart soldier finds himself more often than not replaced by a braggart-citizen, with fewer and fewer links to the military establishment. The German writer Andreas Gryphius dramatizes the conflict of soldier-turned-citizen in his *Horribilicribrifax* (1663). Although Horribilicribrifax suffers tremendous frustration and humiliation as he attempts to deal with his fallen status in a postwar period, he does ultimately marry (though well beneath his aspirations) and is not totally ostracized at the end of the play.

Although the braggart in this literary period is notably less militaristic, he continues to dwell on his physical attractiveness and overall courageousness, qualities that he generally lacks but which he nevertheless believes he possesses. This emphasis on appearance and posturing tends to take the satirical edge off the character, rendering him more comic than contemptible. From the braggart-dandy in Francisco de Rojas' *Entre bobos anda el juego* (*Sport for Simpletons*, 1638) and in Guillén de Castro's *El narciso en su opinión* (*He Thinks He is Narcissus*, 1625), to the sympathetic, occasionally admirable braggarts of Calderón de la Barca (*El principe constante*, *La vida es sueño* [*Life Is a Dream*, 1635]); Lope de Vega (*La Francesilla* [1596], *El perro de hortelano* [*The Dog in the Manger*, 1618]); Guillén de Castro (*Los enemigos hermanos* [*The Hostile Brothers*, 1625]); Pierre Corneille (*Le Menteur* [*The Liar*, 1643], *La suite du menteur* [*Sequel to the Liar*, 1644); Francisco de Rojas (*No hay amigo para amigo* [*True Friends Do Not Exist*, 1636]) and especially of Shakespeare (*Henry IV*, 1597–1600; *The Merry Wives of Windsor*, c. 1600), the traditional stock character tends to evoke spectator complicity as he incessantly opts for the relative over the absolute in choosing life over ideals.

In Shakespeare's *Henry IV*, Falstaff, a comic hero whose indefatigable wit, irrefutable logic, and linguistic flexibility assure him a place in literary history, nearly single-handedly breaks the traditional stereotypes of the braggart's role. Falstaff is not a mercenary, but an unwilling recruit; he is not a coward, though thoroughly committed to prolonging life for as long as possible; he is not a hedonist, but he is nevertheless endowed with a strong aversion to the ascetic life. Falstaff, in fact, sees himself as a kind of poor man's hero. For him, heroism is not a matter of accomplishment, but of style; exaggeration is not an escape from reality, but a means of artistically re-creating reality in one's own fantasy-ridden image. For Falstaff, linguistic flexibility, an agile wit, and verbal legerdemain constitute the surest means by which the average man can display an enormous range of talents and accede to a kind of heroism previously denied to those of non-noble fiber.

The seventeenth century saw the birth of another legendary literary type: Don Juan, in Tirso de Molina's *El burlador de Sevilla* (*The Libertine of Seville*, 1630). The two stage personae (braggart soldier and Don Juan) are not without parallels: both use lies and exaggerations to obtain their goals; both indulge in hyperbolic self-assessments; both pride themselves on their looks, attractiveness to women, and sexual virility. Moreover, the traditional Don Juan, a heretical womanizer whose obstinate defiance ultimately angers the gods themselves, is destined to meet his destruction, just as the classical braggart plunges headlong toward his eventual humiliation. Yet, Don Juan is only a "braggart" when overstating his courage, as in Molière's play *Dom Juan* (*Don Juan*, 1665), or when exaggerating the number of his conquests. Nevertheless, these two theatrical archetypes remain inextricably linked in the minds of many, and both undergo curiously similar transformations. Whereas both the braggart and Don Juan are initially negative characters, they become increasingly non-negative, virtually heroic, as they evolve through the modern period.

Although the braggart soldier is essentially a theatrical phenomenon, he occurs in various prose writings as well. The Spaniards were among the first to put the braggart in the novel (*Celestina*; Feliciano de Silva's *Segunda Celestina* in 1534; Sancho de Muñón's *Lisandro y Roselia*; Alonso de Villegas' *Selvagia* in 1554). Braggarts in the novel can be found in the seventeenth century also (see, for example, Cervantes' *Don Quijote* (*Don Quixote*, 1605, 1615) and Agrippa d'Aubigné's *Les aventures du Baron de Faeneste* (1617). In the novel, braggarts tend to elicit more complex responses than in the drama. Don Quixote, for example, seems to deceive others less from an intentional desire to alter the truth than from a fundamentally distorted world vision that affects his perception. Convinced of his own heroic purpose, Don Quixote, in spite of his alienation from fellow characters who regard his "apartness" with contempt, does not strike readers as a scornful figure. He inspires, instead, much loftier opinions regarding his self-assigned mission to right the wrongs of an imperfect world.

The Nineteenth and Twentieth Centuries

It is perhaps inevitable that the braggart should achieve heroic stature in the literature of the Romantics, so religiously dedicated to the cult of individuality, and in the literature of twentieth-century, war-weary pacifists who dedicate themselves to the Brechtian notion that the survivor (though coward he may be) is always right. Thus the braggart in nineteenth-century and modern literature appears more self-conscious, more confessional, and more vulnerable than ever before.

Boastfulness in general is treated as a far more complicated phenomenon than in previous literature. In the novel, although portrayed as an eccentric and atypical personality, the braggart nevertheless manages to evoke the admiration of his fellow characters (the hero in Mark Twain's *A Connecticut Yankee in King Arthur's Court*, 1889; Alphonse Daudet's *Tartarin de Tarascon*, 1872; Théophile Gautier's *Capitaine Fracasse*, 1863). The Russians, who have fashioned a life style out of fabricated anecdotes (*vranyo*), also season their literature with this type of tale-teller, who occurs both in the novel (Dostoevsky's *Idiot* [*The Idiot*, 1868]) and in drama (Gogol's *Revizor* [*The Inspector-General*, 1836]). For the Russians particularly, though not exclusively, this notion of exaggeration and/or pure alteration of reality is perfectly acceptable, and the literary creations who engage in this practice are condemned less than they are admired.

Similarly, the braggart in theatrical representations appears much more sympathetic, complex, even heroic. The self-vaunting, egocentric, less than honest hero figures in the plays of serious dramatists, wherein he appears to be less a comic stereotype than a symbol for rugged individualism, rebellion, and nonconformity. In two plays by Henrik Ibsen (*Peer Gynt*, 1867; *Vildanden* [*The Wild Duck*, 1884]), the hero is both a liar and a braggart, though no less dramatically significant. For the modern hero, exaggeration is but the means used to shape a character, a technique enabling one to alter facts in order to reveal a truth that would otherwise remain only potential or approximate. For example, Christopher Mahon in John Millington Synge's play *The Playboy of the Western*

World (1907) uses linguistic hyperbole and misleading half-truths to break beyond the boundaries of conventional mediocrity, to transform the mythic into the plausible.

The braggart thus emerges in the twentieth century as a kind of rhetorical confidence man whose swollen claims transcend reality by painting it in more vivid hues. Unlike the braggart soldier in classical and Renaissance comedy, this modern-day braggart succeeds to an extent, but only insofar as he continues to appear to others as he wishes to be perceived. In other words, his false façade must remain intact throughout the drama, a constant masquerade that demands sustained dedication. Such is the quasi-tragic price to be paid for having placed one's faith in the belief that a role is in fact the only worthwhile reality after all.

Traditional braggarts, those mocked buffoons whose fundamentally ridiculous nature is ultimately revealed to a hostile cast of characters, reoccur in some Indian literature of the twentieth century. In traditional Sanskrit literature, two figures suggest an approximate parallel with the European braggart: the *śakāra* and the *vidūska*. These are only approximations, however. In modern literature, a closer resemblance can be seen between the comic hero, a newly returned Indian traveler from the West, and the traditional European braggart. In current comic drama in India, the braggart-hero is used to mock the hubris of Western ethnocentricity and technology. Instead of praise, the returning voyager is confronted only with the ridicule of an unimpressed and contemptuous audience who fails to appreciate his new-found wisdom, loss of inhibitions, or brash self-assurance. Thus the braggart comes full circle: from simple clown, to complex hero, and back to clown again, as irrepressibly comical, as efficaciously satirical, as dramatically rich as ever.

See also: Fool, Picaresque.

Selected Bibliography

Boughner, Daniel Cliness. *The Braggart in Renaissance Comedy*. Minneapolis: University of Minnesota Press, 1954.

Fest, Otto. *Der Miles Gloriosus in der französischen Komödie der Renaissance bis zu Molière*. Erlangen: Deichert, 1897.

Graf, Hermann. *Der "Miles Gloriosus" im englischen Drama bis zur Zeit des Bürgerkrieges*. Rostock: 1892.

Grismer, Raymond Leonard. *The Influence of Plautus in Spain before Lope de Vega*. New York: Hispanic Institute in USA Press, 1944.

                                                                    M. J. MURATORE

BUTTERFLIES

The image of the golden butterfly upon a rose in Keats' "Sleep and Poetry" (1816) expresses the universal significance of the butterfly as a symbol of beauty:

"A butterfly, with golden wings broad parted, / Nestling a rose, convuls'd as though it smarted / With over-pleasure" (ll. 343–345). Poets and painters fascinated by the rich tones of butterflies have immortalized their beauty in their works. Even their names reveal the evocative power of these creatures. Swallow-tails, wood-nymphs, white-peacock, orange-tips, pearly-eyes, angel-wings are just a few of the poetic names the human imagination has given them.

Mythology, Religion, and Folklore

There are many myths and legends with the winged creature of the insect world as the central theme. In ancient Greek mythology, the Olympian goddess Psyche is represented with the wings of a butterfly. "Psyche" in ancient Greece also meant the "soul" and the butterfly, through its association with the goddess, came to share this meaning. Psyche's wings of a butterfly conveyed the sense of lightness that a soul was believed to possess. In fact in ancient Greek art a butterfly was often depicted over the body of a dead man to signify the departure of the soul from the body. "Psyche" in Greek thus had a dual meaning; the soul and the butterfly.

According to Greek mythology, Psyche was the beautiful mortal loved by Cupid who later, at Cupid's request, was made into a goddess by Jupiter. In ancient Greek art, Cupid's wings too were often represented in the colors of a butterfly's wings. Artists of ancient Greece, with the myth of Cupid and Psyche in mind, at times depicted the figure of Cupid as burning or caressing a butterfly. The underlying symbolic significance was that Cupid was tormenting or loving the goddess Psyche or the human soul.

The association of a butterfly with a god is found in Hindu mythology too. Brahma the Creator is symbolized at times as a butterfly. In fact, the Hindu wedding ceremony in Bengal begins by paying homage to *Prajapati*, meaning "Butterfly," the symbol of creation. The butterfly's association with weddings is not an isolated incident in India. In China and Japan too, the butterfly is regarded as a symbol of conjugal bliss.

The religious symbolism of a butterfly is evident in Christian art. In George Ferguson's *Signs and Symbols of Christian Art* (1954), there is the observation that in paintings of the Virgin and the Child a butterfly is sometimes in the Child's hand. It is used here to represent the Resurrection of Christ. This concept has its origin in the three stages in the life cycle of a butterfly; the caterpillar, the chrysalis, and the butterfly symbolizing life, death, and resurrection. These three stages may also be seen as a progressive movement toward an ideal culminating in the ultimate transformation of the chrysalis into a butterfly.

In folklore there are various works on the theme of the butterfly. An interesting American Indian folktale describing the origin of butterflies is that related by William H. Howe in *Our Butterflies and Moths* (1963). He tells the story of the Shoshone chief who marries the beautiful Ona-Chee-Wah, meaning the "welcome wind of spring." Wakonda, "the Great Spirit-Creator of the winds, water, mountains and all their inhabitants," asks Ona-Chee-Wah to go to a crevice in the mountains where she will find beautiful gems and precious stones. She was to keep half of the gems and to distribute the other half to the children of the Indian tribe. Instead, she made a beautiful necklace and costume for herself with the gems. One day when she ventured too far into the pool to admire her reflection, to her horror, "each stone turned into multi-coloured butterflies which started flying away from her body." Clutching frantically at them, she loses her balance and drowns. Howe writes: "Her screams were heard by some braves of the tribe, but when they arrived at the water's edge, they saw only myriads of butterflies gliding over the lake, in the same colours as the beautiful stones that had decorated Ona-Chee-Wah's costume" (p. 19).

From the Orient we have the well-known tale related by the Chinese Taoist philosopher Chuang Tzu (c. 4th century B.C.) in a treatise attributed to Chuang Chou, who dreamt that he was a butterfly flitting amongst the flowers, sipping nectar. When he awakes, he wonders if he is in reality a butterfly dreaming that he is the philosopher Chuang Tzu. This experience, of course, leads to a philosophical speculation on dreams and reality. However, Chuang Tzu did believe that he was a butterfly.

The Butterfly in English Literature

Edmund Spenser, in *Muiopotmos* or *The Fate of the Butterflie* (1590), however, actually presents the existence of a butterfly. This mythical poem depicting the intense beauty of Clarion's life, the turn of fortune, and his death has all the elements of high tragedy. Spenser, in the opening lines, prays to the "mournfulst Muse of nyne" for inspiration to relate the tragedy of Clarion the butterfly, the son of Muscaroll and heir to the "Empire of the aire." The poet describes how Clarion would fly into the "Christall skie, to vew the workmanship of heauens hight:" and then he would descend and fly along the "streaming riuers." On a summer's day, Clarion's preparation for his flight is described as that of a warrior wearing his battle attire. When he wears his wings, the intensity of their beauty is realized through the comparisons the poet makes. They surpassed that of "Iris bowe, . . . heaven with manie a twinckling starre, . . . Iunoes Bird in her ey-spotted traine." Whilst expressing the beauty of Clarion's wings Spenser digresses from the main tale to relate another myth associated with the color of the butterflies' wings. Venus, frolicking with her nymphs one spring day, asks them to gather flowers to adorn her forehead. When one nymph gathers more flowers than the rest, out of envy they tell Venus that her son Cupid had given her aid in secret. The goddess, remembering the affair between Cupid and Psyche, is enraged and she turns the nymph into a winged butterfly. All the flowers she has collected are "placed in her wings, for memorie/ Of her pretended crime." Spenser states that from this time on the butterfly bears the flowers in her wings.

After this mythic tale Spenser returns to the main tale where Clarion is now ready for his flight. His flight through woods, rivers, green meadows, and mountains conveys the full beauty of his existence. Spenser comments:

What more felicitie can fall to creature,
Than to enjoy delight with libertie,
And to be Lord of all the workes of Nature,
To raine in th'aire from earth to highest skie,
To feed on flowres, and weeds of glorious feature,
To take what euer thing doth please the eie?
Who rests not pleased with such happiness,

(ll.209–215)

These lines provide an insight into reasons why the human imagination at times entertains the idea of being a butterfly. This moment in the tale is the highest point of happiness for the butterfly. However, Spenser is aware that the wheel of fortune is always turning and that the "unhappie happie Flie" is destined for a cruel fate. The garden was also the abode of Aragnoll, the foe of the butterfly. Spenser digresses from the main tale to account for Aragnoll's malice toward Clarion. Aragnoll's mother was Arachne, a renowned "fine-fingred work-woman," who challenged the goddess Minerva to a tapestry competition. Arachne was convinced of her defeat when she saw the rare workmanship of the butterfly "fluttring among the Oliues wantonly." The outcome of her jealousy was that she was transformed into a grissly creature. Aragnoll, her son, now seeking revenge, wove a fine net about his cave to entrap the "careles Clarion." Ultimately Clarion the butterfly caught in the web is killed by the spider Aragnoll. Clarion's life was so beautiful, intense, and free that this shocking end is indeed tragic. Spenser, through this mythic tale, has brought out the beauty as well as the vulnerability of a butterfly's existence.

The myth of Cupid and Psyche was alluded to by Spenser. Romantic poet John Keats in his "Ode to Psyche" (1819) celebrates the worship of Psyche. "Surely I dreamt to-day; or did I see / The winged Psyche with awaken'd eyes?" (ll.5–6) he asks himself. He describes his vision of Cupid and Psyche in a beautiful natural setting embracing not only with their arms but also with their wings: "Their arms embraced, and their pinions too, / Their lips touch'd not, but had not bid adieu" (ll.16–17). Keats repeatedly refers to the wings of Cupid and Psyche. Through his imagination he sees the "lucent fans" of Psyche "fluttering among the faint Olympians." In this vision Keats is visualizing Psyche as a butterfly goddess. As a worshipper of Psyche, Keats builds a sanctuary by means of his imagination for the worship of the last Olympian goddess.

William Wordsworth has two lyrics addressed "To a Butterfly" (1802). The lyric beginning with the lines "Stay near me-do not take flight!/A little longer stay in sight!" shows how the poet's observation of a butterfly transports him to a moment in time. He calls the butterfly a "historian of my infancy" as the past comes alive for him: "Float near me; do not yet depart! / Dead times revive in thee" (ll.5–6). He recalls the pleasant days when he and his sister Emmeline "together chased the butterfly." The following lines not only convey the fervor of the chase but also bring out the contrasting attitude toward the butterfly that he and his sister possessed:

A very hunter did I rush
Upon the prey:—with leaps and springs
I followed on from brake to bush;
But she, God love her, feared to brush
The dust from off its wings.

(ll.14–18)

Wordsworth has touched on an important issue in the image of the hunter chasing its prey. This is the cruelty involved in the killing of butterflies that forms a part of the collector's hobby. William Shakespeare, in the play *King Lear* (1606), has brought out the element of cruelty in butterfly collecting by making the blind earl of Gloster say: "As flies to wanton boys are we to the gods, / They kill us for their sport" (4.1). These lines indeed call for reflection as we put ourselves in the butterfly's position and relate all the human suffering in *King Lear* to them. In Wordsworth's lyric the image of the hunter highlights the human urge to capture and possess this creature. On the other hand Emmeline's attitude shows an awareness of its frailty. She just looks at it fearing to "brush the dust from off its wings."

In the second lyric, "To a Butterfly" it is, however, Wordsworth who observes the butterfly sitting motionless upon a flower:

I've watched you now a full half-hour,
Self-poised upon that yellow flower;
And, little Butterfly! indeed
I know not if you sleep or feed.

(ll.1–4)

He imagines the butterfly floating among the trees in the breeze. He extends an invitation to the butterfly to use the trees and flowers in their orchard ground as a sanctuary, telling it at the same time that they would "talk of sunshine and of song, and summer days." These words reveal the common association of the butterfly with sunshine, song, and summer days.

The Butterfly and Its Many Associations

Certain qualities have come to be very strongly associated with the butterfly. When Thomas Hood in a poem entitled "No!" (1844) includes the butterflies in his list of negatives, he reveals how in his mind butterflies are associated with warmth, cheerfulness, comfort, shade, sunshine, flowers, spring, and nature. In the month of November he writes:

No warmth, no cheerfulness, no healthful ease
No comfortable feel in any member
No shade, no shine, no butterflies, no bees
No fruits, no flowers, no leaves, no birds,—
November!

(ll.20–24)

Other qualities such as delicacy, beauty, and airiness are also associated with it. These impressions are at times so strong that they come to mind with the very mention of the creature. John Luther Long's novel *Madame Butterfly* (1898), which inspired the creation of the opera by Puccini (1900), does not have the butterfly as a central theme. However, the name "Madame Butterfly" gives the sense of the delicate beauty of the Japanese maiden. A contradiction may be seen in Henri Charrière's novel *Papillon* (1969), where "Papillon" is the name of the protagonist who spends his life in and out of prison. Though wrongfully convicted, he is called "Papillon" in the underworld because of his butterfly tattoo. A poignant moment occurs when Papillon is in his prison cell in Caen and through a crack he sees a blue butterfly fluttering past. To the prisoner the butterfly symbolizes nature, life, freedom; all the elements denied him. He himself states that this vision affects him as life after death. The prisoner, conscious of its beauty, feels the unnaturalness of its appearance in the prison atmosphere. He feels that sheer contact with the atmosphere surrounding the prison should be enough to kill it. This image of the prisoner observing the butterfly from his cell highlights the symbolic significance of the butterfly as a symbol of the beauty of life and freedom. In Leonard Gershe's drama, which has been made into a motion picture and is entitled *Butterflies are Free* (1969), the butterfly becomes a symbol of freedom for Don Baker and Jill Tanner. Strumming on his guitar, Don sings, "Butterflies are free/And so are we."

Nabokov and the Butterfly

One writer whose works contain the motif of the butterfly is Vladmir Nabokov, who was himself a butterfly collector. In *Strong Opinions* (1973) Nabokov, speaking of his own pleasures, states: "My pleasures are the most intense known to man: writing and butterfly hunting." Through Nabokov one can understand the passion of the butterfly collector. In *Speak, Memory* (1966) Nabokov describes "the highest enjoyment of timelessness" as the moment when he is standing among rare butterflies: "This is ecstasy, and behind the ecstasy is something else, which is hard to explain. It is like a momentary vacuum into which rushes all that I love. A sense of oneness with sun and stone." One of Nabokov's favorite specimens was the "Vanessa atalanta," genus "Nymphalidae," the Red Admirable (or Admiral). This particular butterfly appears in several of Nabokov's works (see George Steiner's *Extraterritorial*, 1971). The fictitious poet John Shade in Nabokov's novel *Pale Fire* (1962) celebrates this butterfly: "My dark Vanessa, Crimson-barred, my blest/My Admirable butterfly!" Steiner observes that "a Red Admirable alights on his arm the minute before he is killed." Again, "Vanessa Van Ness," Steiner points out, is the "maiden name of the mother of Humbert's first fatal love, "Annabel Leigh" in the novel *Lolita* (1955). He also views Lolita as being "a member of the Nymphalidae family." An idea of the Red Admirable may be had from the picture Steiner presents in his book.

Nabokov's story "Rozhdestvo" ("Christmas"), written in Berlin at the end of 1924, has the butterfly as an important motif. The central theme is the grief of Slepstov, the father, over the death of his son. His memories of his son, however, for the most part are related to the butterfly. Whilst walking in the snow he remembers his son in this very scene during summer time, "deftly plucking off with his net a butterfly that had settled on the railing." Again, when he enters his son's study the articles belonging to his son's butterfly collection bring back memories that cause him to break into tears. In the desk, Slepstov found "a notebook, spreading boards, supplies of black pins, an English biscuit tin that contained a large exotic cocoon" and a torn net. It is the memory of his son's absorption with butterflies that cause the father to experience his sharpest grief. Whilst looking at the "files of specimens," reminiscences of his son in this very room come back:

On that very desk, his son had spread the wings of his captures. He would first pin the carefully killed insect in the cork-bottomed groove of the setting board, between the adjustable strips of wood, and fasten down flat with pinned strips of paper the still fresh, soft wings (pp. 157–158).

This is a detailed account of the methods used by the collector to display the butterflies. Earlier, we have examined the role of the butterfly collector in an unfavorable light through Gloster's statement in Shakespeare's *King Lear* and Wordsworth's image of the hunter, hunting for his prey. However, Slepstov's appreciation of the butterflies that his son had mounted reveals how the butterflies in their death have been immortalized as objects of art. Slepstov admires "those spectacular Swallow-tails, those dazzling Coppers and Blues, and the various Fritallaries," some of which were displaying their "mother-of-pearl underside." His exclamation, "the moths, the moths, the first Aspen Hawk of five summers ago," points to the fact that the collector kills in order to preserve the beauty. His son, who had collected these specimens, was dead, and yet these Swallow-tails "dazzling Coppers and Blues" live on as objects of beauty for the appreciation of the human eye. Slepstov's grief over his son's death grows in intensity until it reaches a climax when he thinks of suicide. The "earthly life lay before him, totally bared and comprehensible . . . and ghastly in its sadness, humiliatingly pointless, sterile, devoid of miracles." At this point the miracle does happen as the moth breaks the cocoon to emerge. Nabokov makes use of the "great Altacus moth" here, but the butterfly would have served the same function. The sudden snap of the cocoon takes Slepstov's mind away from thoughts of suicide. It was almost as if the creature "had awaited this moment" to unfold to Slepstov the miracles of life. The moth serves a symbolic function as Slepstov, through it, experiences a resurrection after death. Though throughout the story there is a gradual deepening of grief, a change occurs with the emergence of the moth from the chrysalis and the story ends with a celebration of life.

Hawthorne and the Butterfly

Perhaps nowhere is the full essence of the butterfly realized more intensely than in Nathaniel Hawthorne's story "The Artist of the Beautiful" (1844). Owen

Warland, "the artist of the beautiful," was obsessed with the idea of creating a miniature work of art containing a spiritual beauty. He strove to "put the very spirit of beauty into form and give it motion." When Peter Hovenden, himself a retired watchmaker, lifts the bell glass out of curiosity to discover what the watchmaker had been devoting all his time to, he finds "a mechanical something, as delicate and minute as the system of a butterfly's anatomy." Owen was attempting to create something so delicate that the very presence of the "hard, coarse world" in the form of Peter Hovenden threatened its existence.

The artist's creative ideal is again and again presented through the image of the butterfly. Hawthorne not only embodies the pursuit of beauty by all artists through a butterfly chase, but he also shows how half the beauty and mystery is lost in capturing the beauty in art, in giving form to the conception.

Through the butterfly, Owen Warland tries to make perceptible to mortal senses not only the quintessence of beauty but also the soul of an artist of the Beautiful. To the artist, not only is the butterfly supreme of all God's creations, but it is also the symbol of his own intellect, imagination, and sensibility. This ethereal creature is there for all of humanity; for Papillon looking out of his cell as well as the artist of the "Beautiful." It is almost Nature's messenger flitting about and bringing a little joy and beauty to the soul of all mankind.

Selected Bibliography

Ferguson, George. *Signs and Symbols in Christian Art*. 2d ed. New York: Oxford University Press, 1955.

Howe, William H. *Our Butterflies and Moths*. North Kansas City, Missouri: True Color, 1963.

Williams, Charles Alfred Speed. *Outlines of Chinese Symbolism*. 1931. Taipei: Ch'eng Wen, 1973.

APARAJITA MAZUMDER

C
//

CAPITALISM

The word "capital," from the Late Latin word *caput* for head, emerged in the late twelfth century and referred to funds or to interest-bearing money. The term, as Fernand Braudel has shown, was at first used loosely as a synonym for wealth, goods, assets, property, and inheritance, although it was also used more specifically to denote the principal of a loan. In the mid–1700s, "capital" came to mean productive money. In 1867, Karl Marx's *Das Kapital* (*Capital*, 1867–1894) defined capital as the means of production, and this usage has become standard.

The term "capitalist" was created in the mid–1600s to designate the chief holders of capital: the rich, the people of means. Although the term had the narrower meaning of "provider of investment," it was most often used as a synonym for "wealthy" and was, in any event, consistently pejorative. Not until the early nineteenth century did "capitalist" come to mean primarily an investor or an entrepreneur, a person who might be regarded positively.

The term "capitalism," the latest of the three, was not known to Marx; it was first given serious currency by Werner Sombart's treatise *Der moderne Kapitalismus* (1902). The meaning of "capitalism" has been a thorny issue for historians, philosophers, and political scientists, as has the question of how, when, where, and why the phenomenon arose. Capitalism has been defined as an economic, political, and ideological system characterized by private ownership of physical and human resources (the latter including the individual's mind and body); it is seen as opposed to the ownership of these resources by the community at large or by one segment or class of the community to the exclusion of other segments or classes.

Capitalism is generally viewed as a modern and Western institution, germinating in the sixteenth century, moving from Holland to France and England in the eighteenth and nineteenth centuries, and from there to the United States and eventually also to Germany and Japan. Although claims have been made for capitalistic activity in such places as ancient Babylon and Hellenistic Greece, most writers associate capitalism with the salient features of the modern Western landscape: world-scale trade, the rise of the middle class, the growth of technology and industrial production, the increased rate of capital formation. Adam Smith's *The Wealth of Nations* (1776) is often considered the classic defense of the system. The period beginning in the sixteenth century is sometimes referred to as that of "mercantile capitalism," while "industrial capitalism" dates from the nineteenth century. Various interpretations have been offered for the rise of capitalism; cited factors include the class struggle between the burgeoning bourgeoisie and the decadent nobility, the post-Reformation encouragement of mercantilism and the Protestant "work ethic," the distinctly modern climate of rationality and good faith, and the close connection between capitalism and the modern aspirations for political and economic freedom.

The multiplicity of explanations for capitalism testifies, as does the lateness of the term and the variety of activities associated with it, to a certain confusion about what capitalism is—or at least to some flexibility in the use of the term. When a work is identified by its writer or by a critic as dealing with the theme of capitalism, the reader may expect to find therein such elements as materialism and mercantilism, big business and high finance, banking and speculation, industry and technology, invention and exploitation, wealth and poverty, or all of the above.

Capitalism and Literature

As a literary motif, capitalism can be seen as the translation of personal relationships into the language of commerce and exchange, with the attendant transformation of human beings into the objects as well as the subjects of trade. The negative aspect of this practice lies in the risk of ignoring important qualities while assigning a quantitative ranking, and thus reducing a human being to a narrowly conceived utilitarian function (as a medium of exchange). The positive aspect stems from the act of appraisal itself; in asserting the "value" of a human being, one takes on the responsibility of determining and affirming what that person is "worth," and to whom, and for what purpose.

Commercial metaphors have become more prevalent as capitalism has flourished. In *Literature and the Rise of Capitalism* (1973), Raymond Southall detects in sixteenth-century English poetry a new idiom, a new expression of "personal affections in economic terms"; he traces the shift from Sir Thomas Wyatt to Sir Philip Sidney and Edmund Spenser. Women in particular were often seen as amenable to the calculation of a price, from Daniel Defoe's *Moll Flanders* (novel, 1722), whose romantic career is a matter of successful "investments," to Edith Wharton's Lily Bart in the novel *The House of Mirth* (1905), whose lover tries to estimate her "cost," whose friends consider her only in terms of the "profit" to be derived from her acquaintance, who is pressured to "pay up" sexually, and who ends as a suicide, with all her debts paid and with nowhere, emotionally speaking, to go. The commercial perspective pervades such novels as *Vanity Fair* (1847–1848), in which William Makepeace Thackeray borrows Bunyan's image to liken the world to a corrupt marketplace. The whole landscape of Jane Austen, as Alastair Duckworth has shown, can be treated in terms of "the improvement of the estate"; the universe of Henry James is similarly susceptible to description in economic language (saving and investment in *The Spoils of Poynton*, 1897; speculation in *Portrait of a Lady*, 1881; manufacturing in *The Ambassadors*, 1903; trade and purchase in *The Golden Bowl*, 1904, etc.). Perhaps the darkest usage of commercial language appears in Mario Puzo's *The Godfather* (1969), in which "business" is a synonym for mob affairs, and in which a threat against a life is described as an offer that cannot be refused.

Commercial language, however, cannot be construed as a systematic ideological response to the system of capitalism. Although readers may choose to interpret commercial language as a pejorative commentary on the market economy (and those who do so generally exhibit the hostility they believe they detect in the writer), although the writer may even intend the language to reflect opposition to capitalism (i.e., the reduction of human beings to disposable commodities), these negative sentiments are not inherent in the language. There is a great distance from the woman of valor, whose price is above rubies (Prov. 31:10), to the Don's offer that cannot be refused. In adopting the motif of capitalistic language, writers can be negative, positive, or ambivalent.

The same is true, and more clearly so, in the treatment of capitalism as a theme, and it is the task of this entry to trace these three types of responses in literature. Most of the examples will be drawn from modern Western literature, which has provided the most extensive dramatic embodiment and portrayal of the issues and events of what is seen primarily as a modern, Western phenomenon; although other literatures may include factories, wealth, and other elements associated with capitalism, there is little direct attention to the defining characteristic of capitalism: private ownership. A similar limitation applies to the selection of genres; although several poems and plays contain references to business, money, and technology, the vast majority of the works are written in fictional and nonfictional prose, which is more suited to the exposition of ideological issues and to the presentation of a world in which those issues are worked through.

Discussion in the text will also be restricted to works in which the focus on capitalism is direct and apparent; although Igor Webb has said that any British novel from 1780 to 1850 is ineluctably a novel about capitalism (and others have extended the range to other nations and broader time periods), it seems unwise to broaden the context to that extent.

Works will be classified as positive, negative, or ambivalent on the basis of the predominant response to the moral validity and practical value of the private ownership of physical and human resources. A novel that presents a personally admirable captain of industry may nonetheless be ambivalent about capitalism, while one that is procapitalist may portray a single despicable tycoon. The prevailing attitude determines the classification. Nine representative writers will be treated under each category.

Negative Responses to Capitalism

Writers typically attack capitalism in two ways: through protest and through burlesque. The perceived evils attendant on capitalism—the unwholesome spirit of acquisition, the exploitation of labor, the dehumanizing effects of quantification, the basic dishonesty of speculation, the uncontrolled exercise of the profit motive—are the objects of passionate criticism and satiric mockery. The capitalist—also known as the "magnate," "merchant," "tycoon," "businessman," "Robber Baron," "captain of industry," and "Napoleon of finance"—is condemned as the enemy of the people and a cultural ignoramus (or "Philistine," in Matthew Arnold's classic formulation). He or she is greedy, ruthless, unscrupulous, insensitive, uncouth, sexually lax, socially irresponsible, and emotionally maladjusted. The capitalist is rarely presented here as a decent person coerced by impossible choices; that perspective belongs more often to the ambivalent responses. Capitalism and the capitalist are instead seen as mutually reinforcing; the system fosters the development of such people, and the people allow the system to continue to function.

The first half of *Utopia* (1516), a political romance by Sir Thomas More, contains, in dialogue form, an attack on what he saw as the division of the human community into exploited laborers and idle, gluttonous "wealthy men" (by which he meant the nobility and the clergy as well as traders, merchants, and bankers). The workers, he said, derive no profit, while the profit-makers perform no work. He perceived this paradox and this disjunction as characteristic of a distinctly modern social order, the injustice and disharmony of which troubled him deeply, as did such commercial practices as price-fixing and the artificial creation of a scarcity. Although More occasionally refers to usury, which had long been a target for criticism, the focus of his attack here is mercantile capitalism.

Three hundred years later, Thomas Carlyle, who is credited with coining the term "industrialism," extended the attack to industrial capitalism. In *Sartor Resartus* (philosophical satire, 1833–1834), Carlyle blames the machine and the commercial vision for crowding out art, thought, science, and all other values of mind and soul. The theme recurs, with the passion of savage prophecy, throughout his work, notably in his essays, *Chartism* (1839) and *Past and Present* (1843). The defining of human relationships in commercial terms, the brutal ethics of competition, the inevitable law of supply and demand—all these, Carlyle felt, have violated the natural order. The plague, however, was not entirely incurable. If the captains of industry were to reject the "Cash-Gospel" and the "Brute-god Mammon" in favor of the "Spirit-god," then the energy of industrialism might be harnessed to good. It is not the mills themselves that are "Satanic"—to borrow Blake's famous phrase—but the mill-owners when in the power of the cash nexus.

Honoré de Balzac (1799–1850), as Harry Levin observes (*The Gates of Horn*, 1963), "has graphically illustrated Carlyle's strongest contention: that the laissez-faire society of industrial capitalism discounts all obligations except the cash nexus." In a series of novels, known as *La comédie humaine* (*The Human Comedy*, 1842–1850), written over a period of twenty years, Balzac classifies his characters by their financial status, and each character gauges his or her life success in terms of profit and loss. All relationships are transactions, contracts, calculations; this fact, for Balzac, drains the soul of vitality. It is not only the moneylender Gobseck who believes that gold "contains everything in essence and gives everything in reality." The profit motive governs the actions of all of Balzac's characters, from Félix's dedication to greed in *Eugénie Grandet* (1833) to Lucien's capitulation to royalist bribes in *Splendeurs et misères des courtisanes* (*The Splendors and Miseries of Courtesans*, 1830) to Eugène's corrupt stock-market deals in *La maison Nucingen* (*The House of Nucingen*, 1838). Instead of concentrating on the wealthiest and most powerful figures, Balzac broadens the attack to include the whole society.

Herman Melville then extends the field of fire to include the entire universe. In three very different works of fiction, written in the decade following Balzac's death, Melville evokes, despairingly, a connection between capitalism and the devil. In the novel *Moby-Dick* (1851), Captain Ahab's pride leads him to ally himself with Satan, baptizing his harpoon "in nomine diaboli"; he then supervises the activity of a whaling ship that resembles a factory for processing whales. Bildad and Peleg, the major shareholders of the expedition, are implicitly criticized for greed and unearned gain. Wayne Westbrook (*Wall Street in the American Novel*, 1980) writes: "the *Pequod* is an American corporation, stock-owned, ill-managed, and fated for bankruptcy." The narrator of *Bartleby the Scrivener: A Story of Wall Street* (novella, 1853), a lawyer whose idol is John Jacob Astor, appears at first to be a decent man; when his copyist Bartleby, formerly of the Dead Letter Office, announces that he "would prefer not to" fulfill some (and, eventually, all) of his tasks, the employer fires him but allows him to remain in the building. When the lawyer moves his chambers to another building, Bartleby prefers not to leave and ultimately dies of starvation, in jail. Although the lawyer attempts to be kind, the business world is presented as cold, impersonal, confining, isolating, deceptive. The name "Wall Street" is itself a metaphor, and the lawyer is guilty of complacence and stubborn insensitivity, not to be excused even by Bartleby's self-destructive withdrawal. The third work is the novel *The Confidence-Man* (1857). In the course of a steamboat voyage from St. Louis to New Orleans, the protagonist adopts several disguises calculated to obtain something for nothing. His goal is not money per se, but "confidence," fraudulently secured. His swindles involve patent medicine, bogus charities, and a most interesting "World's Charity" organized according to the "Wall Street spirit." With pointed allusions to Eden and a near-paraphrase of a speech in the poem *Paradise Lost* (1667), Melville implies that the confidence man represents the devil let loose on an unprotected world.

A naturalistic depiction of an equally despairing attitude is found in *The Octopus* (1901) and *The Pit* (posthumously published in 1903), the first volumes of an uncompleted trilogy on the wheat business, by Frank Norris (1870–1902). Born Benjamin Franklin Norris, he abridged Franklin's name and failed to share his namesake's regard for the capitalist system. For Norris, as for Melville, the capitalist often belongs to the devil's party, by nature or by choice. Although Norris does not condemn business out of hand, and although he seems to relish the power and energy of the businessman Curtis Jadwin, the titles and governing images of these two novels are telling. In the conflict between the San Joaquin ranchers and the railroad in *The Octopus*, the monopolistic corporation is a monster of destruction, laying waste to land and labor: "the soulless Force, the iron-hearted Power, the Colossus, the Octopus." Curtis Jadwin, a successful real estate businessman tempted in *The Pit* into speculation, attempts to corner the wheat market and thus to direct and control the force of life. His dramatic fall implicitly recalls that of Lucifer. Norris describes the Chicago Board of Trade, which eventually defeats Jadwin, as "a great whirlpool, a pit of roaring waters that spun and thundered, sucking in the life tides of the city, sucking them in as into the mouth of some tremendous cloaca." Norris deliberately differentiated between private and corporate capitalists; his books cannot therefore be taken as blanket indictments of capitalism. Norris' awe of the railroad and the stock exchange, of the Octopus and the Pit, seems, nonetheless, to reflect a fascination with a system perceived as evil absolute.

Plunder (1948), by Samuel Hopkins Adams (1871–1958), can stand for the many antibusiness novels inspired by a crusading zeal. Adams, a muckraking journalist for *Collier's* and *McClure's*, specialized in exposing fraud in medicine, journalism, and government. The chief characters in *Plunder*—described as vultures, tarantulas, snakes, and saurians—spread death through the manufacture of defective airplanes, shells, ships, armor plate. One of them invents "tozerite," designed to protect against atomic gamma rays; its only flaw is that it does not work. The inventor, far from being shaken by the cancer his son-in-law develops while trusting to the protection of tozerite, pursues a new scheme: a plot to purchase the government. In *Plunder* and in other books like it, the rhetoric is florid, the plot melodramatic, and the antibusiness sentiment absolutely clear.

In a career spanning seventy years and eighty-odd books, Upton Sinclair (1878–1968) carried on the muckraker campaign against capitalism with greater knowledge, consistency, and sophistication. An open advocate of socialism, Sinclair attacked the press (*The Brass Check*, treatise, 1920), the coal industry (*King Coal*, novel, 1917), the Teapot Dome scandal (*Oil!* novel, 1927), high finance (*A Captain of Industry*, novel, 1906), and J. P. Morgan himself, whom he accused of causing the Great Panic of 1907 (*The Moneychangers*, novel, 1908). All areas of life, he believed, were tainted by the predatory corruption characteristic of the capitalistic system. In his most famous novel, *The Jungle* (1906), which was instrumental in the passage of the Pure Food and Drug Act, Sinclair compares the workers to the mutilated and processed animals in the stinking stockyard slaughterhouses. The Durham family factory is seen by the protagonist as "a seething cauldron of jealousies and hatreds; there was no loyalty or decency anywhere about it, there was no place in it where a man counted for anything against a dollar." In this novel, which gave rise to the school of "proletarian literature," the worker is a saintly sufferer, an innocent victim, while the capitalists are vicious, dishonest, and generally unattractive. In the series of six Lanny Budd novels (1940–1945), Sinclair applies a Marxist critique to international politics from the beginning of the First World War to the middle of the Second. He remained, throughout his career, committed to socialism and consequently opposed to capitalism.

A contemporary of Sinclair's, living under socialism, expressed suspicion of capitalism from a very different perspective. Iurii Olesha's *Zavist'* (*Envy*), an anticapitalist novel of fantasy, is also an anti-Soviet satire (1927). Olesha (1899–1960), whose fiction and scenarios celebrated the unique moment, the particular person, and the precise sensation, presents in *Zavist'* a successful, pragmatic, and ambitious sausage manufacturer who despises art and worships the very process of mass-production. His young protégé, a famous soccer player with perfect teeth, expresses a desire to become a machine. The manufacturer's opponents in the novel are his near-senile brother, who speaks of organizing a "Conspiracy of Feelings" to protect this endangered species, and a drunken poet, who asserts, in the face of the perfect sausage and perfect machine, the need for love, honor, and self-respect. Olesha, in his sympathy for the brother and the drunkard, protests against the anti-intellectualism and narrow utilitarianism he regretfully finds characteristic of a Soviet society that has borrowed from capitalism its least appealing aspects.

A recent absurdist treatment of capitalism is the novel *JR* by William Gaddis (born in 1922). *The Recognitions* (novel, 1955) included a burlesque treatment of an evil businessman. In *JR* (1975), a sixth-grade boy, after touring the New York Stock Exchange, makes a fortune with a single dummy stock, which he buys and sells from a phone booth near the bathroom at school. Ignored by his teacher and family, uneducated and isolated, he uses his money only to make more money. A parody of the Horatio Alger hero, he works hard, saves money, follows advice (when he eavesdrops in the bathroom of the Stock Exchange), yet derives no pleasure from his paper empire. Decency, truth, beauty, and sensitivity have no place in his world. The vision he saw in his tour of the Exchange—chaos, panic, inefficiency—never leaves him. The capitalist world according to Gaddis is devoid of true value.

Ambivalent Responses to Capitalism

Ambivalence results from a combination of sympathy, suspicion, and reservation. Ambivalent writers are typically concerned about such matters as unscrupulous business practices, class antagonisms, inferior working conditions, poverty, and unemployment; they do not, however, see capitalism as solely responsible, nor do they anticipate that the abolition of capitalism would remedy these matters. While they recognize the growth of capitalism as part of a larger social change, they often seem to want, as John Updike has said in connection with the humble beer can, "Progress with an escape hatch." The escape hatch, for most of these writers, consists of individual moral attention to honor, integrity, and sensitivity. Salvation is at hand without an upheaval of the system. This salvation can take shape through a personal retreat from the world of business or through a personal reform of one's dishonest or exploitative activities. For this reason, the ambivalent responses to capitalism explore the capitalist's psychology more frequently than do the attacks or the defenses of the system. Ambivalent writers are, on the whole, less concerned with class struggle than with character.

Although the novelist Charles Dickens is often identified as an enemy of industrial capitalism, in the spirit of his friend Carlyle, his attitude is more appropriately described as ambivalent. Dickens is indeed responsible for the classic portraits of an embittered, dessicated miser dedicated to the profit motive (Scrooge in *A Christmas Carol* [novella, 1843]) and of a soul-deadening manufacturing environment (Coketown in *Hard Times* [1854]). Evil representatives of capitalism include Ralph Nickleby in *Nicholas Nickleby* (1838–1839), Dombey in *Dombey and Son* (1846–1848), Bounderby in *Hard Times*, Merdle in *Little Dorrit* (1855–1857), and Veneering in *Our Mutual Friend* (1864–1865). They are typically rude and dishonest in both personal and professional dealings. By their side, however, one must place such benevolent figures as the Cheeryble brothers in *Nicholas Nickleby*, Solomon Gills in *Dombey and Son*, Rouncewell in *Bleak House* (1853), Arthur Clennam in *Little Dorrit*, and Jarvis Lorry in *A Tale of Two Cities* (1859). The variety of attitudes demonstrates, as John McVeagh says, that "Dickens may be against capitalism purely considered, as against any purely considered system, but is not against all capitalists." Some readers see Dickens' view as becoming gradually darker and culminating in a vision of social, moral, and intellectual disarray, while others observe that the specifically capitalist forces of evil become progressively less potent. In either event, Dickens located the choice of good or evil within the individual heart and not merely within the system. Although Daniel Quilp's entrepreneurial activities (*The Old Curiosity Shop*, 1840) are suspect, those of the inventor Daniel Doyce (*Little Dorrit*) are admired.

The novels of Elizabeth Gaskell reveal a similar hope for the moral potential of capitalism and a similar sympathy for the victims of the system's abuses. *Mary Barton* (1848), often said to be the first realistic portrayal of the Manchester industrial poor, criticizes both the violence of a working man who murders his employer's son and the arrogance of a mill-owner who is out of touch with his workers; the solution to the strike and to the distance between capital and labor lies in the employers' willingness to seek that solution. In *North and South* (1855), Gaskell traces the moral regeneration of a manufacturer through his repudiation of the cash nexus in favor of material dependence and "actual personal contact"; after a mob rebellion at the mill and a series of conversations with a persuasively humanistic woman, the manufacturer endeavors to respect the independence of his employees by considering not only their welfare, but also their abilities to choose freely the way that this welfare is to be pursued. Gaskell's works express the spirit of reconciliation, as opposed to resolution.

William Dean Howells, whose long career in fiction and criticism encompassed his awakening interest in economics and a consequent broadening of his focus from individual to social ethics, believed that competitive capitalism was dangerous to moral health. Speculation in particular fostered dishonesty, idleness, and exploitation; the moral and financial troubles of Silas Lapham in *The Rise of Silas Lapham* (1885), Jacob Dryfoos in *A Hazard of New Fortunes* (1890), and J. Mills Northwick in *The Quality of Mercy* (1892) are largely due to speculation. Howells, nonetheless, presented a range of capitalists and dealt with each separately and subtly. Jeff Durgin, in *The Landlord at Lion's Head* (1897), a self-made builder of resort hotels, achieves social and financial success without a corresponding moral downfall. Selectively assimilating the ideas of Ruskin, Tolstoy, and the Marxist socialists, Howells gave expression, especially in his later novels, to his fears of economic individualism and his hope that, under Christian socialism, economic security would allow natural goodness to flower. In the utopian romance of *A Traveler from Altruria* (1894) and its sequel, *Through the Eye of the Needle* (1907), Howell contrasts America's economic distress and moral malaise with the happiness and prosperity of Altruria's cooperative commonwealth. Yet Howells also recognized, as he wrote in "The Man of Letters as a Man of Business" (1902), that business constitutes a universal bond, that art too is a commodity, that the artist is not alien to the world of labor and exchange. Silas Lapham, sometimes said to be the first nonvillainous American businessman, is defeated not by personal venality, but by bad luck, tactical errors, and unwise speculation; at the end, he achieves moral redemption along with his financial ruin. Jacob Dryfoos, on the other hand, although chastened by his son's death at a strikers' protest, is unrepentant (unlike the manufacturer in *Mary Barton*). As Basil March, a character in the novel, says of Dryfoos, he "must have undergone a moral deterioration, an atrophy of the generous instincts." March seems to speak for Howells when he adds: "I am not very proud when I realize that such a man and his experience are the ideal and ambition of most Americans." For Howells, however, not all capitalists were the moral equivalent of Jacob Dryfoos—although the system allowed such meanness to thrive.

Another portrait of a capitalist who is admired, denigrated, and closely examined appears in *Memoirs of an American Citizen* (1905), by Robert Herrick. Herrick, a teacher and a writer who frequently decried the shamefulness of "selling out" to commercialism, here provides sympathetic insight into the nature of Edward Van Harrington—industrialist, financier, and United States Senator—by allowing him to speak in his own voice. Believing that "the strong must rule," Harrington sees no need to obey laws, and for this he is criticized by his sister-in-law as "the devil's instrument." He is, indeed, entirely willing to violate secret contracts and to bribe public officials. Yet he will not sell defective goods or foresake his helpless stockholders. He feels loyalty to his work and to his dependents and to no one else. After he buys his seat in the Senate, he meditates on his career and feels satisfied: "These were my plants, my car line, my railroad, my elevators, my land—all good tools in the infinite work of the world. . . . The thought of my brain, the labor of my body, the will within me, have gone to the making of this world." Even if one assumes that Herrick intends Harrington to be read ironically, the heartfelt pride in personal achievement is not entirely vitiated. Powerful and productive, Harrington is honorable in his fashion. He is often described as a prototype of Theodore Dreiser's Frank Algernon Cowperwood.

Theodore Dreiser, whose first novel, *Sister Carrie* (1900), was admired and accepted for Doubleday by Frank Norris, created what Henry March Smith has called "by far the most impressive portrait of a big businessman in American fiction." With a sublime disdain "for the conventional mind" and "no consciousness of what is currently known as sin," Frank Algernon Cowperwood, a wealthy financier and broker, has clawed his way upward from a modest background by obeying "a private law—I satisfy myself." Cowperwood is modeled on Charles T. Yerkes, whose success in a street railways syndicate was based not on the creation of a good product or the providing of a valuable service, but on the bribery of public officials and the shrewd manipulation of watered stocks. In *The Financier* (1912), *The Titan* (1914), and *The Stoic* (posthumously published in 1947), Cowperwood amasses a paper empire in brokerage and adopts a luxurious life style; loses both fortune and freedom when he is caught embezzling money from the city of Philadelphia; sells short on his release from prison during the Great Panic of 1873; rebuilds his fortune in Chicago through land speculation; nearly succeeds in establishing a monopoly of public utilities; leaves, after his failure, for an aimless existence in England, and returns to the United States to die. Cowperwood's energy and voracity extend to the sexual realm as well; as Emily Watts observes, "it is a rare year in Cowperwood's life when he is not sexually active with at least two women at the same time." Dreiser emphasizes Cowperwood's inveterate dishonesty, intemperate promiscuity, emotional paralysis, and unrestrained greed. Yet he also portrays the financier as resilient, uncompromising, and nearly invincible. Although Dreiser explicitly expressed reservations about the modern capitalist in *Hey Rub-A-Dub-Dub: A Book of the Mystery and Terror and Wonder of Life* (1920), his apparent enthusiasm for Cowperwood's power and resourcefulness have led some readers to say (as Blake said of Milton) that he is of the Devil's party without knowing it. His response to capitalism and the capitalist reveals a decided ambivalence.

Thomas Mann, who has been called the last defender of the German bourgeoisie, portrays the decline of this class in his first novel, *Buddenbrooks* (1901). Chronicling the deterioration of a merchant-patrician family, which is prosperous at the beginning of the nineteenth century and nearly destitute by the end of it, Mann clearly admires the rationality, honesty, good humor, and apparent moral stability of this family and of the class they represent. His sympathy for the Buddenbrooks, who can be taken as kind of small-scale capitalists, is increased by the beating they take at the hands of the large-scale capitalists who are accumulating vast fortunes. The family is imperiled, too, by internal weakness; successive generations are less capable of controlling money and more susceptible to the appeal of art and philosophy (which are, in the novel, associated with decadence). Mann has affection for the Buddenbrook family yet sees their decline as inevitable and not entirely undeserved.

Sinclair Lewis shared this interest in the small-scale capitalist and presented in his novels a range of small businessmen. Although his basic attitude is satirical, he also gives reason for hope. Business itself can help inspire life; it constitutes a chance for invention and independence in *The Job* (1917) and a successful, moral undertaking in *The God-Seeker* (1949). In *Dodsworth* (1929), a retired manufacturer goes to Europe to acquire culture, as did Christopher Newman in Henry James's *The American* (1877); with the help of an American widow and his own ability to resist conformity, Dodsworth succeeds. *Babbitt* (1922) gave the language a new word for "a business or professional man who conforms unthinkingly to prevailing middle-class standards" (Webster's *New Collegiate Dictionary*). Babbitt, a small-town realtor and social climber, lacks the demonic energy and evil grandeur of Sinclair's Durham or Norris' Jadwin; his essential decency, however, is diminished by his thirst for conformity, his proximity to corruption, and his primitive apprehension of religion and art. He displays some understanding of his failed life; although his attempted rebellions and retreats do not succeed, he urges his son to escape from the trap he himself cannot leave. Many readers have observed that Lewis' feelings for Babbitt are closer to pity and affection than to condemnation.

The novels of John P. Marquand, while often sympathetic to commerce, also satirize the customs and codes through which the individual is absorbed in the corporation: the renunciation of earlier friendships; the suppression of original thought; the acquisition of the appropriate car, suit, and address. These demands for conformity, however, can sometimes be disregarded. Case in point: Charles Gray in *Point of No Return* (1949), who becomes the vice president of a bank without following the accepted rules and without sacrificing his integrity. Marquand is similarly ambivalent about the qualities of the people engaged in business. Although he ridicules the stumbling intellectual efforts of the protagonist of *Sincerely, Willis Wayde* (1955), who spends fifteen minutes per day with the Harvard Classics, Marquand does not assume that a Philistine is necessarily a fool or a knave. Even the domineering magnate of *B. F.'s Daughter* (1946), in many ways stereotypically hard-headed and hard-hearted, is the object of empathy and admiration. Although Marquand makes fun of the herd instinct he observed in many corporations, he also displays respect for the intricate and productive activity made possible by business and for the people who worked hard to perform well, albeit often at the cost of personal fulfillment.

The Dispossessed: An Ambiguous Utopia (1974), unlike most business novels, is a philosophically complex presentation of the ambivalent attitude toward capitalism. In this science-fiction novel, Ursula K. Le Guin (born in 1929) invents two worlds, both of which are variations on our own: Urras, a fertile planet governed by competition, hierarchy, and a market economy; and Anarres, a barren planet characterized by cooperation, political anarchy, and the absence of private ownership. Anarresti visitors to Urras must adjust to the use of possessive pronouns, unknown in their own language. Each world has advantages and defects. On the capitalist Urras, there is abundance, science, freedom of movement, but little kindness or warmth. On the socialistic Anarres, there is sensitive human interaction, but little progress, comfort, or freedom of choice. The main character, an Anarresti physicist who devises a new theory of time, moves between the worlds, as does the narrative structure. His goal is to "unbuild walls" between the two; after he takes steps in this direction, he decides to return to Anarres. Le Guin, however, does not lock the reader into this choice; the utopia is ambiguous, and the attitude ambivalent.

Positive Responses to Capitalism

The defenders of capitalism generally celebrate what they see as its democratic openness to new blood and new ideas; its encouragement of individual liberty, self-expression, and of such virtues as productivity, prudence, and fair dealing; its role as the fuel of modern civilization; and its function as a setting for heroic action. The capitalist is often portrayed as a Prometheus, taking great risks in order to achieve high goals; as a soldier, whose strength is designed to protect others; and as a loner, a Wild West hero, engaging in adventure for the thrill of conflict, the hope of glory, or the joy of self-sufficiency. These writers are often impatient and angry with the denigration of capitalism as dull and deadening. For the procapitalist writer, capitalism is a benevolent adventure inspired by a zest for life.

With the voice of successful commercial experience, Daniel Defoe (1660–1731), a journalist and a novelist, extolled the glory of the merchant, the heroism of the trader. The manifold operations of commerce seemed to him to demonstrate the ingenuity of the individual and the harmonious cooperation of the many. John McVeagh writes: "Anticipating Adam Smith, but with a different purpose, he sees in the manufacture and distribution of a single pin, the smallest made article, the felicitously combined labour, needs, and recompense, of a multitude of peoples and lands." Defoe saw the new-age trader as a pioneer, an explorer, applying human energies to the goal of improving the human condition through a thorough, systematic, and wide-ranging use of the available natural world. Defoe's novels can be taken as variations on the theme of moral and material self-improvement and profit. The "estate" to be improved may be an island (*Robinson Crusoe*, 1719) or one's marital status (*Moll Flanders*, 1722), as well as the more traditional assets of money and plantations (*Captain Singleton*, 1720; *Colonel Jacques*, 1722). Defoe's capitalism is perforce mercantile rather than industrial; he nonetheless sees the new style of commercial activity as defining a new age, a new class, and new values (unfinished manifesto, "The Compleat English Gentleman," posthumously published in 1890).

In the early years of America, Benjamin Franklin expressed and exemplified a similarly energetic advocacy of free enterprise and private capitalism, which he saw as directly associated with individual liberty (political, intellectual, and religious). In such essays as "Speech of Polly Baker" (1747), "The Way to Wealth" (1758), and "On the Price of Corn, and the Management of the Poor" (1766), he deplored government restrictions on trade and resolutely defended economic independence as the prerequisite for freedom and self-esteem. In his *Autobiography* (written from 1771 on, published in its entirety posthumously in 1868), he chronicles the first half of his life; he explains the methods behind his financial success, the personal qualities he felt the need to acquire, and the services his success enabled him to perform for the community. In addressing the autobiography to his son, moreover, he intended his example as universal advice rather than as a personal boast. In a world that displayed the values of capitalism and that revered the virtues appropriate to it, Franklin believed that others should do as he had done.

Mark Twain, whose numerous business ventures led him into debt and eventual bankruptcy, satirized speculation, which he saw as one of the most dangerous activities possible under capitalism, in such works as *The Gilded Age* (novel, 1874, written with Charles Dudley Warner) and "Sold to Satan" (short story, 1904). In the novel *A Connecticut Yankee in King Arthur's Court* (1889), on the other hand, a nineteenth-century entrepreneur restores sixth-century England to economic prosperity by spearheading a democratic industrial revolution, complete with factories and mines, new systems of education and communication, freedom and equality, and the transformation of knights into salesmen and of the Round Table into a stock board. The Yankee, Hank Morgan, sees himself in the tradition of Defoe; he says: "I saw that I was just another Robinson Crusoe cast away on an uninhabited island, with no society but some more or less tame animals, and if I wanted to make life bearable I must do as he did—invent, contrive, create, reorganize things; set brain and hand to work, and keep them busy. Well, that was my line." Although Merlin's black magic and the knights' political machinations interfere with his "line," the means and ends of Hank Morgan are viewed sympathetically.

Around the turn of the century, Samuel Merwin (1874–1936), often in collaboration with H. K. Webster (1875–1932), produced a series of novels identified by Walter Fuller Taylor as "amoral romances of economic struggle." These novels are "amoral" only in that they assume (and see no need to formally demonstrate) the suitability of the modern industrial setting for excitement, adventure, and the display of such virtues as energy, dedication, and ingenuity. In *Calumet "K"* (1901), Charlie Bannon, supervises the building of a grain elevator; he is beset, on the one hand, by a Wall Street plot to control the wheat market and, on the other hand, by a dishonest labor organization. His victory is due to resourcefulness, long-range thinking, and responsible leadership; individual ability is recognized and valued at all levels of the business system. Merwin and Webster's novels, however, are like their heroes: unreflective and unintellectual, devoted to action rather than thought. As such, they tend to exemplify the values of capitalism without expounding them.

A less concrete and more philosophical, positive view of capitalism was embodied in the character of Merton, a businessman, in the long poem *Conversation at Midnight* (1937) by Edna St. Vincent Millay. One of eight people discussing politics, economics, and art after a dinner party in Washington Square, Merton defends what he sees as the values of capitalism: its broad-minded tolerance, the freedom it fosters, the improved status of workers, the respect for the individual. He is also shown as personally admirable, evincing consideration for nature, art, and the sensitivities of others. He is, furthermore, more articulate in defense of capitalism than is Carl in defense of socialism. Although the poem is abstract (as befits the nature of a conversation), it nonetheless reveals a commendable understanding of the connection between politics and economics.

The writings of the Russian-born Ayn Rand (1905–1982), who admired the spirit of *Calumet "K"*, constitute a more explicitly ideological defense of capitalism. The most significant character in her play *The Night of January Sixteenth* (1935) is an immensely wealthy capitalist for whom the manipulation of money is an act of creative self-assertion. In the novel *Atlas Shrugged* (1957), capitalists withdraw to a private enclave in response to crippling government controls and the collectivist world view of society at large. Rand associates capitalism with such values as rationality, justice, freedom, and self-esteem. Without these values and the people who display them, society collapses rapidly and dramatically. Not all of the people who engage in business, however, are genuine exemplars of capitalism; Rand presents honorable and dishonorable characters in such industries as banking, steel, copper, and railroads. Business per se is not attacked or applauded. In a later series of essays, collected as *Capitalism: the Unknown Ideal* (1966), Rand explains her reasons for seeing capitalism as "the only system geared to the life of a rational being."

Robert Heinlein, who has alluded to Rand in his novels, has expressed a similar confidence in capitalism throughout his career in science fiction. He honors the entrepreneur, the imaginative risk-taker, whose ambitions find fulfillment only in the quest for a new frontier and another new frontier after that. In science fiction, all of space and time is open territory. Bruce Franklin has associated the emergence of science fiction as a genre with the rise of industrial capitalism; the procapitalist stance of Heinlein, "the dean of science fiction," is therefore entirely to be expected. "The Man Who Sold the Moon" (1950) is the clearest exposition of his enthusiasm. In this story, an entrepreneur buys the moon from the nations over which it passes and takes it under corporate control. He does so by various illegal (but not, in his view, immoral) means in order to rescue the moon from the peril of world war ("Damnation, nationalism should stop at the stratosphere!") and to bring the moon within reach.

Several business novels by Cameron Hawley, which spawned a horde of imitators in the 1950s and 1960s, present a similarly uncompromising positive view of the moral and creative potential of a career in business. Hawley, once an executive in a large corporation, published in 1952 the immensely popular *Executive Suite*, described by one reviewer as "a novel which, without loss of perspective or truth, shows business to be an essentially honorable and socially beneficial way in which to spend one's life." In the twenty-six hours following the death of the president of a furniture corporation, the ensuing contest for control dramatizes the ambition and talent of most of the executives involved— and the ability of the system to divest of power the dishonorable. *Cash McCall* (1955) takes gleeful pleasure in the triumphs of a clever entrepreneur. In *The Lincoln Lords* (1960), the protagonist recovers his talents, ambition, and even his sense of honor (giving up financial profits, at one point, for the sake of principle) because he feels responsible to and for his company; business has a redemptive force.

In *Sometimes a Great Notion* (1964) by Ken Kesey, the big-business environment of Hawley's novels is one of the obstacles facing Hank Stamper; his small lumber company in Oregon is threatened by the lower prices asked by larger corporations (whose competition is presented as legitimate, but regrettable), as well as by the demands of a labor union (presented as misguided, power-hungry, and dangerous). Stamper is seen as a throwback to Daniel Boone and the Leatherstocking hero of James Fenimore Cooper; he is also a near-mythical leader, whose strength is the lifeblood of his community. Whereas McMurphy in Kesey's *One Flew Over the Cuckoo's Nest* (1962) expressed his creative individuality and also enabled others to rebel against the oppressive system of an insane asylum, Stamper fulfills a similarly inspiring function in a less unusual setting. Ultimately he succeeds on his own terms; he also makes peace with his younger brother, a doctoral candidate in literature, who had hoped to destroy him. They learn from each other, and the intellectual brother articulates, as Hank could not, the significance of Hank's fierce independence and of the expression it finds in his business.

Conclusions

Although this discussion of the positive and ambivalent responses to capitalism was intended, among other things, to refute the common assumption that art is inevitably inimical to capitalism, this assumption cannot be entirely ignored. It is true that many writers, especially those who are ignorant of the workings of business, resent the wealth, power, and respect that capitalists may seem to enjoy without earning them. It is true that many artists have sensed in the capitalist an ignorance of the workings of art, as well as a thoughtless indifference. William Hazlitt ("On Thought and Action," 1821) wrote that "to the money getter nothing has a real existence that he cannot connect with a tangible feeling. . . . The want of thought, of imagination, drives the practical man upon immediate realities." It is also true that many writers fear and resent their own participation in capitalism through the sale of the works they create. In a poem that appeared only posthumously, Emily Dickinson speaks of publication as "foul," as "the Auction / Of the Mind of Man," as the reduction of the "Human Spirit / To Disgrace of Price." She is not alone.

She does not, however, speak for all writers. For William Dean Howells, as has been noted, the man of letters was also a man of business engaged in exchange. Although there were and are numerous writers who disdained trade (seeing aristocracy as an alternative), deplored exploitation (seeing socialism as an alternative), or objected to other features of the capitalistic system, there were and are others who applauded capitalism in theory and/or practice.

The literary results of the interest in capitalism have varied in quality. It is easy to sneer at the 250 economic novels published in the United States between 1870 and 1901 or the products of the business-novel fad of the 1950s. As a group, though, novels dealing with capitalism are no worse than adultery novels, war novels, or Hollywood novels—most of which do not meet the standards set by Tolstoy's *Anna Karenina* (1877), Crane's *The Red Badge of Courage* (1895), or Fitzgerald's *The Last Tycoon* (1941). Writers may choose to follow stereotypical formulas—the maturation of an innocent, the idealistic knight, the couple separated by obstacles, the great soul that deteriorates, the saintly victim of evil institutions—or they may adapt and renew the formulas. Gifted writers—whether or not their ideas are historically sound or philosophically valid—can apply their gifts and turn capitalism into literary gold, while the hacks of Grub Street, old or new, grind on and on.

See also: Banker, Financier, and Usurer; Money.

Selected Bibliography

Flory, Claude Reherd. *Economic Criticism in American Fiction 1792–1900*. 1936. New York: Russell and Russell, 1969.

McVeagh, John. *Tradefull Merchants: The Portrayal of the Capitalist in Literature*. London: Routledge and Kegan Paul, 1981.

Watts, Emily Stipes. *The Businessman in American Literature*. Athens: University of Georgia Press, 1982.

SHOSHANA KNAPP

CAVE

The words "cave," "cavern," and "grotto" apply either to natural underground chambers or artificial ones, although the word "grotto" has been especially connected with man-made "pleasances" in gardens, built for recreation and aesthetic enjoyment. Fascination with caves is clearly archetypal and can be directly connected with polar feelings of attraction-repulsion toward the Earth itself as universal womb-tomb.

The Cave in Antiquity

In Western literature, the cave has had and continues to have symbolic values derived from a tradition that originates in Homer's epic *Odysseia* (*Odyssey*, c. 8th century B.C.) and that is given its most striking expression in Plato's Myth of the Cave (*Politeia*, 7 [*Republic*, dialogue, c. 380 B.C.]), where slaves, chained at the bottom of a pit, take shadows on the wall for reality. For Plato, as for Homer, the cave represents illusion, ignorance, possession by the passions, primitivity, simplicity, life at an animal level, privation, austerity, darkness of the soul. A number of these connotations are sometimes given a positive significance, whenever primitivity and simplicity are considered virtues.

Plato's equations darkness = ignorance; light = knowledge, truth, goodness and beauty seem to be part of man's archetypal awareness of his existential condition. The prisoner's progress up from the earthy womb parallels the basic Greek (and Judaic) idea of man's origins, struggling up from autochthonous beginnings (Adam, whose name means "earth"; the dragon's teeth; Deucalion and Pyrrha's stones) into the free air. From darkness, he rises into light, moving from low to high. This, too, is an archetypal idea in which one who has climbed above others is thought to incarnate wisdom and power.

Along with the metaphoric field in general, Homer's *Odyssey* furnishes archetypal material on the cave, exploited in a similar pattern to the one later followed by Plato. In each of the adventures in which Odysseus encounters a cave, he is able to escape it through the power of intellect, either his own or that of his patroness, Athena, goddess of Wisdom. The *Odyssey* contains three types of caves that will continue to occur with variations throughout Western literature to our own day. These are: (1) Polyphemus' cave, in which the monstrous Cyclops traps the hero and twelve of his best men and where they are devoured raw one after another until Odysseus invents a means of escape; (2) the Nymph Calypso's cave on the island of Ogygia, where she imprisons Odysseus for seven years as her consort, promising him eternal youth if he would be content to stay with her. He escapes through Athena's intervention; (3) the cave of the Nymphs in book 13, at the mouth of which Odysseus is put ashore on his native Ithaca after his long years of wandering are over. He and Athena hide his possessions in the cave and pray to the Nymphs before he goes on to challenge the suitors who have invaded his home.

These three caves are reducible to basic types that will be carried foward in the literary stream: Polyphemus' cave provides the prototype of (1) the monster's cave; Calypso's cave, with its heavily sexual connotations forms the basis for (2) the cave of love; the Nymphs' cave is a variety of (3) the sacred grotto. These categories, with many variations, accretions and erosions, continue to appear in an unbroken series that crosses all boundaries of genre, language, and culture.

Developments of the cave of love come down to us as part of the *locus amoenus* tradition. This type of cave was favored in Greek and Roman lyric poetry, as in Theocritus' *Idyll* 7 (*Eidyllia*, c. 270 B.C.), where three shepherds pause to sing of their respective loves in a beautiful glade beside a spring gushing forth from a cave. Six hundred years later, Claudian's "Epithalamium" (poem, 398) of Palladius and Celerina uses and develops the same idyllic material, only here the cave serves as shelter for the goddess Venus. Both of these poems celebrate the passions of love without negative connotations. The "anatomy" of the love cave, especially in Homer and Claudian, is frankly sexual; female anatomy "writ large."

The cave as *locus amoenus* can become a snare for the unwary, as in Virgil's epic poem *Aeneis* (4.165–172 [*Aeneid*, 19 B.C.]). Dido and Aeneas take refuge in a grotto from a sudden and violent storm and are driven to mate by the plotting of Venus and Juno, who engineered the storm. The negative connotations of giving in to the "lower, animal" passions are clearly brought out. Dido, who, after coupling with Aeneas in the cave, lives only for her love, is portrayed as scorched by fire or as wandering aimlessly like a wounded doe. Striking examples of the cave as sexual snare are to be found in epics such as Apollonius of Rhodes' *Argonautika* (*Argonauts*, epic poem, 3d century B.C.), and in Ovid's *Metamorphoses* (epic poem, c. A.D. 2–17), where Diana's grotto becomes a death trap for Actaeon. Lyric poetry, too, contributes examples, such as Horace's "Ad Pyrrham" ("Ode to Pyrrha," c. 23 B.C.), where the lovely Pyrrha (whose name connotes fire) reclines on a bed of roses in a cave, consuming one lover after another with the fire of her love and the pain of her rejection.

The monster cave is always a death trap, exuding overwhelming horror, though the victim may be unaware of this until it is too late (as in the case of Odysseus and his men, who complacently awaited the return of the Cyclops). The monster, dweller in darkness, is destroyed by a hero from the upper world, who brings life, hope, and light. Among the most prominent of the horror stories in antiquity involving caves is the tale of the Minotaur and the Cretan Labyrinth. The story is told among others by Apollodorus (3.1.4; 15.8) and by Ovid in *Metamorphoses* (7.136; 152–176).

The labyrinth represents the attempt to "bury" unspeakable obscenities that lie hidden in human nature. These do not die in their tomb but continue to exert a powerful undertow, making themselves felt constantly by those aspects of the personality that exist "in the light of day." These are all too often dragged down to the lower level and "devoured," as the myth tells us.

Other monster caves are to be found in Virgil's *Aeneid* (8.193–99). Vulcan's son Cacus steals some of Hercules' cattle. This monster, half human, half volcano, is the scourge of the countryside and a devourer of men. Hercules destroys the monster and throws the dark lair, tomb for so many, open to air and sunlight. As in the Minotaur myth, the lower power is overcome by the higher bringer of life and light. Whereas the Minotaur incarnates unbridled lust, Cacus incarnates another passion: ambition, leading to aggression and war.

The sacred cave tradition in antiquity derives from a very early stage of Mediterranean religion that was organized around the subterranean power of the

Great Earth Mother. The sexual and uterine import of many sacred grottoes is thus of great importance and survives in many myths and practices. The interior of the Naiad Nymphs' cave in the *Odyssey* is described in terms of flesh; Odysseus, who is placed ashore while in a deep sleep, awakens at the mouth of the cave as if newly born from it. Caves play an important role in the nurturing of many young gods. Zeus was supposedly born in a cave on Crete and nurtured there; Dionysus was cared for by the nymphs of Nysa in a cave; Maia conceived and bore Hermes in a cave high on a windy mountain. Part of the nurturing function is education, and caves play a prominent role in myths of instruction. Demeter brings up her daughter in a grotto; Chiron the centaur educated Asclepius, Jason, Achilles and many others in his cavern. In oracles, the wisdom of the Great Mother is imparted by exhalations from caves and crevasses in her flanks. Although Apollo became the controlling force in oracular caves, the prevailing myths about Delphi make it clear that he usurped the oracle, which originally belonged to Gaia. In any event, masculine Apollo cannot function without the intermediacy of female prophetesses like the Delphic priestess or the Cumaean Sibyl. The oracular cave is perhaps the type of sacred grotto that most influences later literature. This is undoubtedly because of the survival of much Greek literature concerning Delphi and the popularity of Virgil's *Aeneid*.

It is significant that so many of the important gods of antiquity should be born and nurtured in caves. The cave-womb furnishes a beginning for these deities, but it is transcended and abandoned. If the spiritual power of light fails to transcend the cave, it is devoured and destroyed; the womb becomes tomb.

The Middle Ages and Renaissance

The metaphoric field of the cave remains relatively unchanged in its basic motifs, despite the vast upheavals in politics and religion, as the Roman Empire crumbles and feudalism and Christianity become dominant. One new thread is introduced through the Old Testament tradition, which becomes vital now as Christianity dominates other religions. The cave serves the realistic function of shelter from the desert heat or as a refuge for persecuted Israelites (David hid in a cave from King Saul). Caves serve as tombs for notable persons like Sarah, Jacob and, of course, Jesus of Nazareth. In early Christianity, caves frequently serve as habitats for holy men and women in the wilderness, or, like the catacombs, simultaneously as tombs and dwellings for the living in hiding. In this connection, they connote purification from worldly luxury and a closer approach to God's unadorned creation.

The Celtic tradition contributes as well to medieval literature involving caves. They are dwelling places of great necromancers and supernatural powers like Merlin. The cave is a place of power that works ambiguously for good or ill. It is a place of transition, too, between life and death, and is good or evil according to the direction of travel. The treasure cave exhibits this ambiguity. While the treasure is itself wholly desirable, it is perilous because of its great power. Treasure caves are generally inhabited by monsters, often dragons, who act as guardians and who must be overcome if the treasure is to be taken. The claimant, even if successful, is often destroyed if he is not foreordained to possess the treasure or has not the stature to wield it for the good purposes for which it was intended. Examples of treasure caves abound, in the epic *Nibelungenlied* (c. 1200) and in Welsh legends of Merlin and Arthur. The treasure grotto is a lowly starting point, symbol of primitive acquisitive urges that the hero must overcome and bend to a higher purpose. These attitudes often parallel those in Plato's Myth, but the highest power of man is no longer the light of reason, but the light of faith. The medieval hero's victory is rarely due (like Odysseus') to his "teeming brain," but rather to strength of arm alone, as in Beowulf's victory over Grendel, or to strength coupled with faith and the grace of God. This devaluation of the intellect is still characteristic of prevailing attitudes in the West. Siegfried, dim-witted but brawny, follows the instructions of the magical bird (a figure for soul and/or grace) and slays Fafner, who is guarding the treasure in his cave. Siegfried in all his primitivity becomes a paradigm of the hero in the Western world.

The sexual cave survives in many forms, such as caves where perfect lovers are entombed in a perpetual embrace, the cave serving as a reliquary (Robert de Boron's *Suite de Merlin*, romance, end of the 13th-early 14th centuries), or, in Gottfried von Strassburg's *Tristan* (romance, c. 1210), where the two lovers unite in the *Minnegrotte*, sacred to the goddess of love. This grotto is the most fully and lyrically described of all the love caves, and has in itself no negative connotations. In it, the idealized lovers consummate a perfect union, which is fragile and doomed to destruction. Less perfect is the *locus amoenus*/snare where Nivienne, the beautiful but dangerous witch whom Merlin passionately desires, plots to entrap and kill him. The virtue that will be buried and destroyed by the cave trap has become moral strength and physical self-control in the Christian Middle Ages, whereas it had been, primarily, intellectual power and mental self-control in antiquity.

The monster cave survives in other forms than the treasure cave guarded by a dragon. In *Sir Gawain and the Green Knight* (romance, c. 1370), it serves as habitat for the formidable Green Knight, who has proven his immortality by surviving decapitation. It fits the monster cave category. Its name, the Green Chapel, indicates that it participates in sacred qualities as well. The Chapel, "naught but an olde cave," is consecrated to the powers of the material world as opposed to the spiritual; it will reveal itself as a place of purification, initiation, and revelation about the weaknesses in even the best of human nature. Here, again, the lower passions must be controlled and dominated. The cave serves as a device that teaches Sir Gawain, whose symbol is the sun, how best to live as a hero of light.

The sacred cave in the Middle Ages frequently derives from the Judeo-Christian tradition and is often a chapel or a hermit's dwelling. In the Merlin tradition, the cave-tomb, in which he is trapped by his blind passion for the witch to whom he had taught all his lore, gradually changes until it becomes a place where suppliants may come and ask about their future. The death trap evolves into a sacred, oracular grotto from which issues the voice of the great necromancer, whose soul lives on after his body has decayed. This tradition evolves in the romances *Lancelot-Graal* (13th century), *Palamède* (13th century), Robert de Boron's *Merlin, Merlin ordinaire*, and the *Suite de Merlin* (end of the 13th-early 14th centuries) and culminates in Ariosto's colorful version in *Orlando furioso* (epic poem, 1516), cantos 2–3.

The Sixteenth and Seventeenth Centuries

The cave-topos as used in the Renaissance and baroque periods is characterized by self-conscious or playful manipulation of ancient archetypal material rather than by acceptance of the conventions for straightforward and serious development. Cervantes epitomizes this tendency in the novel *Don Quijote*, 2, 22–23 (*Don Quixote*, 1605, 1615), on the cave of Montesinos. Wonder caves had been regularly a part of the Celtic and chivalric traditions throughout the Middle Ages. Don Quixote visits such a cave, and finds it, on the surface, to conform to all the "authorities" he has read and to his fondest fantasies. According to his report, it contains a delightful meadow and a crystal palace, habitat for the venerable Montesinos, the brave knight Durandarte, his lady Belerma and her attendants, and the three worker women whom Sancho had earlier identified as Dulcinea and her ladies-in-waiting.

Cervantes plays a subtle game with his characters and his reader in this cave passage. The cave, in accordance with its tradition, signifies illusion or delusion. Don Quixote, unlike Plato's slaves, has not been in the cave from infancy but enters it from the upper world. He has sunk into the darkness of illusion from a state where he was able to perceive the light of the sun. In this way, the adventure parallels the hero's plunge into the madness of his knightly fantasies. The realities seen by daylight are uniformly grim and ugly. The mouth of the cave is choked with weeds and brambles, and the knight must cut his way through. He disturbs flocks of crows and bats, creatures of ill omen that knock him flat by their sudden outward rush as he rouses them. In like manner, the hero's fantasies have lain him low repeatedly, flying out of the cavern of his illusory life (cf. the defeats and beatings he suffers in *Don Quixote*, 1). When he has arrived at a resting place within the cave, a side cavern into which distant light is filtering through cracks, he falls asleep (by his own admission) and passes through yet another gate of illusion into a dream world. Yet, even here, his previous experience of reality penetrates sufficiently to disturb the beauty of the delusory idyll. The knight Durandarte's hand is hairy and sinewy, hardly that of the typical Apollo-like knightly beauty. Montesinos recounts in disgusting detail how he had cut out Durandarte's heart with an augur or awl instead of a knife, hence he had a difficult time; his tears were so copious that they washed his hands of all the blood that covered them from groping around in the knight's innards; he wiped the heart on a lace cloth and sprinkled it with salt to keep it from stinking; when he presented it to Lady Belerma, it was mummified. Belerma, too, is described in lurid detail. Her complexion is yellowish; she has dark circles under her eyes beneath eyebrows that meet, a snub nose, a large mouth with long, widely spaced teeth; her bad color is not due to menstruation, Montesinos guilelessly explains, since she has not menstruated for years. When Sancho and the primo ask if Don Quixote had eaten in his fantasy world, the knight replies that no one sleeps or eats in the enchanted state and hence has no excrement, though fingernails, hair, and beards do grow. Dulcinea and her two ladies appear in the crass vulgarity of field hands, and Dulcinea asks Don Quixote for a loan, using a short skirt as security.

The high-flown fantasy in which Don Quixote had lived during the first half of his adventures is disturbed and adulterated. His illusory world (his private cave) is being infiltrated by beams of distant light as if through cracks in the cave wall. It is entirely consonant with Cervantes' pessimism that the light of truth not be the Platonic *sursum corda* of Goodness and Beauty, but the reality of ugliness; of basic physical functions; of sickness, death, and decay. The entrance into and exit from the cave constitute the sign of a turning point for Don Quixote. He knows (but does not want to know) that what he saw is an illusion. Afterward, he is more apt to see inns as inns (not castles) and to flee from danger.

Parallel to Don Quixote's cave is Sancho's *sima* (abyss, cavern, *Quixote*, 2.55), into which he and his donkey fall after he has left his governorship of the "island" Barataria. In each case the cave resembles the personality and state of soul of the individual who enters it (in conformity with the metaphoric tradition of caves). Whereas Don Quixote had painted his cave with his fantasy as being full of (flawed) marvels and crystal palaces, Sancho's *sima* is what it is: ugly, dark, cold, and damp. On emerging from his cave, Don Quixote is nearer regaining his sanity; on being rescued from his, Sancho has left behind his ambition and now follows his master not out of self-interest, but for friendship and loyalty.

Cervantes uses the metaphoric complex in accordance with tradition, but with great delicacy coupled with bitter irony; he subverts the traditional view of reality. Ideas, Ideals, Forms exist only in the cave of illusion. Reality is the scent of decaying blood, the sight of withering beauty, crooked teeth, and snub noses.

Calderón de la Barca's extensive use of the cave epitomizes baroque sensibility. The cave dwellers of his theater fall into several categories, according to the type of cave they inhabit. They can be savage chained captives (Segismundo, La hija del aire, Aquiles [Achilles]) dressed in animal skins as an outward sign that they exist primarily on the level of the animal soul. This category clearly embodies Plato's deluded slave, chained at the bottom of the pit, ignorant of all but shadows of reality. Then there is the Merlinlike magician. In *La exaltación de la cruz* (*The Exaltation of the Cross*, written 1648), Anastasio magically projects images of real events on the cave wall. Calderón rarely needs to depict a monster in the cave unless it be the Devil himself (*El mágico prodigioso* [*The Wonderful Magician*, 1637]). Most often, the "monsters" are the unenlightened or unredeemed souls of those who dwell within: Segismundo, Semiramis, Heraclio and Leonido, Aquiles, and so on. Their monstrosity is generally underscored by their speech, as in Segismundo's first monologue (*La vida es sueño* [*Life Is a Dream*, 1635]), where he calls himself a human monster and a beast among men and is dressed accordingly in animal skins. The cave of love is rare in Calderón, since scenes of adulterous and explicit sex were taboo to his theater. One of his closest approaches is in *Los dos amantes del cielo* (*The Two Lovers of Heaven*, 1636), where the chaste lovers are buried in a grotto that becomes a type of reliquary for the saintly pair. The sacred cave is present in both its antique and medieval guises: as oracular cave in *La gran Cenobia* (*The Great Zenobia*, c. 1634), where the prophetess, like the Delphic oracle, foretells the future of everyone who passes the cave's mouth. The medieval Christian use of the sacred grotto is epitomized in *El José de las mujeres* (*The Female Joseph* written c. 1640–1644), where it serves as a refuge for persecuted Christians. Sometimes the cave, like a flaw in character, provides a means by which more exalted values are betrayed, as in *Amar después de la muerte* (*Love after Death*, 1633), where Galar, a hilltop city, is penetrated and destroyed by enemy forces who enter through a shaft that undermines the city's perch.

The Eighteenth Century

In the self-proclaimed "Age of Enlightenment" the cave, logically, does not play a leading role. Montesquieu's "troglodytes" (Greek: "those who creep into holes") in the *Lettres persanes* (*Persian Letters*, 1721) are deliberately contrasted with their classical forebears in Plutarch and Pomponius Mela. The latter-day troglodytes, although morally bestial, are not furry like bears, do not whistle to communicate, and have two eyes. Neither do they live in caves.

A real cave appears in Jean-Jacques Rousseau's *Confessions*, 3 (1781–1788), where the author admits to having exposed himself obscenely to some women of Turin coming to fetch water. The coincidence of the urge to commit an act of this sort and the milieu in which it is done testify to the archetypal power of the cave.

Diderot makes passing use of Plato's Myth of the Cave in the *Supplément au voyage de Bougainville* (*A Supplement to Bougainville's Voyage*, 1796). While glorifying the natural, commonsensical lives of Tahitians, he contrasts the misery of civilized man, who incarnates both cave dweller and artificial man. Within the cavern, the two selves struggle ceaselessly against each other; the poor monster is continually tortured and torn apart. In his reversal of Plato, Diderot clearly prepares the way for the romantic revolution of values.

Fingal's cave, immortalized by Mendelssohn-Bartholdy, is drawn from the Ossian poems (1760–1763), originally claimed to be translations from ancient Gaelic, but actually composed by James Macpherson. This cave and a host of others (the Maid of Lulan's, Conban-carglas', Oithona's, Morna's, etc.) serve as stage sets for countless battles amid the rising mists of the Scottish heath. Along with roaring waves, echoing rocks, bending oaks, and so on, these stage props provide inspiration for the landscape description of later, romantic works, such as Bernardin de Saint-Pierre's novel *Paul et Virginie* (*Paul and Virginia*, 1787), Chateaubriand's *Atala* (novel, 1801), and Lamartine's *Méditations poétiques* (*Poetical Meditations*, 1820).

The Romantic Literature

The cave complex remains on the whole a negative metaphoric field, standing for those forces in the human personality and in life that are brutal, stultifying, and primitive and are therefore to be avoided and overcome. The romantic revolution brings a reversal. The sign of the field now becomes positive. Two examples will suffice to illustrate: Chateaubriand's *Atala*, and Stendhal's novel *Le rouge et le noir* (*The Red and the Black*, 1830). In *Atala*, the hero Chactas and the chaste Atala, his beloved, have fled from hostile Indians through vast wilderness wastes. To the accompaniment of a violent thunderstorm, they are about to consummate their illicit passion, when a thunderbolt strikes nearby. They are rescued by the heroic Father Aubry, who has come to live in a cave and minister to a flock of Indians. The grotto, located high on a mountainside, contains only the barest necessities of life, a tamed serpent, and, on a rock, a crucifix and Bible. From his cave radiates the idealized goodness of Christianity that, combined with the noble qualities of the Indian tribe, constitute Chateaubriand's version of utopia. The best qualities of the noble savage are combined with the best of the civilized world. The serpent/dragon, chthonian cave-monster, has been reduced to a pet snake. Evil has been rendered harmless, almost "cozy." The sparse furnishings, cross, and Bible mark this as a sacred grotto, the hermit's traditional cave. It is raised up high on the mountainside, combining the simplicity of a return to nature with rejection of civilization's corruption. The two wanderers emerge to contemplate the storm (of their passions) in retreat, while in the west, three suns shine together: the Platonic sun has become a Christian trinity.

Thirty years later, Stendhal uses the cave in a similar way, although for anticlerical ends. It is an antidote to civilization, a place of liberation and joy. Hidden in a crevasse in Nature's flank, Julien Sorel feels safe from attack by his fellow men and truly free, liberated from the weight of his hypocrisy. In his high cave he can be a simple human being, a child of nature unburdened by the Tartufferie imposed on him by civilized society. At the novel's end, after his execution, Julien is buried in his cave, near the peak of one of the highest mountains in the Jura. He had been elevated at intervals throughout the book (as Harry Levin observes) on platforms, ladders, in high rooms, to indicate his superiority to other men. Julien's final exaltation combines height with the cave, now a sign that, after having plumbed the depths of civilized depravity, he has been purified of his passion of ambition and has found the true meaning of life. He has achieved a utopian state of harmony between his soul and nature.

The Twentieth Century

Cave symbolism continues relatively unchanged except for the conscious manipulation of Freudian dimensions. E. M. Forster, in the novel *A Passage to*

India (1924), uses the cave to illustrate the fundamental clash between genteel English culture and the primeval power of India as an engulfing force. A visit to a cave reduces Mrs. Moore's life experience to the same echo that she had heard inside the grotto: "ou-boum": the Great Mother has swallowed and brought down all things to the same primitive level. Miss Quested, her companion, enters another cave and believes that she has been sexually assaulted. For her the cave combines the monster's lair, negative love cave, and snare. Forster uses the cave realistically and yet symbolically, in a traditional way, yet with the malicious irony of one criticizing both cultures of which he is writing.

Christa Wolf, in *Kassandra* (novel, 1982), uses the cave as antidote to the sterile, inhuman world of masculine dominance. The citadel of Troy is a police state, waging an unnecessary war against the Greeks and "purging" anyone who disagrees with its policy. Certain women and the best of Trojan men take refuge in the caves that honeycomb the cliffside. Here, in this quintessentially feminine environment, a genuine society—sincere, simple and comradely—is formed. The cave is a healthy alternative to "masculine" political scheming, coercion, and war.

Both Forster (writing in the second decade of the century) and Wolf (writing in the 1980s) have used the cave in a manner consonant with the romantic reversal. In both cases, the cave is a corrective to a type of excess. In its simplicity, it represents Truth, for good or ill. This Truth destroys the representatives of overgenteel English society; it allegorizes the feminist revolt. Plato's light has been rejected in favor of the cave. The intellect has been subordinated to other, less easily definable human values that dwell in darkness rather than the light. Through all changes in its use, however, basic cave symbolism remains the same.

See also: Horror, Monsters, Tower.

Selected Bibliography

Kerényi, Karl. *Labyrinth-Studien*. 2d ed. Zürich: Rhein-Verlag, 1950.

Neumann, Erich. *The Great Mother: an Analysis of the Archetype*. Trans. Ralph Manheim. 1955. Princeton, N.J.: Princeton University Press, 1974.

Onians, Richard B. *The Origins of European Thought about the Body, the Mind, the Soul, the World, Time and Fate*. 1951. New York: Arno Press, 1973.

Rahner, Hugo. *Greek Myths and Christian Mystery*. London: Burns and Oates, 1963.

FLORENCE WEINBERG

CHRISTIAN HERO

A Christian hero is a person who engages in the practice of charity for Christ's sake. There are, roughly speaking, four classes of Christian hero. In the first class we find those people who bear witness for Christ under conditions that will cost them their friends, wordly goods, secular esteem, and, perhaps, life itself. Such persons "die to," that is, mortify their flesh—their carnal rights and expectations—and humble their spirit in favor of the teachings and promises of Christ. People of this class, whether they be killed for the Faith or made to suffer extreme hardship for the espousal of Christ's cause, are called "martyrs." The second class of Christian hero consists of confessors. The confessor leads an ordinary kind of life, but it is lit from within by charity, which holds all things and people dear for Christ's sake. A third class of Christian hero is comprised of converts and penitents, whom it costs a great deal to acknowledge the sovereignty of Christ in their lives. Quite often, these people have to resist and vanquish the most intimate and obdurate of enemies—the ego, with its anxieties and addiction to enticing vanities. The fourth class of Christian hero is composed of fighters and missionaries. These heroes put their lives at risk so that Christendom may not be overrun by aggressive infidels and that, in keeping with the command of Christ, the Word be preached to everyone.

Most Christian heroes are historical figures, but many also appear in the pages of literature. In a very real sense, the Bible itself not only relates history but recounts inspired stories forming part of what Northrop Frye calls a divine code (*The Great Code: The Bible and Literature*, critical exposition, 1982). In what follows, the concept of the Christian hero will be applied not only to wholly fictional characters but also to historical figures adapted by authors to suit a literary purpose. Hagiography that purports to be only history is ruled out.

The Early Christian Period and Middle Ages

In his *Ho bios . . . tou hosiou . . . Antoniou (Life of St. Antony*, c. 370), Athanasius, bishop of Alexandria, recounts the witness for Christ of one of the earliest Desert Fathers, who confessed his faith as a hermit in the Thébaid. In 1874, Gustave Flaubert turned his attention to this Christian hero and produced *La tentation de St. Antoine* (*The Temptation of St. Antony*, prose poem), a phantasmagoria that betrays its author's hysteria instead of the saint's splendid example, for the spirit that incited Flaubert was modernism, not Christianity.

A convert from Manichaeism, St. Augustine wrote two masterpieces that have influenced poets, dramatists, and novelists to this day: *Confessiones* (*Confessions*, autobiographical account of his conversion, c. 397–400) and *De civitate Dei* (*The City of God*, socio-theological contrast of the earthly and heavenly cities, 413–426). Boethius wrote *De consolatione philosophiae* (*The Consolation of Philosophy*, c. 524) in prison while awaiting execution. He presents himself as a Christian Stoic who perceives that Jesus is the "friend behind phenomena." For him, Fortune is God's servant. She reminds us that here we have no lasting home. We learn patience and are reoriented toward God. In *Waltharius* (*Walter of Aquitane*, verse romance, c. 910), attributed to Ekkehard I of St. Gall, the eponymous Christian hero is depicted as keenly martial, and the number of knightly retainers is fixed at twelve. Hrotswitha of Gandersheim (935?–after 973), a nun, composed *Pafnutius*, a morality play about a monk who, disguised as a lover, converts a harlot. With the customary modernist ironic twist, Anatole France patterned his novel *Thaïs* (1890) on this play. The converted harlot becomes a saintly eremite, but the monk is destroyed by his lusting after her. The Canadian Morley Callaghan utilizes the same theme in his major novel, *Such Is My Beloved* (1934), dealing with a Roman Catholic priest's attempt, which leads to his destruction, to convert two prostitutes.

The anonymous story *Le jongleur de notre dame* (*Our Lady's Tumbler*, 12–13th century) tells of how a humble tumbler is rewarded with a gracious smile from the Queen of Heaven, whose statue, in front of which he is piously somersaulting, comes alive. No doubt, Victor Hugo was inspired by this story when he wrote his novel *Notre Dame de Paris* (*The Hunchback of Notre Dame*, 1831).

Geoffrey Chaucer gives us two Christian heroes of the confessor class in the "Prologue" to *The Canterbury Tales* (c. 1380–1400): the Parson, "A bettre preest I trowe that nowher ys" (line 524), and the Plowman, described as "Lyving in pees and parfit charitee" (532) "For Cristes sake" (537). The epic poem *La divina commedia* (*The Divine Comedy*, c. 1320) of Dante Alighieri, which is the crowning achievement—for which reason it is fitting that this section be concluded with a reference to it—is crowded with Christian heroes (*Paradiso* [*Paradise*]), all of whom reflect Piccarda's words (*Paradiso*, 3, 85): "e la sua volontate è nostra pace" ("and His will is our peace").

The Renaissance and Seventeenth Century

There was great confusion in the minds of Christian writers during the Renaissance. With the revival of humanism and classical studies, an insufficient distinction was made between Apollo and Christ.

In the seventeenth century, the French wrote many epic and other poems about Mary Magdalene, a Christian hero of the convert-penitent class; among them are Charles de Nostre Dame's *Les larmes de Sainte-Madeleine* (1606), M. A. Durant's *La Magdaliade* (1608), Rémy de Beauvais' *La Magdeleine* (1617), F. d'Arbaud's *La Magdeleine pénitente* (1627), Charles Cotin's *La Magdeleine au sépulchre de Jésus-Christ* (1635), Pierre Sautel's *Divae Magdalenae ignes sacri et piae lacrymae* (1663), Pierre de Saint-Louis' *La Madeleine au désert* (1668), and Desmarets de Saint-Sorlin's *Marie-Madeleine* (1669). The Italians also wrote about La Maddalena: Giambattista Andreini's *Maddalena lasciva e penitente* (*Magdalene Lascivious and Contrite*, drama, 1612), F. Pona's *Galleria delle donne celebri* (poetry, 1633), and A. G. Brignole Sale's *Maddalena peccatrice e convertita* (romance, 1642).

Non-Magdalene Christian heroes of the fighter class included Jean Chapelain's *La pucelle, ou la France délivrée* (*The Maid, or France Delivered*, heroic poem, 1656) and Père Le Moyne's *Saint-Louis ou le héros chrestien* (heroic poem, 1653). Writers began to Christianize Old Testament and pagan figures: C. Perrault's *Adam* (Christian poem, 1647), Bernard de Lesfargues' *David* (heroic poem, 1660), M. de P. Calages' *Judith* (holy poem, 1660), Jean de Coras' *Jonas* (sacred poem, 1663), *Samson, Josué*, and *David* (sacred poems, all 1665), and Jean Racine's *Iphigénie* (drama, 1674) and *Phèdre* (*Phaedra*, drama, 1667).

In England, John Milton made Christ the hero of his epic poem *Paradise Regained* (1671). John Bunyan named the hero of *The Pilgrim's Progress* (allegorical novel, 1678) Christian. The second part of *The Pilgrim's Progress* (1684) shows Christian's wife and children on their way to Paradise.

The Eighteenth Century

In June 1700, Richard Steele severely wounded an Irishman, Kelly, in a duel. Repenting, he composed a devotional manual, *The Christian Hero* (1701). It was popular with the public, but Steele's comrades regarded it as incompatible with his military calling. Samuel Richardson astonished his readers by calling the rape and social ruin of his Christian heroine (*Clarissa Harlowe* [novel, 1748]) "triumphant" instead of "tragical." Richardson observed (Letter to Lady Bradshaigh, December 15, 1748), "A writer who follows Nature and pretends to keep the Christian System in his Eye, cannot make a Heaven in this World for his Favourites: or represent this Life otherwise than as a State of Probation." This statement is in keeping with Richardson's Puritan conscience. The shell of the worldly heart must be broken before God can enter in. Pointedly, the villain who "ruins" Clarissa has a Cavalier name, Lovelace.

In Germany, Gottlieb Klopstock made the life, sufferings, death, and resurrection of Christ the subject of his *Der Messias* (*The Messiah*, epic poem, 1748–1773). In Goethe's drama *Iphigenie* (1787), the main character is decidedly Christianized and achieves her goal not through deception, as in Euripides, but through truthfulness and purity. Nor is Orestes saved by way of a mechanical device only, as in the Greek play, but through the love of a saintly sister and the Christian conception of repentance and faith. In Gotthold Ephraim Lessing's *Nathan der Weise* (*Nathan the Wise*, dramatic poem, 1779), the patriarch exemplifies those clergymen whose "religion" excludes both man and God. In contrast, the humble Christian lay-brother, when he hears Nathan's painful but heart-warming story, exclaims (lines 3067–3068): "Bei Gott, Ihr seid ein Christ!/ Ein bessrer Christ war nie!" ("By God, you are a Christian!/ A better Christian there never was!").

The Nineteenth Century

Under the onslaught of the German Higher Critics and their French and English allies, the gospel image of Jesus grew blurred. He became a prankster, a swindler, a *charmeur* (Ernest Renan, *Vie de Jésus* [*The Life of Jesus*, 1863]). Scientific findings controverted the literal authority of the Old Testament. Rising to meet the challenge, Christian writers honed their instrument more finely. Alfred Lord Tennyson wrote poems: "St. Agnes' Eve" (1837), "Saint Simeon Stylites" (1842), "Morte d'Arthur" (1842), "Sir Galahad" (1842), "The Vision of Sin" (1842), *In Memoriam* (1850), "Lucretius" (1868), and "Crossing the Bar"

(1889), in which the Paraclete as psychopomp appears subtly (lines 1–2): "Sunset and evening star,/ And one clear call for me!"

An exponent of "muscular Christianity," Charles Kingsley wrote *Hypatia* (novel, 1853), a brilliant picture of early Christianity in conflict with Greek philosophy at Alexandria, and *The Heroes* (stories, 1856). Gerard Manley Hopkins presented Christ metaphorically as a stormy kestrel ("The Windhover," poem, 1877), a "chevalier" (line 11) who "Rebuffed the big wind" (line 7).

In Victorian England there are many Christian heroes, ranging from George Eliot's Dinah Morris, the Methodist woman preacher (*Adam Bede*, novel, 1859), to Lancelot Smith, the fox-hunting, heart-hungry hero of Kingsley's *Yeast* (novel, 1848 in *Fraser's Magazine*, 1851 as a book). But it was from Russia that the underground movement of Christian man in a nihilistic, Modernist world was to come. This Christian hero discovered that he was a new Desert Father in a new Thebaid, and we find him/her in Dostoevsky's novels, *Zapiski iz mёrtvoqo doma* (*Memoirs from the House of the Dead*, 1860–1862), *Zapiski iz podpolīa* (*Notes from Underground*, 1864), *Prestuplenie i nakazanie* (*Crime and Punishment*, 1866), *Idiot* (*The Idiot*, 1868), *Besy* (*The Possessed*, 1871–1872), and *Brat' īa Karamazovy* (*The Brothers Karamazov*, 1880).

In the United States, in Nathaniel Hawthorne's novel *The Scarlet Letter* (1850), the embroidered 'A' that Hester is forced to wear to mark her as an adulteress gradually takes on a *felix culpa* alpha quality, which culminates in the omega of Christian regeneration through expiation. Herman Melville's novella (1819–1891) *Billy Budd* (1929, published posthumously) presents a Christ-like young man who must hang in order to preserve discipline on the Indomitable.

The Twentieth Century

Joris-Karl Huysmans' (*Sainte Lydwine de Schiedam* [St. Lydwine of Schiedam], literary biography, 1901) powerfully depicts the sufferings of an expiatory saint. On the other hand, we have Gilbert Keith Chesterton's (1874–1936) mild-mannered confessor of the Faith, Father Brown, whose avocation is detecting and whose aim, as a fisher of men, is always to "catch" the soul of the criminal, if at all possible. Father Brown's deeply charitable relationship to his foes foreshadows the innocent conflict between Giovanni Guareschi's (1908–1968) Don Camillo (a priest) and Pepone (the Communist mayor, but loyal to the church in his way). There are many other priest and nun detectives in French, English, and American literature.

San Manuel Bueno, mártir (*Saint Manuel Bueno, Martyr*, novel, 1933) by Miguel de Unamuno portrays a country priest who is tempted, every day of his life, to commit suicide, because he does not believe that he believes. He stays alive out of compassion for his parishioners. What he does not realize is that he needs them every bit as much as they need him. Under such circumstances, charity is a Christian Mystery. Georges Bernanos' country priest in *Journal d'un curé de campagne* (*Diary of a Country Priest*, novel, 1936) is less fortunate in his flock. He tries to serve the poor but they abuse him. A loser in everything but Christian grace, absolved by an unfrocked priest, he dies. Bernanos is a subtle and powerful writer. *Sous le soleil de Satan* (*Star of Satan*, novel, 1926) and *L'imposture* (*The Deception*, novel, 1927) vibrate with Christian intensity. In *La joie* (*Joy*, novel, 1929), the main character, a joyous saintly girl, is murdered by a Russian chauffeur who then kills himself. His suicide brings the priest back to the Faith. Out of the wreck of evil, good emerges.

The Christian hero in the novels of François Mauriac is not a person; it is grace. *Le désert de l'amour* (*The Desert of Love*, 1925), *Le nœud de vipères* (*The Vipers' Tangle*, 1932), and *La pharisienne* (*A Woman of the Pharisees*, 1941) are bleak affairs; but it is a tribute to Mauriac's genius that grace is lambent within each of them. The title of Mauriac's first mature novel, *Le baiser au lépreux* (*A Kiss for the Leper*, 1922), suggests that grace is like the kiss Francis of Assisi bestowed upon a leper.

Grace betokens the presence of the Christian hero in Evelyn Waugh's novel *Brideshead Revisited* (1945). Touched by the moral decay and death of various members of the Flyte family, especially Julia's adultery with him and subsequent repentance and Sebastian's curiously forlorn alcoholism, Charles Ryder is converted. Mysteriously, the Flytes have somehow gained sufficient grace for him. Grace characterizes the Christian hero in the novels of Graham Greene as well. In *The Power and the Glory* (1940), a whisky-priest, the father of a bastard, is the only person who can administer the sacraments in a Mexico that has prohibited both Christianity and alcohol. He is dogged by a Judas figure whom he charitably recognizes to be no more than he is. Betrayed, his last word before he is executed by a firing squad is "Forgive." Forgive them? Forgive him? It makes no difference, because they are one, united by a charity so humble that it is not self-conscious. In the novel *The Heart of the Matter* (1948), Major Scobie, entangled in an adulterous relationship, keeps on receiving the Eucharist to prevent his wife from guessing the truth. Finally, aware that he has been insulting God by his sacrilegious communions, he commits suicide. This peculiar gallantry transcends his powers of appraising the import of the situation. Because he does not understand but simply, as a believer, does, Scobie attains to grace. In an abject, complex world, there is only one Christian hero, it would appear, equal to the task of salvation—the One Who died on Calvary in order to keep on saving us, as unworthy as ever, today.

Christ as a sort of humanistically universal and charitable Pan-Dionysus is the subject of Nikos Kazantzakis' novels *Alexis Zorbas* (*Zorba the Greek*, 1946), *Ho teleutaios peirasmos* (*The Last Temptation of Christ*, 1960), and *Ho phtō-choulēs tou Theou* (*Saint Francis*, 1962). In *The Last Temptation of Christ*, Kazantzakis heightens Thomas à Becket's temptation to martyrdom in T. S. Eliot's *Murder in the Cathedral* (drama, 1935) to Christ's temptation to proclaim himself God, just as Eliot himself had heightened Dostoevsky's ideas of crime and punishment to sin and expiation (*The Family Reunion*, drama, 1939). Agatha is Eliot's spokesperson in this play.

The Christian hero is often so subtly proposed that he impresses the reader as an anti-hero. Nothing could be further from the truth. Jake Barnes in Ernest Hemingway's novel *The Sun Also Rises* (1926) is a case in point. A well-meaning bumbler, castrated by a war injury, he is set in a milieu of graceless souls that careen down dead ends. Connected to Christianity in a way that is ineffable to his associates, he goes into the cathedral to pray even for his enemies while they remain outside valuing the edifice, only as an item of art history.

See also: Birth of Hero, Christianity versus Christendom, Hermit, Scapegoat, Social Status of Hero.

Selected Bibliography

Butler, Alban. *The Lives of the Fathers, Martyrs, and Other Principal Saints 1756–59*, 4 vols. New York: Kennedy, 1956.

Croce, Benedetto. "La Maddalena." *Letteratura italiana del seicento*. Bari: Guisseppe Laterza, 1949, 192–201.

Olschki, Leonardo. *The Grail Castle and Its Mysteries*. Berkeley: University of California Press, 1966.

Williams, Ralph C. *The Merveilleux in the Epic*. Paris: Champion, 1925.

NATHAN A. CERVO

CHRISTIANITY VERSUS CHRISTENDOM

In everyday parlance, "Christianity" encompasses three distinct things: (1) the acts and sayings of Jesus; (2) the interpretation of these by his followers, notably Paul, and the consequent erection of a systematic theology and an institutionalized church based on "the Christ"; (3) the values of individuals and societies denominated "Christian." In an ideal world, all three would be congruent; in this one, they are not. The question has been raised by thinkers and scholars during the last two centuries whether Paul adapted the ideas of Jesus to his own purposes— whether therefore Jesus would have any more rapport with Christian thinkers than Plato would with Platonists, Marx with Marxists, or Freud with Freudians. A question far older and more important with reference to literature is, Do the individuals and societies called "Christian" actually bear witness either to the life of Jesus or even to the doctrines of the church erected in his name?

The problem is rendered acute by that which makes Christianity unique. For in any movement a discrepancy exists between the ideal espoused by the leader and the implementation of it by the followers. The Jesus of the Gospels, however, appears to be an ad hoc, nonsystematic rebel against a ritualized, mechanical, overly systematic religion. Thus any attempt to establish a systematic religion on the basis of Jesus' rebellion runs into inherent contradictions. This dilemma constitutes nothing less than a central theme in Western literature. "Christianity vs. Christendom" is, moreover, merely a more acute case of the redefinition of "religion" in general which the Renaissance, Enlightenment, and, especially, romantic writers made.

Antiquity and the Middle Ages

The problem is posed as early as in the New Testament itself. A naturalistic reading of that work reveals Jesus to be a solitary figure, an Emersonian rugged individualist. The conventional view, of an opposition between the Christians (i.e., Jesus and his followers) and the Jews or the "establishment" (i.e., Pharisees, priests, elders, Romans), overlooks the fact that in all four Gospels the disciples—the first Christians—are portrayed as, though having made the right choice, being in over their heads. They are usually mystified by Jesus' sayings; they are periodically rebuked by him; they are weak in flesh and spirit, violating some of his precepts or scrambling for pride of place; and the greatest of them, Peter, lets his master down at three key junctures. The seminal Christian work, then, strongly suggests that commitment to Jesus is easy but living the life he adumbrates is hard, that understanding does not readily follow conversion, and that "Christendom"—that is, being a a self-described follower of Jesus—is in conflict with "Christianity"—that is, doing what Jesus wants.

In the polemics of the early Middle Ages, this distinction has a special dimension. As numerous sects lay claim to being followers of Jesus, albeit with sharply differing interpretations and dogmas, an accepted term of abuse is "Jewish" or "pagan" (and, later, "Turkish"). This represents a recognition forced on the disputants that people, notably the wicked heretical sects being attacked, may call themselves Christians and yet subscribe to heterodox values and that segments of Christendom are at war with Christianity. On that last point, at least, all the sects would agree.

Confronted with the task of bringing the inspiring but sometimes amorphous and self-contradictory sayings of Jesus to bear on the quotidian life, medieval literary artists go through some curious intellectual contortions. Thus the epic poem *Beowulf* (c. 8th century) is written or adapted by a Christian who manages the feat of leaving out of account every single Christian doctrine (or even reference to Jesus) as if, in order to bring the martial Vikings to Christendom, he is prepared to sacrifice Christianity itself—a Nordic exercise in selfcensorship for the sake of harvesting "rice Christians." Still, when Christianity does gain entry into other works, one is not sure if the result is an improvement: In the epic poem *La chanson de Roland* (*Song of Roland*, c. 1100), Bishop Turpin is a spokesman for a muscular Christianity who blesses the shedding of infidel blood and himself lives avidly by the sword. Though the sensibility of a later era might find such behavior somewhat inconsistent with what Jesus stood for, the author clearly does not.

More detached and urbane is Gottfried von Strassburg (*Tristan*, romance, 1210). His Isolde avails herself of a ruse in order to be technically correct when she swears that she lay with no man other than her husband King Mark. This legalism, so redolent of the Judaism Jesus was rebelling against, elicits from the narrator some wry observations on how accommodating Jesus can be in the hands of Christians. The Arthurian romances of this period were in fact portraying, with the ascension of the courtly love tradition, a serious new defection of Christendom from Christianity. *Sir Gawain and the Green Knight* (c. 1370) dramatizes the immense self-control required of a pious knight who finds himself in a society ostensibly Christian but devoted to the fashionable cult of adultery. In Malory's *Morte d'Arthur* (c. 1469) (and the continental works it is based on) an attempt is made at a synthesis; Lancelot and Guinevere have their day of love and glory—*adulterous* Christians who yet remain dignified and exemplary knight and queen—and then enter religious orders to die in an aura of repentance and sanctity—adulterous *Christians*.

Even without the courtly love tradition as an irritant, making it as a Christian is shown to be hard. In Wolfram von Eschenbach's epic *Parzival* (c. 1210), the hero is a Christian in a Christian society who, however, must (in a tradition established by St. Augustine's *Confessiones*, [*Confessions*, c. 397–400]) undergo a crisis of faith, a spiritual surrender and conversion, a literal handing over to God of the reins of his horse, before finding himself as a born again or real Christian. If in chivalric literature, the reprobates are knights and aristocrats unbaptized in the heart, in nonchivalric literature rascality extends to the rulers and particularly the clergy. Dante is quite busy populating hell with not a few popes and bishops; the papal seat he refers to as the place where Christ is bought and sold every day, a suggestion that, notwithstanding a famous crackdown, the money changers were back at their old stand, albeit in different garb. In Boccaccio's *Il Decamerone* (*Decameron*, novellas, c. 1350), monks and nuns tumble in and out of bed with acrobatic skill and few scruples. Above all, Chaucer (*The Canterbury Tales*, c. 1380–1400) presents a survey of representatives of many social classes; the knight turns out to be one of the few practising Christians, while most of the clergy, far more than the lay people, displays an artful variety of misbehavior. The Dantesque Chaucerian indictment is continued by such lesser literary lights as the author of *Piers Plowman* (poem, c. 1362–1387), W. Langland, and, in the Renaissance, by Erasmus (*Moriae encomium* [*The Praise of Folly*, essay, 1511] and *Colloquia* [*Colloquies*, treatise, 1516]), who presents pilgrims as an ignorant, superstitious lot that might as well be followers of King Tut as of Christ the King.

The Renaissance and Enlightenment

In Thomas More's *Utopia* (political romance, 1516), the wise Raphael gives as clear an expression of the problem as anyone and adds a modern dimension by introducing an idea usually overlooked in more than a millennium of Christian literature: the continuing radicalism of Jesus' ideas. If men are to be guided by fear of the unconventional, Raphael says, "we'll have to hush up, even in a Christian country, practically everything that Christ taught.... Most of His teaching is ... at variance with modern conventions." The reason is that "His doctrines have been modified by ingenious preachers," and Christian ethics has been adapted to human behavior rather than vice versa.

No less revealing is the nearly contemporary critique in Rabelais's *Gargantua et Pantagruel (Gargantua and Pantagruel,* novels, 1532–1564). The author's savage attacks on the clergy, the papacy, and, by inference, the church, are medieval; his insistence on the beauty of Scripture, together with his intimation that organized Christianity is a distortion rather than fulfillment of Jesus' vision, differs with medieval masters like Dante and Chaucer perhaps more in nuance than in content; but his celebration of worldly beauty and of physicality looks ahead to Blake and modern thinkers by introducing, however tentatively or unconsciously, a new issue. For he suggests thereby that the problem is not only that Christendom is at odds with Jesus by not living up to His, and its own, goals, but that the church itself—organized Christianity—misunderstands in the first place what Jesus really meant. And not only misunderstands but perverts; for, writing a generation later, from the vantage point of an intolerable civil war between Catholic and Protestant, Montaigne (*Essais [Essays,* 1580–1588]) perceived the special affinity that "subterrestrial conduct" has with "supercelestial thought"; Jesus' idealism being peculiarly, and paradoxically, vulnerable to infection by its opposite, Christendom is perpetrating horrors in the name of Jesus that cannibals would shrink from, as if being right gives one license to be wrong.

Shakespeare does not often overtly concern himself with Christian issues. The *Henry VI* (c. 1590–1592) plays intimate that being a studiously Christian prince in a Christian world is not, because of the corruption of Christendom, as conducive to social stability as is being Machiavellian—a vision fleshed out in *Henry V* (1600), in which a ruler manages to synthesize Jesus and Machiavelli and in the process lead a manipulative clergy by the nose. What this worldly wisdom has to do with Jesus is blithely ignored by Shakespeare. No less ambiguous is *The Merchant of Venice* (c. 1595), in which Jew and Judaism are triumphantly arraigned for narrowness of vision, but Shylock is not brought down without, curiously, first exacting a dialectical pound of flesh. His accusations leveled at Christian bigotry, prodigality ("Christian ducats"), debauchery, slavery, and double standards of judgment, when taken together with the duke's implicit concern with money and legalisms rather than Antonio's life and his forcing the conversion of the Jew, leave at least the modern reader wondering if the plague is not being wished on both houses. In the only Christian play of Shakespeare's, as Santayana, with only some exaggeration, calls *Hamlet* (c. 1600), the hero is a pious, real Christian living in a society whose Christian credentials are so taken for granted that the contents of no one's mind are disturbed by anything so distressing as a Christian thought—except for the "churlish priest," whose ritual worries about the burial of Ophelia turn out, ironically, to be more "Judaic" than Jesus-like.

No less intriguing is the way Cervantes touches, in the novel *Don Quijote (Don Quixote,* 1605–1615), indirectly on the theme. The protagonist fantasizes about being an ideal knight and proceeds to behave somewhat in a Jesuslike fashion. The "real" world—the world of Christendom—goes about its normal business, treating the Jesus-like man with, by turns, apathy, incredulity, hostility, derision, and manipulativeness. Not until the very end is there recognition by anyone that their society has been graced, through his presence, with a revelation of some sort.

Ben Jonson and John Milton are in the early medieval tradition of excoriating the sects of fellow Christians for serious deficiencies. The Anglican Jonson, in the *Alchemist* (play, 1610) and especially *Bartholomew Fair* (play, 1614), vents his fury on the Puritans for being self-righteous and Judaizing, while the Puritan Milton returns the favor by lambasting (mainly in his prose works but also briefly in several sonnets) first the Anglican clergy and then the Presbyterians for corruption, spiritual pride, tyranny—and, of course, Judaizing. The description of Belial in the poem *Paradise Lost* (1667), a god without a temple, is clearly aimed at places like the court of Charles II, a nominally Christian locale where men are devoted to debauchery and the Christian "priest turns atheist" that is, remains in the fold, though acts like men living in the period Before the Law. The survey of history in books 11 and 12, as well as the haughty elitism of the young Jesus in the poem *Paradise Regained* (1671) and the disillusioned tone of the later prose works, intimate that Milton placed little trust in self-styled "Christians." The character of Abdiel—the angel who stood up to Satan—adumbrates the role in subsequent history of the solitary individual (Enoch, Noah, Abraham) who keeps the faith. This vision simultaneously looks back to one reading of the New Testament—as the story of a solitary whom no one truly understood—and reflects Milton's personal experience. For, starting as an Anglican, he swung ever leftward until, as has been remarked, he belonged to a church with a membership of one, John Milton. Yet he considered himself a pious enough Christian to write a long, complex, private tract on Christian doctrine, *De doctrina christiana*(c. 1645). He thus dramatized in his writings as well as life the ultimate incompatibility between the Christian individual and the Christian society.

Milton's fellow Puritan, John Bunyan, anticipates the modern conundrum as to what would happen were Jesus to return to a Christian society. The heroes of the prose allegory *Pilgrim's Progress* (1678–1684), Christian and Faithful, are "born again" and set out on their pilgrimage to salvation. Their trip takes them through Vanity Fair—the Christian world at large—where they are arrested as subversives. Faithful is guilty of making the Thomas More-like assertion that, as Envy puts it, "Christianity and the customs of our town of Vanity were diametrically opposite and could not be reconciled." For this, he—like dissident Christian sects and, of course, Jesus himself—is persecuted and martyred. The irony is that the hostile society has long been now not Jewish but Christian; Christ's advent has Christianized the world and changed nothing.

Molière's *Tartuffe* (play, 1664) dramatizes the extent to which a representative member of Christendom (or of Christianity, of Christ's church)—one of More's "ingenious preachers"—can, by adapting his words and gestures to Christian ethics, adapt Christian ethics to human, all-too-human motives. Swift (*An Argument against Abolishing Christianity*, 1708) marshals his tremendous powers of irony to rebut the case for ending Christianity. The revival of "real . . . Primitive" Christianity being out of the question, the persona settles for a defense of "nominal" Christianity and shows how the progress expected from abolishing even this attenuated version has been greatly exaggerated. The satire is directed as much at worldly-wise Christians embarrassed by its archaic flavor and moral constraints as at secularists and atheists. His essay *Modest Proposal* (1729) is a reductio ad absurdum addressed to a ruling class and nation, both overtly Christian, treating the Irish peasantry in so rapacious a manner that they might as well literally eat the Irish babies for all the moral difference it would make.

The Romantic and Modern Periods

At the end of the eighteenth century, a major change takes place in the Western sensibility. For nearly two millennia, virtually every major writer either in his compositions or his life subscribed to the Christian idea. However critical they might be of Christendom or clergy, they at least implicitly acknowledged Jesus as the Savior, the validity of the Bible, and the existence of a Christian moral order. From now on, most great writers work from without the Christian system. Thus Thomas Paine in the essay *The Age of Reason* (1794–1795) rejects the Bible as barbarous, Christianity as merely another myth foisted on mankind by those with vested interests. A somewhat different rebellion was undertaken by Paine's contemporary, William Blake. For him, Christianity came to be a life-denying religion, one in which love and desire were proscribed and "thou shalt not" had precedence over "thou shalt." Jesus was, in this view, someone who asserted the role and power of the passions but whose name was used for the erection of a system that did precisely the reverse. In this vein, nineteenth-century writers like, among many, Renan in France and Carducci in Italy discard the traditional savior—divine, ascetic, and proscriptive—in favor of an inspired, life-celebrating Jesus. For Emerson (1803–1882), whose discoveries caused him to leave the church, Jesus was a rare Great Man, in tune with the Oversoul and aware that the secret of life lay wrapped in mystery, spontaneity, intuition, and awe but cursed with followers who insisted on—and superimposed on his career—road maps, abstractions, rules, dogmas, easy answers.

Kierkegaard is, however, one of the giants of thought who remained within the fold. This did not diminish the severity of the critique which he, like his deist, agnostic, and atheist predecessors and contemporaries, mounted against Christendom. In his last works, essays in the journal *Øjeblikket* (1855), he attacked "official" Christianity and gave one of the most scathing descriptions of the gulf separating Christianity from Christians. Christianity stands for poverty, isolation, suffering, hatred of family and of worldly ties, and Christendom knows only material comfort; Europe is a "Christian" continent in which few Christians can be found. The making of everyone officially Christian, the automatic awarding of Christian identity cards at birth, abolishes Christianity itself. A Christian political entity is a self-contradiction. Being Christian is now merely a game, a union card, a guarantee of a worldly career, a means of disguising and furthering one's old-fashioned selfish desires. The New Testament has been cancelled de facto, and Christians are now indistinguishable from Jews. In this uniquely radical vision, Christianity and Christendom seem permanently irreconcilable. No less savage were the writings of Nietzsche, an avowed atheist with an ambiguous response to the components of "Christianity": for Jesus, a grudging respect; for Christianity, notably Paul, virulent hatred; for Christendom, contempt.

The Kierkegaardian vision was dramatized by Ibsen in *Brand* (1866), the story of an earnest Christian minister whose "all or nothing," uncompromising interpretation of the gospel sets him at odds with town and family, costs the lives of wife and son, leads to ostracism and exile at the hands of the parishioners, and ends in death by avalanche at the hands of the "God of Love" he serves. The self-destructive agony of being a Christian in the environment of a comfort-seeking Christian community has rarely been so sharply delineated. If members of Christendom seem often to seek an easy way out of being Christian, the problem is exacerbated in a modern world committed to technology and progress, that is, to the proliferation of creature comforts and hedonistic endeavors. Hawthorne's *"Celestial Railroad"* (short story, 1843) shows that the technological quick fix, symbolized by the building of rail networks, may greatly ease travel on earth but will do nothing for the ultimate trip through outer space to heaven.

Even while it ceases to engage the emotions of the writer or to constitute the framework for his tale, Christianity continued to reenforce the narrative by providing recognizable symbols. In Melville's *Bartleby the Scrivener* (novella, 1853), both the protagonist—with his haunting response to all requests and orders directed at him, "I would prefer not to"—and the narrator (his employer) exhibit Jesus-like traits. Bartleby resembles Jesus in his refusal to engage himself in any of the mundane routines of life; in his implicit questioning of the meaning of man's quotidian, money-oriented existence; his mysterious other-worldy air; and his meek, polite, cheek-turning yet definitive manner of undertaking this rebellion. The employer resembles a good Christian, if not Jesus himself, by the Samaritan compassion he has for one who irritates him, upsets the routine in his office, and imperils his livelihood. Without spouting any religious rhetoric, he acts out the Christian principle of being his brother's keeper and, against all his own interests and habits, becomes solicitous for Bartleby's welfare to the very end. It is therefore significant with reference to our theme that the Christianizing (or interiorizing) encounter with Bartleby results in the employer's diminution of ritual observance. At the very time that he feels drawn to Bartleby by "the bond of a common humanity," he desists from going to church: "Somehow the things I had seen disqualified me for the time from churchgoing." Yet he is still pious enough, or made more pious, as to betake himself to a reading of theologians and to seeing Bartleby as a mysterious emissary from God. The suggestion is strong that church attendance is merely an item on the social calendar, a matter for the swells on parade every Sunday along fashionable Broadway, or an occasion for the appreciation of the oratory of "a celebrated preacher.'' (Cf. St. Augustine's worries over the estheticism lurking in his own response to church music.) The religious experience sought in vain in that hotbed of Christendom, the church, rather accosts one unexpectedly at one's work place during a weekday; living as a Christian cancels, even goes against, the need to ritualize one's Christianity by means of formal prayer on a day set aside for Jesus.

Melville's other cryptic parable of Christianity, *Billy Budd* (novella, 1891), has as hero a man of purity and innocence who strikes out at the evil that would victimize him and dies a martyr—to the Law. Billy is only indirectly a Jesus-like figure, but two of his traits point to a worldly, almost Machiavellian reading of his career against the background of ecclesiastical history: his inarticulateness and, in the consequent frustration, his inadvertent killing. The usual view of Jesus is of someone highly articulate and highly passive, if not pacifist. Could Melville be suggesting, given the tension between Christianity and Christendom traced here through the centuries and given the harm wrought by Christians—who, not understanding the Founder or unable to live up to His ideal, shed much blood in his name—that Jesus must be adjudged inarticulate and inadvertently a killer after all; that he must be judged not merely by what he stood for but by how relevant and viable his message was to a mankind sunk in lethargy, depravity, and ignorance; and that from the perspective of this worldly judgment and of the melancholy historical consequences of his life, he is left as vulnerable and culpable as Billy Budd? If something like this interpretation is lurking in the story, Melville is preparing the ground for Dostoevsky's Grand Inquisitor parable.

Similar in subject—employer versus employee—to *Bartleby* is Tolstoy's "Khoziain i rabotnik" ("Master and Man," story, 1895). Vasili, a wealthy merchant and church elder, is a good Christian Pharisee, sure of his place in the universe, contemptuous (and, not so incidentally, exploitative) of his servant Nikita, the village reprobate. But when they are projected by a blizzard into an extreme situation, the roles are reversed and the true nature of their souls is revealed. The master is helpless, and selfish to boot, while the servant, wise in the ways of nature, takes control and acts humbly and altruistically. At the climactic moment, the master, with motives humanly mixed yet in part altered by the meek and poignant example of his servant, is propelled into a gesture of communion and brotherhood. His realization that they can survive the storm only by combining the heat from their bodies is not only based on a biological fact but is also a metaphor for the essence of Christianity as a vision of the oneness of man, the mutuality of the human enterprise. Having deluded himself all his life that he is a Christian—and that his servant is not—he dies embracing one who is both his servant, his Jesus-like ideal, and, mysteriously, his savior. In a paradox worthy of Jesus, the master, long having been cooped up in the chamber of his egotism and selfishness, rejoins the universe in the very act of dying. The merely formal commitment to Christianity, symbolized by his being an elder of the church, is part of the "Christendom" of the living and is cancelled by the "Christianity" of the manner of his death.

Dostoevsky operated, like Kierkegaard, from within Christianity and, again like the Dane, his critique of Christianity was if anything sharper than that of many an outsider. The *Idiot* (*The Idiot,* 1868) is in the *Don Quixote* tradition (as was Fielding's Parson Adams in *Josepeh Andrews* (novel, 1742) and Dickens' novel *Pickwick Papers* [1836–1837]) of portraying a saintly, Jesus-like figure whose innocence and ineffectiveness makes him a stranger and a fool in a corrupt, hardened, urbane Christendom. The novel *Prestuplenie i Nakazanie* (*Crime and Punishment,* 1866) explores as no other work the profound Christian paradox, rooted in St. Augustine's *Confessions* (and revived by some romantic writers), that only the terrible sinner, by confronting his own depravity, can become a Christian. Raskolnikov is a murderer and Sonia a prostitute, but the knowledge of having touched the moral depths opens the door to regeneration for them, while his mother and sister are bland Christians, offended by the very presence of Sonya, sure of their respectability, ignorant of how the sister had in fact prostituted herself by marrying someone merely in order to be able to have the money with which to send Raskolnikov to college. They err doubly: in confusing respectability with Christianity and in not seeing that the respectability is a cover for spiritual prostitution. They represent a Christendom that, despite its good intentions and its respectability, is beyond the reach of grace because it lacks all self-awareness.

The novel *Brat' ia Karamazovy* (*The Brothers Karamazov,* 1880) is one of the supreme treatments of the theme. Dmitri has developed a bad, and deserved, reputation in the eyes of the townspeople because of his erratic life, but, like Raskolnikov, he is placed on the road to redemption by adverse events—in this case, conviction for a parricide he did not commit—which force him into self-scrutiny. He has been preceded in his pilgrimage by Father Zossima, who had been a worldly, macho military officer until an untoward incident crystallized his guilt feelings and propelled him into the church. There he lived a saintly life, yet his imitating Jesus aroused in many people, even in the bosom of his church, suspicion, envy, back biting—not respect or love.

The major intellectual challenge in this novel, however, is presented by Ivan's parable of the Grand Inquisitor. Jesus returns to earth while the inquisition is in progress. The Grand Inquisitor, who rules in Jesus' name, treats the Savior as an interloper, as a hopeless idealist whose demands are far in excess of what human nature can bear and whose message must be modified and refracted by a ruling class that, better in touch with man's low capacity, knows how to control men even while, because of vague human gestures in the direction of idealism, invoking the name of Jesus. Furthermore, the parable takes the somewhat cynical idea of More's and others' that "Christianity" is the "ingenious preachers" self-serving manipulation of "Christ" and gives it a complex, altruistic dimension, for the Inquisitor has the tormenting burden of keeping mankind free from the dangers of anarchy, while shouldering all alone the terrible truth that men must live by daily lies and that Jesus is doomed to be forever misunderstood and irrelevant. Seen in this way—as a doctor keeping secret the fact that the patient is terminally ill—the Inquisitor is a tragic, not an exploitative, figure. This endlessly suggestive parable is the strongest presentation of the threefold distinction among Jesus, Christianity, and Christendom. As a paradigm of a hopeless cleavage at the heart of the Christian religion and of the contradictions built into Jesus' life, it is the progenitor of the oft-repeated paradox in twentieth-century folklore (especially during Civil Rights days) that if Jesus returned to earth today he would be crucified all over again. This time by Christians. And in the name of Christ.

The idea that people make their gods and heroes in their own image has never been truer than of Jesus—witness the tendency of all sorts of groups to "Kidnap Christ," turn him into their founding father, and make him bless their cause—or more shocking than in modern times. Hence for the Fabian socialist G. B. Shaw, Jesus was the first socialist (or "communist") and for the prophet of sex, D. H. Lawrence, Jesus celebrated the biological urge.

In the long preface to *Androcles and the Lion* (play, 1916), Shaw presents Christianity as an unholy alliance of John the Baptist and Paul working in conjunction with the Barabbas-like church and state to form a Christendom wholly averse to Jesus. His system not yet having been tried because the "respectable world" is still "Barabbasque," Jesus cannot be deemed a failure. In Shaw's version of the Gospels, Jesus emerges once more as a solitary, misunderstood figure. Where John the Baptist was a melancholy ascetic, a "salvationist" with a martyr complex, Jesus was a civilized, pleasure-loving artist and bohemian who, indifferent to rituals and dogmas, stood for the "enrichment and intensification of life" and who would have agreed with the proverb "the nearer the Church, the farther from God." An "anti-Clerical," he affronted all states and churches and was hardly one for establishing new ecclesiastical systems. His preachments against private property, money, judging, punishing, and family entanglements can be realized only now by means of universal suffrage and modern political measures. Such progress had been doomed in the past because "Christianity was slain with Jesus," and he had been followed by apostles who, unlike him, were filled with malice and vindictiveness. Paul, especially, was an anti-Christian, a hysterical and egotistic revivalist, using Jesus' name as a facade for his own brand of repressive religion, which was a reversion to the melancholy salvationism and superstition of John the Baptist that Jesus had rebelled against. To this Paul added his own hatred of life, fear of sex, and submission to church and state. "The conversion of a savage to Christianity is the conversion of Christianity to savagery." If it be objected that this naturalistic version leaves out of account the broader metaphysical claims put forth in the later chapters of the Gospels, Shaw has a formula with which to dispose of the problem. The gay, charismatic Jesus had his head turned by adulation, became insane (like

Swift, Ruskin, and Nietzsche), and began spouting deluded nonsense about being the son of God.

Without reinterpreting the Gospels in detail, D. H. Lawrence was operating in the Blakean tradition of seeing the passions in general and sexuality in particular as among the good things of life; of Christianity as a desiccated, life-denying system; and of Jesus as no "Christian" but a celebrator of the body who was assimilated by the very system, and the systematic view of life, that he had set himself against. In his parable *The Escaped Cock* (novel, 1929), Jesus, instead of going to heaven, returns to earth and has sexual intercourse with a priestess of Isis.

One of the greatest twentieth-century novels, Joyce's *Ulysses* (1922) is not overtly about Christianity but suffused with Christian symbolism and values. Leopold Bloom is a lapsed Jew and, paradoxically, with his dignity, humility, and readiness to help out the son of an acquaintance, the only Jesus-like figure in Christian Dublin. This despite having a mind rife with sexual fantasies (shades of Lawrence), some of which are carried out, for Bloom is a most unusual saint— modern, post-Freudian. Scorned by Dubliners, victimized by his wife and her lover, not too successful in his vocations, futilely mourning his long-dead infant son and growing estranged from his daughter, he is, like Jesus, a solitary, a man passive and ineffective in the eyes of the world, but filled with the milk of human kindness (and socialist velleities—shades of Shaw).

Through his efforts at salvaging another human being, the only communication—or communion?—between two persons in the novel takes place, however brief and ambiguous. Bloom has no religious affiliation, and Stephen is in the throes of a guilt-ridden rebellion against the church. In the worldly perspective of Christendom, or even Christianity, theirs is a sordid, drink-sodden, meaningless coming together begun beyond the pale of respectable society in the bordello section of Dublin and issuing in a rambling, barely coherent conversation filled with blank spots and misunderstandings; for such is human intercourse. In the perspective of Jesus, however, theirs is, like the coming together of Tolstoy's master and man or the solicitousness of Melville's employer, a momentary glimpse of something spiritual caught through the doorway of the material, quotidian world, a doorway Jesus appeared to have opened but the access to which remains a matter of considerable acrimonious dispute in the vales of Christendom.

See also: Christian Hero.

Selected Bibliography

Frye, Roland M. *Perspectives on Man: Literature and the Christian Tradition*. Philadelphia: Westminster Press, 1961.

Jarrett-Kerr, Martin. *Studies in Literature and Belief*. Freeport, N.Y.: Books for Libraries Press, 1954.

McFague, Sallie. *Literature and the Christian Life*. New Haven, Conn.: Yale University Press, 1966.
Scott, Nathan. *Modern Literature and the Religious Frontier*. New York: Harper, 1958.

MANFRED WEIDHORN

CINEMA

Cinema is the art or technique of making motion pictures; the industry engaged in this art or technique; the motion pictures collectively. Cinema as an art or technique entails distinct devices for transitions (dissolve, wipe, continuity cutting, dynamic cutting, cross-cutting, iris-in and iris-out), for focus (deep, selective, soft, follow, and search), and for shots (high-angle, low-angle, close-up, dolly, pan, tilt, tracking, long, and zoom). The cinema as an industry includes the contributions of numerous professionals: producers, writers, directors, actors, editors, cinematographers, composers, designers of sets and costumes, and so forth.

Cinema as a Theme and a Motif

Cinema as a theme has inspired literature that deals with the subjects of filmmaking and film-viewing. Works as diverse as Luigi Pirandello's *Si gira* (*Shoot,* novel, 1914–1915), John Hollander's "Movie-Going" (poem, 1960), and Arthur Miller's *After the Fall* (play, 1964) have examined several of the following concerns: the social/economic/intellectual environment in which films (real or invented) are produced; the impact of particular films, or of film-viewing in general, on the audience; the interaction between the people engaged in the making of films; the source of cinematic excellence, and its price. Numerous significant issues have been discussed and dramatized: the difficulty of apprehending reality while one is occupied with creating illusion; the artistic compromises that frequently accompany the quest for commercial success; the tragic consequences of failed aspirations; the exhilaration of exercising creative control; the hypnotic attraction of chronic and repeated film-viewing; and the tendency of life to imitate art, as well as vice versa.

Cinema as a motif—or the cinematic perspective—entails the use of literary devices analogous to film devices. If a literary work conveys a strong sense of directed visual effects (a wide-ranging view, for example, followed by a close-up focus on one aspect of the landscape) or of forceful transitions (such as abrupt scene changes, back-and-forth movement, or manipulation of chronology), the work may be labeled "cinematic." This label, to be sure, can sometimes be the foundation of a negative criticism; when Virginia Woolf referred to Compton Mackenzie's *Sylvia Scarlett* (1918) as a "movie novel," she meant to attack the novel's rapid succession of truncated scenes. More often, though, the word "cinematic" is applied honorifically, to indicate features such as temporal distortion, shifting point of view, ellipses in narrative continuity, thematic and stylistic superimpositions, and freedom from linear progression–qualities that characterize the modern novel. It is in this sense that Virginia Woolf's own novels (*Mrs. Dalloway*, 1925; *To the Lighthouse*, 1927) have been considered cinematic.

The issue of the reciprocal influence of literature and film has frequently been raised but rarely settled. Several positions have been expounded. The cinema, say some, has strongly influenced literature, or vice versa; the two forms, say others, are essentially independent, with similarities that are merely coincidental; literature and film, say still others, resemble each other primarily because they developed in parallel ways. Although this complex issue will not be adjudicated here, the relevant remarks of two artists will be cited. In the famous preface to his novel *The Nigger of the Narcissus* (1897), Joseph Conrad wrote: "My task which I am trying to achieve is, by the power of the written word to make you hear, to make you feel—it is, before all, to make you see." The filmmaker D. W. Griffith, in an apparent echo, proclaimed: "The task I'm trying to achieve is above all to make you see." The resemblance is suggestive. The literary texts, furthermore, often seem to compel the critic to adopt the vocabulary of the cinema. It has been observed, for example, that parts of Gustave Flaubert's novel *Madame Bovary* (1856) sound like a screenplay. The cinema is sometimes a natural point of reference.

The term has indeed been used loosely to refer to any work displaying qualities that recall film devices, whether or not the writer consciously intended to imitate cinematic techniques. This loose usage has led to discoveries of the cinematic aspects of works as early as the Bible and the epic poem *Beowulf* (c. 8th century), as well as later classics such as the play *Macbeth* (1605–1606) and the poem *Paradise Lost* (1667). Overhead shots have been detected in H. G. Wells' *The War in the Air* (novel, 1908); other discoveries include reverse-angle shots in Baroness Orczy's *The Scarlet Pimpernel* (novel, 1905), zoom shots in Alessandro Manzoni's *I promessi sposi* (*The Betrothed*, novel, 1827), establishing shots in James Fenimore Cooper's *The Prairie* (novel, 1827), cross-cutting in Frank Norris' *The Octopus* (novel, 1901), camera obscura in George Du Maurier's *Peter Ibbetson* (novel, 1891), flashbacks in Thomas Mann's "Tonio Kröger" (story, 1903), and a multiperspectivist *mise-en-scène* in John Galsworthy's *The Man of Property* (novel, 1906). The apparent proliferation of "cinematic" devices suggests that all writing is potentially in some way cinematic—at which point the term ceases to be useful. Studying the devices that can readily be identified, however, sometimes helps to analyze the aesthetic strategies and stylistic patterns of writers who depart—consistently, strikingly, and significantly—from literary traditions and contemporary norms. Referring to the cinema is particularly appropriate—to the point of being essential—when dealing with writers who deliberately invoke film techniques, apparatus, and terminology, writers such as John Dos Passos, with his "Camera Eye" segments in the *U.S.A.* trilogy of novels (1930, 1932, 1936).

Among those writers for whom the cinematic perspective is critically useful is Manuel Puig, for whom the cinema is both a literary theme and a literary motif. Puig employs cinematic devices while addressing the subjects of film-making and film-viewing. Writers have often chosen to become involved with film in several ways. Some writers who have used the cinema as a subject or as a stylistic model have also been screenwriters (e.g., Alain Robbe-Grillet, F. Scott Fitzgerald, and Arthur Miller) or critics (e.g., James Agee, Vachel Lindsay, and Graham Greene); some, with varying degrees of success, have had a large proportion of their works adapted to the screen (e.g., Charles Dickens, John Steinbeck, and James Joyce). The interaction between literature and the cinema has been long, complex, and various.

Cinematic Writing without Major Cinematic Indebtedness

D. W. Griffith claimed that Charles Dickens had been his source for the innovative device of parallel cutting, that is, moving back and forth between two stories or between two parts of the same story. In "Dickens, Griffith, and the Film Today" (essay, 1944; reprinted in *Film Form,* 1948), Sergei Eisenstein, another major early director and theorist, argues that Dickens' novel *Oliver Twist* (1837–1838) contains the prototype of Griffith's exposition through montage, as well as the literary equivalents of fades and dissolves. Although later critics have questioned the assertion (on the part of both Griffith and Eisenstein) of Dickens' direct influence on Griffith, Eisenstein's demonstration of correspondences between the two artists remains persuasive. It is not surprising to find anticipation of the cinema in the work of a writer who had strong theatrical interests (in melodrama, pantomime, and the music hall) and whose novels and stories have later been frequently adapted for films. (There are many more adaptations of his works than of those of contemporaries like William Thackeray, George Eliot, and even the sensation-writer Wilkie Collins.) Among the works most often cited as cinematic are "The Cricket on the Hearth" (short story, 1845), *Bleak House* (novel, 1853), *A Tale of Two Cities* (novel, 1859), and *Our Mutual Friend* (novel, 1865). Cinematic devices that have been found in Dickens include the close-up, the flashback, slow-motion, fast-motion, parallel action, recurring images, shifting point of view, and the modification of emphasis by a change in focus that is analogous to the use of special lenses.

Thomas Hardy's *The Dynasts: An Epic Drama of the War with Napoleon* (1903–1908) has also been seen as an anticipation of the cinema. Hardy apparently had trouble choosing the proper form for his panoramic work, which was intended to demonstrate the effects of the "Immanent Will" on the lives of both well-known historical personages and more obscure figures (private soldiers, English farmers, minor diplomats, ladies-in-waiting, and camp followers); he considered, as possible genres, a Homeric epic, a sequence of ballads, and a grand historical drama. The form he was searching for may indeed have been that of a film; his epic drama sounds at times like a screenplay, or even a shooting script, particularly in the elaborate stage directions that Hardy calls the "Dumb

Shows.'' Cinematic devices include the following: shifting point of view (as if the camera were on a crane), wide-angle shots, tracking shots, and close-ups. When Hardy writes, ''The eye of the spectator rakes the road from the interior of a cellar which opens upon it,'' he is manipulating the field of vision (or the frame) in a way that can be taken as cinematic.

James Joyce, unlike Dickens and Hardy, was quite familiar with the cinema. He was a regular moviegoer and an admirer of Sergei Eisenstein (who, Joyce said, was one of the only two directors capable of transferring *Ulysses* to the screen). His use of cinematic techniques, however, predates his familiarity with films, and it is therefore likely that he developed, independently, innovations such as limited point of view, fragmented narrative, and abrupt transitions. The novel *Ulysses* (1922) is cinematic in its montage structure (''mosaics,'' in Joyce's phrase), fluid imagery, striking juxtapositions, dissolves, slow-motion, fast-motion, close-ups, flashbacks, and cross-cutting (in time and in space). The novel *Finnegans Wake* (1939), although much less visually oriented, uses cinema as a theme. It includes many references to the language, devices, and history of film, and to the names of several actors and directors; an extended sequence, furthermore, is written as a film script. For Joyce, apparently, the cinema was an analogue, rather than an inspiration. Perceiving in the cinema a creative vocabulary and procedure parallel to his own, he found that references to film and its devices helped him define more precisely his own imagination and work.

Marcel Proust's sixteen-volume novel *A la recherche du temps perdu (Remembrance of Things Past,* 1913–1927) displays a similar interest in camera vision and in the loving detail of slow-motion—analogous to that of the cinema, yet without direct indebtedness (as is also the case with Dickens, Hardy, and Joyce). The devices he uses (such as discontinuous, introspective narrative and the condensation of time) are cinematic, yet seem to have preceded the development of the cinema itself, which was, at the time, much less sophisticated. Proust himself, however, was already pondering the nature of the new medium with its new way of seeing. In a remarkable passage in *Le côté de Guermantes (The Guermantes Way,* 1920), he contrasts human vision (tingling with emotions, bristling with memories) with camera vision (alienated and objective). Pirandello's novel *Si gira* also stresses the coldness of the camera eye.

Early Literary Responses to the Cinematic Perspective

One of the earliest important treatments of cinema as a theme is Luigi Pirandello's novel of 1914–1915, *Si gira (Shoot),* later retitled *Quaderni di Serafino Gubbio operatore (Notebooks of Serafino Gubbio, Cinematograph Operator).* Roughly contemporaneous with Proust's masterpiece and rendered into English by the same translator, the novel presents a cameraman's descent into detached impassivity. Initially outraged by ''the machine that mechanizes life,'' by the reduction of people to automatons, by the restless tempo of frantic progress, Gubbio ultimately comes to affirm his task: to operate the machine, to serve it with his hand (if not his soul), to record the spectacle of chaos and disintegration.

This horrifying spectacle is visible on screen and off, in the work and lives of the managers, directors, extras, and stars. The technique of the novel is itself cinematic; the "notebooks" include captions, scripts, close-ups, montages. In the final scene, when an actor shoots an actress instead of a tiger (who then proceeds to attack him), Gubbio keeps turning the handle of his camera, impassively and objectively; he has to be forcibly separated from his machine. The meaning of life, for him, lies in the silent operation of his camera, welcoming and contemplating all people and all things in a paradoxical spirit of "tender compassion."

John Dos Passos, who claimed to have been influenced by both Eisenstein and Joyce, found creative inspiration in the cinema and its camera eye. His important works include *Manhattan Transfer* (novel, 1925) and the *U.S.A.* trilogy of novels —*The 42nd Parallel* (1930), *1919* (1932), and *The Big Money* (1936)— works that are cinematic in style, structure, and subject matter. Fictional actors are among the leading characters, and historical screen stars appear in sketches. Cinematic devices include cross-cutting, tracking shots, shifting point of view, and fragmented chronology—in general, a sort of montage construction. The plot of the *U.S.A.* trilogy is organized in four ways: (1) traditional narrative, (2) stream of consciousness ("the Camera Eye"), (3) short sketches of people or institutions, and (4) collages of headlines and news items ("Newsreel"). Although the novels do not proceed in a linear fashion, thematic continuity is present nontheless, in spite of stylistic disparity. After "Newsreel" announces Valentino's death, for example, his biography is sketched; in the following section, which happens to be a straight narrative, Margo Dowling (later a film star) departs for Cuba with a Valentino-like gigolo. Dos Passos, like Eisenstein, is able to construct the narrative by juxtaposing fragmentary, yet related, materials; to understand the story, the reader is compelled to formulate the continuity that is implicit in the association of word and image. The act of reading this sort of cinematic novel is designed to be a strenuous struggle, rather than simply a surrender to hypnotic manipulation. The reading experience is not one in which everything is done for the reader; reading this "film" is, perforce, active and demanding.

Delmore Schwartz also relies on the tension between the active construction of experience and the passive submission to it. In his story of 1939, "In Dreams Begin Responsibilities," the nameless narrator imagines himself watching, on the screen, the events of the afternoon on which his parents became engaged and subsequently quarreled. Schwartz uses the present tense in this story for the actions and thoughts of both the spectator-narrator and the characters he views on the screen. The narrator occasionally refers, however, to something outside the spatial and temporal frame of the film (saying, for example, that his mother's brother is upstairs studying, "having been dead of rapid pneumonia for the last twenty-one years"). Three times the narrator interrupts the film: when he is overwhelmed by the sight of the sun and the ocean at Coney Island, to which his parents are indifferent; when his parents, to his horror, agree to marry

("Nothing good will come of it''); when they argue about consulting a fortune-teller and come close to parting in anger ("What are they doing?''). The usher, in turn, asks him, "What are you doing?'' and reminds him that everything he does matters "too much.'' The narrator awakes from the dream-film, on his twenty-first birthday, to begin his life as an adult, the life that has resulted from the events he had tried to treat as a film.

Vladimir Nabokov admired this story and saw a connection between it and his own "The Assistant Producer'' (1943), although he wrote his short story nearly twenty years before he read Schwartz's. "The Assistant Producer'' is told as if it were a film made by a German company, employing Russian émigré actors. The complicated plot involves Nazis, Soviets, and White Army double- and triple-agents; other players include a celebrated singer and, as narrator, a "venerable but worldly priest.'' The story is based on a 1938 kidnapping. The true subject of the story, however, is not the historical kernel, but is the cinema itself: its devices, its magic, its romantic clichés, its treatment of Russia and Russians. Cinematic techniques—slow-motion, tilted perspective, meticulous analysis of the visual space—appear in many of Nabokov's works, as do allusions to movies, particularly the devices of anarchic comedy (silent and sound) and *film noir*. His most cinematic novels are *Korol', dama, valet* (1928; translated and revised as *King, Queen, Knave,* (1968) and *Kamera obskura* (1932; translated, revised, and retitled *Laughter in the Dark,* 1938). "Kartofel' nyï elf'' ("The Potato-elf'', short story, 1924) has, as he says, "a cinematic slant'' in its "structure and recurrent pictorial details.'' (The story had its origin in an unproduced scenario.) In 1960, Nabokov wrote a four-hundred-page screenplay for Stanley Kubrick's film of Nabokov's novel *Lolita* (1955); although the director omitted most of Nabokov's material, some was retained. Nabokov was later offered the project of adapting for the screen Nathanael West's novel, *Day of the Locust* (1939), a commission he refused. The results of the confrontation between Nabokov's desire and West's despair are an intriguing might-have-been.

The Hollywood Writers

Day of the Locust is one of the best (and best-known) of the Hollywood novels. Nathanael West, who spent much of his time in Hollywood writing "B'' pictures, describes in this novel the painful failure of the search for beauty and romance, which are promised by the movies, yet delivered in counterfeit form only—a disappointment to those who watch movies, to those who make them, and to those who live in their shadow (gamblers, pushers, prostitutes, etc.). West's technique here is also cinematic, with camera-eye focus and rapid cutting between scenes. The characters are grotesque, from Faye Greener (obsessed with pathetic film-based fantasies) to the child actor Adore (an eight-year-old boy whose voice vibrates with "sexual pain''). The novel ends with a riot at a film premiere; Adore throws a rock and is attacked, after which the crowd turns on his attacker. The images of the riot and those of the earlier episodes and characters of the novel blend, in one character's mind, with the flaming angels of a painting of the Apocalypse. In *Day of the Locust,* West examines and indicts the myth of Hollywood glitter, a myth he replaces with a vision of sterility and corruption. His screen work bought him time for writing, and it also gave him, perhaps, his greatest subject.

F. Scott Fitzgerald, whose years in Hollywood yielded only one screen credit (from the nineteen projects on which he worked) and considerable attendant frustration, felt, nonetheless, a consuming interest in the cinema, which he once called "the greatest of all human mediums of communication." Much of his fiction deals with actors, directors, producers, and screenwriters, notably *The Beautiful and Damned* (novel, 1922), "Crazy Sunday" (short story, 1932), *Tender Is the Night* (novel, 1934), the Pat Hobby stories (serialized 1940–1941), and *The Last Tycoon* (novel, incomplete when Fitzgerald died in 1940, published in 1941). Monroe Stahr, the last tycoon, is modeled on the wunderkind Irving Thalberg. Stahr is a brilliant executive: a man of intelligence, taste, and the strength to use his abilities decisively and responsibly. If he is, perhaps, too paternalistic, too much in control, he is also the last of his breed, a potential victim of the forces of finance and the class struggle. In this novel about the cinema, Fitzgerald employs cinematic techniques such as parallel editing, rapid cutting, and shifting point of view. Thematically, the novel reveals a respect for the cinema and an awareness of the threat posed by short-range commercial considerations, a threat Fitzgerald believed he suffered from personally.

A major source for the belief that Fitzgerald's years in Hollywood were entirely futile and frustrating is the thinly disguised portrayal of him in a *roman à clef, The Disenchanted* (1950), by Budd Schulberg, a screenwriter and the son of a Paramount film producer. Manley Halliday, the protagonist, is a novelist, once successful and esteemed, who loses his talent and his self-respect under the pressures of Hollywood and alcohol. A key episode in the novel refers to an actual incident. In February 1939, Schulberg and Fitzgerald flew to Dartmouth to acquire background for the film *Winter Carnival.* Fitzgerald's drinking led to his causing embarrassing incidents at the college and ultimately to his being admitted to a hospital after being refused accommodations at several hotels. Schulberg's memory and reconstruction of these events perpetuated the legend of the artist destroyed by drink and the Hollywood system. In an earlier novel, *What Makes Sammy Run?* (1941), Schulberg recounts the rise to power of an aggressive film magnate, obsessed with the quest for success, driven by the fear of failure, ruthless in his lack of concern for such values as loyalty, justice, and sincerity. This vision of Hollywood as a jungle has been popular and inflammatory.

Arthur Miller, a writer with direct experience of Hollywood, is best known for the work he has done outside it. A playwright who has also written for the screen, he has created several cinematic plays. Among the qualities of the movies that have influenced the writing of plays (his and those of others), he has identified "their swift transitions, their sudden bringing together of disparate images, their effect of documentation inevitable in photography, their economy of storytelling and their concentration on mute action.'' *Death of a Salesman* (1949)—with its twenty-four time-sequences, linked by dissolves and fades (analogous to those of film), as the past clashes with the present—is an attempt to convey, in a distilled form, the tension between a subjective past and a present that can be approached and conveyed both objectively and subjectively. In *After the Fall* (1964)—in which the chief female character is a film actress—the technique is again cinematic. The transitions between scenes depend not on chronology or logic, but on an association of ideas and images. Much more fragmented than *Death of a Salesman,* the later play seems to employ rapid, cinematic montage as the basis of its dramatic structure.

Cinema and the Modern Novel

Alain Robbe-Grillet—screenwriter of *L'année dernière à Marienbad* (*Last Year at Marienbad,* 1961) and director/screenwriter of, among others, *L'immortelle* (*The Immortalist,* 1962) and *Trans-Europe Express* (1966)—is at the center of the movement known as *le nouveau roman* (the new novel), several characteristics of which can be described as cinematic: fractured chronology, emphasis on precise visual description, attention to surface at the expense of character development. Robbe-Grillet does not wish to label his novels ''cinematic,'' in that the New Novelist is far more subjective than the camera; the novels themselves, however, reveal an extraordinary focus on the object, although they may not in fact be objective. Characters, dialogue, and even pronouns are eliminated as far as possible, in *La jalousie* (*Jealousy,* novel, 1957); knives, hands, clothes, bread, and meat, however, are meticulously described. *Projet pour une révolution à New York* (*Project for a Revolution in New York,* novel, 1970) includes direct references to the cinema with secret movie cameras, stock footage from detective films, and a well-rehearsed scenario in which the reader is encouraged to participate.

Walker Percy's *The Moviegoer* (novel, 1961) examines the transformation of an apathetic stockbroker who finds new purpose and commitment, largely through love for his neurotic cousin. His initial state is conveyed by his ability to enjoy any movie, even a bad one, and by his tendency to treasure memorable moments in movies rather than special experiences in his life. His passion for movies rarely affects his daily life; although he speaks of keeping a ''Gregory Peckish distance'' from his secretary, he is not interested in imitating his movie heroes or in meeting the actors who portray them. Film-viewing for him represents a passive attitude toward experience, as if life were arranged for his contemplation rather than for his participation. By the end of the novel, he has taken a firm step away from this passivity and the despair it entails.

The association of passivity with film-viewing is present in the work of Guillermo Cabrera Infante, a writer who has come to literature by way of the cinema. A film critic and screenwriter who says that film-viewing has taught him more about writing than has literature itself, Cabrera Infante has identified his purpose in *Tres tristes tigres* (*Three Trapped Tigers,* novel, 1964) as the expression of the philosophy of life embodied by the Marx Brothers. In this multilayered collage of documentary, fantasy, and film references, he constructs a confusing and amusing picture of night life in Havana under Batista before the revolution. Many of the characters are habitual film-viewers; Silvestre even sells his father's books, by the pound, to buy tickets to the movies. The cinema is a substitute, not only for literature and other forms of culture, but for reality itself. Characters rely on the cinema for a common language and a common background of experiences; daily life becomes little more than an intermission between the movies that are the sole source of excitement and vitality.

The novels of Manuel Puig—a director turned writer—also portray a world in which the cinema molds the lives of people who find in film their heroes, their vocabulary, their values. In *La traición de Rita Hayworth* (*Betrayed by Rita Hayworth,* 1968), Toto (born, like the writer, in 1932 in a small town in the pampas of Argentina) thinks and expresses himself in terms of the stars he idolizes and whom he imagines to be pursuing a romantic life style off screen as well. *Boquitas pintadas: folletín* (*Heartbreak Tango: A Serial,* 1969)—a montage of newspapers, letters, photos, diaries, police records, and tape recordings—also chronicles the fragmentary lives of characters whose naive expectations are inspired by movies, several of which are quoted in epigraphs. In *Buenos Aires Affair: novela policial* (*The Buenos Aires Affair: A Detective Novel,* 1973), each chapter begins with an epigraph from a classic Hollywood film, in which an actress (e.g., Garbo, Dietrich, Veronica Lake, Rita Hayworth) expresses herself in powerful melodramatic clichés that form an ironic contrast to the behavior of the protagonist, Gladys, who is sexually frustrated and emotionally repressed. The novel also features flashbacks, fantasy sequences, and camera-eye descriptions. *El beso de la mujer araña* (*The Kiss of the Spider Woman,* 1976) is composed largely of conversations between two prisoners: Molina (a middle-aged, apolitical, homosexual window-dresser, who turns out to be a police plant) and Valentin (a Marxist student). Molina recounts to Valentin—at length and in loving detail—the plots of several films, notably *Cat People* and *I Walked with a Zombie.* The films touch on the matters central to the prisoners at this time: love, freedom, beauty, fear, the bizarre. The film fantasy, as in Puig's other novels, ultimately replaces the bleak reality.

In his novel *Gravity's Rainbow* (1973), the elusive Thomas Pynchon uses the cinema as both a theme and a motif, to depressing ends. The book includes manifold references to actors (e.g., Tyrone Power, Cary Grant), directors (e.g., Orson Welles), specific films (e.g., *King Kong, The Wizard of Oz*), groups of films (e.g., German expressionist films of the 1920s), and the conventions of various genres (e.g., pornographic films, horror films, musical cartoons, Hollywood melodramas). Although the allusions to the Marx Brothers and W. C. Fields seem to endorse enthusiastically the refreshing spirit of anarchy, many of the references to film and to the experience of film-viewing seem to suggest passivity, stereotype-bound thinking, and the folly and cowardice of living life at second hand. The novel itself is a kind of film—framed as a World-War-II

movie, characterized by a cinematic direction of the reader's point of view—
and it includes, as significant fictional events, numerous episodes of fantasizing
and moviemaking. In an encyclopedic novel that gathers subject matter from
fields as diverse as physics, linguistics, law, and economics, a network of allusions to the cinema is not out of place. The novel concludes with an apocalyptic
vision, as the screen turns dim and dark, and the audience of "old fans who've
always been at the movies" is invited, just before the rocket brings death, to
sing the words indicated by the bouncing ball. The end of the film, in one of
the most sustained film-novels, is the end of the world.

Selective Bibliography

Cohen, Keith. *Film and Fiction: The Dynamics of Exchange*. New Haven: Yale University
     Press, 1979.
Murray, Edward. *The Cinematic Imagination: Writers and the Motion Pictures*. New
     York: Ungar, 1972.
Spiegel, Alan. *Fiction and the Camera Eye: Visual Consciousness in Film and the Modern
     Novel*. Charlottesville, Virginia: University Press of Virginia, 1976.
Welch, Jeffrey. *Literature and Film: An Annotated Bibliography, 1900–1977*. New York:
     Garland, 1981.

SHOSHANA KNAPP

CITY

The city and literature are contemporaneous; indeed the creation of urban life
may antedate literature. The city of Jericho (8,000 B.C.), with its estimated
population of 2,500, was fully urban. (One must recall that when Goethe arrived
in Weimar in 1775 it had a population of only 6,000.) The form and size of the
city have varied from the time of the original Jericho to the 20th-century megalopolitan centers, but they all have in common the effort of a community of
men to transform or overcome the givens of nature. An important factor in their
success has been the invention of literacy and the creation of literature. While
myth, saga, religion, and law have their roots in oral traditions, a literary culture
assisted in the creation of the complex social organizations that characterized
urbanism and the elaboration and transformation of the oral tradition.

The transition from the hunting and gathering cultures that had characterized
homo erectus for at least 500,000 years to the neolithic cultures of 10,000 B.C.
produced important changes in man's symbolic register, changes that have determined literary symbolization of the garden and the city down to the present
time. The domestication of plants and animals, the invention of smelting and
forging, the development of irrigation, and the creation of urbanity radically
transformed the religious and symbolic life of these neolithic cultures. The
experience of hunting and gathering cultures over a period of 500,000 years did
not vanish in a night, and that cultural resistance is reflected in the image of the

city as the center of alienation, the loss of freedom and innocence, the corruption of the individual, and the cause of the onset of human decadence. God made nature, man made the city. The city, viewed from the pastoral tradition, is the concrete affirmation of man's presumption and rebellion against God. The Old Testament is pervasively and persistently anti-urban. The story of Cain and Abel is a parable of pastoral virtue as opposed to neolithic agriculture. The story of the fiery destruction of Sodom and Gomorrah is an attack upon the urban morality of the cosmological monarchies. The pastoral tradition manifests itself particularly in the prophetical office in the Old Testament.

Myth and symbol, on the other hand, as developed in the new cultures, depicted the city as the creation of the gods and the king as a divine monarch. City plans were a symbolic map of the cosmos. In the city the order of the cosmos becomes the order for human societies. From the Renaissance onward this conception of civic order is humanized and rationalized and secular utopia replaces mythic cosmological order. Perfected human life and perfected society are dominated increasingly by the image of the city.

The success of the cosmological monarchies of the Nile and Euphrates river valleys led to increasing demands by the Hebrews for the creation of a Jewish monarchy on the Near Eastern model. The establishment, consolidation, and extension of the Davidic Kingdom, with its brilliant court life and elaborate temple priestly cult, was completed by the death of King Solomon in 933 B.C. From this time onward the Old Testament is filled with the tension between a pastoral prophetic tradition and a royal, priestly, urban culture. This tension is reflected in the various images of the city that animate later Western literature.

The *Historiai* (*History*, 5th century B.C.) of Herodotus provided the only extensive literary accounts of the cities of the cosmological monarchies surviving into the present. Herodotus deals fleetingly with the great cities of Egypt. Only Babylon is given extensive descriptive treatment. This description, which antedated the archeological discoveries of the nineteenth and twentieth centuries, provided an image of the ancient non-Hellenic city to later writers.

The city of Troy, fleetingly and obliquely presented in the epic *Ilias* (*Iliad*, c. 8th century B.C.), was to exert great shaping power on the idea of the city, as Virgil in his epic poem *Aeneis* (*Aeneid*, 19 B.C.) made it the ancestor of Rome, and Dante and the Florentine humanists believed the city of Florence to be a Trojan foundation.

The idealized view of the Athenian *polis* (city state) presented by Pericles and reported by Thucydides in book 2 of his history of the Peloponnesian War (*Historiai*, c. 400 B.C.) has served as the model conception of the democratic city. This oration pronounced over the dead of the first year of the war presents the population of Athens as a tolerant, democratic, and civically responsible citizen body devoted to the life of reason and the arts but none the less willing to participate in government and the defense of the polity. "I declare our city is an education to Greece," and we might have added an inspiration to cities of the Western World that followed in the wake of Athens.

Nonetheless, it was this same Athens that sacked the city of Melos and executed Socrates. Plato, seeing in Athens the exemplar of democratic excess and decadence, wrote his dialogue *Politeia* (*The Republic*, c. 380 B.C.) in order to contrast the ideal, utopian city with the Greek and particularly the Athenian reality. It must be conceded that the city as conceived by Plato became the model for authoritarian and "closed" societies.

By the end of the fourth century B.C., however, the Greek city-state as contrasted with the cities of the cosmological monarchies was in its death agony. *The Republic* by Plato and Aristotle's essay *Politika* (*Politics,* 4th century B.C.) must be regarded as normative rather than descriptive accounts of the *polis* in spite of the fact that Aristotle in his *Politics* carefully analyzes existing city-state constitutions. Alexander the Great (356–323 B.C.) brought the Mediterranean world within the compass of the cosmological monarchies. The cities founded by Alexander and his successors, particularly the city of Alexandria, even though they contained remnants of the constitution of the Greek city-states, were modeled on cities of the cosmological monarchies. Alexandria, with its divine ruler and its megalopolitan form and population, anticipated the Rome of the Caesars and Byzantium. Alexandria came, because of the research foundation connected with the museum and the library, to symbolize the encyclopedic, overripe, and sterile intellectuality of decadent urban cultures. In reaction to the artificiality of city life, it gave rise to the work of the pastoral poets and the fantasies of the first novelists. In the Hellenistic era a number of utopian novels depicting ideal cities appear; Euhemerus' *Hiera anagraphē* (c. 3001 B.C.) and shortly after 250 B.C. a utopian novel by an otherwise unknown author named Iambulus, the content of which is preserved by Diodorus Siculus. These conceptions of the utopian city anticipate Sir Thomas More's *Utopia* (1516) and Tommaso Campanella's *La città del sole* (*City of the Sun,* 1602).

Even though the Old Testament contained a very strong anti-urban component, the Hebrews of the ancient diaspora were increasingly urbanized. They settled in the cities of the Hellenistic world, particularly Alexandria, and after the conquest of the Mediterranean world by Rome, a large Jewish population found its way to the imperial capital. Christianity was far more unambiguously an urban religion. After the destruction of Jerusalem by Titus in A.D. 70, Christianity's center of gravity shifted to Rome where both the Apostles Peter and Paul found martyrdom. Paul proclaimed himself a Roman citizen (Acts, 25–26), and appealed to Roman justice. For many Christians Rome became the symbol of providential order, and it is not difficult to understand how the city of the Caesars became the city of the popes. Not all Christians accepted this view of Rome and urbanity, however. St. John denounces Rome in the Book of Revelations as "Babylon," the very symbol of the power of wickedness and vice, and the hermit tradition of the "Desert Fathers," out of which monasticism developed, was anti-urban in its conception.

The city of Rome had itself given rise to a providential conception of historical development in which the foundation of the city and its triumph is seen as the work of the gods, particularly Venus; its destiny and mission were believed to be messianic, and its endurance eternal. The concrete manifestation of the ideology of urban Rome is to be found in the Roman History of Livy and the great poem of Rome's foundation and mission, Virgil's *Aeneid*. It was entirely natural that the providential-messianic vision of the city of Rome and her mission as it is presented by Livy and Virgil should be grafted onto the Hebrew-Christian idea of a providential-historical process. Such indeed is the animating idea in Western medieval and Byzantine conceptions of the role and image of the city of Rome. As Arnold Toynbee observed (*Cities of Destiny,* 28), "Will any of the historic peaks [of urban culture] still stand out above this already man-made morass? If any do, we may guess that these survivors will be cities that have become holy cities after their material power and glory have come and gone." "Eternal Rome" only became "eternal" through the reverence and piety of Christian writers.

Roman authors have given us two contrasting visions of the reality of Roman urbanism. These notions have been associated with capital cities generally. Cicero, Livy, and the fragmentary literature of early Rome, particularly the figure of the censor, Cato the Elder, present us with a picture of urban patriotism and civic and moral virtue as having been associated with republican institutions. Rome is depicted as a city of ascetic, pragmatic, and virtuous peasants gradually corrupted by contact with the outside, particularly the eastern Mediterranean world. The loss of Rome's innocence and virtue is paralleled by the decline of republican institutions.

The writers of the imperial era reinforce this image by equating imperialism with the onset of decadence and depravity. The *Carmina* (poems, c. 84–54 B.C.) of Catullus, the *Satyricon* (novel, A.D. 60) by Petronius, the *Satirae* (*Satires* c. A.D. 100–127) of Juvenal, and the *Epigrammata* (*Epigrams,* A.D. 86–101) of Martial, together with comments of the Christian apologists, particularly St. Augustine in the treatise *De civitate Dei* (*City of God,* 413–426), depict Rome as a capital city of depravity, utterly lacking in civic virtue, with a polyglot population more Asian than Roman, contemptuous of the gods, effeminate, cultureless, dependent upon public welfare, and wholly decadent. Nineteenth- and twentieth-century apocalyptic visions of the city on the eve of the "fall" draw exhaustively upon this literature and the equation of republicanism with virtue and imperialism with decadence.

Nonetheless, the Rome of the Antonines (A.D. 98–180) has been considered by most modern writers to have embodied all the elements of ideal city life. Rome's one million inhabitants achieved a level of civic order and prosperity unequaled until very recent times. Edward Gibbon, fascinated above all by the city of Rome, wrote in *The Decline and Fall of the Roman Empire* (1776–1788), that, "If a man were called to fix the period in the history of the world during which the condition of the human race was most happy and prosperous, he would, without hesitation, name that which elapsed from the death of Domitian to the accession of Commodus." The imperial capitals of the twentieth century and those writers who have dreamt imperial dreams have quoted liberally from this golden era.

Gibbon's vision of Rome was essentially a reply, somewhat belated, to St. Augustine's *City of God*. Augustine distinguishes sharply between the city of God and the city of this world. Augustine uses the witness of the Roman writers to depict Rome as a sink-hole of iniquity based upon murder, robbery, and rapine. It is the city of this world, and the calamities that befell Rome in the late imperial period were due, Augustine asserted, to the vengeance of a just and outraged God. Gibbon, assuming the role of the pagan apologist, "the philosopher," paints a happier and brighter picture. The contrasting images of the city as "sin city" and "the Big Apple" have their roots in the dialectic of these two antithetical visions.

From the fall of Rome to the twelfth century, Constantinople provided the model of the city and inspired European notions of urbanity. Lindprand of Cremona as ambassador of Otto I and Otto II visited Constantinople in 949 and again in 968–969. His account of the marvels of the city and the splendor of the court were typical of the response of Western Europeans to Constantinople. Venice fell under the sway of Byzantine culture and mirrored in a lesser way the glory of Constantinople.

Technological mastery, intellectual sophistication, exotic sensuality and splendor, a government dominated often by women and eunuchs, cruelty that matched the bright mosaics of its churches in its obtrusiveness, a religion that was formal and magical, and a melancholy spirit; all these appealed to the symbolist writers of the late nineteenth and early twentieth centuries. The historiographic rediscovery of Byzantium in the nineteenth century culminates in William Butler Yeats' poem "Byzantium" (1930).

Until the eleventh century the decay of urbanity in the Christian West was nearly complete. Then quite suddenly the cities of Italy revive, and northern Europe is dotted with urban centers. These new cities, of which Paris was the greatest, are characterized in literature and in their influence on literature by freedom. This freedom was based upon mercantile prosperity, communal liberties won from king and feudality, the spirit of rational enquiry fostered by the university, especially that of Paris, the skeptical pragmatism of the bourgeois mind, and the heretical movements that were so often fostered by the urban environment. Once more the founders of monastic orders (Carthusian and Cistercian) fled to the wilderness in order to avoid the worldliness fostered by the city.

Paris, the nineteenth-century "city of light," first lays claim to that title in the twelfth century because of the fame of its university. From the High Middle Ages onward the city is in literature the center of intellectual and political freedom. It is characterized not only by rational enquiry but by revolutionary tumult and heretical fervor. The combination of urbanity and intellectuality in the Paris of St. Thomas Aquinas was a determinative influence on all later conceptions of the city.

By the end of the Middle Ages the antithetical conceptions of the garden and the city, the natural and the urban, have begun to merge. St. Francis of Assisi (1181–1226), founder of the new monasticism of the mendicants, perceives his new order in terms of an urban mission and urban location. At the same time his poetry and his life style are indicative of a new feeling for nature and a responsiveness to God as he reveals himself in the created order. Dante, in the epic poem *La divina commedia (The Divine Comedy,* c. 1320), completes this synthesis. The *Inferno (Hell)* depicts a city in which nature is either excluded or inverted. It is man-made and its order is the order of the City of Man. The *Purgatorio (Purgatory)* is the God-made realm of nature in which man's way-wardness is corrected. In the *Paradiso (Paradise)* the City of God and the realm of nature are conflated in the image of the mystic rose. This reconciliation of the natural and the urban provides one of the most powerful literary symbols in Western literature. This is especially true in its secularized utopian form and in the late nineteenth-century conception of the "garden city."

Although elements of cosmological order are prominent in Renaissance ideas of the city, rational civic conceptions, a scale based upon human dimensions, and the conquest of chaos and anarchy through planning become the dominant sources of urban symbolism. While Renaissance civic humanism was not utopian, it was certainly optimistic about man's ability to construct an urban environment capable of satisfying both human needs and desires. "The divine science of perspective" and the ideal of harmony achieved through the correct relationship of all the component parts was not only the ideal for human relationships, painting, literature, and stage design, but also for architecture and city planning. Platonic and Orphic conceptions of cosmic order are reflected in Renaissance notions of the ideal city. Above all the writers, painters, and architects sought through a revival of Roman republican civic virtue the renaissance of Roman urban institutions.

By the end of the fifteenth century, republicanism in the city states of Italy was dead and the princes were triumphant. The darkening mood of the sixteenth century significantly transforms the conception of the city. What men had sought through reason, through obedience to cosmic order, through congruence with human measurement is now sought through magic, through illusion and man-neristic trickery. The city becomes a gigantic stage set on which the rituals of power and the illusion of paradise are enacted. The court and the city become one and the same. The baroque quest for the infinite replaces the measured elegance of the Renaissance. Increasingly, the tension between the court and the country becomes a literary pivot. Alternatively the utopian city, as in Campanella's *City of the Sun,* is projected.

In Germany by the middle of the eighteenth century the baroque princely court is being replaced by a new conception of the city-state. It combines German Bürgertum with the humanistic ideals of the Hellenic city-state. The Weimar of Goethe, Herder, and Schiller, as it is reflected in their literary works, is the most perfect expression of this ideal. The reality was short-lived but the ideal is the basis of classical German literature and culture.

A new city life, however, was developing in the great mercantile centers of Europe, particularly London. The London of Adam Smith is the London of William Hogarth. Daniel Defoe, Henry Fielding, and Tobias George Smollett precede Smith by one long generation. For these writers mercantile London is opportunity, freedom, luxury, corruption, the antithesis of provincial innocence. The education of the hero, the journey through which the self is defined, now takes place in the hero's encounter with the city. The picaresque hero, a Ulysses of the commonplace, makes of the city's lanes and streets a substitute for the grand tour. Stephen Daedalus exploring the cosmos of James Joyce's Dublin is a figure who has at least some of his roots in the eighteenth century.

The tension between the country and the city, innocence and virtue as opposed to urban corruption, is a constant eighteenth-century theme. Civility is artifice and decadence for Jean-Jacques Rousseau. Sparta and Geneva are the city-states Rousseau most admires, and the noble savage, according to the *Discours sur l'origine et les fondements de l'inégalité parmi les hommes* (*Discourse on the Origin and Bases of Inequality among Men,* 1754), is far happier than the modern sophisticate.

From the middle of the eighteenth century onward, a new symbolic representation of the city becomes increasingly important in art and literature. The devastated city, whether its ruins are due to time's erosion, war and bombardment, or pestilence, as in Albert Camus' novel *La peste* (*The Plague,* 1947), becomes an urban symbol for failed hope and the flawed human condition. The romantic cult of ruins; Gibbon's *Decline and Fall of the Roman Empire,* Giovanni Battista Piranesi's etchings of the ruins of Rome, the excavation of the ruins of Pompeii and Herculaneum all contributed to the cult of cities of lost splendor and ghostly streets. Life among the ruins is a favorite literary theme of the twentieth century, and often the ruined city is treated as an analogue of the ruined human mind.

In the nineteenth century, more often than not, the symbol of the city was not death but that of diseased and uncontrolled life and growth. Pathological vitality is the characteristic of Charles Dickens' London; of the Chicago of James Farrell, Nelson Algren, and Saul Bellow.

The genius of Dickens and Balzac transcends any easily established categories. Dickens' London and Balzac's Paris are so fraught with mystery, adventure, delight, and surprise; so filled with vital and extraordinary personages that their narratives are akin to the Arabian Nights. At the beginning of the twentieth century a much less talented writer, O. Henry, writing of Bagdad on the subway, depicted New York in much the same terms. Few writers have dealt with the city as a magical vortex of adventure and alienation more compellingly than Thomas Wolfe. Wolfe especially depicts New York City as the home of the polyglot and inchoate masses.

By the late nineteenth century the city represented, above all else, the power of money. London and New York, Paris and Chicago were the capital cities of the kingdom of gold. Everything was for sale and speculation was the road to riches and power. Anthony Trollope, in *The Way We Live Now* (novel, 1875), and Upton Sinclair, whose novels are now of interest only to the social historian, depict the dissolution of traditional values and the corruption of the political order by the power of money. The city was the realm of gold.

Although the overwhelming bias in American literature has been pastoral, and the city has usually been presented as fouled and degraded, Walt Whitman, in his praise of Manhattan and Brooklyn, presented the city as essentially American. Henry James found his ideal city elsewhere. For him Paris was the city of light and culture; the reality of the American city was superficial, flat, and vapid by comparison.

From the end of the nineteenth century the city has been viewed increasingly as fatality, the historical destiny of a fatally afflicted civilization. Flaubert's novel *Salammbô* (1862) sets the tone, and Oswald Spengler, in *Der Untergang des Abenlandes* (*The Decline of the West* 1918–1922) and *Der Mensch und die Technik* (*Man and Technics* 1931), offers the historical rationalizations. The city is seen as technical achievement, as the decadent pleasure ground of a dying civilization. The masses dominate the architectural forms and the intellectual life of the city as Ortega y Gasset argued in *La rebelión de las masas* (*The Revolt of the Masses,* 1929). Megalopolis, whether in the form of Fritz Lang's silent film (1927), Berlin in films of the Weimar Republic (1919–1933) or Chicago in Saul Bellow's novels, is both attraction and fatality. It is the final form of the 10,000-year-old revolt against civility, the sophisticated expression of the old folk story of "Country Mouse and City Mouse."

See also: Arcadia.

Selected Bibliography

Pike, Burton, *The Image of the City in Modern Literature*. Princeton, N.J.: Princeton University Press, 1981.

Thompson, David. *The Idea of Rome*. Albuquerque: University of New Mexico Press, 1971.

Toynbee, Arnold, ed. *Cities of Destiny*. London: Thames & Hudson, 1967.

White, Morton, and Lucia White. *The Intellectual Versus the City*. Cambridge, Mass.: Harvard University Press, 1962.

STEPHEN J. TONSOR

CLOTHING

Every day civilized people don and doff their clothes. Yet it is surprising, as Carlyle first noted, that little thought has been given to so homely an item and to the fact that man "is by nature a Naked Animal" and "his Vestments and his Self are not one and indivisible." Though formal philosophy has left this territory fallow, poets and imaginative writers, more responsive to the diversity of trivial and quotidian phenomena, have from time to time touched on the subject, and their professional aptitude for seeing "a world in a grain of sand" has enabled them to discover significance in the wearing of apparel. These poetic insights have usually been peripheral; clothing has been treated metaphorically or as a jumping off point for meditations on other matters. But "rightly understood," dress may be found to include "all that men have thought, dreamed, done and been."

Antiquity and the Middle Ages

According to the Bible, not only did God make man and man make clothes, but man's making of clothes grew directly out of the way God made man. Before the Fall, man was naked and happy; then God tested his imperfect creation, and one of the first results of the latter's failure was his shame. Only borrowings from vegetation (and later from animals) could even partially alleviate that feeling. Thus the idea of clothing is established early, as necessitated by the sense of modesty and the consciousness of lust. While no such etiological tale is to be found in Greek mythology, one may note that in the epic poem the *Odysseia* (*Odyssey*, c. 8th century B.C.) the hero, finding himself naked on the isle of the Phaiacians, needs to avail himself of vegetation before approaching some young ladies at the seaside. Later, with Circe, he fears being unmanned by her if he goes naked to bed with her.

Certain articles of clothing mark a man in Scripture, as Joseph's coat of many colors and Jesus' seamless coat. If the Old Testament story of Adam and Eve implies that clothing, like language, was a prerequisite for the formation of civilization, later Christian antiquity advanced a different idea. Clothing had come in various societies to be associated with immodesty and excess, with conspicuous consumption and sexual arousal. Hence the spirit that is responsible for phenomena as diverse as the Mosaic strictures on dress and the sumptuary edicts in the reigns of Augustus or Elizabeth I caused men like the Desert Fathers, in rejecting the world, to return to nakedness as a Christian value, in a definition of saintliness akin to the iconographic representation of the Truth as naked. Diogenes the Cynic had, nearly a millennium earlier, arrived at a similar conclusion from a pagan vantage point and, from a post-Christian vantage point, Nietzsche (*Also sprach Zarathustra* [*Thus Spoke Zarathustra*, prose poem, 1883–1892]) would, millennia later, speak of the gods as actually ashamed of clothes.

Chaucer's *Parson's Tale* (c. 1380–1400), in particular, contains an extended tirade against the superfluity, gaudiness, vanity, and immodesty in the dress of both men and women. On the one hand, excess clothing is wasted on rich people, who trail it in the dung of the streets, while poor people have not even enough to protect them against the elements; and, on the other hand, paradoxically, amid all this excess, the rich people's clothing is often scandalously scanty when it comes to covering the shameful parts of the body. The *Roman de la rose* (*Romance of the Rose*, didactic poem, c. 1230, 1275) addresses to women the moral strictures on clothing, specifically woman's weakness for immoderation in dress. A character cries out at his wife's apparel for its expensiveness, its uselessness most of the time, notably at night, and its obstructive role whenever he is erotically attracted to her during the day.

Yet a third function of clothing is suggested by several medieval romances of a ruler who, on misplacing his attire when bathing, found himself without authority and identity. Such a Kafkaesque predicament reminds one that clothing is a key indicator of social status. As Pascal would later suggest in the *Pensées* (*Thoughts, 1670*), magistrates and physicians, dealers in imaginary sciences, would never have duped the world but for their elaborate dress. Aware of that fact, Gibbon (*Decline and Fall of the Roman Empire,* 1776–1788) criticizes the Emperor Julian for adopting the Diogenes (or "hippie") mode of dress and cleanliness; yet he concedes that, though most rulers, when stripped of their clothes, would disappear in the crowd, Julian's personal endowments would have been pre-eminent in any circumstances or any outer garb.

An archaic function of clothing is exhibited in folklore and in literary works heavily dependent on it: to render one invisible or invincible. If Plato spoke of the legend of the ring that made its wearer, Gyges, invisible, the *Nibelungenlied* (epic poem, c. 1200) has Siegfried wear a magic cloak endowed with similar powers. So also the hero of *Sir Gawain and the Green Knight* (romance, c. 1370) yields to the temptress's blandishments only to the extent of accepting and wearing a green girdle that will preserve his life in the upcoming reunion with the mysterious and fearsome knight clad all in green.

The Renaissance

The voyages of exploration during the Renaissance brought Europeans into contact with human beings for whom clothing played a minor role. This encounter was unsettling. The rationale for clothing that occurs to most people—to preserve us from the extremes of weather—was suddenly called into question. Montaigne (*Essais* [*Essays,* 1580–1588]), noting that some people in the "lately discovered nations" lived in the same clime as France and yet were naked, concluded that wearing clothes was a custom rather than an innate need, that its etiology was psychological or sociological rather than physiological. (Cf. Fielding's *Joseph Andrews,* novel, 1742.) Clothes perhaps had more to do with demarcating class than with insulating the body, for there was a greater difference between Montaigne's own dress and the peasant's—between social classes living in the same climate and locale, that is—than between the peasant's dress and the savage's nakedness.

Montaigne also, of course, subscribed (at least overtly) to the traditional view of clothing as part of the restraint of modesty placed on men by the Creator. Thus in the preface to his works he said that, were he a member of those "said to live still in the sweet freedom of nature's first laws," he would assuredly have portrayed himself "entire and wholly naked." The savage's nakedness, in other words, stands for a candor about inmost thoughts, a freedom from European, Christian notions of modesty; clothes are a concomitant of civilization. Hence the tremendous ironic conclusion to his essay on the cannibals (1, 31), where after showing the many ways in which the admittedly imperfect "savages" appear morally superior to the boastful Europeans, Montaigne can reassure his reader that in the final analysis the Europeans remain superior in the one matter that counts: the cannibals "don't wear breeches." The joke turns on the European's smug assumption that, more than cultivation, morality, and piety, "clothes make the man"—wearing clothes rather than being naked and, additionally, wearing the particular type of clothes that happens to be stylish. Montaigne's implicit distrust of clothing had been, as it were, institutionalized by Thomas More, who, in his *Utopia* (political romance, 1516), did away with tailors and fashions by having everyone (rather as in Mao's China) wear the same type all-weather, loose-fitting, work-oriented, practical dress.

Shakespeare, as might be expected, brings his rich imagination to bear on the subject. For one thing, he makes ready metaphoric use of it in his plays. Throughout *Macbeth* (1605–1606) runs an image pattern of clothes as embodying kingship and dignity, for Macbeth, having obtained the crown by evil means and ruling through a reign of terror, finds the clothes of power too big for him. Some of the other Shakespearean tragic heroes wrestle with the question of the relation of literal clothing to personality, with the function of vesture as a revelation of character. Though Hamlet (c. 1600) insists that his black mourning suit, unlike everyone else's, expresses his mood, he must soon dissimulate by disordering his clothing. Coriolanus (1607–1608) significantly does not "know himself" when he wears the election-time obligatory "gown of humility" and later is not known by others when he wears "mean apparel" as a *turncoat*. Antony's (c. 1607) decline as warrior-politician is symbolized by his donning Cleopatra's clothing during a drunken fit. Lear and Edgar have to lose their identity by going in rags until order and sanity are restored in realm and self.

King Lear (1606) in fact contains a most searching study of clothing. At first, Lear had complained to his daughters that, by granting him only what was necessary for subsistence, they would be rendering "man's life . . . cheap as beast's." But when the outcast king, maddened by his daughters' ingratitude and railing at the world, comes upon the naked Edgar, also a victim of evil forces, he changes his mind and readily accepts the image of man's beastlike quality. Owing nothing to the animals and vegetation from which clothes have been fashioned, naked "unaccommodated" man is "the thing itself," "no more but such a poor, bare, forked animal." He tears at his own raiment as though to halt all pretense and to live according to his nightmarish vision.

In his moments of insight amid madness and suffering, Lear comes to see the unfortunate effects that dress has in the administration of justice: "Through tattered clothes small vices do appear;/Robes and furred gowns hide all." Garments not only render visible the hierarchy of society but also pervert Justice; the law is administered with reference not to the individual's guilt or innocence but to the lavish or mean raiment covering his body. No wonder the repentant, newly-perceptive Lear prays for the "poor naked wretches" of whom he had taken too little care in the days of his reign, when he had deferred too much to men of the cloth (in every sense of the word).

The social function of vesture, beside signaling social class and vocation, operates as well in the intercourse of individuals, where, to be sure, it is modified by esthetic considerations, by the sense that the body, even if naturally beautiful, can have its attractiveness heightened by the proper ornament. This notion may generate a competition between individuals rather than a demarcation between classes, and Castiglione accordingly devotes a section of his *Il cortegiano* (*The Courtier*, treatise, 1528) to the subject of the clothing that best defines the courtier as an individual as well as a functionary. Early in *Lear*, the still untutored hero, fighting for his right to keep his hundred knight-attendants, confronts the argument of necessity. Asked by the two evil daughters why he needs even one knight, Lear ceases to question, plead, or bargain, and begins to think: "If only to go warm were gorgeous/Why, nature needs not what thou gorgeous wearest/ Which scarcely keeps thee warm." There is a clash of functions: the desire to dress herself erotically or to flaunt her corporal beauty conflicts with the desire to shelter the body—and the latter loses out.

The Seventeenth and Eighteenth Centuries

The paradox that people sometimes dress for reasons of immodesty is at the heart of lyrics by Herrick and by Lovelace (mid-17th century). Men and women spend much time, money, and effort on their wardrobes in order to attract each other to the point of undressing for each other; ornate apparel in effect exists in order to ultimately efface itself. But sometimes such excess is counterproductive, and less is more. Hence Lovelace's advice to the lover: "Strive not, vain lover, to be fine, / Thy silk's the silkworm's and not thine." Similar, albeit more erotic, is the advice given in Ben Jonson's "Simplex munditiis (1609)" and Herrick's "Delight in Disorder," (poem, 1648), where casualness in apparel is held to be more arousing than ornateness and perfection.

To the detached observer, the difference between a naked aborigine and a clothed Western man is likely to be culture, progress, civilization itself. To the anthropologist guardedly refraining from value judgments, the difference is merely one between two kinds of social organization. To the devout Christian it is the Fall of Man. In book 4 of the poem *Paradise Lost* (1667), introducing us to Adam and Eve, Milton rhapsodizes over nakedness, especially the exhibition of the genitals, which nowadays are covered by "dishonest shame / Of nature's works" and hypocrisy. The sense of shame—arising after the Fall and regarded now as a becoming sign of modesty—is no source of satisfaction to Milton.

The narrative proceeds: after the Fall, innocence is gone, and they are "naked left/To guilty Shame: hee cover'd, but his Robe/Uncovered more." Their eyes see more because their minds see less. The richness of experience has been so curtailed that they must classify it with rigid categories of good and evil. Adam suggests to Eve the expedient of the fig leaf, as the "mysterious parts" of nature have suddenly become conspicuous, obscene. Adam foolishly thinks that the villain Shame can be warded off by apparel. From this melancholy vantage point, Milton looks yearningly back to the innocence that was: "Vain covering if to hide/Their guilt!" and "O how unlike to that first naked glory." The makeshift does not even work. Their "shame in part/Covered" but they obtain "no ease of mind," even as for the children of Adam and Eve vesture is, under the aspect of eternity, a necessary evil, a temporary, odious, and useless resort, a "troublesome disguise," as well as a metaphor for hypocrisy, for "dressing up" of the simple, naked truth, and for misbehavior behind the facade of holiness in dress.

The contemporary Restoration writers knew these vices at first hand. One figure of literary attention was the fop, an early version of the dandy. Etherege's *Man of Mode* (play, 1676) contrasts the hero Dorimant, who, with worldly good sense and moderation, loves "to be well dress'd, Sir, and think it no scandal to my understanding," with Sir Fopling Flutter, whose excellency, in his own eyes and those of society, lies in "neatly tying of a Ribbond or a Crevat," in imitating French fashions and in making his clothes pay court to the ladies. Most galling to Dorimant is that his own former mistress responds to the fop, a lapse in taste worse (to him) than is prostitution.

In book 4 of *Gulliver's Travels* (satire, 1726), Swift celebrates the continuing moral import that dress has in our lives. Gulliver, living amid the rational Houyhnhnms, is discovered once without his clothing. He protests he must keep it on for two reasons: "As well for Decency, as to avoid the Inclemencies of Air." The Houyhnhnm has trouble understanding the word "decency" and Gulliver's unwillingness to uncover "the parts that Nature taught us to conceal"; why would nature teach one to conceal what she herself gave? Then, one fine afternoon, Gulliver removes his attire in order to bathe in a stream and is nearly raped by a female Yahoo. The incident dramatizes the role of vesture in keeping somewhat under control the human libido. (The suppression of the libido, or an acute case of modesty, prompts the heroine of Bernardin de Saint-Pierre's *Paul et Virginie* [*Paul and Virginia,* novel, 1787] to choose death by drowning rather than to unclothe herself for the purpose of saving her body.)

Furthermore, Gulliver, trying to evade acknowledging the proximity of man and beast that is all too obvious to him, takes pains to hide from his host the fact that his attire, rapidly becoming frayed and torn, is removable. "I concealed the secret of my Dress, in order to distinguish myself as much as possible from that cursed Race of Yahoo. "His sense of dignity now literally hanging by a thread, Gulliver is trying to keep the truth from himself as much as from the Houyhnhnms. When he eventually accepts the truth, he lapses into self-hatred. Thus we see depicted another important function of vesture: to dignify man, to distinguish him from the beast. In the *Memoirs of Martinus Scriblerus* (1741), written in part by Swift, a young nobleman is urged, in order to be cured of love and affectation, to "survey himself naked, divested of artificial charms, and he will find himself a forked straddling animal.'' (The image and the counsel look back to the Socrates of Diogenes Laertius via *King Lear.*) Neither practical nor moral, this function of dress is philosophical or esthetic, depending on whether our brutishness or ugliness in in question.

Some authors forwarded a philosophical explanation for clothing, a motive for dressing of which people are not but perhaps should be conscious. Clothing is a symbol of many realities, of the different sorts of garments in the universe. One of the oldest and most commonly referred-to analogies, for instance, is the one between raiment and the body it covers. In an elegy urging his mistress to bed with him, John Donne (c. 1590s) praises nakedness and tries to legitimize a profane act—undressing for the act of love—by the sophistic use of traditional sacred language: ''As souls unbodied, bodies uncloth'd must be,/To taste whole joys.'' Using similar sophistry to a different end, Swift, in his *Tale of a Tub* (allegorical satire, 1704), mischievously described a group which believed that man was an ''animal compounded of two Dresses''—the body was the natural ''inward clothing,'' while the soul was the outward ''celestial suit.'' The clothing image could be used not only of the human body but also of the church. Perhaps the most famous example is the extended allegory in that work, in which church history is set forth in terms of the metaphor of coats—the bare coat being Calvinism, the adorned one, Rome.

Gibbon, observing in the writings of Pliny and others signs of the decadent Roman fashion, especially among women, of dressing in clothes of fine-spun silk in order to reveal rather than conceal, considers the adoption of this by the Emperor Elagabalus as sullying the dignity of both the office and the man. Still, if most writers and moralists decry the vanity and foppery of fashion, Bernard Mandeville (*The Fable of the Bees,* poem, 1714) is not among them; he sees it as conducive to prosperity in society and contentment in the individual. Clothing, which ''our boundless pride'' has made for the end of ''ornament,'' is merely a salient example of private vices making for public benefits. To be sure, in the various uses of and attitudes to clothes we often see the triumph of custom, vanity, illusion over reason, nature, and common sense.

The Nineteenth Century

In the nineteenth century, two writers had much to say on this subject, Carlyle and Thoreau. The former's *Sartor Resartus* (philosophical satire, 1833–1834) is the most philosophic and wide-ranging discussion of clothing. Carlyle contrasts the fortunate horse, with its perennial rainproof suit, and the man who must daily surround himself with the stealings from animals and plants. Vesture is a warm, movable house (like the snail's), in which ''that strange Thee of thine'' sits snug, defying all variations of climate. Without it man would be nothing; ''here truly was the victory of Art over Nature.''

The social function of clothing is apparent in considerations of status as well as of propriety and etiquette. Carlyle observes that we treasure mere shells, husks; we revere the fine broadcloth, not the straddling animal with bandy legs that it contains and makes a dignitary of. A lord in a tattered blanket fastened with a skewer would be ignored by everyone. Thus the body often appropriates what by right belongs to the cloth. The king and the cart driver are quite the same; it may even be that the latter is wiser. Their difference is due solely to attire. Imagine a ceremonial occasion attended by all strata of society, at which, as in a dream, vesture magically disappears. "The whole fabric of Government, Legislation, Property, Police, and Civilized Society, are dissolved. . . . Lives the man that can figure a naked Duke of Windlestraw addressing a naked House of Lords?" Clothes are the "visible emblems" of the bonds tying men together. In that sense, apparel, making society possible, is an instrument of a spiritual life force.

Clearly the use of clothes for adornment and social self-aggrandizement has little to do with material things like the weather and comfort. Wild people paint and tattoo themselves even before they initiate the use of garments, if ever they do. "The first purpose of Clothing is not warmth or decency," Carlyle declares, "but ornament." That is, if Gulliver worried that his dignity was compromised by propinquity to the beastlike Yahoos, others see the problem as being instead one of insufficient propinquity. A visit to a zoo or bird sanctuary reminds one to what an extent man stands out in his plainness and colorlessness. So that if a Christian theologian speaks of a fall from grace remediable only by faith, works, and study, the philosopher of clothing might see in dress an unspoken anxiety that the fallen state consists rather of the loss (during evolution) of plumage and color, a fall remediable by donning vesture—at that, vesture made of materials taken from the very animals who, lower on the evolutionary tree, in one way appear superior and unfallen.

Carlyle's imagination was also kindled by the thought that much in everyday life is a form of apparel. The 39 Articles are raiment for the religious idea; church clothes are symbolic of the church, which in turn invests the divine idea with a sensible body woven by society. Other institutions—guilds, armies, police, Magna Carta, the pomp of the law, the sacredness of majesty—are forms of vesture. Language is the garment of thought; and all symbols, all forms whereby spirit manifests itself to sense, are vestures. Man himself is an apparel for the divine Me cast down from heaven. In this universe with meaning, everything functions as a veil or cloth for something else. Man, in short, puts on clothes because the universe does.

Thoreau, in the essays *Walden* (1854), taking a less metaphysical approach, established the utility of clothing by a scientific experiment. When he retired to Walden in order to ascertain what were the essentials of life, he found them reducible to four categories, one of which was clothing. It retains internal heat; distinguishes man from beast; helps distinguish man from man; and, if of the appropriate kind, gains its wearer respect. Thoreau laughs at a woman's remark that she "was in a civilized country where people are judged by their clothes"— rather as Montaigne had laughed at society with his remark on breeches. Again like Montaigne, Thoreau noted also that most of our apparel seems indispensable only because of habit. And like Carlyle, Thoreau would have garments reflect the character of the wearer. Respect should go only to the man who, like the true philosopher oblivious of fashions ("The head monkey at Paris puts on a traveler's cap, and all the monkeys in America do the same"), utilizes simple, patched, unadorned raiment that fits the body and its work. The man with something to do can do it in an old suit. "Beware of all enterprises that require new clothes, and not rather a new wearer of clothes."

The apparel may in fact become such an extension of the wearer's self that, for the hero of Gogol's poignant story "Shinel' " ("The Overcoat," 1842), a man's dignity rests on his possession of a new overcoat, or, in Büchner's *Woyzeck* (play, c. 1837), the melancholy captain begins to cry every time he sees his own coat hanging on the wall. Clappique, in Malraux's *La condition humaine* (*Man's Fate*, novel, 1933), discovers that a change of clothing changes the world and throws the existence of the essential self into question. William James (*Principles of Psychology,* 1890) adopted the old saying that the individual consists of three parts—soul, body, and clothing, for the importance of the latter is proved by the fact (or surmise) that most people would rather be ugly and dressed elegantly than handsome and dressed shabbily. So had Kierkegaard remarked (*Sygdommen til døden* [*Sickness unto Death*, 1849]) that people know themselves, no less than others, only by externals, of which clothing is the most obvious example, and Ibsen's hero, in the play *Peer Gynt* (1867), found that for entry into Troll society he had only to change clothing, not his putative Christian faith, for it is "dress and its cut" that Trolls are known by. As Pirandello's *Enrico IV* (play, 1922) asserts, "One's dress is like a phantom that hovers always near one." This holds true of a society no less than of an individual; a colonel in Gogol's novel *Mërtvye dushi* (*Dead Souls,* 1842) "was ready to stake his head that the level of culture and trade would rise and that a Golden Age would dawn in Russia as soon as half the Russian peasants had donned German trousers."

Dress is so important for one's dignity that Dmitri, in Dostoevsky's novel *Brat'ĩa Karamazovy* (*The Brothers Karamazov,* 1880), under false suspicion of having murdered his father and forced to undress during the preliminary investigation, feels guilty or despicable because he is naked amidst clothed people. And in Gottfried Keller's novel *Kleider machen Leute* (*Clothes Make the Man,* 1874), the humble tailor Strapinski is, in good part because of the clothes he wears, mistaken for an aristocrat and treated with great deference by the townspeople. On the other hand, in Hans Andersen's "Kejserens nye kloeder" ("The Emperor's New Clothes," 1835), a brief fairy tale with rich psychological overtones, the association of dignity with clothes is so intense as to survive even nudity; that is, as long as everyone pretends that a man is clothed, life is untroubled. Clothing has here become an example or symbol of fashionable ideas and an expression of mankind's herd mentality and need to conform. (So too in Cervantes' *Don Quijote* [*Don Quixote,* 1605, 1615], the Don's archaic and flimsy garb had startled those he met, even while functioning in his own reveries as lordly gear; yet at one point at least, the sheer magnetism of his personality had coerced others into calling a barber's basin Mambrino's helmet, to the distress of the barber who, unlike Andersen's emperor, stood to lose more than gain from the deception.)

The Twentieth Century

The theme of clothing and dignity is continued in modern literature. Chesterton confidently attacks nudists *(All Is Grist,* essays, 1931), and Wyndham Lewis in World War I would reach for his boots when the shells began to fly at night: "Clothing and its part in the psychology of war is a neglected subject. I would have braved an eleven inch shell in my trenchboots, but would have declined an encounter with a pip-squeak in my bare feet." Hence, after the terrible battering administered to the human condition in Beckett's play *En attendant Godot (Waiting for Godot,* 1952), the plaintive assertion that "We are men. . . . We have kept our appointment," is movingly symbolized by Vladimir's thrice-expressed laconic closing line, "Pull on your trousers." But Yossarian, in Joseph Heller's novel *Catch-22* (1961), tends to show up naked on various official occasions, ostensibly out of a sense of horror over having had a slain colleague smeared all over his uniform during a combat flight and actually as a Diogenes-like way of declaring his alienation from the Air Force and, ultimately, from human society.

The modern writer does not forget earlier insights into the paradox of clothing and sex. One work, Anatole France's *L'île des pingouins (Penguin Island,* 1908), dramatizes the way in which what was meant to contain the sexual drive has been turned into an expression of that drive. The transition from innocent nudity to clothed sophistication is marked by a Thoreauvian experiment, a Miltonic paradox, and a Swiftian sexual assault as the attempt to put one of the penguins into apparel and under the moral law generates wild male fantasies and female deceptiveness with the resulting pride, hypocrisy, cruelty. Raiment "betrayed the penguin modesty instead of helping it."

That betrayal was celebrated by the sensual baron in Isak Dinesen's *Seven Gothic Tales* (1934), who noted that in the old days, the mass of material under which women were buried and compressed had the aim of disguising, keeping the body a secret, creating a mystery that it was a privilege and joy to solve. Now, unfortunately, women's clothing exists for the sake of the body, adheres to its contours, and has no career of its own other than to reveal. So also did Robert Musil, in *Der Mann ohne Eigenschaften (The Man without Qualities,* novel, 1930–1933) find clothing the "civilized erotic," as sexually expressive as nature's plumes; the complicated women's dress of Victorian times, forming a surface five times as large as the body's, constituted a "many-petalled, almost impenetrable chalice loaded with an erotic charge" and concealed "at its core the slim white animal that made itself fearfully desirable, letting itself be searched for." The association of clothing with the erotic could reach idiosyncratic proportions, as in Sacher-Masoch's *Venus im Pelz (Venus in Furs,* novel 1870), in which sexual arousal and its concomitant, male self-abasement, are catalyzed by the woman's wearing furs.

For the keen student of man as a social animal, clothing often takes on a disproportionate, even ludicrous, importance. Thus when Marcel's grandmother is dying (Proust's *Le côté de Guermantes* [*Guermantes Way,* novel, 1920]), the normally loyal and sometimes perverse servant Françoise frequently absents herself from the sickbed in order to see a dressmaker about a new mourning dress; in the lives of most women, the narrator observes, even the greatest sorrow becomes a matter of "trying on." But not women alone, for, in one of the most dramatic literary moments, the duke and duchess of Guermantes, late for a social occasion, have no time to speak to their old friend Swann, newly revealed to be dying, yet abruptly find the time for her to change, at the duke's behest, from black to red shoes to match her red party dress. Nor is clothing solely a part of the external, social creature. It may just as much be associated with the internal, subjective self. If in the first volume, the ingestion of food catalyzed the involuntary memory, in *Sodome et Gomorrhe* (*Cities of the Plain,* novel, 1921–1922) the removal of apparel does that. The death of the grandmother whom Marcel has outgrown remains a superficial event in his consciousness until one day a year later at Balbec he takes off his boots in the same room in which, long ago, his grandmother had helped his sickly youthful self do that; the similarity, bringing home sensuously the meaning of death and the permanent absence of the once deeply loved grandmother, opens the floodgates of emotion in one of the most poignant (and, some say, self-indulgent) passages in Proust.

Thorstein Veblen's *Theory of the Leisure Class* (1899) analyzed the social function of raiment. The expenditure on attire, because of its advantage in being always in evidence, was for him the best illustration of the "rule of conspicuous waste of goods." Clothing is social-esthetic or decorative, exhibiting the wearer's respectable appearance, affluence, elegance, fashionableness, and possession of leisure. The point made by Lear and by Thoreau is expanded by Veblen. People will undergo great privation in necessaries and comforts for the sake of their conspicuous consumption, often going in bad weather "ill clad in order to appear well dressed." Ladies' bonnets, French heels, corsets, hoop skirts, long hair are all devices to mutilate the woman and hamper her from fulfilling any useful domestic task. The gain is in reputability, and insofar as the reputability of the expensive textiles used is more important than the mechanical services they render to the body of the person, apparel is (as Carlyle declared it to be) an expression of man's higher "spiritual" need. For, as the protagonist of Virginia Woolf's novel *Orlando* (1928) observes, clothes wear us; they mold our hearts and brains to their liking.

Selected Bibliography

Brooks, Cleanth. *The Well-Wrought Urn.* New York: Harcourt, Brace & World, 1947.

Fussell, Paul. *The Rhetorical World of Augustan Humanism.* Oxford: Clarendon Press, 1965.

Hollander, Anne. *Seeing through Clothes*. New York: Viking Press, 1978.
Weidhorn, Manfred. "Clothes and the Man." *Connecticut Review* 3 (1970): 41–57.

MANFRED WEIDHORN

COMEDY (COMIC SPIRIT)

For most people most of the time, life is serious; getting through each day's tasks requires, or is accompanied by, solemnity, reverence, gravity. Laughter seems to betray a lack of commitment or cooperativeness, a spirit of irreverence, malingering, irresponsibility. Yet some men long have intuited that moral vacations from seriousness and application are, if not a more correct assessment of reality than is tragedy's, at least necessary for the better discharge of the serious tasks. The result is the comic spirit in literature, that is, works that end happily and that arouse amusement, ranging from the smile on the lips of one reading in a room or library to the communal experience of the belly laugh, in which some bodily controls become dangerously slack.

Horace Walpole said that the world is a tragedy to those who feel and a comedy to those who think. Comedy, in short, works when the audience withholds its sympathy from the victim. "Hard" comedy (e.g., the Marx Brothers or Monty Python), in which the withholding is complete, approximates sadism; "soft" comedy (e.g., Charlie Chaplin or Woody Allen) engages some of our emotions periodically. Another important distinction is between laughing *at* or *with* a character; in Shakespeare's play *Much Ado about Nothing* (c. 1598) we laugh with Beatrice and Benedict (most of the time) over their witticisms and at Dogberry over his stupidity and pompousness. Yet comedy remains in a close relationship to tragedy, for to see life as a joke, or as a lot of jokes, is hardly optimistic; hence it is often said that the clown has a laughing face but a weeping heart and that, as Byron put it, "I laugh that I may not weep."

Antiquity and the Middle Ages

Homer's epic poem *Odysseia* (*Odyssey*, c. 8th century B.C.) has comedy's obligatory happy ending, but the first writer imbued with the spirit of irreverence was Aristophanes. His comedies are firmly wedded to the tight little community that was ancient Athens, where everyone knew everyone else and policymaking was (or seemed) a communal effort. As a result, topical references abound, and contemporary prominent individuals are held up for derision in plays that are politics by other means. Part of the comedy rests on punning and word play; part on caricature; that is, the carrying of visible or well-known traits to an extreme; part on numerous indecorous references to body functions, as if comedy serves to remind man of his animal nature. Above all, Aristophanes' comic dynamism is fueled by a political and cultural point of view. For he is a conservative, perhaps a reactionary. He dislikes innovation, democracy, and rationalism, the latter even when, as in the hands of Socrates, it is put at the service of old values. From Aristophanes one learns that one rich source of comedy is a radical dislike of the status quo, but whether the ensuing critique is mounted in the name of a superior past (the conservative view) or a superior future (the liberal or radical view) is a matter of personal preference.

One type of caricature was established by Aristophanes, the reductio ad absurdum, that is, the tactical adoption of assumptions that are then carried to their logical conclusion in order to show them to be untenable. If this is done on a large enough scale, the result is fantasy, the replacing of the world we know with one that can exist only in man's dreams. The basic Aristophanic dialectic can be seen most clearly in his greatest play, *Ornithes* (*The Birds,* 414 B.C.)— see also *Lysistratē* (*Lysistrata,* 411 B.C.); *Ekklēsiazousai* ([*Women in Parliament,* 392 B.C.]; *Ploutos* [*Plutus,* 388 B.C.]—: (1) life is irrational and unjust (2) a far-fetched plan is put into effect to remedy things; (3) the results, though amusing, are dubious. The fantasy having shown that, given human nature, things can be no different, the impact made is a conservative justification of the status quo and, paradoxically, a tragic view of life; "whatever is, is right." What helps retain the comic atmosphere in a play with a potentially pessimistic logical conclusion is the writer's blithe disregard of reality.

The comedies of Plautus and Terence ignore the public, political life and rather deal with another area of human experience, the private life—with the relations of men and women, parents and children, masters and slaves. Conventional thoughts like gaining access to a beautiful courtesan displace fantasies about building an ideal society in the sky. The comedy turns now not so much on wit and pratfalls but on situation, character, and plotting (in both senses). Such plays also establish certain types that were long to recur in comedy, as that of the vain, boasting soldier who is a coward in a crisis or the parasite who lives by flattery and sycophancy. In one of the best of these plays, Terence's *Adelphi* (160 B.C.), three themes are sources of comedy: the eternal debate over permissiveness versus discipline; the eternal debate over town versus country; and the comic exploitation of the boorish farmer's loss of contact with reality.

If Aristophanes handles political and communal matters while Plautus and Terence handle private, familial matters, then Lucian's dialogues (2nd century) handle cosmic, under-the-aspect-of-eternity matters. Where Aristophanes gives a clear, if critical, picture of the Athenian society of his day, Lucian, writing more than a half millennium later in an entirely different milieu, is more cerebral, detached, universal, less culture bound. One can hardly tell that he dwells within the confines of the Roman Empire. Nor does he deal with the specificities of the private life, as do the two Latin writers. To Aristophanes writing a play is a form of making a speech in the assembly on a burning issue; Lucian, remote from any decision-making process, living in a corner of a vast empire, deals with timeless matters like gods, philosophies, death, and money. Aristophanes is coarse, Lucian genial. Aristophanes parades his firm convictions and values, Lucian deflates all philosophies and values. Lucian's greatest feat is putting the dialogue, virtually invented and perfected by Plato, to comic, satiric use. The comedy takes a variety of forms: autobiographical, biographical, and pseudo-biographical tales; travel fantasies; dialogues of the gods or of some great men of the past; scenes from the next world; the "Persian Letters" effect, i.e., everyday reality seen from an objective outside perspective. What he shares with Aristophanes and not with the Romans is the wrenching of orientation, the use of surrealism and fantasy in place of everyday reality.

Petronius (*Satyricon,* novel, A.D. 60) probes into the depths of the private life, but not the conventional family situation, nor heterosexual matters only. Love, an irrational element mainly absent in Homer and Greek tragedy or disposed of in an orderly, responsible way by a man of piety in Virgil's epic poem *Aeneis* (*Aeneid* 19 B.C.), is shown here as contagious, comical, chaotic, corrosive. This is a realistic work about an erotic drifter and his nonheroic adventures on the road, among people of different classes, vocations, sexual orientations. The comedy comes from beholding the follies of people in three major areas: (1) language, oratory, poetry, in which writers veer into rant, pretense, turgidity; (2) love, in which man is a fickle erotic animal, always becoming involved in triangular relationships and in squabbles as a result of which someone is left behind; (3) money and the many things people will do to amass it or flaunt it as part of conspicuous consumption.

Apuleius (*Metamorphoses* [*The Golden Ass,* novel, c. 150]) turns the comic material of earlier writers into a serio-comic novel by means of bawdy (Milesian) tales and a quasi-Platonic pilgrimage to sanctity. As with the *Satyricon,* we have an Odyssey in which the heroism of Odysseus is replaced by something less dignified, in this case donkeyhood. The overall theme is serious enough, but the individual tales and incidents contain the levity and sexual escapades associated with comedy.

In the Middle Ages the comic spirit is at play in earthy popular works, such as in the beast fable *Roman de Renard* (*Romance of Reynard,* 12–14th centuries) of Reynard the Fox, which reaches its finest expression in Chaucer's "Nonnes Priestes Tale" (c. 1380–1400), but not in most major literary works, as if the solemnity of the Christian vision crowded out the earthier, less intense view that comedy entails. When Dante titled his humorless epic poem *La divina commedia,* (*The Divine Comedy,* c. 1320), he meant only a tale in which one moves from an adverse condition (being lost morally, touring hell) to a happy one (reaching heaven and the beatific vision). Not so is the case with the man who wrote a human or earthly rather than divine comedy, Boccaccio (*Il decamerone,* [*Decameron,* novellas, c. 1350]). His comic vision turns on adopting, like Dante, the idea that love makes the world go round but interpreting it as Eros rather than Agape or Caritas. Man is a copulative animal. Moreover, by favoring Nature over Revelation, Boccaccio reverts, from the dominant guilt or sin culture, to a pagan shame culture. What is troublesome is not sexual misbehavior itself, which begets no agonies of conscience, but being caught at it and shamed before others. Boccaccio's love of life, friskiness, and amorality give serious themes a comic dimension. Sex is not part of procreation or sacrament but, as Shaw would put it, something with "transient" pleasure and "ridiculous" posture. Especially so if the fornicating couples are, as often in Boccaccio, monks and nuns—human beings who made something special of abjuring sex. Desire is notably comic when we pretend to wish it away, resort then to ingenious stratagems to fulfill it after all, and, finally, in Boccaccio's utopian vision, suffer no consequences—no pregnancy, venereal disease, abortion, infanticide, jealousy, psychological stress, adultery, murder. All that is necessary is secrecy (to keep others content) and rationalization (to keep oneself or one's partner content). This is one of the most optimistic, hedonistic, and subversive of all books, written though it be at the height of what is called "The Age of Faith."

Boccaccio's English disciple, Chaucer, is also blessed with the comic spirit. The *Canterbury Tales* (c. 1380–1400) contain beast fables, dramatized folktales and jokes, and Boccaccio-like tales of sexual misbehavior. The characters exhibited in the General Prologue, while fearsome to those who had dealings with them, are presented in an objective, nonjudgmental fashion that makes for risibility, for the author is less concerned with their moral capital than with their proficiency at whatever roguery they have chosen. Their shabby dealings are usually described in a jovial, life-celebrating, ironic, amused tone.

The Renaissance

The Renaissance saw an expansion of comedy in major literature. In *Orlando furioso* (epic poem, 1516), Ariosto took the medieval chivalric romance and self-consciously pushed it into the realm of comic fantasy, writing as if making no demands on the reader's credulity, enjoying the tales for their own sake and not for any seriousness of theme or character. More overtly comic is Erasmus' *Moriae encomium* (*The Praise of Folly,* essay, 1511), written in an ironic mode. What makes life possible and motivates man is Folly, which turns out to mean (1) stupidity; (2) self-deception, i.e., even if intelligence is present, people do not utilize it fully because of emotional roadblocks; (3) deception, i.e., limiting others' access to knowledge in order to prosper by victimizing them, a mode of action that is, because of factors (1) and (2), counterproductive. A major target of Erasmus' is the superficial religion of most people, including clerics and theologians, a religion centered on rituals and superstitions instead of awe and reverence. One of the comic ironies at the conclusion is that the more spiritual and other-worldly one becomes, the more mad and foolish one appears to the world.

Machiavelli wrote several stage comedies, one in which his principles of political science are applied to domestic and erotic matters. If in *Clizia* (1520) a conspiracy punishes a man's sinful desires and returns him to a moral norm, in the more Machiavellian (and Boccaccioesque) *Mandragola* (*The Mandrake,* c. 1512–1520), a conspiracy subverts the moral order by fulfilling sinful desires and yet keeping everyone content. Machiavelli's revolution in thinking on public, political affairs is paralleled by Rabelais' (c. 1494–1553) in private affairs. The consequence is an explosion of comedy, as nearly every aspect of human existence is subject to fantasy and raillery, and the physical side of man is acknowledged, celebrated, laughed at. What had been initiated in different ways by Aristophanes, Lucian, Petronius, and Boccaccio, is here brought to an uproarious climax that would not be matched until Joyce's novel *Ulysses* (1922).

Rabelais uses five main sources of comedy: (1) hyperbole; (2) incongruity, especially the discrepancy between the pettiness of man and his large ambitions; (3) coprology and obscenity; (4) playing with words and languages; (5) parody, or playing with style. Scattered among these five are such typical Rabelaisian devices as huge catalogues and lists, false etymologies, bizarre names (especially of noblemen), reversals of proverbs, tall tales, mock precision and science, mock sermons and oratory, gigantism, caricature, sexual fantasies, and practical jokes. Here is comedy as the sense of play; here is joy in verbal acrobatics, joy in discovering the plastic possibilities in language, joy in the Babel of languages, joy in the writer's God-like powers of creating new worlds through words alone even as contemporary Renaissance explorers discovered new worlds by means of their voyages. Books, sciences, and religions are constructs of language, which is itself a convention—relative, vulnerable, malleable. In action and plot, Rabelais is an extreme example, along with Aristophanes, of "hard" comedy; corpses abound, and sentiment is nonexistent. His comedy liberating from conscience and compassion, he wallows in "sadism" and laughs instead of agonizes. Much is childish and cruel, for this comic-strip world with philosophical overtones is also a vacation from normal adulthood and maturity. The Rabelaisian laughter is deep, philosophic, life embracing, and anarchistic.

The next great master of comedy is Shakespeare. His ebullient comic spirit spills over into the genres of tragedy and history. *Titus Andronicus* (c. 1594) is only unintentionally funny, but Mercutio and the nurse (*Romeo and Juliet*, c. 1596) express the sexual, cynical, and comical underside of the theme of love seen only from a noble and solemn vantage point by the main characters. *King Lear* (1606) has tragicomic scenes of the old man discovering reality, scenes in which one does not know whether to laugh or cry. *Coriolanus* (1607–1608), with its central character who would rather blow up than grow up, is less a tragedy than a curious anticipation of Molièrian comedy. But in *Hamlet* (c. 1600) the prince is his own clown and "fool" or wit, and one of the most amusing things in Shakespeare. His only rival for comic greatness, Falstaff, appears in the other noncomic genre, the history or chronicle plays (*Henry* IV, 1599, 1600). He is nothing less than one of the greatest comic characters in literature, the spirit of comedy itself, in all its irresponsibility, joyousness, spontaneity, creativity, plasticity, commonsensical side, and liberating effect. He has to be dismissed at the end, for the comic spirit is at odds with the spirit of governing and of worldly achievement; however great a drinking companion, he would make a terrible lord chief justice or privy councillor. But had it not been for his presence, Hal might have been little distinguishable from his cold, solemn brother John and might have lacked the best liberal arts education to be had, in or out of school walls. In *The Merry Wives of Windsor* (c. 1600) one sees a shrunken

Falstaff, the victim of a monomania (lechery), as he at his greatest could never be. *Richard III* (1591–1594) is in the first half, amusing. Richard may be a villain, but, like Iago later, his communing wittily with the audience makes him winsome; at least, like Chaucer's misbehaving clerics, he has panache and ability.

In comedy proper, Shakespeare is many-sided. The *Comedy of Errors* (c. 1594) alternates between dated topical references and word play, on the one hand, and the special if amusing case of multiple misunderstandings caused by a pair of twins. *The Taming of the Shrew* (c. 1594) is Shakespeare's one venture into hard comedy, funny and brutal. *Love's Labor's Lost* (c. 1594) squeezes amusement out of the taking of platonism too seriously and out of the lubricity of language. *The Two Gentlemen of Verona* (c. 1594) and *A Midsummer Night's Dream* (c. 1595) have as their text the vagaries of love and are the equipoise to the contemporary *Romeo and Juliet*. The *Merchant of Venice* (c. 1595) begins with a comic treatment of the clash of religions and of cultures but, in trying to humanize the traditional one-dimensional Jewish comic butt and then in ridding himself of the resulting embarrassment by means of forced conversion, Shakespeare has, at least for modern audiences, taken leave of his comic senses. So also are the "problem comedies" too immersed in tragic overtones (*Measure for Measure*, 1603–1604), philosophic disquisitions (*Troilus and Cressida*, 1601–1602), or archaic plot conventions (*All's Well That Ends Well*, 1601–1604) to satisfy the traditional notions of comedy.

The "sunny comedies," Shakespeare's finest, are about the comic anomalies, irrationalities, and incongruities of love; but what they add to *A Midsummer Night's Dream* is warmth, a view of love from within, as if they were the product of the synthesis of the *Dream* with its polar opposite, *Romeo*. In *Much Ado about Nothing* the theme of misplaced suspicion, to be soon rendered tragically in Othello, is subordinated to the comedy of the mutual chaffing of a man and a woman who love each other and are the only ones in the world not to know it. In *As You Like It* (c. 1599) sentimental pessimism (Jaques) and optimism (the exiled duke and Orlando) are played off against unsentimental pessimism (Touchstone) and sentimental realism (Rosalind); love and lovers are mocked as never before and as they well deserve to be—by one herself deeply in love. The clash of the extremes of moral idealism (Olivia, Malevolio) and Falstaffian earthiness (Toby Belch) finds in *Twelfth Night* (c. 1600) its resolution in a moral center that is stronger in sentiment (Viola) than in intellect (Beatrice and Rosalind); the comic weather here is therefore a shade overcast.

Shakespeare's contemporary, Ben Jonson, picked up ideas from Latin comedy and other antique models to construct some early plays built on the concept of "humors", that is, neuroses, obsessions, hobby-horses. Only when he liberated himself from these textbook demonstrations did he come into his own with some of the finest comedies in the language. *Volpone* (1606) is in the vein of Richard III and Iago, with an added twist. One laughs, edgily, at the way Volpone and Mosca outwit the money-hungry gulls, and laughter turns to relief when the two schemers fall out and destroy each other, in the fashion of the thieves in Chaucer's

Pardoner's Tale (The Canterbury Tales). A trio of conspiring rascals achieves even greater triumphs of plotting, profiting, and laughter in *The Alchemist* (1610) before also falling out. This time, a note of unsettling realism qualifies the comic ending of the work, as one of the rascals gets off scot free and remains in his master's good graces. *Epicoene* (1609) also revolves around disguises and deceptions, but the heart of the comic vision here is rather in the banter and repartee of young men about town, as Jonson nearly single-handedly invents what would become the core of Restoration comedy.

One of the greatest expressions of the comic spirit was produced at this very time in Spain, in Cervantes' novel *Don Quijote* (*Don Quixote*, 1605–1615). The work is in many ways a poignant one, as comedy often is once one scratches the surface. The central character is at least half deranged, a deluded aging man who toys dangerously with his own dignity. The main theme is only the most important and serious of all themes: how we live with our values. This novel is a parable about belief. Yet rich comedy is extracted as the reader suspects he sees his own vulnerability in the rickety way the Don puts together his armor and his theories. To validate his initial beliefs, which are held on to, not because they mirror reality but because they mirror fiction, the Don builds a superstructure of theories and commentaries that can absorb any adverse fact. The most elementary and universal principles of psychology—the devil theory of history, the scapegoat factor, the kill the messenger principle, the self-fulfilling prophecy, the idealist's magisterial indifference to facts, issues, and consequences—are intricately tied together and dramatized in the most natural-seeming realistic plot.

The Seventeenth and Eighteenth Centuries

The ambiguities of the idealist are explored in the masterpiece of the next great comic playwright, Molière's *Le Misanthrope* (*The Misanthropist*, 1666). Alceste, like Quixote, is more responsive to the way the world should be than to the way it is. He is a comic figure because, despite his posture of integrity, he has a normal admixture of egotism and self-regard. He is the individual in every group who feels compelled to stand out, no matter how outrageously. The comedy depends on three things: (1) the delicate question of where egotism ends and altruism-idealism begins; (2) the way in which a shocked world reacts to the charge that it is mediocre, as much because the charge is true as because it is tactless; (3) Alceste's falling in love with the one woman who is most unlike him and who, the cynosure of this corrupt and mediocre society, stands for everything he hates. His love is more than just a neat dramatic ploy by an adroit author. Rooted in profound psychology, it embodies the principle of ambivalence and intimates that Alceste is deeply attracted to the very society he so excoriates.

The *Misanthropist* is actually a mutation among Molière's plays. The norm is a pattern used by Jonson in his humor comedies and by Shakespeare in *Coriolanus* and *Merry Wives:* the monomaniac. The hero is a hypochondriac and wants his daughter to marry a doctor (*Le malade imaginaire* [*The Imaginary Invalid*, 1673]); a miser who wants his daughter to marry money (*L'avare*, [*The*

Miser, 1668]); a nouveau riche man who wants his daughter to marry nobility (*Le bourgeois gentilhomme* [*The Would-Be Gentleman,* 1670]); an overly pious soul who wants his daughter to marry a cleric (*Tartuffe,* 1664). The common sense of relatives and maids is ridden roughshod over. The man laughed at has hold of one piece of reality and not much else.

Restoration comedy (notably William Wycherley's *Country Wife,* 1675; Sir George Etherege's *Man of Mode,* 1676; William Congreve's *Way of the World,* 1700) seems limited in class and scope, especially compared with Shakespeare. It lacks politics and wars, yet gives us emotional corpses and brittle repartee. A fast society crowd combining rough play with intrigue, revenge, and verbal brilliance—that situation is universal enough. The controversy over whether one is meant to identify with or reject the philandering main characters is beside the point; instead of falling into the either/or trap, one should entertain the possibility of a serene impartiality in the apportioning of the laughter. One laughs with the Horners and Dorimants as they outwit the fools and sleep with the women; one laughs also at them as one sees them discomfited or compromised by their overreaching at certain junctures.

Pope's poem *Rape of the Lock* (1712) has as its central theme the idea that men of different periods and life styles share a common emotional and moral spectrum. Thus a fight in an eighteenth-century drawing room among spoiled young people of an affluent class over the cutting off of a lock of hair is not so different from the Trojan War fought long ago and far away by exotic heroes over the abduction of the beautiful Helen. The comedy, here technically called the "mock heroic," turns on the incongruity of having language traditionally applied in epics to great men and events now being applied to small ones. If a minor social incident generated Pope's classic, nothing less than the historic rivalry of England and France prompted the writing of Swift's satire *Gulliver's Travels* (1726). When the war between Lilliput and Blefuscu turns out to be over which end of the egg to break, however, we clearly have entered the timeless. The laughter is at the expense not just of Briton and Frenchman, or even Catholic and Protestant, but of what Freud was to call the "narcissism of small difference," the tendency of human beings to differ most virulently with precisely those with whom they share the largest number of values. History has turned into psychology, observations on current events have turned into universals of human nature. Many incidents in book 1 show the human race, represented by the tiny Lilliputians, as being indeed petty (Fr. *petit* = small)—vindictive, irrational, confusing means and ends, ungrateful. In the land of the giants in book 2 the comedy takes a more savage turn as, by means of a quasi-Platonic dialogue between the king and Gulliver, man's depravity is established through irony and laughter. In book 4, the satire becomes more metaphysical and is aimed at nothing less than man's delusions of superiority when he in fact is more nearly akin to the beastlike Yahoos than to the rational horses, the Houyhnhnms.

Swiftian satire and comedy appears in Voltaire's brief *Micromégas* (tale,

1752). His *Zadig* (novel, 1747) and especially the novel *Candide* (1759) (like Dr. Johnson's *Rasselas* [novel 1759]) represent the *Gulliver* pattern modulated into the philosophical tale. A young man is thrown by adversity into a series of adventures that bring him in contact with many forms of evil, with different peoples, cultures, and values. Philosophical ideas about the meaning of life and the problem of evil are tested by experience. These works are comic in the sense that the heroes undergo and witness some of the most horrible atrocities and yet remain cheerful and unscarred; man's depravity is distanced and laughed at rather than bemoaned. The rivers of blood and mounds of hacked limbs have all the reality of a painting or cartoon, as if exotic creatures on another planet were being studied in a telescope. Satirized above all are philosophies and theologies— all the attempts to wrap everything up in tidy little intellectual boxes—and the ability of man to adhere to his theories in the face of numerous adverse facts.

The pattern of the naïve young man who takes to the road and encounters many people and experiences is one of the streams that went into the making of the modern novel. It is at the heart of Fielding's *Joseph Andrews* (1742) and *Tom Jones* (1749). The comedy turns partly on the style, partly on the persona of the narrator holding intimate discourse with the reader on the periphery of the narrative, and partly on the amusing incidents. Disasters are not allowed to overwhelm the hero's fortunes, hurt his handsome body, distort his career, or twist his emotions, but only to deepen—at least on the author's say so—his wisdom. In Sterne's *Sentimental Journey* (1768) there is also a young man travelling, but the narrative structure is haphazard, self-conscious. Comedy, in other words, takes a new turn, as the outside world becomes secondary to the sensibility of the young man moving through it; clear narrative is subordinated to evocation of states of mind; events become fewer and less definite; dialogue becomes monologue. All of this is carried to extreme lengths in Sterne's *Tristram Shandy* (1759–1767), a bizarre comic masterpiece that looks back to Lucian and Rabelais and ahead to Proust and Joyce. Here digressions are central; a presumed autobiography becomes bogged down in its first pages over the name of a grandfather; even the typography is toyed with for the sake of comic effect.

The Nineteenth and Twentieth Centuries

On the whole the comic mode did not flourish in the nineteenth century, with some notable exceptions. Jane Austen excels in an ironic style, richly portrayed eccentrics, and happy nuptial endings. Among poets the order of the day is high seriousness, the only exception being Byron, who wrote a goodly number of neoclassical satires and, signally, the long, sparkling *Don Juan* (epic satire, 1819–1824). The comedy in it turns on the formless form, the apparently random thoughts, the conversational tone, the playful moods, the narrator's banter, as well as on the discrepancies between people's moral and religious aspirations and their quite worldly actions. Marriage, love, religion, even poetry itself are looked at with a good natured skepticism and cynicism.

The great master of the comic and grotesque in human behavior was Dickens, who sometimes reaches almost Shakespearean proportions. *Pickwick Papers* (1836–1837), his first major and his most comic novel, brings a Don Quixote figure into a corrupt early-nineteenth-century England. His other novels become grim but never lose their humor. Memorable and varied character types—the nouveau riche, the vain patriot, the sycophantic hypocrite, the dreamer waiting for the great breakthrough, the expert on child-raising whose household is chaotic—are etched by a style rich in irony, hyperbole, copiousness, and caricature. Among French novelists, the later Flaubert, in *Bouvard et Pécuchet* (*Bouvard and Pécuchet,* 1881) and especially the *Dictionnaire des idées reçues* (1881), lampoons the bland presuppositions of the middle class that is coming into possession of the political and cultural life of Europe.

In Russia, Gogol satirizes dull provincial life, the eccentric landowners, and the inefficiency, corruption, and petty tyranny of the local governing bodies in the *Revizor* (*The Inspector General,* drama, 1836) and *Mërtvye dushi* (*Dead Souls,* novel, 1842). Dostoevsky's early *Dvoĭnik* (*The Double,* novel, 1846) has as central character a paranoiac anti-hero who goes from one faux pas to another. The man is certifiably insane by story's end, but the comedy rather than the pathos of the situation is central. A similar situation is in *Zapiski iz podpol'ia* (*Notes from Underground,* novel, 1864), written nearly two decades later. This is one of the tragicomic masterpieces of literature, and the reader hardly knows whether to feel for the protagonist—identify with him or pity him—or laugh at him, or repel him in disgust, so self-contradictory and self-defeating, so hectoring, irrational, outrageously paradoxical, and elusive is he.

An entirely different sort of comic spirit is at work in the Alice books of Lewis Carroll (1832–1898). Characters like the Mad Hatter, the Queen, and Humpty Dumpty embody one trait or aspect of real people separated from all the other traits. The works are comic in that they are vacations from quotidian reality; logical riddles are worked out in comic sketches by a kind of nineteenth-century Monty Python. A trio of major comic writers thrived at the turn of the century. Oscar Wilde (1854–1900) specialized in the epigram, the witty sally, and the paradox. The laughter he arouses comes from the discovery that opposites do not merely attract but are equal and that what appears is often the opposite of what is. This vein of comedy was carried on, from a Catholic and sometimes reactionary perspective, by G. K. Chesterton (1874–1936), for whom paradox was at times the only mode of expression, and, from an anomalous Nietzschean-socialist perspective, by G. B. Shaw (1856–1950). The latter especially enjoyed outraging the bourgeois, the pious, the moralistic, the liberal, the conservative by showing their conventional views of the basic sacred cows—God, the family, the state, the church, property—to be laughable.

Chekhov's plays (1860–1904) have a subtle comic streak, not in language or plot but in character portrayal. Though the main characters are usually failures (whether as writer, parent, actress, professor-scholar, doctor, lover), their coming to terms with themselves causes the reader to laugh at them gently, because part of their predicament is of their own making (hence the laughter) and part beyond their control (hence the pathos). His "soft" comedy is at the other extreme from the "hard" comedy of Aristophanes and Rabelais. Marcel Proust (1871–1922) is usually known for his style, his subjectivity, his character portrayal, his exhaustive method of treating a subject, notably artists, love, and states of mind. Yet no less powerful is his comic sense and his satire, especially when applied to people at social gatherings in or near high society. Hardly anyone is spared his derision—aristocrats, social climbers, novelists, Jews, servants. Joyce's *Ulysses* is a classic of comedy as well as of the novel. The comic spirit triumphs in the portrait of Bloom, a modern Everyman swaddled in "soft," sympathetic humor; in the collection of parodies of the major English prose styles of the past; in the endlessly inventive manipulation of the novel's structure, with the daring of Rabelais and Sterne; and in the at once poetic and realistic use of stream of consciousness to depict human inconsistency and perversity.

Faulkner's fine sense of humor ranges from the sarcastic, self-pitying stream of consciousness of the Jason section of the novel *The Sound and the Fury* (1929) to the casual tone and the rural Southern tall-tale tradition in the novels *As I Lay Dying* (1930) and *The Hamlet* (1940). Another kind of ethnic humor is found in the novels of the Jewish-American school of writers—in Moses Herzog's (Saul Bellow's *Herzog,* 1964) writing unsent letters to the world while trying to put his private life together or Alexander Portnoy's quest for identity (Philip Roth's *Portnoy's Complaint,* 1969) after a childhood filled with the obsessive solicitousness of a Jewish mother. In Nabokov's *Lolita* (1955) comedy is created by a bizarre case of sexual infatuation, by satire of American folkways, and by the urbane, ironic narrative style, while *Pale Fire* (1962) turns on a parody of the scholarly presentation of a text, the comic portrayal of the diffident anti-hero, and the wit shaping a richly allusive style.

Lastly there is the comedy developed since World War II (sometimes called Black Humor), which is based on the idea that life is absurd, surrealistic, insane. The progenitor of this school of writing is Kafka (1883–1924), in whose fiction the terror of existence is balanced with a bizarre sense of the comic. Perhaps the most representative of the works expressing this outlook is Joseph Heller's *Catch-22* (1961), set in World War II Italy. The war, its causes and issues, its participants, as well as many other details that would be plentiful in a realistic novel, are absent. Instead we have reality perceived mainly from the vantage point of a hero who is half paranoiac and half the object of the hostility of individuals, social institutions (mainly the U.S. Air Force), and, above all, the universe. Nazism does not appear, for it is implicitly everywhere in life; Nazism is merely us without the veneer of civilization and democracy. Once such an unusual vantage point is achieved by the writer (helped to it by the examples of the Underground Man and Kafka's protagonists), everything is going to look askew and provide a rich harvest for laughter. Hence the double talk, the hypocrisies, the racketeering, the petty tyrannies, the Air Force bureaucratese—all written in a fresh, uninhibited vein and with Dickensian gusto. The normal anomalies and irrationalities of society are multiplied under the pressures of war,

and a society of warriors becomes a microcosm for the human enterprise itself, all of it shown to be hopelessly—and therefore laughably—at odds with itself.
See also: Comic Hero, Laughter, Tragicomic Hero.

Selected Bibliography

Corrigan, Robert, ed. *Comedy: Meaning and Form.* San Francisco: Chandler, 1965.
Feibleman, James K. *In Praise of Comedy.* New York: Macmillan, 1939.
Lauter, Paul, ed. *Theories of Comedy.* Garden City, N.Y.: Anchor Books, 1964.
Wimsatt, William Kurtz, ed. *The Idea of Comedy.* Englewood Cliffs, N.J.: Prentice-Hall, 1969.

MANFRED WEIDHORN

COMIC HERO

In its broadest, if least useful, sense, "comic hero" may loosely designate the protagonist, or indeed any leading character, of a comic work of literature, dramatic or other, even when he or she is negatively portrayed as an object of ridicule or contempt. In a more interesting, and recently a more prominent, sense, which gives full weight to both potentially opposed terms, this character is a "hero" who boldly affirms, even in defiance of ridicule by others, festively "comic" values of physical exuberance or imaginative freedom often implicitly or overtly at odds with the everyday rules and regulations by which his society is governed. In this sense (with which the present entry will be concerned), the comic hero is not a fixed character type, but appears throughout the ages in multiple guises reflecting different relationships, from open opposition to seeming accommodation with those who make up the more or less antagonistic world to which he belongs. And since to be a comic hero means to be perceived as such by audience, readers, or critics—and their perceptions have varied widely—the comic hero's history, more than that of most other characters in literature, must take into account the ways in which he or she has been seen. One person's comic hero will remain the fool or knave of another.

Conceptions of the Comic: The Classical Tradition

The comic hero is an ancient and durable character in Western literature; recognition of the comic hero on the other hand, has been relatively new, retarded by the dominant conception of comedy as satire or ridicule that prevailed in the Western critical tradition from Aristotle's *Peri poiētikēs* (*Poetics,* 4th century B.C.) to Henri Bergson's essay *Le rire* (*Laughter,* 1900). Although the word "comedy" (Gk. *kōmōidia*) almost certainly derives from *kōmos,* the "revels," and although Aristotle himself associates the origins of comic drama with phallic songs, the brief but immensely influential Aristotelian treatment of comedy by no means emphasized its festive aspect as a celebration of vital impulse. (Nor did the *Tractatus Coislinianus,* a papyrus manuscript discovered in the nineteenth century and regarded by some as a synopsis of a lost second book of the *Poetics* purportedly devoted to comedy.) On the contrary, Aristotle regarded the laughable or ridiculous as a subdivision of the ugly and differentiated comedy from tragedy in that it represented men as worse, not better, than in actual life; even the writers of the iambic lampoons from which comedy arose were, in Aristotle's view, of a meaner or more trivial sort than their epic or tragic counterparts.

This conception of comedy and laughter, which prevented the comic character from being viewed as a hero, was echoed throughout antiquity. Cicero, for example, in his dialogue *De oratore (On the Orator,* c. 55 B.C.), has Julius Caesar restrict the field of the laughable to "turpitude and deformity," which the orator, no less than the comic dramatist, artfully exposes to ridicule. Only toward the end of the classical period, in the treatise "De fabula" (now attributed to a certain Evanthius) at the beginning of Donatus' commentary on Terence (4th century), did significantly different distinctions of comedy from tragedy find prominent expression: among them, the movement of comedy toward a joyful, not a funereal, outcome, and its affirmation of life as something to seize hold of, not to flee.

Medieval writers, though adopting the joyful ending as a prime criterion of the comic, ascribed little value to laughter or to the affirmation of life in this world; and the humanist scholars of the Renaissance, after the rediscovery of the *Poetics* in the sixteenth century, chose to reaffirm, in didactically moralized form, Aristotle's criterion rather than those of Donatus. Thus Giovanni Giorgio Trissino writes in his *Poetica (Poetics,* mid-16th century) that comedy "teaches through scorn and censure of the bad and ugly," and for Sir Philip Sidney, in his posthumous *A Defence of Poetry* (1595), "the comedy is an imitation of the common errors of our life, which he representeth in the most ridiculous and scornful sort that may be, so as it is impossible that any beholder can be content to be such a one."

This satirical, indeed punitive, conception of comedy, endorsed by such leading dramatists of the seventeeth century as Ben Jonson (1572–1637) and Molière (1622–1673), prevailed throughout the neoclassical period, precluding the very possibility that a comic character might be viewed as heroic. And even as recently as 1900, Bergson, in his essay *Le rire,* defined "something mechanical encrusted on the living" as the principal source, from the perspective of his vitalistic biology, of the comic character's inferiority, and found in laughter "an unavowed intention to humiliate, and consequently to correct our neighbor." Laughter remained a sort of *social gesture* that pursued "a utilitarian aim of general improvement," policing society's values by exposing their violators to censure.

Conceptions of the Comic: New Perspectives

In all this long tradition there is very little to suggest any kind of heroic potentiality in the comic. Evanthius, who in contrast to Aristotle regarded Homer's epic *Odysseia (Odyssey,* c. 8th century B.C.) as a paradigm for comedy, was almost unique in placing both the comic genre and its characters on a par with the tragic; to others the inferiority of one or both was self-evident. Since the end of the eighteenth century, however, certain major writers, such as Friedrich von Schiller in *Über naive und sentimentalische Dichtung* (*On Naïve and Sentimental Poetry*, 1795–1796), have proposed a more positive conception of comedy, which by freeing the mind of passion and engaging the understanding aims, in Schiller's view, at a higher purpose than tragedy. And in the twentieth century a new awareness has arisen of the affirmative values and heroic dimensions of comedy as the expression of a popular viewpoint fundamentally opposed to the aristocratic outlook of the dominant classical tradition.

Sigmund Freud, for example, in *Der Witz und seine Beziehung zum Unbewussten* (*Wit and Its Relation to the Unconscious*, 1905), emphasized the insurrectionary character of popular humor directed against institutions and "dogmas of morality or religion, views of life which enjoy so much respect that objections to them can only be made under the mask of a joke," obliquely affirming "that the wishes and desires of men have a right to make themselves acceptable alongside of exacting and ruthless morality." Such an attitude, as folklorists and anthropologists had been discovering, is characteristic of the tricksters, knaves, and buffoons of popular stories and legends throughout the world: of Brer Rabbit, Punch and Judy, or Till Eulenspiegel, among countless others, all of whom express in word or in deed a reckless disregard for any social order that impedes the preservation and the uninhibited expression of self. These characters, like their modern counterparts in animated cartoons or Chaplinesque comedies, transcend ridicule by the persistence with which they triumph over all who oppose them; they suggest a conception of comedy whose predominant feeling Susanne Langer described in *Feeling and Form* (1953) as one of "heightened vitality, challenged wit and will, engaged in the great game with Chance" whose "real antagonist is the World."

The popular perspective thus rehabilitated by psychoanalysis and folklore opened new fields for the understanding of literary comedy also. For in this perspective the comic character may be viewed not merely as the hapless butt of justified ridicule—a character worse than ourselves, such as no beholder could wish to be—but as an indispensable hero stubbornly celebrating vitally human, festive values in the teeth of concerted opprobrium from a workaday world alarmed at his possibly contagious example. Among the major studies that have contributed most to this important new understanding are Francis M. Cornford's *The Origin of Attic Comedy* (1914) and Cedric H. Whitman's *Aristophanes and the Comic Hero* (1963), Mikhail Bakhtin's *Tvorchestvo Fransua Rable . . .* (*Rabelais and His World*, 1965), and C. L. Barber's *Shakespeare's Festive Comedy* (1959).

Greek and Roman Antiquity

To look back at early works of Greek and Roman literature in the light of a concept so seemingly new and so utterly foreign to the Aristotelian interpretation of comedy is neither so arbitrary nor so anachronistic as it might appear. Evanthius' classification of the *Odyssey* as an exemplary *comedy* suggests dimensions of the term current in ancient times though largely neglected by Aristotle. Not only does the poem move, in contrast to its sister epic, *Ilias* (*The Iliad*, c. 8th century B.C.) toward a joyful outcome for Odysseus, his family, and his loyal subjects, but no hero in literature has been more distinguished for his firm adhesion to life and determined avoidance of death. In physical endurance as in mental and verbal agility, Odysseus, who ascends from the world of the dead, who rejects immortality with a sea nymph for the perils of returning to wife and home, and who adopts the lowly guise of a beggar in order to vanquish his more numerous and more powerful opponents, remains a paradigm of the versatile comic hero throughout antiquity and beyond.

Nowhere has the sharp division between opposing conceptions of the comic throughout the ages been more graphically illustrated than in responses to Aristophanes, the only writer of Athenian Old Comedy whose plays survive in more than fragmentary passages. In the classical tradition Aristotle seems to have ignored him, Plutarch scathingly condemns him in *Ēthika* (*Moralia*, essays, c. A.D. 100) for vulgarity and immorality, Ben Jonson in *Timber* (criticism, 1640) considers his plays an "insolent and obscene" perversion, and Voltaire, in the article on atheism in his *Dictionnaire philosophique* (*Philosophical Dictionary*, 1764), disdains him as unworthy to give farces at the local fair. But his very unrestraint is among the qualities, as Cornford and Whitman both stress, that most associate his outrageous comedy with the *kōmos* of its origins; some of his choruses, indeed, still wore the leather phallus linking them with the phallic fertility rites mentioned in passing by Aristotle. His heroes, like Dicaeopolis in *Acharnēs* (*The Archanians*, 425 B.C.), Peisthetaerus in *Ornithes* (*Birds*, 414 B.C.), and Lysistrata in *Lysistratē* (*Lysistrata*, 411 B.C.), are typically engaged in a contest or *agōn* on behalf of peace and life against the proponents of war and death—a struggle that may still reflect, as Cornford believed, the primordial ritual combat of Summer against Winter. Despite the opprobrium they regularly incur (and dispense), their regenerative triumph in this heroic if not always dignified contest is normally cause for joyful celebration in the revelry of the plays' festive endings. In all its countless permutations, the movement from *agōn* to *kōmos* that is central to Aristophanes remains the underlying pattern of all heroic comedy.

The open celebration of flagrantly antisocial values in comedies presented at public festivals during wartime caused repeated difficulties for Aristophanes, and in his last plays both abuse and festivity were greatly muted. In the romantic and sentimental New Comedy that arose in the fourth century B. C. exemplified by *Dyskolos* (*The Grouch*, 317 B.C.) and other plays of Menander, young lovers repeatedly triumph over the opposition of their curmudgeonly elders not by their own wits and actions but through discoveries and reversals brought about by beneficent Fortune. The virtues of cultured society are never challenged, and where there is no true contest there are likewise no true comic heroes. European comic drama would henceforth consist in significant part of variations on the themes of Menander.

In Roman literature the sacrosanct values of the state—the *res publica,* or "public thing"—allowed small scope, at least outside the farcical mines of popular entertainment, for comic dissidents, who make a marginal appearance only near the beginning and near the end of the classical period. In the comic dramas of Plautus, unlike those of the younger Terence, characters such as the courtesan Philocomasium in *Miles gloriosus (The Braggart Soldier,* 204 B. C.) and the slave Pseudolus in *Pseudolus* (191 B. C.) achieve their limited triumphs not by Menandrine dependence on the workings of Fortune, but by swift footwork and artful deceptions that outwit their duller opponents. And in the novel *Metamorphoses* of Apuleius *(The Golden Ass,* c. 150) the hapless hero Lucius, transformed into an ass by his own reckless folly, gradually learns through painful yet often hilarious indignity and misfortune to renounce the animality of the human condition by throwing himself on a higher power, the goddess Isis, who restores him to a purified and chastened humanity.

The Middle Ages and Renaissance

The medieval Catholic church was no more sympathetically inclined than the Roman state to the comic hero's brazen affirmation of the dissident values of self, yet throughout the Middle Ages in Western Europe a robust popular tradition of carnivalesque festivity and even of sacramental burlesque (as in the braying Ass's Mass) continued to flourish, providing a vent for this-worldly impulses flagrantly antipathetic to monastical virtues. This assertive irreverence found literary expression in the Latin songs of the Goliards, or "wandering scholars," beginning in the eleventh century and in frequently scatological French *fabliaux* (verse tales) of the twelfth and thirteenth. But the latter in particular are too cynical to give rise to heroes of any kind, nor do characters in dramatic farces like *Maître Pierre Pathelin* (c. 1470) succeed in articulating distinct comic values amid the general ludicrousness of their world.

Apart from a few vivid portraits of spirited dissidents from received morality, like Trotaconventos in Juan Ruiz's *Libro de buen amor (Book of Good Love,* poem, 1343) and the Wife of Bath in Geoffrey Chaucer's *Canterbury Tales* (c. 1380–1400), it was mainly in animal stories, and above all in the immensely popular international saga of Reynard the fox, which first took written vernacular form in the early "branches" of the French beast epic, the *Roman de Renard (Romance of Reynard,* twelfth to fourteenth century), followed by versions in German, Flemish, and English, that the comic hero found scope for full self-assertion. Here the scandalous fox, in outrageous travesty of chivalric tradition, unabashedly usurps the privileges and enjoys the wives of his dull-witted neighbors in spite of their leagued opposition and solemn condemnation.

The medieval tradition of carnival survived into the High Renaissance, as Bakhtin stressed, in the four books of François Rabelais' *Gargantua et Pantagruel (Gargantua and Pantagruel,* 1532–1564), whose heroes, both giant and human, amalgamate humanist learning and popular folklore and in so utterly festive a world easily rout the various foes who ineffectively oppose their triumphant progress. In the romantic comedies of Shakespeare, such gentle but determined heroines as Portia in *The Merchant of Venice* (c. 1595), Rosalind in *As You Like It* (c. 1599), and Viola in *Twelfth Night* (c. 1600) contribute by their patient wisdom and humane intelligence to effecting the transformation of a divided world into one again united, however momentarily and precariously, by the spontaneity and love that had reigned in a fabled Arcadian age. In the less fabulous surroundings of a merely historical world, on the other hand, Shakespeare's most boldly assertive comic hero, Falstaff in the two parts of *Henry IV* (1597–1600), finds his triumph thwarted when neither corporal gusto nor exuberant imagination can extend his sovereignty from the tavern at Eastcheap to the kingdom of England, where other—in the end, incompatible—values prevail.

In Cervantes' novel *Don Quijote* (*Don Quixote*, 1605, 1615), the hero's triumph is also foiled by the intractable conditions of his "real" world, and from this conflict a new paradigm of comic heroism arises for the centuries that follow. In contrast to comic heroes from Odysseus to Falstaff, Don Quixote sets forth not to preserve or affirm the endangered self but to benefit his fellow men at great personal risk: not to challenge the prevalent values of his age but to defend them and thus to uphold in practice what others only proclaim in words. Inasmuch as his initially involuntary madness becomes increasingly an act of deliberation and will, courageously adhered to in defiance of a reality that falls hopelessly short of his transformative imagination, Don Quixote—like his faithful squire, Sancho Panza, who admires and even comes to resemble him—carries the comic heroism of the Christian age to its pinnacle of achievement and triumphs in his very willingness to invite the defeat that destroys him.

The Seventeenth and Eighteenth Centuries

Self-consciously classical playwrights like Ben Jonson in England and Molière in France considered comedy, as we have seen, to be essentially ridicule of human foibles condemned by reason of good sense, not celebration of alternative comic values; to the degree that practice accords with theory, theirs will accordingly be plays without comic heroes. Even so, the titular knaves of Jonson's *Volpone* (1606) and Molière's *Tartuffe* (1664), among others, embody an energetic verve that makes these resourceful villains far more impressive than most of their victims (to say nothing of largely irrelevant spokesmen for conventional virtue), and even such foolish gulls as Sir Epicure Mammon in Jonson's *The Alchemist* (1610) and Monsieur Jourdain in Molière's *Le bourgeois gentilhomme* (*The Would-Be Gentleman*, 1670) frequently engage the sympathy of viewers by their almost heroic persistence in folly.

Molière's most nearly heroic characters are perhaps those who transcend ridicule by artlessly or deliberately rejecting society's values, like Agnès in *L'école des femmes* (*The School for Wives*, 1662), when she follows not the self-serving moral precepts of her intended husband Arnolphe but the spontaneous impulse of love for another, or like the truculent Alceste in *Le misanthrope* (*The Misanthropist,* 1666), who scornfully repudiates the criteria by which his society scorns him. Alceste, who was no doubt a figure of ridicule for Molière and his contemporaries, became an exemplar of heroic integrity for ages that followed, even if, in so doing, he virtually ceased to be comic.

English Restoration comedy is far from heroic in temper, yet even here young protagonists like Mirabell and Millamant in William Congreve's *The Way of the World* (1700) affirm the comic value of love through resolute opposition to the frivolous dupes and cynical knaves whom they adroitly excel at a game they would rather not play, and a similar triumph of natural sentiment over artificial contrivance distinguishes the hero of Pierre de Marivaux' *Les fausses confidences* (*The False Confessions,* 1737). But the classic theater remained for the most part a bastion of aristocratic values; it was rather in picaresque fiction, during these centuries, that representatives of the unprivileged classes began to articulate desires potentially in conflict with the established order of things.

The *pícaro* of the Spanish tradition descending from *Lazarillo de Tormes* (novel, 1554) was forced to rely on native ingenuity no less than the comic heroes of ancient times, but instead of challenging a world antagonistic to his needs or reshaping it in his own image he learned to adapt himself to it and to do as others did. The ingenuous hero of Hans Jakob Christoffel von Grimmelshausen's novel *Des abenteurliche Simplicissimus* (*The Adventurous Simplicissimus*, 1669) does indeed voice open dissent from the destructive brutality unleashed by the Thirty Years' War, but in the end his one alternative to it is the otherworldly renunciation of the Christian hermit. In other novels in the picaresque tradition, like Alain-René Lesage's *Gil Blas* (1715–1735) and Daniel Defoe's *Moll Flanders* (1722), the resourceful protagonist is generally content to reach a favorable (and a thoroughly unheroic) accommodation with things as they are.

Only within prudent limits could the prevalent moral values of a deeply traditional social order be openly questioned without severe condemnation in these centuries before the French Revolution. The impetuous young hero of Henry Fielding's novel *Tom Jones* (1749) challenges their authority not by calculation or cunning but by the uncontrollable overflow of his initially undisciplined animal spirits, yet this morality of spontaneous feeling and good nature was sternly condemned by those (including Samuel Richardson and Samuel Johnson) whose morality was of a more conventional and less flexible kind. By persisting in his temperamental opposition to the hypocrisy and artifice that surround him and in his generous impulses toward the unfortunate, Tom becomes a comic hero not of the head but of the heart who is able in the end, thanks less to his own devices than to Fortune's benevolence or his author's good humor, to moderate his reckless imprudence and reconcile himself to a world whose essential values he has felt no need to call into question.

Even in France, where challenges to existing society were more radical, the hero of Voltaire's novel *Candide* (1759) ends by cultivating his garden, and the paradoxical lackey of Denis Diderot's posthumous *Jacques le fataliste (Jacques the Fatalist*, novel, 1773) complacently continues to serve the baffled master whom he so easily dominates. Only on the eve of the revolution did the impudent Figaro of Beaumarchais' *Le mariage de Figaro (The Marriage of Figaro*, comedy, 1784) state the superiority of his mental endowments in terms sufficiently explicit to alarm a king, and even so his potential rebelliousness could be resolved—at least on the stage—by a marriage that left the order of society intact if no longer unquestioned.

The Nineteenth and Twentieth Centuries

The comic heroes of earlier times had frequently drawn strength from the more or less tragic counterparts to whose heroic deeds they presented their spirited alternatives. Thus the scamps of Aristophanes battened on Greek tragedy, Reynard the Fox parodied Tristan or Lancelot, Don Quixote emulated Amadis of Gaul, and even Tom Jones instinctively reacted against the venal morality embodied in Richardson's heroically determined Pamela. But with the fall of Napoleon and the spread of the Industrial Revolution the nineteenth century increasingly came to see itself as an age with no heroic values against which comic heroes could react in forming their own.

In the early decades of the century Jane Austen's Elizabeth Bennet, in the novel *Pride and Prejudice* (1813), could still preserve her essential integrity while critically dissenting from the narrow conventions of a provincial society partly redeemed by her chastening recognition that she has shared in its vices. But in later novels, like Austen's *Persuasion* (1818), the melancholy heroism of nonconformity seems painfully remote from the comic; and in Stendhal's novel *La chartreuse de Parme (The Charterhouse of Parma,*1839), only naïvely rebellious youth can momentarily sustain the high comedy of heroic illusions soon destined to become a reproachful memory for the penitent anchorite that Fabrice, in the end, becomes. With the loss of heroic ideals in a society perceived as artificial and false, the spontaneous passion of youth becomes the principal impetus for comic heroes like the insouciant lover of Byron's *Don Juan* (poem, 1819–1824), who are therefore continually threatened, in the absence of firmly held and clearly articulated comic values of their own, by aimlessness and corruption such as those that undermine the ebullient visions and ambitions of youth in Henrik Ibsen's verse drama, *Peer Gynt* (1867).

Nineteenth-century fiction is rich in comic characters, but few of these are heroic, as Odysseus or Peisthetaerus, Falstaff or Don Quixote were, in affirming and enacting values at odds with those that prevail in their worlds. Unlike many scandalous precursors the affably benevolent Mr. Pickwick, in Charles Dickens' novel *The Pickwick Papers* (1836–1837), violates no taboo and gives no offense either to readers or to fellow inhabitants of his fairy-tale world; and once reality has grimly intruded, in Dickens' later novels, comic characters are seldom heroic or heroes comic. Pip, in *Great Expectations* (1860–1861), is perhaps uniquely, if very imperfectly, heroic in his ruefully retrospective acknowledgment of the unintended comedy of his own blindly misguided actions. In an age that could deplore society's vices but not question its virtues the scope of comic heroism was very severely restricted. Only in a rare and seemingly eccentric work like Gustave Flaubert's uncompleted last novel *Bouvard et Pécuchet* (*Bouvard and Pécuchet*, 1881) do comic characters ridiculed by all venture to challenge directly the basic values on which their society complacently rests, even if by so doing they appear to leave themselves no alternative but to return, after the failure of all their grandiose dreams, to the desperate *pis aller* of copying books "as in the old days."

With the wholesale destruction of traditional values in the twentieth century, the comic dissident, in the virtual absence of all tragic counterparts, has been the authentic hero of our time, tenaciously sustaining, like the "modest, unrecognized hero" of Jaroslav Hašek's novel of World War I, *Osudy dobrého vojáka Švejka* (*The Good Soldier Schweik*, 1920–1923), the invincible underdog's determined adhesion to life in the midst of death. Unlike more audacious predecessors in antiquity and the Renaissance, comic heroes of the collectivist twentieth century have frequently been constrained to take a very low (if not an invisible) profile, but their stubborn affirmation of basic comic values of body, mind, and indomitable selfhood is no less heroic, and all the more essential, for being lost upon others who remain oblivious and impervious to them.

The heroes of two of the foremost comic novels of the modern age, James Joyce's *Ulysses* (1922) and Thomas Mann's *Felix Krull* (1954), reenact, in terms appropriate to their different times, the exploits, respectively, of Homer's Odysseus and of the thievish Greek trickster-god Hermes. Like his classical prototype, Joyce's Leopold Bloom is an "allround man" who despite his retiring temper and inconspicuous demeanor is repeatedly compelled, as a Jewish convert in fanatically Catholic and nationalistic Dublin, to assert and defend the values fundamental to his existence: his humble bodily pleasures, his inquisitive imagination and sensual fantasy, and above all the compassionate kindness that most essentially sets him apart from his many derisive detractors. At the funeral of Paddy Dignam, Bloom reaffirms, in the depths of Hades, the comic hero's immemorial allegiance to "warm fullblooded life"; in the hateful Cyclops' den of Barney Kiernan's tavern he declares his solidarity with his persecuted people and his dedication to "the opposite of hatred," the love "that is really life"; and after he has befriended his fellow outcast, the morose Stephen Dedalus, it is fittingly to Bloom, the true hero of this mock-heroic world, that the drowsy thoughts of his finally faithful Penelope turn in the passionate epithalamium of the ending. Bloom, who sleeps with his head at Molly's feet, remains typically unaware of his crowning moment of triumph.

Felix Krull is a far less modest comic hero, yet one who makes himself, through consummate artistry, no less inconspicuous in his fashion than Bloom. This fortunate "Sunday child" rehabilitates the long discredited arts of the trickster, but far from being a hard-boiled rogue in the picaresque tradition, he is an authentic comic hero employing illusion and make-believe, like Odysseus, Falstaff, or Don Quixote, as creative means of discovering or inventing the truth of his nature. His confident sense of himself as a natural aristocrat, even a godlike avatar of the Hermes of ancient myth, heightens his critical awareness of the arbitrariness of a society in which he remains a servant to others, and only after he undertakes to impersonate a marquis and journeys to Lisbon in company with the starry-eyed Professor Kuckuck does he again experience the "vast expansiveness" of resurrected childlike wonder in the boundless possibilities of the world that he had once known as "The Great Joy." The jubilation of spontaneous union with Kuckuck's unexpectedly passionate wife in the aftermath of a bullfight, with which the extant "first part" of Krull's memoirs (completed in Thomas Mann's eightieth year, forty years and two world wars after he began it) suddenly culminates, crowns his disciplined art of living with a suitably ecstatic *kōmos* of exhilarant freedom.

By their insistent if unassuming assertion of a drastically constricted and continually imperiled physical and imaginative freedom, Joyce's modern Ulysses and Mann's modern Hermes, along with the countless other comic heroes of modern fiction—Gulley Jimson in Joyce Cary's *The Horse's Mouth* (1944), for example, or Yossarian in Joseph Heller's *Catch-22* (1961), or McMurphy in Ken Kesey's *One Flew Over the Cuckoo's Nest* (1962)—bear witness to the essential and finally irrepressible humanity whose bold and difficult celebration, in the century of Auschwitz and Hiroshima, has become, more perhaps than ever before, a task of truly heroic dimensions.

See also: Birth of the Hero, Comedy, Social Status of Hero, Tragicomic Hero.

Selected Bibliography

Jauss, Hans Robert. "On Why the Comic Hero Amuses." *Aesthetic Experience and Literary Hermeneutics*. Trans. Michael Shaw. Minneapolis: Univ. of Minnesota Press, 1982.

Lauter, Paul, ed. *Theories of Comedy*. Garden City, N.Y.: Doubleday-Anchor, 1964.

Torrance, Robert M. *The Comic Hero*. Cambridge, Mass.: Harvard, 1978.

Whitman, Cedric H. *Aristophanes and the Comic Hero*. Cambridge, Mass.: Harvard, 1964.

ROBERT M. TORRANCE

CRIPPLING

Crippling in literature is so multi-faceted that it can mean nothing or anything, and so an overview must necessarily be suggestive rather than seek to be all-encompassing; a survey would take several volumes per language. Thus this entry will mention representative examples in the text; there will be no attempt to list all the cripples in literature.

Crippling includes lame characters from Hephaistos to Melville's Ahab and

Tennessee Williams' Laura Wingfield, Carson McCullers' deaf-mute and dwarf (*The Heart is a Lonely Hunter*, novel, 1940; and *The Ballad of Sad Cafe*, novel 1951); blind individuals from Tiresias and biblical Tobit to Beckett's Hamm in *Fin de partie* (*Endgame*, play, 1957); people with speech defects from Moses to Melville's Billy Budd (novella, 1891) to the tongueless Ellen Jamesians in *The World According to Garp* (1978). Maimed figures would include grotesques from Caliban and Hugo's Quasimodo to John Irving's characters in *Garp*, the shinless man who walks on his hands and the one-eyed, one-armed painter who marries a transexual; they would include Kafka's Gregor Samsa in "Die Verwandlung" ("Metamorphosis", story, 1915)—certainly being changed into an insect is physically debilitating, even before Gregor injures his side and legs— Boris Vian's Schmürz (*Les bâtisseurs d'empire* [*The Empire Builders*, play, 1959] and Edward Albee's emotionally crippled *American Dream* (play, 1960). And if we include the socially and economically crippled characters of Hugo's novel *Les misérables* (1862) or most of Dickens' novels, if we include the mentally crippled, what literary works could we exclude, other than Eleanor Porter's novel *Pollyanna* (1913) and some Disney fables? What literary work of any darkness does not have someone deformed by pain, want, or suffering? The extreme broadness of this category precludes any definitive statement but does allow for a number of suggestions.

There have been inspirational accounts of the lives of handicapped individuals who have not only coped but surmounted their physical difficulties, fictional ones such as the title character of *Porgy* (novel, 1925) by DuBose Heyward or club-footed Adam Rosenzweig in *Wilderness* (novel, 1961) by Robert Penn Warren; autobiographies such as Helen Keller's *The Story of My Life* (1902) and *The World I Live In* (1908); and biographies such as E. G. Valens' *The Other Side of the Mountain* (1975).

Often, particularly in those literary eras when symbolism was not frequently used or in many minor works, crippling is a plot device for recognition—a larger, more visible scar, such as Black Dog's missing fingers in Stevenson's novel *Treasure Island* (1883). Sometimes it would seem to be a required part of an exotic background, especially in pirate lore: the missing limbs of Capt. Hook in Barrie's *Peter Pan* (play, 1904) and Long John Silver. It is a necessary and accurate part of all postwar literature from lame Rafe Damport in Thomas Dekker's *The Shoemaker's Holiday* (play, 1600), the disabled soldiers of Oliver Goldsmith's "On the Distresses of the Poor" (1760), to the myriad cripples found in postwar European literature, such as the lame and legless in Wolfgang Borchert's *Draussen vor der Tür* (play, 1947) or Heinrich Böll's *Wanderer, kommst du nach Spa* . . . (*Traveller, If You Come to Spa*, (stories, 1950). Frequently, however, authors purposely use cripples as an objective correlative for a land deformed by war. The lame and impotent medieval Fisher King of Chrétien de Troyes' *Li contes del Graal* (*The Story of the Grail*, romance, c. 1190) is the primary example of someone whose crippled state reflects on the land he inhabits, and his presence is felt, to cite just post-World War I examples, in

T.S. Eliot's poem *The Waste Land* (1922), in impotent Jake Barnes of Ernest Hemingway's novel *The Sun Also Rises* (1926), and impotent, wheel-chair-ridden Clifford Chatterley of D. H. Lawrence's novel *Lady Chatterley's Lover* (1928), among others.

Beyond this obvious relationship between wasteful and destructive war and those left behind broken in body, there are other widely varied meanings. Still on the literal level, a wound may be a punishment, a sacrifice, or both. Loss of an eye or a limb was, and still is, a Middle Eastern punishment, and in Shakespeare's play *King Lear* (1606), for example, Cornwall blinds Gloucester as punishment. Zeus compensates Tiresias with second sight, the gift of prophecy, when Hera deprives him of his vision; Odin sacrifices one of his eyes for a drink from the Well of Wisdom and, to gain the knowledge of Runes, he consents to endure hanging nine days from a tree, as Jesus endured the agony of the cross for the sins of mankind.

Literal cripples are also the product of mechanization. In John Steinbeck's novel *Of Mice and Men* (1937), for example, Candy loses a hand to a farm machine. As the century progressed and mechanization became increasingly intrusive, authors suggested through numerous prostheses the extent to which people became machines themselves: in Friedrich Dürrenmatt's *Der Besuch der alten Dame* (*The Visit,* play, 1956), Claire Zachanassian loses a left leg in an automobile accident and replaces it with an artificial one, a right hand in an airplane crash and replaces it with ivory; in Thomas Pynchon's novel *V* (1963), V, at the time of her death, is composed of a glass eye with a clock-shaped iris, gold-slippered artificial feet, false teeth, and a sapphire sewn into her navel.

The least literal, most symbolic, cripples are those whose wounds are a sign of divinity: sacred cripples. Most of these are lame. Early sacred kings, participants in fertility marriages, and symbolic rulers of lands whose fertility depended on theirs, were marked by wounds that caused lameness or dressed or acted to mimic limping. Thus, among early mythic heroes, Oedipus has pierced ankles, Odysseus has his boar-scarred thigh, Anchises mates with Aphrodite and is lamed by lightning, their son Aeneas suffers a broken hip in the epic poem *Ilias* (*Iliad*, c. 8th century B.C.), Achilles is shot in his vulnerable heel by Philoctetes, who is bitten in his heel by a serpent, Jason comes hobbling into Iolcos wearing only one sandal—and Dionysus, whose name means lame god, was born from Zeus's thigh. In wrestling with an angel, Jacob—the eponymous father of Israel—has his thigh dislocated, making it awkward or impossible for him to touch his heel to the ground (Gen. 32:25–32), an ironic situation for one whose name means "to catch by the heel." (Sir J. G. Frazer, in *The Golden Bough* (essay, 1890–1915) records many examples of actual practices in which a sacred heel was protected from touching the ground.) Modern authors who are students of the Bible and classical literature have embodied this sense—crippling as a sign of fertility—in some of their characters: D. H. Lawrence, *The Man Who Died* (novel, 1929); Tennessee Williams, *Cat on a Hot Tin Roof* (play, 1955); Bernard Malamud, *The Assistant* (novel, 1957); Saul Bellow, *Henderson the Rain King* (novel, 1959). A further category of quasi-divine cripples would be those literary works in which the devil appears in human disguise; since the devil of folk-lore is cloven-hoofed, in human form he sometimes limps: for example, Mephisto in Goethe's play *Faust* (1808).

See also: Dwarf, Fool, Lameness.

Selected Bibliography

Hays, Peter L. *The Limping Hero*. New York: New York University Press, 1971.

PETER L. HAYS

D
//

DAEMON

The *Oxford English Dictionary* defines "daemon" as a "supernatural being or force of a nature intermediate between the divine or mortal." Although a simplistic view would distinguish between demons and angels as malevolent and beneficient beings, respectively, the daemon can bode ill or well, depending on one's intimacy with supernatural power. Morally ambiguous outside an orthodox Christian context, the daemonic has associations with force, uncanniness, a paradoxical melting of awe and fear. Rather than having exclusively evil coloration, the daemonic can provoke a more positive emotional response. An occult source of power, the daemon can instill sensations of mystery, fascination, energy, or vehemence; in its ancient context, it was often positive and active, rather than diabolical, in its implications. Ancient daemons populated a vast, invisible world; they were worshiped, for example, as potent spirits animating the four elements of earth, air, fire, and water. The classical daemon has been revived in almost every subsequent literary epoch, most extensively by the Romantics of the early nineteenth century.

Classical Background

Belief in beings or forces midway between the divine and mortal permeated ancient culture. According to popular belief, misfortune did not result merely from physical disaster but from daemonic interference that might draw victims into error. Furthermore, the experience of ill fortune might provoke a desire for divine or supernatural justice, such judgments often meted out by daemons. Daemons thus acted as intermediaries between gods and men in their distribution of fate or destiny.

In addition to reflecting popular attitudes, the daemonic received philosophical sanction, most notably in the Platonic dialogues. In the *Symposion* (*Symposium*, dialogue, c. 384 B.C.), for instance, Socrates claims that everything daemonic exists midway between the divine and mortal, the separation into discrete states evolving from a condition of primal unity. Plato views the creation of the universe in daemonic terms: in the *Timaios* (*Timaeus*, dialogue, 4th century B.C.), the Demiourgos creates the universe and lesser gods, then turns over the task of creating mortals to subsidiary beings or daemons. Mortals, in a sense, complete the universe and carry in their souls a remnant of the immortal principle. They remain inferior, however, to mid-world creatures or daemons. Plato's cosmology stands at the beginning of a tradition in which the division of the universe among daemons corresponds to the distribution of the earth into seats of power for various gods. Daemons, in short, compartmentalize function. The *Timaeus* is more notable for its presentation of the daemon as a lofty guardian, a tutelary spirit allied with pure reason. When subsequent writers allude to Socrates being moved by his daemon, they usually refer to this notion of spiritual guidance or higher reason. Far from being assigned an evil role, Socrates' daemon is an inner voice of conscience or moral control. The positive attributes of the daemon receive ampler expression in the *Symposium* in which Diotima says of Eros: "He is a great spirit or Daimon." Love is thus seen as an intermediary force between god and man.

Of somewhat lesser scope but still of significant influence, earlier discussions in the writings of the pre-Socratics provide alternative characterizations of daemonology. Heraclitus' oft-quoted maxim that man's character is his daemon establishes an identification between a person's individuality and his destiny. Empedocles provides a more ambivalent statement, indicating that man's initial possession by a transmigratory daemon contrasted with his more ordinary, fallen condition. Once as whole and complete as a perfect sphere, the human self faces troubling division and harrowing recriminations. The Empedoclean tradition presents the daemon, at one time the repository of man's divine spark, as the carrier of guilt and self-doubt.

Aeschylus' plays reflect a world permeated by belief in daemons. According to the messenger in the *Persai* (*The Persians,* 472 B.C.), Xerxes is tempted by an "alastor" or evil daemon. In the *Agamemnōn* (458 B.C.), characters see only a daemonic world plagued by malignant forces, while the dramatist sees events as the inevitable working out of moral law. Greek playwrights often develop a complex dramatic irony, also exploited by later writers, in which what appears to be the action of fiendish forces turns out to be the inexorable meting out of cosmic justice.

Although characters in the epic *Odysseia* (*Odyssey,* c. 8th century B.C.) ascribe events to daemonic agency, Homer places little serious emphasis on the subject. Hesiod (8th century B.C.) identifies daemons with souls of those who lived in the Golden Age and thereby sees them as invisible guardians of mankind. Both Aeschylus (*The Persians*) and Euripides *Alkēstis (Alcestis,* play, 438 B.C.) refer to the souls of the dead as daemons. Sometimes acquiring a role in prophecy, daemons highlight future events, as in the *Rhēsos* (*Rhesus,* play, c. 455 B.C.) attributed to Euripides, in which the Muse suggests that the title character shall find concealed rest in a cave as a man-demon. Projected as agents of vengeance or anger, daemons could bring punishment to an entire family (Aeschylus, *Agamemnon*) or give vent to *atē* or indignation (Euripides, *Mēdeia* [*Medea,* play, 431 B.C.]). Pindar, in the *Pythia* 10 (*Pythian Odes* 498 B.C.), gives memorable expression to the notion of the guardian spirit when he says: "The mighty purpose of Zeus directs the daemon of those he loves."

E.R. Dodds provides a helpful recapitulation by discerning three types of daemons in the literature of antiquity. Conforming to widely held superstition, they often function as tempters of mankind. Secondly, they serve to translate abstract concepts into situations more understandable in human terms. For example, the concept of evil can easily be made concrete by portraying malicious spirits. Such a facile translation of the abstract into the concrete can often receive subtle artistic treatment as when Euripides' daemons come to represent psychological doubts or pangs of conscience. Finally, daemons can be attached to individuals, that is, they can become part of a person's destiny. The Heraclitean connection of individuality and daemonic destiny was anticipated by the elegist Theognis (fl.544–541 B.C.) when he lamented that more in life depended on one's daemon that one's character. In all three manifestations, nevertheless, ancient writers could use the daemon to examine the vicissitudes of human fate.

Postclassical Manifestations

Under the aegis of Christianity, the emanations of ancient theogonies reappear in ways that account for God's relationships to his angels and mankind. The daemon, nevertheless, continued to have a significant, if muted, role. In Dante's epic poem *La divina commedia* (*The Divine Comedy,* c. 1320), daemons fulfill the somewhat stereotyped role of souls of the dead. In *Purgatorio* (*Purgatory*) and *Paradiso* (*Paradise*), however, intermediary powers inhabit the spiritual world above the Mount of Purgatory; in more general terms, conflict between angelic and diabolical agencies in *The Divine Comedy* becomes a contest between good and bad daemonic influence.

During the Renaissance, the widespread belief in ghosts, spirits, and magic suggested that behind the sensible world lay suprasensible essences that manipulated the materials of the physical world. Daemons were often seen as spirits unattached, even by historical circumstances, to bodies moved by divine agency. Even those writers who explicitly rejected daemonology grudgingly acknowledged its intellectual importance. Sir Francis Bacon, in *The Advancement of Learning* (treatise, 1605), claims that a knowledge of daemons is "no small part of spiritual wisdom." Similarly, Robert Burton, marking "A Digression of Spirits" in *The Anatomy of Melancholy* (essay, 1621), finds daemonology an important part of human learning.

Elizabethan drama was informed by pneumatology, most spectacularly in Christopher Marlowe's *Doctor Faustus* (1604) and Thomas Kyd's *The Spanish Tragedy* (c. 1585), the former influenced by the daemonological work, *Das Faustbuch* (*The Faust Book*, 1587). Whether one interprets the witches in Shakespeare's *Macbeth* (1605–1606) as daemons or symbols of subjective evil, his plays display an abundance of animistic material in their treatments of ghosts and magic. The daemon of Renaissance drama in particular was preserved in so-called witch plays and satire. Daemonic elements appear in *The Birth of Merlin* (1662) by William Rowley, *The Virgin Martyr* (1622) by Thomas Dekker and Philip Massinger, and *The Devil's Charter* by Barnabe Barnes (1607). For the most part, Renaissance authors clearly distinguished among supernatural agents as either blessed or damned. A notable exception to these orthodox restrictions was George Chapman's play *Bussy d'Ambois* (1607), its famous conjuring scene presenting Behemoth, a daemonic name for "a good aerial spirit." A related work in Continental drama is Pedro Calderón's *El mágico prodigioso* (*The Wonderful Magician,* play, 1637), in which a daemon forges the hero's destruction, challenged by the good daemon love in the guise of a virtuous woman.

To the extent that Neoplatonism flourished in the sixteenth and seventeenth centuries, the morally ambiguous character of the daemon could not be expunged by orthodox strictures. Renaissance writers often portray love as a mysterious intermediary force between god and man. The atmospheric locale of "faerie land" evoked by Edmund Spenser (*The Faerie Queene,* epic poem, 1590–1596) and others presents knights and ladies as inhabitants of a spirit world performing fated actions. Milton's Satan (*Paradise Lost,* epic poem, 1667) is clearly an evil figure, but his daunting character suggests a power that cannot be circumscribed by purely moral categories. Even the pious John Bunyan's daemons (*Grace Abounding,* spiritual autobiography, 1666) suggest a fiery force, a sense of being carried away as if in a whirlwind.

Although the daemon suggests an uncanny, volatile energy, this force, in the literary domain, came to be compartmentalized, constricted, or limited in function. Many sublime poems of the eighteenth century incorporate allegorical agents or daemons, often called "engines" or "machines," each serving a particular purpose in the grand scheme. Contributing energy in a network of sublime or epic machinery, daemons reflect the division of the world into separate areas of control. For example, James Thomson (*The Castle of Indolence,* poem, 1748) personifies indolence as "the smooth demon," wizard of "delicious harms." William Collins, in his odes ("Ode to Fear," 1747), directly addresses abstract qualities as if endowed with daemonic power. Chaotic and nightmarish, Alexander Pope's *The Dunciad* (mock-epic, 1728–1743) transforms epic machinery into a farrago of daemonic confusion. The dangers and misfortunes of Daniel Defoe's *Robinson Crusoe* (novel, 1719) sensitize the title character to the invisible world; while his visionary fantasies alert him to God's providence, his privations suggest a variety of daemonic possession.

Romantic Rediscovery of the Daemon

Romantic exaltation of terror over composure and preference for uncanny subjects over tidy, accepted ones encouraged a fascination with the daemonic.

Rejecting the mechanistic world view widely adhered to during the Age of Reason, romanticism held that nature was organic and changeable. For a "new" mythology that would support an organic vision of the world, many romantic authors turned to Platonism with its array of supernatural machinery. Daemons of Platonic lore could be good, bad, or indifferent, and their capricious variety conformed to a vision of nature in a constant state of flux and change.

Committed to daemonology for other reasons than amateur dabbling in occult lore, the Romantics were fascinated by the concept of genius as a kind of daemonic urge. If Socrates were guided by a personal daemon (as Percy Bysshe Shelley notes in journals), his example showed that a supernatural force held sway over human understanding.

Continental works manifest a vital spirit world pervaded by sentience and energy, with Baron de La Motte Fouqué's *Undine* (tale, 1811) and Christoph Martin Wieland's *Oberon* (poetic romance, 1780) asserting a wide influence outside their countries of origin. Informed by ancient religion, Wieland's *Peregrinus Proteus* (*The Adventures of Peregrine Proteus*, novel, 1791), available in an English translation by John Horne Tooke, presents man suspended between heaven and earth, yet yearning for a mystic vision of "eudaemony." Goethe provides both a theoretical and an artistic rendering of the daemon: his *Dichtung und Wahrheit* (*Poetry and Truth*, autobiography, 1811–1832) follows an ancient tradition by defining the "Dämon" as a riddling power, a fearful energy residing in selected individuals. This amoral power receives full artistic expression in *Faust* (play, 1808), in which spirits of love and beauty reside in higher realms while Mephistopheles functions as a daemonic tempter. Goethe also follows an Empedoclean tradition in which the inner force of the daemon challenges the moral order, gearing an individual for immolation rather than salvation.

Absorbing material from Plato as well as from their Continental forebears, British Romantics ardently reinstated the daemon to a place in the literary pantheon. Sir Walter Scott, in his *Letters on Demonology and Witchcraft* (prose, 1830), acknowledges that the pagan deities possessed daemonic power, though he seems more interested in quirky case studies and folkloric sources. Seriously immersed in the writings of Plato and also influenced by Calderón, Shelley views daemons, not as figures of devilish imprint, but as guardians of mankind. In *Prometheus Unbound* (lyrical drama, 1820), daemons act as agents of destiny, possessing oracular charge of divine will. When Prometheus, addressing Jupiter in the opening speech of the play, refers to gods and spirits, he also speaks to Asia, a daemon of love and beauty borrowed from Plato's *Symposium*. In *Queen Mab* (poem, 1821), entitled *The Daemon of the World* in its abridged form, Shelley's revolutionary spirit is a kind of world soul permeating the entire universe. Shelley here harks back to the Platonic doctrine that the soul, in its pre-existent state, was immaterial. A similar mixture of daemonology and Platonism is found in "Adonais" (poem, 1821) in which Urania, a figure of love, appears in aerial form. *Alastor* (poem, 1816) also records the human pursuit of love, but the hero is himself pursued by an evil genius or *cacodaemon*. "Epipsychidion'' (poem, 1821) humanizes the daemon as a woman whose love leads the poet to Intellectual Beauty. Although his reliance on Plato freed Shelley from a moralistic treatment of the spirit world, his lyrics and *Prometheus Unbound* mark a continuing battle between good daemons impelling man to heights of love and bad daemons driving man to sensuality and selfishness.

No less impressed than Shelley by Platonic lore, John Keats included daemonology in a gallery of his works: ''Sleep and Poetry'' (poem, 1816), *Endymion* (poem, 1818), ''The Eve of St. Agnes'' (poem, 1820), *Lamia* (poem, 1820), and ''The Poet'' (poem, 1816). In *Endymion,* what appears to be an ideal quest—the hero's love for Cynthia—becomes a frenzy that overwhelms him. Showing the ambivalence of daemonic experience, Endymion's possession disguises itself as heavenly aspiration. A love amounting to possession is also evident in ''La Belle Dame sans Merci'' (poem, 1820) and *Lamia*, the former presenting a daemonic, wild-eyed fairy child, the latter exposing its hero to an amour that makes human affection seem tame. Referring in ''Ode on Indolence'' (poem, 1818) to ''my demon poesy,'' Keats never calls attention to the term's non-Christian meanings. Nevertheless, here and in ''The Poet'' Keats presents poetry as a means by which to surmount the barriers to transcendence. For Keats, poetic inspiration, a visionary coalescence of terror and beauty, approaches daemonic possession.

Other British Romantics also display an interest in ancient daemonology. William Blake's sense of the inadequacy of a ''god without thunder'' led him to explore the mixture of dread and fascination in religious experience, often making it difficult to discern the divine from the daemonic. Coleridge's comment that ''opium was the avenging demon of [his] life'' places him in an Empedoclean line, tyrannized by what he regarded as a vengeful spirit. His poems ''Kubla Khan'' (1816), ''Christabel'' (1816), and ''The Rime of the Ancient Mariner'' (1798) clearly contain daemonic implications. The title character of Lord Byron's *Manfred* (dramatic poem, 1817) is not intrinsically evil; rather, he becomes a spirit beyond human limitation and solace, confirming Goethe's insight that ''all the combined forces of convention are helpless'' against individuals of daemonic proclivities. Thomas De Quincey presents perhaps a fusion of the affirmative and darker traditions of the daemon in ''Levana and Our Ladies of Sorrow'' (prose fantasy, in *Suspiria de Profundis,* 1845). The three sisters bring tears, sighs, and darkness as part of love's curse at the same time that they unfold the possibilities of blessed vision.

In uncovering the daemonic implications of the prose and poetry of the major English Romantics, the impact of the Gothic novel should not be underestimated. To the extent that Gothic fiction encouraged incursions into the nonrational areas scorned by the Enlightenment, the literature of terror provided a fair field for the daemonic. An abundance of Gothic properties—moving statues, genii, talismans, doubles—enhanced an atmosphere of dreadful anxiety, the sense of sinister fate being particularly strong in Horace Walpole's *The Castle of Otranto* (novel, 1764).

Transferred to the American scene, the Gothic tradition afforded ample opportunities for appearance of daemons. Sometimes labeled a facile exploiter of
lurid Gothic claptrap, Edgar Allan Poe often gives positive expression to the
daemonic. His "Al Aaraaf" (poem, 1829) presents daemonic messengers along
the lines of those in Shelley's poem *Queen Mab* (1813). Similar agents inhabit
his fictional fantasy "The Power of Words" (1845), and his entire tale "Silence—A Fable" (1839) is recounted by a figure referred to only as "the Demon." Other works by Poe—his poems "Alone" (c. 1829), "The Raven"
(1845), and "Ulalume" (1847) and his tales "MS. Found in a Bottle" (1833)
and "The Black Cat" (1843)—provide darker treatments of daemonic obsession
accompanied by a sinister atmosphere of fate or destiny.

Although Ralph Waldo Emerson spoke for most Americans in calling daemonology "a midsummer madness," writers like Poe and Herman Melville
found it a useful tool in exploring moral and psychological ambiguities. Fedallah,
the Parsee daemon in *Moby-Dick* (novel, 1851), appears with his dusky companions as if "fresh formed out of air." He acts as an apostle of darkness to
assist Ahab, whose Byronic grandeur suggests his assumption of a higher order
of experience. Melville, who had read the section in Goethe's autobiography on
"The Daemonic," portrays Ahab as a figure whose daemonic proclivities separate him from human aid and comfort.

Although the daemon was occasionally used as more than a device during the
Victorian period—Thomas Carlyle refers to Teufelsdröckh as a man of "angelic-
diabolical" nature in *Sartor Resartus* (philosophical satire, 1833–1834)—the
romantic era marked the most extensive revival of its ancient meanings. By
making poets their key figures, as in *Alastor* and "The Poet," Shelley and Keats
show the essential fascination that the Romantics found in daemonic experience.
The Greek notion of daemonology became particularly attractive to the Romantics
because of its associations with skill or knowledge. In the artist-centered world
of romantic poetry, the poet could be literally or metaphorically possessed. He
could soar to discover the secrets of the universe as in Keats' "The Poet," or
descend into slavery to passion, as in Shelley's *Alastor*. Whether for Keats'
persona or Shelley's hero, the daemon serves to symbolize the adventurous poetic
imagination. To the mythic and Platonic lore of the ancients, the Romantics
added unique symbolic effects to describe a world potentially charged with poetic
inspiration. This portrayal of the possessed artist probably accounts for the
survival of the daemon among the so-called decadent writers. Oscar Wilde's
fairy tales and stories reflect a daemonic universe, and Walter Pater was similarly
fascinated by the strange beauty of daemonic experience.

Modern Daemons

As one traces the literary progency of the daemon to refinements in the modern
period, one notes widely disparate significances for philosophers and thinkers.
In *Die Geburt der Tragödie* (*The Birth of Tragedy*, philosophy, 1872), Friedrich
Nietzsche cites Socrates' interest in writing poetry in prison as an expression of

his poetic daemon; he thereby finds an exemplar in his developing theory of exceptional human beings. A more orthodox religious thinker, Paul Tillich, distinguishes between the satanic as a force of utter destructiveness and the daemonic as a principle that puts a different order on human experience. Both elevating and terrifying, neither benevolent nor malevolent but often beneficent, the daemon, in its diverse manifestations, presents all manner of enigmatic dualities and rich ambiguities.

William Butler Yeats, perhaps the foremost purveyor of the daemon in modern literature, propounded in *A Vision* (prose, 1925) a mythology that accounted for the development of exceptional character. He applied the term daemons to those illustrious figures who played determining roles in human history. In *Per amica silentia lunae* (essays, 1918) Yeats mentions the daemon as part of his personal quest for identity, his attempt to resolve the antinomies of his own nature. His poetic sequence, "Meditations in Time of Civil War" (1923), harks back to Plato in imagining the beginning of the universe as in a "daemonic rage."

Less systematic than Yeats in their exploitation of the daemon, other writers have used it according to personal predilection. Linking the daemon to personal character as did Heraclitus, John Crowe Ransom (*God Without Thunder,* essays, 1930), acknowledges that in the ancient past, "each daemon stood for the secret, or ineffable, or transcendent individuality of some individual and private person." Some of his poems wittily comment on modern man's separation from a world imbued with "the ghostly retinue" of ancient myth and belief. Modern novels sometimes attempt to resurrect this atmosphere, as do Mary Renault's *The King Must Die* (1958) and C. S. Lewis's *Till We Have Faces* (1956). Franz Kafka's "Kuriere" ("Couriers," 1935) represents an ironic parable of daemons as divine messengers.

Ransom's *God Without Thunder* laments the disappearance of the ominous from modern life. In the face of the ancients' response to a vital, sentient natural world, some modern authors deride the overtaking of that old vision by a dry, rational sterility, as does John Ciardi in "Daemons" (poem, 1966). Rudolf Otto's *Das Heilige* (*The Idea of the Holy,* philosophy, 1917), noting the complementarity of the holy and daemonic, signifies a similar desire to restore a sense of the numinous. Whether one subscribes to the psychological theory that daemonology reflects the release of pent-up frustrations or to the alternative view that it results from social upheavals, the human appetite for the numinous is not easily quenched. J.V. Cunningham's epigrammatic "To My Daimon" (poem, 1947) serves as a fitting tribute to those mysterious recesses of the human psyche that heighten man's quest for self-knowledge amid the ambiguities of modern life.

See also: Demonic Music, Demonic Musician and the Soulbird, Descent into Hell, Evil, Incubus and Succubus, Pact with the Devil, Shadow.

Selected Bibliography

Dodds, E.R. *The Greeks and the Irrational.* 1951. Berkeley: University of California Press, 1968.

Fletcher, Angus. *Allegory: The Theory of a Symbolic Mode*. 1964. Ithaca, N.Y.: Cornell University Press, 1984.

Patterson, Charles I. *The Daemonic in the Poetry of John Keats*. Urbana: University of Illinois Press, 1970.

Stock, R. D. *The Holy and the Daemonic from Sir Thomas Browne to William Blake*. Princeton, N.J.: Princeton University Press. 1982.

KENT LJUNGQUIST

DANCE

The dance falls into three indistinct categories, all of which figure in literature: ritual, social dance, and performance. One might expect the three major genres— drama, the epic/novel, and the lyric, respectively—to correlate with the principal kinds of dance. The Japanese Nō drama, for example, originated partly in Shinto ritual dance; the social dance provided the novel with a useful device for developing romantic relations in social contexts; and the solitary dance performer figures in late-nineteenth-century poetry as an important metaphor for the aesthetic act. There are many significant exceptions, however, to a global pairing of ritual and drama, social dance and the novel, and performance and the lyric. Thus the medieval lyric, which is far less concerned with the subjective voice than with expressions of communal experience, develops the social dance into a metaphor for the lyric as encounter. Later poets, such as Rimbaud in the prose poem *Une saison en enfer* (*A Season in Hell*, 1873), have sought the vitality of ritual dance for the poetic voice. Similarly, novelists have incorporated ritual dance for its mythic connotations and communal bonding (one thinks of Kate's dance with the Quetzalcoatl in D. H. Lawrence's *The Plumed Serpent*, 1926) and individual dance performance as a moment of radically subjective experience (Lawrence's *Women in Love*, 1920, when Gudrun dances before the bulls). Dramatists have frequently imbedded a dance performance into a play's significance (Ibsen's *Et dukkehjem* [*A Doll's House*, 1879], and Strindberg's *Dödsdansen* [*Dance of Death*, 1901], for example). And social dance has figured in the dramatic arts at times much as it has in the novel; at the most extreme, in a play such as Schnitzler's *Reigen* (*Merry-Go-Round*, 1900), the danced encounter may inform the entire work as a structural principle.

Suzanne K. Langer, in *Feeling and Form* (1953), describes two aspects of dance that are particularly relevant to its uses in literature. She argues that all dance generates a "virtual realm," a kind of magic circle in which a virtual world is inscribed by the dance movements. Secondly, she notes that all dance is gesture, but that its only function is to be expressive. The dancer as an individual psyche (or speaking subject) is of no importance; only the movements are in force, and they generate a metaphorical or virtual being or group of beings in their own imaginative space. Dance performance clearly embodies the qualities

Langer discusses; the performance presumes an observer as well as a participant, with the two worlds (actual and virtual) in tension. The ritual dance, by contrast, involves participants whose ecstasy *(ec-stasis,* being outside of themselves) is a part of the ritual's power. Social dance relies on a virtual realm not for its power but for its freedom. Participants enact a courtship for which they are not responsible—unless they take it beyond the dance.

Because literary works, too, are concerned with the process of creating virtual beings and worlds, they may draw on dance as a metaphor for that process. Writers exploit the difference in medium between word and gesture in a wide variety of ways. What follows cannot presume to completeness, since the dance is ubiquitous in literature; it is meant to describe exemplary cases and to provide a scant historical framework. Most egregiously missing is any discussion of the dance in oral and in non-Western literature, with the exception of Indian literature, where the dance is extremely important.

Greek Antiquity

The first point to make about the place of dance in ancient Greek literature is that certain literary forms are unthinkable without it. Much of what we regard as lyric was actually composed to be sung by choruses of unprofessional men, boys, or maidens dancing either in procession or choreographed patterns to the accompaniment of flute or lyre, in certain instances even using interpretive hand gestures to enhance the words. Alcman (fl. 654–611 B.C.), Simonides (c. 556–468 B.C.), Pindar (518–438 B.C.), Bacchylides (5th century B.C.) and—in part—Sappho (c. 612–557 B.C.) were such choral poets (see H. W. Smyth, *The Greek Melic Poets,* 1900, for a complete discussion). Beyond this is the fact that drama—tragedy, comedy, and satyr-play—developed out of choral activity, and, throughout the fifth century B.C. at least, choral dance remained an integral part of dramatic structure (later it became mere interlude). Dance could be such a matrix for "literature" because along with song (from which it was inseparable) it had a large place in religious life, a much broader sphere for the ancients than for us, for it included all formal commemorations of civic or communal life. The ritual sense of the Greeks in the early period, at least (i.e., until the 3d century B.C.) was highly aesthetic and gave great scope to the arts. Poets, who were at the same time musicians and choreographers, contributed importantly to religious festivity; it was their responsibility therefore to address central collective concerns, to articulate cultural ideals (the good, the wise, the beautiful), to resolve underlying tensions, in short to define the community's place in the cosmos.

As a theme in Greek literature dance has three principle symbolic functions: the celebratory, the ecstatic, and the spectacular. Under "celebratory" we include religious dance-observances, combining what we now would call ritual and social dance; such observances express a sense of harmony in man's relation to the gods—thus even funeral dances accompanied by dirge confirm a sense of well-being, of appropriate modes for dealing with the crises of life. We also include festive dancing (such as the wedding dance simulated by Odysseus in Homer's epic poem *Odysseia* [*Odyssey,* c. 8th century B.C.] and the revels that celebrated the victory of a local family in the games). The famous description of a harvest dance depicted on Achilles' shield (*Illias* [*Iliad,* epic poem, 8th century B.C.]) portrays the happiness and beauty of a world at peace (a stark contrast to the main activity of the poem). It is by such joyful expressions of harmonious prosperity that human life approximates the divine. Dance and song especially exemplify the freedom from care that is the chief attraction of the Greek divinity, as in the lovely description of Apollo leading the gods in dance in the Homeric hymn *Eis Appollōna* (*To Apollo,* c. 7th century B.C.). In the poetic vision of Pindar the celebration that crowns athletic victory is a transfiguration of mundane existence into something ideal and immobile. Song and dance are the vehicle of the divine radiance that effects the transmutation. A cosmic perspective is reached in the *Pythia* (*Pythian Odes,* c. 470 B.C.) in which the heavenly lyre of Apollo and the Muses is seen as the archetypal source of music, signaling the recitations of bards and the accompaniments of the dances on earth. Much later, after Plato's notion of music of the spheres had become a commonplace (*Politeia* [*The Republic,* dialogue, c. 380 B.C.]), writers like Lucian would speak of the motions of the planets as a cosmic dance, and therefore the archetype of all terrestrial harmony (Lucian, *Peri orchēseōs* [*On Dance,* dialogue, 2d century]).

The ecstatic function is best seen in Euripides' *Bakchai* (*The Bacchants,* c. 405 B.C.). One of the central concerns of tragedy generally is the tension between the ordered sphere of civilized values and the irrational forces of a wilderness whose locus is either beyond the city's periphery or at the base of human emotions. In the *Bacchants* Dionysus is the prime representative of an elemental life-force that demands recognition and reverence from the civilized order at the risk of annihilation otherwise. In general Greek literature expresses an integrative attitude toward the irrational when it is understood as a religious force, but its danger was never minimized. Plato, in fact, remained profoundly mistrustful of the irrational (he would not permit Bacchic dance in his ideal state), all the while acknowledging that philosophy itself was a kind of madness (*Symposion* [*Symposium,* dialogue, c. 384 B.C.]). After Plato intellectuals tended to neutralize the danger of an orgiastic cult by allegorization of its features. Ecstatic dance remained a poetic topos into late antiquity, with poets often striving for sensational effects. In fact Dionysiac poetry developed an interesting subgenre in the Dionysian epic culminating in the forty-eight books of Nonnus' *Dionysiaka* (*Story of Dionysus,* c. 5th century), which many classical readers have judged the last great extant poem of antiquity.

By the "spectacular" function is meant dance as exhibition. We see already in Homer that certain dancers were exhibited especially for their dexterity, which was often a form of acrobatics (e.g., *Odyssey* 8.370 ff.). In classical times (490–322 B.C.) and thereafter "professional" dancers (slaves or courtesans) performed for symposiac entertainment. Xenophon's *Symposion* (*Symposium,* fiction, 4th century B.C.) contains long passages describing the performances of a troupe of two girls and a boy, which included tumbling within a circle of upturned swords and an erotic mime of the love of Dionysus and Ariadne. The dichotomy that developed in the attitude to such displays can easily be understood: on the one hand marvel at physical skill, on the other disgust for the lurid taste they often indulged. Gradually such dance became emblematic of moral degeneracy. In Athenaeus' encyclopedic *Deipnosophistai* (*Sophists at the Dinner Table*, c. 192), book 14, we find a representative collection of passages deploring the deterioration of the ideal of grace and modesty in movement.

Roman Antiquity

Rome appears never to have had the aesthetic sense of dance in ritual celebration that was natural to the Greeks. Consequently, although dance had a certain place in ritual (e.g., some of our earliest scraps of Latin verse are ritual invocations made by the *Salii* or dancing priests), it was rather in the more austere form of processional that it stood as public expression of the community's status vis-à-vis the gods. Certain choral verse forms were still cultivated, but apparently on a purely literary basis (e.g., the two hymeneals of Catullus, c. 84–54 B.C.). Horace's *Carmen saeculare* (*Century Hymn*, 17 B.C.) commissioned by Augustus, is the notable exception, sung by two choruses (boys and girls) before the Palatine temple of Apollo to celebrate the inauguration of a new era under Augustus. Roman drama, though containing dance, was never a communal expression (actors and dancers were professional, as in postclassical Greece, whence Rome adopted drama in the late 3d century B.C.), and tragedy, at least, by Seneca's time (c. 5 B.C. -A.D. 65) was predominantly a literary exercise.

In general, dance functions in Roman literature as it does in Greek, though there is now the added note (proper to "sentimental" literature, in Schiller's sense) of nostalgia. We can see this in the pastoral genre (Bucolica), which, though borrowed from Hellenistic Greece, becomes a symbol of Rome's lost peasant innocence. Rural festivals are fondly recalled in other poetry too as the vestige of a pious Golden Age (e.g., Virgil's *Georgica* [*Georgics*, 29 B.C.] 2.458 ff. or Tibullus' elegiac poems [c. 27–20 B.C.] 2.1).

Horace best expresses the familiar Greek topos of the poet as spokesman of the Muse. It is his felt status as fellow lyrist in the chorus of poet-priests (*vates*) (see *Carmina* [*Odes*, c. 23 B.C.] 1.1 and 4.3) that confers on him the authority to speak—somewhat in the manner of Pindar, but with the infusion of moral philosophical systems such as Stoicism and Epicureanism—as the conscience of the community. The sphere of Horace's influence was probably rather limited in his own time, though through the ages he has remained paradigmatic for a balance of moral and aesthetic sense in an environment generally hostile to cultivated thought and taste. One indication of how remote dance as festive symbol was from dance as cultural phenomenon is the notorious remark of Cicero that "nobody dances unless he is drunk or unbalanced mentally, whether alone or in moderate and honorable society" (*Pro Murena*, oration, 63 B.C.).

The ecstatic aspect of dance is most profoundly treated in Catullus, poem no. 63, the strange portrait of Attis' (the archetypal devotee of the Phrygian mother-goddess Cybebe) self-castration in frenetic dance and its aftermath. Here the orgiastic dance is treated as a threshold to a sacral realm completely alien to normal life. The focus is on the human emotion of loss: Attis can never return home (across the sea), never know the naïve joys of family life, never return even to former sexual status (in the process of the poem "he" becomes "she"). The value of religious experience is left unexamined, however, which separates it from the Euripidean treatment in the *Bacchants*. In the *Metamorphoses* of Apuleius (*The Golden Ass*, novel, c. 150), Lucius, who has been turned into an ass by witchcraft, falls into the hands of a troupe of mendicant worshippers of this same Phrygian goddess, who are nothing but quacks and thieves. But this cynical portrayal serves only as a foil to the true religious initiation that caps the work.

Especially notable in the Roman treatment of dance in its spectacular aspect is its almost complete loss of prestige. The "Trimalchio's Feast" segment from Petronius' novel, *Satyricon* (A.D. 60), possibly a scathing lampoon of the Neronic court, provides a graphic illustration of the degradation of symposiac entertainment in an age when ostentatious wealth had brutalized the aesthetic sense. Moralists such as Seneca and the satirists Martial (c. A.D. 40–104) and Juvenal (c. A.D. 60–130) saw the popularity and (worse) high social rank of pantomimists (the movie stars of late antiquity) as one of the many signs of an absurd social order. Apuleius, in book 10 of the *Metamorphoses,* gives a detailed description of an elaborate masque of the Judgment of Paris on the occasion of a celebration of military triumph, which was to be capped by the execution of a caged woman criminal condemned to sexual intercourse with the story's ass while being devoured by a wild beast. However, the fact that this scene is placed immediately before the culminatory initiation into the mysteries of Isis, whereby the hero regains his human shape, seems to indicate Apuleius' understanding that even a sordid decadence is also a stage in the soul's discovery of its sublime station.

India

Indian drama, like the Greek, grew out of dance (though out of the formalized gesture-narrative of professionals rather than choral poetry in its communal context), and dance remained an intrinsic part of dramatic performance. In classical Sanskrit poetry, dance, always a performing art, expresses the elegance of court life, finding its prototype in the carefree pastime of Apsarases and Gandharvas (celestial dancing "nymphs" and their musician consorts), as in the *Mālavikāgnimitra* (*Mālavikā and Agnimitra*) of Kālidāsa (fl. 400), a drama in which the principal characters are an Apsaras and a legendary monarch. In the less elegant (though still Sanskrit), mythicized, sectarian corpus of Purānic literature (4th–11 century) we find dance used in two striking instances as "theological" symbol. First, in the Vishnu and Bhāgavata Purānas, Krishna's nocturnal round-dance (called *rāsalīlā*) with the wives of the cowherds of Vrindāvan is meant as a symbol of the soul's need to surrender fully to the intoxication of God's love (the illicitness of the adulterous state only serving to express the totality of surrender). Second is Śiva as Natarāja (Lord of Dancers) whose dance is fully cosmic; that is, he dances the world into existence, maintains it in equilibrious motion, then brings it to the frenzy of destruction (cf. Kūrma Purāna). Destruction, however, is understood mystically as the evaporation of the illusion that keeps the self from experience of its absolute status. This helps explain the paradox of devout love for a god who is of largely terrible aspect. Vernacular devotional poetry, going back to the Tamil collections of the Ālvārs and Nāyanārs (beginning as early as the 6th century) and still thriving, goes much farther than the Sanskrit in elaborating the meaning in emotional terms of these two potent symbols, the erotic round-dance and the cosmic dance in its triple aspect.

Medieval Treatment in Dance-Songs

Little is known about religious and liturgical dance-songs in the medieval period because they were generally frowned upon; records of censorship suggest that a good many once existed. Early wedding songs especially incorporate dance both actually and metaphorically; dance is a metaphor for both human union and divine harmony, the counterpart in movement to the celestial music of the spheres, which was so important in medieval thought and iconography. Thus a Latin wedding-hymn from Spain, the *Tuba clarifica* (*A Fanfare of Trumpets*, 9th century), depicts dance as an earthly reflection of the divine harmony whose first manifestation is the Redemption. In general, however, during the medieval period ritual and spectacular dance forms separated from the social dance and receded in importance.

The medieval lyric functioned as entertainment and frequently accompanied dancing and other festivities, both secular and religious. Dance as a theme is thus closely allied with dance as an accompaniment to music in some lyrics. Examples are the dance-songs from the *Carmina Burana* (13th century), which provide some of the earliest secular lyrics and which take as themes courtship, pleasure, and celebration. Medieval dance-songs such as the carol, the rondeau, and the *estampie* often, but not invariably, refer to the dance that they accompany. One Provençal *estampie*, the "Kalenda maia" ("Mayday," 12th century), of which numerous versions exist, is a comic song cleverly incorporating dancelike rhythms. It celebrates at once the May-dance, the singer's own courtly love, and the foolishness of jealousy; and it figures in a dancelike scene in the Provençal narrative, *Flamenca* (c. 1250). Dance-songs commonly incorporate a chorus, soloists, and their movements, without necessarily developing the theme of the dance beyond a celebratory, enacted framework.

At once the classic and a unique expression of dance in the medieval lyric is Walther von der Vogelweide's "Nemt, Frouwe, disen Kranz" ("Take, Woman, This Wreath") (c. 1200). The speaker offers his wreath in the traditional gesture inviting a woman to dance. He then imagines finding the woman of his dearest fantasies and slips into a reverie in which he is with her in a *locus amoenus,* among the birds and the flowers. As a theme the dance here first establishes the public context of his search for a woman, then becomes a vehicle for his private desires, the means by which the fantasy world—a "virtual realm" of the imagination–unfolds. The poet moves via the dance from the evoked social setting of the dance to a pastoral one, and the poem draws its effect equally from both realms and the tension between them. The mimetic setting of the dance establishes one aspect of his ideal woman: her accessibility, both social and physical. Walther thus departs from the artificial distance of courtly love even as he draws on its vocabulary.

A successor of Walther, Neidhart von Reuenthal, wrote dance-songs, in some of which the dance figures thematically. Neidhart's earthier lyrics form a reaction to the polite dance-songs of the declining courtly mode. In one, "Sinc an guldîn Huon" ("Sing, Golden Hen," early 13th century), the speaker tries to woo by dance a simple young girl who gives her attentions to another; roughhousing interrupts the dance, and the speaker's rival, in his crude way, carries the day. The song incorporates dance as a means of courtship that is one step more refined than outright seduction, but the poet pokes as much fun at that refinement as he does at the characters' rougher ways. The poem's effectiveness as satire depends to some extent on the dance's ineffectiveness as seduction.

When Sebastian Brant, in 1494, published his satirical poem *Das Narrenschiff* (*Ship of Fools*), no trace of the courtier remained in his treatment of the dance. Brant claims the devil invented the dance, and much evil comes of it—but he teasingly stops short of describing exactly what evil. Dance, for him, is primarily a social, quasi-erotic pastime.

The Renaissance and Eighteenth Century

One medieval topos associated with the dance, that of the enactment of cosmic harmony in orderly movement, sustained its importance through the Renaissance and later. Sir John Davies' "Orchestra, or a Poeme on Dancing" (1596) depicts the cosmic order as one vast dance; it proposes that the first dance occurred at the origin of the world, when the four elements ceased their discord to move in measure (a classical topos). The poem then compares all events in the world to the forward and backward whirling steps of Fortune and enjoins the reader to imitate the stars in their dance, thereby becoming one with the world's order. Finally, the poem superimposes the order of the celestial dance on that of Elizabeth's court; the queen dances in the center, and her courtiers circle around her.

Davies' poem aptly summarizes the most important aspect of the dance in the Renaissance: as a theme invoking corresponding orderly systems, compressing ritual, social, and spectacular dance in one organized movement. A complementary function of the dance is to invoke and censure disorder, the Dionysian dance and all it leads to. It is in the English masques of the Elizabethan and Jacobean court that this contradictory nature of the dance most clearly appears.

The masque was to pay homage to royal authority as well as to amuse and instruct; and it led to general social dancing on the part of those present. Originally a spectacle with few literary pretensions (as in the Italian commedia dell'arte) the masque developed into an art form that fused music and dance thematically with the poetry accompanying them. The most literarily rich masques are by Ben Jonson, whose *Pleasure Reconcil'd to Vertue* (1618) exemplifies his synthesis of dance, poetry, and homage. In it the wild dance of the antimasque yields to the stately dancing of the masque, and Daedalus' song at the end weaves a complex metaphor out of the dance movement: "all actions of mankind / are but a Laborinth [*sic*]," he says, which the dances enact in such a way that "men may read each act you doo . . . " Dance, with its labyrinthine measures and steps, is the great reconciler of Pleasure and Virtue. Many other masques by Jonson, Carew, Campion, Nabbes, Shirley, and others incorporate and to varying degrees thematize dance.

Traces of the contemporary masque appear in Shakespeare, who thematizes dance throughout his opus, but especially in the comedies. Indeed, Shakespeare's comic resolution resembles (in the movements of his wit) and often includes a social dance, enacting a reconciliation of opposing tensions; and the absence of a dance may be as telling as its presence. *As You Like It* (c. 1599) and *Much Ado about Nothing* (c. 1598) both conclude with a celebratory dance in anticipation of nuptials. But *Love's Labour's Lost* (c. 1594), with its more somber conclusion, has no dance at the end; and part of the last act's somber quality is the ladies' continued refusal to dance with their wooers. The dance must be postponed till after the gentlemen have proved their mettle and the princess is out of mourning. The profound comic resolution must embrace an awareness of suffering and death. Nowhere is this clearer than in *The Tempest* (1611), where Prospero breaks off a celebratory masque just as the actors are concluding their dance. Their enacted harmony is premature, as Prospero remembers Caliban's plot to kill him. It vexes Prospero to terminate the dance for such a purpose, and he gloomily recalls it is an insubstantial pageant, "whose baseless fabric," like life itself, must fade—his most famous speech. And while the masque has been going on, Ariel has had Caliban's plotters dancing to a different tune, up to their ears in muck. They too are part of the pattern. The plays present life as an artificial dance of approach and retreat, of tenuously honored hierarchies, and of temporary harmonies.

In Italy and France, meanwhile, masquelike entertainments also developed around the court. Molière wrote *Les fâcheux* (*The Impertinents,* 1661), the first of twelve *comédies-ballets* that he was to produce for Louis XIV, all incorporating dance, poetry, and music. As in the English masque, the dance serves here to reinforce the social order and its hierarchies. In Molière's most famous *comédie-ballet, Le malade imaginaire* (*The Imaginary Invalid,* 1673), a dance interlude takes place between the acts, reminding the spectators that the play is an illusion (just as it is about illusion); and the ballet with which it concludes, during the invalid Argan's promotion to doctor, again recalls the illusory quality of social pretenses and behavior, even as it enacts in conventional terms the comic resolution of conflict.

It is Milton's *A Maske Presented at Ludlow Castle* (1634) that best illustrates the masque as a literary genre. The work uses dance as part of its festive as well as structural resolution. It involves a young lady, who, separated from her two brothers in a dark wood, encounters Comus, son of Bacchus and Circe. He tries to seduce her in the guise of offering a potion that would turn her into part animal, as it has others before her. The lady is saved, and the siblings return home for a celebration—dance and song. Dance here incarnates the translation of sensual pleasure into aesthetic artifice. It is a community celebration directly opposed to Bacchic wildness but in some sense too encompassing it. There remains in the play an unresolved tension between Comus' lusty love of life in all its manifestations and the lady's chastity, much-touted, but surrounded by wonderful sensuality right down to the nymph that saves her. The two forms of dance present in the work enact this tension.

After the hey-day of the masque, the dance recedes in importance as a theme. In English Restoration drama the dance often signifies the risqué, and, on the other hand, mastery of it is also a sign of good breeding. The topos of the dance instructor-turned-seducer brings together these two aspects; see, for example, William Wycherley's play, *The Gentleman Dancing-Master* (1672). Because the Puritans in England had frowned on dance and outlawed the masque, some Restoration works make dance the focus of satire. Thomas Shadwell's *The Volunteers* (play, 1692) satirizes the Puritans Major General Blunt and Colonel Hackwell, but it pokes even more fun at Sir Nicholas Dainty, who takes with him to the army "twelve rich Campaign suits, six Dancing suits, and twelve pair of Dancing shoes." Shadwell's play celebrates its comic resolution of tensions with a general dance.

Romanticism

Although the Romantics clearly invert the order of values, pursuing a Bacchic intensity rather than a patterned equilibrium in dance, it is most difficult to generalize about the dance in romantic works. Not even within the individual genres is there consistency. To move from Byron's "Waltz: an Apostrophic Hymn" (poem, 1821), a satirical spoof on the lusty pleasures of the waltz (Byron anticipated the satire in "English Reviewers and Scotch Bards," poem, 1810) to the wild, seething dances of life in Blake's visionary epics *Milton* (1804) and *The Four Zoas* (1797), is to encounter a radical change of tone. Underlying both is the sense of life-force exhibiting itself, barely contained, in vibrant movement. A similar sense informs the dance of the hours in Shelley's *Prometheus Unbound* (lyric drama, 1820), with the added dimension of music accompanying the dance as a metaphor for the linearity of time within life's plenitude. In Baudelaire's "Harmonie du soir" ("Evening Harmony," poem, 1857), the "valse mélancolique et langoureux vertige" ("melancholy waltz and languid vertigo") is a metaphor for the sounds and odors circling together in the evening air. The dance, a kind of unrestrained movement, signifies both the perceived phenomena and the state of mind to which they correspond, the melancholy languor informed by mingled perceptions and memories.

Baudelaire may be playing off the French Romantic topos of the morning after the dance; Hugo, in his famous poem "Fantômes" ("Phantoms," 1828) gives the topos its quintessential expression: "Quels tristes lendemains laisse le bal folâtre" ("What sadness does the wild ball leave to the morning after"). Instead of providing the resolution, the dance here provides the problem, the excess from which the poet finds he cannot derive a new equilibrium. Other poets who reworked the topos include Gautier in "Après le bal" ("After The Ball," 1834) and Sainte-Beuve in "A Alfred de Musset" (1828). The ball's inebriation and the subsequent melancholy—to the point of invoking death—are both necessary to the full romantic consciousness.

Writers of the romantic period often use the dance, especially the circle dance, to inscribe the domain of the fantastic. Perhaps the most famous example is the dance of the elf-king's daughters in Goethe's "Erlkönig" ("Elf-King," poem, 1782); other salient examples are Burns' dance of the demons in "Tom o'Shanter" (poem, 1790) and Scott's "A Dance of Death" (poem, 1815). Goethe also uses a fantastic dance in the Walpurgisnacht scene of *Faust* (drama, 1808); there Faust and Mephistopheles each dance in a circle with a witch—one young and lovely, the other old and coarse. Their dance implies not only Faust's entrance into their supernatural domain, but also his concession to the temptations of lust. He steps out of the dance only when, conscience-stricken, he espies Gretchen's ghost.

Many of Poe's poems allude to the dance, but he makes the most interesting use of it in his tales. In "The Masque of the Red Death" (1842), there are two related kinds of dance. Prince Prospero's guests waltz through the sealed chambers in which they seek to isolate themselves from the pestilence and to forget its horrors; and we are told that quantities of dreams dance about, "causing the wild music of the orchestra to seem as the echo of their steps." This is no social dance, but a private, mental spectacle, and the dance is an analogue to the impulses of madness. The metaphor is more explicit in "The Fall of the House of Usher" (1839). There an allegorical song describes a house, within which dancers at first move in an orderly pattern, then break into a wild frenzy. The house is analogous to an individual mind, and the dances correlate to states of mind. Poe leaves open the possibility that the dance not only resembles madness, it gives rise to it. It can be argued that his works sometimes imitate hypnotic, dancelike movements, structurally and stylistically. They have inspired numerous actual ballets.

In Novalis' fragmented narrative *Heinrich von Ofterdingen* (*Henry of Ofterdingen,* 1802) the protagonist, an aspiring artist, first meets his fantasy lover at a festive entertainment, where instead of speaking with her he dances with her. At that moment the prose becomes increasingly fragmented and fantasylike; the dance movement mimetically correlates to the protagonist's imaginative experience, the scene containing in microcosm the narrative's movement as a whole toward increasing fantasy.

The Novel

Novalis uses the dance as both a poetic and a narrative device; many other novelists use it as an integral, thematically important part of their narrative. Beginning in the late eighteenth century, the ball is an important episode for the display of social networks (and, often, their underlying economic tensions) and for the dignified erotic encounter. Goethe's *Die Leiden des jungen Werthers* (*The Sorrows of Young Werther*, 1774) makes classic use of the dance by having the protagonist first meet the woman he is to fall in love with when they both attend a country dance. The fact of its being rural in nature is significant in this novel. In contemporary works the ball in an urban setting often emblematizes decadence; in *Werther* the country dance is all innocent seduction, and its power is deeply linked to the natural forces that everywhere creep into the narrator's prose. The moment of Werther's waltz is one in which he loses his head, his actual dizziness enacting his emotional state. He is of course forewarned that Charlotte is engaged to another, but the dance brings him into a kind of communion with her, which he will seek, vainly, to retrieve and complete. It is only a virtual courtship; outside the dance it cannot be. Yet its power extends beyond those boundaries. The episode serves as a template for countless subsequent novels.

In Jane Austen's *Pride and Prejudice* (1813) dance is important not for its erotic undertones and power, but for its symbolic meaning, its status as a public sign. Again and again, the matter of who dances with whom bears distinct relation to who marries whom; the dance is an enactment of the continual approach and retreat of courtship that pervades Austen's novels. The story opens with a ball, at which the newcomers Mr. Bingley and Mr. Darcy make themselves known: both by dancing (or not dancing) with significant women, and by being talked about as prospective husbands, their desirability as cavaliers being directly related to their income. Darcy's pride manifests itself in his refusal to dance, and we know, later in the novel, that it is on the mend when he seeks Elizabeth Bennett out for a dance. But as his pride retreats, her prejudice advances. There is constant talk in the novel of balls, as the characters come together to observe themselves, their patterns of connection, and seek to rearrange them. The characters' movements on the dance floor enact every significant aspect of their relations to each other. And the orderly quality of Austen's dances reflect the order-within-movement of her novels' universe (see David Daiches, "Jane Austen, Karl Marx and the Aristocratic Dance," *American Scholar* 17 [1947–1948]: 289–298).

Later novelists develop the dance as a metaphor both for erotic encounter and for the pattern of social relations. Over the nineteenth century the dance becomes increasingly a vehicle of disorder rather than of orderly pattern. Flaubert, in

Madame Bovary (1856) and his other novels, narrates numerous dances that are nexuses of dramatic action. Emma Bovary first becomes decisively unhappy with her marriage and her provincial bourgeois life when she attends a ball and waltzes there with a viscount. Her glimpse there of previously unknown elegance and luxury locks her into a pattern of adultery and extravagance that leads to her downfall. As in *Werther,* the waltz "turns her head," working as a decisive moment in her life. It has a complement in a wild, masked dance at Rouen shortly before Emma's suicide; there, rather than simply observing most of the time (as she did at the first ball), Emma is at the center of the Dionysian dance, her identity given over to its excesses.

In the novels of Thomas Hardy the dance also is more than a metaphor, it is an informing principle. The many dances performed by his characters seem like so many steps in a predetermined pattern (see J. Hillis Miller, *Thomas Hardy, Distance and Desire,* 1970). The characters submit to the exigencies and movements of dance as they do to the narrative principles governing their relations to each other. In Hardy the dance almost invariably has erotic undertones, often, but not always, with negative implications. The characters' relation to dance is always revealing. Thus Tess is at her most beautiful when moving through a simple country dance, as she does when her nemesis, Angel Clare, first meets her (*Tess of the d'Urbervilles,* 1891); Eustacia Vye and her lover Wildeve, when they meet at night, break into a strange dance "like an irresistible attack upon whatever sense of social order there was in their minds" (*Return of the Native,* 1878); and, at the end of *Jude the Obscure* (1896), Jude dies alone and embittered while his thoughtless and relentlessly sensual wife waltzes at a huge celebration, the noise of which Jude hears through his window—in death, as always, estranged from the crowd. It is a tragic inversion of comic resolution.

D. H. Lawrence, in contrast, conceives of the dance more positively, even when it enforces disorder—or especially so. In *The White Peacock* (1911), Lawrence distinguishes between social dances, which enforce class distinctions, and more spontaneous dance, which may have a primitive power. In *Sons and Lovers* (1913), the protagonist's father is a superb dancer, a quality that first attracted his better-educated wife to him and which is part of his often-destructive "sensuous flame of life." In other novels, the ways and circumstances in which characters dance often "reveal the dancers' relationship to the life process" (Elsbree); and Lawrence uses rhythms in his prose to enact the state of mind that inheres in the ecstatic dance.

The Postromantic Lyric

For symbolist and related poetry of the late nineteenth century, the dance is an important, even central image. Yeats' famous lines in "Among School Children" (1927), "O body swayed to music, O brightening glance,/How can we know the dancer from the dance?" powerfully culminate a period in which the dance had increasingly figured as a metaphor for all creative acts. The line also condenses Yeats' own understanding of the dance as an unself-conscious act bringing together organic life and aesthetic statement into an enactment of cosmic harmony, a constantly moving pattern of conflicts in balance. The temporal aspect of Yeats' metaphor—the fact that the body and glance and the dance are only united in an extended moment—is, perhaps, the aspect most anticipated by earlier, symbolist poets. Arthur Symons, for example, returned again and again to the theme of the dance; in "Prologue: Before the Curtain" (1895) the poet distinguishes between the eternal gesture and the shadows who pass it on, and in "Prologue: In the Stalls," (1895) he claims to see himself in the dancer. Other poets of the 1890s explore the image, such as Olive Custance in "The Masquerade" and John Barlas in "The Dancing Girl." Also characteristic of the period is the juxtaposition of the dance with death. Thus Oscar Wilde in "The Harlot's House" (1885) combines dance as a metaphor for lust with the dance of death in a poem whose weary, urbane tone anticipates T. S. Eliot, despite the decadent themes. Yeats, too, associates the dance at its most intense with death, as in "Byzantium" (1930), in which "blood-begotten spirits" are "dying into a dance," undergoing an aesthetic transformation at great sacrifice for great beauty. Yeats also closely associates beauty with the supernatural, and dance often, especially in his dramas, is the means for bringing the unreal into being and disclosing its domain; see, for example, his play *At the Hawk's Well* (1917), written under the influence of Nō drama. It is impossible to summarize briefly the complex role of the dance in Yeats' works as a whole; it is an important theme throughout, in every genre in which he wrote.

Rilke, too, draws on the dance in his poetry as a metaphor for aesthetic transformation. The language of some of his *Sonette an Orpheus* (*Sonnets to Orpheus*, 1923) resembles that of Yeats. In number 18 (second part), the first phrase speaks of dance as transforming transcience into movement: "Tänzerin: o du Verlegung/Alles Vergehens in Gang:" Rilke is especially concerned with movement's inscription in time and its relation to the poetic voice. In number 25 (first part) he describes a dancer who pauses to listen, "als göss man ihr Jungsein in Erz,"—as though her youth were being poured into a mold, the dance taking on a being of its own (as the poem does after it is written). Rilke also sees, like Baudelaire, a confusion of senses in the dance: in number 15 (first part) he cries, "tanzt den Geschmack der erfahrenen Frucht!" Like Yeats, Rilke compares the dance to a tree, whose fruit is part of its being. For both poets the tree and the dance are not far from the poet's voice, always a silent third term in the metaphors. A poet's written words have a permanence that the dance cannot have; but its being only comes to fullness in the virtual time of an ideal reader, who, so to speak, enacts the poem in reading.

In Thomas Hardy's poetry he uses and revises many symbolist themes. Countless of his poems describe a dance. Often the dance has thematic significance as a moment of fusion in which the movement (fused with the poem's rhythms) yokes disparate, discrete moments from a remembered life; such is the case in

"Leipzig" (1878), "The Self-Unseeing" (1901), and "One We Knew" (1909). In "Seen by the Waits" (1914) a widow's secret solitary dance before a mirror, witnessed by a group of Christmas carolers, embodies, implicitly, both her anguish at solitude and a new sense of freedom and desire. "Reminiscences of a Dancing Man" (1909) uses the dance as a metonymy for a process of decline through history, a decline the speaker mourns. Dance is, for Hardy, the sister art that is closest to poetry's temporal and visceral qualities (see Joan Grundy, *Hardy and the Sister Arts,* 1979).

In many ways Rilke, Yeats, and Hardy culminate romantic uses of the dance. A more distinctly modern sensibility such as T. S. Eliot, looking for an austere equilibrium, retrieves some of the qualities of the dance in the masque. (Joyce too pursues such a strategy with a dance of the hours in his novel *Ulysses* [1922] and the dance of the rainbow girls in the novel *Finnegans Wake* [1939].) In *The Four Quartets* (1943), dance is a central metaphor of harmonious resolution, one which embraces both tradition and the contemporary reader. At the same time Eliot borrows from Yeats the image of a dance in a purifying fire, in which the dancer yields himself to a violent intensity in order to achieve renewal. The dance, the poet says, is at "the still point of the turning world," that place and moment of "complete consort" to which the poem aspires. The poem's movement relies on formal pattern, on the life's blood ("the dance along the artery") of earth-bound humanity, and on the refining and destroying fire—all of which a dance enacts—in order to generate its durable virtual world at the still point and to bring the reader into it.

Among contemporary poets, Robert Duncan has used the dance extensively in his poetry as an image of desire in movement; Duncan plays at times with the literary tradition of the dance (and with Eliot in particular). "An Interlude" (1963) concludes, "The dancers come forward to represent unclaimed things," with the suggestion that the dance is proper as a pattern of renewal, rather than as an abstract, virtual point. Like Eliot, Duncan uses the dance as an image of human communion on a cosmic scale; unlike him, he develops the erotic aspect of dance into a complex metaphor for the poetic act ("the bright tongues of two/languages/dance in the one light"). Duncan's use of the dance as a metaphor is typical of contemporary poetry to the extent that the metaphor's terms are often oblique and elusive; the dance is attractive precisely because it is nonverbal, and its quality of unspeakable movement is best captured by the metaphor whose *tertium comparationis* the reader cannot verbalize.

See also: Dance of Death, Masque or Mask.

Selected Bibliography

Brissenden, Alan. *Shakespeare and the Dance*. Atlantic Highlands, N.J.: Humanities Press, 1981.

Lawler, Lillian. *The Dance in Ancient Greece*. London: A. and C. Black, 1964.

Orgel, Stephen. *The Jonsonian Masque*. Cambridge, Mass.: Harvard University Press, 1965.
Salmagundi 33–34 (1976). Special Issue: *Dance*.

SARAH WEBSTER GOODWIN
R.E. GOODWIN

DANCE OF DEATH

The dance of death is a literary or pictorial representation of a dance or procession in which death as a skeleton leads his victims to the grave. The living figures are arranged in order of social or ecclesiastical precedence, and death may be portrayed either as an individual skeleton leading his living counterpart or as a single allegorical figure of Death as a skeleton leading a group. The purpose of the representation is often didactic, both satirizing the meaningless distinctions of social rank in the face of death and warning individuals preoccupied with worldly activities of the inevitability of death. Originating in the fourteenth century, the Dance of Death reached its peak of popularity in the fifteenth, but figurative adaptations of the dance have appeared in literature and art up to and in the twentieth century.

The Middle Ages

It is not known for certain whether the pictorial representations of the Dance of Death inspired the descriptive verses that accompany them or whether the verses brought about the corresponding paintings. The earliest known painting of the Dance of Death was at Klingenthal, Little Basel, in 1312, and other early versions were widespread throughout Europe. The most famous and influential version appeared in the Cemetery of the Innocents at Paris in 1425. The fresco painted there on the walls of the charnel house was accompanied by explanatory verses. This mural, now lost, has been preserved in the illustrated edition printed by Guyot Marchant in 1485.

These murals show fifteen pairs of figures, clerical and lay, ranging in order from pope and emperor to peasant and child. Each living figure is led by the hand of a bony skeleton in a long processional chain. The accompanying verses are in the form of a dialogue, with each living person speaking his piece about his own impending death.

The earliest reference to the Dance of Death as Danse Macabre occurred in a poem written in 1376 by Jehan le Fèvre, "Respit de la mort". One line in this poem about his own death reads: "Je fis de macabre la dance." Marchant borrowed the term for the title of his rendition of the Dance of Death. There has been much speculation about the origin of the word "macabre" (also spelled "macabré" and "macabrée"). According to one theory, it derives from the word "Maccabees," who had been regarded as patron saints of the dead because they were believed to be originators of intercessionary prayers for the dead. Another suggests that it is based on a surname, perhaps of the original poet or painter of the theme. A recent theory posits its derivation from the slang word "mac-chabe" meaning corpse.

When the English poet and cleric John Lydgate visited Paris in 1426, he became interested in translating the verses accompanying the murals of the Dance of Death in the Holy Innocents. By 1433 Lydgate's poems had been placed with the appropriate pictures of a Dance of Death in the cloister of St. Paul's. Un-fortunately the entire work was destroyed in 1549 when the Protector Somerset ordered the building torn down in order to provide him with materials for con-structing his own palace. Lydgate's translation survives in twelve manuscripts and an early (1554) printed version. As the poet explains in the text, his is not a word for word translation but rather an imitation of the substance of the original French. The last of Lydgate's living figures to speak is the pathetic child, who laments that he was born but yesterday yet is pursued by hasty death.

Several historical factors spurred the popularity of the poetic and pictorial Dance of Death in the fourteenth and fifteenth centuries. Most significant were the recurring epidemics of the plague, or black death, which wiped out almost half the population of Western Europe. The grim spectre of death was an ever-present reality. To an anxious population haunted by the fear of sudden death, churchmen preached the attitude of *contemptus mundi*, or contempt for the world, in favor of contemplating a heavenly afterlife. There were also at this time sects of maniacal dancers who danced themselves to exhaustion and even to death on the streets of European cities. No period in Western history has been quite so obsessed by the physical fact of death.

Death is overwhelmingly physical in the Dance of Death theme. The tone of the verses is notably lacking in either tenderness or sentiment. Instead it is often mocking and concentrates on the horror of physical decay. In the pictures, the facial expressions of the living do not reveal either sorrow or anger but rather a blend of surprise and resignation. Ironically the portrayal of the skeletal dead is often rhythmic and full of movement, while the living person is stationary, as if stunned into immobility.

While Lydgate's verses are probably the best-known example of the Dance of Death in medieval English literature, the best-known artistic rendering is the masterfully wrought woodcut series by Hans Holbein the Younger. These vivid illustrations were made by Holbein after a visit to Basel, and they are accom-panied by brief verses in French. For Holbein, death is a personified abstraction who enters into the daily lives of unsuspecting people. There is mordant humor in the portrayal of death in varied poses and even costumes to fit the individual situation. This death is also a practical joker, as when he forces drink down the throat of a drunkard. The scenes are realistic, and all of the victims are taken completely by surprise.

Whereas in both France and Germany artistic examples of the Dance of Death survive without any poetry, in Spain the most important medieval example is the *La dansa general de la Muerte* (c. 15th century), which comes down to us without any illustrations. The Spanish poem is also distinguished by a vividly conceived personification of death rather than the typical series of the individual dead as counterpart to the living. In this long poem, which has seventy-nine strophes of eight lines each, the living victims called to dance with death are not passive about their summons but dispute their fate. Relentlessly, however, in the last line of each strophe Death interrupts to call the next victim.

The French poet François Villon (1431–?) was influenced by paintings at the Cemetery of the Innocents. In his poems about the lords and ladies of yore, he laments the brevity of life and formulates a verbal procession of the dead. He realizes that his father is dead, and his mother will also die. Equally certain of his own impending death, he consigns his body to his grandmother earth. Observing several bodies hanging from the gibbet and suspecting that he too will be hanged, he mordantly observes that soon the rain will wash and the sun dry the corpses. A touch of grim humor characterizes Villon's imaginative vision of his own dead body.

The Renaissance

The Dance of Death theme continued in sixteenth-century literature. In the novel *Don Quijote* (*Don Quixote,* 1605, 1615), Cervantes describes a meeting between the hero and a travelling company of actors who perform a Dance of Death play in towns along their way. The passage describes the costumes worn by the actors. The driver of the cart appears as a devil, and another of the actors represents Death with a human visage. Sitting near Death in the cart are an angel with painted wings and the god Cupid, with bow, quiver, and arrows. Two other actors represent an emperor with a gold crown and a knight with a plumed hat.

The Dance of Death survives primarily in dramatic form in the Renaissance. In Spain it is the subject of several plays, including *Farsa de la muerte* (c. 1536) by Diego Sanchez de Badajoz, *Farsa llamada danza de la muerte* (1551) by Juan de Pedraza, and *Las cortes de la muerte* (1557) by Micael de Carvajal and Luis Hurtado de Toledo. The last is a long and elaborate play with twenty-three scenes in which Death holds court and receives complaints from its victims, who range from the highest to the lowest in the social scale. In addition to plays there are also several allegorical poems based on the Dance of Death theme in sixteenth-century Spanish literature.

The spirit of the macabre also figures prominently in drama on the English stage in the sixteenth and early seventeenth centuries. Many of these plays feature scenes involving a death's-head, the most famous of which is the graveyard scene in *Hamlet* (c.1600), in which the hero addresses his soliloquy to the newly unearthed skull of the jester Yorick. One of the most extremely macabre in mood of the English playwrights at this time is Cyril Tourneur, whose two tragedies include extensive portrayal of the Dance of Death theme. The hero of *The Revenger's Tragedy* (1607), a melancholy and embittered young scholar seeking revenge, somewhat resembles Hamlet. The play opens with his sombre speech to the skull of his beloved, who was driven to suicide several years ago by the persistent advances of the lustful ruling duke. As he addresses the skull, members of the duke's family pass by in a procession. Enjoying their decadent, luxurious lives now, they will all be dead by the end of the play.

In a vivid, emblematic scene that recalls the Dance of Death murals, the revenger dresses up a skeleton in garish courtly garments and annoints its mouth with poison. He places it in a dark corner where its dimly visible gorgeous attire lures the duke into giving it a fatal kiss. The revenging hero then watches with cruel delight as the poison first eats away the duke's mouth, then kills him. The final act of the play offers a kind of Dance of Death processional. A banquet celebrating the accession of the new duke is suddenly interrupted by the entrance of disguised masquers. Catching the revelers completely off guard, the masquers draw weapons and kill them all. In performance the masquers are dressed in black robes as agents of Death.

Tourneur's later play, *The Atheist's Tragedy* (1611), is also rich in macabre scenes and events. One entire scene takes place in a graveyard, with episodes and dialogue recalling the macabre setting of the Cemetery of the Innocents in fourteenth-century Paris. Like the Parisian graveyard, this one serves as an assignation place for lovers, but in the play grisly reminders of death thwart the sexual intentions of the characters. In one case the hopeful lover has gone to the graveyard to meet his mistress but becomes confused in the dark and almost makes love to the corpse of a recently murdered man. In the other, the virtuous hero and heroine do meet, but honor their chastity and seek only rest. They lie down in the charnel house, each with a death's-head for a pillow and lament the transitoriness of life.

Shakespeare's comedy *Love's Labours Lost* (c. 1594) includes a brief but interesting echo of the Dance of Death tradition. In the last scene of the play, the messenger who enters abruptly to announce the death of the princess' father is named Mercade, a variant on the spelling of macabre.

Other lesser known plays of the time, like Thomas Dekker's *The Honest Whore* (1604) and Henry Chettle's *The Tragedy of Hoffman* (1631) also contain skull scenes, reflecting the continuity of the Dance of Death tradition on the stage.

The Eighteenth and Nineteenth Centuries

Concern with death and the transitoriness of life occupies several prominent poets of the eighteenth century, among them André Chénier and Edward Young, but on the whole the tone is more reflective than macabre. In the nineteenth century, however, several poetic imitations of the Dance of Death theme renew the macabre spirit, with its obsessive awareness of physical decay and its grimly mordant humor. A satiric style characterizes many of these. In 1800 *The Dance of Death Modernized,* with designs by G. M. Woodward, offers twenty-four caricatures of worldly individuals in a variety of social roles facing the invitations of death. The miser offers to go willingly if his money is spared; the fine lady protests that she is too exalted a person of fashion to go with such a filthy wretch. Also satiric in import is the two-volume *The English Dance of Death from the Designs of Thomas Rowlandson with Metrical Illustrations by the Author of Doctor Syntax* (1815–1816). The seventy-two drawings, based in part on those of Holbein, are caricatures of different social classes and professions.

In 1832 Paul Lacroix published a novel *Danse Macabre* which is set in the year 1438. The protagonist, named Macabre, is a thin, bony man who lives in an ossuary at the Cemetery of the Innocents with his wife, who sleeps in a coffin. He has gained wealth both through selling clothing he has taken from the dead and through directing a play about the Danse Macabre. The novel has many scenes involving burial of both dead and living, and in the end Macabre's living counterpart, Benjamin, dies of the plague. The audience laughs with extremely macabre glee in one of the final scenes when a friar is pushed into a cauldron of boiling oil.

Although an element of humor is indeed part of the macabre spirit, much of the Dance of Death literature is grimly serious. One of the rare totally humorous treatments of the theme is the poem *La danza ovvero il Ballo della morte* (1888) by Ferdinando Gorè, which is actually a series of comic dialogues between Man and Death. In another short, humorous poem by Goethe, called "Der Totentanz" ("The Dance of Death," 1813), the living person tricks the dead rather than the usual reversed situation. When the skeletons leave their graves at midnight to disport themselves for an hour, their movements are inhibited by the little short shirts they wear, and they put the garments aside temporarily. The night watchman steals one of the shirts and hides it in a tower as a prank. The deprived skeleton tries to retrieve it before he must return to the grave. He is unable to enter the door of the tower where it is hidden, because of the sign of the cross and tries unsuccessfully to scale the wall instead. Promptly at the stroke of one, the skeleton falls to the ground, broken to pieces.

In 1850 Thomas Beddoes published a play, *Death's Jest Book, or The Fool's Tragedy*. Set in Egypt in the thirteenth century, the play has a political theme, but two scenes directly concern the Dance of Death. In the third act a group of conspirators meets in the churchyard of a ruined cathedral where the walls contain a painting of the Dance of Death. In the fifth act in the same setting the figures of the dead come out of the wall, and some seat themselves at a table where guests are about to sit. When the guests come, most of the dead retire to their places, but one remains and joins the feasting company. When one of the living proposes a toast to the health of Death, the dead member of the party poses a startling question. Which are the living and which are the dead? All of the dead come from the wall and begin to dance together.

Also morally serious in tone are the short stories, *Todtentänze,* written by Franz Pocci in 1857. Recalling the Holbein scenes, these tales show death visiting a number of people going about their daily lives. In some cases death acts as an instrument of justice, as in the tale where a woman and a child are cruelly refused assistance by a miser. Death takes the miser. Probably the best known short story writer to use the Dance of Death theme is Edgar Allen Poe. In three of his stories with a medieval setting—"Shadow" (1835), "King Pest" (1835), and "The Masque of the Red Death" (1842)—Poe develops a plot ending in death by plague, that is, the red death. In the "Masque" the prince has gathered his followers together in his abbey, with all the doors locked against the plague ravaging the countryside. Deluded into feeling safe, they have a masqued ball at which a tall, gaunt figure dressed in black suddenly appears. The prince falls dead in approaching him, and when the guests look more closely at the ghastly figure, its garments are revealed to be empty. All succumb to the red death.

Walter Scott and Robert Browning also wrote on the theme. Scott's "A Dance of Death" (1815) describes a soldier's vision of a phantom Dance of Death by those who are about to die in battle on the next day. The figures in the dance are hand in hand, wildly gesturing, and their movements are accompanied by thunder and lightning. In Browning's "Dance of Death" (c. 1826) five abstractions—Fever, Pestilence, Ague, Madness, and Consumption—display their skills as they vie for the achievement prize of Death.

The theme was not limited to painting and literature in the nineteenth century. Camille Saint-Saëns' symphonic composition *Danse macabre* (1874) is probably the most famous example of program music dealing with the theme, but in 1849 Franz Liszt also composed a *Totentanz* for piano and orchestra. Nor was the theme limited to art. In life as well as the arts the tradition of concentration on the artifacts of physical death retained its immediacy. Sarah Bernhardt, the well-known actress, had a coffin installed in her room in Paris. She lay in it while learning her parts and often slept overnight in it as well. Perhaps in keeping with this custom, the poet Victor Hugo also wrote verses to the actress inscribed on a skull.

The Twentieth Century

A number of pictures, poems, plays, and stories testify to the continued popularity of the Dance of Death theme in the current century. At the turn of the century (1898) Hugo von Hofmannsthal wrote a one-act play called *Der Tor und der Tod (Death and the Fool),* in which death appears in a more benign manner, playing a violin. The young man visited by death is nonetheless filled with horror, but death convinces him that his life has so far been in fact a kind of death. Death summons a pageant of his victim's closest friends and relatives, who confirm that he has not really lived. The young man then accepts his fate, hoping that death will bring him a new life.

August Strindberg's play *Dödsdansen (Dance of Death,* 1901) also suggests that life and death may be mistakenly identified with each other. The protagonist is a Coast Guard captain whose unhappy married life he characterizes as a living hell, in which he and his wife have been sent to torment each other. Outwardly unafraid of death, the captain is actually terrified of its imminence. A failure as a human being, he perverts the lives of his associates into a wretched living death.

Death appears as an attractive young woman in a pale green dress in Algernon Blackwood's story "The Dance of Death" (1927). The protagonist of the story is an ailing man who has suffered a severe heart attack. At a party he forgets his weakened condition and dances with the mysterious young woman in green all evening. Somewhat after midnight he glides out into the darkness with her. His death at 2:00 A.M. is subsequently reported.

In these works of Hofmannsthal, Strindberg, and Blackwood, death is not depicted as a skeletal figure. In some recent works, however, the conventional medieval image recurs. One of the most successful of these medieval imitations is the sonnet series by Merrill Moore called *The Dance of Death in the 20th Century* (1957). Moore's sonnets are published to correspond precisely with the forty-nine woodcuts of Holbein. Opposite each woodcut is a sonnet describing a modern scene. Some of the parallels are quite obvious, like the sonnet opposite Holbein's "The Physician," which is called "Doctors Are Not Different from Anybody Else." Some offer a satiric portrayal in keeping with the mood of the woodcut. Holbein's "The Duke" is matched with a sonnet about a wealthy man named Cardigo who lived sensuously and luxuriously until death seized him. Some are impressionistic, as the one matched with Holbein's "The Old Man," called "In the Forest the Invisible Dead Men Sang Harmoniously throughout the Rainy Night." Throughout this interesting collection the modern idiom is effectively sustained alongside the medieval macabre tone.

The graphic and the dramatic qualities of the theme have kept it aesthetically effective through the centuries. The stark contrast of body and skeleton, the abrupt encounter of an active person with his own death's-head, the mocking humor of the dancing posture, the sharply satiric perspective on social class, and the rhythmic interaction of living and dead are dynamic ingredients in plastic and narrative arts. In the twentieth century the Dance of Death motif has also functioned vividly in film. Ingmar Bergmann's film, *Det sjunde inseglet* (*The Seventh Seal*, 1957), set in medieval Europe, includes the figure of Death, who in the opening scene plays chess with a knight. The closing scene offers a striking view of a processional of death on the horizon. Death leads a group of people over the ridge of the hill off into the distance. The Dance of Death theme thus continues to be both imitated and modified in the contemporary artistic awareness.

See also: Dance, Death and the Individual, Masque or Mask.

Selected Bibliography

Clark, James M., ed. *The Dance of Death by Hans Holbein*. London: Phaidon Press, 1947.

Kurtz, Leonard, P. *The Dance of Death and the Macabre Spirit in European Literature*. New York: Columbia University Press, 1934.

Warren, Florence, ed. *The Dance of Death*. London: Early English Text Society, 1931.
Whyte, Florence. *The Dance of Death in Spain and Catalonia*. Baltimore: Waverly Press, 1931.

CHARLOTTE SPIVACK

DEATH AND THE INDIVIDUAL

To think about one's own death is to think about one's own potential annihilation or immortality, and the mythic structure prevailing in one's culture is what provides the individual with an imaginative vocabulary within which to consider these. The individual's contemplation of death is ubiquitous in literature as in life. It has had its own peculiar evolution in Western literature, which also appears cyclical. Christian literature from the earliest times to the Renaissance marks the center point of this conceptual cycle, where the mythological framework acts as a model of eternal life to which individuals might realistically aspire, and by which they learn to degrade earthly life, favoring instead the alternative of a permanent life after death. Within this Christian framework, as in all mythic contexts, there is, of course, a range of possible attitudes toward one's own death.

Faith is what traces the texture of the veil that conceals everything we do not understand. Thus, the individual's faith or lack of it (each tending to reflect the theological inclination of the period in which a given work is written) defines the two major approaches of the individual in the contemplation of his or her own death. The individual's approach is either an essentially religious one, which we will define as any attitude that presumes some kind of ongoing personal existence after death, or a practical one. The practical approach we will define as any attitude that presumes both the final, physical death of the body, as well as the absolute and permanent extinction of the individual, body and soul. Under these two general categories fall six more specific attitudes toward death: fear, honor, piety, communion, acceptance, and indifference.

Since death is nearly omnipresent as a literary theme, what follows is merely an attempt to sketch the salient works and typical terms of understanding at different periods. The chronological framework can belie authors' actual concerns, however. There is no more a single Elizabethan or romantic understanding of death than there is a modern one. Attitudes toward death expressed in literary terms are by nature complex, an unbounded synthesis of the kinds of contradictions philosophical discourses on the subject have needed to distinguish rather than synthesize. While knowledge of death is properly a philosophical problem and has a history in such discourse, it remains an intransigently creative and intuitive concern as well, pressing at the limits of what we think knowledge to be.

The following could not intend to be an all-inclusive study; instead, it is a historical outline with representative examples and addresses Western literature exclusively.

Greek Antiquity

In the Homeric epic, the way an individual dies is as significant to his personal history as the way he lives. The heroes in the epic achieve what they consider to be the most significant kind of immortality available to them through fame, as celebrated and embraced by literature. Since only the gods enjoy physical immortality, and the spiritual immortality of men is conceived of as being an eternal incoherent shadow of their former selves—except Teiresias the prophet, the only dead man "whose senses stay unshaken within him,/to whom alone Persephone has granted intelligence/ even after death" (*Odysseia* [*Odyssey*, c. 8th century B.C.])—the Greeks, as represented through the epics, live and die for the place they will enjoy in history. In Homer's *Ilias* (*Iliad*, c. 8th century B.C.), Sarpedon urges Glaukos into battle as he delineates the value of at least attempting to win glory in the face of death—he explicitly expresses the idea that glory is only significant to mortals and could easily be foregone and abandoned in exchange for immortal and ageless life.

The Greek legendary schema represents the fantasy of a people who considered themselves great and longed for immortality to perfect that greatness. Epic poetry enjoyed an exalted position in that it was considered as immortal as the gods themselves. The immortal Muses speak through Homer, according to Homer himself. A primary and astonishing faith in history, expressed both explicitly and implicitly, prevails in the epic. The word, as employed in the service of this faith, is an integral aspect of it. Meaninglessness (or a radically different form of devotion) would prevail without language. All that humanity ever was or ever will be is inextricably woven into the fabric of the poetic art, and immortality is achieved literally through the word.

In the Greek pattern there is no heaven for mortals (except the deliciousness of immortality achieved through fame), but there is judgment by Minos the son of Zeus; the dead are allotted either a form of hell appropriate to their misdeeds in life or else an eternal nonlife as mute, fluttering shadows. In any case, myth fosters acceptance by replacing fear; and good or bad, death is at least transformed from its original status as intangible unknown. Further, myth merges with honor (in the service of fame, which is also in many ways a prime ingredient and product of myth), to mitigate the horror of death experienced by a people who considered themselves godlike.

In spite of this, and allowing for Odysseus' choosing his homecoming, and therefore death, over immortality offered him by Circe, the prevailing stance toward death in the epic is one of deep sorrow and bitterness, "for Hades gives not way, and is pitiless, and therefore he among all the gods is most hateful to mortals" (*Odyssey*).

The mythological framework in the tragedies is essentially the same as in the epics, but it functions differently. The gods are much more remote, even though what happens is casually attributed to them. When they do appear, they seem more a product of dramatic convenience than living, acting, palpable beings. In tragedy death becomes more predominantly the "great equalizer" in the service of both the moral order and the tragic itself. It denies itself as an avenue of escape from a cruel life as it does for Oedipus, and it takes away the lives of innocents to castigate the crimes or wrong-headedness of others. Because the tragic character is left so completely destitute, he or she will often look to death as a release from suffering. The individual looks forward to that time when "he hath crossed life's border, free from pain" (Sophocles' *Oidipous tyrannos* [*Oedipus Rex,* c. 429 B.C.]) From this feeling are engendered the ecstatic and sometimes erotic aspects of death. The ecstatic experience, which is essentially the flight from physical being, is what Polyxena chooses in Euripides' drama *Hekabē* (*Hecuba,* c. 424 B.C.) because, she explains, "a maiden marked among her fellows, equal to a goddess save for death alone, but now a slave! That name first makes me long for death, so strange it sounds."

The erotic union achieved through death appears perhaps most notably in Sophocles' *Antigone* (c. 441 B.C.). Cursed since birth by her father's fate, Antigone sees herself "compassed about by evils" and considers her earthly life as nothing but painful. She thus turns to the underworld in innocent faith, hoping from it wisdom, witness, judgment, reunion with her curse-sharing but beloved parents, and even union; she, "whom the lord of the Dark Lake shall wed." The combination here of "Tomb, bridal-chamber, eternal prison in the caverned rock, wither I go to find my own" establishes the erotic death motif that is one of the resilient death-related motifs in Western literature.

Aeschylus' *Promētheus desmōtēs* (*Prometheus Bound,* c. 450 B.C.) enacts the inherent conflict between the dominance of religion and the creative fruition of humanity in art which mitigates the individual's personal encounter with death. All the characters in this play except one are immortal, making the play's intent and significance loftier at the outset. It arbitrates between art and the omnipotent and remote (to humanity) status of religion that ultimately signifies the ongoing existence of mankind. It seems that art and religion cannot coexist harmoniously, but rather struggle to embody a distinctive definition of reality. Explicitly, "all human arts are from Prometheus." His gifts give to individuals such an understanding of their world, themselves, and their potential, as to render the need for a deistic framework for faith obsolete, especially because through Prometheus (or creativity, or self-fulfillment) "mankind ceased to foresee death. . . . Blind hopes I made to dwell in them." Art overwhelms necessity and humanity becomes god, overcoming death.

The theatrical effects used in tragedy, like the wearing of masks and other devices to make the actor's stature more impressive and the religious festivals that the plays celebrated are two of the factors that suggest that art was being summoned to re-create a mythic context that presumably had to some extent deteriorated. But the struggle between art and religion is by no means resolved in *Prometheus Bound,* as apparently in Greek consciousness. Art is threatened with defeat, making the spectre of death loom large; and meanwhile, confusion prevails and faith is homeless.

The fame or immortality that the tragic hero then achieves through legend acts more to instruct the living than to edify or even significantly immortalize the individual. Tragedy illustrates just how brutal and merciless life can be, and the tragic hero wins a place in history as an exemplar of life's cruelty. The role that a sense of honor then plays differs vastly from that in the epic because the individual dies with everything that was precious and meaningful stripped away.

The Bible

> O death, where is thy sting?
> O grave, where is thy victory?
> The sting of death is sin; and the strength of sin is the law.
>
> (1 Cor., 15:55, 56)

The mythology of the Bible is a closed and multiple entity that signifies all meaning. Within it the concepts of beginning and end—of the world and of human life—take shape in a uniquely rich eschatological vision.

The first attitude expressed toward death in the Old Testament is one in which death is virtually synonymous with an eternal cycle of servitude. The expulsion from the Garden of Eden is a cautionary measure to exclusivize power: "Behold, the man is become as one of us, to know good and evil: and now, lest he put forth his hand, and take also of the tree of life, and eat, and live for ever" (Gen. 3:22). Adam and Eve are allowed to eat of the tree of life as long as they are innocent or benign and pose no threat to the region of power. Having to die is thus essentially to have to serve and never to be free to actualize the potential inherent in the discovery of good and evil. Ironically, it is later that the milk or text of God "delivered them, who through fear of death were all their lifetime subject to bondage" (Heb. 2:15).

The expulsion is the first instance of God's plan that "when I begin, I shall also make an end" (1 Sam. 3:12), and is exemplary of the eschatology that informs all aspects of biblical life and mythology. The concept of apocalypse is ubiquitous in the Old Testament, but expressions of resurrection and immortality are not consistently encountered, and in many of the books make no appearance at all. In many of the Old Testament books, when an individual dies, he or she "returns to the earth to sleep with his fathers." We learn only gradually through scattered references that "sleep" is to be taken literally. When the Christian vision unfolds its elaborate revelation in the New Testament, it includes the aspect of apocalypse as paradigm and goal of the individual's own death. This gives each individual's life vision and to each individual's death potential resurrection. The signs of apocalypse also creatively cause death to die: God will "swallow up death in victory" (Isa. 25:8).

The Christian model is remarkable for its striking semblance of having so well accounted for death and for its resiliency to both discredit and time. However, as elsewhere, an important and characteristic duality concerning the nature of death prevails. Death can be a resting place until Judgment Day for those who have found favor in the sight of the Lord; but physical death, which robs humanity of posterity and condemns it to be carrion for dogs, is the worst punishment that God can administer to the individual. God's ominous declaration "when I begin, I shall also make an end" suggests that "all life is a mask of death" (Aries' phrase), and it embodies the ambiguous meaning of death. The presence of Job and Ecclesiastes is a psychologically apt part of the biblical text. It allows a special place for doubt to wrestle with itself, for the ambiguity inherent in the mythological model in which the mysteries of death or human destiny remain unrevealed.

In the Christian relationship to Christ's death, we encounter the second most significant attitude toward death in the Bible: the imaginative act of the devotee conceiving the ecstatic sacrifice of himself to his omnipotent Lord. At the most extreme, it is through the powerful transport of imagination that the individual learns the ecstatic aspect of death and learns to experience death vicariously, but positively, since it represents communion with God.

In the Old Testament, the law applies virtually exclusively to the body of the individual (i.e., what one may or may not do with it, where one may or may not go with it, etc.). Because of this physical emphasis, the law becomes predominantly associated with the deathlike and the death-leading. "For I was alive without the law once: but when the commandment came, sin revived, and I died. And the commandment, which was ordained to life, I found to be unto death" (Rom. 7:9, 10, 11, 14). In the New Testament, the law takes on a more spiritual association. The Word undergoes a transformation from signifying law to signifying spirit. The letter of the law, the carnal, piety, sin, and death become analogues here as do their counterparts: the spirit of the law, the spiritual, communion, salvation, and life. From this Neoplatonic dichotomy, the metaphysical conclusion that "the things which are seen are temporal; but the things which are not seen are eternal" (2 Cor. 4:18) takes its place as part of the foundation of the Christian model.

The difference between the typical styles of mourning encountered in the Old and New Testaments clearly illustrates the change of attitude toward death that this revised framework produces. Upon the death of a loved one in the Old Testament, a man would ritualize his emotion of worthlessness and express the feeling of despair at the meaninglessness of life in the face of mortality. He would wear sackcloth, shave his beard and hair, cut his hands, rent his clothes, and give offerings and incense. At his own death he would turn his face to the wall. With the new emphasis on the immortality of the spirit in the New Testament, the living are for the living and the dead for the dead, and Jesus can casually say to the disciple who asks Him if he may first go to bury his father before he follows Him. "Follow me and let the dead bury their dead" (Matt. 8:22). Anything that has to do with the physical realm is thus summarily rejected and so degraded. Death is a physical phenomenon that is irrelevant until Judgment Day arrives and gives it meaning, and in this way the individual's encounter with his or her own destiny (real death or immortality) is postponed, along with its associated fear.

Christianity is apparently the only Western religion where the God is murdered for the atonement and salvation of the people. "For it is not possible that the blood of bulls and of goats should take away sins. . . . We are sanctified through the offering of the body of Jesus Christ once for all" (Heb. 10:4, 10). The extreme enacted in this achievement is possibly the only conceivable means by which life after death could be proved. If Christ, sent to earth in human form, the Son of God and the son of man, was resurrected, then so could any individual do the same. "After two days will he revive *us:* in the third day, he will raise us up and we shall live in his sight (Hos. 6:2). Christ dies to show, to prove, in the supreme act of selfless or masochistic love, that faith saves, that the imaginative act can be pushed over the threshold that divides the idea and the enactment of it. Christ is to the people what the people are to God, and thus the created move into league with the creator. The sacrifice and the shedding of blood are the sine qua non of human creativity, making possible a flight from a death over which the individual has no control and which carries terrifying implications. The need for faith in immortality and purpose (or morality) is the result of this fear, and this need itself engenders the vocabulary of creativity. Christ's assertion of immortality reflects this deepest of wishes: "For I have not spoken of myself; but the Father which sent me, he gave me a commandment, what I should say, and what I should speak. And I know that his commandment is life everlasting" (John 12:49, 50).

Late Antiquity and the Early Medieval Period

The Christian attitude that fears and denies the physical world, and thus death, is in many ways opposed to the attitude encountered in one of the great literary works of the early Christian period. Apuleius' narrative *Metamorphoses (The Golden Ass,* c. 150) climaxes in a conversion. Isis initiates Lucius into her cult. In this model the physical aspects of the world are exalted and adored, since Isis is their informing spirit. The mythology of Isis embraces and succors nature; life is wonderful for its own sake, and as meaningful as eternity itself.

Still, Lucius is told that the initiation amounts to a voluntary death; and what that death signifies for the individual is left ambiguous. Lucius says of the initiation's mysteries, "I approached the very gates of death and set one foot on Proserpine's threshold, yet was permitted to return, rapt through all the elements." We find here a religion in which the initiated achieve status by the witness of death. As in the Greek model and in the New Testament, whatever death is, it becomes palatable when it can be confronted directly with the specific intervention of a god. By this process, the individual becomes absorbed into an immortal power, and personal death recedes in importance. In the case of Isis, death loses its sting in two ways. She claims the underworld will be more pleasant for her initiates, and she claims the "power to prolong your life beyond the limits appointed by destiny." The fear of personal death is then overcome by witness and by initiation into the priesthood of a religion in which the goddess of life is also the goddess of death. Life and death thus become almost interchangeable aspects of experience.

In contrast to Apuleius' Isis, St. Augustine's God is one that demands faith with no witness. There is no tangible revelation of the meaning of death for him. His search is largely a matter of guesswork, an inner dialogue carried on so diligently and so passionately that it proves the reality of the listener, God, by its mere existence. He must by faith overcome the fear of death, concluding that its most frightening implications are "unthinkable." Since everything in the physical world is subject to decay and death, he decries this world, defining a new one in which death is positively linked to judgment and can therefore be avoided. This is how he "die[s] to death and become[s] alive to life" (*Confessiones* [*The Confessions,* autobiography, c. 397–400]).

St. Augustine reached the conclusion, from biblical doctrine via Neoplatonism, that that which is corruptible (the flesh by decay and death, and so many other aspects of the material world) is far inferior to that which is incorruptible. His search for a religious solution is a flight from death, and he expresses this explicitly in *The Confessions:* "What is man to do in his plight? Who is to set him free from a nature thus doomed to death? Nothing else than the grace of God." "Nothing prevented me from plunging still deeper into the gulf of carnal pleasure except the fear of death and your judgment to come."

Since Augustine's conversion is a thoroughly Christian one, it marks the culmination of a process through which he found and defined increasingly more aspects of the material world as deathlike and death-leading. Thus to err is to experience a kind of death ("you alone, are the life that recalls us from the death we die each time we err"). To trespass against any of God's commandments is to insure that "in justice we have been delivered to the author of sin, the prince of death, because he has coaxed us to make our wills conform with his."

Augustine's confession concerns itself with a stripping away, a degradation of mortal life. In contrast, *The Golden Ass* is a building process in structure; its nature (the telling of stories) is a celebration of life. It creates a lively and colorful framework of moral myth. Still, the *Confessions* and *The Golden Ass* coincide thematically in what is perhaps the most significant way. They each describe a conversion from a despairing condition in which death is abhorred and feared and from which escape is sought. They each achieve a deeply longed for and genuine faith by which personal fear of death is mitigated through communion with the eternal. And they each use the individual's death as a metaphor for a conversion to a new life.

The Middle Ages

The Christian church thrived in the Middle Ages as it experienced the zenith of its influence. Pope Innocent III (1161–1216), as one of its representatives, advocated a Christian scorn of physical life. His *De miseria humanae conditionis* (*On the Misery of the Human Condition,* meditation, 1195) is a fascinating and exemplary instance: "We are forever dying while we are alive; we only cease to die when we cease to live. Therefore, it is better to die to life than to live waiting for death, for mortal life is but a living death."

For Innocent, any individual desire for autonomy and personal expression signifies a kind of death wish; even the private and innocent expression of dream life is death-leading in that it is conceived of as the expression of sin. The body is perceived as signifying the vocabulary of sin—or death—and is therefore repulsive and easily compared to a rotting corpse: "in life he produced lice and tapeworms; in death he will produce worms and flies. In life he produced dung and vomit; in death he produces rottenness and stench."

The church preyed on the commonplace of death by disease in the Middle Ages, using it to transform physical values into spiritual ones. The individual's death—especially because of its frequently grotesque effects (plagues, consumption)—became God's direct retribution for the sins of the flesh.

About eighty years after Innocent, Dante synthesized a world in which the manifestations of the sinners' corruption in life became his or her perpetual and eternal punishment in the *Inferno* (*Hell*) of his epic poem *La divina commedia* (*The Divine Comedy*, c. 1320). But to exist as a physical being did not inherently corrupt and spell death for the individual. Innocent sees in mankind only pathetic weakness and insidious corruption; and more wretched still, humanity is "born only to die." Dante envisions the noble, creative, and responsible aspects of men and women, made possible by the gift of grace bestowed by God. Life itself is a gift and investment of God and is therefore both precious for its own sake and given meaning by the realm of the immortal.

Dante's journey in the *Divine Comedy* is a pilgrimage into the meaning of death necessitated by his straying "within a dark wood where the straight way was lost" (canto 1), which results in his conflict and his "pitiful weeping" in the face of "the death which combats him on the flood that is not less terrible than the sea" (canto 2). It begins with his passage through hell in all its dreadful aspects. But this is the first travelled and hence the most superficial realm of the dead. The illumination and conviction of salvation or eternal life become clearer and stronger the farther he moves away from hell. While Innocent stresses Peter's warning that the just man shall "scarcely be saved" (1 Pet., 4:18), Dante reveals, by faith in the creative act, the grace of God that leads the just individual out of the precincts of damnation and eternal death.

The genres to which each of these works belongs indicate much about the role of creativity in the shaping of the elements and meaning of the individual's death. Innocent's book is ostensibly an expository document on the nature of humanity and on its certain destiny decreed by the wrathful God. His writing is the articulation of a long sigh of despair as well as of a morbid fascination with death, which was one of the remarkable characteristics of early medieval culture. Dante, on the other hand, writing inspired and complex poetry, celebrates human creativity by that very act, and with an extraordinary mixture of faith and invention insists on the importance and legitimacy of the individual's very real role in shaping the meaning of his own death. His art acts directly for the salvation of the soul. Through it he is afforded the opportunity of witnessing death directly without dying and then having that experience shape and direct his heart, mind, and the rest of his life.

The theological preoccupation with death, which made it a subject for discursive writing of all kinds in the Middle Ages, also translated into a concern for death in the epic and the lyric. In both instances the death of others is more prominent than the individual's own death: the German epic, which gives pride of place to the *Totenklage* or death lament, for example (see especially the *Nibelungenlied* [c. 1200] anon., stanzas 1002–1072, 2357–2379; *Tristan* [c. 1210], Gottfried von Strassburg, ll.1680–1875; *Parzival* [c. 1210], Wolfram von Eschenbach, parts 250–255; and others); and the *ubi sunt* topos, exemplified in the later Middle Ages by Villon's "Ballade des dames du temps jadis" ("Ballad of the Women of Yesteryear," 1461), a popular topos in the lyric. Although both the death lament and the *ubi sunt* are overtly concerned with the death of others, both exhibit typically a powerful, melancholic undercurrent, a mood that is implicitly inward-turning.

In later medieval works the concern often becomes more overtly a matter of the speaker's own death. Villon's long poetic testament (*Grand testament* [*The Great Testament* 1461]) is often playful, but also includes serious meditations on his own life and death. William Dunbar (Scottish, writing c. 1500) also wrote in both playful and serious veins; one of his most moving poems ("I That in Heill Wes and Gladnes") transforms the *ubi sunt* topos into a confession of death's power and the speaker's fear of it (its refrain reads, from the Latin liturgy, "Timor mortis conturbat me," "the fear of death shakes me").

Dunbar's poem draws on two other contemporary traditions, those of the dance of death and the *memento mori*. In the dance of death—a visual motif with a parallel literary tradition—Death appears to the living and leads them off in a dance. A preacher often frames the dance with a sermon exhorting the observer to prepare him- or herself for death. The motif's popularity reached its height across Europe in the fifteenth century (roughly when a related motif, instructions on the art of dying well, was popular in the graphic arts); it was followed by the rather less spooky, more philosophical *memento mori,* in which the individual typically contemplates a skull that reminds him of his own death to come. The differences between the dance of death and *memento mori* are many and profound. In the former, Death is an ominous and often gruesome presence; in the latter, it is a physical process, related more to scientific knowledge and self-conscious meditation than to the obscure mysteries of God's will.

Chaucer departs radically from the powerful and ubiquitous medieval obsession with death; he rarely even treats the subject. When he does treat it (as in the *Pardoner's Tale* [*Canterbury Tales,* c. 1380–1400]), it serves more as allegory relevant to life than as an exploration of death itself. In this way, Chaucer is an obvious precursor of the Renaissance treatment of death.

Chaucer's *Pardoner's Tale* virtually amounts to a satire on the individual who attempts to sidestep or slight death. Death is elusive and does not lose his game. The three rogues who set out to slay death are corrupt, yes, but more significantly, they are splendidly stupid. They manage to kill each *other,* out of greed and selfishness, under the tree where the old man tells them he has seen Death recently. Death refuses to favor the old man in the story who longs to die, and this is a bittersweet corollary to the idea that death is anarchic, elusive, unpredictable, and therefore untouchable; a far cry from Dante's vision. The story is really a lesson in life, and in this allegory we see an example of death as a rhetorical device that was to become a significant feature of Renaissance narrative.

The Renaissance

During the Renaissance, the collective faith of the community that the mythology of Christianity had engendered and maintained was beginning to break down. With the weakening of the communal faith, the contemplation of one's own death became a much more private and intimate experience. Hope in immortality was suspect—or at least secondary—for many artists, so that the importance of the image and the symbolic qualities of death as simply literary or rhetorical devices became markedly heightened over the imaginative exploration into the meaning of death. Dante certainly used images of death as a medium for poetic expression in *The Divine Comedy,* but this work is explicitly the imaginative solution to the mysteries of a genuine and deep faith. In contrast, Hamlet's consideration of death in his famous soliloquy, (Shakespeare's *Hamlet,* drama, c. 1600) does not grow out of a meditative faith, but out of an emotional dilemma. Life is a burden for him; he considers the possibility of escaping it by death; he concludes that he is too cowardly for this because as far as he knows death could be even worse than life. In short, Hamlet is really weighing the value of life, not death. Even in the sonnets, where Shakespeare frequently treats the subject of death, death seems to serve primarily as a kind of boundary, like practical limitations to the artist. Thus, Shakespeare holds as ideal a dignity in the encounter with the ravages of time, and vows, "This shall ever be,/I will be true despite thy scythe and thee" (*Sonnet* 123, 1609).

The range of meanings assigned to individual deaths in Shakespeare's dramas is as rich as his range of characters. From Prospero's benign view that "our little life is rounded with a sleep" (*The Tempest,* 1611) to Lear's stark association of death with madness in an orderless world, Shakespeare relates the individual's understanding of death to his sense of meaning in life.

Rabelais flippantly treats death as a formalized rhetorical encounter by which he can display his satirical joviality. (See, for example, Panurge in the incident of the sheep dealer, *Gargantua et Pantagruel* [*Gargantua and Pantagruel,* narrative, 1532–1564], book 4). Although this cynical but fun-loving humor represents a practical and accepting attitude toward death, the treatment is not mimetic by any means but rather farcical; Rabelais' characters are having such a good time with their rhetoric, philosophizing, and bawd that the bleaker aspects of death naturally recede in importance. Besides, there is not much need for worry, as Pantagruel suggests, because "I believe that all intellectual souls are exempt from the scissors of Atropos. . . . They are all immortal, whether angelic, daemonic, or human."

Montaigne, in his *Essais (Essays,* 1580–1588), places death at the center of his writing: "Cicero says that to philosophize is nothing else but to prepare for death," and "to teach us not to be afraid to die" *(Essais* 1, 20, "Que philosopher c'est apprendre à mourir" ["That to Philosophize is to Learn to Die"]). While attending to the problem of death directly and relentlessly, he releases faith from his vocabulary, and intellectual pleasure or a certain joie de vivre takes its place. "I enjoy it [life] twice as much as others, for the measure of enjoyment depends on the greater or lesser attention that we lend it." By this same means he accepts death and presumably can even enjoy the thought of it, like an acquired taste: "Let us rid it of its strangeness, come to know it, get used to it. Let us have nothing on our minds as often as death. At every moment let us picture it in our imagination in all its aspects." Montaigne carries on a rhetorical dialogue with the spectres of death in order to be able to live free of the fear of death.

To dwell and fawn on death is a way of lyricizing it, of giving it a sweeter taste. To write about it at all is to place the structure of lyric or narrative between oneself and death. Milton achieves this structure self-consciously and explicitly in his elegy "Lycidas" (1637). By the end of the poem, seemingly having exposed the limits inherent in the elegiac intent, "he rose, and twitched his mantle blue:/Tomorrow to fresh woods, and pastures new." Obviously, this last is also an affirmation of the inevitability of life being for the living, though he solicits immortality for Lycidas through the medium of poetry, or the immortal Muse. Still, the ambiguity expressed toward death is significant and disturbing. The reconstruction of life in the face of death that the poem achieves is a poetic act in language, where poetry's life (and God's) is found. Physical death becomes elided from the vision. Still, the poem emphasizes the struggle between instinctive knowledge about death and the Christian appeal to faith, with a kind of literary immortality in language entering as a third, deeply felt possibility.

Never content at the periphery of experience, John Donne seeks the absolute involvement of consummation, which sets him immediately into the great arena of death. For him, the contemplation of death and of love are usually indistinguishable, and he artfully exploits the seventeenth-century commonplace metaphor of death for the consummation of sensual love. In "The Canonization" (poem, 1635), he implies that the act of love-making is such a complete surrender to—and participation in—life, as to include death. Of course, this is only a temporary and symbolic death, but when he speaks about resurrection, his allusion is to the phoenix; the resurrection of Christianity has no place here.

But Donne's later poetry embodies an exciting union between love and death, death and Christ, and Christ and union (See *Holy Sonnets,* c. 1633, 5.18). In the *Holy Sonnets* Death becomes cloaked once again with the dreamy allure of sleep until resurrection on Judgment Day when Death itself will die. Donne's plea, like the hungry infant's cry, is a desperate one. He has recognized that to look at God, for him, is to die. He wishes to be in the presence of God, but to avert his face; he loves life more than Christ. But Donne finally lays his soul in the lap of Christ, and in the poem "Hymn to God My God, in My Sickness," in spite of the still ambiguous tone, he needs to believe in Christian salvation.

It must never be forgotten that fear is an attitude toward death that prevails almost everywhere in its consideration. It is this fear itself that produces many of the conflicts and creations encountered in the evolution of literature and thought; as Edgar exclaims in Shakespeare's play *King Lear* (1606), "O, Our lives' sweetness!/That we the pain of death would hourly die,/Rather than die at once!"

The Enlightenment

The practical attitude toward death that becomes more prevalent with the Enlightenment and represents implicitly (though usually not explicitly) a departure from the Christian solution to the problem of death is exemplified by Jonathan Swift in *Gulliver's Travels* (narrative, 1726). In this work, Swift comments on the false illusions harbored by anyone who wishes for immortality, by his exposure of the Struldbrugs, who are the unfortunate few of the citizens of Luggnagg born with the curse of immortality. These individuals are physically decrepit, senile, bored, foul-tempered, and desire nothing more than to die.

Further dismissing the ideal of immortality, when Gulliver has the opportunity to summon before him the dead to converse with them, he never asks them what it is like to have died and to be dead. They are interesting to him only as pieces of history and representatives of a certain stage of biological and historical evolution; life is for the living. The Houyhnhnms, whom Gulliver reveres and wishes to imitate, do not mourn their dead or for their own death. Their acceptance of death shows Gulliver's—and Swift's—recognition of the sweetness of a peaceful and balanced life without that extreme of despair, the unspeakable grief that is real mourning. The Christian solution no longer affords an escape from confrontation with death, and Swift's ironies imply desire for acceptance without achieving it. Still, *Gulliver's Travels* does not linger over fears of death; like many Enlightenment works, it is life-centered.

A major Enlightenment essay on death and the arts is Lessing's essay "Wie die Alten den Tod gebildet" ("How the Ancients Depicted Death," 1769) in which the author argues that death was conceived in antiquity not as a horror but as the benign brother of sleep. Lessing criticizes the depiction of death in Christian art as being morbid and argues that to consider death as punishment and as grotesque is simply not reasonable. Lessing's essay had considerable influence on contemporary notions of the appropriate attitude toward death in the arts. As Schiller was to write in *Die Götter Griechenlands* (*The Gods of Greece*, poem, 1788), "No gruesome, skeletal corpse/Haunted the deathbed in those days." A Greek ideal is invented that seeks to banish the macabre from the arts.

One major eighteenth-century poem that does take death as its subject is Edward Young's *Night Thoughts on Life, Death, and Immortality* (1742–1745). Young, who was a priest, writes a theologically "correct" meditation on death, in a way that makes it seem at times more a rhetorical tour de force than a serious meditation. When he writes that at death we "spring to life,/The life of gods, oh transport! and of man," we are less convinced of his sincerity than when he transforms death into Time, using a traditional image: "Each moment has its sickle, emulous/Of Time's enormous scythe."

A fascination with death is one hallmark of the preromantic sensibility. Death may be invoked to inform a mood, as in Thomas Gray's "Elegy Written in a Country Churchyard" (1750–1751) and other poems of the contemporary "graveyard school" of poetry; "the paths of glory lead only to the grave," Gray proclaims, moralizing but pensive, as he seeks in poetry a means as much to understand as to express the universality of death. William Cowper attributes his condition of living death to Christian values in his "Lines Written During a Period of Insanity" (1782): "I, fed with judgment, in a fleshly tomb, am/Buried above ground"; he uses death here as a metaphor for power and extremity, without developing an attitude toward his actual death that might grow out of a rejection of the Christian paradigm. Charlotte Smith creates a fantasy in her poem "Pressed by the Moon, Mute Arbitress of Tides" (1786), where the dead become at once compatible with and immune from the violence of nature, and the poet's stance is one of envy and awe even while she describes the dead by their scattered remains.

In Goethe's *Die Leiden des jungen Werthers* (*The Sorrows of Young Werther*, 1774) a different but related fascination with death appears. Werther's suicide for love is part of the novel's densely constructed mood, but it also poses a solution to the metaphysical dilemma of ontological insufficiency.

Goethe's novel *Wilhelm Meisters Wanderjahre* (*Wilhelm Meister's Travels*, 1829) much more subtly traces the death in life and the death of its heroine Makarie, whose embodiment of the ideal of feminine selflessness is so extreme and so actual that it truly represents a death in life; as Gilbert and Gubar have pointed out, she has no real story, and therefore no real life.

Romanticism

That morbid sensibility undergoes a transformation in romantic works; indeed, a preoccupation with death is one of the defining features of European romanticism in all the arts. The continuing breakdown of the communal aspects of Christian faith now meant that not only was one's mode of faith more personal, but also both the letter and the spirit of religion were becoming more open to individual interpretation. Now Christianity could be made to submit to virtually any structure of perception, and with its rich iconography and resilient model of prophecy, it could complement and inform the romantic vision even at its most subjective, providing a mythic framework for the quintessentially romantic subject, the contemplation of death.

William Blake is one of the most remarkable and agile interpreters of Christian text and vision. For this very reason the spectres of death become as pliant to the poet's manipulation as any other aspect of life that is treated poetically and creatively. Since to Blake "all reality is a mental construction," the consideration of death is a creative act, and as such takes on mythic qualities; the imaginative act transforms death into what the imaginer wants it to be or into the sum of the signs that inform the vision of the individual. The ruddy and colossal products of Blake's myth-making seem impervious to death, as the threshold between life and death is one that the mind may cross and recross in its visionary terrain. There is virtually no *fear* of death in his poetry.

In romantic poetry death becomes increasingly associated with eroticism, as the polar opposition between death and life shifts into a desired fusion. In Blake, for example, the knowledge of death and that of the erotic are linked in his idea of Experience (*Songs of Innocence and Experience,* 1794); but more importantly, his notion of a higher Innocence embraces both death and erotic love in a synthetic vision. The German writer Novalis gives expression to a characteristically romantic longing for death in his "Hymnen an die Nacht" ("Hymns to the Night," 1800) in which death, known imaginatively through night, represents a victory over time and space as well as a quasi-erotic unity of being. Novalis writes within an imaginatively charged Christian vision, as Christ fuses with a longed-for lover and with death.

An important vehicle for meditation on death in romanticism is the elegy; but here, as in Shelley's "Adonais" (1821) or Hugo's poems of mourning for his daughter (1844–1847), knowledge of one's own death is subordinate to, or achieved through, grieving for another. In Wordsworth's *Lucy* poems (1800–1807), the elegiac mode seems to exist primarily as a framework for conveying a knowledge of death's blankness—a knowledge that can only be articulated in the simplest, most barren language possible. Here there is no mystical fusion, no eroticized longing, no moodiness or despair: just a simple and powerful, fully imagined knowledge of death.

Among the many romantic works that center on death, Keats' poems are significant for their synthesis of personal meditation with external images. Keats returns repeatedly, in a variety of tones, to the subject of death. Perhaps the most perfectly balanced poem about death is his ode "To Autumn" (1819), in which death is everywhere present but nowhere mentioned. Images of ripeness and harvest, subtly eroticized, slowly transform death's processes into a larger process, of which the poetic art is an organic part.

Attitudes toward death in romantic poetry remain closely linked to faith. The deep sense of loss that Wordsworth feels and traces in "Ode: Intimations of Immortality" (1807) impresses on the poet his mortal aspect and seems to be the catalyst for his urgent desire to discover and to create the indestructible. His quest is a conscious desire to escape death; "We will not grieve, but rather find strength . . . in the faith that looks through death." This faith is highly personal, but it still echoes the Christian solution to the problem of death since it is also predicated on faith, though not explicitly a Christian faith.

The Later Nineteenth Century

For many artists, doubt and faith continue their turbulent marriage in the human psyche. Tennyson's poem "The Two Voices" (1833) directly addresses the duality of his conviction about the meaning of death; and his elegy "In Memoriam" (1850) traces the map of conflict that he experiences in this struggle, throughout a period of about sixteen years. It expresses an ongoing relationship between the emotion of horror at the idea of death—that is a tendency of youth— and the acceptance of death—a tendency of maturity that is usually attended by some kind of faith.

Perhaps Emily Dickinson's idea that "The abdication of belief/Makes the behavior small—/Better an ignis fatuus/Than no illume at all—" ("Poem 1551," posthumous, 1945) helps in understanding how an artist like Tennyson should finally engage into the machinery of Christianity and in denial of death and of the unknown, after a number of ambiguities have arisen over the course of the very long poem, and conclude, for many unconvincingly, "Whereof the man that with me trod/ . . . That friend of mine who lives in God, that God, which ever lives and loves,/One God, one law, one element,/And one far off divine event,/To which the whole creation moves" ("In Memoriam").

The death theme in "In Memoriam" also, of course, serves a formulaic function as well, as it does in many other writings; George Eliot's "The Lifted Veil" (short story, 1859) as well as Mary Shelley's "The Mortal Immortal: A Tale" (short story, 1834) would also fall under this category; in both stories, death is an overt subject, but is more importantly a vehicle for other social and psychological issues.

Emily Brontë's "[No coward soul is mine]" (poem, 1846) represents an instance of faith that is so large "There is not room for Death." But her poem "The Night-Wind" (1850), which focuses on the relationship between night, death, and the imagination, affirms that the mystery and elusiveness of death remain a powerful metaphor for the imagination. As Gilbert and Gubar show, Christina Rossetti's "mortuary verses" like "After Death" (1862) and "Dead before Death" (1862) mourn the limitations of the range of creative alternatives available to women.

For Baudelaire in *Les fleurs du mal* (*The Flowers of Evil*, poems, 1857) death has a kind of power for the imagination that is related to his constant pushing toward a new and impossible knowledge. In "Le voyage" ("Travel") he pushes beyond ennui, seeking "the abysmal depths of the Unknown,/to find the *New!*" Baudelaire's sense of death as something peculiarly desired—a recurrent attitude of which traces can be found in every period and which Freud labeled a "death wish"—influenced two generations of poets in France, England, and Germany;

there is, in Baudelaire's poetry ("Une charogne" ["A Carrion"], for example) a medievalistic revelling in decaying flesh, and an archromantic fusion of death and eroticism; but later poets, such as Mallarmé, Verlaine, and Rimbaud found in his idea of death an embodiment of poetic imagination at its most unbounded. Mallarmé's "azur" in "Renouveau" ("Renewal," 1866) is a direct descendant of Baudelaire's "nouveau." Hugo von Hofmannsthal's *Der Tor und der Tod* (*Death and the Fool*, play, 1898) is fully marked by a Baudelairean sensibility, as Death is aligned with poetic beauty, and the dying esthete expresses an intense ambivalence. English Decadent poetry reflects a less successful fusion of death with estheticism, as in Ernest Dowson's "Dregs" (1899), for example. But at its best the late-Victorian morbidity is psychologically powerful, as in Swinburne's "The Triumph of Time" (1866).

In the realist novel, direct meditation on death is supplemented by narrative in which death may play a significant role. Tolstoy's work is especially exemplary in this context. In many of his stories, Death seems to wake the somnambulist individual, who has proceeded through life in a kind of living death. *Smert' Ivana Il'icha* (*The Death of Ivan Ilyich*, 1886) is the classic example of this, where Death is a sort of moral overlord who extracts recognition, confession, and forgiveness (of self and others) by its very nature. Also, there is almost never an image of death without a startling image of life by its side in Tolstoy, often minimizing and sometimes even justifying death (see, for example, *Tri smerti* [*The Three Deaths*, story, 1859]). Dorothy Richardson's short story "Death" (1924), like *Ivan Ilyich*, focuses on the belated questioning of the significance of life, especially, in the narrator's case, a hard life of constant and difficult work in the face of death. She concludes "Life ain't worth death."

Of peculiar significance in the history of the novel is the number of stories that end with the suicide of the heroine. Tolstoy's *Anna Karenina* (1877) is, of course, an example, as is Flaubert's *Madame Bovary* (1856); but the most telling example may be Kate Chopin's *The Awakening* (1899), which makes it clear that such deaths seem an inevitable closure for the life of the extraordinary woman, or for the woman who seeks some way out of the confining roles available to her. Death is implicitly tragic here, not attractive, though it may come to seem attractive to the woman to whom other avenues are closed.

However, many women writers claimed a large portion of death's powerful realm, albeit in the "lesser" genre of consolation literature. Barred from many of the fulfilling areas of human endeavour, women marked off the shadowy region of death for themselves, as the only world to which they alone had knowledge, expertise, and rite of entry within the life period. In contrast to the seventeenth and early eighteenth centuries that had no real cult of mourning, in the later nineteenth century the genre of consolation literature was extremely popular in England and America and was part of the "domestication of death" that women created as Ann Douglas has shown in *The Feminization of American Culture* (1977).

The "angel of death" figures prominently in the nineteenth-century literature of both men and women writers and is represented by characters such as Dickens' Little Nell and Harriet Beecher Stowe's Little Eva. (See Gilbert and Gubar's *The Madwoman in the Attic*.) As angels of death, they embody a constant *memento mori* and simultaneously enact a quasi-erotic union with the realm of the dead; their relationship with that world represents an inner and ecstatic flight from the way they are seen and therefore created by men, as well as from the responsibility of that vision. Escape and compliance thus characteristically merge and blur. An austere personality, delicate health, and ready tendency to "decline" at the slightest of reasons appear as ideals in these female characters. Such traits signify the innocuous realm of powerlessness to which these women were relegated, but also their own longing to die, their own lonely, private, and morbid romance with death.

The Twentieth Century/Modern Period

Twentieth-century Western literature is largely concerned with living and creating in a godless universe. This is a dramatic change for humanity, a painful break from the "illume" of hope provided first by Christianity and then by variations and reinterpretations of its model. Eventually, the legacy of Christianity is culturally legible only in pieces of "broken images." These pieces function appropriately as disconnected but still symbolic shards in a collage of little and not lofty meanings. Many writers comment on the now inadequate Christian solution to the problem of death and explore possibilities for the role of a timid and haggard but nevertheless existent faith; that "fragile ship of courage, the ark of faith . . . upon the sea of death, where still we sail/darkly, for we cannot steer, and have no port" (D. H. Lawrence, from "The Ship of Death," poem, 1928). Recognizing that faithlessness "makes the Behavior small"—makes humanity petty and inarticulate—artists and thinkers have been and continue to be involved in a process of shaping a vision into which faith can breathe life. Some, like Beckett, have been resigned to presenting a world that is essentially dead, is inhabited by living dead, and in which hope flickers miserably in the symbolic and awkward gestures of compassion indulged in pseudo-nostalgically by the various characters. In such a world, death has no more meaning than life; and, for writers in the existentialist tradition such as Sartre and Camus, both life and death have only the meaning appropriated for them by an act of will.

The priest in T. S. Eliot's *Murder in the Cathedral* (drama, 1935) says that the church is "supreme as long as men will die for it." But who can die for it now? Not Eliot's own "Son of man," who "cannot say, or guess for you know only/A heap of broken images, where the sun beats,/And the dead tree gives no shelter, the cricket no relief,/And the dry stone no sound of water" (*The Waste Land*, poem, 1922). Eliot himself had to look beyond this vision, which nevertheless remains powerfully emblematic of one modern sensibility. Even in later Eliot, the fear of death makes individuals live timidly, "men and women who shut the door and sit by the fire." The void is too huge, the will too disappointed, art inadequate. There is not an idea that is worth dying for, he suggests; and we are perhaps not even yet on the threshold of being able to conceive of an ideal that does not require the shedding of blood.

The martyrs whose blood "shall enrich the earth, shall create holy places" gave meaning to the individual's death once, gave it direction and purpose, even glorified it as the dying individual fell into the embrace of God. Now the damned dead only "Rave on the leash of the starving mind" (Sylvia Plath, "November Graveyard," poem, 1956); we have recognized that the best symbols are empty, and we have tried for a long time to fill them. It now seems we must discard them altogether.

For some writers, death still may inform the individual's life in a significant way. Thus it is a premonition and a warning from death that motivates Aschenbach in Thomas Mann's *Der Tod in Venedig* (*Death in Venice,* novelle, 1912) to break out of the emotional and physical repression that has kept him all his life from exploration, from color. From death Aschenbach learns passion and self-knowledge. Similarly, in Gide's *L'immoraliste* (*The Immoralist,* novel, 1902) death initiates Michel to love, appreciation of life, and to self-knowledge. In Joyce's *Dubliners* (short stories, 1914), another example of classically modern narrative, death resonates as an emblem of what it is to be alive in the stories' world, from which there is no relief or escape except into artifact. And in Proust's *A la recherche du temps perdu* (*Remembrance of Things Past,* novels, 1913–1927), the narrator's approaching death provides an unspoken destination—though not one necessarily replete with meaning—for the entire work. Death thus provides the reason for art, if not a meaning for it.

For other writers death is more than an inevitable destination, it is a veritable homecoming, the only realm to which they sense and express a feeling of belonging. This death as homecoming theme is particularly, though not exclusively, encountered in women's writing. Sylvia Plath's "I Am Vertical (But I would rather be horizontal)" (poem, 1961) expresses the poet's feeling of alienation even from nature (with which as a woman she has traditionally been associated), and the sense that only after death "The trees may touch me for once, and the flowers have time for me." Anne Sexton's poem "Sylvia's Death" (1965) sympathizes with and reiterates this theme: "what is your death/but an old belonging." For women writers, death also serves thematically to signify the death in life that has been seen as representative of the silent and domesticized or frivolous and complacent female voice that is a significant aspect of female history. An example is Muriel Rukeyser's poem "More of a Corpse than a Woman" (1938). In a variation of this theme, the poem enacts an arduous, prolonged death of a male precursor or a male mythic vision of women (as in Adrienne Rich's poem "I Dream I'm the Death of Orpheus," 1968), before female creativity can act healthily and with relative freedom.

For writers in another modern tradition, perhaps best represented by Beckett and Kafka, the scaffolding on which narrative logic has rested becomes exposed; death holds no more sense than any other inexplicable event. The landscape of

Beckett's *Fin de partie, (Endgame,* drama, 1957) is a world hanging by a thread between action and inaction, between life and death, between fear of life and fear of death. Hamm requests, "Put me in my coffin." But there are no more coffins, no more choices available. One cannot (does not) give significance to one's own death; one must accept instead the inherent potential and hope of inaction. Beckett's attitude pushes the problem of death to an extreme that seems to demand attention, but it cannot be denied that his world not only works formally, but is often absolutely poetic; there is a certain acceptance in the completeness and thus perfection of this world.

See also: Afterlife, Dance of Death, Demonic Musician and the Soulbird, Descent into Hell, Grotesque, Horror, *Liebestod,* Terror, Vampirism.

Selected Bibliography

Ariès, Philippe. *The Hour of Our Death.* Trans. Helen Weaver. New York: Vintage Books, 1981.

Choron, Jacques. *Death and Western Thought.* New York: Macmillan, 1963.

Gilbert, Sandra M., and Susan Gubar. *The Madwoman in the Attic: The Woman Writer and the Nineteenth-Century Literary Imagination.* New Haven, Conn.: Yale University Press, 1979.

Higonnet, Margaret. "Suicide: Representations of the Feminine in the Nineteenth Century." *Poetics Today* 6 (1985): 103–118.

PAMELA CASWELL
SARAH WEBSTER GOODWIN

DEMONIC MUSIC

The belief that evil can exist in music has been prevalent in many cultures. But it was in ancient Greece that the idea of musical evil was refined into a theory that would have profound literary and philosophical significance. Those mainly responsible for this development were the Pythagoreans, a group of philosophers and mathematicians who were convinced that music's mysterious ability to affect the emotions of its listeners was the result of what it expressed.

Their conclusion was based upon a distinction between harmony and discord that contained a moral judgment. They thought musical discord expressed the unlimited or chaotic void that had always existed and which had once ruled the entire universe before being pushed back, while harmony was a divine creation that expressed the triumph of order over chaos, good over evil, limit over limitlessness.

The basis for this distinction that set them apart in the ancient world was the discovery of a mathematical relationship between tones, based on physical measurement. Though sound itself could not be measured physically, they found a way to measure sound through its source. For example, it was possible to produce an octave by plucking two musical strings, one twice the length of the other.

By such means, they were able to conclude that the mathematical ratio of the octave is 2:1. They discovered, moreover, that the most harmonious tones of a scale, the consonants, had simple mathematical ratios—2:1, 3:2, 4:3—and that the scale was responsible for the underlying, invisible structure of music. Using these discoveries, it seems, they made a leap of imagination to a musically oriented cosmology that divided the universe between order and chaos. Our planetary system represented order structured by a cosmic scale. The lengths of planetary orbits, for example, were determined by the ratios of the scale. In contrast, chaos represented the absence of a self-limiting structure like that provided by the scale. Out of these conceptions came the opposing positions of harmony and discord; harmony belonged to the cosmic scale, while discord belonged to chaos and existed primarily outside of the scale. The Greek worship of order and the tendency to associate the lack of order with disintegration and destruction appear to have prompted the judgment that discord was evil (Plato's *Timaios* [*Timaeus,* dialogue, fourth century B.C.]).

Since their cosmology was based primarily on music and numbers, it is not surprising that they saw a connection between primal discord and harmony and earthly music as well as with the mind, which could compose music. Nonetheless, such a bold assertion would seem to be not just unprovable but illogical. The universe was immense and distant. What possible connection could it have with music and the soul? Their answer was that music, cosmology, and the soul were linked through mimesis. The human soul was an imitation of the universe, a microcosm that contained both harmony and "an element of discord, a jarring note caused by a flaw in the numerical order of our souls—or to put it in yet another Pythagorean way, an element of the unlimited as yet unsubdued by the good principle of Limit." (*A History of Greek Philosophy,* vol. 1, 1962). Similarly, music was a vibration or motion of the air, which through its harmony and discord could imitate the revolutions of the soul. The existence of mimetic harmony and discord in music and the soul made it possible for the Pythagoreans to explain how music affected the soul and to identify its source of evil. Music could, at least temporarily, affect the soul through its kindred motion. Discord, whether it originated within or came from outside, could cause the soul to wobble out of its harmonious orbits onto paths that were irregular or irrational. Irregularities in the soul would then be translated into behavior that was evil, vice-ridden, or mentally aberrant.

This proved to be a powerful theory that soon gained in influence and began to expand as it was taken up by other philosophers, most notably by Plato. Plato, who would exert a major influence on Western thought, appears to have taken their ideas about music further than the Pythagoreans did. He saw a political danger in music, which he chose to emphasize. He accused the innovative musicians of his society of inspiring the multitude with "lawlessness and boldness" through compositions that showed "no perception of what is just and lawful in music." And he warned his readers to handle this art, which imitated the revolutions of the soul, with extreme care. "For," he said," if a man makes a mistake here, he may do himself the greatest injury by welcoming evil dispositions" *Nomoi* (*The Laws,* dialogue, c. 350 B.C.).

In support of his accusations, he singled out specific practices he felt had a bad effect upon individual behavior and thus ultimately upon the health of the state. In the process he seems to have expanded the Pythagorean concept of discord. High on his blacklist was the mixture of music and gesture appropriate to free men with that relegated to slaves. In the same category was the disregard for boundaries separating men and women reflected in the mixture of music that expressed the character of men with that which suggested femininity. He also deplored the practice of combining man-made music with bestial sounds. He clearly thought that disregard for "natural" divisions could, by example, threaten the social order.

The mixing of different melodic lines represented yet another kind of misalliance, one which appears to mark a significant innovation. Ancient Greek music was traditionally monodic. It joined a melodic line with modest accompaniment. But during Plato's time, poets began to separate the line they sang from the notes they played, a practice that Portnoy believes was an early attempt at polyphony. Plato condemned the practice on the grounds that it created confusion. His strong desire to keep composers from separating text from music was shown also in his objection to instrumental music, the use of which, he believed, "leads to every sort of irregularity and trickery" (*The Laws*). Tonality and timbre were other elements of music in which he saw deviation. Perhaps his best-known statement about music concerned the intoxicating, enervating, or lascivious effect Ionian and Lydian modes have on the personality and behavior of the listener. As for timbre, the sound of the flute was particularly disturbing to him. He associated it with the Bacchanals and their wild festivals (*Politeia* [*The Republic,* dialogue, c. 380 B.C.]).

Plato's use of Pythagorean cosmology to support his attacks on innovation and change in music was of particular importance since it colored the way in which music was perceived. Innovation and change in music were not thought of as necessary and natural but as deviant and potentially dangerous. In the centuries to come Plato's opinion would be frequently echoed.

Medieval Influences

The first great literary period to explore and modify the Greek concepts was the Middle Ages. Just how heavily influenced it was by Plato's Pythagoreanism is not always easy to access directly. But Plato's interpretation of evil in music was perpetuated in most of its essentials, undoubtedly because medieval writers agreed with Plato's underlying distrust of innovation and his fear that changes in music could affect the stability of the state. What the Middle Ages itself contributed thematically was the belief that demonic music was a sinister expression of the bestial, material world. By implication, it was demonic music's association with instincts and desires that made it evil. This view is evident in the medieval treatment of music in cosmology. The harmonious music of the planetary system described by the Greeks remains as a Christian expression of divine hegemony. It reflects a universe without chaos that is rigidly structured. But significantly, cosmic discord has been moved, taken out of this universe entirely, and placed unceremoniously in the realms of earth and hell, the realms of physical desire, sin, death, and the devil.

The dark association of demonic music with bestial appetites and ignoble desires was not only suggested through cosmology. In medieval literature demonic music was frequently associated with the sound of beasts and thus by implication with instinct and desire. It is, for instance, compared by Caesarius von Heisterbach, a thirteenth-century writer, to the grunt of a pig.

For more complicated reasons, the breakdown in the relationship between notes established by scales or church modes was also an indication of the nature of demonic music. Music that did not make use of the structure of the scales was thought to defy reason and therefore to overturn the hierarchy of reason, passion, and will, which brought harmony. The role of reason and the consequences of defying it are clearly outlined in Chaucer's "Parson's Tale": "God sholde have lordshipe over resoun, and resoun over sensualitee, and sensualitee over the body of man . . . whan man synneth al this ordre or ordinaunce is turned up-so-doun." (The Canterbury Tales, 1380–1400). By defying reason, the sinning man subjected himself to the dominance of his evil, material body. By defying reason, music became an instrument of the devil in his struggle against the spirit.

The sound of unregulated instruments such as horns without stops was an example of sound that defies reason. The tritone or diabolus in musica was condemned by the same criterion. Because it possessed three whole tones in its interval, it broke down the hierarchical pattern established by the modes. The prejudice against the tritone is particularly noteworthy since it lasted well beyond the Middle Ages. Bach could still utilize the tritone in his cantatas to symbolize evil, death, sin, or the devil. Mozart used it in Don Giovanni (1787) to suggest Leporello's fear that the stone statue he confronts is a demon. And Beethoven sounds the tritone in the drums when Florestan is thrown into a dark dungeon by his evil captors (Fidelio, 1805).

The medieval criterion also seems to have been extended in later centuries to chromatic tones, which exist outside the scales or keys used in classical music. Milton suggests in "At a Solemn Musick" (1637) that musicians leave "out those harsh chromatic jars/Of clamours sin that all our music mars." And he appears to have chromatic tones in mind when he remarks "disproportioned Sin/ Jarred against Nature's chime, and with harsh din/Broken the fair music that all creatures made." The medieval charge against demonic music that it can unseat the reason was also leveled against chromatic notes by Alexander Pope, who wrote "chromatic tortures soon shall drive them hence/Break all their nerves and fritter all their sense."

The condemnation of "improper" relationships between notes coincided with a condemnation of larger musical structures. Plato's distaste for the practice of playing one thing and singing another echoes in an early medieval aversion to polyphony that was later abandoned. Typically, an attempt to bring early polyphonic pieces into the church was condemned by the twelfth-century bishop of Chartres, John of Salisbury, as a wanton, bestial defilement of the religious service.

Like tone and structure, rhythm was scrutinized for diabolical, material influences. Dante uses the image of dance and of cross rhythms to convey the idea of conflicting desires among hoarders and wasters in his epic poem *La divina commedia* (*The Divine Comedy*, c. 1320): "Just as the surge charybdis hurls to sea/crashes and breaks upon its countersurge,/so these shades dance and crash eternally." And, by implication, he contrasted their chaotic dance with the stately, ordered dance of the angels inhabiting the celestial spheres of paradise.

Demonic dancing, suggesting a "rhythmic chaos," was one of the favored pastimes of hell. In a French-Norman legend of the thirteenth century, a deceased witch is led dancing to hell where a final grotesque dance of homage is performed before Satan himself. In the *Mystère de Sainte Barbe* (*The Mystery of St. Barbe*, 15th century), the pagan king Dioscurus, after slaying his Christian daughter, slips into hell, where he and the devil dance a branle (a dance characterized by its swaying motion).

On earth the demonic rhythms tended to be more seductive and less grotesque. In Jehan de Meung's *Roman de la rose* (*Romance of the Rose*, didactic poem, c. 1275), for example, a physically suggestive dance is performed to the sound of a bagpipe for the purpose of luring sinners into the clutches of the pagan demon Venus. Among witches, leaping, frenzied sabbath dances were favored according to Margaret Alice Murray who, in *The Witch-Cult in Western Europe* (1921), connects them with ancient fertility rites. The dances were reportedly accompanied by a mass sexual orgy as well as an inverted mass in which hymns were sung to Satan and a feast eaten without salt (since salt preserved "meat" from decay).

The Middle Ages also shared with Plato the belief that certain instruments were suspect. The number of instruments actually maligned at one time or another was quite large. However, they do fit into identifiable albeit overlapping categories. The condemned included those instruments whose timbre was considered to be enticing or otherwise disturbing, those that had allegorical significance, those that seemed unnatural or grotesque in appearance, those whose sounds could not be regulated, and those that were used to parody divine instruments like the harp.

Among instruments whose sound was disturbing, wind instruments were often prominent. The sound of flutes and bagpipes came in for special abuse. The bagpipes' association with the physical or material world and therefore with the devil was suggested by a nickname given to its melody as Robert Eisler recalls in "Danse Macabre": "A bag-piper's melody is called (chant) macabre because it sounds like the grave-digger's dirge. The devil is called "macabret" because

he is believed to fetch the sinner like the grave-digger in the Dance of Death"
(*Traditio* 6 [1948]).

Among instruments that had a special allegorical or symbolic significance,
the bagpipe also had a place because of its resemblance to male sex organs.
This resemblance is grotesquely ridiculed in Bosch's painting of a musician's
hell (*The Garden of Lusts,* 1504), where the bagpipe is treated as a symbol of
lust. Chaucer helped to delineate the lustful character of his miller, furthermore,
by giving him a bagpipe. And he said a great deal about the pilgrimage to
Canterbury when he let the miller, playing his bagpipe, lead the procession out
of London. Like the bagpipe, the tympanum was condemned for reasons other
than sound alone. In the medieval mind, it was a short step from the literal fact
that members of the drum family were made of skin to the belief that the drum
heads symbolized the flesh or "the song of the flesh."

Probably the best-known demonic instrument was the fiddle, which was a
parodic, demonic counterpart of the harp. Like the voices of the sirens, the
devil's fiddle was supposed to be irresistible. In a typical account of its powers,
Satan is said to play the violin with such skill that with it he "could send whole
cities, grandparents and grandchildren, men and women, girls and boys to dancing, dancing until they fell dead from sheer exhaustion" (Rudwin, *The Devil in
Legend and Literature,* 1931).

The concept of demonic music developed in the Middle Ages remained essentially unaltered until the late Renaissance. Then, in the sixteenth century, a
revolution began that would force changes in the perception of music.

The Copernican Revolution

This revolution was the Copernican revolution in astronomy, which successfully challenged the medieval Christian belief that the earth was the center of
the planetary system. The triumph of science was to have a profound effect upon
critical thinking about music in the seventeenth century. The concepts of divine
harmony and demonic discord, which had been associated with the old cosmology, were disputed. And a clear trend toward the demystification of music's
influence on its listeners emerged. As John Hollander commented in *The Un-
tuning of the Sky* (1961), "here we have indication of a new phase in the history
of musical thought. The older tradition of world harmony and its consequences
for the effects of music upon individuals are . . . specifically repudiated, and the
powers of music are accounted for in terms of a quasi-mechanistic model."

But the mechanistic interpretation of music that sought to replace "superstition" with logic was soon to be affected by the struggle developing between
science and religion. While philosophers like Descartes maintained that human
reason was capable of fathoming nearly all the mysteries in the universe, chal-
lengers, often religiously motivated, raised increasing doubts. The mathematician
Pascal, for example, spoke of the universe in *Pensées* (*Thoughts,* 1670) as an
ocean of infinite space whose very immensity was beyond our comprehension.

His doubts complemented those of Kant, who asserted that the essence of things lies beneath a "veil" that reason cannot penetrate. The doubts about reason helped to foster a backlash against it, which was epitomized in Goethe's play *Faust* (1808) by Faust's dissatisfaction with a life consecrated to the intellect and by his yearning for spontaneous, unpremeditated, undefinable experience.

The turn away from reason in favor of a more intuitive and mystical approach to universal questions coincided with a rise in exotic claims about music. The trend toward demystification lost support, and by the late eighteenth century (Alfred Einstein, *Music in the Romantic Era*, 1947) a palpable change had taken place. Music had become "a medium through which the ineffable could be made palpable to sense, through which the mysterious, magical, and exciting could be created." It became fashionable to speak of being stimulated by music to see ineffable images, many of which were images of a strange, chaotic universe. Some were apocalyptic in form, like the demonic vision of chaotic nature that Heine said he had while listening to Paganini's music.

Observations of this sort were accompanied by significant changes in music itself, some of which seemed especially to capitalize upon the yearning for the ineffable. It could hardly be coincidence, for instance, that Wagner introduced what he called "infinite melody" during a period when artists were fascinated with the unimaginable immensity of space.

The trend toward mysticism during a period of transition is the context in which the fate of demonic music in literature needs to be viewed. The conception of the universe as unlimited, mysterious, and untenable to reason, the regard for what the senses and emotions offered beyond the dictates of rational thought, and the dramatic changes occurring in music itself, all contributed to the thematic re-evaluation of demonic music that followed.

The Romantic Era and the Rise of Materialism

It is possible to speak of trends dealing with demonic music from the late eighteenth to the late nineteenth century, though there were crossover ideas. One trend was toward preserving the remnants of traditional (medieval) beliefs; another reflected a rebellious new attitude toward music.

The more traditional writers found material for their stories in the historical changes music was undergoing and in the flamboyant behavior of certain performers and composers. Real music and real composers were even sometimes mentioned. Wagner was a favorite subject of abuse. James Huneker, though writing after this period, reflected typical criticism in *Bedouins* (1920) with his suggestion that *Parsifal* (1882) is really Wagner's "version of the Black Mass" and that "Wagner admired the Devil in Music" because the devil "created the chromatic scale."

Reflecting a wariness toward musical innovation, experimentation with music in traditionally oriented stories could get a musician into a lot of trouble. When E.T.A. Hoffmann's Kreisler sits down to improvise, for instance, in "Kreislers musikalisch-poetischer Klub" ("Kreisler's Musical-Poetic Club," 1814), he finds his mind often filled with terrifying, demonic images. At one point he sees devils dancing on graves, while at another he is convinced that sound, like a devil, is digging its claws into his heart. The experiments of Balzac's Gambara convince him he is creating divine music while in reality a hideous discord rules most of his compositions and is regarded by those around him as evidence of his madness (*Gambara*, novella, 1837). Musical improvisation and experimentation are linked to madness in Poe's "The Fall of the House of Usher" (story, 1839) through the poetic rhapsody Usher invents. A poem accompanying the rhapsody gives a glimpse into Usher's mind as he plays. At the beginning of the poem, Usher describes a paradisiacal vision, a throne room brightened by light from "two luminous windows" and inhabited by spirits who dance to a "lute's well-tuned law." But as the music Usher plays grows more wild and uncontrolled, this poetic vision, meant to represent his mind, begins to change. "Evil things" enter the palace. The throng of dancers becomes hideous and fantastic. The well-tuned music of the lute is replaced by "a discordant melody," and the two luminous windows change into red litten windows that might suggest the eyes of a demon. The ancient ideas that connected evil to mental disorder and musical discord are here clearly in evidence.

The counterpart to stories of musicians who are victims of their own musical madness were stories of fictive and historical musicians who use music in the diabolical manipulation of others. Typical of the demonic seducer is the dark gypsy in Keller's novella *Romeo und Julia auf dem Dorfe* (*The Village Romeo and Juliet*, 1856) and the fiddling devil in Lenau's dramatic poem *Faust* (1836–1840). A somewhat more disguised demonic musician is Du Maurier's Svengali, who gains control over a vocally talented but musically deaf young singer forcing her to act as his musical instrument. Du Maurier's story is noteworthy particularly in that inhuman perfection of tone and timing rather than discordant sound help betray the evil of Svengali's "creation" (*Trilby*, novel, 1894).

Stories of musicians who are victimized by music or who use music to victimize others are the most easily identifiable types to make traditional use of demonic music. But whatever the story line, the stories that relied on traditional images had in common a thematic portrayal of demonic music as detrimental and destructive in effect and as being drawn from sources that would be considered evil both within the context of the story and within Christian cosmology.

The nontraditional portrayal of demonic music, in contrast, challenged Christian values and often parodied the persisting remnants of medieval Christian symbolism. As with more traditionally oriented writings, non-traditional ones often fit into prominent categories. Two are based on outlook and might be designated as optimistic and pessimistic.

An example of the optimistic portrayal of demonic music can be found in E.T.A. Hoffmann's *Der Goldene Topf* (*The Golden Pot*, 1814). Like many of his more traditional tales, this one abounds with Christian symbols of good and evil: witches, snakes, celestial music, discord, an edenic world, a hellish one, charms and potions, black cats and apples. Yet Hoffmann manipulates the symbols in a revolutionary manner. The framework remains, but the picture is turned sideways. As the story progresses, the snakes, who are musical, appear more and more divine in nature. For the main character, the student Anselmus, their enchanting music enables him to understand primal nature in a way that defies reason. Though the alteration in the identity of the snakes and their music from evil to divine makes no sense in Christian or Platonic terms, it is understandable, given the romantic preference for passion, intuition, and will over reason. The snake or serpent of Eden had symbolized, since Chaucer's time, precisely that reversal of the hierarchy of reason, passion, and will that the more optimistic among the rebellious romantics were now extolling.

The pessimistic interpretation also defied Christian conventions. Mark Twain's story *The Mysterious Stranger* (1916) is a case in point. Like Hoffmann, Twain uses demonic and divine Christian symbols but only to create contradictions, as he illustrates in his description of the music the boy Satan plays with expertise. "And he always was playing to us on a strange sweet instrument which he took from out of his pocket; and the music—but there is no music like that, unless perhaps in heaven, and that was where he brought it from, he said."

Ambiguity continues throughout the work, even at points when it seems indisputable that Satan is the devil. For instance, the demonic attributes of the boy who says he comes from heaven first appear when he has exercised his most godlike power, the power to create. To the surprise of a group of boys for whom he has created a miniature village of people, he remorselessly crushes the tiny humans to death and then, using the strange sweep instrument he keeps in his pocket, causes the boys to dance on the graves of the slain. The demonic power of the music in this situation seems evident. Yet Twain, playing with ambiguity and irony, interrupts the narrative to comment "he brought the dance from heaven, too, and the bliss of paradise was in it."

The question of what kind of music Satan plays is inextricably bound to the question of his identity. And in fact he is through much of the story a volatile mixture of divinity and evil that mocks both. He is a satirical figure who amuses himself by enlightening the boys as to the preposterous notion the villagers have of God and how that notion serves their own self-interests. He is self-abnegation that takes the alteration of identity to the point of annihilation. Through him the mythic framework of harmonic and discordant music, good and evil, cosmic order and chaos, explodes. And what is left of the world, of the universe, of life is nothing but "fiction." That is the higher understanding the new artist/ musician has to offer in Twain's deeply pessimistic work. The world is too absurd to exist outside a dream. It is the figment of an erratic imagination, the sensation, images, music, and insanity of thought.

Supporting these nontraditional approaches to demonic music were attempts to fit demonic music into a new cosmology. Arthur Schopenhauer in *Die Welt als Wille und Vorstellung* (*The World as Will and Representation,* 1819), for example, created a non-Christian metaphysics that became the basis for a reinterpretation of demonic music. In an extreme but logical extension of romantic perceptions of the universe, he argued that the unlimited universe was essentially chaotic and irrational. It was governed by a blind instinctive force called "the will" or, in living things, "the will to live." The universe dominated by the will was to Schopenhauer essentially evil because the will was responsible for the most basic evil of life, the need of living things to destroy and consume other living things in order to survive. Schopenhauer theorized that music, the least visual of the fine arts, represented, as Plato supposed, an imitation of interior reality. But it was an imitation not of mental or even cosmic motion but of the desire and passions of the will. This concept of music as a form of mimesis led logically to Schopenhauer's idea of evil in music. Since music copied the will, and since the will was the author of primal evil, it followed that music was inherently demonic.

Another more optimistic interpretation was proposed by Nietzsche in *Die Geburt der Tragödie* (*The Birth of Tragedy,* 1872). He too thought that music expressed the will. But he concluded that the demonic, Dionysian music of the Greeks, when joined with the Apollonian image found in their tragedies, brought men to a higher understanding of the world and ultimately reconciled them to life by converting the horrible into the sublime.

The interpretations of demonic music by optimistic and pessimistic Romantics were at the forefront of the rebellion against traditional Christian attitudes until the development, in the nineteenth century, of yet another influential trend, the trend toward materialism. Materialism, which challenged the whole Platonic/ Christian realm of transcendental reality, encouraged the demystification of music once again by casting doubt on its cosmic roots. Yet in virtually ruling out a primal, metaphysical origin for music or for the gods and demons associated with it, materialism also set speculation in a new direction. It left only one place in which demonic music could originate, the mind. With the musical domain restricted, psychology began to exert an influence on the concept of evil in music. One psychologist whose speculations about the origins of music and of demons became very important to literature was Carl Gustav Jung. Jung argued that the old demonic and divine images arose in a collective unconscious that we all inherit as human beings. And thus in a single stroke he moved the ancient cosmologies or rather their representatives into the mind. The macrocosm became a microcosm within the unconscious.

By originating cosmic myth in the unconscious, Jung made it possible to view demonic musicians as archetypes. In fact he listed a demonic musician among the primary archetypes or images to arise from below the threshold of consciousness. This was the siren. He interpreted her mainly as a dark figure whose presence could indicate psychic disturbance. Like the Homeric sirens to whom Ulysses dared to listen, she offered through her musical words a knowledge that could affect the destiny of a man. To hear her while unprepared was to run the risk of hastening the approach of madness or the complete disintegration of personality. To listen while prepared as Ulysses was, however, could promote self-knowledge.

If the demonic musician was an archetype, music according to Jung was a representation of those movements of feelings that cling to unconscious processes. It expressed in sound what fantasies and visions expressed in images (Letter to the Director of *Polyphonie*, 1950).

Like the trend toward mysticism in the late eighteenth century, the trend toward materialism and the rise of a psychology that dealt with the unconscious mind were paralleled by new developments in music, which would be again exploited by writers. The new sound, which can be traced successively from Wagner to Debussy, from Mahler to Strauss, Stravinsky, and Schoenberg, was increasingly primitive, nightmarish, and discordant, quite distant from the harmonious sound of seventeenth- and eighteenth-century classical music.

The Twentieth Century Inheritance

Despite the challenges that Christianity and Platonism underwent, the traditional as well as nontraditional views of demonic music survived into the twentieth century, but not without accommodation to new ideas. The decline in metaphysics and the impact of psychology could not be ignored. How twentieth-century writers have coped with their contradictory inheritance is perhaps best exemplfied in the work of Thomas Mann and Hermann Hesse.

Of the two, Mann favored the more traditional approach, which in his most ambitious story of music and evil, *Doktor Faustus* (1947), he skillfully blended with elements of modern psychology. The basic story line of *Faustus* is not unlike that of a nineteenth-century author. A fictive composer, Adrian Leverkühn, makes a pact with the devil in return for musical genius. But Mann maintained an ambiguity in the story, the need for which separates him from his predecessors. He never actually resolves the question of whether Leverkühn sees the devil or whether the composer is subjected purely to hallucinations caused or aggravated by a disease he contracted from a prostitute. Working within this ambiguity, Mann was able to credibly use traditional associations between demonic music, the devil, and perverted genius and to connect the music with madness.

What separates Mann still more from his nineteenth-century predecessors though is his purpose for using traditional images. Mann wanted to show a cultural relationship between experiments he saw going on in classical music and the creation of the Nazi state in Germany. An indication of what he is up to is found in his description of the second section of Leverkühn's "The Apocalypse." The section opens with the "music of the spheres," which is described as icily clear, brittle dissonances of unearthly beauty. In conception, the music is meant to turn the Pythagorean and Christian notions of spherical music upside down. Here is no humble glorification of a harmonious or divine universe but rather the depiction in music of a desolate, clockwork universe of perfect, rigid order. In creating discord from a carefully ordered musical pattern, Leverkühn, with mocking irony, contradicted the ancient belief that out of cosmic order came harmony. In his apocalyptic vision he said, in effect, that from order can come discord or chaos, and this is precisely what his cosmic music reflects and forecasts. Discord contained within a rigidly controlled, mechanistic structure described not only Leverkühn's revolutionary experiment but also the totalitarian state that would be erected soon after his death.

In contrast to Mann, Hesse in *Der Steppenwolf* (*Steppenwolf*, novel, 1927) chose a decidedly nontraditional approach to demonic music and to the character who is caught up with it. The difference is reflected in his choice of jazz rather than contemporary classical music as his demonic music. Unlike the cool, nihilistic music Leverkühn created, the jazz music that fascinates Haller (Steppenwolf) is "hot and raw as the steam of raw flesh." Haller's attitude toward the music more than the music itself is at issue, moreover. And that attitude reveals an acceptance of the Christian dichotomy between flesh and spirit in which the flesh and the physical world are considered evil, sinful, and mortal.

In common with the optimistic Romantic, William Blake, Hesse found the Christian dichotomy unhealthy. And his treatment of jazz even in the early stages of the novel shows his anti-Christian bias. Haller's rejection of jazz is made to seem like a rejection of life based upon a fear of death. The music of the flesh represents then for Hesse's troubled hero an invitation to a new level of understanding and acceptance of himself and his destiny.

Hesse, in essence, thematically followed the heretical line of thought developed by the early optimistic Romantics to the conclusion that demonic music can promote spiritual growth, integration, and wholeness; whereas Mann turned to the more traditional argument that demonic music encourages as well as reflects dissolution and vice.

Both visions mark a historical continuity. They belong characteristically to the late nineteenth and the twentieth centuries in their preoccupation with the metaphysical crisis, with nihilism, and with the absurd, while at the same time they sum up much of what came before. In them the tension between the older Platonic/Pythagorean ideas and modern psychology is apparent. The beleaguered relationship between music, the cosmos, and the soul is still recognizable along with the belief that evil music has a subterranean connection with political upheaval, mental disorder, religious or spiritual malaise, and creative struggle. And yet the myths of creation and dissolution in which demonic music had a part have been changed. They have become reflections of the mind, indicators of the basic human fear of and fascination with death, dissolution, and evil as well as with the human desire for immortality and self-creation.

It is difficult to predict in what direction writers may take the theme of demonic music or whether it will even continue to survive. But the likelihood is that it will continue to turn up in literature in new and interesting contexts. For it has shown a stubborn persistence and a remarkable resilience in the face of change.

See also: Daemon, Dance, Demonic Musician and the Soulbird, Evil, Universe.

Selected Bibliography

Guthrie, William K. C. *A History of Greek Philosophy,* vol. 1. Cambridge, Mass.:
    Cambridge University Press, 1962.
Hammerstein, Reinhold. *Diabolus in Musica (Studien zur Ikonographie der Musik in
    Mittelalter).* Bern and Munich: Francke, 1974.
Meyer-Baer, Kathi. *Music of the Spheres and the Dance of Death: Studies in Musical
    Iconology.* Princeton, N.J.: Princeton University Press, 1970.
Rudwin, Maximilian J. *The Devil in Legend and Literature.* London: The Open Court
    Publishing Company, 1931.

SUZANNE LEPPE

DEMONIC MUSICIAN AND THE SOULBIRD

Antiquity

There is strong evidence linking the demonic musician in Western folklore to
the soulbird of ancient Greek and Middle Eastern myths.

A familiar figure in ancient Greek and medieval folklore is the demonic
musician who entices or guides his intended victim into the underworld. There
is some strong evidence that this figure reflects an ancient concept of the soul.
The connection between the soul and the demonic musician seems to have evolved
from speculations about the soul's relationship to air.

It was natural for ancient writers to associate the soul with air. For the soul
seemed to flee the body or to be extinguished with the breath. The Greeks and
Hebrews were particularly attracted to this idea. Plato suggested that the soul
disturbed the air like a vibration. Aristotle attributed to some Pythagoreans (not
mentioned by name) a more specific vision of air or rather motes of air as the
essence of the soul. And Sextus ascribed to the Pythagoreans the belief that the
breath of the cosmic soul pervades the universe, giving it a vitality that unites
man to brute beasts and to supernatural beings alike.

The Pythagorean concept of the soul as something belonging to air was shared
by other Greek philosophers such as Anaximenes, a predecessor of the medieval
alchemists. And Chrysippos believed with other Stoics that *pneuma,* a mixture
of air and fire, entered the universe, permeated its substance, and through *tonos*
(tension) drew it into a cohesive living unit.

Breath or air was important to the Hebraic story of creation as well. God did
not arouse Adam to life, as Michelangelo's painting suggests, by transmitting
the spark of life through an outstretched hand. Rather "the Lord God formed
man of the dust of the ground, and breathed into his nostrils the breath of life;
and man became living soul" (Gen. 2:7). The relationship between the creative
act and the living soul God produced is captured in the word *spiritus,* which
literally means breath.

The identification of the soul with air or with something of the air has initial importance to the concept of the demonic musician in that it provides a link between the soul and music. A parallel between the animation of man in Genesis and the animation of a musical instrument is pointed out by Meyer-Baer in *Music of the Spheres and the Dance of Death* (1970). "A wind instrument," she writes "sometimes, indeed of clay is brought to life by the breath of the player, and a tune 'dies away' if the breath lessens and finally stops." Just as the pipe receives the breath of the piper, in other words, so man receives the breath of life from God and is animated. Music was described by Plato more directly as a vibration or motion of the air "akin to the revolutions of our souls" (*Timaios* [*Timaeus,* dialogue, 4th century B.C.]). Implicit in this conception of music was the suggestion that the soul itself is a kind of music or is something that creates music by its motion. This suggestion is strengthened in the Platonic dialogues by references to the soul's courses as either harmonious or discordant and by the idea that music can be used medicinally "to correct any discord which may have arisen in the courses of the soul" or used diabolically to instill vice by causing discord in the soul (*Nomoi* [*Laws,* c. 350 B.C.]). In the Middle Ages, this close tie between music and the soul was celebrated in the words *musica humana,* which loosely translated means "human music" or "music of the (human) soul."

The interrelationship of soul, air, and music that is suggested so far through images of breath, inspiration, and creation was complemented by a similar interrelationship that brings the soul closer to the demonic realm. This variant interrelationship was based on death, dissolution, and chaos and took shape in certain myths dealing with the soul as the body slips from life into death. What sets these myths apart from the previously mentioned speculations on the soul is their particular aerial imagery. The soul is no longer associated with breath (since breath is too much a symbol of life) but is seen rather as a thing of the air, a birdlike creature. The Chaldeans, for instance, allude to the human soul as birdlike in their myth of Ishtar's descent into hell. They justify the form of the soul that seems to be out of place in hell itself by portraying the soul's journey at death as one which must be traversed through air. The soul had to fly several days in order to reach the western gate of the underworld where a siren or Nereid waited to guide it the rest of the way.

The Egyptians and some Greeks expressed similar beliefs. Greek amphoras dating from the fifth century B.C. depict the soul in flight as a birdlike creature with a human face. The soul is identified by its face, the features of which are identical to those of the dead or dying hero from whom it flees. The Egyptian *Book of the Dead* (c. 25th to 16th century B.C.) tells of the arrival of human soulbirds in the underworld. They are depicted gathering about a great sycamore tree, which was the Egyptian tree of life.

Music became attached to the dead soul too partly as a result of the belief that souls need guidance if they are to find their way in the hereafter. Iamblichus, a fourth-century biographer of Pythagoras, tells the story of the young shepherd who while passing the tomb of Philolaos (another Pythagorean) heard singing.

The gist of the story is that Philolaos, on his journey of purification through the celestial spheres, was guided by music. As he arrived at each sphere, he heard the voice of the inhabitant intoning a note, which he produced. The tones were like beacons telling anyone who listened where Philolaos was in his travels.

Significantly this story demonstrates not only a relationship between music and the dead soul but between the soul, music, and the soul guide; that is, the celestial beings show a likeness to the human souls both in appearance and in their ability to emit musical tones that human souls are capable of reproducing.

The tendency to describe the soul guide as birdlike was not restricted to Iamblichus' story. The Egyptians had a nonmusical soul guide called "Ba" who was also birdlike in appearance. And in the myth of Isthar's descent into hell, the Babylonians or Chaldeans described the rulers of hell as creatures who like birds were covered with feathers. In a variant story, "The Vision of Er," Plato tells of celestial sirens who resemble the soul guides in appearance and who inhabit the spheres. Like Iamblichus' guides, they are also musical. Each one voices "a single tone. The eight together form one harmony" (*Politeia* [*The Republic*, dialogue, c. 380 B.C.]).

With the supernatural guide closely identified with human souls, through its birdlike form and through its association with air and music, the myth of Iamblichus comes close to producing a demonic musician guide from a concept of soul. Other ideas still would have to be added, however, before the guide would clearly be viewed as a demonic personage. He would have to guide the souls to the underworld and not up through the celestial spheres, and he would have to appear malevolent in his intent.

A figure who comes closer to filling these requirements is Hermes. Besides being a musician, Hermes was the inventor of musical instruments, a patron of alchemists, and, of course, the Greek god who guided souls to the underworld. He could be identified with dead souls through the winged staff that he carried or, judging from Ovid's account of Hermes (Mercury) in *Metamorphoses* (epic poem, c. A.D. 2–17), by his wings.

His role as an inventor of musical instruments also suggests his association with the tradition that brought air, music, and soul together. His implication with demonic forces, however, is indirect and comes later. Two of the instruments that he invented, the syrinx, or pan's pipe, and the kithara (kitharody), a stringed instrument, came to be associated with creatures whose appearance was similar to that of Satan after his fall. These were Hermes' son Pan and the Satyrs. With their cloven hooves and their long tails, the kithara loving Satyrs present a particularly striking prototype of the devil playing a lute or violin as depicted in medieval iconography.

Neither Hermes nor Pan was by any standards a full-fledged demonic musician. The associations that surround them offer only tantalizing suggestions of what might have been a pervasive, folkloric notion of the soul that antedated Pythagorean cosmology and that could have influenced it. But there was another guide in antiquity who was already a demonic musician in the full sense and not unexpectedly a being related to the soulbird. That was the Homeric siren. With Homer's sirens, the idea of the birdlike soul guide receives a sinister twist, for these malevolent demons used music to guide living souls rather than dead ones to the eternal abodes of the underworld: As Circe warned Odysseus in the epic *Odysseia* (*Odyssey* c. 8th century. B.C.):

> First you'll come to the Sirens
> Enchanters of men. Whoever in ignorance comes near them
> And hears their song, never again returns
> To rejoice at home with a welcoming wife and small children.
> With the clear liquid tones of their song, the Sirens betwitch him,
> As they sit in a meadow mid the moldering bones of men,
> Great heaps of them, round which the skin is still shriveling.

Homer did not describe the appearance of the sirens, but Pollard and Meyer-Baer have shown from amphoras of the sixth century B.C. on that the Greeks conceived of the sirens as birdlike creatures.

Etymological evidence presented by Gabriel Germain in "The Sirens and the Temptation of Knowledge" (*Homer: A Collection of Critical Essays,* 1962) also suggests that they were conceived of as creatures of the air, but, more than that, it provides other clues as to how the sirens might have been perceived in the popular imagination. The Greek word for siren was very similar to the word *seioēn,* which Aristotle used to denote a species of wild bee, and it was even closer to the biblical Latin word *sir'a,* which in the Septuagint is rendered "bee" or "wasp."

Significantly, both these insects were associated with the underworld. The etymologically unrelated Latin word for "wasp," *vespa,* was used as a slang term for "undertaker" or "body snatcher," while the word *sphēkia,* from the Septuagint according to Germain, came to denote creatures who were endowed by the populace with demonic power. Another closely related word, *melissa,* or "bee" (goddess) also had connections with the underworld. It was the title conferred on Persephone, who was queen of the Greek underworld as well as daughter of the harvest.

It should be noted again in passing that the sirens had a divine aspect as well as a demonic one. Plato's depiction of them in "The Vision of Er" makes each into a clear representative of divine order through her voice. For like the angels of later medieval cosmology, they made the harmony of the spheres audible through their voices.

The Middle Ages

The various connections made in antiquity between sirens, demonism, the soul, air, and music serve as background for the medieval view of the demonic musician as siren. The medieval writers tended to see the demonic musician as a supernatural character who tempted his or her victims with carnal or mundane pleasures rather than with the prophetic knowledge that the Homeric sirens offered in song. The Homeric siren was actually included among these musicians but with some alterations. Frequently, each of the medieval sirens represented a separate vice, and possibly to emphasize their separate symbolic identities, each was given a different musical instrument to play. Honorius Augustodunensis, for example, depicted lechery as a siren playing a stringed instrument and avarice as a singing siren. In addition, he added a third siren, a pipe player, to represent boasting. Whether by design or coincidence, the instruments given to the sirens were related to those Hermes gave to Pan and the Satyrs.

Bechorius, in his allegorical rendering of the siren episode from *The Odyssey*, largely reiterated what Honorius had said. On the other hand, the *Gesta Romanorum* (*Deeds of the Romans*, a collection of morally instructive stories believed to have been written c. 13th century) associated the sirens with wealth, worldliness, and lust and with a different set of instruments: they were the *vox humana* of the devil, the cithara of the world and the lyre of the sinning flesh. The *Physiologos* (*Physiologus*, 2d century), which was probably first translated from the Greek in the fourth century and served the medieval Latin and French bestiaries, was content to call the sirens the "delights of this world." In general, the sirens were seen as the "mis"guiders of the soul, whose worldly, melodious music was the very embodiment of seduction.

The characteristics of the demonic sirens that link them with the soulbird and soul guides also tied them to Satan. The medieval Satan developed in the popular imagination into a misguider of souls who like the sirens could entice his victims with music. Maximilian Rudwin relates the perfect allegorical picture of Satan as pied piper leading the unwary souls (like rats) to their destruction with the aid of his hypnotic music (*The Devil in Legend and Literature*, 1931). There was in Satan's appearance a further connection. Satan was a fallen angel, and in some medieval depictions of him, he still possesses wings. Dante, in his epic, for example, explains the existence of a frozen wasteland in the depths of the *Inferno* (*Hell*, *La divina commedia* [*The Divine Comedy*, c. 1320]) as a result of a chill produced by Satan's "batlike," beating wings.

The assimilation of the sirens into Christian cosmology and the invention of sirenlike demons during the Middle Ages were accompanied by renewed interest in the sirens' appearance. Some bestiaries continued to represent them as birdlike creatures with human faces. But others visualized them as harpies with human heads and the bodies of winged serpents or as mermaids, half fish, half women. An engraving after Mantegna done in the fifteenth century marks the culmination of this process of transformation. Here Christian and non-Christian conceptions of the enticing demons appear for the moment to converge. The three winged, serpentine, fish-finned devils that hover above the entrance to hell in the engraving are clearly composite forms reflecting those found in the bestiaries. Their connection with the sirens, aside even from their appearance, is apparent in their use of music to greet the damned as they enter hell. Here the satanic demons appear again as the embodiment not only of the soul guides of myth but of perverted music itself, which Plato and the Pythagoreans long ago associated with the *anharmostia* or discord of the soul.

By and large, however, the alterations in the sirens' appearance had to obscure their ancient image and their connection to the soulbird. Since the Middle Ages, the soulbird has largely disappeared from literature about the demonic musician and more generally. There are still hints of it, for example, in Dracula's transformation into a bat or in the presence of malevolent birds that ruin a town in Hitchcock's classic film *The Birds* (1963), but the demonic musician has led a largely separate existence and the sirenic demonic musician is more apt to appear either human or snakelike than in the perverted image of a bird.

See also: Afterlife, Daemon, Death and the Individual, Monsters, Siren, Universe.

Selected Bibliography

Germain, Gabriel. "The Sirens and the Temptation of Knowledge" *Homer: A Collection of Critical Essays,* ed. George Steiner and Robert Fagles. Englewood Cliffs, N.J.: Prentice-Hall, 1962.
Meyer-Baer, Kathi. *Music of the Spheres and the Dance of Death.* Princeton, N.J.: Princeton University Press, 1970.
Pollard, John. *Seers, Shrines, and Sirens.* London: Allen and Unwin, 1963.

SUZANNE LEPPE

DESCENT INTO HELL

A universal mythic theme, the descent into hell represents an essential stage in the development of the hero. The descent involves a literal or symbolic journey to the underworld, or the dark kingdom of the dead. The purpose of the journey may be to retrieve someone from the dead, to complete a task, or to bring back some precious gift of wisdom. After the hero accomplishes the rescue, completes the task, or attains the valuable knowledge, he, an enriched and spiritually transformed human being, returns to the upper world of the living. By psychological extension the descent to the underworld may also be construed as a descent to the dark realm of the unconscious.

Myth

The descent into hell, or the underworld, is a feature of various mythologies all over the world. Although the word "hell," which derives from the Norse underworld called *hel,* is associated primarily with the Christian mythos, the idea of an underworld journey is both much earlier and much more universal than Christianity. In ancient Babylonian and Sumerian mythology the goddess Ishtar (or Inanna) desires to travel to the nether world to find her lover Tammuz.

As Ishtar is goddess of light and life, so her elder sister Ereshkigal is sovereign over the realm of darkness and death. The sisters are bitter enemies, and Ishtar fears for her life on the journey. Her ultimate precaution to assure her safe return is to ask her most trusted messenger to invoke the aid of Enki, god of wisdom, if she does not come back in three days. When Ishtar arrives in her sister's dark domain, her worst fears are realized. Forced to kneel naked before Ereshkigal, she is then struck dead and her corpse is hung from a stake. She remains dead for three days and nights, after which her messenger seeks the aid of several gods, all of whom refuse except Enki. The god of wisdom ingeniously devises two mysterious creatures, the *kurgarru* and the *kalaturru,* who travel to the underworld to deliver the food of life and the water of life to the corpse of Ishtar. After they sprinkle the food and water on her sixty times, she revives and is able to reascend to earth.

The descent undertaken with the purpose of reclaiming someone from death is not always successful. In Germanic mythology the attempt fails to restore the god Balder, slain through the trickery of the evil god Loki. His brother Hermodr makes the nine-day journey to Hel to ask for the return of the slain Balder, most beloved of the gods. The response to his request is that if every single creature in heaven really mourns Balder and wishes him alive, then he will be returned to the gods alive. Hermodr goes back to enlist everyone's acquiescence in the mission. Messengers are sent to every corner of heaven asking every living being, even the stones and earth, to weep Balder undead. Every one does, but when the messengers return to report their success, they pass by a cave where sits an old witch, who refuses to shed a tear to help Balder. Because of this one exception, who is probably not really a witch but the trickster Loki in disguise, Balder must remain in Hel. That even an apparently successful rescue can go wrong is demonstrated in the Greek myth of Orpheus. In this tragic tale Orpheus travels to Hades where he pleads with its queen Persephone for the return of his beloved wife Eurydice. The queen of darkness, unable to resist his enchanting lyre, grants him the wish under one condition. He must not look back at Eurydice as she follows him upward out of the dark kingdom. As the reunited couple approach earth, the loving husband fleetingly looks back to make sure that Eurydice is still behind him, but as he does so, she fades back into the darkness. His mission to restore his wife has failed, and he is distraught with grief at her second death.

Greek mythology offers other successful rescues. Dionysius rescues his mother from Hades, which he reaches by diving under a lake, a way shown him by an admiring guide. Hercules also succeeds, although he follows the path taken by the disappointed Orpheus. This hero's exact mission, the twelfth labor imposed on him by his master, is to return from the underworld bearing the terrible three-headed guard-dog Cerberus. Once in the kingdom of Pluto and Persephone, he also requests permission to bring back Theseus. As the powerful Hercules proves himself strong enough to seize the savage dog, he is also permitted to take Theseus with him on his return.

Celtic mythology is rich in the theme of a journey to the underworld. Unlike the Greeks, who saw death's kingdom as a grim and gloomy place populated by shades, the Celts envisioned a glorious underworld, a rich and colorful counterpart of the living world. In one of the important myths recounted in the *Mabinogion* (medieval Welsh tales), the young prince Pwyll undertakes the descent at the request of the ruler of the underworld. Pwyll exchanges places with the lord for a year and a day. During that time he nobly resists the temptation to make love to the wife of Death, a strikingly beautiful woman who seems to regard him as her husband. Sometime after this episode, Pwyll goes on another journey to the underworld in search of a wife and returns with the goddess Rhiannon as his bride. In the first descent the young prince gains courage and strength of character. In the second, although he ultimately gains a wife who will bear him an heir, he also is sorely tested and forced to prove his heroic nature.

Similar myths of the hero's descent may be found in the mythologies of Asia and North America as well, but perhaps the most famous mythic descent in the Western world is recounted in the apocryphal New Testament. This highly successful spiritual mission is undertaken by Jesus during the three-day period between the Crucifixion on Good Friday and the Resurrection on Easter Sunday. Jesus travels to hell for the purpose of redeeming Adam and the prophets and patriarchs of the Old Testament, all of whom died before his miraculous birth made their salvation possible. At the gates of hell the Redeemer encounters fierce opposition and is forced to scourge the devils in order to enter. This dramatic episode of the confrontation before the gates of hell was adapted by the scriptural drama of the Middle Ages, when the guilds staged several so-called Harrowing of Hell plays in their cycles of mystery plays performed processionally in the streets on church holidays. In these plays a comic porter at the gates is reluctant to let Jesus enter, an episode that is later adapted by Shakespeare for a comic scene in the tragedy *Macbeth* (1605–1606).

Epic

The heroes of the classic epics, Homer's *Odysseia* (*The Odyssey,* c. 8th century B.C.) and Virgil's *Aeneis* (*Aeneid,* 19 B.C.) undertake the descent into hell in episodes important to their respective stories. Odysseus, warrior hero of the Trojan War, has been struggling homeward since the end of that conflict, but he has been lost and has encountered extreme difficulties. Desperate to learn what will happen to him, he needs to consult the shade of the prophet Tiresias in order to learn his destiny. He undertakes the requisite journey to the land of the dead in book 11 of *The Odyssey.* First he makes the necessary sacrifice of sheep, pouring their blood into the open pit that leads down to the underworld in order to attract the spirits of the dead. Although legions of shades hover about the blood, all eager to communicate with the living, Odysseus protects it from all but the prophet in order that he may readily learn his fate. Tiresias drinks the life-renewing blood and informs the hero that he will reach Ithaca eventually in spite of the enmity of the gods who have beset his journey with obstacles. The prophet also warns Odysseus that he and his men must not tamper with the magnificent sheep of Helios the Sun-god, when they anchor on his island. The seer finally prophesies that after the wandering hero returns home he will set sail one more time until he comes to a land where the people do not know the sea and do not season their food with salt.

After he receives the message of his own destiny, the hero then converses with the shade of his beloved mother, whose death he had not known about during the war. His mother consoles Odysseus that his father is yet alive and that his wife is faithfully waiting for him. Odysseus is emotionally moved by the sad conversation and strives three times to embrace his mother's shade, but each time he finds himself clasping nothing. She explains that after the death of the body the soul has no substance that can be touched, but rather hovers like a dream. Melancholic yet enlightened, the hero prepares to leave the abode of the dead, a grim place where all lament the loss of life, and to rejoin the happy world of the living. The episode is one of the most touching in the epic, and it clearly demonstrates that for the life-loving Greeks of the Homeric age, the land of death is a place of utter misery.

Aeneas, hero of Virgil's epic poem *The Aeneid,* also makes a descent to the underworld to learn his own destiny. The sybylline prophet warns him in advance that the journey is fraught with danger but informs him that the golden bough plucked from a tree growing near Lake Avernus will permit him to achieve his mission by consulting with the shade of his father Anchises. The Sybil accompanies Aeneas on his fearsome journey, and the way they follow is filled with horrors. Along the shadowy road they see the frightful forms of Disaster, Care, Hunger, Discord, and War. When they finally reach the river where Charon rows the souls of the dead to the farther bank, they behold hundreds of distressed souls who are not admitted to the ferry because their bodies have not yet been properly buried. The golden bough persuades Charon to ferry the two living voyagers across the river, and Sybil is able to pacify Cerberus with a piece of cake. Farther on, in the Fields of Mourning, Aeneas weeps to discover Dido, whom he abandoned and thereby drove to suicide. Sybil and Aeneas continue on their way until the road divides into two paths. From the left sounds of groaning and of clanking chains signal the realm of Rhadamanthus, who punishes the wicked for their misdeeds. To the right are the Elysian fields, where all is cheerful and attractive. Here in the sunlit green meadows live the good and the heroic, among them Anchises. Father and son have a tearful but happy reunion, and Anchises proceeds to tell the young man of the glorious destiny awaiting him. He shows his son a vista of his descendants who will be renowned throughout history. He also advises Aeneas about settling his new home in Italy. The parting between father and son is not sad, as in the case of Odysseus and his mother, for they know that they will meet again.

The most ambitious and complex descent into hell is the first book of Dante's medieval epic *La divina commedia* (*The Divine Comedy,* c. 1320), which was influenced by Virgil's poem. Dante's *Inferno* (*Hell*) relates the poet's descent with the Latin poet, Virgil, as his guide. Although literarily influenced by the Latin model, Dante's epic is a Christian work, and he times his fictional journey to parallel Jesus' harrowing expedition between Good Friday and Easter Sunday. Dante's precise geography places hell underground, a funnel-shaped region with its bottom point at the very center of the earth. Dante begins his journey at age thirty-five, the mid-point in his life, when he suddenly finds himself lost in a dark wood. Although he can glimpse the rising sun, he finds his way out of the forest blocked by three beasts, a leopard, a lion, and she-wolf, allegorically representing the sins of incontinence, violence, and fraud. The shade of Virgil appears to him, offering guidance on the downward path through the nine circles of hell, which Dante will explore with the object of better understanding the nature of those three categories of sin, which also constitute the major divisions of hell. The descent is thus for Dante a learning experience based on his need to recognize his own sins in order to regain the true way through the remaining half of his journey in life.

The actual descent begins on the evening of Good Friday. The gate at the entrance to hell reveals the terrifying message: Abandon all hope ye who enter here. In each of its nine circles a particular kind of sin receives symbolic retribution, usually an intensified and unrelieved form of the sin itself. In a vestibule just inside the gates are the opportunists, those who refused to choose either good or evil. It is their fate for ever to chase after a continually shifting banner, pursued by stinging wasps and hornets. Circle one contains the virtuous pagans, those who died before the birth of Christ, now punished only in their inability ever to see God. Circle two reveals the carnal, rather sympathetically exemplified by Paolo and Francesco, illicit lovers doomed ever to be blown about by tempestuous winds and never to touch each other. The third circle shows the gluttonous who in life wallowed in food and drink and now wallow in fetid garbage for all eternity. In the fourth circle the hoarders and the wasters punish each other for their mutual excesses. The fourth circle completes the sins of incontinence, and the fifth introduces the sins of violence with images of the wrathful who perpetually attack each other and the sullen who complain endlessly beneath the foul waters of the Styx. In circle six Dante and Virgil encounter the heretics when they enter the formidable City of Dis, capital of hell. Circle seven exposes the violent against neighbors, the violent against themselves, and the violent against God, nature, and art. Circle eight introduces the sins of fraud. A great circle of stone, it is subdivided into ten ditches, each with sinners guilty of a different kind of simple fraud. Circle nine, at the bottom of the hellish funnel, is the frozen Lake of Cocytus, where those guilty of compound fraud are punished. At the center of the lake is Satan himself, pictured as a grotesque parody of the trinity with his three mouths, each holding a traitor: Judas in the center mouth and Brutus and Cassius in the side mouths. Climbing up the body of the devil in order to emerge from hell, the poets find, on looking back, that the body appears upside down, for they have now passed the center of the earth.

Their descent thus completed, they now begin their ascent to the surface of the earth.

As Dante explains, his poetic vision of the descent into hell can be interpreted on four levels of meaning. Beyond the first, literal meaning of the narrative itself, the poem can be read for its allegorical, tropological, and anagogical meanings. The allegorical meaning is relevant to political and social behavior, the tropological concerns the moral life of the individual, and the anagogical refers to its religious meaning. On the literal level, Dante's hell is a remedial vision of sinful life in this world. Allegorically it depicts the living hell characteristic of sinful behavior in society. Tropologically it explores the private hell deep in the psyche of every human being. Anagogically it probes the metaphysical meaning of evil.

Of these four levels of interpretation, the tropological comes the closest to contemporary interest in the psychological meaning of human evil. Reading Dante's account as an inward journey to the depths of evil within one's self is a universally valid experience quite apart from personal religious beliefs. Hell is not a merely medieval phenomenon but an image of the continuing confrontation of evil. The descent into hell is a necessary stage not only for the hero but for everyone's psychological and spiritual development.

The Eighteenth and Nineteenth Centuries

Emanuel Swedenborg's visionary accounts, *De coelo et inferno ex auditis et visis* (*Heaven and Its Wonders and Hell*, 1758), might be considered theology rather than literature, but in either case the vivid description of the afterlife by this remarkable engineer turned mystic has the imaginative power of literary writing. In his vision of a literal trip to both heaven and hell, Swedenborg considers each precise matters as "What Hell Fire Is" and "What the Gnashing of Teeth Is." Lacking the artistry and the moral intensity of Dante's vision, this work is nonetheless highly moving as an inspired personal experience. The nineteenth century offers three major literary examples of the descent to the underworld. The earliest occurs in part 2 of Goethe's *Faust* (play, 1832). In this mysterious episode Faust departs from his diabolic companion Mephistopheles to undertake a visit to the "mothers." Before he descends, he is given a magic key by the devil. At first Faust seems to arrive in a misty void, where shapes drift in deathlike fashion, but when he sees a strange tripod he touches it with his key, and from the swirling mists emerge the shades of Paris and Helen. The "mothers" do not appear as such, but their entire underworld habitat suggests the pregnant darkness of the womb. On one level they may be seen as the shadowy goddesses of primitive religions, but on the level of Faust's own spiritual development they seem rather to represent the mystery of creativity. This episode is brief but highly evocative.

A protagonist who communicates directly from his underworld is the narrator of Dostoevsky's *Zapiski iz podpol'iã* (*Notes from Underground*, novel, 1864). Beginning his frank account with "I'm a sick man, a mean man," he goes on to castigate himself and all of mankind for its evil propensities. Like Dante he envisions the vicious side of humanity, and also like Dante, he realizes that this dark, irrational side cannot be ignored nor overcome by reason alone. The embittered voice from the underground does not emerge at the end of the tale, but succeeds in communicating his discovery that the utopian crystal palaces based on the doctrine of social amelioration will not work. In this work the descent into hell is a psychological one, a movement from consciousness to the unconscious, from the material to the psychical realm. The experience involves an encounter with ideational images, not three-dimensional objects or persons. The underworld is not a literal place of death but the inner world of the imaginative mind.

In the same year as Dostoevsky's story of a psychological descent, Jules Verne sent forth a trio of underground explorers on a relentlessly physical descent in his novel, *Voyage au centre de la terre* (*A Voyage to the Center of the Earth*, 1864). Professor Lidenbrock with his nephew and his guide follow an ancient Icelandic map, which leads them to the bottom of an extinct crater, burrowing through underground corridors of rock, swimming in underground oceans, and suffering streams of boiling water, and eventually coming out through the open mouth of erupting Mt. Etna, but landing safely on the mountainside. Verne's tale of descent is thrillingly detailed as sheer adventure.

Modern Literature

Modern literature offers many examples of the descent into hell theme. James Joyce's *Ulysses* (novel, 1922), with its narrative structure based on the Homeric epic, contains a journey to the dead in the form of a funeral procession to a graveyard taken by protagonist Leopold Bloom. Two German novels, Thomas Mann's *Der Zauberberg* (*The Magic Mountain*, 1924) and Hermann Hesse's *Steppenwolf* (1927), both contain effectively realized episodes of descent.

In the Hesse novel the voyage takes the form of a visit to a masquerade ball in an underground room. At the ball the protagonist encounters disparate fragments of his own personality dancing wildly. Before this confrontation with his dismembered self, he had been on the edge of committing suicide, but after the symbolic descent to his inner hell he is able to reintegrate his psyche. He can literally pull himself together.

An outstanding dramatic example of the descent into hell appears in George Bernard Shaw's play, *Man and Superman* (1903). Actually an interlude in the long play, often performed independently as "Don Juan in Hell," this episode features Don Juan Tenorio, with a clear hint that he is also the play's hero, John Tanner. In hell, Don Juan encounters the devil, with whom he engages in witty debates about morality, and the statue of the man he killed, a refugee from heaven, a boring place. Static in terms of physical action, the episode is one of Shaw's most delightful pieces, with sparkling dialogue and sharp characterization. Mozartian music fills in the background of this most appealing scene in hell.

The descent into hell has become a standard feature of contemporary myth-based fantasy fiction. In these works, set in a secondary world and involving magic and wizardry, the hero undertakes a quest that almost inevitably includes a descent to an underworld, usually but not always a land of the dead. Ursula Le Guin's *Earthsea* trilogy (1977), for example, culminates in the visit of the wizard Ged and his apprentice Arren to the land of the dead. The final volume of the trilogy, *The Farthest Shore*, (1972) is devoted to their westward quest for the place of the dead. Their purpose is partly to fulfill a prophecy and partly to close the door between the realms of the living and the dead, for it has been opened by a misguided sorcerer who had foolishly hoped to achieve immortality. Instead of perpetuating life, the open passage has turned all life into a living death. When the voyagers finally arrive, they find a dry and dismal land where stars shine but do not twinkle, where shadows meet but do not recognize each other, and where there is only dust to drink. Ged succeeds in closing the door by using a powerful rune, but his effort exhausts him, and he cannot complete the journey back without the aid of Arren. Although his physical powers are spent, and he abandons his staff of wizardry, Ged has gained wisdom from the experience. At the end of the book he flies off on the back of an ancient dragon, a heightened spiritual being since his return from death. Like many other mythic images to the landscape of the dead, Le Guin's is accented by references to dryness, dust, and darkness. Most underworlds are literally elemental—fluid, dusty, fiery, or ethereal, rather than of the normal mixtures of earthly existence. In J.R.R. Tolkien's influential fantasy *Lord of the Rings* (1954–1956), each of the major characters takes the descent for one or more of the traditional reasons, that is, completing a task, accomplishing a rescue, or learning something of crucial importance. Gandalf the wizard achieves the most dramatic descent. As he accompanies his fellows on their mission to destroy the evil ring of power, he finds himself locked in mortal combat with a fiery monster, the balrog, on a bridge over a deep chasm. The combatants fall together into the abyss, and the wizard's friends are convinced of his death. In fact, however, Gandalf not only survives the fall but climbs the spiral stairway that leads to the surface of the earth, then continues farther up to the top of a mountain where he lies unconscious for several days. When he awakens, he has been transformed. He had been Gandalf the Grey, but now he is Gandalf the White, and his formerly anxious and irascible nature is now calm and confident. The wizard has undergone a symbolic death and rebirth. Not only has he destroyed the fiery monster, but with his renewed spiritual energy he will be able to lead the forces of good to victory over the evil forger of the ring of power.

Whereas Gandalf's descent enabled him to complete a task, the journey to the underworld taken by Aragorn, heir to the throne, is largely for the purpose of rescue. Aragorn takes the terrifying Paths of the Dead, where he enlists the services of the dead, whom he heroically musters to follow him. When he emerges from the eerie paths with the grey company, he appears stronger and more kingly than ever before. Along with Aragorn and Gandalf, the gentle hobbit

Frodo also takes a journey to the underworld before he achieves his final mission to destroy the ring. His descent into the mines of Moria resembles a period of death, for he is seriously wounded and believed dead by his companion. A more symbolic form of the descent occurs when Frodo is wounded by the weapon of the Ringwraiths, for the wound places him partly into their own shadowy world. All three of these heroic characters—wizard, man, and hobbit—thus undergo a descent into hell as part of their development in this fantasy, which resembles the traditional epic in style and structure.

A fantasy novel of a wholly different sort, theological in its meaning and not epic in its narrative, is Charles Williams' *Descent Into Hell* (1937). In this highly complex work of fiction, Williams offers a variety of descents to the underworld among his several characters. Indeed, as the title indicates, the theme of the book is the universal nature of the descent. The central figure is an historian named Wentworth, whose gradual but steady moral degeneration provides the main plot line. His deterioration is caused in part by his frustrated infatuation for a woman much younger than himself. Unable either to rationalize his attraction or to admit his failure, he accepts as substitute a succubus-like creature of his own imagination. Withdrawing ever more into himself, he eventually loses contact with reality altogether. His moment of damnation comes when he falsifies historical facts, no longer caring for truth. In the end he is described as being forever drawn downward through the bottomless circles of the void.

Wentworth has a recurring dream of climbing down a rope, which is both a symbol of his own decline and a link with another character, a young man who has committed suicide. For the suicide, the rope is the very instrument of his death, but after death he continues to climb down the rope. Perturbed in death as he had been in life, the unfortunate soul seeks a communication that he had never known, but which he finally achieves in a remarkable scene in which the dead and the living meet. Three female characters also undertake a descent into hell. Pauline, a sensitive and loving young woman, is often disturbed by the sight of her double, which seems an omen of her own death. She does not die, as it turns out, but instead she steps into the world of death in order to comfort one of her ancestors who is about to be burned at the stake. On this strange spiritual quest, she inspires the condemned man with courage to face his fiery ordeal without terror. Pauline's grandmother, herself near death, has visions of the spirit world beyond and advises the young woman on her mission to relieve her ancestor's fears. In one crucial scene, as the elderly woman lies on her bed, she undertakes the descent and communicates with the dead, including the lonely suicide. The third female character to take the descent into hell is herself a creature from the underworld, Lily Sammile, or Lilith. Temptress and witch, she is a dangerous force but is ultimately destroyed when the graves open and the dead arise.

In this unusual novel, part thriller and part theological fiction, the descent into hell is at once the major theme and a recurring structural device. As in the traditional epic pattern, it is a necessary stage in the development of the hero, followed by a rebirth or reawakening. In a larger sense, it is also the necessary prelude to self-discovery on the part of every human being. The descent on the rope may lead to simple physical death, to ultimate damnation, or to an ascent toward renewed spiritual existence. Modern and contemporary literature thus offers many differing examples of the descent into hell. In some cases it represents a stage in the progress of the hero, and in some an essential step in psychological and spiritual maturation. The underworld may be depicted literally as a hell, a place of torment and damnation, or it may be simply a place of the dead, usually conveyed through imagery of dryness and darkness. It may also be envisioned as a journey to the unconscious, a dreamlike visitation to the spectral world of psychic images, a dark night of the soul leading to illumination.

See also: Afterlife, Death and the Individual.

Selected Bibliography

Campbell, Joseph, *The Hero with a Thousand Faces.* 2d ed. Princeton, N.J.: Princeton University Press, 1968.
Henderson, Joseph L., and Maud Oakes. *The Wisdom of the Serpent: The Myths of Death, Rebirth, and Resurrection.* New York: Collier, 1971.
Jung, Carl Gustav. *Symbols of Transformation.* Trans. R.F.C. Hull. New York: Pantheon Books, 1956.
Spivack, Charlotte. "The Journey to Hell: Satan, the Shadow, and the Self." *The Centennial Review* 9 (1965): 420–437.

CHARLOTTE SPIVACK

DETECTIVE

Attempts have been made to establish the antiquity of the literary detective and the detective story by tracing both back to such plays as *Hamlet* (c. 1600), Oidipous tyrannos (*Oedipus Rex,* c. 429 B.C.), and the biblical account of Susanna and the elders. If, however, Howard Haycraft is correct when he writes, in *Murder for Pleasure,* that "there could be no detective stories until there were detectives," the first detective story cannot be much more than a century and a half old. For the detective profession is a complex and formal one, and if we define it rigorously as an organized system for the exposure and apprehension of criminals, we can reasonably say that it has not been in existence for much more than 150 years. Indeed, the *Oxford English Dictionary* cites no use of the word "detective" earlier than the nineteenth century, and no even rudimentary professional detective appears in English or American history before the middle of the eighteenth.

The detective was in large part a product of the growing industrialization of eighteenth- and nineteenth-century society. As masses of people began to move from country villages to big cities to be nearer mills and factories, the old informal police system of night watchmen and part-time constables personally acquainted with a small, stable population of neighbors and friends began to fail. Instead, what the larger, more mobile, and increasingly anonymous crowds of industrial Europe now required for the control of crime was a trained and expert corps of professional police.

But such a professional force took long to develop. Many of the first eighteenth-century police spies, informers, and thief-takers got their jobs because they were themselves former criminals; as one magistrate of the time put it: "While the present system continues, and while robberies and burglaries are so frequent, without the means of prevention, there is no alternative on many occasions but to employ a thief to catch a thief" (I. Ousby's *Bloodhound of Heaven*). Not surprisingly, these earliest detectivelike figures often could not be distinguished from the lawbreakers they were hunting. They frequently used questionable and even illegal methods to earn the large rewards offered for important criminals and regularly perjured themselves to get convictions at a time when even minor offenses were punishable by death. Add to this the fact that, when they were not acting as agents of a frequently unscrupulous and oppressive government, they were often in the employ of wealthy private citizens bent on personal revenge, and it will be clear why during these years, as one critic has put it, "the aversion to police appeared to be even greater than the aversion to crime" (Ousby, 8). Indeed, the great eighteenth-century folk heroes were much more likely to be thieves and rogues than thief-takers and "detectives."

For the reputation of these first "detectives" to improve, people needed some sign that those chosen to be police officers were themselves morally respectable, that the detective force existed to serve not its own self-interest but something in the nature of an abstract ideal of justice. The government too would have to learn over the years to protect the civil rights of individuals through those fair courtroom procedures and impartial rules of evidence on which true detection and abstract justice depend; but in the meanwhile, separate efforts could be— and were—made to do something about the scandalously bad police system.

Among the best known of these efforts was novelist Henry Fielding's establishment, in 1753, of the Bow Street Flying Squad. Five years before, Fielding had been commissioned a police magistrate in Bow Street, Covent Garden, at the very center of London's criminal activities, and on his own he decided to train half a dozen of his cleverest constables in criminal law and the basic principles of investigation. These Bow Street Runners, as they later came to be known, persisted as an organization for more than three-quarters of a century, "the ancestors," E. F. Bleiler calls them, "of detective police in Great Britain," or as he also puts it, "the Scotland Yard of its day" (*Richmond*, 1976).

The Runners were a colorful group, experts in matters of crime, clever and daring in action, and they did much to improve the image of the police in the public's mind. But they also had their less attractive side. Many of them had joined the force after at least quasi-criminal careers of their own, and the fact that they were paid a fee for each case they accepted inevitably raised doubts about their disinterestedness and objectivity. Thus they eventually had to be augmented by the London Metropolitan Police, a paid professional force created by Robert Peel in 1829. These "peelers" or "bobbies," as they were soon being called, generally came to their new jobs from military rather than criminal backgrounds, and because they drew adequate official salaries they were less inclined to accept bribes or indulge in other irregularities. The Bow Street Runners continued to perform detective functions for another dozen years, but in 1842 they were finally replaced by the Detective Department, an eight-man professional investigative organization that further increased the respectability and public acceptance of the police system.

All during this approximately one-hundred-year period, works of literature recorded the changing attitudes toward crime and the police, and it is among these works we must look for a tale to be designated the first piece of detective fiction. But such a work should meet certain reasonably strict criteria. Two eighteenth-century novels of crime and detection, for example, published half a century apart, reflect the then prevalent public hostility toward police investigation and so cannot be considered founders of the modern detective story tradition. Henry Fielding's own satiric *Jonathan Wild* (1743) recounts the career of a spectacular private thief-taker who was at the same time a master criminal and who ended his life on the gallows, and William Godwin's *Caleb Williams* (1794) is a book which, according to Julian Symons, "denies all the assertions to be made later through the detective story. In the detective story, the rule of law is justified as an absolute good; in Godwin's book it is seen as wholly evil" (*Mortal Consequences*, 1973). In the words of one criminal in the novel, "We, who are thieves without a license, are at open war with another sort of men, who are thieves according to law."

In the period from 1827 to 1829, two books were published that approach more closely to true detective fiction. Both are really collections of short stories, though presented as memoirs, and both display their detective heroes in a more generally favorable light than either Fielding or Godwin do theirs. *Richmond: or, Scenes in the Life of a Bow Street Officer* (published anonymously by Thomas Gaspey in 1827), called by E. F. Bleiler "the first collection of detective stories in English," records the life of a young man who decides to make up for a misspent though not criminal youth by joining the Bow Street Runners. In the book, the Runners are described as an adventurous but essentially honest band of detective police, their cases calling for them to display considerable courage and some cunning. One year after *Richmond* appeared, *Mémoires* (*The Memoirs of Vidocq, Principal Agent of the French Police,* 1828–1829) was published in Paris and almost simultaneously in an English translation in London. Vidocq's career harks back to the earlier tradition of the thief turned thief-taker, but the book is able to capitalize on its subject's undoubted successes as a detective and his many years as first chief of the French Sûreté. Nevertheless, it would be difficult to argue that the memoirs of either Richmond or Vidocq contain anything that could be properly called "the first detective story." Neither work shows much literary distinction, and though both contain certain features that would later be more fully worked out in police procedural and hard-boiled detective fiction, it is unlikely that anyone could have predicted, on the basis of these two books, the future development of the detective story.

A quarter of a century still later, literature about the detective police had become even more flattering. The hero of William Russell's *Recollections of a Policeman* (1852), though he joins the Metropolitan Police in desperation after a life of "reckless folly," is clearly presented to the reader as a member of a respectable profession, while the depiction of the sleuth in Charles Dickens' several articles on the subject in his periodical *Household Words* amounts at times to simple hero-worship. Despite so much support and even celebration of the detective, however, neither the Dickens nor the Russell pieces can be said to qualify as the first detective story. Missing from them is any feeling for the detective as the possessor of an extraordinary mind, any sense of the part that must be played in a model detective story by the pure and powerful force of intellect. Clearly, Dickens' Field and Russell's Duhamel, like Wild and Vidocq, are remarkable people, but it is no genius of theirs for ratiocination that makes them special, and it is just such genius that the detective story demands. Yet even if the Dickens or Russell works had displayed notable genius of this kind, they would have come too late to be considered the first detective story. For nearly ten years before even the earliest of them was published, that memorable first story had already appeared.

Poe and the First Detective Story

Like all literary professionals who must live by their writing, Edgar Allan Poe discovered early the need to satisfy public taste in poetry and fiction, an exercise in which he was sometimes quite successful, as the enormous contemporary popularity of "The Raven" (poem, 1845) and "The Gold-Bug" (story, 1843) makes clear. And the fact that he considerably increased the circulation of the several mass-audience magazines he edited is further proof that the author, though hardly the most practical of men, understood very well the popular literary market of his time and was both willing and able to work in it and write for it.

Poe's talent for giving artistic shape to commercial literary materials is nowhere more clear than in his handling of the popular elements of mystery and detection. The writer knew Vidocq's memoirs well and followed with interest the success other authors were having with crime fiction. In a famous review of Dickens' *Barnaby Rudge* (1841), for instance, Poe tried to solve the murder mystery that is an important part of the novel's plot, and his considerable success is supposed to have caused Dickens to remark of him that "the man must be the devil."

The extraordinary attraction of the detective story for Poe lay in the fact that it appealed both to his preoccupation with horror and death and his fascination with reason and logic. Poe's tales of pure horror are too well known to need any comment here. Perhaps a little less familiar is his intense interest in codes and ciphers or his clever ratiocinative article (1836) attempting to expose the mystery of Maelzel's celebrated chess-playing automaton. So curious a combination of interests was a fateful one for the history of detective fiction. For it permitted Edgar Allan Poe to bring together elements from such diverse literary forms as the gothic novel, the popular philosophical essay, and the memoir of thieves and thief-takers, to mark them with his own special vision, and to fashion from them the first detective story.

On April 18, 1841, "The Murders in the Rue Morgue" appeared in *Graham's Lady's and Gentlemen's Magazine,* a popular periodical of which Poe was then editor. It is this tale, introducing super-sleuth C. Auguste Dupin, which is most often named as the first detective story and the single most influential work in the history of detective fiction. During the next four years, Poe wrote two more stories about Dupin, "The Mystery of Marie Rogêt" (1842) and "The Purloined Letter" (1845), and two additional stories, " 'Thou Art the Man' " (1844) and "The Gold-Bug" (1843), sometimes also included in his list of detective fiction. These five stories may not at first seem an impressive achievement set beside, for example, John Creasey's almost six hundred novels of crime and detection, but as a group they anticipated nearly every element employed by mystery fiction during the next century and a third and by themselves formed a virtually complete catalogue of the genre's principal techniques and devices.

Robert A. W. Lowndes, in his essay "The Contributions of Edgar Allan Poe" (*The Mystery Writer's Art,* ed. Francis Nevins, Jr., 1971), finds no fewer than thirty-two such elements and devices in the Dupin stories alone, twenty of them in "The Murders in the Rue Morgue." These include the eccentric private detective with a genius for applying pure inductive and deductive reasoning to human behavior, the less acute friend who narrates the story, an extraordinary crime such as, in this case, a locked-room mystery, the open display of clues giving the reader a fair chance to solve the puzzle before the detective does, the need to relieve an innocent person of suspicion, the detective's visit to the scene of the crime, the battle of wits with the official police, and the final summary scene in which the surprising but satisfactory solution is revealed.

"The Mystery of Marie Rogêt" and "The Purloined Letter" contribute, as Lowndes calculates it, another dozen devices to the list, such elements as the police coming to the detective to implore his help, the detective studying only official data and newspaper accounts of the case and solving the mystery without leaving his "armchair," and the sleuth having a personal score to settle with the culprit. To these items, J. R. Christopher, in "Poe and the Tradition of the Detective Story" (*The Mystery Writer's Art*) adds the concept of psychological detection, the ultra-obvious place of concealment, the planned diversion of the criminal, and the involvement of the detective in state affairs, as well as, from " 'Thou Art the Man,' " the device of the least likely suspect, and from "The Gold-Bug," the concept of the detective story as a cryptogram. It may be possible, of course, to trace one or more of these elements to sources other than Poe. Indeed, Poe worked by converting just such elements of popular literature to his own uses. But certainly no earlier writer ever thought of gathering these diverse and unusual elements together into a single group of stories, and it was by doing this that Poe was able to create, in little more than a hundred pages, the whole, rich, and elaborate genre of detective fiction.

Conan Doyle and Sherlock Holmes

As influential as Poe's stories were to be, that influence did not make itself felt for some time. Nearly half a century passed between the publication of "The Murders in the Rue Morgue" and the first appearance of Sherlock Holmes in *A Study in Scarlet* (1887), and in the meanwhile, the detectives who continued to appear in contemporary fiction owed much more to the vigor and cunning of Richmond and Vidocq than to the pure ratiocination of C. Auguste Dupin. The considerable improvement in the reputation of the police by the middle of the nineteenth century may have reflected the period's growing faith in material progress. But that faith began to recede during the second half of the 1800s, and the detective began at the same time to lose some of his new glamour.

It was not that he returned to his old role of barely reformed criminal; with the increased institutional controls of the profession, those days were largely behind him. It was rather that writers now began to recognize and depict the limitations of the detective just as they were depicting the limitations of science and technology generally. Even Dickens, who, in his magazine writing, consistently praised the London detective force, frequently used the sleuth in his novels to demonstrate the narrow boundaries of human reason and will. Indeed, in *Bleak House* (1853), even Inspector Bucket, modeled on the much-admired Inspector Field, becomes a symbol of the ultimate futility of detection. After some false starts, Bucket manages to solve the novel's murder mystery, but as he is about to lead the culprit away, the killer turns on him and says, with several sarcastic nods, "Listen, you are very spiritual. But can you restore him back to life?" Bucket's rueful reply, "Not exactly," makes Dickens' point clear. Even where the detective succeeds, his triumph is frequently trivial in the face of the criminal's victory; the murderer may be undone, but never the murder. Mr. Bucket may be a successful solver of puzzles, but true mysteries—like the grand mystery of death—will always elude him.

Other mystery novelists of the period also concentrated on what seemed the necessary failure of the detective. In *The Moonstone* (1868), for example, Wilkie Collins used an actual criminal case as the basis for his fictional one, in the retelling of which, however, he made an important change. For where in the real murder investigation, the police detective's deductions proved sound, in the story, the otherwise formidable Sergeant Cuff blunders badly in his interpretation of the facts and is forced to admit that he was wrong. Unsuccessful sleuths also appear in the works of less well known writers of the period like James Payn (*Lost Sir Massingberd*, 1864), Mary Elizabeth Braddon *(Henry Dunbar,* 1864), and Mrs. Henry Wood (*Mrs. Halliburton's Troubles,* 1862). The failure of the detectives in such novels makes, in part, a metaphysical point. In a universe ruled by the irrational force of chance, these stories seem to say, the power of human reason to solve mysteries is dramatically limited.

The major French practitioner of the detective story during this period was Emile Gaboriau, whose sensational crime and mystery fiction was colored by France's continuing suspicion of its own police. Gaboriau plainly modeled the career of his principal detective, Monsieur Lecoq, on that of Vidocq, alluding to Lecoq's shady past prior to his joining the Sûreté and representing him as vain and ambitious, willing on occasion to connive and cut corners in order to get ahead in his profession. At the same time, he portrayed Lecoq as an imaginative and skillful sleuth, expert at disguises and capable of brilliant deductions from such physical clues as the first plaster casts of footprints ever to appear in a detective story. Gaboriau had done considerable research in French police courts, morgues, and prisons before beginning the Lecoq series, and novels like *Le Dossier No 113* (1867) and *Monsieur Lecoq* (1869) are full of the sort of accurate technical details about the legal system and evidence collecting that were later to be employed regularly by writers of police procedural fiction.

Dupin, Bucket, Lecoq, Cuff—these were the literary detectives on whom the young Arthur Conan Doyle could draw for precedents when in 1886 he set out to write his own first mystery novel. Doyle himself particularly mentions Poe and Gaboriau as authors who had influenced him, and it is possible to read the early Sherlock Holmes short stories as an elaborate homage to C. Auguste Dupin. Lecoq too contributed to the portrait of Sherlock Holmes, though the Great Detective himself once called the Frenchman "a miserable bungler." (He had previously disposed of Dupin as "a very inferior fellow.") Skill at disguise, a Lecoq specialty, is one of Sherlock Holmes's most prominent traits as well, and the French sleuth's ability to draw startling conclusions about people from a few brief observations and deductions is also a memorable Holmesian talent.

Such ability was shared by Dr. Joseph Bell, one of Conan Doyle's medical instructors at Edinburgh University and a man whom the writer always credited with being the principal model for the character of Sherlock Holmes. But Doyle was quite capable of duplicating some of his instructor's detectivelike achievements. Once, visiting a hospital, he paused beside a young baby and almost immediately said to the infant's mother, "You must stop painting the child's crib." Questioned about his instant analysis of the case, Doyle smiled and explained, "The child looked pale but well fed. He was listless and his wrist dropped as he tried to hold a toy. The mother was neatly dressed, but she had specks of white paint on the fingers of her right hand. Children like to sharpen their teeth on the rails of a crib—so lead poisoning seemed a likely diagnosis." (William Baring-Gould, *The Annotated Sherlock Holmes*, 1967).

This talent of Conan Doyle's for putting the principles of pure reason to practical use may help account for the great success and influence of the Sherlock Holmes stories. We have seen that the detective in literature was almost from the start treated as a historical figure, one who, in the hands of Fielding, Godwin, Vidocq, Russell, and Dickens, could be employed as an instrument of political, economic, and social commentary. For entertainment value, these detective stories generally offered dramatic depictions of the sleuth's courage and cleverness, but even such virtues had their limits, and the stories also portrayed the detective as morally and intellectually fallible, not necessarily superior to the criminals he pursued and sometimes indistinguishable from them.

With Poe, the detective story entered a new phase, one in which the sleuth became the embodiment of pure and abstract reason operating in a world where such reason always triumphed. But the fact that these stories took so long to influence the genre suggests that readers may have found Poe's universe too abstract, too unhistorical to be entirely convincing. The world of everyday reality is, after all, one in which ratiocination seems to fail as often as it succeeds, one in which pure logic is often defeated by chance. At any rate, it is such a world that continued to be depicted in detective fiction long after Poe had completed his own work.

What Arthur Conan Doyle was able to do, with the creation of Sherlock Holmes, was to bring these two strands of the detective story tradition together. As a scientist, a doctor, and a student of Joseph Bell, Doyle firmly believed that the purest and most abstract reasoning was also the most practical, and as a writer, he set out to invent a detective character who, like Bell, would demonstrate that such reasoning could be successfully employed in the world of everyday reality. Sherlock Holmes clearly inhabits that kind of world. Where Dupin lives in a visionary Paris of Poe's imagination, Holmes's London is impressively solid; feels, in fact, so much like the world actually inhabited by the reader that when reason triumphs in it, that triumph is convincing. The nature of Holmes' appeal, then, is plain. While mid-Victorian detectives warned disappointingly of the limitations of human reason, Sherlock Holmes offered practical proof that no such limitations exist.

The Early Twentieth Century

If the detective fiction genre developed slowly in the two quarter centuries from Poe to Gaboriau and Gaboriau to Conan Doyle, it virtually exploded into creative activity following the first appearance of Sherlock Holmes. That intense activity may in part reflect the growing importance of the short story as a literary form during the period. Short fiction tends to encourage innovation, and major artists like Rudyard Kipling, Joseph Conrad, D. H. Lawrence, Katherine Mansfield, and James Joyce wrote some of their best work in the medium. Sherlock Holmes did first appear in two novels, *A Study in Scarlet* and *The Sign of Four* (1890), but it was the *Strand Magazine* short-story series, later published as *The Adventures of Sherlock Holmes* (1892), that was really responsible for the detective's international popularity and inspired so many other writers to produce mystery fiction, much of it in short form.

In 1894, for example, in order to help satisfy the enormous appetite for detective fiction aroused by the Sherlock Holmes series, *The Strand* published half a dozen stories about Martin Hewitt, a new detective character created by Arthur Morrison. Morrison, who had previously been known as the author of a group of naturalistic stories collected under the title *Tales of Mean Streets* (1894), created in Hewitt a detective plainly influenced by Holmes through, as E. F. Bleiler puts it, "the identity of opposites. . . . Whereas Holmes is tall and gaunt, Hewitt is of medium stature and plump; whereas Holmes is egotistical and arrogant, Hewitt is pleasant and unctuously affable; whereas Holmes scorns Scotland Yard, Hewitt is grateful for its cooperation. . . . Holmes's adventures are set in a high key; Hewitt is deliberately low key" (from the introduction to his Dover collection *Best Martin Hewitt Detective Stories,* 1976). Bleiler regrets that London's "mean streets," which Morrison knew well from personal experience, were so rigorously excluded from the Hewitt stories, stories that would then have anticipated the *Black Mask* mystery school by a generation. Nevertheless, with just eighteen short tales and a single longer serial, Morrison managed to secure his reputation as one of the major writers of the detective story in the era of Sherlock Holmes.

While Martin Hewitt is portrayed by Morrison as a quite ordinary person, other fictional detectives of the period, again under the influence of Sherlock Holmes, were depicted as memorable eccentrics. Holmes's famous quirks— nonstop violin playing, indoor target practice—clearly have their own origins in C. Auguste Dupin's fondness for the dark or Sergeant Cuff's passion for roses, and by the turn of the century, the notion that a literary detective ought to display certain peculiar habits or character traits had become well established. Among the most bizarre detective figures created during these years was M. P. Shiel's Prince Zaleski, an exiled Russian nobleman who lives in an exotic London apartment with his faithful Ethiopian servant Ham, indulges in an obscure but potent Mohammedan drug, and solves mysteries by combining intense concentration with inductive reasoning and intuition. Of his strange sleuth Shiel once wrote: "There is no detective but *the* detective and the father of detectives, the 'Dupin' of Poe, of whom this Zaleski is the legitimate son, and the notorious Holmes the bastard son." Other eccentric detectives of the period include Baroness Orczy's Old Man in the Corner, who clears up baffling mysteries from his chair in a London tea shop while tying and untying intricate knots in a piece of string, and Jacques Futrelle's "Thinking Machine," Augustus S.F.X. Van Dusen.

Dr. John Evelyn Thorndyke, created in 1907 by R. Austin Freeman, is a criminal investigator who elaborates on another of Sherlock Holmes's notable characteristics, the great detective's skill as a laboratory scientist. It is Holmes, the discoverer of a new test for hemoglobin in *A Study of Scarlet,* with whom Dr. Thorndyke has most in common, and in the eleven novels and forty-two short stories in which Freeman's detective appears, emphasis is consistently placed on the solving of crimes through technologically sophisticated examinations of physical evidence. In such matters as the analysis of dust, the preservation of footprints, or the classification of blood, Dr. Thorndyke, who is never without his well-stocked green research kit, often anticipated actual police techniques of his day, and Freeman was equally careful and accurate in his depiction of courtroom scenes, rules of evidence, and other legal procedures.

One distinct innovation in the Dr. Thorndyke series is what Freeman himself called the inverted detective story, a work in which the reader is first shown the crime being committed, with all the facts, even the identity of the criminal, frankly revealed. "It would have seemed," Freeman wrote in his esay "The Art of the Detective Story" (1941), "that after this there was nothing left to tell, but I calculated that the reader would be so occupied with the crime that he would overlook the evidence. And so it turned out. The second part of the story, which described the investigation of the crime, had to most readers the effect of new matter," "The Case of Oscar Brodski" (1929), in which the technique of the inverted detective story is notably employed, is today considered a significant contribution to the history of detective fiction.

The quarter century following the publication of *A Study in Scarlet* came to a memorable conclusion with the first appearances in 1911 of two major detective characters, G. K. Chesterton's Father Brown and Melville Davisson Post's Uncle Abner. In many ways the two new sleuths were products of the enormous popularity of Sherlock Holmes, but in one very important sense they reached back beyond Holmes to explore issues that had been raised earlier by mid-Victorian pessimism about detection and ratiocination. Conan Doyle himself had dealt with such matters in a small way, matching, for example, the murderer's metaphysical challenge to the detective in *Bleak House* with Holmes' own anguished question at the end of "The Adventure of the Cardboard Box" (1893): "What is the meaning of it, Watson? What object is served by this circle of misery, violence and fear? It must tend to some end, or else our universe is ruled by chance, which is unthinkable. But what end? There is the great standing perennial problem to which human reason is as far from an answer as ever."

What Conan Doyle did only occasionally in his stories, however, Chesterton and Post did regularly in theirs, quite deliberately exploring the complex relationship between the sort of mysteries that can be solved through the application of human reason and the sort that cannot. The two sleuths were themselves divided over the issue; Catholic priest Father Brown worked hard in his cases to keep these two kinds of mysteries distinct from one another, while early American fundamentalist Uncle Abner argued that the attempt to solve any mystery of human behavior inevitably becomes an inquiry into the profoundest religious questions. The effect of both the Chesterton and the Post series, however, despite their differences, was to make of the detective story an instrument for examining serious philosophical questions, and it was clearly this fact that attracted William Faulkner to the genre and helped him to create his own detective, "Uncle" Gavin Stevens, in the spirit of Post's Uncle Abner.

The Golden Age

The period roughly following the one we have just been discussing is often called the Golden Age of the detective story, though for a number of reasons no precise definition of that term has ever been firmly established. For one thing, the brief history of detective fiction, together with the gratifying longevity of many mystery writers, has made it difficult to label the several eras of the genre rigorously. *The Casebook of Sherlock Holmes* (stories, 1927), for instance, was published by Conan Doyle several years *after* the appearances of such major Golden Age sleuths as Hercule Poirot, Reggie Fortune, Superintendent Wilson, and Lord Peter Wimsey. In addition, the desire to choose an exact date for the start of the Golden Age frequently clashes with the effort to establish the key attributes of the works published during the period. Sometimes stories and detectives with "wrong" dates perfectly represent the ideals of Golden Age fiction, while just as often writers who belong chronologically to the period display few characteristics of the Golden Age detective story.

Ellery Queen has listed some of these characteristics of Golden Age detective fiction as "ingenuity and complexity of plot, including the 'locked room,' the 'miracle problem,' and the 'impossible crime'; subtle and legitimate misdirection of clues—poetic license—but always with complete fairness to the reader; and often a stunning surprise solution. In a phrase (R. Austin Freeman's), 'an exhibition of mental gymnastics' " (*Masterpieces of Mystery: The Golden Age—I*, 1977). These attributes clearly describe some works of the period more accurately than others, but there is no denying that the quarter century ending in World War II was a time of enormous richness and vitality for the genre, and that just among writers central to the Golden Age tradition can be found some of the major figures in the history of the detective story.

The publication in 1920 of Agatha Christie's first book about Hercule Poirot has made that year a convenient one from which to date the Golden Age; even more convenient because in the same year a first collection of short stories appeared about a detective who was to become the most popular literary sleuth in Great Britain between the two world wars. The volume was H. C. Bailey's *Call Mr. Fortune,* and the detective was the aristocratic Reginald or "Reggie" Fortune, a practicing physician and surgeon who advises Scotland Yard on medical matters, solves difficult murder mysteries through intuition and a "simple faith in facts," and between cases likes to spend time in his laboratory or garden. Bailey depicts Fortune as a plump, cherubic, middle-aged gourmet who expresses great sympathy for the "common people" while driving around in a Rolls-Royce, and this characterization of the detective as a snobbish, mannered intellectual was to have great influence on such other famous sleuths of the 1920s as Dorothy L. Sayers's Lord Peter Wimsey, S. S. Van Dine's Philo Vance, and the early Ellery Queen. The complexity of H. C. Bailey's puzzles and the willingness of the author to play fair with the reader make the Reggie Fortune stories prime examples of Golden Age mystery fiction.

To match this collection of affected private sleuths, the Golden Age also produced an assortment of successful if somewhat less colorful police detectives, including Freeman Wills Crofts's Inspector Joseph French, G. D. H. and M. I. Cole's Superintendent Henry Wilson, and Georges Simenon's Inspector Jules Maigret. Crofts came late to fiction when his career as a railway engineer was interrupted by a serious illness during which he took up writing to pass the time.

The book that resulted from this therapy, *The Cask* (1920), quickly achieved the status of a mystery classic. Crofts's best-known sleuth, Inspector (later Superintendent) French of Scotland Yard, first appeared in the 1925 novel *Inspector French's Greatest Case,* where he is described as a clean-shaven, easy-going, tweedy man, fond of good food and travel and inclined to discuss his cases with his wife. A number of the parallels here with Simenon's Maigret are striking, but where Maigret succeeds as a detective principally by entering intuitively into the psychological states of the criminals he pursues, Inspector French achieves his remarkable record of never having failed to solve a case through the dogged collection and shrewd interpretation of physical evidence. Inspector French is clearly the product of an authorial mind formed by the study of engineering and mathematics, and of the Crofts stories, as well as those about Superintendent Wilson, Julian Symons has written rather unsympathetically: "They fulfill much better than S. S. Van Dine his dictum that the detective story properly belongs in the category of riddles or crossword puzzles" (*Mortal Consequences,* 1972). This remark is very frank about defining the detective story, and particularly the Golden Age story, as a game, an ingenious diversion having as little as possible to do with the serious concerns of "real" life. S. S. Van Dine makes the point even more openly in his essay "Twenty Rules for Writing Detective Stories" (1946), where he announces that in tales of detection "there must be no love interest . . . no long descriptive passages, no literary dallying with side issues, no subtly worked out character analyses, no 'atmospheric' preoccupations." But such restrictions clearly disturbed those Golden Age writers who, without losing sight of the mystery story's primary obligation to entertain by puzzling, felt that the suppressing of all other literary and social values was a mistake. The creators of Ellery Queen (Frederic Dannay and Manfred B. Lee, also known as Barnaby Ross) developed their work from a story like "The Mad Tea Party" (1929), which cleverly exploits children's literature in the manner of S. S. Van Dine's *The Bishop Murder Case* (1929) or Agatha Christie's later *And Then There Were None* (1939), toward the greater seriousness of such novels as *Cat of Many Tales* (1949), an exploration of the phenomenon of mass hysteria, and *The Glass Village* (1954), a study of McCarthyism. Rex Stout largely avoided the pitfall of triviality in his Nero Wolfe stories by concerning himself from the start much more with character than with plot, just as earlier Ernest Bramah had relied on a brilliant style to deepen his books about blind detective Max Carrados. Meanwhile, the development of the suspense tale and the crime novel during this period provided authors with still other ways of escaping the inevitable sterility of a purely mechanical puzzle story.

The Black Mask School

The most influential literary alternative to Golden Age mystery fiction and all it represented first appeared in the United States, its principal outlet being a pulp magazine called *Black Mask.* Founded by H. L. Mencken and George Jean Nathan, *Black Mask* began publishing in 1920, coincidentally the very year in which Christie's *The Mysterious Affair at Styles,* Crofts's *The Cask,* and Bailey's *Call Mr. Fortune* were inaugurating the Golden Age in Great Britain. Under the editorship of Captain Joseph T. Shaw, the magazine developed what is now familiarly referred to as the hard-boiled detective story: fast, tough, cynical crime fiction in which believable characterization counts for more than ingenious plotting and from which every element is excluded that does not contribute to violent physical excitement. By the 1930s, other pulp magazines, so called because they were printed on cheap, untrimmed wood pulp paper, had arrived to challenge *Black Mask*'s near monopoly of the genre, and into the 1940s, publications like *Dime Detective* and *Detective Fiction Weekly* went on presenting stories about the tough, resourceful private eye who was the major achievement of the *Black Mask* school of mystery fiction.

One of the first of these private detectives to appear in *Black Mask* was Carroll John Daly's Race Williams, a fearless, sometimes brutal figure who lives by a primitive code of good and evil that frequently requires him to act as both judge and executioner in his cases. In this he is a forerunner of Mickey Spillane's Mike Hammer as well as a throwback to the morally ambiguous thief-takers of early detective fiction. Williams' opponents in these stories are often such stock villains as Communists and sinister foreigners, a fact that confirms criticism of Daly's work as lacking in strong characterization. Full of fast-paced action, however, the Race Williams stories made Daly one of the most popular of all *Black Mask* writers.

The early Race Williams stories preceded by only a few months the first appearance in *Black Mask* of perhaps the greatest of all hard-boiled detectives, Dashiell Hammett's Continental Op. There is no doubt that the extraordinary influence the *Black Mask* school has had on the literary detective, an influence which continues to be strongly felt today in television and films as well as in fiction and which has led to the virtual disappearance of the puzzle-solving gentleman sleuth of the Golden Age, is largely the result of Hammett's genius for powerful character studies and lean, Hemingwayesque prose. From the comparatively crude Op stories of the early 1920s, Hammett went on to refine his narrative skills until, in 1930, he published *The Maltese Falcon,* the novel that introduced detective Sam Spade and which, both representing and transcending its genre, has come to be accepted as an important work of American literature.

Other writers who contributed to the success of *Black Mask* in its early days were Raoul Whitfield, who published his Jo Gar stories under the pseudonym Ramon Decolta; and Erle Stanley Gardner, now best known for his Perry Mason novels but in the 1920s the proprietor of such miscellaneous heroes as Speed Dash, the human fly, and Sidney Zoom and his police dog, Rip. In the 1930s, a second generation of pulp contributors arrived, including George Harmon Coxe, creator of the Flashgun Casey series; Frank Gruber, who later recounted his experiences as a struggling young author in *The Pulp Jungle* (1967); Cornell Woolrich, whose work emphasizes the terror of the everyday; and the most highly regarded of the hard-boiled writers after Hammett, Raymond Chandler.

Chandler, whose reputation in fact rests on his much admired Philip Marlowe novels rather than on the novelettes that appeared in *Black Mask* starting in 1933, also became the most influential theoretician of the hard-boiled school when in December 1944 he published an essay called ''The Simple Art of Murder'' in *The Atlantic Monthly*. The essay, still controversial, describes the principles and ideals of *Black Mask* fiction, comparing them with those of the Golden Age detective story. Had Chandler been content merely to list the differences between these two approaches to the mystery, his article would hardly have caused much of a stir. But he went further, vigorously and wittily condemning the majority of Golden Age stories as artificial and absurd, and it was this judgment that evoked the long series of critical responses, including the important one in Barzun and Taylor's *A Catalogue of Crime* (1971), which have helped establish Chandler's ideas as a major force in the study of detective literature.

In his essay, Chandler singles out for particular attention A.A. Milne's *The Red House Mystery* (1922), and in a long analysis reminiscent of Mark Twain's ''Fenimore Cooper's Literary Offences,'' rebukes the British author for reckless inattention to realistic detail. The essence of the criticism is contained in the writer's comments about the novel's principal sleuth: ''The detective in the case is an insouciant amateur . . . with a cheery eye, a nice flat in town, and that airy manner. He is not making any money on the assignment, but is always available when the local gendarmerie loses its notebook. The English police endure him with their customary stoicism, but I shudder to think what the boys down at the Homicide Bureau in my city would do to him.'' In this passage, Chandler mocks the implausibility of many Golden Age detectives, and to the extent that he exposes genuine absurdities in the plot of *The Red House Mystery,* his essay is convincing. But implicit in his remarks about Milne's sleuth are two questionable premises: first, the idea that reality is to be defined as whatever may seem real at any given moment to a Los Angeles policeman; and second, the notion that for a work of art to be successful it must limit itself strictly to that reality.

Most critics of the essay have noted the weakness of such reasoning and have turned the writer's own arguments against him. Jacques Barzun and Wendell H. Taylor, for example, find Chandler's detective, with his carelessness about money and his willingness to absorb frequent beatings and shootings, quite as implausible as Milne's, and others have seen in Chandler's romantic portrait of the private eye as a modern knight ''in search of hidden truth'' an artificiality as great as anything in Golden Age fiction. Ross Macdonald, who did not begin publishing until *Black Mask* had gone out of business but who is clearly one of the most important heirs to the hardboiled tradition, wrote an essay of his own, called ''The Writer as Detective Hero'' (1973), in which he praises Chandler for just that ''tender and romantic sensibility'' which an L.A. cop might find unrealistic and artificial. What Barzun, Taylor, Macdonald, and the others are saying, at least by implication, is that all literature is artificial, even when its object is to appear real; that the strength of the *Black Mask* school lies not in the fact that it mindlessly and mechanically reproduces some actual reality, but that like all other successful movements in the history of detective fiction, it creates a world so exciting and authentic as to become a reality of its own.

The Limits of Detection

Of course, to the extent that every literary form tries to create its own reality, every literary form is limited; for every invention, every work of art, every idea, the moment inevitably comes when too much is asked of it and it can no longer function. Often the study of such a moment can be illuminating. We have already seen how mid-nineteenth-century writers explored the limitations of the detective, constantly pushing him to the point of failure in order to be able to distinguish between the things he could do and those he could not. The question "Can you restore him back to life?" in *Bleak House* describes one such limit; at the same time, it reveals the even broader interest of the period in exploring the boundary between science and religion.

A growing tendency during the last fifty years to question the value of technology and ratiocination has made the theme of the failed detective a prominent one in the works of recent writers not usually associated with the genre of mystery fiction. For example, Eugène Ionesco in *Victimes du devoir* (*Victims of Duty,* play, 1953), Friedrich Dürrenmatt in *Das Versprechen* (*The Pledge,* novel, 1958), and Alain Robbe-Grillet in *Les gommes* (*The Erasers,* novel, 1953) all see in the limitations of detection a metaphor for a culture that has exhausted the possibilities of rationalism. Perhaps the best known and most incisive of these writers of "metaphysical" mystery fiction is Jorge Luis Borges, whose key symbol is the labyrinth and who titled one of his near-detective stories "El jardín de senderos que se bifurcan" ("The Garden of Forking Paths," 1941). Borges' work is haunted by a universe of infinite alternatives among which human beings are unable to make a significant choice, and in his short story "La muerte y la brújula" ("Death and the Compass," 1944), for example, the writer portrays a sleuth who, incapable of dealing with life's multiplicity, reaches the ultimate limit for a detective, death at the hands of the criminal he is tracking. But in the world of infinite alternatives that Borges describes, even death is not final. Instead, it must be gone through over and over again, each time in a slightly different way, until every combination and permutation of it has been experienced. Obviously, for a century like the present one, plagued by the nightmare of uncontrolled growth in a hundred forms—urban sprawl, population explosion, cancer—"Death and the Compass" is a representative story and its defeated detective a representative man.

One result of the work of Borges and others is that the genre of detective fiction has itself become a kind of "garden of forking paths." On the one hand, novelists, playwrights, and filmmakers such as Michel Butor, Jules Feiffer, Stanisław Lem, and Anthony Shaffer employ the figure of the detective in their work to symbolize the arrogance of any search for final truth. On the other hand, traditional mystery fiction, in a wide variety of forms, continues to thrive. According to a recent survey, one out of every four books sold in the United

States is a work of mystery fiction, that term covering such subgenres as the tale of ratiocination, the police procedural, the spy novel, the private-eye story, the so-called Gothic, the crime story, and the novel of suspense. *Ellery Queen's Mystery Magazine*, which began in 1941 as a reprint publication, is today almost entirely devoted to new stories, offering some dozen of them each month, and the popularity of the detective on television and in films is further proof of the on-going vitality of the genre.

(Abstracted by the author from his introduction to *The World of Mystery Fiction*, Del Mar, Calif.: Mystery Library, 1978. Used by permission.)
See also: Horror.

Selected Bibliography

Cawelti, John G. *Adventure, Mystery, and Romance*. Chicago: University of Chicago Press, 1976.
Gilbert, Elliot L. *The World of Mystery Fiction—A Guide*. Del Mar, Calif.: The Mystery Library, 1978.
Haycraft, Howard. *Murder for Pleasure: The Life and Times of the Detective Story*. 1941. New York: Carroll and Graf, 1984.
Ousby, Ian. *Bloodhounds of Heaven*. Cambridge, Mass.: Harvard University Press, 1976.
                                                                ELLIOT L. GILBERT

DIALOGUE

A dialogue is a conversation—two or more people talking to each other. Literary dialogue is the written representation of a conversation, whether that representation is later recited, as in a play, or read silently, as in a novel.

Literary dialogue is, first, a method of portraying in writing two or more people talking, that is, the whole complex of verbal exchange—tone of voice, gesture, inflection, and so on. Secondly, dialogue is a literary genre itself with a long history. Finally dialogue is a theme when the possibility, limits, and use of oral dialogue are made the subject of a literary work that attempts to portray those concerns, not merely discuss them. The dialogue genre has had a decisive impact on the culture of the West, and an outline of its history will clarify how dialogue can operate as a method and theme.

Studies of the dialogue have distinguished three main forms and four phases of its history. These forms are the philosophical dialogue, the expository dialogue, and the ironic or burlesque dialogue; its phases of development are classical, medieval, Renaissance, and modern. The three forms are frequently identified with their representative classical authors: Plato with the philosophical dialogue, Cicero with the expository, and Lucian with the ironic. In the Middle Ages, the pedagogic dialogue and the *débat* developed, both scholastic variants of the expository dialogue. Later, the rediscovery of Lucian combined with the

DIALOGUE

tradition of the medieval pedagogic dialogue to create a new kind of pedagogic dialogue used by humanists to foment their educational goals. Even during the seventeenth and eighteenth centuries, the dialogue retained its vigor and was a favorite genre of Enlightenment writers.

The written dialogue originates with Plato. Plato presents his philosophy in the form of conversations among interlocutors. His chief spokesman is Socrates, the Athenian philosopher who was Plato's own teacher. Plato's philosophy emerges from the dramatized conversations. It is useful to ask why Plato wrote dialogues at all, rather than just expository essays. The answer is that he wanted his own philosophy to affect his readers in ways similar to those that Socrates' conversations produced upon his listeners. Plato wrote dialogues because he conceived philosophy as working in an oral context. Plato was the first philosopher to note the difference between oral and written ways of thinking and how writing can control the way minds work. He formulated the written dialogue as a way of using writing to convey philosophy within an oral setting.

The oral qualities of the dialogue depend first upon "scene." The dialogue not only occurs somewhere and sometime, but it is usually accompanied by some event that is either problematic (e.g., a lawsuit or a trial) or celebratory (e.g., a festival in honor of the gods, or a banquet). The participants in the dialogue are brought together by some event that either invites or demands mutual interrogation or interrogation of the event. Plato's use of scene relates philosophy to a situation.

Within the dialogue's dramatic context, Socrates interrogates not only the problem but the persons as well. He addresses questions to the others and elicits answers from them in the well-known Socratic method.

Other characters may question, but Socrates interrogates. He knows what he wants to know and seeks to find it without distraction. He stimulates, interrogates, and produces the answers from his interlocutors. The metaphors with which Socrates refers to himself—the gadfly and the midwife—refer to his effects upon others. His dramatic role is that of a teacher—not a philosopher in the modern sense.

Socrates does not present a body of knowledge; he has a disconcerting effect upon his listeners. His probes upset the certitude of the other characters. This is Socrates' role as gadfly. He challenges intellectual certitude. He also interrogates the intellectual underpinnings of his interlocutors' behavior, making doubtful not only their opinions, but also their actions. To do this, Socrates induces in his hearers a condition of uncomfortable ambivalence, a recognition that their deepest convictions might be wrong. After his interlocutors reach this point, Socrates can elicit a recognition of another, deeper truth that must, if given assent, alter conduct. This is Socrates' role as "midwife."

The ignorance of Socrates' interlocutors results from their inability to ground their opinions. Socrates' real target is unreflective adherence to popular opinions. In Greek the word for opinion, *doxa*, also connotes the decision of a governing council. It is against the authority of opinion that Socrates puts his method to work, and the method is essentially personal and interrogative. Truth is not objectified nor depersonalized, rather it is sought in a way so personal that individual obstructions vanish. Truth emerges from the communal effort of the interlocutors, who are led to the proper questions in the proper spirit. The truth emerging from the Socratic dialogue is thus "objective" in the sense that it is independent of the egos of the interlocutors.

The chief technique that Plato employs to achieve his desired effect is irony. Irony allows the reader to participate vicariously in the dialogue and prevents him from identifying with either Socrates or other interlocutors. When a character says "Indeed how could it be otherwise," the reader is prodded to think how *could* it be otherwise, lest he simply swallow Socrates' statements and appropriate them as another form of *doxa*.

The dialogues of Plato are the most philosophical use of the genre. To read them is to engage in the search for value that can only occur between persons. Plato uses the dialogue to portray this dialectical activity and to allow the reader to share it vicariously. The effect of the dialogue cannot be separated from its content. It is not simply an expository vehicle.

This intense union between form and content is much less noticeable in the Ciceronian dialogue. Cicero's dialogues are organizational structures that develop ideas according to deductive rules, not according to the dialectics of an actual conversation.

The Ciceronian dialogue is seldom rooted in a concrete situation that gives the topic immediacy. Rather the dialogues are presented as speculative investigations of broad topics, which occur in a serene and placid setting. Usually the dialogue concerns some general problem (e.g., how to educate youth) and thus reduces the reader's involvement with any of the interlocutors. This speculative and undramatic quality is the major difference between the Ciceronian and Platonic dialogue. Plato's dramatic quality serves to involve the reader dynamically in a search for truth conducted in the tension of personal encounter. This tension is provoked by the Socratic method and its art of relevant questioning. The leader of the Ciceronian dialogue, however, already possesses a body of knowledge that he expounds in response to the questions of his interlocutors. This exposition is logical rather than dramatic, and the interlocutors accept their teacher's views because of their logical and persuasive force.

The control of the Ciceronian dialogue resembles the style of Cicero's orations and the logic of the Ciceronian sentence itself. That style, in each instance, requires the possession of truth before its articulation, and, in fact, the style is directed to reinforcing the notion that the speaker, whether orator or dialogue leader, has this truth in his possession and thus speaks with authority.

Platonic and Ciceronic dialogue represent different views of the nature of philosophy. The dialectical qualities of the Platonic dialogue expressed the essence of Plato's idea of philosophy, and the undramatic and logical exposition of Cicero's dialogues presumes a speculative view of philosophy. Cicero's method is exactly that; a method. Characterization is not essential, nor is dramatic encounter. Cicero's method is best suited for presenting a received truth or complex body of opinion in a way that wins intellectual assent. It is, in short, an expository method in which truth can be not only presented but defended. It is more "logical" than "dialogical."

The third form of dialogue is the ironic or Lucianic dialogue. This form is, in fact, an ironic treatment of the serious philosophical dialogues discussed here. The Greek-speaking rhetorician Lucian wrote comic dialogues. These works, however, were lost and not recovered until the fifteenth century. Lucian was one of the luminaries of the Second Sophistic. He was an orator and teacher of rhetoric. He employed the dialogue ironically to satirize the evils and follies of the decaying Roman world. These ironic dialogues borrow comic techniques from Roman comedy and Menippean satire, but are not "dramas." They appear to have been written to be acted or read by a single speaker and thus form a new kind of drama-dialogue hybrid.

Because the dialogues were read aloud, the dramatic setting and change of scene had to be incorporated into the dialogue thematically. Frequently the dialogue is interspersed with narration which "fills out" what cannot be adroitly put in the mouth of the characters. The characters themselves frequently burlesque the characters in a philosophical dialogue. Lucianic dialogues are populated with wise fools. Rather than having acute intellects that destroy false certitude, they have an unlearned common sense that throws false virtue into shame and confusion. The "wise fool," using forensic techniques, exposes vice and folly. Unlike the Socratic questioner, the wise fool neither seeks truth himself nor assists others in finding it. He is rather a moral witness whose testimony against the wicked is all the more damning because he does not possess their sophistication. Thus the Lucianic dialogue is one which burlesques Platonic techniques to achieve satiric ends.

The dialogue's three main forms, philosophical (Platonic), expository (Ciceronian), and satiric (Lucianic) were products of the Classical Age. Because Lucian's dialogues were lost shortly after his death, they played no part in the literary experience of the Western Middle Ages. Likewise, few scholars knew Plato's dialogues. But the Ciceronian dialogue entered the Middle Ages in Cicero's own dialogues and through the writings of St. Augustine and the Fathers.

The dialogue had entered the patristic period in sermon literature. The declamatory style of patristic preaching frequently led to sermons in dialogic format. The frequent use of *inquit,* "he said," in patristic sermons shows the marked tendency of patristic preaching to increase dramatic tension by presenting the other voices "within" the voice of the preacher. The patristic preacher, however, was not interested in presenting a search for truth or a logical exposition of ideas. Rather he portrayed the drama of response and commitment, the conflict between flesh and spirit, good and evil. This kind of conflict-dialogue is the primitive ancestor of the medieval *débat*.

The *débat* was disputation carried on by two speakers, frequently allegorized, for example, the body and the soul. The *débat* was a give and take between these two speakers, usually in the spirit of the scholastic disputation.

The other dialogic form developed in the Middle Ages was the catechism. The catechism combined Cicero's didacticism with the conflict between good and evil. The catechism was a teaching device and not a literary form. Its format was rigidly logical; its purpose was to "prove" or "explicate" doctrine, not to interrogate it. The catechism had no personae or characters, just a question and answer format.

One final form of medieval dialogue combined the catechism and the *débat:* the pedagogic dialogue. One of the most popular pedagogic dialogues was the *Colloquium* of Aelfric (c. 955–1020), a Latin textbook in dialogue form. This text had its precedents in the treatises of Alcuin (735–804) on grammar and rhetoric. While not strictly speaking dialogues, these treatises developed their subject matter logically yet with an admixture of argumentation and humor. Pedagogic dialogue can be found quite early in medieval literature and became the channel through which the dialogue reentered the mainstream of European intellectual life during the Renaissance.

The Renaissance saw the re-emergence of the dialogue as a literary genre whose complexity and subtlety was adequate to that of the new learning. The dialogue, however, did not re-emerge as a simple replica of the classical forms. Its most popular and significant appearance came as a new type of pedagogic dialogue. The Ciceronian format became more specialized, and the Lucianic and Platonic forms were remodeled by the intellectual forces of the Reformation.

This new pedagogic dialogue owed its existence both to the rediscovery of Lucian in the fifteenth century and to the genius of Desiderius Erasmus. Erasmus adopted Lucian's humor and irony to the pedagogic dialogue in order to create models of Latin prose that would both "teach and delight"—the Renaissance educational ideal (adopted from Horace). The *Colloquia* (*Colloquies*, 1516), as he titled them, were immensely popular and went through hundreds of editions all over Europe. For generations thousands of school boys learned their Latin by reading and imitating Erasmus' witty and sometimes pious dialogues. The dialogue, along with the oration, became the controlling genre of humanist education. The enforced familiarity with the dialogue was responsible in large part for its immediate adoption as a preferred format for theology and propaganda during the Reformation.

The Reformation dialogue was closer to the spirit of Lucian and Plato than to that of Cicero. The religious writers were attempting to *convert* their readers, not just inform them. Hence the personal commitment of Plato and the moral indignation of Lucian were more congenial models than the cool and magisterial Cicero. Lucian was particularly dear to the Reformers, who used his techniques to pillory the excesses of the Roman church. A typical example of such a writer was the German Ulrich von Hutten. His dialogues, some written in Latin, others in German, attacked the wealth and pomp of the Roman church. Erasmus himself had satirized excesses of the Roman clergy in his *Colloquies,* but he eventually withdrew from the polemical wars when he could no longer support the Reformers' theology.

The Catholic apologist, Sir Thomas More (1478–1535), utilized both medieval and Renaissance forms in combatting the Reformers. His *Responsio ad Lutherum* (published 1969) is in the form of a medieval *débat* that savagely attacks Martin Luther. The work is akin to the medieval disputation; it is in Latin, it controverts texts and authorities, engages in logical analysis, and is permeated by a spirit of intellectual hostility. On the other hand, More's *Dialogue Concerning Heresies* (1528) is in the form of a Platonic dialogue written in English for the edification of English Catholics who might have been distressed or in doubt because of the new doctrines of the reformers. The work is dramatic, rambling, genial, full of witty stories; most importantly, it evokes and dramatizes a growing relationship between the interlocutors, a relationship that in fact comes to play a prominent role in controlling the outcome of the discussion. The *Dialogue Concerning Heresies* is widely regarded as the best artistic example of the polemical dialogue.

The polemical dialogue flowered between 1510 and 1650. Wherever religion was disputed, the dialogue became the genre of choice. Hundreds of these works were written by controversialists of every persuasion throughout Europe. However, this enormous production did not by any means exhaust the dialogue's uses in the Renaissance. Although the controversialists used the Platonic and Lucianic forms, the Ciceronian dialogue was reborn in the calm intellectualism of the Renaissance.

Before the Reformation, Italy witnessed the Ciceronian dialogue's rebirth. Within the academies and literary societies Ciceronian dialogue was the preferred expository format, not least because its speculation, carried on in leisure, seemed a model for the kind of life the Renaissance humanists wanted to live. A host of these dialogues were written; the best known is undoubtedly Baldassare Castiglione's *Il cortigiano* (*The Courtier,* 1528). A group of enlightened Renaissance interlocutors discuss the proper qualities of the perfect courtier. The work is expository, well modulated, civilized and well informed. The sustained popularity of the Ciceronian dialogue is evidenced by Galileo's choice of it as the vehicle for his discoveries. The *Dialogo sopra i due massimi sistemi del mondo* (*Dialogue Concerning the Two Chief World Systems,* 1632), published a century after *The Courtier,* displays the same urbanity, control, and polish of Italian predecessors and, indeed, of its Roman models. Giordano Bruno (1548–1600) wrote a series of dialogues on cosmology and morals. These dialogues are remarkable literary creations, many satirizing the theology, morals, and intellectual pedantry of Bruno's opponents and of society in general.

French and German writers never raised the Ciceronian dialogue to the heights it achieved in Italy. French philosophy developed its own characteristic genres: the meditation and the essay. These genres are monologic and are distinct from, and perhaps opposed to, the dialogic format. While some critics have called the meditation and the essay "interior dialogues," such a comparison ignores the fact that the dialogue requires two or more interlocutors *who are persons*. The meditation and essay are dialogic only in the sense that they posit a divided self.

In Germany the religious dialogue may have seriously discredited the genre as a vehicle for nonpolemical objectives. Few would argue that Germany in the late Renaissance and early modern period produced any significant literature in the dialogue form.

During the Enlightenment the dialogue made its last appearance as a serious literary and philosophical genre. In both England and France writers found the Ciceronian and Lucianic modes congenial to the philosophy of the Enlightenment, although the dialogue was now competing with other expository methods, for example, the "discourse."

In England John Dryden cast the *Essay of Dramatic Poesy* (1668) as a Ciceronian dialogue. His characters discuss the nature of tragedy while floating on a boat moored in the river. The discussion proceeds logically, and each character represents a particular theoretical viewpoint. George Berkeley drew on the Ciceronian tradition for his *Three Dialogues Between Hylas and Philonus* (1713).

The most ambitious dialogues of the period are David Hume's *Dialogues Concerning Natural Religion* (1779). While these dialogues appear to be Ciceronian, Hume's irony pervades the work, calling into question his real intentions. The dialogues are actually composed within a narrative structure. Hume's control of voice, that is, the tone and inflection implied in the speakers' words, makes the piece a marvel of vocal representation. This sense of voice creates many possible interpretations of the author's meaning and intent, some ironic interpretations, some not ironic. The ostensible Ciceronian format is constantly called into question by the possible irony implied by the speaker's voices. Critics still disagree on which character, if any, represents Hume's own views. The *Dialogues Concerning Natural Religion* is the supreme achievement of the English philosophical dialogue, a work whose subtlety depends upon a deliberate manipulation of the Ciceronian and the Platonic dialogue formats.

While the Ciceronian dialogue never achieved a full rebirth in France, the Lucianic dialogue was congenial to the irony of many Enlightenment writers. Denis Diderot cast his philosophy in such dialogues. His *Jacques le fataliste* (*Jacques the Fatalist*, novel, 1773), *Le rêve de d'Alembert* (*D'Alembert's Dream*, 1769) and *Le neveu de Rameau* (*Rameau's Nephew*, 1762–1784) are the best examples of the French ironic dialogue.

Contemporary Developments

The dialogue ceased to be a serious philosophical instrument for the nineteenth century and remained in limbo throughout the twentieth century. Use of the printed book may have gradually divorced philosophy from the spoken word while locating dialogue in "literature." The printed representation of conversation became imbedded in fiction, particularly the novel. The portrayal of verbal exchange thus enters a fictional world; an entire social and historical context was created in each novel to control and develop the speech of its characters.

Increasingly the portrayal of dialogue was adapted to a culture of readers rather than of speakers.

Written dialogue became encapsulated in the novel, the genre most responsible for its further development. Daniel Defoe may be credited with originating the eighteenth-century novel. He, along with Fielding and Richardson, tended to handle dialogue in a literate and sophisticated style, giving even supposedly illiterate characters complicated ways of talking, reflecting and perhaps flattering the literacy level of his readers. During the nineteenth century, literary realism, in the novels of George Eliot, Emile Zola, and Flaubert, and in the dramas of Ibsen, attempted to portray "life" as it is. Charles Dickens introduced into his novels characters who spoke slang, cockney, and regional dialects. His handling of dialogue reflected more the living speech of his contemporaries and indicated that the reading public was now extended beyond the upper middle classes. Realism, from its origins until the end of the nineteenth century, developed the use of dialogue within narrative or dramatic frameworks as a mode of revealing character, intensifying and complicating the tension of the plot, and inducing the reader or viewer to accept the author's work as a credible representation of human life.

Until the modern era dialogue remained a method of prose fiction and the drama, even if it no longer was a genre itself. In the modern era, however, dialogue itself became thematic, that is, human dialogue became a subject of modern literature, and that theme was treated by manipulating dialogue in completely new ways, exploiting its long tradition for new effects.

James Joyce's novel *Ulysses* (1922), T. S. Eliot's poem *The Waste Land* (1922), and Ezra Pound's epic *Cantos* (1925–1969) each moved away from realistic portrayal of dialogue. These works weave together voices and characters from other literary works to create a kind of dialogue that transcends the limits of realism. On the Continent the dramas of Hugo von Hofmannsthal (1874–1929) and the dramas and fiction of Arthur Schnitzler reflected the artist's growing concern with the problems of dialogue and the inability of everyday language to penetrate psychic depths. Schnitzler's plays *Reigen* (*Merry-Go-Round*, 1900) and *Der grüne Kakadu* (*The Green Cockatoo*, 1899), as well as his novelle *Der blinde Geronimo und sein Bruder* (*Blind Geronimo and His Brother*, 1902), address the way conversation does not reveal interior states but rather is at the mercy of the unconscious.

In France, Eugène Ionesco wrote about the futility of dialogue to achieve any sort of real intimacy. His drama *La cantatrice chauve* (*The Bald Soprano*, 1950) addresses this issue frontally, but the futility of human dialogue is a theme in many of his other plays, for example, *Le rhinocéros* (*Rhinoceros*, 1960), *Les chaises* (*The Chairs*, 1952) and *Tueur sans gages* (*The Killer*, 1958). Finally, Samuel Beckett, writing in both English and French, explored the existential dimensions of dialogue. His plays *Fin de partie* (*Endgame*, 1957) and *Krapp's Last Tape* (1959) portray the isolation of modern man and the futility of dialogue in a life controlled by absurdity.

While dialogue in fiction and drama was becoming more and more problematic, the concern with the shortcomings of realism and realistic dialogue stimulated a new interest in the philosophical dialogue. The last thirty years, philosophical dialogue has reclaimed some of its former significance as a critical and hermeneutic tool. The revival of interest in dialogue stems, first, from the resurgence of verbal/oral communication via electronic media, and, secondly, from the continuing significance of psychoanalytic and other therapeutic methods. The former has alerted us to the difference between literacy and oral-dominated consciousness, and the second has continuously explored those areas of meaning and relation that are present in oral communication. Finally, our increasing contact with and, in some cases, dependence upon, less literate cultures has encouraged us to pay attention to dialogue as a significant cultural phenomenon.

Dialogue has lately become an important concern for critics and cultural historians. Among the most significant modern studies of dialogue are those of Walter Ong. His *Ramus: Method and the Decay of Dialogue* (1958) traces the gradual erosion of dialogic thinking in the West and its replacement by thought processes controlled by the printed word. Ong has written several other books exploring the relation of dialogue and orality to thought. Dialogue has also been studied by Marxist critics who see in it the roots of dialectic. The role of dialogue in Marxist theory is explored most systematically in Mikhail Bakhtin's *Voprosi literatury i èstetiki* (*The Dialogic Imagination,* 1975). Bakhtin traces how dialogue has been represented in writing and explores the implication of those representations for Western thought.

The dialogue thus began as an attempt to put talking into writing in a time when thinking was primarily conversational. Dialogue has now become a conceptual tool to reinsert into thinking and writing those oral significances that the classical philosophers considered the essence of human thought.

See also: Language.

Selected Bibliography

Hirzel, Rudolf. *Der Dialog: Ein literarhistorischer Versuch.* 1895. Hildesheim: Georg Olms, 1963.
Merrill, Elizabeth. *The Dialogue in English Literature.* New York: Holt, 1911.
Niemann, Gottfried. *Die Dialogliteratur der Reformationszeit.* Leipzig: R. Voigtländer, 1905.
Ong, Walter J. *Ramus: Method and the Decay of Dialogue.* Cambridge, Mass.: Harvard University Press, 1958.

JOHN D. SCHAEFFER

DIVINE TUTOR

A divine or superhuman being who undertakes to educate a youth—usually a young man—to prepare him for some purpose or role is a divine tutor. The motif of a divine tutor (d. t.) appears primarily in nonrealistic fiction. It is found in religious literature—including mythology, the Bible, and apocalyptic literature. It is popular in didactic literature and in philosophical stories, where it provides a spokesperson of authority for a viewpoint. In philosophical literature, the "god" may present the philosophical point of view of the author, or may represent the antagonist who is to be surpassed—for example, a traditional viewpoint that is being attacked. In the modern era, the d. t. is a frequent motif in science fiction and fantasy, where the tutor is usually an advanced alien or alien race trying to rescue earth from ruin.

The d. t. may be present throughout the hero's education and experiences or may appear from time to time to rescue, instruct, or provide reflection on the meaning of the youth's experiences. To some extent, the presence of the tutor is a function of the teaching style or purpose. The d. t. may serve directly as preceptor for the youth, presenting instruction through arguments and precepts to be learned. More often, the teaching style is less structured; the d. t. makes possible experiences that serve to prove and shape the character of the young person. The instruction may be aimed at the individual who is expected to take a leadership role in society, as king or high priest. In apocalyptic literature, the d. t.'s instruction is aimed through the pupil at the people, so that the pupil serves as a medium for the god's message, rather than an individual to be trained.

The d. t. motif usually appears in a voyage setting. Most often, the pupil must leave behind the comfortable, familiar settings of his childhood to enter a new, challenging world. The voyage may be either physical or spiritual; it may combine the two, or the reader may never be sure which is happening. It may involve a transformation of the pupil into some other kind of being, more often it does not. The voyage may be overtly allegorical and symbolic; it may represent "real" places and people, whose experiences offer the opportunity for action and reflection.

There has been a change in the identity of the d. t. over the years. In the Greek myths and most of the earlier stories, the tutor is a god or a goddess. In most of the stories written since the middle of the twentieth century, science fiction and fantasy, the d. t. is an alien from a very advanced civilization. In Judeo-Christian works, the d. t. is often an angel sent from God to speak to the prophet and reveal truth. In certain works, the d. t. seeks not so much to train the youth as to corrupt him. In the Faust legend, Mephistopheles is a type of d. t. In Jean-Paul Sartre's *Les mouches* (*The Flies*, play, 1943) the d. t. stands as a powerful spokesman for the traditional ways of responding to situations, but as one to be resisted by the young Orestes who is coming to a new understanding of the universe. The d. t. may be allegorical or symbolic, but this is not necessary.

The d. t. is a major subplot in Homer's epic poem (*Odysseia* (*Odyssey,* c. 8th century B.C.), where Athena decides to express her affection for the hero Odysseus by preparing his son Telemachus for adulthood. Disguised as old family friends, she arranges with him for a sea voyage where he proves himself with his father's friends and prepares to receive the long-lost hero. Athena treats

Telemachus with respect, but as a child. Primarily, she provides opportunities for growth rather than teaching by precept and proposition.

The Bible provides a number of models of the d. t. theme. In the older writings of the Torah, the patriarchs are on very intimate and personal terms with Yahweh. Both Abraham and Moses receive God's promises and learn to trust those promises as they grow in faith. Both enjoy a very intimate relationship with Yahweh, even to the point of arguing with an angry God in order to intercede for the people.

There are differences between them. Abraham receives God's promises because God loves him; even the promise of many descendants is linked to his individual relationship with God. He receives little direct instruction, but learns through experience to trust God's love. Moses, on the other hand, is called and trained to be a leader of the chosen people. He has a specific mission—to bring the people out of Egypt and prepare them for the Promised Land. In consequence, Yahweh teaches him not only through experience, but with very detailed and explicit law. Moses acts as a conduit, receiving instruction to be a blessing on the people.

The biblical prophets—especially the apocalyptic prophets, Daniel, Ezekiel, and John of Revelation—relate to God as pupils receiving instruction for the people. Although they remain God's allies, they have no intimacy or authority with God. They are often, indeed, like puppets under the influence of the Holy Spirit, which supports and transports them. Their tutors—angels or other marvelous figures—explain to them the meaning of visions or experiences so that their instruction becomes ordered and unified. All of them travel miraculously to receive the revelations of God. The Spirit takes Ezekiel to Jerusalem to visit the Temple (Ezek. 8:3ff is one example); and it transports John the Seer into the Heavenly Court (Rev. 4:1–2).

In Hermas' *Poimēn* (*The Shepherd,* allegorical treatise, 2d century), the d. t. appears in much the same way as in the apocalyptic prophets. However, in Hermas, there is a succession of tutors: the church, symbolized by a woman who grows younger; the Angel of Repentance; the Archangel Michael, who is also the Son of God. These tutors begin by treating Hermas with scorn and disdain, but as he grows they change their attitude to one of respect. The put-downs the narrator receives from his tutors are consistent with the theme of repentance, which inspired the book, and the growing respect introduces a sense of hope. Moreover, a tone of tenderness and love underlies the rough treatment Hermas receives from his tutors. Like the biblical prophets, Hermas is trained to carry God's message of repentance to the church; he seems to have been chosen because he is already a leader in the church. Hermas' voyages are rather mundane; even though they get him out of the house, they take him only as far as the woods or his own garden.

Although the tutors who lead Dante through the epic poem *La divina commedia* (*Divine Comedy,* c. 1320) are human (or once were human), they both appear as superhumans, exemplars of what humanity can achieve. Both Virgil and

Beatrice treat the protagonist with love and respect as they prepare him for the vision of God's presence. Dante's education takes place as he witnesses and experiences the different "fates" of humankind—making a voyage from the world through the depths of hell, up the mountain of purgatory and finally into the heavens. Before Virgil leaves him, Dante has grown to the point where the guide is willing to allow him to take the initiative in certain encounters.

The immediate and universal popularity of Fénelon's novel *Les aventures de Télémaque* (*The Adventures of Telemachus*, 1699) made the d. t. theme common in the eighteenth century. It appeared both as the subject of many works and as a subtheme in others.

Fénelon's novel was published as a training manual for the young duke of Burgundy, grandson and heir apparent of Louis XIV. In it, Homer's brief account of Telemachus' initiation into adult society expands into a voyage of adventures that rival those of his fabled father. Athena guides the youth so that he experiences different forms of government first hand and has a concrete understanding of the consequences of the attitudes of the ruler. She has chosen him because he is the heir to Odysseus' throne and she guides him with affection and respect as he reflects on the different possibilities of government personal behavior. She is not afraid to correct him harshly or to let him suffer painful consequences on occasion. Athena/Mentor even acts jealously when Telemachus is tempted by Venus, a rival goddess, to abandon the search for his father.

One of many borrowings from the *Telemachus* occurs in Voltaire's novel *Zadig, ou la destinée* (*Zadig,* 1747), where Zadig, on one of his adventures, encounters a hermit going his way. As the two travel together, the hermit seems to reward the rich and evil while punishing the poor and virtuous who welcome the travelers. The hermit refuses to allow Zadig to interfere with his actions and will give him no explanation until the end of their journey, when Zadig is ready to leave him in great anger and disgust. Then, the old man reveals himself as the angel Jesrad and tries to convince the hero of the justice of his actions. In vain, Zadig is still shouting "But... " as the angel ascends to his heavenly home, leaving the mortal-like Job to submit to divine judgment without final proof.

In the nineteenth century, both Nodier and Dickens returned to a perception of the d. t. that centered on the individual. Both Nodier's fairy tale *La fée aux miettes* (*The Crumb Fairy,* 1832) and Dickens' novel *A Christmas Carol* (1843) portray the relationship of d. t. and pupil as one involving personal salvation: the improvement of the life of the hero rather than the preparation of a leader or communicating with the people.

The Crumb Fairy is a whimsical tale told by an inmate in the insane asylum at Glasgow. He identifies his protector, tutor, and spouse as an ageless old woman (literally, she claims 4 or 5,000 years). The Crumb Fairy has taken him on an amazing voyage among animals who speak and govern, where he has become a carpenter king and where he prepares to marry her. From the very beginning, she treats him with a mother's love and with respect. Her magical powers are used to give him a sense of self-worth, confidence, and peace.

Dickens' *A Christmas Carol* has three d. t.s, the ghosts of Christmas, who bring the old skin-flint Ebeneezer Scrooge to a new understanding of life and its treasures. Through voyages into the Christmases of the past, the present, and the future, Scrooge learns what is vitally important to him and he is prepared to let go of the poor fortune he held so dear. Although Scrooge obviously symbolizes an English social class, his education is not overtly aimed at anyone but himself. Morley's apparition indicates that this grace comes to him through his expartner's intervention rather than because of his place in society.

Examples of the d. t. abound in twentieth-century fiction, especially science fiction and fantasy. The theme was popular in the 1930s as a group of religious writers, led by C. S. Lewis, frequently involved divine figures in their stories. Lewis' own novel, *Out of the Silent Planet* (1938), describes the training of the hero who is transported to Mars to learn about the reality of life, which cannot be seen on the shadowed world of Earth. Madeleine L'Engle's *A Wrinkle in Time* (novel, 1968) has a similar theme. The tutor in *Silent Planet* is revealed to be an angel of light, whose rebellious counterpart is keeping the Earth in shadow so that it cannot learn of God's love.

T. H. White, writing near the end of the decade, included the d. t. theme in *The Sword in the Stone* (1939) in the person of Merlin, the strange and mysterious magician. Merlin's preferred methods of training the "Wart" depend on experience, including the experience of becoming different animals and making short "voyages" into the different worlds (of the animals and outlaws) very near his own home. Although Merlin teaches very little by precept, the animals to whom he sends his charge are the real teachers, and they give instructions and advice in many ways, including very specific precepts. Merlin is unusual among d. t.s in that he is a comic character who is not always sure what his magic is going to accomplish.

The d. t. theme is one focus of A. C. Clarke's novel *2001: A Space Odyssey* (1968). The mysterious black monolith is obviously a tool for instruction and it is linked to the progress of the human race. At the end of the novel, the hero David Bowman is obviously retrained to become the savior for his race. This mysterious transformation is clarified and pursued in the sequel *2010: Odyssey Two* (1982). In both these novels, the d. t.s are an alien race so advanced that their machines carry out the training (or retraining) in their absence.

Richard Adams' novel *Shardik* (1974) describes the training of a poor hunter who becomes the high priest to a god in the form of a great bear. The bear leads Kelderek into many experiences that the young man is left to sort out by himself. His human mentor, the Tuginda or high priestess of the cult, is pushed aside when she challenges his plan to use the bear Shardik in a plan of conquest. Kelderek follows the bear from the heights of power through the depths of degradation and despair, until he is finally shaped to undertake the task of the god. Although the novel leaves little doubt about the god's intentions, ambiguity about the role and function of religion permeates the book. This ambiguity arises out of Kelderek's blind attempts to understand the intentions of the god who is symbolized by the great bear and by others who willingly and hypocritically use the superstition of the followers of the bear to enhance their own fortunes.

The d. t. also represents a major theme in George Lucas' *Star Wars* movies (1978–1983) that were so popular in the early 1980s. In this case, the d. t. is embodied in the Jedi knight Obiwan Kenobi and in the 800-year-old Yoda. Although both of these are human and mortal, their study of the illusive Force and the power they derive from it raise them above the level of humanity into a new range of being. This transformation is expressed in the first movie in Obiwan's threat to Darth Vader during their battle to the death. It is illustrated by the "ghostly" reappearance of Luke's tutors at critical moments in the story. Instruction in the *Star Wars* saga comes primarily by experience with encouragement and reflection provided by the tutors. Even Luke's period of more formal instruction with Yoda during the second movie follows this pattern. Luke's training takes him over much of the galaxy in search of himself and of understanding of the Force.

The d. t. does not always appear as a righteous defender of the innocent. In certain authors and stories, the d. t. becomes a corrupter, trying to make the protagonist abandon the path of virtue for a darker way. In *Revenge of the Jedi*, Darth Vader and the emperor can be seen in this way, although they are not portrayed as divine. In Goethe's interpretation of the Faust legend in his play *Faust* (1808), the dissatisfied doctor conjures up a tutor to complete his damnation. The purpose of Mephistopheles is to encourage Faust's abandonment of God and to keep him directed toward self-destruction. Jean-Paul Sartre's *The Flies* portrays the god Zeus as a tempter for young Orestes, trying to woo him away from duty and revenge in the name of vague fears and conventional morality.

See also: Apocalypse, Religion in Science Fiction, Travel.

Selected Bibliography

Alfred, Joseph R. "Telemachus in French Prose, 1700–1750: An Objective Approach to a Theme." Diss., University of Florida, 1974.
Eckart, Charles W. "Initiatory Motifs in the Story of Telemachus." *Classical Journal* 59 (1963):49–57.

JOSEPH R. ALFRED

DRAGONS

Thought to be derived from the second aorist stem (*drak-*) of the Greek verb *derkomai* meaning "to see clearly" or "shining from the eye," the word "dragon" generally denotes a large animal, ophidian or reptilian in shape, with either two or four legs, a long tail, sometimes scales, sometimes wings, sometimes fiery breath. It lives in caves, clouds, deserts, mountains, forests, and the sea. Regarded by most as a creature of malevolence, the dragon is invariably described as a being of power and mystery and can appear in literature as either a real or a fabulous animal. The freedom we allow in the definition of "dragon" does much to account for the ubiquity of the motif. The Middle Ages saw the most serious treatment of the dragon in Western literature.

Mythology

Dragons are found in many mythologies of the world, even when we limit the meaning of mythology to stories involving the creation of the cosmos. The creatures also appear in many early legends that we more loosely call mythology. One of the oldest occurrences of the dragon in mythology is the Babylonian creation myth, the *Enuma elish* (*War of the Gods,* epic poem, 2225–1926 B.C.), in which Tiamat, the dragoness of chaos, is bound by Marduk and has her body split to form the heavens, earth, and sea. Early Canaanite myth has Baal (later the Judeo-Christian Bel, as in the biblical story of Daniel and the dragon of Dan. 14:22), whom scholars associate with Marduk, fighting a seven-headed dragon. An early Chinese flood myth has a dragonlike creature, Kung Kung, a weather deity, as dragons often were in myth, in combat with a champion. The familiar Eastern dragons, lizards in shape, horned, whiskered, four-legged, wingless, with four or five claws, often accompanied by a ball or pearl, and in some way controlling water, were at times considered benevolent creatures. The motif in Eastern literature and art differs substantially from its Western counterpart, notably in its strong equation of dragon and king. Interlocked dragons also have been known to represent sexual intercourse. Harbingers of good luck or rain, these dragons, often emblems of the East, may have been influenced by the nagas of India, which were brought to China by the Buddhists.

The nagas were supernatural serpents who carry both good and evil connotations. They are creatures with kings and families similar to the Chinese dragons. The individual combat between dragon and champion, however, is found in the Indian myth of Vritra, the gigantic serpent who encompassed the waters of chaos and kept them from flowing, and Indra, the weather-god and champion. This story is told throughout the Rig Veda (hymns), composed c. 1500–1200 B.C. and compiled c. 1000 B.C.

The Egyptian serpent Sito was thought to encircle the world and the giant serpent Apep (Apophis) battles the sun god Ra each night. Hittite myth tells of the fight between the storm god and the dragon. The Old Norse giant serpent Iormungandr encircles the world in the manner of Sito and the biblical Leviathan. Norse myth also describes the flying dragon Níðhǫggr who lives under the tree of life gnawing at its roots. The Germanic dragon combat myth relates the defeat of the treasure-hoarding Fáfnir by the champion Sigurð/Siegfried. A Celtic legend has a hero Fraoch defeating a sea-serpent who defends a magical tree. Even the

Mayans and Mexicans told tales of a Gucumatz/Kulkulcun or Quetzalcoatl who was often represented as a giant plumed serpent.

More integral to the study of the dragon in Western literature, however, is the creature's appearance in Greek mythology. According to Ovid, the foremost authority of ancient myth for over a millennium, dragons played a significant role in the beginnings of our world. His *Metamorphoses* (epic poem, c. A.D. 2–17) tells of the Python (a giant serpent) and Apollo; Cadmus and another giant cave-dwelling snake; Andromeda and her sea monster; Typhon, the huge fire-spouting half-serpent; Jason and his tree-guarding dragon; the child Hercules and his giant serpent; the grown man Hercules and the Hydra; and later Hercules and his sea monster. Dragons also draw heavenly chariots, and Ladon is the dragon who guards the golden apples of the Hesperides.

Dragons in mythology, although at times differing vastly in physical appearance and intent, have a few recurrent traits worth noting. They are often pitted against a highly powerful and eventually victorious champion. They are often bound in some way during the combat, and often they guard something valuable (rain, golden apples, gold itself), but of no use to themselves. Quite frequently they are weather divinities, associated with water and/or chaos, and represent mankind's chief obstacle to civilization or riches.

Antiquity

Some of the earliest dragons recorded in Western writing were of a very different sort. These were the wild and dangerous creatures reportedly encountered by the Greek travellers to the Eastern realms. Herodotus' *Historiai* (*History*, 5th century B.C.) tells of Arabian winged snakes and small-winged serpents who guard spice trees. Later travellers (Ktesias, Megasthenes, 4th century B.C.) relate tales of giant worms. Lucan in his *Pharsalia* (epic poem, c. A.D. 62) describes flying golden dragons in Libya.

Some of these accounts and many others gained almost scientific authenticity in Pliny's *Naturalis Historia* (*Natural History*, c. A.D. 77), which includes over thirty references to *dracones*. Well over half of these clearly indicate a large snake or fish, but the remaining dragons have magical traits such as the medicinal dragon's stone, which must be removed from the animal's brain. Later encyclopedists accepted everything in Pliny as fact, and much of his extraordinary work proved to be just that.

At this time dragons, or at least the creatures referred to as *dracones* in Roman writing, were finding a place in more fictive accounts. Latin fables acquaint us with the fox who comes upon a dragon with buried treasure, the dragon who promises a farmer wealth and good fortune and the rich dragon who tests a man's friendship with an egg supposedly essential to the dragon's life. Influenced by myth and natural scientific accounts, the dragon motif can be found as early as Cicero (*Philippicae* [*Philippics*, speeches, 44–43 B.C.] 13.5.12) as a symbol for greed or guardianship when he berates someone to be so bold as to hold on to his master's patrimony as a dragon does to its treasure.

Perhaps the most consequential treatment of the dragon can be found in the Bible. Over thirty references are made to the beast. The apocalyptic dragon corresponds to the cosmological creature in myth. Again the dragon is bound for the good of mankind. Other references to the dragon show that it was understood to be the largest animal of creation (Ps.148:7) and a creature inhabiting wastelands (Isa. 34:13).

The Early Middle Ages

Biblical commentary by the Christian fathers, read simultaneously with the Scriptures, gave added dimension to the symbolism of the dragon in the Middle Ages. In its various references, the biblical dragon was interpreted as the devil, consummate animal power, secret attack, open attack, pride, a pursuer of chastity, and a venomous tryant.

In the seventh century, Isidore of Seville's *Etymologiae* (encyclopedia) defined the dragon as the large flying creature of Ethiopia and India who lives near rocks and kills even elephants. Reworked ancient travel accounts of Alexander the Great and others circulated throughout Europe in these centuries reasserting the existence of dragons in uninhabited wastelands.

Hagiography of the time occasionally mentions the defeat of dragons by saints (such as Matthew and Margaret) and even the rare occurence of the dragon as a servant of the saint as seen in a Life of St. Erasmus and the biblical account of Aaron's magical rod transformed into a *draco* (Exod. 7:12–15).

In Old English poems (c. 9th century), the dragon is frequently a symbol of the devil as in the *Panther,* Cynewulf's *Elene,* and *Solomon and Saturn.* In the latter, dragons also occur as the menacing beasts of a far-off land, and in *Christ and Satan* they are guardians of the gates of hell. *The Anglo-Saxon Chronicle* (annals, c. 891–1154) reports fiery dragons, sometimes interpreted as meteors, flying over Northumbria in 793.

In the epic poem *Beowulf* (c. 8th century), the dragon receives full treatment. Here is a large-scaled, winged, fire-breathing creature, living in a cave by the sea, defending an ancient treasure, and revenging the theft of part of that treasure. The hero of the poem single-handedly attacks the creature after it has ravaged the coastline of his kingdom. The battle echoes earlier dragon fights, and the poem evokes many of the symbolic interpretations of dragons including pride, chaos, and the devil. The poem ends with both the dragon and the hero slain.

The Later Middle Ages

After the year 1000, dragons became more and more common in written works. Biblical exegeses continued to interpret the creature, but, for the most part, not to cast doubt on its existence in the real world. The great encyclopedias of the thirteenth century continued to define the dragon based on Isidore's and Pliny's accounts and to locate it in India and Africa as the world maps of these centuries indicate. The mythical Eastern kingdom of Prester John boasted dragons, and Mandeville's journal, complete with dragons, was translated into many languages throughout Europe. By this time, the dragon was a standard entry in the medieval bestiary, picture books describing animals and translating each into a spiritual symbol. The dragon was always seen as the devil, powerful and treacherous. In this it was not alone. The Middle Ages wrote about and believed in other monsters and beasts (like the similarly unseen giraffe) because they were attested to on good authority. Some were also interpreted as devils.

In these centuries, the Old Norse sagas were pitting their champions against trolls, cat-like monsters, and dragons. In the account of Danish history of Saxo Grammaticus (*Historia Danica*, c. 1200), two separate heroes battle dragons for treasure. These dragons had no spiritual connotations, which was true for the majority of dragons found in medieval romances.

The Arthurian romance cycle demonstrates a far more secular use of the motif than found in hagiography and bestiaries. Geoffrey of Monmouth (*Historia regum Britanniae* [*History of the Kings of Britain*, c. 1136] expands the story of Merlin's interpretation of two dragons found fighting in a pit below a tower into an almost mystical account of beasts and monsters, particularly dragons, representing England and other political entities and personalities. Dragons, for the most part, appear in dreams in Malory's fifteenth-century version (*Morte d'Arthur*, prose romance, c. 1469), often representing Arthur himself. Malory also writes of the knights (Lancelot, Bors, Tristan, Percival) defeating dragons in individual combat. For these knights (with the exception of Percival, who has a spiritual dream), the dragon is not the devil, but a huge adversary, sometimes magical and portentous. The great French romances that Malory bases his tales upon, as well as the English metrical romances, use the motif in this way. The German hero Wigalois defeats his dragon Pfetan in a world of Celtic myth. Although scholars might be tempted to read the apocalyptic dragon in all medieval dragons, the symbolic treatment of the motif in romances can be seen to be far more subtle, if present at all, compared to its treatment in saints' lives.

In the twelfth century the story of the dragon fight was added to the legend of George, the soldier-saint. The addition demonstrates the tendency in hagiography of this period to embellish a saint's life by supplying a victory over the *antiquus serpens* himself in the form of a dragon. Some saints' lives, like that of Martha and, of course, Michael the archangel, tell detailed stories of the creature and battle, but as the genre became more popular, the dragon became a standardized symbol of the saint's spiritual prowess just as it had become a symbol of the knight's military prowess. Iconographically, well over seventy saints are associated with the dragon.

Although Lydgate repeats the story of St. Margaret and her dragon/devil, he, as well as other major poets, does not write at length about the creature. Chaucer's most interesting reference is when the Wife of Bath tells how her husband, echoing the Bible, instructed that better your habitation be with a lion or foul dragon than a woman prone to chiding.

The Renaissance and After

By the sixteenth century, picture books describing monstrous creatures, including dragons, were circulating around Europe. These creatures were at times even more monstrous than their predecessors, and the collections often exploited freakish births. During this century, Ludovico Ariosto wrote his Italian epic poem *Orlando furioso* (1516) in which his hero, Rogero, defeats the sea dragon Orke in an episode hearkening back to Perseus' battle with the monster threatening Andromeda. Spenser perpetuates the late medieval satanic dragon tradition not only in the creature that Redcrosse (St. George) defeats at the end of book 1 of *The Faerie Queene* (epic poem, 1590–1596), but also in such composite creatures as Errour.

More fictional accounts involving dragons, however, were becoming rare. The decay of the encyclopedic treatment of monsters is evident in Thomas Browne's *Vulgar Errors* (treatise, 1646), which seriously questions the existence of basilisks, griffins, amphisbaenae, and the phoenix. Advances in exploration and the natural sciences drove the dragon more and more out of the classification of real animals. Hagiography, romances, and allegories gradually made room for Renaissance and neo-classical literary tastes. Writers continued to use the motif for an allusion to the exotic or portentous. Marlowe has Mephistopheles first appear to Doctor Faustus (*Doctor Faustus,* play, 1604) in the shape of a dragon. Shakespeare refers to *Merlin* and dragons in a speech about omens in his play *Part 1 Henry IV,* and has a scale of a dragon added to the witches' brew in the play *Macbeth* (1605–1606). Milton describes his Satan as a huge winged Leviathan-like creature when cast down to hell, and when further punished by God in book 10 of the poem *Paradise Lost* (1667), the inhabitants of Pandemonium are transformed into monstrous serpents and Satan himself is "dragon grown." The dragon thus remained as a sign of the devil, but its loss of substance in the real world made it less interesting to the more literal leanings of the times.

The Nineteenth and Twentieth Centuries

With the advent of literary realism, the dragon was banned from the mainstream of serious literature. Interest in Gothic tales helped to hold the door open for the supernatural, but dragons were confined to more obscure fantasy stories, short tales that, if known at all, were usually assigned to juvenile readers because of their unrealistic characters.

Knowledge of the dragon was kept alive through centuries of popularity in the plastic arts, heraldry in particular. A familiarity was also necessary to understand and compare mythologies of the world. Vladímir Propp (*Morphology of the Folktale,* 1968) speculated that the very archetype of Russian fairy tales would involve a dragon kidnapping a princess. The creature became the stuff of nightmares, and because of its close kinship with the serpent, Freud interpreted the dragon as a male, aggressive principle. Jung, on the other hand, saw the beast as representative of the female, more of a nurturing figure. Both interpretations stem from attributes of the mythological dragon.

Although the dragon's intent toward mankind is often a crucial point in any treatment of the motif, writers have also been intrigued with the legendary wisdom of the creature. In some accounts, Fáfnir speaks to Sigurð; the taste of Fáfnir's blood gives the hero the power to understand the speech of birds. Not only wisdom, but treachery was attributed to dragons. The Beast of the Apocalypse speaks with the voice of the red dragon, Satan. The creature's magical qualities recommend it to stories of transformation.

In the first half of this century, Yeats told us that now our "days are dragon-ridden" and the Old English scholar J.R.R. Tolkien wrote *The Hobbit* (1938) and *Lord of the Rings* (1954–1956), his four-volume fantasy based on characters loosely drawn from northern folklore. His dragon, Smaug, a malign, scaled, winged, fire-breathing creature, defends a treasure from the hero. The popularity of these books, along with a general increase in quantity and quality of science fiction and fantasy in this century, has provided a new literary environment for the dragon motif. One adaptation of the traditional dragon appears in Anne McCaffrey's novels about the planet Pern (*The Dragonriders of Pern,* 1968–1978), where the creatures, with many of their usual powers, relate telepathically and cooperatively to humans who ride them. Horror films often exploit the serpentine awe of the traditional dragon. Portrayed by some as threatening, by some as almost humorous, dragons in literary works over the centuries have been used to challenge the distinctions we are accustomed to make between man and animal, good and evil, natural and supernatural, and real and unreal.

See also: Christian Hero, Monsters, Unicorn.

Selected Bibliography

Fontenrose, Joseph. *Python: A Study of Delphic Myth and Its Origins.* Berkeley: University of California Press, 1959.

Hartland, Edwin Sidney. *The Legend of Perseus: A Study of Tradition in Story, Custom and Belief.* 3 vols. 1894. New York: AMP Press, 1972.

Lee, Peter H. *Songs of Flying Dragons: A Critical Reading.* Cambridge, Mass.: Harvard University Press, 1975.

Ploss, Emil. *Siegfried-Sigurd, der Drachenkämpfer: Untersuchungen zur germanisch-deutschen Heldensage.* Cologne: Böhlau, 1966.

LESLEY KORDECKI

DREAM

The experience that the imagination undergoes while the senses and reason are apparently inactive during sleep has been a subject of great interest to thinkers from the earliest times until the late seventeenth century and again from the late nineteenth century on. There were in the earlier period four basic theories of the dream. The most primitive was that dreams are caused by God or gods, angels or demons, spirits of the dead or living, in order to warn, teach, threaten, aid, urge, beg, reveal, or especially, prophesy. Belief in such "objective," supernatural dreams, implicit in Homer and the Bible, was explicitly expressed by pagan writers of late antiquity and received new impetus from the church fathers and Scholastics.

In contrast to this was the belief in a "subjective" dream caused not by a deity but by an internal power, by some suprarational, occult faculty of the soul that enables man to get beyond his limitations and obtain important information not available through reason and waking consciousness. This theory was in one form or another enunciated by Plato, the Stoics, the Neoplatonists, and by some church fathers. A third kind of dream was somatic or physiological—generated and shaped by the inroads of the body on a consciousness rendered passive by sleep. This theory was adumbrated by Democritus and developed by Hippocrates, Galen, and the great Arab physician Avicenna. Fused with the reigning medical theory of body "humors," it obtained through the Middle Ages down to the seventeenth century. According to a fourth tradition (intimated by the Pre-Socratics, Herodotus, the writers of the Bible, and articulated by writers of late antiquity) dreams reflect in some way the waking thoughts of the individual. These four basic approaches coexisted, and conscientious writers on the subject would refer to each in turn but leave the reader at a loss as to how to classify a given dream.

In the Enlightenment, thought about dreams shrivelled into an attenuated version of the last two of the four theories; then Freud, in the greatest revolution in the history of this subject, put new life into the second and fourth theories while ignoring the other two. To many thinking people nowadays, the dream, among the most revealing of psychic incidents, has its roots deep in the individual's past and reveals a person's secret life. If earlier ages extracted from it hints of future physical or moral well-being, we extract from it hints of past psychic illness.

The literary work of the earlier periods is especially rich in prophetic and monitory dreams, as well as in the inevitable debates over whether a given dream belongs to one category or another, as drama is made out of the limitations of human understanding. In modern fiction, by contrast, dreams express anxiety rather than prophesy events, but prophetic overtones of a more subtle, psychological sort can sometimes be discerned. Note should also be taken of the lavish use, in all periods, of the dream as a metaphor, often for the transcience of life.

Antiquity and the Middle Ages

In one literary dream genre, a major character is urged during sleep into battle by a divine figure. Thus is it with Zeus and Agamemnon in the epic poem *Ilias* (*Iliad,* c. 8th century B.C.) by Homer and Allecto and Turnus in the epic poem *Aeneis* (*Aeneid,* 19 B.C.) by Virgil. But where an amoral Zeus is deceiving the Greek king in order to mollify Thetis by indirectly advancing Achilles, a hostile Juno is trying to disrupt the moral order celebrated in the Latin work. The latter example becomes the norm in medieval literature, as Satan, or a satanic figure who is a literary offshoot of the Virgilian Juno, tries to deceive a good knight or tempt a saint. A variant of the objective dream is the licit monitory dream: the dead Patrocles entreating Achilles in sleep to bury his body, or Mercury prompting Aeneas to abandon Dido for bigger things.

Another genre is the symbolic or allegorical premonitory dream, often subjective, that is, not caused by external agency. In Homer's epic poem *Odysseia* (*Odyssey*, c. 8th century B.C.), Penelope tells of having seen in sleep an eagle kill twenty geese; this is a representation of Odysseus' imminent return and killing of the suitors. Veiled but ominous prophetic dreams of a similar sort appear in Aeschylus' *Persai* (*The Persians*, play, 472 B.C.) and *Choēphoroi* (*Libations Bearers*, play, 458 B.C.), Ovid's didactic poem *Ars amatoria* (*The Art of Love*, c. 1 B.C.), as well as to Joseph in the Bible. Dreams with prophetic, indeed political, import abound in the ancient historians Herodotus, Tacitus, Suetonius, Plutarch, Dio, Ammianus Marcellinus—but not, interestingly, in the "scientific" Thucydides and Polybius.

A third genre is the eschatological dream-vision. A character in the *Gilgamesh* epic (c. 2000 B.C.) has a vision in sleep of the afterworld. Centuries later, Cicero, in his *Somnium Scipionis* (*The Dream of Scipio*, 51 B.C.), converted Plato's story of the vision of Er (itself a variant of a dream) into a sleeping vision of last things. Many medieval works, however encyclopedic, are framed by dreams lacking any verisimilitude; among the better ones are the *Roman de la rose* (*Romance of the Rose*, didactic poem, c. 1230, 1275) and Chaucer's poem *The Book of the Duchess* (1369), *House of Fame* (c. 1379), *Parlement of Foules* (c. 1382), and *Legend of Good Women* (c. 1386). Langland's *Piers Plowman* (c. 1362–1387) is a large poetic vision in which eschatology is displaced by allegorical satire of contemporary moral and political evils. And, according to one interpretation of ambiguous lines near the end of the work, Dante's epic poem, *La divina commedia* (*The Divine Comedy*, c. 1320), the greatest of all medieval works, is a vast eschatological dream vision.

Yet a fourth genre is the love dream, common in lyric poetry—for example, Propertius (late 1st century B.C.), Heinrich von Morungen (early 13th century), Petrarch (1304–1374)—and in romances such as Ovid's *Metamorphoses* (c. A.D. 2–17), Longus' *Ta kata Daphnin kai Chloēn* (*Daphnis and Chloe*, 2d century?) and Chrétien de Troyes's *Cligès* (c. 1160). Sleep, instead of bringing oblivion to waking concerns, provides a vision of beauty that alters the sleeper's waking hours, exacerbates the lover's yearning, or fulfills his fondest wish. Thus important dreams occur at the inception of a love affair in Valerius Flaccus' *Argonautica* (poem, c. A.D. 80–93), at the end of one in the *Aeneid*, and at the center and turning point in Gottfried von Strassburg's *Tristan* (romance, c. 1210).

The natural, realistic dream, reflecting waking sorrow or representing a wish fulfillment, was not unknown in early literature. Hector's condition while being pursued by Achilles is likened to the common nightmare in which one wants desperately to run but feels paralyzed; the abandoned Dido sees herself in a sleeping vision wandering alone in a desert. There is, however, also a less physically enervating kind of anxiety dream, which differs in quality from the utter nightmare; early writers used it and accounted for it rationally. These are the dreams that reflect immediate waking concerns. Aristotle (*Peri enupniōn, Peri psychēs* [*De somniis, De anima*, mid-4th century B.C.]) had analyzed this phenomenon, as did Cicero (*De divinatione,* c. 44 B.C.), Lucretius (*De rerum natura* [*On the Nature of Things,* 1st century B.C.]), Petronius (*Satyricon,* novel, A.D. 60), Claudian (early 5th century). In the Anglo-Saxon lyric *The Wanderer* (c. 8th century), the lonely protagonist dreams of being reunited with his vanished community and awakens to the grief of solitude. Wolfram von Eschenbach's hero in *Parzival* (epic poem, c. 1210) suffers a turbulent, debilitating dream during a night in the Grail Castle.

Great skill is shown by some writers in the use of interrelated dreams in a single work. In the *Aeneid,* Dido's dream of her assassinated husband parallels Aeneas' dream of Hector, as each is impelled by a recent victim and confidant to flee and make a fresh start in life. Then, in turn, after Aeneas' and Dido's destinies have merged as a result of these dreams, the hero explains his need to leave her by telling of dreams he has had of Anchises and Mercury. In the work of Virgil's Christian disciple, Dante *(The Divine Comedy),* dreams appear at key junctures and evenly spaced intervals during the pilgrim's ascent in the *Purgatorio (Purgatory)*— dreams that mingle realism (they are generated by heat or flight), moral symbolism (the pilgrim's growing purification), and allusions (to pagan mythology and Christian theology).

Because of the uncertainty as to the meaning of dreams, writers made drama out of conflicting interpretations proffered by individuals with differing temperaments or with vested interests. Thus Agamemnon's dream is misinterpreted by Nestor and results in a Greek defeat. Subsequent writers continued the discussion of this dream. Plato (*Politeia,* [*The Republic,* dialogue, c. 380 B.C.]), accepting the falsity of the dream, made the blasphemous incident of which it is part a ground for barring poets like Homer from his ideal state. Nearly a millennium later, Synesius (c. 400) and Macrobius (c. 400) resorted to sophistry in order to shift the blame from Zeus and Homer to Agamemnon.

A more extensive debate takes place within the tale itself in Boccaccio's *Filostrato* (poem, c. 1338) and its English version, Chaucer's *Troilus and Criseyde* (poem, c. 1385). Troilus has several nightmares, which Pandarus first dismisses as worthless and then, inconsistently and incorrectly, shows to foreshadow a happy outcome to Troilus' love. In Chaucer's "Nonnes Priestes Tale" (c. 1380–1400), the cock dreams that he will be seized by a fox. His mistress, Dame Pertelote, blandly explains dreams away as caused by somatic imbalance. Chauntecleer, ignoring her theory, insists that dreams are mantic. Carried away by uxoriousness and exhibitionism, he nevertheless flies into the farmyard to his unfortunate rendezvous with the fox. The human uncertainty about the meaning of dreams causes the couple's squabble, delineates their personalities, and results in a great literary creation.

The Renaissance and Seventeenth Century

The dream-vision genre survives in the Renaissance in the prose satires *Ignatius His Conclave* (1611) by Donne and *Los sueños (The Visions,* 1627) by Francisco de Quevedo, or in the pious, quasi-medieval *A Cypress Grove* (prose work,

1623) by Drummond of Hawthornden. The greatest of these works is Bunyan's *Pilgrim's Progress* (1678–1684), a Protestant prose allegory in which what is unlike everyday reality can be accepted by the literal-minded Christian without fear of contamination by fiction, for dreams are notoriously strange.

The love lyric dream appears in nonerotic contexts in "neoplatonic" and "stoic" poetry by Chapman, Lord Herbert of Cherbury, and Shakespeare, and in erotic contexts, whether genteel (Ronsard, Herrick, Milton's 23rd sonnet and the two dreams he assigns Adam in *Paradise Lost* [poem, 1667]), ratiocinative and satiric (Donne), or voluptuous (Jonson, Herrick, Dryden). In a neat reversal of the common conceit, Donne's "The Good Morrow" (c. 1590s) suggests that falling in love is an awakening that makes all prior amatory experience seem to have been only dreams.

Shakespeare's plays are replete with dream material. Wish fulfillment or "vocational" anxiety dreams, beside being wittily described by Mercutio, occur to Hotspur, Shylock, Tullus Aufidius, and Caliban. Ominous dreams appear in many plays, notably *Romeo and Juliet* (c. 1596) and *Macbeth* (1605–1606). The most dream-haunted of Shakespeare's plays is *Richard III* (1591–1594), containing such tours de force as Clarence's premonitory anxiety dream, which is rich with lyricism and an under-the-aspect-of-eternity view, as well as with nuances about his own treacherous career and his imminent victimization by his brother; Richard's recurring guilt-ridden dreams; and the vast oneiric experience—part objective and part subjective (like the dream at the beginning of Aeschylus' *Eumenides* [play, 458 B.C.]), part recapitulation and part prophetic, part moral and part poetic—shared concurrently at different ends of the battle scene (and the stage) by Richard III and by Richmond.

The proverbial idea that life is a dream receives extended treatment in *A Midsummer Night's Dream* (c. 1595), in which the lovers' claiming reason as the officiating power over their falling in and out of love makes dubious the notions of constants, certainty, essence, and human rationality. It also receives brief though memorable expression in *Henry IV* (1597, 1600) (Henry V speaks of having dreamed of such a man as Falstaff), *Measure for Measure* (1603–1604) ("and our little life is rounded with sleep . . . an after dinner's sleep dreaming"), and the *Tempest* (1611) ("we are such stuff as dreams are made on") (Cf. the conclusion of Mark Twain's *Mysterious Stranger* [story, 1916.])

A more methodical exploration of the metaphor appears in Calderon de la Barca's *La vida es sueño* (*Life is a Dream*, 1635). Central here is not the traditional prophetic dream at the beginning of the play but the placing of the hero, Prince Segismondo, in different circumstances—first an upbringing in solitary confinement, then an interval of freedom on the throne, then back to confinement—while making him think that what he recollects are not prior experiences but mere dreams. That the play, along with its Catholic affirmation of free will and moral responsibility, has a happy ending does not distract one from the unsettling questions raised about the dreamlike unreality of life. These questions first broached by Plato in his dialogue, *Theaitētos* (*Theaetetus*, c. 368

B.C.) and by Chuang Chou in the treatise attributed to him, *Chuang Tzu* (c. 4th century B.C.), were resurgent in the contemporary writings of Sir Thomas Browne, Hobbes, Descartes, Pascal, (Cf. also the induction to Shakespeare's *Taming of the Shrew,* c. 1594).

The tradition of the objective admonitory dream is continued in Tasso's *Gerusalemma liberata (Jerusalem Delivered,* epic poem, 1581), which has a Christianized "diabolic" version of the dream in the *Iliad* and the *Aeneid.* Such a dream serves, in lieu of modern psychology and sociology, as a primitive explanation (as is often seen in Herodotus) of actions that seem inconsistent or incredible—in this case, that Christian knights would turn against their pious leader. A similar dream appears in the Portuguese national epic, Camões' *Os Lusíadas (The Lusiads,* 1572), when Bacchus, disguised as a Mohammedan priest, inflames the Moors against Vasco da Gama. In Spenser's epic poem *Faerie Queene* (1590–1596), Archimago tries to separate the Red Cross Knight, in quest of holiness, from the lady Una (Truth) by instilling in him a false dream of the lady as lascivious. This dream is at once a common male erotic (or "wet") dream and an allegorical rendering of the idea that evil triumphs when holiness is made impossible through one's separation from the Truth.

In yet another version of the diabolic dream, in Cowley's *Davideis* (epic poem, 1656), Envy, sent by Lucifer, urges Saul to murder David; its counterpart, the angelic dream of posterity granted to a hero like Aeneas, is experienced by a joyous David. Milton continues the diabolic dream tradition in his poems *In quintum novembris* (1626) and *Paradise Regained* (1671), but it is *Paradise Lost* that exhibits one of the greatest such dreams in all literature. In it, a disguised Satan leads Eve through a dress rehearsal of the temptation, eating of the fruit, and Fall. This version triumphs because it combines realistic physiological details (the sensation of falling), narrative requirements (foreshadowing, character consistency), psychological verisimilitude (the wish fulfillment of someone operating under a prohibition), theological-moral correctness (Eve is given advance warning and therefore exercises free will when awake), echoes of the great literary tradition (Homer, Plato, Virgil, Spenser, Tasso), and allegorical and prophetic overtones. Milton uses so much skill and subtlety that scholars have been arguing for decades as to whether Eve is already fallen in the wake of the dream.

At the end of the epic, Adam and Eve are granted divine prophetic dreams that sum up human history and destiny, while throughout the narrative Milton suggests that his own poetic inspiration for the work comes to him in sleep— as, according to Bede, happened to the semilegendary first English poet, Caedmon, and would happen to Coleridge and R. L. Stevenson.

The problem of the interpretation of dreams is depicted with renewed vigor by Rabelais in his Gargantuan novels (1532–1564), as Panurge, resorting to every form of divination in order to ascertain whether to marry, has an ambiguous dream about horns. Pantagruel sees in it a prefiguration of infidelity and marital squabbles, but Panurge insists on seeing rather references to the cornucopia and to erections. Marriage certainly need not entail harmony; one of the things that husband and wife quarrel over is the interpretation of a dream. So is it in Shakespeare's play *Henry VI, Part 2* (1590–1592), when the duke of Gloucester and Eleanor exchange descriptions and exegeses of the dream each has had; in *Julius Caesar* (c. 1599), when Calpurnia's ominous dream dissuades Caesar from going to the Forum until Decius persuades him, by using the venerable principle of contraries (evil dreams portend happy events and vice versa), to ignore dream and wife; and in *Paradise Lost,* when Adam, like Pertelote and Pandarus, dismisses the dream as of benign import, and, like them, is proved incorrect by events.

The Eighteenth Century to Modern Period

Thanks to the materialist explanation and dismissal (notably by Bacon, Hobbes, and Locke) of dreams as the rags and tatters of waking thoughts, theorizing about the phenomenon fell into abeyance among serious thinkers for two centuries. That dreams still preoccupied thoughtful people, however, can be seen from the numerous anxiety dreams recorded in Samuel Pepys's *Diary* (1660–1669). In literature proper, the eighteenth century produced mainly pallid allegorical visions, like those in Addison's *Spectator* (essays, 1711–1712). Objective and somatic dreams disappear from major works, except in a mock epic like Pope's *Rape of the Lock* (1712). In his story "Celestial Railroad" (1843), Hawthorne uses the old-fashioned dream-vision work to good effect, but in his "Young Goodman Brown" (1846) and "My Kinsman, Major Molineux" (1851), the dream frame is ambiguous, realistic, "modern." Lewis Carroll's two Alice classics (1865–1872) are traditional extended dream-visions with, perhaps for the first time, overtly absurd dreamlike content (as well as dreams within dreams) that is nevertheless rich in mathematical, philosophical, and psychological insights.

Concurrently with the changing cultural climate, drugs enter the literary scene, and with them a new literary genre, the artificially induced dream. The most detailed description of "real" dreams in all literature is in Thomas De Quincey's *Confessions of an English Opium Eater* (1822). Moreover, as a result of the growth of interest in the unconscious during the latter half of the nineteenth century, a current of which Freud's writings constitute the climax, dreams regain importance, albeit in the works of psychologists rather than philosophers. Thus the opening sections of Nietzsche's *Die Geburt der Tragödie* (*The Birth of Tragedy,* 1872) discuss "the joyous necessity of the dream experience" and relate it to Apollo, tragedy, Greek culture. In *Menschliches, Allzumenschliches* (*Human, All Too Human,* 1878), Nietzsche traces metaphysics—including the belief in a soul, a hereafter, and in the gods—to the misunderstanding of the dream experience, thereby extending to Christianity an analysis that Hobbes (*Leviathan,* essay, 1651) had applied, at least overtly, solely to "the Religions of the Gentiles."

The major nineteenth-century novelists, anticipating and later articulating the new interest in the unconscious, artistically exploited the anxiety and the symbolic dreams and endowed it with a greater degree of verisimilitude and "surrealist" feverishness. Of such a nature are the vivid nightmares in, for example, Dickens' novel *Great Expectations* (1860–1861), Tolstoy's novels, *Voĭna i mir* (*War and Peace*, 1865–1869) and *Anna Karenina* (1877), Dostoevsky's novels *Prestuplenie i nakazanie* (*Crime and Punishment*, 1866) and *Brat' ĭaKaramazovy* (*The Brothers Karamazov*, 1880). The other dream genres—the divine, diabolic, monitory, and allegorical—have apparently been banished for good from the domain of serious literature.

In Proust's novel *Du côté de chez Swann* (*Swann's Way*, 1913)—which also contains on its opening pages the finest description of the twilight zone between sleeping and waking, an experience first portrayed in Hawthorne's "The Haunted Mind" (story, 1835)—the protagonist's waning infatuation with Odette culminates in a long, richly suggestive dream, as if the love itself had been an elusive, enigmatic dream. The novels of *A la recherche du temps perdu* (*Remembrance of Things Past*, 1913–27) contain numerous (and some repeated) dreams that help resolve the emotional crises of the dreamer; explore the subconscious, preverbal animal self; deal with intellectual and esthetic problems; endow the past with an enhanced reality; teach lessons not available from the waking consciousness; reflect the emotions, which constitute the real self of the individual; and substitute for or re-enforce Proust's theory of a waking involuntary memory.

In Thomas Mann's novel *Der Zauberberg* (*The Magic Mountain*, 1924), the hero recuperates at a sanatorium while undergoing a crash course in the history of Western civilization. Caught in a blizzard, he has a feverish dream of sunny Greece, the locale of youth, love, and joy, as well as of bloody rituals like child sacrifices. This vision constitutes the only possible answer to the question of human destiny so much worried over by the discussants in the book—namely, that there is no discursive answer or panacea, only a sensuous, enigmatic, and elusively dreamlike apprehension of life.

In the twentieth century, Freud and his school have made dreams of central importance to thinkers. Even writers untouched by Freud have written essays on the subject—for example, Stevenson, Chesterton ("Dreams are like life, only more so"), and, often, Borges. More important, a major alteration in modern culture has been the rise, under the joint influence of Freud and of romantic writers (Coleridge, De Quincey, Baudelaire, Rimbaud) fascinated by dreamlike states, of artistic tendencies that go beyond the mere use of dreams embedded in a story or of a dream-vision frame around a series of incidents, to the total imitation of the dream state (which Hawthorne had wanted to achieve). The creations of the Surrealist painters de Chirico, Ernst, Dali, and Magritte have been matched by those of writers. Central works in this new genre are two plays of Strindberg's expressionist phase, *Ett drömspel* (*A Dream Play*, 1901) and *Spöksonaten* (*The Ghost Sonata*, 1907); virtually all the stories of Kafka, which constitute a collection of nightmares, signally *Der Prozess* (*The Trial*, 1925) and *Das Schloss* (*The Castle*, 1926); the short stories of Jorge Luis Borges

(1899–1986); and Joyce's vast epic of the unconscious, *Finnegans Wake* (novel, 1939). These works imitate the dream state so fully as to verge on obscurity and incoherence. Further than that imitation cannot go. Such creations are, in effect, the old dream-visions but with frame and dreamer absent. These impersonal, disembodied dreams iterate the old life-is-a-dream metaphor—as exploited by Shakespeare and by Calderón—but with a thoroughness and intensity that seem to deny the existence of any waking reality or the possibility of heuristic experience.

The change in climate is manifest also in the way the epithet "dreamlike" has become honorific in criticism of literature, drama, cinema, and painting. Such works and changes reflect their age. The unimaginable man-made catastrophes of the twentieth century, paralleling—and, as some surmise, the result of—the loss of belief in another, eternal world has paradoxically diminished for many thinkers the possibility of belief in the existence of this temporal world, which heretofore was considered as at least an emanation from, reflection of, or anteroom to something permanent and definitive. But those readers who cherish the enchantment and mystery of dreams that punctuate a clearly demarcated, fairly predictable waking life can still turn to dreams in the literature of earlier centuries.

See also: Anxiety, Apocalypse, Psychoanalysis of the Self, Utopia.

Selected Bibliography

Bell, William Stewart. *Proust's Nocturnal Muse*. New York: Columbia University Press, 1962.

Messer, William Stuart. *The Dream in Homer and Greek Tragedy*. New York: Columbia University Press, 1918.

Steiner, Hans Rudolph. *Der Traum in der "Aeneis"*. New York: Columbia University Press, 1952.

Weidhorn, Manfred. *Dreams in Seventeenth-Century English Literature*. The Hague: Mouton, 1970.

MANFRED WEIDHORN

DWARF

A person who deviates from the norm through an extremely diminutive stature, generally being under four feet in height is defined as a dwarf. Dwarfs may be achondroplastic, often with large heads and torsos on shortened limbs, sometimes with accompanying deformities, such as a hunched back, or ateliotic (midget), with normal proportions in a miniature frame. Literary portrayals of dwarfs draw both from history and from folklore. In function they often blend with jesters, fairies, and hunchbacks. They are especially plentiful in medieval literature and in modern fiction.

Background in Myth and History

Dwarfs appear in the folklores of many nations as small, mythical beings with supernatural abilities. Almost universally, they are represented as remnants of an earlier race that once populated the earth; this belief is found not only in Europe, but among the Yucatecs of meso-America and the people of the South Seas. In Celtic myth, dwarfs are related to the fairy tradition. They can be extremely beautiful or else hideous in appearance. They usually dwell in subterranean kingdoms. They possess great wealth and are often generous hosts to human visitors. Often they possess supernatural strength, magical weapons, and powers of clairvoyance. In Germanic tradition, too, dwarfs are frequently guardians of treasure. They are intelligent beings created from maggots and dwell beneath the surface of the ground. Some are friendly to man, some hostile. As industrious and skilled goldsmiths and metalworkers, they constructed both weapons and ornaments for the Germanic deities. In later Germanic folklore they are given a variety of trades, which they then teach to human beings. They are portrayed as hoarders of gold, as miners and goldsmiths in Snorri Sturluson's prose *Edda* (narrative, 1220) and in "Rumpelstilzchen" ("Rumpelstiltskin") and "Schneewittchen" ("Snow White"), both fairy tales collected by the brothers Grimm and published in 1812–1814. In August Kopisch's poem "Die Heinzelmännchen" ("The Heinzel Men", 1836) we see dwarfs practicing a variety of trades for the benefit of mankind. In northern mythologies dwarfs appear as water, forest, and house spirits. Forest dwarfs are also common in African mythology. In meso-America, pot-bellied dwarfs were frequently represented in Olmec art. Deformed dwarfs are also associated with the god Quetzalcoatl.

Historical reports of dwarfs also go back far in time. Herodotus (485?–425? B.C.) gives a fairly accurate description of pygmies; Pliny the Elder (A.D. 23–79) describes several dwarf races. Dwarfs figure in the paintings of Pompeii and are common in Egyptian art. Egyptian statuary includes a figure of the dwarf Shumhotep, dating from the fifth dynasty. The Egyptian pharaohs treasured dwarfs as awesome creatures with special spiritual powers. Romans, on the other hand, appear to have kept deformed dwarfs as creatures who would deflect ill-fortune from the family onto themselves. Romans even practiced the art of artificial dwarfing to increase their supply of these unfortunate creatures. As court oddities, pets, and jesters, dwarfs were desirable acquisitions for European royalty and for the higher nobility down into the eighteenth century. Velázquez (1599–1660) painted portraits of the court dwarfs of Philip IV of Spain; marble statuary in the gardens adjoining Salzburg's Mirabell palace preserve the features of deformed dwarfs of the baroque age. Beginning in the late eighteenth century, dwarfs have been popular as carnival attractions, circus performers, and clowns, the most famous perhaps being Charles S. Stratton, who toured under P. T. Barnum as General Tom Thumb.

Antiquity and the Middle Ages

Homer's heroic poem *Ilias* (*Iliad*, c. 8th century B.C.) makes a passing allusion to pygmies who suffer death and destruction through the attacks of migrating cranes. This reference to warring cranes and pygmies was a familiar one among Greek and Roman authors, and the tale travelled eastward to the Arabs and Chinese. One of the better-known Arab versions appears in Mūsā Ud-Damīrī's *Hayāt ul-Hayawān,* a fourteenth-century treatise on animals of the Koran; here a nation of dwarfs has lost its eyes to the cranes, but a normal-sized visitor to the dwarf kingdom rescues them by attacking the cranes with his club. Several American Indian tribes have the same tale.

Philostratus Lemnius (b. c. A.D. 191) in his *Eikones (Pictures,* narrative prose) relates the tale of Hercules being attacked upon his right and left hands by tiny pygmies while he sleeps; Hercules laughingly conquers them by rolling them up in the skin of the Nemean lion. This tale is a partial inspiration for Jonathan Swift's world of the Lilliputians.

During the Middle Ages dwarfs were common figures in Arthurian literature. Sometimes they appear as boastful, arrogant retainers. In Chrétien de Troyes' romance *Erec et Enide* (c. 1160), an offensive dwarf retainer first whips Guinevere's maid and then lashes out at an unarmed Erec. He is described as "rude and mean," with "no equal for villainy." This ugly and ignoble dwarf contrasts sharply with the handsome royal dwarfs who become Erec's friends. The king Guivret the Little is described as "very small of stature, but very courageous of heart" and proves himself a worthy opponent in battle as well as a gracious friend and host. Bilis, king of the Antipodes, attends Erec's marriage with a number of other dwarf kings; they are all "very perfect gentlemen" and are treated with esteem by their hosts.

Other romances of the period make the same distinctions between good and bad dwarfs. In the Middle English romance *The Turk and Gowin* (late 14th-early 15th century), a dwarf leads Gawain to the Isle of Man and helps him to perform enormous feats of strength. In the *Nibelungenlied* (heroic epic, anonymous, c. 1200) Siegfried defeats the evil dwarf Alberich and wrests from him a magic cloak of invisibility. In the Dutch *Roman van Lancelot* (anonymous epic, early 14th century) Gawain and a dwarf king become fast friends, and both ride disguised as dwarfs to Arthur's court in order to test the fidelity of their wives, a reflection of the notion, perhaps, that dwarfs have difficulty satisfying the sexual desires of their larger, human wives. In Gottfried von Strassburg's *Tristan* (c. 1210) a malicious, spying dwarf named Melot le petit endeavors to betray Tristan and Isolde to the king. One of the most interesting portrayals of a dwarf occurs in the anonymous *Huon de Bordeaux (Huon of Bordeaux,* epic poem, c. 1200) where Oberon, the fairy king, proves the most loyal of friends in supplying Huon with the magical implements necessary in achieving his military triumphs. Oberon remains faithful to Huon even when the brash young hero disregards his warnings, and his wisdom and loyalty assure a happy ending to the tale. Oberon is described, in traditional dwarf terms, as a figure with a child's proportions, but with grey hair and an old man's face.

The Sixteenth and Seventeenth Centuries

Oberon was to reappear in Shakespeare's drama *A Midsummer Night's Dream* (c. 1595) as king of the elves, but his appearance is now more human, and his magic is less potent. The prankster Puck, a "shrewd and knavish sprite," acts as his servant. In the drama *The Tempest* (1611) the spirit Ariel is tiny servant to Prospero and demonstrates loyal obedience until, at the end of the play, he is released from further service. Fairies, elves, and dwarfs figure, too, in Edmund Spenser's *The Faerie Queene* (poetic allegory, 1590–1596). Meanwhile, in France, Charles Perrault (1628–1703) kept the fairy tradition alive through his compilations of fairy tales (*Contes de ma mère l'Oye* [*Mother Goose Tales,* 1697]).

Courtly festivals, pageants, and masques sometimes featured dwarfs in minor supporting roles, often as servants, sometimes as representatives of evil, demonic forces. The *Pas de l'arbre d'or,* staged for the Burgundian court at an extremely early date (1468), had already featured a number of dwarf attendants. In *Les plaisirs de l'île enchantée,* a three-day spectacle mounted at Versailles in 1664, dwarfs and giants were part of an army conjured up by an evil enchantress. In a theatrical production at a tournament in Kassel in 1596, one of the characters of the drama was a pygmy king "Piper from Greenland," who was held captive and, under a magic spell, served as watchman for the villain. A Carolian shrovetide masque of 1631, Ben Jonson's *Chloridia,* employed a dwarf to satirize the unpleasant underworld of the royal court. Because most theatricals of this period preferred figures from classical mythology to Germanic folk figures, dwarfs generally served fairly straightforward "functional" roles as human characters.

The Eighteenth Century

During the eighteenth century, popular English chapbooks featured several dwarf heroes. One, Jack Horner, was reportedly under thirteen inches in height. He was an adventurer-prankster whose accoutrements included a coat that could render him invisible and pipes which, when played, forced all who heard them to dance themselves to exhaustion. He lives on today in a Mother Goose rhyme.

Another common chapbook hero was Tom Thumb; he was reportedly an inch high and the product of Merlin's magic. As a member of Arthur's court he proves his courage in numerous ways. Beloved by the fairy queen, he is also resurrected several times, returning to court to continue his life of adventure and narrow escapes.

Henry Fielding, in 1730, made this diminutive hero the subject of his satiric drama *The Tragedy of Tragedies; or, The Life and Death of Tom Thumb the Great.* In this drama Tom is loved and wooed by all the women of the court, and his courageous deeds are the wonder and envy of all. The ridiculousness of the drama reaches its climax as Tom is swallowed by a cow and the members of the court respond to this bad news by murdering each other. The plot is little more than a vehicle for Fielding's mockery of literary critics; this mockery is contained in the lengthy, pedantic notations liberally sprinkled throughout the drama.

Jonathan Swift, too, incorporates little people into the first part of his four part novel *Gulliver's Travels* published anonymously in 1726. Here Swift uses his tiny figures to satirize English statesmen, political parties, and the shams of court. Swift's rich, imaginative treatment of Gulliver's adventures among the Lilliputians, who measure about six inches tall, quite deflects the readers from Swift's major goal, which was "to vex the world rather than divert it."

The Nineteenth Century

A number of British authors of the early nineteenth century turned away from the tiny midget heroes of their predecessors and examined again the deformed dwarfs of a real world. In *The Black Dwarf* (novel, 1816) Sir Walter Scott based his title figure on a real dwarf, David Ritchie, who stood just under three and a half feet and was named "Bow'd Davie" because of his deformity. Scott's figure, Sir Edward Mauley, the "Wise Wight of Mucklestane Moor," is a sullen, bitter misanthrope, who has turned to a hermit existence because of betrayal by his friends. At the close of the work, the dwarf's natural charity reasserts itself as he rescues the lovely daughter of the woman he had once loved. Scott confessed that he rushed the conclusion of this novel because a critic had convinced him that the hideous dwarf was too revolting a figure to hold readers, and he noted that he had "perhaps produced a narrative as much disproportioned and distorted as the Black Dwarf who is its subject."

In George Soane's tragi-comedy *The Dwarf of Naples* (1819), the deformed dwarf is the bastard brother of a noble count. Out of spite and envy he tries to destroy the count and the woman who loves him most. Yet here, as in Scott's novel, the dwarf's fierce behavior has a cause. As one sympathetic character puts it, "he has been teased by contempt and mockery into what he is." The dwarf is described as "wise, learned, valiant . . . everything but good."

The fairy tradition reasserted itself in the finer children's literature of the nineteenth century. Hans Christian Andersen, in "Tommelise" ("Thumbelina," fairy tale, 1835), created a female counterpart to Tom Thumb. Carlo Collodi's *Le aventure di Pinocchio* (*The Adventures of Pinocchio*, 1882) recreates a Jack Horner figure in this small, living puppet. In *Alice's Adventures in Wonderland* (1865) Lewis Carroll has Alice shrink to midget size and narrowly avoid drowning in her own puddle of tears. In all of this children's literature, dwarfs are as children themselves and must use their wits to survive numerous harrowing adventures. Midget figures also appear as fairies and elves in more adult literature of this period—in Johann L. Heiberg's 1827 drama *Elverhøj* and Henrik Ibsen's monumental play *Peer Gynt* (1867).

Toward the close of the century, the more realistic dwarfs in literature came to symbolize degeneration. Gustave Flaubert's *La tentation de Saint Antoine* (*The Temptation of Saint Anthony*, 1874) is a fantastic prose poem that surveys all the conflicting philosophies of the romantic age through visions of violent metamorphoses. Among the strange shapes and horrible monsters of the work, many of them images of death and decay, there is a large-headed dwarf, a grey-haired child, which is itself a representation of deformed nature. In Knut Hamsun's *Mysterier* (*Mysteries*, novel, 1892) the hero regards the unsightly, spineless midget as an object of pity; later, however, this midget double reveals a greater capacity for life than the hero and assumes frightening, demonic dimensions in the hero's mind. H. G. Wells' visionary novel *The Time Machine* (1895) shows a future world in which capitalists and workers have degenerated into complementary midget creatures. The former, called Eloi, are characterized by childlike naïveté and ineffectualness, while the latter, the subterranean Murdocks, are brutal creatures of the night, who live from the meat of their former masters. These midget races set a common standard for twentieth-century science fiction, so that it is now common for creatures from other worlds to be portrayed as humanoid dwarfs.

In his early story "Der kleine Herr Friedemann" ("Little Mr. Friedemann," 1898), Thomas Mann's title hero has become a deformed dwarf through a fall suffered as an infant. The last of a once healthy line, Friedemann is characterized by extreme sensitivity and by refined epicurean tastes. He is destroyed by the cruel attentions of an attractive, married woman.

The Twentieth Century

The split between fantastical dwarfs and realistic dwarfs continued in twentieth century fiction. The fantastical side includes the Leprechauns of James Stephens' *The Crock of Gold* (novel, 1912), the munchkins in L. Frank Baum's *Wonderful Wizard of Oz* (1900), the hobbits, dwarfs, and elves of J.R.R. Tolkien's *Lord of the Rings* trilogy (1954–1956), and, more recently yet, Pierre Culliford's *Smurfs* (books and cartoons, since 1958) and Wil Huygen's *Leven en Werken van de Kabouter* (*Gnomes*, 1976). Sir James M. Barrie's drama *Peter Pan* (1904) introduces a child who refuses to grow up, an idea adopted by Günter Grass in his own later dwarf novel *Die Blechtrommel* (*The Tin Drum*, 1959).

Walter de la Mare's novel *Memoirs of a Midget* (1921) presents a sensitive portrayal of a female midget's perspectives on the normal-sized world and on her relationship with a deformed dwarf. The midget's life is a tiny mirror of the conceits and vanities of human life around her; just as her larger human friend turns vain and cynical and capriciously leads her lover to his death, so, too, does the delicate midget alienate her closest friends and bring despair, disgrace, and death to her devoted dwarf. Pär Lagerkvist's novel *Dvärgen* (*The Dwarf*, 1944) is also a first-person narrative by the title figure. Here the dwarf mirrors only the malicious evil of the court around him; he is unable to comprehend love, peace, and beauty. In several scenes the dwarf assumes the role of anti-Christ as he abuses the court, degrades the princess, and poisons the prince's guests at what he describes as "my somber communion feast where they have drunk my poisoned blood." Of the dual nature of man he notes, "they are deformed though it does not show on the outside. I live only my dwarf life. . . . I have no other being inside me." Just as Lagerkvist's dwarf embodies in his deformity the evils of the Italian Renaissance courts, so Oskar Matzerath, the dwarf narrator of Günter Grass' novel *Die Blechtrommel*, embodies the amoral, destructive nature of wartime Germany. Throughout the World War II years, he remains a well-proportioned three-year-old child, who maintains an innocent demeanor while acting with deliberate, adult malice. After the war he "grows" into a slightly larger, hunchbacked dwarf, whose deformity reflects the postwar capitalist society of West Germany.

In twentieth-century fiction it is often the human qualities of the dwarfs that make them such grotesque and frightening characters. In Katherine Anne Porter's short story "The Circus" (1934) a small girl is terrified when a dwarf, dressed like a fairy-tale elf, reacts to her temper tantrum with "a haughty, remote displeasure" reminiscent of her father, and she realizes with shock that the golden-eyed creature before her is human. This split between appearance and reality assumes ironic dimensions in Frank Wedekind's 1903 drama *Hidalla, oder Karl Hetmann der Zwergriese (Hidalla, or Karl Hetmann the Dwarf-Giant)*. Here the crippled hero preaches a new order of perfect beauty and free love. His Nietzschean doctrine of perfection would make of him a giant, but his crippled body and the actions of a few influential people around him make of him a dwarf. Temporarily confined to an insane asylum, the "prophet" is finally offered a job as circus clown, a gesture that drives him to suicide.

In *La tía Julia y el escribidor (Aunt Julia and the Scriptwriter,* novel, 1977) Mario Vargas Llosa's writer of radio soap operas, Pedro Camacho, is a dwarf whose physical appearance reflects his disproportioned radio scripts. As a parody of an artist Camacho's demonic features are part of a Pinocchio-like body: "His posture, his gestures, his expression seemed the very contradiction of spontaneity and naturalness and reminded one of a marionette, of puppet strings." In John Irving's novel *The Hotel New Hampshire* (1981) the midget Lilly Berry is also a writer, but her writings are better proportioned, like her own midget figure. Irving describes her first, successful novel as "only a euphemism for trying to grow." She is not up to a sustained career as a novelist, however, and commits suicide, leaving behind the cryptic message "Just not big enough."

Katherine Anne Porter's 1962 novel *Ship of Fools* portrays human cruelty to dwarfs. Here the dwarf is so deformed that he appears "to have legs attached to his shoulder blades, the steep chest cradled on the rocking pelvis, the head with its long dry patient suffering face lying back against the hump." The dwarf's name (Glocken), his extreme hunched back, his gargoyle grin recall Victor Hugo's hunchback of Notre Dame (*Notre Dame de Paris,* novel, 1831); like Quasimodo he is taunted and chased by women and children who know they "need never hate or fear him, his disease was not contagious, his bad luck was strictly his own." The Tod Browning film *Freaks* (1932, based on the Tod Robbins' tale *Spurs* [1926]) carries this abuse even further. Here a moneyed dwarf is wooed, then murdered, by a beautiful but greedy woman. And in Fernando Arrabal's film script *Guernica* (1975) dwarfs are victims of Spanish Nationalist persecution. In one bizarre scene the dwarfs become the objects of a brutal "bullfight," and their deaths are applauded by members of the clergy, the army, and the upper classes.

In recent years dwarfs have become part of the stock cast of science fiction novels (as in Steven Spielberg's *Close Encounters of the Third Kind,* 1977), tales of horror (as in the Daphne Du Maurier short story "Don't Look Now" [1966]), and adventure thrillers (Trevanian's 1979 spy novel *Shibumi*). It appears that dwarfs have never been so popular in literature, and we may expect to see many more in the future, sometimes as symbols of perversity, sometimes as images of innocence, sometimes as figures from an estranged world.

See also: Crippling, Fool, Masque or Mask.

Selected Bibliography

Harward, Vernon Judson, Jr. *The Dwarfs of Arthurian Romance and Celtic Tradition.* Leiden, Netherlands: EJ Brill, 1958.

Keightley, Thomas. *The World Guide to Gnomes, Fairies, Elves and Other Little People.* New York: Avenel Books, 1978. [Originally published in 1878 as *The Fairy Mythology*.]

Scobie, Alex. "The Battle of the Pygmies and the Cranes in Chinese, Arab, and North American Indian Sources." *Folklore:* 86 (1975):122–132.

Wood, Edward J. *Giants and Dwarfs.* London: R. Bentley, 1868.

BEVERLEY D. EDDY

DYSTOPIAS

From Plato's *Politeia* (*The Republic,* dialogue, c. 380 B.C.) to Sir Thomas More's *Utopia* (political romance, 1516) and B. F. Skinner's *Walden Two* (novel, 1948), utopian fiction spans almost the entire literary history of Western Man. It remained for the twentieth century to conceive its dark opposite: the dystopian (Greek., *dys-,* bad + *topos,* place) world of the future. So rapid has been its growth, so disquietingly exciting its effect, that writer Karl Meyer declared, "Utopia is no more," replaced by "a new kind of imaginative society which, instead of evolving the possibilities of earthly bliss, serves only as a lens through which every barbarity of our age is magnified" (1954). Meyer calls the new society "Futopia" (future and futile); Lewis Mumford calls it "Cacotopia"; Erich Fromm, "negative utopia"; many simply, "anti-utopia." V. L. Parrington's "Dystopia" has come to be the most generally accepted term. But call it what one may, the nightmare world of the future is one of the facts of modern fiction and, in a span of some sixty years, has established itself as a literary genre.

That such a genre should emerge so soon after Edward Bellamy's *Looking Backward* (novel, 1888) and the dozens of utopian stories it inspired, so soon after H. G. Wells's novels *A Modern Utopia* (1905) and *Men Like Gods* (1923), is solidly grounded in the events of history. The Second World War (1939–1945), which so soon followed the First World War (1914–1918)—"the war to end wars" (Wells's phrase); the threat of nuclear extinction; the rise of the modern totalitarian state; the ecological crisis; the often questionable benefits of technological and social innovations; these, among other calamities and dangers, have persuaded many to envision a darker future. Once this century's most ardent champion of the scientific utopia, H. G. Wells recognized that "these new powers, inventions, contrivances and methods are not the unqualified enrichment of normal life that we had expected. They are hurting, injuring, and frustrating us increasingly. . . . We are only beginning to realize that the cornucopia of innovation may perhaps prove far more dangerous than benevolent." Later, in *Mind at the End of Its Tether* (novel, 1945), he bitterly complained, "The end of everything we call life is close at hand and cannot be evaded." The despair of those words moves one deeply with their personal melancholy and despair for humankind, for they issue from a man who earlier had written, "I saw a limitless universe throughout which the stars and nebulae were scattering like dust, and I saw life ascending, as it seemed, from nothingness toward the stars."

Many of the dark visions reflecting the Wellsian pessimism are contained in modern science fiction (here more appropriately called "speculative fiction"), although general fiction too addresses them. They spring largely from man's disappointment in the promise of a scientific utopia and his fear that "progress" will debase his values and reduce him to some absurd or hellish condition. The dystopias depicted in such fiction often reflect both man's subconscious and conscious apprehensions regarding threats to his integrity and well-being, threats made all the more possible by the awesome physical and social instruments increasingly dominating his life.

While "dystopian" and "anti-utopian" may be used synonymously, many dystopias have a character best captured by the fuller meaning of "anti-utopian." What is abhorrent in such societies is a product of their utopian programs. Such societies usually achieve their specific utopian goals but at the cost of a dehumanized citizenry or a perverted natural order, or both. The word "anti-utopian" applied to such societies describes both the society and the conviction of the writer. He *is* an anti-utopian—that is, against utopia. He believes that utopian success in one area opens a Pandora's box of anti-utopian reactions. He believes that even if a perfect world could be realized, such perfection would erode the moral qualities that make man man: creativity, courage, humility, righteous anger, charity, perseverance . . . for these root only in the imperfect man in the imperfect world. A perfect world of "unman" is not utopia. To the anti-utopian writer the more utopia becomes itself, the more it becomes its opposite.

The corruption or annihilation of man by the sophisticated inventions of modern science or a power elite armed with them constitutes one of the dominant themes of dystopian fiction. The sobering realization that in conquering nature science is also conquering man evokes longings for an Edenic past when nature and science tendered gifts outright. When an inventor in William Golding's humorous *Envoy Extraordinary* (long tale, 1957) offers the emperor of ancient Rome his newly discovered marvels—the steam-powered ship, gunpowder, and the printing press—the monarch wisely refuses them. The galley slave protests his loss of function in the world; the captain of infantry fears that gunpowder will doom glorious close combat; and the emperor, knowing how rare is a

Sophocles or a Horace, foresees the world drowning in the biblio-babble of mere
scribblers, the main beneficiaries of the printing press. An anti-utopian before
the existence of the word, the emperor sighs: "Oh, you natural philosophers.
Are there many of you, I wonder? Your single-minded and devoted selfishness,
your royal preoccupation with the only thing that can interest you, could go near
to wiping life off the earth as I wipe the bloom from this grape."

The anti-utopian hostility to science follows from the belief that a critical
point exists in the interplay of man and science beyond which man loses the
savor of life and control of the course of events. Yet neither scientists nor their
inventions are the essential target of this antiscientism. Rather than presenting
either as incarnately evil, writers stress the incompatibility of scientific or technological ultimates with the ideals of humanness. Aldous Huxley's *Ape and
Essence* (novel, 1948) symbolically depicts scientists as the leashed pets of
baboons, whose nuclear war has ravaged the earth. The captive "Einsteins,"
unaware that in their amoral pursuit of Truth they had prostituted themselves to
the "organizers of the world's collective schizophrenia," government, complain,
"It's unjust. . . . We, who lived only for Truth." But Huxley reminds them of
Pascal's maxim: " 'Truth without charity is not God, but his image and idol,
which we must neither love nor worship.' You lived for the worship of an idol.
But, in the last analysis, the name of every idol is Moloch."

In work after work, the dream of a scientific utopia, whether based on physical
or social innovations, fails because it makes mechanism the shaper of man. But
the flaw in the utopian scheme is usually not in its mechanism but in its failure
to understand and respect the essential qualities of human nature. Though anti-
utopians are far from satisfied with man as he is, they strongly protest his
unmaking or remaking to fit a utopian design. In such a protest in the trilogy of
novels *Out of the Silent Planet* (1938), *Perelandra* (1943), and *That Hideous
Strength* (1945), C. S. Lewis combines antiscientism with religious moralism
to argue that the satanic powers of the universe are attempting to establish a
reign of evil incarnate on earth and are using the scientific community as the
instrument of their grand design. Motivated by a hostility toward traditional
moral values, a worship of soulless, efficient mechanism, and the ambition to
regiment the human race by now-applicable or potentially feasible methods, such
as biochemical conditioning, a scientific group attempts and fails to produce an
unfeeling, programmed, objective, technocratic, and robotic new man to su-
percede the old.

The devaluation of man by science and its methods and machines has thoroughly rebutted the postulate of H. G. Wells's *A Modern Utopia* and *Men Like
Gods* that a qualitative utopia can be automatically realized once machinery has
solved the quantitative problems and scientific clear-sightedness has solved the
social ones. Kurt Vonnegut's *Player Piano* (novel, 1952) depicts an automated
twenty-first-century America controlled by a hierarchy of technical and mana-
gerial Babbitts, who lead affluent but stale lives. In solving quantitative problems,
machinery has brought not freedom but an industrial police state, not equality

but a rigid two-class society, not culture but mechanical toys, not creativity but sapping idleness or dulling labor for the masses and the status struggle for the masters. Frederik Pohl's satire on the technological society, "The Midas Plague" (story, 1954), follows one of the major paradigms of dystopian fiction. A condition, which in the ideal situations of utopian fantasy brings happiness, brings misery instead. So productive is Pohl's goods-glutted technocracy that, while the few "rich" relax in preindustrial simplicity, the "poor" are sentenced to lives of hectic mandatory consumption.

Technology as a source of anxiety and discord, as revealed by Vonnegut and Pohl, represents only one type of threat. Another view has technology sapping human vitality to such a degree that man becomes dependent or degenerate. That, after conquering nature, unchallenged man might evolve into a species like the frail, docile, childlike Eloi in H. G. Wells' *The Time Machine* (novel, 1895) has become an increasingly popular theme in speculative literature. After humanity's technological achievements have brought social stability, degenerate and trivialized societies have evolved from the earlier pioneer strain in Frederik Pohl and C. M. Kornbluth's *Search the Sky* (novel, 1954) and Robert Sheckley's *The Status Civilization* (novel, 1960). In E. M. Forster's "The Machine Stops" (story, 1909) mankind has become a wasted inmate living in the bowels of a world machine, each person remaining almost permanently isolated in a sustaining cell equipped with communication devices and servomechanisms. Land, air, sun; movement, touch, laughter; adventure, passion, creativity—these are outside the bounds of possibility and propriety. Forster's influence is especially noticeable in the "cocoon" dystopias of the midcentury. Isaac Asimov's *The Caves of Steel* (novel, 1954) renders a comparable portrait of stifled humanity, as earth's billions live in vast subterranean hives, a turbulent, tenuously self-sustaining underworld machine of housing cells, factories, tunnels, and life-support systems. In Paul W. Fairman's *I, The Machine* (novel, 1968) a rigid, softened, contemptible society, valuing pleasure, ease, and security above all else, vegetates under the care of servo- and psychomechanisms. In Antony Alban's *Catharsis Central* (novel, 1968) the world stagnates in a peace produced by a nightly worn "catharsis cap," a device that neutralizes human aggressiveness and anxiety. People in Edmund Cooper's *Deadly Image* (novel, 1958) play out their lives in a succession of pointless social amusements and romantic liaisons, having been relieved of worthier pursuits by intelligent robots. Jack Williamson's "With Folded Hands" (story, 1947) raises the spectre of man's virtual imprisonment by "humanoids"—benevolent robots who take him against his will into protective custody to better serve him, but deprive him of even the most ordinary enjoyments and freedom. These dystopias rebut the utopian dream of a golden age in which technology elevates the quality of life and the race, presenting instead the sterile decadence of its opposite.

Important midcentury advances in psychopharmacology and electronics have furnished the seminal ideas for dystopias of synthetic experience. Their principal characteristic is the synthesization of experience so extravagant that people evacuate their own lives, their self-awareness obliterated or diminished by chemical and electrical manipulation. Aldous Huxley established the model of the dystopia of synthetic experience in *Brave New World* (1932), the half-human carnival world of electro-chemical satisfactions. In Frederik Pohl's "What to Do Till the Analyst Comes" (story, 1956) a nonaddictive, harmless euphoric turns the populace into a carefree and careless riot of incompetents; the story broaches the disturbing idea that if man could escape into a euphoric state of mind he might willingly let civilization crumble. Characters in Philip K. Dick's *The Three Stigmata of Palmer Eldritch* (novel, 1964) find relief from their painfully boring lives by hallucinating themselves into a playworld of children's dolls. Beyond relief from self lies another alternative—relief in or through the self of another. The experience recording and projecting machine is the centerpiece of D. G. Compton's *Synthajoy* (novel, 1968), a device that makes the sensations and emotions of a recording "artist," be they aesthetic, sexual, or spiritual, available to those who would share it. In Dean R. Koontz's *The Fall of the Dream Machine* (novel, 1969) the controllers of the experience machine assume political control of the world through a television program capable of transmitting not only sight and sound but, again, the emotions and sensations of any performer with whom the viewer empathizes. Other variations of the synthetic experience are treated in Shepherd Mead's *The Big Ball of Wax* (novel, 1954) and Philip Wylie's *The End of the Dream* (novel, 1972).

While exotic physical innovations are often instrumental to the dystopias of speculative fiction, they are seldom the thematic focus. The issue of man and society dominates these books. Many involve the failure of the utopian planners to anticipate the flawed results of their programs to restructure their human material. Bernard Wolfe's *Limbo* (novel, 1952), Anthony Burgess' *A Clockwork Orange* (novel, 1962), and Leonard C. Lewin's *Triage* (novel, 1972) all detail programs that would eliminate certain human faults or faulty humans. The crack-brained scheme in Wolfe amputates arms and legs, the presumed seats of aggression and war, and replaces them with ingenious prosthetics; in Burgess the criminal mind is reconditioned by Pavlovian techniques into a timid one; in Lewin social "deadwood," drug addicts, the infirm, the chronically poor, are exterminated by private killing groups seeking to purify society. But all goes awry. Amputation makes a truncated spirit but does not stop violence; the reconditioned criminal is pitiable in his impotence; and purification by private murder, besides leaving nobody safe, virtually redefines man by making productivity and social acceptability the price for the right to live.

Not satisfied with the elimination of a vice or frailty, fiction's more ambitious utopian planners envision a more positive and comprehensive renewal. B. F. Skinner's *Walden Two* describes what the author, himself a utopist and psychologist, believes is an achievable utopia. The key to the success of his happy community is its employment of the science of "behavioral engineering," which protects one from the shocks of life while at the same time promoting psychological strength, personal satisfaction, and communal security and efficiency.

Yet Skinner's critics have denounced his community as a dystopia, charging that behavioral engineering, in relegating man's autonomy and freedom to a mere delusion, sees him only as material to be shaped by the masters of his conditioning; furthermore, behaviorism holds this human material incapable of having original preferences and values, for these come only from external stimuli. A society in which man has the soul of a laboratory rat, say Skinner's critics, is a dystopia.

Such an unintended dystopia as Skinner's, however, is not common in modern speculative fiction. Most dystopias are so by the author's design. Rex Gordon's *Utopia Minus X* (novel, 1966), R. A. Lafferty's *Past Master* (novel, 1968), and Colin Anderson's *Magellan* (novel, 1970) present failed utopias—societies whose utopian success is synonymous with their failure. Gordon's utopian planners have succeeded so well in assuring problem-free, civilized, gently hedonistic lives for all that they decree that the search for knowledge must end, for to go beyond utopia is to leave it; but because the abolition of striving man is not utopian but dystopian, the more vital members of the stagnant utopia choose harsh exile. Similarly Lafferty and Anderson portray dystopias that have met their physical challenges and stand on the brink of reaching their ultimate goal: finalized humanity—the merging of all mankind into a single organism; but here too multitudes are fleeing such a consummation, choosing instead to live and suffer as man.

The major argument of utopia's critics is that utopian successes are attained at the cost of diminishing man and producing a dystopia; the attempt to achieve perfection sets in motion unconsidered counterforces, which spoil the perfectionist scheme. Michael Young's *The Rise of the Meritocracy: 1870–2033* (novel, 1958) well illustrates this principle and without the science fiction exotica that so many fictional dystopias employ. Young's twenty-first century England has regained her pre-eminence among nations by supplanting her democracy with a meritocracy. Her program demanded a single-minded effort to separate the intellectually gifted from the ungifted and install her new elite in all the seats of national power. But in her worship of intellect she has disregarded the unmeasurable qualities of humanness—courage, sensitivity, kindliness, imagination—and faces a revolt of the underclass. Demonstrated once again is the folly of victimizing one part of our selves to another, the folly of not living with the whole being.

George Orwell's *1984* (novel, 1949) is the composite political dystopia. So definitive a hell it is that previous fictional totalitarian societies seem but anticipations and later ones variations of Orwell's. Its prominent dystopian features are: (1) the dictatorship of "the Party," whose object is power; (2) the denial of the self—self-awareness, self-esteem, self-assertion, self-fulfillment—and servility to the group; (3) the execution or brainwashing of dissidents; (4) the destruction of the capacity to think, through the perversion of language and the rejection of empirical evidence; (5) the divorce from the values and memory of the past; (6) the installation of the Party as the sole judge of truth; and (7) the maintenance of cultural stasis.

The opposition to freedom and individuality, which most characterizes the political dystopias of speculative fiction, is not directed toward the issue of how man, being what he is, shall be governed; rather, it is directed toward making him other than what he is. The state hatchery's spawn of customized classes in Aldous Huxley's *Brave New World,* their preconditioned biology suited nicely to their controlled environment, inhabit a political dystopia despite their adjustment to it. The inmates of Evgenii Zamiatin's nightmare land in *My* (*We,* novel, 1924), whose national goal is to become as unfree as a machine, reach their robotic ideal by a brain operation that destroys the center for fancy. The hero of Ayn Rand's *Anthem* (novel, 1946) liberates himself from a dystopia whose single purpose is the psychological extinction of the self, when he discovers the great secret: that "I am. I think. I will"; that god's name is "I" and the sacred word is "ego." The full police power of the state converges on one heretic in David Karp's *One* (novel, 1953). The heresy: that he possesses a private and indefinable identity whose welfare is separate from that of the state. One assault on identity in L. P. Hartley's *Facial Justice* (novel, 1960) is a mandatory operation that leaves all women with the same face. Consistently the making of a political dystopia demands the unmaking of man.

The economic boom of the 1950s and 1960s in the United States and the phenomena that attended it—corporate expansion, sophisticated advertising and merchandising techniques, television, increased consumer buying power—suggested the eventual mercantile dystopia to speculative writers. So despoiled is the world run by advertising moguls in Frederik Pohl and C. M. Kornbluth's *The Space Merchants* (novel, 1953) that nonsynthetic food, clean air and water, wood, and living room have become luxuries even for the successful. In *Gladiator-at-Law* (novel, 1955) Pohl and Kornbluth depict an America that is little more than a playing field for corporate giants, a society in which the masses subsist in crumbling core cities while the commercial managers luxuriate in affluent suburbs. Corporate conglomerates dissolve the nation, partition it among themselves, and tyrannize the populace to promote sales in Damon Knight's *Hell's Pavement* (novel, 1955). Kurt Vonnegut's *Player Piano* exposes the major features of the mercantile dystopia: the assault on creativity, dignity, and freedom by a business-dominated police state and the stratification of society into a commercial-technical privileged class and the manipulated masses.

The possibility of nuclear war has infused the eschatological vision of speculative fiction with a measure of grim reality. The postnuclear war story, such as Aldous Huxley's *Ape and Essence* and John Wyndham's *Re-Birth* (novel 1955), commonly shows societies that have descended into savagery, superstition, and repression. Furthermore, Huxley's dystopia, Walter M. Miller, Jr.'s *A Canticle for Leibowitz* (novel, 1959), and Mordecai Roshwald's *Level 7* (novel, 1959) rekindle, in a nuclear context, the argument that a scientific utopia is a contradiction in terms. They assume that the gulf between politics, armed by a prostitute science, and conscience is unbridgeable and nuclear war unavoidable. Miller's once-ravaged world, rebuilt and reindustrialized, is inevitably rearmed and powerless to avoid its second nuclear holocaust. Roshwald reveals earth's last men, facing extinction in their missile-control catacombs after having extinguished all life above, as mere push-button gods, emotionally sluggish and socially indifferent—the apotheosis of technocratic man. Implicit in much nuclear catastrophe fiction is the belief that, in view of man's incorrigibility with dangerous toys, the weakening of moral values and the uncritical urging of materialistic ones is a dystopian threat to a healthy society and life itself.

The spate of prenuclear and postnuclear dystopias beginning at midcentury has been matched by those caused by an ecological crisis—especially the population explosion. The authors of population dystopias submit that much of mankind will suffer anything rather than bridle its procreative power by known, simple, and accessible methods. The world of James Blish and Norman L. Knight's *A Torrent of Faces* (novel, 1967) groans under a cubicle-housed population of one trillion, with Chicago burrowing toward Canada and the Ohio, and London, supported by pillars, spilling into the sea. To contend with the unmanageable glut of bodies, scientists have produced a rocket to transport some to distant planets and a gilled human to occupy the oceans. In short, the story presents one of the classic conditions of dystopian fiction: the triumph of ingenuity over common sense. Another example of fatuous ingenuity is seen in Robert Bloch's *This Crowded Earth* (novel, 1968), in which, to relieve the forced touch, throb, heat, and trample of people, everywhere, scientists create a mutant three-foot human. The New York City of Harry Harrison's *Make Room! Make Room!* (novel, 1966) is a thirty-five million miserable people fleshball plagued by cubicle housing, barely palatable food, rationed drinking water, and social breakdown. Here again, as in the sardine-can dystopias mentioned here, the causes of the calamity remain unaddressed: the unwillingness of the overbreeders to practice reproductive discipline; the timidity and ineffectiveness of leaders in addressing the problem with practical solutions; and the false notion that room can be made on a finite planet for our redoubling breed. However, while most overpopulated dystopias present the spectacle of lunatics bailing into the lifeboat, that of Anthony Burgess' *The Wanting Seed* (novel, 1962) addresses its problem, though cruelly and perversely, with population police, the encouragement of homosexuality, cannibalism, and "extermination sessions" whereby conscripted men and women butcher each other in a bogus war. In all, these dystopias describe man's inevitable strangulation by overbreeding or a substitute disaster by some frightful circumvention.

A sizable body of dystopian speculation deals with an obsessional catastrophe. Some compelling motive—obeisance to the gods, the search for certainty, the relief from strain, the fear of death, the drive for knowledge, the will to dominate—may urge a society to abandon prudence and contort itself to pursue its obsession. In Clifford D. Simak's *Why Call Them Back from Heaven?* (novel,

1967) the quest for physical immortality, through cryogenic arrest and eventual revival, poisons the living present and condemns earth's billions to both economic and emotional impoverishment. The world of Robert Silverberg's *The World Inside* (novel, 1971) has abandoned horizontal space for thousand-floor, million-person, vertical "urbmons," great hives of mindless hedonism and conformity. The oblivion of death through the sacrament of suicide becomes the passion and religion of the Western world in Gore Vidal's dusty dystopia, *Messiah* (novel, 1954). The obsession with progress, that baneful idea that Aldous Huxley claims, in *Ape and Essence*, is "the theory that you can get something for nothing, the theory that you can gain in one field without paying for your gain in another," has brought nuclear devastation. Progress again, in John Wyndham's *Consider Her Ways* (novel, 1957), here a laboratory virus to exterminate the troublesome brown rat, promises the extermination of earth's males, despite warnings of such a catastrophe. Generally speaking, man's reckless, hubristic, and ignorant pursuit of progress is the founder of most dystopias. Writers of dystopian fiction seem to be saying that if man can do something preposterous and hurtful to himself he will likely do it; they warn us to pause before the treacherous terrain of innovation and resolve which paths must not be taken, what deeds must not be done.

See also: Science, Utopia.

Selected Bibliography

Amis, Kingsley. *New Maps of Hell*. New York: Ballantine Books, 1960.

Berger, Harold L. *Science Fiction and the New Dark Age*. Bowling Green, Ohio: Bowling Green University Popular Press, 1976.

Hillegas, Mark R. *The Future as a Nightmare: H. G. Wells and the Anti-Utopians*. New York: Oxford University Press, 1967.

Walsh, Chad. *From Utopia to Nightmare*. New York: Harper and Row, 1962.

HAROLD L. BERGER

E
———— // ————

EATING

Eating is one of the activities that man shares with the animals. Perhaps for that very reason, religions have from early on attached special importance to it, as though to say that the similarity is superficial and that something spiritual is involved. Some primitive peoples ate the corpses of their parents; others ate their gods; most attach benedictions to eating and limit the permissible table of fare. Literature has found that, far from being merely a biological action, eating may offer insights into moral, psychological, sociological, and metaphysical truths— even in secular periods, when eating no longer is sacrament or deadly sin.

Antiquity and the Middle Ages

The Old Testament, while reminding us that man does not live by bread alone, is fully cognizant of the socializing role of breaking bread in human affairs. Men signal their belonging to a community of some sort, their respecting each other's humanity, their own generosity and the guest's dignity, by putting food on the table. Thus it is that when angels visit Abraham, he first of all offers them a meal. Eating also has an important social-political role. Esau sells his birthright for a lentil soup. Pharaoh's dream of the fat and lean kine is interpreted by Joseph as auguring years of affluence to be followed by years of famine, and that dream interpretation begins Joseph on the road to fame and power and concurrently establishes his domestic political policy of saving food during the good years for the bad years. The years of famine bring his father and brothers to Egypt, causes the family reunion, and begins the long, fateful adventure of Israel in Egypt. If man did not need food, none of this sacred history would have taken place.

When God liberated the Israelites and made a new convenant with them, he set down a most detailed list of dietary laws. The understanding is that God will look after His people if they, in turn, are careful about, among other things, what they ingest. For the human body is a temple to be kept purified for the Lord and (as the recent cliché had it) "You are what you eat." Though the modern rationalist explains these laws as a primitive form of hygiene, the Orthodox interpretation is that the dietary laws have no rational basis other than the setting of necessary limits and the testing of man's willingness to obey God even at the cost of indulging in behavior considered "irrational." The earliest reference to eating, after all, and a most consequential one, is to the forbidden fruit (that it is an apple is a later tradition and in dispute). Eating turned out then to be the only test of man's obedience, as God gave Adam and Eve everything except that one item. One consequence of the transgression is that a host of foods had to be forbidden. As the voice of piety says in Flaubert's *Bouvard et Pécuchet* (*Bouvard and Pécuchet,* novel, 1881), "We must groan as we eat, for this is the way man lost his innocence." Man is a spirit that became an animal; so important and tragic was, and is, eating.

The Bible also narrates the departure from Egypt, the years of travail in the wilderness, and the institution of holy days to commemorate these events. Hence the customs of the special Passover meal and of eating in homely sheds during the feast of Succoth. The former meal, called the "Seder" (meaning "order"), is a highly ritualized mixture of recitation and ingestion. And on some holy days, like the Day of Atonement, the Israelite abstains from eating entirely, his sinfulness requiring him to at least temporarily set his body and its needs aside.

The New Testament naturally modifies these traditions. Jesus signals his special role at some junctures by providing the food or drink so necessary at gatherings, especially of the poor. When the Israelites in the desert had complained of hunger to Moses and looked nostalgically back to the fleshpots of Egypt, God had provided manna, a food that fell from heaven and tasted like whatever food the individual wanted; so in turn, when the disciples complained of the many people and the paucity of food, Jesus made a few loaves and fishes feed thousands (or turned wine into water). In the Old Testament, moreover, the eating of the forbidden fruit is merely a tale among many and not referred to again later on. In the New Testament it takes on importance and is periodically referred to. By the time of St. Augustine it becomes The Fall, the Original Sin, and is an obsession.

A similar transformation involves the Seder. As a Jew, Jesus, while remarking that ritual purity of food and washing of hands before eating is futile if accompanied by defiled mouth and heart (speech and thoughts), participated in the Passover ritual. This one meal, the single most famous one in history, is filled with irony. It commemorated a liberation, but for Jesus it was the setting for the revelation of human treachery and consequently of his own imminent death. The meal of freedom and life had turned into one of sorrow. At the same time, however, insofar as the same death of Christ made possible the salvation of mankind and the undoing of Adam and Eve's forbidden repast, it paradoxically reverted to what it had been, a meal of liberation (from damnation) and of life (salvation).

The Last Supper also marks another important confluence of ideas. When he declared the bread to be his body and the wine his blood, Jesus was (consciously or not) converting the unleavened bread and sacramental wine of Jewish ritual into the Sacrament of the Eucharist, one of the two central Christian rituals. Christianity here goes behind Judaism to incorporate even more primitive rituals of the eating of one's god, as if by putting a part of the divine into one's body, one rises above one's sinful, beastly, material self, a self symbolized by normal ingestion. Having undergone a fall by inappropriate eating, man now could rise again by a ritual eating that compensates and redeems. No significance can be assigned to any act that would for importance match this one of eating the God of the universe and achieving thereby (perhaps) an eternity of bliss.

In Homer's epic poems (c. 8th century B.C.), *Ilias (Iliad)* and *Odysseia (Odyssey)*, as in the Bible, eating is a ritual and social matter. Thus Achilles, grieving over the death of his friend Patrocles and abusing his own body, refuses to partake of food. For a while, the Greeks tolerate it, but when the commonsensical Odysseus urges the hero to let at least the Greek warriors eat, for a man cannot fight on an empty stomach, Achilles relents to that extent. The association of eating with human intercourse is never so poignantly portrayed as at the climax, when the humbled Priam suddenly appears in Achilles' tent and throws himself at the Greek's mercy in order to request the corpse of Hector. After his initial surprise, Achilles, moved by the old man's shrewd but poignant reasoning, yields, and the agreement is sealed by a meal served to them even though Achilles has just concluded his dinner. Under the shadow of common grief and mortality, Trojan and Greek break bread together by way of celebrating their temporary insight into their common humanity and doom.

In the *Odyssey* the hero could safeguard himself from Circe's ability with adulterated food to turn men into swine, by ingesting the magical plant moly. More modern and understandable is the capacity of food to alter consciousness, as intimated in the story of the Lotus eaters, those early drug addicts, who have not only changed their Weltanschauung as a result of their eating but have become addicted as well. Drug-taking, then as now, is common even at the highest social level: Helen mollifies the sufferings of the past by putting a potion into the drinks of Menelaus and his guests.

Received genially by the Phaeacians at the court of Alcinous, Odysseus asks, before telling the story of his adventures, to be allowed to eat and drink in the banqueting hall, for the shameless, dictatorial belly insists (as he had also told Achilles), even when one is exhausted, sorrowing, and suffering, on being filled. In the story he later tells, he comes to a climactic incident which, like the Bible, involves the eating of forbidden foods. He had been told under no circumstances to eat any of a flock of sacred cattle on one of the islands they stop at. But his men, running out of licit food and heeding the grumbling of a rebellious one— that hunger is the worst way of dying—turn during the hero's sleep to the prohibited cattle. For their act, all the participants are destroyed, and the opening lines of the poem blame them for their inability to return home.

When Odysseus alone returns to Ithaca, gathers his information and forces, and begins to take revenge, the action symbolically enough begins in the middle of a banquet, for the suitors are presented throughout the work as literally eating him out of house and home. Disguised as a beggar, he has had to eat the scraps of food the suitors contemptuously throw him, his own food in his own house. Odysseus first kills the leading suitor, Antinoos, in the very act of lifting a golden goblet of wine; the end of the exile of the hero and of the oppression by the unjust suitors is nicely symbolized by the dropping of the goblet, the scattering of "all the good food . . . bread and baked meats together." For the suitors, the party is over.

The correlation, in Seder or Eucharist, of eating with spirituality is also made in pagan society by the evolution of the symposium or banquet, from an occasion for breaking bread together, accompanied with entertainment and good conversation, to the occasion for the highest philosophical discourse, the supreme example of which is Plato's *Symposion (Symposium,* c. 384 B.C.). In some circles, no such evolution took place. In the "Trimalchio's Dinner" section of Petronius' *Satyricon* (novel, A.D. 60), eating becomes a form of conspicuous consumption. The dinner displays the vulgarity of the newly rich, the smugness of the self-made man, the grotesque forms that (thanks to human ingenuity in choice and presentation of foods) the humble procedure of filling one's stomach can take, along with the accompanying droll entertainment and conversation. This is Plato's *Symposium* rendered Latin, vulgar, nouveau riche, realistic.

In Apuleius' *Metamorphoses (The Golden Ass,* novel, c. 150), eating has another venerable effect: transformation of self and body. Mistakenly altered into a donkey, the hero, after undergoing many adventures and much suffering, returns to human form when he eats a rose, which is associated with holiness. Here one sees dramatized an idea found as early as in Pythagoras' urging men not to eat animal food and in the teachings of Socrates and other philosophers that the amount, kind, and circumstances of eating bespeaks the moral state of a man. (So too God has Gideon choose the few authentic warriors on the basis of whether they drank from a river with dignity or bestiality.) Folktale motifs about magic foods merge with philosophical prescriptions on spare dieting. Food can either dehumanize one or start one on the quasi-Platonic climb up a ladder of holiness and spirituality.

Or it can take one into deep experience that is neither bestial nor angelic: In Gottfried von Strassburg's *Tristan* (romance, c. 1210), the motif of food changing one's body and fortunes is given a special application under the auspices of the courtly love tradition. Tristan and Isolde are mere acquaintances, he taking her on a boat to be married to Tristan's uncle and chief, King Mark. Accidentally drinking the love potion intended for Isolde and her husband-to-be, they fall in love and undergo the full course of adultery, duplicity, and ultimate tragedy.

In Virgil's epic poem *Aeneis (Aeneid,* 19 B.C.), as in the *Odyssey,* eating is associated with one of the ordeals that the Trojans underwent in their attempt to reach the future Rome. They come to a place where, when they sit down to eat, harpies appear and befoul their food and where the prophecy is made that before they reach their goal they will out of hunger eat their very tables. The first ordeal is reminiscent of that of Tantalus, as described in the *Odyssey*, whose food becomes unavailable just as it reaches his mouth. The tortures are repeated in Dante's *Inferno* (*La divina commedia* [*The Divine Comedy*, epic poem, c. 1320]). Count Ugolino, executed by being made to starve in a cell along with his sons, now gnaws at the skull of his enemy Ruggieri.

In St. Augustine's *Confessiones* (*Confessions*, essay, c. 397–400), the personal forbidden fruit becomes a bunch of pears. What is normally the simplest of actions—the stealing of fruit for the pleasure of eating them—becomes in the hands of a febrile moralist, acute psychologist, and grand stylist, the occasion for pages of analysis in an attempt to separate the various strands that go to make up human evil. Eating or hunger turns out to be the least of the reasons. Still, in the Middle Ages, gluttony—excessive eating—became one of the Seven Deadly Sins, and in early medieval hagiography one of Satan's favorite devices is to tempt the Desert Fathers with sumptuous banquets or dreams of them. Chaucer's Monk (*Canterbury Tales*, c. 1380–1400), for one, seems guilty of gluttony. A more morally subtle rendering of the ambiguity of eating is the portrait of the Prioress, whose delicate mingling of worldliness and piety is nicely brought out by her fastidious, decorous manner of eating. Her moral limitations are hinted at by her giving the best sort of bread to dogs, not to beggars.

The Renaissance

The Renaissance's revival of interest in things of this world is expressed in Rabelais' novels *Gargantua et Pantagruel* (*Gargantua and Pantagruel*, 1532–1564) by, among other things, a riotous celebration of eating and drinking as joys in themselves. This is brought out not only by the heroes' huge diet but also by one of those Rabelaisian endless catalogues, this time of foods. The catalogue is an implicit blessing of both the plenitude of God's creation and of man's ingenuity in concocting so many varied dishes. Renaissance epicureanism is carried on, albeit in typically more muted, mellow form, by Montaigne (*Essais* [*Essays*, 1580–1588]), who, as part of his self-portraiture and as part of his later acceptance of the simple pleasures, lists his preferences in foods—a discussion of the putatively trivial that is probably unprecedented in literature.

The Rabelaisian influence is perhaps less crucial in Shakespeare's portrayal of Falstaff (*Henry IV*, play, 1597, 1600)—that Gargantuan mountain of a man who likes his food and his sack wine—than the old-fashioned Christian outlook, for Falstaff's gluttony is associated with his irresponsibility and selfishness. Elsewhere in Shakespeare, food symbolism is common. In the play *The Tempest* (1611), Prospero obtains his revenge by among other things reviving the harpy incident: His victimizers are served large banquets that are immediately withdrawn. In the play *Coriolanus* (1607–1608), which is rich in imagery of eating and devouring, the political troubles begin with the corn riots; that is, the people are hungry, and the republic, lacking the cunning of the emperors in a later age, has offered them neither bread nor circuses. Hunger therefore leads to structural political changes, like the establishment of the people's tribunate. In a famous metaphor stolen from Plutarch, an old patrician speaks a parable in which the state is analogized to the body; the belly represents the aristocracy, whose jcb it is to govern, that is to apportion the food.

In *Macbeth* (1605–1606), the disruption caused by Macbeth's murder of Duncan is symbolized by the banquet scene, which occurs in the very middle of the play, as though to suggest that the heart of society has been wrenched. Macbeth would feast with his people, has even invited the important Banquo. The image of a communal and festive partaking of food is reminiscent of the society in the mead hall in the epic poem *Beowulf* (c. 8th century). A banquet (like its religious counterpart, the Seder) is the occasion not for eating like an animal but for the celebration of community, the manifestation of hierarchy, order, stability. But a secret evil haunts this one; Macbeth agonizes over one murder even as he plots another. A ghostly visitation harrows him. The anarchy he has brought into the body politic is symbolized by the manner in which the banquet unexpectedly ends. "Stand not upon the order of your going,/But go at once," orders Lady Macbeth. They who had entered in ritualized procession and taken their seats according to a clear and respected hierarchy now are to betake themselves to the exits like people fleeing a fire in a theater.

The protagonist of Jonson's *Volpone* (play, 1606) evokes exotic dishes as part of his attempt to seduce the beautiful Celia; tactile pleasures may be induced or heightened by antecedent gustatory ones. Wanton sex follows exotic food also in Milton's *Paradise Lost* (1667), which recapitulates in great detail the biblical story. An entire ten-thousand-line epic in strict classical form revolves not about the anger of Achilles, the noisy fall of Troy, the difficult trip home of a warrior, the long voyage in quest of a divinely promised land, or the founding of Rome, but about the eating of a fruit! ("The basis of Christianity is an apple!" exclaimed Flaubert in *Bouvard*.) This making central something that had been regarded heretofore as relatively trivial manifests the impact of the monotheistic idea that an all-powerful, all-knowing God worries as much about the eating of a fruit as whether His chosen people should be ruled by judges or kings. Also harking back to biblical and epical material is the generous manner in which Adam invites the angel Raphael to a meal, as Abraham did his angelic visitors and Achilles did the emissaries in book 9 of the *Iliad*. Milton seizes the occasion to divagate on how even angels eat (albeit spiritual food) and how in fact everything in the universe in a sense eats or ingests; "of Elements/The grosser feeds the purer." Eating has become cosmic and metaphysical, a central trait of existence itself.

Eighteenth Century to Modern Period

The hero of Swift's satire *Gulliver's Travels* (1726) discovers on his fourth adventure that Nature can be "easily satisfied" with a diet of mainly ground oats, some honey, and no salt and that much which he had thought necessary was but a matter of conditioning. That point is explicitly explored by Thoreau (*Walden,* essays, 1854), who finds that "man may use as simple a diet as the animals" and dine satisfactorily on purslane and ears of green sweet corn.

Certainly food is a correlative of wealth and power. According to Swift (*A Modest Proposal,* essay, 1729), the ruling Protestant Anglo-Irish class, having, by its indifference, figuratively devoured the Irish peasantry, is morally free to literally devour as well the Irish babies. Pope notes (*The Rape of the Lock,* poem, 1712) how justice is aborted because of the corporal needs of those administering it: "The hungry judges soon the sentence sign,/And wretches hang that jury-men may dine." Similarly, Voltaire (*Candide,* novel, 1759) has an escaped black slave describe his awful life at the sugar mill: "This is the price of the sugar you eat in Europe." The affluent are, of course, oblivious of any such price because they do not pay it and because of the psychological principle illustrated elsewhere in the story—that Candide, after a good dinner and in spite of his many adverse experiences, inclines to the optimistic philosophy of life espoused by Pangloss. A full stomach is a great moral anaesthetic.

The Rabelaisian celebration of the banquet of life, literal and metaphoric, recurs in Fielding's novel *Tom Jones* (1749); eating, dismissed by some sages as "extremely mean and derogatory from the philosophic dignity," is, according to the narrator, something that even heroes do, and with gusto; Ulysses was in fact the best eater in "that eating poem of the *Odyssey.*" In a comic scene written as a mock heroic combat, Tom is so preoccupied with eating and drinking as not to notice Mrs. Waters' intense attraction to his physical charms. Here the gustatory effaces the tactile-erotic. The joy of eating, especially the Christmas dinner, recurs in Dickens' novels, and, in a definitive version that, together with conversation and partying, symbolizes the feast of life framed by anxieties over alienation and mortality, in Joyce's "The Dead" (story, 1914). At the other extreme, Knut Hamsun's novel *Sult (Hunger,* 1890), dramatizing the experiences of a down-and-out writer, gives a graphic and surprisingly rare account of the biological and psychological dimensions of not having anything to eat most of the time.

One of primitive man's great breakthroughs is the discovery of cooked food. The hypothetical event is sketched whimsically by Lamb ("A Dissertation upon Roast Pig," essay, 1823). One day a house burned down and a pig was burned in it; the accidental touching and tasting of the carcass caused the discovery that meat tastes better when cooked. But Lamb is shrewd in showing how difficult it is for prescientific man to get his facts straight, for there follows a wave of house burnings; only gradually do men discover that the flame alone, not what feeds it, causes the succulence and that one need not literally eat oneself out of house.

In Ibsen's *Vildanden (The Wild Duck,* play, 1884), Hjalmar is a lachrymose, vain person, whose posturing is nicely brought out by the way, in the wake of disaster, he gorges himself on thickly buttered bread; he pretends to be a special person, living on a higher plane, but in this scene his coarseness asserts itself. As is typical of much modern literature, eating has become less a function of religious symbolism that of psychological realism.

Thomas Mann's novel *Der Zauberberg* (*The Magic Mountain*, 1924) contains a detailed description of the five square meals a day that some people eat. This would be like the Rabelaisian celebrations of life in *Tom Jones, Pickwick*, and "The Dead," were it not that the people are tuberculosis patients in a sanatorium undergoing a prescribed regimen. The eating therefore is highly ambiguous. It is partly the core of a rest cure; as such, its results are dubious. It is partly a narcotic, a distraction from one's illness, as eating perhaps was for Hjalmar. It is also, along with the flirtations and other empty-headed games, an expression of the boredom and vulgarity of most of the patients; and, not least, it expresses the desire of people under sentence of death to compensate by eating doubly, as though to make up for the years of eating they will not have.

In Mann's *Der Tod In Venedig* (*Death in Venice*, novel, 1912), von Aschenbach eats some overripe strawberries which may very well have given him the cholera that kills him. Their overripeness suggests Venice itself; his own stage of life; the quality of life in Venice, especially the atmosphere of sexual decadence; the lateness of the summer, and the onset of the socially corrosive cholera epidemic.

A secularized version of the mythic, sacramental, magical role of eating takes place in a famous scene in Proust's novel *Du côté de chez Swann* (*Swann's Way*, 1913). The narrator eats some madeleine cakes dipped in lime tea, as he used to in childhood, and, through what he calls the "involuntary memory," childhood locales and experiences are suddenly recalled in all their original vividness. The idea that trivial sensuous experience rather than cerebration is intertwined with the deepest emotional and spiritual sources of one's being is partly romantic and partly based on the psychology of associationism. That the experience in question involves food ties it to folklore motifs of magic potions (as seen in the *Odyssey, The Golden Ass, Tristan*), to biblical tradition, and, specifically, to the Sacrament of the Eucharist. But it appears here, shorn of all such traditional associations, in the midst of a secular, realist-impressionist modern novel.

Eating pervades that other supreme example of the modern novel, Joyce's *Ulysses* (1922). Early in the book, Bloom purchases and cooks kidneys for his lazy wife's breakfast. In the course of the day's journey, he purchases a sandwich and a glass of wine at one tavern—where he meditates on the human crassness of eating animal flesh—in a chapter named after the cannibals in the *Odyssey* and filled with images of the repulsiveness of eating. But the climactic scene involves his coming together with Stephen Dedalus, whom he has helped out of a fix in the Nighttown brothel district. They go to an all-night cabstand for a snack and then to Bloom's home for a communion of sorts over a homely beverage. Whatever communication is possible between human beings takes place often in connection with the ingestion of food, whether at formal feast, religious rite, or the simple coming together of two individuals. Thus the love of Bloom and Molly had once been sealed by their sharing a seedcake in their mouths, and thus now Bloom and Stephen briefly break out of their isolation over a cup of cocoa.

Selected Bibliography

Cyril, Ray. *The Gourmet's Companion*. London: Eyre & Spottiswoode, 1963.
Mercadal, José María. *La cocina y la mesa en la literatura*. Madrid: Taurus, 1962.
Smith, M. R. *The Epicure's Companion*. New York: D. McKay, 1962.

MANFRED WEIDHORN

EMBLEM

An emblem is a combination of *inscriptio* (motto), *pictura* (picture), and *subscriptio* (poem or prose passage) used collectively to expound some moral or ethical truth. The *inscriptio*, a short motto or quotation introducing the emblem, is usually printed above the picture. The *pictura* may depict one or several objects, persons, or events, either real or imaginary. Beneath the *pictura* appears a quotation from a learned source or by the emblematist. An additional explanatory poem or prose commentary often follows the *subscriptio*. Technically, all three parts must be present to create an emblem. However, occasionally "naked" emblems, text that describes and explicates an emblematic scene but does not include the *pictura*, occur.

The word derives from the Greek *emblēma*, meaning not symbol or allegory, but mosaic or low-relief decoration. Mario Praz distinguishes emblem from the imprese or devise, which combined a simple, often epigrammatic *mot* (text) and design disclosing the bearer's purpose. While emblems resemble the heraldic or armorial device, they are not so personally attached to the bearer. Rather, emblems carry a general didactic message for all readers. The terms, however, become considerably confused in the sixteenth century. Equally confusing is the practice of using the term "emblem" to indicate both a rhetorical ornament and a genre. The emblem enjoyed its vogue in the sixteenth and seventeenth centuries, where its hybrid nature and homiletic capacity accommodated a variety of uses. Praz's bibliography of emblem books lists over six hundred authors, most of whom produced several emblem-books. Besides numerous collections of military, amorous, moral, and religious emblems, Renaissance men and women saw emblems in book colophons; heraldic devices; allegorical figures appearing in masques, plays, pageants, and processions; decorations of clothing and jewelry; and especially in seventeenth-century lyric poetry.

The Relationship of *Pictura* to *Scriptura*

Critics generally agree that the combination of picture and word creates an emblem's meaning, and that the emblem may have a cryptic or riddle-like quality. This emphasis upon the enigmatic nature of the *pictura*, which must be deciphered by the *subscriptio*, derives from the tradition of medieval exegesis and an inaccurate understanding of Egyptian hieroglyphics, as well as from a Renaissance attraction to occult or hermeneutical literature. Another alternative suggests a philosophical basis for interpreting emblems, using the system of Albertus Magnus. Thus, the emblem's *inscriptio* presents general or abstract meanings; the *pictura*, concrete and visual particulars; and the *subscriptio*, the application of the general idea. Whichever the preferred interpretation, it seems necessary to distinguish the emblem's *pictura* from a merely descriptive or ornamental accompaniment to the text on the one hand, and on the other, from an elaborate allegorical message-bearer that speaks independently of accompanying text and context.

The most important recent theories about the emblem are the contributions of German critics who argue that the emblem has the dual function of representation and interpretation. The emblem is both *Kunstform*, a descriptive art form, and *Denkform*, a form of thought, a system of correspondences between things and their cosmic meaning. Much of this untranslated work is ably summarized in the critical studies of Peter Daly.

The exact nature of the relationship between word and picture was a concern from the beginning of the emblem's development. In prefatory material to *Dialogo dell' imprese militari e amorose* (1555), Paulo Giovio offers five requirements for the imprese: a just proportion between the "soul" (motto) and the "body" (figure); a meaning neither too obscure nor too obvious; a pleasing appearance; no depiction of the human body; and a brief motto, preferably in a foreign language. In *Le imprese illustri* (1566) Girolamo Ruscelli adds the rule that the figures and motto only have meaning through their mutual connection. That addition, with most of Giovio's guidelines, englished in Samuel Daniel's 1585 translation (*The Worthy Tract of Paulus Jovius*), governs imprese-making in Italy to the end of the seventeenth century, and influences, though less rigidly, the creation of emblems in the rest of Europe.

The rediscovery of ancient texts during the Renaissance brought again to light the pictorialist doctrine "ut pictura poesis," attributed to Simonides by Plutarch. Poetry's analogy with painting is consistently acknowledged by Italian critics, among them, Castelvetro, Minturno, and Robortello. J. C. Scaliger declares that "every oration consists of image, idea, and imitation, just like painting" (*Poetices*, 1561). In England statements on the connection between picture and poetry appear in Ben Jonson's *Timber* (1640), George Puttenham's *The Arte of English Poesie* (1589), in Spenser's argument to the February eclogue of *The Shepheardes Calender* (1579), as well as in Sidney's definition of mimesis, "a representing, counterfeiting, or figuring forth; to speak metaphorically, a speaking picture'' (*A Defense of Poetry*, 1595). Both structurally and aesthetically, then, the emblem genre epitomizes the blending of verbal and visual arts so characteristic of the Renaissance.

Backgrounds in Antiquity and the Middle Ages

The material and form of emblems derive primarily from three sources: Egyptian hieroglyphics, Greek epigrams, and medieval bestiaries, lapidaries, and allegories. Renaissance humanists regarded Egyptian hieroglyphics as ideographical writing that contained divine wisdom, a belief also common in Greek antiquity. Marsilio Ficino, leader of Florence's Platonic academy, explained hieroglyphics as a symbolic system of pictures that reflected divine ideas. Knowledge of hieroglyphics came to Europe in the *Hieroglyphika* (*Hieroglyphics*, c. A.D. 4th century[?]) of Horapollo, a Greek translation of a Coptic text discovered by a Florentine priest in 1419 and printed in Venice in 1505. The first Latin translation appeared in 1515, followed by numerous vernacular editions. Of Alexandrian provenance, the *Hieroglyphika* lists and explains 189 picture-sign equivalents, among them lion = anger, phoenix = soul or rebirth, and fire and water = purity. Even before they became part of the literary tradition, hieroglyphs influenced the graphic and plastic arts of the Renaissance in the decoration of architecture, paintings, medals, and coins.

Greek epigrams, a second source, were found in the *Greek Anthology*, compiled by Cephalas (A.D. 10th century). To compose the first emblem book in 1531, Andrea Alciati made use of approximately fifty of these epigrams, which verbally described objects and their significance. To this ready-made material for the *subscriptio*, he simply added appropriate illustrations. Greek interest in hieroglyphs was also recorded in references made by Plato, Plutarch, Pliny, Clement of Alexandria, Plotinus, Lucan, and Diodorus. Egyptian picture signs accorded well with the Platonic theory of ideas. In the Renaissance, commonplace books, particularly Erasmus' *Adagia* (*Proverbs*, 1500), a collection of Greek and Latin epigrams, provided material for emblematists.

Finally, typological exegeses of the Middle Ages, which assumed an ordered universe wherein God revealed his plan of salvation, had much in common with the emblematic method of interpreting phenomena. Allegorical interpretation was commonly performed upon the words of Holy Scripture, of course, but in fact became a standard feature in the instruction of rhetoric. The practice, transferred to the courtly and military worlds, produced the art of heraldry. To interpret the world of nature, the tradition produced bestiaries on the order of the *Physiologos* (*Physiologus*, 2d century), a collection of symbols suggested by animals and ascribed to the Alexandrian Epiphanius. As a striking union of traditions, the *Hieroglyphica* (1556) of Pierio Valeriano explains hieroglyphics by means of Christian allegory. Valeriano brings the symbolism of medieval bestiaries and lapidaries, as well as of the *Physiologos*, to the interpretation of Egyptian picture-signs. In part, then, the diversity of the emblem's origins accounts for the diversity of its expression.

The Development of the Genre

Charting the dissemination and popularity of emblem-books is helpful in gauging the effect of the emblematic mode upon literature. Books of an allegorical nature were composed before the sixteenth century, most notably Sebastian Brant's satire *Das Narrenschiff* (*The Ship of Fools*, 1494), of which two English versions appeared in 1509. The allegory of a ship bearing and piloted by fools bound for a fools' paradise exposed, in particular, abuses of the church and prepared, in that way, for the Protestant Reformation. But 1531 is usually cited as the first appearance of the emblem-book. Italian Andrea Alciati's *Emblematum libellus* (*Emblem-Book*) saw over 100 editions, often expanded and enlarged, in the sixteenth century. Ironically it was Alciati's publisher who added pictures to the text—the familiar emblem form, thus, created by the collaboration of author and engraver. A publishing explosion of emblem-books followed Alciati's. Expanded and revised editions, translations, and polyglot versions of popular texts, but most of all the widespread borrowing from emblem-makers' predecessors and contemporaries quickly familiarized Europeans with the emblematic mode.

In France, Guillaume de la Perrière's *Le théâtre de bons engins* (1539) and Gilles Corrozet's *Hécatomgraphie* (1540) chose subjects similar to Alciati's: morals derived from fables, histories, allegories, proverbs, astonishing occurrences, and riddles of love. Lyons, the publishing city for Claude Paradin's *Devises héroïques* (*The Heroicall Devises*, 1551) and Maurice Scève's *Délie* (*Delia*, 1544), a volume of verse with emblematic pictures incorporated, also brought to print the first Protestant emblem-book, Georgette de Montenay's *Emblèmes, ou devises chrestiennes* (1571). Even in this sample, however, one notes the increasing specialization of emblem-books—from Paradin's heraldic devices, to Scève's morals, to de Montenay's Protestant coloring of Christian virtues.

Most of the books produced in Italy did not develop particular themes, but were treatises and collections of related arts—devices and iconography. Besides the previously mentioned Ruscelli, Gabriello Simeoni influenced the art of devices with his *Imprese eroiche e morali* (1559). Luca Contile's *Ragionamento sopra le proprieta delle imprese* (1574) is the most detailed treatise on the history of the imprese, and Cesare Ripa's *Iconologia* (*Iconology*, 1593), a comprehensive allegorical dictionary of the virtues, the arts, and the parts of the world (including America) became the eighteenth century's reference text for symbolism.

Dutch emblem-makers, on the other hand, became known as specialists in love emblems, drawn from Ovidian material and lyric poetry of the Provençal and Latin poets. The *Emblemata amatoria* (1600) of Daniel Heinsius and *Amorum emblemata* (1608) of Otto Vaenius are good examples. Dutch emblem-books are also significant for the quality of their emblem engravings. Jacob Cats took the inspiration for his collection of love emblems, *Silenus Alcibiadis* (1618), from proverbs and depicted his emblems in everyday life scenes that owed a good deal to Dutch genre painting. Dutch emblem art stood in good company with the woodcuts of Johannes Sambucus' *Emblemata* (1564) and the copper plates cut by Johann de Bry for Jean Boissard's *Emblematum liber* (1593). Since the art of emblem-books generally overshadowed their poetic merits, illustrations made collectors' items out of emblem-books and undoubtedly later influenced the creation of seventeenth-century metaphors and conceits.

Foreign language and translations of Continental emblem-books were making regular appearances in England in the late sixteenth century. Particularly important for the growth of information about emblems was Samuel Daniel's translation of Giovio previously mentioned *The Worthy Tract*, which includes prefatory material with wide-ranging references to current emblem literature and a description of the emblem/imprese genre. The first treatise on the subject by an English Renaissance writer was Abraham Fraunce's *Insignium, armorum, emblematum, hieroglyphicorum et symbolorum* (1588). And the first English emblem-book was Geoffrey Whitney's *A Choice of Emblemes* (1586), a composite collection of previously published emblems drawn from the work of Alciati, Hadrian Junius (*Emblemata*, 1565), Sambucus, and Paradin. Another popular collection of emblems that included the work of Paradin, Simeoni, and others (*The Heroicall Devises of M. Claudius Paradin and . . . others*), appeared in 1591. The first English emblem-book professing independence of foreign models was a Protestant emblem-book in Latin and English, Andrew Willet's *Sacrorum emblematum centuria una* (1591). A later text not claiming originality was *Minerva britanna* (1612) by Henry Peacham, who produced both illustrations and verses of this collection of heraldic and moral emblems. He is perhaps more important for contributing *The Art of Drawing with the Pen* (1606), which contained sections on the treatment of allegorical themes and on heraldry. This, as well as Thomas Blount's 1646 translation of Henri Estienne's *L'art de faire les devises* (*The Arte of Making Devises*, 1646), provides a detailed description of the nature and function of emblem and imprese-making.

Both Mario Praz and Barbara Lewalski (*Protestant Poetics and the Seventeenth-Century Religious Lyric*, 1979) detail the development of sacred or divine emblems. Lewalski finds five categories: the first, general collections of discrete emblems on diverse subjects of moral or Christian significance, include Peacham's *Minerva britanna*, Cats' *Silenus Alcibiadis*, and George Wither's *A Collection of Emblemes* (1635). Within this group might appear the collections that derive from the tradition of the political-philosophical "mirror of princes," such as the Jesuit Andrea Meno's *Principe perfecto* (1642) and Joannes de Solórzano Pereira's *Emblemata centum, regio Politica* (1651). The second group contains emblems labeled sacred or Christian, usually employing biblical quotations or allusions in motto or inscription. Georgette de Montenay's collection is a good example. A third category, using discrete emblems ordered around a central theme, was particularly popular with Protestant emblematists. An example is the work of Francis Quarles, *Hieroglyphikes of the Life of Man* (1639), which uses the candle motif to depict the growth and testing of faith, as well as the decline of life. The Jesuit Georg Stengel, however, also offered *Ova Paschalia* (1672), one hundred egg-shaped emblem plates depicting the egg's association with Easter and with a Catholic theological world view. Texelius, finally, devoted his emblem-book *Phoenix visus et auditus* (1706) to the mythological bird, a popular image in emblem-books.

The fourth category, one more popular with the Jesuits, an order that produced much emblem art, transferred love emblems from secular to sacred subject matter. Vaenius easily adapted the character of Eros and Anteros in his *Amorum emblemata* to Divine Love and Anteros, with the addition of haloes and wings to the figures, for the emblems in his new collection, *Amoris divini emblemata* (1615). Besides transforming secular texts, Protestant emblematists reworked emblem-books that the Jesuits were producing as instruments of instruction for the young nobility. Francis Quarles took the works of two Jesuits to produce the Protestant text, *Emblemes* (1635). The Catholic versions, *Typus mundi* (1624), attributed to Phillippe de Mallery, which presented emblems of earthly versus divine love, and *Pia desideria* (1624) by Hermann Hugo, a narrative of Anima's (the soul's) progress to Divine Love and salvation, enjoyed much popularity in both their original and pirated versions. The work of Quarles is also significant in that it imported to the Protestant tradition symbols that represent the individual experience of the human soul in its search for sanctity, with surprising psychological acuity.

The fifth category of sacred emblem-books, of particular importance for religious lyric poets, represents the human heart undergoing progressive purgation from sin to renovation. Emblems featuring the heart had already appeared in de Montenay's text and in Daniel Cramer's *Emblemata sacra* (1624), both Protestant collections. The Jesuit Benedictus van Haeften provided an emblematic narrative of the characters Anima and Divine Love working to cleanse the heart of Anima in *Schola cordis* (*The School of the Heart*, 1629). This emblem-book was organized according to the stages of Ignatian meditational exercises. Christopher Harvey adapted van Haeften's work to produce a Protestant version of *Schola cordis* (1646). However, other Catholic texts, such as Etienne Luzvic's *Le cœur dévot* (1627), which was translated by the English Jesuit Henry Hawkins (*The Devout Heart*, 1634), and texts of Marian devotion, such as Hawkins' *Partheneia sacra* (1633), were not subjects of Protestant borrowing. In general, this variety of sacred eblem collections made readily available a visual symbolic mode that could be evoked in the religious verse of the seventeenth century, particularly in that of George Herbert.

The Emblem in Literature

Although the sixteenth and seventeenth centuries are appropriately designated the Emblematic Age, emblem-hunting in the literature of the period must be judicious. Of course, Renaissance writers who acknowledge their indebtedness to emblem-books are easy subjects. Ben Jonson, for example, cites Ripa's *Iconologia* as a source for the material of several masques. Moreover, Spenser's epic poem *Faerie Queene* (1590–1596) and *The Shepheardes Calendar* (1579) seem clearly influenced by the emblem tradition—the latter particularly by its *pictura-scriptura* form as well as its content. But the influence of emblematic thought and expression upon literature is too pervasive, often, to be able to pin a specific emblem to specific literary passage, as Henry Green attempts to do (*Shakespeare and the Emblem Writers*, 1870). Certainly not every strong trope in seventeenth-century lyric poetry is an emblem. It is not so much the presence of iconographical figures or the striking visual metaphors as it is the intention, structure, and technique of the literature that derives in part from the emblem.

Emblematic Drama

Because it combines a visual experience of silent tableau and active scene with a verbal experience, the drama is the most emblematic of all literary arts. Dumb-shows, for example, function as the emblem's *pictura*, and significances not easily apparent are explained by the commentary of a Presenter or of those watching the show. The anonymous play *Locrine* (1595) features dumb-shows explained by the figure of Ate, who prefaces her explanations with a Latin motto. The action following each dumb-show further explicates meaning, so that the play's structure literally imitates emblematic organization. Renaissance drama-tists made frequent use of dumb-show variations; Shakespeare has Gower in *Pericles* (1609) presenting dumb-shows and Hamlet interpreting the dumb-show before the mousetrap play, but other instances are numerous. English civic pageantry also used the emblematic method in creating and staging processions. Scaffolds held allegorical scenes and figures, that were either identified with scrolls above their heads or who spoke revealing lines of verse upon the arrival of the honored personage at the tableau. Descriptions of the coronation entry of English kings and queens to London suggest both the celebratory and didactic uses to which these emblematic tableaux were put.

The masque, another collaboration of spectacle and verse, offered elaborately ornamented and symbolic tableaux with a thin plot line but a rich interpretive setting. Ben Jonson's stage directions and the sketches of Inigo Jones's scenery reveal an elaborate network of symbolism in the costumes and staging. Jonson's *Hymenaei* (1606), for example, employs characters from Greek myths, allegor-ical personifications (among them, Reason, as guide and interpreter), and em-blematic stage properties (lamps, a sword, a golden chain). Since many dramatists, including Francis Beaumont, George Chapman, and Thomas Mid-dleton, also wrote masques for the court, it is not surprising to see the same emblematic elements appearing in Renaissance drama as well. Shakespeare em-ploys emblematic meanings of natural phenomena (sun imagery in the historical plays) and maxims or sententiae as commentaries upon a play's action (the comments of Kent and the Fool in *King Lear* [1606]). Occasionally, characters will function as emblems, the subject of others' commentary (the mutilated Lavinia, the murdered Duncan, the villainous Shylock). The last plays seem particularly given to emblematic tableaux and characters (*Pericles*, *The Winter's Tale* [1611], and *Henry VIII* [1613]).

Emblematic Narrative and Devotional Prose

Narrative and sermonic prose also adapted emblems to appropriate fictional, didactic, or devotional purposes. John Bunyan, the author of a children's emblem-book (*A Book for Boys and Girls*, [1686]), clearly used emblematic forms or referred to the emblematic world view in both *The Pilgrim's Progress* (1678–1684) and *Solomon's Temple Spiritualized* (1688). In this way Puritans could safely isolate and interpret objects to symbolize spiritual truths without being in danger of worshipping papist icons. Christian's journey to the Celestial City, thus, is strewn with emblematic symbols and episodes. Another variation on the Everyman theme is Daniel Defoe's *Robinson Crusoe* (1719), where the episodes of realistic struggle for life are emblems of Crusoe's tormented spiritual struggle. The eighteenth century may have in part derived the episodic, emblematic structure and often didactic nature of its novels from seventeenth-century emblematic practice.

Clearly the Protestant and Catholic arts of preaching also reflect the influence of emblematic thought. The outline of the presentation and interpretation of scripture in William Perkins' *The Arte of Prophecying* (1612–1613) shows the similarity of sermonic to emblematic form. The four steps, reading the text, giving its sense and understanding, gathering points of doctrine from the text, and applying those points to ordinary life, resemble the "reading" of an emblem. The meditations and devotions of the metaphysical poets employ a form that has both meditational and emblematic qualities. These exercises focus upon a particular event or experience that is then interpreted, with references to theological or biblical paradigms. John Donne's *Devotions upon Emergent Occasions* (1624), Henry Vaughan's *The Mount of Olives: or, Solitary Devotions* (1652), and Thomas Traherne's *Meditations upon the Six Days of Creation* (written c. 1669–1674) are representative. The sermons of American Puritan Edward Taylor offer a final graphic example of the emblem's influence. In *Christographia* (written 1682–1725), a collection of fourteen sermons, Taylor offers a verbal engraving or portrait of Christ. Preachers drew from divine emblems as well as Protestant meditations, sermon theory, biblical tropes, and typological symbolism. With each of these, the graphic imaging of and meditating upon a significant event or scene precipitates the interpretations and analysis of the religious mysteries therein contained.

Emblematic Poetry

Emblematic thought and expression from the turn of the seventeenth century onward seem to have strongly affected English poetry. From occasional images in the sonnet sequences of Shakespeare (written 1593–1600; sonnet 116) and Samuel Daniel (*Delia*, 1592; sonnet 15), emblems acquire increasingly important roles. Spenser's *Faerie Queene* uses emblems particularly of temperance to lend thematic continuity to the poem; Milton employs the image of the phoenix to mark the hero's spiritual turning point in *Samson Agonistes* (play, 1671). The poetry of William Blake, more than a century later, is also reminiscent of the emblematic method. Blake's habit of engraving his poems in plates and surrounding these with illustrations seems to suggest his familiarity with the emblem's union of visual and verbal media. Moreover, the complicated personal mythology in *Visions of the Daughters of Albion* (1793) or symbolism in the *Four Zoas* (1797) may perhaps be said to share some similarity with the enigmatic origins of the emblem. Blake knew and admired Albrecht Dürer's sixteenth-century emblematic woodblocks and engravings more than, for example, the naturalistic depictions in eighteenth-century landscape painting that increasingly influenced neoclassical and romantic poets.

From the emblematists of the seventeenth century, the metaphysical poets noted the personal trend developing in emblem collections, which emphasized the psychological concerns of the individual over the public moral responsibilities of mankind. They also noted the emblem-book's use as an aid to meditation. Like the emblem, meditation offers a visual description, an analysis of its significance, and a more personal application of the lesson to the reader's life. George Herbert's poems "Love-Joy," "The Church-floore," "The Collar," and "The Pulley" (*The Temple*, 1633), as well as John Donne's "A Jeat Ring Sent," "The Flea," or "Valediction: Forbidding Mourning" (compass image), published posthumously in 1633, offer visual images that are then often startlingly elaborated into metaphysical conceits: a *subscriptio* for the *inscriptio* of the poem's title. Lewalski identifies as emblematic the divine poems of Donne's, which are traditional meditations either on religious symbols ("The Crosse"), on feast days ("Upon the Annunciation and Passion"), or on events in Christ's life ("La Corona" sonnets). The conventional spiritual emblem, however, yields in each poem to the speaker's personal statement or imprese reflecting his spiritual or psychological state. Similarly, Praz calls George Herbert's *The Temple* a mute emblem-book, wanting only the plates, while Lewalski notes that Herbert's dominant patterns (the Christian as God's husbandry and the temple in the heart) are drawn from visual emblems in contemporary religious emblem-books, particularly Cramer's *Emblemata sacra* and the Protestant *Schola cordis*. In addition, some poems from *The Temple* ("The Altar," "Easter-Wings," "Paradise," and "Deniall") are complete emblems; they provide not only verse commentary but also visual embodiment of the title in the poem's shape. This type of figured or patterned poetry, which first appears in the *Greek Anthology*, was practiced as an eccentric exercise in seventeenth-century England as well as Germany, in Johann Helwig's *Die Nymphe Noris in zweien Tagzeiten vorgestellet* (1650) and Catharina Regina von Greiffenberg's *Geistliche Sonnette, Lieder und Gedichte* (1662).

The poetry of Richard Crashaw offers a striking contrast to the intellectual rigor of Donne and Herbert. Moreover, Crashaw, a convert to Catholicism, relies upon emblematic sources different from those of the Protestant and consequently produces poetry that stresses sensory stimulation and church ritual (rather than scripture) as the means to devotion. In *Carmen Deo Nostro* (1652) appear the Saint Teresa poems, "The Weeper," and "Prayer: An Ode," which all recall the motifs of the Jesuit emblem collections *Pia desideria*, *Typus mundi*, and *Schola cordis*. Crashaw's liturgical hymns to the Virgin recall Hawkins' *Partheneia sacra* as well. It is also possible that the work of the earlier recusant poets Robert Southwell, William Alabaster, and Henry Constable reflects the influence of Jesuit emblem-books.

Although greatly influenced by Herbert's *The Temple*, the *Silex scintillans* (1650–1655) of Henry Vaughan does vary in its use of emblems. The controlling metaphor of his collection is the Christian pilgrimage, but Vaughan is most indebted to the emblem tradition for his representations of creatures—animals as well as objects of nature. The emblem-books of Valeriano, Cats, Peacham, and others are Vaughan's sources for "The Palm-Tree," "The Bird," "The Timber," "The Rain-bow," and "The Water-fall"— creature meditation poems from which didactic lessons are derived. Elsewhere in the collection are poems elaborating upon biblical metaphors and upon icons, many of which appeared in Quarles's *Hieroglyphikes* and Ripa's *Iconologia*. Both Vaughan and Thomas Traherne reveal a Neoplatonic strain in some of their imagery, but emblematic influence is generally much less pronounced in Traherne's poetry. As Vaughan emphasized the theme of pilgrimage, Traherne evokes a regressive pilgrimage to infancy's bliss in the collection *Divine Reflections on the Native Objects of an Infant-Ey* (vol. 1 of *Poems of Felicity*, published posthumously in 1910), which uses the eye motif to unify the poems. His celebration of youthful innocence leads Traherne to make emblems of remembered childhood experience in "Shadows on the Water" and "On Leaping over the Moon." On the order of the occasional meditation and of the emblem, these events are visualized, described, and then interpreted for their spiritual significance.

According to Lewalski, American Edward Taylor is the most self-consciously and overtly emblematic of the metaphysical poets. In the poems accompanying the *Christographia* sermons, Taylor emblematically embellishes several biblical metaphors. While the poems of *Preparatory Meditations* (written 1682–1725) are not precisely structured as emblem-poems, they describe such objects as the rainbow, the Ark, and heavenly manna in visual detail and interpret their significance. Taylor's Canticle series within *Preparatory Meditations* comments upon the emblematic nature of metaphors associated with Bride and Bridegroom (the Church and Christ); several poems are reminiscent of the Anima-Divine Love emblem sequences of Vaenius, van Haeften, and Harvey. Unlike Donne, Taylor rarely unifies an individual poem by using a single striking image. Nor does he, like Herbert, assemble a collection of lyrics that develops a single theme. Rather, Taylor draws from a wide range of biblical metaphors, habitually developing these through a cluster of related or contrasting images or figures. In this way the emblematic strain in the poetry, though diffused, is also pervasive.

There is a difference in British and American uses of emblems in this period, however. While Donne, Herbert, Vaughan, and Traherne use emblems to suggest the immediacy of the divine in nature and in the life of the Christian, Taylor uses emblems to represent the failure of the speaker's imagination and language to bridge the gap between human and divine. This tension is often depicted in the juxtaposition of two contradictory emblems within a poem. "The Ebb and Flow" offers two emblems of the speaker's heart, one inspired with heavenly flame, the other deceived by an ignis fatuus. Elsewhere Taylor combines domestic images in a complicated emblem of regeneration. In "Huswifery," Taylor offers himself as God's spinning wheel (the Holy Word = distaff; affection = the flyers; soul = the holy spool), then as a loom upon which the Holy Spirit may weave heavenly cloth, in which he may finally be clothed.

The use of emblematic devices for moral teaching, increasingly modified to serve the uses of the author instead of the demands of the tradition, had a long life in English poetry. Milton's *Paradise Lost* (1667) presents Archangel Michael instructing Adam and Eve about the future history of mankind by presenting before them a series of tableaux (book 11, 423ff.). The emblematic form influenced as well some features of the third Earl of Shaftesbury's 1732 edition of *Characteristiks of Men, Manners, Opinions, Times* (1711). Though his essays are primarily typological or theophrastian in influence, Shaftesbury does include in book 3 "The Judgment of Hercules," a tablature or emblematic *pictura* of Hercules and allegorical characters. The accompanying text explains the significance of the picture. The character portraits that became so popular in the late seventeenth and eighteenth centuries were certainly relatives of the earlier emblem-books.

By the Restoration emblematic method was turning to the service of social or political satire. John Dryden's *Absolom and Achitophel* (1681) is a political allegory graphically portrayed and accompanied by the author's pointed interpretive comment. The author's habit of both dramatizing and then interpreting the story lends the poem its emblematic character. As the master of pictorial personification, Alexander Pope satirizes with his portraits of Spleen and her handmaidens Ill-Nature and Affectation in *The Rape of the Lock* (poem, 1712) and of women in "Of the Character of Women," epistle 3 of the *Moral Essays* (poems, 1731–1735).

Yet another emblematic motif characterizes the poetry of the eighteenth century: the use of landscape or of garden as a natural or ordered environment. In *The Seasons* (1726–1730) James Thomson personifies nature, investing the seasons with appropriate insignia. Later, Oliver Goldsmith's *The Deserted Village* (1770) makes the dying community, which was once in harmony with nature, a bleak emblem of the future. It seems plausible that the eighteenth century's interest in formally patterned and iconographically composed gardens, as well as the passion for landscapes at the end of the century, may reflect artists' responses to the *pictura* of the world with increasingly personal, emblematized meanings. The imaginative, idealizing version of natural scenery took on for the romantic poets the nature of philosophical emblems. In the late seventeenth and eighteenth centuries, however, the idea of emblem is so diffuse as to become almost untraceable. For every easily identified instance, such as Augustus Toplady's hymn, "Rock of Ages," (*The Gospel Magazine*, 1775), which drew its metaphors entirely from Quarles's *Emblemes*, there are five times as many that are merely suggestive.

Emblems, as an artistic and literary form, are less innovative than preservative. Emblem-books of the sixteenth century were handbooks of the age's *sententia*, to which were attached certain symbolic representations that became the shorthand of heraldic, artistic, religious, and literary expression. In addition to acting as a compendium of materials for writers and artists, the emblem-book tradition remained faithful to its original premise: that, contained within the microcosm of the *pictura* could be found keys to understanding the macrocosm—of the poem, of an entire book, of the human or political condition, or of the universe itself. The emblem celebrates, in short, the human intellect's ability to discover its message.

See also: Hieroglyphics, Masque or Mask.

Selected Bibliography

Daly, Peter M. *Literature in the Light of the Emblem*. Toronto: University of Toronto Press, 1979.

Henkel, Arthur, and Albrecht Schöne. *Emblemata, Handbuch zur Sinnbildkunst des xvi. and xvii. Jahrhunderts*. Stuttgart: J. B. Metzlersche, 1967.

Praz, Mario. *Studies in Seventeenth-Century Imagery*. Rome: Edizioni di Storia Letteratura, 1964.

ELLEN M. CALDWELL

EPISTEMOLOGY

Epistemology is the branch of philosophy that deals with the question of how we know what we know. Insofar as all works of literature deal with the discrepancy between reality and appearance, they touch upon that question. Certain literary works, however, have as a major theme the protagonist's difficulty in ascertaining the truth, or his being caught up between two equally persuasive visions of reality. These constitute literature's graphic, dramatic contributions to the abstract discussions of philosophers.

Antiquity and the Middle Ages

Although the Homeric epic makes no direct statement on this theme, some of its overtones are relevant. Thus Agamemnon in the *Ilias* (*Iliad*, c. 8th century B.C.) unwittingly undermines his war effort by offending Achilles, yet the incident will eventually bring about the fall of Troy. Similarly, when he has a dream in book 2, he is unsure of its interpretation, and the advice he obtains from Nestor proves to be worse than no advice at all. Man clearly operates in an uncertain world. And in the epic poem *Odysseia* (*Odyssey*, c. 8th century B.C.) the basic mystery of paternity is raised: "Nobody knows his own father." The theme first becomes central in Sophocles' play *Oidipous tyrannos* (*Oedipus Rex*, c. 429 B.C.), which is, of course, the seminal detective story. Oedipus initially wants to find the cause of the blight in Thebes and, then, the murderer of his predecessor. Conflicting stories emerge, but through patient sifting, he arrives at the truth. At least there is a truth to arrive at; on the other hand, the fact that Oedipus does everything he can to avoid the fulfillment of the oracle and only brings it about bespeaks a deep pessimism about man's ability to know his future and shape his destiny. Sophocles' *Antigonē* (c. 441 B.C.) does not even provide the consolation of arriving at a truth. The play balances (as had Aeschylus' *Oresteia* [458 B.C.], albeit with less philosophical uncertainty) the claims of individual conscience and familial duties against public authority and raison d'état. Antigone goes to her doom, followed by her lover and his mother; furthermore, she exhibits (notably in her treatment of her sister) a stridency, egotism, and vanity that coexist uneasily with her idealism. Still, if there is something finally repellent about her, one finds little rest with Creon. His vision muddied by denial, egoism, sexism, ageism, and paranoia, he is powerfully rebuked by his son for blindness to the facts, and the ending of the play leaves him a punished and beaten man. Here, then, for the first time in literature, is a portrayal of a clash not between right and wrong, as one usually likes to perceive clashes, but between two rights. Insofar as one leaves the theater or library with a sense that each antagonist had only a partial answer or that the truth is elusive, one confronts the epistemological problem.

Euripides explored this new territory even further in his plays. Theseus, like Othello, quickly jumps to the wrong conclusion (*Hippolytos* [*Hyppolitus*, 428 B.C.]). In *Mēdeia* (*Medea*, 431 B.C.), the jilted woman is given a chance to poignantly plead her case, while the jilter is shown up as smug and insufferable. When Medea, however, takes her revenge by killing the couple's children, the audience turns against her. Who is there left to turn to? Who was right? In *Iphigeneia hē en Aulidi* (*Iphigenia in Aulis*, c. 405 B.C.), Agamemnon is caught up between his public and his private roles, between the need to sacrifice his daughter if he is to retain this leadership position and the Greeks are to thrive and, on the other hand, his love for Iphigenia and his devotion to his family. Though he decides to go through with the sacrifice, the problem seems insoluble. This play also introduces another dimension to the theme by the way in which the word "mad," or any of its many variants, is bandied about. The accusation of lunacy is an important element in the epistemological problem. To be mad is to be out of contact with reality, and to so designate someone is therefore to be making assumptions about what is real and about one's own hold on it. In this play, the accusation of madness is a statement by proponents of the priority of Agamemnon's public or private life not about sanity but about the correctness of the other side's assumptions.

These uncertainties become central in the *Bakchai* (*The Bacchants*, c. 405 B.C.), in which the new cult of Dionysus is sweeping Thebes. Some join it, dress in new ways, change life style, carouse, and dance. To those like Pentheus, the ruler of Thebes, who cling to traditional ways, these converts, even if they be worthies like Cadmus and Tiresias, are mad. But to the converts, who feel that, after a lifetime of delusion, they have achieved the truth, men like Pentheus, refusing to change, are the mad ones. The conclusion is ambiguous. If Pentheus is at first reactionary, intolerant, dogmatic, ruthless, and, at last, a voyeuristic transvestite, Dionysus turns from being a persecuted god into a harsh vengeance-taker who ruins even innocent bystanders and followers. Should one adhere with integrity to the old or open-mindedly follow the new? Is the new a legitimate religion or a perverse cult? On which side does "civilization" depend? These are the epistemological questions the play raises without answering, and the exchange of accusations about being "mad" becomes even more heated and unsettling here than elsewhere.

At the border of literature and philosophy, some of the early dialogues of Plato present the epistemological theme in its most explicit and clearest form by raising questions that are shown to be insoluble. Such is the case in the *Euthyphrōn*, (*Euthyphro*, c. 390 B.C.), on what is piety, and the *Theaitētos* (*Theaetetus*, c. 368 B.C.), on what is knowledge. At the end of the latter, note is taken of the inconclusiveness of the discussion, which, Socrates suggests, is a healthy experience. Plato went on to erect his own vast philosophic system, as did his pupil Aristotle, but one school of ancient philosophers, the Pyrrhonists, made the epistemological question the central issue of philosophy by teaching the impossibility (or improbability) of ever arriving at any certainty.

Although Cicero gave the Pyrrhonists' view a complete airing, Roman writers are on the whole less concerned with this theme. Some scholars nevertheless find in the epic poem *Aeneis* (*Aeneid*, 19 B.C.), which overtly celebrates the Pax Romana, numerous details—the sympathetic treatment of the deaths of Dido and of Turnus, the claims of the victimized peoples, the growing ruthlessness of the pious hero, the fact that the vision of Roman destiny passes through the ivory gates of sleep through which false dreams are sent—that suggest that Virgil was not as sure of the official philosophy he is promulgating as one might think.

But with the coming of Christianity all that fell by the wayside. The confidence of a Plato is replaced by a far stronger faith. Even if Plato in a weak moment conceded that the guardians of the ideal republic would need an admixture of myths in their education (a need that modern writers were to universalize), the gospel writers were confident that the truth shall make one free. Though some men, like St. Augustine (*Confessiones*, [*Confessions*, essay, c. 397–400 B.C.]), may have to take much time, undergo emotional turmoil, know many zigs and zags, one can with endurance reach that divinely revealed truth. The actual motives for the stealing of the pears in Augustine's youth remain, after much self-analysis, a mystery, but about the depravity of the act and its perpetrators no doubt exists. There is therefore no important epistemological problem at the heart of the medieval literary classics.

The Renaissance

But with the Renaissance and the inauguration of the "modern" (in the broad sense) world, with the beginning of the erosion of Christianity, the epistemological theme first comes into its own. One literary master who made gigantic use of it was Montaigne (*Essais* [*Essays*, 1580–1588]). By in effect reviving Pyrrhonism, he almost single-handedly put it on the agenda of major Western literary works. In numerous passages he indicates the uncertainty of what we know, the smug assurance of contending parties who are oblivious to the fact that their mutual fanaticisms cancel each other. Though he remained a Catholic in the contemporary civil war between Catholics and Protestants, he makes clear that his is only a pragmatic, passive choice and that intellectually one side is as strong or weak as the other.

In the "Apologie de Raymond Sebond" ("Apology for Raymond Sebond," 2.12), he set out to defend a medieval theologian but made such a definitive case for skepticism that scholars are still arguing over what he thought he was doing. Did he subvert the original goal or merely misplace it? Did he grow with the essay or merely become swamped by it? The growing literature of reports on primitive tribes in the New World, moreover, made accepted truths questionable from another angle and, as in "Des cannibales" ("Of Cannibals," 1.31), raised the complex problem of relativism. How is it, Montaigne often asks, that rules and laws thought to be universal and immutable end on this side of the mountain range? The savages are not morally superior, but neither are they as inferior as smug Europeans think; they have their own dignity. Though they may not be perfect, neither are Europeans. Reason is, in any case, a two-edged sword that (like examples and facts) can be used to prove anything.

Shakespeare and Cervantes in their separate ways may be thought to have fleshed out these ideas. In the play *A Midsummer Night's Dream* (c. 1595) (as in Calderón's play *La vida es sueño* [*Life is a Dream*, 1635]), sleeping and waking experiences are hardly distinguishable. In *Much Ado about Nothing* (c. 1598) people hear and see things but, because of presuppositions, interpret them idiosyncratically, sometimes running into calamities, sometimes into love. The play being a comedy, all comes out well; the tragedies take up the same issues in greater depth and with less optimism. Of the major tragedies, three are centrally concerned with the epistemological theme. Is the ghost in *Hamlet* (c. 1600) bona fide or, as was believed from ancient times on, the Devil disguising himself as a loved one and telling lies in order to prompt Hamlet to kill an innocent person and so damn himself? Wrestling with this uncertainty, Hamlet does not discover the truth until half way through the play. But once emerging from one tunnel he runs into another, because of the complexities of the epistemological theme. When he had the capacity and the opportunity to act, he had not the knowledge, and now that he has the knowledge, he has not the opportunity. This basic rhythm of the play, which imitates a common perception ("if only I knew then what I know now!"), presents a variant of the epistemological theme: not that the truth is unavailable—the skeptics position—but that it is available late and attenuated, on unacceptable terms; that it exacts a heavy price; that it is so elusive that it might just as well not be available.

Othello (c. 1604) makes the epistemological theme even more complex. The happily married general is caught up between, on the one hand, the beautiful image of the gentle Desdemona and his intuition of her probity and, on the other, the proven reliability of Iago, his reputation for guileless bluntness, the hesitation with which he imparts unsavory information, the care with which he amasses the evidence, the apparent absence of any malice. *Hamlet* and *Othello* nicely complement each other. Both dramatize the problem of having the truth stare one in the face and yet not being accepted as the truth. Hamlet delays in order to validate the truth before acting and pays the penalty of having thereby lost the opportunity to act; Othello does the reverse, acting peremptorily and paying the penalty of having decided prematurely and incorrectly. Together the two plays leave one with the bleak view of "You're damned if you do and damned if you don't." Hamlet would have benefited from Othello's peremptoriness, and Othello from Hamlet's scrupulousness. The target is that while one knows that there is a time to act and a time to delay, one never knows when either is appropriate or how to go about ascertaining that.

In *King Lear* (1606), the father trusts two deceptive daughters who are horrors and shuts his heart to the one daughter in whom he could put his trust, merely because she did not conform to the ritual he had established. The play adds to the epistemological theme by clarifying some of the psychological factors that predispose one to ignore the truth and to jump to the wrong conclusions. Among them are a naïve tendency to trust what people say or write; to trust the assertions made even when conflict of interests come into play, such as when we offer rewards to those saying something we want to hear; to take ceremonial commitments as reliable, as outer symbols of inner grace; to quantify love; above all, to expect to hear the truth when one is the cynosure of the realm, a mistake Lear later acknowledges. Shackled as man is by these weaknesses, is it any wonder that the truth has a hard time getting through to him?

Francis Bacon (*Essays*, 1597–1625) touches on the epistemological theme when he iterates that men's lives would be shrivelled things were all lies removed from their minds. That becomes the key to understanding the novel *Don Quijote* (*Don Quixote*, 1605, 1615). Cervantes, like Montaigne and sometimes Shakespeare, at least overtly accepts the Christian vision of reality and its social concomitant of an institutionalized religion and a stratified society. But, also like Montaigne and Shakespeare, he undermines that religious framework in numerous ways in a work that is ultimately about how one lives with his own values. *Don Quixote* is, among other things, one of the grandest treatments of the idea of the relativity of sanity, of the difficulty of defining madness. For, in one sense, the Don is out of step with the mores of his society and therefore seems unhinged. In another sense, he embodies the ideals that people pay lip service to but blithely ignore in their quotidian lives.

The epistemological theme comes up in various other ways. The barber who insists that what the Don wears is not Mambrino's helmet but a barber's basin finds himself outvoted by the others present. Unbeknownst to him, they are merely humoring the Don, but that leaves the poor barber disoriented, isolated, and wondering about his own sanity. In an inn, the Don's fantasies about invisible, malicious enchanters bring about such a pandemonium that Sancho begins to wonder if the Don is not right after all about the existence and malevolence of such creatures. In another scene, the Don confesses revealingly that if he did not believe that enchanters worked against him he would have to see himself as a dolt and a coward; in other words, man needs (as Bacon observed) to live by lies. Above all, in one scene the Don makes the ambiguous but pregnant agreement with Sancho that he will respect Sancho's account of his trip on the magic flying horse if Sancho will respect the Don's account of what he saw in the Cave of Montesinos. All these vignettes dramatize the idea that what we know is a matter of perspective, consensus, environment, not of objective fact, and that what we think, for good subjective reasons of our own, to be so is not what is actually out there. In this uncertain world, therefore, civilization rests on mutual tolerance. The numerous epistemological riddles rotate around the central one. Who is mad? Who is closer to reality—the idealistic, fanatical, ludicrous, grotesque, unforgettable Don, or the worldly wise, passive, forgettable normal people with their everyday routines and assumptions? Never has the epistemological question been posed so pervasively, dramatically, at once comically and poignantly.

Even a story within the story, "The Too Curious One," sheds light on a corner of that theme by raising the question of which is the true person, the wife who has been faithful in the normal course of life or the same wife who, tempted and nagged by the machinations of the foolishly worried husband, finally succumbs to the blandishments of the friend the husband has been urging on in the interest of testing her virtue? Is the essence of a person what he/she is in daily life or what he/she has the potential of doing—and actually does under the duress of an extreme situation?

Like Cervantes, Molière deals with monomaniacs, and *Le misanthrope* (*The Misanthropist*, play, 1666) raises the now familiar question as to who is in contact with reality—the fanatical, idealistic, quixotic Alceste or his extraverted sweetheart Célimène and his *raisonneur* friend Philinte? The epistemological theme is, however, sounded boldly and clearly in *Tartuffe* (play, 1664). Everyone in Orgon's family, except Orgon himself and his mother, knows that Tartuffe is a hypocrite and swindler. The audience, granted a God-like certainty about the situation, can better see how human beings fool themselves—Orgon in this case, and the audience itself on all matters other than the one under discussion on stage. This is a French and comic version of the issues raised in Shakespeare's three major tragedies. We watch the floundering of a man in possession of the wrong interpretation of the facts. Family members inform him of his error; he is too smart to let mere words separate him from his convictions. To account for the apparent slander of the good man Tartuffe, he imputes envy, guilty conscience, vindictiveness to the others. And he is right up to a point, for such sordid motives often cause people, even "good" ones, to calumny someone innocent.

Since words based on mere intuition are not good enough for Orgon, the son comes up with some facts that prove to everyone's satisfaction that Tartuffe is duplicitous. Bur Orgon, having begun with the assumption of Tartuffe's piety, as Othello does with Iago's honesty, can blithely dismiss such alleged facts as the distortions of others, since he did not witness anything himself. It is easier for him to disinherit his son (or for Othello to cast off his wife, and Lear his daughter) than believe a story that would take away the comfort of the intellectually familiar, of being right, of having an unimpaired judgment. To believe the son would mean nothing less than having to start all over again the complicated process of locating oneself in the universe.

His arrogant dismissal of his son shows that he must be made to perceive with his own senses. So the shrewd servant Dorine arranges affairs in such a way that Orgon will witness Tartuffe misbehaving and, at that, toward Orgon's own wife. The upshot is an extreme situation, the only kind by which he could be jolted into reality, one in which he has to choose between believing his eyes or having his wife virtually raped. It takes indeed a long time for him to bestir himself, as if at first he is as willing to distrust his senses as he had been Dorine and his son. But finally his love of his wife overcomes his delusions about Tartuffe. The story would seem to be over, but now comes an added comic twist. Orgon's mother refuses to believe *her* newly enlightened son just as he, Orgon, has before refused to believe his. Her position is the same as his had been; she has not seen Tartuffe misbehave and can therefore, as he did earlier, dismiss all evidence as hearsay, can now rather believe Orgon to be a party to, or a dupe of, a conspiracy than that she herself had erred. It is as keen and comic a parable of the epistemological problem as *Don Quixote*, but in more compact form.

The Eighteenth Century to Modern Period

Eighteenth- and nineteenth-century literature is not as stimulating on this theme as had been that of the seventeenth century. Sterne's novel *Tristram Shandy* (1759–1767) is perhaps more mystification than exploration of the subject. The detective or murder story, as seen in high literature in Poe, Dickens, Dostoevski, raises the question only to dispose of it tidily. But in a twentieth century abounding in skepticism, relativism, and lack of religious faith, the epistemological theme becomes crucial. Isabel Archer in Henry James' novel *The Portrait of a Lady* (1881) discovers that culture, refinement, and manners may go with moral hollowness. In the novel *Washington Square* (1881), James takes the age-old situation of a father and daughter at odds over her choice of husband and gives it an ironic twist. The man chosen turns out to be a scoundrel; the father is thereby vindicated and yet, though right, is shown to be inhumane, and the daughter, though technically wrong, is sympathetic. This suggests that merely being correct as to the facts is not the whole story. Similarly, in Ibsen's *Vildanden* (*The Wild Duck*, play, 1884) Gregers Werle is technically correct in imparting the truth to Hjalmar about the latter's wife and daughter but in a broader context is adjudged destructive and mean-spirited in the way in which he misuses the truth. Dr. Stockman (*En folkefiende* [*An Enemy of the People*, play, 1882]) is in the Quixote- and Alceste-like position of telling the truth and incurring the wrath of the community. He also appears somewhat ludicrous, pugnacious, self-centered, naïve, and irresponsible. These works imply that the truth has its own psychology and politics. Modern literature in fact tends to dismiss the Christian idea that the truth shall make one free; it shows man needing illusion for survival. Illusion, that is, or pluralism. If Milton, in his mid-seventeenth-century prose pamphlets argued for freedom of expression for all Protestant sects because of the absence of an objective, definitive Christian reading of the Bible, J. S. Mill (*On Liberty*, essay, 1859) calls for a toleration of even the most outrageous propositions and private personal conduct because modern man confronts the elusiveness of the truth on most, perhaps all, questions, not merely exegetical ones.

Private personal conduct is indeed at issue in Henry James's novel *The Ambassadors* (1903). Lambert Strethers goes to Paris to free the Newsome lad from the clutches of a femme fatale and bring him back to his good senses, family responsibilities, and righteous living in Massachusetts. A brief stay in Paris and some glimpses of the young man, his lady, and his milieu, however, are enough to throw all of Strether's New England Puritan values into question. How can he ever explain that change to the folks back home, for will they not see him as Pentheus sees Cadmus, Orgon sees his son, and Orgon's mother later sees Orgon?

Proust's Swann (*Du côté de chez Swann* [*Swann's Way*, novel, 1913]) finds himself in an emotional hell as he falls in love with a woman whose heart he cannot read and whose past he cannot know. Doubts, rumors, and insinuations hound him; he imagines the worst things; he wishes he were terminally ill or dead. Then when he finally seems to find out the truth, his love appears to have waned—and he marries her! The normal assumption is that love and marriage go together and that both rest on a foundation of truth; Proust's point is that all three have little to do with one another. Swann's love, moreover, is a paradigm of the loves of Marcel, first for Gilberte and then for Albertine, and the theme running through all of them is that it is impossible for the lover, trapped in the isolation of the ego, to fully know the beloved, to possess her heart.

If love in modern literature becomes increasingly enigmatic, corrosive, or elusive, literary surveys of the state of modern knowledge are hardly more encouraging. The protagonists of Flaubert's *Bouvard et Pécuchet* (*Bouvard and Pécuchet*, novel, 1881) throw themselves into one discipline after another, only to be disillusioned by contradictions and uncertainties among the experts. In Mann's novel *Der Zauberberg* (*The Magic Mountain*, 1924), modern medicine, like its earlier counterparts in the writings of Montaigne and Molière, seems to know much and understand little, while the long, often heated debates between the liberal, rational, optimistic Settembrini and the reactionary Naphta over the meaning and direction of history are inconclusive, being transcended by the arrival of the "vitalist" Peeperkorn, the suicide of Naphta, and the outbreak of World War I.

The one modern writer to make the epistemological theme the very center of his plays is Luigi Pirandello. In *Enrico IV* (1922) a nobleman acting in a play within a play has an accident and thinks himself to be actually the medieval monarch he had pretended to be. As in *Don Quixote* the reader's conventional assumptions about what is sane and what is the true self are under challenge here. *Sei personaggi in cerca d'autore* (*Six Characters in Search of an Author*, 1921) raises the question as to who is more real—the fleshy, mortal person (like those constituting the audience) or the disembodied fictional but immortal character in a work of literature. The most telling presentation of the theme is in *Così è, se vi pare* (*It Is So, If You Think So*, 1917). A man and his mother-in-law give conflicting stories of what happened between them. The townspeople eagerly set out to find out who is telling the truth; only the choral character Laudisi sits back and laughs at their futile quest. Each act ends with the evidence amassed only to have it dispersed again, against the background of Laudisi's laughter. At the climax of the play, the answer appears in the form of a veiled woman, a somewhat crude symbol for the elusive truth and a dramatic version of Frost's epigram, "We dance round in a ring and suppose, / But the Secret sits in the middle and knows." The difficulty of choosing among divergent versions of the same event is at the heart of Akutagawa Ryūnosuke's stories, "Yabu no naka" ("In a Grove," 1921) and "Rashōmon" (1915), and Lawrence Durrell's *Alexandria Quartet* (1957–1961).

The epistemological problem is as much political as psychological. Orwell's novel *1984* (1949), initially about modern totalitarianism, turns finally into a dramatization of the notion that what is the truth depends on what one assumes and that what one assumes depends on conditioning. Our assumptions are like fingers desperately holding onto the window ledge of a part of reality, which we hope is the main or saving part. Brainwashing, which (like education) consists of replacing one set of assumptions with another, is someone kicking at the fingers and prying them loose. There being no definite Truth or revealed religion, only many contending truths and religions, the modern totalitarian state steps into the vacuum and provides bearings by issuing metaphysical ukases. Once the state propaganda machine is accepted as an oracle, black can be made to be white, just as Tartuffe can be a saint. If in a totalitarian state, a man becomes a nonperson and is erased from the history books, he in a sense never really existed. All politics is about truth, all contentions over the truth are a form of politics; belief and unbelief determine not only religious faith but also good citizenship and treason.

In various modern works, a central detail is left deliberately nebulous as if to dramatize the idea that human beings act on the basis of surmises rather than facts. What was Raskolnikov's motive (*Prestuplenie i nakazanie* [*Crime and Punishment*, novel, 1866]) in killing the pawnbroker? Motives are, Dostoevsky seems to say, beyond human understanding. Did Molly Bloom (*Ulysses*, novel, 1922) have affairs with dozens of Dubliners, both prominent and obscure, as her husband thinks, or is the affair with Blazes Boylan a first? In Kafka's *Das Schloss* (*The Castle*, novel, 1926), K. claims to be a Land Surveyor, but whether that is a fact, a fabrication, or an aspiration is never made clear. Was Albertine (Proust's novel *A la recherche du temps perdu* [*Remembrance of Things Past*, 1913–1927]) enmeshed in lesbian relationships, or do Marcel's endless speculations on the matter spring from his own neuroses? (In fact, this uncertainty is only a salient example of the larger Proustian principle that all "other" people are—like indeed the self—fragmented and beyond understanding, "possession," or integration.) Did Faulkner's Joe Christmas (*Light in August*, novel, 1932) have black blood in him? Everyone acts as if he did, though the facts are deliberately left shrouded; if everyone thought he did, it is as if he did. Similarly, the protagonist of Max Frisch's *Andorra* (play, 1962) was not Jewish; yet people thought he was (for adventitious reasons), found supposedly genetic Jewish traits in him, and he began to act Jewish and suffered a Jew's martyrdom. A host of issues are left unresolved in Ibsen's *Bygmester Solness* (*The Master Builder*, play, 1892).

Ionesco's *Le rhinocéros* (*Rhinoceros*, play, 1960) is, consciously or not, an updating of Euripides' *The Bacchants*. An allegory of moral epidemics— perhaps fascism was in the author's mind, but the subject could as well be communism, early Christianity or Islam, witch hunting, or the latest fad—it shows how at first only a few persons opt for the new. They are considered by the others as deluded and foolish; then, when conversions accelerate, people begin to view the converts as noble souls ahead of their time. Soon the people left in human form are few, isolated, and perturbed. Ionesco takes sides—the rhinoceros is a peculiarly ugly, stupid animal, and Bérenger, the last human being, has his dignity—in a way that Euripides and other writers do not. But that only makes him the more pessimistic when he portrays the way in which people persuade themselves that they are doing the right thing. The audience may know that they are wrong, but they themselves do not, and, insofar as they represent what all too often in history has been the majority of mankind, they dramatize the fact that the truth is elusive still and that epistemology is a problem remaining untouched by the knowledge explosion and the march of science.

See also: Anti-Intellectualism, Reason, Science.

Selected Bibliography

Glicksberg, C. I. *The Literature of Nihilism*. Lewisburg: Bucknell University Press, 1975.
————. *Modern Literary Perspectivism*. Dallas: Southern Methodist University Press, 1970.
Kurrik, M. J. *Literature and Negation*. New York: Columbia University Press, 1979.
Spitzer, Leo. "Linguistic Perspectivism in the 'Don Quixote'." In *Linguistics and Literary History*. Princeton, N.J.: Princeton University Press, 1948.

MANFRED WEIDHORN

ESCAPE

The theme of escape can have many different kinds of implications in literary works. In its simplest sense, the term refers to the act of eluding or getting away from danger, pursuit, captivity, or other immediately threatening circumstances. This kind of escape occurs frequently in suspense and adventure narratives as well as in more serious literature. Another type of escape is departure from a situation, such as a family, a job, a community, or a country, that has become in some way oppressive or intolerable. Escape can also be psychological or spiritual in nature and can take the form of daydream, fantasy, or some other mental activity that provides relief from inner conflict, anxiety, guilt, or from uncongenial external circumstances when physical escape is not feasible. The significance of an escape can be positive, negative, or ambiguous. In some contexts, an escape is seen as admirable, as evidence of a character's courage, skill, or self-realization; in other contexts, it takes on connotations of evasiveness or escapism and indicates weakness, cowardice, dehumanization, or failure to cope with reality. Escape recurs frequently as a plot element in literature of all periods, but it is most common as a major theme in the nineteenth and twentieth centuries, particularly in times of social upheaval and transition.

Antiquity and the Middle Ages

Escape has been an important plot device as long as mankind has enjoyed exciting, suspenseful narratives, and escapes from danger or imprisonment are commonplace in mythology and folklore. The nature and significance of an escape can reflect the prevailing beliefs or attitudes of a particular era. In ancient literature, escape is usually treated on a physical rather than a psychological level. Ancient man viewed his universe as perilous and insecure; his welfare was dependent on the benevolence of unpredictable and mysterious supernatural forces. A successful escape was often seen as the result of divine favor or intervention as well as the heroic capabilities of the escaping individual or group. Failure to escape could result from divine antipathy or a predestined fate or curse. Several escapes recounted in the Old Testament are manifestations of God's will toward His people. Noah is chosen to escape the flood in order to begin a new, less corrupt race of men, and the Israelites escape bondage in Egypt because they are God's chosen people and He has promised them a homeland.

Ancient Greek literature often attributes an escape to the intervention of a god or goddess and/or to the extraordinary traits of the hero. Homer's epics (c. 8th century B.C.) contain numerous escapes, either from death in battle (*Ilias* [*Iliad*]) or from other kinds of danger (*Odysseia* [Odyssey]). Odysseus is particularly adept at escaping from difficult situations, as in the Cyclops and Circe episodes. His escapes are evidence of Athena's favor toward him and of his own shrewd and wily nature, which distinguishes him from other Greek heroes. In contrast to *The Odyssey*, Virgil's epic poem *Aeneis* (*Aeneid*, 19 B.C.) illustrates the Roman ideal of sacrificing personal gratification for duty and service to the state. Aeneas escapes from the fall of Troy and from Dido's love so that he may fulfill his destiny as founder of the Latin race.

Greek tragic drama powerfully embodies the concept of predestination, and characters such as Oedipus often try heroically but unsuccessfully to escape their fate. A successful escape is dramatized in Aeschylus' *Hiketides* (*The Suppliants*, 463 B.C.), which concerns the flight of the fifty virgin daughters of Danaos from Egypt to Argos to avoid marriage with their fifty violently lustful cousins. In deciding whether to offer them protection, the people of Argos must face a conflict between divine and secular retribution—a dilemma characteristic of the ancient Greek consciousness. A parallel is also drawn between divine and human affairs, as the suppliants see a resemblance between their escape and the escape of the goddess Io from Hera's jealous torments. Escape from marriage and sexuality was to become a fairly common version of the escape theme in later literature.

Because medieval man viewed the world according to fixed and ineluctable Christian doctrines, escape seldom occurs as a major theme in this period. Earthly suffering was seen as preparation for the afterlife, and men were expected to resign themselves to their lot rather than to seek escape. Escapes from danger do occur fairly often in the chivalric romances, which were the adventure stories of the day. According to the chivalric code, a knight's ability to escape from adversaries, monsters, dungeons, and other challenges was an outcome of the testing process that proved his worthiness. Escapes are also common in the animal fables or romances, such as the *Roman de Renard* (*Romance of Reynard*, 12–14th century) and Chaucer's "Nun's Priest's Tale" in *The Canterbury Tales* (c. 1380–1400). In these stories, the escape proves the animal's cleverness at outwitting his captor and often conveys a moral lesson as well. Some of the major medieval story collections incorporate escape into the narrative framework, so that the escape becomes the occasion for the storytelling. In Boccacio's *Il decamerone* (*Decameron*, novellas, c. 1350), for example, the storytellers have withdrawn from Florence to the country to escape the Black Death.

The Renaissance and Seventeenth Century

In the Renaissance and seventeenth century, escape continues to be a relatively minor theme. The inspiring rediscovery of secular life and of the potential and dignity of man brought a determination to live as fully and heartily as possible, and in such an atmosphere escape was not an urgent preoccupation. During this period the chivalric romance evolved into more sophisticated forms in which escape is still a common plot device. Two very different forms of this development can be seen in Spenser's epic poem *The Faerie Queene* (1590–1596) and Cervantes' novel *Don Quijote* (*Don Quixote*, 1605, 1615). Spenser uses the chivalric world of knights and marvels to depict in idealized form the deepest conflicts of the human mind, between good and evil, order and disorder. The escapes from enemies or beasts often represent the precarious and temporary triumph of virtue or inner strength over forces of chaos and negation. In *Don Quixote*, Cervantes parodies the chivalric romances by placing them in the context of contemporary life. Don Quixote is an ambiguous figure as he escapes from his home to pursue his chivalric quest and extricates himself with irrepressible determination from his many mistakes and follies; he is at the same time an absurd lunatic and an idealist trying to better a corrupt world.

The escape theme is occasionally prominent in Renaissance and seventeenth-century drama, for example, in Lope de Vega's *Los locos de Valencia* (*The Madmen of Valencia*, 1620). Perhaps the most substantial treatment of the theme occurs in Shakespeare's play *The Tempest* (1611). Prospero has escaped his brother's treachery to find refuge on his island; he in turn arranges for his brother and friends to escape from an illusory shipwreck, and he manipulates the survivors in order to punish them for past wrongs, to test their worth, or to bring out their better selves. Prospero's world of magic is like the world of art, where fantasy and illusion lead to a deeper understanding of the truth. The illusory experience of escape provides a second chance or new opportunity for the characters to right some wrongs and restore order and harmony to their lives.

The religious literature of the seventeenth century depicts the conflict between virtue and sin, belief and doubt, in a more dynamic and intense way than medieval literature does. Personal faith becomes more important than doctrine, and escape from doubt and temptation is often achieved only after a long, difficult struggle. Bunyan's *The Pilgrim's Progress* (prose allegory, 1678–1684) treats escape in a manner that typifies the religious allegory of the period. Christian's flight from the City of Destruction and his escapes from various allegorized traps and obstacles on his journey are carried out in a mood of uncertainty and discouragement; his success at escaping evil and achieving salvation comes only after a protracted effort.

The Eighteenth Century

During the Enlightenment, escape usually serves a rational rather than an emotional or spiritual function. Escapes are often used as elements of satire and social commentary. Marvelous or implausible escapes help to establish an ironic contrast between fantasy and reality in prose satires such as Swift's *Gulliver's Travels* (1726) and Voltaire's *Candide* (1759). Both works parody the travelogue or exotic adventure narrative that was a popular genre in the seventeenth and eighteenth centuries. Gulliver's escapes from the various lands he visits are important devices in the narrative framework, as they enable him to survive and continue his travels. The pseudo-scientific tone in which highly implausible escapes are narrated contributes to Swift's irony. The circumstances of the escapes often demonstrate a point about human folly or treachery, as when Gulliver's own men mutiny against him at the beginning of book 4. Escape gradually takes on more realistic, negative connotations as it becomes increasingly evident that Gulliver is a malcontented escapist, unable to stay at home for long or commit himself to anything. By the end of book 4 he has become a bitter misogynist who escapes from the company of his wife and children to pass his time in the stable. The escapes in *Candide* are usually marvellous or magical in nature and are related to the characters' miraculous recoveries from serious injury and the coincidental meetings with long-lost friends. By giving his work a fantastic quality, Voltaire satirizes the optimistic reliance on reason in the philosophy of Leibniz and others; he draws an ironic contrast between the resilient fairy-tale world and the painful real world, where escape and recovery are not always possible.

Escapes in the eighteenth-century novel are usually more realistic than in the prose satires, though they are still sometimes implausible. Typical novels of the period, such as Defoe's *Moll Flanders* (1722) and Fielding's *Tom Jones* (1749), relate a long series of adventures and predicaments from which the protagonists must escape. In both novels, the protagonists are at odds with society, and their often-comical escapes provide opportunities for satire or commentary on various aspects of contemporary life. Moll Flanders' adeptness at evading capture and confinement for her criminal acts is evidence of her shrewd, amoral, opportunistic nature and her powerful survival instinct; she is a product of the class distinctions and injustices of her society. Tom Jones and Sophia escape from the bleak conventional prospects their families plan for them and then must escape from amorous snares and other dangers before Tom receives his rightful inheritance and they can rejoin society in triumph. They are admirable for their strong determination in resisting and escaping from inimical social conventions.

The Nineteenth Century

Beginning with the romantic movement, escape becomes a much more significant and persistent literary theme. The romantic preoccupation with emotion, the inner light of imagination, and contact with nature was accompanied by increasing alienation from society and a consequent need to escape for self-realization or renewal. Escapes take a variety of forms during this period: escape into nature and solitude; escape through voyages to mysterious, exotic lands; escape into an imaginary world. The romantic hero was typically seen as emotionally intense and weighed down by inner conflict. Escape filled a primarily emotional rather than rational need, and it was often precipitated by a longing for peace. Chateaubriand's *René* (novel, 1802) describes the continual efforts of a romantic hero to escape through travel and solitude from society, from his own sadness, and from his incestuous feelings for his sister. René's exotic voyages bear some resemblance to voyages in earlier works, but he differs from earlier adventurers in his emotional intensity, personal anguish, and responsiveness to nature. As a virtuous man in an evil world, he is engaged in a religious quest, but a much more subjective and individualized one than that of Christian in *Pilgrim's Progress*. He finally escapes from European society completely to live with the Indians in America. *René* had a widespread influence on romantic writers in France and elsewhere. George Sand's *Consuelo* (1842–1843), for example, is a highly romantic novel describing a talented young opera singer who is innocent and pure in heart, like René, and who flees the immoral life in Venice, where she has been exploited and betrayed, to begin a new life in Austria.

English Romantic poetry expresses in a number of ways the longing to escape: for example, escape through exotic travel in such poems as Coleridge's "The Rime of the Ancient Mariner" (1798) and Byron's *Don Juan* (1819–1824); escape from the pain of mortality into an immortal world of the imagination in Keats' "Ode to a Nightingale" and "The Eve of St. Agnes" (1820). Many English novels of the period were influenced by Gothic literature, which describes nightmarish efforts to escape from gloomy castles or from pursuit by a mysterious enemy. Charlotte Brontë's *Jane Eyre* (1847) contains many melodramatic and Gothic elements. Jane must escape from the dark secret in Mr. Rochester's house, and later he barely escapes from the house as it burns. Brontë goes beyond the Gothic tradition, however, by using the escapes as stimuli for her characters' emotional and psychological growth.

The escape theme is especially prominent in the American Romantic movement and in later American literature. A pattern of escape is an integral part of American culture, as seen in our tradition of moving on to a new territory or frontier when life becomes too difficult or burdensome. Thoreau's escape from a society he viewed as materialistic and inequitable to Walden Pond, described in *Walden* (essays, 1854), exemplifies the romantic ideal of solitude in communion with nature and at the same time exemplifies the "Yankee" spirit of independence and self-sufficiency. A similar spirit of confidence and optimism is expressed in the poetry of Walt Whitman. "Song of the Open Road" (1856), for example, invites the reader to escape from the evils of society and to share in the life of the open road, symbolic of freedom, openness to new experience, and a democratic comradeship with people of all races and classes. Escapes are also abundant in American fiction of the period. The Gothic/suspense genre is continued in the stories of Poe. Terrifying escapes from danger are recounted in stories such as "A Descent into the Maelström" (1841) and "The Fall of the House of Usher" (1839). Escapes are important occurrences in the sea narratives of Melville. They often carry a moral significance, as in "Benito Cereno" (1856), a harrowing story about the mutiny of a cargo of slaves against a white captain and crew and their subsequent escape. Melville's treatment of the situation probes the potential for evil in the white men as well as the black. Poe and Melville explore the dark side of the human mind and are consequently more pessimistic than Thoreau and Whitman; in their work the escapes, though ostensibly successful, are often followed by lasting nightmarish memories of the event.

Many of the great realistic novels of the later nineteenth century contain escapes as plot elements, and in some the escape theme acquires considerable significance. In this period escape is often a consequence of the repressiveness in Victorian society. Such factors as a rigid class structure, smug materialism, exploitation of the poor, sexual prudery and discrimination, and religious and racial intolerance created strong pressures to escape among various kinds of people. The urgent need to escape results sometimes in healthy self-fulfillment, but at other times in moral bewilderment, self-deception, and despair. Among the most noteworthy treatments of the escape theme in English fiction is Dickens' *Great Expectations* (1860–1861). Despite the realistic mode, the plot has many features in common with the mystery story and fairy tale, and it includes several kinds of physical and psychological escape that parallel or counterpoint each other: the escape of the convict at the beginning that haunts the imagination of young Pip; Miss Havisham's escape from reality and human involvement to the sterile fantasy of her wedding-day; Pip's escape from his humble origins to a life of social climbing and dissipation. A reversal occurs when Pip makes the humiliating discovery that the convict is his unknown benefactor, and he risks death to help him escape again. Pip is restored to his better self, but he cannot return to his former simple existence, and he finally flees from England for a long period of exile. What Pip ultimately escapes from is surrender to the false, corrupting, and exploitative values of Victorian society.

Escapes draw attention to the faults of American society in Mark Twain's masterpiece, *The Adventures of Huckleberry Finn* (1884). Huck's escape from his father's abuse and Jim's escape from slavery bring them together for a dramatic series of adventures as they travel down the Mississippi River. Many successful escapes occur along the way, from criminals, feuding families, con men, and other such representatives of American life. Huck exhibits characteristically American quick-wittedness and self-reliance in planning the escapes. An ironic contrast is established between the real comradeship that Huck and Jim have shared through their common experiences of danger, and the unintentional cruelty in Tom Sawyer's bookish romantic game of pretending to help Jim escape from captivity. Huck's final escape is to the "territory," away from "civilization" and everything it represents.

Similar kinds of escape recur in Russian and European novels of the period. Escape from capture or imprisonment is a persistent theme in the work of Dostoevsky. His autobiographical account of his own prison experience, *Zapiski iz mërtvogo doma* (*Memoirs from the House of the Dead*, 1860–1862), describes the convicts' dream of escape and an actual escape attempt. In *Prestuplenie i nakazanie* (*Crime and Punishment*, 1866), Raskolnikov tries to escape the legal consequences of murdering an old woman, but he cannot escape the psychological burden of guilt, and he is finally compelled to confess. Dostoevsky suggests that suffering and atonement are necessary stages in the soul's quest for peace. Tolstoy's *Anna Karenina* (1877) narrates the effects of the two protagonists, Anna and Levin, to escape from the destructive influence of Russian upper-class society. Anna seeks escape from her loveless marriage through her affair with Vronsky, but the censoriousness of her social circle and her own guilt destroy her moral fiber. Levin escapes the extravagance and superficiality of urban high society by living simply, like a peasant, on his country estate, rediscovering the joy of hard work and contact with nature.

One of the greatest Spanish novels of the century, Pereda's *Peñas arriba* (*The Upper Peaks*, 1893), also treats the common nineteenth-century theme of escape from the city to the country. Like Tolstoy, Pereda views the simplicity of country life as an antidote to the evils of urban civilization. When the protagonist Marcelo leaves Madrid to live with his uncle on a mountain farm, he is at first contemptuous of country life but gradually becomes attached to it. After his uncle's death he takes over his leadership role in the community. His escape to the country restores his idealism and his faith in himself. The novel contains some Gothic elements; Marcelo undergoes several narrow escapes from danger, which demonstrate his courage and resourcefulness, his worthiness to be a leader.

The realistic drama of the late nineteenth century treats the escape theme in ways similar to its treatment in fiction. Several important plays of the 1880s and 1890s dramatize the conflict between the demands of society for conformity and respectability and the individual's need to break free of the social mold in order to fulfill himself. The note of rebellion was sounded in Ibsen's *Et dukkehjem* (*A Doll's House*, 1879), which challenged Victorian assumptions about the role of women in marriage. Nora's controversial decision to walk out on her husband and children rather than conform to his view of her as a helpless, irresponsible "doll," was a seminal event in the development of modern literature. Shaw's *Arms and the Man* (1894) challenges cherished assumptions about patriotic duty and heriosm in war in its satirical portrayal of a soldier who escapes from the enemy by hiding in a young woman's bedroom.

The Twentieth Century

The escape theme is perhaps more characteristic of the modern period than any earlier one. The early decades of this century, and especially the World War I years, brought profound and radical alterations in man's view of himself and his relationship to his world. The severe alienation of individuals from a universe perceived as relativistic and absurd and the social disorder and anarchy resulting from the loss of communal values caused an intensified, sometimes desperate, need for escape. The theme recurs with particular frequency during the 1920s and 1930s. This was the era of the "lost generation," a generation of young writers from several countries who were deeply disillusioned by their experiences during World War I and embittered toward society after the war. Many rejected all social involvement and spent long periods in exile.

Twentieth-century poets were strongly influenced by the French Symbolist poets of the late nineteenth century, whose poetry often provided escape into exotic fantasy worlds created by an innovative use of images and symbols. Two of the major modern poets, Yeats and Eliot, reflect the influence of the Symbolists but treat the escape theme in highly individualized ways. Yeats' early poetry often exhibits a tendency toward escapism. Like Keats, he expresses a longing to escape from the pain of mortality into an imaginary world: typically, the fairyland of Celtic mythology. This conflict is found in an early play, *The Land of Heart's Desire* (1894), about a young wife's decision to leave her husband and live with the fairies, as well as in poems such as "The Wanderings of Oisin" (1889) and "The Man Who Dreamed of Faeryland" (1893). In his later poetry the impulse to escape is still powerful, but it is counterbalanced by a more vigorous confrontation of social and personal realities. In many poems the impulse to escape is overcome after a struggle—for example, "A Dialogue of Self and Soul" (1933)—but occasionally escape is seen as the more desirable alternative, as in "Sailing to Byzantium" (1927). Eliot creates in some of his poems personae who surrender to their escapist temperaments; they symbolize the emotional and spiritual poverty of modern man. The male speakers in both "The Love Song of J. Alfred Prufrock" and "Portrait of a Lady" (1917) seek escape from amorous involvements with society women. Prufrock escapes to a subjective fantasy world, and the young man in the latter poem flees abroad. They are escaping not only from a society they perceive as superficial and hollow, but from their own self-doubts as well.

A considerable number of modern stories and novels are concerned in some way with escape. Many of these belong to the category of light adventure stories—detective and spy fiction, for example—but the theme also recurs in serious fiction from many countries. Throughout the century there has been a proliferation of novels about individuals who abandon their family and business obligations to "find" themselves; for example, Wells' *The History of Mr. Polly* (1910); Giraudoux' *Aventures de Jérôme Bardini* (*The Adventures of Jerome Bardini*, 1930); and Simenon's *La fuite de Monsieur Monde* (*The Flight of Mr. Monde*, 1946).

The national literature in which the escape theme is most prominent is probably the Irish. Since the mid-nineteenth century emigration has been a major factor in Irish life, and in the early twentieth century circumstances such as fanatical nationalism, repressive and puritanical religion, and social intolerance and anti-intellectualism created strong pressures to escape. The most outstanding Irish treatment of the theme occurs in Joyce's autobiographical novel *A Portrait of the Artist as a Young Man* (1916). The protagonist, Stephen Dedalus, decides to flee Ireland for Paris, to escape the stifling forces or "nets" in Irish society that would prevent his full development as an artist: family life, religion, and nationalism. Personal, subjective values take precedence over social obligation and involvement, because Irish society is regarded as moribund and absurd.

Similar disillusionment and preoccupation with escape are expressed in the fiction of the twenties, thirties, and forties, most notably in the stories of Frank O'Connor and Seán O'Faoláin.

A modern English novel that clearly delineates the forces impelling escape is Lawrence's *Kangaroo* (1923), an autobiographical work about a nomadic writer who settles for a while in Australia. As he reflects on the war years in England, it becomes clear why he left the country in disgust; he and his wife came under heavy suspicion and were harassed by the draft board and others because of his wife's German nationality. They were finally driven by local officials from a country home that they loved. His disillusionment is so deep that he refuses to become involved with any social causes, and he leaves Australia to avoid being caught up in local political conflicts. Like many writers of his generation, he chooses a life of wandering in order to dedicate himself fully to his writing, the only activity that has meaning for him.

Escape and exile is also the protagonist's choice in many American "lost generation" novels. Perhaps the most representative is Hemingway's *A Farewell to Arms* (1929). A recurrent pattern of escape is integral to the plot, which incorporates several dramatic and suspenseful escapes from danger or pursuit, as well as escape in a broader sense. Frederick Henry has left American society, which he finds uncongenial, to serve in the Italian army during the war; he flees from his own comrades, who, made desperate by defeat, turn against him because he is a foreigner. He becomes increasingly more isolated while he evades capture as a deserter and finally flees in a small boat to Switzerland with his beloved Catherine. Her death in childbirth leaves him confused and alone; he has followed a pattern of flight from society and from the war and has tried to live only for love, but human vulnerability has deprived him of even this consolation. Another common American theme, escape from the boredom and narrowness of provincial life, is exemplified in two short-story collections, Anderson's *Winesburg, Ohio* (1919) and Wescott's *Goodbye, Wisconsin* (1928).

The theme of escape from provincialism is also developed in a novel of modern Italy, Silone's *Il seme sotto la neve* (*The Seed Beneath the Snow*, 1940). Pietro, the grandson of the matriarch of a once-prominent family in a provincial town, has had to flee abroad to escape the authorities because of his radical political views. He has secretly returned to hide in his grandmother's house but flees a second time to help a deaf peasant friend and finally surrenders himself to save his friend from a murder charge. Pietro is portrayed as an innocent, Christ-like figure in conflict with the jealousy, maliciousness, and greed of Italian provincial life. More committed than many modern protagonists, he believes in brotherhood between people of all classes and exemplifies the Christian ideal of losing oneself in order to find oneself.

French novelists of the postwar generation were significantly influenced by Gide, in novels such as *Les nourritures terrestres* (*The Earthly Livelihoods*,

1897). His rejection of tradition and nationalism for a life of wandering and an attitude of receptiveness to new ideas, his idealization of personal sincerity over social involvement, appealed to a generation that was disillusioned by the futile sacrifice of the war. Drieu la Rochelle's *Drôle de voyage* (*The Travelling Scoundrel*, 1933) portrays a Gidean hero who flees his engagement to a wealthy woman and becomes a kind of Don Juan, moving from one amorous involvement to another. What he is actually trying to escape is the decadence of modern society, manifest in such symptoms as sexual perversion, overintellectualism, and the decadence within himself. He undergoes the characteristically modern conflict between a desire to commit himself and a fear of doing so.

Modern drama deals with escape in sometimes traditional, sometimes innovative ways. A humorous, fairly traditional treatment can be found in Galsworthy's play *Escape* (1926). The escape of a well-bred gentleman from Dartmoor Prison, where he has been wrongfully confined, leads to encounters with several different types of English citizens, most of whom take the side of the dashing, gentlemanly convict. Galsworthy lightly satirizes the romantic British attitude toward daring criminals, especially upper-class ones. As we might expect, escape is also a significant theme in modern Irish drama, where it is characteristically given a tragicomic treatment. A woman's escape from her mean-spirited husband, for example, is the subject of both Synge's *In the Shadow of the Glen* (1902) and O'Casey's *Juno and the Paycock* (1924).

Two of the best-known innovators in the European theater of the absurd, Pirandello and Anouilh, treat the escape theme in the context of somewhat hallucinatory or nightmarish situations that are often highly implausible and melodramatic. Pirandello's *Come prima, meglio di prima* (*As Before, Better Than Before*, 1920), is based on the familiar subject of escape from an unhappy marriage, but in this case the wife returns to her husband after many years of wandering in the company of various men. She pretends to be a second wife so that their pure young daughter will not be shamed, but the situation proves impossible and she leaves again. The bizarre pretense and role-playing make an implied comment on the strict Sicilian-Victorian moral code. Escape from a painful past is also the subject of Anouilh's *Le voyageur sans bagage* (*The Traveller without Baggage*, 1937), about a soldier who lost his memory during the war. After many years in an institution, he is reclaimed by his respectable family, only to learn that he was formerly a brutal and sadistic adolescent. He escapes from his family and his former self by grasping at a fictitious identity offered to him by chance, but traces of his old self are evident in him. Ahouilh raises the question of the relationship between past and present in human identity and suggests that no one can fully escape his own former personality.

See also: Alienation, Arcadia, Marriage.

Selected Bibliography

Bluefarb, Sam. *The Escape Motif in the American Novel*. Columbus: Ohio State University
    Press, 1972.

DEBORAH M. AVERILL

EVIL

Broadly speaking, evil is simply the difference between the way one wishes the
world to be and the way the world is. The vision of the ideal world will vary
from person to person, but the sense of a large discrepancy is universal. The
philosopher's "problem of evil" arises from the unwillingness to accept evil as
a salient and permanent part of life and the consequent attempt to theorize as to
its origin and possible elimination. The problem becomes particularly acute for
exponents of the Judeo-Christian tradition. How can a God who is both omnipotent and benevolent create a world in which evil exists? If He is all-powerful,
He should be able to prevent the evil (and if evil creeps in from without, for
example, from Satan, then He is not omnipotent); and if He is all-merciful, He
would want to prevent evil. Standard replies about evil being needed as a foil
for good or as a test of man merely beg the question of why God could not have
achieved these goals more painlessly.

Three, and only three, sources of evil exist. (1) Evil may come from the
cosmos, from an adverse deity, from Satan and his demons, from miscellaneous
natural and supernatural forces. Such a view was widely held by primitive people
imbued with a sense of a hostile universe (and by a few latter-day writers who
think God a tyrant or sadist). (2) It was replaced by the view that evil originates
in each individual, the evil in society being but the sum of its constituents. This
is basically the Christian outlook. "Original sin," the name for individual evil,
is responsible for even the adversities (earthquakes, hurricanes) springing from
nature or the sublunary world. (3) This view in turn has been in good part
replaced by the modern, secular, liberal, rationalist one, that the source of evil
is society. Man is born good or neutral but is somehow turned out bad by the
environment (schools, social institutions, rascals in power).

In speaking of evil originating in nature or the cosmos, one should keep in
mind that nature can be viewed in three different ways: as hostile (as it was by
primitive peoples); as beneficent (as it was briefly by the Romantics); and as
indifferent (as it is by modern thinkers). And in speaking of evil originating in
the individual, one should recall that it can spring from two sorts of individuals,
the fool and the knave. The fool's heart is in the right place, but he lacks
intelligence; the knave is intelligent but has no heart. The ascription of evil to
the individual need not, furthermore, entail universal condemnation; some see
men in terms of "black and white," others in terms of "shades of grey." The
first outlook (sometimes regarded as immature but widely held) divides the world

into "we" and "they," good people and bad people, friends and enemies. The second and more mature and sophisticated outlook is that there are no villains, only imperfect, sometimes pathetic, human beings. Personifications of evil have typically been Satan (= malice or gratuitous evil) and Fortuna (= chance, randomness, fate) in a cosmic context; and Caesar (= worldly power), Mammon (= wealth, avarice), and Venus (= sex, love) in a social context. Theologians and philosophers have long wrestled with the insoluble problem of evil, but it is also, at least implicitly, at the heart of all literary works—sometimes explicitly, dramatically so, especially in connection with Christian theodicy.

Antiquity

The Old Testament addresses itself almost at once to the problem of evil. The story of Adam and Eve, in the wake of the Creation, intimates that early in "history" man ruined a good thing wrought for him by God and has been suffering for it ever since. Later commentators tried to answer all sorts of philosophical questions that this story raises and, most importantly, were to associate Satan with the troublemaking serpent. That interpretation meant that evil sprang in part from within man and in part from hostile, supernatural forces at war with God; if primitive man blames evil on the gods, and civilized man on himself (whether on the individual or on society), this biblical tale therefore comes from a transitional phase. The Fall also establishes for the rest of the Bible a theocentric reading of adverse events, a direct relationship between man's actions and their fortunes. When men, or later the Israelites or their rulers, fear and obey God, they prosper; when they backslide and whore after alien gods, they suffer affliction. This theory of history, as well as the problem of evil in general, is addressed explicitly and philosophically only in the Book of Job. The protagonist, conscious of his righteousness, rejects his friends' contention that the evil he experiences is a divine retribution for his alleged wickedness. Despite all appearances to the contrary, he retains faith in the justice of God. The actual reason for his suffering—God's testing and proving of man's worth—remains unknown to Job and, by extension, to all men. Faith and Revelation is all that man has.

Homer's epic poem *Ilias* (*Iliad*, c. 8th century B.C.) shows a complex reading of the nature of evil. The gods visit tribulations upon those men who do not defer to them (as does Apollo to Agamemnon at the beginning). Yet (Achilles informs Priam) they also, though unscathed themselves, destined *all* men to suffer. The choice offered Achilles (by them or by an overarching Fate) between a long obscure life and a short glorious one suggests, as Thetis laments, "the bitterness in this best of child-bearing," the ubiquity of sorrow for even the best-endowed human being. As to particular evils, the actual schism and disaster in the Greek camp is caused by a common, unavoidable clash between two forms of authority, that based on martial prowess and battlefield accomplishments and that based on leadership and strategic oversight (also known in World War I as "Brass" vs. "Frocks"). Achilles emerges from the clash with a sense of dishonor, of shame before his peers; this arouses his anger and a need for revenge, which in turn leads to excess or hubris, overweening pride. He later admits his own responsibility for having been carried away by honeylike anger, whereas his opponent, Agamemnon, blames his own loss of temper on Zeus, Destiny, and atē.

The *Iliad* also sketches at least three ways of avoiding or overcoming evil. One passage, containing the earliest glimmer of ethical monotheism, intimates that Zeus sends adversity to those who act unjustly. Numerous passages depict sympathetically the *amor fati*—the stoic resignation, the acceptance of what is to be, including death—of the heroes, notably Achilles. And, finally the entire work portrays what has been called the principle of disguised blessings. For the schism in the Greek camp and the many Greek deaths caused by it brought about unwittingly, by luring the newly emboldened Trojans out of the citadel, the death of Hector and consequent fall of Troy. So, paradoxically, the very evil that seemed to spell disaster for the Greeks proved in fact to be the doom of Troy, and "all's well that ends well"—though at a terrible price. We have here the root of the *felix culpa* concept of Christianity, which attaches a happy ending to the grim story of man, and the strife of Agamemnon and Achilles is analogous to the stubbornness of Pharaoh and the treachery of Judas.

If the *Iliad* portrays no villains, the epic poem *Odysseia* (*Odyssey*, c. 8th century B.C.) contains the repulsive suitors. Overcoming them occupies the hero in the second half of the book. In the first half, evil originates within the hero himself. Having outwitted the Cyclops, he could not resist boasting aloud; this is understandable (and, according to Aristotle, even necessary for true revenge), but then, in the face of the Cyclops' dangerous reaction and of his crew's urging prudence on him, Odysseus (who often found anonymity a means of survival) persisted in crowing and even gave away his own real name and address. The consequence was that, in response to the Cyclops' prayer for revenge, his father Poseidon became hostile and protracted the hero's trip for years. Odysseus has taken a good thing, which defined his heroism—the desire for fame—and carried it too far. The resulting evil is met and overcome by foresight, prudence, anonymity, endurance, and a resistance to the various opportunities for opting out into forms of permanent ease.

In Aeschylus' *Oresteia* (trilogy of plays, 458 B.C.), the evil principle is the primitive *lex talionis* by which violence begets violence in an endless cycle, and suffering is the lot of man. But the work is optimistic in its portrayal of the replacement of the familial or tribal retaliation ethic by ideas of communal justice and of courtroom juries adjudicating cases and assigning impersonal punishment. Optimistic also is the consequent view that suffering leads, under the guidance of Zeus, to understanding, justice, and civilized forms of behavior. In *Promētheus desmōtēs* (*Prometheus Bound*, play, mid–5th century B.C.), human vulnerability is attended to by Prometheus' beneficent intervention, but this act only brings down on the hero the wrath of Zeus, who is aided and abetted by Force and Violence, by the "good German" Hephaistos, the trimmer Ocean, and the toady

Hermes. The ubiquity of unmerited suffering is underlined in the play's last words; in the trials of the innocent Io; in Zeus' gratuitous hatred of men and the god's enigmatic cruel ways; and by the fact that men, pitiful to start with, remain miserable after being helped by Prometheus. Though civilizing, his gifts are "too great for mortals, a thankless favor" done to a race with feeble, short, dreamlike lives. Evil is truly pervasive.

In Sophocles' play *Oidipous tyrannos* (*Oedipus Rex*, c. 429 B.C.), the hero tries to avoid his fate in every way and merely thereby fulfills it. This suggests that man has neither comprehension of the consequences of his actions (as was true in the *Iliad* also), nor ability to shape his destiny. The hero had answered a riddle, been amply rewarded for it, and established his own identity and man's identity as a rational, problem-solving, destiny-mastering animal. Now he discovers that his worldly power, his sense of self, and the definition of man were all illusory. The evils that he grappled with by means of intelligence can in the end be met only with endurance. He takes responsibility for his actions but blames his agonies—the brutal scenario of life—on Apollo; for indeed adding to the sense of evil is the Kafkaesque mystery of the design of the gods. In the play *Antigone* (c. 441 B.C.), evil is presented as a tragic conflict between social order and individual will. A similar conflict takes place in Euripides' play *Hippolytos* (*Hippolytus*, 428 B.C.), one between the vindictive goddesses Aphrodite and Artemis, between the two meanings of "venery," between a man's need for love and his need for a vocation. The gods, moreover, tolerate each other's desires but unfairly strike back at each other's human followers. Thus Hippolytus, "holy, . . . reverent, . . . pure, . . . guiltless of these sins," is, along with bystanders, struck down by a slighted Aphrodite. Her human instrument is Phaedra, who precipitates the crisis, for a woman scorned may resort to treachery and slander. This is also the motive force in the *Mēdeia* (*Medea*, play, 431 B.C.), in which a woman is jilted, and the *Bakchai* (*The Bacchants*, c. 405 B.C.), in which a god is persecuted. In these two plays especially, the audience is first made to sympathize with the victim and then alienated as the victim strikes back ruthlessly. Euripides thus suggests that the middle way, the moderation so much beloved of moralists and philosophers, is often nonexistent in human affairs. That a nation, for example, goes from the tyranny of the czars to the tyranny of the commissars is typical of a human race for whom the swing of the pendulum from one violent extreme to another is the norm. These plays on the *lex talionis* are in effect pessimistic rejoinders to Aeschylus' *Oresteia*.

For Aristophanes, evil is social, the overtaking of Athens by a set of knaves and fools. The knaves are demagogic warmongers like Cleon and Sophists like Socrates (or whomever Socrates in the *Nephelai* [*The Clouds*] of 423 B.C. is supposed to represent). The fools are innovators of all stripes, signally the "modern," "realist" tragedian Euripides. The typical Aristophanic play (*Ornithes* [*The Birds*, 414 B.C.]; *Lysistratē* [*Lysistrata*, 411 B.C.]; *Ekklēsiazousai* [*Women in Parliament*, 392 B.C.]; *Ploutos* [*Plutus*, 388 B.C.]) begins with a problem, offers a fantasy solution, discovers new problems arising therefrom, yet ends happily in a curious blend of the conservative, tragic view of life with the concessions at the end necessitated by the conventions of comedy and fantasy.

Plato (*Politeia* [*The Republic*, dialogue, c. 380 B.C.]) sees worldly, material evil as nugatory. A tyrant with all the possessions and achievements one could wish for would be hag-ridden by his conscience, while a virtuous man subjected to every torture imaginable would be contented. The real evil is, therefore, the soul's immersion in the material world and its forgetting of its origins above and of the realm of ideas. For Aristotle and Lucretius, evil is mainly within man, not external to him. Aristotle (*Ēthica Nikomacheia* [*Ethics*, mid–4th century B.C.]) finds it in extremes of behavior, and Lucretius (*De rerum natura* [*On the Nature of Things*, 1st century B.C.]) in superstitiousness—the absurd fear of gods who are in fact the creation of men's minds and the unwillingness to face the fact that all reality consists of atoms in collision.

Virgil presents a complex vision of evil. At the beginning of the epic poem *Aeneis* (*Aeneid*, 19 B.C.), he asks how a divinity could cause so much suffering to a hero. The monotheistic version of theodicy is being approximated. That the hero is explicitly and often described as a good man—something that cannot be said of Achilles or Odysseus—heightens the tension. Specifically three sorts of suffering are dramatized. That of the Trojans, first in the treacherous fall of their city and then in Aeneas men's wanderings, all because Juno favored Carthage and took offense over the judgment of Paris. She, Satan-like, sets herself alone (like Poseidon in the *Odyssey* and unlike the complex roster of the gods in the *Iliad*) against Jupiter and the large historical design, of which Roman hegemony is the core. Only after obtaining revenge and exacting concessions from Jupiter does she submit to fate. A second suffering is that of the people who inadvertently get in the way of the Trojan rendezvous with destiny (Dido, Turnus, Queen Amata, the Latins) and who, along with the Trojans, know the painful necessity of war, the impossibility of achieving peaceful compromises. Although the futility of wars is eloquently pronounced by a Diomedes who had been a hawk during the Trojan War, each generation, unable to learn from the others' experience, must discover that truth for itself. All of this is alleged to be redeemed by the Roman mission, but with how much enthusiasm or demurral on the part of the sensitive Virgil is a subject of scholarly controversy. The third and most important sort of suffering is undergone by the pious and melancholy yet valiant hero, sorely tempted to go down fighting at Troy or to live with Dido at Carthage but always pushed on by the gods.

Lucian is, curiously, one of the first to deal directly with theodicy in a discursive (albeit comical) fashion. His *Prometheus* (2d century) arraigns Zeus for administering punishment far in excess of the crime and of what human justice would administer. Creating man was a blessing for the gods, but the reward Prometheus gets for that deed is crucifixion, not a medal. In *Zeus tragōdos* (*Jupiter tragoedus*, dialogue, 2d century), Zeus is worried that the idea of the gods' nonexistence may be proved and spread by philosophers. Momus replies that, considering all the suffering in the world and the fact that the gods care only for a steady flow of animal sacrifices from men and nothing for human welfare or morality, the strange thing is not that some philosophers deny the existence of the gods but that anyone still sacrifices to them at all. In the human debate that ensues, the atheist scores many points, and the gods' defender is encouraged by Zeus to resort to name calling and cursing.

The Middle Ages and the Renaissance

In the New Testament two key sources of evil are the recalcitrant refusal of the Jews to acknowledge their redeemer as well as their adherence, in the face of his tutelage, to a fleshly, this-worldly, materialistic way of reading the Law, the meaning of the Old Testament, and the promise of a redemptive messiah. Subsidiary evils are the glaring weaknesses of even the most devoted followers of Jesus, the treachery of Judas, and the presence of a Satan or adversary, who had been referred to nebulously in the Old Testament. But all is resolved by the promise of the redemption of mankind and of a new heaven and earth. Complex also is the *Confessiones* (*Confessions*, c. 397–400) of St. Augustine. If Adam had his apple, the saint has his pear. The youthful stealing of pears from an orchard causes him years later to seek a motive. He finds it to be peer pressure and gratuitous love of breaking restrictions, the latter of which is paradoxically both cause and effect of original sin. Over the middle and later years of St. Augustine's life, evil hovers in a different form. The pride of intellect in himself, in Manichaean seers, and in pseudo-Christian philosophers presented an obstacle in his quest for the truth; worldly wisdom proved, as Paul had said, to be a stumbling block to faith. Finally, in strictly philosophical terms, St. Augustine (*De civitate Dei* [*The City of God*, treatise, 413–426]), perhaps the first to wrestle at length with the vexing monotheistic form of theodicy, attempts to resolve the issue by concluding that evil does not exist, being simply a nonentity, a defection from God, the absence of God. This raises, of course, more questions than it answers.

In the epic poem *Beowulf* (c. 8th century) evil is an external agency, something in the universe, for society and individual are (except briefly for Unferth) good. First come incursions by the monster Grendel, motivated mainly by Envy and perhaps also by something gratuitous, and then, in the wake of Grendel's death, comes Grendel's Dam, motivated by revenge. One man's physical prowess and courage keeps the community from dissolution. Evil is human in the epic *Chanson de Roland* (*Song of Roland*, c. 1100), with its clear black and white, we and they. The Moslem hosts are damnable, and Bishop Turpin blesses the just war against them. Within the Christian camp, however, are defects too: the treason of Ganelon and the pride of Roland, which prevents him from blowing his horn until it is too late. And in the morality play *Everyman* (c. 1500) evil is in the individual. According to the play's Christianized and simplified Platonism, evil is man's immersion in quotidian existence and obliviousness to death and the hereafter. The imminence of death enables him to regenerate himself and to confess only just in time.

Dante's *La divina commedia* (*The Divine Comedy*, c. 1320) in one sense contains no problem of evil because it presents last things all in order. During the pilgrim's journey, though, one finds details suggestive of evil. Dante himself had, like Everyman, turned to false loves (women and/or pagan philosophy), which could lead him to damnation, and Hell is indeed populated with sinners who set themselves against God and were unrepentant. Meeting them produces a secondary sense of evil insofar as Dante is moved in certain cases to compassion, to implicitly lament that God's judgment has fallen on some (e.g., the lovers Paolo and Francesca or the sage Brunetto Latini) who had a beauty about their earthly lives. The great pagan poets, likewise, are doomed by theology to hell, so Dante modifies the topography by granting them a refuge in a globe of light insulated from the tortures of the damned. The most evil beings, traitors deserving righteous wrath, are Lucifer, Judas Iscariot, and, because of Dante's theory of the Roman Empire as a second chosen people, Brutus and Cassius. *Purgatorio* (*Purgatory*) contains some rather sinful people, but, having repented in time, they are on the path to redemption. And the *Paradiso* (*Paradise*) offers the traditional response to the question of theodicy. The structure of the universe is partly an expression of God's mercy and partly an object of the Christian's faith and love.

Evil in Gottfried von Strassburg's *Tristan* (romance, c. 1210) is the problem caused by Cupid's blindness—love does not run in the channels established by marriages dictated by convenience or politics. The precipitation of the love by a potion is a metaphor for its irrationality and unpredictability. However beautiful, love also is asocial, and the lovers soon find themselves the victims of backbiting, spying, intrigue. Celebrated in *Tristan*, the fashionable new cult of adultery is entirely the source of evil in *Sir Gawain and the Green Knight* (poem, c. 1370). Yet the pious knight passes the various tests more or less successfully. Malory's *Morte d'Arthur* (prose romance, c. 1469) depicts a world in which the nobility and beauty of a courtly love tradition now accepted—it transforms even the greatest in the realm, Lancelot and Guinevere—nevertheless brings about (with the help of the noble Gawain, the cursed Mordred, and a stroke of bad luck) the downfall of Arthur's reign and Round Table—of an entire civilization. For Boccaccio (*Il decamerone* [*Decameron*, novellas, c. 1350]) and Chaucer (*Canterbury Tales*, c. 1380–1400), evil is partly the hypocrisy and chicanery of those who should be bearers of a cure for evil, the clergy; partly Christian asceticism; and partly avarice.

Clerical hypocrisy is also a main source of evil in Rabelais' vision (*Gargantua et Pantagruel* [*Gargantua and Pantagruel*, novels, 1532–1564]). Human striving for earthly fulfillment, a prime evil for Plato and early Christianity, is becoming prized. Warmongers like Picrochole are likewise evil, yet the just war is not ruled out. In the proto-Marxist view of Thomas More (*Utopia*, political romance, 1516)—or at least one side of him—private property and its concomitants—

greed, luxury, vested interests, nonrational social arrangements—result in injustice and inequity, while for Erasmus (*Moriae encomium* [*The Praise of Folly*, essay, 1511]), stupidity in all its forms takes the place of hubris, knavery, or original sin as a monocausal explanation of human adversity. Machiavelli (*Il principe* [*The Prince*, essay, 1532]) offers a transvaluation. Christian morality, being for him irrelevant to the survival of the state, is dubious, and "immoral" acts may become necessary. In fact, Christian virtues, insofar as they play into the hands of evil politicians, are actually responsible for evil, while stern measures, when adopted by men with the welfare of the state at heart, are in the long run the truly merciful ones, for a little violence judiciously and early applied prevents a lot of indiscriminate violence later. Machiavelli thus agrees with Christian thinkers that human nature is depraved but finds that therefore credulity, trust, acts of caritas, far from being the answer Christianity would have them be, are self-destructive. Likewise condemned is the much-honored middle way; for example, in uncovering conspirators, a ruler either eliminates them peremptorily or forgives them generously, but to punish mildly is to leave disgruntled people in one's midst. Yet a third source of evil is Fortuna, chance, luck. Foresight, calculation, prudence, *virtù* are somewhat useful in combatting it, but in a crunch sheer intuition may be best of all.

For Montaigne (*Essais* [*Essays*, 1580–1588]), evil is neither materialism, original sin, Satan, hypocrisy, or private property, but human vanity and intellectual pride, as notably exhibited by dogmatists of all sorts, the zealotry of both sides in the Catholic-Protestant Civil War, and by European man's smug sense of superiority vis-à-vis the Indians of the newly discovered American continent. Bacon (early 17th century) carried this view of false pride further by seeing all evil as originating in the fact that most men believe in the wrong ideas arrived at in the wrong way. The resulting superstitiousness and misery could be done away with only by a new scientific, empirical approach to reality. Marlowe's hero (*Doctor Faustus*, play, 1604) used an old approach when he allowed himself to be seduced by Mephistopheles into signing an evil pact; though he can repent to the very end, the momentum of experience hardens his heart. Faust's predicament is like Everyman's except that he is an intellectual, he seeks unusual powers and experiences, and he is unable to regenerate himself. That the knowledge he gained proves, by opening the door to contact with Satan, to be deadly is an inadvertent parable of the predicament of modern man, whose scientific breakthroughs may yet turn out to be a forbidden knowledge.

Shakespeare's plays give a complex picture of evil. For one thing, he offers various hypotheses or scenarios. If Hamlet is a good man in a corrupt society, Macbeth is a corrupt man in a good society; if *Julius Caesar* (c. 1599) contains neither villain nor saint, *King Lear* (1606) contains numerous individuals who are either all bad or all good. Among the protagonists, a major source of inner evil is the difficulty of harmonizing knowledge with action (Brutus, Hamlet, Othello), feeling with ambition (Macbeth, Antony, Coriolanus), or reality with perception (Othello, Lear, Timon). Romeo and Juliet alone are victims of external fortune. But the defects in the protagonists are often matched, magnified, or exploited by external evil—as embodied in villains rather than supernatural beings or natural disasters. These individuals form a varied lot: the vacillators and exhibitionists, as much fools as knaves (King John, Richard II); the ambiguous ones redeemed either by Shakespeare's fertile imagination, his ability to articulate their vision (Falstaff, Shylock) or, fortuitously, by changes in the social structure and politics, which render them the object of modern sentiment rather than Elizabethan satire (Kate, Shylock, Malevolio); the humane ones, who either originally have, or come to have, a conscience (Claudius, Macbeth, Lady Macbeth); the ambitious ones, who will stop at nothing to gain power (Richard III, Edmund); and the envious, vindictive, or gratuitous ones (Aaron, Don John, Iago, Tullus Aufidious, Iachimo, Caliban). Outstanding among these are Caliban, at once bestial and pitiful; Macbeth, who changes from being a tempted good man to a conscience-driven evildoer and finally to a hardhearted shell of a man; and Iago, the most diabolic and fascinating of all.

King Lear is the one play in which theodicy is handled explicitly and memorably. Different interpretations are offered both by characters within the play and, later, by critics of it. The characters' views range from the eventual pessimism of Gloucester, who comes to see the gods as sadists, and the atheism (or Epicureanism) of Edmund, to the piety, unshaken by adversity, of Kent and especially Edgar. In the middle is the complex response of Lear, at first smugly sure that the gods are ready to do his bidding but later lapsing into a metaphysical (and perhaps agnostic) silence on the subject. Among the critics, some believe that the play dramatizes in the figure of Lear the growing bankruptcy of pagan culture and the growing readiness of man, through a *via negativa*, to accept an imminent Christian revelation. According to another reading, it dramatizes the way in which evil and suffering bring a man to Christian values (patience, endurance, renunciation of revenge) irrespective of revelation and dogma; it shows those values to be eternal truths and not the peculiar property of any one confession. But the dominant interpretation in our century is that, because of the Elizabethan taboo on the dramatization onstage of theological matters, Shakespeare was forced to use indirection, and when he speaks of "gods" he means God. On trial and found severely wanting, therefore, is the Christian God.

In Ben Jonson's major plays, unlike nearly all of Shakespeare's, avarice and Puritan canting are the main targets. The problem of evil is implicit in Cervantes (*Don Quijote* [*Don Quixote*, novel, 1605, 1615]). A quotidian world sunk in habit, custom, and worldliness can greet a naïve idealism only with incredulity, laughter, and buffets. Who is insane, the visionary Don or the practical, corrupt, obtuse society? In Calderón's play *La vida es sueño* (*Life is a Dream*, 1635) (as in *Oedipus Rex*) an ominous prophecy is fulfilled, despite all attempts by the father to evade it. The evil is threefold: man's attempt to tamper with the future by abnormal means; the beastliness that the stars predicted and which Segismondo (and, by extension, mankind) found in himself, whether or not precipitated by the father's preventive measures; and, above all, man's inability to differentiate waking reality from dreams. The solution to the latter problem is to assume the worst and to act one's best.

Milton's poem *Paradise Lost* (1667) is one of those major works that make the problem of evil explicit: "To justify the ways of God to man." The answer is that the main source of evil is cosmic and external (as it is also in the masque *Comus*, 1634, and the epic poem *Paradise Regained*, 1671). It is Satan. He is motivated, like the supernatural monsters in *Beowulf*, by envy and revenge. The blame is, however, shared with mankind as represented by the first couple. Their commission of original sin results from Eve's narcissism, which clouds her judgment and precipitates folly, and from Adam's uxoriousness, which diverts the will from reason to passion. (Yet according to Milton's *De doctrina christiana*, c. 1660s, the eating of the fruit actually involves every sin imaginable.) This convergence of three diverse but representative states of mind generates the melancholy course of human history, with suffering piled on suffering. Since the final result is the triumphant intervention of Jesus, the original sin turns out to be a *felix culpa* or disguised blessing. In *Samson Agonistes* (dramatic poem, 1671), the evil is solely individual, internal. Samson is, like Adam, uxorious, but Dalilah is unlike Eve, being wily and later mendacious rather than credulous and weak.

The Neoclassical, Romantic, and Modern Periods

In Molière (1622–1673), the main characters are usually fools, and each's folly is caused by a monomania (over money, health, aristocratic status, a secure marriage, or total sincerity). The only knaves are Don Juan, an atheist, a sadistic seducer, and something of a gratuitous villain, and Tartuffe, a hypocrite motivated by lust for money and perhaps power. Pope's *Essay on Man* (poem, 1733–1734), like *Paradise Lost*, addresses the question of theodicy, but, in conformity with the tendencies of the Enlightenment, does so by means of discursive, ratiocinative, generalizing, optimistic couplets rather than by means of a blank-verse narrative based on scriptural story and cast into classical epic form with tragic atmosphere. Its conclusion, "Whatever is, is right," echoes the thesis of the recent *Théodicée* (*Theodicy*, 1710) of Leibniz (that God created the best of all possible worlds), derives from the old Christian idea of the Fortunate Fall and looks ahead to the secular resolutions of Adam Smith, Hegel, Marx—and the satire of Voltaire's *Candide* (novel, 1759). In Pope's *The Dunciad* (poem, 1728–1743), rampant stupidity brings darkness down on the world, a vision also implicit, though with much more cheer, in the *Spectator*'s (essays by Addison and Steele, 1711–1712) task of attacking folly rather than vice. For Swift (*Gulliver's Travels*, satire, 1726), vice or villainy is, for once in this age, central. Evil stems from man's pettiness, vindictiveness, vanity, irrationality, and destructiveness. Nor is folly left out, and in book 3 it expresses itself in the seemingly ludicrous endeavors of the early scientists. Here, given the ensuing Scientific Revolution, the last laugh may be on Swift, although the verdict must be postponed until we know whether the explosion of scientific knowledge will or will not have ended with a definitive nuclear explosion. This selection is, nevertheless, a landmark. Marlowe had shown the dangers of forbidden knowledge, and Milton had in the last books of *Paradise Lost* and especially in *Paradise Regained* launched into a Pauline, Jeromian, Augustinian, and medieval attack on worldly, secular knowledge, particularly the venerable Greek and Roman wisdom he himself had been attracted to. But Swift is the first major writer to focus on modern scientific knowledge as more baneful or at least ridiculous than beneficial or dignified; thus a new source of evil enters the human catalogue. In something of this spirit, Wordsworth will assert a century later (and not only of the "meddling intellect") that "we murder to dissect."

What Johnson's *Rasselas* (novel, 1759) and Voltaire's own *Zadig* (novel, 1747) did on a small scale, the latter's *Candide*, another work centered on theodicy, does on a large scale. Evil is both cosmic or at least natural (earthquake) and social (wars, brutality, rape, torture). As if rampant insecurity and villainy were not enough, folly, masquerading as expertise and wisdom, compounds the mess. For philosophers and theologians like Pangloss, in a self-deluding attempt to make words efface deeds and events, tell themselves and others that pain and evil are not real. The next landmark in the changing delineation of evil is Rousseau's *Confessions* (1781–1788). Here, for nearly the first time, the Christian vision is moribund. Satan, original sin, hell, the church as either catalyst for regeneration (as in *Everyman*) or hotbed of hypocrisy (as in the *Decameron*) are gone. Full blown is the secular, liberal (and, by turns, rationalist, romantic, modern) vision of the sensitive soul at bay in a corrupt, unfeeling society, of nature as beautiful and restorative, of the individual born good or neutral and spoiled by that center of iniquity, the city. (This reading of reality informs likewise Wordsworth's *Prelude* [poem, 1799–1805]). Also modern (or proto-Freudian) is the correlation of childhood experience and mature concept. The infliction of injustice and injury on the young Rousseau awakens his consciousness to general social injustice and initiates the thinking processes that will lead to his mature philosophical and revolutionary writings. (Yet he seems to pay unwitting tribute to original sin by acknowledging certain bizarre, self-destructive tendencies within himself.) Secular solutions to the problem of evil are also provided discursively by writers like Mandeville (*Fable of the Bees*, poem, 1714), Adam Smith (*The Wealth of Nations*, essay, 1776), Hegel (*Philosophy of History*, 1823–1827), and Marx (mid–19th century), who hold that what is considered evil in the individual's perspective or the short run becomes good when placed in the context of community or the long run. Instead of God and the *felix culpa*, the ruling principle is, variously, "private vices, public benefits" or "the invisible hand" or "the cunning of Reason" (and "the unfolding of Spirit") or "the historical process."

In Goethe's *Faust* (play, 1808), the hero, like Marlowe's, is disillusioned by the discovery that all his studies have nugatory results. The devil he then spends time with lacks the traditional infernal aims, being rather witty, satiric, urbane, mocking, skeptical, "modern." The pact they make lacks the clarity and formality of Marlowe's and in any case has more to do with the antithesis of eternal striving (for knowledge, creation, self-realization) and complacent contentment than with good deeds versus sins or salvation versus damnation. The basic difference is that Marlowe's hero is a sage who, by venturing beyond the limits assigned to man, damned himself—the twenty-four years of worldly mastery, licentiousness, and rebellion against God being a mere interlude—whereas in Goethe the possibility of damnation is secondary and ambiguous while the immersion in experience, the substance of the twenty-four years, is primary.

Another landmark development at this time is the proclamation of a new source of evil: nothing less than Christianity. Boccaccio, Chaucer, and Rabelais had distinguished misbehaving clerics from mother church. But in the poems of Burns and especially Blake (late 18th century) the church itself as an institution and as an interpreter of Christ's message is the source of evil. If Rousseau accused society of being the culprit, Blake accused Christian society. In short, religion, from having been, as a revelation of reality, an antidote to evil was becoming a crucial part of that very evil. Some thinkers spelled out how that evil worked, as, in the absence of God, two of the older seven deadly sins— avarice and lechery—became the basis of modern monocausal explanations of human motivation (and, therefore, of evil) by Marx and by Freud. For Marx religion was intellectually distracting and politically an instrumentality of the ruling classes in a world where money rather than spirit was the basic reality; for Freud religion was intellectually a fantasy and psychologically a source of repression and pain in a world where the libido rather than spirit, or money, was the basic reality. The idea, subscribed to by the severely Christian Kierkegaard no less than by the pagan Shelley, Byron, and Keats, that a good deal of evil lies in organized Christianity itself, was forwarded with unique vehemence by the anti-Christian Nietzsche. The latter, however, also saw capitalism, social Darwinism, nationalism, liberalism, feminism, socialism, and meliorism as other social evils.

In Flaubert's novel *Madame Bovary* (1856) and Tolstoy's novel *Anna Karenina* (1877) (cf. Ibsen's *Hedda Gabler*, play, 1890), the heroines seek in adultery a meaningful experience they lack in conventional marriage. In these works, as in many others of the realist school or movement, evil is now completely social; no Satan, monster, or earthquake intervenes, nor does the hero or heroine carry the burden of original sin; "God" is a polite formula rarely heard. In the novels of Dickens, for instance, social evil takes the form of victimization of children, the power of money, the obsession with facts and efficiency, and the desire to climb socially by any means. *Great Expectations* (1860–1861) also gives a memorable portrayal of a psychological evil, the fact that fulfillment comes short of expectation, that the achievement of anything we work long for is usually followed by disillusionment (cf. *Macbeth* [play, 1605–1606]).

The sense of malaise and social injustice that haunts Russian literature is symbolized by the squalor, inertness, and misery of that large substratum of society, the serfs, or later the peasants (Gogol's *Mërtvye dushi* [*Dead Souls*, novel, 1842]; Turgenev's *Otĩsy i deti* [*Fathers and Children*, novel, 1862]; Chekhov's *Muzhiki* [*Peasants*, story, 1897]). Sometimes a similar indolence overtakes the master (Goncharov's *Oblomov*, novel, 1859). Social injustice is at the heart of Kleist's *Michael Kohlhaas* (novel, 1810) and Hugo's *Notre Dame de Paris* (*The Hunchback of Notre Dame*, novel, 1831) and *Les misérables* (novel, 1862). Turgenev's novel introduces a new element as a response to social evils—ideology and revolution. The other protagonists strove for personal fulfillment either through individual rebellion (Kohlhaas), amatory encounters (Emma Bovary, Anna Karenina), or entry into the social rat race albeit with higher consciousness and moral autonomy (Stendhal's Julien Sorel, Balzac's Eugène de Rastignac, Gogol's Chichikov). Turgenev's Bazarov does none of these; to a society rotten with injustice, romantic sentimentality, and superstition, he brings reason, science, utility, revolution, and reconstruction.

Such idealists haughtily lecturing a corrupt and recalcitrant society may seem to some to be more the problem than the solution. (Bazarov's self-assurance is indeed checked by love.) Idealism of one sort or another is shown to be a source of evil in Hawthorne's "The Birth-Mark" (story, 1846) and *Scarlet Letter* (novel, 1850), in which it is Christian or Puritan idealism, as well as in Melville's novel *Moby-Dick* (1851). It becomes a tortured issue in Dostoevsky's writings; in *Besy* (*The Possessed*, novel, 1871–1872) it is flabby or gruesomely exploited. And the novel *Prestuplenie i nakazanie* (*Crime and Punishment*, 1866) contains a sense of evil one might have thought had left the literary agenda for good: original sin. The murder of the pawnbroker, which the hero tries to rationalize by identifying himself with Napoleon and by blaming society, issues only in a confrontation with the reality of evil within. (For original sin from a new angle there is the portrayal of overt sadistic and masochistic impulses in Lise, in *Brat' ĩa Karamazovy* [*Brothers Karamazov*, novel, 1880] several decades before Freud was to theorize about them.) Dostoevsky is therefore carrying on a two-front war: on the one hand, with those Western liberals, or westernizing Russians, much satirized in his major works, who locate evil in society, in a tradition-bound society at that, and who see a utopia arising as soon as liberalism and rationalism wipe out the remainder of "superstition"; and on the other hand (like Kierkegaard) on the members of conventional Christian society, who think they solve the problem of evil by subscribing to the right magazine and by, as do Raskolnikov's mother and sister, snubbing prostitutes.

Another of the small number of major works devoted mainly to theodicy is Dostoevsky's *Brothers Karamazov*. Old man Karamazov and his bastard son Smerdyakov are, like Caliban, something animallike, invincibly depraved, an evil fact of life that (whether explained by original sin or social corruption) liberals are unable to come to terms with. His sons are something else; Alyosha is pious and Dmitri, like Raskolnikov, must make a detour through sinfulness on the way to faith. Only Ivan the intellectual has the capacity and the will to challenge the design of things. His conclusion is that the world God made is unacceptable and that life is absurd. Yet the mere thought of complicity in his father's death deranges him; if Dostoevsky seems to be breaking this noble butterfly on the torture rack, the cause is not mere authorial religious zealotry and a literal acceptance of Jesus' dictum that thought (e.g., lustful ones) are as real as acts (e.g., adultery). For one thing, that Ivan, having proclaimed that if God is dead all is permitted, suffers a nervous breakdown over a mere thought, dramatizes the perfectly valid if novel psychological observation that men's intellect develops late and moves much more daringly than their feelings, which are shaped very early. Most men do have difficulty living their own ideas, Christian or not; the same point is dramatized contemporaneously by the anti-Christian Ibsen (*Rosmersholm*, play, 1886), and it explains the undoing of Bazarov and of Kurtz (Conrad's *Heart of Darkness*, novella, 1902). For another, Dostoevsky is in the tradition, originating with Paul, which holds that mere worldly wisdom is not enough to get one through life. Dmitri, like Everyman, finds grace; Ivan, like Marlowe's Faust, does not. For the latter two, being intellectual proved to be a stumbling block (as it almost had for St. Augustine and Dante).

Dostoevsky, however, sometimes wrote deeper than he knew. In Ivan's parable of the Grand Inquisitor, he locates evil in an entirely different place, rather as do the very liberals, agnostics, and secularists he often rails against. For that story suggests that, regardless of whether God exists or who Jesus was, mankind is too weak, dumb, and vulnerable to receive any spiritual message. Jesus and all he stands for must be ejected while a diluted version of his message enables unruly, inchoate mankind to be ruled by a class of clerical guardians who (as Plato had counseled) must administer a dose of myths (e.g., lies about the hereafter) to keep them in line. A mankind that, in T. S. Eliot's words, "cannot bear very much reality" needs bread and circuses in the modern form of authority, mystery, and miracle. This idea—that, given the cosmic evil of an empty universe, man must live in illusion—was, after first being attacked by the playwright Ibsen in the name of liberating truth in *Samfundets støtter* (*The Pillars of Society*, 1877) and *Et dukkehjem* (*A Doll's House*, 1879), voiced implicitly in *En folkefiende* (*An Enemy of the People*, 1882), explicitly in *Vildanden* (*The Wild Duck*, 1884). (Different is the theme in *Hedda Gabler*, whose heroine is, along with Iago, one of the greatest portraits of the gratuitous villain.) The elusiveness of truth and reality as the basic evil in life is also the main theme of, among numerous modern works, Pirandello's *Così è, se vi pare!* (*It Is So, If You Think So*, play, 1917) and *Enrico IV* (play, 1922), as well as of O'Neill's *Long Day's Journey into Night* (play, 1956) and *The Iceman Cometh* (play, 1946).

If in Ibsen's *Doll's House* and *Gengangere* (*Ghosts*, play, 1881), the sins of the fathers are visited on the sons physically, in Lawrence's novel *Sons and Lovers* (1913) the process is psychological, emotional. A virtue one could not have too much of in traditional society, the mutual love of mother and son, proves to be psychically crippling; evil originates in the family rather than in society or the individual, and what happens in one's earliest years, especially in amatory matters, will affect one, often adversely, in adulthood. According to this vision, evil is caused by folly rather than knavery, and knaves themselves are pathetic victims. And indeed the first-rate early modern classics—the plays of Chekhov, the stories and novels of Henry James, Lawrence, and Joyce, the vast novel of Proust—lack villains. The modern wisdom is that in a world of skepticism, relativism, and uncertainty, as well as of the discoveries of psychology, there are no good and bad people, only individuals struggling, poignantly or comically, to come to terms with their fragile lives. Nor do these works concern themselves with theodicy or give any simple reading of the problem of evil. From their complexity one extracts only at great hazard such oversimplifications as in, for example, Proust (A la recherche du temps perdu [Remembrance of Things Past, novels, 1913–1927]), that evil flows from the selfishness, insincerity, and snobbery of high society people, the hopeless entrapment of the lover in the prison of the self, the elusiveness of mutual love, the flux of reality, and the impossibility of knowing anyone. Also noted in the works of these masters is the virtual absence of the Christian vision and its view of evil, except for an occasional Christian symbol used for secular, that is, psychological, purposes.

The scientific revolution of the seventeenth century had led to the Industrial Revolution—the application of science to the reordering of the material world. Most thinkers at first hailed this change as progress, as a way to remedy at last the hitherto permanent problem of evil. Yet Swiftian doubts soon began to rise about this panacea. The baleful impact of the Industrial Revolution was taken note of as early as Blake (''dark Satanic mills'') and, later, by Dickens. For three writers, especially, modern technology was creating vast new problems or adding to the old problem of evil. Lawrence, notably in the novel Lady Chatterly's Lover (1928), presents industrialization as a disease that, in conjunction with cerebration and avarice, is destroying nature, tenderness, humaneness, body consciousness. In Huxley's novel Brave New World (1932), technology has made possible a society based—not, like Plato's on justice; Aristophanes', on quietude; Jesus', on truth and freedom; More's or Swift's (the Houyhnhnms), on reason; the Grand Inquisitor's, on illusion; but on pleasure. Everyone has all needs promptly attended to in a society that, stratified and orderly, is built on creature comforts, labor saving devices, instant gratification, the evasion of painful truths like death and solitariness. Yet it is so dehumanized thereby that a heresy springs up in favor of old evils like suffering and tragedy. Orwell's 1984 (1949) presents the new world blessed with technological progress as being blended with the equally new world blessed with social meliorism to form an unprecedented nightmare—a society based not on pleasure but fear and terror and giving its rulers power over their subjects beyond the wildest dreams of a Hitler or Stalin.

If the belief in progress proves to be as illusory as the belief in God had been, writers must come to terms with the consequences, with what is the modern version of the problem of evil: the apparent absurdity of human existence. That is the task, overt or implicit, in such diverse works as Kafka's Der Prozess (The Trial, novel, 1925) and Das Schloss (The Castle, novel, 1926), Sartre's La *nausée* (*Nausea*, novel, 1938), Camus' *L'étranger* (*The Stranger*, novel, 1942) and *La chute* (*The Fall*, novel, 1956), Beckett's *En attendant Godot* (*Waiting for Godot*, play, 1952) and *Fin de partie* (*Endgame*, play, 1957). The Kafka works in particular have become paradigms of the modern condition in their treatment of the impossibility of finding justice or ingress or explanation, their picture of man as a solitary alien in a cold, bizarre, mysterious world. And Beckett, looking back to Augustinian and Kierkegaardian ideas about life as ennui, tedium, waiting, offers a parable of two seedy, clownish men killing time while expecting someone to keep an appointment with them. This individual, with the curious name of "Godot," seems to hold the promise of curing evil that the Messiah, the Second Coming of Jesus, the Revolution, or Progress through technology and capitalism held for others. He never does show up.

See also: Daemon.

Selected Bibliography

Bataille, Georges. *Literature and Evil*. Trans. Alastair Hamilton. London: Callder and Boyars, 1973.
Carus, Paul. *History of the Devil and the Idea of Evil*. Chicago: Open Court, 1899.
Lovejoy, A. O. *The Great Chain of Being*. Cambridge, Mass.: Harvard University Press, 1936.
Wiegand, Anke. *Die Schönheit und das Böse*. Munich: Pustet, 1967.

MANFRED WEIDHORN

EXISTENTIALISM

Narrowly defined, existentialism is a philosophical and literary movement that emerged during the post-World-War-II decade in Paris and is associated with the writings of Jean-Paul Sartre, Simone de Beauvoir, and Albert Camus. It is noteworthy that only Sartre and de Beauvoir, albeit reluctantly, accepted the label "existentialism," a label given to them by French journalists in 1945. Yet the term is now used to refer to an entire movement that is rooted in the nineteenth-century revolt against the legacies of the Enlightenment, that is, essentialism, rationalism, and the rise of a secular, bureaucratic, and conformist mass society.

As a movement, existentialism is best defined as a confluence of themes and a set of shared influences rather than a body of doctrines. A fundamental feature of all existentialists is their revolt against any form of essentialism that identifies human reality with a priori philosophical, scientific, or religious concepts. On the essentialist view, individuals derive their meaning, values, and justification from the parts they play in a larger scheme of events or purposes (e.g., the cosmos, a divine plan, universal history). Thus, "humanity" itself is understood as having an essence that is prior to and independent of the existence of any particular individual human being. Existentialists reverse the traditional relationship between essence and existence and claim that "existence precedes essence." Accordingly, existentialists begin their analyses of the human condition not with a scientific or metaphysical inquiry into objective essences but rather with a description of the immediately experienced reality of an embodied, living, willing, feeling subject. Having rejected the idea that the universe is a closed system with a pre-established meaning, they place the burden of creating meaning on the free individual who is thrown into the world without knowing why. The only existential certainties are that one is a "being there," that is, a situated being who is born, will die, and must choose. This experience of "thrownness" ("facticity") often leads to nihilism or to feelings of despair, alienation, anxiety, and absurdity—all of which are recurring existentialist motifs. The ordinary response to facticity is to avoid it by conforming to already established social norms and escaping into an everyday routine in which existential anxiety is covered up. Indeed, existentialists often emphasize the importance of extreme psychological states and situations (e.g., anxiety, being-toward-death) in bringing us to an awareness of our freedom and responsibility. They challenge us to choose our freedom and to act authentically by accepting responsibility for our choices. For the existentialist life becomes an adventurous, risk-taking, and dramatic search for personal identity in an indifferent universe.

Existentialist's literary techniques often express their metaphysical outlooks. Because they want to portray a living, choosing, situated individual, they often express their views in novels or plays rather than philosophical prose. Since they tend to eschew rigid doctrine and to emphasize the extent to which existence is more an open question than a set of answers, existentialists do not seek disciples, but rather attempt to invoke in their readers a sense of existence as a being toward possibilities. Thus, they often employ indirect communication through the use of fictional characters, pseudonyms, and ironic detachment.

Nineteenth Century European Origins

The genealogy of twentieth-century French literary existentialism is Germanic. It begins with Søren Kierkegaard's critique of the abstract metaphysical and logical system building of the nineteenth-century German philosopher Hegel. In his *Afsluttende uvidenskabelig efterskrift* (*Concluding Unscientific Postscript*, essay, 1846) Kierkegaard claimed that an existential system could not be formulated since it would require an infinite perspective unattainable by any finite existing individual. While God understands the overall systemic interrelations between individual moments of existence, the individual experiences his or her own existence as a "fragment of life." (The fragment becomes an important symbol in existentialism insofar as it conveys the idea of a part cut off from the whole. Other existentialists such as Nietzsche and Kafka write in an aphoristic or fragmented style.) Kierkegaard's starting point was the existing individual who is cut off from God and must find his or her own moral and religious truth through radical choice.

In his pseudonymous work *Enten-eller* (*Either/Or*, diary, letters, lectures, lyrical notes, 1843), Kierkegaard portrayed two possible ways of being that an individual might choose, the aesthetic and the ethical. As a Christian, he believed that the most authentic choice for an individual involves a leap of faith toward an "absurd" God. The religious choice is represented in his essay *Frygt og Bæven* (*Fear and Trembling*, 1843) by the biblical character Abraham. Abraham's God is an absurd God, since he commands Abraham to sacrifice his only son, the son that God had promised him. Abraham grasped the fact that God's will is not comprehensible in human terms and made the radical choice. Isolated, uncertain, and free, he is the model of the knight of faith who understands that God can only be reached through passionate commitment and soul-searching. What makes Kierkegaard's religious perspective an existentialist one is the fact that he placed God in relation to the existing individual and not within a body of rational doctrine. Kierkegaard was very critical of the religious hypocrisy in his day; he attempted to make religious faith a central part of the individual's everyday life. His authorship is devoted to the tasks of showing how difficult it is to become a true Christian in Christendom.

Kierkegaard rejected the use of speculative philosophical treatises like those of Hegel in favor of a literary form more adequate to stressing the individual subject in the process of self-discovery. *Enten-eller* contains a series of first-person pieces by four fictitious authors. The use of a pseudonymous authorship in many of Kierkegaard's aesthetic and ethical writings serves several functions. In the first place, it distances the author's religious point of view from the aesthetic and ethical perspectives. Secondly, it exemplifies Kierkegaard's view of the relationship between self and others. Each individual is an isolated consciousness limited to seeing others only as objects from outside. Each character is an aesthetically created possibility accessible to others only through what he says and does. Direct (subject to subject) communication is portrayed as impossible. There is always the possibility of irony, deception, and misunderstanding in the individual's relationship with others. Accordingly, Kierkegaard rejects the possibility of an omniscient author in favor of an aesthetic presentation of a multiplicity of individual perspectives.

Like Kierkegaard, Friedrich Nietzsche also opposed philosophical system building. He regarded system building as a mark of intellectual dishonesty insofar as any system must rest on unproven assumptions. He also found academic philosophy too abstract and removed from life. For Nietzsche, the test of any set of beliefs was one's ability to live by them affirmatively and creatively. His diagnosis of the modern age was that the Christian ideals by which it lived had ceased to be creative and represented instead a symptom of decay, world-weariness, and nihilism. Nietzsche proclaimed the death of God and called for a transvaluation of Christian values. Human beings must become godlike creators themselves and establish their own values in order to overcome moral nihilism and resignation. He was severely critical of the self-deception, other-worldliness, submissiveness, and conformism that he found to be characteristic of his times. His own values were aesthetic and his heroes artistic geniuses such as Goethe.

Nietzsche's first book, *Die Geburt der Tragödie* (*The Birth of Tragedy*, essay, 1872) contains a highly original theory of the birth and death of Greek tragedy. Nietzsche's theory eventually replaced the prevailing view of the Greek spirit as one of cheerful optimism with a more complex analysis of the Greek's affirmation of the value and beauty of existence despite their awareness of the terror and destruction in nature and history. Thus, Greek tragedy is regarded as an aesthetic response to and conquest of the suffering in existence, that is, as a synthesis of the Apollonian impulse toward individuation, restraint, and harmony and the Dionysian impulse toward primal unity, cruelty, and the transgression of boundaries. For Nietzsche, life was justified as an aesthetic phenomenon.

Also sprach Zarathustra (*Thus Spoke Zarathustra*, prose poem, 1883–1892) is usually considered Nietzsche's magnum opus. It is his only major fictional work. *Zarathustra* tells the story of the prophet, Zarathustra, who descends from his spiritual solitude on the mountain tops to the world of ordinary humans. The work is preoccupied with the Dionysian theme of rebirth and focuses on the process of individuation. It is an attempt to answer the question, How does one create an integrated, whole, healthy individual out of spiritual and earthly elements?

Zarathustra teaches the ideals of the *Übermensch*, the will to power and eternal recurrence. *Übermenschen* are those who continually strive to overcome themselves, to give form to their passions. They are so life affirming that at any moment they can will the eternal recurrence of the same. Thus, they can will to eternalize becoming and thereby overcome the hierarchical dualisms of spirit and flesh, eternity and temporality, being and becoming, and good and evil, which, according to Nietzsche, are symptoms of decadence in the history of Western metaphysics.

In Spain, Miguel de Unamuno, inspired by the writings of Kierkegaard and Nietzsche, founded Spanish existentialism. His novel *Paz en la guerra* (*Peace in War*, 1897) has been called the first existentialist novel. Later he wrote his masterpiece *Del sentimiento trágico de la vida* (*The Tragic Sense of Life*, lyrical essay, 1913), in which he explored the conflict between faith and reason as it is experienced by the "man of flesh and blood" in search of comfort in an anguished world. Unamuno's essays, novels, and poems emphasize the importance of feeling over intellect, the individual over society and the committed life.

Nineteenth Century Russian Origins

During the nineteenth century Russia was rapidly absorbing Western Enlightenment culture and ideals. At this time there emerged a class of intellectuals, Dostoevsky among them, who were uniquely placed to comment on the dislocation and upheaval that had resulted from efforts to scientifically engineer a rational society. Dostoevsky's most incisive attack on Enlightenment rationalism, particularly its utopian socialist form, is found in the short novel *Zapiski iz podpol'ĩa* (*Notes from Underground*, 1864). Its protagonist and anti-hero, the

Underground Man, a petty clerk in a Russian bureaucracy, inveighs against the Crystal Palace, a symbol of the possibility of a scientific and rational ordering of everyday existence. The Underground Man embodies the frustration, resentment, and whimsical, petty, malicious revolt that, according to Dostoevsky, such a project must inevitably produce in the ordinary individual whose one defining characteristic is not reason but freedom. Dostoevsky's later novels, most notably *Prestuplenie i nakazanie* (*Crime and Punishment*, 1866) and *Brat'ïaKaramazovy* (*The Brothers Karamazov*, 1880) continue to explore the problem of how to preserve free will without unleashing its destructive aspects.

A remarkably different Russian approach to existence is found in the fiction of Leo Tolstoy. In sharp contrast to Dostoevsky's preoccupation with the abnormal and monstrous features of human existence, Tolstoy's novels depict the normal events of life. His characters are often average middle-class men and women who, in rare moments, get glimpses of existential truth. His short novel *Smert'Ivana Il'icha* (*The Death of Ivan Ilyich*, 1884) had a significant influence on later existentialist treatments of death. It is a powerful portrayal of a middle-class judge, Ivan Ilyich, whose encounter with death exposes the inauthenticity of his common life.

The Twentieth Century

Several developments in the German tradition in the early twentieth century had a significant influence on later French existentialists. First there was the introduction of phenomenology by Edmund Husserl. Husserl's phenomenology was a method for discovering the structures that are essential to any possible experience. It involved a description of the consciousness of a knowing subject, which constitutes meaningful objects through its intentional acts. Existentialist philosophers Martin Heidegger, Karl Jaspers, and Jean-Paul Sartre utilized phenomenology to support existentialism. But they shifted their attention away from the knowing subject to the acting, willing, choosing subject in order to define the structures of human being in the world.

In addition, Franz Kafka's novels and short stories appeared around this time. Kafka was moved by his reading of Kierkegaard. Like Kierkegaard, he was attuned to the significance of extreme psychological states for revealing existential truth—particularly the experience of dread or anxiety, that is, an objectless fear in which the familiarity and meaningfulness of the world slips away and one enters a state of alienation that, for Kafka, often takes on surreal qualities. Thus, we find Gregor Samsa's alienation in "Die Verwandlung" ("The Metamorphosis," story, 1915) represented by his transformation into a dung beetle. Whereas Kierkegaard envisaged some salvation from anxiety through commitment or a leap of faith, the protagonists in Kafka's novels *Der Prozess* (*The Trial*, 1925) and *Das Schloss* (*The Castle*, 1926) are portrayed as cogs in a machine whose purpose they do not understand. His characters are condemned to live in the tension of an absurd relation to the world, that is, their demands for transcendence and justice are always frustrated, their efforts to find a meaningful place in the world blocked, their attempts to communicate meaningfully with others thwarted. *Der Prozess* is an especially poignant treatment of the experience of guilt and judgment in a world where God is absent, a theme that becomes so important in French existentialism. Kafka's love for the fragment and the rich ambiguity of his symbols effectively display the isolation, confusion, and alienation that characterize the human situation.

Another early twentieth-century German existentialist is the poet Rainer Maria Rilke. Rilke's *Die Aufzeichnungen des Malte Laurids Brigge* (*The Notebook of Malte Laurids Brigge*, fictitious diary, 1910) is the diary of a Danish aristocrat who ponders death, solitude, anxiety, and inauthenticity in a series of fragmented notebook entries. This work is a model of the existential anti-hero's search for identity and an authentic life into which death is meaningfully integrated. *Malte* is a prototype of Sartre's existentialist novel *La nausée* (*Nausea,* 1938). Rilke's masterful *Duineser Elegien* (*Duino Elegies*, poem, 1923) reflect his Nietzschean affirmation of life and the earth. Although the language of these poems is religious, they reject otherworldly Christian asceticism and celebrate an earthly spirituality. Martin Heidegger called Rilke's *Elegien* a lyrical version of his philosophical treatise *Sein und Zeit* (*Being and Time*, 1927).

Heidegger's *Sein und Zeit* constitutes an important event in the history of existentialism. In this work Heidegger attempts to reintroduce the problem of being in modern thought, to resurrect the sense of mystery and awe of being that he found to be a feature of early Greek thinking. According to Heidegger, modern humanity, immersed in a world of objects, has lost sight of the question of what it means for anything to be at all. Human being (Dasein) is a being for whom being is a matter of concern. Thus Heidegger begins his analysis of being with an analysis of Dasein. For Heidegger, Dasein (literally, "being there") is not a substantive ego, but a moving field or region of being through which a meaningful world is disclosed. Dasein's most fundamental mood is one of anxiety in the face of a finite existence. Death is encountered as the limit, the nothingness, the abyss that surrounds being. An authentic encounter with death as one's own can free Dasein to make a resolute commitment and to fall into the world without falling away from itself. Heidegger's analysis of Dasein played an important role in the development of Sartre's existentialism.

French Literary Existentialism

It is in the novels, plays, biographies, and essays of Jean-Paul Sartre that we find literary existentialism most fully developed. Sartre's existentialism has often been considered the product of a post–1945 mood of crisis and despair in Europe. For Sartre, involvement in the Resistance to the Nazi occupation of France brought home the terrifying freedom, guilt, and responsibility that characterize the human condition. Freedom is at the core of Sartre's philosophy. But it was before the war that he first layed out his theory of freedom and the spontaneity of consciousness. His first novel, *La nausée*, is written in the form of a diary. Roquentin, the author-hero of the diary, records events as they happen, thereby giving the reader a strong sense of a present moving toward an unknown future. The diary tells of Roquentin's discovery of the nausea that permeates his existence. Nausea is the symbol of the disgust that Roquentin experiences as the contingency of existence, a dizzying vertigo of possibilities. For Roquentin, existence is "de trop" (superfluous). There are no necessary relations between events or things, no necessary unfoldings of events in his own life or in the life of the Marquis de Rollebon, whose biography he is writing. Things overflow their boundaries, words refuse to attach to them, and nothing can be assimilated or digested, not even one's self. Indeed, Roquentin discovers that his self and his past have no fixed nature. His character does not lie behind his actions as their cause, but rather ahead of him as a possibility to be chosen. His consciousness is experienced as a meaning-endowing relationship to the world, which is spontaneous and undetermined.

The setting for the story is Bouville ("Mudville"), a symbol of the sliminess of being that entraps freedom and leads to the inauthenticity of the bourgeoisie, who in a spirit of seriousness and bad faith allow their existences to congeal by never questioning given values. According to Sartre, we all desire to be like objects, fixed and necessary, but since consciousness is always not what it is conscious of, and since consciousness is the permanent possibility of nonbeing that constitutes our freedom, to try to become like an object is to flee our freedom. Roquentin's only relief from the nausea that is produced when he becomes aware of his contingency comes during those moments when he hears a jazz melody whose notes follow one another in necessary progression. At the end of the novel, the protagonist abandons the historical project of writing a biography and resolves to write a fictional work instead. The suggestion is that all efforts to retell a life, whether one's own or another's are fictions insofar as they place an order on events that, when lived, are lived toward an open future. Roquentin's diary is his effort to capture moments as they are really lived through, to describe naked existence. With Roquentin's decision to write fiction, Sartre suggests that one can find salvation from contingency in art and imagination.

With the onset of World War II and Sartre's involvement in the Resistance, the moral dimensions of individual freedom were highlighted. The impulse to escape freedom and responsibility for others is a central theme in many of his works from this period.

For example, *Huis clos* (*No Exit*, drama, 1944) is a very successful study of "bad faith," that is, flight from freedom toward thinghood or becoming an object for others. The three characters in the play are situated in Hell (portrayed as a living room) where their punishment consists in torturing one another by refusing to see the other as he or she would like to be seen. Each character is left with no further possibilities of action, condemned to be an object in the eyes of the others eternally. Each desires to possess the freedom of the other, to fix his or her image once and for all. The play reveals the deathlike quality of an inauthentic life.

After the liberation of Paris in 1944, Sartre rose to fame as an existentialist.

Although existentialism developed a reputation as a philosophy of isolated individuals in despair, Sartre's work focused more and more on the importance of political commitment and struggle with others. This emphasis on struggle and social change was reflected in his theory of literature as well. In 1946 Sartre distinguished between the theater of characters and the theater of situations. (Sartre's analyses of the "situation" is adapted from Heidegger's notion of situated being, or *Dasein*.) According to Sartre, the purpose of prewar drama was to create and display character types, that is, the coward, the ambitious man, and to focus on the psychology of the protagonists. In contrast, the existentialist writer must reject a literature of character because it portrays the individual as determined by a ready-made character rooted in heredity or the environment. As we have seen, Sartre's view that the human being is free at every moment to rechoose him- or herself, coupled with his experience of the moral dilemmas of life during the Resistance, contributed to the development of his idea of a literature of extreme situations. Extreme situations are utilized to highlight the heroic choices that face ordinary individuals living toward an open future. Sartre's characters often face life-and-death-situations, which make painfully obvious the burden of freedom and responsibility that we all bear.

The idea of a literature of extreme situations is also connected to Sartre's view that literature is a mode of action. Literature is *engagé* or committed. The purpose of the writer should be to change the world, that is, to move the reader to reflect on society and its injustices and to assert his or her freedom. In an early formulation of his view on literature and commitment in *Qu'est-ce que la littérature?* (*What is Literature?*, essay, 1947), Sartre claimed that poetry (he refers to the poets Rimbaud and Mallarmé) could not be a vehicle of social change since it uses language to refer to itself and not as a translucent instrument of communication. In poetry, according to Sartre, the poet's freedom is engaged in a flight from reality. Later, in *Les mots* (*The Words*, autobiography, 1964) he acknowledged that prose can be equally as opaque as poetry, and he began to analyze the failure of language in general.

Sartre's trilogy *Les chemins de la liberté* (*Roads to Freedom*, novels, 1945–1949) is perhaps the best example of a committed literature of extreme situations. In these works Sartre addressed problems such as being for others, authentic action, and liberation. These three volumes trace the development of Mathieu Delarue, a philosophy teacher who discovers his freedom in France during the time of the rise of Nazism and the impending fall of France to the Germans. Having found his freedom, he must discover what to do with it, that is, how to act authentically. He is contrasted with Daniel, who constantly tries to escape his freedom by being for others, and with Brunet, a committed Communist who is faithful to the party and always acts without reservation. Unlike Daniel, Mathieu wants to act in good faith, and unlike Brunet, he experiences conflict over every decision, particularly if he is unsure whether his political ends justify his means. When he finally does act (instead of handing himself over to the advancing Germans, he dies in a defiant moment of rebellion), it is still not clear whether he has acted authentically. The problem of authentic political action is unresolved in the novels. Indeed, questions concerning the possibility of authentic political action and the problem of "dirty hands" remain central in the writings of all of the French existentialists in the postwar decade.

Sartre also developed the outlines of a theory of existential psychoanalysis. His method is illustrated in existential biographies of Baudelaire (*Baudelaire*, biography, 1947) and *Saint Genet, comédien et martyr* (*Saint Genet: Actor and Martyr*, essay, 1952). Although there are similarities between Sartrean and Freudian analysis, Sartre rejects libido theory and any form of determinism. Instead, he introduced the notion of an original choice, which constitutes an individual's basic orientation toward being in the world. For example, the decisive event in Genet's life is the moment when, at age ten, he is caught stealing. Henceforth, he sees himself as a thief condemned to remain outside the realm of "good" society. Sartre's notion of original choice is not deterministic in any final sense, since the individual is always free to change direction. Radical freedom of choice remains at the core of his psychoanalysis.

Finally, it is important to note that Sartre's work in the late fifties and sixties is preoccupied with the project of reconciling Marxism and existentialism, that is, showing how individuals freely create themselves out of situations that condition but do not determine their choices. Another biographical study, *L'idiot de la famille* (*The Idiot of the Family*, 1971), is an attempt to synthesize an existentialist analysis of Flaubert's life with a Marxist analysis of the historical structures in which Flaubert was situated.

Simone de Beauvoir's literary and philosophical writings are the product of her lifetime collaboration with Sartre. Much of her early fiction was inspired by her effort to work out in concrete detail the abstract principles of Sartre's existialism. But she also contributed to the development of Sartre's philosophy, focusing particularly on the project of laying out the ethical implications of existentialism. She stressed the importance of political liberation as a condition for self-determination and was also especially effective at showing the interrelationship between the personal and the political.

De Beauvoir's novel *Le sang des autres* (*The Blood of Others*, 1944) is a sustained reflection on the individual's responsibility for others, the source of guilt and the meaning of death in both personal and political terms. Set during the Nazi occupation of France, the novel describes the evolution of Helene, the mistress of a Resistance leader Jean Blomart, from flights of bad faith in which she loses herself in her lover and refuses to accept her responsibility for political events in Europe, to an authentic choice to join the Resistance movement, for which she eventually dies. Her lover Blomart, who must send her on the heroic mission in which she is fatally wounded, is the prototype of the existentialist hero who honestly accepts his freedom and responsibility, but is plagued with moral dilemmas that arise when one's free decisions are made in life and death (extreme) situations. The novel explores the theme of political violence and social change as well as the guilt that is an inevitable accompaniment of freedom in an unjust situation. De Beauvoir skillfully characterizes the dilemmas that face political actors who do not want to destroy the present for an unknown future but who recognize that political action is necessary even in the absence of a perfect solution to injustice.

De Beauvoir's most successful novel, *Les mandarins* (*The Mandarins*, 1954) is a further exploration of political violence and authenticity but also a remarkable treatment of the possibility of good faith in personal relationships. Thus it represents a significant contribution to Sartre's existentialism insofar as Sartre, himself, gave much less attention to the possibility of authentic love relationships and was often criticized for his cynical portraits of love as the desire to possess the freedom of the other.

Despite the fact that he consistently refused the label "existentialist," Albert Camus is well placed as a member of the literary existentialist movement. His starting point is the experience of the individual in a world without access to transcendent meaning; he emphasizes absurdity and the human being as a creator of values; and he responds to and is influenced by many figures in the existentialist tradition including Nietzsche, Kierkegaard, Kafka, and Sartre.

Absurdity and revolt are the basic themes around which Camus' writings revolve. His philosophical essay *Le mythe de Sisyphe* (*The Myth of Sisyphus*, 1942) contains a description of the absurd sensibility, that is, the experience of being born into a world that is not explainable in human terms and does not respond to human desires for transcendent meaning. Camus rejects suicide as an adequate response to our godforsaken existence and gives us a picture of existence as a Sisyphean task. Sisyphus is the absurd hero par excellence. With dignity and a life-affirming attitude, he accepts the challenge of his fate, which consists in the eternal task of pushing a boulder up a hill in full knowledge that it will roll back down. Thus, his dignity consists in his ability to affirm the value of life in full awareness of the truth of absurdity. Camus rejects the Kierke-gaardian leap of faith as an escapist philosophical suicide that deifies the absurd.

Camus' first novel, *L'étranger* (*The Stranger*, 1942), is a literary illustration of the absurd philosophy. Through the use of a first-person narrator, the *passé simple* tense, and an avoidance of causal language, Camus succeeds in giving the reader a direct encounter with the experiences of an absurd hero, Meursault, whose life consists in a succession of present moments over which he has little control. Meursault's estrangement is evidenced by his unwillingness to exaggerate his feelings (even at his mother's funeral) and his moral indifference. The novel portrays the inauthenticity of society that, in passing judgment on Meursault's honest moral indifference, finds a scapegoat for its own dishonest indifference. Condemned to die, Meursault refuses the metaphysical comfort that a priest offers him and affirms the value of his life in the face of an indifferent universe.

Whereas in his early writings Camus tended to advocate a hedonistic response to the absurd situation, in two later works, *La peste* (*The Plague*, novel, 1947) and *L' homme révolté* (*The Rebel*, essay, 1951), he introduced the theme of social responsibility. He also explored the problem of evil, both metaphysical and social, the humanist failure of Marxist revolutionary politics, and most importantly, the theme of rebellion against absurdity. Camus maintained that the individual's defiant rebellion against the scandal of absurdity reveals that something in humanity to which absurdity is an offense, namely, the value of individual life. His belief in the integrity of the individual made him critical of Sartre's willingness to apologize for left-wing violence and oppression. Camus called for a politics of moderation and of limits although he also supported leftist political goals. His play *Les justes* (*The Just Assassins*, drama, 1950), an example of the theater of extreme situations, was an attempt to portray the authentic revolutionary as one who recognizes that his or her moral integrity is violated by the killing of innocents, regardless of political ends. Camus was very critical of abstractions such as "humanity" and "justice" and demanded that these ideals always be understood in relation to concrete situations.

Later Developments

The theater of the absurd is a later development in theater that had a philosophical basis in existentialism. Eugene Ionesco's *La cantatrice chauve* (*The Bald Soprano*, drama, 1950) and Samuel Beckett's *En attendant Godot* (*Waiting for Godot*, 1952) present absurdity not only in content, as do their existentialist counterparts, but also in form. Thus, they ignore or distort conventions of structure, plot, and characterization and exemplify the failure of language in their dialogues in order to portray helplessly confused beings in an incomprehensible universe.

See also: Alienation, Anxiety, Nihilism, Theatrical Absurdity, Time, Underground Man.

Selected Bibliography

Barnes, Hazel. *Humanistic Existentialism: The Literature of Possibility*. Lincoln: University of Nebraska Press, 1959.

Barrett, William. *Irrational Man: A Study in Existential Philosophy*. Garden City, N.Y.: Doubleday, 1958.

Goldthorpe, Rhiannon. *Sartre: Literature and Theory*. Cambridge: Cambridge University Press, 1984.

Kern, Edith. *Existential Thought and Fictional Technique: Kierkegaard, Sartre, Beckett*. New Haven, Conn.: Yale University Press, 1970.

JANA SAWICKI

F

—————— // ——————

FAMILY

Classical Background

A sequence in Homer's epic poem *Odysseia* (*The Odyssey*, c. 8th century B.C.) shows the classical Greek understanding of the family. Homeless for ten years as punishment (by Zeus) for war crimes he committed in Troy, Odysseus returns from the Trojan War to Ithaca and there finds his wife Penelope under siege by greedy suitors attempting to take over his kingdom as his son Telemachus tries to fight them to protect it. In this homecoming Odysseus wears several disguises to avoid detection (even from his son), meets with his aged father, passes the public test of drawing the string of a great bow, and tells the secret of Penelope's wedding bed (it is constructed on the trunk of an olive tree). Odysseus, thus, rejoins "family" life by re-establishing specifically political alliances with his son, father, and wife. Foremost, however, is that he must kill the invading suitors and then make peace with their relatives so as to avoid continual feuding in the future. In this sequence, so-called family interests are interwoven almost completely with religious, political, and moral concerns, with the Greek sense of the morally "right" action in every aspect of one's life. Scarcely evident are any purely "familial" concerns, no view of the family as an entity in itself, the modern family as representing life set apart from strictly social experience. Rather, in evidence here is the Greek world's family—not a private sanctuary (the modern "haven in a heartless world") but a direct expression of the moral and public life.

The *Odysseia* yields the further assumption that the family in classical literature develops and extends itself along blood lines, most prominently from father to son. Telemachus, for example, saves Odysseus' "place" in Ithaca so that he himself as a son may later rule and head a family. There are hints in *Odysseia*, however, of another order, a new one made explicit later in Aeschylus' *Oresteia*

(458 B.C.). In this play Orestes is exonerated by the gods for killing his mother, Clytemnestra, to avenge his father's death. Instead of automatically taking further revenge for murder, the gods institute a new family principle—a new rule about the family as an institution in society. Henceforth, in the post-Orestean world the community's authority does not pass primarily through blood ties—thus, Orestes will be judged for his crime and will not be killed automatically by the Erinyes—but through adherence to a cultural law that binds humans and gods alike in a communal partnership (a legal agreement) of ajudication and social trust. Forever after, the law (any law) belongs to the community, not to the family, and familial, private justice, including automatic revenge for blood crimes, is outlawed.

With the advent of such cultural law in the post-Orestean world, the family, as separable from communal or strictly social interests, can be a creature independent of the social community only as an outlaw. The new outlaw family is shown in a number of classical plays, Sophocles' *Antigone* (c. 441 B.C.) and Euripides' *Mēdeia* (*Medea*, 431 B.C.) prominently among them. Sophocles' *Oidipous tyrannos* (*Oedipus Rex*, c. 429 B.C.) crystallizes the possible estrangment of family from community when Oedipus the king pursues his father's murderer for the community's sake, to end a plague. The subsequent discovery that the king has killed his own father and married his own mother surely serves the community's interests by bringing the truth to light, and it also brings the destruction of Oedipus' family. Similarly, in *Oidipous epi Kōlonō* (*Oedipus at Colonus*, c. 406 B.C.), Oedipus is exiled for the crimes he committed in *Oidipous tyrannos*, and the question debated throughout the play concerns the degree to which his family's rights conflict with Theban society's welfare, the community's need to strengthen the law and please the gods, all the while taking further revenge for previous family crimes. This split between community and family is apparent, too, in Euripides' *Trōades* (*The Trojan Women*, 415 B.C.) where the Greek's manner of vengefully ending the Trojan War, most dramatically in little Astyanax's brutal death, underlines that the foreign Trojan family relationships are officially noncommunal, asocial concerns—illicit and able to be dismissed.

The most savage conflicts in the separation of community and family, perhaps in all of literature, occur in Latin revenge tragedies in which illicit (private) family justice operates in complete independence of the larger community. This withdrawal into a private and closed family sphere is evident in Seneca's *Thyestes* (c. A.D. 45–55), a play about the cursed house of Atreus. Here Thyestes first commits adultery with Atreus' (his brother's) wife. In private revenge Atreus then kills, cooks, and serves Thyestes' sons at a banquet in Thyestes' honor. In this cannibalistic sequence familial justice has become an isolated, demonic sphere unrelated to the values of the larger society.

Thus, patent in classical literature is already a complex view of the family as both living in harmony with society *and* suffering from its isolation. Plato, for example, noting these different family views, speaks about a substratum of irreconcilable division in the family, a barrier between what he describes as daytime rationality and nighttime audacity—between the family's human and the bestial impulses. In book 4 of *Politeia* (*The Republic*, dialogue, c. 380 B.C.), he says, in possibly his most direct familial commentary, that the "rational and tamed" part of the soul normally can keep a person's appetites under the control of reason (social law), but when it slumbers "the wild animal part . . . becomes rampant" and "does not shrink from attempting in fancy unholy intercourse with a mother" or "hesitate to commit the foulest murder." The Platonic gasp at scandalous "unholy intercourse" and family "murder," the family's substratum of conflict, depicts the family as inherently split. In this regard, Orestes' decision in the *Oresteia* to destroy a family in order to avenge a family (killing his mother to avenge his father's death) shows the depth of the family's division. So does Oedipus' destruction of a family to gain a family (slaying his father and marrying his own mother) in *Oidipous tyrannos*. Both heroes—and this is not a solvable problem for Plato—profoundly want and do not want familial ties, simultaneously embrace and reject the family. This deep conflict, the family radically at odds with the larger community *and* itself, is a significant dimension of classical literature.

The gradual emergence in medieval Europe of a middle class is accompanied in literature by a growing sense of the family as a separate entity with its own fortunes. A foreshadowing of this development are the medieval romances, works that show the beginnings of an idealization of sexual relations—the coupling of martial valor and romantic success—that will be infused in the family more strongly later. Particularly Guillaume de Lorris' *Roman de la rose* (*Romance of the Rose*, didactic poem, c. 1230, continued by Jehan de Meung, c. 1275) heralds a kind of exotic sanctity inherent to sexual intimacy. The *Roman de la rose* argues, in effect, that a man and woman live in a private realm (in a potentially outlaw sphere) of their own and that sexual intimacy is self-justifying—outside of society.

A major conduit of this tradition is Geoffrey Chaucer's *Troilus and Criseyde* (poem, c. 1385). The lovers in *Troilus* join together nearly oblivious to the concerns of war and politics. The Trojan War eventually intrudes and separates them; thereafter, the poem's narrator condemns their illicit (private) union in Christianity's name. Chaucer's *The Canterbury Tales* (c. 1380–1400) further explores idealized romantic relationships in the "marriage group" of tales, especially in the *Knight's Tale* and *Wife of Bath's Tale*, in which sexual union (and the family that results) is depicted as a sphere separate from but not necessarily violating the bounds of the larger community.

The Renaissance

In the sixteenth century the gradual decline of monarchy, aristocracy, and classical learning helps to center the bourgeois family as an especially important institution. This century includes epics that further idealize (with some irony) romantic and familial union in connection with martial valor, such as Ludovico

Ariosto's *Orlando furioso* (1516) and Torquato Tasso's *Gerusalemme liberata* (*Jerusalem Delivered*, 1581). Toward the century's end the family is being idolized as a private realm that is (or should be) respected by the larger community. Such works as Edmund Spenser's *Epithalamion* (poem, 1595) and William Shakespeare's plays *Romeo and Juliet* (c. 1596) and *Much Ado About Nothing* (c. 1598) mark this trend to idealize family relations and the family sphere, as do Philip Sidney's *Arcadia* (prose romance, 1590), Spenser's epic poem *Faerie Queene* (1590–1596), and Shakespeare's comedy *The Merchant of Venice* (c. 1595).

The last of the sixteenth and beginning of the seventeenth centuries also show serious concern about the family as an independent order and asks what in an increasingly secular world enfranchises the family. What supports it? Why (in effect) is there a family? These questions are asked with dark overtones in revenge tragedies such as Thomas Kyd's *The Spanish Tragedy* (c. 1585), Shakespeare's *Hamlet* (c. 1600), and—most grisly of Renaissance revenge plays—John Ford's *'Tis Pity She's a Whore* (1633). Less violent are domestic tragedies where an imbalance or exaggeration of certain family ties, principally between husband and wife, causes the family to fly apart; Shakespeare's *Othello* (c. 1604), *Macbeth* (1605–1606), and *King Lear* (1606) exemplify the destructiveness of such weak and, conversely, overly strong (in either case, inappropriate) family ties.

The seventeenth century is an age of rational and critical examination of the family as one social construct among others. Pierre Corneille's *Médée* (*Medea*, 1635) brings back a famous family tragedy of betrayal and infanticide for a somewhat dispassionate analysis. John Milton's *Areopagitica* (pamphlet, 1644) inadvertently argues for the secular independence of the family by making the case for divorce—thus moving the family perceptibly away from the indissolvability of being an exclusively divine contract. Milton's *Paradise Lost* (poem, 1667), likewise, implicitly argues for a kind of divine sanction of marriage—but only in the context of its secular administration; Adam and Eve are on their own to make a success of the family institution. In much activity in the remainder of this century the family is held up to rational scrutiny, as if being tested for durability; in comedy see Molière's *Tartuffe* (1664), and in tragedy Racine's *Phèdre* (*Phaedra*, 1677). John Bunyan's prose allegory *Pilgrim's Progress* (1678–1684) is a late-seventeenth-century Puritan effort, the last major one in literature, to reappropriate the family out of its own sphere—to blend the family, in effect, into a larger (in this case, Christian) community. What we see in this period overall is the family's continuing emergence as a problematical institution, essential to social order and the community's survival and yet a fragile matrix of complex relations, a precursor of the modern family as a problem.

The Enlightenment

In the eighteenth century the family becomes a central concern for literature, and the deepest ties are forged between the family motif and newly emergent middle-class values in regard to work, religion, and sexuality. Voltaire's *Œdipe*

(*Oedipus*, tragedy, 1718), for example, reintroduces the deep familial crisis of the Oedipus legend but does so in middle-class terms (with a middle-aged lover for Jocaste). Daniel Defoe's novel, *Robinson Crusoe* (1719) explores the bounds of filial obedience and retribution. Likewise, Samuel Richardson's novels *Pamela* (1740) and *Clarissa Harlowe* (1748) focus on the relationship of familial and romantic ties and a woman's position and power in the course of family formation. Typical of the temper of the mid-eighteenth century are Henry Fielding's novels *Joseph Andrews* (1742) and *Tom Jones* (1749), works that scrutinize and deflate family pride, particularly the snobbism of wealth, and satirize weak families in an effort to strengthen the family as a secular institution.

In the remainder of the eighteenth century the family virtually comes into its own as a literary structure, more than just as a motif, but as an actual structuring principle in literature. For example, a measure of the eighteenth century's willingness to place cultural phenomena in a secular context is Denis Diderot's *Encyclopédie* (1751–1772), one of the greatest and most influential scholarly projects of this period. Diderot approaches the family with the same dispassionate approach in his plays, *Le fils naturel* (*The Natural Son*, 1757), *Le père de famille* (*The Father of the Family*, 1758), and his satire, *Le neveu de Rameau* (*Rameau's Nephew*, 1762–1784). A natural prime concern in this period's acceptance of the family as an entity in itself is education, in effect, the process of relating children to their parents *and* to society. Accordingly, in this period several estimates are taken of possible ideal education schemes, for example, in Voltaire's *Candide* (novel, 1759) and Jean-Jacques Rousseau's *Emile* (novel, 1762)—also, in its own way, in Rousseau's *Du contrat social* (*The Social Contract*, treatise, 1762).

The novels of Laurence Sterne (*Tristram Shandy*, 1759–1767) and Oliver Goldsmith (*The Vicar of Wakefield*, 1766) represent two treatments of the family typical of the later eighteenth century. In *Tristram Shandy* the life of Tristram and the adventures of his Uncle Toby constitute a virtual carnival of familial attachments and probings—an anatomy and handbook of family experience informed by much wit. *The Vicar of Wakefield* depicts much the same expanse of familial experience, but it does so to emphasize the precariousness of the family as a middle-class institution: in some ways self-sustaining as a unit but also dependent on social fathers (rich and powerful men) who control the larger society with questionable beneficence and dole out its economic rewards. Like Samuel Johnson's *Rasselas* (novel, 1759), *The Vicar of Wakefield* examines the gulf still remaining between the familial and private sphere and society and foreshadows the modern dilemma of attempting to bridge that gulf—and of finding it even wider than it appeared to be.

The Nineteenth Century

Nineteenth-century literature encompasses great extremes in the family's development. At one end, nearly eighteenth-century in its idealism, is Johann Rudolph Wyss' *Der schweizerische Robinson* (*Swiss Family Robinson*, 1812–

1827), a novel in which a shipwrecked family sustains itself exclusively through love and cooperation. Equally idealized, though more sophisticated, are Jane Austen's novels, particularly *Pride and Prejudice* (1813) and *Emma* (1816), in which there is a romantic conception of the family as a closed sphere only marginally threatened by the newly industrial and urban world. In Charles Dickens' novels the encroachment of the industrialized city is a fact, and the family is beleaguered as a result. Dickens' *Oliver Twist* (1837–1838) and *A Christmas Carol* (1843) depict the family sentimentally as a bastion of feeling, a circle of innocence threatened by the cruelty of the outside world. In other of his novels, *Bleak House* (1853), for example, more prominently *Hard Times* (1854) and *Great Expectations* (1860–1861), the commercial world seems to triumph as the family as an institution nearly collapses altogether.

This sense of a desiccated family sphere, of a collapsing private world— common in the nineteenth century as it develops—is strong in William Makepeace Thackeray's novel *Vanity Fair* (1847–1848), where a truly vital person, Becky Sharp, is destroyed by her inability to live within the narrow bounds of family experience. The same situation exists in Nathaniel Hawthorne's *The Scarlet Letter* (novel, 1850), in which Hester Prynne, in all of her creative luxuriousness, can survive only as a family pariah *and* as a social outcast. The most ironic, and possibly most vivid, portrait of family failure in this period is Gustave Flaubert's novel *Madame Bovary* (1856), in which familial sterility is the assumption behind Emma Bovary's equally empty romantic desires to transcend all that is familiar to her.

In much remaining nineteenth-century literature family values and the family as an institution are held up for intense scrutiny and analysis. In Dostoevsky's novel *Prestuplenie i nakazanie* (*Crime and Punishment*, 1866) a would-be "superman," in attempting to transcend and crush familial ties, accomplishes a critique of familial and private relations in the light of spiritual growth and community responsibility. On an even grander scale, in the novel *Brat'ia Karamazovy* (*The Brothers Karamazov*, 1880) Dostoevsky examines the nature of paternal authority and underpinning of family relations against perennial human needs for order and revealed truth; this is seen in Ivan's discussions with the Grand Inquisitor. Along this line is George Eliot's *Middlemarch* (novel, 1871–1872) in which family roles are analyzed in several ways, as conventional responses to human and communal needs. Casaubon, for example, is a conventional patriarchal figure but a poor husband for Dorothea. Such analysis of women's place in the family is of particular interest at mid-century and later, as is shown in the plays of Henrik Ibsen. In *Et dukkehjem* (*A Doll's House*, 1879) Nora, a bougeouis housewife, examines her family only to find in it an assemblage of outmoded conventions; thereafter, she leaves the family. The same desperation about the family as an adequate negotiator of individual needs and social demands is also expressed in Ibsen's *Vildanden* (*The Wild Duck*, 1884) and *Hedda Gabler* (1890).

One late-nineteenth-century response to this perceived family crisis is a revolutionary gesture, like that of *Prestuplenie i nakazanie*, Emile Zola's *Germinal* (1885). This novel shows the family's collapse within a picture of social evolution—in this case, the very gradual ability of mine workers to understand the economics and politics of their oppression and to break free of traditional familial and cultural ties. The misogyny of August Strindberg's *Fadren* (*The Father*, play, 1887), wherein women are the cause of the family's collapse, is another response to the family's disintegration. As the century closes, as is seen most clearly in Thomas Hardy's novels, the family-as-a-sanctuary seems actually to collapse. In *Tess of the D'Urbervilles* (1891) and *Jude the Obscure* (1896) impulses to create families (as the fortunes of Tess and Jude show) are seen as parallel or even identical to destructive forces—impulses to pain and to death. The family becomes a singular problem in literature, a site of human betrayal and a focus of what loosely is called the "modern crisis."

The Twentieth Century

In the twentieth century the family and its concerns tend to articulate a truly modern crisis. The subtitle of Thomas Mann's novel, *Buddenbrooks, Verfall einer familie* (1901), "a family's fall," indicating a scenario in which the family persists but is unstable and possibly unviable, begins to indicate the complex modern response to the family in literature. For example, common in modern literature are dark dissections of the family, explorations of it as decadent and possibly anachronistic, a hollow and compromised institution. August Strindberg's *Dödsdansen* (*Dance of Death*, play, 1901) dramatizes the family as stagnant, generally poisoning those within it, but particularly a disaster created by women. This drama of family failure is evident in works so diverse as Samuel Butler's *The Way of All Flesh* (novel, 1903), Anton Chekhov's *Vishnëvyĭ sad* (*The Cherry Orchard*, play, 1904), John Galsworthy's series of novels, *The Forsythe Saga* (especially *The Man of Property*, 1906; *In Chancery*, 1920; and *A Modern Comedy*, 1929), and Marcel Proust's novels *A la recherche du temps perdu* (*Remembrance of Things Past*, 1913–1927). But the most intense indictment and analysis of the family in this period is Franz Kafka's story "Die Verwandlung" ("The Metamorphosis," 1915). In this work, to be a family member is virtually to be monstrous, and Gregor Samsa is a monster insect—figuratively a family member caught between worlds with no defenses or ability to change.

Most influential in the twentieth century, however, is not the family as tragic or even absurd, but, rather, the family as a more generally symbolic and ironic construct, a manifold assemblage of potentiality and restraint. A key text in this regard is James Joyce's novel, *Ulysses* (1922), in which the family is cast self-consciously in mythic, folkloric, historical, biological, legal, political, psychological, religious, and philosophical dimensions—more or less all at once. In this modern (symbolic) version the family is a creation within the literary tradition, not in any way a natural development of culture but a symbol (still a cultural product) with connections to many areas of meaning. This deliberately complex view of the family is common to modernistic novels such as Virginia Woolf's *To the Lighthouse* (1927) and William Faulkner's *The Sound and the Fury* (1929), *Light in August* (1932), and *Absalom, Absalom!* (1936)—all novels in which the family has a deliberately symbolic status. Often this modern depiction of the family is called "mythic," but examination of a complex work such as Jean Giraudoux's *Ondine* (play, 1939) shows that this is so only if "mythic" means an intended multiplicity of meanings.

While this modern version of the family dominates twentieth-century literature, there are significant experiments in other depictions of the family. John Steinbeck's novel *The Grapes of Wrath* (1939) explores specifically political responsibility within the family, particularly in relation to Steinbeck's idea of a biological life urge. William Faulkner's novels *The Hamlet* (1940), *The Town* (1957), and *The Mansion* (1959) follow the cultural transformations, in part from country to city, in the modern American South. Albert Camus' *L'étranger* (*The Stranger*, novel, 1942) focuses on a familial disruption at a level thought to exist as fundamentally prior to political, cultural, or psychological experience—an existential level of alienation that seems to preclude beneficial family experience.

It is a paradox of modern literature that the family—seemingly overtaxed and fragmented as a motif, pulled in too many different directions of meaning—is still a rich source for literary innovation. The midcentury depiction of the family (perhaps emblematic for twentieth-century literature) is captured by Eugene O'Neill when he describes *Long Day's Journey into Night* (1956) as a play "in which things occur which evoke the whole past of the family and reveal every aspect of its interrelationships. . . . At the final curtain, there they still are, trapped within each other by the past, each guilty and at the same time innocent, scorning, loving, pitying each other, understanding and yet not understanding at all, forgiving but still doomed never to be able to forget." This depiction of the family as a trap and yet still a nurturing source belongs equally to Bernard Malamud's *The Assistant* (1957) and *A New Life* (1961) and Günther Grass' *Die Blechtrommel* (*The Tin Drum*, 1959)—novels with ambivalent, divided views of the family.

After midcentury, the era called "post-modern," there are several important depictions of the family. John Updike's "Rabbit" trilogy of novels (*Rabbit, Run*, 1960, *Rabbit Redux*, 1971, and *Rabbit is Rich*, 1981) shows Rabbit and Janice Angstrom's family nearly destroyed by personal tragedy and by the cultural and political tensions of the 1960s and 1970s—and also its resurrection. The same pattern of familial disintegration and resurrection is apparent in Edward Albee's play *Who's Afraid of Virginia Woolf?* (1962), where the hopeful reintegration of the family occurs in a mood uncharacteristically sentimental for the twentieth century. Along side these realistic family stories are postmodern novels such as Thomas Pynchon's *The Crying of Lot 49* (1965), where Oedipa Maas attempts to understand family and personal ties, her own and those of her community, within the disturbingly complex matrices of computer technology and contemporary information theory. Equally postmodern in its treatment of the family is García Márquez's *Cien años de soledad* (*One Hundred Years of Sol-*

itude, 1967) wherein the Buendía family (like a strand in a Möbius strip) winds through history disappearing and reappearing, always changing but never really leaving behind what has come before—the family as irreducibly complex and paradoxical, a unity divided against itself.

Literature and Family Studies in the Twentieth Century

Eugene O'Neill's tableau of the family as a problem of warring relations comes from the recognition of a former world, as Peter Laslett (*The World We Have Lost*, 1965) explains in a sociological context, that the modern world has lost. The lost world, conceived either as a state of mind or as a social situation, was one in which "the whole of life went forward in the family, in a circle of loved, familiar faces, known and fondled objects, all to human size." Having lost it, as Laslett says, we are "very different from our ancestors." Whether the loss is historical or mythological, the price of self-knowledge has come to be unrelieved conflict in self and society. This cultural burden T. S. Eliot depicts in *The Waste Land* (poem, 1922) as "A heap of broken images, where the sun beats,/And the dead tree gives no shelter," and it is a burden weighted with every concern—psychological, social, and political—the word "family" touches. For this reason the family as a problem, as a sphere of conflicting loyalties, expresses much about the modern world. And this recognition of an unalterable division in human nature mirroring that between family members is what the work of T. S. Eliot, James Joyce, Sigmund Freud, and many others suggests. Finally, then, a principal emblem of modern culture, particularly of the late nineteenth and twentieth centuries, is a Picasso-like tableau of a family like O'Neill's, lately arrived to stand before a wasteland, in mourning or in reverie, living with a cultural awareness of the past that allows for no future.

With this modern sense of loss and lost innocence, however, has come the gain in knowledge that accompanies a fall. Theoretical understanding, for example, advances dramatically when Marx and Engels investigate the family by laying bare its ideological foundations within a context of class struggle. From that moment onward the family is not the main drama of human behavior but a single play in a large repertoire. Then, following Marx and Engels in a different universe of discourse, Freud shows a familial pattern beneath economic and social life and, thereby, deeply undercuts the primacy of the economic critique of the family. And certainly the questions Marx and Freud raise are still in conflict. Does the power of economics and of the historical dialectic shape people and their familial relationships, as Marx believes, or does the Oedipal situation, with its cultural determinations, structure social and economic life at every level, as Freud believes?

Between these poles, between Marx and Freud and their respective critiques of power and of culture, most significant investigation of the family takes place. And as the family discussion in the twentieth century has become more complex, the power/culture debate has divided into discrete areas of study—economics, political science, and sociology, on the one hand, and depth psychology, literary criticism, and culture studies on the other. And since the 1930s there has taken root in the gaps between disciplines the development of family-centered studies. These family studies suggest the possibility, as Christopher Lasch notes, of providing "the missing link between cultural and intellectual history" and "politico-economic history," or, more simply, "between the study of culture and the study of . . . power." Additionally, there is the profound familial meditation of the *sciences humaines*, connected with the French rereading of Nietzsche, Hegel, Saussure, Freud, and Heidegger, and there are the anthropological studies and family histories of Claude Lévi-Strauss, Philippe Ariès, Simone de Beauvoir, Peter Laslett, Edward Shorter, Juliet Mitchell, and Lasch himself.

To understand more fully what O'Neill's picture of the modern family means, we need to ask fundamentally what the literary family is. We know that the family may be seen as the destroyer and creator of culture. In an essay on modern drama, Arthur Miller describes the literary family as a regressive tendency in literature, a tendency to rely on the depiction of familiar emotional responses and associations. "Society" (as a term), on the other hand, as opposed to "family," means a direction in literature to explore and seek out new truths. Miller suggests that "family" and "society" are inherently in conflict (*The Theater Essays of Arthur Miller*, Robert A. Martin ed., 1978). Even Freud, who defines culture in terms of the family, sees the same conflict. In *Das Unbehagen in der Kultur* (*Civilization and Its Discontents*, 1930), he says: "One of the main endeavours of civilization is to bring people together into large unities. But the family will not give the individual up. The more closely the members of a family are attached to one another, the more often do they tend to cut themselves off from others, and the more difficult it is for them to enter into the wider circle of life." This Freudian view is reflected in Miller's idea that the family is (as modern literature shows it) the child's shelter that becomes the adult's prison.

The Miller view of the "family" as a circle of innocent but restrictive relationships set against "society's" bold exploration exists, as poststructuralist critics have shown, in relation to further assumptions. The family has a structure related to capitalism and to the other institutions of the West and, thus, to a structural intention expressed in the father figure. Just as Thomas Sutpen, in *Absalom, Absalom!* excludes all who seek to enter his family "design" without pure (white) blood and a paternal sanction, the familial concept depends on the power both to exclude and to contain and on the enforcement of a paternal line of influence that originates with a founding patriarch. Subsequent generations are thought to be extended expressions of his authority. As the family constitutes a trap for those within it, family members do not cross the father's "line"— regarded by all with love and hate because it divides people from each other even as it groups them within familial boundaries. Furthermore, a family member, like Quentin Compson, must sustain conflicting responses to authority, succumbing to neither, or else fail in the family and die in exile from it. Thus, while Miller understands the family in terms of its inherent opposition to society, the problematic nature of the family exists within the family itself. That is, just as Quentin Compson's dilemma is an inability to respond to the deep division of familial attachments, O'Neill's portrait shows the family existing on a fault line, in light and dark divisions of its own making. Thus, in the Miller view the family/society opposition is an outward expression of a conflict *within* the family, the family as "guilty and at the same time innocent," as O'Neill says. Membership in the family, therefore, brings at the same time a sense of bondage within the paternal prohibition.

This picture of the father is helpful. Yet stopping here means understanding the family solely in terms of the male line. Sandra M. Gilbert (*Cornell Review* 6 [1979]: 54) shows that this is not correct. Regarding the family in literature, Gilbert grants that "of course the patriarchal notion that the writer 'fathers' his text just as God fathered the world is and has been all-pervasive in Western literary civilization, so much so that, as Edward Said has shown, the metaphor is built into the very word, *author*, with which writer, deity, and *pater familias* are identified." Gilbert stresses, however, that as phallic authority exists in literature there is a complementary relationship with a female authority (the mother) characterized as "The Solemn—Torrid—Symbol—/The lips that never die." Presenting this image of uniquely female authority, Gilbert elaborates Mary Shelley's depiction in her "Author's Introduction" to *The Last Man* (1826) of the Sybil's cave: "a dim sea-cave that was nevertheless *open* to the sky"— that is, it has " 'an aperture' in the 'arched dome-like roof' which 'let in the light of heaven.' " In the cave are "leaves, bark and 'a white filmy substance,' " living icons of a "specifically sexual texture" that stand for a "Goddess' power of maternal creativity." What Gilbert proposes here is a serious assertion of female power along side the father's—a true bond of reciprocity between mother and father. As the mother is a source of "primordial power" and creativity, she is a principle of familial structure along with the father. In this way Gilbert brings the mother into the family and, implicitly, into the scene of conflicting desires that O'Neill portrays.

So, O'Neill's portrait begins to fill out as a coupling of paternal and maternal authority and a source of strong attachments that, consequently, may be judged in a variety of ways. At one extreme in a range of critical judgment is a view of the family as contained within a superstructure of ideology and class conflict. This view generally asserts the potential for social analysis through literature and focuses on the workings of political and economic power as it appears analogously in literary structures. Literary criticism from this perspective on power often sees the family as a curse on social relations since the family's stabilizing tendency in society, the same that Miller notes, impedes "social" aims that are extra- or even anti-familial in intent. This view would show, for example, that the family metaphor prominent in Dickens' *Hard Times* is set against and obscures conflicts in the novel between workers and bosses—"real" social issues. *Hard Times* proposes and then collapses real political conflicts while superimposing the (false) reconciling metaphor of child-parent relations, as if mine workers could be called children and the mine boss a father. On the other hand, as Catherine Gallagher has shown (*Arizona Quarterly* 36 [1980]: 70–96), Elizabeth Gaskell's *North and South* (1855, novel) is a rejection of the family metaphor in favor of an argumentative comment on fictionally depicted working-class issues analogous to those in the workaday world. Thus, from this viewpoint, by abandoning the familial metaphor for social criticism, Gaskell's novel attains a degree of political relevance and responsibility. Confined to its proper sphere, as this Marxist position claims, the family metaphor can be almost innocuous. Left to dominate literature, the exclusive family focus trivializes real social content and makes mere entertainment of literature.

At the other extreme of critical response is a view of the family as a generator of culture, a view in which all fictional relations repeat variations on the Oedipal situation (child, mother, father) in which the child internalizes the mother's nurturing capability and the father's "law," what Gregory Bateson (*Steps to an Ecology of Mind*, 1972) calls "a difference which makes a difference." That is, the child must not merely repeat the Oedipal experience but incorporates its meaning. This psychoanalytical approach to literature derives its authority not so much from an examination of an author as a psyche behind the text but from the structure (internal workings) of texts themselves.

With the valuation of the family as an essential determinant of culture, another boundary of critical response to the family is set. Between this Freudian meditation on culture and the Marxist meditation on power, critical response is limitless and, of course, need not be derived solely from either side. For historical and theoretical reasons, however, Freud and Marx are convenient signposts for the literary criticism that actually is being done on the family. Within their bounds the most influential approaches are those that examine myth and those that concentrate on the role of women in literature.

Myth criticism, exemplified by Northrop Frye's *Anatomy of Criticism* (1957), neither depends entirely on social reference for its authority nor sees the family as an all-encompassing structure. Frye's version of the "quest" contains a "descriptive" phase in which social issues are relevant. It also contains a symbolic marriage. In neither reference, however, does society or the family give exclusive definition to the quest. So, on the one hand, Frye's myth criticism may describe familial influence without referring to a world outside of literature. Along the same line, for Harold Bloom (*The Anxiety of Influence*, 1973) it is a "strong" poet like John Keats who "fathers" poetry in Wallace Stevens and with whom the descendant poet must struggle. Myth criticism, then, because it can draw directly on society in its approach to the family in literature, can be situated to the left of psychoanalytical criticism, but is still a good distance from the Marxist approach that subordinates the family (and literature itself) to a social or economic reality.

Further to the left in this spectrum is the majority of literary approaches that focus on the role of women in the family. From Simone de Beauvoir's *Le deuxième sexe* (*The Second Sex*, essay, 1949) to Kate Millet's *Sexual Politics*

(1970), Shulamith Firestone's *The Dialectic of Sex* (1970), and Sandra M. Gilbert and Susan Gubar's *The Madwoman in the Attic* (1979), the feminist approach analyzes the literary family for a reflection of women's psychological and economic status in society. Such feminist approaches, often strongly mimetic in their orientation, are at times identical to a Marxist criticism (clearly so in the case of Shulamith Firestone) in assuming literature's immediate service to and comment on social reality. Although some feminist approaches depend less on a reference to a world "out there," in feminist criticism the family often is investigated and judged according to a standard of social verisimilitude.

Now, standing back from these critical approaches, we can see certain rough lines that blend into a single perspective on thought about the family in literature and family studies. First, whether seen from the viewpoint of Marxism, feminism, myth criticism, or psychoanalysis, the family occupies the place, structurally, of an origin. This is true whether the family is an origin of capitalistic, exploitative society; of the patriarchal dominance of women; of the separation of ego from the (Jungian) Great Mother; or of the inauguration of the Oedipal situation. Second, in each case, this origin in a later stage becomes a shelter for the individual who must venture out unsheltered and into a realm of experience in a different key, as it were. From the Freudian and mythic perspectives, the family-as-shelter is Edenic, or, at least, like King Lear's court before his abdication, a world in which desire and satisfaction are separated by little. From the feminist and Marxist perspectives, the family shelter is often a necessary evil and a fact of historically verified oppression, a plague, like Gregor Samsa's family in Kafka's "Die Verwandlung," or, like Sutpen's family in *Absalom, Absalom!* a circle of pain and death. Third, in all four approaches the experience of the individual's shelter gives way to one of "exposure" or of opening forth. In the Freudian and mythic views this exposure is a fall from Eden and a discovery of pain, like the strife Lear finds on the heath. The family in effect splits internally along the lines of desire and satisfaction. In the feminist and Marxist views, the opening forth is, rather, a loosening of chains, an unbinding of Prometheus, and a promise of restitution. In the literary moment when the family is sloughed off, Ibsen's Nora leaves her house and her husband's domination, and the proletariat becomes it own ruler. Fourth, after the initial loss of the family as a shelter, which necessitates a transition to exposure, the first relationship with the shelter is reclaimed as knowledge *about* the family—the family being an origin to be lost ("the world we have lost") and, thereafter, to be refound through recollection as knowledge. Therefore, although the valuation of the family as a literary structure is divided between Marxists and feminists, who tend to emphasize the restrictiveness inherent to the family, and myth critics and Freudians, who tend to emphasize the family as an essential metaphor in literature, the family metaphor as a complex of "origin," "loss," and "exposure" is a structure implicit in the whole range of critical thought.

This taxonomy for the family metaphor in literature may seem to play down the differences within and among the four views. However, the differences that distinguish between feminist views or between psychoanalytic approaches, for example, are highlighted in this contrast, which emphasizes different initial assumptions. In fact, it is only by placing these possibilities within a range of response that the question of approach has any real significance. It follows that the study of the family in literature at some point must be a study of approaches.

We can stand back farther yet from perspectives on the literary family and an even wider picture comes into focus. For—and in this we are taking the critical range itself as a text—in the separation of Marx and Freud is a telling estrangement of the political group from the individual psyche. This division, which makes little critical sense because group and individual are conceptually dependent on each other, is one that authorizes a political view of the family in literature, on the one hand, and a psychological view, on the other. The appearance of separation between group and individual, then, must be a useful illusion allowed by the absence of a mediating third term, a term that unites both, contains both, and yet is identical to neither. The third term, furthermore, would have to be a structure that expresses the possibilities of critical response that are not defined strictly in terms of group and individual, those that exist within the wide boundaries of power and culture.

The mediating term is evident when we realize that between collective, political existence and personal, psychic life is, in fact, the family, a system wherein psychic life is founded in a relationship with others. It need not be argued that this mediation perfectly reconciles Marx and Freud, but only that structurally the family is the mediation for terms that do not exist unconnected. Accordingly, in the different views of the family, as in O'Neill's family portrait, is an expression of ambivalence in the Marxist "no" to family structure and in the Freudian "yes"—in effect a somewhat abstract but accurate manifestation of family structure. Further, in the imagery of "origin" common to all four approaches is the maternal "primordial power," and in the common expression of "loss" is the paternal prohibition, the law. Thus, the pattern of origin and denial emerges as the structure of the family in literature and also as the pattern that unites the various perspectives on the family.

From this new vantage point the Platonic gasp at unholy intercourse and the division between nighttime audacity and daytime rationality (a division that in O'Neill's vision becomes *ambivalence*) are once again pertinent. We return to Plato's depiction because, as Freud explains, the drama of ambivalence is re-enacted in us as we watch Oedipus, or any character, male or female, enact "unholy" experience. In that character, as Freud says, "our wishes of our [own] childhood have been fulfilled, and we shrink back from him with the whole force of the repression by which those wishes have since that time been held down within us." Similarly, amid perspectives on the family the encounter of power/culture, Marx/Freud, group/individual is a re-enactment of the crisis of ambivalence depicted in all family scenes. Therefore, the discussion about the family in literature itself expresses a familial discourse wherein unities are sundered and then rediscovered, and where power and culture alternately fold into each other in a sheltering and then an opening forth. In essence, a discussion about the family—in a very broad sense—repeats the familial pattern it sets out to isolate and to objectify. This rather startling but unavoidable puzzle, wherein the literary family and discussion about the literary family get entangled, and wherein one seems to become the other, seriously threatens to efface the commonsense separation of critical discussion *about* literature from literature itself. And yet this whole investigation tends to suggest that there is indeed a kindred, familial bond between perspectives on the family and the thing called the family.

See also: Adolescence, Great Father, Incest, Oedipus Complex, Parents and Children, Psychoanalysis of the Self, Search for Father.

Selected Bibliography

Ariès, Philippe. *Centuries of Childhood: A Social History of Family Life*. New York: Knopf, 1962.

Armens, Sven. *Archetypes of the Family in Literature*. Seattle: University of Washington Press, 1966.

Lasch, Christopher. *Haven in a Heartless World: The Family Besieged*. New York: Basic Books, 1977.

Tobin, Patricia. *Time and the Novel: The Genealogical Imperative*. Princeton, N.J.: Princeton University Press, 1978.

ROBERT CON DAVIS

FEMINISM

Feminism is both an ideology and a political movement. As an ideology it is complex, historically variable, and necessarily reticulated with contradictory contemporary ideologies. Long before feminism became an organized political movement in the nineteenth century in most parts of the world, literature had already inscribed many of the conditions of women's lives against which feminism protests. Centuries of worldwide male domination of written culture have produced a perennial interest in the nature and place of women and intermittent periods of recognition that women are more capable and various than is generally acknowledged in the dominant culture. Heroines capable of critical verbal and behavioral resistance to the oppression of women appear, for instance, in the literature of China's T'ang Dynasty (A.D. 618–905) and of fifth-century Athens. A feminist theme, however, is not only characterized by sympathetic recognition that women's lives are seriously limited in a male-dominated world. It also entails recognition that relations between men and women and ideas about women and the options allowed to them ought to be changed. Although the definition of the predicament of women and the vision of what should and can be changed varies greatly with time and place, the literature informed by feminist insight and reaction to it reveals the development and continuities of feminist ideology.

The Renaissance

The "querelle des femmes," starting in France around 1400, is the most clearly marked beginning of European literary feminism. For at least two centuries France witnessed a continuous outpouring of literature about the relative merits of women and men, frequently based on interpretations of the Christian creation myth and arguments drawn from classical sources. The most significant early feminist participant in this crucial quarrel is Christine de Pisan. Her many works include the long poem *L'épistre au dieu d'Amours* (*Epistle to the God of Love*, 1399) and *La cité des dames* (*The City of Ladies*, 1405). Though she does not thoroughly challenge the hierarchical relations between men and women, Christine de Pisan exposes the failure of men to treat women according to the courtly and Christian ideals they espouse and analyzes the reasons for the virulently expressed lies of the misogynist tradition. By summoning historical and legendary images of learned, faithful, and strong women, she institutes the now time-honored feminist strategy of displaying positive female role models in order to refute men and to bolster female identity.

Christine de Pisan's emphasis on female moral and intellectual capacity is echoed by later fifteenth-century writers such as Teresa de Cartagena in Spain and Laura Cereta in Italy. In an autobiographical defense of her controversial theological writing, *(Admiraçión operum Dey*, c. 1450), Cartagena disclaims belief in the equality of the sexes but asserts that it is proper for women to write. In her letters Cereta challenges the notion that female inferiority is ordained, enjoining women to concentrate on learning rather than appearance. Unlike other learned women humanists of her time, she also aggressively responds to male attacks and condescension. However, some writers during this period went even further. In order to honor Eleanora of Aragon in Ferraro, a number of treatises, poems, and orations went so far as to celebrate female superiority. But the opportunistic exaggerations of works honoring a female ruler only partially constitute a feminist theme. The examples of Cartagena and Cereta announce the primary emphasis of the first two centuries of literary feminism. Repeatedly we encounter male and female defenses of exceptionally learned women.

Because he was widely translated and wrote many books about women, Desiderius Erasmus may be the most important European feminist of the first part of the sixteenth century. Primarily through dialogues between traditional misogynists and defenders of women, he develops arguments that are rather advanced for his time, even though they include predictable contradictions. He generally rejects a double standard in education and sexual morality, praises women for some areas of equality with men, and softens the authority of husband over wife. Nonetheless, his vision of increased liberty for women rests on the belief that education will develop in them the self-control and virtue they lack. Furthermore, although it works to improve certain opportunities and images of women, Erasmus's writing does not question women's economic dependence and exclusion from public activity. In this respect and in his justifications of education for women he typifies early feminism as it is voiced by men. In works that are often autobiographical, women writers emphasize the personal satisfaction of learning as a virtue in itself and as an alternative to marrying and child-bearing. Sympathetic male writers are likely to be motivated more by the desire to apply social meanings and controls to revisions of women's roles that might have revolutionary effects if they are not integrated into established institutions and affective structures (Lula McDowell Richardson, *The Forerunners of Feminism in French Literature of the Renaissance, Part I,* 1929).

The Seventeenth Century

Louise Labé is an instructive example of the unfolding of feminist themes in sixteenth- and seventeenth-century France, for her introduction to a volume of poems (1555) suggests the suitability of women experiencing and rendering love and sensuality. By the seventeenth-century women rendered scarcely anything else in France, the development of salon society and Neoplatonist emphases having led to the expectation that women would temper their learnedness with gracefulness. Both the absence of such restraint and the existence of female pedants are attacked in several plays by Molière, a very engaged contributor to the stock antifeminist theme of mockery of female intelligence as superficial, virile, and unnatural.

In contrast, in Spain María de Zayas y Sotomayor includes in her love stories narrated by multiple male and female speakers not only protests against the educational deprivation of women but also against male conspiracy to deceive women sexually. Female powerlessness to control abusive fathers and husbands also figures in her list of grievances. Probably the first Spanish feminist, in *Novelas amorosas y exemplares* (*Amorous and Exemplary Novels,* 1637) de Zayas tells stories about love in such a way that female readers can receive an education in how to survive and male readers an education in how to reform.

A feminist defense of the amorous and scholarly engagements of women also is made by the Mexican writer Sor Juana Inés de la Cruz. Her autobiographical *Respuesta a Sor Filotea de la Cruz* (*Reply to Sister Filotea de la Cruz,* 1691) describes the debilitating effects of denying women education and of isolating those women who do earn acknowledgment of their learnedness. In reaction to a tradition that defines sexual activities as triumphs for men and transgressions for women, that is to say the double standard, her poems include witty denunciations of men for eliciting from women behaviors that are then excoriated. Such poetic jibes at men also appear in the works of a number of women writing in the late seventeenth and early eighteenth centuries in England. They also wrote verses deliberately praising other women and dispraising aspects of marriage, the education available to women, and male receptions of writing by women. Aphra Behn's poems are notable early examples of the ironic appropriation of male forms and themes in order to allow distinctively female experience and feminist perspectives to be heard. Apologies for writing, discrete pleas for understanding, and sometimes more spirited defiance characterize many of these works written at a time when for a woman to write at all was still an act of protest that itself may be a feminist gesture.

The Spanish medieval debate about the relative superiority of men and women, often referred to as feminist, was followed by a more distinctly feminist theme in Golden Age drama of the seventeenth century. Many plays feature the *mujer esquiva,* a woman strongly resistant to love and marriage. They introduce female characters who explain why female identity is threatened by close association with men and take dramatic steps to improve their position or that of other women. Pedro Calderón de la Barca's *Afectos de odio y amor (Feelings of Love and Hate,* 1657) is notable for the presence of a female ruler who makes provisions for the entrance of women into public roles. The eruption of feminist ideology in such works, however, is almost always contained by denouements in which the reluctant heroine is conquered or humiliated by love, which represents nature's refutation of unnatural female pretensions to equality with men and self-sufficiency.

In contrast, heroic women resist pressure to conform in some seventeenth-century Chinese literature. P'u Sung-ling's (1640–1716) "The Lady Knight-Errant" from *Liao-chai chih-i (Tales of the Unusual from the Leisure Studio,* 1679) is one of many tales about the woman-warrior, this time including a woman who willingly loves a man while refusing marriage and asserting her right to avenge her father's enemy.

The Eighteenth Century

Eighteenth-century China witnessed the eruption into literature of an entirely indigenous feminist theme: Yüan Mei (1716–1797) used poetry to protest footbinding.

An undercurrent of feminist themes also can be detected in the eighteenth-century novel in England and France. Indeed, it has been argued that there is a symbiotic relation between the rise of the realistic novel and the rise of feminism, for from its beginnings the novel appealed to female audiences by representing versions of female subjectivity previously elided and showing aspects of female experience that may lend legitimacy to feminist responses. Literary expositions of female poverty, vulnerability to the vagaries of the marriage market, and subjection to stern male authority figures can be read as expressions and provokers of feminist consciousness, though at the same time the prominence of heroines who die or enter conventional marriages indicates the novel's participation in traditional ideology. It has been argued that despite the punishment suffered by the female protagonists, the sexual freedom and cynical knowledge of Antoine-François Prévost's *Manon Lescaut* (1731) and Madame de Merteuil in Choderlos de Laclos' *Les liaisons dangereuses (Dangerous Acquaintances,* 1782) suggest that women need not be slaves to love and the unwitting victims of rakish male machinations. Daniel Defoe's heroines defy the pervasive law of the English novel that the loss of female chastity leads to the loss of life. Furthermore, it has also been argued that the conventional plots and sentiments of many works by women of this time screen a subtext of virtually feminist protest. Certainly many such works include indictments of female education and male behaviors. But on the whole few writers come close to the commanding despair and rage of Mary Wollstonecraft's incomplete novel *The Wrongs of Woman: or, Maria* (1798). In this novel, a justly disobedient woman is imprisoned in an asylum by her husband and consequently meets a cleaning woman whose life story points to the shared oppressions of women of various classes. This emphasis on women as a class does not become prevalent until the twentieth century.

Within the safety of forms that do not have to propose consequent social change, drama contributed to the loosening of restrictive ideas about women. For example, English comedy of the eighteenth century parades a number of female characters who wryly describe their position in the system of courtship. Unlike critics of the same time, playwrights could stage the possibility of female independence of mind without suggesting structural changes in male domination. A similar dilution of progressive currents occurs in eighteenth century Spanish dramas in which the justness of women having a say in choosing husbands is acknowledged at the same time that only the most self-effacing heroines are rewarded with husbands deserving of love. Such literature exemplifies a notable literary capacity for making currency out of historical changes in the freedom allowed women only to reinvest it in the message that social order depends on the continuing subordination of women in the family. In this way historical perceptions of necessity continually interact with feminist themes in literature. In contrast, the iconoclastic, sensationalist English writer Mary de la Riviere Manley includes in *Secret Memoirs and Manners of Several Persons of Quality, of Both Sexes from the New Atalantis* (1708–1711) what may be the first lesbian utopia, a genre that burgeons in the twentieth century.

The Nineteenth Century

Early in the century the Chinese writer Li Ju-chen wrote an enchanting narrative about imaginary voyages, *Ching-hua yuan* (*Romance of the Flowers in the Mirror,* c. 1827). In addition to providing frequent examples of the equality of the sexes, the book includes a visit to "the country of women," where men are treated like ornaments and must suffer bound feet under the rule of a female king. Feminist writers frequently have employed such role reversals to expose the unnaturalness of many restrictions imposed on women.

A number of cultural and economic changes in the nineteenth century helped to make possible an increase in the articulation of women's grievances and in the imagination of possibilities for women. Sensitive thermometer that it is, literature recorded many of the changes in the climate of opinion. Most of the feminist themes that matured in the nineteenth century survive in the twentieth century because similar conflicts and dreams still characterize images of women.

Building on centuries of defenses of woman's capacity and right to learn, nineteenth-century writers began to resist the idea that female characters should choose between the alternatives of love and learning. In France in particular, once it became possible to assume that a woman is capable of exercising imaginative intelligence, her right to exercise self-defined, sexual femininity as well could become a prominent issue. In *Corinne ou l'Italie* (*Corinne, or Italy,* novel, 1807), Madame de Staël dramatizes what is now a favorite feminist theme: the conflicts between genius and womanliness. Similarly, George Sand created heroines who consciously and successfully defy their assigned roles. They protest against the double standard and also exercise the male prerogative of sexual freedom. In addition, Sand creates more typical nineteenth-century heroines, those who are tormented by the disjunctions between the ideology and reality of female existence.

Much nineteenth-century European literature noted the ways women in particular are stifled by the rules of courtship and marriage, the double standard, and enforced economic dependency. Realism and naturalism were marked by a concern with exposing the difficulties of individual lives, including the lives of women affected by divorce and custody laws and attitudes toward illegitimacy and poverty. Gustave Flaubert's novel *Madame Bovary* (1856) is only one of many texts that expose a woman's fatal boredom with bourgeois marriage. In conjunction with concern for the exploited in general, novelists such as Emile Zola represent the intersections between the economic and sexual oppression of female workers. Though such literature usually does not propose feminist solutions or project alternative images of the nature of women, it underscores the same circumstances of women's lives addressed by feminism. Outside of Europe, in the novel *Sab* (1841) the Cuban writer Gertrudis Gómez de Avellaneda y Arteaga dramatizes what became a standard feminist parallel between the positions of slaves of both sexes and all women. The popularity of the theme of the fallen woman in the nineteenth century exemplifies the impossibility of completely separating feminism from other reformist impulses or even from a tradition of representing victimized women so that sympathy and respect coincide with titillation.

The Norwegian writer Henrik Ibsen wrote several plays with feminist themes. Though predictably embedded with contradiction, *Rosmersholm* (1886) dramatizes the connections between nineteenth-century liberalism and feminism. Without reaching any clear conclusion, it calls into question the legitimacy to both men and women of the faith of the fathers, including the faith that one person can rule a household wisely without seeking consensus and equality. Ibsen thus embodies the historical, ideological, and literary intersections in the development of democracy and feminism. Furthermore, the play summons the popular and sometimes accurate association of feminism with free love while indicating that resistance to sexuality is also an important aspect of nineteenth-century feminism. Similar themes emerge in Spain in the novels of Emilia Pardo Bazán. Her ambivalence about female capacities does not keep her from powerfully indicting the inequities of absolute paternal power over female marital choice and the differential treatment of illegitimate children according to their sex. She also shows very sympathetically and systematically how the capacity for creating change is inhibited in women of all classes by the myths of romantic love.

The less violently revolutionary Anglo-American nineteenth-century world also includes significant continuations of feminist themes. A number of texts explore the circumstances of aspiring, special young women whose lives are cramped by gender. Many of the novels advertise the heroine as completely pure; more complicated novels attribute the sufferings of heroines to their needs for recognition from men and to the culturally constructed frustration of that need. English novels especially emphasize the plight of middle-class women whose obligations to earn livings, frequently as governesses, reveal the contradictions in an ideal of domesticity that was not only experienced as deficient by some participants but also was not available to everyone. The scandalous vehemence of Charlotte Brontë's influential novel *Jane Eyre* (1847) and the approval given a woman abandoning an abusive husband in Anne Brontë's novel *The Tenant of Wildfell Hall* (1848) are examples of midcentury feminist tones and themes in English literature.

The strong American women's movement is also reflected in that country's literature in the nineteenth century. In *Work: A Story of Experience* (novel, 1872–1873) Louisa May Alcott deplores the lack of work for self-supporting girls. This was another important theme of nineteenth-century feminism, which usually responded to the plight of unmarried women in dire circumstances without envisioning women combining domestic and public work. Nonetheless, like Madame de Staël, in *The Story of Avis* (novel, 1877) the popular American writer Elizabeth Stuart Phelps exposes the problems of a woman trying to be creative and free while married. Elsewhere Phelps also dramatizes a woman's pride in being able to choose to sacrifice her ambitions for her family, thus pointing to a side of the feminist theme often lost in discussions of literature of protest and reform.

The peculiarly Anglo-American obsession with the Angel in the House appears to be consistently antifeminist. In fact, it is highly overdetermined, for nineteenth-century feminism included an insistence on the separate spheres and moral capacities of the sexes. A number of feminist utopias written at the time in America envision a world dominated by the attributes associated with maternity. Women nurse the world and clean up the messes left by men in such works as Mary Griffith's *Three Hundred Years Hence* (novella, 1836). In other more standard realist texts, to recognize feminist themes the reader must be prepared to hold on to a paradoxical sense of the disharmonious continuity linking feminism and convention, feminism and the perennial "woman question."

Male as well as female writers influenced by egalitarianism and romantic yearnings for freedom created, however ambivalently, strong female characters who articulate feminist protests or embody in their circumstances the conditions against which feminists had begun to fight by the 1860s. By the end of the nineteenth century and continuing through 1920 many novels about the New

Woman recognize the righteousness of feminist protest, though many novels
about the New Woman also include skepticism about feminist methods and hopes.
The English writers Sarah Grant and George Egerton and the South African
writer Olive Schreiner joined a number of other women writers in analyzing
female self-destructiveness as a consequence of a socialization that cultivates
parasitic, frustrated relations with men. The theme of an inherent antagonism
between the sexes enacted in the body and in the social order is prominent in
such works of women's suffrage propaganda as Elizabeth Robins' popular play
Votes for Women (1907). By this point in literary history a substantial number
of women writers deliberately wrote sensational novels about abusive men and
feisty but flawed women in order to raise the consciousness of middle-class
female readers. Furthermore, many women writers began to insist that only
women could tell the untold stories of women's lives because male writers were
too biased to do so. (Elaine Showalter, *A Literature of Their Own: British Women
Novelists from Bronte to Lessing,* 1977).

At the same time a number of writers used the image of the New Woman to
present feminism as a negation of society rather than an attempt at re-creation.
The strength of many representatives of the New Woman is undercut considerably
by a tendency toward self-destructiveness and violence toward others that comes
out particularly in tortured resistance to marriage for the sake of an emancipation
that is figured as almost without content. Though on the surface their grievances
are legitimate, the women are presented as so neurotic it is hard to believe they
are capable of living up to the opportunities they demand. Thomas Hardy's Sue
Bridehead in *Jude the Obscure* (novel, 1896) is an example of this use of the
figure of the New Woman.

Henry James's *The Bostonians* (novel, 1886) is one of the finest examples of
literary suspicion about the unnaturalness of feminism, which is understood
variously as man-hating, utopian, masochistically obsessed with the sufferings
of women, and prone to ignore the wider context of human suffering. Portraying
the forums used by feminists and by the other reform movements with which
they were associated, James represents feminism in part as a rhetorical vaudeville
act. At the same time, *The Bostonians* aptly includes an equally extreme example
of the explicit demands made by men against which feminists arrayed arguments
and alternative female communities. Some of the more anxious attacks on feminism through the image of the New Woman assume that marriage and liberation
cannot be combined and so conclude it is primarily neurotic women, ill-adapted
to their sex role, who are raising all this furor within themselves as well as
between men and women.

The Twentieth Century

In H. G. Wells's infamous *Ann Veronica* (1909) feminism is also a significant
theme. The heroine is shown justly rebelling against her father's authority,
discovering how hard it is to find work that will allow a young woman to be
independent, and joining a suffrage demonstration. But ultimately her feminism

is subordinated to an almost mystical biologism that involves the woman finding happiness in home, family, and her husband's work. Such a novel implicitly proposes a more egalitarian ideal of marriage as the alternative to feminist agitation. In *Ann Veronica,* as in many other works with feminist themes, feminism is presented as an outside force intruding on individuals rather than as a force growing from within women's consciousness of their circumstances.

In contrast, feminism is the voice of reason and hope in Sibilla Aleramo's novel *Una donna* (*A Woman at Bay,* 1906). Threatened by madness and even death, the heroine leaves her brutal, confused husband and dearly loved child. The anguished personal voice of this Italian novel insists on one woman's desire for sexual awakening; outlines the contradictions between her oppressive married life and her feminist writing, in the process informing the reader about early twentieth century Italian feminism; and reports provincial customs that protect a woman's honor by depriving her of experience and mobility.

The absence, dwindling, obliteration, or troubled development of a sense of purpose are as much feminist themes as the somewhat mistaken but still meaningful sense of the historical value of her individual life that characterizes the New Woman. Edith Wharton and Kate Chopin dramatize female anguish about the uselessness of women in genteel society. In the second decade of the twentieth century in England, May Sinclair contributes several fine novels powerfully focused on the attempts of women to define themselves despite the effects of stifling families and stifled sexuality. Sinclair's *The Tree of Heaven* (1917) in some ways exemplifies a significant turning point in feminist literary themes early in the twentieth century in the Anglo-American world. Dismay at feminist violence and skepticism about the possibility of transforming society through public activity led a number of writers to posit a pastoral female world or a distinctly female preoccupation with consciousness as an antidote to a male-dominated public world. In her novels, *Night and Day* (1919) and *Mrs. Dalloway* (1925), by representing suffragettes as pitifully limited personalities, Virginia Woolf echoes this modernist preference for female personalities whose inner lives can be evoked lyrically.

With an acute consciousness that women had been defined as Other and might experience themselves as such, many modernist women writers explored the existential and ontological meanings of feminism, whether or not they publicly affiliated themselves with the movement. Their works include Dorothy Richardson's attempt in the eleven volumes of *Pilgrimage* (novels, 1915–1935) to convey one feminine consciousness exhaustively; Hilda Doolittle's (known as H.D.) autobiographical fictions, which wrestle value out of interludes of debilitating intoxication with men, and her lyrical revisions of such legendary female figures as the Virgin Mary and Helen of Troy; and Edna St. Vincent Millay's sometimes perfectly glib and sometimes eloquently serious poems about affairs. In these works reticence and propriety are often relinquished so that women can challenge androcentric notions of which literary topics have universal significance.

In such works the question of women's rights often becomes embroiled with questioning of what it means to be a woman through exploration of a female consciousness of precious inwardness. Though such literature is obviously a product of various literary currents, it also registers an anxious response to specific historical circumstances: an increase of opportunities for women at the same time that certain structural dilemmas persist.

One of the dilemmas that especially haunts the feminist imagination early in the century is that the increase in sexual freedom for women is both liberating and debilitating, as can be seen in the poems of Yosano Akiko (1878–1942). Though the Japanese can cherish the remarkable achievements of women writers during the Heian period (794–1185) and a tradition of strong samurai heroines, feminist themes do not clearly make their way into Japanese literature until Hiratsuka Raichō founded the magazine *Seitō* (*Bluestocking*) in 1911, in part as a forum for feminist literary efforts. As the most famous poet associated with the magazine, Yosano Akiko wrote deliriously sensual poems that celebrate a woman's right to her feelings while revealing the depressing as well as exhilarating effects of preoccupation with love. Later in the century the same themes can be found in the early work of the Iranian poet Forugh Farrokhzad, whose poems often evoke the squandering of female sexuality on unworthy men, the sexual politics of passion, and the persistence of desire. A tendency to savor sensual experience as a source of knowledge that may also be a deprivation of identity is a feminist theme in that many writers have seen it as a problem peculiar to independent women. It is reflected in an almost worldwide production of what might be called the masochistic love lyric or, at least, the politicized lyric of loss.

The theme surfaces in novels as well, notably but less impacted with depression in the work of France's most significant woman writer of the early twentieth century, Sidonie Gabrielle Colette (1873–1954). Though literature frequently has represented feminists as male impersonators, Colette is a prototype of the writer whose feminist themes emerge out of an unabashed self-identification as feminine. Many of her heroines are women who strive to combine strength of character with the vulnerability attendant on sensuality. The problems of reconciling love and independence, managing to leave paternalistic men or to find psychological balance while involved in love triangles, and cherishing female bonding in itself and as a protection from suffocating involvement with men are all significant twentieth-century feminist themes addressed by Colette.

A similar concern with how women maintain their individual identities in the midst of passionate attachment to others emerges in *Liubov'pchel trudovykh* (*Love of Worker Bees,* novel and short stories, 1923) by Aleksandra Kollontai, an important Russian feminist. One of the reasons the desire for the love of a man may be seen as especially problematic is considered in the trilogy *Mujer y hombre* (1955) by the Spanish writer Elena Soriano, in which we see a classic example of a woman who desires both spiritual and sexual communication with a male lover who is incapable of imagining a fusion of body and spirit. A belief that male and female patterns of intimacy differ so sharply that female dissatisfaction is almost guaranteed persists as a feminist theme today.

Of course, this self-conscious grappling with new options while feeling persistent internal constraints expresses a kind of privileged confusion. It is usually not a theme in literature about poor women and married women with children. The stories of women with no sense of choice, no liberal education that might enable resistance to the tug of custom, are also included in the feminist theme. In *La amortajada* (*The Shrouded Woman*, 1938), the Chilean María Luisa Bombal tells the story of a woman whose life is tragically disappointing because she accepts the reigning belief that every woman can be fulfilled by investing all her hope in love of her husband and children. *Balún-Canán* (*The Nine Guardians*, 1957) by the Mexican writer Rosario Castellanos is also a representative example of the admonitory tale with strong feminist themes. In addition to defending indigenous Indian populations, the novel records the tragic effects of the repression of female sexuality, including guilt, fearfulness, and a sense of unreality. Also, like the Argentine poet Alfonsina Storni, Castellanos writes poems critically describing women's role in Spanish American society (Lucia Fox-Lockert, *Women Novelists in Spain and Spanish America*, 1979).

Though the depression and World War I witnessed some erosion of interest in the women's movement, a number of American writers in the 1930s produced fiction intertwining the themes of feminism and socialism. Using traditional narrative forms, Josephine Herbst, Tess Slesinger, and Agnes Smedley point to the contradictions in the lives of working-class heroines and other women committed to labor reform. They show these women struggling politically and personally with men whose radicalism does not extend to an analysis of family and sexual relations. Today the same themes appear notably in the work of the American novelist and poet Marge Piercy.

Similar themes appear in twentieth-century Chinese literature. During the modern period in China many writers assimilated elements of Western values sharply in conflict with traditional expectations for youth, including young women. Furthermore, because Chinese women lived under many of the revolutionary circumstances leftist feminists around the world are trying to create, feminist heroines often are women for whom the possibility of total commitment to social action empowers irreversible repudiation of traditional female roles. Before she was beheaded in 1907 at the age of twenty-eight, Ch'iu Chin wrote straightforward poetic demands for the emancipation of women through their participation in nationalist struggles. In *Zai heianzhong* (*In the Darkness*, short stories, 1928), Ting Ling (or Ding Ling) interrogates the conditions of oppression as well as women's responsibility for their submission, particularly through romantic obsession. (see Yi-tsi Mei Feuerwerker, *Ding Ling's Fiction: Ideology and Narrative in Modern Chinese Literature*, 1982). Pa Chin's novel *Chia* (*The Family*, 1931) features an unflinching picture of a young woman first driven to suicide attempts because of beatings and belittlement from her mother-in-law and husband but finally liberated by her efficacy as a village leader. Similarly, in "Meng Hsiangying Stands Up" from *Li Yu-ts'ai pan-hua* (*The Rhymes of Li Yu-ts'ai*, 1943), Chao Shu-li exposes the violent absurdity of traditional expectations for women and models new possibilities for resistance through revolutionary activity.

In the twentieth century, stories about the diversity of women have proliferated alongside the unabated production of literature in which women characters are seen only through the way they inspire or undermine men. With the resurgence of the women's movement in the late 1960s and throughout the 1970s, we begin to see again a number of texts that address a feminist perspective. As in the past, romantic impulses and the forces of socialization are significant aspects of the feminist theme.

Representations of the tragic repressiveness of marriage and sexual relationships characterize many works of literature, of course. This theme is feminist when the perspective is that women are especially constrained by the institutions and rituals of heterosexuality. They are not given many alternatives to marriage and are invited to define themselves exclusively as wives, mothers, and caretakers by a process of socialization that cultivates romantic dispositions. Furthermore, this socialization consists of suppressing one's own desires with a zest and spontaneity associated with the male expression of self. Though communication between mates is at best intermittent, sexuality is an arena of contest, and relationships are often presented as ego destroying rather than generative; women find it hard to leave their men in most versions of this feminist theme.

In *Les stances à Sophie* (*Cats Don't Care for Money*, 1963), Christiane Rochefort presents this theme with an economy of words and wonderful wit. A spirited heroine, contented that her life is going in no particular direction, drifts into marriage because of what she uncertainly calls love and because her lover wears her down with the logic of the male bourgeois. After a stint as a resigned housewife, she erupts into humorous cynicism about wifedom as prostitution and joins in a playful dialogue with another "wife," who becomes her lover. As she unravels herself from the fabric of married life, she remarks on the synergism of sexual politics, language, and the economic and political orders.

Rochefort's radical suspicion that what men and women do together threatens female identity is one of the many contemporary feminist themes in the important work *Novas cartas portuguesas* (*The Three Marias: New Portuguese Letters*, 1972) by María Isabel Barreno, María Teresa Horta, and María Velho da Costa. Frankly describing the pleasures and dangers of female sexuality in the context of other discourses on female oppression, this work models in its very structure one feminist solution. Its joint authorship, by three women accepting and helping to complete one another's thoughts, gives a priority to the attachment to one another that is supposed to disrupt patterns of complete bondage to love and men. A related emphasis on the importance of female friendship appears in Christa Wolf's *Nachdenken über Christa T.* (*The Quest for Christa T.*, novel, 1968), which is structured by one woman's devoted investigation of the choices made by another woman. The interdependence of different types of women is also a feminist theme in Irmtraud Morgner's novel *Leben und Abenteuer der Trobadora Beatriz nach Zeugnissen ihrer Spielfrau Laura* (*Life and Adventures of the Trobadora Beatriz as Chronicled by Her Minstrel Laura*, 1974), just as it is in the science fiction novel *The Female Man* (1975) by the American Joanna Russ. Russ is one of many authors, frequently published by small women's presses, whose treatment of female friendship extends into representations of lesbian relations, a highly significant contemporary feminist theme.

In the 1970s the United States witnessed the publication of numerous tales about unhappy marriages and the process of liberation. The stories women told each other in consciousness-raising sessions made it into print. Imprisoning suburban marriages have been presented from the perspective of wives who are neglected by gallivanting, obsessively ambitious husbands who are more comfortable being authoritative than they are being introspective. The things women give up and have to put up with are emphasized. This description explains their descents into madness or depression or fuels their discoveries of feminist impulses. In texts such as Marilyn French's *The Women's Room* (novel, 1977) the talk of women redescribes reality and allows women to redefine themselves. Often women in such novels take action, determined to imitate the more liberated women they meet, to avoid the fates of others, to help themselves and other women. Sometimes the women leave marriages and find rewarding careers and unconventional relationships. Frequently, women leave boyfriends and marriages, but they have no place to go. Their new-found liberty is given little content; what they walk away from is represented more fully than what they walk toward. Repeatedly we see details about female sexuality, the frustrations of discussions with husbands and lovers, the ritualized humiliations of the unskilled woman's job search, the unacknowledged labor of housework and child-care, and the intense ambivalence of feelings about mothers.

After feminism began successfully to draw attention to rape, wife abuse, and sexual harassment, the number of straightforward foregroundings of these themes also increased. In *The World According to Garp* (1976) John Irving powerfully depicts a woman's rage at the violence of rape—an act that has been eroticized by many writers. The most internationally notorious rendering of a woman's difficult choice of abortion occurs in the novel of Oriana Fallaci, *Lettera a un bambino mai nato* (*Letter to a Child Never Born*, 1975). The formerly taboo topics of wife abuse and incest are treated in Alice Walker's searing *The Color Purple* (1982). This novel explores a number of differences with which feminism grapples, including those of class, sexual preference, and race. Walker also uses her narrative to trace parallels between sexism and imperialism.

Many of the major themes of twentieth-century feminism are embodied in the works of a number of contemporary writers from the Middle East. The protest against the faithless husband who has withdrawn from his family appears with a specificity that reflects conditions in much of the Middle East in the work of

Ilfat Idilbi, an internationally known Syrian writer particularly concerned with
the lives of women. An angry husband unaware of the separate consciousness
of his wife and eager to throw her aside is presented as well by the Moroccan
writer Leila Abouzeid. Middle-Eastern women writers with a feminist consciousness also depict the debilitating consequences of male independence from
family life and control over decisions. The theme of female friendship tested by
class differences and differing commitments to tradition and a husband is exhibited poignantly in a novel by Emily Nasrallah, a highly acclaimed Lebanese
writer. The problems facing women committed to revolutionary struggles alongside male comrades who choose traditional women as lovers are depicted by
Daisy Al-Amir, an Iraqi writer whose four volumes of short stories bear titles
that announce the conjunction of traditional and feminist concern with love. (See
Elizabeth Warnock Fernea, ed., *Women and the Family in the Middle-East: New
Voices of Change,* 1985).

Just as Western and Middle-Eastern writers have made a feminist theme of
their native marital customs, in Africa literature written from the perspective of
women includes description of marriage and related activities. The Nigerian
writer Buchi Emecheta's novel *The Joys of Motherhood* (1975) includes many
of the themes already discussed but with differences that reflect aspects of some
African cultures. The title of the novel is both straightforward and ironic, for
we see a major protagonist whose only joy and identity come from being the
mother of nine children: a grueling position that includes being taken for granted,
being treated as a commodity as she is sold to an unknown husband for a bride
price, listening to her husband make love to a second wife, and being harassed
for barrenness in a first marriage and for excessive fertility in the second. The
novel also specifies the effects of modernization and urbanization on women
who thus lose the protections, status, and productivity allowed in traditional
communities. Furthermore, Emecheta indicates how Western colonization, particularly through the introduction of Christianity, destroyed Nigerian appreciation
of independent, strong women. The willingness to sacrifice everything for the
education of male children and nothing for girl children compounds the problem
because it is clear that the girls are being raised for obsolescence. Emecheta's
writing is a literary primer on international feminist issues as well as issues
indigenous to Africa. Equally powerful novels about traditional women tormented
by severe patriarchal authority have appeared in Japan. *Hanaoka seishū no tsuma
(The Doctor's Wife,* 1966) and *Ki no Kawa (The River Ki,* 1959) by Ariyoshi
Sawako and *Onnazaka (The Waiting Years,* 1949–1957) by Enchi Fumiko are
examples.

Though for centuries the feminist theme in literature necessarily has been
articulated with bitterness and has tended to emphasize the tragic limitations
of the place of women under patriarchy, it also includes an imaginative vision of alternatives. Many feminist writers have revived and revised images
of women from the past. Amazons and goddesses as well as such historical
figures as Harriet Tubman are the subjects or muses of poems. For instance,

Ch'iu Chin, mentioned before, attempts to inspire women with the figure of Joan of Arc. A number of contemporary Chicana writers, appalled by all the animus directed at Malinche, the Indian woman Cortes used as interpreter and mistress during the initial stages of the conquest of Mexico, have written eloquent revisions of her meaning in Mexican history and of her life as a woman.

Just as the first stage of the organized women's movement inspired the production of numerous utopias, the contemporary women's movement has promoted visionary literature. The influential novel *Häutungen* (*Shedding*, 1975) by Verena Stefan follows the exposure of a woman's dissatisfaction with typical heterosexual routines with her stripping away of the layers of acculturation smothering her essential self. Through loving other women and herself she arrives at states of being and consciousness that are meant to depart from those modes that aid patriarchy. Similarly, the American Sally Miller Gearhart's *The Wanderground: Stories of the Hill Women* (1978) associates sensual plenitude and coordination of mind and body so that special powers can be exercised within all female communities. A more physically violent and concrete utopian feminist image is offered in *Les Guérillères* (1969) by Monique Wittig. In that novel the feminist theme of women asserting power, in part through recovery of past power, coincides with experimentation with language motivated by the assumption that linguistic organizations shape an oppressive reality at least as much as material and psychological forces.

The pervasiveness of feminist concerns is also clear in literature in which they are not a dominant theme and, of course, in the literature of backlash. Suddenly the feminist appears as the ultimately desirable pal and sexual partner in detective fiction. At the same time, one sees fiction in which the female characters are described as valuable because they are not man-hating careerists. Just as there are numerous works of fiction that explore the possibilities, dilemmas, and social changes wrought by feminism, there are many texts, written mostly but not exclusively by men, which protest the effects of feminism on male characters or on the family or on social life in general. We can certainly anticipate that for many years feminism will continue to be a theme struggling within world literature.

See also: Alienation, Amazons, Lesbianism, Utopia.

Selected Bibliography

Gilbert, Sandra M., and Susan Gubar. *The Norton Anthology of Literature by Women: The Tradition in English*. New York: Norton, 1985.

Miller, Beth, ed. *Women in Hispanic Literature: Icons and Fallen Idols*. Berkeley: University of California Press, 1983.

Morgan, Robin, ed. *Sisterhood Is Global: The International Women's Movement Anthology*. Garden City, N.Y.: Anchor Press/Doubleday, 1984.

Resnick, Margery, and Isabelle de Courtivron. *Women Writers in Translation: An An-notated Bibliography, 1945–1982*. New York: Garland, 1984.

MARY M. CHILDERS

FOOL

Although the history of the figure of the fool is a long one covering probably all cultures in one variation or another and appearing through all known time in differing forms and functions, its most impressive literary manifestations for the West were from late medieval times until the beginnings of the Enlightenment. The figure appeared again in the late nineteenth and early twentieth centuries, especially strong in the plastic arts where the figure was generally called "clown" rather than fool. One of the most difficult aspects of describing the phenomenon of the fool is the immediate certainty that the concept is so broad and diverse that one is foolish to think it can be stabilized in a description. It could be helpful, therefore, to consider the figure as a set of fairly distinct yet related phenomena rather than as a coherent and stable concept to be described linearly.

The shamans and performers among certain American Indian tribes are not like the fools found in the Bible, nor are either of these the same as the holy fools of Moslem societies. And Folly, the creation of Erasmus, is neither an inhabitant of London's Bedlam nor a counterpart to Lord Rochester's monkey, although one could surely establish filiations between all these examples, including even some figures from ancient Egyptian paintings, which have traits quite similar to those found in the mentioned examples.

In attempting this overview of the fool figure in literature, some of the divisions and general structure of Enid Welsford's early, masterful, and comprehensive study, *The Fool: His Social and Literary History* (1935), will be followed. Some attempt to differentiate kinds of fools through the ages is necessary, even though such categories will never be exclusive. First, there are court fools, usually individuals with some peculiarity or deformity, who have learned to protect themselves from the cruelty of society by making fun of themselves (and often of others), discovering in this experience how sense and nonsense can be used to their advantage by amusing others and turning society's cruelty against itself. These practitioners may well have been sound of mind, ones who counterfeited foolishness, and could be called artificial fools. The village fool, on the other hand, is commonly a natural fool, or simply a "natural," that is, a person with some skill and sense, but one clearly in need of protection, one whose mental abilities are faulty but who has learned to adapt to protective surroundings. Some court fools, of course, could also be "naturals," but one would hardly find an artificial fool playing the village fool. In country festivals that date from early Christian times (and some no doubt even from pre-Christian cultures), fools often played a part; in fact at festival time there was license for the general population to play the fool. As these practices became more organized and self-conscious, some of them grew into controlled performances and became sources for secular theater.

In ancient Greece and Rome, there is evidence of people with deformities, usually dwarfs, who were household pets in the houses of the wealthy. In the Egypt of the Pharaohs, as later in Moslem societies, there were dwarfs and others with physical deformities who held positions of some importance, and to call these individuals fools would be misleading because physical deformities do not necessarily mean mental deficiencies. Also, however, in Near Eastern societies, those who are mentally deficient are considered to be under divine protection. Given, therefore, the special treatment that these people have had at different times and in many places, one is led to recognize that physical and/or mental deficiencies could be taken as signs of special gifts, which made these people mysterious since they seemed not fully human and existed on that line of demarcation between one being and another. The tradition of divine protection for them fits with Paul's remarks in the Epistles to the Corinthians where fools along with women and children are given special access to salvation. In addition, there is evidence of the related belief that people with certain deformities (given beliefs in the sympathetic qualities of magic) had the power to ward off the evil eye, an almost universal opinion among Mediterranean peoples. For these reasons, it is not difficult to see relationships between divine protection for the deformed and foolish and the view that these people could in both cases have special gifts. It was thought that they had a gift of seeing further, of understanding more profoundly, than ordinary humans.

The artificial or court fool, like the fool in literature, will have different appearances but will keep many of these fundamental traits of the fool. Whether artificial or natural, his presence usually afforded entertainment, by his wit or by his antagonism, or by his being the butt of his own or others' jibes. The fool, whatever his particular appearance, seems always to have that ambiguous position of being inferior and superior, and while he can inspire both ridicule and fear, he needs protection but can also protect others against evils.

From the beginning the figure seems to include some of those opposing character traits that remain even today. They are simulacra of humans but ones bereft of right reason and unable to maintain acceptable behavior—qualities that define humanity. They are outcasts yet familiar, repulsive yet able to charm and entertain, even to amaze with unexpected wit. Their relationship with the other world (or worlds) was recognized in most places, but especially in the Near East, where they were seen as the chosen, the touched by God, the empty vessel through whom the powers beyond could transmit messages. This is, however, not the attitude taken in the Hebrew Wisdom literature of the Old Testament, where the words "fool" and "folly" are the contrary of divine wisdom. The words characterize that stubborn blindness of humankind that refuses to accept that we can conform to the divine laws that are imprinted in us. The quotation from Proverbs, "The fear of Jehovah is the beginning of wisdom, but the foolish despise wisdom and instruction," indicates how the concept in this culture could be expressed without the ambivalence it will so often carry elsewhere.

Despite the breadth and variety of this topic, the figure of the fool retains sufficient coherence to allow general agreement on a set of his characteristic traits. In the broadest sense, the figure of the fool could be considered as one possible symbol of partial or temporary disorder, one that is allowed to exist for a variety of reasons within the seats of order. If the fool seems ubiquitous, it also seems to be true that he appears more readily in societies where order is more rigid. And the figure is ambivalent. Fools are chiefly male, and although female fools have appeared through history, a common trait of the figure is that it can be sexless or androgynous so that either sex may counterfeit the other. The following list offers other ambivalences to be found in the figure: he was at once safe and dangerous, child and adult, servant or slave yet with special privileges, attractive and repulsive, human yet not quite so, free and enslaved (both physically and mentally), agile and awkward, petted and abused. This short list of opposing qualities could be helpfully reduced to three more inclusive pairs: divine and diabolical, not fully part of a culture yet not simply held by nature, and finally an unpredictable mixture of folly and wisdom, in action as in thought. Such a description of the fool may, of course, evoke in the reader an echo of what we like to think of as its opposite, the human being, making the fool therefore simply the distillate figure of humanity or of the human condition. In the medieval image, "nobis est et speculum" (he is our mirror).

The Ancient World

In both Greece and Rome, there was a long tradition of entertainers called mimes who seem to have acted individually or in groups, in theaters, in the streets, and in the houses of the great. They were thus known by all strata of society, but because their art seems to have been practiced with few words, much of it done ex tempore, our knowledge of it is largely conjectural. A further conjecture is that this tradition continued in folk activity, making a possible link between the ancient mime and the later figure of the fool in the medieval world. Probably by Roman times, the mime actors had taken already some of the traits that will become standard for the figure of the fool by medieval times. Allardyce Nicoll finds descriptions of Roman mimes with shaven heads, asses' ears, and a stick or wooden sword (which may be a mock sceptre), and who communicate with the audience by dance and gestures, often obscene ones (*Masks, Mimes, and Miracles*, 1931). By dance and gesture, they could play stories silently that their artistic movements made comprehensible to the spectators.

In the formal theater of Greece and Rome, which has come down to us, we find slaves and servants who carry some of the characteristic badges of the fool, but really none of the personae of this theater fit the comprehensive character of the fools that will be found later in theater and other literary works. The assumption, therefore, is that the figure of the fool survived in folk activity, which makes the lacunae in the tradition understandable.

E. K. Chambers notes in *The Mediaeval Stage* (1903) that most players during the early Empire were slaves and that even those who had been freed had many of the rights of citizenship abrogated because they exercised this profession. Although these strict rules were later relaxed, the fact of being a player, or even of being descended from a family of players, remained a stigma for centuries. Some of these censures were strengthened as the power of Christianity grew, an explanation of the fact that as late as the seventeenth century actors were still technically excommunicate and could be refused burial in consecrated ground.

As Rome came under the influence of invading and conquering barbarians, the Roman stage, with its relative sophistication and obscenity, was out of place and out of favor. As a formal part of the life of Romans, it ceased to exist. Then, as the tribes consolidated their power and adopted cultural aspects of the former culture, singers and entertainers found places in these new courts where the more democratic mores of the Germanic tribes made the singer one of the group, allowing even the princes to take part with them in the entertainment.

The Middle Ages

The Middle Ages knew the fool as a literary convention, especially in the religious and secular theater that was already flourishing by the twelfth century. In religious theater, we find that the role of the devil carries many of the attributes that have already become standard as symbols of the fool: the cap, long ears, a stick or a club. The devil in the medieval theater might be seen as the fool or sinner in the Old Testament who is now fixed in his character.

The influence of St. Francis of Assisi (1181–1226), writer and founder of the Franciscan Order, revolutionized practices of piety, especially among the lower orders of people. He was the holy fool, the Fool of Christ, and his followers were called the Players of the Lord *(joculatores Domini)*. In his poetry he sang the love of Mary, poverty, and all living things in God's creation. Writings about Francis began to appear immediately after his death—biographies as well as an allegorical romance called *Sacrum commercium beati Francesi (Sacred Love* [trans. in Marion Habig, ed., *St. Francis of Assisi: Writings and Early Biographies*, 1973], 1227, authorship disputed), in which Francis pursues Lady Poverty as the lord pursued his lady in traditional romances.

Dante wrote of Francis and the Franciscans in the epic poem *La divina commedia (The Divine Comedy,* c. 1320), praising the ideals of Francis and his early followers, and castigating the Order for falling later from the unworldiness of its founder *(Paradisio [Paradise],* cantos 11 and 12). Among the wealth of writings on Francis, some modern writings are Hermann Hesse, *Franz von Assisi* (biography, 1904); G. K. Chesterton, *Francis of Assisi* (biography, 1924), written before he became a Catholic; Laurence Housman, *Little Plays of Saint Francis* (1924); Nikos Kazantzakis, *Ho phtōchloulēs tou Theou (Saint Francis,* novel, 1956); and Joan Erikson, *Saint Francis and His Four Ladies* (novel, 1970). Lawrence Ferlinghetti, in *A Coney Island of the Mind* (1958), has a poem that reads, "they were putting up / a statue of Saint Francis" which catches comically in a brief scene several events taken from stories about Francis that point to contrasts between him and the world (see L. S. Cunningham, *Saint Francis of Assisi,* 1976).

In the fifteenth century, and perhaps somewhat earlier, a kind of play developed in France called *sottie,* a type of allegorical farce in which "the traditional virtues are rejected by everyone, because it is the only way to survive" (Alan Knight, *Aspects of Genre in Late Medieval French Drama,* 1983). Many of the players are dressed as traditional fools *(sots)* and all, deceivers as well as deceived, live in folly. Performed at festival times, especially near the Feast of Fools (December to early January), these plays represent a world turned to ridicule, with no power that can be a source of moral judgment. Folly is rampant and her wise remarks serve only to emphasize and castigate the surrounding corruption (Heather Arden, *Fools' Plays: A Study of Satire in the Sottie,* 1980). The *sots* (fools) of the *sotties* amuse with their unusual twists of language and their physical agility, operating within their disguise to expose truths and to conceal their seriousness. Their satirical comments can give rise to the notion of a different world, past or present, where venality would not be the rule, but there is no feeling of striving toward change, as if it were known that the times were not propitious.

The Renaissance

It is, however, at the end of the fifteenth and the beginning of the sixteenth centuries that the figure of the fool makes its most enduring appearance in Western Europe. We find him (or her) portrayed in two broadly influential works: Brant's *Das Narrenschiff* (*Ship of Fools,* satire, 1494) and Erasmus' *Moriae encomium* (*Praise of Folly,* essay, 1511). Sebastian Brant was from the area called Alsatia, and spent his life between Basel and Strasbourg; he had a birthplace, a family, a settled life. Erasmus was a foundling whose country might simply be called *humanitas* and whose family was the church (often a cold bosom). He seemed to consider the print shop his home, and in his travels he was often the guest, the parasite, of both the wealthy, the powerful, the arrogant, and also of the poor, the hungry, the desperate. Erasmus, thus, knew the many facets of folly before re-creating her as Folly in something akin to his own image.

Both the *Ship of Fools* and the *Praise of Folly* were immediately popular and were soon known as widely throughout the populace as a literary work could be. Although both were popular, each played somewhat different roles. Where Sebastian Brant's work was moralizing and therefore fitted better with some traditions of medieval Christianity, Erasmus' work put much of the tradition into a new mold that allowed him to use that constructive satire which became his hallmark. They even chose different languages, which helps explain some more fundamental differences. Although Brant chose the vernacular, a choice that put him in the modern camp, the popularity of his work has never approached that of Erasmus' work. Erasmus, on the other hand, made what looks to be a traditional choice by using Latin. But he used that new structure, Renaissance Latin, an artificial language that he was helping to create. Both books were quickly translated into other languages (Brant's into Latin also). While both carry moral dicta, the *Ship* is more traditionally didactic and broad in intent, while *Folly* is rhetorical and satiric, a comic form that Erasmus invested with a spirit that carried the work far beyond the life of its creator.

The fool in Brant's work has fewer facets than Folly in Erasmus. Brant's fools are those who act sinfully or in error, tempted often by the attractions of the world, which will lead them to forsaking the right path, the path to salvation. Lure and error are two parts of foolishness, but the essential distinctions of good and evil are kept quite clear in this work and remain generally unmixed opposites.

Erasmus' work differs from Brant's also by changing the emphasis from a moral and religious view of mankind to an ironic handling of all the higher levels of human endeavor. The intent and form are thus broadened in ways that make the work a literary piece of great and enduring influence. Folly speaks the oration, creating instantly the ambiguity: "Are we to take this fool seriously?" which she answers properly with: "Of course not, unless you recognize her words as consonant with your own experience." The personage Folly is witty and wise enough both to recognize folly in human activity and to express its two (or more) faces. In the most general terms, foolish actions can be a result of necessity, as well as a sign of wisdom higher than one expects, and finally they can be seen as foolish attempts to break the limits of necessity (almost always done in egotistical ardor or mania). Thus, this Folly created by Erasmus breaks the bounds of categories to show the reader that people of importance are as foolish in their actions as the rest of us and compound their folly with hypocrisy.

No one, not Erasmus himself, is untouched by the barbs of Folly, whose aim is constantly directed at those who would be, by one petty distinction or another, raised above others. Does the person elevated to bishop or bishop's woman, to professor or regent or either's wife or mistress, to king or to queen, does this person lose any of the qualities of humanness? Folly says, of course, "no," and says also that any such pretentions make these titled or elevated persons all the more foolish. The public charge and responsibility they have received would properly make them humble and sensitive to the possibility of human error. When they forget that humility is a necessary aspect of authority and believe rather that their power raises them above others, they become fools and sources of laughter to others.

Erasmus ends his work with a section of several pages in which he slowly transforms Folly into the Christian fool. Radical though this metamorphosis is, it continues Paul's remarks in the Epistles to the Corinthians. And closer in time to Erasmus, similar religious and humanist themes were expressed by Thomas à Kempis in *De imitatione Christi* (*Imitation of Christ*, essay, 1418) and by Nicolaus Cusanus in *De docta ignorantia* (*Of Learned Ignorance*, essay, c. 1440), both of whom found "Christ the Fool" a very powerful weapon in the fight against growing human arrogance. By relying on these predecessors, Erasmus can end the oration with this powerful and recognizable paradox. The oration becomes a statement of faith in the human condition when considered from the viewpoint of Christianity. "Folly" can take on the meaning of "salvation" because what the world sees as foolishness can be excellence from the perspective of the divine. The fool can show at times powers that are superior to ordinary human powers while still keeping his character as an inferior human. This basic paradox is what makes the figure so useful in such varying ways.

After Erasmus and Brant, the figure of the fool explodes, and the Renaissance can take him as its insignia. Rabelais' novels contain not only several characters who fit the description of fool, but include also a list of different kinds of fools numbering almost two hundred. Rabelais' most notorious fool is Panurge, a character introduced in the first volume (*Pantagruel*, 1532) of his four (or five) volume work. Panurge combines the clever, the wise, the scurrilous, and the cowardly in his experiences through this series of novels. At his appearance, he amazes and wins the constant love of his prince, Pantagruel, by expressing his urgent needs in a number of various languages, some of which were his inventions, and none of which Pantagruel understood. The performance convinces Pantagruel that Panurge is a resourceful and agile companion who will fit his needs for education and entertainment. A short time later, Panurge replaces Pantagruel in a debate with the learned Englishman, Thaumaste, whom Panurge defeats in a speechless dialogue where communication is effected by signs— many of them obscene, others seemingly without meaning.

As with many fools, Panurge's self-confidence, his willingness to try anything (the etymological meaning of his name), derives as much from his lack of self-criticism as from his skill. Self-love dominates him, leaving him free to act as he wants because he cannot imagine any need more imperious than his own.

In book 3 of the work (1546), he begins by wasting profligately the land and people Pantagruel gave him to govern. Pantagruel's criticism elicits the specious and sophistical praise of debtors and lenders, which has the fool's mixture of sense and nonsense. Then Panurge, the aging seducer of the wives of others, decides that he ought to marry but expresses his fear of being cuckolded in turn. The rest of the book involves posing two questions to a series of authorities: "Ought I marry? Will my wife be faithful?" The answers he receives all indicate his foolishness in trying to know or control the future; yet Panurge persists in twisting each answer sophistically to mean what he wants to hear.

He refuses to accept the fact that humans must learn to live with the troubling uncertainty of human decision, just as he refuses also to recognize that his cleverness blinds him to the only meaningful knowledge available to humans— the Socratic imperative: Know thyself.

Barbara Swain finds a shift in attitudes toward the fool in the course of the sixteenth century and the early part of the seventeenth century, in some countries earlier, in others later. The growing importance of Stoicism, strongly influenced by ideas from Epicureanism, tended to make the "natural man" a source of goodness and basic wisdom, a shift from the picture Brant gave of man's nature as faulty, and foolishness as a sign of the sinner. For example, in the *Essais* (*Essays*, 1580–1588), Montaigne can speak of some actions and judgments that the world calls foolish as being decisions based on good sense. For example, the world calls public actions glorious and private actions of little worth, a judgment he disputes. He explains that victory and defeat are not so easily judged as we think, because victory may be gained by accident (thus not be a sign of one's virtue), while defeat may be suffered with great courage. Another support for such a shift of opinion is that the figure of the fool does not appear in the *Essais*. The reader can find several narratives in which people act in a variety of foolish ways, but there is not a story or an example in the *Essais* involving a fool. The closest example might be the thief (3.2) who survived in his youth by selective thefts that he repaid after achieving a comfortable situation in his later life. Montaigne's comments on this thoughtful thief are that he was certainly guilty of wrong actions in his youth but that his later calculated repayment righted the earlier wrongs. Montaigne expresses approbation, almost admiration, for this honesty, which the world could call foolishness.

Shakespeare's fools come in such variety that they fill the spectrum from the lighter fools of the early comedies to the deep wisdom that Lear and his Fool share on the cold and dark wind-blown heath. The rustic players of *Midsummer Night's Dream* (c. 1595) clown through a production of *Pyramus and Thisbe* that mirrors comically the noble lovers of the drama, indicating the foolishness of human activity, while their own production of the play offers its mix of folly and wisdom. The unsavory Thersites of *Troilus and Cressida* (1601–1602) demeans any grandeur claimed by the great that surround and eclipse him. This is one duty of the fool, and bitter Thersites fulfills it with the filth that is his own. Also unsavory, but perhaps venal rather than evil, are Mistress Overdone and Pompey and other frequenters of her tavern and brothel in *Measure for Measure* (1603–1604). If the whole of this play is crowded with characters who show the faulty sides of human life, Overdone and Pompey offer heartening comic comment with their frank self-awareness of their worth. As does even Lucio, who begs for mercy after hearing his sentence to die by being pressed to death. The duke offers to commute the sentence on condition that Pompey marry the whore. Pompey's answer is in character: ''Marrying a punk, my lord, is pressing to death.''

Fools play different roles in many of the other plays; some are court fools, others natural fools, while some of the protagonists play the fool in attempts to achieve their goals. If Lear's Fool is among the most famous, there is also Yorick who, though not exactly a player, gives rise to discussion between Hamlet and the grave-digger, which helps define different attitudes toward the fool. And when Laurence Sterne picks up the name one hundred and fifty years later to use as the alter ego for the narrator in *Tristram Shandy* (novel, 1759–1767), we certainly find a brilliantly learned fool.

Cervantes gave the world two quite different fools in his novel *Don Quijote* (*Don Quixote*, 1605, 1615), where the protagonist and his servant Sancho Panza mirror the foolishness in each other as they constantly speak and act as if the one's views and desires would be understood by the other. But the idealist cannot imagine seeing the practical concerns of the world, and the practical man is unaware that another concern than the belly could exist.

Neoclassicism: The Seventeenth and Eighteenth Centuries

In seventeenth-century France, the satirical literature shows as fools both generalized examples of human behavior and also very personal lampoons of religious and political figures. The fool in neoclassical literature changes character, losing some of the power that we have seen him holding heretofore. In a general way, it is as though folly is reduced to a description of self-delusion. Although the fool, the self-deluder, can still attract sympathy in some cases, he has become the defeated hero, the scapegoat rejected by a society that no longer has the security to allow his ambiguities, his wisdom, his deeper than usual sense of right. Now vanquished by social and practical norms, whether still to call him a fool becomes a question.

In the theater, Molière puts a series of types on stage, types such as the Miser, the Misanthrope, the Aged Lover, the Bigot, and others who act foolishly, that is, contrary to the norms. Many of these same types shift to the English stage later in the century, when that monarchy is restored (1688). In the Molière versions, the fools are generally those who think that they can change some aspect of human behavior or some social convention by an act of will or by persuading some others of the rightness of their case. For the most part, they will fail.

Taking two of Molière's protagonists as examples, Arnolphe (*L'école des femmes* [*The School for Wives*, 1662]) and Alceste (*Le misanthrope* [*The Misanthropist*, 1666]), we are made aware in the exposition how each is acting foolishly. Arnolphe is not sympathetic, yet we can understand his temptations, even if with misgivings. Alceste is sympathetic and in many ways laudable in his decision to speak directly rather than politely. Yet both will fail to attain their desires. Society will not allow Alceste such deviance, and human nature and society militate against Arnolphe's attempts to control another in an action so essential both to society and human nature.

Molière shows the spectator how each protagonist fails to understand that his actions are ambiguous because they do not in fact correspond to the positions each avows. Arnolphe is a man who has taken joy at watching cuckolds suffer and who has never learned that love is an essential element in marriage. His decision to marry, therefore, indicates his foolishness. As the play unrolls, we see the proper frustration of his plans and at the same time the success of his antagonists—Horace, the young lover, and Agnès, his young ward, whom he had planned to marry.

In *Le misanthrope*, we learn eventually that Alceste's decision is based not on some rational principle of honesty but on an attempt to correct Célimène's practice of accepting the attentions of all her suitors rather than choosing Alceste as the one she loves. As a young widow, Célimène is enjoying the first taste of freedom that her society offers, and she refuses to cede to Alceste's impatient demands, expecting him to understand and to wait. Alceste's desire, therefore, expressed as a war on society's superficial politeness, is a ruse to force Célimène's hand. We understand that such actions will not change the accepted manners of the society; whether it will convince Célimène is left unanswered by Molière at the end. This can be known only in time lying outside the play.

These protagonists act foolishly, but their lack of deeper wisdom makes them unlike the fools we have been considering. This was the century of Descartes, where the fool is out of order, and where paradox is no longer an acceptable expression of truth. The search for different criteria of truth has begun, and Erasmus' Folly can find no room within Cartesian rules.

Other French writers in this century also portray foolishness, but few with the control Molière used. La Rochefoucauld and La Bruyère show the social games that human interest devises to hide itself from others, often from the self. The fabulist La Fontaine, drawing from Aesop's Greek, from Phaedrus' Latin, and from a wealth of Near-Eastern fables, created a broad range of fools, often like Molière's fools, who wanted to change some aspect of themselves or the world. But since the stratum of seventeenth-century France for whom this literature was written was a small and controlled society, the fool in it is the one unable or unwilling to adjust to control by the society.

The eighteenth century, rich in satire, also portrays the fool as outcast, the one unwilling or unable to adjust to the dictates of a society more and more rigid—perhaps because the century felt itself under attack by shifting economic and political realities. But in addition to the castigated fools of the satire, there appear also in this century sympathetic fools, such as those in Fielding's novels, whom we laugh at and who enjoy their worlds with a simplicity of nature that some could find enviable, but few would want to imitate. Yet the fools Alexander Pope creates in his satirical poem *The Dunciad* (1728–1743) are arrant ones, meant to attract our derisive laughter but not our sympathies.

Voltaire and Diderot created fools, Voltaire creating perhaps a larger number of them, but Diderot creating a more radical kind who could in fact expand the accepted boundaries of sense. In *Le neveu de Rameau* (*Rameau's Nephew*, satire, 1762–1784), one of the interlocutors in the dialogue throws into question most of the traditional limits of morality. And in *Le rêve de d'Alembert* (*D'Alembert's Dream*, 1769) a work difficult to categorize, the bounds of waking and sleeping, of genius and fool, are exploded. The speakers of the dialogue, d'Alembert, Dr. Bordieu, and Mlle de l'Espinasse, examine in the most radical ways the accepted ideas of the age. The latter is able to speak without reserve because she is of course only relating what she has just heard d'Alembert mumbling in the restless sleep of one recovering from an illness. He cannot, therefore, be held to account for what might be only the result of fever on the mind, a kind of madness. But Dr. Bordieu is intrigued by the brilliant ravings while Mlle de l'Espinasse is amazed at the kind of sense that Bordieu finds in what she thought might be

dangerous or only nonsense. The reader is guided by the remarks of the interlocutors to hear these disjointed ravings as the workings of the mind of a genius
when it is not controlled by social conventions.

In Voltaire's works, especially in his philosophical tales (*Candide*, 1759,
L'ingénu, 1767, and some dozen more), the fools are broad and general human
types. The truly dangerous ones are supporters of or actual members of the ruling
institutions—church or state. And there are the ordinary scoundrels who are
dangerous when one cannot outwit them. Most of the rest are simply unaware
fools who give others the opportunity to laugh. Another group, calling themselves
philosophers, are fools claiming to have special knowledge and who, consequently, give rise to even greater laughter. Finally, there is the rare holy fool,
the Anabaptist in *Candide*, who truly follows Christian precepts and who will
suffer early a hero's death.

Romanticism: The Nineteenth Century

As romanticism developed, the nineteenth century saw the birth of a slightly
changed fool. The artist and the intellectual began to see themselves as superior
members of the society that often excluded them out of jealousy or fear or
misunderstanding. The artist will become in varying ways the scapegoat, the
saint, the prophet, the fool, and even the savior of mankind who may be sent
into exile when society finds his foolishness dangerous.

In Russia, Dostoevsky's novel *Idiot* (*The Idiot*, 1868) shows the suffering of
the protagonist Mishkin, an epileptic, as he learns progressively the reality of
spiritual concerns and the diminishing power of society to rule his reactions.
What society views as his naïve foolishness, Mishkin understands as the way
of salvation, for himself and for the world. He is the "holy fool" whom we
saw in the Middle Ages.

The Modern World

Baudelaire's works show his constant concern with the fool, who for him is
the social outcast, the prophet, poet, genius who can see beyond the ordinarily
accepted realities of the world. He is most often the clown, the circus entertainer,
someone at the lowest social level. He (or she) is ambiguous and expresses
contradictory feelings and reactions. This is a fairly common figure in certain
levels of art during the second half of the nineteenth century, continuing perhaps
(with variations) until the Second World War, or in other terms, until the end
of the Great Depression of the 1930s. His most prominent appearance might be
in the early works of Picasso, during his blue and red periods. He, she, they
are the silent figures who express with great economy the conditions of humankind—pain, loss, strength, wisdom, sensuality, joy, vice, struggle. They indicate
the full life whose facets are myriad. They stand in contrast to the economic
development of the West as it drives toward increasing consumption and waste.

The clown in Bavaria and Austria was a folk figure appearing as early as the
sixteenth century with various names such as Hanswurst, Pickelhering, Harle-

quin, and Casterle. Deriving from the *Singspiel* traditions, he is the masked jester figure who personifies and also makes fun of the dull-witted German. Mozart used this figure in two of his operas, *Die Entführung aus dem Serail* (*Abduction from the Seraglio,* 1782) and *Der Zauberflöte* (*The Magic Flute,* 1791). In Thomas Mann's novel *Zauberberg* (*The Magic Mountain,* 1924), we find a similar clown, Hans Castorp, who plays the pupil-fool to the learned Settembrini, a closet Jesuit. In general, this German-language jester is an innocent as well as a figure of goodwill. He can be coarse and harmlessly satirical in the popular theater, and Mozart uses them (e.g., Papageno and Papagena) as oppositional figures to the elevated characters of the drama. The jester allows us to see that others—the great—are not so powerful as they want to appear. The clown achieves the stature of humanity in these works as he lowers somewhat the stature of the learned.

In America, the works of Steinbeck, Hemingway, and Faulkner portray this figure—the generous prostitute, the compassionate farm worker, all those simple and displaced persons who care for others, usually with some loss of money or time or effort to themselves but receiving the pay of abundant grace. In France, Anouilh gives the reader adolescents with great purity and little experience, but with instincts that will lead them to special insights and often to death. The creators of the greatest modern clowns are Charlie Chaplin and Samuel Beckett. Both of them continue the work of Baudelaire and Picasso in figuring for the public the special strength and wisdom of the clown, of the modern fool. Chaplin is closer to the clown/fool, as he is known in early twentieth-century literature— pathetic, lacking the belief in progress and the betterment of mankind, but showing this lack in comic and therefore postive ways. The viewer can identify with the feelings of powerlessness that he embodies while laughing at him at the same time.

Beckett, however, created a variation that was surprising enough to produce troubled reactions in the spectator. His clowns come too close to a deep sense of absurdity in our lives to allow easy laughter. Chaplin's clown softened the common blows of fate, and his comedy offered the fulfillment of the expected happy ending. When the clown walks off at the end of the episode without the pure and lovely girl as his wife, someone else has married her, and he is satisfied that he has left her in proper hands. He seems to say that his loss is minimal if he has succeeded in bringing happiness to deserving youth. Beckett, on the other hand, refuses such traditional fantasy and belongs to a different time with a different view of humanity.

Although Beckett's theater can be called "comedy" from certain points of view, his world is not the traditional one of comedy. It does not work on wish fulfillment; its laws are ineluctable; the endings are often repetitions of the beginnings, with only small changes. The events during the time of the action could be understood as having taught the characters, for example, that they have no power to change the laws that they have come to know by experience. The nature of human beings may be to try to change these necessary laws of the universe, and human learning may precisely mean learning that such laws are not subject to change. That the spectator sees generally all the figures as fools is an acceptable assumption. They are usually of the lowest classes, persons so denuded of what we take to be the necessities of Western human life, persons whose language is either so elemental or so preposterous that the readers or viewers have some difficulty taking them seriously. At first, they seem so distant that we, the real people, are out of danger. Then at some point, Beckett makes us realize that they are us and we are them. The human family is complete and comprehensive. Their foolishness mirrors our own, but theirs is at such an elemental level that we need some time and determination to be able to see that. Beckett's fools are transcendent at the unexpected end of the spectrum.

In Heinrich Böll's *Ansichten eines Clowns* (*The Clown,* novel, 1963), is the following exchange: " 'What kind of a man are you?' he asked. 'I am a clown,' I said. 'I collect moments. Strangely enough, I like the kinds to which I belong: people.' " The speaker here (the narrator Hans Schnier) is announcing his profession and his relationship with the subject of his work. Hans Schnier is a professional clown but carries many of the marks of the natural fool—single-mindedness in his prejudices and in his ability to criticize others as well as to state his own faults. The naturalness of his reactions to what he considers hypocrisy and self-serving rationalizations is the source of most of the comedy. His reactions come so immediately from his concerns that the reader is convinced of their appropriateness when they are set in opposition to the abstract and often veiled concerns of those who are trying to convince him to act and believe as though his world were theirs. He is a fitting figure with which to close this discussion because his extreme reasonableness seems so correct yet also so self-defeating in the world of convention. We know that he is right as we know that he will not win as the world knows winning.

See also: Anti-Intellectualism, Dwarf, Picaresque, Scapegoat, Stupidity.

Selected Bibliography

Swabey, Marie. *Comic Laughter.* New Haven, Conn.: Yale University Press, 1961.
Swain, Barbara. *Fools and Folly during the Middle Ages and the Renaissance.* New York: Columbia University Press, 1932.
Welsford, Enid. *The Fool: His Social and Literary History.* London: Faber & Faber, 1935.

PAUL BURRELL

FORTUNE

The goddess Fortune represents, above all else, the role of chance in human affairs. Literary portrayals of Fortune have generally placed predictable and appropriate emphasis on her inconstancy; but this inconstancy has two aspects.

For those who see the universe ruled by moral order, Fortune serves that higher power, and her fickleness is illusory. For those who reject or cannot perceive the existence of this universal moral order, she is both fickle and all-powerful. Because she seems to grant favors to the wicked and withhold them from the good, Fortune is often depicted as blind or wearing a blindfold. She is commonly portrayed in art as standing on a globe, a symbol both of her instability and of the world over which she holds sway. The most popularly used attribute of Fortune, however, is the wheel, for an endlessly turning wheel dramatically exemplifies the inconstancy of her favors. She raises the fallen and then plunges them back downward. Although the image of Fortune is found in literature without interruption from classical antiquity to the present, she is employed most frequently and most prominently in works from the Middle Ages and the Renaissance.

Background in Classical Literature

Classical literature abounds in references to Fortune. In Greek literature *Tychē* remains primarily an abstract concept; the personified deity who would capture the imagination of the Middle Ages and Renaissance emerges from Roman literature. For both the Greeks and the Romans the concept of Fortune is closely associated with that of Fate. Both the theme of Fortune and its connection with Fate are introduced into Greek literature in the seventh century by the lyric poet Archilochus, who declares that "Fortune *(Tychē)* and Fate *(Moira)* give a man all he has." In subsequent Greek literature *Tychē* is used in a variety of meanings. Sometimes it means little more than luck, good or ill. Most often, however, it refers to the unaccountable external power that controls men's happiness and unhappiness. As Sophocles says in the *Antigonē* (c. 441 B.C.): *"Tychē* raises and *Tychē* overturns the happy or unhappy from day to day. No man can prophesy concerning those things which are established." The tragic poets, in particular, stress the subordination of *Tychē* to the higher power operating in the universe. In Aeschylus' dramas can be seen the earliest development of the paradox that good fortune is an evil, for good fortune can cause misery by leading men to greed and dissatisfaction. Sophocles' tragedies, particularly the *Oidipous tyrannos (Oedipus Rex,* c. 429 B.C.), are filled with references to *Tychē;* but his emphasis is upon the reaction of self-conscious individuals to events that they can neither predict nor control. Euripides too makes considerable use of *Tychē.* Although in his dramas there is less sense of a providential order governing human affairs, several of his dramas, for example the *Helenē (Helen,* 412 B.C.) and *Iōn* (c. 415 B.C.) are centered on the struggles of heroic characters with the vicissitudes of *Tyche.*

The tension between the power of chance and the possibility of self-determination becomes a major issue in Greek historical and philosophic interpretation. The historian Thucydides (457–401 B.C.), for example, draws a distinction between events that are unpredictable and those that are unaccountable; for him, events that are seemingly the result of random *Tychē* are in fact events for which we simply have not yet discovered the causes. Aristotle (384–322 B.C.) argues that chance exists only in the sublunar realm and is necessary for the concept of free will. The vision of a morally ordered and understandable universe deteriorates in later Greek thought, however; and the Epicurean position, that "Chance, not Wisdom, rules the life of men" becomes increasingly widespread.

For the Romans, *Fortuna* (Fortune) was a more important goddess than was *Tychē* for the Greeks. The Italian goddess was originally associated less with chance than prosperity. She was worshipped extensively in Italy from the earliest period and had numerous shrines. The symbols most commonly associated with her are the cornucopia and the rudder, corresponding to her roles as bringer of abundance and controller of destinies. This original Italian *Fortuna* is not the fickle goddess of literary tradition but a stable divinity worshipped as *Fortuna manens* (Stable Fortune). Later, as her cult became associated with that of *Tychē*, she was more frequently pictured standing on a ball, symbolic of the uncertainty of her favor.

The greater popularity of the cult of *Fortuna* in Italy explains in part the greater degree of personification of Fortune in Roman literature. In general, Roman literature of the Republic and early Empire views Fortune as subordinate to Fate; but with the increasing skepticism and loss of confidence of the later Empire comes a view of Fortune as the capricious and dominant ruler of human life. The stable goddess of Italian religious tradition gives way to a figure who, like the Greek concept of *Tychē*, represents instability and the power of unpredictable chance.

At the height of their power and self-confidence, Romans were inclined to explain their extraordinary rise to prominence in terms of Fortune and Virtue. The two powers were seen as complementary, for, as Livy says in his history of Rome (*Ab urbe condita libri*, c. 27 B.C.–A.D. 14), "Fortune helps the brave" ("*eventus docuit fortes Fortunam iuvare*"). Cicero stresses the subservience of Fortune to effort, arguing in *De officiis* (*On Duties*, 44 B.C.) "misfortunes and failures . . . although they involve an element of luck" owe more to cooperative effort. In general, for the Romans, Fortune, acting in the service of the Fate that predestined Roman greatness, offered opportunities for the demonstration of Roman *virtus* (excellence).

Not surprisingly, Fortune is a dominant force in Roman comedy. In this usage, the Romans followed the practice of Greek "New Comedy." A fragment from a play by the Greek comic playwright Menander (c. 300 B.C.) states "For the righteous-minded *Tychē* is an ally." In the comedies of the two great Roman playwrights of the second century B.C., Plautus and Terence, Fortune is frequently paramount. Plautus, prefiguring the same theme in Cicero and Livy, stresses the importance of the ability to make use of the opportunities presented by Fortune. In *Pseudolus* (191 B.C.), for example, the clever slave argues that "each man's excellence lies in the use he makes of Fortune."

Roman literature of this period also contains striking uses of the theme of Fortune to emphasize the uncertainty of life. The lyric poet Horace (65–8 B.C.), for example, devotes an entire ode to Fortune (1.35) and gives her a prominent role in several poems. He emphasizes her fickleness:

Fortuna saevo laeta negotio et
ludum insolentem ludere pertinax
    transmutat incertos honores,
    nunc mihi nunc alii benigna.

(Fortune, happy in her savage business and
persistently playing her cruel game
shifts her uncertain honors,
kind now to me, now to someone else.)

Later Ovid, banished by the Emperor Augustus, would write in his *Tristia* (*Songs of Sadness,* A.D. 9–12) of Fortune's "uncertain steps" and changing visage. Fortune is the principal divine force in Lucan's epic poem *Pharsalia* (c. A.D. 62). Lucan portrays Caesar as "Fortune's child." With the literature of the later Empire comes greater emphasis on both the power and the fickleness of Fortune. Pliny complains in his *Naturalis historia* (*Natural History* c. A.D 77) of his contemporaries' obsessed fascination with the goddess, who is "the sole object of our thought, our praise and our abuse." In his tenth satire (c. 100–127), Juvenal equates the rising interest in the cult of the goddess with the Romans' loss of *prudentia.* In Apuleius' *Metamorphoses* (*The Golden Ass*, novel, c. 150) worship of and service to the goddess Fortune is symptomatic of a mistaken absorption in worldly matters.

Finally, Roman literature contains numerous references to a turning wheel of Fortune. In his oration against Piso (*In Pisonem,* 55 B.C.), Cicero declares that his enemy fears Fortune's wheel. Later, Seneca's tragedy *Agamemnon* (c. A.D. 60) pictures Fortune "turning the precipitous falls of kings" ("ut praecipites regum casus / Fortuna rotat"); and the historian Ammianus Marcellinus makes several references to the wheel of Fortune in his *Rerum gestarum libri* (*The Chronicles of Events,* A.D. 378).

Medieval Literature

When the Roman Empire was converted to Christianity, the goddess Fortune was entrenched in both popular religion and literature. Neither the goddess nor the concept, however, had a place in Christian thought. St. Augustine composed several detailed attacks upon the concept of *Fortuna.* The basis for his rejection as argued in *De civitate dei* (*The City of God,* A.D. 413–426) is that "everything must be referred to divine wisdom" ("omnia revocanda ad divinam pruden- tiam"). For Augustine, chance events are merely events the reason and cause of which are hidden from human understanding. Augustine articulates the basic Christian argument for the repudiation of the existence and power of *Fortuna.* Both Fortune and her rule are illusory.

The most detailed attack upon the concept of Fortune in late antiquity appears in *De consolatione philosophiae* (*The Consolation of Philosophy,* c. 524) by the philosopher Boethius. Written while Boethius was in prison awaiting execution, *De consolatione* recounts a dialogue between the author and Philosophy, who visits him in his cell. Like a physician, Philosophy cures Boethius of his obsession with worldly success and leads him toward a deeper understanding of true goodness. Among the principal themes of the *Consolatione* is that men mistakenly value temporal goods, thus placing themselves in the power of Fortune, to whom are attributed the inevitable alternations of worldly prosperity and adversity. Boethius describes Fortune as blind and having a changing face ("caeci numinis ambiguos vultus"). Constant only in her inconstancy, she is always playing her game: turning her wheel, sending what is at the bottom to the top and what is at the top to the bottom. Although Philosophy argues that Fortune, strictly speaking, is an illusion, since nothing really happens by chance in a divinely ordered universe, paradoxically the portrayal of her in the *Consolatione* provided an inspiration and model for countless authors during the next thousand years.

In medieval literature the theme of Fortune has three main aspects. Above all, she is a symbol of the mutability of worldly goods. To be in her power is symbolic of a misplaced concern with those worldly goods. Finally, the turning wheel is commonly used as a motif in political history to explain and symbolize the cyclical rise and fall of empires. All three thematic uses have their basis in *De consolatione*.

Fortune is a ubiquitous figure in medieval literature. She stands for the unpredictable occurrences of life. In Gower's words (*Confessio amantis*, poem, 1390): "The chaunces of the worlds also / That we Fortune clepen so." Dante sees her in Hell, and learns from Virgil that her constantly turning wheel is part of the scheme of divine providence (*La divina commedia* [*The Divine Comedy*, epic poem, c. 1320]). Indeed, so fixed in the popular imagination does the image of Fortune's wheel become that when, in Malory's *Morte d'Arthur* (prose romance, c. 1469), the king dreams "that him seemed he sat upon a chaflet in a chair, and the chair was fast to a wheel," the allusion to Fortune and Arthur's imminent fall would have been unmistakable. Chaucer, who had translated Boethius' *Consolatione* into English (c. 1375), makes the fickleness of Fortune a major theme of several works. She is invoked specifically in the moralistic discussion of the falls of such heroes as Julius Caesar and Alexander that appear in the *Monk's Tale* (*The Canterbury Tales*, c. 1380–1400):

> O worthy, gentil Alisandre, allas,
> that evere sholde fallen swich a cas!
> empoysened of thyn owene folk thou weere;
> thy sys Fortune hath turned into aas,
> and yet for thee ne weep she never a teere.

The reference here to dicing is typical of medieval descriptions of Fortune as playing various games. The fall of Alexander is imputed to Fortune also in Gauthier de Châtillon's epic poem *Alexandreis* (1178–1182), one of the most widely read and translated Latin works of the twelfth century.

Boethius suggests that Fortune plays a central role in the literary genre of tragedy. In *De consolatione,* Philosophy declares "What does the outcry of tragedies lament but the overthrow of happy realms by the random blows of Fortune?" The most elaborate development of this theme in medieval literature is to be found in the *De casibus virorum et feminarum illustrium (The Falls of Famous Men and Women,* c. 1355–1360) by Boccaccio.

The influence of Boethius' portrait of Fortune in his *Consolatione* is evident, moreover, in numerous medieval narratives that recount dream visions. In William Langland's *Piers Plowman* (poem, c. 1362–1387), for example, Fortune takes the author to the "londe of Longynge." The most elaborate use of Fortune in a vision narrative occurs in the Scottish poem *The Kingis Quair (The King's Book,* 1424).

In medieval literature, characters who invoke Fortune or seek her aid are by that very act revealed as having inadequate values. Thus when the hero Walter of Aquitaine, in the ninth-century Latin epic poem *Waltharius,* calls on Fortune, the reader knows that he cannot be intended as a positive heroic model. Similarly in Chaucer's poem *Troilus and Criseyde* (c. 1385), Troilus laughs when, as he ascends to heaven, he understands how foolishly he had acted when he had placed himself in Fortune's power by his love for Criseyde.

The rule of Fortune was thought to extend particularly over lovers. In the eleventh century Hildebert of Lavardin, in *De infidelitate fortunae et amoris,* connects the faithlessness of love and Fortune. The power of Fortune over lovers is emphasized by Guillaume de Lorris in the allegorical *Roman de la rose (Romance of the Rose,* c. 1230). In a later imitation, the *Livre du cueur d'amours espris (Book of Love,* 1457) by René, duke of Anjou, the lover's subservience to Fortune is symbolized by his drinking from her spring, *la fontaine de Fortune.* In one of the stories of the collection known as the *Gesta Romanorum (Deeds of the Romans,* late 13th century) Fortune is said to have two streams; one has the power to make barren land fruitful, the other makes fruitful land barren. Fortune's "drink," another common motif, is said to be both sweet and bitter (*Monk's Tale*: "Fortune hath in her hony gall").

Fortune plays a role in love with greatest frequency in lyric poetry. In the thirteenth-century anthology of poems known as the *Carmina Burana,* a series of lyrics on the fickleness of Fortune precedes and prefigures those on the theme of love. The first poem in that collection begins with a comparison of Fortune with the moon ("O Fortuna velut luna/semper variabile"), but one example of an extremely popular motif.

Finally, the association between Fortune and love can be seen in medieval depictions of her dwelling place. The first full account of the house of Fortune appears in the twelfth-century allegorical poem *Anticlaudianus* by Alain de Lille, who took many of his details from earlier descriptions of the abode of Venus. Fortune's house is constructed partly of rich and partly of shabby materials. It has a garden in which grow both fruitful and barren trees. It has two streams—one sweet, one bitter. Alain de Lille's description begins a long tradition. It is imitated by, among others, Jehan de Meung in the second part of the *Roman de la rose* (*Romance of the Rose,* allegorical poem, c. 1275).

The Renaissance

Fortune's use as a literary theme wanes only slightly during the Renaissance. The continuing popularity as well as the symbolic nature of Fortune and her traditional attributes are made clear by the character Fluellen in Shakespeare's *Henry V* (play, 1600):

Fortune is painted blind, with a muffler afore her eyes, to signify to you that Fortune is blind; and she is painted also with a wheel, to signify to you, which is the moral of it, that she is turning, and inconstant, and mutability and variation; and her foot, look you, is fixed upon a spherical stone, which rolls, and rolls, and rolls; in good truth, the poet makes a most excellent description of it: Fortune is an excellent moral.

Renaissance treatments of the theme of Fortune do not differ markedly from those of the Middle Ages. The emphasis on her fickleness remains, as do most of the traditional elements in her description: for example, the wheel and the globe or spherical stone.

The theme of Fortune appears with particular power and frequency in Elizabethan tragedy. Not only Shakespeare but also Thomas Kyd, Christopher Marlowe, and a host of lesser writers were influenced in this regard by the popularity of Boccaccio's *De casibus,* which had been translated into English (*The Fall of Princes,* 1440) by the monk John Lydgate. Lydgate had used a French translation and expansion of Boccaccio's work composed in 1409 by Laurent de Premierfait.

The traditional use of Fortune as a motivating force in comedy continues also through the Renaissance. Typical in this regard is the English romantic comedy *The Rare Triumphs of Love and Fortune* (1583), which may have provided some material for Shakespeare's *Cymbeline* (1610). Italian comedies, as, for example, Ariosto's enormously popular and often translated *I suppositi* (*The Pretenders,* 1509), similarly imitate the Roman practice of making Fortune and her random favors central to the plot.

The theme that "Fortune favors the brave," which was articulated by Livy, finds renewed emphasis in Machiavelli's treatise *Il principe* (*The Prince,* 1532). Machiavelli likens Fortune both to a raging river and to a woman. The goddess of chance, he argues, must be taken by storm, for she will not be conquered by cautious strategy. The notion of resisting Fortune occasionally finds literary expression in the image of an individual seeking to turn her wheel. In Marlowe's *Tamburlaine the Great* (play, 1588), for example, the hero boasts "I hold the Fates found fast in iron chains / And with my hand turn Fortune's wheel about." Such statements of resistance to Fortune and her power are more common in Renaissance than in medieval literature. In Shakespeare's *Henry VI, Part Three* (c. 1590–1592) Henry declares "Though Fortune's malice overthrow my state / My mind exceeds the compass of her wheel." For the most part, however, Fortune and her wheel are portrayed as unconquerable. Elsewhere Marlowe

writes (*Edward II*, play, 1593) "Base Fortune, now I see that in thy wheel /
There is a point to which when men aspire / They tumble headlong down."
The inexorably turning wheel was used primarily as an image of the imperman-
ence of worldly wealth and success. It is thus used, for example, in Ariosto's
Orlando furioso (epic poem, 1516) and Spenser's *Daphnaida* (elegy, 1591).

A second motif associated with Roman rather than medieval literature revived
during the Renaissance is that Fortune provides opportunity for the demonstration
of heroic excellence. An allied development in the visual arts is a renewed
interest in the figure *Fortuna manens,* the stable and favorable goddess of the
Roman republic who is pictured with a cornucopia and ship's rudder.

The Seventeenth through Twentieth Centuries

In the succeeding centuries, there has occurred a steady decline if not total
eclipse of the goddess Fortune in literature. Although allusions to Fortune continue, most writers show little interest in the goddess herself. The continuing
popularity of Fortune as a theme in love poetry is typified in James Thomson's
(c. 1745) lines "For ever, Fortune, wilt thou prove / An unrelenting Foe to
Love?" In narrative, writers of picaresque tales often cite Fortune as a divine
justification for their use of coincidence as a plot device. Henry Fielding uses
Fortune as the divine machinery in *Tom Jones* (1749); and since his novel is a
comedy, Fortune ultimately works for the victory of the good.

Nineteenth- and twentieth-century allusions almost invariably emphasize either
the wheel of Fortune or her proverbial fickleness. Thus in *Middlemarch* (novel,
1871–1872) by George Eliot, the sister of the poor clergyman Farebrother attributes his not being rich, in part, to Fortune, stating "They say Fortune is a
woman and capricious." The use of Fortune as a major principle is generally
limited to consciously medievalizing works: for example, Dante Gabriel Rossetti's *The King's Tragedy* (poem, 1880), which is based on *The Kingis Quair*.

Modern literature, however, has often been unkind to Fortune. In *L'assomoir*
(*The Dram-Shop,* novel, 1877) by Emile Zola, a picture of Fortune shows her
as "a fat woman in red." Tennyson makes use of the image of Fortune's wheel
only to deny its power when, in *The Marriage of Geraint* (1872), the hero Enid
sings: "Turn, Fortune, turn thy wheel with smile or frown; / With that wild
wheel we go not up or down... / Thy wheel and thee we neither love nor
hate." The twentieth century has been even less kind. Phelps Putnam's *Hymn
to Chance* (poem, 1927) celebrates chance as the creative force of the universe,
but sees that force as masculine ("We have insulted you as Lady Luck"); and
W. H. Auden trivializes the image of the wheel when he begins his poem *In
Time of War* (1939): "Abruptly mounting her ramshackle wheel, / Fortune has
pedalled furiously away." So low has Fortune fallen that a recent literary role
of the once proud divinity is that of Mommy Fortuna, owner of a travelling
carnival, in Peter S. Beagle's fantasy novel *The Last Unicorn* (1968).

It is a paradox worthy of the goddess Fortuna that while her fascination as a
character for writers has been steadily diminishing, the concept of Chance, which

she symbolizes, has become increasingly important as a subject of modern philosophic and scientific discussion. Much contemporary literature is pervaded by the implications of the loss of belief in a providential moral design in the universe. Jacques Monod, winner of the Nobel Prize in 1965 for his work in genetics, argues in *Le hasard et la nécessité* (*Chance and Necessity*, 1970) that homo sapiens itself is the result not of any evolutionary plan or pattern but of chance genetic mutation. Monod's theories have greatly influenced the work of contemporary novelist Jerzy Kosinski. In his novel *Being There* (1970) Kosinski personifies randomness not as a female but as the male gardener Chance, who rises to world prominence through a series of accidental occurrences and misunderstandings.

Recent developments in quantum physics have also had a profound influence on the concept of chance. According to Heinz Pagels (*The Cosmic Code*, 1982) the quantum theory implies that to know the world we must observe it, but in the act of observation uncontrolled and random processes are initiated in the world under observation. Modern physics thus has made chance a basic principle of the universe. This rejection of sure knowledge, first posited as the Uncertainty Principle by the physicist Werner Heisenberg, has strongly influenced recent literature. For example, the novels of Thomas Pynchon are in part applications of modern concepts of randomness and the Uncertainty Principle to literary narrative. His *The Crying of Lot 49* (1965) and *Gravity's Rainbow* (1973) dramatize the futility of the human attempt to see meaning in what ultimately may be merely random events. Fortune, then, may be at the bottom of her own wheel; but the concept of chance that she personifies has become entrenched momentarily at the top.

Selected Bibliography

Bush, Douglas. *Mythology and the Romantic Tradition in English Poetry*. Cambridge: Harvard University Press, 1937.

Greene, William Chase. *Moira: Fate, Good and Evil in Greek Thought*. Cambridge: Harvard University Press, 1944.

Patch, Howard. *The Goddess Fortuna in Medieval Literature*. Cambridge: Harvard University Press, 1927.

Pickering, Francis P. *Literature and Art in the Middle Ages*. London: Macmillan, 1970.

DENNIS M. KRATZ

G
//

GREAT FATHER

Classical Background

The figure of a "great father" in Western literature owes much to Greek mythology's depiction of Zeus as the father of all humans—"great" in the sense that alone of all beings (human or divine) he bows to no higher power and himself holds the classical world together. His privileged stature dates to the overthrow of Kronos (his father), the figure whose name is often linked in false etymology (but with good reason) to "time." Prior to being overthrown, Kronos relentlessly ate his own newborn children. Zeus managed with the help of his mother Rhea to survive his father and then forced Kronos to regurgitate his brothers and sisters and let them live. In so doing, Zeus guaranteed children's survival, that is, a temporal existence. And, in effect, by rebelling Zeus established a sanction for the family and virtually created it as a viable institution. In this way his "law" established the principle of dominance, but not destruction, based on priority in time—parent over child, king over subject, and so on. Zeus, thus, is the patron of children, who accept subservient status and yet are protected, *and* parents, who either let children live or else cease to be parents. The full extent of this "great" paternity—Zeus as familial/cultural sponsor—is shown dramatically in Homer's epic poem (*Ilias (Iliad,* c. 8th century B.C.) at the moment when Zeus reminds all on Olympus that he—without opposition and whenever he so desires—can retract the entire "golden line" of the familial/cultural world to himself and let it "swing in midheaven" as a plaything "tied around Olympus' top."

Implicit in this characterization of a "great" paternity is that underlying patriarchal authority is culture itself—rather, the manner in which culture is engendered and maintained. In this regard Greek culture and paternal authority are synonymous. Human laws, thereafter, incorporate or reflect Zeus's law and promote the indispensable institutions of community, most centrally the family and the legal system that protects it. Such power is dramatized in *Ilias,* Sophocles' play *Oidipous tyrannos (Oedipus Rex,* c. 429 B.C.), and elsewhere, as inexorable authority. In Homer's epic poem *Odysseia (The Odyssey,* c. 8th century B.C.) the cultural link with paternity is particularly evident. Odysseus managed to help overturn the gods' sanction of Troy, and that city fell to the Greeks. In thus challenging the gods, Odysseus violated the covenant by which the gods enfranchise and protect cities—human culture. Thereafter, as a penance for committing this crime, Odysseus is sentenced to travel the Odyssey's route in order to rediscover community's engendering principle, the "law." His circuitous journey abroad and the specific manner of re-entering Ithaca, in various ways, re-enact in great detail the meaning of Zeus's rebellion against Kronos. In this Odysseus reaffirms the cultural (and paternal) priorities according to which family and communal law are possible—the cultural rule that was temporarily lost in Troy's defeat. When paternal rule is reaffirmed—temporal priority as a basis for relationship rather than as a mode for certain destruction–Odysseus re-enters his kingdom. And only then can Ithaca—its king in place—thrive again as a (re-) civilized culture. In this way cultural and paternal authority, virtually indivisible in the *Odysseia,* reflect a major preoccupation in the whole expanse of classical literature.

The Renaissance and Seventeenth Century

In the Renaissance paternal "greatness" is vastly diminished and the father figure becomes increasingly a mere representation of the law, less an absolute power and more an indicator of authority. In the wake of the idealized chansons de geste and romances of chivalry in the Middle Ages—works such as *La chanson de Roland (The Song of Roland,* c. 1100) and *Girart de Roussillon* (ca. 1150), in which heroic and epic endeavors support a paternal communal order—are plays in the Renaissance like Shakespeare's *Hamlet* (c. 1600) and *Macbeth* (1605–1606) in which father figures pointedly fail to guard communal life, and the representatives of paternal authority are vastly diminished in stature compared to their Greek predecessors. In *King Lear* (1606), for instance, the king abdicates his throne, and his paternal power soon withers in his old age. Thereafter, the tie between communal and paternal authority is broken, and the community itself is diminished and tentative. *King Lear,* in short, is the frightening drama of a reversion of civilization to a precommunal (nearly primordial) state. The panic of this period, especially as shown in the drama, is that paternal failure depicts an impending community failure, an uncivilized disruption in the Great Chain of Being—a world increasingly felt to be (as Hamlet says) profoundly "out of joint."

Miguel de Cervantes' novel *Don Quijote (Don Quixote,* 1605, 1615) decisively challenges the remaining idealism about a social order whose causes are championed by heroic father surrogates. Quixote fights the traditional battles to sustain ideal communal order, but his efforts are all misspent. In the fledgling Renaissance "novels" of Thomas Deloney (see *Jacke of Newbury*, 1597, and *Thomas of Reading*, 1598) there is by contrast a fragile optimism—quite different from the attitude in the same period's drama and in *Don Quixote*—that social and economic "fathers" (representatives of an ideal community) can articulate the abstract (communal) rule of law in the newly secular world of prose fiction. This optimism about paternal and cultural benevolence—tied strongly to bourgeois culture and middle-class economic advances—marks many early novelistic experiments. Typical and revealing here is the nearly doctrinal passivity of the "son" figure in prose fiction. Speaking of this passivity, Merritt E. Lawlis (*Apology for the Middle Class*, 1960), for instance, says of the tradesfolk (especially the men) in Deloney's proto-novels,

They reward virtue and punish vice, but they themselves are allowed only a possible role in the action of the story. Young Jacke of Newbury is wooed by a designing widow; Simon Eyre achieves great wealth through a rather shady plan engineered by Mistress Eyre. In each case the hero reaches a desired goal without having to turn a hand. Presumably if he had turned a hand, he would have soiled it.

Jacke, a subject of Henry VIII, is subordinate to the king and yet manages to exploit that relationship for economic and social advancement. And although Jacke has a number of relationships—to his two wives, to his employees, and to his peers—his shrewd attitude about economic prosperity, defined by the king's authority, is the one that defines his character (limited as it is). The "passivity" Lawlis speaks of, that is, complete acceptance of what the king stands for, is an essential (if somewhat ironic) aspect of Jacke's character—an indicator of the "law's" benevolence here.

In the political and social turmoil of the interregnum and the Restoration, the seventeenth century goes on to define the character of a more "stern" paternity, the father as a harsh figure against whom "children" hurl themselves (most obviously in revenge tragedy) in bloody debacles of incest, murder, and self-immolation. This stern father, exacting and punishing, is depicted in great detail as God in John Milton's poem *Paradise Lost* (1667), a parent not fully pleased with his fallen creation. In France in this period, the irony of community falling away from an ideal paternal order is examined comically by Molière (see *Tartuffe*, 1664) and tragically by Pierre Corneille (see *Médée* [*Medea*, 1635]) and Jean Racine (see *Phèdre* [*Phaedra* 1677]). Here, as with John Milton, the human community is estranged from a stern set of values associated with paternity and is urgently in need of reason and moral analysis to maintain any semblance of civilized life in the world as a fallen sphere.

The Eighteenth Century

At the century's beginning with Daniel Defoe's *Robinson Crusoe* (1719), the stern father materializes in fiction as a truly harsh authority, nearly as severe as he had appeared in earlier Renaissance drama. *Robinson Crusoe* shows this preoccupation with inflexible authority. Crusoe goes to sea for commercial gain and moves in a spiral away from his tyrannical father in London, until at last, farthest away from home, he turns to seek forgiveness from God-the-father. At last, he has to face a father for the first time in his life. In this religious rebirth he accepts a father (God) as representing the law. This same pattern occurs in Henry Fielding's *Tom Jones* (1749). Tom runs from Squire Allworthy but eventually swings back to take up a new relationship with him, a father-son relationship different from before and more stable. In this movement Tom certainly is not static. His social identity changes as the secret of his birth is revealed, and his temperament changes as the result of gaining Sophia Western's love. In making these changes, Tom is ostracized by his father-figure, hunted down, and nearly hanged. Allworthy, on the other hand, is impassively static—the same at the end of Tom's journey as he was at its beginning. A projection of virtue as social and economic reward, Allworthy is simultaneously an obstacle Tom must move around in order to reach Sophia and to overcome the evil Bliful forces. Like the fathers in *Jacke of Newbury* and *Robinson Crusoe,* Alworthy is a paternal object—both an obstacle and the prize for getting over the obstacle. Without Allworthy as paternal object, this novel's world means nothing. There is a similar but more severe situation in Samuel Richardson's novel, *Clarissa Harlowe* (1748). Clarissa is raped and otherwise tortured because she will not obey a father's strict command to marry an old man (a father figure) she does not love. In this instance the paternal object kills. In Oliver Goldsmith's *The Vicar of Wakefield* (novel, 1766), paternal authority is as absolute, but it splits into double fathers, "good" and "bad" (Sir William Thornhill and Squire Thornhill), and the Reverend Dr. Primose's family is buffeted to the extremes of fortune and ill-luck depending upon which father is influential at any one moment.

In each case the father (again a composite figure), represents communal values and unbending authority. What begins with Deloney in the last of the sixteenth century as exuberance about a generous king, here cools in the eighteenth century to ambivalence about a father with irreconcilably "good" and "bad" sides. In France, too, the sense of a potential communal tragedy under a harsh paternal task master is clear in Voltaire's *Œedipe* (*Oedipus,* tragedy, 1718), with the addition of a middle-aged lover for the suffering Jocaste, and *Candide* (novel, 1759), which satirizes eighteenth-century optimism, belief in a deistic (paternal) sanction of community. Denis Diderot's *Le neveu de Rameau* (*Rameau's Nephew,* satire, 1762–1784) explores the converse of optimism, the Mephistophelean world of roguery and dissolution under the eighteenth century's version of a Great Father. Typifying the attitude of this period, as does Diderot's plays, *Le père de famille* (*The Father of the Family,* 1758) and *Le fils naturel* (*The Natural Son,* 1757), is his great *Encyclopédie* (1751–1772), an attempt in a world of questionable (paternal) authority to establish fact and reason as moral guides on the basis of what, during the same years, Jean-Jacques Rousseau called *Du contrat social* (*The Social Contract,* treatise, 1762).

The Nineteenth Century

In the nineteenth century, the father turns either starkly malevolent or excessively weak and is no longer the protector of children. As if to counter this development Jane Austen, early in the century, shows a distrust of any social attachments that cannot be contained in her pastoral world; her greatest fear is that the continuity of personal history may be lost if that pastoral world (protected by "fathers") is contaminated. Her most authoritarian father figure, Mr. John Knightly, in the novel *Emma* (1816), is a shadowy but commanding figure whose judgment is the last word on all matters of morality and decorum. He makes doctrine of the decree that it is foolishness for anyone to venture beyond the Highbury arcadian existence. Accordingly, the figures close to Emma and Knightly deeply distrust the characters, especially Jane Fairfax, who have fallen under influences outside of Highbury, notably commercial London, and who, therefore, cannot be constrained by the limited paternal authority Knightly embodies. Fear of contamination among the devotees of Highbury is so great that all unpredictable activities, carriage rides (within Highbury), walks in the countryside (Jane Fairfax insists on her walks to the post office), and encounters with outsiders are avoided if possible and otherwise undertaken with great caution. And yet there is no suggestion in *Emma* that these strictures or Knightly would have any significance outside of Highbury, in London or beyond. As patriarch, Knightly is a precious object—strong in appearance and yet fragile—to be guarded in a safe place (Highbury). An even more sentimentalized version of paternal authority in this period is Johann Rudolph Wyss's novel *Der schweizerische Robinson* (*Swiss Family Robinson,* 1812–1827), in which a Swiss family is shipwrecked and survives primarily through affirmation of the familial order, particularly the father's preeminence in this small sphere.

Less sanguine, but more typical of nineteenth-century literature, are Charles Dickens' novels, wherein the crisis of paternal authority intensifies. All of Dickens' children are virtually "orphans" competing with each other for a benediction the father in this world no longer administers. Without family support, without the guidance of a trustworthy mentor (one "allworthy"), without the personal resources to repulse a morally corrosive world, the orphaned child in Dickens is an embodiment of panic over father loss. If the father and what he stands for are gone, really gone, then there is no place for anyone to turn. Pip, for example, in *Great Expectations* (1860–1861), is lured from a world that, like Highbury, is relatively safe from the encroachment of the dangerous world outside. Joe's farm and the tradition of folk wisdom and family loyalty that Joe represents are possible only in a community where mutual dependence perpetuates personal debt, continually retying the community members together. The bait that brings Pip to renounce Joe's farm is the promise of sonship under an anonymous, idealized sponsor (really Magwitch) not bound by personal history. The fantasy of Pip's great expectations is that of erasing paternal authority by erasing the past. Joe and Magwitch, "good" and "bad" fathers for Pip, both fail as teachers or representatives of the "laws."

Also, typical of Dickens' failed fathers is John Jarndyce of *Bleak House* (1852–1853), who is powerless to act but retains the appearance of paternal strength. Like Knightly in *Emma,* Jarndyce represents humanistic and communal values in a too narrowly circumscribed world, which Bleak House represents. The unredeemable corruption of authority in Chancery taints and condemns all such communal relations so that attempts to form ties in the world beyond Bleak House cannot succeed. Jarndyce has the power merely to offer Esther sanctuary from the world at large. When she refuses what would amount to incest with her father-figure, he offers her and her husband hardly an alternative, Bleak House II. The impossibility of exchange between Jarndyce's sphere of influence and the world beyond is a condition that gives Jarndyce (as a father figure) an "orphan" or unsponsored status of his own. The sentimentality of *Bleak House,* however, and of many other Dickens' novels, is the move to prolong an impossible situation by placing the endangered species, the apparently strong father, in a kind of cage (Bleak House) for safe keeping.

In *Hard Times* (1854) Dickens goes a step beyond this panic and toward resignation about paternal weakness to caricature even the possibility of paternal authority. All of its fathers are pretenders, authorities with no authority, guides capable of no guidance who instead advocate the debasement of all communal ties and the elevation of isolated "facts." M'Choakumchild, most flagrant of Coketown's failed fathers, harangues the children of his classroom to renounce all "knowledge" outside of a dictionary definition. Bounderby, the industrialist, brags about his lonely climb to "success" and lies about the true ease of his childhood. The two most interesting failed fathers are Thomas Gradgrind, Sr. (the outwardly wise educator who sponsors the teaching of "facts") and Signor Jupe (the circus-clown father). Gradgrind is a powerful figure with no understanding of children, and Signor Jupe (who runs away) is all sentiment and understanding with no ability to act.

On a grander scale than Dickens' work are the seventeen novels by Honoré de Balzac, under the corporate title of *La comédie humaine* (*The Human Comedy*)— most notably *Eugénie Grandet* (1833) and *Le père Goriot* (*Father Goriot,* 1834)—in which Balzac introduces over two thousand characters in an implied comparison between "zoological species" and the "social species." In Balzac's human zoo, without paternal and communal authority, money motivates and rules all in near chaos. Ivan Turgenev's novel, *Otisy i deti* (*Fathers and Children,* 1862), in contrast, begins with the assumption of a failed patrician class, a failed paternal order, and exhalts the nihilist Bazarov as a powerful common man (as if a potential "new" father) who could revitalize his society through decisive action. Father failure in the nineteenth century is treated most famously in Johann Wolfgang von Goethe's novel, *Die Leiden des jungen Werthers* (*The Sorrows of Young Werther,* 1774). But it is in Goethe's masterpiece

Faust (play, 1808) that the Mephistophelean nature of paternal authority—in this play literally a satanic "father"—is explored.

The failure of paternal authority is equally a fact in the nineteenth-century American novel, certainly touching on the same moral and social themes as Continental literature. In America, however, there is a fascination, fetishistic in intensity, with the disappearance or absence of fathers that is mesmerizing in its effect. For this we can turn to the white whale in Herman Melville's novel, *Moby-Dick* (1851), as Charles Olson notes (*Call Me Ishmael,* 1947), to which Ahab attributes supreme paternal authority; the whale in size and power is a kind of god that commands all at sea and in the exercise of its great will is inscrutable. Coming out of the water, which Melville says is "the key to it all," the whale (in the symbol system of this book) is the embodiment of nature's will. Ahab's strategy, in trying to kill the whale, is to overcome the natural and cultural orders and himself be God-the-father. *Moby-Dick's* fascination with the whale as a paternal object, for reasons apparent as far back as *Jacke of Newbury,* where a father figure is the mere representative of the law, turns out to be a fascination with the necessary failure of father figures to encompass the law they stand for—in effect, a fascination with the inevitability of father failure.

In Mark Twain's novel *Huckleberry Finn* (1884), Huck Finn is no maniac of Ahab's proportions, but his obsessive interest in father failure, in a sense in the father as a lost object, is considerable. Of the principal authority figures of Huck's experience—Tom Sawyer, Judge Thatcher, Jim, and Pap—it is Pap whom Huck describes physically with an intensity indicating obsession:

His hair was long and tangled and greasy, and hung down, and you could see his eyes shining through like he was behind vines. It was all black, no gray; so was his long, mixed-up whiskers. *There warn't no color in his face, where his face showed; it was white; not like another man's white, but a white to make a body sick, a white to make a body's flesh crawl—a tree-toad white, a fish-belly white.* As for his clothes—just rags, that was all. He had one ankle resting on 'tother knee; the boot on that foot was busted, and two of his toes stuck through, and he worked them now and then. [Italics added]

Particularly revealing here is the attention given to Pap's whiteness, "a white to make a body sick." As with Ishmael's concern with the whale's whiteness, Huck is struck by the multiple associations for white in his father's face. What appears to him as grotesquerie is the same quality of multiple reference that is overwhelming for all who attempt to grasp the phenomenal nature of the white whale. Huck's father does later die, but already in this description father loss is evident in Huck's fascination with the elusive nature of his father's appearance. The mesmerizing force of whiteness here, as in *Moby-Dick,* suggests that the father is an object breaking up and disappearing before one's eyes.

Such paternal loss and absence in nineteenth-century American literature is expressed in the controlled desperation of Henry Adams' *The Education of Henry Adams* (1907). Adams (as a character within this fiction), with sympathetic intelligence, with superb education, possessing the best the nineteenth century has to offer, looks to history and to what the culture is becoming as few others are capable and, by his own admission, seems "to know nothing—to be groping in darkness—to be falling forever in space." A historian in a historical crisis, his "historical neck [is] broken by the sudden irruption of forces totally new." Adams' concern about the loss of the "father" (cultural authority) in America, really in all modern culture, suggests Yeats' anxiety that the center of culture in the twentieth century will not hold. It is this crisis of fin de siècle malaise in the "sudden irruption of forces totally new" that most immediately captures the impact of father loss as reflected in *Huckleberry Finn, Moby-Dick,* and in various other works such as Nathaniel Hawthorne's novels *The Scarlet Letter* (1850), *The House of the Seven Gables* (1851), and "Benito Cereno" (1855–1856), and Mark Twain's novel *A Connecticut Yankee in King Arthur's Court* (1889).

How far this sense of paternal loss may be intensified before it is incorporated into a new literary awareness altogether is shown in two novels, Dostoevsky's *Brat' īaKaramazovy (The Brothers Karamazov,* 1880) and Thomas Hardy's *Jude the Obscure* (1896). In Dostoevsky's novel paternal authority is sharply divided between father Karamazov, a blustering and ineffectual clown, and Father Zossima, a pure soul not of this world. Ivan Karamazov's existential agony over "truth" and "goodness" is symptomatic of this paternal projection of an irreconcilable contradiction of values in this novel. Even more intensely, in Hardy's novel the nineteenth century ends with an unflinching gaze into the crisis of father absence. Jude Fawley is a tragic version of Job who listens for but never hears a call to duty; he is desperate to be a protégé to church or university fathers but can find none. He is initially no different from Robinson Crusoe and Tom Jones, who begin their quests fatherless, unsponsored. And like them, Jude is at first "living in a world which did not want [him]," —a world that is a stark, empty space. Unlike them, however, Jude finds no authority who may be served. Never finding the relationship that Crusoe discovers as true deliverance, Jude remains figuratively fatherless and eventually returns to Marygreen with a sense of futility and disgust. At the novel's end his feeling of displacement and self-revulsion grows to tragic proportions. With no calling to respond to, his life is simply a series of missed opportunities.

Father absence, a transformed and diminished version of the great father, here surfaces as a motif with a vengeance. Prominently in *Jude,* as in much other literature of the later nineteenth century, the absent father (the motif representing lost authority) rises like a titan awakening to claim a central place in literature. In a way literature can barely cope with (after *Jude,* for example, Hardy refuses to cope with novel writing), the absent father comes to dominate literature and makes stringent demands on its formal integrity. Given this dramatic development in literary form, one can assume that literature reaches, with *Jude* and with other works of the century's end, the conclusion to one line of development. The twentieth century, thereafter, is given the opportunity—in fact, the necessity—of developing a new sense of what the great father can become.

The Twentieth Century

A number of twentieth-century works recapitulate the nineteenth century's concern with paternal authority and the family. Samuel Butler's *The Way of All Flesh* (1903) is an English *Bildungsroman* that surveys the various crises of lost paternal authority. This is also the terrain of Thomas Mann's novel *Buddenbrooks* (1901) and John Galsworthy's Forsythe Saga, particularly *The Man of Property* (1906), *In Chancery* (1920), and *A Modern Comedy* (1929)—novel chronicles that explore family and communal life in which all authority has been displaced. More indicative of twentieth-century treatments of a new version of the great father is John Millington's Synge's play *The Playboy of the Western World* (1907), where the father figure becomes a self-consciously folkloric and mythic presence, the father as a mere character or role in a psychological and mythic story—not so much a figure as purely a symbol.

This symbolic father emerges even more distinctly in 1922 with James Joyce's novel *Ulysses*. This new father encompasses father absence, the sense of loss, but does so without the obligatory tragic assumptions that accompany father loss in *Jude*. The appropriateness of singling out *Ulysses* for its new version of paternity is an indication of why Joyce's novel occupies a place, as Harry Blamires says (*The Bloomsday Book*, 1966), as "the major imaginative work in English prose of the present century." Leopold Bloom in this work is simultaneously and very deliberately a religious, philosophical, cultural, historical, and psychological representation of paternity. This new (symbolic) father is a decisive turn in literary development from which subsequent directions are taken. For instance, just as Aeschylus' play, *Oresteia* (458 B.C.) is a new testament of the post-Orestean world in which paternal authority is not passed through blood from father to son, but through adherence to the cultural law that binds humans and gods alike in a partnership of trust, *Ulysses* in its presentation of the symbolic father is a testament of modernism that finds beneath the multiplicity of the twentieth century a principle of structural continuity. That structure, the symbolic father, binds humans and gods, also the dark gods even if the whole relationship is not circumscribable.

In the symbolic father's rise in the twentieth century, Greek mythology's great father is almost completely transformed. No longer a privileged and powerful image of authority, the father henceforth represents one possibility for order among others. Here the father, in an important sense, has joined the family. This new fictional father (the symbolic father) can be seen in modernist novels such as William Faulkner's *Absalom, Absalom!* (1936), a novel wherein literal patriarchs are completely ironic figures—fathers whose privileged status is undercut by a general dispersion of authority to other family members. Almost the whole development of *Absalom*, for example, is the revelation that patriarchal Thomas Sutpen is simply the composite body of all who know him. The dispersion can be mythic in a clearly religious sense, as in T. S. Eliot's depiction of the fisher king in *The Waste Land* (poem, 1922), or surrealistic (magic realism), as in García Márquez's novels *Cien años de soledad* (*One Hundred Years of Solitude*, 1967) and *El otōno del patriarca* (*Autumn of the Patriarch*, 1975).

The advent of this symbolic father tends to direct emphasis to the symbolic authority of fiction itself—of narration as a significant structure not dependent in any direct way on something outside of itself. This development can be seen in a rather conventional and realistic novel, John Steinbeck's *The Grapes of Wrath* (1939), where an emerging socialist order begins to subsume an old regime of paternalistic capitalism. Here the family's authority, in a very broad, communal sense—as embodied particularly in Ma and Tom Joad's character development—is far more important than the father's. Especially in later postmodern fiction, however, such as Donald Barthelme's novel *The Dead Father* (1975) and Robert Coover's *The Public Burning* (history, 1977), vestiges of power are stripped from father figures and other manifestations of patriarchal authority. What is left after the dissolution of the great father is the symbolic father in a symbolic family, a complex set of relationships on various levels of literary development simultaneously. The great father in the twentieth century is simply a family member with complex ties to the other members.

The Theory of the Father

The twentieth century has produced many different understandings of the father in literature, principally mythic and psychoanalytic in the early part of the century and Marxist and feminist in more recent developments. The great body of theory that most nearly encompasses such diverse approaches, that in fact is assumed and subsumed by them, can be called a theory of sacrifice, an ancient tradition of dialectical thought that existed prior to—but has been codified in—the Judeo-Christian tradition. An introduction to this thought serves as an introduction to the theory of the father in literature.

A useful focus of this tradition is the treatment of sacrificial theory in the Catholic church, a complex development that leads eventually to the institution of the Mass. From the first century A.D. through modern times, for example, the church has invested its claim to philosophical authority in its ability to mediate the opposition of father and son. The result of the mediation is that Christ, a dispensation or accommodation of God to man, bridges the distance between humans and the Father. In the paradox of Christ's two-fold position as son of man and of God, the principle of mediation between father and son is contained, a principle that Augustine expressed as a paradox of difference and identity, wherein the Father and the Son "are two different things, [and] still there is no difference in their substance . . . but to the relation, and the relation is no accident because it is not changeable." The central mystery of the Trinity, for instance, is the existence of opposition within mediation, a construct Augustine expresses in the distinction he makes between a "panel and the picture painted on it." Both "are together called image, but [only] on account of the picture painted on it, the panel is at the same time called an image." In other words, the nature of the Trinity as a structure is reflected in a complex of relationships and cannot be reduced to the status of an object.

Behind the horizon of the risen Christ who reconciles humans with the Father is a long working out of the father-son relationship in terms of sacrifice, which becomes the Mass—a symbolic, nonbloody sacrifice in narrative form. The philosophy of the church, in fact, begins with the simple assumption that the opposition of father and son is in need of mediation. In the early Catholic church the concept of atonement was conceived as a ransom paid to keep away the devil, but with the gradual development of Christology and the identification of Christ with sinful humanity, a shift occurs so that what was formerly a ransom paid to a threatening, dark father becomes much less of a burden. As the concept of atonement develops in the thought of the church fathers, especially as elaborated by St. Paul, satisfaction gives way to justification by faith, where, as E. O. James explains, "the victorious death and resurrection of Christ [produces] a new status of sonship by securing justification and reconciliation" with the father. Thus, the development of the church's conception of God has been from the angry father who could be bought off only for the moment, to the benevolent father for whom one wishes to be a good child.

This relationship with God finds primary expression in sacrifice, a symbol of the son's mediation with the father, for which there is a pre-Christian or primitive, mode and a Christian or totemic mode. Sacrifice "in its primitive mode of expression," as E. O. James explains (*Sacrifice and Sacrament,* 1962),

is devoid of any moral and ethical qualities in the modern sense, but nevertheless, although sin is regarded as a ritual defilement, its expiation is a sacramental process of restoration of the state of religious purity and non-moral holiness on which the continuance of divine beneficence depends. Its purpose is to raise mankind either in an individual or corporate capacity to a higher spiritual status in which the transcendent exercises control over the physical and human, and the eternal over the temporal, but always through human agents and material instruments employed as the vehicle of purifying efficacy.

At the origin of primitive sacrifice seems to be an initial act of doubling, where a single god (generally a father) with a single spirit in some sense becomes two. By traveling outside of himself to constitute the being of another, the god renounces his own sacred body in order to bring "about the existence of things." Thus, the first sacrifice is a kind of narrative act of creation *and* a god's suicide, the god committing suicide through the offspring in the other self; thereafter, the world comes into being. This manifold act of doubling and suicide, which constitutes an origin story, may overcome the difficulty of explaining how a powerful god can be slain by presenting the god "in the guise of an evil spirit [so that] it is the spirit who is put to death, and from it emerges the god." In any case, the commemoration of the god's suicide is signified by a reenactment of suicide in sacrifice, where "a part of the self is made into an 'it' for the seeming preservation of the remainder."

In pre-Christian sacrifice a father actually gives his first-born son to god-the-father so that he himself will be maintained in a connection with what is holy. In this bloody version of sacrificing a child resides an attempt to be atoned with god-the-father through the obliteration of the very opposition between father and child. The latent motive of this sacrificial act must be, as Kierkegaard pointed out (*Frygt og bæven* [*Fear and Trembling*, 1843]), hate for the child, in that the father performing the sacrifice desires the son's death so that he can stand free of any such opposition without a rival before god. Through the infanticidal wish the father removes the son and obliterates the structure of opposition the son represents in order to place himself in the preeminent position of being the sole "son" to god-the-father. Such infanticide does overcome opposition, although there is a deep contradiction involved. Without a son the father ceases to be a father, and in so being denies the validity of sonship, a state that has meaning only as a development in relation to fatherhood. So, in killing his son, the father necessarily has killed himself as a son and, thus, has destroyed his own father's fatherhood. In this cycle of child killing, god himself is even destroyed *as a father*. In effect, by seeking the role of preeminent son to god-the-father, the father tries to usurp god's position. Infanticidal sacrifice, in this way, is an act of paternal insurrection that spreads suicide and patricide over three generations and ends finally as an act of theocide.

In the Judeo-Christian tradition it was sometime after the destruction of the Temple in A.D. 70 that sacrifice became a kind of totemic expression of God's suicide. "The ancient blood ritual" of sacrifice, according to E. O. James, "underwent a fundamental change in character so that the concept of life-giving became that of self-oblation, the sacrifice of the lips instead of the calves." Whereas human and animal sacrifice commemorated, in the form of ransom, God's suicide when he created the world, the "sacrifice of the lips" becomes a symbolic expression of the giving over of a whole life as love for God-the-Father. That is to say, by taking in the Host, the communicant signifies in a narration, through symbolic participation, an act for which God is the only authority. In communion, the communicant accedes to the death of God as a Spirit in the world. So, through voluntary ingestion of the Host (Spirit) a circle of love is completed in that a human mediates the opposition of Father and Son by returning love to the Father who first gave love to humans through the Son. Therefore, through love the subjectivity of life in the world, where Christ lived, is returned to its object, toward whom all life and love travels as, in Augustine's words, "a kind of life which couples together or seeks to couple some two entities, the lover and the loved."

The theory of sacrifice inherent in the Catholic Mass is a theory of totemism in which the opposition of Father and Son is mediated by the mutual recognition of a dead father, an absent father. Whereas in pre-Christian sacrifice the father killed his father by killing his son, in communion a father recognizes that his father, God, has already died by taking the image of the Son, and a bloody sacrifice need not be repeated. In fact, the full recognition is that God has died twice. He died first when he left his solitary state to create the possibility of love in the Son, and he died again when the Son died for humans, a sacrifice made so that through divine retribution the Holy Spirit would be infused into the world. In each case the accommodation of God, in the incarnation of Christ, and in the commemoration of Christ's death in the ingestion of the Host—thus Christ's dual sonship—is focused on a totem that signifies the process of the sacred falling into time. The incarnation and communion are part of, in James' words, ''a sacramental system in which the [totemic] material is the instrument and channel of the spiritual.'' Through the agency of the so-called material totem of sacrifice, the signifier of the dead father Freud refers to, a timeless primal unity that is lost can be signified in time by the operation of what is essentially a narrative. The Mass is, thus, a narrative (actually a story) that articulates the totem in time and in so doing signifies the absence (or death) of the Father. It follows that the Father's death is necessary for the totem to have its significative function. It also follows that father absence should be a recurrent concern of literature from antiquity through the present.

Striking here is that the totemic system of sacrifice in the Mass, especially as seen in relation to its development from blood sacrifice, depicts the production of narration (of storytelling)—a process that operates in part according to a paternal principle, the functional element implied by the great father. This narrative process certainly can be described in other ways, without this strong paternal bias, and literary theory from 1965 on has been engaged in doing just that. In fact, it has been a major point here to show that literary works in the nineteenth and twentieth centuries tend to show a decisive transformation of the great father, and certainly there are deep theoretical implications in this shift. In the twentieth century the great father is dismantled and his authority redistributed among various family members for various reasons. The current tendency is to recast the great father's importance to the point that his greatness is merely historical, clearly a fact of Western literature but not a reality of twentieth-century writing or of theory about that writing.

See also: Adolescence, Family, Oedipus Complex, Parents and Children.

Selected Bibliography

Armens, Sven. *Archetypes of the Family in Literature*. Seattle: University of Washington Press, 1966.

Davis, Robert Con, ed. *The Fictional Father: Lacanian Readings of the Text*. Amherst: University of Massachusetts Press, 1981.

Malinowski, Bronislaw. *The Father in Primitive Psychology*. New York: W. W. Norton, 1927.

Tobin, Patricia. *Time and the Novel: The Genealogical Imperative*. Princeton, N.J.: Princeton University Press, 1978.

ROBERT CON DAVIS

GROTESQUE

Fabulous or imaginary creatures of pagan origin, grotesques were regarded as both threatening and benign, such as primitive deities or fantastic beasts. In

Christian cultures, grotesques were also the images of the devil, demons, condemned souls, having ludicrous and horrific qualities from the belief that the devil mocked and tortured mankind. Conversely, the Christian grotesque is carnivalesque, festive, or comedic activity through which destructive forces are imitated and transformed to benevolent powers. In literature, the grotesque is a disjunctive image, scene, or larger structure, composed of comic-horrific elements or otherwise irreconcilable parts. It is also a fictional world that appears to be absurd. Bestial types or stock characters of farce are called grotesque, as are fictional portrayals of harsh and deformed reality and the sordid characters of such worlds.

Background In Antiquity

The grotesque has its origins in the preliterary festivals of Dionysus, which were celebrated with sacrifice and solemnity as well as feasts and revels. The celebrants dressed as satyrs and sang abusive songs in the belief that degradation and destruction would assure birth and renewal. Grotesque presentations of the later Dionysia are known to us through the satyric drama and Old Comedy of Aristophanes (444–388 B.C.). *Ornithes* (*The Birds*, 414 B.C.) presents the absurd world of Cloudcuckooland where all the actors wear feathers and discuss wild political dreams; *Lysistratē* (*Lysistrata*, 411 B.C.) is realistic, but the world is topsy-turvy, for women ridicule the masculine ethos of war and withhold sex from their husbands until they agree to make peace. In Aristophanes' grotesque, ribald and abusive language is imposed on the serious concerns of men, and human affairs gain heightened significance from the fusion of destructive themes with the comedic mode of renewal.

Very little is known about Greek comedy in the fourth century B.C., but fragments from plays of Menander suggest that the grotesque was reduced to a much milder form. Improvised farces *(Atellanae)* played by Roman youths from about the third century B.C. to the middle of the first century B.C. may have been grotesque, as was the mime theater that followed and which subsumed techniques of the *Atellana*. The mime *Atellana* employed stock characters— Bucco (Fatty), Dossenuus (Glutton), Pappus (the *senex* or old father), and Maccus (the fool)—and presented farcical plots dealing with lovers and adulterers. Apparently, the actors wore bestial masks and used exaggerated gestures, grimaces, and obscene body language. These were probably the plays that Horace attacked in *Ars poetica* (*The Art of Poetry,* treatise, c. 19 B.C.) when he set rules for comic action that was to avoid "violence or the supernatural which occasion disgust and disbelief."

The Middle Ages

The mime, buffoon, or itinerant player seems to have survived church suppression of the Roman theaters; entertainers and amateurs in fantastic masks gave wild performances at carnival time and other calendar festivals. Twelfth-century records indicate licentious games were played as seasonal fetes in which social and religious decorum was overturned by mock-ordinances and mock-masses, and where carnival foods, having sexual significance, such as pig and black sausage, were consumed, or dice were played on the church altar. On other occasions, mumming plays and morris dances were performed in masks and wildmen's costume, suggesting ancient fertility rites and demonic exorcisms that were intended to appease the destructive forces in nature. Literary forms of the grotesque are extant in twelfth-century fables and in bawdy tales and roguish jests of the thirteenth century. These achieved artistic form in *Il decamerone* (*Decameron*, novellas, c. 1350) by Giovanni Boccaccio, in which elegant youths attempt to escape death by plague through seclusion in the country. There, they symbolically exorcize fear of death by telling festive tales of trickery, cheating, and adultery, which reflect a primordial amorality toward such matters. An English masterpiece in a similar "frame-tale" genre is Geoffrey Chaucer's *The Canterbury Tales* (c. 1380–1400), where some of the most memorable comic sinners or grotesques in fiction come alive in such verbal portraits as the drunken Miller, the ulcerous Cook, and the gap-toothed Wife of Bath. Their images convey animalistic qualities harbored within the varied forms of mankind, while their tales of tricksters, dupes, and transformation celebrate the baser forms of human behavior.

Owing to the dualism of Christian thought, which held that both tragedy and comedy originated in the fall of Lucifer and the loss of Eden, sinners were perceived darkly, but also as ludicrous and absurd for daring to defy God. Early mystery plays present the characters of Herod, the Devil, Belshazzar, and other scriptural villains in extravagant comic roles. Herod ranted and raved; the Devil jumped and tumbled or ran about like a wild man, evoking ludicrous horror among the spectators, as was expected from this barbaric style of acting.

Death was closely associated with the Devil, and stories circulated among the people about meetings with demons and ghouls. A legend told of St. Macarius may account for the grotesque danse macabre or dance of death theme, popular from the fifteenth century to modern times. In this comic-horrific genre, Death is figured as a skeleton who dances off with the souls of the living. There is good evidence that the Renaissance harlequin was an incarnation of an old French demon *Herlequin* or *Hellequin*, or *familia Herlechini*, who had commerce with the living. His descent has been traced from the eleventh-century history by Ordericus Vitalis to a Latin manuscript of 1514 and a commedia dell'arte plot of 1585, by which time he is a lusty, comic devil who consorts with lascivious women and bawds.

In fifteenth-century literature, the grotesque figures are demons and giants, villainous knights, and wicked elves who do the work of the devil but are foiled by chivalrous knights. Many may be found in the romances of Sir Thomas Malory's *Morte d'Arthur* (c. 1469). Evil and monstrosity or natural deformity are contrasted with the good and the beautiful in the chivalric romance and bear little resemblance to the grotesque-farce portrayed in riot scenes of contemporary morality plays, such as *Mankind* (c. 1475) and *Everyman* (c. 1500). The grotesque element shared by both types of literature, however, derives from the war of good and evil waged within characters in the moralities and between heroes and monsters in romance. Scottish poetry in the "eldritch tradition" and John Skelton's (c. 1460–1529) images of beastly hags in "The Tunning of Elinour Rumming" also reflect fifteenth-century taste for comic-horror.

The Renaissance (1500–1660)

Grotesque mingling of the fantastic and the real, the sordid and the ideal, the comic and the horrific that is characteristic of most medieval popular literature is also manifested in the great burlesque exaggerations that appeared in the sixteenth century. This period is remarkable for its achievement in comedy, much of it an earthy realism, accompanied by grotesque reversals or burlesques of medieval romance and epic conventions, the intrusion of farcical interludes in serious drama, an inordinate interest in the sordid—in bawds, servants, crime—and a delight in reporting the worm's eye view of hypocrisy in the privileged classes. The prevalent impulse of the age was carnivalesque, which was applied to almost every branch of art. Comedic joy and brutal social conditions, naïve and barbaric conduct, are reflected in especially horrific-comic style, made possible by the linguistic irruption of contemporary vernaculars in the age of print.

The century opened with Spain's first Renaissance tragicomedy, *La tragico-media de Calisto y Melibea* (*Celestina or The Spanish Bawd*, 1499–1502) partially attributed to Fernando de Rojas. This prose work, written in dialogue and twenty-two acts, mingles demonic elements with the grotesque world of servants and the ideal but tragic world of great lovers, creating far greater interest, however, in its grotesque realism than in the virtues of enduring love. In Italy, Ludovico Ariosto produced his comic romance-epic in verse *Orlando furioso* (1516), where the hero of popular legend goes mad; his wits are taken to the moon and returned later in a bottle, whereupon he goes off to his famous victory. In France, François Rabelais created the world-favorite "demon of thirst," *Pantagruel* (1532), followed by "the most horrific life" of *Gargantua* (1534) and by sequels to these novels as well as new editions throughout the century.

Grotesque images of the body are pervasive in the Rabelaisian style, and the entire tone is carnivalesque; the language of excrement and fertility, destruction and regeneration, reflects the deep ambivalence of grotesque logic, in which life-death-birth are fused as single concepts. A primal knowledge of nature's perversity collides with civilized values, which are reversed, destroyed, and renewed in such episodes as Gargantua's strange birth or Panurge's trick on the Parisian lady. The legendary demon Pantagruel is inflated to burlesque proportions as a giant of drinkers and philosophers, and his enormous thirst and evacuations may be taken for the Renaissance thirst for intellectual freedom and nature's destruction of the obsolete. With its genius for bizarre, zany, and earthy invention, the Rabelaisian style has become synonymous with the grotesque.

In the same era, Spain issued its first *novela picaresca* by Francisco Delicado:

Retrato de la lozana andaluza (*Lozana of Andalusia,* 1528), a novel of social protest, in which the female protagonist is a realistic type of the lowest class who, in serving many masters, is able to describe bourgeois and upper-class hypocrisy from within. Grotesque realism marks the style of this and subsequent picaresque, such as the anonymous and more popular *Lazarillo de Tormes* (1554). Picaresque violence and atrocity, deeply associated with demonic forces, were brought to the English novel by Thomas Lodge in *Robert of Normandy* (1591) and Thomas Nashe in *The Unfortunate Traveller* (1593). Nashe's literary style, recently described as "Elizabethan grotesque," is low and Rabelaisian, both in its rhetoric of detraction and its body imagery, which are either repulsive, or exuberant, or both. Shakespeare's Falstaff, who appears in the two parts of *Henry IV* (1597; 1600) and *Henry V* (1600), is probably the finest example of Elizabethan grotesque embodying in language, style, imagery, and the multiple worlds he occupies in the plays, the efforts of an entire century to organize, assimilate, and unify the disjunctive grotesque elements of Renaissance experience. The same may be said of a work in a different genre, the Spanish picaresque-epic-romance novel *Don Quijote* (*Don Quixote,* 1605, 1615) by Miguel de Cervantes. In this masterpiece among grotesque novels, the mad hero turns ordinary reality into idealistic vision, while his picaresque squire Sancho Panza follows his master with blind loyalty, experiencing the same events with the "obtuseness" of common sense. This clash of perceptions creates uneasy disjunctions throughout the novel and are unified only by Cervantes' comic point of view.

In such diverse works, the grotesque is the unifying vision of the century. It is a comic perspective, applied with more visible exaggeration than ever before, to honored conventions of literature, spiritual concerns, and social realities. This grotesque vision provides compelling evidence that the Renaissance, having revived the classics and disseminated the ancient rules, had also produced a school of writers who protested vehemently against them.

Commedia dell'Arte and Farce (1500–1850)

Among the forms of comic expression that arose in the middle of the sixteenth century was the commedia dell'arte, an extemporaneous theater, known to us through scenarios or plot outlines and through engravings, paintings, and contemporary descriptions, all of which make clear that it was not only a popular nonliterary form for nearly three centuries but a permanent influence on the literary grotesque.

The commedia began as popular parody of commedia erudita, Latin plays that had been revived or adapted for production during the first half of the sixteenth century. It borrowed stock character types from the classical plays (the *senex,* the parasite, servants, lovers, the braggart soldier), gave them regional dialects and names (Pantalon was a merchant of Venice; Zanni was a Neapolitan servant), and portrayed them in an exaggerated style of ancient and medieval farce. Except for women and lovers, all the characters wore demonic, bestial, leering masks;

early commedia players wore leather phalluses that might be stuffed full for the Zanni or hang limp for the Pantalone; later ones carried a sword and pouch in place of genitalia, and the Bawd carried a purse as a sign of her business or a rosary when she played a hypocrite. Commedia scenarios were usually farcical and fantastic; pastorals, especially, employed magicians, satyrs, nymphs, and monsters. Harlequin was often beaten or abused but also rewarded for his tricks, which helped foil obstructive characters and unite lovers. In this popular grotesque, fear was amplified to heighten the fantasy, and fun was assured by the grotesque truism that all will be set right in the end.

The rise of Italian commedia may be indebted to the taste for native farce that prevailed in most countries of Europe in the early Renaissance. In France, human comedies like *Maistre Pierre Pathelin* (*Pathelin*, c. 1470) were performed near the end of the fifteenth century; in England, adaptations of French farces were made by John Heywood in *The Pardoner and the Friar* and *John John, the Husband, Tyb His Wife and Sir John the Priest*, both published in 1533. The human comedy of beggars and merchants in *Tragedia żebracza* (*The Beggar's Tragedy*, pre-1551) was popular in Poland. Like the fantastic commedia, these native farces are distinguished for their carnivalesque humor, where social codes are suspended and riotous and indecorous behavior is allowed.

Literary farce of the late Renaissance focused on social satire but borrowed wholesale from commedia. From the graciosos of Lope de Vega (1562–1635) and Tirso de Molina (1583?–1648) in Spain, to Ben Jonson's *Volpone* (1606) in England, Molière's *Tartuffe* (1664) in France, and the scenarios by Carlo Goldoni (1707–1793), in Venice, "humours" types, or stock characters, or masks played pious lechers, would-be cuckolds, frustrated and endangered lovers, and zanies who introduced chaos and disorder to the plots.

Commedia influence was also strong in the courtly masque, a glittering genre of the Baroque period, in which grotesque interludes or "entrées," usually performed by professionals, portrayed wild, fantastic creatures from pagan myth, commedia types in lewd antics, or lower-class types in rustic revels. Ben Jonson's *Irish Masque* (1613–1614), written for King James I, is essentially a grotesque interlude of comic dialogues and dances by Irish servants, and the apparitions in his masque *Vision of Delight* (1617) are ribald and grotesque shows of a pregnant she-monster, lecherous Pantalones, and a host of monstrosities that represent carnival symbols of a belly and no face, or a face with the bill of a shovel. Such dehumanized types, employed in the comic masques of Florence and France, are found in the grotesque engravings of *Balli di Sfessania* (1622) by Jacques Callot, in which commedia characters are seen in bird-visors, feathered headdresses, and animalistic, although graceful, postures of the grotesque dance. Louis XIV entertained visiting dignitaries of Europe with such masques, and the Duke Anton Ulrich of Braunschweig adapted them to his own court. He was himself the author of *Ballet der Diana* (1663), which contains numerous interludes or "entrées" for drunkards, craftsmen, and milkmaids. While the drinkers provide rough and tumble fun, the workers praise the virtues of sobriety.

Poland too followed the trend, as shown in the commissioned carnival enter-tainment *Z chłopa kro'l (Peasant into King,* 1637) by Piotr Baryka. In this play, the carnival motif of drink and riot substitutes for the real thing. A peasant is found sleeping off his drink and is dressed as a king by some bored soldiers looking for amusement. The peasant is baffled by his treatment but takes ad-vantage of the opportunity to consume huge amounts of beer and cabbage, to the despair of the soldiers who must provide the "king's" needs. Commedia influence on Polish literature extends into the nineteenth century with the play *Zemsta (The Vengeance,* 1834) by Aleksander Fredro, in which a braggart soldier wears exaggerated dress, assumes ridiculous refinements, and uses high-flown language in an impossible hope to win a rich heiress in marriage.

The Eighteenth Century

After the Restoration and the reopening of the theaters in England, commedia farce gained dominance over the popular stage for its ability to evoke laughter at the animal antics and vices of the lowest orders in society. While grotesque comedy pervaded the burlesque poetry and satires of the period, its presence in the musical theater was far more spectacular, reaching its highest achievement in John Gay's musical satire *The Beggar's Opera* (1728), which gave tragicomic emotion to the underworld grotesque in such characters as Polly, Peachum, and Macheath.

Such realistic types also appear in picaresque novels, *Joseph Andrews* (1742) by Henry Fielding, *Peregrine Pickle* (1751) by Tobias Smollett, *Candide* (1759) by Voltaire, and *Tristram Shandy* (1759–1767) by Laurence Sterne, which rely on grotesque incidents and style in varying degrees. These novels deal with naïfs, rather than rogues, who survive a brutal and carnivalesque world, usually with their innocence intact. Grotesque import is conveyed by the juxtaposition of barbarous events and the protagonist's unfailing virtue. Sterne's novel is unique in that the grotesque is achieved, not through the disjunctivism of comic-horror, but in the lighter mixtures of styles and concepts, tragicomic interruptions, and prurient interpolations. All the novels are marked, to some extent, by Rabelaisian style.

Gothic-Grotesque (1770–1850)

While the English, on the whole, entertained themselves with genuine gro-tesque, in which comic-horrific elements maintained balance, a somber mood was cast over the German grotesque. Commedia was banned in 1770, and foreign troupes were forbidden entry to the country. German playwrights continued to use commedia techniques, however, in tragicomic plays of a reform movement, named for Friedrich Klinger's *Sturm und Drang* (1776). According to Wolfgang Kayser, Klinger introduced a third genre, in which the fusion of grotesque elements created the impression of confusion, anticipating the modern theater of the absurd. In *Sturm und Drang* commedia acting style, eccentric language, and tragic events are fused in a single play. By the tail end of the movement, in Georg Büchner's *Woyzeck* (c. 1837), comedic techniques are put to tragic purpose, and the old carnival fun is replaced by the threatening quality of the grotesque.

The magical and ribald grotesque of "Merry England" turned Gothic in the romance novel that gained preeminence in the 1790s and emphasized the uncanny and the erotic over the fantastic and the ribald. Whereas picaresque writers had handled primitive bawdy material overtly in farcical style, the Gothic novelist dealt with these themes covertly, setting action in underground vaults of eerie castles and in demonic landscapes. The playful seducer of commedia with his bestial mask become a dangerous sadist or decadent spirit from hell. Novels such as *The Old Manor House* (1793) by Charlotte Smith, *The Mysteries of Udolpho* (1794) by Ann Radcliffe, and literally hundreds of imitations present virtuous heroines entrapped by human demons who haunt the libidinous grottoes of the human psyche. In the other gender, *la belle dame sans merci* or the beautiful witch served as the symbol for sexual sin.

The horrific mood of Gothic-grotesque is heightened by the inversion of carnival joy in the romantic view, which held that laughter and sensuality were temptations of the Devil who mocked at men in their pleasure. The Faustian hero of Goethe and the Byronic hero of *Manfred* (dramatic poem, 1817) live full and sensuous lives, harbor unspeakable horror in their souls, and are claimed by demons in the end. In this view, the carnival or masquerade spirit is to be feared. The mask does not emulate the beast in order to appease it but hides the Devil within man. In Bonaventura's (pseud.) *Die Nachtwachen* (*The Night-watches*, novel, 1804), when the nightwatchman calls "eternity" instead of the hour, all the respectable people unmask, revealing themselves as human beasts; the Master of Revels in the Russian play *Pir vo vremia chumy* (*The Feast during the Plague*, 1832) by Alexander Pushkin, defies the power of death and accepts damnation; and in "The Masque of the Red Death" (short story, 1842) by Edgar Allan Poe, one of the revellers is Death himself.

Among the Romantics, there are exceptions to this Gothic mode. William Blake's devils turn theology inside-out, introduce chaos to conventional order, and destroy rationalism for imaginative rebirth. In Blake's poetry, grotesque fusions are metaphysical events; the Devil gains the upper hand in comic dialogues with the angel in *The Marriage of Heaven and Hell* (1790), and passion (Orc) becomes reason (Urizen) in *The First Book of Urizen* (1794). Blake's topsy-turvy cosmos equates the angel with sterility, and diabolic perversity with the primal, creative forces in life. Samuel Taylor Coleridge may also have achieved the grotesque in "Kubla Khan" (poem, 1816), where creative light and dark meaning are joined in the "stately pleasure dome"; in the Abyssinian maid and her demon lover; in Alph and the measureless caverns of Xanadu. But the reconciliation of comedic and dark forces is rare in romantic writing.

Where grotesque dualities are acknowledged as inevitabilities, they are employed with reference to the grotesque-absurd world, as in *Leyendas* (*Legends*, short stories, 1870) of Spain's Gustavo Adolfo Bécquer. In "La creácion," the world is an "animated absurdity," constructed on principles of death and destruction, life and reconstruction; it is a "deformed, rachitic, dark world" and a source of cosmic laughter for its infantile creators. This is not the carnivalesque vision of Rabelais, nor of the early Harlequin, nor of Falstaff who are assimilated into the world's zany design. Rather, it is a despairing vision of natural law and anticipates the new perception of the absurd that would come forward in the twentieth century.

Postromantic Grotesque (1820–1900)

A type of macabre humor became popular in the 1820s, along with the illustrated verse books that were published in the course of the nineteenth century. In these works, cheerful caricatures of dehumanized types convey images of greed, vanity, and folly but also direct harsh satirical comment against industrial society in which man is merely a body with detachable parts and an irrelevant soul. The social satires of poet-illustrator Thomas Hood run along distinctly grotesque lines in *Whims and Oddities* (1826), where the ballad "Faithless Nelly Gray" tells of the legless soldier Ben Battle who finds himself on "another footing" with the girl he left behind. Carnivalesque ribaldry is figured as grotesque dismemberment in Victorian nonsense verse, where legs signify genitalia and are often made impotent. In *Bab Ballads* (1867–1869), written and illustrated by W. S. Gilbert, jealous mermen dismember Capt. Clegg because the mermaids have admired his fine legs. The same macabre wit is turned against bourgeois manners in the self-illustrated verses of *Eispeter* (*Ice-Peter*, 1864) by Wilhelm Busch where grieving parents store their son's remains among the preserves in their cellar.

Prose fiction, as it developed in the postromantic period, was not without grotesque quality. The German prose writers employed a "ludicrous demon" in their gothic reflections, and Russians dealt with evil and death in strange fantasies. Nikolai Gogol's story *Vĭ* (*Viy*, 1835) portrays the demon named in the title with eyelashes extending to his toes and earth-covered limbs. His realistic novel *Mërtvye dushi* (*Dead Souls*, 1842) about the rogue Chichikov is a grotesque novel that dehumanizes its characters in accordance with their spiritual vacuities by likening them to plants, animals, and things. Similarly, the caricatures of Charles Dickens in *The Pickwick Papers* (novel, 1836–1837) distort human forms to emphasize folly and vice. Taken as a model of grotesque realism for his interest in sordid life, Dickens has also been noted for the grotesque intrusions of farcical scenes and for imparting comic quality to repulsive villains like Fagin in *Oliver Twist* (novel, 1837–1838) and Mr. Squeers in *Nicholas Nickleby* (novel, 1838–1839). The realistic novel *Idiot* (*The Idiot*, 1868) by Dostoevsky is structured on the grotesque transformation of its protagonist, and painful scenes are reported as farcical incidents, especially the final ones where a wedding turns into a riot, and a death watch ends in the final conversion of Myshkin to a raving lunatic.

Although fiction in the latter decades of the century became increasingly naturalistic, there were continual outbreaks of grotesque invention, mainly in romantic literature. E.T.A. Hoffmann (1776–1822) had explored the bizarre nature of dreams in his collection of tales *Fantasiestücke in Callots Manier (Fantasy-Pieces*, 1814–1815) and *Nachtstücke (Night-Pieces,* 1817). Poe's *Tales of the Grotesque and Arabesque* (1840) had offered horror stories of psychological disturbance. These gothic studies set loose an interest in psychosis from Robert Browning's grotesque portraits in *Dramatic Romances and Lyrics* (poetry, 1845) to Sherwood Anderson's *Winesburg, Ohio* (short stories, 1919) where the "grotesques" are severe neurotics seen against a background of an ordinary American town. At the close of the century, themes of madness, perversion, and black magic remained prevalent; *Là-bas* (novel, 1891) by J. K. Huysmans is an example. And science fantasy, such as human transformation in *The Invisible Man, a Grotesque Romance* (1897) by H. G. Wells, is an update of the theme of Mary Shelley's *Frankenstein* (novel, 1818). Rarely are comic factors at work in this Gothic-grotesque.

Modern Grotesque (1900–1944)

The Expressionist movement, on the other hand, gave rise to new comic horrors. In *Dödsdansen (Dance of Death,* 1901) by the Swedish dramatist August Strindberg, psychological warfare between man and wife is represented with painful horror and comic implication that is often lost in translation and interpretation. "The Dance" is the love-hate relationship between the sexes and also the dance of life. The couple takes pleasure in tormenting each other, much in the manner of the tramps in Beckett's *En attendant Godot (Waiting for Godot,* play, 1952). *Ett drömspel (A Dream Play,* 1901) re-creates the surreal effect of dreams; events are disjointed; characters multiply and split, creating an absurd world that represents life without intellectual superstructures. German Expressionist poets drew hideous and often ludicrous images of man; poets like Gottfried Benn and Jakob van Hoddis resorted to the grotesque to express a view of nature as malevolent and impotent. Simultaneously, entertaining tales of terror *(Schauerliteratur)* proliferated in Germany, and a group of narrators, including H. H. Ewers and Gustav Meyrink, wrote in the uncanny mode which is often mistaken for genuine grotesque.

Comic-horror, in the sense in which Strindberg perceived it, is the central aesthetic of modern grotesque, where absurd worlds are created or mimetic forms are rendered to suggest grotesque significance at many levels: biological, psychological, historical, and metaphysical. This grotesque mode is found in the German-Czech writer Franz Kafka, whose uncanny tales play on fear but rise to a profound comic perspective of the world as an absurd and dehumanizing place. Kafka's treatment of the comic changed the Gothic tale of terror into genuine grotesque that is now often described as "Kafkaesque." His best-known story "Die Verwandlung" ("Metamorphosis," 1915) deals with Gregor Samsa's transformation into an insect, and his family's treatment of that event is handled as burlesque. In the novels *Der Prozess (The Trial,* 1925) and *Das Schloss (The*

Castle, 1926), nonspecific settings and stilted characters provide eerie frame-works for the protagonists' sufferings, while Kafka's matter-of-fact style creates chilling effects when the painful events are rendered as farcical scenes. Absurd scenarios pervade the Kafkaesque, producing severe tensions between the protagonist and his maddening world and raising questions about the human condition that are never resolved.

This disjunctive Kafkaesque world is also found in Italy's *teatro del grottesco,* founded by a group of playwrights who saw modern implications in their native commedia dell'arte. In *La maschera e il volto (The Mask and the Face,* 1916), Luigi Chiarelli revived stock types of the adulterous wife, a cuckold, a deceptive friend, and put them to serious purpose in social criticism. In *Sei personaggi in cerca d'autore (Six Characters in Search of an Author,* 1921) by Luigi Pirandello, the master of *grottesco,* six characters play actors who rehearse a play *al improviso.* Frequent disturbing dislocations occur, and puzzling scenes are created out of commedia tradition, as when the comic Madame Pace suddenly appears in a fright-wig and scares off all the characters, thereby changing the "pace" of the action.

Parallel with the *grottesco* school came the Spanish grotesque theater, which grew out of that country's long tradition of black humor and its tendency to social satire through a disgusted but comic focus on cruelty and deformity in nature. Grotesque fusions of comic and repulsive images recur in the realistic plays of Ramón Valle-Inclán: *Divinas palabras (Divine Words,* 1920) centers on a hydrocephalic idiot; in *Luces de Bohemia (Bohemian Lights,* 1924) the audience watches a man die and his corpse decay. The surrealistic films, made in France by Luis Buñuel—from *Un chien andalou (The Andalusian Dog,* 1928) to *Le fantôme de la liberté (The Phantom of Liberty,* 1974)—juxtapose blasphemous and sexual images in social satires of Spanish repression. And in the absurd theater of Fernando Arrabal, also produced in France, war, religion, human ignorance, and cruelty are treated in the grotesque mode of comic-horror. Some of the best examples of Arrabal's grotesque may be found in *Pique-nique en campagne (Picnic on the Battlefield,* 1954), *Oraison (Orison,* 1957), and the multimedia event *Le ciel et la merde (Heaven and Shit,* 1970), where Arrabal replicates a religious ceremony in order to satirize it.

Cast in an equally satirical and disturbing mold are the works of the Anglo-Irish writer Samuel Beckett, another expatriot in France, whose grotesque novels and theater of the absurd strive continually for new modes of literary disruption that, simultaneously, disturb conventional views of religion, human dignity, and social order, as in the novel *Watt* (1953) or the play *Waiting for Godot.* In this same French school of the absurd, neurotic personal searches are expressed in the grotesque situations of the plays, *La parodie (The Parody,* 1950) by Caucasian-born Arthur Adamov and *Les nègres, clownerie (The Blacks, a Clown Show,* 1958) by Jean Genet.

A somewhat more festive grotesque is found in early modern fiction that protests and attempts to disarm social and political dangers of this century.

America's grotesque has been more hopeful than that of the absurd theater, particularly the works of William Faulkner. Southern writers tend to perceive their region affectionately as a "confederation of dunces" who breed violence out of perversity. Faulkner's characters are often simpletons, perverts, or criminals who cause social upheavals that are treated farcically and are all the more horrifying for their comic treatment. Arbitrary injustice, gratuitous violence, and matter-of-fact absurdity in Faulkner's fictional works betray and affirm life in the South. The affirmation resides in strong lyrical qualities that Faulkner imparts to his fictional world. When upheavals subside, balance in nature is always restored. A child is born, on the one hand; on the other, a murderer is brutally executed after a farcical bicycle chase (*Light in August,* novel, 1932); or a fusion of underworld perversion and the hypocrisy of respectable society is achieved in *Sanctuary* (novel, 1931) that restores normalcy to daily life. Such transformations speak for the slow but creative progress that imperfect humanity makes.

Postwar Grotesque (1945–   )

In postwar Holocaust literature, violence is universalized; fear is no longer nameless; and evil has concrete reality, even though fictional worlds are often no less absurd than Faulkner's. Comedic affirmation is lyrical more often than funny. The imagery of grotesque poetry embodies memories of living skeletons and atrocity, but also expresses an idealistic longing for salvation and harmony, as in Paul Celan's *Ausgewählte Gedichte* (*Speech-Grille and Selected Poems,* 1970) or Nelly Sachs' *Das Buch der Nelly Sachs* (*The Book of Nelly Sachs,* poems, 1968). The postwar novel *Die Blechtrommel* (*The Tin Drum,* 1959) by Günter Grass recreates the historical period leading to the war, which is seen as a symbolic act, and the comic element is both aggressive and defensive. The reader is mocked and provoked by the perceptions of an amoral dwarf whose exuberant will is asserted in his comic-horrific visions of war, death, atrocity, insect life, potatoes, the fields, and nature's continuity. Grass's *Hundejahre* (*Dog Years,* novel, 1963) deals with the same prewar Nazi and postwar decades in Danzig, recounted by three narrators who contradict each other, creating ambivalent effects. Other postwar novels evoke comic-terror in defensive-aggressive reaction to holocaust atrocities. These include John Hawkes' *The Cannibal* (1949), whose title gives focus to symbolic and literal events in Germany between 1914 and 1945; Joseph Heller's *Catch-22* (1961), where the soldier Yossarian witnesses death almost daily, each time in a new ridiculous way; and *A Canticle for Leibowitz* (1959) by Walter M. Miller, Jr., where the planet Earth goes up in atomic smoke, which is perceived as "the visage of Lucifer," and the sole survivor is a new Eve with sacred instincts and a gleam in her eye.

In this modern grotesque, the ebb and flow of history and myth are re-created by juxtapositions of life and death imagery and in fused symbols of destruction and continuity. The narratives are disorderly, horror reaches inordinate proportions, comic infusions seem objectionable and barbaric, endings are ambiguous and threatening. Intimations of primal harmonies are granted by the cyclical structures of these works, where upheavals are temporary, and ploughs bite the earth in momentary renewals. But the promise of recurrence ever remains their horrific implication.

See also: Daemon, Evil, Horror, Masque, Monsters, Picaresque.

Selected Bibliography

Barasch, Frances K. *The Grotesque, a Study in Meanings*. The Hague: Mouton, 1971.

Kayser, Wolfgang. *The Grotesque in Art and Literature*. New York: Columbia University Press, 1981.

Kern, Edith. *The Absolute Comic*. New York: Columbia University Press, 1980.

Thomson, Philip. *The Grotesque*. London: Methuen, 1972.

FRANCES K. BARASCH

H
//

HERMIT

The hermit, or eremite (Gr. *erēmos*, "desolate," "solitary"), is a religious character with an ancient and honorable history. He is distinguishable from the anchorite, recluse, and loner, the latter two being secular counterparts to the anchorite and hermit. Whereas anchorites were frequently immured, albeit willingly, in small, cell-like buildings attached to churches, hermits pursued the vocation of the solitary life as a career. Neither monks nor friars, they were free agents who chose to renounce the distractions of social communities and dwell apart. They did, however, as a rule, respond to the needs of others when called upon to do so or when magnanimity prompted such activity. Hence we find in history hermits who built bridges, roads, and lighthouses, and who served as guides, particularly to river travelers. In legend, St. Christopher was such a hermit. Old Semyon ("Preacher") in Anton Chekhov's "V ssylke" ("In Exile," short story, 1892) operates, in effect, as such a hermit. That hermits not only could but did take the lead in large-scale movements is borne out by Peter the Hermit (1050?-1115), French preacher of the first Crusade.

Three distinct stages in the hermit's literary development are recognized (Weaver, p. 7): "(1) the religious, including saints' legends and pious tales; (2) the semi-religious or social, including the hermit in social service roles in the medieval tales of chivalry; and (3) the unreligious or philosophic, including the hermit in the variable capacity of counselor."

Historical Background

Not all hermits were Christian. Hermits appear frequently in the two great Indian epics, the *Ramayana* and the *Mahabharata* (c. 5th century B.C.–A.D. 4th century). In the former, Rama himself turns hermit. In the sacred *shastras* of the Hindus, it is proposed as an ideal that the middle part of a man's life should be spent as a *Banaprastha* (forest recluse or hermit). According to W. E. Griffis

(*Corea, the Hermit Nation*, rev. ed., 1911), Korea was given the name "The Hermit Kingdom" in 1637 because it had no traffic with the West. However, there were Korean recluses before and after this date. Among the Greek philosophers, the asceticism ("discipline") often associated with the eremitic life found champions in Pythagoras and Plato. The Therapeutae and the Essenes, Jewish sects antedating the Christian church, forsook their wives, children, and property and lived in sequestered cells principally in the mountains of Nitria. With the advent of Christianity, many Gnostics and Manichaeans practiced asceticism, which often entailed their dwelling apart from others. The same is true of many Montanists. The charge is still made of Alfred Lord Tennyson's St. Simeon Stylites, in the poem by the same name (1842), that, although canonized by both the Western and Eastern churches, he is really a yogi or a Gnostic.

Among the first great hermits of Christendom are the Desert Fathers, many of whom situated themselves in the desolate area outside Thebes (the Thebaid). The first Christian distinguished by the name "hermit" was Paul of Thebes (died c. A.D. 325). Next in the order of the ancient hermits is St. Anthony of Egypt, the subject of Gustave Flaubert's *La tentation de Saint Antoine* (*The Temptation of St. Anthony*, prose poem, 1874), which with its rationalistic irony, foreshadows *Il santo* (*The Saint*, novel, 1905) by Antonio Fogazzaro and *Thaïs* (satiric novel, 1890) by Anatole France, in which the hermit Paphnutius is fictively exposed as an "Arian." Hrotswitha of Gandersheim (c. 935–973) had treated the story of a harlot converted by a hermit disguised as a lover in her drama *Pafnutius* (n.d.). A variation appears in Edith Wharton's *The Hermit and the Wild Woman and Other Stories* (1908).

St. Patrick (d. 464) is reputed to have been a hermit; likewise Palladius, the quasi-legendary converter of the Irish Scots; and the Welsh St. Ninian Dubricius, a legendary contemporary of both St. Patrick and King Arthur, after serving as both bishop and abbot of Llandaff, ended his days, according to tradition, as a hermit. Hermits of this type appear in Sir Walter Scott's historical novels, for example, *Ivanhoe* (1819), *Quentin Durward* (1823), and *The Talisman* (1825). The same ideal of spiritual warfare generally accompanied by magnanimous deeds of active charity that characterized the Desert Fathers inspired the British hermits Cuthbert, Guthlac, Roger, Godric, Robert of Knaresborough, and Richard Rolle of Hampole, and diabolic insults and attacks are described in accounts of them. In *Hermits* (cultural history, 1868), Charles Kingsley describes the eremitical impulse as "a passion akin to despair, which ended in a new and grand form of suicide."

Counterfeit, self-seeking "town" hermits (the "hermit" qua confidence man and schnorrer) soon made their appearance. Bishops sought to control hermits "at large" by regulations that prescribed them to hear Mass daily, if possible, and to be houseled once a week. The excesses of the town hermit ("loller": Lollard), licensed to beg, led to the type of ecclesiastical cheat against whom William Langland inveighed in his poem *Piers Plowman* (c. 1362–1387). In *Morte d'Arthur* (prose romance, c. 1469), Sir Thomas Malory confirmed the decay of the sincere religious solitary from one who offered hospitality to opportunistic cadger. In England, the hermit's cell, as a recognized part of the chantry system, was doomed at the Dissolution of the Monasteries (1536–1539); and if any solitary remained in his cell, he was almost inevitably homeless after the Suppression of the Chantries (1546). The Reformation finished off hermits in other countries as well. (For Protestant disdain for monasticism of any kind, see Augustus Neander, *General History of the Christian Religion and Church,* tr. from German by Joseph Torrey, 1851, 2:227–75.) Gradually, the traditional hermits were supplanted by romantic visionaries and cantankerous seers who appropriated their prophetic powers; for example, by Zarathustra in Friedrich Nietzsche's *Also sprach Zarathustra* (*Thus Spoke Zarathustra,* prose poem, 1883–1892).

The Dark Ages

Bede's *Historia ecclesiastica* (*Ecclesiastical History,* 731) gives biographical accounts of several eremitical saints. The hermit in Cynewulf's poem "Guthlac" (9th century) wastes his youth in rapine and debauchery. Having retired from the world, he is assailed by devils from whom Guthlac's guardian, St. Bartholomew, "shining with heavenly brightness amidst the dim darkness of the black hell" to which the demons had transported the hermit, saves him. With the poem "Guthlac" we enter definitely and unmistakably the field of the hermit in English literature. Among hermit source books are *Historia regum* (Simeon of Durham, fl. 1130), *Historia de Sancto Cuthberto* (author unknown, of uncertain date), *Gesta regum anglorum* (William of Malmesbury, c. 1120–1128), *De genealogia regum anglorum* (Ailred of Rieveaulx, d. 1166), *Chronica majora* (Matthew Paris, d. 1259), and *Chronicle of England* (John Capgrave, d. 1464).

The Middle Ages

The commemorated deeds of the saints (*Acta sanctorum*) made their way from a brief passage in the Liturgy before the Epistle, with a brief exposition of the legend first, to a reading at the close of Prime of a chapter of the acts of the saint for the following day, and then to introduction into the Nocturnes, where they developed from concise notices to elaborated accounts. Many hermits were among the saints thus remembered. As a result of these conditions there developed the *Proprium sanctorum,* or legendary—a cycle of saints' legends. Such legends were sometimes added to a homily cycle, as was the case of the Northern Homily Cycle, the earliest manuscript belonging to the early fourteenth century; and sometimes there is a complete fusing of homily cycle and legendary, called a "festial," such as the *Festial* of John Mirk, author of the *Instructions for Parish Priests* (c. 1400). Mirk's *Liber festivalis* (published 1486) illustrates the hermit's position in the legendaries. (See C. Horstmann, *The Early South-English Legendary,* 1887.)

In the life of Thomas à Becket (1118?–1170), the hermit is presented in an altogether new role, as protector of the weak and the pursued. In the life of St.

Brendon, Paul the Hermit epitomizes asceticism, hospitality, and the great longevity often attributed to hermits in literature. Blaze the Martyr also appears in the *Liber festivalis*. Born in Cappadocia, Blaze lived as a hermit in the desert in preternatural harmony with the animals, a state of affairs a secularist like Honoré de Balzac thoroughly perverted in his infamous short story "Une passion dans le désert" ("A Passion in the Desert," 1833). St. Blaze blesses all the animals. On one occasion he makes a wolf bring back a pig he has carried off.

The earliest collections of these spiritual tales are ascribed by some authorities to the Cistercian Odo de Ceritona (or Shirton), an English monk of the twelfth century, and entitled (1) *Parabolae,* (2) *Homiliae,* and (3) *Brutarum.* Others attribute the earliest collections to Hugo de St. Victoire, a Parisian who mixed a great variety of pious and profane history with Aesopian fable. The most complete collection of hermit stories is *An Alphabet of Tales,* a fifteenth-century English translation of the *Alphabetum narrationum* attributed to Étienne de Besançon. Others are to be found in *The Pilgrimage of the Life of Man* (Englished by John Lydgate, 1426, from the French of Guillaume de Digulleville, c. 1330). These stories, forty-eight in number, may be grouped under five heads: (1) Hermit Counsel, (2) Hermit Virtues, (3) Hermits and Animals, (4) Hermit Doubts, and, by far the most numerous, (5) Hermit Trials. One story from the *Alphabet of Tales,* "The Devil Tempts an Anchorite," appeared more suitably, in much briefer form, in the *Ancren Riwle* (*Rule for Anchoresses,* ed. from a semi-Saxon 13th century text by James Morton, 1853). There are no hermits in Chaucer, though one does appear in the source-version of the *Pardoner's Tale,* "Here is the Story of a Hermit, who, as he was Walking through a Forest, found a very great Treasure," in a collection of tales probably antedating Boccaccio, but printed in 1525, *Cento novelle antiche.* Giovanni Boccaccio salaciously recounted in *Il decamerone* (*Decameron,* novellas, c. 1350) how the monk (hermit) Rustico "put the devil into hell seven times," a tone toward such matters François Rabelais (1494?-1553) adapted. In *La divina commedia* (*The Divine Comedy,* epic poem, c. 1320), holy hermits are given a very high place in Paradise. Peter Damiano repines at having to leave the solitary life of contemplation in order to "wear the hat" (*Paradiso,* 21, 106–26).

The Age of Chivalry

Wolfram's *Parzival* (epic poem, 1210) and Grimmelshausen's *Simplicissimus* (novel, 1669) contain the most important portrayals of the hermit in German literature prior to the eighteenth century. These two works are in themselves the most important single literary expressions of their ages, the age of chivalry and the baroque age. In the former, when Trevrizent describes the folly of Anfortas and the consequences of it, the reason for his own withdrawal and the purpose in his life as a hermit are made plain. In England, of the semireligious romances of chivalry there appear to be but two well-defined examples, though their influence is quite strong in many of the later pure romances: (1) *The History of the Holy Grail* (Henry Lovelich, author of *Merlin,* c. 1450), which presents, among other aspects, the devil-possessed hermit; and (2) *Robert le Diable* (*Robert the Devil,* verse romance, late 12th century). In the sixteenth century a metrical version appeared, as well as a prose romance by Thomas Lodge, printed in 1591. In *Robert the Devil,* a hermit who is the Pope's own "goostly fader" hears Robert's confession, appoints his penance, and sets him on the path of virtue as a brave soldier of the cross.

In the secular romance of chivalry, the hermit partakes of both the secular and the religious. As a secular character in these romances, he is (1) the dispenser of hospitality to strangers; (2) the healer of wounded knights; and (3) the burier of the dead. As a religious character, he is (1) the ideal father confessor for knights errant; (2) the most approved of counselors and interpreters of dreams and visions; (3) the most potent and revered defender of the weak; and (4) the perfect penitent in the eyes of all classes for every form of wickedness. Hermits frequently live to a very great age in the romances. Pergambu, for example, in *Perce-forest* (F. W. Schmidt, *Wiener Jahrbücher der Literatur,* 1825), a fabulous history of Britain preceding the age of Arthur, lives for a number of centuries.

In two of the most conspicuous illustrations of hermit hospitality the host proves to be no true hermit. In Sir Edmund Spenser's *The Faerie Queene* (epic poem, 1590–1596), the necromancer Archimago poses as a hermit. An outlaw does the same in *The King and the Hermit* (*Ancient Metrical Tales,* 1829; ed. from imperfect original manuscript, Ashmole 6922, by Hartshorne). When Arthur is wounded (Malory, *Morte d'Arthur* bk. 1, ch. 25), he is carried by Merlin to "an ermyte that was a good man and a grete leche." Sometimes in these romances (as in bk. 18, ch. 12) it appears that the hermit maintained a large retinue of assistants and had established a reputation for healing wounded knights. In book 18, chs. 21–22, Lancelot, when wounded, seeks out a hermit (located nearby) who heals him. The wounded Guy of Warwick likewise seeks the aid of a hermit (*Guy of Warwick,* metrical romance, c. 1300). Hermit sepulture occurs in both these works. A hermit acts as father confessor to Gawain, Lancelot, Bors, and Ector in *Morte d'Arthur.*

The hermit protector appears in *Sir Degare* (metrical romance, probably 1325); and Blase plays such a role in *Arthour and Merlin* (metrical romance, not later than 1325). A hermit serves as protector in *Ywain and Gawain* (metrical romance, c. 1300–1350) and *Chevalere Assigne,* the only representative of the cycle of legends about Godfrey of Bouillon in English before the fifteenth century.

The hermit penitent appears in *The Tale of Melusine* (trans. from the French of Couldrette before 1500), *The Right Pleasant and Goodly Historie of the Four Sonnes of Aymon* (trans. from French by William Caxton and printed by him about 1489), and *The Knight of the Swanne,* the prose version of *Chevalere Assigne.* Both Sir Bedivere and Lancelot end their days in hermitages (*Morte d'Arthur,* bk. 21, chs. 6, 10). In a prose source-version of Robert Greene's play, *Friar Bacon and Friar Bungay* (1594, appearance of earliest quarto), Friar Bacon turns hermit as an act of penance.

The hermit as disappointed lover occurs in *The Squyr of Lowe Degre* (c.

1450), composed in short couplets, and George Gascoigne's *Tale of Hermetes the Hermit* (1575), as well as, much later, Oliver Goldsmith's ballad "The Hermit, or Edwin and Angelina" (1765).

The Secularization of the Hermit: 1500–1660

The religious hermit suffered extinction as a historical figure during this period. Chivalry, in the medieval sense, was gone, but not forgotten; it continued to exert its influence albeit in sentimentalized fashion. A new literary type of the hermit appeared in *Euphues and His England* (1580) by John Lyly. Unlike his predecessor who dwelt apart, his chief function is telling tales with moral intent, such as warning the young not to travel abroad. The moralizing "Dutch uncle" hermit appears in Robert Greene's *Arbasto, The Anatomy of Fortune* (prose romance, 1584) as a kind of self-satisfied sage-poet. The hermit as exotic furniture appears in Emanuel Forde's *The Most Famous Delectable and Pleasant History of Parismus, the Renowned Prince of Bohemia* (prose romance, 1598). He is situated on a "desolate Isle" which features an "enchanted castle." The hermit of this type makes his stage debut in a masque by George Gascoigne, *The Tale of Hermetes the Hermit*, where Hermes seems to replace *erēmos* as the etymon for hermit, and he is lost in a welter of gods, goddesses, magic, and enchantment about which he speaks in recounting a knightly narrative. A hermit plays a similar role in a royal pageant written by the dramatist George Peele, *The Hermit's Speech* (c. 1581). A number of isolated references occur in Shakespeare's plays. In all, "hermit" is used eight times, "hermitage" twice, and "anchor" (anchorite) once. The hermitage, as the essence of forlorn and cheerless nakedness, appears in *Love's Labor Lost* (5.2.805 [c. 1594]), *Richard II* 3.3.148 [c. 1596]), and *Hamlet* (3.2.229 [c. 1600]). The hermit as "loller," a skillful beggar, occurs in *Titus Andronicus* (3.2.41 [c. 1594]) and *Henry IV* (5.1.71 [1597]). The great age of hermits is mentioned in *Love's Labor Lost* (4.3.242) and *Henry VI* (2.5.117 [1590–1592]). The friendly office of hermits in love affairs is personified by Friar Laurence in *Romeo and Juliet* (c. 1596).

Hermits and hermitages are alluded to and the joys of the sober recluse described in "A Farewell to the Vanities" (poem, uncertain authorship, appearing in Izaak Walton's *The Compleat Angler, or the Contemplative Man's Recreation* [1653]); "To Althea, From Prison" (poem, Richard Lovelace, 1649); "Il Penseroso" (poem, John Milton, 1632); and in a song inserted in the opening of the Fourth Day's account in the third edition (1664) of *The Compleat Angler,* the first words of which Samuel Butler quotes in *Hudibras* (verse satire in three parts, 1663, 1664, 1678), part 1, canto 2: "Like hermit poor in pensive place."

The Mid-Eighteenth Century

Henry Beers observes (A History of English Romanticism in Eighteenth Century, 1899):

The first peculiarly medieval type that contrived to secure a foothold in eighteenth-century literature was the hermit—a figure which seems to have had a national attraction, not only for romanticizing poets like Shenstone and Collins, but for the whole generation of verse writers, from Parnell to Goldsmith, Percy and Beattie, each of whom composed a *Hermit,* and also for the authors of *Rasselas* and *Tom Jones,* in whose fictions he becomes a stock character, as a fountain of wisdom and of moral percepts.

The hermit-philosopher is revived in James Beattie's *The Minstrel* (poem, 1771–1774), the purpose of which was to "trace the progress of a poetical genius born in a rude age" in the person of a young shepherd, named Edwin, who "lived in Gothic days."

In Germany, the laicization of the hermit proceeded apace. Gotthold Lessing's little tale in verse, *Der Eremit* (1749), satirizes both hermit and the society with which he comes in contact. The hermit illustrates Lessing's aphorism "When the devil and a hermit live together for a long time, either the devil becomes a hermit, or the hermit becomes a devil." In Lessing's *Nathan der Weise* (*Nathan the Wise,* verse drama, 1779), the *Klosterbruder,* who has retreated from the world in order to preserve his ideals, listens to Nathan's tale, then cries out "By God, you are a Christ!/There was never a better Christ!"

Late Eighteenth Century Romantic Solitaries

In Goethe's *Satyros* (verse drama, 1773), the hermit is the exponent of a true understanding of nature and is wronged and persecuted both by Satyros and the misled Arcadian community. The traditional hermit garden appears in Goethe's *Erwin und Elmire* (operetta, 1775), but Erwin retires to mountain peace not to save his soul but because his love has been spurned by the coquettish Elmire. In Jakob Lenz's *Die Kleinen* (dramatical fragment, 1775), the hermit informs Engelbrecht that he has fled to the wilds in order to preserve the ideal of friendship, which could not have endured in an intriguing society. Lenz's *Der Waldbruder* (novel, 1776) presents a hermit, Herz, who removes himself to the Odenwald out of an idealistic love for Gräfin Stella. His lofty passion assumes the form of *Liebesschwärmerei* (enthusiasm for love), and he retires from the world to preserve his ideal emotion from the sophisticated criticism of courtly society. In Friedrich Maximilian von Klinger's *Die Zwillinge* (drama, 1776), Grimaldi expresses the desire to become a hermit but lacks the moral strength to do so. He lives in devotion to an ideal love in a world of his own. In Klinger's *Sturm und Drang* (drama, 1776), Blasius decides to reject the world in favor of hermithood and the deeper eternal world of nature. The hermit in *Fausts Leben, Thaten, und Höllenfahrt* (*Faust's Life, Deeds, and Journey to Hell,* novel by Klinger, 1791) is assailed and destroyed by the devil Leviathan who desires to show to Faust the hypocrisy, superficiality, and perverse nature of man. Although a clerical figure, he is otherwise traditional in conception—a refugee from worldly evils who wishes to save his soul by devoting his life entirely to God. Yet, because of his isolation and asceticism, he is vulnerable to evil forces. Extreme asceticism and godliness are transformed by temptation to mad voluptuosity. Even in isolation the hermit, as in Annette von Droste-Hülshoff's (1797–1848) *Walter* (epic poem, 1818), is sought out and martyred by forces of evil in the world. The hermit Hyperion in Hölderlin's *Hyperion* (novel, 1797–1799) is consciously dedicated to a religion of nature. Other German hermit works of this time are Gottfried August Bürger's "Der wilde Jäger" ("The Wild Hunter," ballad, 1778); Christoph Martin Wieland's *Oberon* (poetical romance, 1780), in which the hermit Alfonso's *Todessehnsucht* (yearning for death) is a major romantic theme; Clemens Brentano's *Godwi* (novel, 1800); Novalis' (Friedrich von Hardenberg) *Heinrich von Ofterdingen* (*Henry of Ofterdingen*, novel, 1802); Friedrich Schiller's *Die Braut von Messina* (*The Bride from Messina,* drama, 1803); Ludwig Uhland's "König Eginhard" (ballad, 1809); Justinus Kerner's *Die Heimatlosen* (poem, 1811); Adelbert von Chamisso's *Peter Schlemihl* (novelle, 1814), in which Schlemihl becomes a hermit after losing his shadow to the devil; Ernst Theodor Amadeus Hoffmann's *Serapion* (tale, 1818); Nikolaus Lenau's "Die Marionetten" (poem, 1832); and Joseph Freiherr von Eichendorff's "Eine Meerfahrt" (poem, 1835). The affinity between the hermits presented by these writers and the great English Romantics and the Pre-Raphaelites is apparent.

On the American scene, hermit figures haunt the literature of the American Renaissance, among them the hermit as "town" derelict, personified by Herman Melville's *Bartleby the Scrivener* (novella, 1853). A variant of this figure begins to pervade American literature. The hermit derelict appears in Edwin Arlington Robinson's "Mr. Flood's Party" (poem, 1921), climbing toward "the forsaken upland hermitage / That held as much as he should ever know / On earth again of home."

Modern Times

The keynote for the modern hermit is sounded by Matthew Arnold in "Stanzas in Memory of the Author of 'Obermann' " (poem, 1852): "A wounded human spirit turns, / Here, on its bed of pain." In *Obermann* (Rousseau-like confessional meditation-revery, 1804), by Étienne Pivert de Sénancour, the hermit figure, plagued by universal doubt, retreats from society through nature to eternity by means of a melancholic sensibility. The traditional religious conception of the hermit is wholly absent from Eugène Ionesco's *Le solitaire* (*The Hermit,* novel, 1973). A nondenominational therapeutic asceticism is celebrated in Seamus Heaney's "The Hermit" (poem, *Station Island,* 1985).

Conclusion

The word "hermit" is derived from Greek *erēmia* ("solitude, desert, loneliness; helplessness; absence, want") and *erēmos* ("lonely, solitary, desert, desolate, waste; helpless, abandoned, needy, destitute"). Whenever one of these ideas is touched upon in literature so, technically, is the motif of the hermit, as in T. S. Eliot's "The Love Song of J. Alfred Prufrock" (poem, 1917; 1.4): "Let us go, through certain half-deserted streets." Strictly, however, the hermit motif develops historically in Western literature from the Desert Fathers, the religious "dwellers apart" who, mortifying their flesh and observing the evangelical counsels of chastity, poverty, and obedience, contemplate God within the framework of orthodox mysteries and yet magnanimously remain responsive in practical fashion to the needs of others. Under the successive shock waves of the Renaissance, Reformation, Enlightenment, and modernism, the traditional hermit has gradually been stripped of his authentic traits, and even of a place to roost, and increasingly subjected to sardonic contempt. In his place, the wistful solitary, or mystic, has arisen. Among the less metaphysically or transcendentally inclined, the loner is viewed extremely, either as sociopath (for example, Captain Ahab in Melville's *Moby-Dick,* novel, 1851) or a kind of existential anti-hero, dwelling apart and authentically in an otherwise universal desert, or wasteland, of absurdity. Alienated by his awareness of ploys that seek to engulf him, the hermit-loner first participates, as existential anti-hero, in the sloughing off process that is the sense of Sartre's *La nausée* (*Nausea,* novel, 1938) and Camus' *L'étranger* (*The Stranger,* novel, 1942), then, bored and disgusted with conventional artifice, decides to "dwell apart," as does the secular solitary in Ionesco's *The Hermit,* who withdraws into total solitude, barricading himself in his apartment. Since religion itself would impress such a man as a ploy or dodge, he "deserts" the outside world completely by inferentially perceiving that nothing in it has any value at all. He may be said to continue to exist, indeed to begin to exist in the first place, only by virtue of his uncompromising probity, which he asserts by means of his peculiar "hermithood."

*See also:*Alienation, Christian Hero, Retreat.

Selected Bibliography

Clay, Mary Rotha. *Hermits and Anchorites of England.* London: Methuen, 1914.

Fitzell, John. *The Hermit in German Literature (From Lessing to Eichendorff).* Chapel Hill: University of North Carolina Press, 1961.

Veuillot, Eugène. *Les vies des Pères des déserts d'Orient, Leur doctrine spirituelle et leur discipline monastique.* 2d ed. 6 vols. Paris: L. Vivès, 1869.

Weaver, Charles P. *The Hermit in English Literature from the Beginnings to 1660.* Nashville, Tenn.: G. Peabody College for Teachers, 1924.

NATHAN A. CERVO

HIEROGLYPHICS

The characters or mode of writing used by the ancient Egyptians or, by transference, other ancient peoples, consisting of figures of objects representing syllables or letters, but also occasionally directly or figuratively representing words and concepts (picture writing) are known as hieroglyphics. By extension, the definition includes a picture standing for a word or notion, especially one which it does not directly figure; hence a sign having some hidden meaning; a secret or enigmatical symbol, an emblem. Often hieroglyphics thus understood have some religious meaning. The adjectival form sometimes means obscure or illegible, especially in French.

Background in Antiquity and the Middle Ages

When Champollion deciphered the Rosetta Stone (discovered in 1799) in 1819, it at last became apparent that Egyptian hieroglyphics were mainly phonetic signs, even though they could, on occasion, be ideogrammatic. According to Iversen, this was true almost from the beginnings of hieroglyphic writing around 3200 B.C. While hieroglyphics survived more or less unchanged through the 4th century A.D., their influence declined and their use became more restricted over the centuries. The decline began around 1550 B.C. as the origin of some signs was forgotten and attempts were made to bring the system into closer conformity with linguistic evolution. With the foreign occupation of Egypt, hieroglyphics came to be used only in religion and ended up as the exclusive domain of the priests. Eventually, after 525 B.C., new transferred meanings, often dependent on subtle mythical or speculative explanations, were attached to the old signs, and their use was increasingly restricted to sacred and official inscriptions. During this period of decline, the hieratic and demotic forms of cursive script emerged to replace hieroglyphics in other kinds of writing. By late antiquity, a fourth kind of "writing" was developed in Alexandrian Egypt for use in magic and in the expression of philosophical ideas with cryptograms. The sources of such "enigmatic hieroglyphs" can be found in the ancient body of animal lore and fables where behavior was governed by a certain dominant characteristic of the animal's nature. The *Physiologos* (*Physiologus*, anecdotes, 2d century) and the whole medieval bestiary tradition can be traced to the same origin.

During antiquity, interest in Egyptian hieroglyphics seems to have occurred in two stages. First, the Greeks were interested in the Egyptians as the inventors of writing. However, they did not understand the magical foundations of Egyptian thought and so persisted in seeing the hieroglyphics as a kind of picture writing in which the sign symbolized some thing. Later, in the period between approximately 200 B.C. and A.D. 200, the rapid spread of the cult of Isis throughout the Greco-Roman world did much to popularize all things Egyptian and keep the hieroglyphic tradition alive, but the tradition survived in a corrupt form. Obelisks, for example, became fashionable in Rome, and inscriptions were considered to make them particularly attractive. So when imported Egyptian obelisks lacked them, the Romans simply added "hieroglyphic" inscriptions. Authentic hieroglyphics were used on Domitian's obelisk (c. A.D. 96), but this was an exception, and knowledge of the hieroglyphics was gradually lost as Egypt first became Christian (Coptic) and then Moslem (640). Memory of the hieroglyphics was lost in the Western Middle Ages, which did not have access to most of the ancient texts where they were discussed, and it was mainly in the work of Byzantine scholars that some knowledge of them survived.

In 1419, the Florentine monk, Christoforo de' Buondelmonti, brought back to Italy a manuscript he had purchased on the island of Andros in the Aegean. This manuscript contained Horapollo's *Hieroglyphika (Hieroglyphics)*. The find was greeted enthusiastically by Buondelmonti's humanist friends, Nicolo dei

Nicoli and Poggio Bracciolini; Nicoli immediately recognized a possible relationship with the hieroglyphics engraved on the Roman obelisks(!) that so intrigued Renaissance antiquarians, and Bracciolini had just discovered (1416) a manuscript of Ammianus Marcellinus' *Rerum gestarum libri* (*The Chronicles of Events*, histories, 378) in which obelisk hieroglyphics are described and discussed. The origins of this Greek text remain obscure; it has been impossible to identify Horapollo with certainty, or his Greek translator, Philippus. It is believed the collection originated in the 4th century A.D., and the compiler must have had some knowledge of Egyptian hieroglyphics. Over half the signs presented are authentic hieroglyphics, more or less correctly interpreted, even though they are presented as ideogrammatic rather than phonetic signs.

This work generated such excitement because it provided key corroboration for the numerous ancient references to the hieroglyphics by other Greek and Roman writers, most notably Plato, Clement of Alexandria, Iamblichus, Plutarch, and Plotinus. Although Plato's description of the mythological origins of Egyptian writing in the *Phaidros* (*Phaedrus*, 4th century B.C.) is critical, this dialogue was crucial for the later understanding of hieroglyphics among the Neoplatonists because of its stress on the primacy of sight in cognition. Hieroglyphics later became central to Neoplatonic thought when Plotinus (A.D. 205–269/270) posited relationships between hieroglyphics, intelligible forms, and beautiful works of art. He used the word *agalma* to designate all three, and the word was still being used in the sixteenth century as a synonym for "emblem." Plotinus saw hieroglyphics confirming his conception of the allegorical nature of things, and he was the first to link them to art. Plotinus believed that the Egyptians had used hieroglyphics to express entire concepts with a single sign that put the wisdom of that concept before the eye of the beholder to be understood in an instantaneous intuition rather than through discursive analysis; such, he thought, is the way the gods apprehend ideas. More than any other single text, the famous passage in the *Enneades* (*Enneads* c. 300–305) 5.8, where Plotinus explains this idea prepared the way for the Renaissance conception of the hieroglyphics.

Still, other ancient texts were also important in forming the Renaissance idea of the hieroglyphics. Philo Judaeus (A.D. 1st cent.) laid the foundations for the allegorical interpretation of the Bible, and Saints Basil and Ambrose (4th century) retold the biblical story of the creation in their *Hexamera (Commentaries on the Six Days of the Creation)* in such a way as to present the universe as a kind of "natural Bible." In the same vein, Clement of Alexandria (2d-3rd century) made the first attempt to integrate pagan wisdom with Christian belief. In his *Stromata (Miscellanies)*, Clement tried to show how Greek and Egyptian philosophy was derived from the Bible. These precedents laid the groundwork for the later expansion of the idea of the hieroglyphics into the area of Christian symbolism.

Clement probably had a more accurate idea of the hieroglyphics than any other ancient writer, but he was influential because he believed hieroglyphics contained hidden wisdom that could help initiates interpret the Bible. The variant notion that wisdom must be hidden from the simple-minded and the unbelievers may also be found in the *Corpus hermeticum* (*The Hermetic Writings,* c. 100–300). In these writings, the magic power of the Egyptian language is extolled because it is supposed to be able to produce the things it names. There, the hieroglyphics are called *stoicheia*, meaning either elements of nature or elements of writing, thus signalling the belief that through this kind of writing men came to possess the elements of nature themselves.

Perhaps Plutarch's discussion of the hieroglyphics in his essay *Peri Isidos kai Osiridos* (*On Isis and Osiridos*, c. A.D. 120) summarizes the Greek misunderstanding as well as any. For Plutarch, the hieroglyphics were pictorial rebuslike expressions of divine ideas and sacred knowledge; indeed, the Greeks actually referred to Egyptian writing as "sacred letters." Plutarch also saw many other types of animal symbolism as hieroglyphic following a trend in Greek thought that was confirmed by the enigmatic hieroglyphics. Finally, for the first time, we find the hieroglyphics described as symbols of moral wisdom as Plutarch discusses the mystery that shrouds Egyptian wisdom. This discussion was very important for Renaissance thinkers and artists because it provided models for the kind of "hieroglyphic" imagery they were trying to produce in a way that Horapollo did not do, for although his hieroglyphics provided the central body of material for building a system of such signs, Horapollo never gave moralizing interpretations.

The Renaissance

Renaissance humanists became interested in hieroglyphics principally because of the renewed interest in Neoplatonism; hieroglyphics seemed to provide a vehicle for redefining the symbolic process within the context of Neoplatonic thought. One of the earliest and most influential Renaissance statements on hieroglyphics is found in L. B. Alberti's *De re aedificatoria,* 8.4 (*On Architecture,* 1452). There he talks about hieroglyphics as fitting decoration for carved tombstones, and by pointing out the pleasing ornamental character of the hieroglyphics, he paved the way for their entry into Renaissance art. Alberti also characterized hieroglyphics for the first time as a universal language. But this pictorial language is universal for Alberti in a very special way; he believed that hieroglyphics can be understood in all nations, but only by initiates.

The Renaissance conception of the hieroglyphics, which would remain largely undisputed until the eighteenth century, was based primarily on Marsilio Ficino's (1433–1499) understanding of Plotinus' discussion of the hieroglyphics. They were, in this view, a divinely inspired Egyptian invention, a unique form of symbolic writing. Although the individual signs appeared to be ordinary pictures of material objects, they were really symbolic entities revealing their true meaning only to initiated readers by means of a divinely inspired process of intuitive intellection. Being a mediator between the human intellect and divine ideas, the hieroglyphics provided insight into the very essence of things and were also supposed to reflect and illustrate the dynamic process of divine thought. Through his translation and commentary on Plotinus, it becomes clear that hieroglyphics are the perfect symbols for Ficino. They are the Platonic ideas made visible through the correspondence of sensuous form and pure idea. Later in the fifteenth century, Pico della Mirandola expanded the use of this conception of hiero-glyphics into areas of mysticism and hermetic philosophy through his attempts at syncretism in the *Heptaplus* (1489).

Given such an exalted conception of the hieroglyphics in the Renaissance, together with their decorative value, it is not surprising that artists almost im-mediately began to make extensive use of Horapollo's hieroglyphics and interpret other symbols according to the same conception. Mantegna, Pinturicchio, Giulio Romano, and Leonardo da Vinci all used Horapollo to some degree in their work. Dürer was probably influenced more than any other artist by the hiero-glyphics. He did illustrations for Willibald Pirckheimer's unpublished translation of Horapollo (c. 1514), where we find the first version of his portrait of Max-imilian surrounded by symbolic animals, which he was to take up again in his elaborate and highly hieroglyphic *Ehrenpforte* (*Triumphal Arch,* 1515) for the emperor. The best-known work from this period of the tradition was Francesco Colonna's *Hypnerotomachia Poliphili* (*The Dream of Poliphilo,* novel, 1499). This "dream of love" contains numerous beautifully stylized illustrations of ancient monuments and ruins inscribed with hieroglyphic messages that are transcribed and deciphered in the text. As a result, it provided one of the pro-totypes for the emblems that were developed early in the sixteenth century.

Aldus published the Greek text of the *Hieroglyphics* in 1505, and Latin trans-lations soon followed (Trebazio, 1515; Fasanini, 1517; Mercier, 1548, 1551). The first published vernacular version was French (1543); other vernacular trans-lations followed quickly, and a second French translation was even published in 1554. Erasmus maintained a lively interest in hieroglyphics, as is clear from his discussion of Augustus' *Festina lente* ("Hasten slowly") motto (*Adagia* [*Proverbs,* 1500]). Hieroglyphics were well known at the French court from the beginning of the reign of Francis I (1515). Horapollo and *Poliphilo* were already influencing French artistic production during this period, and the French awe of hieroglyphics surfaces in Geoffroy Tory's essay *Champ fleury* (*Flowered Field,* 1529) and Rabelais' novel *Gargantua* (1534), where he contrasts the revered hieroglyphics with the contemptible fad of rebus devices. Hieroglyphics were soon being used in the decorative schemes for courtly festivals such as the Paris and Lyons entrées of Henry II in 1549. Maurice Scève was one of the collab-orators on the Lyons entrée, which, like its Paris counterpart, featured obelisks inscribed with hieroglyphic symbols. Scève's *Délie* (*Delia,* poems, 1544) con-tains many symbols from Horapollo (basilisk, viper, salamander, phoenix, etc.). These developments, together with the publication of a French version of the *Hypnerotomachia Poliphili* (1546) and Nostradamus' translation and commen-tary of Horapollo (1545), suggest that hieroglyphics enjoyed their greatest vogue in France during the 1540s.

The development of emblems is also closely related to the vogue of the hieroglyphics. Colonna's book and Horapollo provided models and materials for emblems. The Milanese jurist Andrea Alciati published the first group of emblems in 1531 *(Emblematum libellus),* but he had probably been working with the idea for about ten years. In a statement published in 1530, he compares his emblems to the hieroglyphics of Chaeremon and Horapollo. Despite the massive influence of the epigrams of the *Greek Anthology* (Cephalas' *Anthologia,* 10th century) on the formation of the emblems, it is not surprising that Alciati should also see the hieroglyphics as a source of his idea, for one of his teachers was Filippo Fasanini, the translator of Horapollo. And several of his emblems do show the influence of spurious hieroglyphics from Horapollo's second book. Later, other emblematists also traced the origin of the genre to the hieroglyphics to give added prestige to their own compositions, but in fact the origins of the emblem are very complex, and its development probably owes more to medieval thought and art than to the hieroglyphics.

Hieroglyphics also provided the impulse for the compilation of iconographies that began to proliferate in the second half of the sixteenth century. The first of this generation of anthologies of symbols is Pierio Valeriano's *Hieroglyphica* (1556). This vast compendium is a very heavily annotated Latin version of Horapollo, where the author draws on the whole range of ancient symbolism, both pagan and Christian, in a vast experiment in syncretism. He justifies this contamination by reference to his learned uncle Urbano Valeriano, who claimed that hieroglyphics could be interpreted only by having recourse to the whole body of ancient symbolism. This compendium and others based on it (Pierre Langlois, *Discours des hiéroglyphes aegyptiens,* 1583; Cesare Ripa, *Iconologia* [*Iconology*], 1593; Pierre Dinet, *Cinq livres des hiéroglyphiques* [*Five Books of Hieroglyphics*], 1614) were handbooks for artists and writers throughout the seventeenth century, but it contributed mightily to the confusion over what hieroglyphics really were. The term lost its primary connection with Egypt; it came to refer to symbols in general and especially Christian symbols.

Later in the century there was a renewed interest in hieroglyphics in France. Du Bartas used several hieroglyphic symbols in his epic poem *La semaine (Divine Weeks and Workes,* 1578), and there are several references to them in Guillaume Bouchet's *Sérées* (stories, 1584). In 1600 Béroalde de Verville published a new French version of the *Hypnerotomachia Poliphili.*

The Seventeenth and Eighteenth Centuries

In the early seventeenth century there was more interest in hieroglyphics in England than elsewhere. Ben Jonson knew Horapollo and the mythographers and relied heavily on them in his *Masques* (1605f.). For the metaphysical poets, with the exception of Abraham Cowley, hieroglyphics were always related to religion. For Donne they figured the mystery of Christianity in which two levels of meaning are as one; for Henry Vaughan, they were a symbol of the gap between man and God. Throughout the seventeenth century, poets in the Neo-platonic or mystical traditions tended to see hieroglyphics as mysterious, necessary symbols, usually related to religion. Understood this way, they became more closely related to religious emblems as in Francis Quarles' *Hieroglyphikes of the Life of Man* (1639). Even Bacon was claiming that hieroglyphics are "congruous" or necessary symbols because they bear some resemblance to the thing signified.

Meanwhile, other writers were preparing an attack on the hieroglyphic tradition. In France Isaac Casaubon attacked Ficino's chronology of the hermetic tradition in a philological demonstration that cast doubt on the antiquity of much of that wisdom (*De rebus sacris* [*On Sacred Matters,* 1614]). At the same time, Thomas Browne (1605–1682), who approved of hieroglyphics if not taken literally, was pointing out their inauthenticity in relation to the findings of natural science. Also in the first half of the seventeenth century, Athanasius Kircher was laying the foundations for modern Egyptology by studying the relations of the hieroglyphics, which he still believed to contain immanent signs of Christian revelation, with the more accessible Coptic language (*Obeliscus Pamphilius,* 1650). Such attempts to understand the hieroglyphics on scientific grounds highlighted the difficulty in deciphering them and led to a change in usage, at least in France, where the word began to mean obscure or illegible (Mme de Sévigné, Cyrano de Bergerac, Corneille).

In the eighteenth century the situation changed again. First, Shaftesbury, in his *Second Characters* (1713), redefined the emblem in such a way as to exclude hieroglyphics not only from the emblem, but also from visual art in general. This attitude, and others like it, point the way to Lessing, and may help explain why people lost their awe of the supposed wisdom of the Egyptians. Nevertheless, a keen interest in Egyptian archaeology and antiques developed with an attendant interest in the real inscriptions they contained. Explorations began around 1735 and produced many travel-book descriptions of Egypt and its monuments.

The theoretical understanding of the hieroglyphics was beginning to change too. Giambattista Vico (1668–1744) felt the Egyptians had no monopoly on hieroglyphics, but that they were a natural first step in writing that was taken by many ancient peoples, that indeed, these "natural significations" are at the origin of language. Following Vico, William Warburton (1698–1779) claimed the Egyptians took this process one step further by limiting the number of necessary pictures; they made the pictures into hieroglyphics or combinations of both figures and characters. Warburton claimed that, in making them, the Egyptians used three kinds of contractions. The simplest way was using the principal circumstance of the subject to stand for the whole. The second way was to make the instrument stand for the thing itself, as the eye was made to mean God's omnipotence. Finally, the most advanced way was through analogy or resemblance. Warburton insisted further that hieroglyphics were not mysterious, but practical; he also contributed to detaching the hieroglyphics from Neoplatonism.

Most followers of the Enlightenment took little interest in hieroglyphics; they were even used in satire. The rebuses used for political satire in the English

"Hieroglyphical Letters" (1761–1830) were called hieroglyphics, and Horace Walpole composed a satire of mysticism and the hermetic tradition (*Hieroglyphic Tales*, 1785). An exception is Diderot whose *Encyclopédie* (1751–1772) article on the hieroglyphics is an interesting summary of eighteenth century thinking based largely on Warburton. In his *Lettre sur les sourds et muets* (*Letter on the Deaf and the Dumb*, 1751), Diderot used the term to characterize "energetic expressions" that combine a simultaneity of saying and representing, and claimed that these are the basis of all poetry.

Preromanticism and Romanticism

In Germany, hieroglyphics were still related to the mystical tradition, and Goethe was exceptional in his use of the term; for him, they are incomplete sketches which only suggest, leaving much unsaid and open to interpretation. Winckelmann in his *Versuch einer Allegorie* (*Study of an Allegory*, 1766) returns to an earlier aesthetic, concluding that pictorial art needs "poetic images" in order to transform thoughts into figures; he also insists that allegorical images should not need explanation, but should contain the distinctive qualities of the thing signified. He laid the groundwork for the revival of hieroglyphics by Hamann and Herder, who saw Nature as an important means of access to God, as providing the only true revelation of God. But Nature needs to be interpreted by man through a symbol-creating process; the symbols created are called "hieroglyphics" because of the necessary relation between the symbol and the thing symbolized. The hieroglyphics are intended to teach man, but they also hide part of their meaning.

Hieroglyphics were central to Swedenborg's law of correspondences, which was the basis for his interpretation of the Bible and his visions (*Clavis hieroglyphica* [*The Hieroglyphical Key to Natural and Spiritual Mysteries*, written 1741]). He saw these correspondences as hieroglyphical because of the necessary relation between signifier and signified. His theory of the three "churches" parallels the three stages in the development of language as described by Vico and others; in both systems, hieroglyphics correspond to the second stage.

Throughout the romantic period, the term "hieroglyphic" would refer to the symbolic expression, based on the law of correspondences, of the basic religious truths revealed not only to Christianity, but also to the other religions of antiquity. Novalis saw Nature as one vast hieroglyph and the oldest art as hieroglyphical. When Novalis used the term, he usually meant "symbolic," or simply "artistic," but with that degree of mystery which he believed must surround every poetic creation (*Fragmente*, 1795–1800). In his writings on art Friedrich von Schlegel asserted that every true painter must paint hieroglyphics, that is, paintings which indicate symbolically the divine secrets. Only genius, moved by a divine spark, he claimed, can produce hieroglyphics, either in art or in poetry. In his *Philosophische Lehrjahre, 1796–1828*, he used the term *Hieroglyphe* to refer to a special type of poetry or as the highest type of poetry, or as a very special religious poem. His preoccupation with hieroglyphics can be traced to his ardent belief in the Neoplatonic conception of the unity of the universe. Later, after Champollion's discovery, he contended that the phonetic symbols retain their "hieroglyphical nature" in such a way that Champollion's discovery actually proves rather than disproves his conception.

The romantic mythographers like Kanne, Görres, and Creuzer made much use of hieroglyphics in their attempts to explain ancient myths as symbols of natural phenomena. Everything on earth is a hieroglyphic expression of the Deity; Görres even talks of animal language as hieroglyphic. Creuzer believed that thought began with symbolic activity, and saw hieroglyphics as one of the most important examples of this kind of thought.

In nineteenth-century America, hieroglyphics figured prominently in the metaphorical vocabulary of many writers. Emerson was influenced by the American Swedenborgians, and he used the metaphor of hieroglyphics to talk about man's condition and nature (e.g., *Nature,* 1836; *Representative Men,* 1850). It also informs Thoreau's description of the thawing of a sandbank in spring (*Walden,* 1854) as well as parts of Whitman's poem "Song of Myself" (*Leaves of Grass,* 1855). Perhaps Whitman even conceived *Leaves of Grass* at one point as a hieroglyphic Bible, one of those illustrated anthologies of biblical verses for children that date back to the seventeenth century and in which key words are replaced by pictures.

Edgar Allan Poe saw the self as a hieroglyph of which the work is the decipherment, and Champollion's intuitive deciphering of the hieroglyphics served Poe as a metaphor for the question of origins and for interpretation in general. The key to "The Gold-Bug" (story, 1843) turns on the deciphering of a phonetic hieroglyph of a proper name, Captain Kidd's "hieroglyphical signature"; these themes all come together in their most complex form in the *Narrative of A. Gordon Pym* (novel, 1838).

For Hawthorne and Melville, the hieroglyphics served as a metaphor of the ambiguous external world whose shape could sustain many interpretations. In *The Scarlet Letter* (novel, 1850), Pearl was the "Living hieroglyph" that revealed the secret Hester wished to hide, while in "Monsieur du Miroir" (story, 1837), Hawthorne calls the mute expressions on the double's face "visible hieroglyphics." In Melville's novel *Moby-Dick* (1851), the metaphor figures mainly indeterminacy. He described Queequeg's tattoos as "hieroglyphic marks" because Queequeg was a "riddle to unfold." In the same way, he describes the markings on the sperm whale as "hieroglyphical." After Champollion, the hieroglyphics were always used metaphorically, usually to figure problems of interpretation, mystery, the quest for origins or indeterminacy, as Mark Twain clearly summarizes it in his short sketch "As Concerns Interpreting the Deity" (1905).

In France, hieroglyphics enter into Victor Hugo's discussion of the development of mankind as the secret meaning of the oldest architecture (*Notre Dame de Paris* [*The Hunchback of Notre Dame,* novel, 1831]).For Delacroix, the forms in painting are hieroglyphics of "mysterious and profound sensations" (*Journal,* 1853). For Baudelaire, who took his system of correspondences from Swedenborg, everything is hieroglyphic, and all metaphors are drawn from the inexhaustible reserves of the universal analogy. So hieroglyphics is a metaphor for the necessity of symbolism (*Réflexions sur quelques-uns de mes contemporains* [*Reflections on Some of My Contemporaries,* 1868]). The symbolists were also interested in hieroglyphics; Mallarmé used the term metaphorically as did Gide in his essay *Traité du Narcisse* (1891).

After the early years of the twentieth century, the metaphor seems, for the most part, to disappear.

See also: Alchemy, Emblem.

Selected Bibliography

Dieckmann, Liselotte. *Hieroglyphics. The History of a Literary Symbol.* St. Louis: Washington University Press, 1970.

Horapollo. *The Hieroglyphics.* Trans. George Boas. Bollingen Series 23. New York: Pantheon Books, 1950.

Irwin, John T. *American Hieroglyphics. The Symbol of the Egyptian Hieroglyphics in the American Renaissance.* New Haven: Yale University Press 1980.

Iversen, Erik. *The Myth of Egypt and Its Hieroglyphics in the European Tradition.* Copenhagen: Gad, 1961.

DANIEL RUSSELL

HIPPIE

Basically, literary movements take two distinct directions. Simplistically speaking, these are realistic or imaginative. Among the imaginative genres we might place such offshoots as utopian (Bellamy, Orwell); evangelic (Mather, Luther); science fiction (Wells, Verne); surrealist (Baudelaire, Rimbaud); and such similar modes whose impetus comes more from the idea, which is then, so to speak, made flesh as literary works. Among the realistic offshoots, including realism itself, we may include naturalism, historical writings, memoirs, documentations, and the like, which essentially are recordings *after* the event, or flesh transmuted into idea. The pertinence of this dichotomy is to note the fact that hippie literature generally recorded an actual way of life and as such was historic, documented, realistic.

In its ideal sense the hippie life style and its literature had as its bases no leaders; life lived as an exciting balance between playful gamesmanship, communality, and concern for a cosmic hereafter; expansive sexuality; nature-oriented meshing of time/space; individual autonomy within a tribal communality; more efficient and joyous usage of planetary bounties—including drugs—as purposeful to increased physical and spiritual consciousness; necessary—that is, meaningful, and only meaningful—labor; flexible and fluctuating incorporation of mysticism and the like eucumenicalisms; rejection of empty-shell remnants of cadavered religions; refusal to subject nature to human foibles and vice versa;

escape from superficial sit-com bawdway musical/escapisms; spurning of quas-isolving Cold War paranoias; balking against pie-in-the-sky and similar and/or corelated concocted fantasies; and, finally, embracing the seemingly apolitical stances of shunning traditional socio-economically based doctrinaire power politics.

It was a tall order; in fact, too tall, and so, subjected from within to the diseased infestations acquired from its predecessors and from without to a society historically terrified of joyousness, peace, and love, it was toppled.

Of course, and though indeed a realistic literature, like most, the hippie literature also reflected spiritual concerns. These concerns included the incorporation of Christianity, Buddhism, Hinduism, and so on, and esoteric commentaries on the *Cabala,* Ouspensky, Blavatsky, *I-Ching,* Tarot, alchemy, yoga, theosophy, as well as others. The reasoning here, according to Theodore Roszak (*The Making of A Counter Culture,* 1969) was "the alienated young are giving shape to something that looks like the saving vision our endangered civilization requires."

As an example of one of their own uniquely created religions here follows a flyer circulated by the League of Spiritual Discovery which utilized the psychedelic drug, LSD, as part of its sacrament (Ethel Grodzins Romm, et al., *The Open Conspiracy,* 1970, p. 72).

L.S.D.

The seal for the League of Spiritual Discovery is a mandala reminding us of the seven levels of consciousness, the seven Paths to God.

LOVE!?

1. The physical or solar consciousness is seen in the center and in the radiant overall design.
2. The four-fold central lotus surrounded by a spherical field is nuclear or cellular on a level of consciousness.
3. The mental or somatic level is seen in the intertwined triangles; the union of male and female.
4. The intuitive or sensory level. . . .
5. The angelic or symbolic-social level. . . .
6. The archangelic level. . . .
7. The celestial level, the void, the somnambulant is found in the disordered space outside everything.

In a somewhat similar vein (Romm, p. 48), expressive at the same time of the hippie sacred seriousness of purpose and paradoxically, its hi-jinks comedics, is this curious Alice-in-Wonderland-like call to arms:

Ringing the Pentagon

At the Pentagon on October 21, we will witness the death of the old Liberal war protest and beginnings of a new scene. The old protestors are coming to the ultimate war protest to end protests. They are probaby going to do their own thing and make speeches, carry pickets and so on but they are also going to meet newcomers to the scene who will be involved in street or guerrilla theater and a religious exorcism ritual. The multitude assembled will represent the largest coalition of dissident elements since the depression. The participants will read like a Magic Menue of Shamens, Indian Medicine Men, Wizards, Priests, Rabbis, Black Power, White Power, Mothers Strike for Peace, Sane, Artists, Diggers and thousands of Mr. Nobody's sick of senseless killing. All will perform in a spontaneous happening and religious rite to exorcise the traditional and actual symbol of evil—The Pentagon.

It is a citadel of propaganda, corruption and mistrust. A totalitarian, drab crypt ironically configured in a symbol which appears in many religions and cultures as the symbol of evil. To ring a Pentagon is to render it impotent. We will ring it many times over with thousands of people celebrating, defying, dancing and praying.

That there is, relatively speaking, a rather slight body of scholarly work regarding hippie literature may be, in part, explained thusly. First, the more florid hippie expressions of music, clothing, drug-usage, audacious life-style, communality and such more firmly captured both the popular mind and the media than its literature. And second, accultural antecedents, historic karma, socio-economic design or some tenuous combination thereof greatly restricted scholarly and academic considerations. Such negligence is both unfortunate, narrow, and, again, whether by accident or design, verges on the censorious and repressive. Such neglect appears unwarranted. Even though in point of time the hippie phenomenon was extremely brief and transient, covering a scant handful of years, its influence was immense and profound and, even if only from a rather ironic point of view, is still being felt via both the dominant culture's counteractions and assimilations thereof.

The hippie movement, quite loosely, lasted from 1963 to 1969. Its history led from its first stirrings along San Francisco's Haight-Ashbury area to its heyday peaks—the Human Be-in of 1967, through to the Woodstock Summer of Love of 1969—and finally to its symbolic demise at the infamous Altamount Concert of December 1969.

If we view society as a sprawling case study of economic conflicts and cumulative psychoses, then the "flower-power" hippie pockets in California, on New York City's East Side, and in the various smaller colonies in Cleveland, Chicago, New Orleans, and so on, might well have been seen as demilitarized zones. These pockets, more or less, ranged from within America's largest cities and Europe's greatest capitals finally filtering down to towns, hamlets, and villages where there might have been as few as two or three "long-hairs." Besides whatever their actual number may have been, there were millions who partook, to some degree, of the hippie phenomenon if only through such superficial and surface accoutrements as longer hair and freer attitudes toward jewelry, cosmetics, and clothes. Because such basically intangible crosscultural influences are immeasurable, neither the fleeting nor permanent effects of the "laid-back" hippie life-style is likely ever to be accurately known. As noted, even the repressive actions by the dominant culture such as legislative cut-offs of college tuition monies (since these institutions were viewed as hotbeds of incipient neohippieism), though negative, are clearly influences. Thus, by the dominant culture's so doing, the suddenly economically debauched middle class, which had been briefly sparked by the black civil rights, the anti-Vietnam and the hippie movements to demands for improvements in quality-of-life, became once again distracted by said manufactured terrors and reverted back to their cautious nose-to-the-grindstone/hand-to-mouth existences. In his autobiographical novel *Ringolevio* (1972), Emmett Grogan, a significant hippie figure at the time "watched Nixon squash the prosperity that spawned the country's counterculture."

Regardless of appearances and protestations, all thought and all action is political, moral, ethical and affects all. From that perspective, even at its start, the hippie movement was always political and as such always mobilized both enemies and allies. Those who saw it as a *threat* to their life style decided on a three-fold form of combat: attack, obfuscation, and indifference. Perhaps, with whatever other purposes, those who saw fit to implement this policy had seen how much the media had done to publicize, enhance, and romanticize the earlier beat movement and to make its spokespersons, especially Allen Ginsberg and Jack Kerouac, formidable molders of polarizing public opinion. Thus, the dominant culture minimized the essential hippie philosophy and in its stead perpetuated the less complimentary image of hippies as lazy, shiftless, nonproductive, and malingering. That the dominant culture also opted to focus on the hippie surfaces—long hair, flamboyant clothing patterns, sexual mores, and drug activities—instead of its ideals, such as they were, suggests at best slovenly and sluggish perceptions, slipshod documentation, and at worst, a censorship motivated by callow desires to maintain their real and/or presumed threatened power base.

It was in this harsh socio-economic climate that the hippie movement arose, briefly found its voice, and shortly thereafter in part was silenced, in part faded. The hippie movement is generally acknowledged to be an outgrowth of the late 1950s beat movement. These Beats, through such writers as Ginsberg, John Clellon Holmes, Charles Potts, William Burroughs, Jack Kerouac, Gregory Corso, Charles Foster, Gary Snyder, Diane di Prima, Hugh Fox, Charles Plymell, and others most profoundly reached an American youth that, like any generation of youth not yet encumbered by the "realities of life," still sought justice, logic, ethics, equality, and a diminishment of the superfluous constraints against joy. The beat movement itself may be said to have begun on August 6, 1945, when the first atomic bomb was spewn on Hiroshima, when World War II in effect ended and human beings realized the suicidal edge to which traditional politics had brought humanity. At that point, life no longer could be taken for granted. And its official close could be said to have been January 1, 1967, when at the San Francisco Human Be-in the beats passed their torch to the hippies.

The difference between the beats and the hippies was more in degree than essence. This essence was quite accurately mirrored in the beats except that the hippies were *more* youthful, outrageous, spiritually-drug-myth-sexually oriented, politically aloof, and culturally rebellious against a raucous society whose main tenets included excessive repression, a continuous cycle of paranoic socio-economic panics, blind obedience to blind purpose, a ceaseless plethora of debt-ridden "joys;" unending confrontations with nature; the acceptance of self-torturing life styles, and finally, facile promises of ecstasies perpetually postponed, then ruthlessly eradicated as "unpayable" at death.

In this philosophical sense the beats took that uniquely American vision of Manifest Destiny to its ultimate in such works as Holmes' *Go* (novel, 1952), Kerouac's novel *On the Road* (1957), Ginsberg's poem *Howl* (1956), and Burroughs' novel *Naked Lunch* (1959). In fact, it was the beats, with their mad rushings seeking human joys and pleasures, who discovered the bankruptcies of such efforts and in turn, prodded the hippies to their searches within. Thus, after the beat failure (along with the inevitable de rigueur societal repressions) to find joy, the hippie resorted to the more internalized spiritual and psychic planes. From the vantage of the average person, such hectoring hippie indolence was even more threatening than that of the gadabout beats, whose frantic scurryings were at least more comprehensible than those of "zombielike drug fiendish navel-contemplating" hippies.

What, more precisely, was hippie literature? To begin with, a literature is more than a dilettante's best-seller list of escapism. A literature is a concretization of a philosophy, and as such hippie literature had as its philosophy the aforementioned goals of ridding itself of superfluous repression; greater enjoyment of karmic incarnation, and simultaneously, working toward a nirvanic bliss. To discuss hippie or any other literature in merely aesthetic terms is to demean it, muddy it, and subvert its purposes. Too frequently, rigid and overzealous considerations of aesthetics, like "proper speech" and "dress codes" are merely subtle forms of oppression and censorship. Hippie literature sought to "decode" this world and its bizarrely alternating showpieces of Dachau and Rockefeller Center; Hiroshima and Harvard; Buchenwald and the British Museum. Nor was hippie literature willing to accept as 'practical realities'—pogroms, massacres, racism, famines, addictions-to-addictions, encouragement to brutal and ruthless self-aggrandizements, corruption, bribes, distortions, institutionalized ignorance and psychotic greed. Certainly, whatever else hippie literature may or may not have been, at least in its own terms its purposes were serious, noble, and dignified and as such justified demands that it be considered in serious, noble, and dignified terms. Hippie journalist Tom Forcade loosely defined the concerns of hippie literature as "radical theater, sexual freedom, the taboo against knowing who you are, communes, anarchy, draft resistance, light shows, peace and freedom, hashish and a thousand other things and non-things, real and imagined, ridiculous and sublime" (Robert Glessing, *The Underground Press in America*, 1970, p. 107).

Of course, there were contrary viewpoints. The generally considered ultra-conservative John Birch Society saw hippie literature as "a Marxist message blanketed in sex and drugs. This is kneaded with four letter words, malapropped with polysyllables, and stirred with corny revolutionary slogans that would have embarassed an East Side anarchist of 1910. It is mixed with 'hip' language taken from the lexicons of Marx, Lenin and Chairman Mao, along with the weird vernacular of the Hindu mystics. Served with a quart of self-righteousness, the above recipe produces the nicest litle revolutionary stew you ever saw'' (Glessing, p. 106). Such divergence about the same phenomenon certainly denied of anything like a common ground from whence meaningful dialogue might occur. And since most Americans held more to the John Birch view, both the Hippies and, of course, their literature suffered neglect, distortion, and attacks that eventually helped end them.

Hippie literature may be said to be of two categories. Because the hippie movement lasted for so short a time and had come from what Marshall McLuhan had defined as the Gutenberg print culture, much of its literature had not divested itself of its traditional dominant culture canons, orthodoxies, and aesthetics. Thus, the two basic modes of hippie literature were those that expressed hippie thought in wilder hippie terms and aesthetics and those that expressed hippie thought but in the traditional print culture methods. As ready examples of hippie thought immersed in print culture mannerisms, one might place such works as Emmett Grogan's *Ringolevio;* Timothy Leary's *Confessions of a Hope Fiend* (1973); Abbie Hoffman's *Steal this Book* (1971), and *Woodstock Nation* (1969); Jerry Rubin's *Do It! Scenarios of the Revolution* (1970); Tom Wolfe's *The Electric Kool Aid Acid Test* (1968); and Jeremy Larner's *Drive, He Said* (1964).

On the other hand, literature that more closely expressed hippie philosophy in terms of hippie aesthetics was to be most readily found in its magazine and small press newspaper outlets; in large part because these were autonomous to decision making by hippies rather than by tradition bound, print-culture book publishers and newspaper editors. In this context, Thorne Dryer, a spokesperson for this hippie phenomenon, noted: ''Every day millions of sheets of gray print come off the big commercial presses of America. Every day these gray sheets find their way into American homes, American minds. But into this sea of gray came a colorful splash—the underground press'' (Glessing, p. 49). Again, the hippie journalists could do this because they were their own bosses. Further, they had particular allegiance neither to the earlier print culture nor to its basic tenets. In fact, it was instead quite antithetical to this sea of gray that affected the American eye and the American mind. The television-weaned hippies were much more comfortable with, even conditioned to, a tribal-visual-aural experience. Furthermore, they did not have to hold back their most creative expression for advertisers or a readership easily offended, easily herded, easily lulled. Thus, they were able to achieve an intellectually and visually stimulating literature; as Robert J. Glessing called it, ''a psychedelic rainbow'' (p. 49).

As a literature that denied the merits of its dominant culture, it was more concerned with escape rather than escapism. Hippie literature, much of it either manifesto or near-manifesto, rejected the temporary escape of Broadway musicals and the like, acceptable to those who felt the socio-political system was basically proper and correct and/or the best available. According to its lights, hippie literature sought a real, profound, and permanent plan of escape from those conditions it found oppressive. Presuming its validity, genuine escape would eliminate not only any further need for escapism but for escape itself. In terms of analogies, once one had escaped from a prison, both escapisms and escape itself became obsolete, pointless, moot. Abbie Hoffman, one of the lynchpins of the later hippie movement, described the future as he saw it happening: "I took a trip to our future. That's how I saw it. Functional anarchy, primitive tribalism, gathering of the tribes. Right on! What did it all mean? Sheet, what can I say brother, it blew my mind out! . . . If I had to sum up the totality of the Woodstock experience I would say it was the first attempt to land a man on earth. It took an awful lot of people to pull it off, but pull it off we did. Welcome to the Aquarian Age" *(Woodstock Nation,* p. 9).

Much hippie literature, especially that which the hippies themselves published, was brief, rambling, used interwoven print-visual techniques, and was loosely linear. The rationale behind this aesthetic was life was to be lived and excessive obeisance to Art was as foolish and time-consuming as any other addiction or careerism. It was this aesthetic, in part, that explained hippie ephemera, which released publications often inundated with traditional print-culture bugaboos: "misspelled works, unnumbered or misnumbered pages, and captionless pictures" (Glessing, p. 48). Indeed a limited and inexperienced staff, inferior machinery, tight-money and concern for interference on real and/or trumped up charges by the dominant culture authorities and yahoo vigilante groups were also factors. Nonetheless, at least relatively, hippie literature strove to re-create what might be called fourth dimensional extrasensory perceptions both in terms of text and technique. The Hippie "underground" newspapers—*Berkeley Barb, Oracle,* and others—virtually by definition, flowed more freely than the traditional print-culture *New York Times/Washington Post,* which was tied both by philosophy and technology to the "reality" dimensional rigidities of time-space-weight. Because of this freedom, much hippie literature was paradoxically timeless, while being ephemeral. Its timeless qualities came of concerns for the soul, for sacred and spiritual values, while its ephemeral qualities were reflected in the technical transience of their publication.

The general public, for its own reasons, mostly shied away from hippie literature, expecially the ephemera from such underground journalistic sources as *Rat, Baltimore Free Press, Berkeley Barb, Distant Drummer, Bandersnatch* and several hundred other such endeavors rooted throughout the United States and Europe. The public's major source of information regarding hippies came from its traditional media sources—newspapers, television, periodicals—with a smattering of images coming from films and television melodramas, most of which unilaterally cast the long-haired hippie "types" as filthy sex perverts, subversive psychopaths, or demented dope fiends. For the more inquisitive, interest gave rise to studies and anthologies of varying excellence and objectivity. Anthologies that attempted to capture some of the Hippie furor and flavor were *The Hippie Papers*, 1968, edited by Jerry Hopkins; *Our Time*, 1972, edited by Allen Katzman; *Our Time is Now*, 1970, edited by John Birmingham; *How Old Will You Be in 1984?*, 1969, edited by Diane Divoky; *The Open Conspiracy*, 1970, edited by Ethel G. Romm, et al.; *Dig-USA*, 1970, edited by Arthur Daigon and Ronald T. LaConte; and *The Sixties*, 1977, edited by Lynda Rosen Obst.

There were other works that strove to consider specifically one aspect of the hippie and related culture through research, studies, surveys, and so on. Such studies included *The Groupies and Other Girls*, 1970, by John Burks and Jerry Hopkins; *Right On, A Documentary of Student Protest*, (1970), by Maryl Levine and John Naisbitt; *Rock and Roll Will Stand*, 1969, edited by Greil Marcus; and *Rock Revolution*, 1976, edited by Richard Robinson.

Those works, which more or less purported to be scholarly studies, ranged from the quite reasoned to the quite strident and included *The Making of A Counter Culture*, 1969, by Theodore Roszak; *The Hippie Trip*, 1968, by Lewis Yablonsky; *The Greening of America*, 1970, by Charles H. Reich; and *Rhythms, Riots and Revolution*, 1966, by David A. Noebel. Again, as a generalization, the more fanciful and shocking, the more acceptable they were to the average American good burghers who sought to corroborate their prejudices that hippies were filthy, decadent, dope fiends; lazy, sexual perverts; Commie dupes; and cadres of Dr. Spock's legions of spoiled brats.

Among those authors who both lived and reflected the hippie viewpoint, although some with a more studied radical political base than its earlier compatriots, were Abbie Hoffman's *Steal This Book, Revolution for the Hell of It*, 1968, *Woodstock Nation*, and *Soon to be a Major Motion Picture*, 1980; and Jerry Rubin's *Do It!* Other such in the main autobiographical works which stayed within the traditional literary modes were the aforementioned Emmett Grogan's *Ringolevio*, a novelized account of his life up to that point with particular emphasis on his hippie experiences on the West Coast. In addition, there was *Goliath*, 1970, by David Harris; *Seed Journal*, 1973, by James Strahs; *Guitar Army*, 1972, by John Sinclair; *The Strawberry Statement*, 1969, by James Kunen; *Decadence*, 1975, by Jim Hougan; *Revolution at Berkeley*, 1965, edited by Michael V. Miller and Susan Gilmore; and *New World Utopias*, 1975, by Paul Kagan; all of which were either mainly personal statements or investigations of a special facet of pre- or post-hippieism.

It must be noted the hippies subsequently yielded up their "apolitical" stance and became more politically active in the traditional sense for a multitude of reasons. Law enforcement harassments, hostile media, illegal attacks from left- and right-wing vigilante elements, legal persecutions, public animus and being vulnerable targets for political and religious hacks were among these. Robert J. Glessing explained the hippie move from a relatively apolitical to a radical activism as being caused, in part, by "the social and political indifference of the Eisenhower years, the youthful involvement in the Southern civil rights movement, the drug culture of the early 60's, the moral resentment of the war in Vietnam, and the bitterness toward a government incapable of solving racial and poverty problems in the world's wealthiest nation'' (Glessing, p. 11).

In any case, the Hippie changed. Those authors who could be viewed both as embracing the hippie life style and utilizing the hippie literary aesthetics, that is, free-wheeling, visual rambling, graphic, spacious, catholic, fluid, floating-world should include Richard Brautigan, Hunter S. Thompson, Tom Robbins, middle-period Ken Kesey, and, of course, all those countless, virtually anonymous and now forgotten writers of the ephemera. Without doubt, some of the best and most singular examples of hippie literature were to be found, unexpectedly indeed, in their underground comics. Here, combining all the hippie techniques of psychedelia—film, drama, cartoon, graphic, surreal, space/time, absurdity, satire and a spasmodic outrageous ultra-neo-proletarianism—some of the most creative and authentic expressions of hippieism were evolved. Talented writer-cartoonists like R. Crumb, whose creations included Mr. Natural; Clay Wilson's Checkered Demon; Gilbert Shelton's Fabulous Furry Freak Brothers and Wonder Warthog; Bill Griffith's Zippy the Pinhead; as well as Robert Williams, Victor Moscoso, Rich Griffin, Willy Murphy, Jay Kinney, Paul Mavrides, Joyce Farmer, Becky Wilson, Roberta Gregory and Kim Deitch in comics entitled *Mother Oats, Flammed Out, Great Diggs, Zap, Young Lust, Snarf, Astral Outhouse, Twisted Sisters, Leather Nun,* and others more than any others personified the gamut of the hippie culture. Certainly, films and plays have been made of cartoon characters: Popeye, Superman, Batman, Barbarella, Hulk, Joe Palooka, Dick Tracy, The Lone Ranger, and others. And much ado has been justifiably made regarding Don Marquis' Archie and Mehitabel, Gary Trudeau's Doonesbury, Walt Kelly's Pogo, as well as Walt Disney/Ralph Bakshi filmed animations, so it is not quite far-fetched to think of these Hippies as dramatists and/or film script writers. After all, since all utilize characterizations, the fundamental difference between the stage, the cinema, and the cartoon pages is only technical. Further, it is quite plausible to surmise that hippies' socially unpopular attitudes rather than offenses against aesthetic absolutes kept these cartoon works from further popularization into films and plays. Instead, due to the ongoing repressive socio-political climate, these hippie cartoons remained rudimentary drawing-board works-in-progress for potential film and theater projects and poignant expressions in the vein of Grotowski's ''Poor Theater.''

In theater, along with the aforementioned cartoonists for whom their comic-book expressions was their stage, the hippies were able to utilize two additional though more traditional dramaturgic outlets. In fact, one of their few crosscultural popular successes was McDermot's *Hair* (1968), a musical that re-created with some veracity the hippie life style. Other traditional stage works and playwrights included Langford Wilson, Sam Shepard, Rochelle Owens, Leonard Melfi, Robert Patrick's *Kennedy's Children* (1973), Kenneth Tynan's *Oh, Calcutta!* (1969), and others. Films, too, though of hazy and somewhat "unofficial" origins, more or less sought to capture the hippie mystique: *The Trip,* 1967 (R. Corman, dir.); *Tribes,* 1970 (J. Sargent, dir.); *RPM,* 1970 (S. Kramer, dir.); *The Strawberry Statement,* 1970 (S. Hagmann, dir.); *Sympathy for the Devil,* 1969 (J.-L. Godard, dir.); *Joe,* 1970 (J. Avildsen, dir.); and *Easy Rider,* 1969 (D. Hopper, dir.) being among the most memorable. Film documentaries, usually of hippie music festivals, included *Fillmore,* 1972; *Woodstock,* 1970; *Jimi Hendrix,* 1972; *Let It Be,* 1970; *Janis* (Joplin), 1975; and *Gimme Shelter,* 1970.

In the arena of poetry, as well, there were, exponents of hippieism. Again, one finds Brautigan, whose collections of poems included *Galilee Hitch-Hiker* (1958) and *All Watched Over by Machines of Loving Grace* (1967). Other poets clearly within the hippie domain were Jim Morrison, Leonard Cohen, Joni Mitchell, Charles Foster, Donovan, Jimi Hendrix, Judy Collins, John Lennon, Neil Young, and d. a. levy. Many of the more renowned hippie poets were musicians whose poems were often an intrinsic part of their songs. There were many reasons for this obviously more aural, spatial rather than linear format. These included the much desired hippie aesthetic of totality whereby the poetry was a component part of the experiential whole. There was also their resistance to the dominant culture's canon that "pure" poetry be confined to the printed page. In addition, the responsive similarity to the rather recently revitalized beat aesthetic of unifying poetry with jazz was a factor. Then, too, the traditional print culture generally closed ranks to its "encroachments." And finally, there were the hippie tribal festivals and communelike life styles where these poet-performers took intertwining roles somewhat reminiscent of traditions involving shaman, Goliard singers, witch-doctors, Homeric singers, Gnostic psalmists, and Druidic bards. Among these part-collective, part-individual poet-performers were such heyday rock-and-roll music groups as Jefferson Airplane, The Doors, The Beatles, The Grateful Dead, Big Brother and the Holding Company, Cat Mother and the All-night Newsboys, Luther and the Hand People, Lovin' Spoonful, Vanilla Fudge, Spooky Tooth, Quicksilver Messenger Service, Joy of Cooking, MC-5, Country Joe and the Fish, Rolling Stones, and others, and such significant recordings as the Beatles' *Rubber Soul* (1965), *Revolver* (1966), *Sergeant Pepper's Lonely Hearts Club Band* (1967); the Jefferson Airplane's *Surrealistic Pillow* (1967); and the Rolling Stones' *His Satanic Majesty* (1967). In fact, ironically, many of these songs such as "Light My Fire," "Norwegian Wood," "Me and Bobby McGee," "Summer in the City," among countless others, continue to be performed long after the hippie phenomenon, which spawned them into being, receded into the dusty side roads of history.

Unlike most other movements that at best encourage only lip-service homage to individuality, the hippie saw everybody as the center of the universe. Thus, the great interest in astrology, numerology, and similar occult works wherein the planet Earth was the center of the universe, the astrological chart, and the individual the center of this center. At the same time and quite conversely, the hippies held great faith in tribal-communal life styles. Here is an example of this:

People:

The national collection of tribes/communities. The tribal-nation. The identity as a people. The merging with the cities and the country. The realization of the urban/rural struggle and the need for flow between them. As people we abolish space and time. We are one wherever we go. The highest form of communal existence: total environment. The creation of our own life, culture, destiny. The revolutionary alternative. The new within the old. The seed within the shell. The form for creation and the vehicle for defense. The armed hip alternative. The new culture and the destruction of the old. The foundation of our vision and its realization (Romm, p. 47).

From whence came the Hippies? According to Abbie Hoffman:

Once upon a time, about a generation ago . . . young people started to congregate in an area of San Francisco known as the Haight-Ashbury. They were sick of being programmed by an education system void of excitement, creativity and sensuality. A system that channeled human beings like so many laboratory rats with electrodes rammed up their asses into a highly mechanized mass of class-rankings, degrees, careers, neon super-markets, military-industrial complexes, suburbs, repressed sexuality, hypocracy, ulcers and psychoanalysis *(Woodstock Nation,* p. 15).

Then the question was frequently asked, why were the hippies, in the main, the youthful, the boisterous, the young? The ready conjecture is that only the young, still unencumbered by the burdens of known civilization, have sufficient latitude of action to struggle against these burdens. To the young, and especially the hippies, maturity, responsibility, and practicality were euphemisms for defeat, decay, and a psycho-spiritual demise. In this sense, certainly for its adherents, the hippie communes were seen as pockets of freedom in a world that was essentially one monstrous and huge concentration camp dedicated solely to main-taining itself, because, like Mallory's mountain peak, it is.

As should be apparent, these considerations have been taken from an ideal point of view. Of course, as with every other movement and human effort, the hippie reach to perfection was but a reach. Obviously, that should not come as any surprise. Due *both* to external repression and internal weakness, the whole of human history is a history of failure, reversals, back-trackings, retreats, and circlings, and the hippie movement, as merely a facet of this human history, by definition, was itself destined to fail. Still, it deserves a study *as if* it had succeeded. Perhaps then one could better obtain a clearer picture of what the hippies, in their heart of hearts, envisioned. Now, only the word remains and certain vague intimations. But it is not unduly remiss to suggest, had the hippie phenomenon succeeded in converting the whole of this planet Earth to its ideal vision, there would have occured some tentative and tenuous easements in the overall plight of its Earthlings.

The fact the hippie movement lasted so short a time might prove, not its failure but success. The hippies so threatened the dominant culture they were rapidly crushed. Their successes were minimized; their failure maximized. Sensing it as a sign of the tip of an iceberg of discontent, the dominant culture and its terrified lackeys quickly moved to stifle it. How was this done? The complete story may never be known but intimations of the existence of agents, dupes, functionaries, turn-coats, fools, idiots, spies, provocateurs, infiltrators, and the like remain. Any considerations of hippie literature must reflect on their defense of the individual's inalienable right to do one's thing . . . drugs, sex, clothes, work, religious practice. Much like the American Transcendentalists, the Harlem Renaissance, the beats, the influence of the hippie movement and its literature likely will never be accurately ascertained. But there is no doubt its influence on world thought in the ideal sense was gentle, lasting, and profoundly spiritual. After the hippies came the punks, but that, more or less, is another story.

See also: Beat Generation.

Selected Bibliography

Birmingham, John, ed. *Our Time Is Now*. New York: Bantam, 1970.
Daigon, Arthur, and Ronald T. LaConte. *Dig-USA*. New York: Bantam, 1970.
Hoffman, Abbie, *Woodstock Nation*. New York: Vantage, 1969.
Hopkins, Jerry, ed. *The Hippie Papers*. New York: Signet, 1968.

JOHN PYROS

HISTORY IN AMERICAN LITERATURE

American literature expresses, with variations and permutations, the two basic attitudes toward history found in American society at large. The first is the American urge to be free of history and the restraints of history, to look not to the past but to the present and the future, to be like Adam, born anew in a new world. This attitude toward history, perhaps best characterized by Henry Ford's comment that "history is bunk," can be found in every period of American literature, from colonial times to the twentieth century.

The second attitude is that history is interesting, valuable, and necessary for self-definition and identity. Many American writers have described the need to rediscover or repossess history, or have sought in history analogies to their own society or answers to the ills of their time. Some of these writers look to English or European history in their literature, some to biblical or classical history, and some strictly to the history of America.

Both attitudes toward history expressed in American literature involve self-consciousness on the part of the writer and choice. As the critic Stephen Spender explains in *Love-Hate Relations* (1974), unlike Europeans, who take their history as a matter of course, American writers are extremely conscious of the choices that have to be made about history. Because America is a land of immigrants, and thus because separation from historical continuity is in the American grain, Americans can choose to remain unconnected with the past and to ignore history. If they choose to connect, they must select from their two (or more) historical lines: American and pre-American. Thus American writers who use history in their literature tend to be subjective, personal, and selective in the periods they choose, and to use history to serve the ends of the present.

The Colonial Period and the Early Republic, 1620–1800

Early American literature, in particular the prose essays, diaries, journals, and letters written during the period, stressed the newness of the New World and detailed the forging or creating of a new history. Early American writers seemed conscious that they were both recording history and making history. Thus the term "history" in colonial literature often meant very recent events, or, as Moses Coit Tyler labelled it, "contemporaneous history."

The explorer John Smith, for example, wrote several enthusiastic and boastful histories of his adventures with Pocahontas and with other aspects of the new land. Smith's *Generall Historie of Virginia, New England, and the Sumner Isles* (1624) described countless new experiences and encouraged like-minded adventurers to forego the restraining traditions of the Old World, to plan new colonies, and begin anew.

Other contemporaneous history was written by such colonials as Mary Rowlandson, who in *A Narrative of Captivity* (1682) described her kidnapping by Indians, thereby being the first American to write what later became a genre of Indian captivity stories; William Byrd, who wrote two versions of *The History of the Dividing Line* (1728, published posthumously, 1841), both an official history of the boundary dispute between Virginia and North Carolina and, in addition, a rather bawdy, privately circulated *Secret History of the Dividing Line* (posthumous, 1841); and St. Jean de Crévecœur, who in *Letters from an American Farmer* (1782) was among the first to describe the American's restless moving from place to place and the repeated process of starting anew.

At the same time that they recorded the creation of history in the colonies, early American writers described a complex relationship with British history. They were British subjects and thus to some degree part of British history, yet they were removed from England, separated from it by a vast ocean, and in many cases felt cut off from much of its customs, religion, and history. For the Mayflower Pilgrims, who called themselves Separatists, history was less a continuation of British history than a new type of biblical history. Like them, many early American writers sought analogies for their experiences in Old Testament history. Thus early American literature described several historical lines running parallel.

In colonial New England, William Bradford in *History of Plimoth Plantation* (1630–1651) and John Winthrop in his *Journal* (1630–1651) recorded the history of their long ocean voyage, their separation from the Old World, and the various stages in the settlement of New England. At the same time, they reached into biblical history for models for their experience. Thus their colony is called New Jerusalem, New Israel, or New Canaan, and the covenant that the Puritans made with God is described as analogous to convenants described in the Bible. Cotton Mather in *Magnalia Christi Americana,* which is subtitled *The Ecclesiastical History of New England from Its First Planting in the Year 1620 unto the Year of Our Lord 1698* (1702), described many Puritan leaders as "types" of biblical personages. John Winthrop, for instance, was called a new Moses, engaged in a holy mission.

These Puritan writers expected that the New England settlement would be the beginning of a new history and a guide for future generations. With such high expectations, it is perhaps understandable that many of their historical accounts end with disappointment over the weakening of the Puritan influence in later generations.

Of the poetry written in the early period, Anne Bradstreet's provides an example of how a colonist gradually relinquished her connection with European history to become part of American history. Bradstreet's early poetry, published in 1650 as *The Tenth Muse Lately Sprung Up in America* and consisting of long, rhyming histories of "The Four Ages of Man" and "The Four Monarchies," was imitative of European models and was apparently written to assuage her feelings of disconnection with England. As she wrote in her letter "To My Dear Children," at first, her "heart rose" up against some of the hardships of the New World, but later she "submitted" to the will of God and joined the new community in Boston. Bradstreet's later poems, those written between 1650 and 1672 and published posthumously in 1678 as *Several Poems . . . ,* are freer, more personal, and more accepting of her place in America. Her fame as a poet is based primarily on these later poems, which include "To My Dear and Loving Husband" and "As Weary Pilgrim." Bradstreet's poetic style as well as her content demonstrate accommodation to the New World.

The period of the Early Republic found many writers determined to turn their backs on England and English history and to celebrate the virtues of the new nation. These writers were equally determined to isolate a uniquely American literature, incorporating uniquely American history, heroes, and subjects. Thus the American frontier, American Indians, and American explorers became the subjects of literature. Joel Barlow's *The Vision of Columbus* (1787) was written as an epic describing American history from the Incas to Barlow's own day and celebrating the founding of America. Timothy Dwight's poems *Columbia* (1793) and *Greenfield Hill* (1794) contrast the European history of war and class inequality with the possibilities in the New World. Hugh Henry Brackenridge's novel *Modern Chivalry* (1792–1815) both describes and satirizes American frontier life, and William Dunlap's drama *André* (1798) celebrates the leadership and judgment of George Washington in punishing traitors to the American Revolution. In Dunlap's play, in poems by Philip Freneau, and by the black slave woman Phillis Wheatley, and in other literature describing the history of the Revolutionary War, George Washington was often described as a godlike hero.

This nationalistic fervor can be seen also in Mercy Warren's poetry and plays, as well as in her authoritative *History of the Rise, Progress, and Termination of the American Revolution* (1805).

The Nineteenth Century: Romanticism and Realism

The nineteenth-century literary movement called romanticism affected attitudes toward history in somewhat divergent ways. Some writers, responding to the romantic emphasis on individuality and independence, called to Americans to be self-reliant, to avoid undue dependence upon history, and to pay heed to the present rather than the past. Representative of these writers was Ralph Waldo Emerson, who in his *Essays* (1841, 1844), especially in "Self-Reliance," pressed Americans to be independent, to refuse to conform to thwarting traditions. In "The Poet" he urged American writers not to dwell on history but to examine and glorify the present. In his essay "History" he asked readers to trust their own experience over experience described in history books and to base their actions on their own intuition, spiritual leanings, and personal feelings. In "The Over Soul" Emerson explained transcendentalism, a philosophy that collapses historical chronology by stating that in the world of Idea or Spirit, past and present merge; thus history is subsumed into an eternal present. In all his works, Emerson preached not ignorance of history, but the proper use and subordination of history.

Like Emerson, Henry David Thoreau in his narrative *Walden* (1854) and Walt Whitman in his long poem *Leaves of Grass* (1855) asserted the American drive for self-reliance and for release from the unwholesome restraints of history.

Other nineteenth-century writers responded to the romantic nostalgia for the past, as well as to the American need for a national literature. Thus America's two-hundred-year-old history was probed, and early American heroes, villains, and events were immortalized and sometimes mythologized in much nineteenth-century literature.

James Fenimore Cooper's five novels, *The Leatherstocking Tales* (1823–1841), depict American frontier history, a history full of rapid changes as settlements were forged out of the wilderness. These novels, which include *The Deerslayer* (1841), *The Last of the Mohicans* (1826), and *The Pioneers* (1823), provide much accurate detail about frontier history at the same time that they romanticize the woodsman-hero, the natural world, and the American Indian.

Washington Irving re-created and often satirized American history. His *Sketch Book* (1819–1820) contains several humorous stories about the picturesque American past, including "The Legend of Sleepy Hollow," which is set in postrevolutionary Dutch New York and reveals how legends are created, and "Rip Van Winkle," a humorous account of the traumatic changes that had taken place in America's short history. Irving's historical satire, *The History of New York* (1809), chronicles the Dutch settlement in America and at the same time spoofs the pedantry of official history books. Irving re-created history also in books about Christopher Columbus, George Washington, and the American West.

Nathaniel Hawthorne chose to investigate his own Puritan ancestry and to re-create Puritan history in such works as *The Scarlet Letter* (novel, 1850) and in several short stories, including "The Minister's Black Veil" (1835), "Young Goodman Brown" (1835) and "The Maypole of Merry Mount" (1836). In these works, which Hawthorne called "romances," he described the legacy of guilt and darkness that Puritan history had bequeathed to later generations of Americans and to him personally.

Henry Wadsworth Longfellow presented an extremely romantic view of the American past. He selected the most dramatic moments in American history as the basis for his poems, sometimes heightening the drama by altering historical fact. Longfellow's *Song of Hiawatha* (1855), a paean to America's prehistory, tells how the Indians prophesied the arrival of the white race, and *The Courtship of Miles Standish* (1858) glorifies Puritan history and virtues. "Paul Revere's Ride," one of *The Tales of a Wayside Inn* (1863), praises the revolutionary spirit in American history, and, despite its inaccuracies (for example, Revere rode to Lexington, not to Concord), the poem set an American legend. It also uttered a call for national unity during Longfellow's time, when America was preparing for a civil war. Thus Longfellow used history to serve an important purpose in his own day.

Although nineteenth-century writers sought to create a uniquely American literature and often looked to American history for material, they also used European history in their works. Some found American history meager when compared to long centuries of European history; others considered their personal history to be both European and American. Longfellow's *Tales of a Wayside Inn* describes not only American historical characters and settings, but also European and classical. Irving wrote not only about New York history, but also about the history of Moorish Spain in *The Conquest of Granada* (1829) and *The Alhambra* (1832). James Fenimore Cooper, in *Notions of the Americans* (1828), stated that Americans share English literary history in such writers as William Shakespeare, John Milton, and Alexander Pope. And, in addition to his *Leatherstocking* novels, which use American history, Cooper also wrote many historical novels using English or European history as background for fictional characters. *The Bravo* (1831), for example, describes Venice during the Renaissance, and *The Heidenmauer* (1832) and *The Headsman* (1833) are set, respectively, in sixteenth-century Bavaria and eighteenth-century Switzerland. Such works demonstrate Cooper's regard for the richness of European history, but also his criticism of monarchy and feudalism. Like many American writers of the romantic era, Cooper preferred American republicanism; for him, America represented an advance in human history, the latest stage in the progression of history.

Besides Cooper, other nineteenth-century writers of historical novels include Herman Melville, whose *Israel Potter* (1855) re-created the period of the American Revolution, and Francis Marion Crawford, who employed European and Oriental history in such novels as *Zoroaster* (1885) and *Via Crucis* (1898).

An important literary genre of the nineteenth century was the Gothic romance, which often called upon remote European history for settings and effects. Edgar Allan Poe's horror stories, such as "The Fall of the House of Usher" (1839) and "Ligeia" (1840) placed characters in ancient castles, dungeons, and crypts, and employed other trappings of medieval history. Another nineteenth-century literary genre that relates to history was the slave narrative. Most notable of these, *The Life and Times of Frederick Douglass* (1881) and the *Narrative* of William Wells Brown (1847), tell the history of American slavery from the exslave's own perspective.

Toward the end of the nineteenth century, as the romantic movement gave way to the realistic, writers became more critical in their approach to history. For example, Mark Twain set several novels in the pre-Civil-War period and exposed the evils of America's history of slavery. Such novels as *The Adventures of Huckleberry Finn* (1884) and *The Tragedy of Pudd'nhead Wilson* (1894), for all their Western frontier humor, included realistic accounts of the slave trade and the evils of the slave system. Other aspects of American history were exposed in these novels as well, for example the practice of dueling, which existed in the eighteenth and nineteenth centuries. Twain's critical barbs were aimed at European history also. In *A Connecticut Yankee in King Arthur's Court* (1889) and *The Prince and the Pauper* (1882) Twain exposed the superstition and ignorance that was part of the European feudal tradition. Twain's *The Mysterious Stranger* (posthumously published, 1916) moves from fifteenth-century Austria to Twain's own day and reveals the bitterness he felt late in life about human history. Whereas earlier nineteenth-century literature described history as a steady progression toward perfection, *The Mysterious Stranger* suggests that history is cyclical, an endless series of wars and other evils.

Other late nineteenth-century realistic writers who dealt with history include Sarah Orne Jewett, Stephen Crane, Ambrose Bierce, and Henry James. Jewett's short stories in *The Country of the Pointed Firs* (1896) describe the local history of a Maine town, decaying after its heyday as a West Indian trading port. Crane's novel *The Red Badge of Courage* (1895) and Bierce's story "An Occurrence at Owl Creek Bridge" (1890) re-create realistic Civil-War scenes and at the same time expose their heroes' tendency to romanticize events. James' novels *The American* (1877), *The Europeans* (1878), and *The Bostonians* (1886) contrast the meager history of America with the rich, although decadent, history of Europe, and James' final, unfinished novel, *The Sense of the Past* (1917), reveals his own preference for Europe and European history.

The Twentieth Century

In the twentieth century, the call for self-reliance—for liberation from confining history and tradition—is repeated and reworded; for example, an early Carl Sandburg poem insists that "the past is a bucket of ashes." The notion that Americans should be like Adam, new people independent of history, persists and is analyzed in R.W.B. Lewis' *The American Adam* (1955) and Daniel J.

Boorstin's *Democracy and Its Discontents* (1974). These scholars find that the American tendency to disown history has resulted in extraordinary progress, innovation, and adaptability, but also, unfortunately, in rootlessness, loss of connections, and anxiety about identity.

These feelings of loss and anxiety were expressed by many writers after the devastation of World War I, when their literature records their search into history for causes, roots, and reconnections. Thus, despite a history-denying tendency in America, a major theme for twentieth-century writers is the search for a "usable past," a term coined by Van Wyck Brooks in an influential *Dial* magazine essay, "On Creating a Usable Past" (1919). Brooks charged that American writers of his era were separated from their vital, usable history—either because they did not know history or because they had been misled by the established history and mythology of America—and he urged writers to uncover or "to create" a past that would explain them as they exist in the present. Although many writers seemed to answer Brooks's call, the search for a usable history was not unified, but rather a series of individual and highly personal searches, some writers finding their history in America and others outside America. Such multiplicity demonstrates Henry Adams's theory, expounded in his autobiography, *The Education of Henry Adams* (1907), that modern history, like the modern mechanical dynamo, involves a dispersion of energy.

A prime example of a writer who found his usable past outside America is T.S. Eliot, whose poetry records the many steps in his search and recovery. In the *Prufrock* volume (1917), Eliot describes the American separated from history, purpose, and vitality; in *The Waste Land* (1922) and in *Ash Wednesday* (1930), he discovers fragments of history and enacts an arduous search for a way to recover and reconnect; finally in *Four Quartets* (1943) he finds reconnection with his seventeenth-century Anglo-Catholic background. By repeating, in reverse, the emigration of his English ancestors, Eliot discovers that history is cyclical and that for him personally, "history is now and England." For Eliot, history, in good part, means literary history, that is, the works of past writers, such as Dante, John Donne, and John Dryden.

Like Eliot, Ezra Pound describes an arduous search for his usable past, eventually, in the *Cantos* (poems, 1925–1969) choosing not a single past but many pasts, American, European, and Oriental. Pound reconnects with history by selecting a number of historical great men, such as Confucius, Sigismondo Malatesta, John Adams, and Thomas Jefferson, and by willfully identifying their struggles and aims with his own.

Other American writers seek their usable past in America—in the history and mythology of America. William Carlos Williams in *In the American Grain* (essays, 1925) and *Paterson* (poetry, 1946–1958), Hart Crane in *The Bridge* (poem, 1930), John Berryman in *Homage to Mistress Bradstreet* (poem, 1956), and Charles Olson in *The Maximus Poems* (1953–1968) all make individual and personal choices about where American history begins or where they personally enter history.

History in some American literature is regional, the history of the writer's own locale. Willa Cather's novels, such as *O Pioneers!* (1913) and *My Antonia* (1918), depict the history of the Nebraska frontier, and Robert Penn Warren's novel *All the King's Men* (1946) and his poem *Brother to Dragons* (1953) delve into the Southern past. William Faulkner's novels are drenched in Southern history, as he attempts to find the origins of modern Southern life and to discover, moreover, the nature and meaning of history itself. *The Sound and the Fury* (1929) and *Absalom, Absalom!* (1936) suggest that only after many historical records and witnesses are probed, assessed, and interpreted can the Southern past be understood, and only then can one begin to understand the present.

Like earlier writers, many twentieth-century writers are drawn to history because they find in it explanations or parables for the present. Arthur Miller's drama *The Crucible* (1953), for example, reenacts the seventeenth-century witch hunt in Puritan New England, but by implication also analyzes and criticizes the "witch hunt" conducted by Joseph McCarthy in the 1950s. By inventing motivations and by probing into the question of guilt by association, Miller expands upon the known historical record. Similarly, Gore Vidal in the novels *Burr* (1973) and *Lincoln* (1984) and William Styron in *The Confessions of Nat Turner* (novel, 1967) imagine character traits, motivations, and conversations between historical persons.

Such imaginative re-creation of history often challenges previous historical records, and while some writers insist that they are merely making history relevant and new, others, such as John Barth in *The Sot Weed Factor* (1960) intentionally debunk and revise previous historical accounts. Barth's novel, set in colonial Maryland and Virginia, posits a chaotic and bawdy picture of historical events, such as the encounter between John Smith and Pocahontas, and intends to correct what Barth considers the tame and orderly arrangement of history in most history books.

History is corrected and revised in the literature of many twentieth-century black and women writers, who attempt to retrieve the history that white, male writers had ignored. Alex Haley's semiautobiographical *Roots* (1976), for example, traces one black American family to its origins in Africa, Alice Walker's *The Color Purple* (novel, 1982) and Toni Morrison's novels *Sula* (1973) and *Tar Baby* (1981) emphasize the historical plight of individual black women, and Emily Toth's historical romance *Daughters of New Orleans* (1983) takes a feminist look at the marriage and career options available to women a century ago.

Toth is one of many twentieth-century writers who have vitalized the historical romance, using historical events as a backdrop against which the domestic lives of characters are described. The most popular twentieth-century work in this genre, Margaret Mitchell's 1936 novel *Gone With the Wind,* depicts the upheavals in the romantic and domestic lives of Southerners during the Civil-War era. Since Mitchell's day, historical romance writers have become more explicit in picturing what once had been considered the private details of their characters' lives. Since the 1970s writers such as Kathleen Woodiwiss in *The Flame and the Flower* (1972), Meredith Tax in *Rivington Street* (1982), and Barbara Chase-Ribound in *Sally Hemings* (1979) have re-created not only historical periods, but also the intimate details of courtship, marriage, birth, and birth-control.

A recent direction taken by some writers who use history in their literature is to blur the lines between fact and fiction, as E. L. Doctorow does in his syncopated novel *Ragtime* (1975), and to question whether one can make sense of history, as John Barth had questioned in *The Sot Weed Factor*. These writers have been charged with "deconstructing" history, with raising questions about whether the past can ever be truly known or whether it can provide answers to the present. Americans have always been of at least two minds about history, however, and most contemporary writers who use history in their literature do attempt to discover the meaning of the past and its relevance to the present.

' A final connection between history and literature has to do not with how writers use history as theme or setting, or how they imaginatively re-create history, but with how literature written in a particular era reveals that era. Many cultural historians point out that one's understanding of a historical period can be enhanced if one penetrates that period's literature. They thus assert that history may be understood *via* literature. This idea, often labeled historicism, requires that the reader see a past society without modern preconceptions and judgments. Morris Wesley's study *Toward a New Historicism* (1972) analyzes several developments in historicism, including the recent attempt to view literature not only for its intrinsic, but also for its extrinsic value—that is, to unite aesthetic and historical studies of literature.

Selected Bibliography

Bremmer, Robert H. *Essays on History and Literature*. [Columbus]: Ohio State University Press, 1966.
Henderson, Harry B., III. *Versions of the Past: The Historical Imagination in American Fiction*. New York: Oxford University Press, 1974.
Levin, David. *In Defense of Historical Literature*. New York: Hill and Wang, 1967.
Strout, Cushing. *The Veracious Imagination, Essays on American History, Literature, and Biography*. Middletown, Conn.: Wesleyan University Press, 1981.

LAURA JEHN MENIDES

HOMOSEXUALITY

Defined as erotic interest, sexual outlet, capacity for intense emotional affection between persons of the same sex; homosexuality here is applied exclusively to males. While the phenomenon of homosexuality has been known in all cultures, its moral acceptance and literary significance vary sharply from era to era and from civilization to civilization—so much so that few generalizations are possible. As Jonathan Katz reminds us, "there is no such thing as homosexuality in general, only particular forms of homosexuality." Perhaps we can say that homosexuality seems to be a problem during periods of social proscription when hostile attitudes prevail against it. The literature of homosexuality, in virtually all periods, testifies to possibilities of love and sensual imagination conceived outside the narrowing of desire to standard forms of heterosexuality. Thus the love and sexuality between persons of the male gender recorded in world literature reflect attitudes of particular ages and cultures but also clarify the universality of the erotic in all its manifestations, incomplete surely without testimony from the largest minority.

The Background in Antiquity

In classical Greece the relationship between males was of primary cultural significance, although historians have acknowledged this fact openly only within the recent past. The definitive example of the homoerotic basis of Greek educational practices is, of course, Socrates as portrayed by Plato (c. 428–347 B.C.). Learning was predicated on an erotic association between the teacher/role-model *(erastēs)* and his pupil *(eromenos);* the younger man learned from the older mentor, who in turn was inspired by the youth's good looks, but rarely, it was assumed, did the pupil give himself to his senior lover/teacher, despite entreaty. Thus emerges the putative basis of so-called Platonic love: arousal but nonconsummation as stimulus to the spiritual ends of beauty, goodness, and truth. As K. J. Dover explains, "the most important aspect of Socrates is his exploitation of the Athenian ethos as a basis of metaphysical doctrine and philosophical method." Socrates himself exemplifies this lesson of discipline in *Symposion* (*The Symposium,* philosophical dialogue on the nature of love, c. 384 B.C.) when he resists the advances of Alcibiades. The situation may be somewhat reversed in Plato's *Phaidros* (*Phaedrus,* dialogue, 4th century B.C.), where Socrates appears to be wooing the young man, taking "delight in close attendance on him."

A mythic source for this kind of relationship is the story of Zeus and Ganymede, the latter a son of Tros, king of Phrygia, and of Callirrhoe, a youth distinguished by his immense personal beauty. Attracted by his considerable physical attributes, Zeus resolved to make Ganymede his favorite and in the form of an eagle swept him up from the plains of Troy to establish him as cupbearer on Olympus. This abduction has often been portrayed symbolically as a form of rape. In the Middle Ages the term "ganymede" became generic for homosexual, much as "gay" has evolved in the twentieth century. In small complement to his frequent and renowned heterosexual liaisons with mortal women, this one episode with a person of his own sex suggests the omnisexuality of Father Zeus.

In a lost play by Euripides (c. 480–407 B.C.) may be found what Professor Dover terms the original Greek mythic example of a person falling in love with a member of his own sex. It concerns Laios, the father of Oedipus, who, becoming enamored of Khrysippos, the son of Pelops, carried him off, apparently less spectacularly than Zeus managed with Ganymede.

Topical allusions to same-sex erotic attachments abound in the comedies of Aristophanes (c. 450–385 B.C.), where they are viewed, in the main, nonjudgmentally, as was the Greek custom in matters of sexual preference, partly because it was assumed that most men developed from lovers of one another to husbands of women, as do nearly all Aristophanic heroes. The numerous references to practices of homosexuality in these comedies perhaps indicate the extent of such behavior in Greece of this time period. Since comedy traditionally deals much more often with local and topical concerns than does tragedy, the sociological interest of Aristophanes' treatment of homosexuality is great. Homosexuality is sometimes presented in the grossest physical terms with much laughter occasioned by the passive role required in the practice of same-sex sodomy, which the Greeks ridiculed along with many later cultures. It must be acknowledged that Aristophanes' perennially most successful play, *Lysistratē* (*Lysistrata,* 411 B.C.), endures with the presumption that there is no true alternative to heterosexuality.

The Hellenistic phase of Greek civilization, sometimes dated from the coming of the Macedonians who fought under Philip II and Alexander and the defeat of the Peloponnesian city-states beginning at the Battle of Chaeronea in 338 B.C., saw the efflorescence of the poetry of male homosexuality. As a poignant sidelight, at Chaeronea, the Sacred Theban Band, the famous regiment of 150 pairs of male lovers (the closeness of military pairs being a mainstay of Greek literature from Achilles and Patroklus, despite Homer's chaste treatment of them) was destroyed, an event that, according to legend, brought tears of grief to their conqueror, Philip. The homosexual verses usually took the form of "epigrams," brief poems customarily of two to five elegiac couplets, which were enshrined in a variety of anthologies of which the most important was the *Garland* of Meleager (c. 80 B.C.). Such poems, plus a number of others in imitation of them, found their way into the so-called *Greek Anthology,* compiled in the tenth century A.D. by Cephalas, which maintained its popularity throughout the Middle Ages and into the Renaissance and beyond. Also during the Hellenistic period, which is thought to extend as far forward as the fourth century A.D., when it was superseded by the Christian Byzantine Empire, philosophical dialogues on love ascribed to Plutarch and Lucian, in which love between men is regarded as morally superior to heterosexual involvements, continue the tradition of Plato.

The Greek obsession, aesthetic, philosophical, and physical, with naked young men was not one of the fashions that the Romans appropriated to any great extent for emulation from their predecessor culture, yet Roman society during the Republic and the first two centuries of the Empire assumed a highly tolerant attitude toward homosexuality, with presentations of love between men offered without censure by poets as diverse and significant as Catullus (c. 84–54 B.C.), Virgil, Tibullus, Horace, and Ovid (all in the Augustan period, 27 B.C.–14 A.D.), and later writers of the Empire such as Petronius, Juvenal, Martial, Plutarch, Achilles Tatius, and Lucian. It was not until the third century A.D. that a series of laws was enacted to regulate various aspects of homosexuality. The Romans preserved until this time insouciance on sexual matters in the belief that most people have the capacity for sexual pleasure with either sex.

While the idealization of love between men associated with Greek homosexuality persists in certain Roman poetry by masters like Ovid, Virgil, and Horace, a new satiric spirit enters the literature of homosexuality in the *Satyricon* by Petronius (novel, A.D. 60), the arbiter of taste for the court of Nero. The hero, or better anti-hero, of this work, Encolpius (whose name, according to translator William Arrowsmith, means roughly "The Crotch"), suffers in mock-epic fashion from the wrath of the god Priapus; he is subjected to repeated bouts of sexual impotence, which affect his relationships not only with women but most especially his affair with Giton, the object of his intense pederastic attention. His restoration to potency is almost incidental to the running satiric commentary on nearly every facet of life in Nero's Rome, but Petronius illuminates the sexual mores of the times along the way, proving that it is not easy in such a milieu to separate the men from the boys.

Breaking the chronology for a moment with a twentieth-century digression and allusion, Marguerite Yourcenar's *Mémoires d'Hadrien* (*Memoirs of Hadrian*, 1951) affords in a brilliant historical novel a sensitive treatment of male homosexuality by a woman with Hadrian's first-person narration of his affection for the beloved boy, Antinous, whose suicide in his early twenties utterly demoralizes the Roman emperor. Both Yourcenar (1903–) and British historical novelist, Mary Renault (1905–) have provided haunting reconstructions of homosexuality in the ancient world for modern readers.

John Boswell, in his recent, much-admired study, *Christianity, Social Tolerance, and Homosexuality: Gay People in Western Europe from the Beginning of the Christian Era to the Fourteenth Century* (1980), opens his chapter dealing with Rome by citing Edward Gibbon's famous remark that "of the first fifteen emperors Claudius was the only one whose taste in love was entirely correct," that is, heterosexual; the latter-day historian takes note of the factual significance that for nearly two hundred consecutive years "the Roman Empire was ruled by men whose homosexual interests, if not exclusive, were sufficiently noteworthy to be recorded for posterity." Negative attitudes toward homosexuality surface finally in works like Suetonius' *De vita Caesarum* (*Lives of the Caesars*) during the second century A.D. By the time of the *Codex Justinianus* (*Justinian's Code*, 529) the strongest antihomosexual attitudes derived from the Old Testament had been written into Eastern Roman law. Apparently the Emperor Justinian I feared that permitting homosexually oriented people to survive would bring down God's wrath to stage a revival in his own kingdom of Sodom and Gomorrah. Notwithstanding the harshness of such civil laws, Boswell shows that church law remained surprisingly tolerant toward acts of homosexuality in the Early Middle Ages.

The Rise and Fall of Tolerance in the Middle Ages

The years 1050 to 1150, according to Boswell, saw the return for the first time since the decline of Rome of what he calls "a gay subculture." Boswell highlights people like Saint Ailred of Rievaulx for whom God is friendship and who encouraged within a Christian context the expression of love between monastics of the same gender. Lyrics of homosexuality are included in the popular *Carmina Burana* such as "I Am Already Changing My Mind," which relates an affectionate argument between two clerics who are also lovers (12th century). In another well-known poem of the period, "Debate between Ganymede and Helen," it is conceded that homosexuality is common among the most important and influential members of society, and, as Boswell notes, "the very people in a position to declare it a sin are involved in it." However, these halcyon years of homosexuality yield to virulent opposition to its practices just as many formerly tolerated minorities such as Jews found themselves caught increasingly in the web of forced intellectual and institutional conformity that burgeoned throughout Europe during the latter part of the twelfth century through the fourteenth century. The freedom enjoyed by the hitherto gay subculture completely evaporated. It was not to be restored until the very recent past in the Western world of the late twentieth century.

Nonetheless, a curiously sympathetic treatment of a supposed sodomite may be remembered in Dante's (1265–1321) famous portrait of Brunetto Latini from canto 15 of the *Inferno*, part 1 of *La divina commedia* (*The Divine Comedy,* epic poem, c. 1320), as well as the compassionate characterization of the three Florentines also charged with sodomy in canto 16. Dante contrasts Brunetto's noble mind and civic excellence with the deficiency of his presumed sexual practices, which constitute sin. The roving bands of sodomites are discovered on the hot sands, reminiscent of the sodomites of the cities of the plain in the Book of Genesis. The most damaging description in canto 15 is registered not against Brunetto but against Dante's old enemy, Pope Boniface VIII, with the reference to "mal protesti nervi," which John Ciardi explains in the notes to his translation as the pontiff's "unnatural organ" erected for perverse purposes. In Dante's presentation of homosexuality, this sexual orientation becomes the temptation not only of intellectuals such as writers, clergy, and students or speculative temperaments like Brunetto, but also of military persons such as the knights evoked in canto 16—Guido Guerra, Tegghiaio Aldobrandi, and Jacopo Rusticucci.

The anti-homosexual attitudes of fourteenth-century medieval Europe did not prevail in the Muslim world of the Middle Eastern countries or in those parts of the Iberian peninsula under Arabic influence. Indeed, much of the prejudice against homosexuality in Europe may be traceable to its association with the Arab world. *Alf Layla wa-layla* (*The Thousand and One Nights* or *Arabian Nights*, 8th to 17th century) featured a number of specifically gay tales. Another well-known example of literary homosexuality from non-European culture is the *Salāmān u Absāl* (*Salaman and Absal*, 1480), composed for the Sultān Ya'qūb by the great Persian poet, Jāmī, in which some of the love quatrains of Omar are addressed at least in part to a young man. It is sometimes thought that the homosexual content of this work accounted for Edward FitzGerald's (1809–

1883) enthusiasm for the poem, which preceded his work on the *Rubaiyat* (1859), itself not without elements of homosexuality in Victorian England.

The Renaissance

Some kind of transition may be possible between the Middle Ages and the Renaissance through the example of Christopher Marlowe's (1564–1593) *Edward II* (1592), a historical drama based on the life of the last overtly homosexual monarch of the Middle Ages (1307–1327) whose passion for Piers Gaveston and later Mortimer leads to his overthrow and death, largely with the assistance of his queen, Isabella, who utters the lament:

> For now, my lord, the king regards me not.
> But doats upon the love of Gaveston.
> He claps his cheeks, and hangs about his neck,
> Smiles in his face, and whispers in his ears;
> And when I come he frowns, as who should say,
> "Go whither thou wilt, seeing I have Gaveston."

Hobbinol's love for Colin in Edmund Spenser's (1552–1599) *The Shepheardes Calender* (essay, 1579) certainly has homosexual overtones, even as Colin manifests heterosexual erotic desires later in the poem for Rosalind. Likewise, Marlowe's description of Leander reveals more conspicuous physical beauty than his portrayal of the female Hero in his poem, *Hero and Leander* (1598). And, of course, we must at least note the possibilities of homosexuality in quite a few of Shakespeare's (1564–1616) *Sonnets* (1609), wherein his two loves "of comfort" and "of despair" take on, respectively, a homosexual aspect and a heterosexual one, even as we admit that such an interpretation remains open and controversial. We can be on somewhat surer ground when we turn to the fifty poems and sonnets of Michelangelo (1475–1564). The former represents impassioned lyrics addressed to the beautiful boy, Cecchino Bracci. Michelangelo's sonnets are addressed to a series of young men, Tommaso Cavalieri, Gherardo Perini, and Febo di Poggio. The poet's contemporary, Aretino, by innuendo, kept accusing Michelangelo of homosexuality without extracting admission of such practice from this Renaissance titan, but the implications of homosexuality, whether or not actually practiced, are very persuasive on the strength of what we know of the artist's life. It is necessary to keep in mind that homosexuality remained a mortal sin and a capital crime during this period. Hence overt endorsements of homosexual relationships were most infrequent. While tolerance slowly began to replace severe oppression and persecution in the next two centuries or so, candor and openness were not to be achieved until well into the twentieth century. Whatever the basis of desire in his poetry, Michelangelo obviously as a sculptor elevated the male nude to new heights of beauty and expressive power.

On the Threshold and into the Modern Age

The Victorian Age in England made hypocrisy a fine art and practiced significant cruelties toward persons who deviated from official norms. The most notable example of social repudiation of the odd man out, to be sure, is Oscar Wilde (1854–1900) whose homosexuality exposed publicly at great personal cost led to the assumption of the closet-persona for numerous fellow-homosexuals who followed him. Jeffrey Meyers (*Homosexuality and Literature, 1890–1930,* 1977) seems to be on target when he explores Wilde's best-known novel, *The Picture of Dorian Gray* (1891), as the unresolved conflict between the author's desire for homosexual freedom and his fear of social condemnation—"the impossibility [for Wilde at least] of achieving homosexual pleasure without the inevitable accompaniment of fear, guilt and self-hatred," embodied objectively in the physical decline of the portrait. Similarly, such fate belongs also to the Decadent's Cupid of Aubrey Beardsley, who embarks on his amatory missions not with a bow and quiver but with a gallows and noose. Wilde's sexuality in the instance of Dorian Gray cannot be redeemed even by art; the Eden of the narcissistic self is transformed into the Hell of self-corruption and self-consumption.

Traditionally twentieth-century British novelists have been diffident or defensively reticent about revealing their sexual nature and experience as sources for the content of their art, if that nature is homosexual, suggesting the legacy of fear from the case of Wilde. One of the most interesting examples of concealment turning to posthumous revelation is E. M. Forster (1879–1970), whose novel *Maurice* (finished 1914; published 1971) resembles in some ways a gay version of Lawrence's (1885–1930) *Lady Chatterley's Lover* (novel, 1928), wherein a respectable British businessman, ordinary in the extreme except for his sexual predilection, runs away with Alec Scudder, a gameskeeper on his friend's estate, to live, Forster wants us to think, happily ever after. It is not an especially good novel, but *Maurice* represents what Forster apparently wanted to write about during much of his life and only rarely managed to do, always without thought of publication during his lifetime.

In his once highly esteemed and now unjustly neglected trilogy, *The Root and the Flower* (novels, 1929–1940), L. H. Myers (1881–1944) offers a serious satirical analysis of a homosexual milieu, modeled somewhat on the culture of Bloomsbury's loving friends whose relationships have so deeply intrigued American literary scholars in recent years. Set in sixteenth-century India of the Emperor Akbar, the first installment of the eventual trilogy, *The Near and the Far* (1929), shows the consequences for society of permitting the trivial and frivolous, represented by the Pleasance of the Arts, the "Camp" of Prince Daniyal, to determine manners and morality. Myers sees in homosexuality the primacy of the aesthetic over the moral with Daniyal becoming "the enraptured lover of Beauty," the exponent of artifice (not genuine art) at the expense of nature; he is presented as a practicing sodomite. Myers' equation of homosexuality with frivolity is a common charge brought against this sexual orientation both then and now. As a biographical footnote of some interest about Myers, R.A.D. Grant notes in "Art versus Ideology: The Case of L.H. Myers," (*Cambridge Quarterly* 6 [1974]: 214–240) that "despite a deep-seated attachment to his wife, he [Myers] had run through a quite staggering number of affairs (of extremely varied quality), and had indulged, if infrequently and experimentally, a sexual ambidexterity at odds with the virulent dislike of homosexuality—or at any rate of the homosexual *milieu*— apparent in his books."

Nearer the present, Christopher Isherwood's (1904–1986) *A Single Man* (1964), though the work of a British-born writer who has been an American citizen since 1946, heralds a new dimension in candor about homosexuality in a line of British fiction. This brief novel traces one day in the life of a single man, George, by birth British but now a resident of California, where he teaches college English, as he attempts to deal with loss of his former lover who has died in an automobile accident. Adept over the years in putting on the psychological make-up necessary for playing the "straight" role in society, George deals honestly with himself and his sexuality during this day in his life. Isherwood achieves compassionate, but not sentimental, universality here, without evading the particularity of George as a homosexual and the special texture of his life. George's homosexuality is simple fact rather than a cross to bear.

Francis King (1923–   ) has written a compelling British novel about unreciprocated homosexual passion in *A Domestic Animal* (1970). Dick Thompson, a successful, middle-aged author, suffers the frustration of falling in love with his boarder, an unremittingly heterosexual Italian philosopher who lodges in his house during a year's residency at an English university. Thompson will not let Antonio Valli, his boarder, be deceived about the nature of his feelings; as King writes: "It was essential, therefore, to maintain the pretence that, though in my friendship there was something eccentric—the result of my loneliness, my singleness, my childlessness—there was in it nothing abnormal. I should have allowed him to maintain that pretence. But I could not do so."

King's matter-of-factness about Thompson's homosexuality contrasts with Thomas Mann's (1875–1955) portrayal of homosexuality as a bizarre vice in *Der Tod in Venedig* (*Death in Venice,* novelle, 1912) in which a somewhat similar unreciprocal relationship exists between a northern European and the sensuousness of the southern European world, the Apollonian Gustav Aschenbach succumbing to the charms of the young Tadzio, the Dionysian recipient of love, the embodiment not of moral excellence but of innocence and beauty, who nevertheless is Polish by birth, though in the novelle Tadzio is inextricably bound to an Italian mystique. In the years between 1912 and 1970, the distance separating Mann and King, the taboo of homosexuality ceased to be the guilty secret with the metaphoric and symbolic significance it could assume in *The Picture of Dorian Gray* or *Death in Venice*.

Twentieth-century French literature affords especially rich examples of homosexuality in the modern world, but for reasons of economy only three large figures in French prose fiction of the century can be evoked: André Gide (1869–1951), Marcel Proust (1971–1922), and Jean Genet (1910–1986). Gide has become synonymous with the literature of homosexuality. After considerable hints but also evasiveness about his sexual nature in earlier works, Gide presented his homosexuality definitively in *Corydon* (dialogues about homosexuality, 1924), *Si le grain ne meurt* (*If It Die,* autobiographical essays, 1926), and in his most forthright homosexual novel, *Les Faux-monnayeurs* (*The Counterfeiters,* 1925). Of earlier works, so-called *récits,* the most revealing antecedent is probably *L'immoraliste* (*The Immoralist,* 1902) with its portrayal of the young husband, Michel, and his attraction to Arab boys, most notably the seductive Moktir, whom he prefers to his wife, Marceline. Like Edouard, the protagonist of *The Counterfeiters,* Gide tries to overcome the hypocrisies and lies whereby so many people pass through their lives superficially, including sexual "counterfeiters." In this novel, Edouard's mother expresses preference for her son to continue a same-sex relationship with Olivier rather than attempt what would be a disastrous marriage with Laura. Thus Edouard does not duplicate the mistake or generate the duplicity of Michel or Gide himself.

It is hard to forget but reasonably easy to refute the observation of a female character in Raymond Chandler's *The Big Sleep* (novel, 1939) about Marcel Proust: "A French writer, a connoisseur of degenerates." In Proust's retrieval of the past, *A la recherche du temps perdu* (*Remembrance of Things Past,* 1913–1927), are the prefigurations for a renewed understanding of art and eros and the many levels of identity that we are only now comprehending. The conundrum that constitutes romantic love, notwithstanding sexual orientation, has never been more fully explored in all its permutations than in Proust. Yet the novelist makes it clear that art and theory may be one thing, and human nature—especially human flesh—quite another; nevertheless, the Proustian style and intelligence shed light on everyone—on Marcel and Albertine as well as on the Baron de Charlus. The intricacy of love and politics cannot be understood, according to Proust, without using homosexuality as a means of analysis. If Gide is to be believed, Proust expressed regret that he exposed the "bad" side of homosexuality without adequately showing the positive side. The mind of the moralist, informed by Judeo-Christian values, colors the *recherche* and finds in love and sexuality a species of enslavement and cruelty that may be attributable to the way homosexuality was seen in the cultural context of Proust's era, as J. E. Rivers (*Proust and the Art of Love,* 1980) persuasively argues.

Jean Genet might have been the creation of Jean-Paul Sartre, if human biology had not anticipated the philosopher; Genet has appropriately been canonized as the perfect avatar of existentialism in Sartre's *Saint Genet: Comédien et martyr* (*Saint Genet: Actor and Martyr,* essay, 1952). Genet's own heroes are the Parisian homosexuals and criminals of his prison realities and fantasies, those people like himself whose vices become, in his moral scale, the greatest virtues—theft, homosexuality, and treason. Genet's homosexuality may have originally been situational, the result of early reformatory life in a monosexual environment,

shown in *Miracle de la rose* (*Miracle of the Rose,* novel, 1946). To some degree
all of Genet's other books duplicate this one; he was a writer of repetition without
much skill at characterization, which is perhaps a corollary to the narcissistic
sexuality he celebrated, although Genet offered a curiously wide-ranging portrayal of homosexuality in a spectrum from masculine to feminine despite the
fact that his "females" can never actually become women. The chief form of
sexuality that Genet immortalized is finally masturbation, inspired by homosexual
fantasy—a not unimportant theme for understanding the literature of homosexuality—as in his novel, *Querelle de Brest* (1947; rev. ed., 1953; trans. *Querelle
of Brest,* 1966), where Seblon fantasizes onanistically about the evil sailor,
Querelle.

Some Relevant Poets

To leave prose fiction for awhile, two quite opposite approaches to the erotic
relations between males inform some significant nineteenth-century poetic examples with the "Calamus" section of the *Leaves of Grass* (first appearance,
1855) by the American Walt Whitman (1819–1892) and the poetry of the French
lovers, Arthur Rimbaud (1854–1891) and Paul Verlaine (1844–1896). Whitman
urges celebration of the need of comrades in great public poems of American
democracy predicated on his own secret of nights and days that strongly imply
a homoerotic basis. To be sure, Whitman denied any such inspiration from
homosexuality in his famous letter to John Addington Symonds, who had per-
ceptively noted the phallic implications of the calamus plant interpreted as "the
token of comrades," the symbol of male-male love, along "paths untrodden."
With the increased recognition of the testimony found in Whitman's diaries, the
homosexual content of *Leaves of Grass* seems often inescapable.

A far more private relationship characterizes the poetry of homosexuality in
the case of Rimbaud and Verlaine, biographically remembered for their sado-
masochistic behaviour that led, perhaps inexorably, to Verlaine's shooting of
his lover, Rimbaud, the boy who had replaced his wife in a new inverted
"marriage," a "drunken boat," as it were, rather than the sanctified order of
holy matrimony. Paul Schmidt, in an important essay, "Visions of Violence:
Rimbaud and Verlaine" (*Homosexualities and French Literature: Cultural Con-
texts/Critical Texts,* eds. G. Stambolian and E. Marks, 1979, 228–242), sees
homosexuality as

a radical denial of all human order, in that it denies kinship and its rules and obligations.
By denying generation, homosexuality denies time, and fruition in time; and it rejects
them in the name of the instant, the instantaneous in perception and experience. . . . It is
thus one with states of trance, of contact with the extraordinary. From this point of view,
homosexuality may well be seen not as a psychological aberration but as a cultural
possibility—a state of permanent quest for vision.

Verlaine's *Parallèlement* (*Parallelly,* 1889) and *Amour* (*Love,* 1888) yield pro-
vocative hints in confirmation of Schmidt's interpretation.

One of the first twentieth-century poets to acknowledge openly his homosexuality was Constantine Cavafy (1863–1933), whose Greek ancestry and sexual proclivities link the world of modern Alexandria to ancient, mythic Hellenism—the veneration of the body, usually male, of and in history. His principal collection written in Greek, *Ta poiēmata (Poems,* 1935, though a good edition of this work did not appear until 1963), connects the homoerotic with the historical, since memory informs the pleasures of both and the art of poetry can thereby give permanence to evanescence as in "Their Beginning":

> The fulfillment of their deviate, sensual delight
> is done. They rose from the mattress,
> and they dress hurriedly without speaking.
> They leave the house separately, furtively; and as
> they walk somewhat uneasily on the street, it seems
> as if they suspect that something about them betrays
> into what kind of bed they fell a little while back.
>
> But how the life of the artist has gained.
> Tomorrow, the next day, years later, the vigorous verses
> will be composed that had their beginning here.

In contrast to Cavafy, W. H. Auden (1907–1973), who admired the Alexandrian civil servant/poet, is far more oblique on sexual matters, as has been characteristic of a large number of distinguished American and British poets of the twentieth century who are reputed to be gay. By means of a declension from Cavafy through Auden to some selected lines by the contemporary American poet, James Merrill (1926–), a latter-day implicit defense of homosexuality through commemoration of the single life and childlessness as conducive to the production of art rather than biological bodies may be made. In *Mirabell: Books of Number* (1978), James Merrill communicates through a Ouija board with the late poet, Auden, who at one point offers the following pronouncement:

> LOVE OF ONE MAN FOR ANOTHER OR LOVE BETWEEN WOMEN
> IS A NEW DEVELOPMENT OF THE PAST 4000 YEARS
> ENCOURAGING SUCH MIND VALUES AS PRODUCE THE BLOSSOMS
> OF POETRY & MUSIC.

These lines attributed to Auden might be used retrospectively as a gloss on some of the more explicitly gay poems in Merrill's earlier Pulitzer Prize-winning collection, *Divine Comedies* (1976).

A Far Eastern Voice of Much Western Acclaim: Mishima

Doubtlessly overrated when compared to other Japanese novelists of the twentieth century like Kawabata, Tanizaki, or Abe Kōbō, Mishima Yukio (1925–1970), with his large output of fiction, proved to be the Japanese writer of greatest fame in the West during the post-World War II years, and he is the Oriental writer who has manifested themes of homosexuality most consistently in his fiction. While Japan has a long history of acceptance of homosexuality, traceable to the tradition of the samurai, warrior-lovers similar to those of ancient Greece, Mishima does not avail himself of this relaxed attitude toward homosexuality, typical of Japan, in his early autobiographical novel, *Kamen no kokuhaku (Confessions of a Mask,* 1949). In this novel his young protagonist, upon discovering his own homosexuality, masquerades as a counterfeit heterosexual in a manner much more characteristic of homosexuality in the United States than of the Orient. Obsessed by pictures of St. Sebastian (as was Mishima), the first-person narrator finds himself a martyr to his own sexuality, re-inventing his existence and his sense of self. From the pressure of solitary uniqueness experienced by the homosexual narrator of *Confessions of a Mask,* Mishima moved to the brotherhood of a homosexual milieu in *Kinjiki (Forbidden Colors,* 1951–1953). The protagonist leads a double life as a married man and as a homosexual, and he finds himself entangled in the vines of homosexuality that Mishima calls, in a brilliant conceit, a ''jungle of sentiment.''

Recent American Gay Literature

The range of gay experiences and attitudes shown in recent American prose fiction militates against any claim that this novel or that novel is definitive of homosexuality in the United States. Some of the most audacious, even outrageous, writing on gay themes has been produced by John Rechy (1935–) whose singular experience illuminates the narcissistic world of the male hustler, beginning with his first novel, *City of Night* (1963) and extending through eight subsequent volumes, principally works of fiction. In *The Sexual Outlaw* (1977), which is nonfiction, Rechy takes an adversarial stance against the straight world, arguing that the promiscuous homosexual male is a sexual and political revolutionary. The author seeks to turn the rage that formerly gays directed against themselves toward their oppressors instead. His recent novel, *Bodies and Souls* (1983), moves away from the primary area of homosexuality to other concerns of ''lost angels'' in the city of Los Angeles, yet the world for which Rechy is famous remains a part of the whole. This novel may be Rechy's bid to gain mainstream status.

The sexual politics of homosexuality likewise figures prominently in Daniel Curzon's (1937–) first novel, *Something You Do in the Dark* (1971), where police entrapment intensifies the self-hatred of the homosexual victims even as it generates new-found militancy on their part in defense of their sexual identity. In *Among the Carnivores* (1978) positive gay consciousness becomes more evident in Curzon's work. Here an openly gay teacher combats with alternate bitterness and humor conflicts with reactionary administrators, closeted colleagues, and homophobic citizen groups.

Stylistically one of the more recondite authors on homosexuality is Edmund White whose first novel, *Forgetting Elena* (1973), won the plaudits of Vladimir Nabokov, and whose more recent *Nocturnes for the King of Naples* (1978) has its own loyal admirers. In the latter White claims that he has done something very religious or very sacrilegious in writing a gay novel in which one of the lovers is God. Not writing realist fiction in these two books, White seems to be a difficult and complex novelist whose highly developed mastery of ambiguity invites comparison with Henry James. In *Forgetting Elena* he juxtaposes something like the gay environment of Fire Island and the hierarchy of medieval Japan as revealed in the Lady Murasaki's eleventh-century masterpiece, *Genji monogatari* (*The Tale of Genji*, novel) exploring thereby the hidden self, as prince and slave, as metaphor of homosexuality, controlled by stricter codes of behavior and a sense of hierarchy than are often supposed. White has turned from these rather mannerist novels to more accessible fiction in *A Boy's Own Story* (1982), an almost classic development novel, now relative to homosexuality, presented in such a way as to render the experience universal for readership irrespective of sexual orientation. In the nameless protagonist's rites of passage comes graduation into the culture at large.

Andrew Holleran's poignant and witty *Dancer from the Dance* (1978) represents an unusual quasi-novel of ideas about a subgroup of homosexuals, the "queens," either deeply effeminate or, less popularly understood, very macho, all primarily a visual people, sick with love in their frenzied dance, who live (and die) for beauty rather than for happiness. Gays here are the last romantics with a kind of spiritual or ritualistic quest similar to the religious, which is not to say Christian, dimension that Edmund White and John Rechy also intimate in quite different styles. Holleran's novel resembles, to some extent, a "gay" *Great Gatsby* (1925 novel by F. Scott Fitzgerald) with his character Malone acting as another latter-day Platonist now in the context of homosexuality.

Circumstances in the United States have not changed greatly since Roger Austen concluded in his pioneering study of the homosexual novel in America, *Playing the Game* (1977) that Americans remain "homophobic to a degree that they are no longer anti-Semitic or racist." Such prejudice may account for the lack of significant mainstream literary works on homosexuality even at a time when the homosexual is much more visible and respectable in American life than ever before. Many years ago Kay Boyle described homosexuality as engrossing as bee-raising and as monotonous to the outsider; that popular assumption is currently being challenged in the commercial success of something like Harvey Firestein's dramatic work, *Torch Song Trilogy* (1981). That recent gay liberation has changed the self-image and social acceptance of homosexuality should have artistic reverberations of some magnitude. The psychiatric, medical categorizing of homosexuality with all its negative associations has recently fallen; what once was thought to be criminal has become a matter of life style, a position that may have a damaging and trivializing effect on the art of homosexuality. Gay men in their artistic endeavors celebrate their special and privileged viewpoint of society and their sexuality in it. Michel Foucault (*The History of Sexuality: An Introduction*, 1978) has shown how in ancient civil or canonical codes the "sodomite had been a temporary aberration" and how in the nineteenth century "the homosexual was now a species." So he remains, speaking on his own behalf without former legal and medical disqualifications. The antecedents and precedents for an honest portrayal of homosexuality exist in history, and artists will bear witness to them in the future, as they have in the past, but perhaps to humane and cultural ends hitherto undreamed of.

See also: Lesbianism, Sex (Heterosexual, Erotic).

Selected Bibliography

Boswell, John. *Christianity, Social Tolerance and Homosexuality: Gay People in Western Europe from the Beginnings of the Christian Era to the Fourteenth Century.* Chicago: University of Chicago Press, 1980.

Dover, K. J. *Greek Homosexuality.* Cambridge, Mass.: Harvard University Press, 1978.

Norton, Rictor, *The Homosexual Literary Tradition: An Interpretation.* New York: Revisionist Press, 1974.

Sedgwick, Eve K. *Between Men: English Literature and Male Homosexual Desire.* New York: Columbia University Press, 1985.

EDWARD T. JONES

HORROR

The Oxford English Dictionary defines "horror" as "a painful emotion compounded of loathing and fear; a shuddering with terror and repugnance; strong aversion mingled with dread; the feeling excited by something shocking or frightful." The terms "horror" and "terror" may be so close together in meaning and connotation that they are often used interchangeably by authors and critics. In *A Philosophical Enquiry into the Origin of Our Ideas of the Sublime and Beautiful* (1757), for example, eighteenth-century aesthetician Edmund Burke suggests that both terror and horror may produce the sublime. In part 1, section 6, Burke says that the "ideas of *pain, sickness,* and *death* fill the mind with strong emotions of horror," while in section 2, part 1, he states that "an apprehension of pain or death" causes fear or terror. Burke goes on to say that because these passions "concern self-preservation" and "turn chiefly on *pain* and *danger* . . . [they] are the most powerful of all passions"; they rob "the mind of all its powers of acting and reasoning." Horror and terror, then, are major sources of the sublime, provided they do not "press too nearly." They are "delightful" when they do not immediately affect the reader.

Ann Radcliffe, on the other hand, who has been called the "Shakespeare of romance writers," makes a clear distinction between the two terms in an article first published in *The New Monthly Magazine* in 1826:

Terror and horror are so far opposite, that the first [terror] expands the soul, and awakens the faculties to a high degree of life; the other [horror] contracts, freezes, and nearly annihilates them. I apprehend that neither Shakespeare nor Milton by their fictions, nor Mr. Burke by his reasoning, anywhere looked to positive horror as a source of the sublime, though they all agree that terror is a very high one.

For a more complete discussion of terror, see the entry on it in this *Dictionary*. Fear of an extraordinary intensity is a characteristic of both terror and horror, and terror often turns to horror. Generally, however, horror is produced by real rather than imagined dangers and is accompanied by less suspense.

Horror has fascinated writers for centuries. It appears in numerous and diverse works where it is put to a variety of uses and creates effects that are often very complex. Horror may be an almost incidental inclusion in some works, while it functions as a dominant theme and principal subject in others. Basically, works that capitalize on horror fall into three categories:

1. Works where horror is treated as a subject itself—the horrors of which man is capable, for example;

2. Works where horror is used to illustrate some other thematic point—where it is functional, but not itself the central subject;

3. Works where horror is used for sensational effects alone.

The origins of horror in literature go back very far, and horror has made an appearance of some sort in every literary age. It was particularly in vogue in the second half of the eighteenth century where it was especially prominent in the German *Ritter-Räuber* and *Schauerromane,* the English Graveyard poems, and the English Gothic novel. American popular fiction and film of the last thirty years reflect a renewed public interest in horror.

The Middle Ages

The horrors that the author of the epic poem *Beowulf* (c. eighth cent.) describes thematically reflect the violence and cruelty of Anglo-Saxon society. To satisfy his "lust for evil," for instance, Grendel smashes thirty men in their beds and runs out of the mead hall with their bodies, "blood dripping behind him." To a twentieth-century reader, the wars described in the interpolated tales are often as senseless and just as violent.

Furthermore, Grendel's mother, "the female horror," becomes a metaphor for what revenge could and did become in that violent society—a monster. In fact, the language the author uses to describe Beowulf's underwater fight echoes that which he uses in the interpolated tale of Finn and Hnaf, which the court poet sings as they celebrate Beowulf's victory over Grendel. After the Danes and the Frisians agree upon a "truce," the poet sings, a funeral pyre was prepared. Then Hnaf's body was thrown into the fire with the other dead warriors, "Wounds split and burst, skulls / Melted, blood came bubbling down, / And the greedy fire-demons drank flesh and bones / From the dead of both sides, until nothing was left." The gory details underscore the savage horror of the story of the Frisians' treachery and the Danes's revenge. The day after Beowulf hears that story, to avenge Aeschere's violent murder, he dives into the hellish lake, its water "bloody and bubbling." He finally kills Grendel's mother by striking her with the giant sword with all his strength. Then in another horrifying scene, which takes place in the present rather than the past, though, he "Caught her in the neck and cut it through, / Broke bones and all. Her body fell / To the floor, lifeless, the sword was wet / With her blood, and Beowulf rejoiced at the sight.'' Finally, after the Geatish hero cuts Grendel's head off, the sword (like the dead Danish and Frisian warriors' bodies in the fire) ''Melted, blood-soaked, dripping down / Like water, disappearing like ice.''

The Renaissance

Despite Ann Radcliffe's claims that William Shakespeare and John Milton avoided horror, it is present in both authors' works. Shakespeare's *Titus Andronicus* (c. 1594) (one of his lesser-known plays), for example, is filled with sensational, horrifying visual and verbal effects that thrilled Renaissance viewers. However, like the author of *Beowulf,* Shakespeare also uses the theme of horror to comment on the violence inherent both in the Romans and in the supposed barbarians, the Goths. As a result of vengeance, civilization breaks down, and the world of *Titus* is one in which mothers ultimately devour their own sons.

The play opens with the barbaric Roman sacrifice of one of Tamara's sons. His limbs are cut off and his entrails ''feed the sacrificing fire.'' The most revulsive visual moment of the play, however, occurs when Lavinia, who has just been raped, enters with her hands cut off and her tongue cut out. Marcus Andronicus cries out:

> ... Why dost not speak to me?—
> Alas, a crimson river of warm blood,
> Like to a bubbling fountain stirr'd with wind,
> Doth rise and fall between thy rosed lips,
> Coming and going with thy honeyed breath.
> But, sure, some Tereus hath deflower'd thee,
> And, lest thou shouldst detect him, cut thy tongue.

These horrors are followed by more. Titus Andronicus cuts off his own hand as ransom to free his sons; he receives instead his own hand back with the heads of his two sons. Despite all the horrors he has suffered, Titus' revenge is equally revolting. He kills Chiron and Demetrius (Lavinia's rapists), drains their blood, grinds their bones to dust, makes a paste with the blood, and bakes them in a pie. Dressed as a cook, Titus serves the pie to Tamara, and watches the ''ravenous tiger'' devour her own sons.

French Baroque poet Agrippa d'Aubigné uses the theme of horror in *Les tragiques* (1616) in order to show truth and to emotionally affect his readers so that they would empathize with Protestant suffering in the Wars of Religion. Thus, he repeatedly describes macabre horrors, like the deaths of the martyrs in *Les feux* (book 4), to illustrate the cruelty of Protestant persecutors and the beauty and suffering of the martyrs.

Les fers (book 5) presents a historical panorama of religious wars, but the central section of the book and of the entire poem is the St. Bartholomew's Day Massacre. The horrors described illustrate d'Aubigné's message: the tyranny of the rulers and the patience of the faithful who suffer and die with serenity. Man, he states, is no longer a man–he has reverted to an animal state.

Like d'Aubigné, John Milton uses horror in his epic *Paradise Lost* (1667) to reinforce a religious theme—in Milton's case, though, to justify the ways of God to man. Horror reinforces the monumental consequences of both Satan's and man's falls. Milton's epic, however, ends with hope for man, rather than despair. Horrors are reserved for Satan, Sin, and Death, who Milton predicts will ultimately be conquered.

In book 4 "Horror and doubt distract" Satan's "troubled thoughts" and stir the hell within him, despite his earlier boast to the fallen angels that he could make a heaven of hell:

> Me miserable! which way shall I fly
> Infinite wrath and infinite despair?
> Which way I fly is Hell; myself am Hell;
> And, in the lowest deep, a lower deep
> Still threatening to devour me opens wide,
> To which the Hell I suffer seems a Heaven.

His prediction comes to pass. After he succeeds in tempting man, he and his followers suffer additional horrors when in book 10 they are transformed into serpents: "They saw, but other sight instead—a crowd / Of ugly serpents; Horror on them fell, / And horrid sympathy, for what they saw / They felt themselves now changing."

Similarly, after the fall horrible consequences unfold upon Adam and Eve and upon mankind. When Adam first learns in book 9 that Eve has eaten the forbidden fruit, "horror chill" runs through his veins. Eve's disobedience and his realization that because he cannot live without her, he too will disobey God are so dreadful to Adam that he responds physically as well as emotionally. More horrid, though, is Death's sadistic reaction to Sin's suggestion in book 10 that they join Satan on Earth:

> So saying, with delight he snuffed the smell
> Of mortal change on Earth. As when a flock
> Of ravenous fowl, though many a league remote,
> Against the day of battle to a field
> Where armies lie encamped come flying, lured
> With scent of living carcasses designed
> For death the following day in bloody fight:
> So scented the grim Feature and upturned
> His nostril wide into the murky air,
> Sagacious of his quarry from so far.

As Adam watches Sin and Death begin their destruction on Earth, he is both terrified and horrified. Fearing death and blaming himself for bringing it to all mankind, Adam cries out: "O Conscience, into what abyss of fears / And horrors hast thou driven me; out of which / I find no way, from deep to deeper plunged!"

Adam's terror and horror intensify when Michael shows him the first murder: "But have I now seen Death? Is this the way / I must return to native dust? O sight / Of terror, foul and ugly to behold, / Horrid to think, how horrible to feel!''

The Eighteenth Century

Although Horace Walpole's *The Castle of Otranto* (1764) is the progenitor of the Gothic novel of terror and horror, signs of English interest in horror are earlier evident in the Graveyard school of poetry. In *The Grave* (1743), for example, to promote virtue and morality, Robert Blair exploits horrifying effects that have since become associated with later Gothic fiction. By emphasizing the repulsive imagery associated with the decaying process, Blair illustrates the vanity of human life—for all men, "Proud Royalty" and the "dungeon slave," will ultimately rot alike. He begins by stating his purpose: "To paint the gloomy horrors of the tomb" where all men will eventually meet:

> . . . The sickly taper
> By glimmering through thy [the grave] low-browed misty vaults
> (Furred round with mouldy damps and ropy slime)
> Lets fall a supernumerary horror,
> And only serves to make thy night more irksome.

Later he imagines a formerly proud "beauty" in her grave, now food for worms: "with thy head low laid; / Whilst, surfeited upon thy damask cheek, / The high-fed worm, in lazy volumes rolled, / Riots unscared. For this was all thy caution?''

Although in his preface to the first edition of *Otranto,* Walpole says that "terror" was the author's "principal engine," horror (i.e., real rather than imaginary dangers) predominates in the novel. Walpole, however, unlike earlier writers, uses horror primarily to entertain his readers, rather than to illustrate a thematic point. The story begins and ends with the violent and shocking deaths of Manfred's children. Conrad is "dashed to pieces, and almost buried under an enormous helmet, an hundred times more large than any casque ever made for human being.'' And later Manfred stabs his innocent daughter, Matilda, in the bosom, jealously mistaking her for Isabella, the young woman for whom he lusts. Throughout the novella there are many other horrifying scenes. Frederic's blood freezes "in his veins,'' for example, when he sees the "fleshless jaws and empty sockets of a skeleton, wrapt in a hermit's cowl.''

Influenced by *Otranto,* a host of English and German romance writers began to exploit horrors to satisfy the growing popular taste for sensationalism. In 1795, directly influenced by the German romances, Matthew G. Lewis published *The Monk* (parts of which are borrowed from and translated from German stories). It became the most popular novel of a class of fiction in which horror, violence, and lust prevail—the *Schauerromane*. Lewis regales the reader with horror on almost every page of the second two-thirds of the novel. But many of the macabre scenes are purely gratuitous—included simply to thrill the reader—like Don Raymond's tale of the bleeding nun.

The horrors involved with the Agnes and Ambrosio plots are more serious, however; they illustrate the evils of monastic life and warn against the sins of pride and lustful self-gratification. Lorenzo's discovery of his half-naked sister, clutching her dead baby in the convent dungeon, is one of the most shocking scenes in the novel. Agnes' narration produces yet more revulsion. In vivid detail she describes her confinement with a worm-covered nun. Insects, toads, and lizards crawled over Agnes' body; but worse than that, she says, was awakening to find "my fingers ringed with the long worms which bred in the corrupted flesh of my infant."

The proud, evil Ambrosio's crimes are, however, the most horrifying parts of the novel. His lust, aroused by the demonic agent Matilda, drives him to kill his mother Elvira and to rape and murder his sister Antonia. The rape, committed "by the side of three putrid half-corrupted bodies," is a dreadful combination of violence, lust, and sadism. Antonia's resistance and her terror of the wicked monk only intensify his desire:

He clasped her to his bosom almost lifeless with terror, and faint with struggling. He stifled her cries with kisses, treated her with the rudeness of an unprincipled barbarian, proceeded from freedom to freedom, and, in the violence of his lustful delirium, wounded and bruised her tender limbs. Heedless of her tears, cries and entreaties, he gradually made himself master of her person, and desisted not from his prey, till he had accomplished his crime and the dishonor of Antonia.

Besides inflicting horrors, Ambrosio also suffers them. Each crime he commits is followed by horrors of remorse; but, later as a prisoner of the Inquisition, he is threatened with physical rather than mental torture. This leads him finally to make a compact with the devil—he escapes from the Inquisition only to be thrown headlong from a precipice. There, covered with insects who feed on him and tormented with a burning thirst, Ambrosio suffers "tortures the most exquisite and insupportable. The eagles of the rock tore his flesh piecemeal, and dug out his eye-balls with their crooked beaks." He languishes that way for six days, fearing to die because of the worse torments in store for him in hell.

Despite Ann Radcliffe's claim that terror, rather than horror was the guiding principle of her art, horrors do find their way into her last novel, *The Italian* (1797). Although the villainous monk Schedoni resembles his predecessor Ambrosio in several ways, Radcliffe's villain is even more horrifying because he (like Milton's Satan) is self-tempted, not deceived as Ambrosio is; and he too falls because of his excessive pride. Radcliffe does not rely as heavily on sensational effects as Lewis to produce horror; but from her first description of Schedoni, there is "something terrible in its [his figure's] air; something akin to super-human"; while his cowl gives "an effect to his large melancholy eye, which approached to horror." But he becomes more horrifying because he exhibits some very human characteristics. He inflicts more pain on himself than he does on others; and through his character, Radcliffe illustrates the complex nature of evil. Like Ambrosio, Schedoni suffers horrors of remorse from his own evil nature, and he too becomes a prisoner of the Inquisition. But, although Radcliff does not describe Schedoni's death as gruesomely as Lewis describes Ambrosio's, the former's unrepentant evil is shocking because he is a more believable character. Triumphant that he has poisoned his enemy and himself, Schedoni utters a demonic sound that horrifies everyone in the room. The sound is "so strange and horrible, so convulsed, yet so loud, so exulting, yet so unlike any human voice," that, "in an agony of horror," Vivaldi asks for medicine to relieve him from what he has witnessed.

The Nineteenth Century

In the first two decades of the nineteenth century, the popularity of the Gothic novel declined. The Gothic villain, however, lived on and continued to evolve psychologically, and writers began to focus on the thematic implications of mental horrors. The Byronic hero was one of the many various forms in which the Gothic villain reappeared. The guilt-ridden Manfred in Byron's play of that name (1817), a character "of deeds good and ill, extreme in both" is tormented by mental horrors. Unlike Ambrosio, who is manipulated by the devil and his agents, Manfred controls and defies evil spirits. None of their tortures, he says, can equal the horrors he suffers from his own guilt. Like Milton's Satan, he carries hell within him:

> What I have done is done; I bear within
> A torture which could nothing gain from thine:
> The mind which is immortal makes itself
> Requital for its good or evil thoughts,
> Is its own origin of ill and end,
> And its own place and time—

Aspects of the Gothic villain also reappear in the character of the "horrible" monster in Mary Shelley's novel *Frankenstein* (1818). Through the innocent monster's suffering, Shelley illustrates man's innate hostility to the ugly or deformed. Immediately after he gives life to the monster, for example, Victor Frankenstein shrinks from his creation: "the beauty of the dream vanished, and breathless horror and disgust filled my heart." Frankenstein's early rejection of the monster, the scientist's detestation and contempt for his creation, and the cruelty the monster faces wherever he goes transform the innocent creature into a vengeful demon. In his revenge, though, the monster becomes the slave rather than the master of his evil behavior. Hence, Frankenstein's description of his dead bride evokes aversion, both for the monster's murderous deed and for the forces that drove him to do the deed: "The shutters had been thrown back, and with a sensation of horror not to be described, I saw at the open window a figure the most hideous and abhorred. A grin was on the face of the monster; he seemed to jeer, as with his fiendish finger he pointed toward the corpse of my wife."

Like Byron and Mary Shelley, Edgar Allan Poe, the master of nineteenth-century American horror fiction, explores the psychological effects of horror. "The Pit and the Pendulum" (1842) is an excellent example of the effects of one horrifying event after another on the mind of the sufferer. Too much horror, Poe suggests, will eventually result in despair. The narrator, who is imprisoned by the Inquisition, doesn't merely refer to the "horrors of his torture"—he describes them step by step so that the reader shares the horrors with him. First, he explores his dungeon in the "blackness of eternal night," and he is horrified when the faint gleam of light illuminates the pit that he barely escaped. He contemplates suicide in the pit, but he resists when he thinks of what he has "read of these pits—that the *sudden* extinction of life formed no part of their most horrible plan." His horror intensifies when he discovers that he is strapped down and that the pendulum above is slowly descending upon him. His thirst from the highly seasoned food and the rats that come up from the pit also add to the horrifying effect. However, when the narrator frees himself from the pendulum, he faces the worst shock of all. The hot glowing metal walls begin to close in on him, forcing him toward the pit: "Yet, for a wild moment, did my spirit refuse to comprehend the meaning of what I saw. At length it forced—it wrestled its way into my soul—it burned itself in upon my shuddering reason.—Oh! for a voice to speak!—oh! horror!—oh! any horror but this!" But just as the narrator stops struggling and despairs because he feels that he totters "upon the brink," he is miraculously saved by General LaSalle, who has overthrown the Inquisition.

Although Charles Dickens cannot be termed a "horror novelist," motifs of terror and horror permeate his works. The interpolated tales in his first, primarily comic novel, *Pickwick Papers* (1836–1837), for example, are Gothic stories in which terror and horror are major themes. Most notable are "The Convict's Return" and "The Old Man's Tale About the Queer Client." They function primarily to entertain the reader as earlier Gothic fiction did. In Dickens' novella *A Christmas Carol* (1843), horror becomes his "principal engine." Like Poe, Dickens deals with the effects of horror on the psyche; but Dickens' theme emphasizes the need for suffering for the salvation of the soul, rather than the body. Unlike the protagonist of "The Pit and the Pendulum," whose life is saved only after he utters "a final scream of despair," Dickens' protagonist reforms morally as a result of his dreadful experience. Scrooge is first horrified by the appearance of Marley's Ghost who removes the bandage from his head and allows his lower jaw to drop to his breast, and later by the monster children, "Ignorance and Want." But his earliest reactions are more akin to terror than horror.

Scrooge's most horrifying experiences are produced by the last Spirit, reminiscent of Milton's Death: "shrouded in a deep black garment, which concealed its head, its face, its form, and left nothing of it visible save one outstretched hand." The Spirit's "Unseen Eyes" cause Scrooge to shudder. But the sight of the woman haggling with the buyer over the personal effects of a corpse (who

Scrooge doesn't yet realize is himself) fills him with "a detestation and disgust, which could hardly have been greater, though they had been obscene demons, marketing the corpse itself." When the Spirit takes Scrooge to the churchyard and points to a neglected grave bearing his name, he is again horrified; but his horrors ultimately lead to a happy end—his repentance.

French short-story writer Villiers de l'Isle-Adam uses horror in "Claire Lenoir" (1867) to illustrate his theme of the disparity between appearance and reality and to suggest that man's rationality is merely a façade. After the narrator, Bonhomet, witnesses several horrifying scenes, climaxed by a vision through the dead Claire Lenoir's eyes, he comes to believe that one's personality lives on after death. The "unimaginable horror" of seeing a monstrous black cannibal (whose face resembles Claire's dead husband Césaire) holding the bloody head of her lover convinces Bonhomet that Césaire learned of his wife's infidelity after his death, and that he was able to influence her, by force of suggestion, from the grave. The narrator concludes that "any microscope is enough to prove that our senses deceive us and that we *can't see things as they are.* . . . But, if we were once to consider it [nature] under its veritable aspect, where everything devours everything, it is probable that we would shiver more with horror than with enthusiasm."

Robert Louis Stevenson's use of horror in *Dr. Jekyll and Mr. Hyde* (novel 1886) is somewhat reminiscent of Mary Shelley's. Like Frankenstein's giving life to the monster, Jekyll's ability to change into Hyde (and vice versa) through drinking a chemical potion is shocking both to the reader and to the character who witnesses the transformation. Stevenson uses Jekyll's alter ego to illustrate his theme of the dual nature of the personality—evil coexists with good; and because evil becomes stronger than good, he suggests that the former is more innate to man. Lanyon, whose "life is shaken to the roots" and who dies soon after he sees Hyde turn into Jekyll, cannot think about what he saw "without a start of horror." But more horrible than the transformation and more horrible even than the evil monster Edward Hyde himself (a being whose "every act and thought centered on self") is his creator, the reputable, apparently "virtuous" Dr. Jekyll. That he created his alter ego because he was tired of being ashamed of satisfying his "impatient gayety of disposition" was shocking to the Victorian reader; but even more shocking is that Jekyll refers to Hyde—who *is* Jekyll—as a separate being, a being who gratifies and stimulates his "lust of evil."

To a lesser extent than Scrooge, Jekyll undergoes a kind of repentance, but only after Hyde begins to take over and Jekyll is unable to reproduce the potion. Jekyll writes that he has become horrified of being Hyde not only because he fears the gallows, but because he fears Hyde's evil nature. Before he dies Jekyll becomes "a creature eaten up and emptied by fever, languidly weak both in body and mind, and solely occupied by one thought: the horror of my other self." Stevenson's horror story challenged his Victorian reader's more optimistic views of human nature.

The most horrifying aspect of Bram Stoker's novel *Dracula* (1897) is that his criminal-monster seeks eternal life by feeding on blood of the innocent, turning them into evil vampires (Un-dead) like him, and robbing them of their souls. His theme is similar to Milton's; good ironically nourishes evil. Like Lewis' Ambrosio, perverse sexuality is also a part of Dracula's evil. Besides Dracula, the only other vampires in the novel are women; for, mesmerized by him, they become willing participants in his "rapes." Dracula's physical lust is merely a means to an end; his more horrifying lust is for eternal life and awesome power.

Two of Stoker's most frightening scenes involve Dracula's two women victims, Lucy Westerna and Mina Harker. The men who love Lucy, in fact, shudder "with horror" at the sight of her arisen from the grave, her lips "crimson with fresh blood," which "had trickled over her chin and stained the purity of her lawn death-robe." Clutching a child to her breast and "growling over it as a dog growls over a bone," Lucy's "sweetness was turned to adamantine, heartless cruelty, and the purity to voluptuous wantonness."

Even more horrifying is Van Helsing's and Seward's discovery of Jonathan Harker in a stupor, while beside him Dracula and Mina are feeding on each other's blood. Mina's

white nightdress was smeared with blood, and a thin stream trickled down the man's bare breast which was shown by his torn-open dress. . . . His eyes flamed red with devilish passion; the great nostrils of the white aquiline nose opened wide and quivered at the edge; and the white sharp teeth, behind the full lips of the blood-dripping mouth, champed together like those of a wild beast. . . . [Mina] had given a scream so wild, so ear-piercing, so despairing that it seems to me [i.e., Dr. Seward] now that it will ring in my ears till my dying day. . . . Her face was ghastly, with a pallor which was accentuated by the blood which smeared her lips and cheeks and chin; from her throat trickled a thin stream of blood.

Later, Mina further horrifies her husband and friends by telling them that she was Dracula's willing victim. "I was bewildered, and, strangely enough, I did not want to hinder him. I suppose it is a part of the horrible curse that such is, when his touch is on his victim."

Joseph Conrad's *Heart of Darkness* (novella, 1902) cannot be described as a traditional horror story. Kurtz's dying words, however, "The horror! The horror!" echo in both Marlow's and the reader's minds. Horror is a major theme of Conrad's novella—the horror of man's recognition of his own capacity to become evil. Though they occupy separate bodies, Marlow and Kurtz are akin to Jekyll and Hyde. When Marlow meets *his* dark side in Kurtz, though, he is saved from going over the brink into "the heart of darkness." Marlow learns that Kurtz (who lacked restraint) exploited the savages, raped their land, allowed himself to be worshipped as a god, and participated in unspeakable rites. The spell of the wilderness, Marlow says, awoke in Kurtz brutal instincts and monstrous passions, and his soul had gone mad. The "horror" of the "heart of darkness" is both Kurtz's self-realization of what he had become and Marlow's recognition that the same thing could have happened to him:

He had something to say. He said it. Since I had peeped over the edge myself, I understood better the meaning of the stare, that could not see the flame of the candle, but was wide enough to embrace the whole universe, piercing enough to penetrate all the hearts that beat in the darkness. He had summed up—he had judged. "The horror!" . . . True, he had made that last stride, he had stepped over the edge, while I had been permitted to draw back my hesitating foot.

The Twentieth Century

American author Erskine Caldwell uses the theme of horror to illustrate the destructive forces in modern society and to examine mankind's indifference to others' suffering and death. The horrifying events in *Poor Fool* (1930) become particularly shocking because of the matter-of-fact, almost simplistic tone of the third-person narration. The novel centers around a simple-minded hero who sees horrors all around him, but never fully understands them. Shortly after Blondy (a second-rate boxer) discovers his lover Louise bathed in blood (her throat cut), he comes under the mysterious power of Mrs. Boxx, a witchlike woman who takes in men whom she uses both to satisfy her strange sexual needs and to help her run her abortion "clinic." Blondy's main duty in the Boxx household is to carry dead (and half-dead) bodies to the basement; it is more profitable for Mrs. Boxx to let the women die because she can sell the bodies for five dollars each. Truly chilling is Blondy's impotence when one of Mrs. Boxx's dying victims begs him to help her. Mrs. Boxx's attempt to castrate Blondy with a pair of scissors is also shocking.

Caldwell's description of Blondy's death, however, is the most horrifying part of the novel. Blondy escapes from Mrs. Boxx only to be brutally shot right in front of the apartment building where he had lived with Louise. Dripping with blood, he struggles up the stairs calling for his dead lover. The two girls who now occupy the apartment are at first frightened, and then, almost routinely, they throw Blondy out the window into the river, horrifying the reader by their nonchalance:

"Who was he?" the younger girl asked.

"I don't know. I never saw him in my life."

"Well, he had a hell of a nerve coming here to die. Why couldn't he have gone home and done it?"

"The poor fool probably didn't have a home," the other said.

As in Caldwell's novel, motifs of horror appear throughout British author Aldous Huxley's *Eyeless in Gaza* (1936). The ultimate horror, though, is the hero's realization (like Conrad's Kurtz's) that he is guilty. Because of his "fear of being afraid," Anthony has become irresponsible—causing his best friend's suicide and almost destroying his relationship with Helen, the woman he loves. He realizes finally that all the horrors he has experienced in his life are alike: "Separate patterns, but everywhere alike . . . in the drunken Mexican's pistol as in the dark dried blood on that mangled face among the rocks, the fresh blood spattered scarlet over Helen's naked body, the drops oozing from the raw contusion on Mark's knee.'' They are all symbolic of Huxley's theme—horror results from one's not feeling a sense of duty to others.

Horror also became a major theme in crime and detective fiction. American novelist James M. Cain focuses on the murderer rather than the victim and uses horror to illustrate the effect of a dreadful crime on the murderer's mind. In *Double Indemnity* (1936), for example, Walter Huff's love for his partner Phyllis turns to hate after the murder: "That's all it takes, one drop of fear, to curdle love into hate." He learns later that Phyllis is "an out-and-out lunatic" who had already killed four others and is planning two more murders. At the end of the novel, the two former lovers who "get away with murder" are placed on a ship to Mexico. Realizing that their lives have become unbearable, though, they plan to throw themselves into the sea to an awaiting shark. In the last scene of the novel, Phyllis, who has grotesquely dressed and made herself up for her death, appears to Huff like Coleridge's "Nightmare Life-in-Death."

In Patrick Quentin's *The Green-Eyed Monster* (1960), the protagonist solves the mystery of his wife's murder and discovers a horrible truth about himself. Quentin suggests that circumstances can drive "innocent" people to become murderers. Andrew Jordan learns that his wife, not his own jealousy, was a "green-eyed monster" and that "Mrs. Thatcher had committed his murder for him. Whatever ordeal lay ahead for her could, but for the grace of God, have been his ordeal." The roles become reversed in the novel, and the real horror is not the gruesome description of the murdered woman, but the fact that "The victim had been the killer, the killer just another victim."

In the past thirty years America has witnessed an influx of horror fiction and films. Two world wars, nuclear power, and bloody assassinations have created more real horrors than earlier writers may ever even have imagined. Television has brought these horrors into the home. Film clips of the attempted assassination of President Ronald Reagan in 1981, for example, were viewed repeatedly by a shocked world, mesmerized by the dreadful violence.

This fascination with horror is especially evident in the large number of popular novels published each year, which both reflect the horrors of the age and provide a temporary escape from them. Comtemporary horror novels repeat various shocking motifs; some deal with the demon, his familiars, or monsters; some focus on children, either evil, possessed, or having extraordinary powers; some center around a haunted house or building; some are variations of the vampire legend.

Stephen King, one of the most popular and prolific American horror writers, has at one time or another included almost all of the mentioned motifs in his novels. All of his novels deal with the unexplainable presence of evil in contemporary society. In *Danse Macabre* (1981) King states that the horror story "is often the tough mind's way of coping with terrible problems which may not be supernatural at all but perfectly real." King's best seller, *'Salem's Lot* (1975), for example, is a vampire tale set in a contemporary New England town. The Marsten house is "haunted," and the first vampire to appear is a child. By providing vivid, realistic details of the townspeople's daily lives, King suspends his readers' disbelief and horrifies them through his mixture of realism and the supernatural. He also shocks his readers, as Matthew Lewis did nearly two centuries ago, with sensational, gory effects. Among the most horrifying moments in the novel are the dead Mrs. Glick's attack on Cody and Mears; Straker's imprisonment of Mark; Ben's hammering the stake through Susan Norton; Barlow's murder of the Petries; and Barlow's transformation after Ben drives a stake through him.

There are also many parallels between *'Salem's Lot* and *Dracula;* and, in fact, several of King's characters indicate that they are familiar with Stoker's novel. The differences, however, add to the horror. Barlow, like Dracula, is destroyed; but he leaves behind him a town full of vampires. The novel ends with unanswered questions. How many other towns in the world has Barlow fed upon? Although Ben Mears and Mark Petrie burn the town, will they be able to locate and ultimately destroy all the vampires? Good does not clearly triumph over evil.

See also: Cave, Grotesque, Monsters, Terror.

Selected Biblography

King, Stephen. *Danse Macabre*. New York: Everest House, 1981.
Tracy, Ann B. *The Gothic Novel; 1790–1830: Plot Summaries and Index to Motifs.* Lexington: University Press of Kentucky, 1981.
Varma, Devendra P. *The Gothic Flame: Being a History of the Gothic Novel in England.* London: A. Barker, 1957.

NATALIE SCHROEDER

HUNT

A hunt involves pursuit of wild game for profit or pleasure, conducted with or without the aid of hounds, lions, or leopards by hunters on foot, horseback, in chariots, or mounted on elephants. Hunters are often accompanied by skilled persons who attend rather as servants than as sportsmen. The quarry sought differs in different parts of the world and ranges in size from the rabbit to the elephant and in type from the deer to the tiger. Some animals are hunted for food, hides, fur, or ivory; predators are hunted because they are a threat to humans or to domesticated fowl or herds. All types of animals may be pursued for the acquisition of tropies.

Regardless of the quarry or method, the hunt is usually governed by a fairly rigid code of ethics and etiquette and in many cases by law. Although in primitive societies all able-bodied men could take part in the hunt, it later became the privilege of the aristocracy, in Western Europe from about 1000 A.D., in China as early as the Chou Dynasty (c. 1027–221 B.C.).

Many countries regarded the hunt, which demands endurance and courage, as well as skill in the use of weapons, as useful training for the military class.

Most hunting today is undertaken for excitement and pleasure rather than necessity and is often not without danger to the hunter as well as to his prey. It may take the hunter from a provident society and make him rely on his own resources for food. The chase can be exhausting and the terrain treacherous, especially for the mounted hunter; those who hunt big game may be prey to their quarry. Far from being a deterrent, these hazards seem to have lent additional attractions to the sport, the risk providing one of its greatest inducements. The excitement of the chase and satisfaction at its success are themes frequently present in literature.

From earliest times, however, man seems to have identified himself with the quarry rather than the hunter. Both basic primitive economies, the earlier hunting-and-gathering and the later agricultural, have contributed to this attitude.

Dependent on the hunt for most of their necessities, hunting societies surrounded it with taboos and made it the focus of magic and ritual intended to ensure a supply of game, to exert power over it, and to appease the spirit of the slain animal or the god who presided over it. Men also disguised themselves as animals to act as decoys and deceive their prey or as part of rituals relating to the hunt or intended to cement the bond between tribe and totem creature. In addition, since the hunter's life depended on the death of his quarry, that death seemed sacrificial, and in it the hunter recognized and accepted his own mortality. Thus he came to perceive, instinctively or consciously, that death was the ultimately successful predator, at whose hands man and beast suffered the same fate.

Although agricultural societies augmented their food supply with game, they hunted wild animals also because they presented a threat to the group's livelihood by eating grain or preying upon domestic flocks and herds. Seen thus, the quarry they pursued was evil and came to be identified with all that is wild and disorderly, including devils and human enemies, but also with unruly elements within the heart of the hunter.

Legend

Hunter-victim is a recurring motif in legend. While hunting, Actaeon spied Artemis bathing. Goddess of chastity as well as hunting, she turned him into a stag to be torn to pieces by his own hounds. Laelaps, a hound fated to catch whatever it pursued, was set to hunt the Teumessian vixen, so fleet no hound could ever catch it. Not wishing either to be defeated, Zeus turned both to marble, trapping them in a never-ending chase. Adonis hunted a wild boar against the advice of his adoring goddess Aphrodite and ended as its victim. The Celtic hero Diarmaid, too, broke a prohibition against hunting boar and, although he killed his quarry, was poisoned by a bristle, the boar being the transformed body of Roc's son, slain by Diarmaid's father.

In a complex fashion a wild boar hunt was also fatal to Meleager, son of the king of Calydon. Artemis had caused the boar to ravage the land because its king had failed to offer sacrifice to her. Accompanied by a large band of hunters, among them Atalanta with whom he had become infatuated, Meleager set out to rid the land of this affliction. When he had killed the boar, Meleager presented the head, prized trophy of the hunt, to the maiden, because she had drawn the first blood. Shamed that a woman should be so advanced above them, Meleager's uncles turned on him and were killed in the ensuing fight. In her grief at her brothers' deaths, Meleager's mother burned the brand she had snatched from the fire at his birth because it was foretold the brand and Meleager would have the same span of years. As it burned, Meleager was consumed by an invisible fire.

The irony of victim-hunter and beloved-slain also occurs in the story of Cephalus and his wife Procris. Jealous of a supposed rival, Procris tracked her husband as he hunted and hid in a bush to watch his encounter with "Breeze" of whom she had heard him speak so lovingly when heated in the chase. Cephalus came and, assuming that the stirring in the shrub where Procris was hiding was caused by a wild creature, flung at it a javelin destined never to miss its mark. Thus to his great sorrow he killed his own wife.

One successful hunt occurs in Celtic myths, that of Arthur's pursuit of the wild boar Twrch Trwyth, also known as Porcus Troit, a king who, transformed for his wickedness, had laid waste a third of Ireland. Arthur followed the boar through South Wales and Cornwall, finally winning the shears and comb between its ears.

Legend, then, enshrines the evil beast ravaging the land and the hunter who becomes the prey. Augmenting this concept of human quarry is Eros, god of love, who stalks victims and pierces their hearts with arrows that compel them to love.

The Bible

Although the hunter figures positively in such passages as "Take us . . . the little foxes that spoil the vines" (Song of Sol. 2:15), the Bible presents the hunt most often from the point of view of the quarry. David sees Saul as hunting his soul (1 Sam. 24:11); Jeremiah laments that enemies hunt his people's steps (Lam. 4:18). The world is filled with evil men who lie in wait for blood and hunt their brothers with nets (Mic. 7:2). Women adorn themselves to hunt the souls of those who come to them (Ezek. 13:18). The Psalmist's soul is among lions, among men whose teeth are spears and arrows, and their tongue a sharp sword (57:4). His soul thirsts for God as the hard-pressed hart for water brooks (42:1).

Man is the hunted, not the hunter, in the warning that the devil as a roaring lion walks about seeking whom he may devour (1 Pet. 5:8). In a similar image, Job thinks God is hunting him as a fierce lion (10:16) and Hosea warns that God will be like a lion to Ephraim and Judah because of their wickedness (5:14). By contrast, the coming kingdom is a place where there is no hunting. The wolf will dwell with the lamb, the leopard with the kid, and the lion, instead of preying on the calf, will eat straw like the ox (Isa. 11:6 and 65:25).

Some hunters are not unattractive. Nimrod is a mighty hunter before the Lord and bequeathed his name to generations of hunters (Gen. 10:9). Samson is so mighty that he kills a lion with his bare hands (Judg. 14:6). However, Esau darkened the name of the hunter by selling his birthright for a mess of pottage, and his strife with his herdsman brother Jacob became an archetype for later fiction (Gen. 25:27–34)

Antiquity

References to the hunt in antiquity are usually figurative, the prey being human. Thus, Homer likens Achilles' pursuit of Hector to a falcon swooping down on a cowering dove, and to a hound tracking a hiding faun by its scent. Agenor standing up to Achilles is like a leopardess attacking a hunter, undeterred by dogs and undiscouraged by wounds. In the *Eumenides* of Aeschylus (play, 458 B.C.) the ghost of Clytemnestra reproaches the Furies for hunting Orestes, the prey, listlessly as in a dream, goading them to pursue him to the death. They later claim that they track him by the drops of his mother's blood as a hound does a wounded faun.

The literal hunt that the protagonist in Euripides' *Hippolytos (Hippolytus,* play, 428 B.C.) follows so ardently, regarding Artemis as the greatest and Aphrodite as the vilest of the gods, foreshadows the huntlike pursuit his father makes for him when he believes Hippolytus has dishonored his stepmother, Phaedra. For her part Phaedra would be relieved to take up the ardors of the deer hunt and be set free from her frenzied passion for Hippolytus in which she sees herself as the prey of the god of love.

A most sustained metaphor of hunting is employed in *Oidipous tyrannos (Oedipus Rex,* play, c. 429 B.C.) in which Oedipus is both hunter and hunted as the action seeks out the slayer of Laius, and Sophocles uses the vocabulary of the hunt as the players track down, follow the spoor, flush out and seek to catch the culprit.

Literal and figurative are mingled in the *Bakchai (The Bacchants,* play, c. 405 B.C.) of Euripides, where the hunter-victim Pentheus orders that Dionysus and his followers be hunted as animals because Dionysus hunts desire with beauty as a lure. The gods, however, wait in ambush for him, and fate quests like a sleuthhound until its relentless hunt has tracked down the godless man. Death and the vengeance of the god are the ultimate hunters when his mother in her fury tears him to pieces, taking him for a desert lion. Thus Pentheus becomes the prey of the Bacchants he has pursued, and his own destruction becomes the quarry his questing has deserved. The hunting society's conception of the relationship between hunter and quarry is suggested in the claim that Pentheus is hunter-victim, sacrificed that the god may be glorified and live. The play may also incorporate the view of the hunt as an attempt to subdue the unpredictable and irrational and the defeat of that attempt by the force of the emotions.

Ovid recommended hunting as one of the remedies of love, explaining that the excitement of the chase drew the lover's mind away from his lady, and the exertion involved tired him so that he would sleep rather than waste the night in thoughts of her (*Ars amatoria* [*The Art of Love,* didactic poem, c. 1 B.C.]). Ovid introduces, too, the notion of the rivalry between Venus and Diana for the devotion of mankind.

The hunt recurs in the epic poem *Aeneis* (*Aeneid,* 19 B.C.). It illustrates the recklessness of youth as the hero's son scorns the hunt of goats and deer that flee before the hunter and longs to tackle the roaring lion and the foaming boar. Dido is wounded by love for Aeneas and is like a doe pierced by the arrow of some hunting shepherd. The chase acts as a guide into a new situation as it takes them to the cave in which the lovers shelter from the storm. The resemblance between the hunt and war is also exploited by Virgil as he pictures Aeneas dogging Turnus, who flies from him as a stag whom the huntsman chases with his baying hounds.

The Orient

The Confucian tradition permitted hunting but condemned aiming at a roosting bird as unsporting and inhuman. As early as the sixth century B.C., however, Lao-tzu had taught that hunting served only to madden the heart of man, revealing that the enemy was within, was in fact desire itself. Such teaching seems to have influenced the poets for they generally reveal mixed feelings in their handling of the hunt.

In the "Kao-t'ang fu" ("Mount Kao-t'ang," poem, 3d century B.C.), Sung Yü describes for the king of Ch'u the glories of the mountain of Kao-t'ang but warns him that if he wished to hunt there he would have to practice abstinence and fasting for a long time, select the proper hour by augury, dress in black, and be carried in an unpainted chair. His banner must be woven of clouds, his streamers fashioned like rainbows, his awnings of halycon feathers. After the hunt the king would deal gently with the lands, grieve at the wrongs of his people; he would promote the wise and good, correct what was wrong. All things would be laid bare to his soul's scrutiny and his strength would eternally endure. The game killed in the hunt thus described is taken by an invisible stroke, and altogether the poem suggests that the ascent of the mountain and the hunt there are symbolic of a spiritual exercise rather than a physical one.

"Tzu-hsü fu" ("Master Nil," 145 B.C.), by Ssu-ma Hsiang-ju, alternates passages of poetry and prose in a fashion that allows the prose to make moral judgments on what the poetry has so glowingly described. The poetry sets forth the splendor and wealth of a variety of game parks and celebrates those that yield the most lavish kill. The prose, however, laments the slaughter of birds and animals, the strife provoked between feudal lords by the hunt's trespassing over one another's lands, and the waste of land reserved for this sport that might be opened for cultivation, to the benefit of the common people.

"Ch'i fa" ("Seven Stimuli," poem, c. 180 B.C.) of Mei Sheng, however, seems to approve of hunting. The heir apparent of Ch'u is ill from surfeiting and a visitor seeks to stimulate him back to health by describing a variety of exotic events. The heir is not attracted by the offer of music, carefully prepared food, the delights of the lofty terrace of Ching-i, or an exciting chariot ride, but when the chase is described to him he begins to show interest. However, the translator, Hans H. Frankel, suggests that the cure is really achieved by words that pile up mental images. The hunt merely catches the heir's attention, and his recovery is brought about by the description of a tidal bore and the passages from the philosophers that follow. As the hunt is described, it is pursued mainly for the pleasure of the chase and the joy of competition among the hunters for game and rewards of gold and silk. It ends, however, with a feast on some of the animals killed, and the aristocracy's tendency toward the display of wanton slaughter is reflected in the poem.

Oriental literature also uses the hunt as an image of the struggle for power. The *Tso chuan (Tso Commentary)* entry for 558 B.C. describes the defeat of the state of Ch'in as resembling the pursuit of the stag, the stag being a royal beast and a symbol of power and liberty. The image was to persist and to occur again in the Korean epic poem, *Yongbi Ŏch'ŏn-ga (Songs of the Dragons Flying to Heaven,* 1447), where it alludes to Hsiang Yü, rival of Kao Tsu of Han for the throne, as the "pursued deer . . . not yet ensnared" (canto 55). The same work speaks admiringly of great hunting feats: one of the "Dragons," King T'aejo, while still a boy, shot five crows with one arrow (canto 86). Canto 43 praises his skill: "two deer / By a single arrow fell," after relating how Hsüan Tsung of T'ang "two boars / By a single arrow shot."

The Medieval and Renaissance Periods

At no time was the literary potential of the hunt exploited more thoroughly than in the medieval period, and some of the courses charted then continued to influence writers in the Renaissance. The hunt provided situations for plot development, images for characters' experiences, and a sure means of communicating information about the characters to the reader.

Enthusiasm for the hunt and knowledge of the rigid code of behavior that governed it were the marks that distinguished the nobly born and bred from baser men. Wolfram von Eschenbach's Parzival (*Parzival,* epic poem, c. 1210) has the zeal for the hunt proper to his noble ancestry but, because he has been brought up remote from the court, begins as a youthful wanton slayer, using the wrong weapon and, in his ignorance, taking home the carcass whole. The romance tradition credited Tristan with bringing hunting to its refined height, although the roots of the strict rules for breaking up the quarry and distributing its various portions may in fact go back to the primitive hunter's sense of obligation to the animal whose death gave him life.

Knowledge of hunting practices was so revealing that when Ipomydon, son of the king of Toyle, is travelling incognito as squire to his mentor 'Tholomew, the princess of Calabria employs it as a test. She is attracted to him but afraid that he may not be of sufficiently high rank for her. She therefore arranges a hunting party. His success and the perfection of his technique in breaking up the deer assure her of his noble birth (*The Lyfe of Ipomydon,* Middle English version of Huon de Rotelande's Anglo-Norman romance *Ipomedon,* c. 1174–1191).

Highly as hunting was esteemed, however, it ranked below battle in conferring prestige. Later, when the ladies of the court believe Ipomydon is hunting rather than taking part in a three-day tournament, they properly scorn him. Only when they discover that the hunting is pretense and he is actually the anonymous knight who has triumphed in the tournament is he vindicated. This motif appears also in Chrétien de Troyes' *Cligès* (c. 1160), Ulrich von Zazikhofen's *Lanzelet* (c. 1194) and *The History of Roswall and Lillian,* a medieval Scottish romance first published in 1663, as well as other romances.

The irony of a hunter who becomes potential prey is a recurring theme in tales where the quarry draws the protagonist away from his companions. This may result merely in a searching of his character, as it does that of Duke Begon in *Garin le Loherain (Garin the Lorrainer,* epic poem, 12th century). Bored because there is no war, the duke resolves to hunt the formidable wild boar of the forest of Vicogne. His rage when it kills his favorite hound proves his capacity for affection. He continues the hunt though his fellows fall away and, single-handed, avenges the hound by killing the boar. A great hart in the middle English romance *Wedding of Sir Gawain and Dame Ragnell* leads Arthur into danger. He is challenged by an armed knight who is only stopped from killing the king when he acknowledges that it would be shameful for a man in armor to fight an unarmed man. Arthur is reprieved for a year but charged to discover in the interval what women love best. It is Gawain rather than Arthur who passes this test as he shows there are no limits to the services he will perform for his liege lord.

Frequently, separation strands the hero in a strange country or in a supernatural situation. Placidas (whose life was first recorded in Greek c. 726 and later translated into Latin, French, and English) follows a splendid stag while hunting. When the beast has isolated him from his fellows, it addresses him. The stag is Christ. As a result of the encounter the virtuous but pagan Placidas becomes St. Eustache, champion of the Christian faith in the fire of adversity. Thus the hunter is captured by his intended quarry, yet gains by the capture. In accepting the suffering that follows, he also takes on aspects of the god who triumphs by being a victim.

Malory's Arthur, too, follows a great hart to isolation as he outstrips his companions and rides after it until his horse drops dead. When the hart thus eludes him, he encounters the Questing Beast, a conglomerate creature whose odd mixture of parts may make him an externalization of Arthur's moral state, unholy hybrid, brother and lover of his sister Margawse. He has thus pursued noble game, but has encountered the evil within himself. Chrétien de Troyes, in his *Erec et Enide* (romance, c. 1160), introduces a variation of the luring-prey motif when Erec, half-heartedly taking part in the Chase of the White Hart, is separated from his more eager companions and strays into a strange land. There he marries Enide and enters upon events that lead to his development and self-knowledge. In Gottfried von Strassburg's *Tristan* (romance, c. 1210), Marke pursues a white stag to the cave where he finds Tristan and Isôt asleep and withdraws believing them innocent of adultery. The white stag here seems symbolic of ideal love, elusive for the ignoble Marke.

Symbolic use of the hunt also occurs in *Sir Gawain and the Green Knight* (romance, c. 1370), where the host's successive pursuit of deer, boar, and fox parallels and defines the hunt his wife carries on in Gawain's bedroom. She seeks to discover the exact nature of her quarry, finding in the end that Gawain cannot be successfully hunted as deer or boar, but can be taken as fox. The detailed, ceremonious breaking up of the kill keeps the reader aware of the beheading, which is the probable outcome of the other game Gawain is engaged in. Unceremonious breaking up of a hart is revealing in the Middle English poem *The Parlement of the Thre Ages,* in which a poacher works with great haste to hide evidence of his crime from the royal forester. Wearied, he falls asleep and sees in his soul a dream of youth, middle age, and old age wasted in pursuit of the values that have brought him to his illegal hunt in the forest.

Shakespeare makes extensive use of the imagery of the hunt, more often drawing on the suffering and fear of the hunted deer or hare than on the joys of the successful hunter (e.g., *Julius Caesar* [play, c. 1599] 3.1.204–210; *Antony and Cleopatra* [play, c. 1607] 4.1.7). Hunters in Spenser's *Faerie Queene* (epic poem, 1590–1596) are led by their pursuits to other adventures, and the devotion of Hippolytus to hunting wins him the friendship of Diana, who later is the means by which his fragmented body is restored to life.

John Denham, in *Cooper's Hill* (didactic poem, 1642), is reminded, as he watches a stag hunt, of King John's tyrannous pursuit of the barons that, unlike the stag hunt, ended not in the death of the quarry, but in their compelling him to sign the *Magna Carta*.

The resemblance between the hunt and seduction, where woman is the prey, had been developed by Ovid in the *Ars amatoria* and was further exploited by Andreas Capellanus in the treatise *De arte honeste amandi* (*The Art of Courtly Love*, c. 1200). It was a figure that was to be used and adjusted by poets for many centuries.

The lover in *Die Jagd* (*The Chase,* poem, c. 1340), an allegory by Hadamar von Laber, pursues a lady as his quarry, but the hounds of Heart and Desire are held in check by restraining Leash and Collar. He rejects the advice of a lecherous knight to uncouple the hound Consummation, refusing to dishonor the stag. On the other hand, he cannot bring himself to slay the hound Perseverence, and is therefore trapped in a perpetual, unsuccessful chase, the victim of his own hunt.

The lady is again the prey in the thirteenth-century allegory *Li dis dou cerf amoreus (The Stag of Love)* but in it the hunter is Love and his hounds are the lady's own desires and emotions. Her death at the end signals the loss of her virginity but her awakening to happiness as Love sends her body as its gift to her lover. Male lovers suffer greatly from the hunting of the god of Love. Gahmuret, in Wolfram's *Titurel* (epic poem, c. 1220), is sympathetic to lovers, having himself been hunted to death by Minne. In a twelfth-century Provençal lyric of Rigaut de Barbezieux, the love-smitten man is a hunted and captured stag. Love's hounds chase another lover from the sheltering thicket of childhood and set on him the relay hounds of the lady's charms and his own desires. These finally bring him down, bleeding and dependent on his lady to whom Love sends his heart and will (Jean Acart, *La prise amoureuse* [*Love's Capture*, allegorical poem, 1332]). As can be seen, customs relating to the proper distribution of the various parts of the prey are often employed by the poet to express his meaning.

Human prey is even more graphically portrayed in one of the poems of Provençal Peire Vidal, "De chantar m'era laissatz" ("I Had Stopped Singing," c. 1194). In it love madness turns the lover into an animal as he dons the skin of a wolf and has himself hunted by the men and dogs. A complex handling of this motif is found, too, in the thirteenth-century Persian poem *Ushshāq-nāmeh (Song of Lovers)* by 'Irāqi in which a man catches sight of a lady out hunting. She flies on in pursuit of her original quarry, unwilling yet to hunt a lover. Wounded to the heart, the man runs with the wild beasts and, when next she hunts, dresses himself in the hide of a slain deer so that he is pursued and eventually killed by her. He accepts death gladly if only he can see her face.

An older man in *Die Jagd* advised the lover to hunt Christ rather than the lady—advice he rejects. However, the hunt had earlier been used as a metaphor for the soul's relationship with Christ. The thirteenth-century lyric poet Mechthild von Magdeburg writes of a soul that hunts the quarry love but is hunted by Love and, paradoxically, finds its great delight in the wound that Love inflicts.

In *The Book of the Duchess* (poem, 1369), Chaucer takes advantage of the English homophones hart-heart using them to guide the reader to a clearer understanding of his meaning. The heart of the Knight in Black is wounded by love, but later waxes glad when fair White grants him her favor. In the parallel hunt of Octovian, the hart has rused and momentarily escaped. With the death of White, the Knight's heart is wounded and his life is endangered but he escapes for the time as does the hart, though the hunter Death will ultimately be successful in both cases.

Led on by Petrarch, Renaissance poets drew on the imagery of the hunt in lyrics portraying the hazards of love. Love lurked in their lady's eyes and hair, and from that vantage point pierced the lover's heart with his darts. The Catalan poet Fra Rocabertí (c. 1451) sees the hunt as like the game of love, and love's captives as moving through a dark forest as do hunted deer. Thomas Wyatt, the sixteenth-century English poet, following Petrarch closely, knows a hart worthy to be hunted but out of bounds because it bears the warning that it belongs to

Caesar. In Shakespeare's *Twelfth Night* (play, c. 1600) the duke, in love with Olivia, is turned into a hart, and his desires like "fell and cruel hounds," pursue him (1.1.22). Rosalind (*As You Like It* [play, c. 1599] 4.3.18) says that Phebe's love "is not the hare that I do hunt."

In a longer exploration, *Vers de chasse et d'amour* (poem, 1597), Jean Passerat pictures himself as a stag tracked by love and harried by hounds named Killing Care, Vain Thought, Burning Desire, and False Hope. When these dogs tire he is set upon by an envious spy as the hart is by the fresh hounds at the relay point.

Passerat dealt, too, with the Adonis myth, using it more as evidence that fate rules all than as a warning against the boar hunt, although Adonis' devotion to the hunt may have in it elements of hubris as had that of Hippolytus. Shakespeare's treatment of the myth deals mainly with the goddess's fierce pursuit of the shy mortal hunter.

The Eighteenth Century

French literature shows a limited interest in the hunt at this time, possibly because literary life centered on the salons of Paris, while in the country the *droit de chasse* excluded all but the nobility from participating in the hunt. Similar laws in Germany curbed interest in it there. *Die Parforcejagd (Coursing)* of L.F.G. von Goeckingk (c. 1771) presents in dialogue the suffering of the hunted animal and also that of the farmer who, his crop overrun and his meadow trampled, does not know where his rent is to come from, while the knightly hunter curses him for his complaint, wishing the prince would hang all such worthless dogs.

In England, however, any man might join the chase, although the various ranks did not mingle socially. Until the mid-eighteenth century little refinement distinguished the manners of even the upper-class hunter, and the boorish hunting squire was already a stock character when Henry Fielding created his Squires Booby and Western. The dullness of the fox hunter's conversation of five-barred gates and broken bones, as well as his pride in drinking deep and his insistence that those in his company do the same, is lampooned in J. Addison and R. Steele's *The Spectator* (essays, 1711–1712), No. 474. Later, the fashionable world took up fox hunting and a spate of minor novels set in hunting country appeared, written by such nineteenth-century authors as R. S. Surtees and "Scrutator" (pseudonym of Knightley William Horlock).

The frisson of the ghostly hunt held some appeal for the Age of Reason. This unresolved hunt in which the hunter is trapped in unending and fruitless pursuit had an extended history, figuring in the chase of Laelaps and the Teumessian vixen, and enriched by Norse legends of the furious host.

This *wütende Heer,* originally led by Woden on a white horse, swept through the air in the stormy seasons of autumn and winter in fruitless chase of a visionary boar, a wild horse, or of wood nymphs called Moss Maidens. The hunters' pursuit of white-breasted maidens had a chance of success once in seven years.

The host still pursued its eerie chase in Christian times but was known as Cain's or Herod's hunt, types of the never-ending restlessness suffered eternally by evil men for their heinous sins. It was also known in France as the Mesnée d'Hellequin and in England as the Herlathin. Charlemagne, Frederick Barbarossa, King Arthur, St. Hubert, and the Grand Veneur de Fontainebleau also succeeded Woden as leaders of the host.

Among many such tales is a subclass dealing with priests or abbots whose love of hunting led them to abandon the Mass they were celebrating on hearing the baying of hounds that had started a hare. Such men were condemned for their blasphemy to continue that hunt forever. The chronicler Ordericus Vitalis records the sighting by a priest near Chartres in 1091 of such wretched souls goaded on by Herlechinus, and according to the *Peterborough Chronicle*, they were also seen in England in 1127. An echo of this ceaseless, unproductive hunt is found in the Middle English lay *Sir Orfeo* where Orfeo in his forest exile sometimes sees the hunt of the fairy king that, though it rides at noon day rather than at night, has the host's ill fate of never achieving any prey.

"Der wilde Jäger" ("The Wild Hunter," 1778), a poem by G. A. Bürger, tells of a count who hunts on the Sabbath as well as other days and ruthlessly disregards the farmer's plea to spare his grain and cattle. Ignoring the advice of his fair companion and obeying that of his swarthy one, he is punished by being condemned forever to take part in the sport he so loved, not as hunter but the hunted, pursued by the dark hunter and his dire hounds of hell. The eerie quality is caught in the English translation of Sir Walter Scott.

The hunt's capacity to alter the character of the hunter is a consistent feature in American literature. A vital source of food for both natives and new-comers, the hunt entered deeply into the life of both communities. Attitudes toward the wilderness in which it took place differed. For the Puritans it was the objectification of their preconversion state and offered those who entered it temptation to throw off the order of civilization for the chaos of the untamed forest. The prey in that correlative of their former unregenerate condition appeared to them as evil itself. Thus in his account of the Indian Wars when the Indian was the quarry, William Hubbard speaks of pursuing the Indian leader Metacom as a savage and wild beast hunted to his den (*The History of the Indian Wars in New England*, 1677).

A century later St. Jean de Crèvecœur deplores the degeneration of settlers who combine hunting and cultivating to the neglect of the latter, allowing their children to grow up half civilized and half savage. His good farmer, however, though compelled to hunt to survive, is diligent in his farm work and careful to employ his children as much as possible in agriculture to counteract the evil attractions of the chase (*Letters from an American Farmer*, 1782).

But change need not be seen as degeneration. The Delaware creation myth presents the hunt as leading to a new and better condition. Their race did not begin in a garden of Eden but in a dark cave under a lake. One day one of their number caught sight of a deer and followed it through an opening into the upper world. He hunted the deer, killed it, and ate its flesh. In that eating his eyes were opened and he saw the beauty of the world he had entered. He returned to the cave, shared the meat with his tribe, and led them from their dismal home into the forest.

Without accepting the myth, white hunters shared a love of the wilderness and of the spiritual satisfaction of the chase and the kill. Daniel Boone, hunter hero of these pioneer days, is pictured by Timothy Flint as taking part in the hunt as a religious experience, changed in that respect from civilized to primitive. Not changed but liberated by the hunt to exercise his latent desire for power and exploitation is the other American hero, Davy Crockett, for whom hunting was slaughter and whose autobiography applied the language of the hunt to both courtship and politics.

The hunted as well as the hunter was subject to change as the legend of Boone's fire hunt reveals. Hunting by torchlight was forbidden but the young Boone attempts it and is eventually rewarded by seeing the eyes of his quarry reflect the light from his torch. At the last moment some impulse restrains him from shooting, and he sees that the deer is a young girl who flees home to tell her family she has been pursued by a panther. The girl later becomes Boone's wife.

The Nineteenth Century

Change of identity continues to be a theme of the more openly fictional works that come later. James Fenimore Cooper's Natty Bumppo becomes Deerslayer (*The Deerslayer,* novel, 1841), taking on a new identity in the initiation rite of killing his first deer. As Leather-Stocking he later confirms this as his true self when he resists the attempt by Judge Temple to impose game laws on hunting. The primitive Bumppo is willing to restrain his desire for the hunt, but only in submission to nature's law that the wild creatures should never be killed except to satisfy the hunter's need for food.

Adoption of the prey's identity is to be found in T. B. Thorpe's account of "The Big Bear of Arkansas" (short story, 1841). In it Jim Doggett tells of his pursuit of the Big Bear, a pursuit so obsessive that he himself becomes its prey. When on one occasion he is sure he has succeeded, he finds that the creature has escaped and he has actually killed a female bear. Finally Doggett triumphs, and he then assumes the identity of his prey, calling himself the Big Bear of Arkansas.

Almost all the motifs connected with the hunt are gathered together in Melville's novel *Moby-Dick* (1851). In it Ahab is changed from family man to obsessed hunter. His prey is the inscrutable face of evil or elements of life beyond the control of reason, and he perverts the religious experience of the hunt into a blasphemous communion rite. With his whale-bone leg he has assumed part of the nature of his quarry, and he finally becomes its victim.

Although fox hunting had become a fashionable pursuit earlier in England and women of good families had become increasingly part of the hunting scene, they did not actually take part in the hunt until the mid-nineteenth century. In *The Eustace Diamonds* (novel, 1873), Lizzie Greystock begins to hunt in order to gain entry into the social world. However, even Trollope, ardent huntsman that he was, seems to have disliked too great a zeal for the sport in a woman, and Lizzie's recklessness is part of his characterization of her as opportunist and gambler, while the exclusive interest in hunting of Mrs. Spooner in *The Duke's Children* (novel, 1880), classifies her as unfeminine, albeit resourceful in an emergency.

Turgenev records the experiences of a Russian hunter in *Zapiski okhotnika (A Sportsman's Sketches,* short stories, 1852), but, though the narrator goes about the countryside with a gun, his real quarries are the nature of peasant life and the oppressive manners of the aristocrats.

A fawn that wishes to be hunted is to be found in "Brüderchen und Schwesterchen" ("Brother and Sister"), one of the folktales of the eighteenth century and earlier, collected by Jacob and Wilhelm Grimm and printed in 1812–1815. The fawn is, of course, the brother transformed, and his strange desire causes him to endure a slight wound so that he leaves a trail of blood by which the king can track him to the cottage where the children are living in exile, and eventually to marriage with the sister.

Francis Thompson is perhaps an only partially unwilling prey in "The Hound of Heaven" (poem, 1893), where he employs the ancient theme of God as the implacable hunter of the prey he pursues out of love.

As the century progressed, opposition to hunting as a blood sport increased and the prey itself became the pathetic hero of literature about it. Louise Colet's *Lui* (novel, 1860), contains a story of the hunting of deer in which she pictures the pathos of their deaths. John Masefield, however, having run with the fox and hunted with the pack in *Reynard the Fox* (narrative poem, 1919) is able to have it both ways by letting the fox we have been following outwit his pursuers, but allowing the hounds to pick up a fresh trail and follow it swiftly to the kill.

The Twentieth Century

American authors found particularly congenial the idea that civilization hides from man his true nature, which he may only learn by risking himself against big game or by making himself dependent on nature for his livelihood. Faulkner's character in "The Old People" (short story, 1942) achieves initiation in the kill: the death of the boy and his birth into manhood. His new self is granted a vision of the great deer, his kin and ancestor. When the veneer of civilization is stripped away from Hemingway in *The Green Hills of Africa* (reportage, 1935), he perceives the true nature of man, akin to wild creatures in his essential violence. The narrator in James Dickey's *Deliverance* (novel, 1970) is delivered from his crippling vision of the uselessness of life when he pits himself against a hunter whose prey he becomes by intruding into his world. Armed with bow and arrow, the narrator experiences the restorative excitement of tracking and killing the one who hunts him.

A very old motif makes its appearance in Galway Kinnell's "The Bear" (*Body Rags,* poems, 1968). Here a hunter who has inflicted on his prey a cruel and lingering death, insensitive to its suffering, wraps himself in the carcass merely to escape the cold. In dream, however, he finds himself taking on the bear's agony and its identity, which he cannot later put off.

The human is constantly prey in *Un homme se penche sur son passé* (*A Man Scans His Past,* by the Canadian novelist Maurice Constantin-Weyer, 1928). Here nature is a monster with blood-stained claws where everything survives by preying on its neighbor, and the hero Monge feels himself a beast tracked almost to death by the cold of Canada's northwest. Returned home, he finds himself the object that his hunting companion Archer is shooting at because he desires to marry Monge's wife. When that attempt fails, the couple flee and Monge tracks them across the thawing northland. The goal of his hunt is to recover his daughter Lucy, but when the child falls ill the persistence of his chase makes it impossible for the pair he is pursuing to give her the care she needs. Thus his hunt brings about her death and she becomes his prey.

In the novel *Harpoon of the Hunter,* by the Eskimo Markoosie (1970), although the young Kamik proves himself a hunter and a survivor in the hunt for a mad bear and resists many temptations to find peace in death, he yields at last to the temptation of suicide when all who are dear to him have died, and his harpoon makes its final kill.

A perversion of the hunter's identification with his prey is contained in the French novel *La dernière harde* (*The Last Hunt,* 1938) by Maurice Genevoix. Its hero is the stag Le Rouge who starts as a yearling orphaned by the first hunt. He is followed through capture and escape, on to triumph as the herd's chief male, then finally to death. Human hunters are mere personifications, among them Le Tueur, who delights in slaughter and leaves the animal's body where it falls because he does not eat venison. His needs are sufficed by milk, the faun's diet in its first encounter with human beings. Le Tueur's real hunger, which he has assuaged by killing the stag Pelerin, is to sleep several feet under ground.

A similar sense of the evil that is man's basic characteristic appears in *How Many Miles to Babylon?* by the Irish author Jennifer Johnston (novel, 1974), although she uses the hunt theme quite differently. For her, hunting the fox is an innocent occupation compared with the carnage of war and the incomprehensible brutality of military discipline.

See also: Bear, Dragons, Lion, Mountaineering.

Selected Bibliography

Campos, Jorge, ed. *La caza en la literatura.* Madrid: Taurus, 1961.

Lee, Peter H. *Korean Literature: Topics and Themes.* Tucson: University of Arizona Press, 1965.

Slotkin, Richard S. *Regeneration through Violence: The Mythology of the American Frontier, 1600–1860.* Middletown, Conn.: Wesleyan University Press, 1973.

Thiebaux, Marcelle. *The Stag of Love: The Chase in Medieval Literature.* Ithaca, N.Y.: Cornell University Press, 1974.

MARGARET J. ALLEN

I

//

INCEST

Incest is defined as the actual or imagined, knowing or unknowing, sexual relations between members or their surrogates of the consanguine or affinal nuclear or extended family. Thus defined, some form of incest is invariably taboo (even within those societies that have permitted some intrafamilial sexual relations). Socially and psychologically the taboo is a negative imperative in both its supposed origins and its probable functions. It is thought to have originated in (1) a natural sexual aversion between family members (Edward Westermarck); (2) a natural sexual love between family members that is suppressed (Freud); (3) a jealousy in matriarchal cultures by mothers for their sons, who to gratify their own sexual desires break away from home (Robert Briffault and in part Johann Jakob Bachofen); (4) a rivalry in patriarchal cultures between husband and son for mother and daughter (Freud); (5) a fear of woman's blood, preventing all who belong to the same totem from inbreeding that would cause dire results (Emile Durkheim); (6) a repudiation of the mother, who personifies two male fears: female as the menstruator—life force—and female as the Other—death force—(Simone de Beauvoir); and (7) an art of equilibration, that is, a holding back of aggressive (patricidal) and sexual (incestuous) responses by young males in the primal horde (Freud), this psychic disposition surviving as a selective biological process (Robin Fox, *The Red Lamp of Incest,* 1980). The taboo is thought to function as (1) a preventative to biological degeneration (Lewis Henry Morgan, Westermarck); (2) a preventative to upsetting family relations and thus confusing roles (Bronislaw Malinowski); (3) a prohibitive law, thou-shalt-not, upon which culture was able to go beyond the family to build larger social and economic units, inter-family structures (St. Augustine, Sir E. B. Tylor, Claude Lévi-Strauss, Talcott Parsons); and (4) a stop sign in its purely modern manifestations to the new sexuality that originated when capitalism destroyed the social and economic alliances between families (Foucault). No matter how it is explained, incest always is used by creative writers as a device for discovery of self or society.

In literature incest takes essentially four forms: mother-son (the Oedipus theme); stepmother-stepson (the Joseph theme); father-daughter (the Cenci theme), and sister-brother (the Amnon theme). Mother-son incest is typically unconscious, biological but not social; stepmother-stepson typically conscious, social but not biological. Father-daughter and sister-brother incest take both conscious and unconscious, social and biological forms. Even when conscious, incest reveals to the individual a hidden self within the self. As a law-breaker, the incestuous one is out of step with his world. Alienated, he searches for self, for identity—the invariable raison d'être for the theme. Frequently the incestuous one is a bastard, the sole survivor of a cataclysmic event, a changeling, an orphan, or in some way separated from his home or family or not at home in his family. He is not recognizable either to himself or to others. Incest, therefore, is tied to the triad: ignorance, discovery, enlightenment. By the formula that what is abominable becomes holy through suffering or knowledge, the incestuous one frequently becomes a savior. Incest never loses its character as the forbidden fruit and so never loses its ability to stun and horrify. But it is rarely used this way—though always present as a substratum—in legitimate literature, which bends the shock value to the philosophical concern of understanding man. Its ability to titillate the senses is exploited in pornography, where incest abounds. Beyond its concern with the self, incest also is the mark of political upheaval, a socially lost world without rule or stability.

Antiquity

Perhaps because of its association with creation, incest was of concern to ancient peoples. The origin of the species was projected into an original mother goddess (see E. O. James, *The Cult of the Mother-Goddess*, 1959) who parthenogenetically gave birth to a son whom she then seduced, or into an original related couple (e.g., Adam and Eve) who mate. Incest is found in the mythologies of all people (e.g., Greek, Uranus and Gaia; Egyptian, Nut and Geb) either because it was considered inevitable to creation or because these ancient people held it to be less fearful. Nevertheless, in more than a third of the myths from all over the world among primitive peoples incest has deleterious results—from blindness in participants to eyelessness in offspring. This range from harmless to harmful effects is catalogued in ancient literature.

Conflicting attitudes are reflected in the Bible. Father-daughter incest in the story of Lot is condoned on the basis of the necessity for preserving the species. Contrary to most later father-daughter relations, here it is the daughters who initiate the act. In the story of Isaac and Rebecca (the granddaughter of Abraham's brother's wife) the marriage is not only accepted but assures well-being; exogamous marriage is virtually condemned. But after the return from Egypt—universally seen in the ancient world as an exemplum of an incestuous culture—

incest is carefully defined, prohibited, and punished by death, excommunication, or divine wrath (Lev. 18, 20).

Two stories in the Bible, Joseph's seduction by Potiphar's wife and Amnon's rape of his half sister (so important to later incest literature) are barely incestuous. Potiphar, as it were, is a father surrogate, telling Joseph as he would a son that he can have all in his house save his wife (Gen. 39.9). Two elements in the story are pivotal: the captivating quality of his youth and virility (the necessity of justification for incest) and his naïveté (the necessity of initiation through suffering). In the Amnon-Tammar story, incest and moral and political dissolution go hand in hand. Amnon rapes his half-sister, while Absalom—his half-brother—avenges her only as an excuse to fight against their father David. Both brother-sister and father-daughter incest demonstrate male power and female passivity. After Amnon rapes Tammar, he dismisses her even though David would have not refused their marriage (2 Sam. 13–19). The link between incest and political corruption is one aspect of the Oedipus theme also and is particularly used from the Renaissance through the eighteenth century.

Greek myth and literature parallel in many ways biblical literature; they connect incest with higher states of knowledge and political dissolution and undergo a similar narrowing of tolerance for it. Myths particularly abound in unions between close relatives of every kind and degree. Such a union is a *hieros gamos* (a divine marriage). In a sense the *hieros gamos* is the model of all incest. Human incest is an act so holy as to be deadly (or as the Freudians would have it, what is desired is repressed: see Otto Rank, *Das Inzest-Motif*). Human incest is at best an exotic custom, like that among the Persians and among the Egyptians. Socrates said that the law against incest came directly from the gods; Plato added that even flouters of civil law respected the *nomos agraphos* (the unwritten law) against incest. Throughout Greek history incest prohibitions were never a part of civil law but of *Themis* (religious law). Perhaps there was no civil code because incest could be prosecuted under other crimes with which it was linked; for example, adultery. Nevertheless, throughout Greek history marriage to a paternal sister is permitted and unions with relatives through marriage do not constitute incest. Even incest dreams never seem to have been repressed. Homer, in his epic *Odysseia* (*Odyssey,* c. 8th century B.C.), has sympathy for the mating of Aeolus' children and pictures Alkinoos, married to his aunt Arete, living in a utopia. But when incest is transferred from the sphere of gods to men, his attitude changes. Homer is outraged by Oedipus' marriage to Epikaste.

It is the story of Oedipus that adds one great motif to the incest theme not present in the Bible—the marriage of mother to son. Sophocles is no less harsh than Homer on mother-son incest. Such incest is not even marriage, and that is what the Chorus seems to mean when it calls Oedipus' marriage an *agamos gamon* (a non-marriage marriage) in *Oidipous tyrannos* (*Oedipus Rex,* c. 429 B.C.) or when Kreon calls such unions unsanctified (*Oidipous epi Kolōnō* [*Oedipus at Colonus,* c. 406 B.C.]). Oedipus foresees that incestuous children are doomed. They will never marry (*Oedipus Rex*); they will have no rights and can only usurp power (*Oedipus at Colonus*). Even Oedipus' paternal authority is curtailed, all rights falling to Kreon. In spite of such an attitude, the incest remains in the background. It might almost be said that these plays—though there is marriage and sexual intercourse between mother and son—do not concern incest at all. The nature of the incest is minimized because the parties have been separated from birth—a constant element in the literature. This is biological but not social incest. The horror—the shock value of incest—occurs only at the moment of knowing; it is a glance into the very depths of human misery. The Chorus is shaken by its revelation *(Oedipus Rex)*. Not only is Oedipus a patricide but incestuous—the unthinkable. Self-discovery is tied to incest in these plays; half of the oracle to be worked out refers to incest. As the plays unfold, Oedipus moves from ignorance to knowledge, from suffering to apotheosis. One stage on the way to this development is reached when Oedipus believes he is the child of fortune, a bastard. Themis treated children of incest as bastards, so his statement looks ahead to the status of his own children. The chorus at this point considers him almost born of the gods, while he feels more than ever the need to find his parents. This theme of the bastard is taken up by André Gide in his play *Œedipe (Oedipus, 1931)*.

The key to the Greek treatment of mother-son incest is that it is unconscious. So it is in Euripides. Jocasta specifically states in *Phoinissai (The Phoenician Women, c. 409 B.C.)* that both did not know. Euripides links in this play an incestuous house with the political fortunes of a state. The fruit of incest is fraternal or civil war, the War of the Seven against Thebes. This version of the Oedipus story is the one carried to the Romans and the Middle Ages.

The propensity for unconscious forms of incest is displayed in the failure to treat the stepmother-son relationship as criminal on sexual grounds. Euripides' play *Hippolytos (Hippolytus, 428 B.C.)* has only the very slightest concern with incest. Phaedra feels shame for her emotions, but only because they dishonor her husband. Her acts are exploited as examples of conscious incest only later in the versions of Seneca and Racine.

Greek versions of sister-brother incest also show that where knowledge pre-ceeds action, the Greeks have little interest in the tragic possibilities of incest. For instance, the Electra-Orestes relationship in the plays of Aeschylus (*Eumenides, 458 B.C.*) Sophocles (*Elektra ([Electra, c. 410 B.C.])*, and Euripides (*Orestes, 408 B.C.*) has hardly any hint of incest compared to the same material in the hands of someone like Eugene O'Neill (*Mourning Becomes Electra*, trilogy of plays, 1931). A cynical attitude toward sister-brother incest seems present in one of Euripides' lost plays, *Aiolos (Aeolus, before 423 B.C.)*. The play concerns the marriage of Aeolus' six daughters and six sons to each other. One of the brothers, Makareus, rapes his sister, Kanake. When she becomes pregnant, Makareus persuades his father to allow his sons to marry his daughters, selecting who shall marry whom by lot. Because Kanake's lot does not fall to Makareus, tragic results ensue, leading to an ending like Sophocles' *Antigone*. Although it is hard to say exactly what Euripides' point of view is, one line of the play about incest shocked his contemporaries: "There is nothing shameful if it doesn't seem so." Euripides here reflects a current opinion–following instinct is natural and what is natural is permissible. Later Sophists, Cynics, and Stoics found no rational basis for the incest taboo. This foreshadows the pastoral settings in which nineteenth-century natural man accepts at least certain kinds of incest.

The Greeks used incest as a means to an end—the investigation of the human condition, the relation of self to family. The Romans used incest as an end—the delineation of a mental condition, how the incestuous person feels, thinks, acts. Greek interest in incest was philosophical; Roman interest was psychological. In Seneca's tragedies *Oedipus* (c. A.D. 50) and *Phoenissae* (a fragment) incest is the "crime of the age"; there is no greater crime that man can commit. In both plays Oedipus rages. Before half of *Oedipus* is over, Oedipus is named murderer and incestuous by his own father, called up from the dead in a chilling scene of necromancy. With that scene before his eyes, he struggles, proving to himself what he already knows. Both Oedipus and Jocasta react to the incest with frenzy; both agree that there is no equivalent to the crime. Death can vindicate patricide, but not incest, Oedipus says. Statius, in his epic *Thebais* *(The Thebaid,* A.D. 91), was no less concerned with the psychological effects of incest and saw them not only in Oedipus and Jocasta but in the whole family and in the War of the Seven against Thebes. Oedipus speaks of experiencing ecstasy in his union with Jocasta (1.68–69). Because passion reigned, the whole household is destroyed; it is the "Oedipodae confusa domus" (1.16–17). One sin is enough to deprave, and the depraved are insane. The balance of love, duty, and morality—*pietas*— that informs the sound household is missing. *Ira* reigns over the house of Oedipus. Like their father Oedipus, Eteocles and Polynice are infected—they also lack *pietas*. Incest is an impulse that sets in motion the destruction of family and state—a view shared by the medieval writers who took up the theme.

In Seneca's tragedy *Phaedra* (c. A.D. 60), the stepmother-son motif all but disappears, for Phaedra is the equivalent of Hippolytus' mother. In one scene, Phaedra even dresses like Hippolytus' mother (hunting clothes with spear) and then proceeds to hunt him throughout the play. She struggles with her passion but not against it. Incest is accepted and its horror enjoyed. At one point she faints, and when he infolds her in his arms she lasciviously enjoys the mock caress. She wants him to call her sister, almost wishing to conquer aging through enjoying his youth. A new motif is added to the repertory of motivations for incest: because of age disparity, parent-child incest is a way to renew one's youth. Phaedra is attracted to Hippolytus because he not only looks like his father but looks like him when he was young.

One curious treatment of sister-brother incest is Ovid's story of "Caunus and Byblis" in his epic poem *Metamorphoses* (c. A.D. 2–17). It is pseudo-incest. Byblis experiences it nightly in dreams only. When Caunus learns of her passion, he leaves home. One of her justifications for incest recalls Euripides' fragment *Aiolus*. She says that all things are right if we believe they are. She even rationalizes her love by using the example of Aeolus' children. What prevents incest is not the lack of natural attraction but only blind fear.

The Middle Ages

Incest in the Middle Ages is equated with original sin, the sin of origin, and is the single crime sufficiently grave to show the glory of God's forgiveness. New motifs are added to the theme: (1) Christian characters (demonstrating religious truths); (2) double incest (demonstrating that man engendered in sin is bound to repeat that sin); and (3) eroticism and paternal love (demonstrating the progress of the crime in the typical rather than the heroic character). But literary condemnation, influenced by church precept, was in conflict with aristocratic practice, which used incest openly to build family power (Georges Duby, *Medieval Marriage*, 1978). While historic cases are rarely of close degree, in literature they commonly are. Mother-son incest predominates; sister-brother incest being the cause or the result of mother-son incest. The representative incestuous figure throughout the period is Oedipus, though in many guises. Judas commits mother-son incest. He is given a biography, in both Jacopo de Voragine's *Legenda aurea* (*The Golden Legend,* c. 1270) and in an episode of Arnoul Gréban's passion play *Mystère de la Passion* (c. 1450), that includes all the major episodes in the Oedipus myth. Judas' crimes against Christ can only be explained by patricide and mother-son incest. Ignorant of both crimes, he discovers the truth in a conversation with his wife-mother, and she advises him to seek out Jesus.

Sibling incest leads to mother-son incest in the widespread story of Pope Gregory. The point of double incest seems to be that man engendered in sin is bound to repeat that sin in himself. In tale 81 of the *Gesta Romanorum* (*Deeds of the Romans,* c. 13th century, first printed, 1473) and in the romance by Hartmann von Aue, *Gregorius* (c. 1195), both stemming from a twelfth-century French poem, *La vie du pape Grégoire,* the lofty pope is humanized. His early life is fully exploited. Left parentless while still children, the mother of the future pope and her brother are stimulated by the Devil to commit incest. A child is born and then exposed. Years later he returns and unknowingly marries his mother. To atone for his sins he undergoes a self-inflicted and strikingly difficult solitary confinement on a remote island. When a pope is about to be selected in Rome, a nobleman dreams of the remote island, finds Gregory still alone, and helps to have him elevated to pope. Gregory's repentant mother is summoned to Rome where both serve God and are sainted. Early in his work, Hartmann remarks that no sin is so great that it cannot be forgiven. Double-incest seems to replace Fate and a loving God the cruel Greek gods.

The double-incest motif is examined in terms of conscious and unconscious sin in Marguerite de Navarre's *Heptaméron,* Third Day, tale 30 (1559). Here rather than sibling incest leading to mother-son incest, mother-son incest leads to sibling incest—or depending on one's point of view—to father-daughter incest. While the mother, conscious of her incest, must suffer guilt and do penance, her son and their child, who meet and marry, unconscious of their relationship, need not even be told of their incest. A legate advises the mother that because the couple are ignorant they have not sinned. The first incest is biological and social; the second only biological. During the medieval period a child of incest was not considered evil, nor was unconscious incest a sin. A striking erotic element in this tale is that once the mother begins sex with her son she enjoys it so much that she forgets who he is.

Erotic love and horror in tale 13 of *Gesta Romanorum* are added to a new form of double-incest: pseudo and then real. A queen entices her young son to sleep in the bed vacated by his dead father (pseudo). This erupts into real incest. The mother becomes pregnant. Finally in a bloody scene, she kills her baby girl. The tales directly concerned with Oedipus pay particular attention to the love between child-parent and husband-wife. The romance *Roman de Thèbes* (12th century) and the works based on it, like the *Romanzo d'Edipo* (14th century) and John Lydgate's moral poem *Siege of Thebes* (1420–1422), add details about Oedipus' early life and devote a great deal of time to the incestuous marriage. All mitigate the patricide by having it occur in a battle, sometimes a duel, and so stress the incest, the cause of all future problems. The *Romanzo* and *The Siege* tackle the problem of conscious and unconscious incest and decide that a marriage of evil cannot be innocently happy—a departure from the French view. In none is the process of coming to know important; therefore all tie awareness to the device of the scars on Oedipus' ankles. What is important—as it was in *The Thebaid*—is the political consequences of personal sin. *The Siege* is a "mirror of princes," and advises princes "teschewe such weddying" lest their fortunes fall.

The Renaissance

Rather than mother-son incest from this period on sister-brother incest dominates. A debate over the justification in Nature for incest begins, and out of this a language of incestuous love is created. The link between internal family breakdown and the collapse of the state continues. But two new motifs preoccupy the period: averted incest, a kind of inside-out Oedipus theme where the supposed incestuous couple turn out not to be related at all; and liberated incest, where the incestuous couple is victimized and imprisoned by society's taboos or where the rejection of the incest taboo is a stage in the rejection of all roles that delimit the self.

Shakespeare's *Pericles* (1609) as well as plays that use the Oedipus theme, like Hans Sachs's *Die unglückhaftig Königin Jocasta* (1550) and Anguillara's *Edippo* (1556), are very different, yet they share one thing. They treat incest in the framework of civil disobedience. Incest is a metaphor for tyranny in *Pericles* and virtuous love a metaphor for the well-regulated kingdom. An incestuous father, Antiochus, usurps the rights of his daughter, creating a condition of jealousy and fear; as king, he usurps the rights of his people, creating a condition of fear and subjugation. Opposed to this is the loving king and father, Pericles, who respects and suffers for his people and for his daughter. In both Sachs and Anguillara a curious detachment of Oedipus' incest from the patricide-regicide is made, thus emphasizing the cause of Oedipus' and his country's suffering not in killing a father-king but in loving a mother. All medieval versions of the Oedipus theme emphasized the incest by making Oedipus utterly justified in killing Laius during a knightly duel or battle. Sachs does the same and further stresses the incest by cutting the oracle to "Layus" in half, only the patricide is mentioned (Sachs does not do this in his poem on the same subject). His tale then is about an innocent Jocasta, ruining herself and her kingdom. She had no desire to marry after Layus' death; she loved him so much she could not love again. But she is forced to marry at the direction of the conquering King Atletes, Corinthian father to "Edippus." Discovering incest is a matter of a personal message from God and a sign–a jewel. Jocasta calls the incest the *unerhörte Schand* ("the unheard of shame"). Edippus says there is no greater evil; he pays not for his patricide but for his incest. Mother and son both are destroyed by their sin, and their sons cause civil war. Anguillara's play communicates the patricide and the incest in two different scenes, thus effectively detaching them. Learning he is a patricide, Edippo calmly asks and is granted forgiveness. Going into exile, he will do what he has always wanted—become a condottiere. Patricide's punishment is disconnected from incest's punishment. When the incest is discovered, thunder breaks loose in a scene filled with insidious prurience. Blood flows. Edippo blinds himself, his blood-filled tears dripping on Antigone; Jocasta kills herself, ripping open her belly on a sword, much like Seneca's Phaedra. Having tried to regulate his personal and public life according to law, Edippo's world falls apart. He had anticipated giving one son Thebes and the other Corinth—and so made a will to that end. But with the discovery of the incest comes the discovery he has no rights to Corinth. His incest is the proximate cause of the fight between his sons and the downfall of the kingdom.

The motif of averted incest, usually between sister and brother, in works like John Lyly's play *Mother Bombie* (c. 1590) and Celio Malespini's *Ducento novelli* (tales written 1595–1605), 2:37 is used to heighten an environment of lust by making a love affair prohibited. Such works invert the Oedipus motif of a foreigner marrying a supposed stranger who turns out to be related and therefore taboo. Instead, supposed relations who are in love but frustrated by the taboo discover they are not related. One of the problems in such plays is that there is no courtly language of incest. So it is with Arbaces, in Beaumont and Fletcher's play *A King and No King* (1619), when he describes how he feels about his sister Panthea: "I would desire her [Panthea's] love / Lasciviously, lewdly, incestuously, / To do a sin that needs must damn us both" (3.3). He wishes to "act such sins" that he fears to think. All is done to arouse, to titillate by holding up what can't be had. Even Panthea feels a passion she won't name, and only that he is a brother stops her. Then the Laws of Nature and of God are brought in. To be incestuous is to follow the beasts and physical desire and thus to overthrow divinity. But to be unable to follow Nature is not to be free. Arbaces' personal dilemma is split into two characters: Mardonius, or Reason, who says that if the king is incestuous then all laws may be broken; and Bessus, or Beastly Nature, who says if the king so desires he may rape even his mother. In the end the laws of God barely are sustained over those of Nature.

Nature in such plays is equated with ferocious beasts and wild passion. Lope de Vega's *La fianza satisfecha* (*A Bond Honoured,* c. 1614) and John Ford's tragedy *'Tis Pity She's a Whore* (1633) consider sister-brother incest from the standpoint of liberation of the self. Lope's play at once looks back to the Middle Ages with its insistence on Christ's ability to forgive all sins no matter how grievous, and looks forward to the twentieth century in creating a character, Leonido, existential in dimensions. Incest becomes a tool to test the self. Before the self can be found, all things that bind the self must be rejected; so incest binds to the rules of the family, religion to the commands of God, nationality to the laws of the state. Each of these is rejected by Leonido. Throughout most of the play he tries to rape his sister. The rape is not motivated by lust or love, but as he puts it, by the desire to defile his blood. As a child he bit his mother's breasts and sucked blood with milk; later he kills his mother a moment after she gives birth; he blinds and kicks his father, renounces his religion, his name, his country. After all is abandoned, he is free to choose who he will be. He has a vision of Christ, accepts Him, and dies like Christ on the cross. No less astounding in its exploitation of shock is Ford's *'Tis Pity*. The incestuous brother brings his sister's heart in on a dagger during the last scene. Incest is justified as natural—the attraction to someone thought beautiful, the enjoyment of pleasure. While Beaumont and Fletcher offered the same concepts, they repudiated them in favor of moral law and social custom. Here it is these very laws that form a barrier between brother and sister and bring them to subterfuge and to death. Incest would have no ill effect if such barriers were not imposed by society. The language of incestous love is here expanded. The incestuous pair kiss and fondle; they make of the taboo a new divinity and a new heaven. Nor will death end their love. If mother-son incest showed how civil upheaval grew out of moral disintegration, now because of rampant civil and moral corruption, the world can be redeemed only by the truth of the senses—including the freedom for incestuous love.

The Seventeenth Century

Little is new in this period, save perhaps for multiple incest (illicit relationships among several members of the same family or incestuous affairs in both the subplots and main plots of plays). Incest does, however, take center stage in all its tender as well as lusty aspects, an outgrowth of the Renaissance's candid treatment of it. Dynastic dramas pivot about an incest issue; fate, detached now from the gods, is put into the camp of man, whose single rule is the familial one concerning incest. Even in the fairy tale incest becomes a legitimate motif; see G. Basile, "La bella delle mani mozze," ("Penta the Handless"), and "L'orsa" ("The She-Bear") in *Il pentamerone,* 1634. The Renaissance debate about incest also continued. Is the taboo a mark of the decayed modern world or a mark of the innocent ancient world? Is blind incestuous love different from any other love?

The works that consider mother-son incest revolve around the Oedipus theme and have in common a detachment of the incest from the patricide, multiple incestuous relationships, and a continuing concern to incorporate incest into the category of love. In both Corneille's *Œdipe* (1659) and Dryden and Lee's *Oedipus* (1679) Oedipus has a sister. She would have been the legitimate heir to the throne had Oedipus, the foreign conqueror, not come to Thebes. Thus both works link the Oedipus theme to dynastic struggles. But in both plays the sister offers fresh love interest and in both cases incestuous love—one a feigned incest and the other a real incest. Corneille keeps the mother-son incest in the background; it hardly creeps out. His Molinist tendencies interfered with the strong relationship between Fate and blind incest. He tries therefore to detach fate from all of Oedipus' acts; for instance, Oedipus' killing of Laius is justified as an act of free will—a single man defended his life against three. Their incest is the single irrational element in the couple's relationship. But their self-punishment surmounts Fate by making man control his fate—in acting morally by self-punishment man puts to shame the gods. How Corneille unlinks Fate from incest is seen by how he treats the love of Dirce, Oedipus' sister, and Thésée. Assuming they are sister and brother, they briefly debate the question of love's relation to incest. Though they condemn incest, they intimate that love is love and if incest is discovered love doesn't change, that love of the senses is always sweet. Dryden also gives Oedipus a sister. The sister gives the opportunity to multiply the incests; she becomes the love target of her uncle, Creon. Thus the dynastic concerns of Corneille in creating the character are transferred to predominately incestuous ones. Incest is forever on the stage. To stress its horror Oedipus distinguishes the crime of patricide and mother-son incest: "embrue my Arms up to my shoulders / In the dear entrails of the best of Fathers / Than offer at the execrable Act of damned Incest." In fact, Dryden does everything possible to make incestuous attraction a matter of free choice rather than fate. Signs, omens, dreams, necromancy are piled up from the start to point out to Oedipus and Jocasta who they are, as Dryden also does in *Don Sebastian* (play, 1690). So that when the discovery is made, Jocasta and Oedipus express a kind of obligatory horror and then almost fall into each other's arms—a triumph of reason over superstition. No less is Racine's *La Thébaïde* (*The Theban Brothers*, play, 1664) filled with incest, structured into every aspect of the play: mother-son incest (Jocasta and Oedipus) versus a son's patricide; sister-brother incest (Antigone and Polynice) versus brothers killing each other; uncle-niece incest (Creon and Antigone) versus a father's hatred for his niece's love, his own son. All relationships originate in the prior incest of Oedipus and Jocasta; all history originates in their incest—manifested in fraternal hatred and civil disorder. The family is fate, and the fate of the family is incest

Stepmother-stepson incest is the subject of Racine's masterpiece, *Phèdre*

(*Phaedra,* 1677). Here he develops his ideas on incest and the family. He substitutes for the classical idea of fate, incest. Incest becomes a projection from the past on the future, and one cannot escape it. Racine makes the incest a part of the very structural fabric of his play. To the other unities he adds the unity of the family. As time and place are contained within the parameters of stage conventions, the characters are trapped in the conventions of the family. In spite of the fact that she struggles, Phèdre cannot free herself from her Cretan past— the monstrous bestiality of Pasiphae. She does not blindly fall into sin, as Jocasta did, but knowing she is doing wrong, she participates in the criminal act. Phèdre clearly sees her sin as incest—not stepmother-stepson incest—but love for a son. Her attraction is at first maternal but turns into lust. It is more than a biological connection; it is social. Racine adds a subplot to the play, the love of Hippolyte for Aricie, the true heir to the Athenian throne. On one level this subplot emphasizes the dynastic problem consistently found in incest plays of this period, but on the other it thrusts Phèdre's incest into higher relief, contrasted as it is with the pure love of Hippolyte and Aricie.

Two of the outstanding plays about sister-brother incest also consider dynastic problems: Tirso de Molina's *La venganza de Tamar* (*Tamar's Vengeance,* c. 1623), from a religious point of view, and John Dryden's *Don Sebastian,* from a secular one. Tirso's play takes up the Bible story of David's children, Amnon, Tamar, and Absalom. The war-love metaphor is used in striking ways. David fights against his enemies while he has foes in his house: Amnon's lust for his half-sister Tamar and Absalom's lust for David's kingdom. Although on a biological level Amnon's desire is for a sibling, on a symbolic level it is paternal. He scales the walls of his father's seraglio, where his father keeps his concubine-wives, and finds there his sister, whom he eventually rapes. At first Amnon argues for a universal natural law to justify his relations with his sister: like is attracted to like. Next he posits that Adam and Eve obeyed the law of necessity, and finally he argues for the Law of Love. Two central qualities that Dryden's *Don Sebastian* shares with Tirso's play are the consummation of the incest and the arguments in defense of the union. Don Sebastian unwittingly marries his sister Almeyda, though—as in Dryden's *Oedipus*—many signs, verging on the absurd, are given to the pair that only the most obtuse would not be forewarned. Upon learning of the incest, they speak of their one night of bliss—"a glorious, guilty night." Just before they separate forever at the end to live in penitence, they—as in his *Oedipus*—almost stay together. They argue that their world is decrepit for preserving such taboos made only for "little man," and that "the vigorous young world was ignorant / of these [incest] restrictions."

The Eighteenth Century

Mother-son incest is almost entirely avoided in the plays that treat the Oedipus theme. While the patricide could be logically explained, the way it had been in the Middle Ages, as a fight for life and therefore reasonable, the eighteenth-century writers found no way to place the incest under the control of Oedipus' will. Even M.-J. Chénier in a late eighteenth-century translation of *Oedipus Rex, Œdipe roi* (posthumous, 1824), cut Jocasta's statement about it not being unusual for men to dream of sleeping with their mothers. For the most part, when incest of every other type was treated, it was rationalized with greater force than ever before as a sanctioned practice of early times, among many peoples of both the prehistoric and the historic periods, and as fulfilling a multiplicity of desires—the capacity of every person to love on several levels at once. Such paneroticism was a mark of the *homme raffiné;* the incest taboo was only a prejudice according to the more literate pornographers of the period. More and more writers portray incest as they thought people would actually experience it and react to it.

Realizing the incompatibility of mother-son incest to their concept of Oedipus as a political leader unswervingly dedicated to the truth, writers used a number of devices to strip him of its taint. Because Voltaire, in his tragedy *Œdipe* (*Oedipus,* 1718), cannot reconcile Oedipus the clear-sighted investigator with Oedipus blindly incestuous, he has Jocasta marry Oedipus without loving him, having only the tender feeling toward him appropriate for a mother. She, meanwhile, fittingly loves another. To completely purify the theme, mother and son have no children. Lamotte-Houdar, in his play *Œdipe* (1730), also will not have Oedipus culpable of incest when it is outside of his will. Oedipus' crime, here, is that having been brought up in the home of a peasant, he marries beyond his class. A half sentimental, half Gothic play, *Oedipus* (1760), by Bodmer exploits sheer prurience in a long scene that takes place around Oedipus and Jocasta's marriage bed. When they try to embrace each other, a ghost—according to Oedipus—or a "blitzender Schatten" ("flashing shadow")—according to Jocasta—steps between them. Like Lamotte-Houdar, Bodmer will have no irrational crime; therefore, both royalty and the people declare the pair innocent (though they do punish themselves eventually). It was easier to fit mother-son incest into a subject other than Oedipus, like the history of the exotic queen Sémiramis, used by a slew of writers. As he had done in his *Œdipe,* Voltaire in his tragedy *Sémiramis* (1748) has the awful relationship discovered before a union is consummated. But in the *Sémiramis* (play, 1717) of Crébillon (père) all the potential of such a prohibited act is fully exploited. Discovering she has made love to her son, Sémiramis is less concerned with incest than with losing a lover. In fact she argues that she feels no maternal instinct, that the gods commit incest, and that it is practiced by members of her class. Crébillon uses incest as a way of saying that no one really knows himself.

Crébillon's incestuous pair are not blameworthy and neither are those in Restif de la Bretonne's *Sara; ou la dernière aventure . . .* (*Sara,* 1783), a tale of father-daughter incest that begins unwittingly and continues even after it is discovered. Incest regenerates; it recalls to the father his mistress in the person of their daughter. The father loves the daughter as a wife "selon les lois de la nature" [according to nature's laws], while the daughter argues her love from the threshold of the multiplicity of feelings it stimulates.

Sister-brother incest is treated by Defoe in *Moll Flanders* (novel, 1722) as a mistake having no lasting psychological consequences; while Sade treated it as a desirable aim having only erotic consequences. Moll marries her brother unwittingly and though she feels "nauseous" upon discovery, she is practical—what would she do, where would she go, how would she live if she told her brother-husband the truth? So she goes on living with him for three years. After she does leave, she never lets the incest trouble her. On the other hand, the brother does deteriorate, but this is more because of her wretched treatment of him during the three years after she found out the truth. Defoe purports to be giving the actual autobiography of Moll; this is the way people really act and feel. When Moll and the son of this incestuous marriage meet years later, they greet each other with an excess of passion and no guilt. Incest of every kind is a staple in Sade's works. He treats incest as stemming from the natural love of relatives taken to its ultimate—passion. For instance, a sister and brother in the novel *La philosophie dans le boudoir* (*The Philosophy of the Bedroom,* 1795) slowly and surely develop their love before it is perversely consummated, only after the sister's marriage. The justifications for incest are historical, anthropological, economic, and psychological: (1) it was practiced of old (e.g., by Adam) as a way to propagate the race; (2) it is universally authorized among many cultures to cement families together for economic and social reasons; (3) it is banned only because of the fear that some families would become too powerful; (4) it is initiated because love is born of resemblances; (5) it is the only love given by nature, for it grows out of family feelings.

The Romantic Period and Nineteenth Century

Mother-son incest concerns few writers who treat the Oedipus theme. When incest is tied to this theme, ghosts, dreams, and visions abound, emphasizing the psychological conditions of incest. Such elements come from the standard repertoire of Gothic literature, which itself used every kind of incest for shock value. Father-daughter incest is also rare and when used becomes a metaphor for tyranny both familial and political, as in Shelley's melodrama *The Cenci* (1819). Sibling incest, both pseudo and real, on the other hand, becomes virtually *the* type of true love. It is pure, touching, and invariably sympathetic. The long and slowly growing justification of this type of incest as natural is solidified and sustained by comparative anthropological and even biological data. But most of all this incest is a way of gaining the matching half of his soul for which the romantic hero always seemed to be searching. Toward the end of the century only the decadents treat incest. The Victorians, for the most part, tried to shun even the word incest, so in Edward FitzGerald's version of Sophocles' *Oedipus Rex* (1880) Creon is castigated for shaming his family by using the word in public.

In the plays that deal with the Oedipus theme, spirits and mystic revelations haunt the characters, stressing the incestuous aspect of the theme. The sexual relations between mother and son, rather than patricide, engender a tense psychological condition. This is true of the plays by C. Alberghetti Forciroli, *Edipo*

(1798), Martinez de la Rosa, *Edipo* (1832), and even those by Prellwitz, *Oedipus* (1896), and Hofmannsthal, *Ödipus und die Sphinx* (1906). The last two particularly consider the Oedipus theme almost in a dream vision that mirrors a mythic world, a time before incest was differentiated as crime and was the final bliss of prehistory. Prellwitz adds to the earlier mythic period, the modern era. Oedipus' self-sacrifice distinguishes the old law of incest from the new law with the taboo.

Rousseau (see *La nouvelle Héloïse* [*The New Heloise,* novel, 1761]) sets the keynote for viewing sister-brother incest in a positive way. The first unions in prehistory were happy, for such unions were strengthened by a sympathetic mental bond of relationship added to a physical one. These first unions, Orou forced *l'aumônier* to admit in Diderot's dialogue *Supplément au voyage de Bougainville* (*Supplement to Bougainville's Voyage,* 1796), obviously did no harm to nature. Sibling relationships in Chateaubriand's novels *Atala* (1801) and *René* (1802) are nevertheless tragically frustrated not by nature but by decadent modern civilization. Besides the divine right of the passions, which these works assume, the standard metaphor they use is Adam and Eve—in a union with a sibling one finds the other half of his soul. Such love is called "amitié fraternelle," where love is deepened by the knowledge of a relationship. Shelley glorified sister-brother incest as the purest and most lasting kind of love in his poem *Epipsychidion* (1821). Incest is a symbol of pristine love in Byron's play *Cain* (1821), which because the work is more concerned with revolt views the incest from that standpoint. Lucifer explains to the sister-wife and the brother-husband, Adah and Cain, that incest will be negatively viewed in later times, for arbitrary law will violate the law of nature. Incest is then equivalent to defiance in the modern world; it is a chosen direction, never blindly entered in Byron. In Melville's *Pierre, or the Ambiguities* (1852), Pierre and his half-sister live together as husband and wife in name only. As the subtitle of the novel indicates, their relationship is ambiguous both to themselves and to the outside world. Their smoldering emotions are continually frustrated because of a taboo they only half acknowledge and half understand. The very bond that holds them together prevents the expression of their love.

Toward the end of the century the theme is colored by sado-masochism, eroticism, and decadence, as in the sister-brother incest in Swinburne's novel *Lesbia Brandon* (1877, not published until 1952). Sister-brother incest heightens an atmosphere of decadence in Elémir Bourges' novel *Le crépuscule des dieux* (*The Twilight of the Gods,* 1884), where it is shamefully nurtured by an evil mistress from its unconscious stirrings in the siblings to its conscious expression.

The Twentieth Century

Interest in Greek mythology and the influence of Freudian psychoanalysis combined to force incest to the very forefront of literature. A group of works treats incest in a mythic setting, trying to find out how it is related to the problem of individual freedom. A second group looks at incest in a psychological setting, examining its emotional dynamics and the geometry of its process as an abnormal condition. Both groups interlock, for Freud is mythologized. His influence is so pervasive that every relationship between a man and and woman is potentially incestuous, a reenactment of the myth of Oedipus.

The extent to which the incest taboo stunts individual growth and inhibits personal freedom is examined in a great many poems, plays, and novels that deal with the Oedipus theme. One group of works projects mother-son incest into a mythic prehistory, much in the manner of Prellwitz and Hofmannsthal. Rudolf Pannwitz's play *Die Befreiung des Oidipus* (*The Liberation of Oedipus,* 1913) is a wild revel, depicting a golden age of freedom when incest was the "unsinful" sin, when only ecstatic song, dance, and music mattered. In Natalia Correia's dramatic poem *O progresso de Edipo* (1957) and Pier Paolo Pasolini's screen-play *Edipo re* (*Oedipus the King,* 1967) mother and son are erotically attracted; the sin of incest is of the head not of the heart, and incest is tantamount to self-discovery. Correia views the mythic period as a time of blindness to such a taboo; Pasolini sandwiches the contemporary period around the mythic, showing how the family is integrated into a universal idea. Alain Robbe-Grillet's novel *Les gommes* (*The Erasers,* 1953) uniquely places incest in a kind of cycle, which he mirrors in the form of the oracle: patricide in the morning, incest in the afternoon, and blindness in the evening. Another group of works finds that to disregard the taboo is to be free, and at the same time to experience it is to deepen love. This paradoxical situation underlies a part of André Gide's play *Œdipe*. On the one hand Oedipus believes he is a bastard. But on the other hand incest is an extension of love—together with conjugal love Oedipus also feels filial love for Jocasta. The Oedipus in Henry Treece's novel *The Eagle King* (1965) must symbolically kill his father and mate with his mother many times if he wants to be free of them. He must get beyond the "smothering" mother; he cannot be great as long as he is a son. Alberto Moravia has his modern Oedipus perform the ancient *Oedipus* of Sophocles in the play *Il dio Kurt (Kurt the God,* 1968). The objective of Kurt, the Nazi commandant-director of the inner play, is to destroy the family and its cornerstone the incest taboo, the only obstacle to freedom. In a Nazi concentration camp a Jewish mother and son are tricked into having sexual relations. When faced with either the death of her son or sex with him, the mother chooses sex and life. The son also chooses life rather than self-blinding after he discovers he unknowingly slept with his mother. The life principle and individual freedom triumph over the taboo. But on another level, since Kurt himself suffers guilt for his own incestuous feeling toward his sister, the taboo triumphs. The whole psychological apparatus of sexual frustration, incestuous dreams, incestuous fantasies, and erotic arousal fills the works of this period. Oedipus flees Corinth in order to suppress his youthful erotic desires for his supposed mother Merope in both Max Croiset's *Oedipoes en zijn moeder* (*Oedipus and His Mother,* 1950) and José María Pemán's *Edipo* (*Oedipus,* 1953). Jocasta, who dominates so many of the works of this period, either desires a young man like her son, dreams of incest with her son, or knows from the start that she is mating with her son, as in Raymond Duncan's *Oidipous* (1927), Jean Cocteau's *La machine infernale* (*The Infernal Machine,* 1934), and Herman Teirlinck's *Jocaste tegen God* (*Jocasta against God,* 1961). In all these plays the gods are culprits, toying with and suffocating man.

Thomas Mann treated both mother-son incest and sister-brother incest in his *Der Erwählte* (*The Holy Sinner,* novel, 1951) and his trilogy of novels *Joseph und seine Brüder* (*Joseph and His Brothers,* 1933–1943). *Der Erwählte* is an ironic retelling of the medieval myth of Gregorius. Incest here is an expression of the uncontrolled Id. First Mann describes the psychological conditions of sister-brother incest; parental permissiveness and continual physical contact allow free reign to the natural feelings of the boy and girl. For example, the very night the father dies the siblings first enjoy intercourse. Next, mother-son incest unwittingly committed occurs because nature only recognizes male or female. The child of the sister-brother incest, Gregorius, after having been exposed and brought up on a remote island, returns and marries his mother. Though unaware they are indeed mother and son, they are aware that their relationship is parental in nature. The unrestrained sexual appetite may only be purged by man's first living as a beast—as Gregorius does when he almost becomes a hedgehog— before he can become human again. In his Joseph epic, Mann again treated mother-son incest in mythic terms, this time following the story of Joseph and Potiphar's wife. The relationship of Potiphar, his wife—here called Mut—and Joseph is shaped in terms of a nuclear family. Mut's neurotic desires for Joseph, Potiphar's impotence, and Joseph's egocentric nature interplay to form a classic family drama. But for the most part Mann sees the incest in larger terms. All events are replicas of previous events and models for future actions. Thus this incest is like the incestuous relationship of Jacob with Leah and Rachel. Indeed, at one point, Mut dresses up like Rachel.

Two extraordinary novels treat father-daughter incest: Julien Green's *Varouna* (*Then Shall the Dust Return,* 1940) and Max Frisch's *Homo Faber* (1957). Divided into three parts, the third part of *Varouna* analyzes the incest of the second part through the eyes of a writer, herself consumed by incestuous desires. A father can only escape from the guilt of incest by shadowing it in magic and necromancy and then finally convincing himself of the transmigration of souls. Thus he believes his dead wife is reborn in his daughter, who in name and looks is exactly like her. At the very point of consummating his lust, he dies, overcome by the weight of repression. In Max Frisch's beautiful novel, the father unknowingly enjoys his daughter. The closer he gets to the solution of her identity the greater is his repression. But repression here is a device to show how modern man ignores the truth of his feelings and instincts, which are held in bondage by the demands of a mechanical and technological society.

Confused family relations mark many of the words that treat sister-brother incest. Children left parentless or a drunken unloving or adulterous parent seem to mark the tense psychological condition in which incestuous siblings grow as in Ibsen's play *Lille Eyolf* (*Little Eyolf,* 1894) and Cocteau's novel *Les enfants terribles* (*The Holy Terrors,* 1929). Incest means an escape from the law of change in Ibsen's play; it insures stability, for a relationship is simply continued. Both in this play and in Robert Musil's novel *Der Mann ohne Eigenschaften* (*The Man Without Qualities,* 1930–1943) love is somewhat narcissistic. Sister and brother are made in each other's image. Iris Murdoch's brilliant novel *A Severed Head* (1961) considers sister-brother incest and various kinds of symbolic incestuous relationships in a world structured on a foundation of misdirected love. Seeing the woman he loves in bed with her brother, a man becomes obsessed with incest, studies it. Incest is the forbidden, the magical—a glimpse into the unknown. It is of the head not of the body.

Other kinds of incest range from the homosexual relationship between an uncle and his nephews in André Gide's novel *Les faux-monnayeurs* (*The Counterfeiters,* 1925) to the aunt and nephew incest in the novels by Ivy Compton-Burnett, *More Women than Men* (1933), and by García Márquez in *Cien años de soledad* (*One Hundred Years of Solitude,* 1967). Márquez's novel sees incest growing out of family traditions of love and caring. For example, from childhood a nephew grows up with his aunt. They undress in front of each other. At first all is natural and innocent. The nephew runs to the aunt's bed when he is afraid of the dark. Next they begin to play kissing games. This turns into passion. Then the aunt realizes that "she was foundering about in an autumnal passion, one that was dangerous and had no future."

See also: Family, Marriage, Oedipus Complex, Rape, Sex.

Selected Bibliography

Glotz, Gustav, and G. Humbert. "Incestum-Incestus." *Dictionnaire des antiquités grecques et romaines.* Ed. Charles Daremberg and Edmond Saglio. 1900. Graz, Austria: Akademische Druk-u. Verlagsantalt, 1962–1963.

Hesse-Fink, Evelyne. *Etudes sur le thème de l'inceste dans la littérature française.* Berne: Herbert Lang, 1971.

Rank, Otto. *Das Inzest-Motiv in Dichtung und Sage: Grundzüge einer Psychologie des dichterischen Schaffens.* 2d ed. Leipzig: Franz Deuticke, 1926.

Thorslev, Peter L. "Incest as Romantic Symbol." *Comparative Literature Studies* 2 (1965): 41–58,

RICHARD FABRIZIO

INCUBUS AND SUCCUBUS

"Incubus" and "succubus" are defined as demons, deities, or spirits, generally malign, which oppress, weigh down, or have intercourse with humans of the opposite sex. Early Latin church fathers used the term "incubus" when dealing with a number of Old and New Testament texts, apocryphal lore and literature, early Jewish commentaries, and Greek traditions in which spirits, gods, angels, or demons oppressed humans of the opposite sex. The term "succubus" was used only after the year 1000 to describe the female of the species (masculine gender; demons were supposed sexless).

Origins in Judaeo-Christian Literature

It is evident that the incubus/succubus is related to the nightmare dream. The dream is usually of an attacker that causes a feeling of complete helplessness, suffocation, and terror as it weighs down upon its victim. The incubus came to describe in particular the nightmare monster who attacked sexually. The seriousness of the theme varied from age to age, but in general, the earlier the account, the more serious the encounter. In the earliest narratives, a visit by a nightmare or incubus could be momentous and tragic. During the Middle Ages, a victim who confessed to intercourse with an incubus could be charged with heresy—allegiance to Satan. From 1300 to 1700, certain authors exploited the comic aspects of dealing with an "incubus," and in more recent times, from 1700 to the present, authors introduce incubi or succubi, or their various manifestations, for symbolic purposes.

The most significant passage for the origin and development of the concept of the incubus/succubus is Genesis 6.1–6, which describes how the "sons of God came in unto the daughters of men, and they bore children to them,"—the Nephilim, men of renown. The "sons of God" were taken by certain writers of the Apocrypha to mean fallen angels, hence the offspring of such unions were extraordinary persons, giants. Several New Testament writers shared this interpretation (Jude 6–8; 2 Pet. 2.4; and 1 Tim. 2.9), but the major support comes from numerous Apocryphal books. First Enoch narrates the story of how certain angels, the "Watchers," originally sent to watch over, instruct, and judge, instead fall in love with the daughters of men. Their offspring are the giants. After these giants die, their evil spirits afflict, oppress, destroy, attack—"rise up against the children of men and against the women" (15.12). The Book of Jubilees (c. 135–105 B.C.) also contains references to the "Watchers" who "went whoring after the daughters of men" (5.1–5; 7.21–25; 10.1–6), as do the Testament of Reuben (5.3–7)(c. 109–106 B.C.), and 2 Baruch (56.10–15)(c. A.D. 50–100).

Early Jewish Tradition

Early Jewish commentators perpetuated the story. Philo of Alexandria (30 B.C.–A.D. 45) gave a quasi-Platonic interpretation of Genesis 6.1–6 in his *Peri Gigantōn* (*On the Giants,* pars. 2, 3, and 13). This was not mythmaking, he wrote, "the air, too, is filled with living beings, invisible to us." They are higher creatures and "have never deigned to be brought into union with any of the parts of the earth." Some of the lower sort, however, enjoyed the pleasures of sex, and thus the giants were conceived and born. As he states in *Ton en Genesei Kai tōn en Exagōgē zētēmatōn te kai Luseōn Biblia* (*Questions and Answers on Genesis,* 1.92), such unions were not entirely felicitous. The offspring may "become zealous emulators of material depravity" and "draw away from paternal virtue." Flavius Josephus (c. A.D. 38–c. 100) also alluded to the stories deriving from Genesis 6, writing in his *Antiquitates judaicae* (*Antiquitates of the Jews,* 1.3.1): "The deeds that tradition ascribes to them [the angels who consorted with humans] resemble the audacious expoits told by the Greeks of the giants."

This tradition of lustful angels continued as a major motif in Jewish literature throughout the early Middle Ages. It is found in the Chronicles of Jerahmeel (c. 1150), which is made up of materials going back at least to the seventh century. The Pirkei de-Rabbi Eliezer, a haggadic midrash dating from the first half of the eighth century, includes a complete chapter on the seduction of angels by the daughters of men, rather than vice versa (so also women seduced the Watchers in the Testament of Reuben). In the thirteenth century, the Zohar, the "Book of Splendor," a compilation of ancient lore and glosses on the Bible, has numerous references to female spirits who came to Adam and had intercourse with him. A certain Rabbi Isaac commented: "This need cause no surprise, because now also when a man dreams in his sleep, female spirits come and disport with him, and so conceive from him and subsequently give birth." According to Rabbi Isaac such demons also consorted with Cain, from whom "originate all the evil habitations and demons and goblins, and evil spirits in the world," and with the sister of Tubal Cain, Naamah, who was "the great seducer not only of men, but also of spirits and demons." These demons, or heavenly spirits, according to Rabbi Hiya, could unite with men in spite of their airy substance because they became "concrete as air" when they descended from heaven (Zohar, "Bereshith," 1.54a–57b; "Leviticus," 5.76b–77a; and Louis Ginzberg, *The Legends of the Jews,* 1925). The prototype of the female demon in Jewish literature, Lilith, appears in earliest Assyrian texts as Lili, a sexually insatiable female demon who roamed at night looking for mortal men to share her orgies. She is a variant of the goddess Ishtar who seduced men and then grew tired of them and turned them into various sub-human forms. Gilgamesh rejected her in no uncertain terms but lost his friend Enkidu in the subsequent quarrel with Ishtar. Lilith in Jewish lore of the early Middle Ages was Adam's first wife, and the result of the union was a race of demons, spirits, and ghosts (Zohar, "Bereshith," 1.54b; "Leviticus," 5.76b).

The Early Christian Era

Early church fathers applied the name "incubus" to these molesting demons. They came to their attention because of Genesis 6 and the numerous traditions of unions between spirits and humans in Jewish and classical lore. Josephus had perceived the similarity between the actions of the sons of God in Genesis 6 and the giants in Greek tradition, and the early church fathers, Justin Martyr (c. 100–165), Tertullian (c. 160–230), Clement of Alexandria (c. 200), Lactantius (c. 240–c.320), and Augustine (354–430) came to the same conclusion. Justin Martyr in his *Apologia* (*Apology,* 1.5, 2.5; c. 160) relates that the fallen angels of Genesis 6: "transgressed [their] appointment, and were captivated by love of women, and begat children who are those that are called demons.'' The ''evil demons, affecting apparitions of themselves, both defiled women and corrupted boys, and showed . . . fearful sights to men.'' To appease these beings, men worshipped them as gods until, Justin writes, Socrates had the courage to deny the error. Tertullian and Lactantius followed the general interpretation of Justin, and it is not until the fourth century that a second view gained ascendency— that sons of God were the sons of Shem and the daughters of man, offspring of Cain. The view that prevailed after the fourth century did not detract from the belief in the existence of demons such as the incubi, but only from the theory that they derived from the union between angels and men. St. Augustine's *De civitate Dei* (*The City of God,* treatise, 413–426) is the *locus classicus* for later interpreters. St. Augustine wrote that he distrusted the Book of Enoch and was not wholly convinced that the ''sons of God'' were angels. He also discussed the ''general rumor'' of the molesting ''sylvans and fauns who are commonly called 'incubi.' '' He finally conceded that ''these attacks are affirmed by persons of such indubitable honesty and credit that it would be impudence to deny it.''

Numerous women and clerics of the early centuries of the Christian era, especially those committed to celibacy, were prone to attacks from night demons of the opposite sex, and the descriptions of these accounts are legion. The male demon attacks a woman committed to virginity in the Acts of Thomas (3.42– 47), and the female demon oppresses St. Anthony ''in the navel of the belly'' in St. Athanasius' *Vita S. Antonii* (*Life of St. Anthony,* first written in Greek c.356, chapter 5). In Renaissance art, the scene of the sleeping St. Anthony being tempted by a number of beautiful women became popular (e.g., Jan Wellens de Cock, c. 1600). The encyclopedist Isidore of Seville (c. 560–636) (*Etymologiae,* 8.11.103–104) equated incubi with Greek classical demons, satyrs and *pilosi* (hairy monster), Celtic *dusii* (spirits), and Latin *fauni ficarii* (fig tree fauns), and their actions, he wrote, are well known: ''[The incubi] often appear immorally to women and accomplish intercourse with them.'' Later encyclopedias, commentaries, and glossaries depended upon St. Augustine and Isidore, and the incubus is usually linked with the *pilosus* and *satyrus.* The female demon is equated with Lilith or the *lamia.*

The Middle Ages

The amalgamation of the classical, Judeo-Christian incubus with generically similar monsters of other cultures continued as Latin influence spread northward. In the various Germanic areas, the *mara/maere* (modern mare—nightmare) equated with the night stalker (*nichtgenga*), and elf oppressor (*aelfadle*), was glossed by Latin authors with *incubus, satyrus, monstrum,* and *pilosus.* The female counterpart, the hag (*haegtis*) and wild woman (*strix*) was glossed with *lamia* and described as man-devouring. These many associations seem to have contributed to the prominence of the incubus throughout the Latin Christian world. By the year 1000, the ''incubus dogma,'' as G. L. Kittredge called it (*Witchcraft in Old and New England,* 1929), became almost an article of faith.

Clerics described in detail the sexual nature of this demon, the potential violence that he was capable of inflicting, his various disguises, and his ingenious methods of propagation. At the same time, the official church position, as stated in the *Canon episcopi* (c. 900), in decretals by Burchard of Worms (1020), Ivo Chartres (c. 1040–1115), and Gratian (1140), was that these night attacks by the incubus, "agrestes feminae" or "sylvaticas," who appear to their lovers and then disappear, had more to do with dreams and visions raised by the devil than with physical night creatures.

Yet even influential churchmen sometimes had first-hand experience with victims, and after 1100 the delusion of the incubus was more pervasive than ever. It is not clear why, in the twelfth and thirteenth centuries, there should have been such pervasive interest in the night demons. A thesis advanced recently by Jeffrey B. Russell (*Witchcraft in the Middle Ages*, 1972) is that the early belief in these dark forces in France, Lombardy, the Low Countries, and Germany resulted from the rise of Aristotelian science and the heresy of the Catharist sects. If the Aristotelians argued that all could be explained by the use of logic and dialectics, then irrational events could be seen as the workings of supernatural forces. It was this closed system of scholastic logic that, according to Russell, reinforced "the trend, already begun within the Augustinian tradition, toward driving magic in the direction of witchcraft." Russell also states that "from 1140 to 1230 the heresy of Catharism was the single greatest influence on demonology and witchcraft." The Catharist dualism, positing an evil opposition to the good, meant that those in league with the devil, heretics, had to be eradicated. In this context, the definition of "heretic" came to include not only religious dissenters, but also sorcerers. Witchcraft, illicit sex with incubi, and certain kinds of magic now were regarded as dissent and heresy, subject to investigation by the Inquisition. The widely reported case of Angele de la Barthe (1275) included charges that she had intercourse for a period of years with an incubus. Intercourse with demons or with the devil was evidence of a "pact" with the devil.

Popular theologians of the thirteenth century who dealt with the subject of incubi and succubi include Caesarius of Heisterbach, William of Auvergne, Vincent of Beauvais, Albertus Magnus, Thomas of Cantimpre, St. Bonaventure, St. Thomas Aquinas (1225–1274), and Duns Scotus. St. Thomas Aquinas (*Summa theologica*, c. 1266–1274) dealt with most of the issues that were current, though his answers were not always the standard. Could the angels of God have stooped to such depths in antediluvian times?—Unthinkable, according to St. Thomas. Were there really such creatures as incubi and succubi?—Yes. Did these creatures take pleasure in their exploitation of men and women?—No, "they delight in human sins in so far as they impede human good." How could these spirits, composed of air, propagate?—They could assume living bodies and do what living bodies could do. The incubus demon could "steal the semen of an innocent youth in nocturnal emissions and pour it into the womb of a woman." Were these ordinary children?—They could be greater and more illustrious than ordinary children because demons could perform the acts at auspicious moments and with exceptional mortals. On the last point, an alternate answer soon became more prominent. The offspring of an incubus were often demonic, and it is through the union of the devil and a woman that the Antichrist himself was to be born. So the Old English writer Wulfstan II, archbishop of York, wrote in his tract on the Antichrist, "Christ is true god and man, and Antichrist is true devil and man." This tradition remained alive through the Middle Ages and Renaissance.

The major compendiums of the later Middle Ages, Johannes Nider's *Formicarius* (*The Anthill*, 1435–1437), Ulrich Molitor's *De lamiis et phitonicis mulieribus* (*Concerning Female Witches and Sorcerers*, 1489), and the most infamous and popular of all, Jacob Sprenger and Henrich Kraemer's *Malleus maleficarum* (*The Hammer of Witches*, 1486–1489), dealt with issues of witchcraft and sorcery in prurient detail. The last was prefaced in the 1495 and later editions with the so-called Witch Bull of Pope Innocent VIII. The attack by Innocent is mainly against witches: "many persons of both sexes, unmindful of their own salvation . . . have abandoned themselves to devils, incubi and succubi" and perpetrated all kinds of crimes. Even Martin Luther (*Tischreden* [*Table-Talk*, 1566]) stated that "there are incubi and succubi." Luther also agreed that the devil could have "illicit intercourse with old whores and weather witches to satisfy their lusts," but he denied that the devil could beget a child, "for only God is the creator." The devil could, however, exchange a child for a "changling"—a mere "massa carnis," without a soul.

Literature in the Middle Ages

Demons of the incubus species are common in various genres of secular literature during the Middle Ages—in Arthurian legends, folktales, ballads, romances, and novellas. In Geoffrey of Monmouth's *Historia regum Britanniae* (*The History of the Kings of Britain*, c. 1137), and in the versions of his successors, Wace, Layamon, and others, the magician Merlin is miraculously conceived in a union between an incubus and a nun. In the *Historia*, a wise man commented on the union: "In the books . . . I have discovered that many men have been born in this way. . . . As Apuleius states in *De deo Socratis* between the moon and the earth live spirits which we call incubi demons." As a result of his father, Merlin had something supernatural about him. In later French and English romances the episode of the conception became greatly expanded and linked to the Antichrist story. *Merlin*, translated from the French, c. 1450 by Henry Lovelich, the London skinner, opens with a conclave of devils in hell shortly after the harrowing. One of them, who has "power for to sowe seede in woman, and make her conceyve," suggests that he breed a rival to Jesus. He chooses a nun for his victim, but is foiled when the nun repents of her deed and prays that her son have "fre choys to do what he wolde." Malory's *Morte d'Arthur* (c. 1469), while lacking the episode of Merlin's conception, includes references to demonesses who attempt to seduce Sir Bors and Percivale. In both cases the cross miraculously preserves the heroes in moments of stress, and the temptresses disappear in smoke or thunder.

The Welsh churchman, Walter Map, in *De nugis curialium* (*Courtiers' Trifles,* c. 1181–1193), retells a number of folktales in which supernatural lovers appear to mortals. Edric Wilde has a child, Aelfnoth (elf-boldness), by a fairy who later disappears into thin air. Such are "demons, incubi and succubi" concludes the storyteller. Henno with the Teeth is another mortal who falls in love with a maiden in the forest at high noon. This supernatural disappeared when Henno's mother discovered that she refused the host and, while alone, metamorphosed into a serpent (the Melusine motif). She also bore offspring and "many children of that demon woman are still alive," according to Map. A third tale tells how Gerbert, later Pope Sylvester (999–1003), falls in love with a "incubus-demon" in the forest at high noon. He stays with her, accepting her gifts of gold and love until near the end of his life when he rejects her supernatural aid and dies, repentant.

There are a number of early ballads and short romances in which an other-worldly fairy—the Celtic version of the German mare and Latin incubus—seduces or tries to seduce men: "Thomas Rhymer," "The Demon Lover," *Thomas of Erceldoune* (c. 2d half of 13th century), *Sir Gawain and the Green Knight* (c. 1370 [with the temptress Morgan le Faye]), *Richard Coeur de Lion* (c. 1300), and the 14th cent. Breton lay, *Sir Gowther* (in which the same demon that sired Merlin is also the father of Sir Gowther).

Theologians or clerics did not underestimate the seriousness of an encounter with an incubus or succubus. The sexual union could result in death or madness, or result in a deformed or demonic child. On the other hand, certain authors after 1300 began to exploit the humor in the situation. Geoffrey Chaucer makes several playful references to incubi or fiends who are thought to molest human victims. His Wife of Bath (*Canterbury Tales,* c. 1380–1400) probably reflects his own view when she states that the only "incubus" in her day is the lecherous friar, who lurks "in every bussh or under every tree". During the same century Boccaccio also found in current mores and superstitions about angelology a great opportunity to develop his wit. In the *Il decamerone* (*Decameron,* novellas, c. 1350), the lecherous Brother Albert seduces Madonna Lysetta by convincing her that the angel Gabriel has fallen in love with her and will visit her in the evening. The visits of "Gabriel" continue until Lysetta cannot keep her love a secret and boasts to a gossip: "He does it better than my husband, and he informs me that they do it up there as well." Lysetta's relatives then set a trap for Brother Albert.

Renaissance Literature and Demonology

During the Renaissance the incubus remained no less prominent in tracts on witchcraft, but literary artists began to use the figure for thematic and symbolic purposes. Thus there were by this time three kinds of interpreters: the rational, who debunked the uncomfortable dream as merely the result of physiological disorders; the supernatural, who took the night oppressors to be physical realities;

and the imaginative, who utilized the legends of the nightmare, and their own experiences, to explore the relationship between the dream world and the real world. There had always been the rational interpreters, even in classical times. Hippocrates, Galen, and Soranus all attributed dreams and nightmares to illness, gastric disturbances, or diet (common beans were the frequent cause). There were skeptics even in the early Middle Ages who saw the cause of the incubus in diet. During the Renaissance the theologian John Wier in Germany began to question the church positions on incubi, and in England Reginald Scot (*Discoverie of Witchcraft*, 1584) rejected out of hand all stories about incubus spirits. As for the nun who bore Merlin, Scot declared that the fable was concocted "speciallie to excuse and mainteine the knaveries and lecheries of idle priests and bawdie monks; and to cover the shame of their lovers and concubines."

Such reasonable analysis was not universal. Demonologists in the late sixteenth and early seventeenth centuries, Jean Bodin, Nicholas Jocquier, Paul Grillandus, Nicolas Remy, Martin Del Rio, Francesco Guazzo, and Pierre de Lancre, maintained the tradition of a rabid antiwitchcraft polemic that had reached a plateau in the *Malleus maleficarum*, and incubus/succubus lore was important to that tradition. Even King James VI of Scotland (later, James I of England) subscribed to a belief in incubi. In his *Daemonologie* (1597), he wrote that these demons were especially prevalent in the northern lands "where the devil finds greatest ignorance and barbarity." The polymath, Paracelsus, wrote a book *De nymphis, sylphis, pygmalis et salamandris* (*On Nymphs, Sylphs, Pygmies and Salamanders* [published in 1566]) which goes into great detail about various demons, including incubus/succubus type. Unions between certain of these demons and humans, he argued, could be fortuitous and result in normal children. A Neoplatonic sect, the Rosicrucians, followed Paracelsus' lead, viewing commerce with supernatural creatures to be a positive good. This thesis was parodied by Abbé de Montfaucon de Villars in the esoteric *Le comte de Gabalis* (1671) and by Pope in his poem *The Rape of the Lock* (1712) but supported at length by the Italian cleric Ludovico Sinistrari in *De daemonialitate, et incubis et succubis* (*Demoniality*, 1701). Sinistrari's basic argument is that "When having intercourse with an Incubus, man does not degrade but rather dignifies, his nature."

Literary artists tended to use the incubus/succubus for thematic purposes, and examples are in the plays of Marlowe (*Dr. Faustus*, 1604), Shakespeare (*Midsummer Night's Dream* c. 1595; *King Lear*, 1606; *Macbeth*, 1605–1606; and *The Tempest*, 1611), Middleton (*A Mad World, My Masters*, c. 1606; and *The Witch*, 1616), Rowley (*The Birth of Merlin*, published in 1662), Marston (*The Tragedy of Sophonisba*, 1606), or in Spenser's epic poem *The Faerie Queene* (1590–1596). Whatever Milton may have believed about the reality of the incubus/succubus, he retells the story of Genesis 6: "False titl'd Sons of God, / roaming the Earth, / Cast wanton eyes on the daughters of men, / And coupl'd with them, and begot a race" (*Paradise Regained*, epic poem, 1671). Asmodeus, who attempted to seduce Sara, he describes as "the fleshliest incubus"; Baalim and Ashtaroth, as spirits which "can either sex assume," versatility that writers in the Middle Ages attributed to demons also; and Belial, as the "most lewd" of those who fell from heaven (*Paradise Lost*, epic poem, 1667; *Paradise Regained*).

1700 to the Present

During the neoclassical age, interest in the subjective, imaginative world of the supernatural gave way to the objective and rationalistic. John Dryden, commenting on Caliban, who was "got by the devil himself" upon the witch Sycorax, wrote that Shakespeare "seems there to have created a person which was not in Nature, a boldness which at first sight would appear intolerable; for he makes him a species of himself, begotten by an *Incubus* on a witch."

The romantic age ushered in a new and different mood. Terrifying dark figures, highly romantic and Gothic settings, and new applications of Neoplatonic mysticism began to appear in Continental, especially German, literature and then in the writings of numerous English Romantics. Scott, Coleridge, Byron, Keats, and Shelley all reflected these trends and drew heavily on the spirit lore of classical, Germanic, and native Celtic traditions. Coleridge's interest in the demon lover and vampire of the Middle Ages at the time he wrote his poems "Kubla Khan" and "Christabel" (1816) is well documented. Byron returned to medieval conceptions of satanic figures that appear to men when he composed his "speculative quartet" of plays: *Manfred* (1817), *Cain: A Mystery* (1821), *Heaven and Earth: A Mystery* (1822), and *The Deformed Transformed* (1824). *Heaven and Earth* owes its inspiration in part to the Book of Enoch. Keats turned to saint's legend, traditional ballad sources, and classical myth for the demon lovers in his poems "The Eve of St. Agnes" (1820), "La Belle Dame sans Merci" (1819), and *Lamia* (1820). Shelley, as did Keats, used the metaphor of sexual union with otherworldly spirits to indicate total comprehension in *Alastor* (poem, 1816), *Epipsychidion* (poem, 1821), and *Prometheus Unbound* (play, 1820).

In art, John Henry Fuseli gained fame and notoriety with two oil paintings (1781–1791) of the nightmare resting on the breast and stomach of a prostrate sleeping woman. In both paintings a supernatural horse peers into the bedroom, demonstrating the confusion between mare, night monster, and the female horse.

Writers up to the present continue to find the theme of the demon lover, the incubus/succubus, a compelling metaphor. W. B. Yeats (1865–1939) referred to the faery world as a source of inspiration—the Virgin's receiving the Holy Spirit and Semele's and Leda's receiving Zeus are allegories of man's periodical need to gain inspiration from the divine. J.-K. Huysmans, in *Là-bas* (novel, 1891), illustrates the intellectual chaos in a world of rampant satanism and presents a history of the succubus as well as the seduction of his protagonist by a "human" succubus. Charles Williams, in *Descent into Hell* (novel, 1937), depicts the quest for meaningful love and the horrors of its opposite with the demonic lilith. Arthur Machen, in *The Great God Pan* (novel, 1894), shows the horror of life without vision, which results when a man who has had part of his brain removed fathers a demonic child. Ira Levin, in *Rosemary's Baby* (novel, 1967), affirms that man will endure in the face of evil as Rosemary comes to believe that her demon son is part of God's plan. Isaac B. Singer and Eve Friedman, in the script *Teibele and Her Demon* (1977), present a comic and tragic story of a credulous Jewish peasant woman who believes it was a demon who impregnated her. Finally, the movie *Demon Seed* (1977), based on Dean Koontz's novel (1973), tries to warn of the horrors of modern technology as a computer assumes the role of the incubus and seduces a woman. The heroes and heroines in these modern works are tormented by the same imaginary, or to some writers real, beings who stalked through the dreams of primitive man and were described centuries ago as the nightmare who "leaps on, oppresses and crushes." The sexual nature was emphasized by the early Christian clerics and remains the major distinction of the incubus even today.

See also: La Belle Dame sans Merci, Daemon, Dream, Evil, Sex (Heterosexual, Erotic).

Selected Bibliography

Dexinger, Ferdinand. *Sturz der Göttersöhne oder Engel vor der Sintflut*. Wiener Beiträge zur Theologie 13. Vienna: Herder, 1966.

Kiessling, Nicolas. *The Incubus in English Literature*. Pullman: Washington State University Press, 1977.

Mack, John. *Nightmares and Human Conflict*. Boston: Little, Brown, 1970.

Roscher, Wilhelm. *Ephialtes, Abhandlungen der philologisch-historischen Classe der königlich sächsischen Gesellschaft der Wissenschaften*. Leipzig: B. G. Teubner, 1900–1903.

NICOLAS KIESSLING

J

//

JEALOUSY

As a troubling companion of love and of ambition, jealousy has been one of the passions most frequently represented in literature. From the oldest accounts of human thoughts to the present, just as often in collective myths and folktales as in individual works, in histories as in narrative fiction, in religious scriptures as in essays on the human psyche, in comedy as in tragedy, jealousy sets sibling against sibling, spouse against spouse, statesman against statesman, leaving behind a legacy of cruelty and death. It could be said that jealousy constitutes one of the primal forces that frustrate man's pursuit of happiness.

Although jealousy is known to afflict animals to some degree (see treatises on animal psychology and, for early records, Robert Burton, *Anatomy of Melancholy*, 1621, part 3 sec. 3., memb. 1), here it will be discussed as a human experience.

Traditionally termed the vilest of all passions, jealousy is multifaceted. The range of emotions it describes in literature is partly due to the etymology of the word. "Jealousy" derives, through French and Latin, from the Greek zēlos meaning "emulation, zeal, rivalry," and thus it may, generally, be described as a zealous and easily offended interest in someone or something. Usage has specified particular meanings of the term. Thus, in its entry "jealousy," the *Oxford English Dictionary* distinguishes five types of feelings. For the purpose of simplification, three main acceptations of the notion will be stressed.

In biblical language, but also in mythological and legendary literature, the notion of jealousy most often denotes the anger or wrath that seizes the divine being when faced with the suspicion or knowledge that his beneficiary is unfaithful (e.g., Exod. 20). The next definition, and the most common in the modern sense of the word—the feeling arising from the "suspicion, apprehension, or knowledge" of rivalry, especially in love—can be traced back to the Provençal *gelos, gilos* (12th century) and therefore to the vulgar and antisocial jealousy of old husbands (see one of the first recorded examples in Marie de France's *Guigemar* [lay, c. 1170]). The fear of being displaced in the love, regard, or favors of a particularly valued person may manifest itself in doubt, anger, and even vengeful murder. William L. Davidson explains that "When I am jealous of a person . . . [it] means that I hate the usurping person, but also that I am annoyed with the other who has allowed him thus to intrude" (*Encyclopedia of Religion and Ethics*, 1928, article "Envy"). In many a country, acts of cruelty perpetrated by an individual under the influence of jealousy are treated with compassion by criminal laws. It has been suggested that the concept of crimes of passion acknowledges jealousy as an understandable—and even rightful—response to marital infidelity.

A third distinct acceptation of the term designates the "resentment or ill will towards another on account of advantage or superiority, possible or actual, on his part." Some authors have argued that this latter acceptation of "jealousy" is more properly named *"envy."* It differs from the feeling of jealousy in so far as it is not concerned with keeping something that is understood to be one's own, but rather with the desirability of someone else's good (possession, wife, honors, reputation, success, etc.). The French moralist La Rochefoucauld made the often quoted distinction: "Jealousy is somehow right and rational since it aims at keeping something that belongs to us, whereas envy is a rage than cannot tolerate possession by someone else" (*Maximes, [Maxims,* 1665]). In fact, many cases of envy suggest that the intrinsic value of the desired good is much less relevant than the mere fact that someone else, a rival, possesses a good. Thus, one may be envious of a good never before desired until observing it in someone else's possession.

Should we distinguish jealousy from envy? While contemporary scholars acknowledge the semantic specificity of "jealousy" and "envy"—"envy" is a derivative of the Latin *invidia,* which has equivalents in most of the European languages (*envie* [Fr.], *envidia* [Sp.], *invidia* [It.]; the German word *der Neid* comes from a Germanic root)—the term "jealousy" appears to be overwhelmingly preferred to its counterpart. Helmut Schoeck, who addresses this question in his 1966 essay *Der Neid (Envy: A Theory of Social Behaviour)* argues that "a genuine instance of repression" of the concept of envy has been in process since about the beginning of the twentieth century. He offers evidence that the phenomenon of envy is taboo in our age, and that the few social scientists or psychologists who examine it prefer to "disguise" it "with concepts such as ambivalence, aggression, tension, rivalry, jealousy and similar indirect descriptions." As far as literature is concerned, it seems that, except for moral literature, which is fairly abundant on this subject, most narrative and dramatic fictions shirk any clear attempt at isolating the two feelings. While a character's initial emotions can be identified, the development will generally include components of the allied feeling. When a work develops the motif of jealousy, the fear of being displaced often nurtures an ever-increasing envy toward the suspected, and often more desirable, beneficiary. Similarly an envious character will find reasons for believing that he has a legitimate, if not better, claim to the desired good than his rival.

From a psychological point of view, the difference between jealousy and envy appears to be difficult to identify. Schoeck, one of the strongest advocates of the proper linguistic distinction, fully agrees with psychiatrists like Sigmund Freud and Ian D. Suttie (*The Origins of Love and Hate,* 1935), who locate the origins of both feelings in the family group. In his essay *Über einige neurotische Mechanismen bei Eifersucht, Paranoia und Homosexualität (Some Neurotic Mechanisms in Jealousy, Paranoia and Homosexuality,* 1922), Freud insists that the type of jealousy that he labels "normal" and which he distinguishes from "projected" and "delusional" jealousy

is by no means completely rational, that is, derived from the actual situation, proportionate to the real circumstances and under the complete control of the conscious ego; for it is rooted deep in the unconscious, it is a continuation of the earliest stirrings of the child's affective life, and it originates in the Oedipus or brother-and-sister complex of the first sexual period.

In *Envy and Gratitude* (essay, 1957), Melanie Klein argues that envy is a developmental step that precedes and leads to jealousy.

Finally, the concept of "rightful claim" advanced in support of this distinction shows little anthropological evidence. Thus, if we take the example of sibling jealousy, who is to say that the child experiencing jealousy has a better claim to his parents' love and attention than does his new-born or his older sibling? Across the varied civilizations of the world, widely diverging and often incompatible sets of socio-cultural conventions and laws further testify to the frailty of the "rightful claim" attributed to *jealousy.* Nothing, perhaps, better demonstrates the relativity of this claim than the practice of cannibalism reported among the Aborigines of Central Australia. To attenuate sibling jealousy, mothers have been said to eat every second child, sharing it with the older child (Ian D. Suttie, pp. 107–110). Yet, in another manner of dealing with sibling jealousy, Indians of Guatemala beat a fowl to death against the body of the older child to absorb his likely hostility toward the new-born (H. Schoeck pp. 63–64). Similarly, the Indian custom of honoring guests by giving them company of one's own wife offers a striking challenge to Western definitions of "normal" cases of jealousy. On the subject, see Margaret Mead, "Jealousy: Primitive and Civilised" (essay, 1931).

In this essay, therefore, representations of feelings for which "envy" could be argued to be a better qualifier than "jealousy" will not be excluded.

Myths of Origins

Jealousy being experienced as an undesirable and yet universal reaction within the structure of familial life, it is no surprise that a number of the myths of creation give it a significant role. Because their representations have provided much of the inspiration of literary works, it is important to emphasize famous depictions of jealousy.

Long transmitted orally, myths of origins have come to our knowledge by means of rudimentary, often conflicting, and moreover randomly preserved, accounts that forefathers of our contemporary folklorists chose to jot down. Perhaps as a result, jealousy receives little or no detailed psychological development. It is presented as a dramatic force that encourages discord and generates significant changes in the shape of the world.

In the Western world, one of the earliest documented narratives to display the cosmogonic effects of jealousy is the story of Horus, Isis, and Osiris, the Triad of Abydos of ancient Egypt. While it is admitted that the narrative dates from the worship of the Triad prominent during the first five or six dynasties (going back as far as 7500 B.C.), there seems to remain no extended account of it previous to Plutarch's *Peri Isidos kai Osiridos (On Isis and Osiris,* essay, c. A.D. 120). As it may be reconstructed from Plutarch's testimony and fragments of papyrus found in several Pharaohs' tombs, it testifies to the disturbing although ultimately beneficient role that jealousy played at the origins of the world according to ancient Egyptian folk literature.

The story of the Triad of Abydos seems to offer the earliest and most socially concerned account of ways to face jealousy in others and in oneself. Seth's jealousy, murder, and mutilation of his brother Osiris cause Isis, Osiris' sister and spouse, to establish not only the bases of proper mortuary care of the dead, thus allowing Osiris to come back from the dead, but also to advocate a loyal, pious and nonvindictive behavior both within the family nucleus and outside it. Indeed, rather than giving in to jealousy when she learns that her late husband fathered a son by Seth's wife, Isis searches for the infant, whom she rescues from the reeds of the Nile and rears. As a result, her efforts to retrieve and to honor her husband's remains succeed. They are crowned with the miraculous conception and birth of Horus, Osiris' son. Isis again demonstrates her loyalty, piety, and lack of a vengeful mind when she learns of Seth's mutilation and dissemination of her husband's body. Years later, although still fervently dedicated to her husband's memory, Isis is nonetheless compassionate enough to free Seth, whom her son, by now a mature man able to avenge his father's honor, had bound after defeating him in a several-day-long battle. The fact that Horus reacts violently at her act—he beheads his mother—could be interpreted as the sign of the inappropriateness of Isis' answer to the plea of her husband's murderer. In any case, the goddess' decapitation is instantanenously undone by the gods. Isis receives the cow-head by which she is known. Osiris' return to life and his subsequent award of the domain of the living and the dead—episodes that close the narrative—seem to suggest that the exemplary manner in which Isis dealt with Seth's jealous destructiveness, as well as with her own possibilities of retaliation, is the very means by which Osiris was able to come back to life, thus establishing the reversibility of death.

In Greek mythology the chief account of creation also rests upon the dynamics

of jealous feelings within the family and more specifically on a conflict—Oed-
ipian in nature—that sets the mother and sons against the ruling father. Contrary
to the Egyptian myth, it does not attempt to promote any exemplary behavior.
Gea, the wife of Uranos and the mother of the six Titans whom her husband
confined in the Tartarus, helps her son Chronos slay Uranos. Chronos, who fears
that a fate similar to that of his father would overtake him, swallows each of
his children as it is born. Rhea, his wife, cunningly substitutes a stone in place
of her last infant, Zeus. When Zeus attains full growth, he resolves to defeat
his father. After a long raging war, Zeus and his party triumph. The subsequent
rule of the Olympian gods, who divide the world among themselves, marks the
end to the bitter father-son struggle for control of the world.

As for the rivalry that later opposes Zeus to his chosen counselor, Prometheus,
it may be understood as another case of jealousy over control of the world, this
time the part inhabited by humans. While it bears features of parental jealousy
over the love of their progeny, it also comprises *phthonēsas,* the Greek word
referring to the jealousy gods feel when humans exalt themselves because of
their great riches, fame, or power and call themselves happy (see S. Ranulf,
The Jealousy of the Gods and Criminal Law at Athens, essay, 1913–1914).

As a result of the spread of Christianity, Cain's jealousy provides the archetypal
motive of sibling rivalry in the Occident. Only a few lines long, the biblical
narrative of Cain's murder of Abel (Gen. 4) is less useful than the commentaries
that scholars, homilists, church fathers, and rabbis have devised. Louis Ginzberg's monumental collection of Jewish scriptural exegeses, *The Legends of the
Jews* (1909), provides several interpretations of Cain's motives. One well-known
interpretation attributes the first murder of the Judeo-Christian tradition not primarily to God's displeasure at seeing Cain's sacrifice, but to the latter's desire
to take Abel's twin sister to be his wife. According to this version, sexual desire
was Cain's true motive. Jealous and envious, Cain waited for the first opportunity—one of Abel's sheep trampling over a newly planted field—to rid himself
of a constant rival.

As Seth's murder of Osiris marked the Egyptian world, Cain's crime had
baneful consequences for both Cain and the whole of nature. After Cain's repentance, insincere as it was, God afflicted the murderer with leprosy to mark
him as a sinner, condemned him to be a fugitive on the earth, protected him
against the wild beasts only by a dog, and stained his descendants with blood-
guiltiness up to the seventh generation. Furthermore, the earth ceased to bear
fruits that tasted like the fruits of Paradise. Trees and plants in the part of earth
belonging to Abel refused to yield their fruits for several generations and never
resumed their former powers. Where there were "nine hundred and thirty-six
different varieties of fruit," there remained only one. There are even a few
interpretations which attribute the origin of mountainous surfaces to God's punishment of the earth for having received Abel's blood.

In other parts of the world, namely among Indian tribes of both North and
South America, a widespread myth of creation attributes the positions of the sun

and of the moon in the universe to jealousy. This myth also attributes to it the origins of pottery clay and of a bird belonging to the North American species of *Chordeiles minor* (Whippoorwill, also known as Nighthawk). As Claude Lévi-Strauss explains in *La potière jalouse* (essay, 1985), the Jivaros, a tribe of the northeast Andes, tell how the sun and the moon were humans who lived upon the earth. They shared the same lodging and the same wife, Aôho, that is Nighthawk. Aôho liked the sun's warm embrace but she feared the touch of the moon, whose body was too cold. Sun thought it humorous to tease Moon about his disadvantage. Moon took offense at this and climbed up to the sky by means of a liana. At the same time, he blew on Sun and eclipsed him. Both spouses gone, Aôho thought herself abandoned. She attempted to follow Moon to the sky, bringing with her a basket full of pottery clay. Moon caught sight of her and cut the liana, which united the two worlds. Aôho fell with her basket scattering the clay all over the face of the earth. It is at this time that she changed into a bird (the nighthawk) and at every new moon, her plaintive cry to her spouse can be heard. As for Sun, he too climbed to the sky with the help of another liana. But Moon continued to flee from him. They have not been reconciled. This is why the sun is seen only by day and the moon only by night.

In the Jivaros' perspective, this cosmogonic account also has consequences on the human scale. Indeed, the Jivaros state that if "the sun and the moon had agreed to share the same wife instead of each wanting her for himself, [they] also could have had a woman in common." It is thus the jealousy and fight of the heavenly bodies that caused the Jivaros to never cease to be jealous of one another and fight over women they want to possess.

The Ancient World

In the abundant corpus devoted to the lives of the Olympian gods and their progeny, jealousy is a fearsome passion that leads to cruel reprisal, if not death.

Zeus's infidelities to his wife, Hera, set the scene for famous portrayals of feminine jealousy. At one point, while spying on her husband's wanderings, Hera discovers Zeus's interest in Io. Although the god changes Io into a white heifer, Hera outwits her husband and gains possession of her rival. When Hermes succeeds in killing the heifer's guard, Hera conjures up before the eyes of the maiden the figure of a Fury so monstruous and bloody that Io, driven mad, plunges into the sea. Hera rejoices in Io's pain, and it takes all of Zeus's power of persuasion to make her renounce her vindictiveness and withdraw her spells. Aphrodite is similarly prone to fearsome fits of jealousy.

Generally speaking, it seems that amorous jealousy is a female affliction with which men, be they gods or heroes like Ulysses or Eneas, must learn to contend. Several classical tragedies could be cited as further examples. In *Trachiniai* (*Trachinian Women*, c. 430 B.C.), for instance, Sophocles presents Deianeira's jealousy over the most recent of her husband's infidelities. Her unusual attempt at restoring Herakles' love by means of magic—she sends her husband the tunic he wore when fighting Nessos—rather than by harming the beautiful Iole is fatal to Herakles. Wracked with pain from the poisoned blood of Nessos, Herakles only succeeds in having Deianeira take her own life in remorse before he dies. A later account of a woman's use of magic to win back her "unfaithful beloved" appears in *Pharmakeutria* (*The Sorcerer*), the second of Theocritus' *Eidyllia* (*Idylls*, poems, c. 270 B.C.). Still in classical theater, Euripides features Medea's devastating jealousy in *Mēdeia* (*Medea*, 431 B.C.). When Jason deserts her, Medea's passionate love is transformed into a desire for vengeance that backs down neither at the killing of her rival nor at that of the two children whom she had with Jason. Medea's jealousy also comprises the fear of being humiliated by mockery, a social concern not depicted in other Greek tragedies.

As for men, they primarily experience jealousy in relation to their sociopolitical status. Homer's epic poems *Ilias* (*Iliad*) and *Odysseia* (*Odyssey*, c. 8th century B.C.) offer Achilles' wrath and Penelope's suitors' stratagems as examples. It even seems that the Greek expeditions against Troy are justified by the need to avenge Menelaus rather than the desire to regain Helen. In the Oedipus cycle, which interested both tragic poets Aeschylus and Sophocles, the double fratricide of Eteocles and Polynices similarly points to the crystallization of men's jealousy over power issues. Aeschylus' tragedy *Agamemnon* (458 B.C.) offers a more complex portrayal of jealousy. Here, the murders of Cassandra and Agamemnon by the illegitimate couple Aegysthus-Clytemnestra arise not only from a desire to retain political power and from the need to protect their own lives, but also from the queen's resentment over Iphigenia's sacrifice and her husband's infidelities while in Troy.

In spite of major literary works where they depicted jealousy and its maddening effects, Virgil, Horace, Ovid, and Seneca did not significantly alter the sexual partition of amorous and nonamorous forms that they had inherited from their Greek predecessors. The case of the *Satyricon* (A.D. 60), a comic and satirical romance written by Petronius, is quite different. Its development of the motif presents the double interest of recounting a homosexual love in a first-person narrative and parodying earlier Greek love-romances that have been lost. Although only parts of Petronius' original text have come down to us, enough remains to show the obsessive passion the narrator Encolpius nurtures for the handsome and loving young servant Giton. The rivalry that develops between him and his companion in roguery, Ascyltus, also enamored of the boy, gives rise to three major burlesque scenes of jealousy. The first one occurs when Ascyltus surprises the narrator and the boy in bed. He seizes a belt and, while shouting insults, vigorously whips his all too-successful rival. In a role reversal, the second scene shows Encolpius' jealousy at the sight of Ascyltus' advantage. Though more violent than the previous encounter, bloodshed is avoided through self-control and mediation. The third scene of jealousy does not take place until the narrator and the boy, at last reunited, face the poet Eumolpus' amorous stratagems. The most dramatic of the episodes, it stages a sequence of three attempted suicides whose theatricality and burlesque resolution provide the parody of jealousy-throes with a remarkable climax. Although prevented from enjoying his reunion with Giton, Encolpius seizes this opportunity to reflect upon, and to apologize for, the violent temper that his jealousy has brought forth. Causes for jealousy are definitively left ashore as the two embark on Lichas' boat under the protection of the old poet.

Although the *Satyricon* is a parody, the first-person narration gives the treatment of jealousy a level of credibility that parody does not destroy. Most effective in that respect is the representation of Encolpius' grief after Giton's defection to Ascyltus. His ego deeply hurt, the narrator offers the reader a recollection of alternating periods of depression, self-pity, anger, and vengeful desires in a style whose comparative understatement suggests a depth of feeling not conveyed in earlier parts of the work.

Sisterly jealousy receives an interesting representation in the Psyche episode (book 5) of Apuleius' *Metamorphoses* (*The Golden Ass,* c. 160). Psyche's sisters succeed in persuading her, by means of cleverly planned suggestions and insinuations, to overlook the promise she made not to attempt to see her husband. Although Psyche's faith in her husband helps her resist her sisters' assaults for some time, she finally gives in to their scheme. The means of persuasion used by Psyche's sisters anticipates those employed by Iago in Shakespeare's *Othello* (play, c. 1604).

Premodern Times: The Tenth To Sixteenth Centuries

In the Orient and especially in Japan, the most influential representation of jealousy is found in Lady Murasaki Shikibu's *Genji monogatari* (*Tale of Genji,* novel, 11th century). The charms, looks, and high station of Genji make him an irresistible lover who moves from one woman to another. Instead of fostering jealousy, he resorts to polygamic arrangements to provide support for the women he has seduced. Nonetheless, as Murasaki reports, the women suffer terribly from Genji's amorous tendencies. The type of triangular relationship that first occurs between Genji and his stepmother inexorably favors schemes of concealment and deceptions on one hand, and suspicions, doubts, spying, on the other. If most misunderstandings begin with the failure to communicate openly, it is because refined innuendoes and ambiguous poems are prized at the Heian court. Interpretation is an elaborate game, particularly when it comes to communication between men and women. Complicated by public life and an often precarious sense of self (Kaoru suspects he is not the son of Genji), characters fear being displaced by rivals or learning of their loss of favor from third parties.

In Europe, medieval literature presents a number of well-known cases of jealousy in chansons de geste, ballads, and courtly romances. Among them are Ganelon's jealousy over the favors that Charlemagne bestows on Roland in *La chanson de Roland* (*Song of Roland,* epic poem, c. 1100); the fierce jealousies nurtured at the court of Siegfried and Kriemhild in the High German narrative poem *Nibelungenlied* (c. 1200); the barons' jealousy of King Mark's nephew, Tristan, and that of Ysolt "aux blanches mains [with the white hands]," in the Tristan romances, poems of the late twelfth and thirteenth centuries. Connected to greed for power, jealousy is portrayed as the main cause of treachery or other evil deeds in epics. Interestingly enough, the jealousy of King Mark's barons is also depicted as a villainy in versions of the Tristan legend. The anomaly (the barons are indeed loyal to their king) points to the courtly conception of love introduced by Provençal troubadours. For them, "zealous love" and "jealousy" are antithetical. While the former sentiment inspires an altruistic, selfless, and devout service of the beloved on the basis of her moral nobility, the latter is a compulsive or ridiculous manifestation of combined pride and miserliness. Possessive, selfish, arrogant, it treats the Lady as a material good. Expectedly, the typical *gilos* is the spouse who considers himself the rightful owner of and only desirable conversation partner for his wife.

No picture of jealousy in medieval literature could be complete without a reference to the great allegorical works and to the vast body of popular narratives in which the age delighted. In Guillaume de Lorris and Jehan de Meung's *Roman de la rose* (*Romance of the Rose,* allegorical and satirical poem, c. 1230 and 1275), Friend (*Ami*) advises Lover (*Amant*) not to behave like the jealous husband who unjustly reproaches his wife for being unfaithful and then physically abuses her. In a good marriage, infidelities of each partner should be discrete and overlooked. The personification of jealousy, however, is foremost that of a guardian of the Rose and of her chastity. She becomes aroused when she hears Slander (*Malebouche*) report the kiss that Lover has given the Rose. After chiding Shame (*Honte*) for her indifference, she builds a castle around the rose trees and locks up Welcome (*Bon Accueil*) in a tower guarded by an old woman. In a distinctly original understanding of the notion, Jealousy is the Rose's shield against Love. In the continuation of the poem, Jehan de Meung turns to satire. He first follows the original story, but becomes more interested in expressing Nature's views and her criticism of the two extremes of love: vice and chastity. Clearly, Jealousy is a maker of old maids and should be recognized as an enemy of the reproductive concerns of Nature.

The Renaissance provided Europe not only with the discovery of many Greek originals but also with literary works that greatly influenced the modern representations of man. Thus, the Italian poet and dramatist Ariosto, expanding on the story of Orlando and Angelica, the heroes of his predecessor Matteo Boiardo (1434–1494), gave jealousy a vivid and, in a sense, preromantic depiction, in *Orlando furioso* (epic, 1516), one of the most influential poems in the age. In a medley of allegorical incidents, dramatic adventures, and intertextual references, passion, rage, and jealousy overcome the valiant Orlando. It takes a sorcerer to bring his wits back from the moon. Dante, of course, recounts tragic cases of jealousy in both *Inferno* (*Hell,* canto 5) and in *Purgatorio* (*Purgatory,* cantos 5, 13, 14, and 17) of his meticulously structured epic poem *La divina commedia* (*The Divine Comedy,* c. 1320). To surmount personal rivalry, jealousy, and envy, the poet advocates *charity,* an attitude preferred to *love,* and a virtue demanded in *Paradiso* (*Paradise*): "essere in carità è qui necesse," "to be in charity is here a necessity." As Piccarda declares to the hero: "Brother, the power of charity quiets our will and makes us will only what we have and thirst for nothing else.'' Jealousy and envy do not belong to the highest sphere of *La divina commedia*.

In comic and parodic genres, jealousy is mostly the problem of avaricious burghers, often craftsmen or merchants, who fear or know the evils of cuckoldry. In a world where love is almost entirely sexual, the infidelity of one's wife taints one's manhood and social respectability. Cuckolded husbands are the laughing stock of a town. Popular tradition assigns them horns, a motif present in all European comic literature of marriage. When women are the victims of adultery, their temper determines whether they elicit laughter or sympathy. One will find various accounts of marital jealousy in Boccaccio's *Il decamerone (The Decameron,* novellas, c. 1350; e.g., 7.4) and Chaucer's *Canterbury Tales* (c. 1380–1400). Other collections of tales, fabliaux, or exempla attest to the prevalence of the motif in the fourteenth-, fifteenth-, and sixteenth-century European narrative entertainment. It looks as if cuckoldry was then a pastime that stimulated creativity, both in real life and in stories. The satirical tone of *Les quinze joyes de mariage (The Fifteen Joys of Marriage,* satire, c. 1400) and of *Les cent nouvelles nouvelles (The Hundred Tales,* c. 1460) yields, more than a century later, to the humor, awe, and even compassion of the stories created by the aristocratic Marguerite, queen of Navarre, in her *Heptaméron* (1559).

Some forty years later, Montaigne's commentaries on jealousy reflect the still widespread prejudices of clerics and learned middle-class men. In his *Essais (Essays,* 1580–1588), Montaigne warns against jealousy as "the most vain and tempestuous malady that afflicts human souls" (3.5). It particularly devastates women. Historical anecdotes prove how ravaging the disease is among them (3.5 and 2.29). The example to follow when victim of "this fever," he advises, is that of "Lucullus, Caesar, Pompeius, Antonius, Cato and other brave men [who] were cuckolds and knew it without stirring up a tumult about it" (3.5). Such a philosophy finds echoes in contemporary parodic and satirical works.

Italian and Spanish writers were to renew British and French views on jealousy. Among the most influential works are Tasso's epic *Gerusalemme liberata (Jerusalem Delivered,* 1581), his pastoral play *Aminta* (1573), and Montemayor's pastoral novel, *La Diana* (1559). A measure of the intertextuality that pervades the European treatment of jealousy can be demonstrated by Spenser's contemporary use of the conventional Italian metaphor for jealousy: *martel d'Amore* (hammer of Love) in his description of Scudamour's restless night in book 4 of *The Faerie Queene* (allegorical epic, 1590–1596). A number of Italian or other Mediterranean narratives likewise inspired seventeenth-century writers to develop similar plots in prose and on the stage.

The Seventeenth Century

At the turn of the sixteenth century, as Europe's sovereigns asserted their control over unruly courtiers, and as the nobility and members of the learned middle class, while participating in complicated intrigues, became interested in the explorations of human nature, jealousy became an ever more fascinating object of attention.

While the views of the late sixteenth and early seventeenth century are partly summarized by Robert Burton in part 3 of *Anatomy of Melancholy* (treatise, 1621), earlier texts introduced the psycho-physical notion of jealousy that prevailed at the beginning of modern times. These texts included comments by the Italian cardinal Benedetto Varchi (1503–1565), translated and better known as *The Blazon of Jealousie,* 1615; *L'académie française* (*The French Academy,* 1577), a symposium on manners and happiness at the court by Pierre de La Primaudaye; and *Tableau des passions humaines* (*Table of Humane Passions,* 1620), a synthetic treatise by N. Coeffeteau. Among the four fluids or "humors" that rule the body, according to the scientific theory of the period, jealousy is linked to the bile, that is, to the choleric humor. However, it is not clear which one takes precedence, that is to say, which one generates the other. Published in 1649, René Descartes' *Les passions de l'âme,* translated in 1650 as *The Passions of the Soule,* located jealousy in a more synthetic and rationalized view of human nature, but it drew less attention than did his predecessors' comments on the subject.

The epitome of the jealousy motif in Western literature (both in Europe and in the Americas) is found in Shakespeare's *Othello.* While episodes of jealousy appear in several of Shakespeare's tragedies—*Troilus and Cressida* (1601–1602), *Antony and Cleopatra* (c. 1607), *Cymbeline* (1610)—and while cuckholdry informs the plot or subplots of several of his comedies—*A Midsummer Night's Dream* (c. 1595), *The Merry Wives of Windsor* (c. 1600), *Much Ado About Nothing* (c. 1598), and *The Winter's Tale* (1611)—the staggering power of *Othello* has remained unsurpassed on the Western stage. In Shakespeare's play, the spectator witnesses the transformation—perhaps the metamorphosis—of Othello, a Moorish general at the head of the Venetian army, whom his ensign, the resentful and suspicious Iago, induces to doubt Desdemona's fidelity. Iago's skills to shape "faults that are not" lead Othello from estrangement to folly, to the murder of his wife, and his own suicide. The treatment of jealousy, the famous "green-ey'd monster, which doth mock / That meat it feeds on" and, "like a poisonous mineral," gnaws both Iago's and Othello's "inwards," is so compelling that, for fear of the reactions of their audiences, some theater directors and later interpreters (e.g., Jean-Francois Ducis, Rossini, and Verdi) adapted the play, either giving it a happy ending or shifting the emphasis from Iago's maneuvers to Desdemona's unjust fate.

Spanish literature's treatment of the motif of jealousy was also influential. New heroes of narrative genres, the rogues or *pícaros,* transformed the representation of jealousy in the novel. Free from moral constraints, they hold jealousy as a laughable feature of aging and ill-suited husbands who married too attractive women. Generally speaking, jealous characters—husbands, wives, lovers—of parodic and satirical novels and novellas are unable to command sympathy from the reader. Whether they are ridiculed or not, they are portrayed as peculiar, anachronistic, or pathetic fellows. The portrayal is not necessarily derogatory, as can be seen in the final twist Cervantes gives to *El celoso estremeño* (*The Jealous Husband*), one of his *Novelas ejemplares* (*Exemplary Novels,* 1613). In order to protect himself against the danger that marriage involves—cuckoldry— Felipe de Carrizales builds a fortified mansion in which he keeps and treats generously his captives—his fifteen-year-old wife, Leonora, her friends, and his female servants. The distress he feels when he discovers Leonora asleep in the arms of a lusty young man who has succeeded in entering the fortress, kills him, but not before he recognizes that he, ''like the Silke-worme, wrought the house wherein I must dye,'' and requests his widow-to-be to ''take felicitie with him whom she seemeth to love so dearly.'' Leonora chooses instead to prove her innocence and becomes a nun in one of the strictest monasteries of Seville.

Jealousy was also staged. Calderón dramatized the extreme jealousy of Herodus, tetrarch of Jerusalem, in his tragedy *El major monstruo, los celos* (1635). Herodus' cruelty had already been the subject of *Mariamne* (1610), a French tragedy by A. Hardy, and it was to appeal to German Romantics (F. Hebbel) and Shelley. Contrary to his contemporary, Tirso de Molina chose to set jealousy in comedies (e.g., *Celosa de si misma* [1627], *Celos con celos se curan* [1633], *El celoso prudente* [1621]).

Perhaps more than any other European educated elite, the French were drawn to jealousy. Madeleine Bertaud has recently argued that the subject had lost some ground in French theater and novels at the end of the sixteenth century (*La jalousie dans la littérature au temps de Louis XIII,* 1981). As a result, when the contemporaries of Louis XIII discovered Italian and Spanish masterpieces whose success at the French court the civil wars had delayed, jealousy was very appealing because of its novelty and socio-political relevance.

Generally speaking, the French classical novels, inspired by the Greek romances of the third century, in particular *Aithiopika* (*An Aethiopian History*) by Heliodorus of Emesa, and the Renaissance Italian epics have their plots built around jealousy. Jealousy is unavoidably elected to complicate the adventures of the young lovers. Suitors or abductors of all sorts, nymphs, or former friends share the task of opposing jealousy, resentment, and envy as obstacles to their happy union. Nevertheless, in accord with the generic character of the romance, the jealous, the slanderers, and the envious are ultimately defeated. Thus, in *L'Astrée* (*Astrea,* pastoral novel, 1607–1628) by Honoré d'Urfé, Semire, the shepherd who inspires jealousy in Astrée and is the cause of Céladon's suicide, dies after he has saved the lives of Alexis and Astrée and amended his fault. Half a century later, with the first modern psychological novel, *La Princesse de Clèves* (*The Princess of Cleves,* 1678), Madame de La Fayette has the heroine's husband die from jealousy. The Prince of Clèves, who is more in love with his young wife than aristocratic mores of the time allow, suffers from a growing and literally poisonous jealousy after the princess confides in him that she has reasons to leave the court. Episodes written from his point of view show the prince obsessed with jealousy and searching for signs that will confirm his suspicions. His ego appears to be both the investigator and the main victim of his qualms. On his death bed, he reproaches the princess for having made her confession ("l'aveu"), thus leaving her with a guilty conscience, which later prompts her to refuse Nemours' love and to retire from the court. Interestingly, the prince is not the only one to experience jealousy. The princess also must deal with her own emotions. At first, jealousy reveals to her that she loves Nemours "like her husband wishes her to love him." Whenever she believes Nemours to be interested in someone, she experiences a state of emotional upheaval. After her husband's death, fear of jealousy may contribute to the princess' refusal to marry Nemours. The ending is far from clear as to the princess' reasons to retire. Jealousy recurs in all the works attributed to Madame de La Fayette. The story of Alphonse and Belasire in *Zaïde* (*Zayde*, novel, 1670) offers a moving first-person description of jealousy. Because of his compulsive jealousy, Alphonse loses his best friend, pushes Belasire, his beloved, to enter religion, thus ruining his own hopes of happiness. The pseudo-memoirs *La vie d'Henriette d'Angleterre* (*Henrietta, Princess of England,* 1670–1671, published in 1720), show many a courtier the victim of jealousy, envy, or resentment.

The treatment of jealousy by French seventeenth-century writers (moralists and religious leaders; novelists like Sorel, Camus, or Gomberville; dramatists like Corneille; state rulers like Richelieu) is too broad to be discussed here. Remarkably influential have been renditions of the motif by Molière and Racine, notably Molière's portrayals of jealous suitors such as Arnolphe and Alceste in *L'école des femmes* (*The School for Wives,* comedy, 1662) and *Le misanthrope* (*The Misanthropist,* comedy, 1666), respectively—his farcical or comic husbands (Sganarelle, le Barbouillé, Georges Dandin) belong to the commedia dell'arte stock characters—Racine's treatment of Hermione's, Nero's and Phaedra's devastating jealousies in his tragedies *Andromaque* (1667), *Britannicus* (1669), and *Phèdre* (*Phaedra,* 1677). Greatly noticed were also La Rochefoucauld's *Maximes* and La Bruyère's *Les caractères* (*The Characters,* essays, 1688), which fueled conversations for several decades. Other works enjoyed temporary fame: Montfleury, *L'école des jaloux, ou le cocu volontaire* (comedy, 1662), Brécourt, *Le jaloux invisible* (comedy, 1666).

Modern Times

The association of jealousy and literature has been and remains very productive. If we accept Denis de Rougemont's thesis in *L'amour et l'occident* (essay, 1939 and 1956), this continued interest results from a Western infatuation with "passion." In an analysis that prepares the path for René Girard's theory of "triangular" desire (*Mensonge romantique et vérité romanesque,* essay, 1961), Rougemont explains the psychology of jealousy by our tendency to revive the "feeling" of love by seeking the possession and love of persons whom others find desirable. A line from a Tibetan poem summarizes the effects of such comparisons: "men and women suffer from jealousy as soon as they pass their threshold."

In Western literatures, and it is particularly true for the period extending from the late eighteenth century to the mid-1930s, many new plays feature jealousy. Titles such as Carlo Goldoni's *Le donne gelose* (*The Jealous Wives,* play, 1752), George Colman's *The Jealous Wife. A Comedy* (1761), William Gardiner's *The Sultana, or the Jealous Queen: a tragedy* (1806), J.F.A. Bayard and P. Laurencin's *Mathilde ou la jalousie* (comedy, 1835), Augustin Daly's *Griffith Gaunt, or Jealousy* (drama, 1867), F. Crommelynck's very successful *Le cocu magnifique* (comedy, 1920), and Sacha Guitry's *La jalousie* (comedy, 1934) are indicative of the appeal that playwrights still saw in the motif. Neither devoid of clichés nor of certain insights, plays of this sort have kept the motif of jealousy attractive to theatergoers. A feminization of the motif may be partly responsible for its enduring success. One has to look for romantic dramas to find masculine jealousy. Taking up again Renaissance and seventeenth-century tragic stories, Schiller, Grillparzer, Büchner, Hugo, and Musset put on the stage the criminal effects of the passion. Among recent interpretations of the motif, *Cat on a Hot Tin Roof* (play, 1955) by Tennessee Williams—and to a lesser degree *A Streetcar Named Desire* (play, 1947)—revives the exploration of jealousy in relation to buried feelings of guilt and personal inadequacy.

Among novelists, contributions to the history of the motif attest to both borrowings from past treatments and interest in a new socio-economic milieux. In *La nouvelle Héloïse* (*The New Heloise,* novel, 1761), Rousseau proposes the exemplary approach to love and jealousy of an enlightened country nobility. Laclos' novel *Les liaisons dangereuses* (*Dangerous Acquaintances,* 1782) shows how the "roués" Valmont and Merteuil use human passions and, foremost, love and jealousy, to reach their goals. Their psychological expertise anticipates the refined calculations of Sade's characters. In *Le lys dans la vallée* (*The Lily of the Valley,* novel, 1835), Balzac depicts the tragic conflict between Madame de Mortsauf's Christian values and her repressed desires. In North American literature, Hawthorne's obsessed, jealous, scholar Prynne besieges the minister of the small colony of Boston when he suspects him of having been his wife's lover (*The Scarlet Letter,* 1850). Several other novels, *Sister Carrie* (1900) by Dreiser, *The Sound and the Fury* (1929) by Faulkner, and *The Sun Also Rises* (1926) by Hemingway, revive the motif of jealousy through well-delineated socio-cultural contexts.

Among the novels that explore the subtle dynamics of love, jealousy, and the sense of self, Proust's *Un amour de Swann* (*Swann's Love,* from *A la recherche du temps perdu* [*Remembrance of Things Past,* 1913–1927]), holds a first place. The nature of Swann's feelings for Odette suggests that jealousy may be independent from love. Swann becomes jealous *before* caring for his mistress. Jealousy has a life of its own, often deeper, more sensitive, and certainly more hermeneutic in nature than love. It provides moments of joy whenever it enables its host to interpret the lies of the unfaithful, but like the octopus of Proust's simile, it takes solid possession of each moment of the day and of each corner of the mind, deeply altering its host. The irreversibility of the change in character is further explored by Simone de Beauvoir in *L'invitée* (*She Came to Stay*, novel, 1943) and by Jorge Amado in his novel *Dona Flor e seus dois maridos* (*Dona Flor and Her Two Husbands,* 1966).

Novelists have been attracted also by the exploration of the margins of sanity and jealousy. Tolstoy gives an extraordinary and disturbing account of the combined progression of jealousy and insanity in *Kreĭtserova sonata* (*The Kreutzer Sonata,* 1889), a novel often regarded as an attempt by Tolstoy to reckon with his own views on marriage and jealousy. The narrator Pozdnishef explains how he has, in his view rightly, escaped the hell of marriage by killing his wife. The narrator's confession, which takes place aboard a train, stresses the contradictions in his attitude toward his wife. Lacking both affection for his wife and self-confidence, he feared and desired to have a rival. Trukhashevsky, whom he introduced to his wife at a gathering of friends, aroused his increasingly maddening suspicions while playing Beethoven's "Kreutzer Sonata" with his wife. Very moved by the music, the narrator started imagining an old complicity between the players. The next day, he was certain to find the musician and his wife together in his Moscow apartment. Indeed, when Pozdnishef enters, he sees his wife having dinner with Trukhashevsky. He coldly murders his wife while she protests her innocence and her guest escapes. Obsessive suspicions are also the subject of the Brazilian novel *Dom Casmurro* (1899) by J. Machado de Assis. Bento Santiago, the protagonist-narrator, examines his adolescence and his married life. He tells of his long-awaited marriage to Capitú, a young and beautiful neighbor he loved since childhood but whom he never expected to wed. He traces to that time the origins of the suspicions he later had concerning his wife's fidelity. After he discovers a resemblance between his two-year-old child and Escobar, his best friend, he becomes obsessed with the idea that Escobar and his wife are lovers. He does not vent his suspicions, grows bitter, and interprets his wife's pain at the funeral of Escobar as a proof of her adultery. The parallel he draws between his case and Shakespeare's *Othello* persuades him to be more severe than the Moor and to banish his wife and son to Switzerland. Tanizaki Jun'ichirō, a prominent modern Japanese novelist, and the author of *Kagi* (*The Key,* 1956), also uses the resources of first-person narrative to render the peculiar dynamics of jealousy in the sexual life of a university couple in their fifties. Yet another first-person narrative of obsessive jealousy is Robbe-Grillet's New Novel *La jalousie* (*Jealousy,* 1957). While no "I" appears in the text, it is generally assumed that the reader is given the point of view of A . . . 's jealous husband. Repetition and variation on scenes from an African plantation reproduce the obsessive state of mind of the narrator, who tries to determine whether A . . . is having an affair with Frank. No novel has better penetrated the inner logic and progression of suspicions. More than knowledge, the fear of rivalry is what inflames jealousy.

See also: Love Triangle.

Selected Bibliography

Bertaud, Madeleine. *La jalousie dans la littérature au temps de Louis XIII. Analyse littéraire et histoire des mentalités*. Geneva: Droz, 1981.

Clanton, Gordon, and Smith, Lynn G., eds. *Jealousy*. Englewood Cliffs, N.J.: Prentice Hall, 1977.

Ellis, Keith. "Ambiguity and Point of View in Some Novelistic Representations of Jealousy." *Modern Language Notes* 86 (1971): 891–909.

Köhler, Erich. "Les troubadours et la jalousie." In *Mélanges de langue et de littérature du Moyen Age et de la Renaissance offerts à Jean Frappier*. pp. 543–559. Geneva: Droz, 1970.

MICHÈLE E. VIALET